Library of Congress Cataloging-in-Publication Data

Craig, Grace J.
  Human development / Grace J. Craig and Don Baucum.—9th ed.
    p. cm.
  Includes bibliographical references and indexes.
  ISBN 0–13–033441–3
  1. Developmental psychology. I. Baucum, Don. II. Title.
  BF713.C7 2001
  155—dc21   2001018514

VP, Editorial director: Laura Pearson
Senior acquisitions editor: Jennifer Gilliland
Editorial assistant: Nicole Girrbach
Editor in chief of development: Susanna Lesan
Development editor: Marilyn Miller
VP, Director of manufacturing and production:
  Barbara Kittle
Senior managing editor: Mary Rottino
Production liaison: Fran Russello
Editorial/production supervision: Bruce Hobart
  (Pine Tree Composition)
Manufacturing manager: Nick Sklitsis
Prepress and manufacturing buyer: Tricia Kenny

Art director: Ximena Tamvakopoulos
Cover and interior designer: Laura Gardner
Cover photos: Top left, Digital Stock, "Faces of the World";
  top right, PhotoDisc 33, "Everyday People 2"; bottom
  left, DigitalVision, "Parents and Babies"; bottom right,
  DigitalVision, "Teenagers Today"
Director, Image Resource Center: Melinda Lee Reo
Manager rights & permissions: Kay Dellosa
Image specialist: Beth Boyd
Photo researcher: Terry Stratford
Line art coordinator: Guy Ruggiero
Artist: Maria Piper
AVP, Director of marketing: Beth Gillette Mejia

This book was set in 10/12.5 Palatino by Pine Tree Composition, Inc. and was printed
and bound by World Color. The cover was printed by Phoenix Color Corp.

Quoted material on pp. 240–241 is from Winnie-the-Pooh by A. A. Milne, illustrated by E. H. Shepard.
Copyright 1926 by E. P. Dutton, renewed 1954 by A. A. Milne. Used by permission of Dutton Children's
Books, an imprint of Penguin Putnam Books for Young Readers, a division of Penguin Putnam Inc.
For permission to use copyrighted photos, grateful acknowledgment is made to the copyright holders
on pages 695–696, which is hereby made part of this copyright page

Printed in the United States of America
10 9 8 7 6 5 4 3 2 1

ISBN 0-13-033441-3

Pearson Education Ltd., *London*
Pearson Education Australia Pte. Ltd., *Sydney*
Pearson Education Singapore, Pte. Ltd.
Pearson Education North Asia Ltd., *Hong Kong*
Pearson Education Canada, Ltd., *Toronto*
Pearson Educación de Mexico, S.A. de C.V.
Pearson Education—Japan, *Tokyo*
Pearson Education Malaysia, Pte. Ltd.
Pearson Education, *Upper Saddle River, New Jersey*

Ninth Edition

HUMAN DEVELOPMENT

Grace J. Craig

University of Massachusetts

Don Baucum

University of Alabama at Birmingham

Prentice
Hall

Upper Saddle River, New Jersey 07458

Brief Contents

Contents

15 MIDDLE ADULTHOOD: PHYSICAL AND COGNITIVE DEVELOPMENT

16 MIDDLE ADULTHOOD: PERSONALITY AND SOCIOCULTURAL DEVELOPMENT

Preface

The story of a human life—in any cultural context—is a rich and compelling drama. The systematic study of human development in context is a challenge for students and researchers alike. *Human Development*, Ninth Edition, draws from many fields (psychology, biology, sociology, anthropology, history, nursing, medicine, and public health, to name a few), to provide an up-to-date presentation of the key topics, issues, and controversies in the study of lifespan development.

In this edition of *Human Development*, I continue to be joined by Don Baucum, an experimental psychologist with clinical training, who draws on his own observations, his eclectic teaching experience, and an engaging writing style to help breathe life and voice into the narrative. We discovered in writing the previous edition that his expertise and mine as an applied developmental psychologist also with extensive teaching experience augment each other well, so Don is now my full co-author. Together, we attempt to provide a sound, often thought-provoking survey of contemporary developmental research and theory as well as applications to everyday life. Because this field is so broad, challenging, open-ended, and controversial, ample opportunities are included for students to consider a wide variety of perspectives and kinds of evidence. Students are encouraged to weigh the evidence against personal experience, and to develop an informed, critical perspective on how we come to be who and what we are as human beings and what each of us can expect in our years to come.

Student Diversity

Today's college students are more diverse than ever. A given classroom may have a cross-section of students who vary widely in age, ethnicity, personal experiences, and outlook. Today's students also vary in academic background, degree of exposure to the social sciences in particular, and career interests. Each of these factors, and more, create "filters" through which each individual perceives human development and life in general. Many students of human development will pursue a future in fields related to human service, including social work, education, nursing, counseling, various areas of psychology, and program administration. Some are already parents, many will become parents in the future; considerable practical advice about parenting is also included for this reason.

We believe that most students by far have a unique and potentially irresistible curiosity about how childhood, adolescence, and adulthood work. This text encourages that curiosity through its emphasis on diversity. *Human Development* presents people as they are in the context of culture and subculture, both within the United States and beyond. Rather than generalize from any one group of people, it makes a special effort to explain how developmental phenomena apply or relate to a wide range of peoples. The contemporary case studies and research efforts incorporated in the text reflect this variety. Hopefully, students will find themselves in the pages of this text, regardless of background, and yet at the same time escape the confines of ethnocentrism.

Chronological Organization

In the field of human development there is always the question of whether to organize developmental research and theory by topical chapters, such as biological, cognitive, language, social, and personality development, or to present child and adult development as it happens chronologically, emphasizing the holistic interrelationships. *Human Development* takes the latter approach and presents child and adult development primarily in chapters devoted to each of the traditional age divisions: the prenatal period, infancy, early childhood, middle childhood, adolescence, and young, middle, and older adulthood. The text opens with two chapters on perspectives on human development and its study, one on the interaction of heredity and environment, and one on prenatal development, and closes with one on death and dying. In between, each age range includes two chapters: one on physical and cognitive development, one on personality and sociocultural development. Given these necessary divisions, we remain alert throughout to the crucial importance of the complex interplay of the many different facets of development through which a *whole* person emerges.

Special Features and Study Aids

Throughout this text, we have woven cultural diversity and personal relevance into the ongoing narrative. Special boxed features extend this emphasis. *A Matter for Debate* explores controversies about human development and encourages thought and discussion. *In Theory, In Fact* focuses on popular concepts about development that are sometimes supported by research and sometimes not. Finally, *A Closer Look* examines important contemporary issues in development.

Within each chapter, the opener is a *Chapter Preview* that poses questions intended to stimulate interest in the main topics to be considered. Each major section of the chapter is followed by a brief *Content Check,* with *True-False* questions and a *Thinking Critically* question; answers and additional questions are provided on the Companion Website discussed below. Throughout, to enhance understanding, Tables present information such as brief summaries of contrasting views, additional terms, and current statistical data; Figures illustrate discussions of complex topics, research materials, and the like, and also present current statistical data in graphical form. The chapter then closes with a *Chapter Revisited,* which summarizes the main topics and issues while requiring that the reader return to the chapter for definitions and the like, followed by *Key Terms* listed in the order in which they appear in the chapter. Key terms are defined in the margins near where they appear; they are also collected in the comprehensive *Glossary.*

Supplements

For the Instructor

Instructor's Resource Manual with Test Item File: Created by Carolyn Meyer of Lake-Sumter Community College, this extensive resource contains chapter outlines, lecture topics, classroom activities, a list of videos available from outside sources and handouts. The Test Item File includes over 1,500 questions in multiple choice, fill-in, short answer and essay formats that test for factual, applied and conceptual understanding of the material presented in each chapter.

Prentice Hall Test Manager: One of the most popular test-generating software programs on the market, Test Manager is available in Windows and Macintosh formats and contains a Gradebook, Online Network Testing and many tools to help you edit and create tests. This program comes with full technical support and telephone "request-a-test" service.

Prentice Hall Color Overhead Transparencies for Human Development: Available in acetate form, or as downloads from our Companion Website, these transparencies add visual appeal to your lectures.

Media Support for Human Development, Ninth Edition

Human Development, Ninth Edition Companion Website at www.prenhall. com/craig: Written by Don Baucum, this online study guide allows students to review each chapter's material, take practice tests that provide immediate feedback, and link to chapter specific web resources to research topics for course projects. Each chapter includes Objectives, Multiple Choice Questions, True-False Questions, Fill-In-The-Blanks Questions, Essays, Web Destinations, and Answers to each chapter's Content Checks.

***ContentSelect* Research Database:** Prentice Hall and EBSCO, the world leader in online journal subscription management, have developed a customized research database for students of psychology. This database provides access to the text of many popular periodicals and peer-reviewed psychology publications. For more information about *ContentSelect,* contact your local Prentice Hall representative.

Online Course Management: For professors interested in using the Internet and online course management in their courses, Prentice Hall offers fully customizable online courses in WebCT, BlackBoard and Pearson's *Course Compass* powered by BlackBoard. Contact your local Prentice Hall Representative or visit www.prenhall.com/demo for more information

For the Student
Study Guide: Written by Carolyn Meyer of Lake-Sumter Community College, this student workbook helps students master the core concepts in each chapter. Every chapter includes a Chapter Outline, Key Terms and Concepts, Key Names, a Pre-test, a Programmed Review, a Post-test, Essay Questions, and an Answer Key.

Psychology on the Internet: Evaluating Online Resources: This "hands-on" Internet tutorial features Web sites related to psychology and general information about using the Internet for research. This supplement is available FREE when packaged with the text and helps students capitalize on all the resources that the World Wide Web has to offer.

Supplementary Textbooks Available for Packaging
The supplementary textbooks are available in specially discounted packages with the textbook or as stand-alone supplements:

Human Development in Multicultural Contexts: *A Book of Readings* by Michele A. Paludi: Designed to be used with a text on Human Development, this collection of readings demonstrates how culture affects development across the lifespan. Each section begins with an introduction and is followed by readings carefully selected and excerpted with the undergraduate in mind.

Acknowledgments

As was true of previous editions, the ninth edition of *Human Development* reflects the contributions of many individuals, beginning with people of all ages that Don and I have met in classrooms, clinical encounters, and interviews; students and research assistants; colleagues, teachers, and mentors; family members and friends. Many of their experiences, ideas, and insights are reflected in this text.

I specifically would like to thank reviewers who read various earlier editions of this text and helped in improving them: Dorothy J. Shedlock, State University of New York, Oswego; Bradley J. Caskey, University of Wisconsin, River Falls; John S. Klein, Castleton State University, Frank R. Asbury, Valdosta State University; Rick Caulfield, University of Hawaii at Manoa; Sander M. Latts, University of Minnesota; Pamela Manners, Troy State University; and Jack Thomas, Harding University.

I would also like to thank the reviewers who read the eighth edition and made helpful suggestions for the ninth edition, many of which are incorporated and constitute distinct improvements. Special thanks also go to our primary researcher, Albertina Navarro-Rios, for her steadfast and conscientious search for basic and applied research. She was consistently juggling several topics at once to keep pace with a demanding schedule. Thanks in no small part to her diligence, together with her insight and thoughtful suggestions, this edition strongly reflects the newer research trends and the contemporary topics of debate.

At Prentice Hall, I would like to thank our principal editor, Jennifer Gilliland, who led the general planning and maintained faith in the final product. Our development editor, Marilyn Miller, performed minor miracles in the early stages of this edition, working with Don on forging a new, more accessible reading style. Her ideas, sense of humor, suggestions, and careful editing got this project off the ground and flowing. Our production editor, Bruce Hobart, deserves special thanks for his long hours of coordinating, juggling, and managing manuscript, artwork, photos, and page proofs, and keeping us all on schedule. For the attractive and student-friendly design and appearance of the text I am grateful to Laura Gardner and Ximena Tamvakopoulos, who created and managed the design, and Terry Stratford, who researched the photos. Finally, Fran Russello deserves special credit for untangling problems, smoothing rough spots, and pulling together the final stages of this project.

GJC

HUMAN DEVELOPMENT

PERSPECTIVES AND RESEARCH METHODS

1

3

CHAPTER PREVIEW

Do you know:

1. The difference between *society* and *culture*?
2. The difference between *socialization* and *enculturation*?
3. What's involved in being *scientific*?
4. That development is always a result of *heredity* and *environment* in interaction?
5. The relationship between *maturation* and *learning*?
6. How what it means to be a *child*, an *adolescent*, or an *adult* differs historically and across present-day cultures?
7. That the makeup of *families* differs historically and across present-day cultures?
8. The advantages and disadvantages of *case studies*, *observational techniques*, *surveys*, *psychological tests*, and *correlation*?
9. The basic research designs used to study developmental *change*?
10. What's involved in conducting a valid and meaningful *experiment*?
11. That there is a strict *ethical code* that must be followed when conducting research with human participants?

These are the main topics of Chapter 1.

omplex and rich, full of quest and challenge, a human life is the product of many strands—the blending of the biological and the experiential, the intertwining of thought and feeling. Consider the people in the picture of a fishing village that opens this chapter. Who are these people? What shapes and molds their lives? What are they thinking and feeling as they go about their day? What are the commonalities of maturation and experience in infancy, childhood, or adulthood that link their lives with people around the world?

Development refers to the changes over time in body and in behavior due both to biology and to experience. Just how much of who and what we are is "built in" and how much is a result of the things that happen to us? How and in what fashion do the many influences interact and help mold us? Conversely, how do we as individuals help determine our development? And how do our relationships with *significant others*—the people who are important to us—influence who and what we become? These questions and a great many more are the concerns of the study of human development.

Development begins with conception and continues throughout life, although developmental change is typically more obvious and more rapid in the earlier years. This is the basic reason why the developmental "periods" and the age ranges that define them, as presented in Table 1–1, are relatively short in the earlier years and become progressively longer as development continues. Note too that the periods of the lifespan given in the table apply best to indus-

development The changes over time in the physical structure, thought, or behavior of a person as a result of both biological and environmental influences.

Table 1-1 The Human Life Span

Note that some age ranges vary considerably across cultures (see text, p. 380) and some vary according to an individual's biology (e.g., adolescence as defined by entrance into puberty, p. 385).

Prenatal Period—Conception to birth

Infancy—Birth to 18–24 months of age

Toddlerhood—12–15 months to 2–3 years of age

Early Childhood—2–3 years to 5–6 years of age

Middle Childhood—6 years to about 12 years of age

Adolescence—about 12 years to 18–21 years of age

Young Adulthood—18–21 years to 40 years of age

Middle Adulthood—40 years to 60–65 years of age

Older Adulthood—60–65 years of age to death

trialized peoples. For example, the table shows that "adolescence" is an extended period that can actually go well beyond ages 18 to 21, and "older adulthood" does not begin until after age 60 or 65 years. However, among some peoples of the world where lengthy education isn't necessary and economic life is demanding, adolescence may be a relatively short period that begins with the attainment of puberty and ends perhaps a few years later. Similarly, in places where earning a livelihood is physically demanding and good nutrition and medical care aren't easily available, older age may occur as early as 45. Thus, the periods and age ranges are not *universally* applicable. Table 1–1 simply supplies an introductory framework used by developmentalists for examining lifespan development. In addition, the table provides the overall organization of this text.

The goal of this text is to examine developmental trends, principles, and processes across many disciplines. We look at the developing human organism with attention to the biological, evolutionary, anthropological, sociological, and psychological forces that directly or indirectly influence development. We pay special attention to family ties and other relationships, because they help define who we are and how we relate to the world around us. Whether sensitive and fragile, sturdy and supportive, stormy and anxious, or quietly comfortable and comforting, relationships normally exert a strong influence on development. Our view is that humans are first and foremost *social* creatures.

At the same time, of course, we consider how people interpret and react to social and other forces, from the perspective that each individual actively participates in how her or his development proceeds. As beings who are at least potentially capable of complex, abstract thinking, we are not simply pawns in a game; we are active participants who help shape our "game." Again, think about the people in the fishing village. They are in part a product of the environment they grew up in, and most of the time they work together in harmony and contribute to the good of the group. At the same time, they are individuals with personal feelings and desires, and they make at least some of their own choices every day. Life isn't always harmonious either—in virtually any group of people, there will at times be disagreements attributable to those personal feelings and desires.

Key Issues in the Study of Human Development

Development in Context

Development is deeply embedded in **context,** which refers to the immediate and extended settings in which it occurs. In the pages that follow, we repeatedly encounter the significance of the social context from perspectives such as family, **society,** and **culture.** Society normally refers to an organized group of interacting people, which can be relatively small or large—a village or a community or a city, a state or a nation. Culture has many possible definitions, but there is general agreement that it refers to the beliefs, norms, practices, language, ethnicity, and other aspects of personal and group identity these interacting people share. Thus, we might say that an individual "belongs" to a society and is "immersed" in a culture. However, such distinctions are somewhat arbitrary; in the larger sense, society and culture are inextricably intertwined.

Developmental Domains

For practical reasons, the human growth and change that occurs within each period are divided into four major *domains* or areas: (1) physical growth and development, (2) cognitive and language development, (3) personality development, and (4) sociocultural development. Development in the **physical domain** involves changes in shape and size, plus changes in brain structures, sensory capabilities, and motor skills. Development in the **cognitive domain** includes acquiring skills in perceiving, thinking, reasoning, problem solving, and the like, as well as the intricate development and use of language. Development in the **personality domain** includes acquiring relatively stable and enduring traits and a sense of self as an individual. Finally, the **sociocultural domain** is comprised of *socialization,* which occurs as we are deliberately taught and trained by parents and others about how to fit in and function in society (with or without formal schooling), and *enculturation,* which occurs as we learn about our culture more or less on our own, by observing and absorbing rather than being taught (Segall, Dasen, Berry, & Poortinga, 1999). As noted by Segall and colleagues, much of what we learn involves socialization and enculturation in interaction. An example they give is language, in that children acquire language skills in part through direct teaching and in part through spontaneous efforts on their own part. It is because of this frequent interaction that the term "sociocultural" is the choice in this text.

Domains are arbitrary segments of development used by developmentalists to take a closer look. Real people are "whole" creatures and not at all compartmentalized. Changes and continuities in each domain interact with other aspects of development in other domains. A baby boy who has just learned to stand (a motor skill) sees the world from a new angle (perceptual skills), may feel proud of his new skill (an emotional event or personality accomplishment), and may well interact with others in new ways (social skills). Similarly, a school girl's cognitive development is interwoven with her social development in many respects, leading to the progressively more sophisticated thinking and reasoning necessary to understanding her physical and sociocultural world. Development is not piecemeal; it is *holistic.*

context The particular setting or situation in which development occurs; the "backdrop" for development.

society An organized group of interacting people.

culture The beliefs, norms, practices, language, ethnicity, and other aspects of personal and group identity shared by interacting people.

physical domain Segment of development involving changes in shape and size, brain structure, sensory capabilities, and motor skills.

cognitive domain Segment of development that includes acquiring skills in perceiving, thinking, reasoning, problem solving, as well as the intricate development and use of language.

personality domain Segment of development that includes acquiring relatively stable and enduring traits and a sense of self as an individual.

sociocultural domain Segment of development comprised of socialization and enculturation.

The Scientific Study of Human Development

In all likelihood, our early ancestors asked questions about development in trying to understand themselves and their children, just as we do today. In past millennia, people found answers in custom, tradition, myth, and folklore. But as far as we know, none of these earlier humans actually *studied* development scientifically, putting the truth of their beliefs to the test. Scientific inquiry is conducted as objectively and systematically as possible. Twentieth-century researchers paved the way in developing specific procedures to achieve objective, verifiable evidence. The latter part of the chapter is devoted to the procedures that make 21st century developmental science possible.

It isn't easy to be objective and systematic when we study ourselves. In contrast to the biological, behavioral, or ecological study of earthworms or frogs, when we study ourselves we are both subject and object. We tend to be influenced by our own values, attitudes, and beliefs. We may make the mistake of seeing people who are like us in a more positive light and misunderstand the behavior people who are unlike us and label it as curious, bizarre, primitive, or ignorant. One of the most important things in studying people is to take an open mind and use systematic, objective procedures that overcome any **ethnocentric bias.**

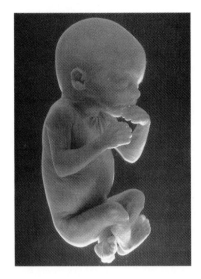

The first stage in the lifespan is prenatal development.

Developmental Processes

Some developmental processes, such as growth during the prenatal period or the onset of puberty or the arrival of gray hair, are primarily biological. Evidence suggests that early language development is also primarily biological, as noted later in the chapter (see also Chapter 5). Other aspects of development, such as learning calculus, navigating the Internet, or acquiring a taste for sushi, may depend mainly on experience. Acquiring the particular speech patterns, vocabulary, and "accent" of the people you grow up with or learning a second language are additional examples of development influenced primarily by experience.

Most development throughout the lifespan, however, is a result of successive *interactions* between biology and experience. Development in general cannot be neatly categorized as primarily biological or experiential; rather, it involves an ongoing, dynamic interplay between the two basic sets of causes. Perhaps, for example, you were born with a certain intellectual potential based on the specific nature of your central nervous system; that is, your biological makeup established a range within which your intelligence might eventually fall. But how intelligent you actually are today is also a function of your childhood nutrition, your experiences at home and at school, and many subtler experiential factors. As another example, perhaps you were born with a certain personality tendency such as shyness or gregariousness. Your present personality, however, is also a function of your lifelong interactions with other people, the sense of self you began to acquire in infancy, the sociocultural contexts you grew up in, and much more.

The days are past when theorists focused on single components of development to the exclusion of everything else, as noted earlier. Similarly, developmentalists no longer argue over whether aspects of cognition and personality are *either* a function of biology *or* a function of experience. Language development clearly occurs as a function of built-in capabilities interacting with experience: All normal human infants are "prewired" with the capacity for

ethnocentric bias   The tendency to assume that our own beliefs, perceptions, customs, and values are correct and normal and that those of others are inferior or abnormal.

acquiring a language. They spontaneously go through a sequence that includes selectively listening to speech sounds, making simple speech sounds, and eventually decoding the words and sentences they hear being used around them (Pinker, 1997). Obviously, however, they must have exposure to a particular language if they are to produce actual words and sentences that others can understand. Infants also spontaneously show emotions such as anger or distress, but they must eventually learn how to handle their emotions within their particular culture—an observation by Donald Hebb (1966) that is particularly noteworthy because it was made more than a third of a century ago.

What theorists do still debate (at times hotly) is *how much* and in *what way* a given characteristic or behavior is a result of biology or experience. Using intelligence as an example, some theorists attribute intellectual ability to biology to the tune of as much as 75 to 80% (see Chapter 9). At the other extreme, some believe that only about 25% is biologically based. So the controversies of the past aren't entirely dead; they remain, albeit with a different emphasis.

Heredity and Environment   Today the issue of biology versus experience is more often cast in the context of *heredity* and *environment*. In Chapter 3, we focus more specifically on genetic factors that might underlie and predispose and therefore set the stage for development, in interaction with specific effects of the individual's physical and social environment. Heredity-oriented theorists assume a power role of underlying biological structures, citing evidence from experiments with animals and statistical procedures with humans to support their case. In addition, they point out that specific genes underlying development and behavior have been identified, emphasizing those that are known to cause conditions such as mental retardation. On the other hand, environmental explanations focus on an individual's experiences pertaining to thinking and reasoning, plus environmental factors such as nutrition and health—each of which can also contribute to mental retardation. As noted earlier, nowadays each view acknowledges the other. Heredity and environment interact, but theorists still disagree over the relative contributions of each and the manner of their interaction. The position they take on this question determines the direction and nature of their research.

The third stage in the lifespan is toddlerhood.

Maturation and Learning   These terms generally refer to the processes of change that act independently or together. Terms like *growth*, *maturation*, and *aging* refer to heavily biological processes. *Learning* is change over time related to practice or experience. When development is considered in terms of maturation and learning, the emphasis often shifts to *timing*. For example, how does skeletal/muscular development, which is biologically based, interact with practice, which is experiential? In particular, what kinds of practice, when, and how frequently result in optimal development of musculature and motor abilities? Similar questions arise in considering cognitive and personality development, where neurological and hormonal maturation interact with experience. How might the individual's experiences during childhood affect the onset of puberty, a biological process? Or how is the biological event of menopause (cessation of menstrual periods due to hormonal changes) affected by a woman's lifestyle, if at all? What are the relative contributions of maturation and learning? Also, are there "critical" periods during which maturation and learning must interact to produce optimal development? Questions like these arise at many points in later chapters.

Critical Versus Sensitive Periods   The question of how maturation interacts with learning naturally leads to a related question: Are there **critical periods** during which certain types of development *must* occur or else will *never* occur? Consider the effects of certain diseases during pregnancy (Chapter 4). If a pregnant woman who lacks immunity for rubella (German measles) is exposed to the virus about 2 months after conception, severe birth anomalies such as deafness or even miscarriage are likely. However, if the same woman is exposed to rubella 6 months after conception, the virus won't affect her developing baby.

Another example comes from the animal world. There is a critical time span several hours after birth during which goslings become "bonded" to the mother goose simply by being in her presence. This is known as *imprinting* (Chapter 6). The goslings will not imprint before or after that critical period. Might there be a similar critical period during which human infants become emotionally attached to their caregivers? More generally, do we have critical periods for acquiring certain types of skills and behaviors?

Theorists disagree. Despite recent evidence indicating that early experiences have a decisive and permanent impact on the architecture of the brain directly and indirectly (Shore, 1997; see also Ramey & Ramey, 1998), the details of the timing are complex. It is often more accurate to think in terms of **sensitive** or **optimal periods** during which certain types of learning and development occur best and most efficiently, but not exclusively. For example, if you acquire a second language during childhood you have a much better chance of using it like a native speaker than if you acquire it after adolescence. Also, you will learn some aspects of the language more quickly and easily as a child than you will later in life. You *can* learn a second language at any time in your life, however, and with enough effort you can learn to speak it almost like a native.

There clearly is such a thing as *readiness*, though, which refers to reaching a maturational point at which a specific behavior can be learned; before that maturational level is achieved, the behavior cannot be learned. For example, no amount of special training will enable a 3-month-old to walk without support; at this level of maturation the infant simply lacks the capability for balance and the necessary musculature for coordinated movement of the legs under the weight of the child's body.

The precise nature of the timing of human development is still not known. What periods are optimal for particular behaviors remain a major focus of research.

Table 1–2 reviews the key issues discussed in this section.

Table 1-2   Key Issues in Human Development

Heredity and Environment

To what extent do specific genetic factors set the stage for development, and to what extent do specific factors in the physical and social environment affect development?

Maturation and Learning

How does maturation, which is biologically based, interact with learning, which is experiential, to shape development?

Critical Versus Sensitive Periods

Are there critical periods during which certain types of development must occur or else will never occur?

critical period   The only span of time when a particular environmental factor can have an effect.

sensitive or optimal periods   The times during which certain types of learning and development occur best and most efficiently, but not exclusively.

CONTENT CHECK
KEY ISSUES IN THE STUDY OF HUMAN DEVELOPMENT

True–False (answers are on the Companion Website)

1. The definition of developmental periods such as childhood and adolescence are universal across cultures.
2. Socialization involves deliberate teaching; enculturation involves learning on our own.
3. Scientific research on human development began in the 1500s.
4. In each developmental domain, heredity alone determines most of human development and behavior.
5. With regard to timing, most human development is better thought of in terms of sensitive periods than critical periods.

Thinking Critically

What do we mean when we say that development is holistic and always occurs in context?

Historical and Contemporary Perspectives on Human Development

In understanding today's developmental perspectives, it's helpful to have some background on where they came from. In this section we trace the origins of childhood, adolescence, adulthood, and family, terms that many of us simply take for granted. In actuality, the way each has been viewed has varied considerably historically and each still varies considerably both across and within cultures.

Images of Childhood

Conceptualizations of childhood and attitudes toward children have varied a great deal throughout recorded history and beyond.

Relatively little is known about prehistoric, primarily agrarian civilizations' attitudes toward children (as opposed to adults), although the agrarian societies of today's Africa can provide some likely parallels. As reviewed by Çiğdem Kağitçibaşi (1996), such societies view children as co-workers and material contributors. At an early age children are assigned household chores and errands, with their workload increasing as they grow older. As early as middle childhood, a substantial portion of a child's day is devoted to work. Strict obedience is also stressed, with an eye toward children's safety in the often-hazardous environments of rural Africa. Perhaps, of necessity, this view of childhood was more typical in prehistoric and early historic agrarian times.

More is known about childhood in some ancient Western civilizations. At least we know what leaders, crusaders, and moral preachers had to say about presumed popular attitudes of the times. Some societies viewed children as material possessions and little more. In parts of ancient Greece, strict obedience and harsh physical punishment were the norm; in ancient Rome, killing undesirable or otherwise unwanted children—or selling them into servitude—was common (deMause, 1974). Parents were free to exploit their children in whatever ways they wished, child sexual abuse was rampant, and children tended to have no rights. Although child-killing was finally outlawed in Christian Europe in the 12th century AD (deMause, 1974), it was not until the end of the Middle Ages (about 1500 AD) that general attitudes toward children began to change significantly.

Along these lines, some 40 years ago Philippe Ariès published a now-classic and controversial book on childhood in medieval and early modern France that was translated into English as *Centuries of Childhood: A Social History of Family Life* (1962). In it, he garnered evidence from paintings and from French memoirs and other documents and concluded flatly, "In medieval society the idea of childhood did not exist" (p. 128). Ariès acknowledged that the French word for childhood was in use long before that—in the 12th century—but he argued that it was used inconsistently and did not connote the lifespan period it does today. Particularly striking in Ariès' opinion were paintings in which children were consistently shown in full adult attire, which seemed to support the idea that after age 6 or 7 they were regarded as "miniature adults." They were expected to work, dined with adults, participated in adult conversations, told and were told adult jokes, and engaged in sexual play (Ariès, 1962; see also Plumb, 1971).

Were Ariès and his supporters correct in their conclusions? Or were they interpreting too much from the artistic styles of the day? The consensus that has formed in the years since is that he markedly overstated the case (e.g., see Pollock, 1983, 1987; Cunningham, 1996). Although there is no doubt that European children were treated differently in the Middle Ages than now, it has been well documented that they were indeed recognized as dissimilar to adults in many respects and that many of Ariès's conclusions were in error. For example, as Hugh Cunningham pointed out (1996), medieval literature contains numerous references to developmental stages during childhood as well as "childrearing advice" to parents.

Either way, scholars agree that after 1500 childhood began to be considered a period of innocence, much as it is today in many cultures—notwithstanding the substantial differences among societies in the extent to which children are expected to work, play, and go to school. Especially in Western societies, parents tried to protect children from the excesses and evils of the adult world. Children were seen less as anonymous members of the clan or community and more as individuals within families. By the 18th century this attitude had gained broad support at least in the upper middle classes, with children assigned a special status of their own (Ariès, 1989; Gelis, 1989).

They were however still viewed by many as "assets," exploited and made to work, and often subjected to severe corporal punishment. In the United States, for example, not until the late 19th century did children gain special rights through the advent of child labor laws and compulsory schooling (Kett, 1977). Laws defining child abuse and limiting the use of corporal punishment came even later. Nevertheless, even today, some forms of corporal punishment are still widely used. In the United States some 80% of parents spank their children at least occasionally (Murray, 1996a). Meanwhile, several nations have outlawed *any* use of corporal punishment with children (Murray, 1996b).

Childhood in the 21st Century At the beginning of this century, the shift continues toward more humane attitudes toward children and child-rearing practices, with legal protection for children's rights now in place throughout most of the world. Even so, conceptualizations of childhood and what is appropriate in childrearing still vary considerably across cultures.

By the 18th century, children were seen as persons in their own right, with their own interests, as illustrated in John Singleton Copley's painting *Boy with Bow and Arrow*.

For example, Japanese children up to 3 years of age tend to sleep with their parents, grandparents, or siblings (Nugent, 1994). This sleeping arrangement appears to have evolved as part of a socialization process that attempts to foster a close relationship between children and their parents and others and reflects a culture that values *collective* harmony. In **collectivist** cultures, which exist in varying degree in many parts of the world, the group takes priority over the individual. Consequently, socialization and enculturation include an emphasis upon learning to belong to the group at levels ranging from the family to the local community to the society or nation as a whole. Cooperation is stressed over competition. Group achievement is stressed over individual achievement, as is the good of the group over the individual, and self-sacrifice is often taken for granted. In all, collectivist cultures foster *interdependence*, which has strong implications for many aspects of personality development— such as personal identity and a sense of self in childhood and beyond.

In contrast, by age 3, U.S. children are likely to be sleeping alone in a separate room—an arrangement that promotes individuality and helps children adapt to a society that values *independence* (Nugent, 1994). **Individualist** cultures such as the United States, which are predominantly Western, stress socialization noticeably different from that of collectivist cultures. Competition tends to predominate over cooperation, and personal achievement is typically valued more highly than group achievement. Overall, individual freedom and choice receive strong emphasis. Yet collectivist cultures and individualist cultures are not exactly "opposites." Getting along with others and becoming a productive member of society are considered extremely important in each—a theme we return to in later chapters.

Economic factors affect attitudes toward childhood in different cultures. More affluent families tend to have fewer children. With fewer children, parents are under less pressure to provide for the basics and therefore have more time to enjoy and educate their children. Those societies with proportionally more children logically, experience pressures to put children in the workforce early rather than keep them in school. Figure 1–1 shows the percentages of the population under age 15 for selected nations.

A more extreme example of childhood's still not being a special and protected time is the forced conscription of hundreds of thousands of children to fight in the brutal ethnic wars that have raged in parts of Africa for more than twenty years as of this writing (see "A Closer Look," p. 15).

So what is childhood? What are children like and how should they be treated? The best answer to each question is "it depends." Consider a few of the culturally based proverbs collected by Jesús Palacios (1996), which mirror some of the conflicting opinions of differing peoples (Table 1–3).

Images of Adolescence

For centuries, popular literature—including that of the Greeks, Romans, Spanish, and Chinese, has referred to an intermediate and relatively short period between childhood and adulthood. Drama, poetry, and fiction have expressed the intemperance and excesses of "youth." *Prolonged* adolescence, as a distinct and major period of development, is a much more recent phenomenon and is largely limited to industrialized peoples. In the 18th, 19th, and early 20th centuries, when unskilled labor was in great demand, most youths became adults quickly and blended into adult life as soon as they were capable of adult work. Then, after World War I, advancing technology in nations around the world, along with rapid social change, made it necessary for young people to stay in

collectivist (culture) A culture where the group takes precedence over the individual. Cooperation and group achievement are stressed over competition and individual achievement.

individualist (culture) A culture where competition predominates over cooperation and personal achievement is typically valued more highly than group achievement; individual freedom and choice receive strong emphasis.

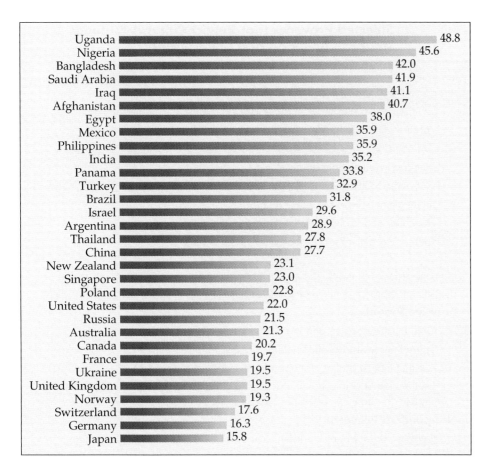

Uganda	48.8
Nigeria	45.6
Bangladesh	42.0
Saudi Arabia	41.9
Iraq	41.1
Afghanistan	40.7
Egypt	38.0
Mexico	35.9
Philippines	35.9
India	35.2
Panama	33.8
Turkey	32.9
Brazil	31.8
Israel	29.6
Argentina	28.9
Thailand	27.8
China	27.7
New Zealand	23.1
Singapore	23.0
Poland	22.8
United States	22.0
Russia	21.5
Australia	21.3
Canada	20.2
France	19.7
Ukraine	19.5
United Kingdom	19.5
Norway	19.3
Switzerland	17.6
Germany	16.3
Japan	15.8

Figure 1-1   Percentage of Children Younger Than Age 15, Selected Nations

Source: Britannica Book of the Year, 1997.

school or other training longer—therein causing them to remain to a large degree financially and psychologically dependent on their parents. Industrialization and the extended education it required for many created adolescence as it is known today. The view of adolescence as a separate period of dependence, rather than self-sufficiency, was noted by G. Stanley Hall as early as 1904. By the mid-20th century other theorists were drawing special attention to this period (e.g., see Clark, 1957; also Erikson, 1950, 1963).

Adolescents tend to be highly sensitive to the society around them—its unwritten rules, its values, its political and economic tensions. They form plans and expectations about their own future, and these expectations depend in part on the cultural and historical context in which they live. For example, Western adolescents who spend their childhood in a period of economic expansion, when jobs are plentiful and family incomes high, expect to find similar conditions when they enter the job market. Expecting their standard of living to be at least as high as their parents', they may be unprepared to accept a lower standard of living if economic conditions worsen when they enter adulthood (Greene, 1990).

Economic and cultural conditions can make adolescence a brutally short prelude to independence, or they can cause prolonged dependence on the family. In 19th century Ireland, for example, potato famines led to widespread poverty and suffering. Young people stayed home because their labor was needed to help the family survive, so their progress toward adult independence was delayed. By contrast, in the United States the Great Depression of the 1930s conferred unexpected responsibilities on young people—adolescents had to grow up as quickly as possible. Many young people took on adult tasks and entered the job market sooner than they might have otherwise.

The sixth stage in the lifespan is adolescence.

Table 1-3 Selected Proverbs that Reflect Cultural Attitudes Toward Childhood and Childrearing

The following are a few of Palacios' proverbs that concern parental attitudes toward childhood and characteristics of children:

"Children are a perpetual millstone around the neck" (Japanese)

"Parents with three children have a happy life" (Japanese)

"You can't put an old head on young shoulders" (Finnish)

"Young dogs think only about playing" (French)

"Out of the mouths of babes come words of wisdom" (Polish)

"Small pitchers have big ears" (English)

"The child who is always led will never walk alone" (Finnish)

"There is no better teacher than time" (Rumanian)

(pp. 82–83)

Palacios also noted that many more childrearing proverbs exist that emphasize punishment than nonpunitive alternatives. Here's a sample of each:

Punitive Proverbs

"Gold must be beaten and the child scourged" (Hebrew)

"Spare the rod and spoil the child" (international)

"A pitiful mother makes a scabby (nasty) daughter" (English)

"Treat the child you love with the rod; treat the child you hate with another cake" (Korean)

Nonpunitive Proverbs

"If you want your pupils to listen to you, forget about the rod" (Rumanian)

"Wine and children must be raised with care" (Spanish)

(pp. 86–87)

Source: Palacios, 1996.

In brief, the social and historical context of development is as crucial to the outcome of adolescence as are individual differences (Jessor, 1993). Just as children do, adolescents come of age in a particular "developmental niche" (Chapter 3) that affects every aspect of their lives, from fads and fashion to economics and educational opportunity, leisure time, health, and nutrition. The developmental niche defines what adolescence is.

Images of Adulthood

In industrialized nations the adult years account for approximately three-quarters of the life span. Again somewhat arbitrarily and with the usual disclaimers about differences both across and within cultures, we distinguish among three age periods: young adulthood (the 20s and 30s), middle adulthood (the 40s and 50s), and later adulthood (age 60 or 65 and up). Age guidelines, however, do not always reflect how individuals see themselves with regard to adulthood. Socioeconomic status, rural or urban setting, ethnic background, historical periods, wars, financial depression, and other life events strongly influence the definitions, expectations, and pressures of adulthood just as they influence childhood and adolescence.

A CLOSER LOOK

WHEN WAR INTERRUPTS CHILDHOOD

War usually has devastating effects on all concerned, but its effects on children are especially tragic. Many children are killed as innocent bystanders, many are instead orphaned and may wind up starving and sick, alone or in often ill-equipped refugee camps. Many are also subjected to sexual abuse. As noted by Michael Wessells (1997), citing an extensive study funded by the United Nations and headed by Graca Machel, as of the mid-1990s there were 27.4 million refugees and 30 million displaced persons; *half* were children.

Other boys and girls find themselves involved in fighting the war. Increasingly, as noted by Neil Boothby and Christine Knudsen (2000) in a *Scientific American* report on the changing face of war, children are serving as soldiers—to an extent unprecedented in the last millennium. Some are conscripted; others choose to join as a means of survival. The younger girls and boys are used as "spies, porters, cooks and concubines" (p. 60), until they are old enough to take up weapons and go into combat.

The use of child soldiers is extensive. According to Jeffrey Boutwell and Michael Klare (2000), in another article in the same report, "More than 100 conflicts have erupted since 1990, about twice the number for previous decades. These wars have killed more than five million people . . . and left tens of millions of refugees and orphans" (p. 48). Based on statistics provided by Amnesty International, Boutwell and Klare list 50 regions around the world that currently are in conflict, in more than two-thirds of which underage soldiers are used—in several cases, children as young as 5 or 6, and in many cases children who have

not yet attained puberty. In all, again from the Machel study (Wessells, 1997), in the mid-1990s there were about 250,000 child soldiers worldwide. If Boothby and Knudsen were correct, that number is now even larger.

What happens to these children psychologically? Aside from obvious effects such as having to live with demoralization, depression, and a chronic sense of fear and uncertainty during wartime, numerous researchers have found high rates of *posttraumatic stress disorder* (PTSD) afterward in those who survive. For example, in a study of Palestinian children who had experienced war, it was found that almost three-fourths had at least mild PTSD symptoms and over one-third had moderate to severe symptoms.

PTSD, as defined in the *Diagnostic and Statistical Manual of Mental Disorders, 4th Edition (DSM-IV)* (American Psychiatric Association, 1994), is characterized by reexperiencing the horrors of an event such as war consciously or in dreams, also by amnesia or deliberate efforts to avoid thinking about the event. There are also disturbances such as insomnia, irritability, difficulty in concentrating, and hypervigilance (being constantly "watchful"). Studies of the aftereffects of war on children have also found various somatic (bodily) complaints, social withdrawal, attention problems, and anxiety (e.g., Mollica et al., 1997; Mollica, 2000). The symptoms may appear immediately afterward, or instead months or even years afterward (Sack, Him, & Dickason, 1999). PTSD may also persist for years (Almqvist & Brandell-Forsberg, 1997), with negative effects on function-

ing that can extend into adulthood (Ajdukovic & Ajdukovic, 1998). Fortunately, however, for most children PTSD gradually subsides over the years that follow (e.g., see Thabet & Vostanis, 2000).

PTSD and other disorders are not the only effects. Perhaps even more tragically, children may be left with bitterness and hatred toward the "enemy." Consider the following observations of Albanian children in post-war Kosovo, which is now purportedly "multiethnic" Albanian and Serbian even though many of the Serbs have left (*Newsweek*, 1999):

> With regard to Serbs leaving, a 7-year-old girl bragged, "Some went on their own, some we forced out."

> Having pulled out a toy pistol from under his T-shirt, a 9-year-old boy was asked by an adult what he intended to do with it. The boy's immediate reply: "Kill Serbs."

> A 15-year-old vows, "Everything [the Serbs] did to us, we will do to them."

The article also described how even small Albanian children were ganging up to throw rocks and shoot pellet guns at elderly Serbs, while screaming Serbo-Croatian curses they had learned from the Serb soldiers that had occupied Kosovo. For many such children in Kosovo and other areas around the world, hatreds born of war may last for life. In all likelihood, sooner or later these hatreds will lead to more wars.

For example, adults who do hard physical labor for their livelihood may reach their prime at age 30 and enter "old age" by the time they are 50. In contrast, in some professions, people need to develop mature analytic ability and self-confidence to reach their prime. Recognition and financial success may not come to them until they are in their 40s or early 50s, and their productivity may continue into their late 60s and beyond. In other professions, like computer and "dot-com" technology, success may come quickly but fade as younger individuals with mental and physical speed take over (Cole, 1999). Periods or stages in adulthood are also determined in part by socioeconomic status; the higher the person's social class, the more likely the person is to delay in moving from earlier stages to later ones.

Development in the Context of Changing Families

Attitudes about family size, structure, and function have changed considerably over the years. So too have the roles and expectations for family members. These roles help shape the development of the individual. For example, until the 1920s many U.S. families (and those around the world) were large, usually including members from three or more generations. Grandparents, parents, and children frequently lived under the same roof and did the same kind of work—an arrangement that still prevails in many parts of the world. Children were expected to stay close to home because their parents needed help in running the family farm, store, trade, or manufacturing concern. Parents had many children, not only to provide more helping hands but also because of the high child mortality rate—attributable primarily to infectious diseases for which there was at the time no cure.

As noted, in the United States and other industrialized nations today many children remain financially dependent on their parents into their 20s. In addition, the high cost of raising children to maturity, the widespread use of contraception, and the growing number of working women have resulted in smaller families. Parents, in turn, make greater and more extended investments in their children. To underline this point, Table 1–4 illustrates how the percentages of young adults living at home or in college dormitories changed from 1960 to 1995.

The attitudes, values, and expectations of children are linked to how they are reared. Even in the same culture, different families can have very different approaches. For example, the child-rearing practices of dual-income families are clearly affected by their social circumstances and their beliefs and values (Jordanova, 1989). If the mother of a large family works outside the home, older children often take care of their younger siblings. In such families children may learn many of their social roles, values, and competencies more from siblings than from parents. Ideally, the older children learn nurturant, responsible behavior, and the younger children tend to develop strong ties to their siblings

Table 1–4 Young Adults Living at Home or in College Dormitories, United States, 1960–1995

YEAR	Male NUMBER	Male PERCENT OF POPULATION	Female NUMBER	Female PERCENT OF POPULATION
1960	1,185,000	11	853,000	7
1970	1,129,000	9	829,000	7
1980	1,894,000	10	1,300,000	7
1985	2,685,000	13	1,661,000	8
1990	3,213,000	15	1,774,000	8
1995	3,166,000	15	1,759,000	8

Source: U.S. Census Bureau, 1997.

and a sense of competence among their peers. Family bonds and affiliation usually become stronger. Social historians of the 20th century have concluded that the small, close-knit, "nuclear" family with mother tending the home, father at work, and an average of 2.5 children is more myth than reality. It is not the norm. If it ever did exist as the norm in industrialized nations, it was only for a brief period in the 1950s (Coontz, 2000).

In sum, families develop their own identity and child-rearing patterns as a result of the historical context in which they live, the cultural contexts shaping them, and the ongoing developmental stages of their members. The form and function of a family exists because of sociocultural necessities and changes to adapt to changes in sociocultural necessities—as does the family itself.

CONTENT CHECK

**HISTORICAL AND CONTEMPORARY PERSPECTIVES
ON HUMAN DEVELOPMENT**

True–False (answers are on the Companion Website)

1. The professional consensus is that during medieval times children were treated as miniature adults.
2. The United States is primarily an individualist culture and Japan is primarily a collectivist culture.
3. Adolescence as a distinct and prolonged period did not exist prior to industrialization.
4. Both within and across cultures, most adults retire in their early to mid 60s.
5. In industrialized nations, the nuclear family is the norm.

Thinking Critically

If you were a child in the United States, would you rather have grown up 100 years ago or nowadays? Why?

Studying Human Development: Descriptive Approaches

The search for reliable, verifiable facts about human development is complex. What are the differences between the evidence of our own personal experience and the researcher's data? At what point does the researcher stop looking for more evidence? Both the casual observer and the researcher must decide what constitutes reliable evidence and when enough evidence has been gathered to support a conclusion. Personal experience can be useful and important, but it must be tested in a more systematic way before others are likely to believe it. In the social sciences, we rarely prove anything with absolute certainty. Nevertheless, if enough researchers gather evidence and reach similar conclusions, we become confident that the conclusions are correct.

In the remainder of the chapter, we discuss approaches researchers use in studying human development. First we examine approaches that primarily involve the observation and description of behavior. Then we explore experimental approaches, which go beyond description and attempt to determine what *causes* what in development and behavior. In both types of approaches, it is important to ask good questions and to observe carefully, systematically, and objectively.

Case Studies

Developmental theorists from the late 19th century to the mid-20th century often used an approach known as the **case study,** which involves compiling often large and intricate amounts of information on an individual, a family, or a community. Through a combination of interviews, observations, formal testing, and the like, considerable information can be obtained. This method is still popular today. The goal is to obtain as complete a picture as possible of an individual, a parent-child interaction, a patient-doctor interaction, a classroom climate, even a cultural event.

The earliest (and much simpler) case studies that took a developmental perspective were called **baby biographies.** Charles Darwin (1809–1882), for example, kept a daily record of his son's early development. Darwin's interest in development during infancy stemmed from his larger work on evolution; he thought that studying the developmental "evolution" of young children might provide insights into human evolution overall. Baby biographies typically focused on what might be called "mini-milestones," such as the ages at which infants first seemed to discover parts of the body such as hands and feet, and later the ages they first achieved creeping (on all fours with stomach and chest off the floor), sitting upright, and eventually walking. However, there were several major problems with this approach. For one, it was never certain whether the "firsts" were accurate or merely the first time the biographer noticed the behaviors. For another, the observations might be highly subjective—whether an infant actually first "recognized" something at a certain age could easily be misinterpreted.

For these reasons baby biographies were soon abandoned in favor of more thorough and systematic case studies. Viennese physician Sigmund Freud (1856–1939) was an early and avid proponent of case studies, which contributed heavily to his psychoanalytic theory (Chapter 2). Many other early personality theorists also relied on case studies because of the intricate detail and occasional insights they can provide. Case studies have also been used extensively in studying relatively rare mental and behavioral disorders; because of the small number of people who suffer from such disorders, other research approaches aren't feasible.

However, the intricate detail that case studies uncover is also a shortcoming. The task of sorting out the detail and making sense of it can be very time-consuming. It is also difficult to determine what causes what. For example, physical or sexual abuse or other emotional trauma during early childhood is almost always found in the case histories of adults with dissociative identity disorder, formerly known as multiple personality disorder (e.g., see Goodwin & Sachs, 1996; Hornstein & Putnam, 1996). Does this necessarily mean that child abuse *causes* multiple personalities within an individual? Maybe yes, maybe no; the evidence is inconclusive. Moreover, if a case can be made for one individual, does that necessarily generalize to all such individuals?

Partly because of these problems, case studies are used infrequently in modern developmental research. They do, however, remain important in modern clinical diagnosis and treatment, because they can provide a rich, descriptive picture of the changing and *whole* individual in a social-environmental context. A case history is almost always the first step for persons entering psychological

case study The compilation of often large and intricate amounts of information on an individual, family, or community through interviews, observations, and formal testing.

baby biography Recording mini-milestones of child development, such as the ages when the child discovers parts of the body, creeps, sits upright, or walks.

or psychiatric treatment. Case studies are also used frequently by anthropologists studying communities and by educational researchers studying the interplay of influences in classrooms.

Systematic Observation

Depending on the setting in which the research takes place, there are two general approaches to observing and describing behavior: **Naturalistic** or **field observation,** in which researchers go into everyday settings and observe and record behavior while being as unobtrusive as possible; and **laboratory observation,** in which researchers set up controlled situations designed to elicit the behavior of interest. Here's a hypothetical example. Suppose researchers are interested in how children play together and share (or don't share) toys. After videotaping the children at play, and having carefully defined the behaviors of interest, observers would then independently record instances of the behaviors and check their results against those of their colleagues to eliminate any errors or subjectivity. In the end the researchers would have an objective record of the target behavior as it naturally occurs, rather than behavior occurring under "artificial" conditions such as in a lab.

Or would they? Aside from practical problems (the behaviors of interest might not even occur), there's the real possibility that the mere presence of an observer—especially with a camera—changes things. Perhaps even young children will play differently when an adult is watching. It may be possible to observe children from the equivalent of a "duck blind" or through one-way mirrors, but such arrangements are often neither possible or effective. Unobtrusive observation is even more of a problem with older children and adults because of their greater self-consciousness. There are also potential ethical problems: While you are observing a group of children, what if one child starts hitting another child in a conflict over a toy? Should the observer intervene and perhaps lose a day's work? If such difficulties can be resolved, however, naturalistic observation can be a very useful method that unearths a rich body of information about what people do in real life.

In a laboratory setting, various techniques are used to elicit the behaviors under study, which can then be observed under highly controlled conditions. An example is the now-classic "strange situation" test devised by Mary Ainsworth and Bell (1970) to study the quality of infant-mother attachment (see Chapter 6). One at a time, infants experience the same events and in the same order: A stranger enters the room, the mother leaves and returns, and the stranger leaves and returns. The observers record the infants' reactions from behind a one-way mirror. Contrast these conditions with what might happen if you tried to study such behaviors in haphazard field settings such as people's homes. There you might have to wait for quite some time to see what the infant does when a stranger happens along, and it would be almost impossible to observe unobtrusively.

But do infants necessarily behave the same way in a homelike laboratory setting as they do in their actual homes? They probably do in research environments such as the strange situation test, but this may not be the case with all behaviors and across all age ranges. There is no way to be absolutely sure. Thus, there's always a trade-off between field and laboratory research, and each has its advantages and disadvantages. When interpreting developmental research, it's always necessary to consider the setting in which the research was conducted and evaluate the findings accordingly.

The eighth stage in the lifespan is middle adulthood.

naturalistic or field observation The method in which researchers go into everyday settings and observe and record behavior while being as unobtrusive as possible.

laboratory observation   The method in which researchers set up controlled situations designed to elicit the bahavior of interest.

The ninth stage in the lifespan is older adulthood.

questionnaire A paper-and-pencil method that asks questions about past or present behavior, attitudes, preferences, opinions, feelings, and so on.

survey A questionnaire administered to a large group.

representative sample A sample that accurately mirrors a population.

random sample A sample selected in such a way that any member of a population has an equal chance of being selected.

Questionnaires and Surveys

The "paper-and-pencil" method employed in **questionnaires** and **surveys** asks questions about past and present behavior, attitudes, preferences, opinions, feelings, and so forth. The distinction between the two approaches is one of scale: A questionnaire may be administered to one individual (typically as a part of a case study) or it may be administered to a large group of people—at which point we have a survey. On occasion, questionnaires and surveys are administered verbally as well, either in person, by phone (in which case they become interviews), or increasingly via the Internet.

Surveys, even ones on large *samples*, are only valuable if they accurately represent the views of the *population* in question. One way to have the best chance of getting a **representative sample** of, for example, all high school students in a city would be to select the sample at random from a list of all students. We might select the first participant at random, and then go through the list selecting every fifthteenth student after that. We would thus have a **random sample,** which is likely to be a representative one.

Most Internet surveys are notoriously inaccurate, as are surveys printed in popular magazines and collected from readers. These surveys are neither random nor representative. How might this be so? Because the respondents "select themselves" instead of being selected by a researcher, and it is quite possible that the people who choose to respond will differ in important ways from the people who don't.

The advantages of questionnaires and surveys are that the information can be objectively and efficiently tabulated, and—in the case of surveys—very large numbers of people can be assessed quickly. Obvious limitations are that the researcher gets only the information that respondents are willing to report and can remember accurately, without the little "distortions" and "revisions" human memory is subject to. It has long been known that people reconstruct memories in self-serving ways, also that memory is dependent upon a person's emotional state while the events were occurring.

A prominent example of the use of questionnaires and surveys is the National Household Survey on Drug Abuse (NHSDA), discussed in Chapter 12. The NHSDA is a confidential questionnaire administered annually by a division of the U.S. Department of Health and Human Services to thousands of people age 12 and over who live at home or in other noninstitutional settings. It is by far the best survey of its kind, providing much detail about drug users according to age, sex, race/ethnicity, educational level, and employment status. Yet the numbers tend to be on the low side. Drug abuse is generally undesirable and largely illegal, which means that some respondents who use or abuse drugs won't tell the truth no matter what assurances they are given as to confidentiality. A related problem, also characteristic of surveys in general, is that not all of the people who are selected to fill out the questionnaire agree to participate (typically about 20% refuse on the NHSDA), and, as a result, more "nonusers" may be included in the results. It each case, drug use might be sharply underestimated.

Psychological Testing

Intelligence testing is frequently used in developmental research. As presented in Chapter 9, it basically involves administering questions and problems that assess an individual's intelligence quotient (IQ)—an approximate measure of current intellectual functioning. Personality tests are also sometimes used in developmental contexts. Personality-related testing with children often takes the form of checklists filled out by parents or other caregivers. Word-association exercises and sentence-completion tests can be used directly with children. For example, children might be asked to complete a thought, such as "My father always . . ."

"Projective" tests are sometimes employed as well: Children might be shown a series of ambiguous pictures and asked to interpret, react to, analyze, or arrange them so as to construct a story. It is assumed that the children will project their thoughts, attitudes, and feelings as they respond. For example, in one study 4-year-olds participated in a game called the bears' picnic. The experimenter told a series of stories involving a family of teddy bears. The child was then handed one of the bears and invited to complete the story (Mueller & Tingley, 1990).

Three considerations should be kept in mind in interpreting findings based on psychological testing. First, tests should be *reliable*: They should yield similar scores from one testing occasion to the next. Second, tests should have good *validity*: They actually measure what they are supposed to measure. Third, the best psychological tests are *standardized*, which means that they have been administered to representative samples of people to establish *norms* to which an individual's responses can be compared. Standardization also includes the provision of instructions and procedures that allow the tests to be administered in the same way every time.

If a test isn't reliable, valid, and standardized, there is no good way to know what the resulting data mean. This is why the American Psychological Association requires that such information be included with standardized tests. Developmental researchers, in turn, tend to use tests that have been shown to be highly reliable and valid.

Developmental Research Designs

Because development is a dynamic and continuous process, developmental studies—in contrast to other types of research—often focus on change over time. How do researchers gather data about developmental change? There are three general approaches, as illustrated in Figure 1–2.

The Longitudinal Design   In a **longitudinal design,** a single group of individuals is studied repeatedly at different points in the lifespan. Researchers might track development in areas such as language acquisition, cognition and intelligence, and physical skills. They might also follow children into adulthood to see whether early personality characteristics persist.

Researchers can look at some developmental processes very closely by studying individuals every week or even every day. For example, a group of 2-year-old children might be tested weekly to create a detailed picture of their language development. Longitudinal designs have also been applied to change across many years. A prominent example is the classic study of "gifted" children initiated in the early 1920s by Lewis Terman (1877–1956), which is still going on. Findings of the Terman study at differing age ranges are discussed at several points in later chapters.

Longitudinal studies have some serious drawbacks, however. In studies of intelligence, for example, participants can become practiced and familiar with the tests and appear to show progressive gains quite apart from those associated with development. Also, in practical terms there's obviously a limit on how many such studies a researcher can conduct in a lifetime. In general, longitudinal research requires a great deal of time from both researchers and participants.

Another problem with longitudinal studies is the possibility of *bias*. Researchers initially select participants who are representative of the population of interest. As the study continues, some participants become ill, go on vacation,

longitudinal design   A study in which the same participants are observed continuously over a period of time.

Figure 1–2
Developmental Research Designs Compared

The longitudinal, cross-sectional, and sequential/age cohort research designs. The diagonal rows (see bottom row circled in red) represent longitudinal studies, and the vertical columns (see left column circled in green) represent cross-sectional studies. The complete illustration is of the sequential/age cohort design, and it shows four age cohorts that are being sudied at four different times.

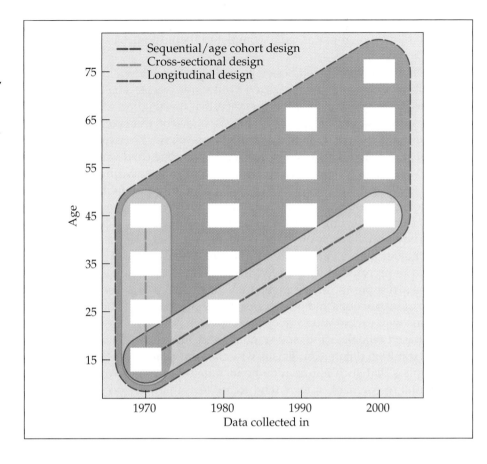

It is usually found within families that variables such as height and weight are positively correlated.

move away, or otherwise stop participating in the research project, with the effect that the remaining participants may no longer be representative of the original target population. For example, a study of personality change might become biased because the remaining participants tend to be the more cooperative and emotionally stable, leading researchers to believe that people generally become more cooperative and stable as they age. Similarly, participants in longitudinal studies may be healthier, wealthier, and wiser than their peers.

Researchers, too, may move away, lose interest, or even die if the study continues long enough. Terman, for example, died in the 1950s, though his study clearly lives on. Several personality studies begun in the 1920s and 1930s have also outlived their researchers. These include the Berkeley Guidance Study of personality, which began in 1928 with 8 to 10-year-olds and continued into the 1990s, and the Harvard Medical School Study of Adult Personality (Brooks-Gunn, Berlin, Leventhal, & Fuligni, 2000). In any long-term longitudinal study the original purposes and methods may become outdated. Often it becomes difficult to incorporate new approaches and still obtain data that can be compared to earlier findings.

Nevertheless, longitudinal studies yield detailed data about individual developmental change that other means cannot obtain, and so it remains a popular research approach. As noted by Jeanne Brooks-Gunn and colleagues (2000), after a gap of many years several new and large-scale longitudinal projects are currently underway in the United States alone. They cover areas such as early head start evaluation, "fragile" families and effects on child well-being, the family income dynamics and child development, the effects of welfare reform on children, and much more.

The Cross-Sectional Design A **cross-sectional design** compares individuals of different ages at one point in time. Although cross-sectional research cannot assess individual development, it is quicker, cheaper, and more manageable than longitudinal research. An example is a study of change in children's understanding of sarcasm, in which third graders and sixth graders were compared to adults (Capelli, Nakagawa, & Madden, 1990). From differences in what the participants attended to, the researchers concluded that younger children tend to miss cues when someone is being sarcastic, such as when the context contradicts what the speaker has said or when the speaker simply uses a different tone of voice. In other words, understanding sarcasm depends directly on a person's level of thinking and language comprehension.

Cross-sectional designs require careful selection of participants to ensure that the results are due to differences in development and not to other kinds of differences between the groups. For example, studies of adult intelligence and changes associated with aging have been plagued by problems of comparability. Is a sample of 70-year-olds, for example, as healthy or as well-educated or from the same ethnic or sociocultural group as a sample of 30-year-olds? Factors such as public health and education have changed substantially in recent decades, so that at any given time adults of differing ages aren't likely to be comparable. Education strongly influences IQ test scores, and the education a person who is now 70 years old began receiving back in the 1930s differs in many ways from the education a current 30-year-old began receiving in the 1970s. Such differences are called **cohort effects**—we would say that the 30-year-old cohort differs in important ways from the 70-year-old cohort. Cohort effects can therefore produce **confounding.** The researcher can't be sure whether any obtained differences or trends are due to development or to historical factors. Thus, early research on intellectual change across the adult lifespan indicated a greatly exaggerated decline in later adulthood (see Chapter 17).

However, cross-sectional research across much shorter age ranges is only minimally subject to cohort effects—if at all. Education and other historical factors tend to change relatively slowly, so that, for example, a comparison of 4-year-olds, 6-year-olds, and 8-year-olds is not likely to be confounded with historical factors. Numerous examples of this kind of research appear in later chapters.

The Sequential-Cohort Design Because of problems with each of the approaches just described, researchers are now more inclined toward a mix of the two, which is called the **sequential-cohort design.** Thus, a researcher might start with a group of 4-year-olds, a group of 8-year-olds, and a group of 12-year-olds and study each cohort every 2 years for 8 years. Comparisons could then be made both longitudinally and cross-sectionally. Examples of this approach also appear in later chapters.

Correlation as a Descriptive Tool

Does watching violence on television make children more violent and aggressive? Indeed it can, though in ways that researchers are still trying to unscramble through experimental research to be discussed later.

Before experimental research on children's aggression began, tests of a possible relationship between televised violence and their aggression often went like this. Measure the number of hours that selected children spend watching violent TV shows. Then apply a second measure, such as a scale for aggressiveness (perhaps a questionnaire completed by parents or teachers). Finally, compare the two. If children who watch a lot of violent TV are more aggressive, and if children who watch little violent TV are less aggressive, a relationship of some kind exists between the two measures.

cross-sectional design A method of studying development in which a sample of individuals of one age are compared with one or more samples of other age groups.

cohort effects Sociocultural differences between people of different age groups.

confounding The problem of not being able to tell if effects noticed between cohorts are due to developmental or historical factors.

sequential-cohort design Research design where several overlapping cohorts of different ages are studied longitudinally.

The statistical technique researchers use to assess such relationships is **correlation.** It yields a number that ranges either from 0 to +1.00 or from 0 to –1.00. The former is called *positive correlation*. In our example, as one variable (watching violent TV) increases, the other variable (aggressiveness) also increases. That is, the two variables "change" in the same direction: Children who spend more hours watching violent TV are also more aggressive on the scale, and vice versa.

To illustrate *negative correlation*, suppose that we instead found that children who watch more violent TV turn out to be *less* aggressive. This might be predicted on grounds that watching violent TV could provide an acceptable outlet for aggressive impulses that might otherwise be expressed in reality (see "In Theory, In Fact" in Chapter 2, p. 43). If so, then more hours of watching TV violence would correspond to *lower* scores on the aggressiveness scale, and fewer hours of TV violence would correspond to *higher* scores. In other words, the measures would be reversed: As one increases, the other decreases, and vice versa. They change in opposite directions, yielding a negative number.

As a general frame of reference, correlations between 0 and .20 or 0 and –.20 are viewed as *weak* or nonexistent; correlations between about .20 and about .60, whether positive or negative, are *moderate*; and correlations exceeding .60, in either a positive or a negative direction, are *strong*.

It is important to bear in mind that correlation tells us absolutely nothing about *causation*, meaning what causes what. Although a large body of experimental evidence has demonstrated that watching violence on television makes children more aggressive than they otherwise would be, we can't know that from positive correlation alone. All correlation tells us is that a relationship exists, nothing more. On the basis of correlation alone, it *might* be true that watching TV violence increases aggressiveness. But the reverse might also be true: Maybe children who are inherently more aggressive prefer to watch violent TV programs. In that case aggressiveness causes such children to watch TV violence. There are other possibilities as well: Maybe the more aggressive children are that way because their parents are violent and punish them harshly (which tends to make children more aggressive) and the parents also select violent TV programs for the family to watch.

In sum, although correlation is not an indicator of what causes what, it is an excellent research tool when used and interpreted appropriately.

correlation A mathematical statement of the relationship or correspondence between two variables.

CONTENT CHECK
STUDYING HUMAN DEVELOPMENT: DESCRIPTIVE APPROACHES

True–False (answers are on the Companion Website)

1. Case studies, systematic observation, and surveys cannot provide conclusive information about cause and effect.
2. In psychological testing, reliability refers to whether a test measures what it is supposed to measure.
3. Long-term cross-sectional designs are highly subject to error because of cohort effects.
4. A correlation of –.50 is weaker than a correlation of +.50.

Thinking Critically

What are the advantages and disadvantages of case studies, observational techniques, and surveys?

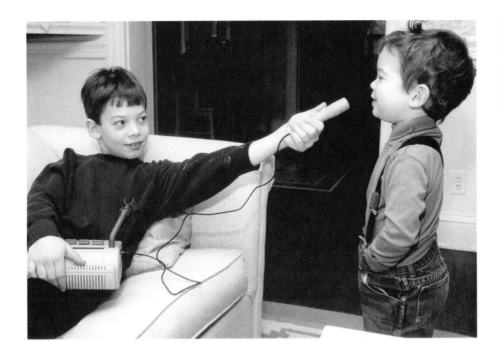

Because they assume that people are reactive beings, strict behaviorists study how individuals respond to their environment rather than investigating what they think or feel about these responses (see Chapter 2).

Studying Human Development: Experimental Approaches

The preceding section implied that only experiments can yield trustworthy information about cause-and-effect relationships. In this section we consider what constitutes experimentation in detail.

The Search for Cause and Effect

Humans have always been curious about how things work. Early humans undoubtedly manipulated and poked and prodded things to see what would happen. Build a raft out of rocks; it sinks. Build a raft out of branches and limbs; it floats. Let the raft get waterlogged, though, and it too sinks. Startle a wildebeest; it runs away. Sneak up on a wildebeest and poke it in the right place with a spear, though, and it doesn't run far. Such simple tests, often driven by survival, would have been among the first experiments.

From this perspective, psychological and other developmental experiments take two basic forms: Those that focus on individuals, whose behavior is studied and assessed one participant at a time; and those in which the focus is on groups of participants assessed collectively by averaging. **Experimental design,** which is a broad term that refers to the many considerations necessary in conducting meaningful experiments, depends on which approach is selected.

Experiments Focusing on Individuals

Single-subject designs are exemplified by the work of B. F. Skinner (1904–1990), whose approach is discussed in detail in Chapter 3. One subject at a time—rat, pigeon, chimpanzee, or human participant—is exposed to **contingencies** that are expected to alter or otherwise affect behavior. A contingency is a relationship between behavior and its consequences. Single-subject designs are most often cast in the context of *conditioning,* which is the application of contingencies to behavior. A demonstration of conditioning typically begins by

experimental design A broad term referring to the many considerations necessary for conducting meaningful and valid experiments.

single-subject design An approach whereby one subject at a time—rat, pigeon, chimpanzee, or human—is exposed to contingencies that are expected to alter or affect behavior.

contingency A relationship between behavior and its consequences.

As in Bandura's research, a child aggresses toward a Bobo doll in ways the child has seen an adult model aggress.

recording specific behaviors as they naturally occur, to obtain what is called a *baseline*. It then proceeds to manipulate contingencies to see how those behaviors change. *Behavior modification* (Chapter 3), which can be a highly effective method of eliminating problem behaviors and establishing desirable ones, generally takes this approach: First, identify and carefully define instances of the behavior and record the baseline rate at which they occur, then supply contingencies such as rewards or punishments and see if the behavior changes for the better.

Experiments Focusing on Groups

Experimental psychologists who study development are inclined to conduct group experiments in an attempt to get at general principles that might apply to all humans. From this perspective, individual differences become a nuisance. For example, it is assumed that human memory basically works the same way for everyone. Yet some people find it easier to memorize information than others do—a difference that may be related to neurological differences or early learning experiences and practice. Such differences get in the way when you are trying to develop general theories.

How do researchers deal with individual differences? Essentially by averaging. That is, they conduct the memory research using groups of people, then average and compare their performance scores.

There are many considerations in conducting group experiments to provide definitive information about development and behavior. The following classic research by Albert Bandura and colleagues on the relationship between children's media exposure and their aggressiveness illustrates these considerations.

Elements of Group Experimental Design   In research by Albert Bandura on children's learning of aggressive behavior through observation and imitation (Bandura, 1965; see also Bandura, 1969), three groups of preschool boys and girls watched a film in which an adult model "beat up" an inflated, adult-sized Bobo doll in specific ways. One group saw the model "rewarded" at the end of the film with praise from another adult. A second group saw the model "punished" by being scolded, and a third group saw the model experience no consequences either way. Thus, there were three different experimental treatments that constituted the **independent variable**—the variable in an experiment that is manipulated by the experimenter to observe what effects it will have on behavior. Also note that the children were **randomly assigned** to the groups. Random assignment can be accomplished in various ways; the simplest involves drawing slips of paper with the children's names on them out of a container or "hat." The hope is that random assignment will produce groups that are, in this case, roughly equivalent on average in initial aggressiveness.

In Bandura's experiment, he and his associates next allowed each child to play with a Bobo his or her own size and counted the number of aggressive acts the children displayed—specific acts that the children had seen the model perform. This was the **dependent variable**—the behavior that is measured to determine if the independent variable had an effect. The results are presented in Figure 1–3, where the blue bars represent the average number of imitated acts for each group at this point in the experiment, which was called the *performance test*. As you can see, the consequences the model received had a marked impact on the children's imitation: Boys and girls who saw the model punished imitated significantly fewer aggressive behaviors. But the levels of imitated behaviors for boys and girls in all three groups differed on the performance test— a finding consistent with differences in socialization of girls and boys that were predominant in the United States in the 1960s (see Chapters 6 and 8).

independent variable   The variable in an experiment that is manipulated in order to observe its effects on the dependent variable.

random assignment   Placing subjects in groups with the hope that these groups will be roughly equivalent, e.g., by drawing names from a container.

dependent variable   The variable in an experiment that changes as a result of manipulating the independent variable.

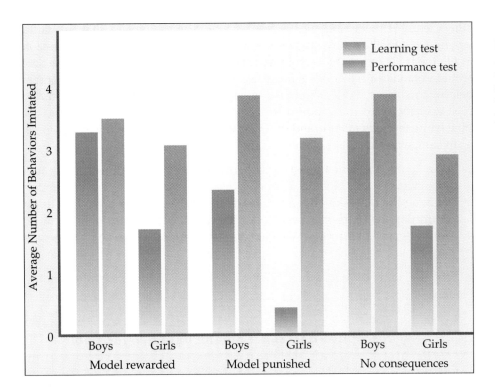

**Figure 1-3 The
Learning–Performance
Distinction**
Children's imitation of an adult
model whom they saw be rewarded, be punished, or experience no consequences for
aggressive behavior toward a
Bobo doll.

Source: Adapted from Bandura, 1969.

In the next phase of the experiment, called the *learning test*, the researchers offered all of the children rewards for reproducing as much of the model's behavior as they could. Now things changed considerably. Look at the green bars in
Figure 1–3: *All* of the children reproduced high levels of aggressive behavior regardless of what they had seen happen to the model, and the previously large differences between boys and girls became minimal—as Bandura concluded, "...
The initially large sex differential... was virtually eliminated (1969, p. 128).
The implication of this observation is that children readily learn how to commit aggressive acts when they watch such acts in films and on TV, whether or
not the children actually display those behaviors at the time.

Was Bandura's experiment a fair and meaningful test? First, most researchers would probably agree that the **operational definitions** were reasonable. Operational definitions "translate" general concepts such as media
violence and aggression into what is actually done in an experiment (or other
research method). Here, watching a model beat up a Bobo was the operational
definition of exposure to media violence, and the children's beating up a Bobo
themselves was the operational definition of aggression. Adding the observations (1) that Bandura's experiment was very carefully conducted so that the
only thing that differed for the groups of children was what they saw happen
to the model, and (2) the groups themselves probably did not differ in overall
aggressiveness because of random assignment as noted earlier, we can then say
that the experiment had good **internal validity.** That is, it seems clear that what
happened to the model *caused* the differences in the children's behavior during
the performance test. In general, internal validity refers to just that—whether
an experiment is conducted in such a way as to allow researchers to draw
meaningful conclusions about cause-and-effect relationships.

Most researchers would probably also agree that Bandura's experiment had
good **external validity:** What occurred in the lab corresponded nicely to what
might happen in the real world; the analogy is straightforward. Although Urie
Bronfenbrenner (Chapter 2) has characterized U.S. developmental psychology as

operational definitions The
actual procedures researchers
use to represent variables.

internal validity Conducting
an experiment so as to allow researchers to draw meaningful
information about cause-and-
effect relationships.

external validity The extent
to which an experiment corresponds to what happens in the
real world.

"the science of the strange behavior of the child in a strange situation with a strange adult for the shortest period of time" (1979, p. 19), this isn't always the case.

On the basis of a single experiment such as Bandura's, however, researchers would not make a sweeping generalization such as saying that watching adults being aggressive increases children's aggressiveness. Rather, they would want to repeat, or **replicate,** the experiment using different children, different kinds of filmed or televised violence, and differing measures of children's aggressiveness.

In sum, experimental research consists of the following steps:

1. Defining the problem and formulating hypotheses (predictions) about what causes what.
2. Definimg the independent and dependent variables.
3. Performing the experiment and collecting data.
4. Analyzing and interpreting the data and drawing whatever conclusions are warranted.

Table 1–5 reviews the research methods discussed in this and the preceding section.

Table 1–5 Descriptive and Experimental Research Methods

Case Study

Through a combination of interviews, observations, formal testing, and gathering of other information, the researcher tries to obtain a complete picture of an individual.

Naturalistic Observation

Researchers go into everyday settings and systematically observe and record behavior while being as unobtrusive as possible.

Laboratory Observation

Researchers set up controlled situations intended to elicit the behavior of interest, which is then systematically observed and recorded.

Survey

Using questionnaires or interviews, researchers ask objective questions about attitudes and behavior, past or present.

Psychological Testing

An individual is presented with a set of questions and problems designed to assess his or her intelligence or personality.

Developmental Research Designs

Developmental change can be assessed through the longitudinal design, the cross-sectional design, or the sequential-cohort design. The first two have both advantages and disadvantages; the latter combines the first two in an attempt to eliminate their disadvantages.

Correlation

Statistical analysis is used to determine the extent to which two variables increase or decrease together.

Single-Subject Experiment

One participant at a time is exposed to contingencies that are expected to cause behavior to change.

Group Experiment

Two or more groups of participants are exposed to conditions that differ in terms of at least one independent variable. If their behavior differs (as assessed by one or more dependent variables), researchers conclude that the difference was caused by the independent variable(s).

replication (replicate) Systematic repetitions of an experiment to determine if findings are valid and generalizable.

CONTENT CHECK
STUDYING HUMAN DEVELOPMENT: EXPERIMENTAL APPROACHES

True–False (answers are on the Companion Website)

1. In group experiments, individual differences are dealt with by averaging.
2. In Bandura's classic experiment, watching an adult beat up a Bobo doll was the independent variable.
3. In experiments that compare groups, participants are typically placed in the groups by random assignment.
4. As discussed, most researchers would probably agree that Bandura's experiment had good internal validity and good external validity.
5. Bandura's experiment by itself provided conclusive evidence that watching adults being aggressive makes children more aggressive.

Thinking Critically

What elements determine whether an experiment is a good one or a poor one?

Ethics in Developmental Research

Most people agree that experiments using humans are necessary, especially if we are to understand and control the impact of potentially harmful events and situations. A recurring case in point is research on the effects of televised violence on children, and more generally, what causes aggression and other antisocial behavior by people of any age. There are many other examples that apply throughout the lifespan: the effects of media inducements for (and against) smoking and use of other drugs, including alcohol; the effects of differing approaches to educating people about sexually transmitted diseases; the effects of child abuse and what causes it; the effects of stress, frustration, being teased or bullied, being the object of prejudice and discrimination, and on and on.

Researchers nowadays must adhere to strict ethical principles when conducting *any* research with human participants, whether it involves things that hurt people or things that help. The most basic principle is that researchers should never knowingly cause significant or lasting harm to anyone, nor should they want to—no matter how important the research topic might be to the understanding of development and behavior or to aiding society at large.

Note the term "cause": Developmentalists can certainly study the very worst of what life sometimes serves up for people by using the descriptive methods discussed earlier in the chapter. They may in turn perform experiments intended to minimize or eliminate maladaptive behaviors, mental and behavioral disorders, and the many more specific variants of human suffering. What developmentalists cannot do—and again, should not even want to do—is to perform experiments that produce or reproduce human suffering. For example (in some parts of the world more than in others), there continue to be numerous cases every year in which children are severely abused or neglected by parents or other caregivers. Researchers study characteristics both of caregivers and children that contribute to abuse, along with environmental factors that increase its likelihood of occurrence (see Chapters 6 and 8). They also devise social or clinical interventions intended to counter the effects of such abuse on children or to prevent its occurrence in the first place. But, obviously, they do *not* conduct experiments that one way or another might cause such abuse to occur—even though research along these lines might be extremely helpful in understanding and eliminating it.

Since the publication of its *Ethical Principles in the Conduct of Research with Human Participants* in 1973, the American Psychological Association (APA) has provided detailed guidelines that have been widely used by researchers in human development and many other disciplines. The current edition, *Ethics in Research with Human Participants* (Sales & Folkman, 2000), goes to great lengths to define what is acceptable and what is not. The Society for Research in Child Development (SRCD) publishes similar guidelines oriented specifically toward research with children (SRCD, 1996). Nor do these guidelines apply only to members of organizations such as the APA and the SRCD; they are backed up by law (see the sections of The Public Health Service Act that are reprinted as an appendix in Sales & Folkman, 2000).

Ethics in Research with Human Participants is based on five moral principles as summarized in Table 1–6. The most salient issues that arise from these principles are discussed below.

Protection from Harm

No research should have the potential for serious or lasting physical or psychological harm, although it is ethically possible to conduct research where participants are temporarily made physically or psychologically uncomfortable. However, whereas serious harm is easily anticipated and avoided, it is often difficult to determine what might produce lasting psychological harm. For example, in studies of obedience, is it reasonable to give people orders to see if they will follow them, when if they do, it may have a lasting effect on their views of them-

Table 1–6   Moral Foundations of Ethical Research with Human Participants

I. Respect for Persons and Their Autonomy

Research participants are persons of worth and their participation is a matter of personal choice. This underlies issues such as informed consent, coercion, deception, confidentiality, and privacy.

II. Beneficence and Nonmaleficence

Possible benefits should be maximized and possible harms should be minimized. In other words, where harm to a participant is a possibility, the research effort should be subjected to a "benefits/costs" analysis and—given other constraints involving protection from harm—conducted only if the ratio is favorable.

III. Justice

Because of the "power differential" between researchers and research participants, safeguards should be in place to ensure that potentially vulnerable groups such as ethnic minorities and persons in institutional care bear a fair share of the burden with regard to their efforts and reap a fair share of the benefits of research.

IV. and V. Trust, Fidelity, and Scientific Integrity

The relationship between researchers and research participants should be one of reciprocal trust, especially with regard to considerations such as informed consent and deception as noted in Principle I. At the same time, in the larger view, scientific integrity is not open to compromise.

Source: Smith, 2000.

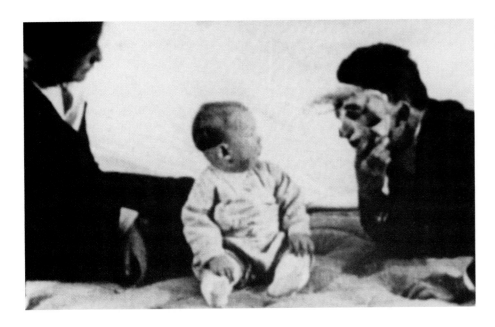

Rosalie Rayner, Albert, and J. B. Watson (see "A Matter for Debate," next page).

selves as "obedient" persons? As another example, suppose a researcher wants to demonstrate that 9-year-olds can understand a particular concept and solve certain problems that 5-year-olds cannot. All of the 5-year-old children will experience repeated failure, most likely having been deceived as to the solvability of the problems (otherwise they might simply give up too quickly). Is it ethical to have children (or anyone) go through the frustration of attempting unsolvable problems? Moreover, when we *debrief* our younger participants afterward and tell them that we didn't actually expect them to be able to solve the problems, will they believe us? Or will they be left with an impression that we were covering up, that they are actually somehow inferior in this respect? After all, we lied to them in the first place, so we might still be lying.

Research organizations now have screening committees, called **Institutional Review Boards (IRBs)** now evaluate all research projects to make sure that the research isn't likely to be harmful to the participants in the long run. Preferably, experiments involve only *minimal risk*—that is, the risk of harm is no greater than that experienced in daily life (a participant could, for example, accidentally trip and get hurt coming into in an experimental room, but the risk of this is no greater in the room than elsewhere).

If justifiable in terms of benefits and costs, and if no alternative procedure is feasible, research participants can be placed *at risk*. At-risk participants are those who will experience some degree of harm—as always, within limits determined by moral considerations and kept to the minimum necessary for the experiment to work. For example, a participant might be angered or otherwise emotionally upset, might be verbally insulted, or might experience mild but painful electric shocks. There are many possible risks. In addition, a participant might experience risks such as ". . . [b]oredom, depression, altered self-concept, increased anxiety, or loss of confidence in others" (Sieber, 2000, p. 15).

Informed Consent

In all cases, people should participate in research voluntarily, be fully informed of the nature and possible consequences of the research, and not be coerced in any way. Each of these is an aspect of **informed consent:** ". . . [a] clear statement of the purposes, procedures, risks, and benefits . . . as well as the obligations and commitments of both the participants and the researchers"

Institutional Review Boards (IRBs) Screening committees of research institutions that evaluate all research projects relative to potential harm to participants.

informed consent A clear statement of the procedures and risks, as well as the obligations of both the participants and the researchers.

A MATTER FOR DEBATE

THE "LITTLE ALBERT" EXPERIMENT

Initially reported in 1920, J. B. Watson (1878–1958) and Rosalie Rayner (1899–1936) conducted the "Little Albert" experiment that has long been a classic in the annals of psychology—it is one of the most widely cited studies ever. It is discussed in nearly every introductory psychology and developmental textbook, typically in the context of conditioning and learning (Chapter 3). Here we consider it from a different vantage point: that of ethics in research with human participants.

The basic experiment went like this: An 11–month-old infant known as Albert B. was taught to fear a white laboratory rat through *classical conditioning*. The child initially had no fear of the rat. Then came repeated "trials" in which one experimenter presented the rat to Albert and another experimenter—behind Albert's back-made a loud, frightening noise by striking a steel bar with a claw hammer. As a result, Albert ac-quired a pronounced fear of the rat and (to a lesser extent) of any white, furry, or fluffy object. Although the actual conditions of the experiment were at times haphazard, and although Albert's fear response wasn't always as predictable or profound as many textbooks suggest, he did acquire reactions consistent with those of a *phobia*—an extreme, unreasoning fear of an object or situation.

Was Watson and Rayner's experiment ethical by contemporary standards? Today we're inclined to answer with an immediate "No!" on a number of grounds. For example, it hardly seems ethical to repeatedly expose a helpless infant to an extremely frightening situation. Moreover, there was considerable potential for lasting psychological harm—once phobias have been acquired, they tend to persist. In addition, it is not clear whether Albert's mother even knew what was going on, much less that she gave informed consent for her child to be subjected to such procedures.

On the other hand, modern ethical standards for psychological research didn't exist at the time, so at least technically, Watson and Rayner aren't culpable. More to the point, relatively little was known about how children acquire phobias and other fears. Thus, it *might* be argued that the potential benefits in understanding the origins of children's fears outweighed the risks to Albert. There was also no way for Watson and Rayner to know that Albert's fear might persist—indeed, that was one of their research questions.

One thing is clear, however: The Little Albert experiment could not and would not be conducted today.

Primary source on the details of the experiment: Harris, 1979.

(Fischman, 2000, p. 35). At-risk participants must sign a consent form that specifies the preceding; minimal-risk participants need not, although most researchers require a signed consent form anyway, just in case. Because infants and young children and people who are mentally disordered cannot provide true informed consent, their parents or other legal guardians or proxies do so on their behalf. Finally, all participants must be free to discontinue their participation in the research at any point, for whatever reason and without attempts being made to prevent them from doing so. This includes not withholding any payment or other compensation that has been offered: If a participant *begins* an experiment or other research project, the participant must be paid in full regardless of whether she or he completes it.

There is a potential conflict, however, between informed consent and the deception that is often necessary in research with humans. Deception is used because participants' behavior may change if they know the true purpose of an experiment—they may try to behave as they think the experimenter wants them to and be "good" participants, or they may deliberately try to defeat the experiment and be "bad" participants. The general rule is that participants cannot be deceived in any way that might affect their decision to participate, although they can be deceived about the specific purposes of the research. In the latter case, however, participants must be thoroughly debriefed afterward and in a timely fashion and told the true nature of the research, with any erroneous beliefs or attitudes dispelled—to the extent that this is possible as discussed earlier.

Issues in informed consent and especially protection from harm are discussed further in "A Matter for Debate," above.

Privacy and Confidentiality

Information obtained in a research project must remain private and confidential. As noted by Susan Folkman (2000), based on citations from other authors, privacy means (1) that personal information about the participant is not divulged without the person's consent, and (2) that the participant is not given information he or she doesn't want—such as information derived from tests the person took or feedback about performance that might distress the person.

Researchers can of course publish their "numbers" and they must include general information about their participants such as age, sex, and other demographics, but names and identifying information about individual participants cannot be disclosed without their written permission. No agencies or individuals except the researchers should have access to participants' records, which may include information about their private lives, thoughts, fantasies, and the like, scores on intelligence or personality tests, and behavior during experiments.

Knowledge of Results

Whether during debriefing or at a later time (such as when the research effort is completed), individuals have the right to be informed of the results and in terms that they can understand. Many people, for example, are unfamiliar with much of the psychological jargon you're learning from this text or have learned elsewhere. When children are involved, these results may be shared with parents.

Beneficial Treatments

Finally, each participant has the right to profit from any beneficial treatments provided to other participants in the study. For example, if a participant is assigned to a comparison or "control" group in an experiment on a new vaccine or a psychological treatment and therefore does not receive it during the experiment, the person is entitled to receive the treatment afterward should it prove effective. In general, researchers must supply any positive benefits of research to all participants in return for their participation, at no charge.

CONTENT CHECK

ETHICS IN DEVELOPMENTAL RESEARCH

True–False (answers are on the Companion Website)

1. With regard to protection from harm, human research participants cannot be made even the slightest bit uncomfortable.
2. Institutional Review Boards aren't necessary where participants are at minimal risk.
3. Informed consent includes the requirement that research participants be free to stop participating at any time and for any reason.
4. Ethical principles include the requirement that a research participant not be given feedback on performance if the participant doesn't want to know.

Thinking Critically

Why is deception often necessary in research with human participants and how is this reconciled with ethical considerations such as informed consent?

CHAPTER 1 REVISITED

■ The study of development focuses on change, beginning with conception and continuing throughout the lifespan.

Key Issues in the Study of Human Development

■ Development always occurs in social and cultural context.

■ Four developmental domains are: physical, cognitive (including language), personality, and sociocultural.

■ What others teach us constitutes socialization; what we learn on own constitutes enculturation.

■ Although domains are convenient concepts, development is not compartmentalized; it is instead holistic.

■ The scientific study of human development began at about the begining of the 20th century.

■ Being scientific means being systematic and objective and avoiding ethnocentrism.

■ Some aspects of development are largely biological, others largely experiential; most development involves the dynamic interplay of biology and experience.

■ Nowadays, the interplay of biology and experience is usually expressed as heredity and environment in interaction.

■ When the interplay of biology and experience is cast as maturation and learning in interaction, the emphasis shifts to timing.

■ In most cases, it is more accurate to consider human development in terms of sensitive periods rather than critical periods.

Historical and Contemporary Perspectives on Human Development

■ Views of childhood vary both historically and across cultures; these include viewing children as co-workers, as property to be sold or traded, as beings without rights, and in most contemporary cultures, as beings with clear-cut rights not to be abused or exploited.

■ It was once thought that children in medieval Europe were viewed as miniature adults; that idea is now viewed as an overstatement at best.

■ Individualist cultures stress independence; collectivist cultures stress interdependence.

■ Adolescence as a prolonged period of dependence came about as a result of industrialization and the increasing need for extended education.

■ How long a person remains an adolescent depends on culture and also social and historical context.

■ How long adulthood lasts and at what point a person becomes "old" varies across and within cultures; one factor is socioeconomic level.

■ Family composition varies across and within cultures; the nuclear family is definitely not the norm.

Studying Human Development: Descriptive Approaches

■ Case studies attempt to create a complete picture of an individual; the earliest developmental case studies were baby biographies.

■ Case studies and other descriptive approaches cannot make conclusive statements about cause and effect.

■ Naturalistic or field observation has the advantage of studying behavior as it naturally occurs, laboratory observation has the advantage of studying behavior under controlled conditions; both have disadvantages as well.

■ Surveys using questionnaires or interviews have the advantage that they can be administered to large, representative samples of people; disadvantages are that people don't always respond or respond accurately.

■ Psychological tests are often used in developmental research to assess factors such as intelligence and personality; the best psychological tests are strong on reliability, validity, and standardization.

■ The longitudinal design can provide accurate information on individual developmental change but is time-consuming; the cross-sectional design is efficient with regard to time but is subject to cohort effects; the sequential-cohort design is a mix intended to minimize the disadvantages of the first two.

■ Correlation is a research tool that assesses the degree and direction of correspondence between two variables; it cannot yield conclusive statements about cause and effect.

Studying Human Development: Experimental Approaches

■ Only experiments can directly assess cause and effect; experiments can involve studying the behavior of an individual under different contingencies or comparing the behavior of groups under different conditions.

■ A group experiment involves randomly assigning participants to different groups, manipulating one or more independent variables, and measuring one or more dependent variables; if the groups' behavior differs, differences in the independent variable are concluded to have been the cause.

■ A good experiment is systematic and objective, uses reasonable operational definitions, and is high in internal validity; high external validity is a plus as well.

Ethics in Developmental Research

■ Ethical principles in conducting research with human participants stem from the necessity of protecting them from lasting physical or psychological harm; many behaviors therefore cannot be studied experimentally, but they can be studied by descriptive approaches.

■ Institutional Review Boards (IRBs) now evaluate all research projects to assess any potential for lasting harm.

■ Additional ethical principles include informed consent, privacy and confidentiality, knowledge of results, and access to any beneficial treatments than may be confirmed by research.

■ Informed consent is a potential problem because deception is often used with human participants; reconciliations are that the participant cannot be deceived about anything that would affect willingness to participate and the participant must be debriefed afterward.

KEY TERMS

development
context
society
culture
physical domain
cognitive domain
personality domain
sociocultural domain
ethnocentric bias
critical period
sensitive or optimal periods
collectivist (culture)
individualist (culture)

case study
baby biography
naturalistic or field observation
labratory observation
questionnaire
survey
representative sample
random sample
longitudinal design
cross-sectional design
cohort effects
confounding
sequential-cohort design

correlation
experimental design
single-subject design
contingency
independent variable
random assignment
dependent variable
operational definitions
internal validity
external validity
replicate (replication)
Institutional Review Boards (IRBs)
informed consent

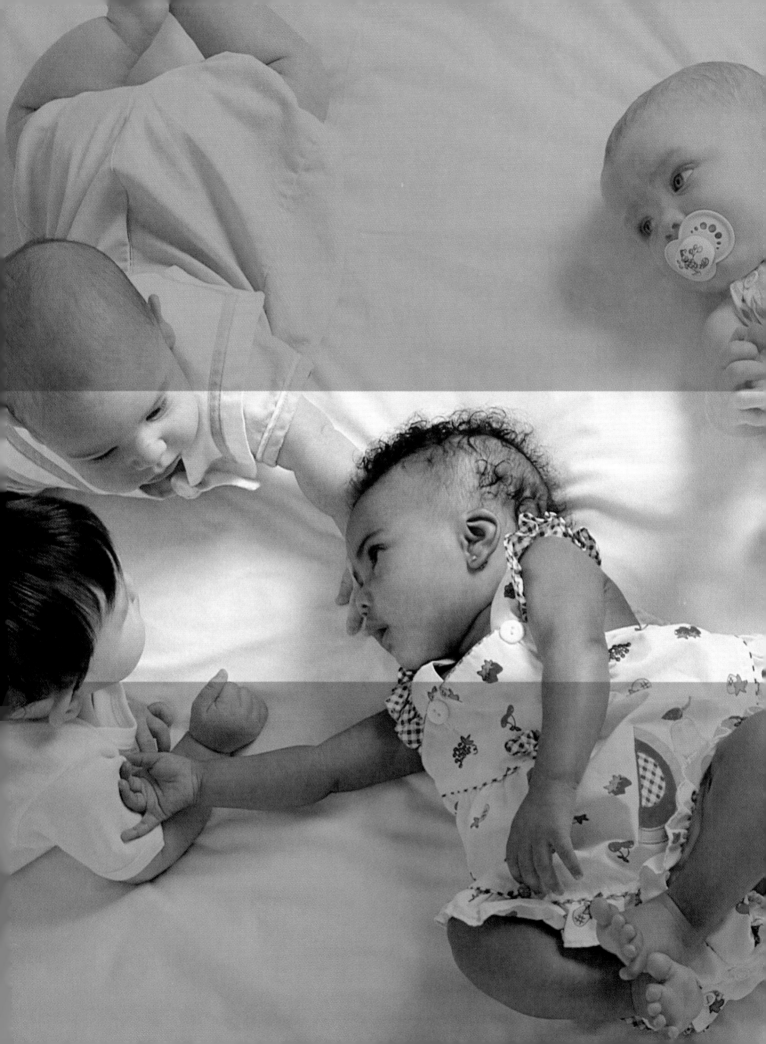

APPROACHES TO UNDERSTANDING HUMAN DEVELOPMENT

2

CHAPTER PREVIEW

Do you know:

1. What constitutes a good *theory*?

2. The distinctions between views of development as *active* versus *passive*?

3. The extent to which meaningful developmental *stages* exist?

4. The *components* of personality and the two *developmental sequences* in Sigmund Freud's psychoanalytic theory?

5. The differences between Freud's *psychosexual theory* and Erik Erikson's *psychosocial theory*?

6. The *stages* in Erikson's lifespan theory?

7. The approaches and methods of *strict behaviorists* such as Ivan Pavlov, E. L. Thorndike, and B. F. Skinner?

8. The approach and methods of *classic learning theorists*?

9. The role of modern *social-learning theory* in understanding development?

10. The basics of Jean Piaget's *cognitive-developmental theory*?

11. The basics of Lev Vygotsky's *social-cognitive theory*?

12. The role of *information-processing theory* in understanding development?

13. The role of *evolutionary theories* such as ethology and evolutionary psychology in understanding development?

14. What *developmental neuroscientists* study?

15. What is involved in *systems approaches* such as contextualism, ecological systems theory, and Urie Bronfenbrenner's *bioecological model*?

16. What it means to be *eclectic*?

These are the main topics of Chapter 2.

A
s we saw in Chapter 1, developmentalists have long grappled with fundamental questions concerning what human development actually is, how it proceeds, how it differs across contexts and cultures, and especially how to go about studying it. As we also saw, the quest continues; some of the many questions have been answered, others remain to be answered, still others to be asked. In brief, the study of human development is truly a challenge, but it is an exciting one that has already yielded a vast amount of knowledge and understanding in a relatively short timespan (a mere century or so) and continues to do so at an ever-increasing pace. Just keeping up is hard enough; getting a solid grasp on the volumes upon volumes of accumulated information can seem overwhelming, particularly when that information appears contradictory and often difficult to reconcile.

This is where *theories* come into play. Theories attempt to give shape to large and otherwise unmanageable collections of information. A good theory provides a framework and then organizes around it, offering explanations—for our purposes, of human development and behavior. A good theory also provides testable *predictions*, which are important in two ways. First, we are always interested in predicting things such as how specific aspects of development will unfold or what a person will do in a certain situation. If we can predict with reasonable accuracy, we become more confident that we understand ourselves. Second, predictions give rise to further research that continues to enhance our understanding by refining or extending theories—or by disconfirming them and causing them to be rewritten either partially or entirely—or on occasion simply discarded.

Actually, you already know a great deal about theories. Whether you can articulate them, you have spent much of your life formulating your own personal theories about how people come to be who they are and why people do the things they do. For example, you almost certainly have theories, or at least assumptions, that center around human nature—such as whether people are basically selfish or unselfish, when people can be expected to behave rationally and when not, and a great many others. Like a scientist, although less formally, you've "built" these theories on experiences with and observations of people and—ideally—you continue to refine and extend them.

This chapter introduces you to a diverse assortment of major theoretical approaches, grouped within broader, more general approaches to understanding and explaining human development and behavior. It is purely an introduction and as such is by no means comprehensive. Consequently, many more specific theories or conceptual frameworks follow in later chapters. The intent here is to provide a background, to set the stage.

Some of the theories in this chapter are classic and are included primarily because of their historical impact, although even the most dated ones still influence modern views of development and behavior indirectly or in part. Most, however, are quite contemporary and directly influential, having survived the testing and revision process implicit in any discipline. Some are relatively recent on the scene, with many of the details still being worked out.

Additional Questions About Development

In Chapter 1 you were introduced to several key issues in the study of human development, including the importance of context, the relative roles of heredity and environment, and the relative contributions of maturation and learning. Here we briefly consider two additional issues that are directly relevant to theories of human development.

Active Versus Passive Development

This question is derived from philosophy, but it turns out to be a very practical issue in everyday life and in education in particular. Especially while we're children, do we *actively* seek knowledge and understanding of our world, of morality, of values, or do we *passively* react to what we experience and what we are "taught"? Do we mold ourselves, or are we molded by others and by the physical environment?

Theorists who emphasize active development—often referred to as "organismic" theorists—argue that we are quite active participants in our own development. We seek to interact with other individuals as well as with events, and we are changed in the process. In turn, we act on those individuals and events and change them too, all while thinking about what we experience and trying to figure it out and understand it for ourselves. Curiosity and the desire to acquire knowledge and understanding are central to development.

Theorists who view development more as a passive process—often referred to as "mechanistic" theorists—see us primarily as reacting to events in our environment. From this perspective, we are driven primarily by our internal drives and motivations in conjunction with external incentives and pressures provided by others and the environment in general. Development is determined largely by rewards and punishments, which shape and mold us. Note that the use of the word *determine* here also implies that everything we know or do is a function of past or present conditions.

So which view is correct?

The best answer is that both are. Much of the time we actively approach the world in all its complexity and construct our own view of it to guide us, yet we often have little choice except to react to what the physical and social world serves up for us. In other words, our active human minds *interact* with the forces of society and nature, and that interaction determines what we do and who we become.

Stages Versus Continuity in Development

As development proceeds, do behaviors and capabilities build continually on each other, so that we gradually accumulate behaviors and skills and knowledge about the world around us? Or does development occur "stepwise" in **stages** that are qualitatively different, so that we achieve new ways of understanding our world quite abruptly?

Some developmental changes are clearly gradual and cumulative, resulting in steadily increasing organization and function. For example, an infant's motor development progresses from random waving of arms and legs to purposeful reaching and grasping. Somewhat later, the ability to use symbols—especially words—develops gradually and progresses steadily toward reading, manipulation of number concepts, and eventually higher-level thinking.

In general, continuity in development throughout the lifespan is the prevailing view nowadays. However, some theorists stress stages of development. Notable among them are cognitive-developmental theorists, who view cognitive abilities as developing in discrete stages during which children see the world in qualitatively different ways compared to adults. To put it simply, children *think* differently than adults do, and there is good evidence for this observation.

stages Discrete periods proposed to have abrupt transitions from one to the next.

In general, though, the truth seems to lie somewhere in between the extremes of gradual continuity and abrupt stages. There is little evidence that people make rapid, abrupt transitions from one stage to the next, even in theories that emphasize stages. Instead, to the extent that stages of development are meaningful, we move gradually from each stage to the next and often go back and forth between them.

CONTENT CHECK
ADDITIONAL QUESTIONS ABOUT DEVELOPMENT

True–False (answers are on the Companion Website)

1. Active development is the rule; passive development is the exception.
2. Organismic theorists view development as active and mechanistic theorists view development as passive.
3. Most aspects of development unfold in discrete stages.

Thinking Critically

How does the active participation of the child or adult interact with the demands of the environment to determine development and behavior?

Psychodynamic Approaches

Viennese physician Sigmund Freud (1856–1939) founded what is now known as the **psychodynamic approach,** which, stated in very general terms, focuses on the often-subtle inner workings of the mind as they play out against external reality. What those inner workings are thought to consist of and how they are seen as interacting with the external social world differ considerably among contemporary personality theorists, but—one way or another—most psychodynamic approaches can be traced to Freud. This applies equally to (1) psychodynamic theorists who sharply criticized his ideas and emphases but retained his basic approach and (2) nonpsychodynamic theorists who rejected his approach altogether but used his frame of reference as their starting point. For example, nonpsychodynamic theorists retained Freud's idea of personality as an organized system, comprised of relatively stable characteristics we now call *traits.*

Freud's impact on the study of personality development has been no less profound, and he clearly ranks high on the list of candidates for the title of first developmentalist. From the late 19th century on, he spent over 40 years researching and writing about how personality works and where it comes from, beginning in infancy. Along with his theorizing about the workings of personality, his ideas about how personality develops have also been criticized and largely rejected. Yet his legacy includes a frame of reference for personality as a system that originates in childhood, is markedly influenced by interactions with parents or other caregivers, and unfolds in an orderly manner—assumptions basic to all ensuing theories of personality development.

We begin with a look at personality development from Freud's point of view. Then we consider Erikson, one of several notable theorists who made major changes or additions to psychodynamic theory.

An elderly Sigmund Freud with his daughter Anna. Anna Freud carried on the psychoanalytic tradition while broadening its emphasis upon the ego and defense mechanisms.

Freud's Psychoanalytic Theory

Freud primarily used clinical case studies of his adult patients—along with recollections of his own childhood—in developing **psychoanalysis.** Psychoanalytic theory refers literally to analysis of the "psyche," with its origins in the Greek word for "soul."

In the clinical work upon which his theory was primarily based, he experimented with various techniques but wound up emphasizing his method of *free association.* A patient would lie on a comfortable couch and, in the early stages of therapy, literally ramble about whatever came to mind. Freud sat nearby but out of the patient's view, taking notes and making only occasional, open-ended comments to maintain the flow. Each aspect of the setting and the procedure was designed to minimize any biasing effects he might have on the patient's choice of topics. If the patient reported dreams (especially recurring ones), he would use dream analysis as an adjunct to free association, again encouraging the patient to take the active role.

As therapy reached a certain point, however (which could take years), things changed considerably. Freud would now have clear-cut hypotheses about what the origins of the patient's problems were and would begin to make his own interpretations and be much more "directive" in keeping the patient focused. Notably, at this point, his interpretations were not to be argued with. Any confrontation, avoidance, or lack of acceptance on the patient's part was deemed *resistance,* and Freud would take such behavior as further evidence that he was on the right track. He could be quite stern and authoritarian—as he was

psychodynamic approach The theory that focuses on the often-subtle inner workings of the mind as they play out against external reality.

psychoanalysis Freud's view of human nature as motivated by innate biological drives and inner dynamics.

with regard to the particulars of his theory as well. Thus, as we provide an overview of Freud's "classical" psychoanalytic theory, bear in mind that the extent to which he was accurate in unscrambling the patient dynamics upon which his theory was built versus simply being good at "convincing" patients (and himself) that he was correct remains unclear.

In any event, throughout his career Freud refined his theory into an extremely intricate view of human nature and development. The basics are covered here; applications of psychoanalytic theory appear at various points in later chapters.

In Freudian psychoanalytic theory there are two developmental sequences that overlap somewhat. The first concerns the structure of personality and its basic components; the second involves stages through which personality development progresses.

Components of Personality   From birth, the infant is dominated by the **id**—the primitive, selfish component of personality (see Freud, 1923/1960, for a succinct discussion of the id and the other components below). That is, the id represents the "animal" within us, and it generates biologically based impulses or *instinctual wishes* that must be reckoned with somehow. These impulses have to do with things like obtaining food and water and other necessities of survival, also sex; together, they constitute the **life instincts,** which Freud called **Eros.** This was his starting point in delineating the driving forces within the id. The life instincts operate according to the *pleasure principle*: They seek immediate gratification and avoid pain. Later, in his more-or-less final formulation of the motivating forces of the id (Freud, 1920/1922), he added the **death instincts,** called **Thanatos,** to round out the picture. The death instincts account for processes involved in each person's eventual death, plus the aggression and destructiveness Freud thought were also instinctive in humans.

Sexual and aggressive impulses dominate much of our lives, in the sense that we must find socially acceptable ways to express them (see "In Theory, In Fact," p. 43). The id is also part of the much larger **unconscious mind** that Freud saw as governing most of our behavior without our direct awareness.

As development proceeds, the **ego** gradually evolves from the id and eventually becomes an essentially separate component of the personality. The ego serves as the "executive agent" for dealing with impulses. It is **conscious mind,** consisting of what we're aware of and thinking about at any given time as well as negotiating between the id's impulses and external reality. If the id sends up an impulse for sex, for example, the ego must deal with it somehow. The ego thus operates according to the *reality principle* and continually tries to reconcile impulses and other unconscious forces with the demands and constraints imposed by the outside world. In addition, the ego is responsible for **defense mechanisms.** A defense mechanism is a way of reducing or at least disguising anxiety. The most basic and we might say most insidious of these is **repression,** the mechanism by which the ego "parks" unacceptable and inexpressible impulses, perceived guilts over past misdeeds, and other personally distressing ideas or memories in the unconscious, where they remain without the individual's awareness but continue to trouble the individual all the same. As toddlers, we are already accumulating repressed material that must be suffered perhaps for life, and the primary goal of classical psychoanalysis is probing the unconscious and bringing this material into the light of awareness where the individual can effectively face it and achieve insight and understanding.

id According to Freud, the primitive, hedonistic component of personality.

life instincts According to Freud, impulses having to do with obtaining food, water, and other necessities of survival.

Eros Life instincts.

death instincts According to Freud, the processes involved in each person's eventual death, plus aggression and destructiveness.

Thanatos Death instincts.

unconscious mind According to Freud, the part of the personality that governs most of our behavior without our direct awareness.

ego According to Freud, the conscious, reality-oriented component of personality.

conscious mind What we are aware of and thinking about at any given time.

defense mechanisms According to Freud, the cognitive "tricks" that individuals use to reduce tensions that lead to anxiety.

repression According to Freud, the mechanisms by which the ego "parks" unacceptable and inexpressible impulses, peceived guilts over misdeeds, and other personally distressing ideas in the unconscious, where they remain without the person's awareness but continue to trouble the individual all the same.

superego According to Freud, the conscience component of personality, which includes the ego ideal.

IN THEORY, IN FACT
CATHARSIS AND AGGRESSION

Many of us have mild emotional outbursts from time to time. But some people are chronically angry and hostile, and their outbursts emerge more as an "explosion" of rage in the form of shouting and cursing, throwing or breaking things, or even physically attacking someone. Such outbursts are especially likely with children, who are still in the process of developing self-control and moral restraints in their dealings with others.

Volumes have been written on how to control aggression and anger and hostility and emotional outbursts, and we return to some of these approaches in later chapters. Here we focus on one notion of such control that has dominated Western thinking since Freud's time: *catharsis*, which here refers to "venting" negative emotions in socially acceptable ways as a means of relieving the pressure and avoiding perhaps devastating outbursts. According to the *catharsis hypothesis*, a caregiver or other adult may encourage a child to beat up a Bandura-style Bobo doll (Chapter 1), an adult may scream and curse in private from time to time, and anyone—adult or child—may beat a punching bag or hit baseballs with a bat, perhaps gleefully imagining that they're doing it to someone for real. For a special few, participating in aggressive sports can be cathartic. For children or adults, playing any of hundreds of murderously violent computer or video-arcade games may do the trick.

Does it work? Popular opinion says it does, based on surveys of people in the United States (as reported by Wann et al., 1999) and in Canada (Russell, Arms, & Bibby, 1995). Even some educators have supported catharsis in justifying intercollegiate football (Bennett, 1991). Flip through the pages of current self-help books on coping with anger and hostility and aggressive impulses, and you are quite likely to find catharsis listed as a viable approach.

However, of the many studies of catharsis that have been conducted over the years, the majority indicate that cathartic techniques either (1) are *ineffective* in reducing aggressive behavior (e.g., Kaplan & Singer, 1978; Moyer, 1982; Goldstein, 1999) or (2) actually *increase* the likelihood of aggressive behavior (see especially Berkowitz, 1970, and Lewis & Bucher, 1992; also Mallick & McCandless, 1967; Nighswander & Mayer, 1969; Green, Stonner, & Shope, 1975).

Why does public opinion favoring catharsis remain so strong? Brad Bushman, Roy Baumeister, and Angela Stack recently conducted a pair of experiments that took an interesting slant on these questions (1999). In part, their reasoning was that public belief in catharsis and media endorsement of it can conceivably produce a "self-fulfilling prophecy": People expect catharsis to reduce their anger and aggressive urges; so they engage in it, and it eases them specifically because that's the outcome they expect. Most revealing was the second experiment of the pair. In brief, one group of participants read a bogus *Science* article that was "pro-catharsis," in which catharsis was lauded as highly effective; another group read a comparable "anticatharsis" article, and a control group read an article unrelated to catharsis. Next, the researchers deliberately angered the participants, who were then given the opportunity to hit a punching bag (the catharsis phase). Finally, the participants engaged in a competitive task designed to elicit aggressive behavior from them. The results were quite clear in their implications: Compared to the control group, the participants who read the procatharsis article responded with significantly *more* aggression in the final phase. Paraphrasing the researchers' interpretation, these participants apparently "chased" cathartic relief, having failed to find it with the punching bag—in other words, becoming more aggressive rather than less.

In sum, consistent with social-learning theory, catharsis usually doesn't work. In turn, consistent with social-cognitive theory, an abiding belief in catharsis can lead people to ever higher levels of anger and aggressive behavior precisely because it doesn't work.

The **superego** begins to evolve from the ego during early childhood. It consists of two parts. First, there is what we call *conscience*, that inner voice that warns us of what we ought not do. In addition, there is an *ego ideal* that contains our self-images and beliefs regarding who and what we should be. The superego can be said to operate according to the *morality principle*. It interacts dynamically with the id and the ego: If, for example, the id produces an impulse for sex and the ego devises a way to gratify it, the superego may intervene if it disapproves of what the ego proposes to do. How might the superego intervene? By threatening and perhaps delivering liberal doses of anxiety, shame, and guilt.

In the context of the personality as a whole, Freud's three components may develop with differing strengths. A person with a "strong" id and a "weak" superego, for example, has little in the way of moral and ethical controls on

According to Freud's theory, infants seek gratification through oral activity. Older children may turn to oral activity in times of stress.

behavior. A person with an "overdeveloped" superego is constantly guilt-ridden and tentative about everything.

Stages in Personality Development   The other developmental sequence consists of the **psychosexual stages** listed and described in Table 2–1. Here, the focus is on *erogenous zones* that shift over the first several years of development. An erogenous zone is an area of the body that produces intense gratification when stimulated. In the first stage—which corresponds to much of infancy—that area centers around the lips and mouth; hence, Freud called it the *oral stage*. Next comes the *anal stage*, in which the erogenous zone shifts to the region around the anus, and during which toilet training typically occurs in most cultures. Then comes the *phallic stage*, in which the erogenous zone shifts to the genitals, where it remains for life. After that there is a *latency stage* during middle childhood when sexual urges become dormant, and finally the true *genital stage*, which begins at puberty when sexual feelings again become prominent. Freud had much less to say about the latter two stages; he put most of his efforts into exploring the first three, perhaps because of his belief that the basics of an individual's personality are formed indelibly during early childhood.

Casual observation of children's behaviors during the oral, anal, and phallic stages do seem to correspond to what Freud emphasized. Infants do interact primarily by "mouthing" objects; toddlers do become concerned with eliminatory functions; and by early childhood children do have at least a primitive sexuality in that they can become sexually aroused. Freud was the first theorist to draw attention to such aspects of children's behavior, although his interpretations of what underlies these behaviors have not fared well.

Freud also proposed that **fixations** can occur during the psychosexual stages and affect the personality for life. Fixations are "arrestments" in development

psychosexual stages   Freud's stages of personality development in terms if erogenous zones.

fixation   According to Freud, and "arrestment" in development that causes the adult to continue to seek gratification in ways that are appropriate only for children.

Table 2–1   Freud's Psychosexual Stages

Oral (birth to age 1 or 1½ years)

Infant derives pleasure and gratification primarily from stimulation of the mouth and lips.

Example fixation: *Oral-incorporate*, in which the individual continues to derive important gratification from activities such as eating, drinking, and smoking.

Anal (age 1 or 1½ to 3)

Child derives pleasure and gratification primarily from eliminatory functions.

Example fixations: *Anal-retentive*, in which the individual's personality is characterized by stinginess and stubbornness, as well as by "emotional constipation" and difficulty expressing feelings; *anal-expulsive*, in which the individual has "emotional diarrhea" and can't keep thoughts and feelings in.

Phallic (age 3 to 5 or 6)

The erogenous zone shifts to the genitals and becomes sexual.

Major issue to be resolved: Oedipus or Electra complex.

Latency (age 5 or 6 to 12)

Sexual impulses are dormant.

Genital (age 12 on)

Primacy of sexual impulses returns with adolescence and puberty.

Primary source: Freud, 1924/1964.

that cause the adult to continue to seek gratifications in ways that are appropriate only for children. If, for example, a child is either over- or underfed during infancy, the child might develop into an adult who excessively chews gum, smokes, drinks, or talks. However, whereas no one denies that early experiences can profoundly affect later personality, research over the many years since Freud formulated his theory has provided little if any support for the long-range influence of early fixations. You may still hear some of the terms in Table 2–1 used in everyday conversation, however.

Freud's dynamics of psychosexual development have been especially controversial, but they are worth noting because they underscore some of the problems of the case-study method discussed in Chapter 1 and of Freud's method in general. On the basis of selected patients' reports and events of his own childhood, Freud proposed that *all* children experience what he called the **Oedipus complex**—so named after the legendary Thebian king who killed his father and unwittingly married his mother. During the phallic stage, Freud believed that the boy develops lustful desires for his mother, then becomes afraid that his father will castrate him for those desires (*castration anxiety*). Eventually, however, he *identifies* with his father and tries to be as similar to him as possible, particularly with regard to moral principles. The idea is that the father won't castrate the boy if the boy is just like the father. The boy's superego thus develops as a result of the Oedipus complex.

Girls also experience the Oedipus complex (at one point Freud considered calling the female version the *Electra* complex, a term derived from a female personage in Greek mythology, but he instead wound up using Oedipus to apply to both sexes). In the female version of Freud's theory, the girl develops lustful desires for her father in conjunction with *penis envy*, which causes her to wish to possess her father's penis. Eventually she resolves the conflict symbolically either by identifying with the mother or through hopes of having a male child. However, according to Freud, penis envy isn't nearly the driving force that castration anxiety is, so girls acquire much less in the way of moral principles and a personal ethic. In effect, women wind up with a weaker superego that is inferior to that of men.

As you might imagine, subsequent research has not confirmed the idea of universal Oedipal conflicts in early childhood and certainly not moral inferiority for women. Evidence to this effect is discussed in Chapter 8 in the context of gender development.

Freud's Contributions Revisited   Freud's psychoanalytic theory was deeply rooted in the Victorian, sexually inhibited culture of 19th-century and early 20th-century Vienna, where he lived and saw patients. Perhaps his greatest error originated in his generalizing from a very restricted sample of case studies to all humans. This problem was reinforced by his own personality that, often described as highly dogmatic, led him to "see" what he wanted to see in the behavior and dynamics of others.

However, despite its subjectivity and overemphasis on sexuality, classical psychoanalytic theory revolutionized how we look at personality and motivation, thereby setting the stage for more objective theories to come. Freud's lasting contributions include his idea of the unconscious mind, which—although not emphasized nearly as much in psychodynamic theory today—remains important. We aren't always aware of the reasons for our actions, and at least some of what we do is a direct result of needs and desires like those Freud attributed to the id. Freud's ideas about ego defense mechanisms such as repression—as extended and clarified by his daughter, Anna Freud (1895–1982)—are

Oedipus complex   According to Freud, during the phallic stage, a boy develops lustful desires for his mother and then a fear that his father will castrate him for those desires; a girl develops lustful desires for her father, but without the driving force of castration anxiety.

also still widely accepted as ways by which we sometimes deal with frustrated impulses and desires, also unpleasant aspects of social life (see Chapter 8).

Erikson's Psychosocial Theory

Erik Erikson (1902–1994) is called a *neo-Freudian* because his theory of personality development derives from Freud's, but with a different emphasis. Erikson, who studied primarily under Anna Freud, devised a theory that didn't directly contradict classical psychoanalysis but that emphasized unconscious forces much less than ego (conscious) functions. Erikson focused mainly on the effects of social interactions in shaping personality; his approach is therefore termed **psychosocial theory.** Based on case studies and thoughtful observations of people in various cultures, Erikson's theory also differs from Sigmund Freud's in that it includes developmental stages throughout the human lifespan instead of ending at entrance into puberty. Underlying the developmental stages are what Erikson called the *epigenetic principle*, a biological concept that there is a "ground plan" built into all living organisms that determines or at least sets the stage for development throughout the organism's lifespan (for his later ideas on epigenesis, see Erikson, 1984).

Erikson became disenchanted with classical psychoanalytic theory because he felt that it dealt only with extremes of behavior. Although he believed that development occurs in stages, with the earlier ones corresponding to those Freud proposed, he emphasized the manner in which social "crises" or conflicts are resolved in each stage (see Table 2–2). This differs markedly from the Freudian emphasis on psychosexual maturation as the primary determinant of personality development. Although Erikson agreed that early experiences are extremely significant, he saw personality development as a dynamic process that continues throughout life. Also, whereas he at least tacitly agreed with Freud that gratification of impulses and drives is a key force in life, he saw ego "synthesis" and the ordering and integration of experience as equally important (e.g., see Erikson, 1959).

The core concept of Erikson's theory is *ego identity*, a basic sense of who we are as individuals in terms of self-concept and self-image. A distinct part of each of us is based on the culture we grow up in, beginning with our interactions with caregivers during infancy and continuing with interactions with others outside the home as we grow and mature. Although Erikson's theory remains descriptive, it is less subjective than classical psychoanalysis. In its emphasis on social interactions, it also suggests what parents and others might actually do in fostering good development—as well as what we might do for ourselves.

Regarding the eight stages in Table 2–2, Erikson proposed that each stage builds on what went before. Although the adjustments a person makes at each stage can be altered or reversed later, the preferable course of development is "positive" resolution of the developmental conflict or crisis at each stage. For example, children who are denied affection and attention in infancy can make up for it if they are given extra attention at later stages. Development proceeds more smoothly, though, if children receive what they need in infancy and start out with a good sense of trust in others and in the world around them. In addition, although each conflict is "critical" at only one stage, it is present throughout life. For example, autonomy needs are especially important to toddlers, but throughout life people must continually test the degree of autonomy they can express in each new relationship.

We will return to each of Erikson's stages in later chapters. They provide an intuitively appealing description of some key concerns at each period of life.

psychosocial theory In Erikson's departure from Freud's theory, which emphasizes stages throughout the lifespan and social interactions as primary.

Table 2-2 Erikson's Psychosocial Stages

Trust versus mistrust (birth to age 1 year)

From their early caregivers, infants learn about the basic trustworthiness of their environment. If their needs are consistently met, and if they receive attention and affection, they form a global impression of the world as a safe place. If, on the other hand, their world is inconsistent, painful, stressful, and threatening, they learn to expect more of the same and come to believe that life is unpredictable and untrustworthy.

Autonomy versus shame and doubt (age 1 to 3 years)

Toddlers discover their own body and how to control it. They explore feeding and dressing, toileting, and new ways of moving about. When they begin to succeed in doing things for themselves, they gain a sense of self-confidence and self-control. If they instead continually fail and are punished or labeled as messy, sloppy, inadequate, or bad, they learn to feel shame and self-doubt.

Initiative versus guilt (age 3 to 6)

Children explore the world beyond themselves. They discover how the world works and how they can affect it. For them, the world consists of both real and imaginary people and things. If their explorations and activities are generally effective, they learn to deal with things and people in a constructive way and gain a sense of initiative. However, if they are severely criticized or over punished, they instead learn to feel guilty for many of their own actions.

Industry versus inferiority (age 6 to 12)

Children develop numerous skills and competencies in school, at home, and in the outside world. A sense of self is enriched by the realistic development of such competencies. Comparison with peers is increasingly significant. A negative evaluation of self as inferior compared to others is especially disruptive at this time.

Ego identity versus ego diffusion (age 12 to 18 or older)

Before adolescence, children begin to learn a number of different roles—student or friend, older sibling, athlete, musician, and the like. During adolescence, it becomes important to sort out and integrate those roles into a single, consistent identity. Adolescents seek basic values and attitudes that cut across their various roles. If they fail to form a central identity or cannot resolve a major conflict between two major roles with opposing value systems, the result is what Erikson called *ego diffusion*.

Intimacy versus isolation (age 18 or older to 40)

In late adolescence and young adulthood, the central developmental conflict is intimacy versus isolation. Intimacy involves more than sexual intimacy. It is an ability to share oneself with another person of either sex without fear of losing personal identity. Success in establishing intimacy is affected by the extent to which the five earlier conflicts have been resolved.

Generativity versus self-absorption (age 40 to 65)

In adulthood, after the earlier conflicts have been partly resolved, men and women are free to direct their attention more fully to the assistance of others. Parents sometimes "find themselves" by helping their children. Individuals can direct their energies without conflict to the solution of social issues. Failure to resolve earlier conflicts often leads to a preoccupation with self in terms of health, psychological needs, comfort, and the like.

Integrity versus despair (age 65 and older)

In the last stages of life, it is typical for individuals to look back over their lives and judge themselves. If, when looking back, people find that they are satisfied that their lives have had meaning and involvement, the result is sense of integrity. If life instead seems to have consisted of a series of misdirected efforts and lost chances, the outcome is a sense of despair.

Source: Adapted from Erikson, 1963.

The positive aspects of the theory as well as its limitations are discussed in more detail in later chapters in the context of each stage. For now, a major problem that you may already have noticed is that the theory is strongly oriented toward understanding personality development in Western and other cultures that stress *individual* identity over *collective* identity. This is ironic, noting that Erikson traveled extensively and based his theory on observations of people in many cultures. Yet this "bias" renders his theory far from being universal.

CONTENT CHECK
PSYCHODYNAMIC APPROACHES

True–False (answers are on the Companion Website)

1. Both Freud's psychoanalytic theory and Erikson's psychosocial theory are psychodynamic theories.
2. In Freud's psychoanalytic theory, the ego operates according to the pleasure principle.
3. In Freud's psychoanalytic theory, adult personality is determined primarily by early childhood fixations.
4. In Erikson's psychosocial theory, the emphasis is upon the ego.
5. In Erikson's psychosocial theory, the stages are determined by crises to be resolved.

Thinking Critically

What do Freud's theory and Erikson's theory have in common, and how do they differ?

Behaviorism and Learning Theories

As noted in Chapter 1, humans have performed experiments throughout the ages. True experimentation, however, was not applied to human development and behavior until the late 19th century—a scientific climate in which the **strict behaviorists** soon became predominent, at least in the United States. In strict (or "stimulus-response" or simply "S-R") behaviorism, only what is directly observable is considered worthy of study. (A *stimulus* is literally any environmental event that an organism is capable of detecting, such as a light or a sound; a *response* is literally any behavior the animal engages in.) Thinking, feeling, knowing, and the like are **covert behaviors** that can't be seen or measured with instrumentation. The premise of strict behaviorists is that researchers must limit themselves to studying **overt behavior,** meaning behavior that can be observed and measured objectively. In their view, this was the only way psychology could become a true science. In turn, they believe that the laws of behavior they discovered were applicable to an individual throughout the entire lifespan. We begin with two early researchers who considered themselves strict behaviorists. Then we trace the evolution of behaviorism into its more modern form—picking up the role of "learning theory" along the way.

Pavlov's Classical Conditioning

Russian physiologist Ivan Pavlov (1849–1936) spent the first part of his prominent career studying animal digestive processes, for which he won the Nobel Prize in 1904. His early researches included preparations in which dogs were *tracheotomized.* A small tube was surgically inserted into each dog's throat. With

strict behaviorism   The view that only observable, measurable behavior can be studied scientifically.

covert behavior   Behavior that cannot be seen or measured with instrumentation.

overt behavior   Behavior that can be observed and measured objectively.

the dogs held stationary in harnesses, Pavlov and his laboratory assistants could accurately measure the amount of salivation that occurred when food was placed in the dogs' mouths.

As it happened, however, Pavlov became sidetracked by his observation that after the dogs became experienced with the procedure they would begin to salivate *before* the food was placed in their mouths—including when they were simply approached by Pavlov or his assistants. The consequences of this detour dominated the remainder of his career. Pavlov became intensely interested in this phenomenon, which he initially called *psychic secretion*—an allusion to some manner of covert mental process. Later, he and the countless researchers to follow who studied what came to be known as Pavlovian, or **classical conditioning** (also called *respondent conditioning*), avoided such terms in favor of explanations based entirely on overt stimuli and responses (for a detailed account, see Rosenzweig, 1963).

Pavlov's experiments on salivation in dogs gave rise to what is now known as classical conditioning.

In classical conditioning, in brief, two or more stimuli are paired and become associated with each other in the subject's brain. In Pavlov's research, dogs were conditioned to salivate and otherwise prepare to receive food in response to sounds such as a bell tone or the click of a metronome. The sound was repeatedly paired with the food until eventually the sound alone produced salivation. Then the experimenters varied things like the timing of the two stimuli and recorded the effects in terms of how quickly the association was learned, how permanent it was, and so on.

Pavlovian conditioning has come to be regarded as a major way that our development and behavior, especially during childhood, are influenced by environmental events—planned or otherwise. We therefore return to the details of classical conditioning and the many behaviors to which it applies in Chapter 3, where we also discuss the modern "cognitive" view of how it works and the behaviors to which it does and does not apply.

Thorndike's Law of Effect

E. L. Thorndike (1874–1949) was a highly respected educator but is perhaps best known for his **law of effect** (1911). Simplified, this "law" states that (1) when behavior is followed by satisfying or pleasurable consequences, it tends to be repeated, and (2) when behavior is followed by unsatisfying or unpleasurable consequences, it tends not to be repeated. As a strict behaviorist, Thorndike defined "satisfying" simply as what an animal freely seeks or does, and "unsatisfying" as what a subject normally avoids or doesn't do. It isn't actually a law, however. Animals—especially humans—do not *always* behave in ways that are determined by satisfying or unsatisfying consequences, which we explore in depth in Chapter 3.

Thorndike formulated his law on the basis of research with animals, typically cats, in "puzzle boxes." The puzzle boxes were cages with various devices (such as a string or a lever) that the cat could manipulate to release the latch on a door, escape the puzzle box, and obtain food. Although we elaborate the use of contingencies in controlling behavior in Chapter 3, it may be helpful to note here that two contingencies were in effect for Thorndike's cats and that both are consistent with the *first half* of the law of effect. First, for a hungry cat, getting to eat food is obviously a satisfying consequence. Second, being confined in a cage is unsatisfying, but then the *consequence* of getting out of the cage is satisfying—again consistent with the first half of the law.

Otherwise, across successive *trials* (instances of a cat being placed in the puzzle box), a cat would come to escape the box faster and faster, until it reached the minimum time possible. Thus, it *learned* how to escape. Thorndike retained

classical conditioning A type of learning in which a neutral stimulus, such as a bell, comes to elicit a response, such as salivation, by repeated pairings with an unconditioned stimulus, such as food.

law of effect A principle of learning theory stating that a behavior's consequences determine the probability of its being repeated.

his strict-behaviorist orientation and called this *trial-and-error* learning, giving the cats no credit for having "figured out" or "solved" the problem cognitively. However, he did use the term learning, which is a covert behavior that again cannot be directly observed. We return to this issue later in the chapter; the key, as with satisfying and unsatisfying, is finding an objective and observable way of defining terms that represent things that can't be seen directly.

Classic Learning Theory

Learning refers to a relatively permanent change in behavior potential as a result of practice or experience. The definition has three key elements: (1) The change is typically permanent and enduring; (2) what actually changes is the *potential* for behavior (the subject may learn something that doesn't affect behavior until later, if ever); and (3) learning requires some kind of experience (for example, it does not result from growth or maturation).

Departing from the work of Pavlov and Thorndike, the early "learning theorists" who dominated U.S. psychology for roughly the first half of the 20th century focused on what they called *instrumental* behaviors, which are behaviors that produce consequences. They studied behaviors such as a rat finding its way through a maze to reach a "goal box" and obtain food, using measures such as how much time it took the rat to reach the goal box across repeated trials. Analogous to Thorndike's research, a trial consisted of placing the rat at the beginning of the maze and then assessing its progress toward the goal box. How many trials it takes the rat to run the maze without making errors (such as going into dead-end corridors) was a major focus of the analysis.

The learning theorists departed somewhat from strict behaviorism by using concepts such as learning, motivation, drives, incentives, and inhibitions, which are covert behaviors. As distinguished learning theorist Clark Hull (1884–1952) argued, such terms are scientific to the extent that they can be defined in terms of observable operations (e.g., see Hull, 1943). An operational definition of "hunger drive," for example, can be stated as the number of hours of food deprivation a rat experiences before an experiment, or as the percent reduction in the rat's body weight below normal. In turn, learning can be operationally defined in terms of the progressive reduction across trials in the time that it takes a rat to reach the goal box (or a cat to escape the puzzle box). The theorists could then pose research questions such as, "Does learning occur more rapidly if motivation in the form of hunger drive is increased?" As it turns out, it does but only up to a point. Subsequently, the rat is too weak to run the maze.

The learning theorists devised formulas for learning and behavior by averaging the behavior of individual subjects, and they eventually produced general "laws" of learning. An example is the *classic learning curve* illustrated in Figure 2–1, which extends readily to many human behaviors. For example, learning a skill such as playing a musical instrument is characterized by rapid improvement in performance at first, then by progressively slower improvement. Suppose a child is learning to play the guitar. At first the child improves rapidly in fingering and plucking strings and making chords; but it will be years before the child becomes a virtuoso, if ever. The learning curve holds up fairly well for many complex human skills, even though it originated in observations about how rats' performance in running mazes improves over time.

Certain other other functions and principles proposed by the classic learning theorists have also readily generalized to human behavior, but many have not, and the search for principles of learning that are universal across all species has

learning   The basic developmental process of change in the individual as a result of experience or practice.

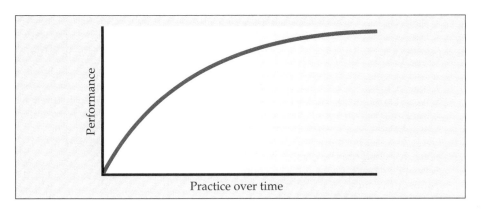

Figure 2-1 The Classic Learning Curve
In learning any complex skill, improvement is rapid at first and then gradually slows down and becomes more painstaking.

Source: Adapted from Hull, 1943.

largely been abandoned in favor of principles that are species-specific. We see examples of "exceptions" in human learning at various points in later chapters.

Skinner's Operant Conditioning

B. F. Skinner (1904–1990) coined the term **operant conditioning** (1938; see especially Skinner, 1953). He maintained that an animal's behavior "operates" on its environment and is repeated—or not repeated—because of the consequences. Consistent with Thorndike's view, those consequences can take various forms, such as receiving rewards for performing certain behaviors or avoiding unpleasant outcomes by performing certain behaviors. Many kinds of stimuli can serve as rewards (food, praise, social interactions, etc.) or as unpleasant outcomes (pain, discomfort). In Skinner's consistently extreme view, *all* of what we do or don't do occurs because of consequences.

In the lab, Skinner studied operant conditioning primarily with rats and pigeons. With rats, for example, an easy behavior to study is pressing a lever or "bar," which a rat can readily learn to do to obtain rewards such as food. Then things like the timing of the food delivery and the regularity with which it is delivered (for example, after every bar press versus after several bar presses) can be varied to see what effects the changes have on the rat's behavior. Skinner then focused on the *rate* of bar pressing as a function of various kinds of contingencies—that is, factors that might cause the rat to press the bar faster, slower, or not at all.

In a sense, Skinner also turned the clock back to strict behaviorism. Throughout his approximately 60-year and highly distinguished career, he steadfastly refused to use terms such as learning, motivation, and anything covert in explaining behavior, on grounds that such terms lead us to believe we understand something when we don't. As Skinner put it,

> When we say that a man eats *because* he is hungry . . . smokes a great deal *because* he has the smoking habit . . . or plays the piano well *because* of his musical ability, we seem to be referring to causes. But on analysis these phrases prove to be merely redundant descriptions. A single set of facts is described by the two statements: "He eats" and "He is hungry." A single set of facts is described by the two statements: "He smokes a great deal" and "He has the smoking habit." A single set of facts is described by the two statements: "He plays well" and "He has musical ability." The practice of explaining one statement in terms of the other is dangerous because it suggests that we have found the cause and therefore need search no further. (1953, p. 31)

B. F. Skinner in his prime, observing the operant behavior of a rat in one of his Skinner boxes. Modern operant conditioning research uses computers instead of the rack of electronic equipment shown in the background and the cumulative recorder shown in the foreground, but Skinner boxes remain the same.

operant conditioning A type of conditioning that occurs when an organism is reinforced or punished for voluntarily emitting a response.

A MATTER FOR DEBATE

ARE PEOPLE INHERENTLY GOOD, BAD, OR NEITHER?

Since classical antiquity, the ultimate nature of humanity has been the subject of debate. Are human beings inherently good at the "core" of personality, with positive motives toward self and others? Or are we inherently bad at the core, in the sense of being exclusively selfish and with propensities toward aggression and conquest? Or are we born essentially neutral in this respect? More generally, and parallel to the discussion of heredity and environment in Chapter 1, how do "nature" and "nurture" interact and what is the relative contribution of each?

Think about your opinion of people in general, based on those whom you know and those whom you've read or heard about in the media. How did they come to be the way they are? Are the altruistic, humanity-oriented, good people of our world behaving that way naturally, or is their behavior merely a "front" for selfish gains? Are those society deems bad—child molesters, rapists, serial killers—inherently good people who were severely warped by society? Or are people the way they are entirely as a result of their rearing and life experiences, having started out neither good nor bad?

English philosopher John Locke (1632–1704) argued that each person is born a *tabula rasa*, a "blank slate." His view follows logically from the *empiricist* position that everything we know and are derives from our experience via the senses. Therefore, nothing could be "built in," beyond the basic bi-ological processes that allow us to develop and function. In the 20th century, J. B. Watson elaborated on Locke's views. A strict behaviorist, Watson repeatedly stated that he could take any normal child and, given complete control over the child's environment, turn that child into any kind of person he wished—skilled or unskilled, good or bad (e.g., see Watson, 1925). From this perspective, society is entirely responsible for who and what we will become. In accordance with the strict behaviorist position that we are passive and molded by the environment, we also don't have much say in the matter.

Meanwhile, another English empiricist, Thomas Hobbes (1588–1679), proposed that people are inherently selfish and, consequently, in need of strict molding and ongoing control if they are to become cooperative members of society. A very similar position underlies Freud's psychoanalytic theory: At the core of both these beliefs is the idea that people have selfish motives for survival, sex, and aggression; there is nothing positive or altruistic in human behavior. These views are also highly consistent with the Christian doctrine of *original sin*, which holds that people have inherent tendencies to be self-serving and to transgress against others in the process. Daily functioning, then, requires that we work at keeping our selfish inner drives and desires in check.

French philosopher Jean Jacques Rousseau (1712–1778) took still another view, holding that people are born in-herently good but often corrupted by the "evils" of society. In a very similar vein, 20th century psychologists Abraham Maslow and Carl Rogers (Chapter 14) argued that our inner core is basically good, with positive motives toward both self and others. We actively seek personal growth and fulfillment, while also being concerned with love, belongingness, and the welfare of those around us.

Which of these three basic views of human beings is correct? There is as yet no clear answer. Caring for others in the form of empathy is clearly present in 2-year-olds (e.g., see Young, Fox, & Zahn-Waxler, 1999), and now-classic research by Martin Hoffman and colleagues has provided evidence that even 2-*day*-old infants sense the distress of others and are disturbed by it (Sagi & Hoffman, 1976, 1994; Hoffman, 1981, 1982; see also Hoffman, 1990). This strongly suggests that empathy is inborn, although it is apparent that very young infants are also keenly oriented toward gaining pleasure and avoiding pain first and foremost. It is also obvious that children must *learn* the specific morals and values of their culture. Whatever inherited predisposition we might have interact with family influences, culture, and society to determine whether we become good or not-so-good members of society, and whether we start out essentially good, bad, or neutral remains a matter for debate.

In other words, such statements are entirely *circular*. How do we know a person is hungry? Because the person eats. Why does the person eat? Because the person is hungry. As numerous theorists have pointed out, however, there are ways out of this trap, ways to retain scientific use of terms that describe inner, covert states or processes. We have already noted one: the learning theorists' use of operational definitions for states such as hunger. The debates continue, however, on the *extent* to which such terms should be used.

Nevertheless, with appropriate limitations and exceptions (especially for humans) as discussed in Chapter 3 in the context of the details of operant conditioning, Skinner's approach has come to be viewed as a major way that environment influences our development and behavior.

Social-Learning Theory

Social-learning theorists such as Albert Bandura recognize that children and adults observe their own behavior, the behavior of others, and also the consequences of those behaviors—as in Bandura's observational-learning experiment in Chapter 1. Even young children can anticipate consequences on the basis of the observations of past situations and events. In turn, people form opinions about themselves and others and then behave in ways that are consistent with those opinions (Miller, 1989).

Social-learning theory received a major impetus from Bandura's research in the 1960s, but it has roots in social psychology and related disciplines that date at least to the early 1950s. In addition, as we see repeatedly in later chapters, since the 1960s social-learning theory has been applied by numerous researchers to the acquisition of a broad range of behaviors, beliefs, and attitudes—both individual and cultural. These include much more extensive research on aggression, as well as prosocial behavior (e.g., helping others), gender identity, prejudice and discrimination, numerous mental and behavioral disorders, and alcohol and other substance abuses.

As with the other approaches discussed in this section, social-learning theory does have its limitations. One is simply that it tends to approach learning as a one-way street, without allowance for ongoing interactions and give-and-take between observer and model. Another is that just as everything we do is not always a result of contingencies, everything we learn is not always a result of observing and imitating others. Some things we figure out for ourselves. Some behaviors we see others engage we deliberately do not imitate—even when the behaviors are appropriate and adaptive. Characteristics of a model that influence whether a behavior will or will not be imitated by an observer are discussed in Chapter 8.

CONTENT CHECK

BEHAVIORISM AND LEARNING THEORIES

True–False (answers are on the Companion Website)

1. Strict behaviorists focus on covert behavior.
2. Pavlov's classical conditioning is an example of strict behaviorism.
3. Thorndike's law of effect laid the groundwork for Skinner's operant conditioning.
4. Classic learning theorists avoided operational definitions wherever possible.
5. Social-learning theory focuses primarily on how consequences affect behavior.

Thinking Critically

What do the approaches of Thorndike, the classic learning theorists, and Skinner have in common?

Cognitive Approaches

Experimental research has come a long way away from the narrow view espoused by the strict behaviorists; developmentalists now often *prefer* to deal with covert processes such as thinking, reasoning, and understanding. However, they still emphasize the need to verify those processes via observable or otherwise measurable behavior.

As with psychodynamic theory and strict behaviorism, the approaches discussed in this section also have roots in the early 20th century; they simply weren't in the foreground. We begin with developmental approaches to studying cognition that began in the 1920s, then introduce a broad area of cognitive study drawn largely from social psychology that also began in the 1920s, and conclude with the highly influential theorizing about cognition based on computer models that began in the 1950s.

Piaget's Cognitive-Developmental Theory

Cognitive-developmental theory focuses on thinking, reasoning, and problem solving, with emphasis upon how such processes develop beginning in infancy. Swiss cognitive theorist Jean Piaget (1896–1980) pioneered this line of research.

Piaget believed that the mind does not simply respond to stimuli and consequences but instead grows, changes, and adapts to the world (1950, 1970). Piaget and some other cognitive-developmental psychologists have been called **structuralists** because they are concerned with the structure of thought and the way in which the mind operates on information (Gardner, 1973). Here, the term "structure" is not to be taken literally, as if it corresponded directly to neural structures in the brain. The cognitive structures of Piaget are instead abstract and hypothetical.

Piaget's investigations grew out of his studies in biology and philosophy. In his adolescence he completed some pioneering work on the adaptive behavior of mollusks (snails and clams) and studied with an uncle the philosophical question of "How we come to know." These two concerns—adaptation and the development of thought—became his life work. One key influence was his early work on intelligence tests in the 1920s (see Chapter 9 for a discussion of the origins of intelligence testing). Hired to help develop the tests, he soon became much more interested in children's *wrong* answers than the correct ones that determine intelligence scores. Children's errors gave him insights into how children think. He saw consistent patterns indicating that children's thinking is *qualitatively* different from that of adults. In other words, differences in child and adult cognition are not confined to how much children know, which naturally is less than adults know; there are also differences in the *ways* children and adults know and go about understanding things. From this perspective, Piaget then conducted "mini-experiments" with his own children, expanded his work to a laboratory, and spent some 60 years studying and writing about cognitive development—at the same time attracting scores of colleagues and spawning a worldwide movement.

As we describe in more detail in the chapters on each age range, Piaget and his colleagues devised a broad range of tests to assess children's cognitive development and provide detail on how children at different cognitive levels think. Based on extensive research, Piaget proposed the stages of cognitive development summarized in Table 2–3.

A key feature of Piaget's theory is that the mind is an active participant in the learning process. If information or an experience the person encounters fits

cognitive-developmental theory An approach that focuses on the development of thinking, reasoning, and problem solving.

structuralists Cognitive-developmental psychologists concerned with the structure of thought and the way in which the mind operates on information.

Table 2–3   Piaget's Stages of Cognitive Development

Sensorimotor (birth to about age 2 years)

Infants learn about the world through looking, grasping, mouthing, and other actions. Intelligence relies on the senses and bodily motion, beginning with simple reflexes that give rise to more complex, voluntary behaviors.

Preoperational (age 2 to about 7)

Children form concepts and use symbols such as language to help them communicate. Such concepts are limited to their personal, immediate experience. Preoperational children possess very limited, sometimes "magical" notions of cause and effect and have difficulty classifying objects or events. They do not hold broad, general theories, but use their daily experiences to build specific knowledge. Preoperational children neither make generalizations about classes of objects (e.g., all grandmothers), nor can they think through the consequences of a particular chain of events.

Concrete operational (age 7 to 11 or 12)

Children begin to think logically, classify on more than one dimension at a time, and understand mathematical concepts, provided that they can apply these operations to concrete or at least concretely imaginable objects or events. Concrete operational children begin to use logic in their thinking, but they may experience difficulty in understanding that a particular animal can be both a "dog" and a "terrier," and they can deal with only one classification at a time. Yet 7-year-olds understand that terriers are a smaller group within the larger group, dogs. They can also see other subgroups such as terriers and poodles as "small dogs" and golden retrievers and St. Bernards as "large dogs." This kind of thinking shows an understanding of *hierarchy* in classification.

Formal operational (age 11 or 12 years on)

Individuals can explore logical solutions to both concrete and abstract concepts. They can think systematically about all possibilities and come up with logical solutions; they can project into the future or recall the past in solving problems; and they can reason by analogy and metaphor. Formal operational thinking no longer needs to be tied to physical objects or events. It allows the individual to ask and answer "what if" questions ("What if I were to say this to that person?"). It allows them to "get inside the heads" of other people and take on their roles or ideals.

Source: Adapted from Flavell, 1985.

within an existing mental framework, it is **assimilated.** If it does not fit, the mind may simply reject it or **accommodate** the new information or experience. Assimilation consists of interpreting new experiences in terms of existing mental structures—called **schemes** or **schemas**—without changing them significantly. Accommodation, in contrast, means changing existing schemes to integrate new experiences. Most learning situations involve an interaction between both processes: We interpret what we experience in terms of what we already know, and because new experiences are rarely exactly like older ones, we notice and process differences as well (Piaget, 1950). Consider learning to drive a car with a five-speed transmission if all you've driven before is an automatic. You'll assimilate things like manipulating the steering wheel and gas and brake pedals, while at the same time you'll be accommodating the clutch and gearshift.

In later chapters, we also discuss how Piaget and other researchers have applied cognitive-developmental theory beyond its initial emphasis on

assimilation In Piaget's theory, the process of making new information part of existing schemas.

accommodation Piaget's term for the act of changing our schemas when a new object or event does not fit.

schemes or schemas Piaget's term for mental structures that process information, perceptions, and experiences; the schemes of individuals change as they grow.

According to Piaget, children learn by actively exploring what is in their environment.

understanding the physical world to areas such as moral reasoning and how we acquire a sense of self. Although it has its critics and its shortcomings as we discuss for each stage, Piaget's theory remains highly influential and continues to be extended.

Vygotsky and Social-Cognitive Theory

According to Piaget, the child is an "active scientist" who interacts with the physical environment and develops increasingly complex thought strategies. This active, constructing child often seems to be working alone at solving problems and forming concepts. Increasingly, however, developmentalists are also emphasizing that the child is a *social* being who plays and talks with others and learns from these interactions as much or more than from figuring things out alone (e.g., see Bruner & Haste, 1987; Lloyd & Fernyhough, 1999a). In a Piagetian lab, children typically work alone in solving the problems given to them by researchers. In real life, however, children have ongoing experiences in the company of adults and older peers, who translate and help make sense of these experiences for them. Thus, children's cognitive development is often an "apprenticeship" in which more knowledgeable companions guide them in their understanding and skills (Rogoff, 1990).

Psychologist Lev Vygotsky (1896–1934) from the former Soviet Union was the first to emphasize the social context in which much of children's cognitive development takes place, as well as the historical development of the community's knowledge and understanding. He posed this central question: How do we collectively make sense of the world around us? Vygotsky incorporated sociology, anthropology, and history into trying to answer this question in the context of individual development. He concluded that we understand our world only by learning the **shared meanings** of others around us (e.g., see Vygotsky, 1935/1978).

Together, people construct shared meanings of objects and events, which are passed from generation to generation through observation as well as through

shared meanings Vygotsky's concept that we understand our world by learning both simple and complex concepts of the culture of others around us.

language. Simple activities like cooking or somewhat more complex ones like playing sports in the particular style of a particular culture are shared. Shared meaning also applies to much more complex things, such as the systematic learning of history, mathematics, literature, and social customs. We develop understanding and expertise mainly through apprenticeship with more knowledgeable learners, which has parallels with social-learning theory as discussed early. This **guided participation** enables us to understand more and more about our world and to develop an increasing number of skills.

Vygotsky defined two levels of cognitive development. The first is the child's actual developmental level, as determined by independent problem solving. The second is the child's level of potential development, as determined by the kind of problem solving the child can do under adult guidance or in collaboration or play with a more capable peer (Vygotsky, 1935/1978; Berk, 1994; Lloyd & Fernyhough, 1999b). This distance between what a child can do alone and what a child can do with help is called the **zone of proximal development.** Vygotsky illustrated this concept by contrasting two 7-year-old children, each of whom had a tested performance level of 7 years. One child, with the help of leading questions and demonstrations, could easily solve problems 2 years above his actual level of development. However, the other child, even with guidance and demonstration, could only solve problems 6 months ahead. Vygotsky emphasized that we need to know both the actual and the potential levels of development in children to fully understand their cognitive development and design appropriate instruction for them.

Experts have also pointed that Vygotsky's and Piaget's approaches are not opposites but instead complement each other in understanding cognitive development as a whole. Just as children (and adults) at times learn from others, they at times learn on their own.

It is also worth noting that the social-cognitive approach launched by Vygotsky is by no means the only theory that looks at the effects of social interactions upon cognition. Indeed, much of the vast discipline of social psychology is built upon the social and cultural origins of our knowledge as well as how that knowledge is structured. Generally referred to as **social cognition,** this approach emphasizes beliefs and attitudes and other "units" of knowledge— along with where they come from. Social cognition also frequently incorporates the term *schema*, with much the same meaning as Piagetian theory does. However, compared to Piaget's theory and the other elaborate theories discussed in this chapter, social-cognitive theories tend to be much more circumscribed and focused on specific aspects of development and behavior. Specific theorizing and observations about social cognition from perspectives other than Vygotsky's appear at numerous points in later chapters.

Information-Processing Theory

As noted, the study of cognition has been around a long time. However, for developmental cognitive theory in particular and cognitive psychology in general, a major advance occurred in the 1950s because of (1) the work of Allen Newell and Herbert Simon (1927–1992) and (2) the advent of the first near-modern computers. Newell and Simon focused on *artificial intelligence*, which refers to programming computers to "think" like humans. Their work, along with the work of countless researchers who have followed, revolutionized the scientific study of cognition through what came to be known as **information-processing theory.** For the first time, researchers had a theoretical model for tracking information into and out of the brain.

guided participation   Vygotsky's concept that we develop understanding and expertise mainly through apprenticeship with more knowledgeable learners.

zone of proximal development   Vygotsky's concept that children develop through prticipation in activities slightly beyond their competence with the help of adults or older children.

social cognition   Thought, knowledge, and understanding that involve the social world.

information-processing theory   A theory of human development that uses the computer as an analogy for the way the human mind receives, analyzes, and stores information.

In contrast to a computer, a human mind is capable of doing more than one thing simultaneously. This woman is monitoring the child's activities while at the same time talking on the phone.

As humans, we constantly process information. You're doing it right now as you attend to the letters and words on this page and filter out irrelevant sights and sounds around you. As you read, you translate words and sentences into facts and ideas, thinking about them and (hopefully) storing them for later reference, such as when you take an exam on this material.

Information-processing theorists use computer analogies in developing models of how memory and other aspects of human cognition work. A computer such as your PC or Mac has hardware—the machine itself—and software—the programs that instruct its operations. By analogy, we also have hardware—our central nervous system—and software—our natural and learned strategies for processing information. Information is input into computers, which then perform certain operations on the information, store it, and generate output. We selectively attend to information and perceive, associate, compute, or otherwise operate on it. The information is then stored in memory and retrieved later as necessary. Finally, "output" may be generated in the form of responses—words and actions.

This is not to say, however, that computers and humans learn and remember things in exactly the same way. For one thing, the electronic hardware of a computer is quite different from the organic human brain; we do not store information in the form of bits (0s and 1s) the way a computer does. For another, computer processing is *serial*, meaning that only one piece of information is processed at a time, even though modern computers run so fast that it's easy to overlook that. Humans, in contrast, can attend to and think about more than one thing at time, using *parallel* processing. If, for example, you're an experienced driver on an open stretch of freeway, you can readily attend to what's necessary to keep the car moving forward while thinking about something else, such as the wonderful time you're going to have with the person you're driving to see.

In general, however, the computer model works well and has generated volumes of valuable research on child-adult differences in *encoding*, the initial processing of information; *storage*, the temporary or permanent retention of information; and *retrieval*, the remembering of information at a later time. We look at differences and developmental changes in memory processes and strategies in each of the later chapters on cognition.

CONTENT CHECK
COGNITIVE APPROACHES

True–False (answers are on the Companion Website)

1. Both Piaget and Vygotsky are considered to be structuralists.
2. Both Piaget and Vygotsky viewed development as occurring in stages.
3. In Piaget's theory, assimilation means understanding new things via existing schemas and accommodation means understanding new things by altering existing schemas or acquiring new ones.
4. In Vygotsky's theory, the zone of proximal development is the distance between what a child can do alone and what a child can do with someone watching.
5. Humans and computers process information in different ways.

Thinking Critically

Is the child an active participant in cognitive development in both Piaget's theory and Vygotsky's theory? Why or why not?

Biological Approaches

For perspective, remember that Freud believed the id to be biological in origin, as Erikson did with regard to epigenesis. In turn, the learning theorists emphasized biology and physiological needs as a primary source of motivation. The idea that biological underpinnings influence many aspects of human development and behavior is not new.

What is new (or at least recent) is the subject of this section. Whereas the earlier theorists took biological processes as their starting point, they had little to say about them after that, preferring to study personality dynamics, learning, and so on. By contrast, biology in one form or another is at the *core* of the approaches discussed here.

We begin with an overview of the origins of biologically based development and behavior, deferring the specifics of the broad area of genetics and heredity to Chapter 3. That is, genetic mechanisms underlie most of the topics discussed here, but it isn't necessary to understand genetic mechanisms to understand their overall impact—just as it isn't necessary to understand how an automobile engine and transmission work to understand what an automobile does. Hopefully, beginning with a discussion of what is accomplished through genetics will make the later discussion of genetic mechanisms more concrete.

Darwin's focus on the adaptive value of inherited characteristics led to important modern formulations about development.

Evolution

The process by which species change across generations is **evolution.** Charles Darwin (1809–1882) is credited with the major work, *On the Origin of Species* (1859/1958), that gave rise to the modern understanding of evolution.

In this work, Darwin proposed the *theory* of **natural selection,** which centers around "survival of the fittest." The essentials are as follows. First, within a given species, individuals vary somewhat in physical and behavioral characteristics that are related to coping with and adapting to their environment. Except in the case of identical twins, just as no two humans are exactly alike, no two members of any species of animal, plant, or other taxonomic category are exactly like.

Then, if the environment changes (either for a species that stays in a given locale or a species that moves to a new one), those members that have characteristics that are better suited to the new environment will survive better and be more likely to live long enough to reproduce, thereby passing their characteristics along to the next generation. Those who are less suited have less of a chance—perhaps no chance if the environmental change is sudden and extreme. Down the line, with successive generations, adaptive characteristics spread to the entire species and maladaptive ones mostly drop out. Often in the history of life on this planet, through this process and given enough generations, species have become transformed into entirely new ones and the original species has become extinct.

Adaptation through natural selection applies to finding food and water, fending off diseases or predators, anything relevant to living long enough to reproduce successfully (and in many species, especially mammals, living long enough beyond that to rear the offspring to the point where they can take care of themselves). Natural selection also applies wherever there is competition for resources such as food. If, as a whole, one species is better than another at obtaining limited resources, the second species will eventually die out if it doesn't either move on to another locale or find a different *environmental niche*. This latter point, Darwin showed, was revealed very clearly by the finches of the

evolution   The process through which species change across generations.

natural selection   Survival of the fittest.

Galapagos Islands that he studied extensively: Presumably one species of finch originally made it to the islands, but over many generations diverse and quite different species of finches developed as they adapted to eating different foods and obtaining food in different ways.

Most theorists now take Darwinian natural selection for granted—it is a very well-established theory, as far as it goes. But there is more to natural selection than Darwin thought, a fact that we return to later in the chapter.

Ethology

Ethology owes its existence primarily to Karl von Frisch (1886–1982), Konrad Lorenz (1903–1989), and Niko Tinbergen (1907–1988), who were jointly awarded the 1973 Nobel Prize for medicine and physiology. Lorenz is perhaps best known for his extensive research on factors in imprinting in geese (Chapter 6) (for overviews of ethology as a discipline, see Lorenz, 1952; Tinbergen, 1963/1996).

Ethologists study evolved patterns of behavior, with emphasis on behavior that is guided by **instinct.** For a behavior to be considered instinctive, it must meet three criteria: (1) It must occur in all *normal* members of a species; (2) it must always occur under the same conditions; and (3) it must occur in essentially the same way every time. Dogs, cats, birds, rats, and most other nonhuman animals have evolved behaviors that meet these criteria. Have humans?

In the strict ethological sense, we apparently do not. For example, we may be tempted to view the universal sequence of language development in infancy—crying, cooing, and then babbling (Chapter 5)—as instinctive, but *preprogrammed* is a better term for these behaviors because infants quickly learn to modify them and to perform them in many different situations. We might also consider women as having a "maternal instinct" that propels them to have children and to take care of their young, but this falls apart in several ways. For one thing, not all women by far want to have children. Does this mean that they are not normal members of our species? Hardly. For another, not all women who have children take good care of them, and of those who do, childcare practices are extremely diverse across cultures. Finally, the concept of a maternal instinct is entirely circular (see also Skinner's argument with regard to internal states, discussed earlier). How do we know that a mother has a strong maternal instinct? Because she takes good care of her baby. Why does she take good care of her baby? Because she has a strong maternal instinct. . . .

Evolutionary Psychology

Sociobiology is an extension of ethology oriented toward the study of evolutionarily based *human* social behaviors. The term was coined by E. O. Wilson in 1975, and the issues that he raised quickly became highly controversial. Although only one short chapter was devoted to humans, it was a provocative one in which he claimed that evolutionary factors play a much larger role in human psychology than most social scientists were willing to accept.

Wilson's main contribution was in pulling together ideas that gave impetus to **evolutionary psychology,** which can be controversial at times as well but endeavors to be rigorously scientific. A central tenet is the concept of **inclusive fitness,** in which evolutionary survival of the fittest comes about in two ways. First, *direct fitness*, which is what Darwin proposed: the survival of the individual long enough to pass adaptive characteristics along to the next generation. Second, *indirect fitness*, which is based on the biological relatedness of parents and children, of siblings, of uncles and aunts and nieces and nephews, even of

ethology The study of patterns of animal behavior, especially behavior that is guided by instinct.

instinct Behavior that occurs in all normal members of a species, under the same conditions, and in the same way.

evolutionary psychology The study of inherited psychological characteristics.

inclusive fitness The concept that evolutionary survival of the fittest comes about through both direct and indirect fitness, where adaptive characteristics are passed along to the next generation and biological relatedness also plays a part.

cousins. As an illustration of the latter, suppose an aunt runs into a burning building to save her niece, and she succeeds but loses her own life in the process. Because of the shared biological heritage of the two, the aunt's characteristics are partly saved to be passed along—even if she doesn't have children of her own. It is in this way that evolutionary psychologists explain how **altruism,** which is usually defined as self-sacrifice without self-interest, might instead be quite "selfish" in an evolutionary sense and have evolved accordingly in humans.

Everything we do is selfish in this sense—whether or not we are aware of it. Our primary motive in life is—one way or another—to pass along our characteristics to the next generation. This is controversial enough, but where evolutionary psychology gets really controversial is in its more recent extensions to possible gender differences in human courtship behavior, which we return to in Chapter 14.

Discussion of evolution and psychology dates back to Darwin and *The Origin of Species*, and was extensive in the writings and research of the ethologists. However, according to Steven Pinker, in his popular book *How the Mind Works* (1997), evolutionary psychology was christened as a discipline by anthropologist John Tooby and psychologist Leda Cosmides (e.g., see Tooby & Cosmides, 1989). Pinker also noted that evolutionary psychology is basically a blend of cognitive psychology and evolutionary biology, with an emphasis on the human mind as an "organ" that has evolved like any other. Thus, evolutionary psychology attempts to delve into the cognitive and emotional processes that underlie human social interactions and reproduction, also culture in general.

In all, evolutionary psychology is still in its infancy and still in need of methodology that will make its propositions about evolved mechanisms in humans more acceptable to the scientific community at large. Nevertheless, it is beginning to make inroads into many areas of human behavior and endeavor. It is also busily spawning subdisciplines, such as the one discussed next.

Evolutionary Developmental Psychology In a sense, the emerging field of evolutionary developmental psychology has its origins in the research of English psychologist John Bowlby (1907–1990) on early infant-to-caregiver and caregiver-to-infant attachment. Bowlby's efforts had their origin partly in ethology and in Darwinian evolutionary theory (Bowlby, 1969/1980; also see Ainsworth & Bowlby, 1991, for a historical account). Among Bowlby's many observations about attachment and its importance was his conclusion that human infants and caregivers alike have evolved predispositions that increase infants' chances of surviving. For example, a young infant's crying distresses most adults and motivates them to approach and try to comfort the infant. Adults also tend to be attracted to a baby's doll-like appearance and other cute features and behaviors such as smiling. For the first month or so of life, crying and smiling are reflexive and convey no meaning, yet adults are induced to approach anyway—on each count suggesting the baby's behaviors and the adults reactions have evolved because of their adaptive value.

Besides examining adaptive functions of a large variety of infant, child, and adolescent behaviors (discussed in later chapters), modern evolutionary developmental psychologists are taking a broader look at the adaptive value of attachment in and of itself (e.g., see Geary & Bjorklund, 2000; Pederson & Moran, 1999; Pietromonaco & Barrett, 2000). They have also begun to theorize about the adaptive value of cognitive and physical immaturity during childhood and the extended period of childhood in humans as compared to other animals (Bjorklund, 1997).

According to evolutionary psychologists, altruistic self-sacrifice such as parents risking their lives to save their children may actually be selfish in origin because it serves to maintain the parents' biological heritage.

altruism Self-sacrifice without self-interest.

Developmental Neuroscience

The 1990s saw a proliferation of research in two allied disciplines, behavioral neuroscience and cognitive neuroscience—both of which seek to establish links between the functioning of brain structures, overt behavior, and the mind. The bulk of this research is conducted with rats and other laboratory animals, because they can be subjected to brain lesions (tiny cuts in neural tissue) to study the effects on behavior, be given powerful drugs, and have their brains dissected in post-mortems—a practice some find highly objectionable, but which is within ethical standards given that the researchers make every effort to minimize the animals' suffering. Researchers can generalize some of the outcomes to humans because of rat-human brain similarities, but much cannot be generalized because of rat-human brain differences—especially when the research is on cognitive or emotional behavior.

Increasingly, however, studies using harmless, noninvasive procedures such as brain scans (Chapter 5) are being conducted on human children, along with studies of children with brain damage and children who died from diseases. Much of this research has a developmental slant—giving rise to a subdiscipline appropriately called **developmental neuroscience.** A primary area of interest has been the development of brain structures associated with different kinds of memory (e.g., Ciesielski, Lesnik, Benzel, & Hart, 1999; Hayne, Boniface, & Barr, 2000; Nelson, 1995; Pascalis, de Haan, Nelson, & de Schonen, 1998; Schacter, Kagan, & Leichtman, 1995), which are described in Chapters 5 and 7.

In its relative infancy, developmental neuroscience has a long way to go in verifying relations between brain structures and functions and behavior and tracking developmental change, but as with behavioral and cognitive neuroscience in general, it is one of the most rapidly growing areas in the study of human development.

developmental neuroscience
The study of the development of brain structures and the relations betweeen brain structures and functions and behavior.

CONTENT CHECK
BIOLOGICAL APPROACHES

True–False (answers are on the Companion Website)

1. Both evolution and natural selection are theoretical.
2. Based on the ethological definition, humans do not have instincts.
3. In evolutionary psychology, altruistic behaviors cannot be naturally selected for.
4. In evolutionary developmental psychology, the emphasis is upon instincts.
5. Developmental neuroscientists study the relationship between brain structures and behavior.

Thinking Critically

Which of the approaches discussed in this section assume that modern human brain structures and functions have come about as a result of evolution?

Systems Approaches

Gradually, over the last several decades, developmental research (and research in the social and behavioral sciences in general) has been shifting to a higher level of analysis that focuses on *systems* and how they change and evolve. For our purposes, a system is (1) an organized and interactive set of components, that (2) operate according to certain principles and (3) serve some function. For example, the human body as a whole is a system: Its components include the head and brain, the sensory organs, the internal organs, the trunk, the musculature, and the limbs, all of which interact through principles such as neural transmission and serve many functions including simply keeping the body alive. At a somewhat finer level of analysis, the brain is a system: The various brain structures are components that interact in systematic ways to produce thought, emotion, and action. On a larger scale, a human family or other social group is a system: Its components are the individuals it is comprised of, it has a structure defined by society and rules particular to the group, and—when it works—it serves many functions ranging from surviving and remaining intact to accomplishing short- and long-term goals. As you can see, the term system can be applied to a broad range of issues and factors in human development and behavior, at a microscopic level, a macroscopic level, or anywhere in between.

However, interest in physiological systems and social groups as systems is not what is new; physiological systems research has been around for centuries, and social systems research has been around for several decades. What's relatively new is the application of systems models to complex *psychological* development and functioning, along with the very heights of complexity systems theory is beginning to achieve. What's also new is the promise systems theories hold for bridging the gaps between disparate and often contradictory theories of human development (Barton, 1994; Lewis, 2000). Systems theorists focus on the *dynamic* interplay between as many variables as possible and at as many levels as possible. In the words of Richard Lerner,

> . . . the person is not biologized, psychologized, or sociologized. Rather, the individual is "systemized"—that is, his or her development is embedded within an integrated matrix of variables derived from multiple levels of organization, and development is conceptualized as deriving from the dynamic relations among the variables within this multi-tiered matrix (1998, pp. 1–2).

Contextualism

The systems view that development and behavior always occur in a specific physical and sociocultural context (Chapter 1) is called **contextualism.** Most aspects of human development are markedly influenced by cultural practices and beliefs and the child-caregiver interactions they produce, consistent with the position taken by Vygotsky as discussed earlier.

Historically, the contextual approach relied on cross-cultural comparisons and the effects of different childcare practices on the child. For example, a popular area of research has been the clear difference in context and the possible outcomes when infants or young children sleep alone versus with one or more caregivers. In a now-classic descriptive study by Gilda Morelli and colleagues (Morelli, Rogoff, Oppenheim, & Goldsmith, 1992), the attitudes of middle-class U.S. families in which no children slept with their mothers after about 6 months of age were compared to those of Central American Mayan families in which all infants slept with their mothers into toddlerhood. In interviews, U.S. mothers stressed the need for early independence training, which is consistent with the predominantly individualist U.S culture as discussed in Chapter 1. In contrast, Mayan mothers saw infants sleeping alone in separate rooms as child *neglect.* They cited benefits of "co-sleeping" such as maintaining a close relationship

According to systems theorists, a family is a complex interacting system in which each member influences each other member with regard to functioning and development alike.

contextualism The view that environmental, social, psychological, and historical factors interact to determine development.

with the child and fostering the child's social awareness. In a detailed review of other research on sleeping arrangements, the authors cite additional benefits of co-sleeping such as increasing the likelihood of the child's survival because of the parent's presence if something goes wrong. This example shows how a traditional contextual approach to studying development via comparisons can yield considerable information that may be overlooked by studying development in only one culture and then generalizing the results to all children.

Nowadays, contextual approaches go further and emphasize the "big picture," namely, how cultural practices and the child or adult *interact* over the course of development and on several levels simultaneously—which brings us to ecological systems theories.

Ecological Systems Theories

The phrase **ecological systems theory** is an umbrella term that covers a variety of emerging approaches to studying development (Lewis, 2000). Each approach holds that human development cannot be understood in a simple, "mechanistic" or cause-and-effect way, as has traditionally been the norm (Dent-Read & Zukow-Goldring, 1997; Sharma & Fischer, 1998). For example, in the preceding study of Mayan versus U.S. sleeping arrangements, the researchers focused on the effects of co-sleeping on the child rather than on the effects on the mother, the father, siblings, or the role of co-sleeping within the community and its culture. Moreover, an ecological systems theorist might suggest that the picture painted by Morelli and colleagues was "static," in that it paid little attention to the role of co-sleeping in the ongoing, evolving relationship between mother and child. Morelli and colleagues did an admirable job of exploring different developmental domains, but from a systems perspective the study simply didn't go far enough.

The Bioecological Model Perhaps the most influential systems model of human development originated with the work of Urie Bronfenbrenner (1970, 1979) and continues to be refined and elaborated (Bronfenbrenner & Morris, 1998; Bronfenbrenner & Evans, 2000). Currently in its fifth reformulation, the **bioecological model** emphasizes that human development is a dynamic, reciprocal process that begins with genetic endowment and unfolds as a result of interactions with the immediate environment. At first this is primarily family members. As the child grows, the child actively restructures what become the multiple environments in which she or he functions, and at the same time the child is influenced by these settings, the interrelationships among them, and external influences from the larger environment. Bronfenbrenner and colleagues picture the sociocultural environment as a nested arrangement of four concentric systems, as illustrated in Figure 2–2. A key feature of the model is the fluid, back-and-forth interactions among the four systems across *time*, which yields a fifth system called the **chronosystem** (not illustrated).

The **microsystem,** or first level, refers to the activities, roles, and interactions of an individual and his or her immediate setting, such as the home, day-care center, or school. These interactions are called *proximal processes.* For example, in the home development may be encouraged by the mother's sensitivity to the child's moves toward independence. In turn, the child's moves toward independence may encourage the mother to think of new ways to promote this kind of behavior. Because of its immediacy, the microsystem is the environmental level that is most frequently studied by psychologists and other developmentalists.

The **mesosystem,** or second level, is formed by the interrelationships among two or more microsystems. Thus, development is affected by the formal and in-

ecological systems theory A theory of child development in which the growing child actively restructures aspects of the environment in which he or she lives while simultaneously being influenced by these environments and their relationships.

bioecological model A model that emphasizes that human development is a dynamic, reciprocal process that begins with genetic endowment and unfolds as a result of interactions with various levels of the environment.

chronosystem Part of Bronfenbrenner's model of the sociocultural environment; the fluid back-and-forth interactions among the four systems (microsystem, mesosystem, exosystem, macrosystem) across time.

microsystem First level of Bronfenbrenner's model of the sociocultural environment; the activities, roles, and interactions of an individual and his or her immediate setting.

mesosystem Second level of Bronfenbrenner's model of the sociocultural environment; the interrelationships of two or more microsystems.

Figure 2-2 **Figure 2-2 The Bioecological Model**

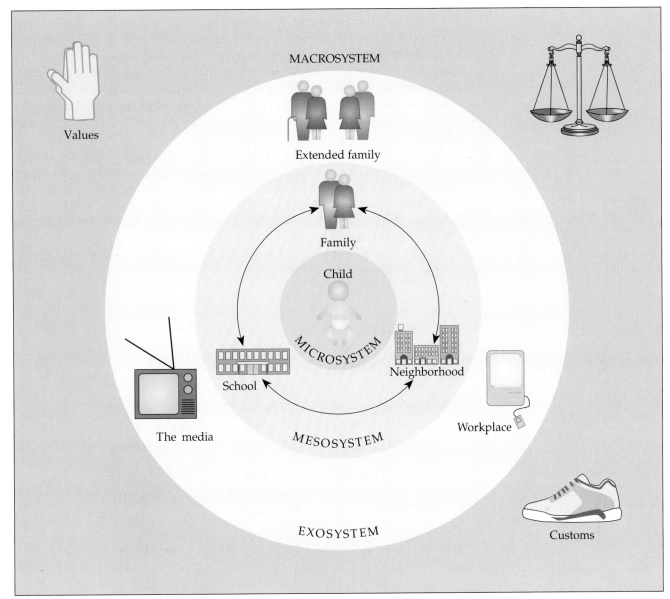

formal connections between the home and school or among the home, school, and peer group. For example, a child's progress at a day-care center may be affected positively by his or her parents' close communication with the teachers. Similarly, the attentiveness of the teachers is likely to benefit the child's interactions at home.

The **exosystem,** or third level, refers to social settings or organizations beyond the child's immediate experience that affect the child. Examples range from formal settings, such as a parent's workplace and the community health and welfare systems, to less formal organizations like the child's extended family or the parents' network of friends. For example, the child's mother may be employed by a company that allows her to work at home two or three days a week. That flexibility may enable the mother to spend more time with her child; thus, it may also indirectly promote the child's development. At the same

exosystem Third level of Bronfenbrenner's model of the sociocultural environment; social settings or organizations beyond an individual's immediate experience that affect the individual.

time, the increased time the mother spends with her child may make her less tense and therefore more productive on the job.

Unlike the other levels, the **macrosystem,** or outermost level, does not refer to a specific setting. It consists of the values, laws, and customs of the society in which the individual lives. For example, laws providing for *mainstreaming*—inclusion of children with disabilities in regular school classes—profoundly affect the educational and social development of both children with special needs and their agemates in these classes. In turn, the success or failure of mainstreaming may encourage or discourage other governmental efforts to integrate the two groups.

Although actions designed to encourage development can occur at all levels, Bronfenbrenner suggests that those occurring at the macrosystem level are especially important. This is because the macrosystem has the power to influence every other level. As another example, government programs like Head Start have had an enormous impact on the educational and social development of generations of U.S. children.

Specific genetic and environmental factors—especially those within the microsystem—are the subject of Chapter 3.

macrosystem Outermost level of Bronfenbrenner's model of the sociocultural environment; the values, laws, and customs of the society in which the individual lives.

CONTENT CHECK
SYSTEMS APPROACHES

True–False (answers are on the Companion Website)
1. Systems theory can be applied to both physiological and social systems.
2. The study of differences in U.S. and Mayan views of co-sleeping is a good example of modern contextualism.
3. In Bronfenbrenner's bioecological model, there are four interacting systems.
4. In Bronfenbrenner's bioecological model, proximal processes occur with the microsystem.

Thinking Critically

Why are systems approaches difficult to implement in developmental research?

Theories in Retrospect

As we've seen, some developmental theories have fared better than others, which raises a significant issue. A theory can never be "proved" or "disproved." Rather, with regard to the social sciences, a theory can be shown to apply to certain people in certain situations—the more people and situations, the better—or it can be shown not to apply. That is, a theory may at times make accurate predictions and at other times not. For example, as discussed earlier, some theorists view us as active participants in our own development, and some of the predictions they make are accurate. We do at times actively seek new knowledge on our own and make decisions that determine the directions our lives take. At the same time, other theorists view us more as passive creatures who are shaped and molded by our experiences, and some of the predictions they make are accurate too. We are at times markedly influenced by conditions that are imposed upon us by others and by the environment at large.

From a different perspective, part of a theory may work whereas part may not. A prime example is Freud's psychoanalytic theory. Much of Freud's theorizing about the dynamics of personality development during childhood has not withstood the test of time. Yet the part of his theory that says that we aren't always consciously aware of the reasons why we do things and that we often engage in mental "trickery" as a way of coping has held up quite well. This insight into Freud's theory, then, underscores our need to be **eclectic,** which means accepting and using those parts of a theory that work—in other words, refusing to discard a theory simply because it isn't accurate in its entirety. Similarly, being eclectic means being willing *and* able to draw upon what works from a broad range of theoretical perspectives. Obviously, the more theories and approaches you're familiar with, the better your chance of understanding development and people in general.

Eclecticism is important in another way. There is as yet no theory of development that qualifies as *the* theory. Indeed, it is unlikely that there ever will be a single theory that can fully account for and integrate the complexities of human development.

eclectic Accepting and using those parts of diverse theories that work; being willing and able to draw upon works from a broad range of theoretical perspectives.

CHAPTER 2 REVISITED

A good theory provides an organized framework, offers explanations, and makes predictions.

Additional Questions About Development

- Orgasmic theorists view development as active, mechanistic theorists view development as passive; both views are correct with regard to different aspects of development.

- Continuity theories view development as gradual change, stage theories view development as distinct progressions from one stage to the next; to the extent that there are meaningful stages, they are apparently not discrete and the progression is not abrupt.

Psychodynamic Approaches

- Psychodynamic approaches focus on the inner workings of the mind as it deals with external reality.

- Much of Freud's psychoanalytic theory has not survived in modern personality theories, but modern theories nevertheless owe psychoanalytic theory a great deal with regard to the idea of personality as an organized system and the importance of childhood events in personality development.

- Freud built his theory primarily on case studies of his patients and self-analysis.

- Freud's primary technique in psychoanalysis was free association; he also used dream analysis and often focused on resistance.

- In psychoanalytic theory, impulses from the id are biological in origin and the id operates according to the pleasure principle; the ego develops from the id and operates according to the reality principle; the superego develops from the ego and operates according to the morality principle.

- Within the id are the life instincts (Eros) and the death instincts (Thanatos), with emphasis upon sex and aggression; the ego attempts to gratify impulses from the id and may deploy defense mechanisms; within the superego are conscience and the ego ideal.

- Freud proposed five developmental stages, based on the shifting of erogenous zones: the oral stage, the anal stage, the phallic stage, the latency stage, and the genital stage.

- Freud believed that fixations during the early stages can affect personality for life.

- The idea of the unconscious mind and the idea of defense mechanisms are among the lasting contributions made by Freud.

- Erikson's psychosocial theory began as an extension of Freud's theory, but wound up bearing little resemblance to it; psychosocial theory places much more emphasis on ego functions and social interactions.

■ In Erikson's lifespan theory, development takes place in stages marked by crises; the stages are trust versus mistrust, autonomy versus shame and doubt, initiative versus guilt, industry versus inferiority, ego identity versus ego diffusion, intimacy versus isolation, generativity versus self-absorption, and integrity versus despair.

Behaviorism and Learning Theories

■ Strict (S-R) behaviorists study overt behavior and avoid consideration of covert behavior.

■ Pavlov was ultimately a strict behaviorist whose classical conditioning is now accepted as a major way we learn about and are affected by environment.

■ Thorndike was a strict behaviorist whose law of effect was derived from research on cats escaping puzzle boxes to obtain food; his view was that the cats learned to escape by trial and error.

■ The classic learning theorists studied instrumental behaviors, based on principles drawn from research by Pavlov and Thorndike; they also made extensive use of operational definitions of covert behaviors.

■ Skinner was a strict behaviorist whose operant conditioning of rats and pigeons and later humans was derived from Thorndike's law of effect; in Skinner's extreme view, all behavior depends upon external contingencies and consequences.

■ Bandura and other social-learning theorists emphasize how observation and imitation influence development and behavior.

Cognitive Approaches

■ Contemporary behaviorists and others often prefer to study covert behavior, but with the requirement that it be verifiable by overt behavior.

■ In Piaget's cognitive-developmental theory, children are active learners who construct knowledge in the form of schemas through assimilation and accommodation; their thinking is also qualitatively different from that of adults.

■ There are four stages in Piaget's theory: the sensorimotor stage, the preoperational stage, the concrete operational stage, and the formal operational stage.

■ In Vygotsky's view, the child is a social being whose cognitive development depends a great deal on acquiring shared meanings through guided participation with adults and older peers; he saw the zone of proximal development as especially important to learning and education.

■ Information-processing theorists use computer models to describe how humans encode, store, and retrieve information; although computers and humans don't process information in exactly the same way, there is enough similarity that information-processing models have been applied successfully to child and adult memory functions and other aspects of cognition.

Biological Approaches

■ In Darwin's view, evolution occurs through natural selection, adaptation across generations, and survival of the fittest.

■ Ethologists focus on evolved behaviors in nonhuman animals that might exist in humans as well; however, their tight definition of instinct largely rules out the existence of instinctive behaviors in humans.

■ Evolutionary psychologists employ what they call direct Darwinian fitness in understanding human development and behavior, but they add indirect fitness to explain behaviors such as altruism; inclusive fitness includes both processes.

■ Evolutionary developmental psychology, initiated by the work of Bowlby, focuses on questions such as how humans might have evolved predispositions that foster early attachment.

■ Behavioral neuroscience, cognitive neuroscience, and the newer area of developmental neuroscience focus on brain-behavior relationships.

Systems Approaches

■ Systems theories focus on how components of development and behavior dynamically interact at various levels; modern contextualism and ecological systems theories are prominent examples.

■ Bronfenbrenner's bioecological model is an ecological systems theory that emphasizes dynamic, ongoing interactions at every level from the immediate environment of the child to the impact of society and culture as a whole.

■ The model begins with consideration of the genetic endowment of the child, then proposes progressive higher levels of reciprocal influence on the developing child: the microsystem, the mesosystem, the exosystem, and the macrosystem, plus time and the chronosystem.

KEY TERMS

stages
psychodynamic approach
psychoanalysis
id
life instincts
Eros
death instincts
Thanatos
unconscious mind
ego
conscious mind
defense mechanisms
repression
superego
psychosexual stages
fixation
Oedipus complex
psychosocial theory

strict behaviorism
covert behavior
overt behavior
classical conditioning
law of effect
learning
operant conditioning
cognitive-developmental theory
structuralists
assimilation
accommodation
schemes and schemas
shared meanings
guided participation
zone of proximal development
social cognition
information-processing theory

evolution
natural selection
ethology
instinct
evolutionary psychology
inconclusive fitness
altruism
developmental neuroscience
contextualism
ecological systems theory
bioecological model
chronosystem
microsystem
mesosystem
exosystem
macrosystem
eclectic

HEREDITY AND ENVIRONMENT

3

CHAPTER OUTLINE

CHAPTER PREVIEW

Do you know:

1. What the implications are of having a *map* of the *humane genome*?

2. What *deoxyribonucleic acid* (DNA) is and what it does?

3. What *single nucleotide polymorphisms* (SNPs) are and why they are important?

4. What *genes* are and how they synthesize the many *proteins* that make life possible?

5. How cells *divide* to produce replicas of themselves and ova and sperm?

6. The role *mutation* plays in reproduction?

7. How genes *express* themselves and help determine physical and psychological characteristics?

8. The roles of genes and chromosomes in *congenital anomalies* (birth defects) and why some anomalies are more common in *males* than in *females*?

9. How *genetic counseling* works?

10. What role *recombinant DNA technology* plays in research on genetics and the search for genetic therapies?

11. The implications of the possibility that humans may someday be *cloned*?

12. How *behavior geneticists* study inheritance of psychological characteristics?

13. The basics and the importance of *habituation*, *classical conditioning*, *operant conditioning*, and *social learning*?

14. How *family systems* dynamically influence child development?

15. How families *transmit* culture to children?

16. How *historical factors* influence development and create generations and cohorts?

These are the main topics of Chapter 3.

On June 26, 2000, Celera Genomics and the Human Genome Project made a joint announcement at the White House that the "correct alphabetical order of the 3.12 billion letters" of the *human genome* had been mapped (Culliton, 2000, p. 1). What they had in hand was a working draft with much remaining to be done in filling in the gaps. It will in fact be many years before the incredibly complex functions of the genome in making and maintaining a living human being are fully understood. Nevertheless, it was an accomplishment that was heralded worldwide as one of the major scientific breakthroughs in all of human history, one with many ramifications. Greater insights into diseases will be achieved, cures for them may be found, and incurable diseases may be prevented in the first place. In addition, there will be new insights into the evolutionary origins of humans.

Highly controversial issues concerning the uses of the genome will no doubt also arise. For example, will it be ethical for parents to have their children screened prior to birth and decide not to have a child with a genome that is merely "undesirable"? What about employers not hiring people with "bad" genomes and insurance companies refusing to insure them (Yamey, 2000)? Such questions will indeed be difficult to deal with, although efforts are well under-way to make genome discrimination and other misuses illegal.

In this chapter we take a detailed look at heredity and environment and how each works, beginning with heredity at the molecular level and then working up to processes that set the stage for conception and development throughout the lifespan. Next we look at environment in detail, beginning with basic learning processes and then working up through family systems and sociocultural processes. We close with a reminder about the interaction of heredity and environment.

Molecular Genetics

Understanding biological development, along with understanding what the human genome is and what it does, begins with understanding the biochemicals that make up all life and what they do. These biochemicals reside in the cells that make up complex organisms such as humans, so that's where we begin.

Human Cells

The human body is comprised of over 200 different kinds of **cells,** which are the smallest self-contained structures. In spite of their diversity, virtually all of our somatic (bodily) cells have some essential things in common as illustrated in Figure 3–1. The outside layer is the *cell membrane*, which is porous to allow nutrients and other biochemicals to enter and the products of the cell to exit. Within the cell is the *cytoplasm*, which is comprised of a host of distinct and highly specialized structures held together by a fibrous *cytoskeleton* in a fluid suspension. *Mitochondria* are the "powerhouses" of the cell; they process nutrients and provide the cell's energy. The *endoplasmic reticulum*, the *Golgi apparatus*, and the *ribosomes* are components of the "assembly line" that produces

cells   The smallest self-contained structures in the human body.

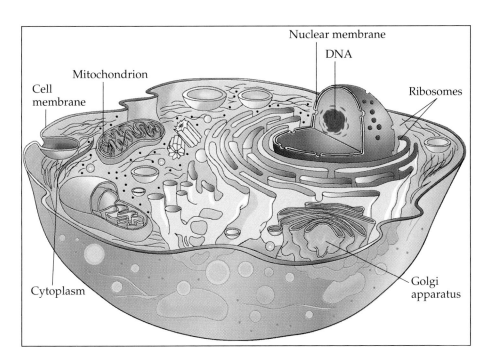

Figure 3–1   **A Bodily Cell**

From Human Heredity: Principles and Issues, 4th edition, *Copyright © 1997. Reprinted with permission of Wadsworth, an imprint of the Wadsworth Group, a division of Thomson Learning. Fax 800-730-2215.*

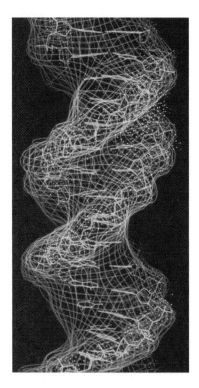

Figure 3–2 **A Computer-Generated Simulation of a Segment of DNA**

deoxyribonucleic acid (DNA)
A large, complex molecule composed of carbon, hydrogen, oxygen, nitrogen, and phosphorus. It contains the genetic code that regulates the functioning and development of an organism.

nucleotides Building blocks of DNA.

base A nitrogen-carbon-hydrogen component of nucleotides.

base pairs A "rung" in the DNA ladder; the base adenine pairs only with the base thymine, the base cytosine pairs only with the base guanine.

single nucleotide polymorphisms (SNPs) Nucleotide variations that occur on average about every 1,250 base pairs.

the many kinds of *proteins* that are essential to the life and functioning of both the cell and the body as a whole. The inner part of the cell is the *nucleus*, which is also surrounded by a porous membrane that separates it from the rest of the cytoplasm while allowing biochemicals to enter and exit. Finally, within the nucleus is most of the **deoxyribonucleic acid (DNA).** DNA serves as the "executive" of the cell and is the basis for heredity.

DNA The structure of DNA was discovered by James Watson, Francis Crick, and colleagues (Watson & Crick, 1953). With a paper merely two pages long and based on logical deductions from the findings of a number of earlier researchers, Watson and Crick revolutionized biology and related disciplines and later received the Nobel Prize. A computer-generated image of the "double helix" structure of DNA is presented in Figure 3–2.

DNA is a highly complex *macromolecule.* It is made up of many smaller molecules that are in turn comprised of atoms. If we hypothetically "unwind" a segment of DNA and visualize it as a ladder (Figure 3–3), we can see the building blocks called **nucleotides.** Each nucleotide consists of a phosphate molecule and a sugar molecule, which form the sides of the ladder, and one of four nitrogen-carbon-hydrogen **bases:** adenine (A), thymine (T), cytosine (C), and guanine (G), hydrogen-bonded in pairs that form the rungs of the ladder. (You can also see this structure in Figure 3–2: The sides or "backbone" are in violet, the rungs in green.)

Which two bases bond to form **base pairs** cannot vary. Because of their chemical makeup, adenine can only pair with thymine, and cytosine can only pair with guanine. There are, however, three important things that can vary: (1) which *side* of the ladder each base comes from, (2) the *order* in which the base pairs occur along the ladder, and (3) the overall number of base pairs. These variations account for differences between species; that is, all living organisms use just these four bases but with different arrangements and numbers of base pairs. For example, the DNA makeup of our closest living relatives, the chimpanzees, is over 98% the same as ours—less than 2% accounts for the marked differences between chimpanzees and us (e.g., see Pinker, 1997).

As noted at the outset, Celera's findings indicate that there are 3.12 billion "letters" of the human genome; what this really means is that there are 3.12 billion base pairs in human DNA. Moreover, the DNA of each normal human being is about 99.9% the same as every other normal human being (Lander, 1999). Only 0.1% accounts for the biological contribution to all of our individual differences in physical and psychological characteristics. One immediate implication of this finding is that it casts doubts about whether the concept of "race" is meaningful, as discussed in "In Theory, In Fact," p. 76).

At the molecular level, a large portion of the 0.1% individual difference takes the form of **single nucleotide polymorphisms (SNPs,** pronounced "snips"). SNPs are nucleotide variations that occur on average at about every 1250 base pairs (Celera Genomics Corporation, 2000), which yields a potential 5 million or so if Celera's data are correct—although it is thought that only about 10 to 20% of these perform meaningful functions. Over half have been identified by Celera and the Human Genome Project as of this writing, and the rate of discovery is such that most or all will probably have been identified by the time you read this. However, as with the human genome overall, it will take much longer to determine what all of these 5 million SNPs actually do. In the meantime, the race is on to determine which of the known SNPs are involved in

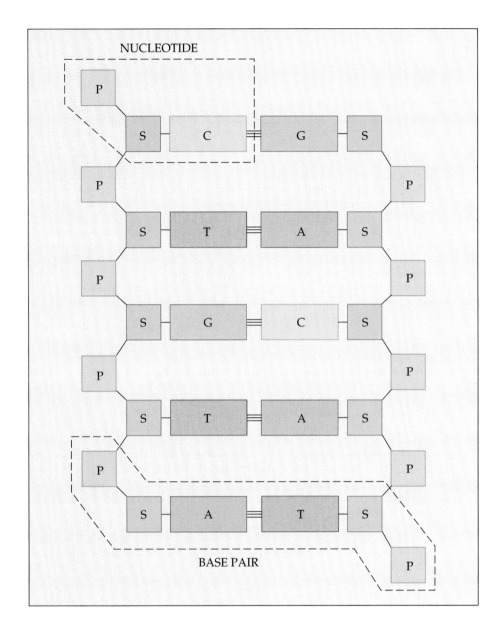

NUCLEOTIDE

BASE PAIR

Figure 3–3 **A Segment of DNA Visualized as a Ladder**
P = phosphate, S = sugar, A = adenine, T = thymine, C = cytosine, G = guanine.

According to Celera's findings, humans are 99.9% genetically identical.

genes The basic units of inheritance.

various diseases and which help explain how individuals respond differently to medicinal drugs.

Perhaps in the long run, the SNPs involved in the biological contribution to intelligence and personality will be identified as well, raising the possibility of benefits as well as risks of misuse.

Genes and Protein Synthesis

The concept of **genes** as the basic units of heredity was around long before the field of molecular genetics could determine their biochemical nature and verify that genes do indeed exist as meaningful units. A gene (which some prefer to call a *locus*) is a delineated segment of DNA that may be several hundred to several million base pairs long. As yet, the total number of genes in the human genome is unknown. Estimates range from 30,000 to 120,000; by combining estimates obtained in different ways, the range can be narrowed to an estimated 65,000 to 80,000 (Strachan & Read, 1999). At this writing, less than 10,000 genes

IN THEORY, IN FACT

RACE AND ETHNICITY

The June 26, 2000 announcement noted at the beginning of the chapter (by Craig Venter, President and Chief Scientific Officer of Celera Genomics) included the following:

> We have sequenced from the genomes of three females and two males who have identified themselves as Hispanic, Asian, Caucasian, or African American. We did this initial sampling . . . out of respect for the diversity that is America, and to help illustrate that *the concept of race has no genetic or scientific basis*. In the five Celera genomes *there is no way to tell one ethnicity from another* (emphasis added). (p. 1)

If race has no biological basis, which is also supported by studies in which differences *within* "racial" groups have been found to be much greater than differences *between* them (e.g., Zuckerman, 1990), is race useful as a construct? Is it meaningful in some sense to think and talk and write about people as being different based on physical characteristics such as skin color, hair color and type, facial features, and other anatomy? Is it meaningful to compare people who are grouped, typically, as "black," "white," "Asian," or "Hispanic"? (The latter is especially problematic, because it covers a truly diverse range of peoples who often don't use the term to describe themselves.)

Although there have been arguments to the contrary (e.g., Eisenman, 1995; Helms & Talleyrand, 1997), it appears that *ethnicity* is a much more useful term than in describing and understanding peoples (Brace, 1995; Dole, 1995; Yee, Fairchild, Weizmann,

& Wyatt, 1993). This is not a new idea; it was proposed back in the 1950s (Montagu, 1951; as discussed by Yee et al., 1993).

Ethnicity "is a concept that incorporates social, religious, linguistic, dietary, and other variables to identify individual persons and populations" (Witzig, 1996; p. 675). Ethnicity, with its roots primarily in culture and to an extent in the social construct of race (in that people may identify with and define themselves according to racial membership), is a much clearer concept. It also gets around a number of problems associated with classifying peoples and studying how they differ and why. For one, if you look around the world you will find peoples that display almost every conceivable combination of physical features thought to reflect race (Segall et al., 1999; Shreeve, 1996). There are darker-skinned people with essentially "white" facial features, there are people with Asian coloration but "black" features, and on and on—all of whom defy simple classification. There are also numerous biracial and multiracial people—people of mixed ancestry—who also defy simple classification.

Focusing on ethnicity also bypasses the notorious "one-drop rule"—the idea that if a person has predominantly white features but has even a trace of black ancestry, the person is black. Similarly, if an apparently white person has a bit of Asian ancestry, the person is Asian. Aside from the clearly white bias of this outmoded idea, it produces marked difficulties for developmental researchers where comparative surveys are concerned. U.S. Census Bureau statistics, for example—which can be quite helpful and are used at various

points in this text—are at the same time often vague with regard to what the statistics actually represent. For example, not all black people are ethnically black even though they may self-identify as black on surveys. In addition, U.S. and other black subcultures can be quite diverse among themselves—being black can mean different things. In the United States, the same observation applies to Asian cultures, which may be Japanese, Chinese, Korean, Vietnamese, and many others, each with quite different beliefs and customs. U.S. white subcultures can be even more diverse, to the extent that they retain elements of their differing European and other cultural heritages, also that they vary geographically.

Many people are proud of what they perceive as their racial or other heritages, and this does have to be taken into account. Many people incorporate this into their feelings of belonging to something and their sense of who they are. In turn, the black experience in particular in the United States has been such that its effects on succeeding generations of black people cannot be ignored. As a friend of one of your authors (GJC) put it, "If you look at me and see me as a black woman, you don't really see me; if you look at me and don't see me as black, you don't really see me either."

Thus, we make every effort in this text to qualify race-oriented data with regard to the limits on their interpretation. Where possible, we also provide subcultural and ethnic information on participants in such research. Some theorists and researchers do provide this, and predictably many more will in the future.

---

have been mapped to specific DNA locations (Human Genome Organization, HUGO, 2000; Online Mendelian Inheritance in Man, OMIM, 2000) and far fewer have been identified with regard to their specific function (or dysfunction).

On a moment-to-moment and day-to-day basis the most significant thing genes do is *protein synthesis*. **Proteins** are molecules that perform a diverse array of crucial functions throughout the body. The National Center for Biotechnology (NCBI) database currently lists over 200,000 different human proteins. *Enzymes* are the most common kind of protein: They serve as catalysts

proteins Molecules that perform a diverse array of crucial functions in the human body; examples include enzymes, hemoglobin, collagen, and hormones.

in the multitude of ongoing biochemical reactions within the cell and through-out the body, which means that they break down or alter biochemicals. They also perform this function in producing other proteins and in replicating or re-pairing DNA. Other proteins in the cell membrane perform functions such as regulating the flow of biochemicals in and out, "informing" the cell about ex-ternal conditions, and recognizing and destroying invaders if possible. The *he-moglobin* in red blood cells is a protein that binds with oxygen, allowing it to be transported to cells throughout the body and especially the brain. Muscles are made up of special "contractile" protein that allows them to move and exert ef-fort. Bones and connective tissues include *collagen*, another specialized, struc-tural protein. Hair and nails are also made of protein. Yet another important class of proteins is the *hormones* that regulate physical growth and development from the prenatal period on, that trigger the adolescent growth spurt and en-trance into puberty (Chapter 11), and that help prepare the body for stress and danger. In turn, abnormalities in proteins or in their rate of production are a pri-mary cause of genetic disorders discussed later in the chapter.

An Overview of Protein Synthesis Of the many thousands of genes, only a small proportion are "active" and synthesize proteins necessary to life. The process begins when a nuclear enzyme attaches to the appropriate segment of DNA and causes the nucleotide bonds to separate. One side then serves as a template and begins attracting free nucleotides in a process called *transcription* that will result in *messenger RNA (mRNA)*. As illustrated in Figure 3–4, the re-sulting "pre-mRNA" strand is a mirror image of the DNA strand, except that the base *uracil* (U) bonds with adenine; mRNA has no thymine. In the next steps, the pre-mRNA strand separates and the DNA strands reunite. The pre-mRNA then undergoes further processing in the nucleus of the cell in which unnecessary nucleotides are removed and the strand is "capped" at the ends, turning it into mature mRNA that is ready to exit to the cell's cytoplasm. Note that each "triplet" of nucleotides is called a *codon*; each of these will *translated* into specific *amino acids*, molecules that are the components of proteins.

Transfer RNA (tRNA) molecules initiate this translation by attaching to the mRNA codons at one end and binding the free-floating amino acids that corre-spond to them—with the help of cytoplasmic enzymes that perform the actual recognition.

In the next phase, a *ribosome*—again with the help of enzymes—starts at one end of the mRNA-tRNA strand and moves along it in steps. At each step, adjacent amino acids are bonded into a string called a *polypeptide chain*; when the ribosome reaches the end, the polypeptide chain is complete and is released. Some proteins consist of a single polypeptide chain; complex proteins consist of several.

Some ribosomes are attached to the walls of the endoplasmic reticulum (Fig-ure 3–1); if one of these performs the translation, the polypeptide chain enters the endoplasmic reticulum for further processing, such as combination with other polypeptide chains to produce a complex protein. The chemical structure may be altered as well; it all depends upon which protein is being synthesized. From there, proteins are "packaged" and sent to the Golgi apparatus for further pro-cessing and eventual secretion through the cell membrane. Other ribosomes are free in the cytoplasm; if one of these does the translation, the polypeptide chain typically becomes activated as a protein immediately and remains within the cell.

Thus, it only takes the four nucleotides that make up the DNA of all living things to produce potentially billions of combinations of the 20 main amino acids, that is, billions of different proteins. As noted, over 200,000 proteins have been identified in humans.

Figure 3–4 The Steps in Protein Synthesis

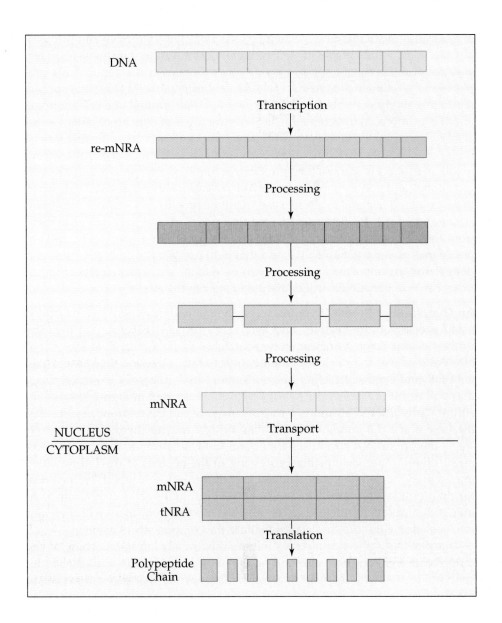

CONTENT CHECK

MOLECULAR GENETICS

True–False (answers are on the Companion Website)

1. Human DNA is based on five nucleotides.
2. All normal human beings are genetically 99.9% the same.
3. SNPs are the basis for individual differences in humans.
4. Enzymes are the most common kind of protein.
5. Protein synthesis begins in the cell's cytoplasm.

Thinking Critically

Why is protein synthesis so important to ongoing life?

Genes, Chromosomes, and Cell Division

Most of the time, DNA is spread throughout the confines of the nucleus. When a cell prepares to divide, however, the DNA assembles into **chromosomes.** Staining and computerized rearrangement of the chromosomes then yield *karyograms* such as the two in Figure 3–5. The "banding" of the chromosomes has been studied extensively, and abnormalities at the chromosomal level can be detected by studying an individual's **karyotype.** In normal humans, most cells contain exactly 46 chromosomes arranged in 23 pairs. Twenty-two of the pairs are called **autosomes** and are numbered for the most part from largest to smallest—the distinction is simply that these are not involved in determining sex. The 23rd pair are the **sex chromosomes:** *XX* in females and *XY* in males.

Cell Division and Reproduction

When a cell is ready to divide and reproduce, the DNA staircase unwinds and the two long chains separate. Each chain then attracts new biochemical material from the cell to synthesize a new and complementary chain, and ultimately new cells.

In the process termed **mitosis,** each cell normally divides and duplicates itself exactly. After the DNA has replicated itself, the chromosome pairs separate and reproduce the former chromosomal arrangement of the original cell. Thus, two new cells are formed, each containing 46 chromosomes in 23 pairs just like those in the original cell, as shown on the left side of Figure 3–6.

Also shown in Figure 3–6 is **meiosis,** which is how reproductive cells (ova and sperm) are formed. This process results in **gametes,** cells that contain only 23 chromosomes (as opposed to 46 in 23 pairs). In males, meiosis takes place in the testes and involves two rounds of division, resulting in four fertile *sperm cells.* On entrance into puberty (Chapter 11), males normally begin producing many thousands of sperm cells on an ongoing basis, and they continue to do so throughout their lifespans. In contrast, meiosis in females begins in the ovaries well before birth and only partly completes all of the roughly 400,000 *ova* a woman will ever have—again in a two-stage process. The process becomes arrested at the point before the final division produces a functionally mature and fertilizable ovum and the second polar body. This final stage does not occur

chromosome   Chain of genes, visible under a microscope.

karyotype   A photograph of a cell's chromosomes arranged in pairs according to size.

autosomes   All chromosomes except those that determine sex.

sex chromosomes   The twenty-third chromosome pair, which determines sex.

mitosis   The process of ordinary cell division that results in two cells identical to the parent.

meiosis   The process of cell division in reproductive cells that results in gametes with an infinite number of different chromosomal arrangements.

gametes   Reproductive cells (sperm and ova).

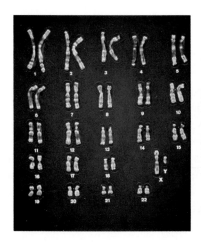 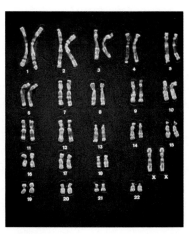

Figure 3–5   Human Karyograms
On the left is a male karyogram; one of the chromosomes of the 23rd pair is much smaller (XY). On the right is a female karyogram; the chromosomes of the 23rd pair are the same size (XX).

Figure 3-6 **Comparison of Mitosis and Meiosis**

Mitosis results in two cells that normally are identical to the original cell. In males, meiosis results in four sperm cells, each of which is genetically different. In females, meiosis results in only one relatively large ovum, plus two small polar bodies that aren't capable of being fertilized. Sometimes the first polar body also divides, yielding a total of three nonfertilizable polar bodies.

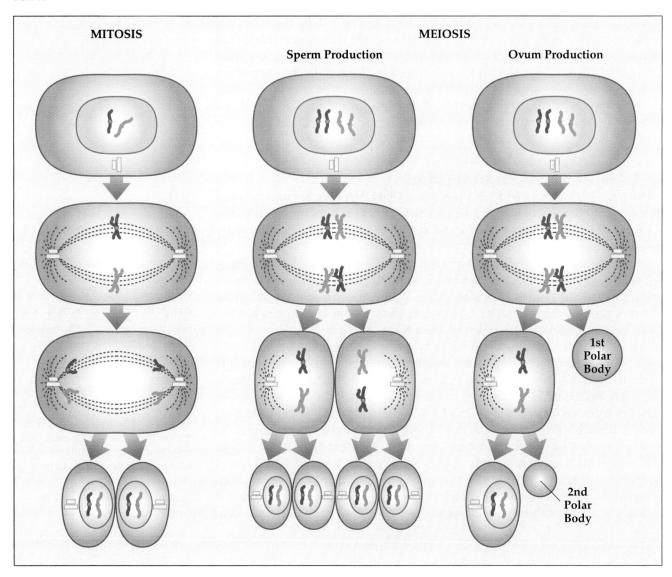

until the female enters puberty; then ova begin completing meiosis or "ripening" approximately once per month.

Meiosis and Fitness Meiosis is the primary reason why children are not exactly like their parents. Individual variation occurs in several ways. First, when the parents' chromosomes separate at the beginning of meiotic division, genetic material often randomly *crosses over* and is exchanged between the chromosomes, resulting in unique new ones. To that, add the possibility of mutations in genetic material. Next, in the final stage of meiotic division, which chromosomes go into which sperm or ovum is determined by chance. (This process is called *independent assortment*.) Similarly, at the time of fertilization and conception, which sperm and ovum unite is also determined by chance. Because of all of these possibilities for variation, it has been estimated that the same two parents could produce hundreds of trillions of unique children—many times the number of humans who have ever lived. We can therefore safely assume that no two people (other than identical twins, Chapter 4) are genetically almost exactly alike.

Mutation

Mutations were once thought to be relatively rare, but molecular genetics research has shown that they are actually quite frequent. At the molecular level, a mutation is an alteration in the DNA that typically occurs during mitosis or meiosis. In most cases mutation is maladaptive and the new cell simply dies (or repairs and eliminates the mutation), but a small number of mutations are *viable*—the cell survives. Many mutations are harmless and have no effect. Others can have pronounced effects. In mitotic cell division, if a viable mutation occurs early in development, it will then be passed along to all cells replicated in subsequent divisions of that cell. The effects may then be detrimental to the developing organism, or they may be adaptive in an evolutionary sense—especially if the mutation occurs very early and later affects the gametes. In meiotic cell division, mutation only affects the ensuing gametes and stops there, unless a mutated gamete happens to be involved in producing offspring—in which case the mutation can be passed along to the next generation and beyond.

Mutations occur primarily at the molecular level, usually during replication (excluding damage from radiation, toxic chemicals, and the like). They take various forms, each in turn potentially affecting gene expression and protein synthesis (Strachan & Read, 1999). *Base substitutions* are the most common type. These include the presence of a wrong base (or several wrong bases) at encoding locations on a gene, which in turn causes the wrong amino acid to be inserted in a protein sequence. Less frequent but especially insidious in their damaging effects are *deletions*, the simple loss of nucleotides during DNA replication, and *insertions*, the addition of nucleotides, sometimes through repetition of nucleotide chains. Mutations can also occur at the chromosomal level.

Regardless of the often deleterious effects of mutations, however, the ones that turn out to be viable and adaptive are the bottom line in evolution (Chapter 2). Without adaptive mutations that get passed along to succeeding generations, natural selection could not occur.

From Genotype to Phenotype

Just as each of the 22 autosomes is a duplicate pair, each of the thousands of genes within each autosome are paired. Alternate versions of a gene that perform the same function are called **alleles;** one allele is inherited from the mother and the other from the father. In turn, all of the pairs of alleles constitute the person's **genotype,** or individual biochemical makeup. In females, because the sex chromosomes are XX, genes all exist as matched allele pairs here as well. In males (XY), there are many genes on the X chromosome for which there is no match on the smaller Y chromosome.

Simple Dominance and Recessiveness   Some inherited traits, such as eye color, are primarily determined by a single gene pair. A child might inherit an allele for brown eyes *(B)* from the father and an allele for blue eyes *(b)* from the mother. The child's genotype for eye color would therefore be *Bb*. What actual eye color will the child display? As it happens, the allele for brown eyes *(B)* is

Hypothetically, the same parents can produce hundreds of trillions of unique children.

alleles   A pair of genes, found on corresponding chromosomes, that affect the same trait.

genotype   The genetic makeup of a given individual.

Gene pairs combine to create taller or shorter people, but environmental factors such as nutrition also help determine height.

dominant   In genetics, one gene of a gene pair that will cause a particular trait to be expressed.

recessive   In genetics, one of a gene pair that determines a trait in an individual only if the other member of that pair is also recessive.

phenotype   In genetics, those traits that are expressed in the individual.

homozygous   Referring to the arrangement in which the two alleles for a simple dominant-recessive trait are the same.

heterozygous   Referring to the arrangement in which the two alleles for a simple dominant-recessive trait differ.

incomplete dominance   Where people with a single recessive gene for a trait show some of the trait along with other normal manifestations; an example is sickle-cell anemia.

codominance   Where neither the dominant nor recessive allele is dominant and the resulting phenotype is a blend of the two; an example is the AB blood type.

dominant and the allele for blue eyes *(b)* **recessive.** When an allele is dominant, its presence in a gene pair will tend to cause that trait to be expressed as the **phenotype**—the displayed characteristic or trait. An individual with the genotype *BB* or *Bb* should therefore have the phenotype brown eyes. However, except in the case of simple physical characteristics (and with possible exceptions here as well), phenotype is more often a result of genetics and environment in interaction.

If the two alleles for a simple dominant-recessive trait are the same, the individual is said to be **homozygous** for that trait. With regard to eye color, a homozygous individual could be either *BB* or *bb*. If the alleles differ, the individual is **heterozygous**—*bB* or *Bb*. So, for example, a recessive trait such as blue eyes can be displayed by a child of parents who both have brown eyes if *both* parents are heterozygous for that trait. What are the chances for heterozygous brown-eyed parents producing a blue-eyed child? Four combinations are possible: *BB, bB, Bb,* and *bb*. Because only *bb* can produce a child with blue eyes, the chance is 1/4, or 25%. Note that if either brown-eyed parent is homozygous, there is no chance of having a blue-eyed child (barring mutation).

Other traits determined by simple dominance-recessiveness include hair color, hair type, skin pigmentation, nose shape, and dimples, plus numerous anomalies and disorders that are genetic in origin.

However, it's important to note that with many phenotypes that involve single gene-pairs, numerous individual variations are still possible (Alper, 1996). For example, with regard to genetic anomalies, a defective or mutated gene may contain thousands of base pairs, and *different* base pairs may be involved in making the gene defective. Different base pairs can mean differences in expression, so that some of the disorders we discuss later in the chapter may not be simply "either-or." Rather, they may lie on a continuum, where some individuals display the disorder to a greater or lesser degree than others, whereas still others with the defective gene may not display the disorder at all.

Incomplete Dominance and Codominance   Dominant alleles can be only partially dominant and recessive ones only partially recessive. The *sickle-cell trait* that occurs at its highest rate in individuals of black African ancestry is an example of **incomplete dominance:** People with a single recessive gene for the trait have a marked percentage of abnormal, "sickle-shaped" red blood cells that interfere with oxygen transport throughout the body, but such individuals have normal (dominant) red blood cells as well. It is believed that the high rate among certain populations is actually due to a prior adaptation: The sickled cells are resistant to malarial infection, so those individuals with the trait would have been more likely to survive long enough to have children in areas of the world where mosquito-borne malaria is highly prevalent.

Sickle-cell carriers tend to experience pain in the joints, blood clotting, swelling, and infections under conditions of oxygen shortage, such as at high altitudes. *Sickle-cell anemia*, however, occurs when an individual inherits both recessive alleles. The symptoms are much more severe, and without blood transfusions many such individuals do not survive past their teens.

Codominance is related but works a bit differently. Neither allele is dominant, and the resulting phenotype is equal blend of the two. The A and B blood types are an example: If an individual gets an allele for each, the result is type AB blood.

Polygenic Inheritance   More complex traits do not result from the alleles of a single gene pair but rather from a combination of many gene pairs. In determining height, for example, several gene pairs combine to create people with taller or shorter phenotypes—although environmental factors such as nutrition also play an important role in determining actual height. The overall system of interactions among genes and gene pairs is called **polygenic inheritance.** Such interactions frequently give rise to phenotypes that can differ markedly from those of either parent.

Polygenic mechanisms are exceedingly complex and largely beyond the scope of this text. For example, a group of genes may express itself differently according to which parent it comes from. Another example is gene "switching," in which one gene or gene group turns another gene or gene group on or off with regard to resulting phenotype. Yet another is gene "silencing," in which a faulty gene prevents the expression of other genes (Baker, 1999).

Sex-Linked Inheritance The 23rd chromosome pair determines **sex-linked inheritance.** Because the X chromosome contains many more genes than the Y chromosome, males are much more likely than females to display recessive traits. If a normally recessive allele appears on the male's X chromosome, there often is no allele on the Y chromosome to offset it, and the recessive trait will be expressed as the individual's phenotype. In contrast, in females the recessive trait will be expressed only if it occurs on both X chromosomes.

polygenic inheritance The overall system of interactions among genes and gene pairs.

sex-linked inheritance Traits determined by genes on the twenty-third chromosome pair.

CONTENT CHECK
GENES, CHROMOSOMES, AND CELL DIVISION

True–False (answers are on the Companion Website)
1. All of the cells of a normal human contain 46 chromosomes.
2. Meiosis is the process by which gametes are created.
3. Mutations that occur during cell division are inevitably harmful.
4. Genotype directly determines phenotype.
5. Psychological characteristics involve polygenic inheritance.

Thinking Critically
Why aren't children identical to their parents?

Genetic and Chromosomal Disorders

In the United States, most babies by far are born healthy and normal, but about 3% are born with **congenital anomalies** (which many still refer to as "birth defects") (Centers for Disease Control and Prevention, CDC, 2000a). Most of these approximately 120,000 infants will live; about 8,000 will die within the first year of life (CDC, 2000a). In turn, congenital anomalies account for almost 22% of infant deaths, making them the leading cause (U.S. Census Bureau, 1999).

"Congenital" simply means present at birth, and these anomalies can arise in two general ways: the genetic and chromosomal abnormalities discussed here, and abnormalities that result from exposure to toxins, diseases, and such during the prenatal period that are discussed in the next chapter. Many such causes have been identified, but more haven't; about 70% of congenital anomalies arise from as yet unknown causes (CDC, 2000a).

congenital anomalies Also called birth defects; abnormalities resulting from genetic and chromosomal problems as well as exposure to toxins, disease, and such during the prenatal period.

Genetic anomalies typically involve problems with specific *metabolic pathways*, which are chains of biochemical reactions. Most involve disruptions in metabolic pathways for protein production, during or after protein synthesis and either directly or indirectly as a result of defective DNA. Because of the sequential nature of metabolic-pathway reactions, even a very simple error at any point can damage the protein or prevent it from having its normal effects. Given this and the 3.12 billion base pairs in the human genome, you might think that errors either through inheritance or mutation would be relatively common, and they are. But as noted earlier, many mutations and other errors are harmless, many can be repaired within the cell, and many do not get passed along during cell division.

Sex-Linked Disorders

Sex-linked disorders can occur either at the genetic or the chromosomal level. Often, sex-linked genetic disorders occur via dominant-recessive patterns. As noted, a recessive gene on the X chromosome is much more likely to be expressed as the phenotype in males because the Y chromosome has no allele that might counteract the gene. Pattern baldness, which can include a receding hairline, loss of hair on the top of the head, or overall hair thinning, is a common example. Many men carry the recessive allele and display pattern baldness as early as their twenties. Many women carry the recessive allele as well, but a dominant allele on the other X chromosome prevents pattern baldness from being displayed. Partial color blindness is also much more common in males for the same reason (see Table 3–1).

Hemophilia is a dramatic example of a usually sex-linked disorder that is more likely to occur in males than in females. Hemophilia is actually a family of disorders, in the sense that different defective genes on the X chromosome (and in one form, on an autosome) disrupt different metabolic pathways that lead to normal blood clotting. That is, one or more different blood plasma factors are missing, depending upon which gene is affected. Each form, however, follows the usual dominant-recessive pattern.

Hemophilia is relatively rare, but it is a severe disorder, with no cure as yet beyond regular transfusions of normal blood. People with hemophilia may bleed indefinitely from a small wound, and any internal bleeding is especially dangerous because it may go unnoticed and cause death. Hemophilia assumed considerable media prominence in the 1980s because of its association with *acquired immunodeficiency syndrome* (AIDS). Before donated blood was routinely screened for the *human immunodeficiency virus* (HIV) that causes AIDS, many people with hemophilia who received blood transfusions contracted the virus.

Extra or missing sex chromosomes occur in a variety of ways. Females may have extra X chromosomes, males may have extra X or Y chromosomes. Females may also have only one X chromosome. Such combinations produce the disorders summarized in Table 3–1.

In addition, *chromosomal breakage* can occur both in males and females. An example is the inherited genetic disorder called *fragile X syndrome*. The term refers to breakage of a small portion of the tip of the X chromosome, which, although it amounts to less than 1%, can have profound effects. Growth abnormalities include a large head, large protruding ears, and a long face. Some babies with this condition also display atypical behavioral patterns such as hand clapping, hand biting, and hyperactivity. Fragile X syndrome is now the most common hereditary disorder associated with mental retardation (Tsuchiya, Forsythe, Robin, & Tunnessen, 1998).

Table 3–1   Examples of Sex-Linked Disorders

Statistics for each of the disorders are based on U.S. live births. For the extra X and extra Y disorders, the symptoms are usually more severe the more Xs or Ys a person has.

GENETIC:

Color-Blindness

Recessive disorder that occurs in almost 1 of 10 males. Genetic X-linked color-blindness is usually partial: that is, the disorder affects the ability to distinguish certain colors but not others.

Hemophilia A and B (see text)

Recessive disorders that occur in about 1 of 5,000 males. These interfere with normal blood clotting and that occur at different loci on the X chromosome. Hemophilia A is usually accompanied by color-blindness.

CHROMOSOMAL:

Fragile X Syndrome (see text)

Occurs in about 1 of 1,200 males and 1 of 2,500 females. Results from a breakage of the tip of an X chromosome. The ratios are different because females have two X chromosomes whereas males have one, so in females a normal X chromosome may partially or completely offset a fragile one.

Klinefelter syndrome (XXY, XXXY, XXXXY)

Occurs in about 1 of 1,000 males. The phenotype includes sterility, small external genitalia, undescended testicles, and breast enlargement. About 25% of men with Klinefelter's are mentally retarded. Physical manifestations can be eased by hormone replacement therapy in adolescence. The testosterone injections must be continued for life, however, to maintain male secondary sexual characteristics.

"Superfemale" syndrome (XXX, XXXX, XXXXX)

Occurs in about 1 of 1,000 females. Although these women appear normally female and are fertile and capable of bearing children with normal sex chromosome counts, the women tend to score slightly below average in intelligence.

"Supermale" syndrome (XYY, XYYY, XYYYY)

Occurs in about 1 of 1,000 males. These men tend to be taller than average, with a greater incidence of acne and minor skeletal abnormalities. It was once hypothesized that supermales are more aggressive and develop differently than males with a normal genotype. However, that conclusion turned out to be exaggerated. The National Academy of Sciences concluded that there is no evidence to support a relationship between an extra Y chromosome and aggressive, violent behavior.

Turner's syndrome (XO)

Occurs in about 1 of 10,000 females. One of the X chromosomes is either missing or inactive. Individuals with Turner's syndrome usually have an immature female appearance—they do not develop secondary sex characteristics. They also lack internal reproductive organs. They may be abnormally short and sometimes are mentally retarded. The disorder is usually discovered at puberty, and hormone replacement therapy can help with a more normal appearance.

Primary sources: OMIM, 2000; Pasternak, 1999.

Because fragile X syndrome involves a recessive gene on the X chromosome, males tend to be more severely affected, once again because they lack a gene on the Y chromosome that might counteract the effects. However, almost 20% of males with a fragile X chromosome do not display the phenotype. More recent research suggests that unstable gene mutation is the culprit: Base pairs of the recessive gene repeat themselves, up to several thousand times. The more the repetition, the more severe the symptoms (Mazzocco, 2000; Sutherland & Richards, 1994; Tsuchiya et al., 1998).

Autosomal Disorders

Like sex-linked disorders, disorders involving the other 22 pairs of chromosomes can result either from defective genes or extra chromosomes. Table 3–2 summarizes selected autosomal disorders.

Down syndrome is the most common autosomal anomaly, and it is the second leading inherited disorder associated with mental retardation. The most frequent type is *trisomy-21*, in which an extra chromosome is attached to the 21st pair. Down syndrome occurs once in every 800 births for mothers under age 35, and the incidence steadily increases as the age of the mother increases (Chapter 4). Individuals with Down syndrome usually have distinctive physical characteristics such as a round face and slanted eyes without eyefolds (which is the reason for the former pejorative label "mongoloid idiot"). Heart abnormalities, hearing problems, and respiratory problems are also common.

However, individuals with Down syndrome vary considerably with regard to the degree of mental retardation associated with the disorder. It is a myth, for example, that no one with Down syndrome can be a functional member in society. The notions that children with Down syndrome are happy and carefree and that adults with Down syndrome are stubborn and uncooperative are also entirely erroneous. Historically, researchers often painted a grim picture of the expected lifespan and adult functioning for individuals with Down syndrome, but those conclusions were based primarily on adults whose education and health had been neglected or who had spent many years "warehoused" in institutional environments. Today special education can make a major difference in the lives of people with this syndrome, and some young adults with Down syndrome can achieve a great deal in work and independent living (Freeman & Hodapp, 2000; Nadel & Rosenthal, 1995; Selikowitz, 1997). The same is true, of course, for persons with other forms of mild to moderate mental retardation.

Prader Willi syndrome (PWS) and *Angelman syndrome* (AS) are disorders that illustrate some of the complexities of genetic mechanisms. **Gene imprinting** refers to a phenomenon in which gene expression and phenotype depend upon *which* parent the gene or genes came from (e.g., see OMIM, 2000; Prows & Hopkin, 1999). The same genes are responsible but are expressed quite differently. In PWS the infant's behavior appears essentially normal although perhaps lethargic for the first year, but then relentless food-seeking and overeating begin. An affected child (or later, adult) will eat just about anything and as often as possible if allowed to, to the point of obesity. Developmental delays and mild mental retardation are also typical. By contrast, in AS an affected infant's behavior again appears essentially normal for the first year, but the infant then begins to display frequent and inappropriate outbursts of laughing, uncontrollable movements, and severe mental retardation.

If the mother's genes are expressed, the result is PWS; if the father's genes are expressed, the result is AS. One way this can happen is simply if one parent's genes are defective, leaving the others to determine phenotype. Another

gene imprinting A phenomenon in which gene expression and phenotype depend on which parent the genes come from; examples are Prader Willi syndrome (PWS) and Angelman syndrome (AS).

Table 3-2   Examples of Autosomal Disorders

Statistics for each of the disorders are based on U.S. live births.

GENETIC:

Angelman's syndrome (see text)

A possibly dominant disorder that occurs in about 1 of 10,000 to 15,000 people. It is determined by a set of mutated genes on chromosome 15, but only if they are the father's; several proteins that affect the functioning of the hypothalamus are not produced.

Cystic fibrosis

A recessive disorder that occurs in about 1 of 2,500 people of white European ancestry; otherwise rare. Among U.S. whites, approximately 1,500 new cases occur each year. A mutated gene on the 7th chromosome fails to function properly, disrupting several metabolic pathways that lead to regulation of the exocrine glands in the pancreas. Excess mucus is produced throughout the body, including the lungs and digestive tract, and perspiration is altered so that the person is subject to salt depletion in hot weather. Death by early adulthood is common. Persons with cystic fibrosis must undergo extensive physical therapy to loosen the mucus several times a day—a fatiguing, time-consuming process. Most males and females are also infertile.

Huntington disease

A dominant disorder that occurs in about 1 of 10,000 people. Huntington's chorea is carried by a dominant gene on chromosome 4 that therefore can be inherited from only one parent. The faulty protein it synthesizes is called *huntingtin*, which is found in numerous cells including the neurons of the brain. There, it causes selective degeneration of neurons, in turn producing dementia, random jerking movements, and a lopsided, staggering walk—symptoms that get progressively worse until the person becomes mute and rigid and eventually dies. The deterioration can last as long as 30 years, although many people with the disease die much sooner of complications such as pneumonia or heart failure. The disease is insidious in that no symptoms appear until about 35 years of age. Thus, people who eventually develop the disease may pass the gene along to children long before they are aware that they are carrying it.

Phenylketonuria (PKU)

A recessive disorder that occurs in about 1 of 10,000 people. A defective gene on chromosome 12 fails to synthesize the enzyme phenylaline hydroxylase, which is responsible for converting the essential amino acid phenylaline from dietary protein into tyrosine, another essential amino acid in a complex of metabolic pathways (but which is also available in food). After birth, when the mother's enzymes can no long convert phenylaline for the baby, the amino acid accumulates and blocks other essential amino acids from entering cells—including brain neurons. The result is brain and other neurological damage and severe-to-profound mental retardation, plus symptoms such as uncontrollable muscle twitches and movements, hyperactivity, and convulsive seizures. All U.S. newborns now receive a PKU screen. Because phenylaline is present in many foods, infants with PKU are immediately placed on a synthetic protein substitute that contains very low but necessary levels of phenylaline. Thus treated, people with PKU have normal life expectancies and can reproduce. However, fertile women with PKU have a very high risk of miscarriage or birth disorders because the fetus grows in an abnormal uterine environment.

Prader Willi syndrome (see text)

A recessive disorder that occurs in about 1 of 10,000 to 15,000 people. It is determined by a set of mutated genes on chromosome 15, but only if they are the mother's; several proteins that affect the functioning of the hypothalamus are not produced.

Sickle-cell trait and sickle-cell anemia (see text)

Sickle-cell trait occurs in about 1 of 12 U.S. blacks; sickle-cell anemia occurs in about 1 of 500. Other groups whose ancestors lived in low-lying malarial wetlands show high rates as well. The defective gene on chromosome 11 produces mutated beta globin, a component of hemoglobin—the oxygen-transport protein in red blood cells. The resulting blood cells break easily and are sticky; breakage results in too few cells and anemia, and the broken cells clog blood vessels. Treatment typically takes the form of blood transfusions or bone-marrow transplants.

Tay-Sachs disease

A recessive disorder that occurs in about 1 of 5,000 people of European Ashkenazi Jewish ancestry; otherwise very rare. Indirect evidence suggests a prior adaptation for heterozygote carriers in resisting tuberculosis. A defective gene on chromosome 15 fails to produce the enzyme hexosaminidase A, which catalyzes the fatty sphingolipids in brain neurons; lethal concentrations accumulate and neurons die. In its extreme form, the child appears normal at birth but begins to show signs of physical weakness and irritability within a few months. Death from brain degeneration or complications such as pneumonia usually occurs by age 3 to 5.

CHROMOSOMAL:

Down syndrome (see text)

Occurs in about 1 in 1,000 live births. Risk increases with maternal age: pregnancies in women over age 35 (5 to 8% of all pregnancies) account for 20% of Down syndrome births.

Primary sources: OMIM, 2000; Pasternak, 1999.

way is *uniparental disomy* (e.g., see Cummings, 2000). Either because of errors in meiosis prior to conception or errors in mitosis afterward, the child winds up receiving both of the chromosomes containing the defective genes from only one parent. Thus, even if the parent who contributes the chromosomes is heterozygous for the defective genes, those chromosomes can still be expressed in the child.

Genetic Counseling

Most recessive genes are not expressed. Consequently, most of us never know what kinds of defective genes we carry—yet we all probably harbor at least five to eight potentially lethal recessive genes besides many less harmful ones.

You can obtain valuable information about your genetic makeup, and that of a potential partner, through **genetic counseling.** This is a widely available resource (although typically not an inexpensive one) that can help potential parents evaluate genetic risk factors in childbearing and enable them to make intelligent decisions. Genetic counseling includes analysis of parental medical records and family histories to construct a genetic "pedigree," maternal and perhaps paternal blood screening, and prenatal screening of the developing child. Parental or prenatal screening can detect many chromosomal or genetic anomalies—including all of the disorders in Tables 3–1 and 3–2 and over several hundred others.

If genetic counseling reveals the presence of a heritable genetic disorder in the parents, the counselor evaluates the couple's risk of having a baby with the disorder, puts the risk in perspective, and suggests reproductive alternatives if the couple decides that the risk is too great. Such alternatives may include adoption or artificial insemination of donor ovum or sperm. Genetic counselors are also trained in supportive and psychotherapeutic techniques to assist the potential parents if necessary, and genetic counseling continues to become a highly specialized discipline (e.g., see Peters, Djurdjinovic, & Baker, 1999). In particular, genetic counselors increasingly pay special attention to diversity and the varying beliefs and cultural backgrounds of their clients—factors that affect both the decisions potential parents make and how they cope with any bad news they receive (Cohen, Fine, & Pergament, 1998; Greb, 1998).

Table 3–3 summarizes characteristics of individuals for whom genetic counseling is recommended.

If a couple has already conceived and there is a potential risk, prenatal screening can then be used to determine whether a genetic, chromosomal, or other disorder is actually present in the developing child. An understanding of prenatal screening techniques requires fairly detailed knowledge of prenatal development and is therefore discussed in Chapter 4.

If a prenatal disorder of any kind is detected, the genetic counselor's primary function is to help prospective parents make an informed decision. The counselor's advice and the direction the interview takes depends on the specific disorder involved. For example, genetic assessment might show that both parents have the recessive gene for Tay-Sachs disease, which is as yet incurable and fatal in early childhood. Parents may decide to terminate the pregnancy once they are informed of the pain and suffering that will probably ensue—both for the child and for themselves. Even in such an apparently clear-cut case, however, there is always the possibility that some variations of the defective gene as discussed earlier might not cause Tay-Sachs to be expressed, making the decision all the more difficult (again, see Alper, 1996). Until molecular

genetic counseling   A widely available resource that can help potential parents evaluate genetic risk factors in childbearing and enable them to make intelligent decisions.

Table 3–3 Indications for Genetic Counseling

FAMILY HISTORY OF:

- Neonatal deaths
- Children with multiple malformations or metabolic disorders
- Children with mental retardation, developmental delays, or failure to thrive
- Children with congenital anomalies such as cleft palate, neural tube defects, clubfoot, congenital heart disease
- Children with unusual appearance, especially if accompanied by failure to thrive or suboptimal psychomotor development
- Any disease that "runs in the family," especially hearing loss, blindness, neurodegenerative disorders, short stature, premature heart disease, immune deficiency, or abnormalities of the hair, skin, or bones

PARENTAL CONDITIONS:

- Known genetic or chromosomal abnormality
- Amenorrhea, aspermia, infertility, or abnormal sexual development
- Prior pregnancy loss or stillbirth
- Mother over age 35, father over age 55
- Father and mother biologically related to each other
- Ethnic background suggesting an increased risk for a specific disorder (see Table 3–2)
- Mother exposed to certain diseases, toxic agents, radiation, illegal drugs, and other potentially harmful agents prior to or during pregnancy (Chapter 4)
- Familial cancer

Source: Adapted from Mountain States Genetics Network (MoSt GeNe), 2000.

analysis determines which mutated variations an anomalous gene will express a disorder and which ones will not, life-and-death decisions based on single genes will always be based on probability.

The counselor's role in advising parents of a child who will have sickle-cell anemia is more open-ended and tends to focus on exploring possibilities, and the parents' decision may be even more difficult. As noted earlier, in its worst form this disorder causes severe pain and perhaps early death. Yet many sufferers can lead relatively normal lives with existing treatments such as blood transfusions and bone-marrow transplants. Sickle-cell anemia is also currently a target for research on gene therapy (discussed next), which means that a less invasive and less costly treatment could be on the horizon. Such parents face a difficult decision indeed, as do many other parents whose developing children have a genetic anomaly for which a breakthrough cure could come at any time given the rapid progress that is now being made in molecular genetics.

Finally, it should be noted that many parents who know their child will have an incurable congenital anomaly choose to go ahead with the pregnancy anyway and make a commitment to caring for and loving the child. This is most likely in cases where the child will be physically disabled but otherwise normal and healthy, also in cases where the child will almost certainly be at least mildly mentally retarded but otherwise healthy. That, for example, is why you see children and adults with Down syndrome on a regular basis. Some parents may not have known, but others did and chose to have the child regardless.

CONTENT CHECK
GENETIC AND CHROMOSOMAL DISORDERS

True–False (answers are on the Companion Website)

1. Congenital anomalies are always the result of defective genes or chromosomes.
2. Disrupted metabolic pathways are the most common cause of genetic disorders.
3. Sex-linked disorders are more common in males because the Y chromosome has more genetic information than the X chromosome.
4. Down syndrome is the most common cause of mental retardation.
5. Couples whose unborn child has a known genetic or chromosomal disorder are usually advised to terminate the pregnancy.

Thinking Critically

If you had a genetic disorder that appears later in life and causes premature death, would you want to know? Why or why not?

Advances in Genetic Research and Treatment

Both the technology of genetic research and our understanding of genetic determinants are advancing rapidly. Aside from the identification, cataloging, and mapping of many genetic anomalies, and of course the breakthrough on the human genome, genetic technology continues to be refined and extended into treatment of genetic disorders.

Within the emergent discipline called **bioinformatics**—the mesh of biology and computer science—the basis for most of these advances is **recombinant DNA technology.** Recombinant DNA techniques surfaced in the 1980s and revolutionized the study of molecular genetics. In brief, the term covers an assortment of highly sophisticated procedures in which DNA is extracted from cell nuclei and initially cleaved (cut) into segments by selected enzymes. Researchers now have a number of these enzymes (extracted from bacteria) that cleave the DNA at specific junctions and maintain the integrity of the DNA. The resulting fragments are then joined to one of an assortment of self-replicating elements researchers have also collected from organisms such as bacteria. These combine with the DNA to form, in essence, functional gene clones capable of producing proteins. They are then placed in host bacterial cells to be maintained and cultured.

From there, numerous directions are possible depending upon the purpose of the research. The cloned DNA can be studied to find out what protein it produces (normal or mutated), which is helpful in identifying the basis for genetic disorders. Or the cloned DNA can be tagged with additional "probe" DNA and recombined with an intact chromosome to see where it winds up, which is useful in mapping locuses one at a time. Or the cloned DNA can be combined with specially engineered synthetic DNA to study specific nucleotide sequences, which will eventually open the way to identification of nucleotide makeups that produce mutant proteins. Cloned genes can also be used in **gene therapy** and in the cloning of entire organisms.

bioinformatics A discipline that combines biology and computer science.

recombinant DNA technology An assortment of highly sophisticated procedures in which DNA is extracted from cell nuclei and cut into segments. The resulting fragments are then joined to self-replicating elements, forming, in essence, functional gene clones. These are then placed in host bacterial cells to be maintained and cultured.

gene therapy An approach to establishing cures for genetic disorders that can be applied at any point from altering the molecular structure of DNA to altering the process of protein synthesis.

Gene Therapy

Researchers are proposing or attempting numerous approaches to establish cures for genetically based disorders. In theory, gene therapy can be applied at any point from altering the molecular structure of DNA to altering the process of protein synthesis. Some of the more active areas of research are discussed here.

In the *indirect* approach to gene therapy that has now become commonplace, missing genes are cloned and inserted into a bacterial growth medium. Their proteins are then harvested and introduced into the patient's system. Examples are the production of human insulin and human growth hormone for persons lacking in the genes that produce these essential proteins.

In a still-experimental approach called *ex vivo* gene therapy, treatment begins with the removal of defective cells from a patient with a genetic disorder. By various means, these are then infused with clones of normal genes, and after being cultured in large numbers are reinstated in the patient. The idea is that these "engineered" genes will then produce normal quantities of whatever protein was either missing or mutated. This approach has been tried with various genetic disorders, but at this point with limited success.

Another, more direct experimental approach call *in vivo* gene therapy takes advantage of benign *retroviruses*—viruses that are capable of penetrating cells but that do not have adverse effects. Some viral genes are removed, a cloned human gene that is normal with respect to a genetic disorder is inserted, and the retrovirus is cultured in large numbers and finally introduced into the patient. Here, the idea is that the retrovirus will penetrate cells and deliver the normal gene. This approach has also met with only limited success, but along with ex vivo gene therapy, it also holds great promise for the future once a number of obstacles are overcome (e.g., see Felgner, 1997; Friedmann, 1997; Ho & Saplosky, 1997; Weiner & Kennedy, 1999). Currently, there is also intense interest in applying gene therapy to the treatment of various kinds of cancer—

Dolly makes a media appearance at the Roslin Institute.

A MATTER FOR DEBATE

HUMAN CLONING AND ITS IMPLICATIONS

In February 1997, Ian Wilmut and colleagues at the Roslin Institute in Scotland announced the first successful cloning from an adult mammal: Dolly the sheep (see Wilmut, 1998; also Wilmut, Campbell, & Tudge, 2000). Not long after that, researchers at the University of Massachusetts refined the procedure and successfully produced a small herd of genetically identical cattle; numerous other mammal clonings have been accomplished in the years since. In addition, conservationists are now attempting to clone endangered species as a last-resort way of keeping them from becoming extinct (Lanza, Dresser, & Damiani, 2000).

Naturally, Wilmut's success immediately revived the issue of cloning humans as well—a topic long popular in science fiction but previously thought impossible by most genetic researchers, all of whom have now been forced to reverse their positions. The cloning of Dolly also prompted worldwide policy statements and attempts at legislation to ban all research on human cloning, citing moral, ethical, and religious grounds. The bans in turn elicited an outcry by the scientific community; researchers feared that genetic research in general would be impeded, and those fears have not been completely resolved. If anything, they have been revived by the news about the mapping of the human genome.

Let's examine some of the issues in cloning humans. The readiest observation is that there are already far too many people on this planet and our numbers are increasing geometrically. Do we need clones too? Another point is that Wilmut's success in cloning Dolly was preceded by hundreds of failed attempts, which would predictably also happen in attempts to clone humans. This raises serious ethical questions, such as what would happen if a "partially" successful procedure produces badly malformed human clones. Wouldn't they, as well as normal clones, have the same right to life that we traditionally conceived humans do? Another possibility is that humans would be cloned to provide perfect replacement organs and tissues, then sacrificed. Ethically unacceptable? Most by far would say yes, but it is not hard to imagine a booming underground industry in human "spare parts" for those who can afford them.

Yet, some argue that cloning might be acceptable in certain cases. A couple could replace a dying child (assuming the child isn't dying from a genetic disorder), infertile couples could clone a child from either partner, a gay or lesbian couple could have their own children. (See Green, 2000, for arguments pro and con on these issues.) Perhaps specific human organs for replacement could eventually be cloned without producing an entire human, thereby eliminating or at least minimizing ethical concerns. Perhaps, and more likely, genetic alteration and cloning of animals such as sheep and pigs will provide human replacement organs in a less objectionable way. Finally, if there ever is a war or a plague or other catastrophe that wipes out most of humanity, cloning might save us as a species.

One thing appears certain: Now that cloning humans is a distinct possibility, efforts in that direction *will* occur—with or without government approval and funding. Thus, perhaps the real issue for debate is how we will deal with human cloning if and when it becomes a reality.

which may or may not have a genetic basis (but see Blaese, 1997, for a overview of obstacles here as well).

Diseases being treated in clinical trials of gene therapy include hemophilia and rheumatoid arthritis. Progress is also being made in the search for AIDS-resistant genes that might account for the observation that many carriers of HIV do not develop AIDS. Advances are being made in other areas as well. One promising strategy is to develop synthetic strands of DNA that can attack viruses and cancers without harming healthy tissue (Friedmann, 1997).

Cloning Entire Organisms

There is considerable controversy at all levels of cloning. Some see any form of genetic engineering as "tampering" with nature, an endeavor that might have a plethora of grave consequences. The cloning controversy reaches its zenith, however, where the cloning of entire organisms—potentially including humans—is concerned.

It is now well established that we can clone animals from the DNA of a single cell. Such cloning is based on transferring the nucleus of a cell from one animal to a recipient cell—typically an unfertilized ovum—and stimulating the newly formed cell to begin developing in a surrogate mother. This is not an easy process to sustain (Wilmut, 1998), in part because it requires coordinating the existing RNA functioning of the recipient cell with the functioning of the new DNA in the nucleus.

The obstacles were finally overcome in 1997, however, and the scientific world was stunned by the announcement of the successful cloning of a sheep. This gave rise to widespread debate over the possibility of cloning human beings (see "A Matter for Debate," on facing page) and generated a controversy that is certain to continue.

CONTENT CHECK
ADVANCES IN GENETIC RESEARCH AND TREATMENT

True–False (answers are on the Companion Website)

1. In recombinant DNA technology, the result is cloned genes that are cultured in bacterial cells.
2. Human insulin is produced via ex vivo gene therapy.
3. Retroviruses are used in in vivo gene therapy.
4. The first human was cloned in 1997.

Thinking Critically

Would you want to be cloned? Why or why not?

Behavior Genetics

Thus far, we have discussed the effects of specific, known genes from the molecular level up, based primarily on the increasingly powerful techniques of molecular genetics. Except for occasional comments as to the interaction of genes with genes and genes with environment, the emphasis has been on single-gene determinants of physical and behavioral characteristics. However, where the unraveling of complex, polygenic characteristics such as temperament, personality traits, intelligence, and mental and behavioral disorders (other than some forms of mental retardation) is concerned, molecular geneticists have barely begun. What we know about the genetics of such characteristics is instead a result of decades of research in **behavior genetics,** an approach that assesses patterns of inheritance at the behavioral level—typically through the use of psychological tests, parental self-reports, or observations of children's behavior.

Modern behavior genetics incorporates the accepted view that complex traits are determined by heredity and environment in interaction. For the most part, the field also takes the view that what is inherited are genetic predispositions, which are expressed in behavior to varying degree (or not at all)

behavior genetics The study of relationships between behavior and genetic makeup.

depending upon environmental influences. For example, you might inherit a predisposition toward severe depression, but whether you actually become severely depressed can depend upon a host of overlapping influences. These influences may include how your parents and others behave toward you, what kinds of living conditions you experience, what positive and negative experiences you have, and so on—including what you make of it all.

The primary tool of behavior genetics is correlation, which here translates into *concordance*: the extent to which biologically related people show similar characteristics. Concordance rates then give rise to estimates of **heritability,** which is the extent to which a trait is inherited versus acquired and therefore has a presumed genetic basis. Two traditional approaches to assessing concordance and estimating heritability are adoption studies and twin studies, which appear at various points in later chapters as well.

Adoption Studies

In the classic and extensive Minnesota Adoption Studies, researchers compared adopted children with their biological parents, their adoptive parents, and the biological children of their adoptive parents (Scarr & Weinberg, 1983). In addition, they compared adoptive parents with their biological children. When test scores of adopted children were compared to those of nonadopted peers, the results indicated that adoptive families influenced the children's intellectual abilities; *as a group,* the adopted children had higher IQs than their nonadopted peers and achieved more in school. But when the researchers analyzed individual differences *within* the group, children's test scores were closer to those of their biological parents than to those of their adoptive parents—indicating heritability as well.

Other evidence supported heritability was that some attitudes, vocational interests, and personality traits are highly resistant to the adoptive family environment (Scarr & Weinberg, 1983). Such a finding is particularly likely if a child's genetic predisposition is at odds with that of the adoptive parents: The expression of genetically based interests and habits may simply be delayed until the child matures and is less influenced by parental restrictions and behaviors.

In the years since Sandra Scarr and Richard Weinberg's research, numerous adoption studies similar to theirs have found at least a moderate degree of heritability for a large variety of psychological traits and characteristics. For example, in a meta-analysis of twenty-four adoption (and twin) studies on the heritability of aggression (Miles & Carey, 1997), the authors concluded that heredity was up to 50% responsible for individual variability, at least with parental self-reports as the way child aggressiveness was measured. In an additional finding the genetic contribution apparently increased with age and the family environment contribution decreased—consistent with Scarr and Weinberg's observations about the resistance of some hereditary characteristics to environmental influences.

As a final example, Robert Plomin and colleagues, who have conducted numerous adoption and twin studies over the past decade in particular, recently used data from the ongoing Colorado Adoption Project to assess whether genetics may partly determine something as subtle as children's adjustment to parents' divorce (O'Connor, Plomin, Caspi, & Defries, 2000). The findings—consistent with most research on the effects of divorce on children—were that following divorce both in biological families and adoptive families, children displayed higher levels of behavioral problems and substance use compared to

heritability   The extent to which a trait is inherited versus acquired, thus presuming a genetic basis.

children whose families remained intact. However, children of divorced bio-logical parents displayed lower scores on measures of achievement and social competence and children of divorced adoptive parents did not. The authors concluded that a *passive genotype/environment interaction* (Scarr & McCartney, 1985) was probably responsible. In essence, besides to providing their children with genes, parents also provide their children with living environments con-sistent with the parents' own genes. Because of this "fit," a breakup of the home would affect children of biological families much more dramatically in the ways indicated.

Twin Studies

Twin studies have repeatedly shown that identical twins show high concor-dance in intellectual abilities and that identical twins show higher concordance than nonidentical twins (Bouchard, 1999). Moreover, such findings have been replicated beyond the United States across cultures such as Japan (Lynn & Hat-tori, 1990) and India (Pal, Shyam, & Singh, 1997). It would therefore seem that from this perspective, as well as from adoption studies, that intelligence has a strong genetic component. Studies of antisocial behavior also indicate high her-itability (Mason & Frick, 1994). Looking across such studies, a consistent esti-mate is that genetics contributes about 50% to intelligence, although—as always—how that genetic predisposition plays out depends a great deal upon environment as well.

Studies show that identical twins are more similar than fraternal twins in personality traits like so-ciability, emotionality, and activity level. But how much of this simi-larity can be attributed to genetic influence and how much to the environment?

Twin studies have also found that a wide range of specific personality traits are at least partly heritable. Three such characteristics are *emotionality*, *activity level*, and *sociability*—sometimes called the *EAS traits* (e.g., Hershberger, Plomin, & Pedersen, 1995; Plomin, 1990). Emotionality is the tendency to be easily aroused to a state of fear or anger. Activity level is simply the frequency and degree to which the person is active as opposed to docile and relaxed. So-ciability is the extent to which individuals prefer to do things with others rather than be alone. Overall, the estimate here is a genetic contribution to personal-ity of about 40% (Bouchard, 1999), or as imminent twins researcher Nancy Segal put it, 20 to 50% (Segal, 2000). More so than with intelligence, similarity in twins' emotionality also seems to last a lifetime, but similarity in their activ-ity levels and sociability diminishes somewhat in later adulthood—probably because of the different life events twins experience when they are apart. (See McCartney, Harris, & Bernieri, 1990 for a meta-analysis of developmental twin studies.)

Although twin studies offer considerable evidence for a genetic influence on different temperaments and personality styles, they are unable to tell us how genes interact with the environment. A quiet, easygoing child experiences a dif-ferent environment than an impulsive, angry, assertive child, and other people will respond differently to a quiet child than they will to an assertive one. The child therefore helps shape her or his environment, which, in turn, limits and molds how the child expresses feelings. In this way a child's personality has a tremendous impact on the environment in which he or she lives (Kagan, Arcus, & Snidman, 1993).

In addition, twin studies that indicate relatively high heritability remain sub-ject to debate. Except when they are adopted into different families, twins share many aspects of the family environment that could elevate apparent heritabil-ity. Moreover, the statistical procedures used to "separate" the effects of genet-ics versus environmental influences are not universally agreed upon. It has also been noted that identical twins share a common maternal environment (Devlin,

Daniels, & Roeder, 1997), which can have profound effects on intelligence and personality. Comparing identical twins to nonidentical twins at least partly eliminates this problem, but it remains a serious one when identical twins are compared to siblings born separately.

At the same time, it should be noted that behavior genetics is starting to merge with molecular genetics in an attempt to overcome methodological problems. This trend is likely to continue, and as it does, the discipline of behavior genetics should come fully into its own.

CONTENT CHECK
BEHAVIOR GENETICS

True–False (answers are on the Companion Website)

1. Behavior geneticists study patterns of concordance and heritability.
2. Adoption studies usually focus on identical twins who are separated at birth.
3. Research indicates that both intelligence and personality are highly heritable and influenced little by environment.

Thinking Critically

What problems are there in interpreting the results of adoption and twin studies?

Environmental Influences and Contexts

Here we turn to environmental factors, starting with basic learning and conditioning processes that directly affect development and proceeding to environmental influences at the level of the family and beyond.

However, note at the outset that environmental factors cannot always be neatly categorized. For example, it is explicit in Bronfenbrenner's bioecological systems model (Chapter 2) that the developing child's environment consists of multiple settings that interact and change over time. By adolescence, environment has moved well beyond the home to the neighborhood, the school, and an ever-expanding world of influences beyond those, all peopled with changing friends and acquaintances. The environment also consists of books, television, movies, and now the far reaches of the Internet.

Because Bronfenbrenner's model provides a convenient framework for looking at environment at its differing levels, we begin with the microsystem and work outward.

Processes Within the Microsystem

By tradition, learning theorists designate four basic types of learning: *habituation, classical conditioning, operant conditioning,* and *social learning.* In a given instance of learning any or all may be occurring in conjunction with each other, which is the reason for beginning this section with "by tradition."

Although some of these processes were derived primarily through controlled laboratory research with animals such as rats and pigeons, they nevertheless apply to a great many situations we as humans encounter in everyday life on a moment-to-moment basis—whether the situations are deliberately contrived by others or occur naturally in our interactions with the physical and social environment. In essence, these processes are the "machinery" of the microsystem.

Habituation

The simplest and at the same time one of the most important kinds of learning is **habituation,** which in its most basic sense means ceasing to attend or respond to irrelevant stimuli. Habituation occurs at several levels, from sensation to perception to higher cognition. Sensory receptors cease to input information as they are repeatedly stimulated—if you are reading this while sitting in a comfortable chair, you aren't consciously attending to the surface of the chair (or you weren't until we brought it up). At the sensory-perceptual level, if you are concentrating on reading this, you also aren't attending to minor sounds occurring around you or irrelevant images in your peripheral vision. Of course, at the cognitive level, you may get so tired of reading that you cease to attend to the content, which illustrates that habituation isn't always adaptive.

Normally, habituation permeates our ongoing lives and helps "filter out" the repetitive and monotonous stimuli that often bombard us. Habituation thus enables us to stay focused and attend to things that are important—even though we can only attend to a limited amount of information at any given time. Habituation is also a key way of studying infant capabilities, as we see in Chapter 5.

The learning-theory explanation of phobias emphasizes early aversive experiences.

Classical Conditioning

Basic experiments on classical conditioning are carried out according to the following procedure. Start with an *unconditioned stimulus (UCS)* that elicits an *unconditioned response (UCR)*. In Pavlov's early research (Chapter 2), the UCS was food and the UCR was salivation, but virtually any "automatic" stimulus-response relationship will do—all that's necessary is that the subject respond immediately and consistently to the UCS, then repeatedly pair the UCS with a novel stimulus such as a sound, a flash of light, or anything that doesn't produce the response in question. Eventually, the novel stimulus alone will produce the response. At this point, the novel stimulus has become a *conditioned stimulus (CS)*, which produces a *conditioned response (CR)*. Pavlov's bell, for example, became a CS that when presented alone (on a test trial) would produce the CR of salivation. The UCR and the CR aren't exactly the same, however; a dog will never salivate as much to the bell as it will to actual food.

Figure 3–7 illustrates this procedure. Note that classical conditioning works best if the CS slightly precedes the UCS. In modern cognitive terms, the CS comes to serve as a *cue* that the UCS is on the way, so the dog begins salivating in anticipation of the arrival of food.

Classical conditioning is a powerful force in our lives, beginning in early infancy. This point is illustrated by a classic experiment conducted by Lipsitt and Kaye (1964). Ten 3-day-old infants were given 20 trials in which a tone CS was paired with a pacifier UCS. The UCR was sucking (a natural response to a pacifier). After the 20 trials, the tone alone consistently elicited a sucking CR.

In everyday life, a cat learns that the sound of an electric can opener might be followed by a tasty treat, a dog learns that the sound of a car in the driveway might be followed by the arrival of its beloved owner, a toddler learns that the word "No!" might be followed by a pop on the bottom. In each case the

habituation Ceasing to attend to respond to repetitive stimulation; occurs at several levels from sensation to perception to higher cognition.

Figure 3-7 A Typical Classical Conditioning Procedure

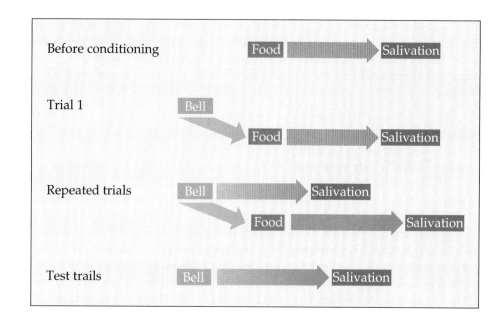

subject learns that one stimulus follows the other, and has an emotional reaction—pleasant or unpleasant. Although emotional reactions aren't always involved in classical conditioning, in many cases they are. As an example, the learning-theory explanation of **phobias** is that they are acquired by classical conditioning: If you have an unreasoning, horrified fear of bees, for example, it could be because you were badly stung as a child. The sight of a bee by itself elicits fear before the bee actually stings you. Similar reasoning applies to phobias for snakes, spiders, heights, tightly enclosed places, and the many other things people sometimes fear to the extent of irrationality.

Positive emotional reactions can be conditioned the same way negative ones are. Reactions of relaxation or pleasure are often associated with previously neutral stimuli, like an old song that brings back memories of a sunny day at the beach or the excitement of a festival. Also, many behaviors associated with eating display elements of classical conditioning, in the sense that we derive a sense of pleasure just from smelling good foods while they're being prepared, or perhaps even from merely thinking about eating them.

Operant Conditioning

In Chapter 2, we noted that Skinner used different terminology in applying Thorndike's law of effect. According to Skinner, the first part of the law—in which behavior is performed in order to achieve a pleasant or satisfying consequence—is called *reinforcement*. The second part—in which behavior is not performed because the consequence is unpleasant or unsatisfying—is called *punishment*. Each of these contingencies can be further subdivided according to whether they're accomplished by *presenting* or *removing* a stimulus when the behavior occurs. This results in four possible contingencies: positive reinforcement, negative reinforcement, positive punishment, and negative punishment as shown in Table 3–4.

In **positive reinforcement,** or *reward training*, the subject receives rewards for behavior, and the behavior predictably increases (becomes more likely). A pigeon pecks a key and thereby gains access to a hopper containing food; a child is praised for sharing toys with another child.

phobia Unreasonable fear of an object or situation.

positive reinforcement Also called reward training; a subject receives rewards for behavior and the behavior increases.

Table 3-4   Positive and Negative Reinforcement and Punishment

	Present Stimulus	Take Stimulus Away
Stimulus is pleasant	Positive Reinforcement	Negative Punishment
Stimulus is unpleasant	Positive Punishment	Negative Reinforcement

In **negative reinforcement,** also called *escape training* or *active avoidance train-ing*, behavior results in something unpleasant or aversive being taken away or simply not occurring; again the behavior predictably increases. A pigeon pecks a key to turn off a mild electric shock to its feet (escape), or it pecks the key in advance to prevent the shock from occurring at all (avoidance). In the operant conditioning view, human phobias are *maintained* by negative reinforcement: A phobic person approaches the object or situation, becomes fearful, and then avoids the object or situation—in effect making it go away. This is why phobias are self-perpetuating if untreated: The person never sticks around long enough to find out that the fear is disproportionate—that bees usually don't sting un-less provoked, that most snakes aren't dangerous, and so on.

In **positive punishment,** also called *passive avoidance*, behavior results in something aversive being presented or happening. A pigeon, having been trained to pick a key for food, now receives a shock instead and soon stops pecking the key. A child is scolded for misbehavior, and—ideally—the misbe-havior stops.

Finally, in **negative punishment,** or *omission training*, the behavior results in something desirable or pleasant being taken away; this should also make the behavior stop or become less likely. In the case of the pigeon, the food hopper now appears regularly *except* when key pecking occurs. In the case of the child who misbehaves, privileges such as TV time are taken away. A popular version of negative punishment at school is the *time-out procedure*. A child who misbe-haves is removed to a quiet room and left alone there for a short period. The logic behind this technique is that children misbehave to get attention from other children or from the teacher, so the attention is in effect "removed."

Two other operant conditioning procedures are important. The first is **shap-ing,** which is how behaviors are established in the first place. Pigeons, for ex-ample, don't normally go around pecking keys, so they must be trained to do so. This is accomplished by means of *successive approximations*, as follows. Using a manual switch, the experimenter briefly triggers the food hopper when the pigeon simply turns toward the area of the key. Then the hopper is triggered when the pigeon approaches the key, then when it accidentally touches the key, and eventually only when a full peck occurs. The same procedure can be used in toilet-training a child: First praise the child for going toward the bathroom, then for actually going inside, and eventually for climbing on the potty and completing the act successfully. Shaping can also be therapeutically effective, as with *autistic* children who don't speak at all and therefore can't be reinforced for communicating: First reward the child for making *any* vocal sounds, then for making sounds resembling speech, and eventually only for actual words (Lovaas, 1977).

The second procedure is **partial reinforcement,** which is more typical of what happens in everyday life than the "continuous" reinforcement discussed so far. In partial reinforcement, only some instances of a behavior are

negative reinforcement   Also called escape or active avoid-ance training; a subject's behav-ior results in something unpleasant or aversive being taken away or simply not occur-ring. Behavior increases.

positive punishment   Also called passive avoidance; a sub-ject's behavior results in some-thing aversive being presented or happening and the behavior decreases.

negative punishment   Also called omission training; a sub-ject's behavior results in some-thing desirable or pleasant being taken away and the be-havior decreases.

shaping   Systematically rein-forcing successive approxima-tions to a desired behavior.

partial reinforcement   A proce-dure in which only some re-sponses are reinforced; produces much stronger habits than con-tinuous reinforcement.

Young children are able to identify their most prized possessions.

behavior modification A method that uses conditioning procedures such as reinforcement, reward, and shaping to change behavior.

reinforced—not every instance. Partial reinforcement can take various forms, but the most powerful version is the *variable-ratio schedule*. Some instances of behavior are reinforced, some not—and unpredictably. The result is that the behavior persists much longer if reinforcement is later discontinued. The effects of a partial reinforcement schedule can be seen in children who throw tantrums in stores in an attempt to get toys or candy. *Sometimes* the parents give in and buy the toy to stop the embarrassing and annoying behavior the child is displaying. The child therefore learns to keep trying, even when the parents don't give in—just because it didn't work this time doesn't mean it won't work next time. The parents may also unwittingly shape longer and louder tantrum behavior by trying to hold out before occasionally giving in.

Conditioning, Behavior Modification, and Life   The shaping of an autistic child's speech is only one of a great many applications of conditioning called **behavior modification.** Phobias can be "desensitized" and eliminated through procedures that include elements of classical and operant conditioning. Difficult, aggressive children can be taught to get along with others through carefully timed reinforcements for appropriate behavior (perhaps combined with limited punishment where the child's behavior is dangerous to self or others). As an aid to eliminating a bad habit, you might write a "contingency contract" with a friend in which you must give your friend money each time you engage in the behavior. A couple who regularly has arguments about and difficulties with who does household chores might negotiate a contract in which when one partner does one chore, the other partner does another chore and thereby rewards the first partner. Particularly with regard to problem behaviors, the applications of conditioning and behavior modification are virtually endless.

More generally, conditioning permeates much of our lives. We acquire preferences and aversions through classical conditioning; we learn to behave in socially appropriate ways at least in part because of operant conditioning in the form of favorable or unfavorable reactions from others. As a student, you may enjoy reading and learning material in a text such as this for its own sake, but it is unlikely that you would spend a lot of time memorizing it if there weren't a payoff in the form of a good grade and, down the line, a college degree. As a worker, you may enjoy your job for its own sake, but it is unlikely that you would get up and go to work every day if you didn't get paid for it.

Conditioning processes are indisputable; they are facts of life. A problem only arises when—as was the case with Skinner—theorists and others attempt to explain *all* behavior in terms of conditioning and take a cold, mechanistic approach to understanding people as "pawns" of their environments. Phobias are an easy example. Rather than being conditioned to become phobic for certain objects, children can become phobic by observing parents or older siblings or friends display phobic behavior. If a parent reacts with terror to snakes, the child will likely be terrified too and may acquire a lasting tendency to react this way. Alternately, based on the observation that a great majority of people are intensely afraid of snakes in particular, evolutionary psychologists argue that a predisposition to such fear might have evolved in our early and much smaller primate ancestors for whom snakes were a constant threat (see Buss, 1999). In general, however, and consistent with Vygotsky's social-cognitive theory and Bandura's social-learning theory, perhaps most of what we learn has nothing to do with conditioning. Rather, we learn by observing others and regularly receiving help from them.

In a larger sense, we always need to consider the active, *thinking* part of human nature in the learning of behaviors. We do not always engage in behaviors strictly for payoffs, as when we help someone and expect nothing in return (notwithstanding the evolutionary psychologists' views of altruism discussed in Chapter 2). Nor we do necessarily accept the controls and payoffs others place before us and behave in the ways they want us to. Depending upon how contingencies are imposed, we may instead resent and resist them and perhaps even behave in ways opposite to others' wishes. As most of the personality theorists in Chapter 2 have repeatedly pointed out, there is much more to human development and behavior than the quest for payoffs.

Social Learning and the Evolving Self-Concept

Social-learning theorists enlarged the scope of learning theory to explain complex social behaviors and patterns. Albert Bandura (1977), for example, pointed out that in daily life people attend to the consequences of their own actions—that is, we notice which actions succeed and which fail or produce no result—and adjust our behavior accordingly. In this way we receive *cognitive* reinforcement in addition to any external rewards or punishments. We think about what behaviors would be appropriate in specific circumstances and anticipate what may happen as a result of certain actions.

As noted, observational learning and conscious imitation of what we see in our social environment play a major role in learning and development. Very early, for example, children begin observing and learning the many aspects of sex-appropriate behavior their culture offers as well as its moral expectations. They also observe others and learn how to express aggression or dependency or to engage in prosocial behaviors like sharing. If anything is universal in human nature, it is the tendency to observe, evaluate, and imitate what we deem appropriate.

In the years that followed Bandura's research on observational learning, he shifted his emphasis to developing a theory of personality based on **self-efficacy** (e.g., see Bandura, 1997), which quickly became an extremely popular research topic and began being applied to improving people's sense of control over their lives. In brief, self-efficacy refers to what we as individuals are actually capable of doing in a given situation. This is contrasted with *perceived* self-efficacy, which is what we think we can do—based on observations of our own successes and failures as well as those of others. If perceived self-efficacy is significantly lower than actual self-efficacy, the individual doesn't try. Hence, major applications of self-efficacy theory have been assisting people in achieving self-control and in eliminating bad habits by working through their erroneous beliefs that they can't do what they actually can. We return to self-efficacy theory in Chapter 14.

Social learning is also intimately involved in developing first a sense of self as distinct from others and eventually a **self-concept.** Self-concept is your aggregate of beliefs and feelings about yourself—that is, about who you are. Self-concept begins with self-awareness. Infants initially are unable to differentiate between themselves and the world around them. Gradually, however, they realize that their bodies are separate and uniquely their own, and much of infancy is devoted to making this distinction. Later, young children compare themselves with their parents, peers, and relatives, realizing that they are smaller than their older brothers and sisters, darker or fairer, fatter or thinner.

In a family system, members often assume specific roles in relation to other members.

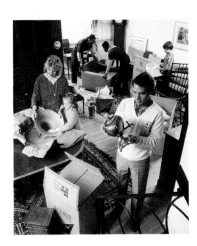

Throughout our lives we adapt to change by using self-concept to filter the impact.

self-efficacy   What we as individuals are capable of doing in a given situation.

self-concept   Your perception of your personal identity.

In expressing self-concept, children demonstrate their capabilities. They also identify their preferences and possessions (Harter, 1988). During middle childhood self-knowledge expands to include a range of trait labels. A fifth grader may describe herself or himself as popular, nice, helpful, smart in school, and good at sports. Self-attributes become logical, organized, and normally consistent as well.

During adolescence self-knowledge becomes more abstract, and adolescents often display considerable concern about how others regard them. This is when they become capable of formulating philosophies and theories about the way things are and the way they ought to be. With this new mental ability, adolescents ideally develop a sense of ego identity—a coherent, unified idea of self as in Erikson's definition of identity. In turn, throughout adulthood there is both continuity and change in self-concept. Major life events, new jobs, marriage, birth of children or grandchildren, divorce, unemployment, war, and personal tragedy cause us to reexamine who we are with respect to our life circumstances.

CONTENT CHECK
PROCESSES WITHIN THE MICROSYSTEM

True–False (answers are on the Companion Website)

1. Compared to operant conditioning, habituation and classical conditioning have little relevance to our lives.
2. In the behaviorist view, phobias are acquired through classical conditioning and maintained through operant conditioning.
3. Positive reinforcement corresponds to the first half of the law of effect and negative reinforcement corresponds to the second half.
4. With regard to establishing behaviors that are highly enduring, the most effective approach is partial reinforcement.
5. Operant conditioning and social learning have in common an emphasis on cognitive processes.

Thinking Critically

Why don't principles of operant conditioning and social learning explain all of human behavior?

Processes That Transcend the Microsystem

As highlighted by the bioecological model, each of the processes within the microsystem is influenced by systems beyond it. What fears a child has stem in part from the fears of parents, which in turn may reflect those of the parents' culture. What food preferences and aversions a child acquires depend in part on what foods the child is given by parents and reflect the culture beyond. What behaviors parents reinforce or punish may be based on their personal beliefs, but they also reflect sociocultural beliefs about what is and is not appropriate. Social learning and the development of self-concept are based on observing others who are going about their business of living in a particular society with a particular culture.

Here we look at some of the ways in which cultural and social factors work their way into the microsystem from the outer systems, beginning with a discussion of the developmental "niche" a child grows up in, then considering family systems and the family as the transmitter of culture, and closing with a discussion of sociocultural influences throughout the lifespan.

The Developmental Niche

The concept of the **developmental niche** grew out of extensive studies by Charles Super and Sarah Harkness of Kipsigis-speaking communities in Kenya (1986, 1994; see also Gardiner, Mutter, & Kosmitzki, 1998). The authors' intent was to clarify interactive processes that affect what goes on within the microsystem, which makes this concept a fitting beginning of our discussion of transcending processes.

The developmental niche includes (1) everyday physical and social settings, (2) childcare and child-rearing customs, and (3) the overall psychology of the caregivers (see Table 3–5). Each of these overlapping components interacts dynamically and reciprocally to determine the unique world each child experiences, as illustrated in Figure 3–8. Even children in the same family do not experience exactly the same developmental niche, and the niche continuously changes throughout childhood and beyond.

Family Systems

At the heart of development is the family, especially when children are young. The family has a tremendous influence on the kind of person the child becomes and on the child's place in society. Indeed, the type of family into which a child is born can dramatically affect the expectations, roles, beliefs, and interrela-

Table 3–5 Components of the Developmental Niche Defined

Note, of course, that not all caregivers necessarily adhere to all culturally prescribed customs.

Everyday Physical and Social Settings

Living conditions, such as size and type of the living space, sleep and eating schedules, and whether children sleep in the same area as the parents or other caregivers; social conditions, such as the size of the family, the presence or absence of siblings or extended-family members, and others the child interacts with in and around the home

Childcare and Child-Rearing Customs

Approaches to the specifics of caring for and rearing children that are normative for families and in a larger sense for cultures, such as the extent of formal versus informal schooling and training oriented toward independence from versus dependence upon others

Overall Psychology of the Caregivers

Culturally based belief systems of the parents or other caregivers, including their expectations about their children's behavior and development and their feelings about what is "right" and what is "wrong," which they in turn impart to their children

developmental niche Interaction of components such as everyday physical and social settings, childcare and child-rearing customs, and the overall psychology of caregivers that determines the unique world of each child.

Figure 3-8 Components of the Development Niche
Double arrows within the inner circle emphasize the reciprocal nature in which the components interact. Single arrows inward from the larger human ecology indicate the role of cultural factors in each component.

Source: Super, C. M. and Harkness, S. in W. J. Lonner & R. S. Malpass, eds., "The Developmental Niche" in Psychology and Culture. *Copyright © 1994 by Allyn & Bacon. Adapted by permission.*

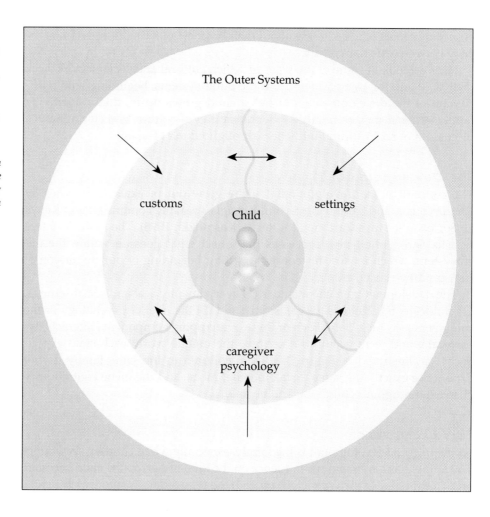

Unexpected events such as job loss can have a profound impact on development.

tionships the child later experiences throughout life (Hartup, 1989, 1995), as well as the child's physical, cognitive, emotional, and social development.

The way people interact in families has an intricate and dynamic impact on development. Each family member may play a specific role in interactions with other family members. An older sibling may be responsible for younger siblings. Each family member may have alliances with some family members but not with others. Two sisters, for example, may frequently gang up against their brother. The network of interrelationships and expectations within the family is a major influence on the child's social, emotional, and cognitive development.

Siblings in the same family may share many similar experiences, such as an overly strict parent or the values of the local neighborhood. Yet there is also a set of *nonshared* experiences and relationships. In one series of studies, relationships between parents and their first born and between parents and their second-born were compared over time (Dunn, 1986). As we might expect, mothers and firstborns often had a close and intense relationship, at least until the birth of the second child. Things then became more complicated. If the first-born child had an affectionate relationship with the father, this affection tended to increase, as did the amount of conflict between the mother and the firstborn. In addition, if the mother gave a good deal of attention to the second child, the conflict between the mother and the first child escalated. And the more the mother played with the second baby, the more the siblings quarreled with each other a year later.

Clearly, members of the same family do not necessarily experience the same environment. When adolescents are asked to compare their experiences with those of their siblings, they often note more differences than similarities. Although they may see some similarities in family rules and expectations, there are many differences in the timing and impact of events such as divorce. Even larger differences occur in how each sibling is treated by the other siblings.

The Family as Transmitter of Culture

Besides integrating the individual child into the family unit, parents interpret the society and its culture. Religious and ethnic traditions and moral values are conveyed to children from an early age. In a cohesive, homogeneous society like the Israeli *kibbutz*, people outside the family reinforce and expand parental teachings. There is little contradiction between the family's way of doing things and the customs of the community. In a more complex, multiethnic society such as that of the United States, cultural traditions often oppose each other. For example, some minority parents struggle to instill their own values so their children will not become assimilated into the culture of the majority. Parents express cultural values to their children in their attitudes toward aspects of daily life such as food, clothing, friends, education, and play.

Transmission of culture is not a simple matter. The more diverse the social fabric, the more pressure the family system experiences. It also becomes more difficult to transmit values when they are unfocused and in transition, and this may be the main challenge families in the United States and other cultures in transition face today. It is important to keep in mind that family units, social environments, and cultures are not fixed entities. An individual's social environment, already complex at birth, changes constantly and dynamically.

Although some cultural characteristics such as incest taboos are nearly universal, a great many others are not. Indeed, with regard to sexuality, incest is just about the only universal taboo. Cultural diversity reminds us of the necessity of avoiding **ethnocentrism**—the tendency to assume that your culture's beliefs, perceptions, and values are true, correct, and factual, whereas those of other cultures are false, unusual, or downright bizarre. It may be especially hard to suspend judgment on cultural differences that are close at hand. For example, it is often assumed that single-parent families are less representative of "family values" than families in which both parents are present. Yet a poverty-level single mother living in a deteriorated part of a city who turns to her own mother for help with child care may transmit as clear a message about the value of family as does a "nuclear" family living in a better part of town. We return to this issue at several points in later chapters—being a financially poor single parent brings many hardships, but it does not equate with being culturally poor or with providing low-quality childcare.

Parental influences are just one element in the larger process of socialization. Socialization is a lifelong process through which individuals are taught to function as members of social groups—families, communities, work and friendship groups, and many others. Becoming a member of a group involves recognizing and dealing with the expectations of others—family members, peers, teachers, and supervisors, to name just a few. Whether they are tense and anxiety producing or smooth and secure, our relationships with others determine what we learn and how well we learn it.

Socialization also forces people to deal with new situations. Infants are born into families; children go to school; families move to new neighborhoods; adolescents begin to date; people marry and raise their own families; older people

ethnocentrism The tendency to assume that our own beliefs, perceptions, customs, and values are correct or normal and that those of others are inferior or abnormal.

retire from jobs; friends and relatives become ill or die. Adapting to such changes throughout life is an essential part of socialization. Throughout the socialization process, the individual's evolving self-concept acts as a filter to moderate the impact of the environment. Unlike a camera, which captures every light image and imprints it on film, the self-concept captures only selected images. As a result, each person experiences the social and cultural environment in different ways.

Sociocultural Influences on Development Across the Lifespan

Here we consider how each individual's development interacts with changing cultural and historical factors, producing identifiable generations and cohorts.

Several classic investigations have focused on the U.S. generation that was born during the Great Depression and that experienced World War II as adolescents. These individuals entered college or the labor market during the postwar boom of the late 1940s and early 1950s, and many served in the armed forces during the Korean War. That war was followed by a period of economic prosperity and relatively low unemployment. Thus, the period during which that generation entered adulthood was significantly marked by specific historical factors (Featherman, Hogan, & Sorenson, 1984). Compare this cohort to the "baby boomers" born in the post–World War II period of 1946 to 1960. That large group enjoyed the benefits of a growing economy in childhood and adolescence and experienced adolescence and adulthood in the turbulent 1960s. Are members of those two cohorts similar? In some ways yes, but in other ways definitely not.

Paul Baltes (1987; Hetherington & Baltes, 1988), who has since moved on to focus on factors in aging during the later years, devised a framework that still provides insights into the interaction of developmental and historical change. He proposed that three basic factors interact. **Normative age-graded influences** are the biological and social changes that normally happen at predictable ages in a given society. Included in this category are puberty, menopause, and some physical aspects of aging, as well as predictable social events such as entering school, marrying, or retiring, which often occur at particular times—again potentially varying from one society to the next. **Normative history-graded influences** are historical events, such as wars, depression, and epidemics, that affect large numbers of individuals at about the same time.

Nonnormative influences are individual factors that do not occur at any predictable time in a person's life. Examples include divorce, unemployment, illness, moving to a new community, sudden economic losses or gains, career changes, even a chance encounter with an influential individual—critical events that may define turning points in an individual's life. Development therefore is more than just a product of age or history; it includes the timing and influence of certain events that affect us as a group or uniquely as individuals.

Baltes proposed that factors like race, sex, and social class *mediate* both the type and the effects of these influences. For example, girls universally experience puberty (an age-graded influence) earlier than boys. In the United States, black males are more likely to experience unemployment (a nonnormative influence) than white males. The effects of divorce may be different in a white family than a black family (Harrison, Wilson, Pine, Chan, & Buriel, 1990),

normative age-graded influences The biological and social changes that normally happen at predictable ages.

normative history-graded influences The historical events, such as wars, depressions, and epidemics, that affect large numbers of individuals at the same time.

nonnormative influences Individual environmental factors that do not occur at any predictable time in a person's life.

although, as always, it is necessary to consider ethnic differences among blacks and among whites that may alter or even reverse such observations (recall "In Theory, In Fact," page 76).

The impact of these influences also differs according to age. Children and older adults are often more strongly affected by age-graded influences. Adolescents and young adults are often most affected by history-graded influences; trying to find a first job during a depression or fighting in a war is more likely to occur at these ages. Nonnormative events can happen at any time, but their effects can be mediated by family or friends. The cumulative effect of these events can be particularly important for older adults. Table 3–6 and Figure 3–9 show how these influences interact at different ages for people in different generations.

Glen Elder and colleagues (Elder, Caspi, & Burton, 1988; also see Elder, 1998) provided another still-useful example of how history-graded and age-graded factors, mediated by sex, interact to produce different outcomes. Two groups of people were studied using an extensive longitudinal design. Members of the first group were infants when the Great Depression began. Members of the second group were of school age (about 10 years old) at the time. It took approximately nine years for real recovery from the Depression to occur, so members of the first group were 1 to 10 years old during the period of economic hardship, while members of the second group were 10 to 18 years old. Elder and colleagues found that boys who were younger during those years showed more negative effects of the stress and deprivation experienced by their families than boys who were older at the time. Indeed, the older boys often worked to help the family survive, thereby further limiting their exposure to the family problems that frequently accompany unemployment and poverty.

Table 3–6   How Historical Events Affect Different Age Cohorts

Historical Events	Year Born					
	1912	1924	1936	1948	1960	1972
1932 (the Depression)	20 years old (starting out)	8 years old (schoolchild)				
1944 (World War II)	32 (parenting/ career	20 (starting out)	8 (schoolchild)			
1956 (Postwar boom)	44 (middle age)	32 (parenting/ career)	20 (starting out)	8 (schoolchild)		
1968 (Vietnam War era)	56 (preretirement)	44 (middle age)	32 (parenting/ career)	20 (starting out)	8 (schoolchild)	
1980	68 (retired)	56 (preretirement)	44 (middle age)	32 (parenting/ career)	20 (starting out)	8 (schoolchild)

Note: Those who started out during the Depression were more affected than schoolchildren, whereas those who established a career during the postwar boom were more affected than those nearing retirement.

Figure 3-9 A Lifespan Profile on Influences
Age-graded, history-graded, and nonnormative influences affect people more directly at different times in their lifespans.

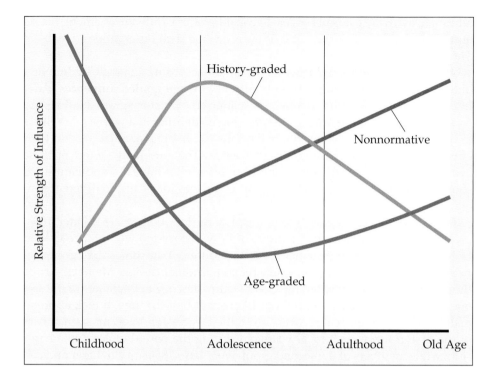

The girls in the study showed a different pattern. The younger girls apparently formed an unusually strong mother-daughter bond while the family was suffering economic hardship. Consequently, the girls who were younger during the Depression were actually more goal-oriented, competent, and assertive than those who were adolescents at the time.

Several conclusions can be drawn from these findings (adapted from Stoller & Gibson, 1994):

1. Development is influenced by an individual's personal characteristics, the life events to which that person is exposed, and the ways in which she or he adapts to these events.
2. Specific personal characteristics influence the opportunities people have during specific historical periods. For example, most black adult males living during the 1950s had far different social opportunities than most white adult males living at the same time.
3. Being born during a specific historical period shapes the experience of development. Gender, ethnicity, and social and economic class also influence the life course.
4. Although historical events shape the experiences of all people born in a particular time period, the advantaged and disadvantaged members of society are affected in different ways.

Donald J. Hernandez (1994) used the concept of the life course in his analysis of how the lives of children have changed over the past 150 years. Hernandez conceived of children's lives as "trajectories distinguished by the specific order, duration, and timing of the particular events and resources experienced in life, and by the number of characteristics, and activities of the family members with whom they live" (p. 1). The following case studies illustrate how the cultural and historical experiences individuals are exposed to at various times in their lives affect their attitudes, values, and abilities:

Ruth was born in Russia in 1913. One of five children in an orthodox Jewish family, she experienced persecution firsthand as soldiers repeatedly tried to kill her and her family because of their religious beliefs. When Ruth was 12, she came to the United States and settled in Kansas City, Missouri, where she started school. After four years, her father, a poor tailor, insisted that Ruth quit school and help support the family, which now had seven children. Despite her lack of education, Ruth was able to earn enough money after several years to move to New York City, where she met and married her husband. They had two children, both of whom graduated from college and became successful professionals. Because of the scarring experiences she had as a child, Ruth spent her married life protected by the cocoon of her family. As she grew older, her husband made all the real-world decisions for the family, and she became increasingly fearful and unable to function outside the home.

Judy was born in 1948, the youngest of three children. Her father was a lawyer and her mother was a homemaker. Judy attended private schools and, like her father, became a lawyer. Asked about her childhood and youth, she remembers fearing the atomic bomb and hiding under the desk during air raid drills in grade school; Judy also recalls the Korean War, the space race, the start of the civil rights movement, the assassination of John F. Kennedy, Vietnam, and Watergate. During the 1960s, she became a student activist, registering voters in the South and protesting the Vietnam War. While attending law school, she married a fellow activist. Both now have government careers and perform extensive volunteer work. Sometimes Judy wonders whether she made the right decision in choosing not to have children.

These two women's values and life experiences were strongly shaped by the historical events of the times in which they lived. The differences between them force us to take a closer look at the relationships between developmental and historical changes over the lifespan, and at how the timing and influence of events affect each person differently.

CONTENT CHECK
PROCESSES THAT TRANSCEND THE MICROSYSTEM

True–False (answers are on the Companion Website)

1. Children in the same family experience essentially the same developmental niche, experiences, and relationships with parents.
2. In multiethnic societies, most families adopt the culture of the majority and transmit this to their children.
3. For the most part, family processes are a one-way street in which the parent or parents influence the child but the child has little influence on the parents.
4. Normative age-graded influences are universal across cultures.
5. Normative history-graded events have profound effects on the life course of the cohorts who experience them.

Thinking Critically

In what ways are family systems dynamic?

A Tale of the Interaction Between Heredity and Environment

Shortly after Leonardo da Vinci died in 1519 at the age of 67, his younger half-brother Bartolommeo set out to reproduce a living duplicate of the great painter, sculptor, engineer, and author. Since he and Leonardo were related, the father that Bartolommeo chose was himself. He chose as his wife a woman whose background was similar to that of Leonardo's mother. She was young and came of peasant stock and had also grown up in the village of Vinci. The couple produced a son, Piero, who was then carefully reared in the same region of the Tuscan countryside, between Florence and Pisa, that had nurtured Leonardo. Little Piero soon displayed artistic talent, and at the age of 12 he was taken to Florence, where he served as an apprentice to several leading artists, at least one of whom had worked with Leonardo. According to Giorgio Vasari, the leading art historian of the period, the young Piero "made everyone marvel . . . and had made in five years of study that proficiency in art which others do not achieve save after length of life and great experience of many things." In fact, Piero was often referred to as the second Leonardo.

At the age of 23, however, Piero died of a fever, and so it is impossible to predict with certainty what he might have gone on to achieve—though there is some indication in that Piero's works have often been attributed to the great Michelangelo. Nor is it possible to say positively how much of Piero's genius was due to heredity and how much to environment. Full brothers share, on the average, 50% of their genes, but Bartolommeo and Leonardo were half-brothers and so would have had only about a quarter of their genes in common. Piero's mother and Leonardo's mother do not appear to have been related, but in the closely knit peasant village of Vinci it is quite possible that they had ancestors in common and thus shared genes. On the other hand, a strong environmental influence cannot be ruled out. The young Piero was undoubtedly aware of his acclaimed uncle; and certainly his father, Bartolommeo, provided every opportunity that money could buy for the boy to emulate him. But Bartolommeo's efforts to give the world a second Leonardo by providing a particular heredity and environment might, after all, have had little influence. Piero possibly was just another of the numerous talented Florentines of his time. (Excerpt from *Humankind*. Copyright © 1978 by Peter Farb. Reprinted by permission of Houghton Mifflin Co. All rights reserved.)

CHAPTER 3 REVISITED

The mapping of the human genome has many ramifications, potentially positive and negative.

Molecular Genetics

▪ The human body has over 200 different kinds of cells; cell components important to an understanding of molecular genetics include the cell membrane, the cytoplasm, the cytoskeleton, mitochondria, the endoplasmic reticulum, the Golgi apparatus, the ribosomes, the nucleus, and deoxyribonucleic acid (DNA).

▪ The building blocks of the DNA double helix are nucleotides, which are comprised of a sugar molecule, a phosphate molecule, and one of four bases: adenine (A), thymine (T), cytosine (C), and guanine (G).

▪ Base pairs of nucleotide bonds are the 3.12 billion letters of the human genome; adenine pairs with thymine, cytosine pairs with guanine.

▪ Single nucleotide polymorphisms (SNPs) occur at about every 1,250 base pairs; this yields about 5 million SNPs in the human genome, over half of which have been mapped but most of which perform no meaningful function.

▪ The total number of genes in the human genome is estimated to be between 65,000 and 80,000; only about 10,000 have been mapped.

▪ The proteins genes synthesize perform numerous crucial functions throughout the body; enzymes are the most common kind of protein.

▪ Protein synthesis begins when nucleotide bonds separate to provide a template; transcription then produces messenger RNA (mRNA); next, transfer RNA (tRNA) attaches to each mRNA codon; finally, ribosomes translate the mRNA-tRNA strands into amino acids, which are assembled into the polypeptide chains that make up proteins.

Genes, Chromosomes, and Cell Division

▪ The 23rd chromosome pairs in humans are visible just before cell division, at which point they can be rearranged to yield a individual's karyotype for assessment; 22 of the pairs are autosomes and the 23rd pair determines sex, XX or XY.

▪ Mitosis produces cell replicas and meiosis produces gametes; meiotic processes (including mutation) are the primary basis for individual differences from one generation to the next.

▪ Gene alleles in interaction with environment determine phenotype; simple dominance and recessiveness, incomplete dominance, codominance, and polygenic functioning are ways in genes are expressed.

Genetic and Chromosomal Disorders

▪ The congenital anomalies that are attributable to genes usually involve disruptions of metabolic pathways involved in protein production, as a result of defective DNA.

▪ Sex-linked disorders involve the 23rd chromosome pair; these are more common in males because the Y chromosome has considerably fewer genes and cannot offset many anomalies on the X chromosome.

▪ Hemophilia and fragile X syndrome are sex-linked genetic disorders; the latter is the leading genetic cause of mental retardation.

▪ Down syndrome is an autosomal disorder in which there is an extra chromosome; it is the second leading genetic cause of mental retardation.

▪ The genetic mechanisms involved in congenital anomalies can be complex; gene imprinting is an example.

▪ Genetic counseling is important if there are indications that parents are at risk for having a baby with a serious anomaly; aside from providing support for parents, genetic counselors assess the degree of risk and assist parents in making an informed decision.

Advances in Genetic Research and Treatment

▪ Recombinant DNA technology is the basis for most of the advances in genetic research and treatment; it typically consists of extracting DNA, then culturing and cloning it in host cells either for study or for use in gene therapies.

▪ The indirect approach to gene therapy is now commonly used; ex vivo and in vivo gene therapies are still experimental.

■ Entire organisms, including mammals, can now be cloned from a single cell, which has generated much controversy because of the possibility of cloning humans.

Behavior Genetics

■ Behavior geneticists study polygenic traits by assessing concordance rates and determining heritability; their most commonly used approaches are adoption studies and twin studies, in which heritability is determined by comparing people who vary in the degree to which they are biologically related.

Processes Within the Microsystem

■ Habituation occurs at the sensory, perceptual, and cognitive levels.

■ Classical conditioning involves the pairing of a neutral stimulus with a stimulus that produces a reflexive or otherwise automatic response; classical conditioning is often involved in acquisition of emotional responses.

■ The four basic contingencies in operant conditioning are positive reinforcement, negative reinforcement, positive punishment, and negative punishment; the first two correspond to the first half of Thorndike's law of effect, the last two the second half.

■ Shaping and successive approximations are used to establish novel behaviors; partial reinforcement establishes behaviors that are extremely enduring.

■ Behavior modification is the application of classical and operant conditioning procedures to behavioral deficits or problem behaviors.

■ Classical and operant conditioning contingencies cannot predict or explain all human behaviors; cognition must be allowed for as well.

■ Social-learning theory incorporates observational learning and underlying cognition, but also cannot explain all human behaviors.

■ Acquiring self-concept often involves social learning.

Processes That Transcend the Microsystem

■ The concept of the developmental niche attempts to clarify processes within and beyond the microsystem; the focus is on everyday physical and social settings, childcare and child-rearing customs, and the overall psychology of the caregivers.

■ Family systems consist of the dynamic network of interrelationships between family members, which have a dramatic effect on children in a family.

■ Each child in a family has nonshared experiences that differ, with differing outcomes for each child.

■ In its role as transmitter of culture, the family attempts to instill its own values and cultural preferences in the child.

■ Avoiding ethnocentrism is important in studying families both within and across cultures.

■ Normative age-graded influences occur at predictable ages in a given society; normative history-graded influences produce differences between generations and cohorts; nonnormative influences are often unpredictable and affect individuals rather than groups.

KEY TERMS

cells
deoxyribonucleic acid (DNA)
nucleotides
bases
base pairs
single nucleotide polymorphisms (SNPs)
genes
proteins
chromosome
karyotype

autosomes
sex chromosomes
mitosis
meiosis
gametes
alleles
genotype
dominant
recessive
phenotype
homozygous

heterozygous
incomplete dominance
codominance
polygenic inheritance
sex-linked inheritance
congenital anomalies
gene imprinting
genetic counseling
bioinformatics
recombinant DNA technology
gene therapy

behavior genetics
heritability
habituation
phobia
positive reinforcement
negative reinforcement

positive punishment
negative punishment
shaping
partial reinforcement
self-efficacy
self-concept

developmental niche
ethnocentrism
normative age-graded influences
normative history-graded
    influences
nonnormative influences

PRENATAL DEVELOPMENT AND CHILDBIRTH

4

115

CHAPTER PREVIEW

Do you know:

1. What the *germinal period*, *embryonic period*, and *fetal period* are and what development takes place during each?

3. What causes *twins?*

4. How many conceptions *fail* to result in birth and why?

5. What *developmental trends* begin during the prenatal period and continue into childhood?

6. What *teratogens* are and when they are most likely to cause harm?

7. The potential effects of maternal *diseases* during pregnancy?

8. The potential effects of maternal use of *alcohol and other drugs* during pregnancy?

9. How childbirth *works?*

10. The differences between *traditional* and *natural or prepared* childbirth and the advantages and disadvantages of each?

11. When *cesarean* childbirth is necessary?

12. What causes *premature birth* and what characteristics premature infants display?

13. What built-in processes and behaviors are involved in a newborn infant's *survival?*

14. How parents must adjust in making the *transition to parenthood* and how *attachment* begins?

These are the main topics of Chapter 4.

A human life is conceived, and in about a week the mother and father of that life may know it exists. A positive test for pregnancy tends to elicit a wide range of reactions, depending to a large degree on the circumstances. For those who are ready for the experience of parenthood, the news that conception has occurred can be a wondrous moment: "We're having a baby!" For those who are not, the news can mean mixed feelings or quite negative ones.

In the United States, about 50% of all pregnancies are unintended. For teens, despite having dropped to a record low in the 1990s, the percentage is even higher—about 66% (Ventura, Joyce, Curtin, Mathews, & Park, 2000). Pregnancy in these circumstances is frequently greeted with more trepidation than joy. Moreover, even for committed couples, the first pregnancy often occurs at inconvenient times, interrupting jobs, careers, studies, and favorite pastimes and straining finances. Second, third, and more children are sometimes carefully planned but even today, in the age of regularly available birth control, they are not totally intended. Even when couples have planned and even waited for this event, the reality of expectant parenthood can seem a bit overwhelming. Aside from the shopping and borrowing spree to get ready for the baby that will characterize much of the next nine months, the prospective parents start deliberating a multitude of issues—especially if it's their first baby. "Life won't be the same around here. . . ." "What kind of parent will I be?" "Will it be a boy or a girl?" "Should we find out or just wait and see?" "We're *actually* going through with it—we're having a baby! Imagine. . . ." "What will she or he be like?"

"Will I be able to manage school and being a parent? "How are we going to manage the finances?" "And what about a name?"

The months before a baby's birth can be stressful as well. First-time parents in particular tend to do a lot of worrying. The mother may imagine having a baby who will be attractive, easy, and smart, and will one day fulfill her dreams, but she may also imagine a baby who is malformed, weak, or ugly, or who may someday wreak havoc on the family (Bruschweiler-Stern, 1997). Fathers are subject to similar imaginings. Prospective parents also wonder whether childbirth will be an ordeal and worry that it will be painful or dangerous. Perhaps it's a good thing that they usually don't fully realize what's in store for them after their baby arrives and immediately starts making demands on their time and energy.

In this chapter we focus on the biologically programmed sequence of events leading up to the birth of a baby, with emphasis on what goes right. The 20th century saw much progress in infant health. During the late 1990s, for example, infant mortality rates dipped to new lows, while the percentage of mothers receiving prenatal care reached record highs—in 1998, the percent of women who began prenatal care in the first trimester rose for the ninth consecutive year to over 82% (Ventura et al., 2000). Moreover, new medical treatments such as neonatal intensive care have caused many babies born prematurely not simply to survive but to lead healthy lives. Better access to health care, environmental interventions, improved nutrition, higher educational levels, and improved standards of living have also contributed to infant health and the drop in infant mortality (CDC, 1999a; Children's Defense Fund, 2000). Things can sometimes go wrong, as we saw in Chapter 3 with regard to heredity and as we discuss in this chapter with regard to the prenatal environment. Normally, prenatal development occurs within a highly controlled and safe environment—the uterus—and follows an orderly, biologically programmed sequence. At the same time, however, the expectations and anxieties, advantages and deprivations, stability and disruptions, health and illnesses of a family into which a child is born affect not only the child's life after birth but also the child's prenatal development. The childbirth process too is a biologically programmed sequence, but the reality of a specific child's birth is strongly defined by the cultural, historical, and family contexts within which it occurs.

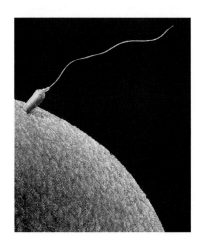

A living human ovum at the moment of conception. Although some sperm cells have begun to penetrate the outer covering of the ovum, only one will actually fertilize it.

Prenatal Growth and Development

The development of a unique human individual begins with fertilization. So tiny that it is visible only under a microscope, a one-celled, fertilized egg carries all of the genetic information necessary to create an entire new organism. Many will not complete the journey to childbirth. An estimated 50 to 70% of all fertilized eggs are lost within the first 2 weeks (Beller & Zlatnik, 1994), and of those that survive, another 25% or so will be lost through miscarriage later in the pregnancy. Even so, many will survive and emerge as healthy babies.

Periods and Trimesters

Prenatal development can be viewed in terms of *trimesters* or in terms of *periods* or stages with regard to the developing child. Trimesters simply break the 9 months of the mother's pregnancy into three 3-month segments. The first trimester lasts from conception to about 13 weeks, the second from 13 weeks to just over 25 weeks, and the third from 25 weeks to birth, which normally occurs around 38 weeks (266 days) after conception. Periods are more specific than trimesters and reflect developmental milestones as discussed next.

Conception and the Germinal Period

As noted in Chapter 3, women are born with all the ova they'll ever have, which usually mature one at a time during a woman's reproductive years. About the 10th day after the start of a regular menstrual period, stimulated by hormones, an ovum enters the final stage of meiosis. By the end of the 13th or 14th day of this growth, the follicle (sac) surrounding the ovum breaks, releasing the ovum. It then embarks down one of the two **fallopian tubes** (see Figure 4–1). The release of the mature ovum is called **ovulation.**

Most of the time, ovulation occurs around the 14th day after the onset of menstruation. A mature ovum survives for 3 to 5 days. A male's sperm cells—which in a normal adult male are produced at a rate of about one billion per day—survive for as long as 2 or 3 days after entering a woman's vagina. This means that there's a "window" of a week or so before and after a woman's ovulation during which conception might occur. If the ovum is not fertilized, it continues down the fallopian tube and disintegrates in the **uterus,** also illustrated in Figure 4–1.

The events leading up to the union of a sperm and an ovum are remarkable. During a male's period of peak fertility in young adulthood, some 300 million sperm are deposited in the vagina during each instance of sexual intercourse. Yet only one of them may penetrate and fertilize an ovum and determine the sex and genetic traits of the child.

For the tiny sperm cells, the trip to a potential rendezvous with an ovum in a fallopian tube is long and difficult. The sperm must work their way upward

fallopian tubes Two passages that open out of the upper part of the uterus and carry ova from the ovary to the uterus.

ovulation The release of an ovum into one of the two fallopian tubes; occurs approximately 14 days after menstruation.

uterus The area that contains and nourishes the embryo and fetus (discussed later in the chapter).

Figure 4-1 Ovulation and Fertilization

The journey of the fertilized egg is shown as it moves from the ovary to the uterus. Fetal development begins with the union of sperm and egg high in the fallopian tube. During the next few days, the fertilized egg, or zygote, travels down the fallopian tube and begins to devide. Cell divisions continue for a week until a blastula is formed. By this time, the blastula has arrived in the uterus. Within the next few days it may implant itself in the uterine wall.

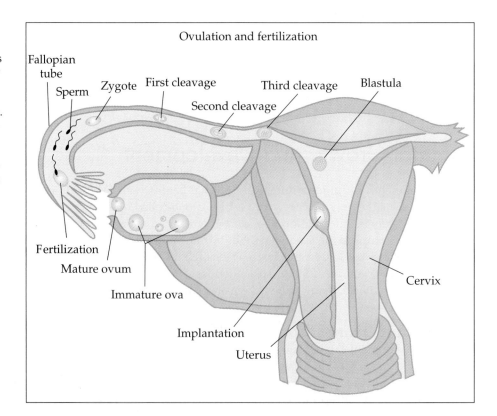

Ovulation and fertilization

Fallopian tube
Sperm
Zygote
First cleavage
Second cleavage
Third cleavage
Blastula
Fertilization
Mature ovum
Immature ova
Implantation
Uterus
Cervix

through a foot-long passageway containing acidic fluids that can be lethal and obstacles such as mucus. Finally, if a sperm arrives at the right place at the right time, it penetrates the cell membrane of the ovum to initiate fertilization. Over the next 24 hours, the genetic material of two individuals "fuses" and is translated into a new living entity (Beller & Zlatnik, 1994) called a **zygote** (from the Greek root for "yoke or join together").

The **germinal period** thus begins with conception and fertilization, and it continues until the developing organism journeys down to the uterus and achieves *implantation,* discussed later. At about 2 weeks after conception, implantation is normally complete.

The germinal period is a time of extremely rapid cell division and organization. About 48 hours after conception, the one-celled zygote divides to produce two cells. Then a second division occurs in each cell, yielding four cells, and so on. The rate of cell division increases, so that by the sixth day more than 100 cells (each one smaller, but containing exact copies of the original zygote's genetic material) have been produced.

What Causes Twins? Sometimes the first division of the zygote produces two identical cells that then separate and develop into two individuals. The result is **monozygotic (identical) twins.** Because they develop from the same cell, identical twins are always the same sex and share the same physical traits.

In other cases two ova are released simultaneously and *each* unites with a different sperm, producing **dizygotic (fraternal) twins.** The genetic traits inherited by fraternal twins can be as similar or as different as those of any two siblings. Fraternal twins may also be of the same sex or different sexes. Certain fertility drugs and techniques such as in vitro fertilization also increase the chance of conceiving fraternal twins or triplets, even sextuplets. It is estimated that about 80% of triplet or more births in 1996 and 1997 were the result of fertility interventions (CDC, 2000b).

Differentiation Toward the end of the first week the dividing cells have developed into a **blastula**—a ball of cells around a fluid-filled center—that has made its way to the uterus. Now the cells begin the process of *differentiation*— that is, they start separating into groups according to their future function. Some of the cells move to one side of the hollow sphere and form the embryonic disc, from which the child itself will develop. The other group of cells begins to develop into the supportive structures that will nourish and protect the embryo. This is also the point at which home urine tests can assess pregnancy: The cells of the supportive structures begin secreting a detectable hormone called *human chorionic gonadotropin (hcg),* which shuts down further ovulation and prevents the next menstrual period (Nilsson & Hamberger, 1990).

Implantation At the same time, the blastula starts to burrow into the lining of the uterus, breaking tiny blood vessels to obtain nutrients. This process triggers hormonal changes that signal the beginning of pregnancy. Within a few days, if all goes well, the blastula is implanted in the uterine wall.

The crucial process of implantation is far from routine, however. Over 50% of blastulas don't implant successfully—some because they are incompletely formed, others because the uterine environment is inhospitable. An unsuccessful implantation may yield what resembles a heavy menstrual period that arrives a bit late, so the woman may not even realize that she was temporarily pregnant.

Identical twins (top) have the same genes and physical characteristics, including sex; fraternal twins (bottom) can be as similar or different as siblings born at different times.

zygote The first cell of a human being that occurs as a result of fertilization; a fertilized ovum.

germinal period After conception, the period of very rapid cell division and initial cell differentiation lasting for approximately two weeks.

monozygotic (identical) twins Twins resulting from the division of a single fertilized ovum.

dizygotic (fraternal) twins Twins resulting from the fertilization of two separate ova by two separate sperm.

blastula The hollow, fluid-filled sphere of cells that forms soon after conception.

The Embryonic Period

The **embryonic period** starts when implantation is complete. It is a time of major structural development and growth that continues until 2 months after conception. (The term **embryo** comes from the Greek word for "swell.")

Two crucial processes occur simultaneously during the embryonic period: (1) The outer layer of cells produces all the tissues and structures that will house, nurture, and protect the developing child for the remainder of the prenatal period; and (2) the cells of the inner embryonic disc differentiate into the embryo itself.

The Supporting Structures   The outer layer of cells produces three structures: the **amniotic sac,** a membrane filled with watery **amniotic fluid** that helps cushion the embryo and otherwise protect it; the **placenta,** a disc-shaped mass of tissue growing from the wall of the uterus that serves as a partial filter; and the **umbilical cord,** a rope of tissue containing two arteries and a vein that connect mother to child.

The placenta, which is formed partly from the tissues of the uterine wall as well, continues to grow until about the seventh month of pregnancy. The placenta provides for the exchange of materials between mother and embryo, keeping out larger particles of foreign matter but allowing nutrients to pass through. Thus, enzymes, vitamins, and antibodies to protect against disease pass into the embryo, while the resulting waste products in the embryo's blood pass out to the mother for elimination. Sugars, fats, and proteins also pass through to the embryo, but some bacteria and some salts do not. Note that the mother and the developing child do not share the same blood system. The placenta permits the exchange of nutritive and waste materials by diffusion across cell membranes, normally without any exchange of blood cells. However, leakage across the barrier can occur in the later months of pregnancy.

Unfortunately, however, viruses contracted by the mother during pregnancy can also pass the placental barrier, as can potentially harmful drugs and other substances ingested by the mother. These are discussed at length later in the chapter.

The Embryo   During the 6 weeks of the embryonic period, the embryo develops arms, legs, fingers, toes, a face, a heart that beats, a brain, lungs, and all the other major organs. By the end of the period, the embryo is recognizably human, as illustrated in Figure 4–2.

The embryo grows rapidly and changes daily. Immediately after implantation it develops into three distinct layers: the *ectoderm,* or outer layer, will become the skin, the sense organs, and the nervous system; the *mesoderm,* or middle layer, will become muscles, blood, and the excretory system; and the *endoderm,* or inner layer, will become the digestive system, lungs, thyroid, thymus, and other organs. Simultaneously, the *neural tube* (the beginning of the nervous system and the brain) and the heart start to develop. By the end of the fourth week after conception (and therefore only 2 weeks into the embryonic period), the heart is beating and the primitive nervous system is functioning. Yet at 4 weeks the embryo is still only about a quarter of an inch (6 millimeters) long.

During the second month all of the structures that we recognize as human develop rapidly. The arms and legs unfold from small buds on the sides of the trunk. The eyes become visible, seemingly on the sides of the head, at about 1 month; the overall face changes almost daily. The internal organs—the lungs, digestive system, and excretory system—are also forming, although they aren't yet functional.

embryonic period   The second prenatal period, which lasts from implantation to the end of the second month after conception. All the major structures and organs of the individual are formed at this time.

embryo   From the Greek term "swell."

amniotic sac   A fluid-filled membrane that encloses the developing embryo or fetus.

amniotic fluid   Fluid that cushions and helps protect the embryo or fetus.

placenta   A disk-shaped mass of tissue that forms along the wall of the uterus through which the embryo receives nutrients and discharges waste.

umbilical cord   The "rope" of tissue connecting the placenta to the embryo; this rope contains two fetal arteries and one fetal vein.

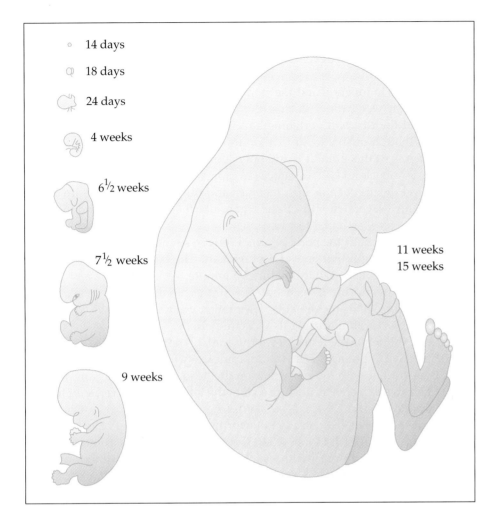

14 days

18 days

24 days

4 weeks

6½ weeks

7½ weeks

9 weeks

11 weeks
15 weeks

Figure 4–2   Growth During the Embryonic Period
This is a lifesize illustration of the growth of the human embryo and fetus from 14 days to 15 weeks.

Spontaneous Abortions   Miscarriages or **spontaneous abortions** occur primarily during the first trimester; almost 90% occur by 12 or 13 weeks, and miscarriages beyond 20 weeks are rare. They are often caused by inadequate development of the placenta, the umbilical cord, or the embryo itself, or by unsuccessful implantation. In addition, many toxic substances can pass through the placenta and cause spontaneous abortion—especially certain drugs and pollutants discussed later in the chapter. Maternal age, health, and nutrition also can be risk factors, as discussed later. Notably, researchers have also found a link between miscarriage and the father's preconception exposure to drugs, chemicals, radiation, and other potentially toxic agents (Friedler, 1996).

The Fetal Period

The **fetal period** lasts from the beginning of the third month until birth—or for about 7 months. During this period the organs and systems mature and become functional. The **fetus** (French for "pregnant" or "fruitful") begins to kick, squirm, turn its head, and eventually turn its body. Even with its eyes still sealed shut, the fetus starts to squint. It can also frown, open its mouth, practice breathing the thin amniotic fluid, and make sucking motions—perhaps even suck its thumb.

During the third month physical structures become more complete. The eyes, still set toward the sides of the head, develop their irises, and all of the

spontaneous abortions   Miscarriage; expulsion of the developing child before it is viable.

fetal period   The final period of prenatal development, lasting from the beginning of the second month after conception until birth. During this period, all organs mature and become functional.

fetus   French for "pregnant" or "fruitful."

nerves needed to connect the eyes to the brain are formed. Teeth develop under the gums; ears start to appear on the sides of the head; fingernails and toenails begin to form. The fetus develops a thyroid gland, a thymus gland, a pancreas, and kidneys. Both in males and females, the sexual organs become complete. The liver starts to function and the stomach to move.

By the 12th week the vocal cords have developed, the taste buds have formed, and the ribs and vertebrae have begun to ossify (harden into bone). The fetus, though unable to survive on its own, has acquired almost all of its body systems. At this point it is still only about 3 inches (7½ centimeters) long and weighs only about half an ounce (14 grams).

Structural details such as lips, toenails, and buds for adult teeth are added during the next several months. Basic organs like the heart, lungs, and the brain mature to the level essential for survival.

In the fourth month the body becomes longer, so that the head doesn't look quite as out of proportion as it did previously. The heart muscle strengthens and starts beating fast—120 to 160 times a minute.

In the fifth month the fetus acquires a strong hand grip and increases the amount and force of its movements. The mother can feel its elbows, knees, and head as it moves around during its wakeful periods.

In the sixth month the fetus grows to about 12 inches in length and weighs approximately 1½ pounds. The eyes are completely formed and the eyelids can open. Bone formation progresses, hair on the head continues to grow, and the fetus begins to straighten its posture so that the internal organs can shift to their proper positions.

Brain development is especially noteworthy during this time. The size of the brain increases sixfold (Moore, 1988). Going into the second trimester, brain waves are virtually absent—with electrical patterns similar to those of brain death in adults. At about 24 weeks bursts of electrical activity begin to occur, indicating that the brain is becoming functional. The foundation is laid for sensing pain and making associations. Brain development also allows for regulation of other body functions, such as breathing and sleeping.

At the end of the second trimester (i.e., after 24 weeks), a healthy fetus reaches the **age of viability.** It now has about a 50-50 chance of surviving outside the uterus if given high-quality intensive care. However, over half of fetuses born at 24 weeks have serious anomalies. In contrast, at 25 weeks nearly 80% survive (69% with no major anomaly); and at 29 weeks over 90% survive with a good outcome, provided again that they receive quality intensive care (Allen, Donohue, & Dusman, 1993). Despite modern medical advances and highly specialized care, however, infants who are born at earlier periods don't fare as well. At 23 weeks, for example, only 15% survive, and five out of six of them have serious medical problems or anomalies (Allen et al., 1993). Specialized care for a very small infant is also extremely expensive.

The Third Trimester   Think of the first trimester as the time when basic structures are formed and the second trimester as a period of maturation of organs, especially the brain, in preparation for basic survival. The third trimester is a time of extensive brain maturation and system "rehearsal." During this trimester the fragile fetus transforms into a vigorous, adaptive baby.

At 7 months the fetus weighs about 3 pounds. Its nervous system is mature enough to control breathing and swallowing. During the seventh month the brain develops rapidly, forming the tissues that become localized centers for the various senses and for motor activities. The fetus is now sensitive to touch and can feel pain, and it may even possess a sense of balance.

age of viability   The age (at about 24 weeks) at which the fetus has a 50-50 chance of surviving outside the womb.

Can a fetus hear at 7 months? Yes. It has long been known that a fetus can be startled by very loud sounds occurring close to the mother, though hardly at all by moderate sounds. This is partly because sounds from outside the mother are muffled, but also because the fetus is surrounded by a variety of sounds occurring *within* the mother. There are digestive sounds from the mother's drinking, eating, and swallowing. There are breathing sounds. There are circulatory system sounds that correspond to the rhythm of the mother's heartbeat. The internal noise level in the uterus in fact has been characterized as being as high as that in a small factory (Aslin, Pisoni, & Jusczyk, 1983; Restak, 1986).

With regard to motor and sensory development, fetuses can grasp and grimace as early as 15 weeks, near the beginning of the second trimester, and reflex movements are elicited if the soles of the feet or the eyelids are touched. By 20 weeks, the senses of taste and smell are formed. By 24 weeks, the sense of touch is more fully developed. Past 25 weeks, responses to sound become more consistent. At 27 weeks, a light shone on the mother's abdomen can cause the fetus to turn its head, and brain scans verify that the fetus reacts. Such reactions—facial expressions, turning, kicking, ducking—may also be purposeful movements that make the fetus more comfortable (Fedor-Freybergh & Vogel, 1988).

In the eighth month the fetus may gain as much as half a pound per week. It now begins to prepare for life in the outside world. Fat layers form under the skin to protect the fetus from the temperature changes that it will encounter at birth. The survival rate for infants born at 8 months is greater than 90% in well-equipped hospitals, but the babies still face risks. Breathing may be difficult; initial weight loss may be greater than that of full-term babies; and because their fat layers have not fully formed, temperature control may be a problem. For that reason babies born at this developmental stage are usually placed in incubators and given the same type of care as babies born earlier.

Fetal sensitivity and behavior also develop rapidly in the eighth month. Around the middle of the month, the eyes open and the fetus may be able to see its hands (although the uterus is quite dark). It is possible that *awareness* starts at about 32 weeks, as many of the fetus's neural circuits are quite advanced. Brain scans also show periods of rest that look like dream sleep.

During the ninth month the fetus develops daily cycles of activity and sleep. Hearing capacity is thought to be quite mature at this point (Shatz, 1992). Throughout the ninth month the fetus continues to grow. It also shifts to a head-down position in preparation for the trip through the birth canal. The *vernix caseosa* (a cheese-like protective coating) starts to fall away, and the fine body hair some babies are born with—called *lanugo*—normally dissolves. Antibodies to protect against disease pass from the mother to the fetus and supplement the fetus's own developing immune reactions. Approximately 1 to 2 weeks before birth, the baby often "drops" as the uterus settles lower into the pelvic area. The fetus gains weight at a slower rate; the mother's muscles and uterus begin sporadic, painless contractions; and the cells of the placenta start to degenerate.

Thus, in about nine months, the initially one-celled zygote normally has developed into perhaps 10 trillion cells organized into organs and systems. Figure 4–3 summarizes major milestones in prenatal development.

Developmental Trends

During the prenatal period (and throughout childhood), physical growth and motor development exhibit three general trends. Although there are individual differences in the timing of various aspects of development and the trends are

Figure 4–3

Major milestones in development: **(A)** A two-cell organism showing the first cleavage a few hours after fertilization. **(B)** The germinal period at 2 days—no cell differentiation exists yet. **(C)** An embryo at 21 days. Note the primitive spinal column. **(D)** A 4-week-old embryo. One can now distinguish the head, trunk, and tail. The heart and nervous system have started to function by this time. **(E)** A 5-week-old embryo. The arms and the legs are beginning to unfold from the trunk. **(F)** A 9-week-old fetus showing the umbilical cord connection with the placenta. **(G)** A 16-week-old fetus showing the umbilical cord connection with the placenta. All internal organs have formed but are not yet fully functional. **(H)** A 20-week-old fetus. At this stage, most internal organs have begun to function, and the fetus is able to kick, turn its head, and make facial expressions.

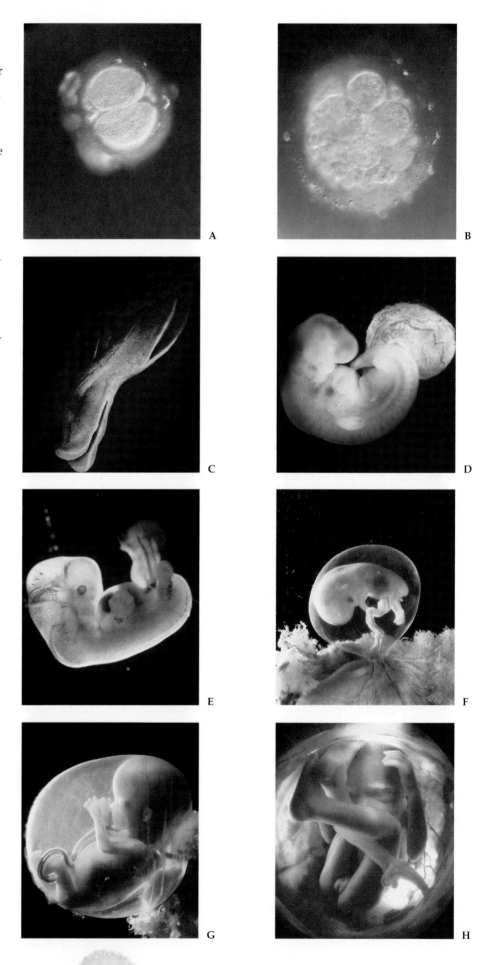

just that (not laws or principles), children tend to follow the same sequences as their bodies grow and their motor skills become refined.

First, development proceeds from the top of the body down, or from "head to tail"; this is termed the **cephalocaudal trend.** During the prenatal period the fetus's head is disproportionately larger than the rest of its body, and it will be years before the rest of the body catches up. (Incidentally, the cephalocaudal trend in physical growth is part of the reason that toddlers "toddle": They're top-heavy.) A similar trend can be seen in motor development: Infants control eye and head movements first, then arm and hand movements, and finally movements of their legs and feet.

Second, development usually proceeds from the middle of the body outward, or from "near to far"; this is the **proximodistal trend.** The inner arms and upper legs develop earlier, and infants reach and grab with their full hand long before they can pick up something like peas and bits of carrot with their finger and thumb.

Finally, there's the **gross-to-specific trend:** A fetus initially reacts to a poke on the skin with gross, generalized, whole-body movements, but after birth and in early childhood the movements become more localized and specific. However, even young children, when learning to write, still often move their whole bodies, perhaps including their tongues. Only later do they confine the action to the fingers, the hand, and wrist motions.

cephalocaudal trend   The sequence of growth that occurs first in the head and progresses downward.

proximodistal trend   The sequence of growth that occurs from the midline of the body outward.

gross-to-specific trend   The tendency to react to body stimuli with generalized, whole-body movements at first, with these responses becoming more local and specific later.

CONTENT CHECK
PRENATAL GROWTH AND DEVELOPMENT

True–False (answers are on the Companion Website)

1. In prenatal development, trimesters are the same as periods.
2. The germinal period is characterized by relatively slow cell division.
3. All of the major structures and organs of the developing child are formed during the embryonic period.
4. Most miscarriages occur during the fetal period.
5. The age of viability is the point at which a fetus has nearly a 100% chance of surviving outside the womb.

Thinking Critically

Why is the union of a sperm and an ovum to produce a human being a remarkable achievement?

Prenatal Environmental Influences

Up to this point we have focused mainly on normal developmental processes that occur under normal environmental conditions. Ideal conditions include a well-developed amniotic sac with its cushion of amniotic fluid, a fully functional placenta and umbilical cord, an adequate supply of oxygen and nutrients, and—equally as important—freedom from invading disease organisms and toxic agents.

Most pregnancies in the United States (92–95%) that make it past the first few weeks result in full-term, healthy babies. However, every year some

The hormonal balance and tissue development in older first-time mothers may be a factor in the higher incidence of prenatal defects or abnormalities reported for this population.

150,000 or more babies (5 to 8% of live births) are born with congenital anomalies. These range from minimal physical or mental anomalies, which may have little impact on the future development of the child, to gross anomalies that spell certain and almost immediate death. Some people mistakenly assume that congenital anomalies happen only in families with defective genes; in reality they can happen to anyone, and only a small proportion are the result of inherited factors. Environmental influences during the prenatal period or childbirth cause the majority of congenital anomalies. Heredity and environment can also interact to produce anomalies.

In this section we begin by considering the mother's age and overall health. Then we discuss the many harmful things a mother can ingest or otherwise be exposed to and how they affect the child developing inside her body.

Maternal Age

The age of the mother interacts with the prenatal development of the child in ways that aren't fully understood. The greatest success rate is for mothers in their 20s. Teenage mothers and mothers over 35 to 40 are at greater risk for having miscarriages, stillbirths, or children with congenital anomalies. For teenage mothers, the likeliest reason for the increased risk is that their bodies may not yet be mature enough to conceive and sustain a healthy developing child. Other risks for teens include socioeconomic factors, as well as immoderate use of alcohol and other drugs (Kalil & Kunz, 1999).

For mothers over 40, one study of over 1.2 million pregancies in Denmark revealed a miscarriage rate of over 50%, and for mothers over 45, the rate was 75%—compared to about 9% for mothers age 20 to 24 (Andersen, Wohlfahrt, Christens, Olsen, & Melbye, 2000). With regard to congenital anomalies, the relationship between maternal age and Down syndrome has been studied extensively; generally accepted figures are that its incidence increases from about 1 in 800 births for mothers under age 35 to about 1 in 25 for mothers 45 or older. Of course, such statistics don't necessarily mean that older women shouldn't have children. As noted earlier, most miscarriages occur early in pregnancy, and though the parents may experience extreme disappointment, the physical effects on the mother tend to be minimal. As for Down syndrome, 1 in 25 is still only a 4% chance. Clearly, however, older women should consider these statistics in deciding whether to have a child.

One theory regarding increased risk with age simply notes that older mothers have older ova (remember that all of a woman's ova were formed before she was born). Through aging alone, ova might be defective in ways that affect development. There is also a greater risk of damage to the ova because aging allows more time for exposure to harmful agents. Of course, older mothers' bodies are older too, which could increase the risk of miscarriage. Finally, the differing hormonal balance of older mothers could be a factor.

Maternal Health and Nutrition

Mothers who begin pregnancy in good health and fitness, eat a balanced diet rich in protein and calcium, and gain about 25 pounds (11⅓ kilograms) are more likely to give birth to healthy babies. Unfortunately, in some parts of the world—including parts of the United States—mothers are undernourished or malnourished and don't gain enough weight during pregnancy.

Fetal malnutrition can be caused by the mother's unbalanced diet and vitamin, protein, or other deficiencies, as well as by deficiencies in the mother's digestive processes and overall metabolism. The most noticeable symptoms of fetal malnutrition are low birth weight, smaller head size, and smaller overall size compared to newborns who have been in the uterus for the same amount of time (Metcoff et al., 1981; Simopoulos, 1983). It has been proposed that significant fetal malnutrition can predispose for adult disorders such as hypertension, coronary heart disease, and thyroid disease (Scrimshaw, 1997), as well as schizophrenia (Brown et al., 1996; Dalman, Allebeck, Cullberg, Grunewald, & Koester, 1999). Malnourished pregnant women also more often have spontaneous abortions, give birth prematurely, or lose their babies shortly after birth.

In regions that have been ravaged by famine or war, the effects of malnutrition on child development are clear. There are high rates of miscarriage and stillbirth, and children born to malnourished mothers may quickly develop diseases and fail to thrive unless immediate dietary adjustments are made. Another unfortunate outcome is that malnutrition can cause reduced brain development both in the late fetal period and in early infancy; this effect is probably never overcome, even with good later nutrition (Chavez, Martinez, & Soberanes, 1995). Even in industrialized nations such as the United States, each year almost 4,000 babies are paralyzed or die from serious abnormalities of the spine or brain. The National Center for Environmental Health (NCEH) has estimated that between 50 to 75% of these cases could be prevented if the mother consumed sufficient folic acid before and during the early weeks of pregnancy (NCEH, 1999a; also see Johnson, 1997). However, some researchers have pointed out that the picture may not be that simple: Supplemental folic acid has been found to markedly increase the spontaneous abortion of fetuses with abnormalities and therefore reduce the number of children born with congenital anomalies this way—thus distorting the statistics (Hook & Czeizel, 1997).

Food supplement programs begun at birth can have major benefits, however. In a large long-term study in Guatemala, the health of children who received food supplements in infancy and early childhood improved almost immediately. Even more striking were the long-term gains produced by a special program of protein-rich supplements. Years later adolescents and young adults who had received the special supplements from birth performed

The effects of malnutrition on child development are painfuly apparent in countries ravaged by famine or war.

significantly better in tests of knowledge, arithmetic, reading, vocabulary, and speed of information processing than peers who had received no supplements before they were 2 years old. The difference was particularly dramatic for individuals in below poverty-level families and those with good primary education (Pollitt, Gorman, Engle, Martorell, & Rivera, 1993).

How does the *duration* of a period of malnutrition affect the fetus? Research with animals has shown that the mother protects the fetus from the effects of short-term malnutrition by drawing on her own stored reserves. She can also protect her own tissues from serious long-term effects. Both mother and fetus thus appear to be capable of recovering from limited malnutrition (Jones & Crnic, 1986). Therefore, if previously well-nourished mothers go through a temporary period of malnutrition during pregnancy, but the baby has a good diet and responsive caregivers after birth, there may be no long-lasting effects (Stein, Susser, Saenger, & Marolla, 1975; Grantham-McGregor, Powell, Walker, Chang, & Fletcher, 1994). Also, if the period of fetal malnourishment has been relatively short, it can sometimes be compensated for by infant nutrition programs or by combined health, nutrition, and child-care programs.

Prenatal Health Care

One of the single best predictors of healthy, full-term babies is five or more visits to a doctor or health-care facility beginning in the first trimester of pregnancy. Good prenatal care usually includes a careful health history, a full medical examination, and counseling about potential risks and the avoidance of alcohol, tobacco, and illicit drugs as well as advice about the value of regular physical exercise (NCEH, 1999b). It also includes assessment and recommendations regarding good nutrition during pregnancy. In addition, reduction in vaccine-preventable diseases such as measles, diphtheria, and type b meningitis have lowered infant mortality (CDC, 1996). Public-health outreach programs to provide prenatal health care to expectant mothers who might not otherwise receive it also have been shown to be effective in reducing infant-mortality and premature-birth rates (Murphy, 1993).

Critical Periods in Prenatal Development

The effects of many environmental influences depend on the point in the developmental sequence when the influence occurs. Tragically, many damaging effects on prenatal development can occur before the woman is even aware that she is pregnant.

Figure 4–4 illustrates *critical periods* of prenatal development, which are periods during which the developing child is at greatest risk for different kinds of abnormalities as a result of **teratogens**—diseases, chemicals from air pollution or water contamination, radiation, or anything else that can harm the child. (The term comes from the ancient Greek word for "monster.") Note especially that major abnormalities of the central nervous system or the heart may occur as a result of diseases the mother contracts or substances she ingests during the early embryonic period. (Prior to implantation, the developing child usually is not susceptible to teratogens because it is not yet connected to the mother's body.) Researchers are also investigating whether periods of vulnerability exist for neurobehavioral impairments associated with maternal stress. For example, early gestation stress was found to be associated with more pronounced and pervasive motor impairments in infant primates than mid-late gestation stress (Schneider, Roughton, Koehler, & Lubach, 1999).

Sometimes exposure of the mother to a specific teratogen inevitably causes damage to the embryo or fetus. Accidentally ingested poisons act this way.

teratogen Toxic agent of any kind that potentially causes abnormalities in the developing child.

Figure 4-4 Critical Periods In Prenatal Development

Green represents highly sensitive periods; blue represents less sesitive periods.

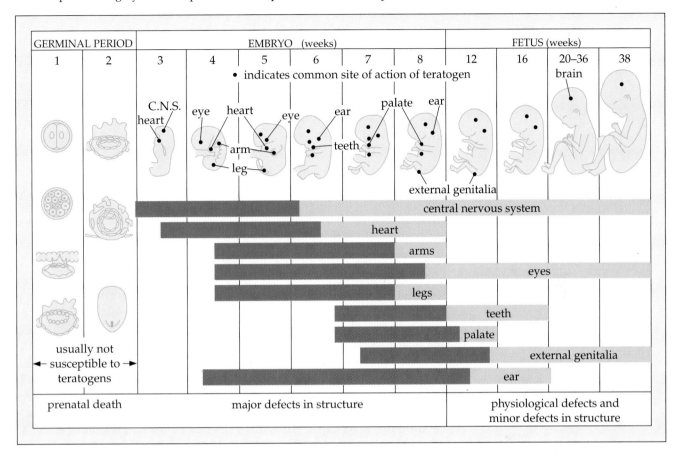

More frequently, however, the teratogen results in *increased risk* of damage, which may occur in varying degree or not at all. Whether there is damage depends on a complex interaction of factors, including the amount and duration of exposure, the developmental stage of the fetus, the overall health of the mother, and genetic factors.

An extreme example involved thalidomide, a mild tranquilizer that was taken by pregnant women in 1959 and 1960 to relieve nausea and other symptoms of morning sickness. The drug was thought to be harmless, but within the next 2 years as many as 10,000 babies were born with severe deformities as a result of mothers' thalidomide use. A careful study of the pregnancies showed that the nature of the deformity was determined by the timing of the drug use. If the mother took the drug between the 34th and 38th days after her last menstrual period, the child had no ears. If she took the drug between the 38th and 47th days, the child had missing or stunted arms, and if she took the drug during the latter part of that time range, the child also had missing or stunted legs (Schardein, 1976).

Amount and Duration of Exposure Small amounts of exposure to a toxic agent may have no effect because a healthy mother's metabolism can often break down or eliminate toxic substances quickly. In many cases, a drug or chemical agent must reach a certain concentration, or *threshold* level, in fetal organs or tissue to have an impact. On the other hand, sometimes even a small amount of a drug can move through the mother's body quickly and with no permanent damage to her, yet be caught in the immature fetal tissue (Hutchinson, 1991).

Teratogens and Their Effects

The variety of environmental factors that can adversely affect prenatal development is staggering. Drugs, diseases, hormones, blood factors, radiation, exposure to toxins in the workplace—such as lead or certain gases,—along with maternal age, nutrition, stress, and type of prenatal care all play a part in the development of the embryo or fetus (Paul, 1997). There may be still other harmful environmental agents whose influences have not yet been determined.

Some drugs and other chemicals can be turned into waste products and be eliminated by the mother's mature body but not by the embryo or fetus. Thus, drugs that cross the placental barrier and are "trapped" and accumulate in the developing child to the threshold level can cause severe damage. From this perspective, almost no drug or chemical—even a normally harmless substance such as aspirin—is entirely safe during pregnancy.

Maternal Diseases Not all diseases affect a developing embryo or fetus. For example, most kinds of bacteria do not cross a normal placental barrier, so even a severe bacterial infection in the mother may have little or no effect on the fetus, provided that she recovers quickly so that it does not markedly affect her overall health. However, smaller organisms such as many viruses—particularly rubella (German measles), herpes simplex, and many varieties of cold and flu viruses—do cross the placental barrier and can inflict harm. Rubella, for example, can cause blindness, heart abnormalities, deafness, brain damage, or limb deformity in the embryo or fetus, depending on the specific period during which the mother contracts it. Some of the maternal diseases and other maternal conditions that can affect an embryo or fetus are summarized in Table 4–1.

In general, diseases may enter the child by one of three routes: directly through the placenta, as occurs with rubella and HIV; indirectly through the amniotic fluid, as sometimes occurs with syphilis and gonorrhea; and during labor and delivery, when there is interchange of bodily fluids and perhaps blood. HIV can also be contracted after birth, through breast feeding.

Maternal infections like influenza and reproductive-tract infections such as bacterial vaginosis, along with and preexisting chronic conditions such as diabetes, hyptertension, and sexually transmitted diseases, may affect the embryo or fetus in a variety of ways. They may produce miscarriage or stillbirth. They may produce defective or malformed tissues and organs, and sometimes they cause death. Or they may produce no effect at all—especially when the mother has antibodies for the diseases.

One of the most devastating viruses that can be transmitted to the embryo or fetus is HIV. Although the number of babies with AIDS in the United States is still low, it has been increasing rapidly. In 1989, 547 infants died of AIDS; in 1993, approximately 1,800 babies were born with the disease (Nozyce et al., 1994). The situation is worse elsewhere, as the HIV/AIDS epidemic continues to spread around the world, with 93% of the 26 million HIV infections occurring in developing nations. Sub-Saharan African has the largest number, with up to 40% of pregnant women infected. Every day about 1,700 babies are newly infected there (Africa News Service, 2000).

It isn't yet understood why some babies born to HIV-positive mothers get the virus but many more don't. Some surveys indicate an average of about 1 in 4; others cite from 15 to 40%, including those infected *in utero*, during labor and

Table 4-1   Effects of Some Maternal Diseases During Pregnancy

Acquired Immune Deficiency Syndrome (AIDS)

AIDS is an incurable, often fatal, but sometimes treatable disease caused by the human immunodeficiency virus (HIV) in which the immune system breaks down and the person dies from what would normally be minor bacterial or viral infections. (See the text discussion on how babies can contract HIV from their mothers.)

Diabetes

Maternal diabetes can cause numerous physical malformations; it also sometimes causes stillbirth. The fetus may grow larger than normal, increasing the chance of birth difficulties. Diabetes is normally controlled through a special diet.

Gonorrhea

Many people carry the bacterial infection gonorrhea but display no symptoms of the disease. Gonorrhea can cause blindness if contracted from the mother during delivery. This is why newborns are routinely given silver nitrate eye drops immediately after birth. Gonorrhea can be treated by antibiotics, although increasingly antibiotic-resistant strains of gonorrhea continue to evolve.

Herpes simplex

The virus that causes genital herpes can cross the placental barrier, but infection is much more common during birth. Risks for the newborn include blindness, neurological problems, mental retardation, and death in a significant number of cases. Cesarean section is recommended if the mother has active herpes at the time that the baby is due to be born. Herpes simplex is currently incurable.

High blood pressure

Chronic high blood pressure can be treated with drugs, but if it is not controlled during pregnancy it can cause miscarriage.

Influenza

The many strains of influenza virus can cross the placental barrier. The most common effects are spontaneous abortion early in pregnancy or premature labor later. Maternal fever, if uncontrolled, can also be fatal to the fetus.

Rh factor

Rh incompatibility between the mother and the developing child is a disease in the sense that a protein component of the mother's blood can cause severe congenital anomalies or death in the fetus. Most women are Rh-positive, but some lack the blood component and are Rh-negative. If an Rh-negative mother has an Rh-positive child and their blood comes into contact through placental seepage or during birth, the mother's bloodstream begins building up antibodies that attack and destroy fetal red blood cells. Although there is usually no danger for a first-born child (and none for the mother), later-born children are highly at risk if they're also Rh-positive. Rh-negative mothers can be treated to prevent the buildup of the antibodies.

Rubella

If the rubella virus is contracted during the first 16 weeks of pregnancy (but after implantation), a frequent recommendation is to terminate the pregnancy because the risks of damage to the embryo or fetus are so great. Nonethless, parents sometimes choose to continue the pregnancy, and some have normal children.

Syphilis

Syphilis is a bacterial infection that normally doesn't pass the placental barrier during the first half of the pregnancy. It is most likely to be transmitted near or during birth. Syphilis can cause premature labor and miscarriage, deafness, and skin sores and lesions. Although syphilis can be treated by antibiotics, the drugs themselves can affect the embryo or fetus. C-section 1 to 2 weeks early is often recommended.

Toxemia of pregnancy

The causes of *preeclampsia* and the more severe *eclampsia* experienced by some pregnant women during the third trimester aren't known. Maternal symptoms of the disorders include elevated blood pressure, blurred vision, and puffy swelling of the face and hands. Eclampsia can cause fetal brain damage or death. Both forms of toxemia can usually be controlled, however, with bed rest and a special diet.

Primary source: The Columbia University College of Physicians and Surgeons Complete Home Medical Guide, 1985.

delivery, or by breast-feeding (Connor et al., 1994). As a result of the use of zidovudine (ZDV or ATZ) during pregnancy, the number of U.S. children with AIDS caused by mother-to-child transmission of HIV fell by 43% between 1992 and 1996 (CDC, 1997a). Even so, until medical researchers come up with a preventive method or cure, AIDS education and community-based outreach programs remain the main ways to stem the spread of and treat the virus in babies, especially in developing nations where ATZ is largely unavailable.

Even light drinking during pregnancy can cause harm to the developing child. If the mother is a heavy drinker, FAS is a likely result.

fetal alcohol syndrome (FAS)
Congenital abnormalities, including small size, low birth weight, certain facial characteristics, and possible mental retardation, resulting from maternal alcohol consumption during pregnancy.

Prescription and Over-the-Counter Drugs Studies indicate that many women consume a wide range of drugs during pregnancy. A Michigan study of nearly 19,000 women found that they consumed an average of three prescription drugs during their pregnancies (Piper, Baum, & Kennedy, 1987). Prescription drugs such as tetracycline, an antibiotic, have been shown to have adverse effects on fetal teeth and bones and can contribute to other congenital anomalies. Some anticonvulsant medications given to mothers with epilepsy can cause structural malformations, growth delays, heart abnormalities, mild mental retardation, or speech irregularities in babies (Vorhees & Mollnow, 1987). Oral contraceptives, which may cause malformation of the fetal sexual organs, provide another tragic example. Mothers who took the hormone diethylstilbestrol (DES) to help prevent miscarriages had daughters with a higher than normal incidence of vaginal cancer or cervical abnormalities, and sons who were sterile or prone to develop testicular cancer.

In addition to prescription drugs, many over-the-counter (OTC) medications can harm the embryo or fetus. Some of these are listed in Table 4–2 along with other substances that can cause harm. Many drugs can harm the developing child when ingested by the mother. There are also industrial chemical pollutants that might find their way into the mother's system and cause damage.

Alcohol The most widely used "recreational" or "social" drug in the United States and many other nations is alcohol, which at the same time has the potential to cause severe and permanent congenital anomalies. It also greatly increases the risk of miscarriage for U.S. mothers, but paradoxically, apparently not for mothers in European nations—an effect not attributable to differences in levels of alcohol use (Abel, 1997). Recent findings show that 1 in 8 women of childbearing age (18 to 44 years old) reported *risk drinking*, defined as seven or more drinks per week or five or more drinks on any one occasion (CDC, 1999). In addition, 1 of every 29 women who knows that she is pregnant reports risk drinking. Congenital anomalies associated with prenatal exposure to alcohol can readily occur in the first 3 to 8 weeks of pregnancy, before a woman even knows that she is pregnant (again, see Figure 4–3).

How much alcohol can be safely consumed during pregnancy—if any— is still unclear, and it also isn't known for sure what prenatal periods are most critical in this respect. Studies have generally found that more than one-third of infants born to mothers who drink heavily have congenital abnormalities. One study found that as little as 2 ounces (60 milliliters) of alcohol daily taken early in pregnancy is sufficient to produce facial deformities (Astley, Clarren, Little, Sampson, & Daling, 1992). In a carefully conducted study of otherwise drug-free women in Ireland, noticeable effects on the newborn were found for women who drank as little as three glasses of beer per week (Nugent, Greene, & Mazor, 1990).

Children of mothers who drink heavily during pregnancy may be born with a severe condition called **fetal alcohol syndrome (FAS).** Fetal alcohol syndrome has 3 primary components: facial abnormalities, growth retardation, and central nervous system (CNS) abnormalities. Children and adults with FAS can usually be recognized by their distinctive facial characteristics. They tend to have a thin upper lip, a poorly developed indentation above the upper lip, a wide space between the margins of the eyelids, and flat cheekbones. Growth retardation may involve low birth weight, a small head, and a smaller-than-average stature throughout life. FAS occurs as often as 1 in 1,000 births and is

Table 4-2 Selected Drugs and Chemicals and Their Effects on Prenatal Development

Air pollutants

Increases in urban air pollutants such as nitrogen dioxide, sulfur dioxide, and carbon mononoxide have been found to correlate with increases in miscarriages (Pereira et al., as reported by Raloff, 1998).

Alcohol

Drinking can cause fetal alcohol syndrome (FAS) and the less severe fetal alcohol effects (FAE) (see text). The effects are the same regardless of which alcohol-containing beverage is consumed: beer, wine, liqueur, or liquor.

Amphetamines

Drugs in the amphetamine family were once widely prescribed as an aid to dieting because they very effectively suppress appetite. Today they're prescribed only rarely, but forms such as *methamphetamine* are widely available on the illegal market. Amphetamine use during pregnancy can cause spontaneous abortion, stillbirth, or prematurity, as well as many of the same effects as those caused by cocaine.

Cocaine

Cocaine ingestion during pregnancy, whether in powder or crack form, can have numerous lasting physical and psychological effects on the child (see text).

Caffeine

The caffeine in coffee, tea, and soft drinks can retard prenatal growth and produces a slightly increased risk of miscarriage if consumed in amounts exceeding the equivalent of about six cups of coffee per day; this is because the developing child lacks enzymes that break down caffeine, allowing it to accumulate to potentially toxic levels (Walling, 2000).

Marijuana

The effects on the embryo or fetus when mothers smoke marijuana (or other forms of the drug such as hashish) still are not fully understood (see text).

Mercury, lead, and other pollutants

Poisoning by mercury, lead, and other industrial byproducts can occur through pollution of the water supply. The pollutants then find their way up the food chain into fish and other food sources. Dangerous chemicals can also be ingested through direct consumption of tainted water or air (Vorhees & Mollnow, 1987) and can cause profound mental retardation and neurological impairment in the developing child. Other potentially harmful chemicals include polychlorinated biphenyls (PCBs), found in electrical transformers and paint (Jacobson, Jacobson, Schwartz, Fein, & Dowler, 1984), as well as food preservatives, insecticides, and even some cosmetics and hair dyes.

Narcotics

In general, narcotics such as codeine, morphine, heroin, dilaudid, and even methadone (a maintenance drug that suppresses narcotics withdrawal symptoms) depress fetal respiration and can cause behavioral disturbances in the infant. Babies born to women who use such drugs regularly are smaller than normal and are less responsive as newborns. The babies show drug withdrawal symptoms—extreme irritability, shrill crying, vomiting, shaking, and poor temperature control. They tend to have low appetite and difficulty sucking, and their sleep patterns are disturbed, at least for the first several weeks. At 4 months, they are more tense and rigid and less well coordinated than normal babies. Up to 12 months, they may have difficulty maintaining attention, and researchers suspect that attention and language deficits may persist well into childhood (Vorhees & Mollnow, 1987).

Over-the-counter (OTC) drugs

Many OTC medications such as analgesics, cough medicines, laxatives, and allergy pills are—at best—unsafe. Aspirin in large doses can lead to excessive bleeding and other problems (Briggs, Freeman, & Gaffe, 1986). Large doses of antacid tablets or cough syrups, especially those containing codeine, may not be entirely safe (Brackbill, McManus, & Woodward, 1985). Even vitamins are risky if taken in excess. Moreover, such substances don't clear from the fetus's system as easily as they do from the mother's.

Tobacco

Smoking, whether cigarettes, cigars, or pipes, and also dipping or chewing tobacco, can cause serious birth problems and congenital anomalies (see text).

Tranquilizers and sleeping pills

Like alcohol, tranquilizers and sleeping pills are central nervous system depressants. Although their effects aren't generally thought to be severe (except in the case of thalidomide, see text), they cause the baby to be born sedated and they increase the risk of respiratory distress and anoxia.

the third leading cause of mental retardation in the United States (Streissguth, 1997). FAS is ten times higher in lower-income U.S. black and Native American families than in the general population (Abel, 1995). Some children suffer less severe damage from alcohol called **fetal alcohol effects (FAE).** Usually these children do not show the classic facial characteristics but do have mild growth retardation and probable CNS abnormalities.

The more alcohol that is consumed during pregnancy, the greater the risk of damage to the embryo or fetus. Even when alcohol is consumed in moderate amounts such as an ounce or two daily, researchers have found higher rates of respiratory and heart-rate abnormalities in the newborn, difficulty in adapting to normal sounds and lights, and lower mental development scores later in infancy (Streissguth, 1997). Other effects include less attentiveness to and compliance with adults during the preschool years, and increased chances of learning disabilities, attention problems, and hyperactivity (Barr, Darby, Streissguth, & Sampson, 1990; Briggs et al., 1986; Mattson & Riley, 1998; Newman & Buka, 1991; Streissguth, Sampson, Barr, Darby, & Martin, 1989). A recently published longitudinal study by Ann Streissguth and collegues revealed that such effects are still present at age 14 years (Streissguth, Barr, Bookstein, Sampson, & Olson, 1999), consistent with the findings of other researchers (Steinhausen & Sphor, 1998). In addition, a recent literature review by Streissguth and colleagues concluded that attachment during childhood and a variety of social behaviors well into adulthood may be disrupted by prenatal exposure to alcohol (Kelly, Day, & Streissguth, 2000).

Even moderate alcohol use may interact with stress (which might lead to alcohol use in the first place). One study of alcohol-consuming mother monkeys found that their infants later displayed significant impairments in attention and neuromotor functioning (Schneider, Roughton, & Lubach, 1997). The effects were greater for infants whose mothers had been experimentally exposed to "mild" psychological stress, which might help explain why babies born to mothers in stress-ridden lower-income neighborhoods have higher rates of alcohol-related congenital anomalies.

So the conclusion about alcohol is easy: *Any* level of drinking during pregnancy is risky. Still, despite extensive publicity about the dangers of drinking during pregnancy, about one-third of childbearing women report alcohol use in the 3 months before becoming pregnant, with 11% being binge drinkers (defined as 5 or more drinks at a single sitting). Most women cut back or quit once they know they are pregnant. Yet roughly 6% report that they are still drinking in the last 3 months of pregnancy; of these 2.9% are binge drinkers (Public Health Service, 2000).

Tobacco In 1998, 12.9% of women giving birth in the United States were reported to have smoked, down from 13.2% in 1997 and 34% in 1989 (CDC, 1999a). Tobacco, with its chief ingredient nicotine, has been clearly linked to fetal abnormalities. Among mothers who smoke heavily, rates of spontaneous abortion (Mills, 1999; Ness et al., 1999), stillbirth, and prematurity are significantly higher than among nonsmoking mothers. Babies born to heavy smokers tend to weigh less at birth than those born to nonsmokers and have delayed growth that can continue for years (CDC, 1999a; Naeye, 1980, 1981; Streissguth et al., 1989; Vorhees & Mollnow, 1987). Children of mothers who smoke regularly also display more cognitive and behavioral deficits and tend to do less well in school than children of nonsmokers (Fried, Watkinson, & Gray, 1998; Olds, 1997; Vorhees & Mollnow, 1987).

fetal alcohol effects (FAE)
Similar to FAS though milder abnormalities due to drinking during pregnancy.

How does smoking damage or even kill fetuses? Research points to the placenta and its role in nutrient exchange. Some forms of damage to the placenta that interfere with nutrient exchange occur only among women who smoke, and others occur more often among women who smoke than among those who don't (Naeye, 1981). Smoking can also constrict blood vessels in the uterus, reducing the flow of nutrients (Fried & Oxorn, 1980). Both effects can reduce the flow of oxygen and cause **anoxia** as well, with potential damage to brain tissue.

Marijuana Smoking marijuana during pregnancy is also inadvisable, although the effects of marijuana use have been less thoroughly studied than those of alcohol and tobacco. The results of a series of studies in Jamaica are noteworthy. In Jamaica marijuana is used in much higher doses among some segments of the population than in the United States. Newborn infants who were exposed to marijuana before birth have relatively high-pitched cries and behave in a manner similar to that of infants experiencing mild narcotics withdrawal. Thus, it appears that high doses of marijuana during pregnancy affect the central nervous system and later the infant's neurological/cognitive control (Lester & Dreher, 1989). Impulse control in particular may be negatively affected (Fried et al., 1998).

Cocaine The 1970s and 1980s saw a dramatic increase in use of cocaine powder and later crack cocaine as recreational drugs. There was a corresponding increase in cocaine-related birth problems. Although cocaine powder and crack cocaine may have equal potency (depending on the extent to which they are diluted by sellers to increase profits), smoking crack causes the drug to enter the user's system and reach the brain and other parts of the body much faster than does inhaling or injecting the powder. Crack therefore produces higher concentrations of cocaine and is potentially more harmful to the embryo or fetus (or to the newborn child via breast milk).

Early studies of prenatal exposure to cocaine found few negative effects (Madden, Payne, & Miller, 1986), and some pregnant mothers, lulled into a false sense of security, used cocaine to ease labor pain. More extensive research has demonstrated clearly that the risk of severe damage to the unborn child is considerable. Mothers who use cocaine experience more labor complications, and their infants have a high risk of prematurity, growth retardation, mental retardation, and neuromotor dysfunction (Bateman, Ng, Hansen, & Heagarty, 1993; Swanson, Streissguth, Sampson, & Olson, 1999). Although research thus far is inclusive, it is also possible that cocaine increases the risk of spontaneous abortion (Mills, 1999; Ness et al., 1999), as do other stimulants such as amphetamines and even caffeine.

Exposed infants also tend to smile less, are harder to console, and suck and root less intensely than normal infants (Phillips, Sharma, Premachandra, Vaughn, & Reyes-Lee, 1996). Many infants born to cocaine-using mothers have difficulty establishing motor coordination, orienting to visual objects or sounds, and achieving normal regulation of waking and sleeping. Research also indicates that other long-term affects of prenatal exposure may include attention problems, impaired language comprehension, and difficulty in regulating emotions and behavior. For example, studies have found that prenatally exposed 4 to 6-year-olds experience higher rates of depression and anxiety, higher rates of delinquent and aggressive behaviors, and greater impulsivity and distractibility (Berger & Waldfogel, 2000; Chasnoff et al., 1998; Lester, LaGrasse, & Bigsby, 1998).

Smoking has been clearly linked to fetal abnormalities.

anoxia Lack of oxygen; can cause brain damage.

A MATTER FOR DEBATE

PROSECUTING VERSUS TREATING CRACK MOTHERS

Crack cocaine use by pregnant mothers can have severe and lasting effects on the developing child, as discussed in the text. The crack "epidemic," which began in the United States in the early 1980s, played a major role in focusing the attention of state criminal justice systems, social services agencies, and especially the medical community on drug use during pregnancy.

Drug-using mothers have often been prosecuted under existing child abuse laws, which can result in felony convictions. Such convictions are hard to obtain, however; they often become bogged down in legal details. For example, in a 1997 case, a major point at issue was whether an existing law regarding child abuse also applies to a fetus. Convictions in several states have been overturned by rulings that such laws do not apply.

In a 1996 survey, the National Court Appointed Special Advocate Association (CASA) studied thirty-five criminal cases in twenty states, most involving charges of child abuse or de-

livery of drugs to a minor. The researchers found that in most of the cases the charges were dismissed or later overturned. Civil prosecutions for abuse and neglect—based on a mother testing positive for drugs when her baby is born—have been more successful, at least in removing the babies from the mother and placing them in foster care. However, even successful criminal or civil prosecutions address the problem of prenatal effects only to the extent that they serve as a possible future deterrent.

Can we instead treat mothers during pregnancy? The first problem is detection: Expectant mothers are not routinely screened for drug use, partly because such screening would cause many to avoid prenatal care rather than risk detection. When prenatal care professionals do detect drug use during pregnancy, mothers don't necessarily accept treatment voluntarily. Mandatory, court-enforced treatment for pregnant mothers may work, although there is a need for further research on

its efficacy. But in many cases treatment is not a practical approach. Drug-abusing mothers-to-be typically lack the resources to pay for treatment, and publicly or privately funded treatment programs for such mothers are scarce. Thus, convicted or civilly committed pregnant addicts are often sent to prison while awaiting treatment. While in prison, they often receive no prenatal care. If they do receive prenatal treatment and abruptly cease drug use, there are increased risks to the embryo or fetus as a result of *in utero* withdrawal—risks that include abortion and premature delivery.

The solution? Because criminal prosecution and incarceration have no proven benefits, the Committee on Substance Abuse of the AAP recommends preventive education programs for *all* women of childbearing age before they become pregnant.

Primary sources: National Center on Addiction and Substance Abuse at Columbia University, 1996; AAP, 1996

The majority of cocaine-exposed infants can be classified as "fragile." They are easily overloaded by normal environmental stimulation, have great difficulty controlling their nervous system, and often cry frantically and seem unable to sleep. After a month they still have difficulty attending to normal stimulation without losing control and lapsing into urgent, high-pitched cries (Chasnoff, 1989). Even years later, after the most obvious symptoms have subsided, children of cocaine-using mothers have much higher rates of attention-deficit disorder; language delays; learning disabilities; impulsive, delinquent, and aggressive behaviors and exhibit higher delinquent and aggressive behaviors (Chasnoff et al., 1998; Lester et al., 1998). Early treatment during prenatal development can often limit the damage. For some children effects may not be as severe if they receive good postnatal care, including referral to early intervention specialists such as home visitors (Berger & Waldfogel, 2000).

Clearly, mothers should avoid even the slightest cocaine use during pregnancy. Moreover, because cocaine use is illegal, some people believe that there should be criminal penalties for mothers who knowingly use it during pregnancy. (See "A Matter for Debate," above.)

Finally, note that the majority of expectant mothers who abuse drugs are *polydrug* users: They consume drugs in combinations that can compound the effects on the developing child. Because drug-using mothers often suffer malnutrition and health problems as well, it can be very difficult to identify the effects of specific teratogens (Newman & Buka, 1991). Nevertheless, it is clear that the more drugs consumed during pregnancy, the worse off the child.

CONTENT CHECK
PRENATAL ENVIRONMENTAL INFLUENCES

True–False (answers are on the Companion Website)

1. Teen mothers are at lesser risk for miscarriages and congenital anomalies than are mothers in their 20s.
2. The effects of fetal malnutrition can be completed reversed by good nutrition during early childhood.
3. The developing child is at greatest risk for abnormalities caused by teratogens during the embryonic period.
4. Exposure to drugs virtually always damages the embryo or fetus.
5. The congenital anomalies that characterize FAE are milder than those that characterize FAS.

Thinking Critically

What are the most dangerous drugs for a mother to use during pregnancy and why?

Childbirth

Although attitudes toward pregnancy and approaches to childbirth vary from one culture to another, the birth of every normal human child follows the same biological timetable. In this section we look at stages of childbirth, differing approaches to childbirth, prenatal testing and monitoring, and complications in childbirth.

Stages of Childbirth

The process of childbirth can be divided into three distinct stages: initial labor, labor and delivery, and afterbirth.

Initial Labor   The first stage is the period during which the cervical opening of the uterus begins to dilate to allow passage of the baby. Although **initial labor** can last from a few minutes to over 30 hours, the norms are 12 to 15 hours for the first child and 6 to 8 hours for later children. Labor begins with mild uterine contractions, usually spaced 15 to 20 minutes apart. As labor progresses, the contractions increase in frequency and intensity until they occur only 3 to 5 minutes apart. The muscular contractions of labor are involuntary, and it's best if the mother tries to relax during this period.

Some mothers experience **false labor** (called *Braxton-Hicks contractions*), especially with the first child. False labor can be hard to distinguish from real labor, but one test that usually works is to have the expectant mother walk around. The pains of false labor tend to diminish, whereas those of real labor become more uncomfortable.

Two other events occur during initial labor. First, a mucus plug that covers the cervix is released. This is called *showing*, and it may include some bleeding.

initial labor   The first stage of labor, during which the cervical opening of the uterus begins to dilate to allow for passage of the baby.

false labor   Also called Braxton-Hicks contractions; contractions that may diminish if the mother walks around.

Second, the amniotic sac may break and amniotic fluid may rush forth, as when a mother's "water breaks."

Labor and Delivery The second stage of childbirth begins with stronger and more regular contractions and ends with the actual birth of the baby. Once the cervix is fully dilated, contractions begin to push the baby through the birth canal. Labor and delivery usually take from 10 to 40 minutes, and like initial labor, they tend to be shorter with succeeding births. Contractions come every 2 to 3 minutes and are longer and more intense than those that occur during initial labor. If the mother is conscious, she can greatly assist in the delivery by controlling her breathing and "pushing" or bearing down with her abdominal muscles during each contraction.

Normally, the first part of the baby to emerge from the birth canal is the head. First it "crowns," or becomes visible, then it emerges farther with each contraction. The tissue of the mother's *perineum* (the region between the vagina and the rectum) must stretch considerably to allow the baby's head to emerge. In U.S. hospitals the attending physician often makes an incision called an **episiotomy** to enlarge the vaginal opening. It is believed that a incision will heal more neatly than the jagged tear that might otherwise occur. Episiotomies are much less common in Western Europe and other parts of the world.

Occasionally, obstetricians use steel or plastic *forceps*, or a *vacuum extractor* (a cup placed on the baby's head and connected to a suction device) to grasp the head and hasten the birth should complications arise. As with episiotomies, forceps and vacuum-extractor deliveries are more common in the United States than in Europe—used in 20 to 30% of births versus only 5% (Korte & Scaer, 1990).

Finally, in most normal births, the baby is born in a face-down position. After the head is clear, the baby's face twists to the side so that its body can emerge with the least resistance.

Afterbirth The expulsion of the placenta, the umbilical cord, and related tissues marks the third stage of childbirth, called **afterbirth.** This stage is virtually painless and typically occurs within 20 minutes after the delivery. Again, the mother can help by bearing down. The afterbirth can be checked for imperfections of the placenta that might indicate damage to the newborn baby.

Approaches to Childbirth

Although the biology of childbirth is universal, the precise ways in which babies are delivered and cared for vary considerably across generations, across cultures, and from one family to another. Some cultures, for example, view childbirth as comparable to an illness. Traditionally, among the Cuna Indians of Panama, pregnant women visited the medicine man daily for drugs and were sedated throughout labor and delivery. Among the !Kung-San, a tribal society in northwestern Botswana, women told no one about their initial labor pains and went out into the bush alone to give birth. They delivered the baby, cut the cord, and stabilized the newborn—all without assistance (Komner & Shostak, 1987).

In some cultures home birthing is still the norm, but in Western nations and in Japan, most births by far now take place in hospitals instead (Misago, Takusei, Noguchi, Mori, & Mori, 2000; Zander & Chamberlain, 1999). The extent to which the father is involved during childbirth also varies considerably both across and within cultures.

Traditional Childbirth A hundred and fifty years ago in the United States, "traditional" childbirth meant home delivery with the assistance of a family doctor or a **midwife**—a woman experienced in childbirth, with or without formal train-

episiotomy An incision to enlarge the vaginal opening.

afterbirth The third and last stage of childbirth, typically occurring within 20 minutes after delivery, during which the placenta and the umbilical cord are expelled from the uterus.

midwife A woman experienced in childbirth, with or without training, who assists with home delivery.

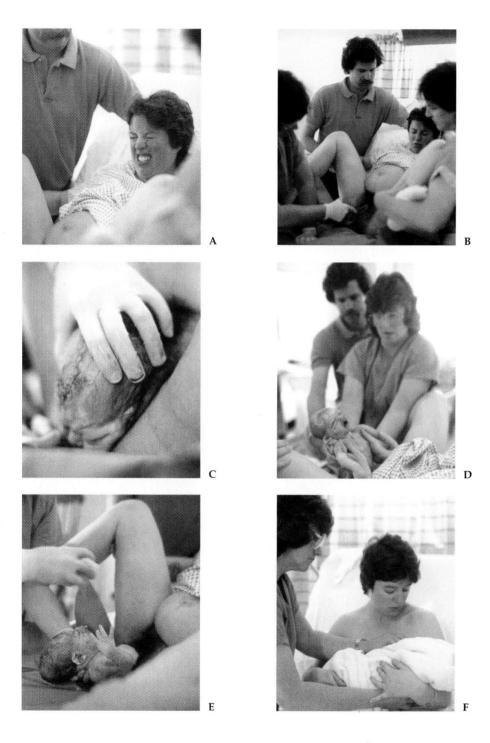

The sequence of childbirth.

ing and in those days more often without. With the advent of sanitary hospitals and modern medicine, birthing shifted to hospital labor and delivery rooms where the mother could be assisted by specialized medical staff and emergency equipment in case of complications. Correspondingly, in most Western nations home births dropped from about 80% in 1930 to a mere 1% in 1990, although the proportion of home births has begun to rise somewhat in the years since (Zander & Chamberlain, 1999). In any event, today when we speak of **traditional childbirth** we're actually talking about hospital childbirth by a medical team.

Until recent decades, traditional childbirth also meant that the father was strictly excluded from the labor and delivery rooms. (Think about those old

traditional childbirth   Hospital labor and delivery.

movies in which the father paces up and down outside the delivery room and finally sees his baby for the first time through the nursery window.) Because childbirth was assumed to be highly painful, the mother was usually anesthetized and sedated. Because such medications easily pass the placental barrier, the baby was therefore also anesthetized and sedated. Although this doesn't necessarily have harmful long-term effects (depending on the drugs used), it does produce babies who are groggy and less alert at birth and therefore are less responsive to the mother and father—with the mother groggy as well. No one disputes the importance of easing the mother's pain, but it is clear that childbirth medications should be used prudently (Broman, 1986).

Contemporary Childbirth Practices In general, the mother's experience of childbirth depends on her mental set and her knowledge about what to expect. This is the basis for what is now known as **"natural"** or **prepared childbirth** that can take various forms but is based primarily on procedures developed by Fernand Lamaze (1958, 1970). Whether or not prepared childbirth is practiced in its entirety, the approach has had a major impact on procedures hospitals use during childbirth.

In prepared childbirth the expectant mother and her coach (father, family member, or friend) attend a short series of classes. They learn about the biology of childbirth, and the mother practices relaxation exercises and control of her breathing with the coach serving as her assistant. (The relaxation exercises help reduce the pain of labor and delivery; the breathing and other techniques help distract the mother from any discomfort she may be feeling.) When the day arrives, the coach is present throughout childbirth to provide support and help the mother stay as relaxed as possible. Medication can be kept to a minimum or perhaps not used at all, so the mother is conscious and alert and actively assists in the birthing process. This is especially beneficial to the many modern mothers who prefer to feel a sense of control or "agency" in their childbirth, as opposed to feeling that they are being treated like a patient with a disease (Rudolfsdottir, 2000).

Generally, labor is shorter and less stressful both for mother and infant if the mother and coach have accurate knowledge about what is happening in each stage (Mackey, 1995; Slade, MacPherson, Hume, & Maresh, 1993). It is also helpful if only limited medication (or none) is used and the mother is able to participate. Mothers also experience less fear and muscle tension when they know what to expect, especially during a first delivery. As a result, both parents feel more in control of the birth process (Leventhal, Leventhal, Shacham, & Easterling, 1989).

Today most U.S. hospitals allow the father or other coach to be present during labor and delivery. In many areas, hospitals also provide more home-like delivery and recovery rooms, or entire **birthing centers** or suites, either within or near the hospital (Kinnon, 1998). Birthing centers are designed to accommodate the entire process, from labor through delivery and recovery. They combine the privacy, serenity, and intimacy of a home birth with the safety and backup of medical technology, viewing the parents' social, psychological, and aesthetic needs to be just as important as medical considerations (Allgaier, 1978; Lucas, 1993; Zander & Chamberlain, 1999). If the birth is uncomplicated, a certified nurse midwife (CNM) delivers the baby, but emergency equipment and obstetricians are available if necessary (Lucas, 1993). Between 1975 and 1998, the percent of births attended by CNMs increased sharply from 1.0% to 7.4 percent, with most of this increase occurring in hospitals (Curtin & Park, 1999). Not surprisingly, it has been found that mothers who view childbirth as natural and normal are more likely to opt for a CNM, whereas mothers who

"natural" or prepared childbirth Childbirth based on procedures developed by Fernand Lamaze, a French obstetrician.

birthing center Place designed to accommodate the entire birth process, from labor through delivery and recovery.

view it as risky and requiring medical technology are more likely to choose an obstetrician (Howell-White, 1997).

Most birthing centers encourage prepared childbirth and an early return home, generally within 24 hours. They also encourage mothers to spend as much time as possible with the newborns to help promote early attachment (Allgaier, 1978; Parker, 1980). This is also the norm in modern hospitals, in contrast to earlier practices in which the baby was whisked away after birth and kept in a nursery perhaps for days.

Most parents find birthing centers deeply satisfying. The centers keep the focus on the family and give the parents the maximum possible independence and control (Eakins, 1986). In all, the philosophy of childbirth has changed. It is now much more likely to be viewed as a natural, nonpathological event during which technological intervention should be kept to a minimum. Cost is another factor in choosing the form of delivery. Home births are the cheapest; hospital deliveries by CNMs are less expensive than if an obstetrician delivers the infant. Most health maintenance organizations (HMOs) cover hospital deliveries by CNMs, with many also covering deliveries in birthing centers; coverage for home birth is more sporadic (Lucas, 1993).

Birthing centers are not equipped to handle everyone, though. They screen out women with high-risk factors or complications. Typical guidelines exclude women over 35 having their first baby, women bearing twins, women suffering from diseases like diabetes or cardiac problems, and women who have had previous cesarean deliveries (Lubic & Ernst, 1978). A hospital delivery is also recommended if there are direct signs of potential problems with the baby or the birth.

Prenatal Screening and Perinatology

Prenatal screening is used to determine whether a child will be "at risk" during childbirth, also whether anomalies attributable to genetics or the prenatal environment are present. Three popular procedures are discussed here; additional procedures are presented in Table 4–3.

Ultrasound is the least invasive and most widely used method of providing information about the growth and health of the fetus. Harmless high-frequency sound waves produce a picture called a *sonogram*. Sonograms can detect structural problems such as body malformations, especially cranial anomalies such as *microcephaly* (extremely small upper head) that are invariably associated with severe mental retardation and perhaps death. Though it has traditionally been done around the 15th week, ultrasound with modern high resolution scanning can now be done much earlier and is routine in some hospitals (McFadyen, Gledhill, Whitlow, & Economides, 1998). For example, early scanning is indicated if doctors suspect an ectopic (tubal) pregnancy, which is extremely hazardous for the mother; they may use ultrasound as early as 3 to 4 weeks after conception to get a picture of the gestational sac.

In **amniocentesis,** amniotic fluid is withdrawn from the amniotic sac with a syringe inserted through the mother's abdomen. The fluid contains discarded fetal cells, which can be karyotyped and analyzed for chromosomal or genetic anomalies (Chapter 3). This procedure too is usually not done until the 15th week of pregnancy (*standard* amniocentesis), although it can be done at the 13th week or even earlier (*early* amniocentesis). Either way, the results are not available for 2 weeks because the fetal cells must be cultured. Amniocentesis during the second trimester may slightly increase the risk of miscarriage, although research thus far has been inconclusive. If performed prior to the 13th week, it apparently greatly increases the risk of miscarriage, stillbirth, or limb

ultrasound   A technique that uses sound waves to produce a picture of the fetus in the uterus.

amniocentesis   The withdrawal and analysis of amniotic fluid with a syringe to obtain cells for testing.

Table 4–3   Prenatal Assessment Methods

Amniocentesis

A procedure for obtaining discarded fetal cells by using a syringe. The cells can be karyotyped and analyzed for major chromosomal and some genetic abnormalities (see text).

Chorionic villus sampling (CVS)

In this procedure, fetal cells for karyotyping are drawn from the membranes surrounding the fetus, either with a syringe or with a catheter (see text).

Fetoscopy

Fetoscopy is used to inspect the fetus for limb and facial abnormalities. In this method, a needle containing a light source is inserted into the uterus to view the fetus directly and withdraw a sample of fetal blood or tissue for the prenatal diagnosis of genetic disorders. Fetoscopy is not usually done until 15 to 18 weeks after conception. The risk of miscarriage and infection is greater than that associated with amniocentesis.

Maternal blood analysis

Because some fetal cells enter the maternal bloodstream early in pregnancy, maternal blood analysis can be a helpful diagnostic tool around 8 weeks after conception. A blood sample is obtained and tested for alpha fetoprotein, which is elevated in the presence of kidney disease, abnormal esophageal closure, or severe central nervous system abnormalities.

Preimplantation genetic diagnosis

Following *in vitro* (outside of the body) fertilization and culturing of a prospective mother's ovum, a single cell is microsurgically removed soon after cell division begins and analyzed for genetic defects. If the DNA is found to be healthy, the developing child will then be placed into the mother's body for implantation. Preimplantion screening is expensive, but it has been used successfuly in detecting genetic disorders such as cystic fibrosis, hemophilia, sickle-cell anemia, and Tay-Sachs disease.

Ultrasound

A procedure in which high-frequency sound waves produce a picture of the fetus called a sonogram. Sonograms can detect structural problems (see text).

The safety and reliability of ultrasound imagery used to inspect the fetus makes this technique popular among the medical professional.

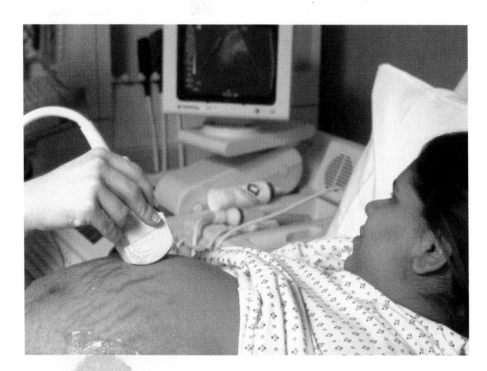

abnormalities (Schreck, 1998). Obstetricians routinely recommend this procedure for women over 35 because of the increased risk of congenital anomalies, especially Down syndrome.

Chorionic villus sampling (CVS) can be conducted much earlier than standard amniocentesis, at around 8 to 12 weeks after conception. In this procedure, cells are drawn from the membranes surrounding the fetus, either with a syringe or with a catheter. Because more cells are collected in this procedure than in amniocentesis, the test can be completed more quickly. However, the procedure involves slightly more risk than standard amniocentesis, with a small percentage of fetuses aborting spontaneously (Wyatt, 1985). Research has also linked CVS with miscarriages and limb abnormalities (Kuliev, Modell, & Jackson, 1992), but the risks associated with CVS are apparently lower than those associated with early amniocentesis (Sundberg et al., 1997).

Because of the added risk, about half of all high-risk mothers wait and use amniocentesis together with ultrasound (Reid, 1990). Those who choose CVS often do so because there is a strong chance that they are carrying a baby with a serious genetic abnormality. Should they choose it, abortion early in the pregnancy (before 12 weeks) is safer and also tends to have less serious psychological effects on the parents than abortion later in the pregnancy. In general, hospitals that perform CVS frequently have greater success in avoiding fetal damage (Kuliev et al., 1992).

High Technology for High-Risk Pregnancies   The branch of medicine known as **perinatology** considers childbirth not as a single point in time but as a span of time that begins with conception and continues through the first several months of life. Perinatologists specialize in the management of high-risk pregnancies and deliveries. They are usually associated with major hospitals that have the resources to support such pregnancies. They monitor the mother and her baby through pregnancy and delivery, using prenatal screening procedures such as amniocentesis and fetoscopy to identify potential problems requiring prompt medical treatment. (See "A Closer Look," p. 144).

In the past quarter-century obstetrical medicine has progressed dramatically. Infants who would not have survived in the 1970s are now thriving in record numbers. For example, today over 80% of premature infants weighing 750 to 1000 grams (1.6 to 2.2 pounds) will survive in a well-equipped intensive care unit for newborns. In 1972, only 20% survived.

The new medical advances include drugs, microsurgery, diagnostic tools, and preventive measures. For example, many hospitals routinely use **fetal monitors,** which can be applied either externally or internally. An *external* monitor records the intensity of uterine contractions and the baby's heartbeat by means of two belts placed around the mother's abdomen. Continuous external monitoring from the beginning of labor is typically used in low-risk births where potential complications such as bleeding during labor, a very long or fast labor, or maternal high blood pressure occurs (Cooper, 1999a).

Internal monitoring is an invasive procedure that records contractions and the baby's heartbeat more directly, plus other critical functioning (Cooper 1999b; Goodlin, 1979). An internal monitor consists of a plastic tube containing electrodes that are inserted into the vagina and attached to the baby's head. It can assess uterine pressure, fetal breathing, head compression, umbilical compression, and poor fetal oxygen intake. Typically, internal monitoring is used only in high-risk situations. The use of internal fetal monitors in low-risk pregnancies, formerly a common practice, is now discouraged by the American College of Obstetrics and Gynecology, partly on grounds that fetal monitors are linked to an increase in otherwise unnecessary cesarean sections as discussed later in the chapter.

chorionic villus sampling (CVS)   In this procedure, cells are drawn from the membranes surrounding the fetus, either with a syringe or with a catheter. Because more cells are collected in this procedure than in amniocentesis, the test can be completed more quickly.

perinatology   A branch of medicine that deals with childbirth as a span of time including conception, the prenatal period, and the first few months of life.

fetal monitor   The external monitor records the intensity of uterine contractions and the baby's heartbeat by means of two belts placed around the mother's abdomen. The internal monitor consists of a plastic tube containing electrodes, that is inserted through the vagina and attached to the baby's head.

A CLOSER LOOK

NEWBORNS AT RISK

In the United States about 90% of babies are born on time and healthy, scoring a 9 or 10 on the Apgar Scale. Only about 10% are born preterm; only 7% weigh less than 5½ pounds; and less than 1% die in their first year. Because of medical advances and health education, infant mortality rates in most of the developed nations have fallen steadily in the last five decades, from 47 deaths per 1000 births in 1940 to an all-time low of 8.1 in 1995 (Children's Defense Fund, 1991; NCHS, 1995).

Despite these optimistic statistics, some infants still face serious risks at birth. Let's take a closer look at the statistics on the roughly 10% of U.S. babies who come into the world struggling to survive. Who are these infants? Can some of their problems be prevented?

Infants in families below the poverty line are more than twice as likely to die in their first year, compared to those in families above. Premature babies or babies with low Apgar scores are far more likely when the mother is under 15 or over 44, poor, or unmarried (NCHS, 1993). Are there any common threads in this pattern?

One of the best predictors of low birth weight is the absence of prenatal care starting in the first 3 months of pregnancy. Teenage mothers, unmarried mothers, and women living in poverty are far more likely to delay prenatal care than are married, more affluent women over age 20 (NCHS, 1993).

Community characteristics rather than demographics may account for these findings. For example, in low-income areas, the incidence of low birth weight among babies of black women born in Africa and in the Caribbean was higher than black women born and raised in the United States. The rate was roughly the same as it was for infants born to white women. "Race" is clearly not the issue. Differences in birth outcomes among women born in other nations may be the result of their early health experiences and other factors that influence those who decide to immigrate to the United States (Schreck, 1999). In addition, some regions lack basic health services for poor families, services that can often remedy maternal health problems like high blood pressure, anemia, or poor nutrition before they become risk factors for the infant. Nor are there educational programs to address potentially harmful behaviors like smoking, alcohol use, and other drug use during pregnancy, as well as the basics of childcare.

Young mothers are particularly at risk. Usually they are physically and emotionally immature and lack the stamina, patience, and understanding to care even for a healthy child. Often a lack of basic education, along with isolation from peers and family, make it even more difficult for them to cope with motherhood. As one social worker reported:

I will never forget the look of fatigue which I saw on the face of a 14-year-old girl who had given birth to twins four months previously. She looked old beyond her years as she sat on the stoop of her parents' house in rural South Carolina. Her mother and brother were away at work, her younger siblings in school, while she remained home to care for her babies and her youngest brother. Her father had tried to be supportive, but now, he had moved several hundred miles away to find work, so the bulk of the childcare fell on her. At an age when her peers were starting high school, dreaming of their futures and beginning to date, it seemed her future had arrived. She was at home, lonely, chasing a toddler, changing diapers, and soothing two restless babies.

Despite improved medical technology, the death rate for U.S. babies with LBW actually rose in the 1990s (Ventura et al., 2000), especially where poverty has increased and drug use and AIDS are widespread. Faced with the prospect of such statistics earlier in the 1990s, Marian Wright Edelman of the Children's Defense Fund asked: "Is this the best [U.S.] America can do?" (1992, preface).

In all, however, the new technology of childbirth is a blessing for many families, especially those facing premature or high-risk deliveries.

Complications in Childbirth

More difficult births occur when the baby is positioned in a **breech presentation** (buttocks first) or a posterior presentation (facing toward the mother's abdomen instead of toward her back). In each of these cases there is potential injury to the mother or anoxia for the infant due to strangling. Figure 4–5 shows two types of breech presentation. Attempts are made to turn the baby to the proper birth position; if they are unsuccessful, the infant will often instead be delivered by cesarean section, although it has been argued that C-section is not

breech presentation The baby's position in the uterus such that the head will emerge last. Assistance is usually needed in such cases to prevent injury to the infant, producing anoxia.

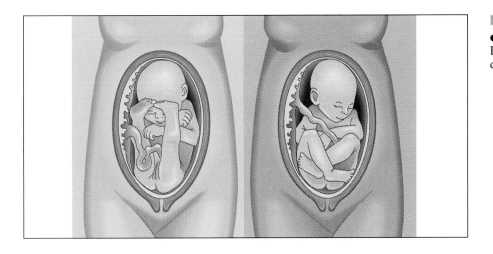

Figure 4–5 Two Types of Breech Presentation
Delivery in this position is difficult for both mother and baby.

necessarily better or safer than vaginal delivery in cases of breech presentation (Hannah & Hannah, 1996).

Cesarean Section   Various other complications may occur during childbirth. In addition to breech presentation, these include early breaking of the amniotic sac without labor (thus leaving the fetus unprotected and vulnerable to infections), failure to begin labor or respond to attempts to induce labor postterm, and fetal distress. In such cases the childbirth team may resort to **cesarean section** surgery, in which the baby is removed through the mother's abdominal wall. This procedure is frequently performed under regional anesthesia so that the mother is awake and aware. Because the procedure is quick, very little of the anesthesia reaches the infant. The outcome for both mother and infant is excellent in most cases.

Nevertheless, many believe that the rate of cesarean births is far too high (LoCicero, 1993). For example, in 1998 the rate of cesarean delivery in the United States was 21.2% (Ventura et al., 2000). C-sections continue to be the most common form of major surgery. A million or so U.S. C-sections are performed each year, with some hospitals performing over 40% of childbirths by this method. Some consumer advocates suggest that the high rate of cesarean births is a result of increased technology in the delivery room, partly as a result of invasive prenatal screening, fetal monitoring, and routine use of drugs to induce labor. Indeed, in the 1990s the American Academy of Pediatrics (AAP) took the position that electronic fetal monitoring should be abandoned in low-risk pregnancies because ". . . this technology hurts women by increasing operative delivery rates. . . . (1999, p. 1037). With regrets, the same statement notes that more than 75% of U.S. births still use this technology.

Why is the high rate of C-sections a problem, given that the procedure is relatively safe? For one thing, it is major abdominal surgery, which requires a much longer recovery period than normal childbirth. For another, it's expensive and puts a greater strain on parents and their health insurance providers. And as noted, the results aren't in on whether it is necessary in many of the cases in which it is used.

Finally, and perhaps most important, the mother's psychological reaction to cesarean childbirth can be quite negative (Waldenstroem, 1999). Many mothers report feeling disillusioned, particularly those who had general instead of regional anesthesia and "missed the event." Repeated studies report that some mothers who have had a C-section are disappointed or even angry, are slow to choose a name for the baby, test lower on self-esteem shortly after giving birth,

cesarean section   Surgical procedure used to remove the baby and the placenta from the uterus by cutting through the abdominal wall.

The Apgar Scale is a quick objective assessment of a newborn's condition.

Table 4–4   The Apgar Scoring System for Newborns

	Scores		
	0	**1**	**2**
Pulse:	Absent	Less than 100	More than 100
Breathing:	Absent	Slow, irregular	Strong cry
Muscle tone:	Limp	Some flexion of extremities	Active motion
Reflex response:	No response	Grimace	Vigorous cry
Color*:	Blue, pale	Body pink, extremities blue	Completely pink

*For nonwhites, alternative tests of mucous membranes, palms, and soles are used.
Source: "Proposal for a New Method of Evaluating the Newborn Infant" by V. Apgar, *Anesthesia and Analgesia*, 1953, 32, 260. Used by permission of the International Anesthesia Research Society.

and have more difficulty feeding their infants (DiMatteo, Morton, Lepper, & Damush, 1996; Oakley & Richards, 1990). There may also be more intense postpartum depression following C-sections than after normal vaginal deliveries (Cohen & Estner, 1983; Kitzinger, 1981).

The Apgar Scale   Not all newborns are equally well equipped to adjust to the changes that occur at birth, and it is essential to detect any problems or weaknesses as early as possible. In 1953 Virginia Apgar devised a standard scoring system that allows hospitals to evaluate an infant's condition quickly and objectively. The **Apgar Scoring System** is presented in Table 4–4. At one minute and again at 5 minutes after birth, the scorer observes the newborn's pulse, breathing, muscle tone, general reflex response, and general skin tone. A perfect Apgar score is 10 points, with a score of 7 or more considered normal. Scores below 7 indicate that some bodily processes are not functioning fully and may require special procedures. A score of 4 or less requires immediate emergency measures. Later, during the first few days of life, a newborn will also often be assessed on the more detailed Brazelton Neonatal Behavioral Assessment Scale discussed in Chapter 5.

Apgar Scoring System   A standard scoring system that allows hospitals to evaluate an infant's condition quickly and objectively.

CONTENT CHECK
CHILDBIRTH

True–False (answers are on the Companion Website)

1. During childbirth, the child first becomes visible during the labor-and-delivery stage.
2. Of the invasive procedures used to obtain fetal cells for karyotyping, amniocentesis is the safest regardless of age.
3. Internal fetal monitoring has been linked to an increased likelihood that cesarean section will be necessary.
4. Birth by cesarean section is generally considered safe for both mother and infant.
5. A score of 7 or more on the Apgar scale means that the newborn infant needs immediate emergency measures.

Thinking Critically

What are the advantages and disadvantages of traditional childbirth in a hospital and prepared childbirth in a birthing center?

Premature and High-Risk Infants

Prematurity

The most common indicator of prematurity is low birth weight. As specified by the World Health Organization, a newborn who weighs less than 5½ pounds (2.5 kilograms) is usually classified as having low birth weight (LBW) and being in need of special treatment and care. As a rule, the lower the birth weight, the greater the need.

Two indicators of low birth weight are frequently confused, however. The first is **preterm status.** An infant born before a gestation period of 35 weeks (or 37 weeks from the mother's last menstrual period) is preterm, and most preterm infants have LBW. The second indicator is **small-for-date.** A *full-term* newborn who is LWB is considered small-for-date. Fetal malnutrition is one cause of small-for-date babies.

Prematurity can occur for a number of reasons. The most common cause is a multiple birth, in which two or more infants are born at the same time. Other causes include diseases or disabilities of the fetus, maternal smoking or other drug use, and malnutrition. In addition, maternal diseases such as diabetes or polio may lead to delivery of a baby before full term. In all, prematurity can result from many of the same causes as miscarriage.

Immediately after birth, premature infants usually have greater difficulty adjusting to the external world than full-term babies do. Temperature control is a common problem: Premature infants have even fewer fat cells than normal infants and have a harder time maintaining body heat. This why newborns with LBW are usually placed in incubators immediately after birth. Another common problem is the difficulty of matching the nutritional environment of the late fetal period. In their first few months, premature infants seem unable to catch up to full-term infants in weight and height.

Many researchers believe that the effects of prematurity can last long after infancy. Historically, studies indicated that premature infants suffer more illnesses in their first 3 years of life, score lower on IQ tests, and are slightly more prone to behavioral problems than full-term babies (Knobloch, Pasamanick, Harper, & Rider, 1959). However, more recent research has found that such difficulties are experienced by less than one-quarter of premature infants (Bennett, Robinson, & Sells, 1983; Klein, Hack, Gallagher, & Fanaroff, 1985). Yet, researchers have also found a high prior rate of prematurity among children who were later diagnosed as having a learning disorder or being distractible or hyperactive.

All such reports must be interpreted with caution. It cannot be concluded, for example, that prematurity *causes* such anomalies. Although premature babies may be less able to adjust to the shock of birth, the relationship between prematurity and later problems may be more complex. For example, prenatal conditions such as malnutrition, faulty development of the placenta, or crowding in the uterus may result in a number of symptoms, only one of which is prematurity. So prematurity is often a *symptom* of an abnormality rather than a cause.

Some of the later problems of premature infants may also arise from the way they're treated during the first few weeks of life. Because of the need to keep them in incubators, they receive less of the caregiver contact normally experienced by newborns. Few premature infants are breast-fed; few are held even while being bottle-fed; and some are unable to suck at all for the first several weeks. Consequently, they miss the social experiences of feeding, which help establish early attachment. Some caregivers may also be less responsive to

preterm status An infant born before a gestation period of 35 weeks.

small-for-date A full-term newborn who weighs less than 5½ pounds.

"preemies" because they are unattractive or sickly or display their characteristic high-pitched, grating cry.

The consequences of limited early contact due to prematurity can be seen throughout infancy (Goldberg, 1979). On average, preterm infants are held farther from the parent's body, touched less, and cooed at less. Later, they tend to play less actively than full-term babies and have difficulty absorbing external stimuli. Even so, many of the differences between premature and full-term babies disappear by the end of the first year, especially when parents actively compensate by spending extra time with them and making extra efforts to get them to respond. In many hospitals parents are now encouraged to become involved in the care of premature infants. They put on masks and gowns and enter the intensive care unit to help with feeding, diaper changes, and other care. They stimulate the baby by gently stroking and talking to it, and the result is better attachment and caregiving when the baby is sent home.

There have been follow-up studies of premature infants whose parents helped care for them in the hospital. The parents learned to be especially responsive to the often subtle behaviors of their infants that might indicate needs and discomforts, and the children improved at each developmental stage. As infants, these babies developed more appropriately in performing social and intellectual tasks (compared to premature infants whose parents did not care for them in the hospital). At age 12, the children showed higher intellectual and social competence (Beckwith & Cohen, 1989; Goldberg, Lojkasek, Gartner, & Corter, 1988).

Some of the detrimental effects of prematurity may also be offset by an enriched environment during the first year of life. In a pilot program for infants who had been born prematurely because of fetal malnutrition (Zeskind & Ramey, 1978), the infants were given high-quality day care in addition to the necessary medical and nutritional services. Most of them reached normal performance levels by 18 months. A matched group of fetally malnourished infants received the same medical and nutritional services but were cared for at home. The latter infants reached normal levels more slowly, and deficits in their performance were still apparent at age 2.

High-Risk Infants

High-risk infants who are born with physical disabilities present similar problems to those of preterm infants with regard to early experience. Such infants are likely to be separated from their parents for medical reasons and often have developmental problems that interfere with their ability to signal their parents and give them positive feedback for good caregiving. The result is often a fussy, unresponsive baby and confused, perhaps overattentive caregivers.

It can be extremely difficult for parents to become attached to a high-risk infant. In addition to problems such as early separation and hospitalization, deficiencies such as visual or auditory impairment may severely restrict the baby's ability to respond. Moreover, parents frequently need to go through a period of mourning over the "perfect" child who didn't arrive before they can accept, nurture, and become emotionally attached to the less-than-perfect baby who did. Support groups consisting of other parents with high-risk infants can be very constructive. Such groups help parents realize that they are not alone, and members who are going through similar experiences can often suggest helpful techniques for interacting with the child.

CONTENT CHECK
PREMATURE AND HIGH-RISK INFANTS

True–False (answers are on the Companion Website)

1. Small-for-date babies are those who are full-term but have LBW.
2. In most cases, special care during the first several years of life cannot eliminate the side effects of being a premature infant.
3. In most cases, special care during the first several years of life can eliminate the side effects of being a high-risk infant with a disability.

The Evolving Family

As we've seen, childbirth is not just a medical event but a psychological and social milestone full of meaning for the family. The family system will no longer be the same. The newborn immediately starts signaling her or his presence, needs, health status, and personal style, and the parents, grandparents, and siblings respond in ways that reflect their personal and cultural beliefs. In this section we consider several factors in the family's adjustment to its new member, beginning with what the new member looks like and does.

First Impressions

The new baby has arrived, and everyone wants to know how much it weighs and who it looks like. What do normal **neonates** (newborns to about one month of age) look like, and how do they react to being born?

Size and Appearance   At birth the average full-term infant weighs between 5½ and 9½ pounds (2.5–4.3 kilograms) and is between 19 and 22 inches (about 48–56 centimeters) long. The skin may still be partly covered with the vernix caseosa and the lanugo hair (which should drop off during the first month).

The newborn's head looks misshapen and elongated because of a process called *molding*. The soft, bony plates of the skull called **fontanelles,** connected only by cartilage areas, are squeezed together in the birth canal to help allow the baby's head to pass through. Fontanelles don't fully harden and fuse the skull until late in infancy, which is why you should never bump or thump an infant's or young toddler's head—if you do, you risk concussion. In addition, a neonate's external genitalia may appear enlarged because of the presence of hormones that passed to the baby prior to birth.

The new parents may initially be shocked by their baby's appearance. It will take three to four months for the neonate to become a smooth, plump infant like those shown on TV and in magazine ads.

Is Birth Traumatic?   Whether birth is "traumatic," and whether, as Freud proposed, it is related to adult anxiety, birth *is* a radical transition from the protected, supporting environment of the uterus to a much less certain, even harsh external environment. No longer will oxygen and nutrients be provided as needed. Newborns must breathe for themselves and learn to communicate their needs and wants in a social world that may or may not be responsive to them.

Mother and father share the joy of admiring their newborn child.

neonate   Baby in the first month of life.

fontanelles   The soft, bony plates of the skull, connected only by cartilage.

Childbirth is remarkably stressful for the newborn. At the same time, a normal full-term baby is well prepared to cope (Gunnar, 1989). In the last few moments of birth, infants experience a major surge of adrenalin and noradrenalin, the hormones that counter stress. The adrenalin also helps counteract any initial oxygen deficiency and prepares the baby for breathing through the lungs. The first breaths may be difficult because the amniotic fluid that was in the lungs must be expelled and millions of tiny sacs in the lungs must be filled with air. Yet within minutes most infants are breathing regularly.

What about pain? Newborns also have relatively high levels of a natural painkiller called *beta-endorphin* circulating in their blood. This, along with the stimulating hormones, causes most infants to be unusually alert and receptive shortly after birth. Many experts have suggested that this period of extended alertness, which may last for an hour or more, is an ideal time for the parents and the infant to start getting acquainted (Nilsson & Hamberger, 1990).

A Period of Adjustment Despite their helpless appearance, full-term newborns are sturdy little beings who are already making a profound adjustment to their new life—from having the mother's body do everything for them to functioning on their own as separate individuals. Four crucial areas of physical adjustment are respiration, blood circulation, digestion, and temperature regulation.

With the first breaths of air, the lungs inflate and begin to work as the basic organ of the child's own respiratory system. During the first few days after birth, neonates experience periods of coughing and sneezing. These often alarm new parents, but they are a natural clearing of mucus and amniotic fluid from the infant's air passages. The onset of breathing marks a significant change in the neonate's circulatory system too. The baby's heart no longer needs to pump blood to the placenta for oxygen. Instead, a valve in the baby's heart closes and redirects the flow of blood to the lungs. The shift from fetal to independent circulatory and respiratory systems begins immediately after birth but is not completed for several days. Anoxia for more than a few minutes at birth or during the first few days of adjustment can cause permanent brain damage.

Before birth the placenta provided nourishment, but now the infant's own digestive system must begin to function. This change is longer and slower than the dramatic changes in respiration and circulation that occur immediately after birth. The neonate's temperature regulation system also adjusts gradually to its new environment. Within the uterus, the baby's skin was maintained at a constant temperature. After birth, the baby's own metabolism must protect it from even minor changes in external temperature. This is why—unless they're in incubators—babies must be carefully covered to keep them warm during the first few days and weeks of life. Gradually, they become able to maintain a constant body temperature, aided by the layer of fat that continues to accumulate during the early weeks.

The Beginnings of Attachment

Attachment is an emotional bond between parents and children. It includes elements such as feeling close and loving. Attachment works in both directions: Ideally, parents become strongly attached to their baby and their baby to them. This reciprocal relationship begins at birth and continues to unfold and change in subtle ways throughout childhood, as we see in detail in Chapter 6.

After the initial birth cry or gurgle and the filling of the lungs, an alert newborn calms down and has time to relax on its mother's chest, if given the opportunity. After a little rest, the infant may struggle to focus on the mother's or father's face. The infant seems to listen as the parents watch in fascination and begin talking to

attachment The emotional bond that develops between child and caregivers. The infant's first bond is usually characterized by strong interdepence, intense mutual feelings, and vital emotional ties.

him or her. They examine everything—fingers and toes, wrinkled but perhaps smiling face, funny little ears. There is close physical contact, cradling, and stroking. Many infants find the breast and almost immediately start to nurse, with pauses to look about. Infants who have experienced little or no anesthesia may display adrenalin-heightened alertness and exploration for an hour or more as their parents hold them close, establish eye contact, and talk to them. In turn, a baby's physical responses trigger physical processes within the mother's body. When babies lick or suck on the mother's nipples, secretion of *prolactin* (a hormone important in nursing) and *oxytocin* (a hormone that causes the uterus to contract and reduces bleeding) increase. The infant also benefits from early breast-feeding: Although milk often is not yet available, the mother produces a substance called *colostrum* that appears to help clear the infant's digestive system and can confer many of the mother's immunities to the newborn (the choice of breast- versus bottle-feeding is discussed in Chapter 5). Early contact is helpful in getting off to a good start, especially for teenage mothers or those who have had little or no experience with newborns, and for mothers of premature and high-risk infants. But parents who adopt children long after the first few hours, days, or weeks after birth can become just as strongly attached to them (e.g., Field, 1979).

Fathers who participate in their child's birth report an almost immediate attraction to the infant, with feelings of elation, pride, and heightened self-esteem (Greenberg & Morris, 1974). Not surprisingly, some studies have found that such fathers are more deeply involved with and attached to their infants than those who do not participate in their infant's birth and early care (Pruett, 1987). New fathers who don't participate in childbirth and do not have early contact with their infants frequently feel more distant from their wives and somewhat ignored when the baby arrives. Often the companionship between husband and wife is sharply reduced (Galinsky, 1980). Altogether, many studies report that fathers who begin a relationship with their newborns early continue to provide more direct care to their infants and play with them more.

Greater involvement by the father has many benefits. For example, such infants were found to be more socially responsive than average (Parke, 1979). Remember, though, that fathers who choose to have early contact with their infants may differ in many other ways from those who do not choose to have such contact (Palkovitz, 1985), so we cannot always be sure that the early contact itself is the cause of the later developmental benefits.

We see evidence for the significance of early attachment again and again in later chapters. We also see the continuing effects of the family environment on development.

The Transition to Parenthood

The transition to becoming a parent begins well before a child is born and continues well afterward. The phrase "we're expecting" carries with it the understanding that expectant parents are making changes in their lives that may involve new roles and relationships. Aside from finding a place for baby in the home, adjusting to parenthood is a major life change for adults—especially with a first child. Major life changes are often accompanied by stress and the need to communicate and solve problems. The new parents must also make economic and social adjustments, and they often need to reevaluate and modify existing relationships. Related factors are the cultural attitudes of the family toward childbearing and child rearing.

Motivations for childbearing vary considerably from one culture to another. In some societies—including in the United States in times past—children are valued as financial assets or as providers for the parents in their old age. In other societies, children represent those who will maintain family traditions or fulfill parents' personal needs and goals. Or children may be regarded simply as a duty or a necessary burden. Certain cultures accept children as inevitable, a natural part of life for which conscious decision making simply isn't necessary. In India, for example, traditional Hindu women want to have children to guarantee themselves a good life and afterlife (LeVine, 1989).

In all cultures, of course, pregnant women must adjust to the physical, psychological, and social changes that come with motherhood. Profound bodily changes occur that can hardly be ignored. Even before the fetus is large enough to cause alterations in a woman's appearance, she may feel nauseated or experience fullness or a tingling sensation in her breasts. Often she may suffer fatigue and emotional hypersensitivity during the early weeks of pregnancy—with direct effects on other family members. In contrast, in the middle stage of pregnancy she may experience a sense of heightened well-being. In fact, some of her bodily systems, such as the circulatory system, may show increased capacity and functioning. Finally, in the last stages of pregnancy some physical discomfort is usual, along with, at times, a feeling of emotional burden. Increased weight, reduced mobility, altered balance, and pressure on internal organs from the growing fetus are among the changes experienced by all pregnant women. Other symptoms, such as varicose veins, heartburn, frequent urination, and shortness of breath, contribute to the discomfort women feel. There are wide individual differences in the *amount* of discomfort, fatigue, or burden women experience during the last few weeks, however. Some women find the last stages of pregnancy to be much easier than do others.

The physical changes of pregnancy affect the mother's psychological state. She must come to terms with a new body image and an altered self-concept, and she must deal with the reactions of people around her. Some women experience a feeling of uniqueness or "distance" from friends, whereas others desire friendship and protection. Pregnancy may also be accompanied by considerable uncertainty about the future. In particular, the mother may be unsure about career plans following childbirth, anxious about her ability to care for a child, fearful of the possibility of congenital anomalies, concerned about finances, or uncomfortable with the idea of being a mother. Ambivalence is common: A woman may be eager to have a child, yet disappointed when she must share her time, energy, and husband with that child (Osofsky & Osofsky, 1984). Women also sometimes wonder whether they will be able to fulfill the expectations of everyone who will need them—the new baby, any older children, the husband, aging parents, close friends, and perhaps also job supervisors and coworkers.

The Father's Changing Role At first glance, the father's role seems easy compared to the major physical and emotional changes that the mother undergoes. Yet that usually isn't the case. Fathers report feeling excitement and pride, but some report feelings of rivalry with the child. Most men report an increased sense of responsibility that can seem overwhelming at times. Some report envy of their wife's ability to reproduce, and some report feeling like a mere bystander (Osofsky & Osofsky, 1984). Fathers worry about the future as much as mothers do. They feel concern about their ability to support the new family and about the role of parent. Fathers also tend to be concerned about whether the child will like and respect them and whether they will be able to meet the child's emotional needs (Ditzion & Wolf, 1978; Parke, 1981). Some fathers take the opportunity to learn more about children and parenting. Others make new financial arrangements. Many attempt to give their wife more emotional support. When there are other children in the family, fathers often spend more time with them and help them prepare for the new arrival (Parke, 1981).

Expectant fathers may also sometimes go through a phase in which they identify with their wife and actually display symptoms of their wife's pregnancy (Pruett, 1987). A somewhat extreme example occurs among the natives of the Yucatan in Mexico, where pregnancy is "confirmed" when the woman's *mate* experiences nausea, diarrhea, vomiting, or cramps (Pruett, 1987). Closer to home, expectant fathers sometimes crave the proverbial dill pickles with ice cream, and they also experience troubling dreams and disturbing changes in sexual desires, just as women sometimes do.

Cultural Prescriptions It's easy to see that *both* parents' attitudes toward pregnancy and childbirth are often shaped by their culture. In the United States, for example, pregnancy was formerly treated as an abnormal condition. A pregnant woman was not seen in public or in school or in an office pursuing a career. But, beginning some 150 years ago, massive changes in family structure, roles, and perceptions of pregnancy took place. Further changes have occurred in this century, particularly during World War II and in the years that followed. There was a rapid increase in the number of mothers working outside the home and a rise in mother-only families (Hernandez, 1994) that continues today—placing more pregnant as well as nonpregnant women in the workforce. Today women are encouraged to work until close to delivery. Ideally, they take the discomfort and fatigue of pregnancy in stride and go on with their normal lives.

In sum, social attitudes, coupled with the expectant parents' needs and emotions, can make pregnancy and early childrearing a period of stress, change, and adjustment. Such conflicts may be more intense for young parents, particularly those who lack the support of family and friends (Osofsky & Osofsky, 1984). None of these feelings will harm the fetus directly, of course, unless the mother suffers severe or prolonged emotional stress. Nevertheless, parental attitudes and stress do affect maternal diet, hormonal levels, rest, exercise, drug use, and resistance to disease, any of which can affect the developing child. They also help create the social environment that the child enters at birth.

CONTENT CHECK
THE EVOLVING FAMILY

True–False (answers are on the Companion Website)

1. The prevailing view is that babies experience severe birth trauma and that this sets the stage for later anxiety.
2. Attachment begins after the first 6 months after birth.
3. Physical contact by the baby stimulates hormone changes in both the mother and the father.
4. Motivations for childbearing are universal across cultures.
5. Some expectant fathers actually display symptoms of their wives' pregnancies.

Thinking Critically

In what ways is maximum early contact important to the formation of attachment bonds between infants and their caregivers?

CHAPTER 4 REVISITED

- About half of all U.S. pregnancies are unintended; the rate is higher for teens.

- Whether a child successfully makes the journey from conception to birth depends on both genetics and the prenatal environment.

Prenatal Growth and Development

- Prenatal development is viewed either in trimesters (1st, 2nd, and 3rd) or in periods (germinal, embryonic, and fetal).

- Each month a woman's ovaries normally release one ovum, which moves into one of the fallopian tubes, where it may be fertilized by a sperm.

- The germinal period begins with conception of the zygote and ends with implantation.

- Monogyzotic twins occur when a zygote divides into two cells that develop separately; dizygotic twins occur when two mature ova are released at the same time and fertilized.

- The embryonic period begins with implantation and continues for two months, during which the outer layer of cells produces the amniotic sac, amniotic fluid, the placenta, and the umbilical cord and the inner layer of cells differentiate to form the embryo.

- During the second month all the structures of the embryo develop rapidly, including the arms and legs, the eyes, and the internal organs.

- During the fetal period the organs and systems mature and become functional and the fetus begins to move; physical structures become more complete.

- Structural details such as lips, toenails, and buds for adult teeth are added during the second trimester, as the body becomes longer and the heart starts beating.

- At about the end of the second trimester a healthy fetus reaches the age of viability.

- During the third trimester the brain matures and the fetus grows rapidly; various behaviors appear and the fetus goes through daily cycles of activity and sleep.

- The three general growth trends are cephalocaudal, proximodistal, and gross-to-specific.

Prenatal Environmental Influences

- Although most pregnancies in the United States result in full-term, healthy babies, sometimes congenital anomalies occur; the majority are caused by prenatal environmental influences.

- The incidence of congenital anomalies is highest among teens and mothers over 35 to 40.

- Fetal malnutrition can be caused by nutrient deficiencies as well as by deficiencies in the mothers' digestive processes and metabolism; malnourished mothers also more often miscarry.

- The single best predictor of healthy, full-term babies is prenatal health-care visits beginning in the first trimester of pregnancy.

- There are critical periods during which the developing child is at greatest risk for different kinds of anomalies as a result of teratogens—diseases, drugs, toxic chemicals, and the like,—that affect the child directly or by gradual accumulation.

- Many viral diseases can cross the placental barrier and cause congenital anomalies such as blindness, deafness, brain damage, or limb deformity; most bacterial diseases cannot.

- Certain prescription drugs and many OTC medications can cross the placental barrier and harm the developing child.

- Heavy drinking can cause extensive damage to the developing child; the symptoms of FAS include low birth weight and physical and neurological abnormalities.

- Smoking has been clearly linked to fetal abnormalities as well as higher rates of spontaneous abortion, stillbirth, and prematurity.

- Infants exposed to cocaine before birth have great difficulty controlling their nervous system and often cry frantically and seem unable to sleep; later in childhood they have higher rates of attention-deficit disorder and learning disabilities.

Childbirth

- Childbirth occurs in three stages: initial labor, labor and delivery, and afterbirth.

- Episiotomies are much more common in the United States than in most other parts of the world.

- The biology of childbirth is universal; approaches to childbirth vary considerably both across and within cultures.

- Traditional childbirth had a much different meaning 150 years ago than it does now.

- With the advent of modern medicine, birthing shifted from the home to the hospital, where the mother could be assisted by specialized medical staff and technology.

■ Today many expectant parents in the United States and other Western nations choose natural or prepared childbirth: They attend classes where they learn about the biology of childbirth, the mother practices relaxation exercises, and the father or a friend serves as a coach during labor and delivery.

■ Birthing centers offer a home-like alternative to traditional hospital childbirth settings; birthing centers often employ CNMs rather than obstetricians.

■ Three popular prenatal screening procedures are ultrasound, amniocentesis, and CVS; perinatologists also use fetal monitoring.

■ Breech presentation is a common reason given for choosing cesarean section; many researchers believe that the rate of C-sections in the United States is excessive.

■ Using the Apgar scale, newborns are evaluated at 1 minute and at 5 minutes after birth to detect any problems or weaknesses.

Premature and High-Risk Infants

■ Infants born with LBW require special treatment and care.

■ Preterm birth may result from a variety of factors; small-for-date birth is often caused by malnutrition.

■ Because premature infants must be kept in incubators, it is more difficult for caregivers to form early attachments with them; hospital care can produce similar problems for high-risk infants who have disabilities.

■ With support for parents and special care for infants over the first two years, premature and high-risk infants can reach normal developmental levels.

The Evolving Family

■ The average full-term infant normally weighs between 5½ and 9½ pounds and is between 19 and 22 inches long.

■ Although childbirth is stressful for the newborn, the baby immediately begins to adjust to its new environment as respiration, blood circulation, digestion, and temperature regulation begin.

■ Attachment is a reciprocal relationship between parents and child that begins at birth; it is fostered by parents having extensive contact with the baby immediately after birth.

■ Attachment is fostered by avoidance of medication during delivery, which allows the infant to enter a heightened state of alertness for the first hour or so.

■ Adjusting to parenthood is a major life change for adults, especially with a first child; parents must make economic and social adjustments and modify existing relationships.

■ Pregnant women must adjust to numerous physical, psychological, and social changes.

■ Fathers also react emotionally to their wife's pregnancy.

■ Both parents' attitudes toward pregnancy and childbirth are shaped by their culture.

KEY TERMS

fallopian tubes
ovulation
uterus
zygote
germinal period
monozygotic (identical) twins
dizygotic (fraternal) twins
blastula
embryonic period
embryo
amniotic sac
amniotic fluid
placenta
umbilical cord
spontaneous abortion
fetal period

fetus
age of viability
cephalocaudal trend
proximodistal trend
gross-to-specific trend
teratogen
fetal alcohol syndrome (FAS)
fetal alcohol effects (FAE)
anoxia
inital labor
false labor
episiotomy
afterbirth
midwife
traditional childbirth

"natural"or prepared childbirth
birthing center
ultrasound
amniocentesis
chorionic villus sampling (CVS)
perinatology
fetal monitor
breech presentation
cesarean section
Apgar Scoring System
preterm status
small-for-date
neonate
fontanelles
attachment

INFANCY AND TODDLERHOOD: PHYSICAL, COGNITIVE, AND LANGUAGE DEVELOPMENT

5

CHAPTER PREVIEW

Do you know:

1. That neonates alternate between predictable *states of arousal*?

2. What *survival reflexes* and *primitive reflexes* infants are born with and what role they play in infant assessment?

3. That the timing of *motor development* varies according to cultural contexts?

4. What *visually guided reach* is and why it's important?

5. What *fine motor skills* and *gross motor skills* are and how they develop?

6. What constitutes *malnutrition* and how extensive it is around the world?

7. The advantages and disadvantages of *breastfeeding* versus *bottlefeeding*?

8. What *sensory* and *perceptual* capabilities infants are born with and how they are studied?

9. How *visual* and *auditory* perception develop during infancy?

10. The extent to which the senses are *integrated* at birth?

11. What constitutes Piaget's *sensorimotor* period?

12. The extent to which infants can *imitate* the actions of others?

13. What *object permanence* is and how it develops?

14. What *symbolic representation* is and how it develops?

15. How infants develop the ability to *categorize*?

16. How *language development* proceeds during infancy?

17. What *universals* there are in language development?

18. What roles *imitation*, *reinforcement*, and *built-in mechanisms* play in language development?

These are the main topics of Chapter 5.

Neonates enter the world quite capable of sensing their environment and responding to it. They can see and hear, taste and smell, feel pressure and pain. They're selective in what they look at. They learn, although their abilities are limited. During the first 2 years of life change is more rapid and more dramatical than during any other 2-year period. It is an amazing transformation, from profound ignorance of the images, sounds, and smells around them to basic understanding of objects and people, of language and customary routines. Some of these changes are obvious. Infants crawl, sit, walk, and talk. Other changes are harder to assess; it is difficult indeed to know exactly what an infant sees, hears, and thinks.

Neonates communicate their needs with a cry, a yawn, or an alert squint, but they have no real knowledge of life, day and night, self and other, mine and yours, boy and girl, mothers and fathers and sons and daughters. Yet just 2 short years later, children are thinking, wondering, and expressing their thoughts and feelings through language. At the same time, language helps them structure what they know and understand. Because of the enormous power language provides, it is considered a bridge out of infancy and a key aspect of cognitive development.

In this chapter we begin with a look at the competencies of the neonate and then discuss what is known about physical, motor, and perceptual development during the first 2 years of life. Then we turn our attention to cognitive and language development.

Neonates

The first month is a very special period because the baby must adjust to life outside the protected environment of the mother's womb. As we saw in Chapter 4, the first month is a time of recovery from the birth process and adjustment of vital functions such as respiration, circulation, digestion, and regulation of body temperature. It is also a time for developing a balance between overstimulation and understimulation in a challenging physical and social environment. How well equipped is a normal neonate for such tasks?

Until the 1960s it was thought that neonates are incapable of organized, self-directed behavior. In fact, it was not uncommon to view the infant's world as a "blooming, buzzing confusion," as William James (1842–1910) described it (1890/1950). Developmental literature stated that infants do not use higher brain centers until they are almost a year old and that newborns see light and shadow but do not perceive objects or patterns. Behavior in the first weeks of life was considered to be almost entirely reflexive.

Subsequent research has shown that newborns' capabilities had been grossly underestimated. We now know that neonates are capable of organized, predictable responses and of more complex cognitive activity than was once thought. They have definite preferences and a striking ability to learn. Moreover, they deliberately attract attention to their needs.

The key to the new understanding of infants is in the development of more accurate and effective ways of observing their behavior. Early studies often put infants at a disadvantage. Even adults who are placed flat on their backs to stare at a ceiling while covered up to their necks with blankets are not their most perceptive or responsive selves. When neonates are placed stomach down on the mother's skin in a warm room, they display an engaging repertoire of behaviors that wouldn't otherwise be seen.

States of Arousal

If you watch sleeping newborns, you'll notice that they sometimes lie calmly and quietly and at other times twitch and grimace. Similarly, when they are awake, babies may be calm or thrash about wildly and cry. Through extensive observation of infants' activity, Peter Wolff (1966) identified six newborn behavioral states that continue to appear valid today: *waking activity, crying, alert inactivity, drowsiness, regular sleep,* and *irregular sleep* (Table 5–1). Theses states are regular and follow a predictable daily cycle.

An infant's responsiveness to others and to the environment depends on his or her behavioral state. In a state of alert inactivity, infants are easily stimulated and react to sounds or sights with increased activity. Infants who are already in an active state tend to calm down when stimulated. At first newborns spend most of the day in either regular or irregular sleep. As an infant matures and the higher brain centers "wake up," the percentages shift. For example, by 4 to

Table 5-1 Infant States of Arousal

Waking activity

The baby frequently engages in motor activity involving the whole body. The eyes are open, and breathing is highly irregular.

Crying

The baby cries and engages in vigorous, disorganized motor activity. Crying may take different forms, such as "hunger" cries, "anger" cries, and "pain" or "discomfort" cries.

Alert inactivity

The eyes are open, bright, and shining. They follow moving objects. The baby is fairly inactive, with a quiet face.

Drowsiness

The baby is fairly inactive. The eyes open and close. Breathing is regular, but faster than in regular sleep. When the eyes are open, they may have a dull, glazed quality.

Regular sleep

The eyes are closed and the body is completely relaxed. Breathing is slow and regular. The face looks relaxed, and the eyelids are still.

Irregular sleep

The eyes are closed, but there are gentle limb movements such as writhing, stirring, and stretching. Grimaces and other facial expressions occur. Breathing is irregular and faster than in regular sleep. Rapid eye movements (REMs) occasionally occur; these may indicate dreaming.

Source: Wolff, 1966, 1969.

8 weeks a typical baby is sleeping more during the night and less during the day. There are longer periods of alert inactivity and waking activity, and the baby is more responsive to caregivers—as well as to researchers.

Much to the delight of parents and other caregivers, by 4 months the average baby is usually sleeping through the night. Gradually the baby settles into the family routine, in the daytime as well as at night.

Reflexes

Researchers have long known that infants enter the world with biologically based behaviors that can be classified as **survival reflexes** and **primitive reflexes.** Survival reflexes are just that: reflexes necessary for adaptation and survival, especially during the first weeks before the higher brain centers begin to take control (see Table 5–2). Breathing, for example, is reflexive although it is also subject to voluntary control after the first few months. Coughing, sneezing, gagging, hiccupping, yawning, and many other reflexes not included in Table 5–2 are also present at birth and throughout life. In contrast, rooting and sucking, which are highly adaptive reflexes for finding a nipple and obtaining milk, are reflexive at first but become entirely voluntary after a few months.

Primitive reflexes do not have apparent survival value and appear unrelated to motor development (Bartlett, 1997), but may have been important at some point in our evolutionary history. The Moro reflex, for example, is the newborn's startle reaction. When newborns are startled by a loud sound or by being dropped, they react first by extending both arms to the side, with fingers outstretched as if to catch onto someone or something. The arms then gradually

survival reflexes Reflexes necessary for adaptation and survival, especially during the first few weeks before the higher brain centers begin to take control.

primitive reflexes Reflexes that do not have apparent survival value but may have been important at some point in our evolutionary history.

Table 5-2   Infant Reflexes

SURVIVAL REFLEXES

Breathing

Infants reflexively inhale to obtain oxygen and exhale to expel carbon dioxide. Breathing is permanently reflexive in that it doesn't require conscious effort, although after the first few months of life we can voluntary control our breathing—up to a point.

Rooting

If you touch an infant's cheek, the infant will turn its head toward the stimulus and open its mouth as if expecting a nipple. This reflex normally disappears after 3 or 4 months.

Sucking

If you touch or otherwise stimulate an infant's mouth, the infant will respond by sucking and making rhythmic movements with the mouth and tongue. This reflex gradually becomes voluntary over the first few months.

Pupillary

The pupils of infants' eyes narrow in bright light and when going to sleep, and widen in dim light and when waking up. This is a permanent reflex.

Eye-blink

Infants blink in response to an object moving quickly toward their eyes or a puff of air. This is a permanent reflex.

PRIMITIVE REFLEXES

Moro (startle)

When infants are startled by loud sounds or by being suddenly dropped a few inches, they will first spread their arms and stretch out their fingers, then bring their arms back to their body and clench their fingers. This reflex disappears after about 4 months.

Palmar

When an infant's palm is stimulated, the infant will grasp tightly and increase the strength of the grasp if the stimulus is pulled away. This reflex disappears after about 5 months.

Plantar

When an object or a finger is placed on the sole of an infant's foot near the toes, the infant responds by trying to flex the foot. This reflex is similar to the palmar reflex, but it disappears after about 9 months.

Babinski

If you stroke the sole of an infant's foot from heel to toes, the infant will spread the small toes and raise the large one. This reflex disappears after about 6 months.

Stepping

When infants are held upright with their feet against a flat surface and are moved forward, they appear to walk in a coordinated way. This reflex disappears after 2 or 3 months.

Swimming

Infants will *attempt* to swim in a coordinated way if placed in water in a prone position. This reflex disappears after about 6 months.

Tonic neck

When infants' heads are turned to one side, they will extend the arm and leg on that side and flex the arm and leg on the opposite side, as in a fencing position. This reflex disappears after about 4 months.

Source: Adapted from Taft & Cohen, 1967.

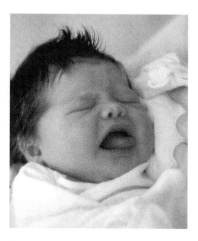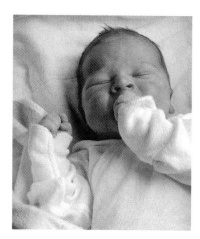

Some reflexes of the newborn: (left) rooting reflex, (middle) stepping reflex, and (right) sucking reflex.

come back to the midline. Thus, the Moro reflex might have had survival value in the distant past: In case of a fall, neonates who grasped their mother's body hair would be most likely to survive. A related reflex is the palmar grasp. When the palm of a neonate's hand is stimulated by an object such as a finger or a pencil, the infant's fingers will close tightly in a grasp. Indeed, some neonates can grasp with enough strength to support their full weight for up to a minute (Taft & Cohen, 1967).

Primitive reflexes normally disappear during the first several months of life and therefore have diagnostic value: If they do *not* disappear more or less on schedule, it may be a sign of neurological problems.

Neonatal Assessment

During the first few days of a baby's life, hospitals perform evaluations that may include a neurological examination and a behavioral assessment. T. Berry Brazelton's Neonatal Behavioral Assessment Scale (BNBAS; first published in 1973, current revision 1995) is used by many hospitals and has also been employed in hundreds of research efforts (Nugent & Brazelton, 2000). The 28 separate measures on the test are grouped into 7 behavioral clusters. As described in Table 5–3, the clusters include habituation, orientation, motor tone and activity, range of state, regulation of state, autonomic stability, and reflexes (such as those in Table 5–2). Thus, although the scale includes the usual neurological tests, it also assesses the newborn's behavioral capabilities and social responsiveness.

Neonates differ in their responses to new, prolonged, or slightly annoying stimuli. Some can easily detect, attend to, and habituate to changes in their environment. Others may be less responsive, still others overly responsive and too easily irritated—behaviors that decrease attention span and adaptability. By assessing the newborn's competencies and patterns of responding, the Brazelton scale supplies early information about a child's potential personality and social development. Parents who observe a physician administer the Brazelton scale become much more sensitive to the capabilities and individuality of their neonate (Parke & Tinsley, 1987). With a "difficult" baby in particular, parents can also receive special training that teaches them what to expect and methods of coping with their baby's behavior over the first several months of life (Nugent & Brazelton, 2000).

Table 5-3 Clusters in the Brazelton Neonatal Behavioral Assessment Scale

Habituation

How quickly does the infant respond to and then habituate to a light, bell, rattle, or pin prick?

Orientation

How readily does the infant quiet and turn toward a light, bell, voice, or face?

Motor tone and activity

How strong and steady is the infant's motor activity?

Range of state

How quickly and easily does the infant shift from sleeping to alertness? To crying?

Regulation of state

How does the infant calm or quiet down? How easily is the infant soothed?

Autonomic stability

Does the infant react to noises with tremors or unusual startles?

Reflexes

Are there appropriate survival and primitive reflex responses?

Source: Adapted from Nugent & Brazelton, 2000.

Learning and Habituation

Learning is readily observable from birth on. Neonates quiet down in response to familiar sounds, songs, or lullabies. A neonate's early ability to imitate facial expressions demonstrates learning. Improved methods of observation have yielded useful information about the infants' ability to learn fairly complex responses.

In pioneering conditioning studies (Papousek, 1961), newborns were taught to turn their heads to the left to obtain milk whenever a bell was rung. For the same reward, they learned to turn their heads to the right at the sound of a buzzer. Then the bell and the buzzer were reversed and the infants quickly learned to turn their heads in the appropriate direction. There were also experiments in which infants learned to turn on a light by turning their heads to the left. Then an interesting thing happened, revealing a key facet of infant habituation. After a while, the infants lost interest in turning on the light, as if they were bored with the game. Their interest could be revived by reversing the problem, but they soon became bored again.

Remember that habituation is a form of learning that involves becoming accustomed to stimuli and then no longer responding to them. Infants need to adapt to or ignore nonmeaningful stimuli like the light touch of their clothing or any repetitive noises in their environment (sounds within or from outside the home). Habituation also gives rise to an important research technique. In the **habituation method,** researchers habituate infants to certain stimuli to study their perceptual capabilities. For example, a newborn's response at the onset of a moderately loud tone is a faster heartbeat, a change in breathing, and sometimes crying or generally increased activity. As the tone continues,

habituation method To study infant perceptual capabilities, researchers habituate infants to certain stimuli and then change the stimuli.

Every day in an infant's life brings new opportunities for discovery.

however, the infant soon habituates and stops responding. Then the frequency of the tone is changed slightly. If responding resumes, it is clear that the infant perceived the difference. The habituation method continues to be used extensively in studying infant capabilities (e.g., see Bornstein & Arterberry, 1999).

Because sucking comes under voluntary control early, it has also been used extensively in studies of neonatal learning and visual preferences. For example, classic research by Jerome Bruner and colleagues (Kalnins & Bruner, 1973) assessed whether infants could control sucking when it was linked to rewards other than feeding. Pacifiers were wired to a slide projector. If the infants sucked, the slide came into focus; if they did not, the picture blurred. The researchers found that the infants—some as young as 3 weeks—quickly learned to focus the picture and also adapted quickly if conditions were reversed. That is, they learned to stop sucking to get the picture into focus. Like the habituation method, what is now sometimes referred to as the *high-amplitude sucking procedure* has also been a popular research tool over the years (e.g., see Floccia, Christophe, & Bertoncini, 1997).

CONTENT CHECK
NEONATES

True–False (answers are on the Companion Website)
1. To a newborn infant, the world is a blooming, buzzing confusion.
2. The BNBAS reflex cluster assesses both survival and primitive reflexes.
3. Soon after birth, infants are capable of conditioning and learning.
4. The habituation method is used to study infant perceptual capabilities.

Thinking Critically
Why is it important to be aware of an infant's states of arousal?

Physical and Motor Development

Infancy is a time of motor discovery. Infants play with faces, foods, and daily routines. They explore flowers, insects, toys, and their own bodies. Every day brings opportunities for discovery of the people, objects, and events in their environment. Such discovery is not merely exciting for infants; it plays a crucial role in their development.

Maturation or a Dynamic System?

For decades, developmental psychologists carefully studied maturational "markers." Arnold Gesell (1880–1961), a pioneer in the field, observed hundreds of infants and children (e.g., see Gesell, 1940). He recorded the details of when and how certain behaviors emerged, such as crawling, walking, running, picking up a small pellet, cutting with scissors, managing a pencil, or drawing human figures. On the basis of the resulting data, he compiled detailed reports of the capabilities of *average* children at different ages.

In the healthy, well-nourished children Gesell observed, the behaviors under study emerged in an orderly and predictable sequence. By knowing the age of a child, Gesell could predict not only the child's approximate height and weight but also what the child knew or could do. He concluded that development does not depend primarily on the environment. Instead, he believed—given a normal environment—that most of a child's achievements result from an internal biological timetable. Behavior emerges as a function of maturation.

Gesell's theory and method had a major shortcoming, however. The children he studied came from the same socioeconomic class and community, so their shared environment may have caused them to develop in similar ways. We now know that children raised in widely different social or historical contexts develop quite differently than those described in Gesell's schedules. For example, contemporary U.S. infants normally begin "free" walking between 11 and 13 months of age instead of at 15 months as Gesell observed, presumably because baby care customs have changed. In the 1930s, infants spent more time resting and lying flat on their backs than they do now, so they did not get as much early practice with the skills leading up to walking.

There are also cultural differences in the onset of walking. On average, black infants walk a few weeks earlier than white infants, although there is considerable variability within each group. West Indian infants, whether in Jamaica or East London, normally walk about a month earlier than other London infants. This is because their mothers use massage and encourage vigorous exercise (Hopkins, 1991). Historically, infants raised in some Guatemalan villages—where they spent their first year confined to a small, dark hut, were not played with, were rarely spoken to, and were poorly nourished—walked months later (Kagan, 1978).

Despite the shortcomings of his research, Gesell's contribution remains substantial. If we use his findings carefully and don't interpret them rigidly, we at least have a baseline of developmental milestones to which we can compare individual infants' development. Gesell's milestones are averages and only that; quite normal children vary widely in the ages at which they develop maturationally based behaviors. Children develop at their own pace and in the context of their sociocultural environment.

Contemporary developmental psychologists have gone well beyond Gesell's studies in analyzing the form and processes of infants' developing competencies. Perceptual, motor, cognitive, and emotional development go hand in hand in a particular social context. The infant reaches out for an attractive object and pulls it in for closer inspection. The baby who has just begun to walk toddles precariously toward the outstretched arms of an eager, encouraging parent. The toddler explores the world from a new perspective. Motor development is intimately related to the infant's perceptual, cognitive, and social development. Body, brain, and experience influence each other (Thelen, 1987, 1989; Thelen & Smith, 1994). Physical and motor developments occur not simply through maturation, but in a dynamic system of evolving competencies that augment and complement each other (Bushnell & Boudreau, 1993; Lockman & Thelen, 1993; Thelen & Spencer, 1998).

An Overview of the First Two Years

The First 4 Months By about 4 months, most infants have nearly doubled in weight. (Figure 5–1 illustrates growth rates for height and weight over the first 2 years of life.) Their skin has lost the newborn look, and their fine birth hair is

Figure 5-1 **Growth Rates for Height and Weight**

The weight and height of about 50% of the infants at a given age will fall in the purple regions; about 15% will fall in each of the white regions. Thus, on the average, 80% of all infants will have weights and heights somewhere in the purple and white regions of the graphs. Note that as the infants age, greater differences occur in weight and height within the normal range of growth.

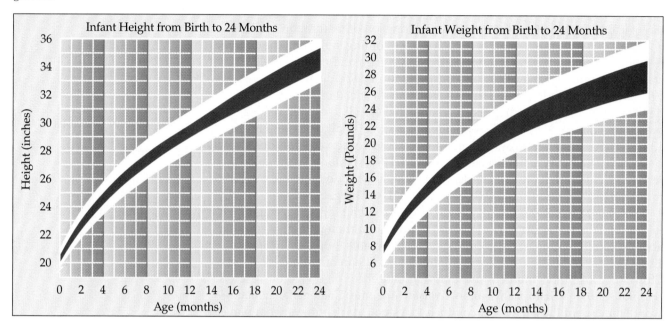

being replaced by permanent hair. Their eyes now focus rather well. When awake, they may coo contentedly and smile in response to pleasant stimuli.

At birth, the size of an infant's head represents about one-quarter of its total body length. Around age 4 months, however, the body starts to grow and lengthen much more rapidly than the head, and the proportions change markedly (see Figure 5–2). By young adulthood, the head accounts for only one-tenth of total body length.

Figure 5-2 **Growth Trends**

The cephalocaudal (head-downward) and proximodistal (center-outward) development that we saw in prenatal growth continues after birth, and the proportions of the baby's body change dramatically during infancy.

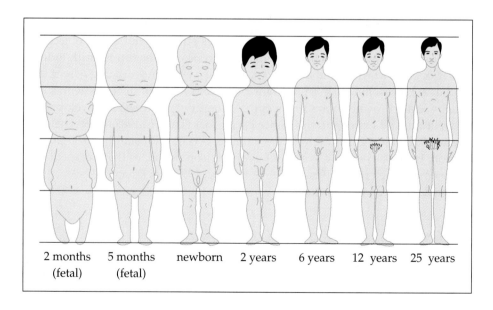

2 months (fetal) 5 months (fetal) newborn 2 years 6 years 12 years 25 years

IN THEORY, IN FACT

IS THERE A SINGLE CAUSE OF SUDDEN INFANT DEATH SYNDROME?

SIDS is defined as the sudden death of an apparently healthy infant in whom no medical cause can be found in a postmortem examination, and over the years there has been an extensive search for "the" cause of such deaths. Sometimes called "crib death," SIDS tends to happen without warning, while the child is asleep. SIDS is the most common cause of death among U.S. infants during the first year of life. Although U.S. SIDS cases gradually declined during the 1990s, they still accounted for about 28% of all infant deaths in 1998 (CDC, 2000c). There are approximately 4,700 such deaths each year.

Various circumstances in which SIDS is more likely to occur have been identified. The risk is increased if the mother was ill during her pregnancy or did not receive prenatal care. Smoking and drug abuse by the mother are often connected to SIDS (Kandall & Gaines, 1991); exposure to second-hand smoke apparently increases the risk. Infants whose mothers smoked during pregnancy and were also anemic are at higher risk (Bulterys, Greenland, & Kraus, 1990). Parental abuse and ne-glect also increase the risk of SIDS, and it is likely that some deaths reported as being SIDS cases are instead the result of maltreatment (Hobbes, Wynne, & Gelletlie, 1995)—or worse.

Many infants who die of SIDS had severe breathing and digestive problems in the preceding week. Second and third children also are at higher risk for SIDS than the average firstborn child. Also, infants who later died of SIDS have been observed to be less active and less responsive than their siblings.

Death frequently occurs at night when the infant is asleep, regardless of its position. Considerable research now indicates, however, that babies who are put to sleep in a prone position (on their stomachs) are at significantly greater risk for SIDS (e.g., see Dwyer, Ponsonby, Newman, & Gibbons, 1991; CDC, 1999b). Because of this and other research linking sleeping position and SIDS, the American Academy of Pediatrics (AAP) recommends putting babies to sleep on their back or propped on their side against pillows (AAP, 1992). Note, however, that this is more important for babies for whom the risk of SIDS is high than for healthy babies.

SIDS seems to occur most often in winter, which implicates possible irregularities in the autonomic nervous system, especially as this relates to breathing and heart functions. Some infants apparently are born with an immature respiratory center. Combined with other problems such as illness, head colds, or exposure to cold air or smoke, this may result in cessation of breathing. Vestibular stimulation by rocking has been shown to be beneficial for premature babies in reducing *apnea* (halting of breathing), which can be associated with SIDS. Recent research suggests that an inherited enzyme deficiency may also be involved in SIDS (Voelker, 1999).

In all, given such disparate findings, it appears unlikely that SIDS has a single, primary cause—a family of interrelated or even separate causes is much more likely. Thus, parents whose children are at risk may have to continue to rely upon special *apnea monitors* that sound an alarm and awake them should their infant stop breathing. Also note that co-sleeping (Chapter 1) apparently reduces the risk of SIDS (McKenna, 1996).

The infant's teeth and bones are also changing. In some children the first tooth erupts at 4 or 5 months. Many bones are still soft cartilage; they tend to be pliable under stress and rarely break. Muscles, however, may pull easily and be injured, for example, if young infants are hoisted by the arms and swung about in play.

Most of the newborn's reflexes normally disappear in the second and third months, gradually being replaced by voluntary actions as the higher brain centers take control. The well-coordinated stepping reflex, for example, is replaced by more random, less well-coordinated kicking (Thelen, 1989). The transition from reflexes to higher brain center control is also the time when sudden infant death syndrome (SIDS) is common (see "In Theory, In Fact" above.)

Self-discovery also usually begins at this time. Infants discover their own hands and fingers and spend minutes at a time watching them, studying their movements, bringing them together, and grasping one hand with the other.

From 5 to 8 Months By 8 months, although babies have gradually gained weight, their general appearance doesn't differ dramatically from that of

Many 8-month-olds start to play social games like peekaboo.

4-month-olds. Their hair is thicker and longer. By this time too, their legs are oriented so that the soles of their feet no longer face each other—an early change that sets the stage for later standing and walking.

By about 5 to 6 months, most infants achieve an important milestone called the *visually guided reach* (Rochat, Goubet & Senders, 1999). They can accurately reach out and grasp an attractive object and bring it to them, even when the object is moving (Wentworth, Benson, & Haith, 2000). In contrast, 1-month-olds will react to an object by opening and closing their hands and waving their arms and perhaps opening their mouths, but they can't coordinate such motions into a complete act. Successful reaching requires accurate depth perception, voluntary control of arm movements and grasping, and the ability to organize these behaviors into a sequence. Throughout the first 5 months, infants use visual information to direct exploration with their fingers (Rochat, 1989). Eventually they combine reaching, grasping, and mouthing into a smooth sequence, and their world is transformed: They can now engage in more systematic exploration of objects—with the hands, the eyes, and the mouth used individually or in combination (Rochat, 1989). **Fine motor skills,** which involve use of the hands and fingers, continue to be refined. By 5 months the infant has progressed from a reflexive grasp to a voluntary scooping grab. Most 8-month-old babies can pass objects from hand to hand, and some can use thumb and finger to grasp. They can usually bang two objects together—often joyfully and endlessly.

Gross motor skills—those involving the larger muscles or the whole body—show progressive refinement as well. Most 8-month-olds can get themselves into a sitting position, and nearly all can sit without support if placed in a sitting position. If they are placed on their feet, many 8-month-olds can stand while holding on to a support. Some may be walking, using furniture for support. By now, all valuables and any small objects that could be swallowed should be placed beyond the infant's reach—it's time for "childproofing" the

fine motor skills   Competence in using the hands and fingers.

gross motor skills   Those skills that involve the larger muscles or the whole body and that show refinement as well.

home. Infants learn to crawl (with the body on the floor) or creep (on hands and knees). Other infants develop a method called "bear walking," which employs both hands and feet. Still others "scoot" in a sitting position.

Especially interesting with regard to infant crawling at 8 months and older is a series of studies by Karen Adolph and colleagues (1997), which demonstrated infants' capabilities when confronted with crawling up and down "slopes" at varying angles. For example, without training, 8½-month-olds "charged up" steep slopes with no hesitation, then—perhaps after surveying the downward side—continued head first and required rescue by the experimenters. In contrast, older infants (walking 14-month-olds) were more discriminating. They walked up the steep slopes and then carefully slid down.

Many 8-month-olds begin to play social games, such as peekaboo, bye-bye, and patty-cake, and most enjoy handing an item back and forth with an adult. Another quickly learned game is dropping an object and watching someone pick it up and hand it back—a source of endless pleasure for some infants.

From 9 to 12 Months   By 12 months most infants are about three times heavier than they were at birth. Girls tend to weigh slightly less than boys.

On average, about half of infants 12 months old are standing alone and taking their first tentative steps toward becoming toddlers. As noted earlier, however, the age at which walking begins varies widely, depending both on individual development and on sociocultural factors.

The ability to stand and walk gives the toddler a new visual perspective. Locomotion allows for more active exploration. Infants can now get into, over, and under things. Their world has broadened once again. Motor development is spurred on by new and exciting things to approach and see. Exploring at new levels and with new skills promotes cognitive and perceptual development (Bushnell & Boudreau, 1993; Thelen, 1989; Thelen & Smith, 1994). Twelve-month-olds actively manipulate their environment. They undo latches, open cabinets, pull toys, and twist lamp cords. Their newly developed **pincer grasp,** with thumb opposing forefinger, allows them to pick up grass, hairs, matches, dead insects, you name it. They can turn on the TV, open windows, and poke things into electrical outlets, which is why relatively constant supervision and a childproofed house remain necessary.

Now babies can play games and "hide" by covering their eyes. They can roll a ball back and forth with an adult and throw small objects, making up in persistence for what they lack in skill. Many children begin to feed themselves at this age, using a spoon and holding their own drinking cup. It isn't yet the neatest behavior, but it is a beginning of independent self-care.

From 13 to 18 Months   An 18-month-old weighs up to four times her or his birth weight, but by this age the rate of increase in weight has slowed. Almost all children are walking alone at this age. Some are not yet able to climb stairs, however, and most have considerable difficulty kicking a ball because they can't free one foot. They also find pedaling tricycles or jumping nearly impossible. Figure 5–3 illustrates motor skills related to walking and typical ages by which they are acquired over the first 15 months for U.S. infants.

At 18 months children may be stacking two to four cubes or blocks to build a tower, and they often manage to scribble with a crayon or a pencil. Their ability to feed themselves has improved considerably, and they may be able to undress themselves partly. Many of their actions imitate what they see others doing—"reading" a book, "sweeping" the floor, or where applicable, "chatting" on a toy telephone.

pincer grasp   The method of holding objects, developed at around the age of 12 months, in which the thumb opposes the forefinger.

Figure 5–3 Motor Skills in Walking
Examples of developmental tasks in infancy. The lower edge of each box represents the age at which 25% of all children perform each task; the line across the box, 50%; the upper edge of the box, 75%.

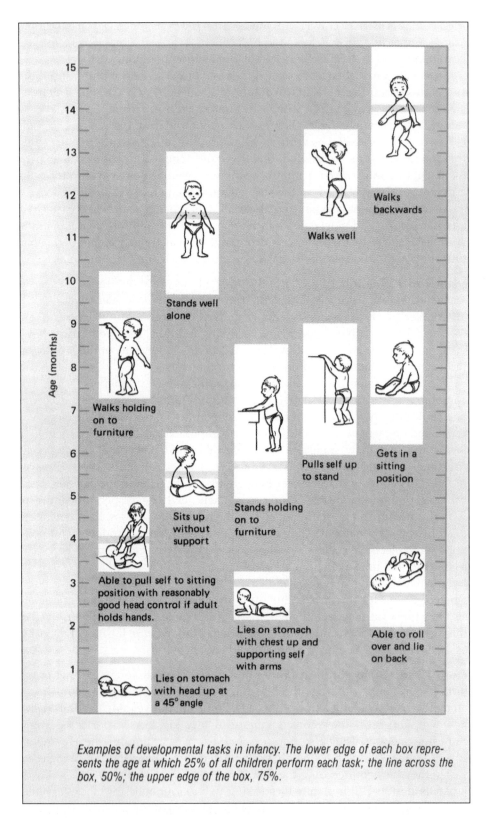

Examples of developmental tasks in infancy. The lower edge of each box represents the age at which 25% of all children perform each task; the line across the box, 50%; the upper edge of the box, 75%.

Source: Adapted from Frankenburg, W. K., & Dodds, J. B. (1967). The Denver Developmental Screening Test. Journal of Pediatrics, 71, *181–191.*

From 19 to 24 Months   By their second birthday, toddlers typically weigh just over four times as much as they did at birth and their rate of growth is continuing to taper off.

Two-year-olds can usually pedal a tricycle, jump in place on both feet, balance briefly on one foot, and throw a ball. They climb up steps. They crawl into, under, and over objects and furniture; they manipulate, carry, handle, push, or pull anything within reach. They pour water, mold clay, stretch the stretchable, bend the bendable. They transport items in carts and wagons. In every way imaginable they explore, test, and probe their physical world. Two-year-olds can also dress and undress with assistance.

If they are given a crayon or pencil, 2-year-olds may scribble and be fascinated with the magical marks that appear. They may stack six to eight blocks or cubes to build towers, and they can construct a three-block "bridge." Their spontaneous block play shows matching of shapes and symmetry.

In sum, physical and motor development during the first 2 years is a complex, dynamic process. For infants to thrive, their basic needs must be met. They must get enough sleep, feel safe, receive consistent care, and have appropriate, stimulating experiences. Each developing system—perceptual and motor skills, for example—supports the others. Brain development, too, depends on the information the child receives from actions and sensory explorations (Lockman & Thelen, 1993). These interacting systems are helped or hindered by the social context in which the infant develops (Hazen & Lockman, 1989; Thelen & Fogel, 1989). Much remains to be learned about how brain maturation and experience interact, in terms of the myriad ways in which experience modifies brain structures—although developmental neuroscientists have made considerable progress. We return to this topic in Chapter 7.

Infant Nutrition and Malnutrition

The United States may be the best-fed nation in the world, but many of its people still suffer from nutritional deficiencies. For example, in 1992 a national program serving low-income families reported that 20 to 24% of their infants suffered from iron deficiency anemia (Pollitt, 1994). Similar figures have been reported for other nutritional deficiencies, and it is likely that cuts in food-stamp programs and related services have increased levels of malnutrition in U.S. low-income families in the years since.

Around the world in many developing nations, the situation is worse. With respect to these nations, the United Nations Children's Fund (UNICEF) has estimated that over 30% of children under age 5 years suffer moderate to severe *stunting* as a result of malnutrition (2000), and the World Health Organization (WHO) has estimated that nearly 30% of humanity of all ages suffer from one or more forms of malnutrition (2000). In turn, almost half of the annual 10 million deaths of children under age 5 in developing nations are associated with malnutrition (WHO, 2000).

Serious deficiencies in the first 30 months of life have effects that are rarely eliminated later. Physical growth may be permanently stunted, resulting in shorter children and adults as well as delays in maturation and learning (Waterlow, 1994). Long-term deficits in brain size, together with deficits in attention and information processing, also occur.

There are two basic types of malnutrition: insufficient total quantity of food and inadequate quantities of foods containing essential vitamins and minerals. With regard to the former, starvation or severe lack of food produces deficiencies in protein and total calorie intake and results in a condition called **marasmus.**

marasmus   Type of malnutrition caused by insufficient total quantity of food where muscles waste away and stored fat is depleted. If duration is short, no long-term negative effects result.

Muscles waste away and stored fat is depleted, although there are no long-term negative effects if the period of starvation is relatively short. Another type of severe malnutrition, called **kwashiorkor,** is caused by insufficient protein. The term, Swahili for "deposed child," refers to an African practice of placing a nursing child in the home of relatives for weaning if the mother becomes pregnant again. Once removed from the mother's protein-rich breastmilk, such children often suffer protein deficiency. The effects of kwashiorkor in the first 3 years of life can be highly damaging in the long run because brain development is directly affected. These and other nutrient deficiencies and their effects on children are summarized in Table 5–4.

For many children, lack of sufficient protein in infancy starts a downward cycle that seriously limits their potential. In Barbados, 129 children who were healthy at birth but malnourished during the first year of life were studied through age 11. With a vigorous public health and nutrition program, the children eventually caught up in most aspects of physical growth, but in academic tests at age 11 they showed an average 12-point deficit compared to matched pairs (Galler, 1984). What went wrong? In a careful follow-up study using parent interviews, teacher reports, and observation of the children, two findings emerged. First, the children's behavior was characterized by impulsiveness and attention deficit. Second, their parents, most of whom had also been through periods of protein malnutrition, had low energy and symptoms of depression. They could not provide a stimulating, focused, or consistent environment for their children (Salt, Galler, & Ramsey, 1988). Parental depression and hopelessness, together with impulsive and inattentive children, are commonly found in studies of protein malnutrition (e.g., Lozoff, 1989).

Even in cases of severe malnutrition during infancy, food supplement programs combined with education can produce dramatic results. In a study in Bogota, Colombia, poverty-level children who were given food supplements for the first 3 years of life showed much less growth retardation and all-around better functioning than comparison groups who did not participate in the pro-

kwashiorkor Type of severe malnutrition caused by insufficient protein. In first three years of life, this can be highly damaging in the long run because brain development is affected.

Table 5-4 **Some Important Nutrient Deficiencies and How They Affect Children**

Iodine deficiency

Mental retardation, deaf-mutism, and goiter (an enlargement of the thyroid gland that results in either hypothyroidism or hypothyrodism, in turn with effects on growth)

Iron deficiency

Anemia, impaired psychomotor development and coordination, decreased activity level

Protein deficiency

Kwashiorkor and stunting (see text)

Protein-calorie deficiency

Marasmus and stunting (see text)

Vitamin A deficiency

Severe visual impairment to blindness and markedly increased susceptibility to common childhood diseases

Primary source: Adapted from World Health Organization (WHO) (2000). "Malnutrition—the global picture." Reprinted with permission from the World Health Organization. www.who.int

gram. The improvement was still evident 3 years after the supplements were discontinued (Super, Herrera, & Mora, 1990). For over a decade now, establishing and maintaining programs that get enough food and the right kinds of food to the children of the world have been top priorities for both WHO and UNICEF.

In the United States, severe forms of malnutrition are rare, but protein and iron deficiencies are quite common. Many people who can afford a good diet often consume too many "empty calories" in the form of foods that are high in carbohydrates but low in protein, vitamins, and minerals. Many people who ingest too few calories cannot afford protein-rich foods. As with peoples of many developing nations, the diets of U.S. people at or below the poverty level also most often lack the other nutrients in Table 5–4 (Eichorn, 1979).

Breastfeeding Versus Bottlefeeding Mother's milk is the major source of nutrients for infants. For women who can nurse, breastfeeding is typically used almost exclusively for the first 6 months; after that, complementary foods are necessary to maintain the baby's health and growth. Breastfeeding together with solid foods then continues for the next 6 to 12 months and in many cases beyond 24 months. Throughout the world many women breastfeed their infants, and the numbers are apparently on the rise as a result of urgings by WHO, UNICEF, AAP, and numerous other organizations concerned with infant health. The U.S. Surgeon General now also recommends breastfeeding. Table 5–5 presents percentages of babies being breastfed in selected developing regions of the world, based on data from 1990 to 1999.

A unified front favors breastfeeding because the breastmilk of a well-fed mother contains a remarkably well-balanced combination of nutrients and other beneficial substances. As noted by UNICEF (1998),

. . . Breastmilk contains all the nutrients, antibodies, hormones and antioxidants an infant needs to thrive. . . . Breastfed infants not only show better immune responses to immunizations, but their intake of breastmilk also

Experts agree that, when possible, breastfeeding is greatly preferable to bottlefeeding.

Table 5-5   Percentages of Babies Being Breastfed in Developing Nations, by Regions of the World

	Exclusively breastfed (0–3 MONTHS)	Breastfed with complementary feeding FOOD (6–9 MONTHS)	Still breastfeeding (20–26 MONTHS)
Sub-Saharan Africa	31	66	49
Middle East and North Africa	41	45	33
South Asia	45	36	68
East Asia and Pacific	59	74	(no data)
Latin America and Caribbean	39	45	23

Source: Reproduced with permission from UNICEF, The State of the World's Children 2000, Table 2, New York, 2000, www.unicef.org.

protects the mucous membranes that line their gastrointestinal and respiratory tracts, thus shielding them against diarrhea and upper respiratory tract infections. (p. 22)

UNICEF went on to point out that in developing nations where infant mortality rates are high, bottlefed babies are 14 times more likely to die from diarrhea and 4 times more likely to die from respiratory diseases such axs pnemonia.

Even a malnourished mother's milk can provide adequate nutrients, although often at a cost to her own health. Breastmilk suits most babies. In addition, breastmilk is always fresh and ready at the right temperature, does not need refrigeration, and is normally sterile. Unless the mother is very ill, has an inadequate diet, or uses alcohol or other drugs, breastmilk is better for a baby's health.

Despite these advantages, many mothers still choose bottlefeeding (again, see Table 5–5). Bottlefeeding causes no hardship or nutritional problems for the great majority of infants in developed nations, but the shift to commercial infant formula has resulted in widespread malnutrition in lower-income nations (UNICEF, 1998). Malnutrition occurs when people lack the money to buy what are for them extremely expensive breastmilk substitutes. In addition, many babies die when commercial formula is diluted with contaminated water, thereby transmitting bacterial diseases to the infant.

Why do some mothers breastfeed and others bottlefeed? It appears that good nutrition is only one of many factors influencing the choice. Obviously, cultural factors, personal factors (such as allocating time to work and child care, social obligations, and the availability of a peer group that accepts breastfeeding), and even national policies may have an effect. For example, until recently the United States lacked a family-leave policy. Many women who returned to work a few weeks after the birth of their child found it difficult to combine full-time employment with breastfeeding, although nowadays an increasing number of companies are providing rooms with lactation equipment and refrigeration to allow mothers to collect their breastmilk during each workday and have it given to the baby the next.

Weaning and Introduction of Solid Foods   Some mothers in industrialized nations begin weaning their babies from the breast at 3 to 4 months or even earlier; others continue breastfeeding for as long as two to three years. Although extended breastfeeding is rare among middle- and upper-class mothers in the United States, two to three years is not unusual among certain ethnic groups.

Normally, at about 3 months infants gradually start accepting strained foods. Usually they begin with simple cereals such as rice, and expand to a variety of cereals and pureed fruits, followed later by strained vegetables and meats. Some infants are allergic to specific foods; others respond well to almost everything nutritious that is offered to them. By 8 months most infants are eating a broad range of specially prepared foods, and milk consumption is usually reduced.

Weaning is a crucial time because of the possibility of malnutrition, as we saw earlier. Particularly vulnerable are 1-year-olds who have already been weaned from the breast in families that cannot afford nutritious foods. Such children may survive on diets composed of potato chips, dry cereals, and cookies—foods that typically provide calories but few nutrients. Even if enough milk or a variety of nutritious foods are available, however, 1-year-olds may be unwilling to drink a sufficient amount of milk from a cup or eat protein-rich foods.

After weaning, infants gradually acquire skills in feeding themselves.

CONTENT CHECK
PHYSICAL AND MOTOR DEVELOPMENT

True–False (answers are on the Companion Website)

1. Most newborn reflexes disappear within the first month of life.
2. Most infants are capable of visually guided reach by the middle of the first year of life.
3. Childproofing the home is not necessary until infants begin to walk.
4. Malnutrition is extremely rare in the United States.
5. Experts agree that in most cases breastfeeding is much better than bottlefeeding.

Thinking Critically

In what ways are physical and motor development a dynamic system?

Sensory and Perceptual Development

Can newborn babies see patterns and the details of objects? Can they see color and depth? Can they hear a low whisper? How sensitive are they to touch? Research indicates that all of the senses are operating at birth. Thus, **sensation**—the translation of external stimulation into neural impulses—is highly developed. In contrast, **perception**—the active process of interpreting information from the senses—is limited and selective at birth. Perception is a cognitive process that gives organization and meaning to sensory information. It develops rapidly over the first 6 months, followed by fine tuning over the first several years of life.

The 1960s through the 1990s saw a profiloration of research on infant perceptual capabilities and development, along with methods to study perception in children too young to talk about what they perceive. Basic research methods and some of the more revealing findings are the focus of this section.

Studying Infant Perceptual Capabilities

Basic physiological measures provide information about infants' reactions to environmental stimulation. Heart activity and the electrical response of the skin can provide information about what infants perceive and understand. Researchers also use highly refined videotapes of an infant's movements—for example, eye movement or hand manipulation. However, technology is only part of the answer. A good research *paradigm* (method or model) is just as important.

Classical conditioning, operant conditioning, and habituation, as discussed in Chapter 3 and earlier in this chapter, have been used extensively in assessing infant sensory and memory capabilities. Simply put, an infant can't be conditioned to respond to stimuli that the infant can't perceive.

An especially useful strategy in measuring infant competencies is the **novelty paradigm,** which is closely related to the habituation method. Babies quickly tire of looking at the same image or playing with the same toy. They habituate to repeated sights and often show their lack of interest by looking away. If given a choice between a familiar toy and a new one, most infants will choose the new one, provided that they can perceive the difference. Among other things, researchers use this approach in setting up experiments to determine

sensation   The translation of a stimulus by a sense organ.

perception   The complex process by which the mind interprets and gives meaning to sensory information.

novelty paradigm   A research plan that uses infants' preferences for new stimuli over familiar ones to investigate their ability to detect small differences in sounds, patterns, or colors.

how small a difference in sound, pattern, or color young infants are capable of detecting.

Another popular approach is the **preference method,** in which infants are given a choice between stimuli to look at or listen to. Researchers record which stimulus the infant attends to more. If an infant consistently spends more time attending to one of the two stimuli, the preference indicates that the infant can both perceive a difference and respond to it. The preference method can also be combined with behaviors such as sucking as discussed earlier. Here, a neonate might be required to suck at a specific rate to produce a preferred outcome, such as hearing a recording of mother's voice instead of that of another woman (e.g., DeCasper & Fifer, 1987).

The **surprise paradigm** is a yet another useful way of studying infants' understanding of the world around them. Humans tend to register surprise—through facial expression, physical reaction, or vocal response—when something happens that they don't expect, or conversely, when something doesn't happen that they do expect. Infants' surprise reactions can be assessed by measuring changes in their breathing and heart rate as well as simply observing their facial expressions or bodily movements.

Variations of each of the above methods continue to be used by many researchers, but a newer approach called the **event-related potential (ERP) method** has become increasingly popular with developmental neuroscientists. In one procedure, a cap with an extensive array of harmless electrodes is carefully positioned on the infant's head to obtain the equivalent of a complex *electroencephalograph*—a graph of brain-wave activity. Through computer analysis, often-subtle changes in brain-wave patterns can then be correlated with changes in the infant's environment to study perceptual and other capabilities—as well as to study specific areas of brain functioning in response to different kinds of stimulation.

Vision and Visual Perception

From anatomical research we know that infants are born with a full, intact set of visual structures. From perceptual research it appears that there is an innate although immature organization of the visual system—a newborn's visual world is in some respects quite coherent (Slater & Johnson, 1998). Although most of these structures and this organization must develop further over the next few months, neonates do have some visual skills. Newborns' eyes are sensitive to brightness; their pupils contract in bright light and dilate in darkness. They have some control over eye movements, and they can visually track (follow) an object such as a face or a doctor's penlight as it moves across their field of vision.

It has long been known that newborns focus optimally on objects at a range of 7 to 10 inches (17.8 to 25.4 centimeters), with objects closer or further away appearing blurred. Thus, they are nearly blind to details of objects on the far side of a room (Banks & Salapatek, 1983). Newborns also lack fine convergence of the eyes, which means that they can't focus both eyes on a single point. They cannot focus effectively until about the end of the second month (Fantz, 1961).

It is clear that newborns can visually perceive their environment, within limits, because they are selective about what they look at. Classic research indicates that newborns prefer to look at moderately complex patterns. They look primarily at the edges and contours of objects, especially curves (Roskinski, 1977). Newborn babies are therefore highly responsive to the human face (Fantz, 1958). It is not surprising, then, that they normally develop the ability to recognize their mothers' faces quite early, which may have had survival

preference method A research plan that gives infants a choice between stimuli to look at or listen to. If an infant consistently spends more time attending to one of the two stimuli, the preference indicates that the infant can both perceive a difference and deliberately respond to it.

surprise paradigm A research technique used to test infants' memory and expectations. Infants cannot report what they remember or expect, but if their expectations are violated, they respond with surprise.

event-related potential (ERP) method A method for testing infants whereby electrodes carefully positioned on the head obtain a graph of brain-wave activity, which is then used to study perceptual and other capabilities and specifics of brain function in response to different kinds of stimulation.

value at some point in our evolutionary history and is still highly adaptive in augmenting infant-caregiver attachment (Chapter 6). An experiment by Genevieve Carpenter (1974) showed that newborns can recognize mother's face as early as 2 weeks after birth, given sufficient interaction. Using the preference method, Carpenter presented each infant with pictures of its familiar mother and an unfamiliar woman; 2-week-olds preferred to look at the mother. In some cases infants turn their heads completely away from an unfamiliar face (MacFarlane, 1978).

One of the more remarkable examples of visual perception in neonates is their seeming ability to imitate facial expressions. Imitation has been demonstrated with infants no more than 2 or 3 days old. Researchers wait for a time when the neonate is alert, calm, and not too hungry, and therefore is most receptive (Gardner & Karmel, 1984). The infant and adult look at each other, and the adult goes through a random series of scripted expressions such as pursing the lips, sticking out the tongue, and opening the mouth. In between, the adult presents a neutral facial expression. Analysis of videotapes reveals remarkable consistency in infants' matching of the adult's expressions (Field, Woodson, Greenberg, & Cohen, 1982; Meltzoff & Moore, 1977, 1989, 1997), as illustrated in Figure 5–4. Although it has been argued that newborns perform

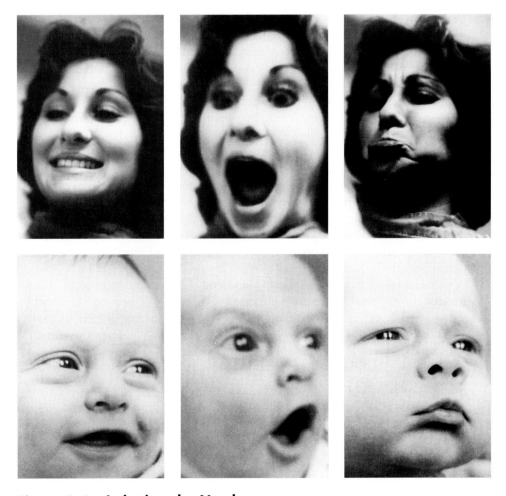

Figure 5–4 Imitations by Newborns
Although some theorists disagree, it seems clear that very young neonates are capable of behaviors that closely resemble imitation.

The coordinating of vision with reaching—the visually guided reach—is one of the milestones in development.

such behaviors in response to a variety of stimuli—or perhaps reflexively—and might not strictly be imitating (e.g., see Jones, 1996), it does appear that they see the stimuli and respond to them in a selective way that at least resembles imitation.

How relevant are infant visual preferences? Early behavioral competencies such as gazing at familiar objects (like the mother's or father's face) and imitating facial expressions are important factors in developing and sustaining early attachment between infant and parents, as noted. A baby who alertly explores the mother's face, or is soothed when held by a familiar father, helps the parents feel competent too.

Early Development of Visual Perception   In the first 4 to 6 months, infants' visual abilities improve rapidly. Even before they can grasp or crawl, they explore their world visually. Focusing ability improves rapidly; 3- to 4-month-olds focus almost as well as adults (Aslin, 1987). Infants' visual acuity also sharpens dramatically (Banks & Dannemiller, 1987; Fantz, Ordy, & Udelf, 1962).

Color discrimination improves steadily during the first year. Although newborns can discriminate some bright colors (Adams, Courage, & Mercer, 1995), they prefer black-and-white patterns over colored ones for the first 1 to 2 months—probably because of the greater contrast. By 2 months, infants pick out more subtle colors like blue, purple, or chartreuse when compared with gray. By 3 months, they can discriminate among most colors (Adams & Courage, 1995), and by 6 months their color perception nearly equals that of adults (Maurer & Maurer, 1988; Teller & Bornstein, 1987).

From the beginning, as noted earlier, infants are selective in what they look at. They prefer novel and moderately complex patterns and human faces. Some preferences change over the first year, however. By 2 months, infants look at internal features of the face such as the eyes. By 4 months, they prefer a regularly arranged face over a distorted one. By 5 months, they look at the mouth of a person who is talking. By 6 to 7 months they respond to whole facial expressions and can discriminate differing expressions such as "happy" versus "fearful" (Nelson & de Haan, 1996). Interestingly, research also indicates that 6-month-olds' brain activity consistently differs in response to faces compared to objects—as does that of adults (de Haan & Nelson, 1999). In addition, researchers have found that 6-month-olds have a preference for "attractive" faces (Rubenstein, Kalakanis, & Langlois, 1999). Because these behaviors occur at too early an age to have been learned, it again appears that much of facial perception is prewired.

Other marked improvements in vision and visual perception occur during the first six months. Older infants are better able to control their eye movements; they can track moving objects more consistently and for longer periods (Aslin, 1987). They also spend more time scanning and surveying their environment. By 3 or 4 months, infants can also use motion as well as shape and spatial positioning to help define the objects in their world (Mandler, 1990; Spelke, 1988).

Depth and Distance Perception   A key aspect of visual perception is seeing that some things are closer and others are farther away. Even with one eye closed (monocular vision), we can determine the approximate distance of objects using the sorts of cues that cartoon artists rely on. For example, objects that are close to us appear larger, and they block our view of more distant objects. In turn, if you close one eye and hold your head still, the view resembles a two-dimensional photograph. But if you move your head, the world comes to life with its three-dimensional aspect. If you use both eyes (binocular vision), you don't have to move your head because the left-eye view and the right-eye view differ slightly. Your brain integrates the two images, giving you information about distance and depth.

A question that has long interested researchers is exactly when infants develop depth perception. Are their brains preprogrammed to integrate the images from the two eyes to gain information about distance or relative size? Can they use the information produced by moving their heads to see the world in three dimensions?

Although lack of convergence of the eyes probably limits neonatal depth perception, it appears that a neonate's brain can integrate binocular images in rudimentary form. Because a newborn's eyes are not well coordinated and the infant has not yet learned how to interpret all of the information transmitted by the eyes, early depth perception is probably not very sophisticated. It takes about 4 months for binocular vision to emerge (Aslin & Smith, 1988).

However, even infants as young as 6 weeks use spatial cues to react defensively. They dodge, blink, or show other forms of avoidance when an object appears to be coming directly at them (Dodwell, Humphrey, & Muir, 1987). By 2 months infants react defensively to an object on a collision course. In addition, they prefer three-dimensional figures to two-dimensional ones. At 4 months, infants can swipe with reasonable accuracy at a toy that is dangled in front of them. By 5 to 6 months, they also have a well-controlled, visually guided reach, as noted earlier.

A classic approach to assessing infants' depth perception uses the "visual cliff" created by Eleanor Gibson and colleagues (Gibson & Walk, 1960) to simulate depth (see Figure 5–5). On one side of the horizontal surface, a heavy piece of glass covers a solid surface. On the other side, the glass is well above the floor, simulating a cliff. Infants 6 months or older refuse to crawl across the cliff. Younger infants who are not yet able to crawl show interest, but not

Figure 5–5 A Visual Cliff Apparatus
Even when coaxed by their mothers, infants 6 months or over will not crawl over the edge of the visual cliff.

distress, when placed on the cliff (Campos, Langer, & Krowitz, 1970). These findings indicate that younger infants are also able to discriminate among spatial cues for depth.

Further studies focused on the factors that determine whether babies will cross the deep side. If the mother is encouraging, the baby can be coaxed to cross the deep side if the depth is relatively shallow (Kermoian & Campos, 1988). However, the same baby will refuse to cross if the mother signals that it is dangerous by speaking anxiously or otherwise expressing fear.

In sum, it appears that an understanding of visual cues for depth perception develops within the first 4 to 6 months (Yonas & Owsley, 1987). The meaning of distance or depth is learned more gradually, however, as the child begins to move about in the environment. Sensory-perceptual maturation and the psychosocial environment interact to guide development.

Audition and Auditory Perception

It is obvious that newborn infants can hear. They're startled by loud sounds. They're soothed by low-pitched sounds such as lullabies, and they fuss when they hear high-pitched squeaks and whistles. How refined is neonatal hearing?

The anatomical structures for hearing are well developed in the newborn. For the first few weeks, however, there is excess fluid and tissue in the middle ear, and hearing is believed to be muffled—similar to the way you hear if you have a head cold. Moreover, the brain structures for transmitting and interpreting auditory information are not fully developed at birth. Brain structures pertaining to hearing will continue to develop until the child is about 2 years old (Aslin, 1987; Shatz, 1992). Despite such limitations, however, newborns can respond to a wide range of sounds.

Infants can also localize the sources of sounds. Even in their first few days of life they will turn their head toward a sound or a voice. Later, somewhat after they develop visually guided reach, they can localize objects in the dark as well by using sound cues (Clifton, Rochat, Robin, & Berthier, 1994; LaGasse, Van Vorst, Brunner, & Zucker, 1999).

Early Development of Auditory Perception   Neonates prefer human voices, and beyond that, mother's voice in particular. This is likely because of neonates' regular exposure to mother's voice prior to birth. Moreover, in studies where researchers had mothers read certain passages aloud prior to the birth of their child, it was found that neonates later preferred those passages over novel ones—indicating an early capability for relatively complex speech discrimination (DeCasper, Lecanuet, Busnel, & Granier-Deferre, 1994; De-Casper & Spence, 1986), which we return to later in the chapter.

Acuity of hearing improves considerably over the first few months. Although it takes several weeks for the fluid in the middle ear to dissipate, neonates show changes in heart rate and breathing in response to moderate tone levels such as those that are typical of a telephone conversation. Infants can also be soothed, alerted, or distressed by sounds. Low-frequency or rhythmic sounds generally soothe infants. Loud, sudden, or high-frequency tones cause them distress. Such behaviors imply that infants have fairly well-developed auditory perception within the first 6 months of life.

As with neonates, the older infant is also especially attentive to human speech. By 4 months the infant will smile more in response to his or her mother's voice than to another woman's voice. By 6 months the infant shows distress on hearing her or his mother's voice if she or he cannot see her, and mother's mere talking to the infant from another room—perhaps while preparing food or a bottle—is no longer an effective soother.

Taste, Smell, and Touch

The senses of taste and smell are fully operational at birth. Newborns discriminate among sweet, salty, sour, and bitter tastes, as evidenced by facial expressions (Rosenstein & Oster, 1988). They react negatively to strong odors and are selectively attracted to positive odors, such as those of a lactating mother (Makin & Porter, 1989). As early as 6 days of age, infants can distinguish the smell of their mother from that of another woman, and they prefer the familiar scent (MacFarlane, 1978; Makin & Porter, 1989).

The sense of touch is well developed even in preterm newborns. Regular stroking of tiny preterm infants in their incubators helps regulate their breathing and other bodily processes. Simply holding newborns' arms or legs is often enough to soothe them. Swaddling has a similar effect (Brazelton, 1969).

Infants have a limited number of behavioral schemes in their repertoire. Looking, mouthing, gasping, and bumping are ways they interact with their environment.

Sensory Integration and Intermodal Perception

Researchers generally agree about the extent to which the individual senses are present and operative at birth or soon after, but there has been much disagreement as to whether neonatal senses are fully *integrated* or coordinated. For example, with regard to audition and vision, does a young infant know that a particular sound comes from a particular object?

Research generally indicates that either the senses are integrated at birth or integration occurs early and rapidly. In one classic study, infants were allowed to suck on either of two different pacifiers, one covered with bumps and the other smooth. When the pacifier was removed and the infants were simply shown each pacifier, they looked longer at the one that they had just felt in their mouth (Meltzoff & Borton, 1979). In another study 4-month-olds were shown two novel films with a soundtrack that matched only one film. The infants preferred to look at the film that matched the sound (Kuhl & Meltzoff, 1988), indicating visual-auditory integration. Compatible results have been obtained with 6-month-olds matching male and female faces with voices (Walker-Andrews, Bahrick, Raglioni, & Diaz, 1991), with 7-month-olds using matched versus mismatched facial expressions and vocalizations (Soken & Pick, 1999), and by numerous other researchers (see Lickliter & Bahrick, 2000). It has even been found that newborns only a few *hours* old can readily learn arbitrary pairings of sights and sounds (Morrongiello, Fenwick, & Chance, 1998).

Sensory and especially perceptual integration must also be learned, of course. Infants must learn which sounds go with which sights, what soft fur feels and looks like, what the noisy puppy looks like, and so on. Nevertheless, it appears that infants have a built-in tendency to seek out such cognitive links. Integration then advances rapidly over the first year. Researchers who compare intermodal perception at different ages during infancy consistently find that older infants are better at it. Research on the visual cliff makes a similar point. Although young infants recognize depth on the visual cliff, they do not necessarily recognize it as unsafe; they are more interested than afraid. Older infants with a higher level of integration are warier of the deep side. Behavior and emotions become integrated over time as a result of the interaction of experience and maturation.

CONTENT CHECK
SENSORY AND PERCEPTUAL DEVELOPMENT

True–False (answers are on the Companion Website)
1. The preference method is closely related to the habituation method.
2. Within about a few days after birth, visual and auditory perceptual capabilities are well developed.
3. Within the first couple of weeks of life, infants can recognize mother's face and voice.
4. Research indicates that the senses are integrated at or soon after birth.
5. The senses of taste, smell, and touch are well developed at birth.

Thinking Critically
What early infant visual capabilities show evidence of prewiring and therefore evolution?

Cognitive Development

Cognition is a set of interrelated processes through which we gain and use knowledge about our world. It includes thinking, learning, perceiving, remembering, and understanding. *Cognitive development* refers to the growth and refinement of intellectual processes. In this section we explore various approaches to studying and describing cognitive development during the first 2 years of life.

The Active Mind

Many theorists believe that infants take an active role in their cognitive development. This was the basic position of Jean Piaget. Piaget saw infants as active, alert, creative beings who possess mental structures called *schemes* or *schemas* (Chapter 2) that process and organize information. Over time, schemes develop into more complex cognitive structures. This occurs in a series of stages that may begin at somewhat different ages but always follow the same sequence.

The Sensorimotor Period

Piaget called the first period of development the **sensorimotor period.** Infants enter the world prepared to respond to their environment with extensive sensory-perceptual and motor capabilities. According to Piaget, basic sensorimotor behavior patterns—which begin as reflexes—enable infants to form schemes through the process of assimilation and accommodation. Ready-made behavioral schemes such as looking, visually following, sucking, grasping, and crying are the building blocks for cognitive development. Over the next 24 months they are transformed into early concepts of objects, people, and self. Thus, sensorimotor behavior is where intelligence begins.

Adaptation Infant schemes are developed and modified by the process that Piaget called **adaptation,** which refers to the general tendency to adjust to and mentally incorporate elements of our environment. As an example, he described how his 7-month-old daughter, Lucienne, played with a pack of cigarettes. Unlike a 2-year-old, who might (regrettably) take out a cigarette and

sensorimotor period Piaget's first period of cognitive development (from birth to about 2 years).

adaptation In Piaget's theory, the process by which infant schemes are elaborated, modified, and developed.

pretend to smoke it, Lucienne treated the pack of cigarettes as if it were any other toy or object that she was accustomed to handling. Looking, mouthing, grasping, and banging were her only toy-manipulating schemes. In other words, she *assimilated* the pack of cigarettes into her existing schemes.

With each new object, children make minor changes in their action patterns. Grasping and mouthing *accommodate* new objects. Gradually, these action patterns become modified and the infant's basic sensorimotor schemes develop into more complex cognitive capacities. Beginning with *circular reactions*, which are simple, repetitive behaviors that are primarily reflexive in nature, much of young infants' learning takes place quite by accident. An action occurs, and infants see, hear, or feel it. For example, babies may notice their hands in front of their faces. By moving their hands, they discover that they can change what they see. They can prolong the event, repeat it, stop it, or start it again. Infants' early circular reactions involve the discovery of their own bodies. Later circular reactions involve how they use their bodies or themselves to change the environment, as in making a toy move.

Sensorimotor Stages   Piaget viewed the sensorimotor period as six fairly discrete stages, which are briefly outlined in Table 5–6. A detailed discussion of each stage is beyond the scope of this book, but we do consider some of the processes and cognitive achievements that occur as Piaget's stages unfold.

Play with Objects   Often-subtle accomplishments in object play are important to children's cognitive development. By 5 months infants reach out and grasp. Such seemingly simple skills—together with advancing perceptual skills—equip infants for progressively more varied play with objects. Infants remember repeated events, match their actions appropriately with various objects, and develop their understanding of the social world through pretending and imitating. Play, in other words, lays the groundwork for further complex thought and language.

Object play goes through identifiable stages, starting with simple explorations at about 5 months (Garvey, 1977). By 9 months most infants explore objects. They wave them around, turn them over, and test them by hitting them

Table 5–6   Piaget's Six Stages of Sensorimotor Development

Stage	Age	Key Features
One	0–1 month	Exercising reflexes: sucking, grasping, looking, listening
Two	1–4 months	Adaptations of basic sensory and motor patterns (e.g., sucking different objects)
Three	4–8 months	Developing strategies for making interesting sights last
Four	8–12 months	Actions become more purposeful; brief search for hidden objects
Five	12–18 months	Active exploration through trial and error (the "little scientist")
Six	18–24 months	Thinking before doing, using mental combinations

Source: Adapted from Flavell, 1963.

By 6 or 7 months, infants are greatly improved in their ability to imitate gestures and actions.

against other objects, although they are not yet aware of their use or function. By 12 months infants examine objects closely before putting them in their mouths. By 15 to 18 months they try to use objects appropriately. For example, they may pretend to drink from a cup or brush their hair with a toy brush. By 21 months, they use many objects appropriately. They try to feed a doll with a spoon, put a doll in the driver's seat of a toy truck, or use keys to unlock an imaginary door. Play becomes even more realistic by 24 months. Toddlers take dolls out for walks and line up trucks and trailers in the right order. By 3 years of age, children may see dolls as imaginary people. They may have a doll go outdoors, chop wood, bring it back inside, and put it in an imaginary fireplace (Bornstein & O'Reilly, 1993; Fein, 1981).

Imitation   It can easily be seen that the object play of 2-year-olds is rich with imitations of the world as they see it. Imitation, however, also has simple beginnings in early infancy.

Within the first 2 months, infants do some sporadic imitation in the context of play with caregivers. As discussed earlier, a neonate may imitate facial expressions. However, early imitations of facial expressions disappear at 2 to 3 months, not to reappear until several months later (Meltzoff & Moore, 1989).

At 3 to 4 months, babies and mothers often begin to play a game of "talking" to each other in which the infant appears to be trying to match the sounds of the mother's voice. Typically, however, the mother begins the game by imitating the infant, and it can be hard to tell who is imitating whom (Uzgiris, 1984). By 6 or 7 months, infants can imitate gestures and actions fairly accurately. The first hand gestures to be imitated are those for which infants already have *action schemes* such as reaching and grasping. By 9 months, infants can imitate novel gestures such as banging two objects together. During the second year, infants begin to imitate entire series of actions or gestures. At first infants imitate only actions that they choose themselves. Later, at the request of caregivers, they imitate cleaning their teeth or using eating implements such as a fork or spoon or chopsticks. Some toddlers even toilet-train themselves by imitating an older child or a caregiver.

Does imitation require a mental representation of the action? Is it thinking? Piaget believed that even simple imitation is a complex mix of behavioral schemes. Thus, he predicted that infants would not be capable of imitating novel actions until they were at least 9 months old. He also believed that **deferred imitation**—imitating something that happened hours or even days before—requires cognitive skills that are not present in the first 18 months.

However, it is now clear that infants can imitate novel actions considerably earlier than Piaget predicted. For example, children of deaf parents begin to learn and use sign language as early as 6 or 7 months (Mandler, 1988). Researchers have also demonstrated that infants are capable of deferred imitation well before 18 months. One study (Meltzoff, 1988a, 1988b) used novel toys, such as a box with a hidden button that would sound a beep and a toy bear that would dance when jiggled with a string. Infants were shown these actions but were not given the opportunity to perform them right away. The researchers found that 11-month-olds could reproduce the actions up to 24 hours later, and 14-month-olds could reproduce them as much as a week later. Subsequent research has demonstrated deferred imitation after a 24-hour delay with infants as young as 6 months of age (Barr, Dowden, & Hayne, 1996; Collie & Hayne, 1999), although these infants require more exposure to the target behaviors than older infants do. It is also worth noting that young infants display apparently stable individual differences in the capability for deferred imitation (Heimann & Meltzoff, 1996): Some are consistently better than others independent of age.

deferred imitation   Imitating something that happened hours or even days earlier.

Object Permanence According to Piaget, **object permanence** is a major accomplishment of the sensorimotor period. Object permanence is the awareness that objects exist in time and space, whether or not they are present and in view. According to Piaget, the development of object permanence is not complete before about 18 months, although infants form an idea of their mother's or father's permanence as early as 8 months. With regard to objects in general, "out of sight, out of mind" seems to be literally true throughout much of early infancy. If a young infant doesn't see something, that something doesn't exist. Thus, a covered toy holds no interest even if the infant continues to hold onto it under the cover.

The development of object permanence involves a series of cognitive accomplishments. First, as early as 2 months infants are able to recognize familiar objects. For example, they become excited at the sight of a bottle or their caregivers. Second, at about 2 months infants may watch a moving object disappear behind one side of a screen and then shift their eyes to the other side to see if the object reappears. Their visual tracking is excellent and well timed, and they are surprised if something does not reappear. However, they do not seem to mind when a completely different object appears from behind the screen. In fact, infants up to 5 months old will accept a wide variety of changes in disappearing objects with no distress (Bower, 1971).

Infants more than 5 months old are more discriminating trackers. They are disturbed if a different object appears or if the same object reappears but moves faster or more slowly than before. Even these older infants, however, can be fooled. Imagine two screens side by side with a gap in the middle. An object disappears behind one screen, say from the left; it does not appear in the gap, but it does reappear from behind the second screen, to the right (also see "A Closer Look," p. 186).

Searching for hidden objects also proceeds through a predictable sequence. Infants less than 5 months old typically do not search or hunt; they seem to forget about an object once it is hidden. Beginning between 5 and 8 months, however, infants will engage in and greatly enjoy hiding-and-finding games with objects. They also like being hidden under a blanket or covering their eyes with their hands and having the world reappear when they take their hands away. The searching abilities of infants up to 12 months old still have limitations, however. If a toy disappears through a trapdoor and another reappears when the door is reopened, they are surprised, but they accept the new toy. Older infants, between 12 and 18 months, are puzzled; they search for the first toy.

Some irregularities persist in 12-month-olds' searching behavior. If a toy is hidden in one place and they expect to find it there, 8- to 12-month-olds will continue looking for it there even when they have seen it hidden in another place. Piaget (1936/1952) suggested that at this age infants have two conflicting memories—one of seeing the object hidden and another of finding it—that, plus an immature object concept.

However, not everyone agrees with Piaget's interpretation of such hiding experiments. The "A-not-B" error (so called because the infant searches for an object that was previously hidden at location A even when it is now hidden at location B) has been thoroughly researched and has proved to be a universal phenomenon, but researchers still disagree on what it implies about infant cognition (Smith, Thelen, Titzer, & McLin, 1999). Do infants know the object still exists even though hidden? Do infants actually believe that the object is still at location A? Esther Thelen and colleagues take a different view, based not on what an infant *knows* but rather on what an infant *does*. In essence, noting that obtaining the effect depends upon first repeatedly hiding the object at location A, they propose

object permanence According to Piaget, the beginning realization in infants at about 8 months that objects continue to exist when they are out of sight.

A CLOSER LOOK

CATS, HORSES, AND TROUBLESOME RABBITS

What evidence is there that young infants have perceptual concepts like squareness, or cats versus tigers, or horses versus zebras, or animals versus vehicles, or male versus female? Some researchers have concluded that infants acquire these categories or perceptual schemas before Piaget predicted they do and well before they acquire productive language.

Peter Eimas and Paul Quinn (1994) studied the formation of perceptually based categories in infants as young as 3 months of age. A viewing box was placed around each infant as the infant sat comfortably on mother's lap. The viewing box displayed two pictures at a time. Six times in a row, the infants viewed two color pictures of different horses while researchers measured how long the infant looked at each picture. The seventh time, the infant was shown two more pictures—one of a new horse, the other of a new animal (a zebra, a cat, or a giraffe). The researchers then observed whether the infants looked more at the new animal.

Eimas and Quinn found that the infants looked longer at the new kind of animal. Similarly, infants who were shown pictures of cats six times in a row looked more at a tiger than a cat on the seventh presentation. In each case, in the view of the researchers, the infants had apparently formed a perceptual category (horses or cats) and then habituated to it. Not all of the infants did so, however; some preferred looking at horses or cats regardless.

Other studies appear to demonstrate inferential processing by young infants. In an experiment conducted by Renée Baillargeon and Julie DeVos (1991), 5½- to 6½-month-old infants sat in an infant seat and watched a short rabbit and a tall rabbit cross behind an opaque screen and come out the other side. The researchers then placed a new screen with a window near the top in front of the infants. As the infants watched, the short rabbit crossed behind the screen and reappeared on the other side. This rabbit was too short to appear in the window, so the infants were comfortable with the sequence. Next, the tall rabbit crossed behind the screen, but didn't appear in the window—an "impossible event." The infants did a double-take and looked back at the window. It was clear, from the per-plexed expression on the infants' faces, that the infants realized that all was not right.

To complicate matters further, the researchers made a small change at the beginning: Momentarily, the infants saw two tall rabbits. Infants who watched the same sequence of events after seeing the two tall rabbits were not terribly perplexed when one of them did not appear in the window before emerging on the other side. Could the infants have concluded that the two tall rabbits changed places—one went in and the other came out? We can't know, but clearly something in their thinking was different.

Experiments such as these indicate that infants are capable of making inferences about what they perceive on the basis of what they have just seen and remembered. They also provide evidence that infants understand some properties of objects before they hunt for them (Mandler, 1992). Could it be that, in some preliminary way, infants have enough conceptual ability to be bothered by impossible events and that they understand object permanence well before Piaget believed they could?

that the memory of repeatedly reaching to that location dominates even when the object is hidden at location B. That is, the error is not a result of immature cognitive structures or lack of the object concept as assumed by Piaget. It is instead attributable to the dynamic interplay of looking, reaching, and remembering, the integration of which is still developing in this age range.

As Renée Baillargeon put it, young infants might fail such tasks because they have ". . . [d]ifficulties associated with the planning and execution of action sequences" (1994, p. 133), not because of limited knowledge of the physical world. Using a variety of tasks that violate physical principles in more direct ways than those used by Piaget, Baillargeon and other investigators have demonstrated that even infants age 2½ to 3½ months possess many of the same basic beliefs about objects as adults do (Baillargeon, 1993, 1994).

Memory The sensorimotor abilities discussed so far generally require some form of memory. We noted earlier that 4-month-old infants prefer to look at novel objects, which shows that they have already established memory for the familiar (Cohen & Gelber, 1975). An infant who imitates must remember the sounds and actions of another person, at least briefly. Infants who search for a toy where they have seen it hidden are remembering the location of that toy.

Very young infants appear to have powerful visual memory (Cohen & Gelber, 1975; McCall, Eichorn, & Hogarty, 1977). Habituation studies have shown that infants as young as 2 months store visual patterns (Cohen & Gelber, 1975). Joseph Fagan (1977) found that 5-month-olds recognize patterns 48 hours later and photographs of human faces 2 weeks later. Subsequent research has generally verified Fagan's pioneering research, especially with regard to early memory for faces (e.g., Nelson & Collins, 1992; Pascalis et al., 1998). A few studies indicate that infants have even longer-term memory, at least for dramatic events. For example, children who participated in an unusual experiment at a very young age remembered it when they were reintroduced to the same setting several months later (Rovee-Collier, 1987). Indeed, in one study, children recalled aspects of an unusual experiment 2 years later (Myers, Clifton, & Clarkson, 1987). Further research has demonstrated various factors that determine the extent to which early memories are retained (Hayne & Rovee-Collier, 1995), notably whether movement and motion are involved when the infants are first exposed to objects later to be recalled. Music associated with an object can also enhance later recall (Fagen et al., 1997).

Children generaly start pretending between 6 and 12 months—particularly if they have the help of an older sibling.

Symbolic Representation During infancy, some of the earliest forms of mental representation are actions. Infants smack their lips before food or a bottle reaches their mouth. They may continue to make eating motions after feeding time is over. They may drop a rattle, yet continue to shake the hand that held it. They may wave bye-bye before they are able to say the words. Such actions are the simplest forerunners of **symbolic representation**—the ability to visualize or otherwise think about something that isn't physically present.

Pretending, as discussed earlier, is also evidence of an underlying process of symbolic representation (Mandler, 1983). Between 6 and 12 months children begin pretending, that is, using actions to represent objects, events, or ideas. Pretending behavior also develops in a predictable sequence (Fein, 1981; Rubin, Fein, & Vandenberg, 1983). The first stage occurs by about 11 or 12 months; most children of this age pretend to eat, drink, or sleep—all familiar actions. In the next few months the range and amount of pretend activity increases dramatically. At first, infants do not need objects to pretend, as when a child pretends to sleep curled up on a rug. As children grow older, toys and other objects are used too. By 15 to 18 months, children feed their brothers and sisters, dolls, and adults with real cups and toy cups, spoons, and forks. By 20 to 26 months, children may pretend that an object is something other than what it is; a broom may become a horse; a paper sack, a hat; a wood floor, a pool of water. Such pretending represents a further step in cognitive development. By noting the rough similarities between a horse and a broom, children combine a distant concept with a familiar one and thus establish a symbolic relationship between the two.

Language, of course, is the ultimate system of symbolic representation. We explore infants' language development in the closing section of the chapter. Before we do, however, it is important to summarize how Piaget's theory of cognitive development during infancy is viewed today and some important topics he overlooked.

Closing Thoughts on Piaget's Sensorimotor Stage

Piaget's theory of infant cognitive development has fueled decades of research and debate. His careful, naturalistic observations of infants have challenged others to look more closely. His emphasis on the interaction between maturation and experience and on the infant's active, adaptive, constructive role in his or her own learning brought a new respect to infant research. For Piaget, the

symbolic representation The use of a word, picture, gesture, or other sign to represent past and present events, experiences, and concepts.

Initially, affordances are limited, but then they become more refined, with babies testing objects for their "suck-ability," "squeeze-ability," and noise-making ability.

toddler is a "little scientist" who tests and discovers the nature of physical objects and the social world.

At the same time, Piaget's findings were not always accurate, as we have seen with regard to imitation and object permanence. Object permanence in particular doesn't occur precisely in the manner that Piaget described. Critics suggest that infants may have more sophisticated knowledge of objects based on their perceptual development but that their motor development may lag, in which case they cannot show through actual behavior that they have acquired the idea of object permanence (Baillargeon, 1987, 1994; Gratch & Schatz, 1987; Mandler, 1990).

Among Piaget's critics are proponents of information-processing theory, who are skeptical of a theory based on qualitatively different stages. They tend to believe that human development, particularly cognitive development, is a continuous, incremental process.

Piaget has also been criticized for paying too much attention to motor development and too little attention to perception. From an early age, infants recognize and remember the regular aspects of their world. Not only do infants learn by doing, they also learn by seeing as they select, sort, and organize the sensory information available to them. Let's look at these developing perceptual abilities in detail, picking up more or less where we left off in our earlier discussion.

Perceptual Organization and Categories

When we look at objects, we automatically consider the possibilities they offer. A cup of coffee or a glass of juice is something to drink. An empty window sill in a crowded lecture hall may provide a place to sit. Eleanor Gibson, whose research on depth perception was discussed earlier, believed that such thinking occurs even in infancy. **Affordances,** the potential uses of objects, depend on the individual's needs at the time, as well as on her or his past experience with and cognitive awareness of the object. An orange, for example, may look different to a thirsty adult, an artist, and a teething baby. Possible affordances of an orange are smelling, tasting, touching, viewing, throwing, and squeezing. Gibson contends that almost from the beginning of life, infants examine what they see and hear for possible uses. The affordances are limited at first but become increasingly refined. Eyeglasses, hair, and ears are graspable; eyes are not. Similarly, babies may test these objects for their suckability, squeezability, and noise-making ability. Babies often squeeze furry objects but suck plastic objects. Such behaviors are considered to be early attempts at categorization (Gibson & Walker, 1984).

Perceptual Categories Research on infant perception indicates that infants may be neurologically wired to perceive some *categories* in the same way that older children and adults do. Here, a category is a grouping of different things that have something in common, such as "food" (different things to eat) or "cat" (different cats and kinds of cats). Some researchers believe that infants may be born with the ability to "carve up" the physical world into categories (Gelman, 1998) well before they can express them in words or solve problems involving putting objects into categories.

In any event, as noted earlier, by 3 months infants can discriminate among the basic colors and many shades and hues. They also seem to have perceptual schemes for more complex categories. They can discriminate between male and female faces and voices almost as well as adults can. They can tell the difference when they look at two versus three objects. This doesn't mean that infants have

affordances The different opportunities for interaction offered by a perception; for example, halls are for moving through.

conceptual knowledge about men and women or that they understand the concept of number, but it does indicate that they notice things in perceptual displays (Mandler, 1992). At 7 or 8 months, for example, infants have at least a global concept of animals versus vehicles and at 9 months they can differentiate between birds and airplanes (in each case, given exposure). Thus, it appears that perceptual analysis is working even in very young infants. They are sorting, organizing, and noticing differences and similarities early on, although, as noted by Lisa Oakes and Kelly Madole (2000), some 25 years of research on infant categorization remains ambiguous and difficult to interpret. That is, we know that very young infants form categories, but as yet we know relatively little regarding how they go about forming them. (Again, see "A Closer Look," p. 186.) Categorization during early childhood is another matter, however, as we see in Chapter 7.

In conclusion, regardless of which theoretical foundations we use in understanding cognitive development during infancy, it is a period during which children must accomplish a great deal in the way of understanding how the physical (and social) world around them works—or they may never accomplish it. In a sense, as scientists we are still in our infancy with regard to understanding how early cognitive development unfolds, whereas babies have been "knowing" what to do since time immemorial. It is important that we understand early cognitive development and foster and enhance it, but healthy, well-nourished, secure infants in a conducive environment will nevertheless observe what goes on in their world and figure much of it out for themselves—whether we ever fully understand how they do it. Language acquisition, discussed next, is a case in point.

CONTENT CHECK
COGNITIVE DEVELOPMENT

True–False (answers are on the Companion Website)

1. In Piaget's theory, sensorimotor development begins with reflexes.
2. Research indicates that Piaget was correct in his assumption that deferred imitation is not possible prior to about 18 months of age.
3. Research indicates that Piaget was correct in his assumption that infants have no sense of object permanence prior to about 8 months of age.
4. Learning affordances involves perceptual categorization.
5. Perceptual categorization begins very early in infancy.

Thinking Critically

What elements of Piaget's theory remain as important contributions to our understanding of infant cognitive development?

Language Development

Even newborn infants communicate, and they are born with an array of perceptual skills that assist them in detecting important features of whatever language they are exposed to (Werker & Tees, 1999). As noted, it also doesn't take them long to discover how to let their parents know that they are hungry, wet, or bored, such as by crying. By about 1 year of age, most children say their first word; by 18 months, they put two or more words together; and by 2 years they have mastered more than 100 words and can have conversations. Their vocabulary may be severely limited and their grammar flawed, but their implicit grasp of language and its structure by the end of infancy is remarkable.

Language is based on the use of symbols for communicating information. The acquisition of language is a complex yet natural process. Perhaps better than any other single accomplishment, it illustrates the range and potential of the human organism.

Elements of Language

Language has three major dimensions (Bloom, 1993; Golinkoff & Hirsh-Pasek, 1999). **Content** refers to the meaning of a written or spoken message. **Form** involves the symbols used to represent that content—sounds and words—along with how words are combined to produce sentences and paragraphs. **Use** refers to social exchange between two or more people: the speaker and the person spoken to. The details of the social exchange depend on the situation, the relationship between the speaker and the listener, and the intentions and attitudes of the participants.

The social use of language is complex and is learned simultaneously with content and form. Children learn to be polite and deferential to their elders, to simplify their language when speaking to babies, to take turns in a conversation, and to understand indirect as well as direct speech. They learn to determine the speaker's intention as well as to understand the actual words. For example, a sentence such as "What's that?" can have different meanings depending on the situation. It can serve as a simple request for information, but it can also be an expression of fear.

In the discussions that follow, it may be helpful to have a frame of reference for talking about language. Table 5–7 summarizes the "language" of linguistics with regard to phonemes, morphemes, semantics, syntax, and grammar.

content The meaning of any written or spoken message.

form The particular symbol used to represent content.

use The way in which a speaker employs language to give it one meaning as opposed to another.

Table 5–7 Linguistic Terminology

Phonemes

The basic units of sound in a language. English, for example, has about 45 phonemes. These include the sounds indicated by the letters of the alphabet plus the variations in those sounds for vowels and some consonants. Distinct combinations such as *th* in words like "the" or "that" and *ng* in "talking" or "thinking" are also phonemes.

Morphemes

The basic units of meaning in a language. A word can be a single morpheme, or it can include additional morphemes such as *-s* for plural, *'s* for possessive, and *-ed* for past tense.

Semantics

How meaning is assigned to morphemes or morpheme combinations. Semantics includes connotation and context, i.e., how word meanings change according to the situation.

Syntax

Governs how words are combined into meaningful statements such as sentences.

Grammar

A comprehensive term that includes all of the above.

The Beginnings of Language

Language development involves learning to speak or produce oral language, learning the meaning of words, learning rules of syntax and grammar, and—in most cultures—eventually learning to read and write. Language development takes two forms. **Receptive language** refers to understanding spoken or written words and sentences. **Productive language** refers to producing language through speaking or writing.

Among the most common first words in an American-English-speaking infant's receptive vocabulary are "mommy," "daddy," "peekaboo," "bye," "bottle," "no," and the child's name. Infants as young as 8 months usually understand such words. The most common first words in children's productive vocabularies are "daddy," "mommy," "bye," "hi," and "uh-oh." Children can generally produce single words like these by the time they're 14 months old (Fenson et al., 1994). Productive and receptive language evolve simultaneously, although receptive language leads productive language. For example, a parent may ask her 14-month-old, "Will you go into the kitchen and bring back the cookies?" The child may be incapable of producing such a sentence, but will return with the cookies. Throughout the lifespan receptive vocabulary tends to be larger than productive vocabulary; that is, we can understand more words than we can use.

Before the First Words Language production begins with undifferentiated cries at birth. Infants soon develop a range of different cries and other communicative behaviors, which mothers and other caregivers learn to discriminate during the months that follow (Meadows, Elias, & Bain, 2000). By about 6 weeks, infants begin making cooing sounds.

With regard to receptive language, classic research indicated that as early as 1 month, infants can detect subtle differences between speech sounds, such as "lip" and "lap" (Eimas, 1975). Early on, it was noted, they can also discriminate among some consonants and vowels. However, more recent research with premature infants now indicates that early in the third trimester fetuses can discriminate some speech sounds—which Marie Cheour-Luhtanen and colleagues posited to be the earliest discriminative response of any kind by the brain (Cheour-Luhtanen, Alho, Sainio, Rinne, & Reinikainen, 1996). Another study found that at age 2 days, as a result of hearing the language of their parents from within the womb during the months prior to birth, French infants could discriminate their own language from Russian (Golinkoff & Hirsh-Pasek, 1999). Thus, even before birth, infants are prepared to respond to and learn language. In turn, during the first three days after birth, researchers have found that neonates can reliably discriminate words based on phonological and acoustic cues, if the words are presented in maternal speech (Shi, Werker, & Morgan, 1999).

By the second or third month, infants can distinguish between very similar sounds such as "b" and "p" or "d" and "t" (Eimas, 1974). In fact, during the first year infants can sometimes detect differences in speech sounds that older children and adults cannot detect (Maurer & Maurer, 1988). This is underscored by a series of studies by Patricia Kuhl and colleagues (e.g., see Kuhl & Iverson, 1995). In one such study, it was observed that 7-month-old Japanese infants were just as accurate as infants in the United States in making the distinction between "r" and "l." Because the distinction does not appear in Japanese, by 10 months of age—as a result of experience—the Japanese infants could no longer make the distinction.

In the first year of life and long before the first words are spoken, infants must learn a great deal about language. Major milestones in the development

receptive language The repertoire of words and commands that a child understands, even though she or he may not be able to use them.

productive language The spoken or written communication of preschool children.

Table 5–8   Milestones in Language Development

Average Age	Language Behavior Demonstrated by the Child
12 weeks	Smiles when talked to; makes cooing sounds
16 weeks	Turns the head in response to the human voice
20 weeks	Makes vowel and consonant sounds while cooing
6 months	Cooing changes to babbling, which contains all the sounds of human speech
8 months	Certain syllables repeated (e.g., "ma-ma")
12 months	Understands some words; may say a few
18 months	Can produce up to 50 words
24 months	Has vocabulary of more than 50 words; uses some two-word phrases
30 months	Vocabulary increases to several hundred words; uses phrases of three to five words
36 months	Vocabulary of about 1,000 words
48 months	Most basic aspects of language are well established

The ages given are strictly averages. Individual infants can differ by days at the younger milestones and weeks at the older ones.

Source: Robert A. Baron, *Psychology,* copyright ©1995 by Allyn & Bacon. Reprinted with permission.

of language are presented in Table 5–8. Three interesting aspects of language learning during early infancy are babbling, receptive vocabulary, and social communication.

Babbling   From their earliest moments infants make a variety of sounds. Often they start with vowel sounds and front-of-the-mouth consonants: "Ahh," "bahh." By 6 months they have a much more varied and complex repertoire. They string together a wide range of sounds, draw them out, cut them off, and vary their pitch and rhythm. Increasingly, they seem to control their vocalizations. They purposefully repeat sounds, elongate them, and pause in a kind of self-imitating precursor to speech called *iteration.*

The earliest vocalizations involve only a few different phonemes. Sound production increases rapidly, however, and by the second month infants are forming a large number of phonemes (as well as clicks, gurgles, grunts, and other sounds). Many of these sounds do not appear in the language of the infant's caregivers. This "random" phoneme production continues to increase until about 6 months; then the range of phonemes infants use begins to narrow, eventually including only those of their native language.

Sometime after 6 months, English-speaking parents may hear something suspiciously like "ma-ma" or "da-da" and interpret it as their precocious infant's first word. Usually, however, these are chance repetitions of sounds that have no real meaning. Babbling takes on inflections and patterns like those of the parents' language and may sound so much like coherent speech that the parents strain to listen and understand, thinking that it is. This **expressive jargon,** a highly developed form of babbling, is the same for infants in all language groups and cultures (Roug, Landberg, & Lundberg, 1989).

How important is babbling? How does it prepare a baby for speaking? A baby's babbling is an irresistible form of verbal communication, and caregivers

expressive jargon   The babbling produced when an infant uses inflections and patterns that mimic adult speech.

throughout the world delight in imitating and encouraging it. In the course of babbling, it appears that babies are learning how to produce the sounds they will later use in speaking. Thus, the sounds or phonemes that babies produce are influenced by what they hear before they use words. Although babbling is a means for babies to communicate and interact with other people, it is also a problem-solving activity. Babies babble as a way of figuring out how to make the specific sounds needed to say words. This may be the reason that babies do not stop babbling when they start producing words. In fact, new words seem to influence babbling, and babbling, in turn, affects the preferred sounds babies use in selecting new words (Elbers & Ton, 1985).

Babies are language *universalists* who can distinguish among all the possible sounds in human language, while adults are language *specialists* who perceive and reproduce only the sounds of their native tongue. In one study, 6-month-old infants were taught to look over their shoulder when they heard a difference in pairs of sounds and to ignore sounds that seemed alike. The babies were able to distinguish variations in unfamiliar languages but ignored the familiar similarities of their own language, indicating that language perception is clearly shaped by experience—and at an earlier age than was once thought. The study also indicated that "conversations" between parents and infants are instrumental in producing spoken language (Kuhl, Williams, Lacerda, Stevens, & Lindblom, 1992).

Comparisons of the babbling of hearing babies and deaf babies also demonstrate the importance of what the baby hears, even at the babbling stage. Although the babbling of hearing babies and deaf babies is the same at first, over time only the babbling of the hearing infants moves closer to the sounds used in their language (Oller & Eilers, 1988). Moreover, the babbling of deaf babies appears to lessen significantly after about 6 months.

Babbling therefore plays a key role in normal babies' learning to use the specific sounds needed to speak the language of their caregivers. For example, a comparison of the babbling of 10-month-olds in Paris, London, Hong Kong, and Algiers found that differences in how the infants pronounced vowel sounds paralleled the pronunciations of vowels in their native languages (de Boysson-Bardies, Halle, Sagart, & Durand, 1989).

Receptive Vocabulary As noted earlier, very young children understand words before they can say them. Infants as young as 1 year can follow directions from adults and show by their behavior that they know the meaning of words like "bye-bye." They also display a beginning understanding of the segmentation of phonemes into words. If an adult says, "Give me the cup," the child may very well hand over the cup appropriately—having learned that words following *the* are important. Research indicates that infants may actually begin such segmentation of single-syllable words as early as age 3 to 4 months (Eimas, 1999).

By eight months babies understand first words such as "mommy" and "daddy."

However, it is usually difficult to identify and describe concepts that very young children associate with specific words. Even when the evidence seems clear—for example, when a 1-year-old follows the instruction "Put the spoon in the cup"—the child's understanding may not be as complete as we might think. It is, after all, unlikely that the infant will instead try to put the cup in the spoon, even if that is what the infant mistakenly comprehended. Also, children may receive clues, such as gestures, that help them perform tasks correctly when they don't fully comprehend spoken instructions.

Social Communication Throughout the first year infants also learn *nonverbal* aspects of communication as part of their "mutual dialogues" with caregivers (Chapter 6). They learn to signal, take turns, gesture, and pay attention to facial expressions. Infants learn a lot about communication while playing simple games like peekaboo (Ross & Lollis, 1987). Indeed, some parents are skilled at structuring social games that teach their infants aspects of conversation in an enjoyable way. They provide a structure for the game that helps the child learn the rules of give-and-take and turn taking (Bruner, 1983). Along the way, they provide a support system for early language acquisition. As mothers and their infants focus together on objects of play ("Look, a kitten"), infants learn the names of objects and activities (de Villiers & de Villiers, 1992). But social communication with the infant goes beyond such games. By 1 year of age most infants are alert to the people around them, including strangers, and they respond appropriately to the emotional expressions of adults (Klinnert, Emde, Butterfield, & Campos, 1986; Nelson & de Haan, 1996).

Words and Sentences

Most children utter their first words around the end of the first year. Their vocabulary grows slowly at first, then much more rapidly. However, there is wide individual variation in the rate at which language learning progresses. Toddlers who seem to progress rather slowly are not necessarily developmentally delayed; they may be preoccupied with other tasks, such as learning to walk. Some children start late but catch up quickly; others seem to be stuck at particular stages for long periods. Regardless of the pace of language learning, however, the language development follows a regular and predictable *sequence* in every language (Hirsh-Pasek & Golinkoff, 1996).

Early Words and Meanings   Around the world, infants' first utterances are single words—most often nouns and usually names of people and things in their immediate environment. At first, children do not have the ability to use words in combination. Instead they engage in **holophrastic speech**—one-word utterances that apparently convey more complex ideas. Thus, in different contexts and with different intonations and gestures, "mama" may mean "I want my mama" or "Mama, I'm hungry" or "There she is, my mama."

What words form an infant's early vocabulary? It depends upon the vocabulary being used around them, but first words do fall into predictable categories. Names—that is, nouns that refer to specific things such as "dada," "sissie," and "home"—comprise much of a child's early vocabulary (Nelson, 1974). However, children in the holophrastic stage also use words that indicate function or relationship, such as "there," "no," "gone," and "up," sometimes before they use nouns (Bloom, Lifter, & Broughton, 1985).

The individual words and the categories of words that a child uses most may also depend on the child's personal speech style. Katherine Nelson (1981, 1996), one of the first researchers to study children's language-learning styles, identified children with a "referential" style, who tended to use nouns, and "expressive" children, who were more inclined to use active verbs and pronouns. By 18 months, when the children had vocabularies of about 50 words, the two styles were distinct. The referential children's vocabularies were dominated by naming words—mostly nouns indicating persons or objects. The expressive children, on the other hand, had learned the naming words but used a higher percentage of words pertaining to social interactions (e.g., "go away," "I want," "give me"). The later language development of expressive and referential children also differed. Expressive children typically had smaller vocabularies than did referential children. In addition, expressive children were more likely to create and use "dummy words"—words with no apparent meaning—to sub-

holophrastic speech   In the early stages of language acquisition, the young child's use of single words to convey complete thoughts.

stitute for words they didn't know. Other researchers have noted even more stylistic variation in children's language usage at the one-word stage (Pine, Lieven, & Rowland, 1997), partly as a function of their mother's speech characteristics.

Categorizing Objects A child's first words are often **overextensions.** Although first words refer to a specific person, object, or situation, the child overgeneralizes them to refer to all similar objects. Suppose a child has a dog named "Pookie." The child may use "Pookie" as the name for all other dogs or even all other four-legged animals. Only after learning new words, such as "doggie," does the child redefine the erroneous categories (Schlesinger, 1982). Children tend to overextend, underextend, or overlap the categories they use to determine what words refer to because they often do not share adults' knowledge of appropriate functions and characteristics of objects. Instead, they may emphasize characteristics that adults ignore (Mervis, 1987). Some examples are given in Table 5–9.

As children learn additional contrasting names for objects, such as "kitty," "cat," "lion," and "tiger," they reassign words to more specific categories (Clark, 1987; Merriman, 1987). In other words, although a lion and a tiger are different, they are both cats. Over time, the child's linguistic categories take on the structure of the linguistic culture in which the child is being raised; children adopt their language's approaches to grouping and sorting objects and concepts. The process of categorizing appears to follow the same pattern as intellectual or cognitive development in general (Chapman & Mervis, 1989). Children's words and their meanings are closely linked to the concepts the children are forming.

Which comes first, the word or the concept? Researchers differ in their interpretations of the evidence. Some, including Piaget, argue that the concept usually comes first. The child forms a concept and then attaches a name to it, whether real or invented. Twins sometimes create their own private language, and deaf children create signs or gestures even when they are not taught sign language (Clark, 1983), which implies that concepts come first. Other researchers emphasize that words help shape concepts. When a young child calls the family pet "dog," the child is simply naming that object. When the child extends and refines categories, the concept "dog" follows (Schlesinger, 1982). Thus, it is

Table 5–9   Examples of Overextensions of First Words

Child's Word	First Referent	Possible Common Extensions	Property
Bird	Sparrows	Cows, dogs, cats, any moving animal	Movement
Mooi	Moon	Cakes, round marks on a window, round shapes in books, postmarks	Shape
Fly	Fly	Specks of dirt, dust, all small insects, crumbs	Size
Wau-wau	Dogs	All animals, toy dog, soft slippers, someone in a furry coat	Texture

Source: Adapted from de Villiers and de Villiers, 1979.

overextensions The young child's tendency to overgeneralize specific words, as when a child uses "chihuahua" as the term for all dogs.

difficult to determine whether concepts precede words or vice versa. The two processes probably occur simultaneously and complement each other.

The Language Explosion At an average of about 21 months of age, and again regardless of language or culture, there occurs a "language explosion" in which children begin acquiring new vocabulary at a much faster rate (Cowley, 1997; Golinkoff & Hirsh-Pasek, 1999). They appear self-motivated to do so, often pointing and asking things like "Whazat?" and wanting to play "naming games" with caregivers and others. They also engage in active imitation of the words they hear. In all, they may begin acquiring more new words per week than they have acquired in all of the months since they began to talk.

The explosion appears to be linked to increasing skills in categorization, in that toddlers assume that each new word is linked to a new category and is therefore important to know. At the same time, adding and sorting the new words improves categorization skills. Increasing attention to the relationship between social cues and words may be a factor as well. Prior to the language explosion, children pay little attention to cues from parents and others as to whether a new word is "meant" for them to learn. When the explosion starts, children now become extremely sensitive to such cues and use them in their rapid acquisition of words. Their reading of social cues isn't perfect, however. As Roberta Golinkoff and Kathy Hirsh-Pasek pointed out (1999), children at this age are also quite capable and willing to learn certain words that definitely are not meant for them and subsequently blurt them out at exactly the wrong time—perhaps causing considerable embarrassment for the parents.

Telegraphic Speech and Early Grammar Around the middle of the second year children begin to put words together. The first attempts typically are two words that represent two ideas: "Daddy see," "Sock off," "More juice." Implicit rules of syntax soon appear, and children use two-word sentences in consistent ways. They may say "See dog" or "See truck" as they point at things. They don't say "Truck see."

What sort of linguistic rules do children use at this stage? When children start putting words together, their sentences are sharply limited. At first they're restricted to two elements, then three, and so on. At each stage, the number of words or thoughts in a sentence is limited; children retain informative words and omit less significant ones. The result is what Roger Brown (1973) called **telegraphic speech.** The informative words, which Brown called *contentives*, are nouns, verbs, and adjectives. The less important words were called *functors* or simply *function words*; they include articles, prepositions, and auxiliary verbs.

The concept of **pivot grammar,** originated by Martin Braine (1926–1996) (1963), describes the two-word phase. In American English, *pivot words* are usually action words ("go") or possessives ("my"). They are few in number and frequently occur in combination with *open words*, which are usually nouns. "See," for example, is a pivot word that can be combined with any number of open words to form two-word sentences: "See milk," "See Daddy," or "Daddy see." Pivot words almost never occur alone or with other pivots (McNeill, 1972). Open words may, however, be paired or used singly. Thus, children follow rules in their two-word utterances; the word combinations are not random.

With the help of gestures, tone, and context, children can communicate numerous meanings with a small vocabulary and limited syntax. Dan Slobin (1972) studied the variety of meanings conveyed by two-word sentences spoken by 2-year-olds. Although the children were from different linguistic cultures (English, German, Russian, Turkish, and Samoan), they used speech in

telegraphic speech The utterances of 1½- and 2-year-olds that omit the less significant words and include the words that carry the most meaning.

pivot grammar A two-word, sentence-forming system used by 1½- and 2-year-olds that involves action words or possessives (pivot words) in combination with open words, which are usually nouns.

the same ways. Among the concepts they were able to communicate by two-word utterances were the following:

Identification: See doggie.
Location: Book there.
Nonexistence: Allgone thing.
Negation: Not wolf.
Possession: My candy.
Attribution: Big car.
Agent-action: Mama walk.
Action-location: Sit chair.
Action-direct object: Hit you.
Action-indirect object: Give papa.
Action-instrument: Cut knife.
Question: Where ball?

In sum, the language development that occurs during infancy sets the stage for the expanding vocabulary, understanding of complex grammar, use of language as a social act, and ability to engage in conversation that occurs during the preschool years. Theorists sharply disagree, however, on what causes it all to happen.

Processes in Language Learning

Over the years, a great deal of research and theorizing has been devoted to understanding how we progress from crying to babbling to speaking an adult language. Although there has been considerable controversy as to precisely how language development works, it is possible to highlight four components: imitation, reinforcement, innate language mechanisms, and cognitive development.

Imitation Imitation plays a large role in many aspects of human learning, and language learning is no exception. Children's first words are obviously learned by hearing and imitating. In fact, most early vocabulary must be learned in this way; children cannot make themselves understood with words they invent. In contrast, the development of syntax is not as easily explained. Although some phrases result from imitation, a form such as "amn't I" is clearly original. So is a phrase like "me go"; it is unlikely that the child has heard anyone speak this way. Even when adults use baby talk or attempt to correct children's errors, the children tend to adhere to their own consistent speech patterns.

Imitation plays an important role in language learning, particularly in the early stages of development.

Reinforcement Conditioning through reinforcement (and punishment) is a powerful learning device, and this holds true for certain aspects of language acquisition. Clearly, children are influenced by the way people react to their speech. Smiles, hugs, and increased attention will encourage learning of words. Also, when particular words produce favorable results, children are likely to repeat them. If an infant calls "Mommy" and she comes, or says "Cookie" and is given one, the infant will use these words again—they have been reinforced. Punishment plays a role too. Uttering certain socially unacceptable words can produce consequences that will cause the child to refrain from using these words again—at least in the presence of adults.

However, like imitation, reinforcement by itself does not explain the acquisition of syntax. Much of children's speech is original and therefore has never been reinforced. Even if some forms are encouraged and others discouraged, it would not be possible to reinforce all correct forms and extinguish all incorrect

ones. Also, especially when children first begin to talk, adults tend to reinforce any speech at all, however unintelligible or incorrect. They are more likely to respond to content than to form. For example, if a child says, "I eated my peas," the parents will probably praise the child—unless, of course, the statement isn't true. In general, research indicates that parents rarely reinforce their young children for correct syntax.

Innate Language Structures Prominent former linguist Noam Chomsky (1959) drew attention to the limitations of imitation and conditioning theory, proposing instead that we are born with cognitive structures for acquiring language. This **language acquisition device** or **LAD** (which is not an actual neurological structure) enables children to process linguistic information and "extract" rules with which they create language. That is, when children hear people talk, they automatically acquire rules and produce their own language accordingly. The process follows a predictable sequence; children can assimilate certain kinds of rules and information before they can assimilate other kinds. According to Chomsky, children are preprogrammed to learn language, and they do it actively if not entirely consciously. Thus, at first they develop simple rules in accord with pivot grammar, then over the first several years of life their syntax gradually becomes more complex and closer to that of an adult as they add "function" words such as articles and prepositions and make other grammatical adjustments.

One piece of evidence for the existence of an LAD is deaf children's ability to develop spontaneous systems of language-like gestures (Goldin-Meadow & Mylander, 1984). Another is the observation that deaf children babble just like hearing children during the first 6 months or so. Yet another is the observation that there are universals that are found in all linguistic cultures; these include the orderly sequence of development of babbling, first words, and telegraphic speech.

Chomsky's approach has been criticized, however. For one thing, as yet there is no neurological evidence of an LAD, beyond the observation that the brain hemispheres specialize in language functions (Chapter 7). For another, Chomsky's reasoning was circular (Brown, 1973; Maratsos, 1983), as we have seen with regard to theorists in other areas: Why do children learn language? Because of the LAD. How do we know there's an LAD? Because children learn language. Yet another criticism involves Chomsky's proposal that a common grammar underlies all languages—theorists have been unable to agree on what that grammar is (Moerk, 1989).

Despite such criticisms, the theory has been useful and has stimulated considerable study of children's language development. Whether there is a innate language device or whether it is better to view the universals in language development more simply as an assortment of prewired strategies (early preference for human speech over other sounds, early abilities to discriminate speech sounds, spontaneous babbling and then refinement, and so on) remains debatable.

Cognitive Development The fourth major approach to language acquisition emphasizes the link between language learning and a child's developing cognitive abilities. This approach stems from the observation that basic grammatical structures are not present in children's earliest speech but develop progressively over time. Learning them depends on prior cognitive development (Bloom, 1970). Thus, a particular speech pattern will not emerge before the child has grasped the concept behind it. Between the ages of 1 and 4½, children are actively constructing their own grammar, gradually approaching the

language acquisition device or LAD Chomsky's term for an innate set of mental structures that aid children in language learning.

full grammar of the adults around them. At any given time, however, children are capable of expressing only concepts that they have mastered.

There are many parallels between cognitive development and language development. At about the time that a child is gaining an understanding of object permanence and is interested in games that involve hiding and finding objects, the child's beginning language reflects these cognitive processes with words like "see," "all gone," "more?" and "bye-bye." Comings and goings and hidings and findings become the focus of language and vocabulary. Later, as children become concerned with possessions, they learn aspects of syntax that reflect the possessive case: "Daddy sock," "baby bed," and eventually "mine" and "Mommy's cup." As discussed earlier, the language explosion appears to be linked to categorization skills. Thus, the development of language and the development of cognition often go hand in hand.

CONTENT CHECK
LANGUAGE DEVELOPMENT

True–False (answers are on the Companion Website)

1. Throughout the lifespan, receptive vocabulary exceeds productive vocabulary.
2. The universal sequence in early communication and language development is crying, cooing, babbling, first words.
3. At first, hearing infants and deaf infants alike babble all possible human speech sounds.
4. Expressive jargon is an example of holophrastic speech.
5. The telegraphic speech of toddlers has its own distinct grammar.

Thinking Critically

In what ways are each of the processes in language learning accurate?

CHAPTER 5 REVISITED

Change during infancy is more rapid and dramatic than during any other two-year period of the lifespan.

Neonates

- James' view of the infant's world as a blooming, buzzing confusion remained popular until the 1960s.
- Infants go through six predictable and distinct states of arousal.
- Neonates display a long list of survival reflexes and primitive reflexes.

- The BNBAS uses 28 measures that are grouped into 7 clusters; the scale is administered during the first few days of life.
- Research has demonstrated that infants are capable of habituation and simply forms of learning from birth on; in turn, conditioning and the habituation method can be used to study infant perceptual capabilities.

Physical and Motor Development

- Classic developmental researchers focused on maturational markers; modern researchers view physical and motor development as dynamic and influenced by cultural context.

■ Infants typically double in weight by 4 months, triple by 12 months, and quadruple by 18 months; after that the rate of growth slows.

■ Most reflexes disappear during the second and third months as higher brain centers assume voluntary control.

■ Visually guided reach is an important milestone that is achieved by about age 5 to 6 months.

■ Fine motor skills and gross motor skills refine progressively throughout the first 2 years and beyond; infants vary widely in the age at which they begin walking, but most are walking by age 18 months.

■ Most infants have a well-developed pincer grasp by about age 12 months.

■ Nutritional deficiencies remain a widespread problem in the United States and more so in developing nations; such deficiencies cause stunting, marasmus, and kwashiorkor.

■ For mothers who can, experts uniformly recommend breastfeeding over bottlefeeding, at least for the first several months; some mothers breastfeed for as long as 2–3 years.

Sensory and Perceptual Development

■ The senses are highly developed at birth; perceptual capabilities are limited.

■ In addition to conditioning and habituation, researchers studying infant perceptual capabilities use the novelty paradigm, the preference method, the surprise paradigm, and the ERP method.

■ Neonates can respond to a variety of visual stimuli; however, they have a fixed focal distance.

■ Newborns are highly responsive to features characteristic of the human face and learn to recognize mother's face as early as 2 weeks of age; some researchers believe that newborns can also imitate facial expressions.

■ Infants' ability to discriminate faces and facial expressions develops rapidly over the first 6-7 months, as do other visual skills including binocular depth perception.

■ Newborns can respond to and localize a wide range of sounds within a few days; early on, they prefer human voices and speech over other sounds.

■ The senses of taste, smell, and touch are well developed at birth.

■ Although researchers have disagreed about whether the senses are integrated at birth, most research indicates that the senses are either integrated at birth or soon after.

Cognitive Development

■ Piaget took the view that infants are active learners; during the sensorimotor period, learning begins with reflexes and becomes more complex through adaptation.

■ Object play progresses in stages throughout infancy and is important to cognitive development.

■ Imitation becomes more sophisticated throughout infancy; research now indicates that infants are capable of deferred imitation by about the middle of the first year, contrary to what Piaget thought.

■ Object permanence develops in stages throughout infancy; an immature object concept is clearly present during the latter part of the first year, if not much earlier.

■ Memory skills are present very early; young infants have especially good visual memory.

■ Symbolic representation, as evidenced by pretending, develops in stages throughout infancy; infants begin pretending at 6 to 12 months of age.

■ Piaget's theory of the sensorimotor periods has been criticized on many grounds, but his views of infants as active learners and cognitive development as based on the interaction of maturation and experience remain important contributions.

■ Affordances are thought to begin early in infancy, as is perceptual categorization.

Language Development

■ Language consists of three major dimensions, which are content, form, and use; in turn, the structure of language is comprised of phonemes, morphemes, semantics, syntax, and grammar.

■ Before infants can produce language, they develop receptive language skills; limited ability to discriminate speech is present prior to birth.

■ Receptive vocabulary exceeds productive vocabulary in infancy and throughout the lifespan.

■ Early communication and language development universally begins with crying, following by cooing, babbling, and first words.

■ At first infants babble potentially all possible human speech sounds; during the second half of the first year babbling narrows to the sounds of their native language.

■ Expressive jargon appears as babbling narrows and is soon followed by first words.

■ Infants often use overextensions during the holophrastic stage.

■ During the telegraphic stage, children use a distinct grammar; the telegraphic stage is also soon followed by a language explosion.

■ Four processes in language development are imitation, reinforcement, innate language mechanisms, and cognition; each explains how certain aspects of language development occur.

KEY TERMS

survival reflexes
primitive reflexes
habituation method
fine motor skills
gross motor skills
pincer grasp
marasmus
kwashiorkor
sensation
perception
novelty paradigm

preference method
surprise paradigm
event-related potential (ERP) method
sensorimotor period
adaptation
deferred imitation
object permanence
symbolic representation
affordances
content

form
use
receptive language
productive language
expressive jargon
holophrastic speech
overextensions
telegraphic speech
pivot grammar
language acquisition device or LAD

INFANTS AND TODDLERS: PERSONALITY AND SOCIOCULTURAL DEVELOPMENT

CHAPTER PREVIEW

Do you know:

1. The difference between *personality* and *temperament*?

2. That there are six identifiable stages in infant *emotional* development?

3. What constitutes *attachment* and how it is studied?

4. How heredity and environment *interact* in explaining attachment?

5. What *stranger anxiety* and *separation anxiety* are and when they occur?

6. The difference between *secure attachment* and three forms of *insecure attachment*?

7. What *responsive caregiving* is and why it is important?

8. How child *abuse* and *neglect* affect attachment?

9. What infants with *disabilities* need to form secure attachments?

10. How *fathers*, *siblings*, and *grandparents* are involved in attachment?

11. How responsive caregiving is important in an infant's development of a *basic sense of trust*?

12. What *social referencing* is and how it influences both behavior and sociocultural development?

13. What principles underlie effective *discipline* with toddlers?

14. When infants become capable of *prosocial behavior* and what fosters it?

15. How *self-concept* and *self-awareness* develop during infancy?

16. How the *social ecology* of child care affects attachment and other aspects of development?

17. Whether *early day care* is good or bad for infants and why?

These are the main topics of Chapter 6.

H uman infants are born into an environment that is rich with expectations, norms, values, and traditions. All of these and more will help shape their **personality**—their characteristic beliefs, attitudes, and ways of interacting with others. From a somewhat different perspective, over the first 2 years infants are enculturated and socialized. They learn and assimilate beliefs and standards for behavior in the form of society's laws, norms, and values, both written and unwritten. They learn to cope with their society's contradictions and hypocrisies as well. At the same time, as they grow older, they help shape their own personality: They actively accept or reject norms and rules, as opposed to being passive recipients.

Newborns are unaware of their relationship to those around them. At birth, an infant apparently has no understanding of self versus others, male versus female, child versus adult. A newborn also has no expectations about the behavior of others; things simply happen or they don't. In other words, at first the infant lives in the present, and whatever is out of sight is out of mind, as we saw in Chapter 5 with regard to development of object permanence.

Dramatic changes occur during the first 2 years of life. Newborns become aware of their environment and how they can interact with it, aware of the re-

personality Characteristic beliefs, attitudes, and ways of interacting with others.

204

sponsiveness or unresponsiveness of the world around them, and aware that they can do some things for themselves or get help when necessary. As they become toddlers, they become more aware of family relationships and of what is "good" and "bad." They become conscious of being a girl or a boy and begin to learn how gender imposes certain styles of behavior.

Babies are not born devoid of **temperament,** however. They come into the world with certain behavioral styles, which, taken together, constitute temperament. Some neonates are more sensitive to light or sudden loud sounds than others. Some react more quickly and dramatically to discomfort. Some are fussy, some placid, some active and vigorous. In turn, most infants still fall in one of three categories proposed by Alexander Thomas and Stella Chess in 1977 (also see Chess & Thomas, 1996): *easy* (often in a good mood and predictable), *difficult* (often irritable and unpredictable), and *slow to warm up* (moody and resistant to attention). Early infant temperament can have a profound effect on the quality of early parent-child interactions.

In this chapter we look at how the infant's personality develops within relationships with caregivers and others. We focus on the first relationships—those that establish patterns for the development of future relationships and for the acquisition of basic attitudes, expectations, and behavior. Specifically, we examine the social and emotional development of infants during the first and second years; the process of attachment between the infant and the primary caregiver (usually the mother); factors that affect the quality of early relationships; the infant's emotional ties with the father, siblings, and grandparents; and the potential effects of maternal employment on personality and sociocultural development.

Social and Emotional Development in Infancy

In the course of a lifetime, most individuals are involved in a number of significant interpersonal relationships. The first—and undoubtedly the most influential—occurs between the infant and the mother or other primary caregiver. The relationship normally becomes firmly established by 8 or 9 months. Since the mid-1960s developmentalists have used the term *attachment* in referring to this first and enduring relationship—a relationship that is characterized by interdependence, intense mutual feelings, and strong emotional ties.

First Relationships

Children go through phases of emotional and social growth that result in the establishment of their first relationship. Whereas the emotional states of newborns are limited and consist mainly of distress and relaxed interest, a range of self-oriented emotions quickly emerges—sadness, anger, disgust, fear, and pleasure. These are nurtured and given meaning in the context of relationships, as parents encourage the development of emotionally healthy children through playful intimacy, games, fantasy, and verbal and nonverbal conversation as well as by learning to read the baby's communications (Greenspan & Lewis, 1999).

Later, primarily in the second year, socially oriented emotions such as pride, shame, embarrassment, guilt, and empathy emerge as the toddler gains greater understanding of self and others. Stanley and Nancy Greenspan (1985)

temperament Inborn behavioral styles.

described six stages in the emotional development of the child during infancy and early childhood with regard to first relationships. These are summarized in Table 6–1. Note, as with other developmental sequences, that the timing varies from one child to another but the order of the stages is necessarily the same—each builds on the ones before.

Table 6–1   Milestones in Early Emotional Development

Self-Regulation and Interest in the World—birth to 3 months

In the early weeks infants seek to feel regulated and calm, but at the same time they try to use all their senses and experience the world around them. Infants seek a balance between over- and understimulation. Gradually they become increasingly socially responsive as they use signaling and orienting behavior—crying, vocalizing, visual following—to establish contact. At this stage infants do not discriminate between primary caregivers and other people; they react to everyone in much the same way.

Falling in Love—2 to 7 months

By 2 months, self-regulated infants become more alert to the world around them. They recognize familiar figures and increasingly direct their attention toward significant caregivers rather than strangers. Infants now find the human world pleasurable and exciting—and they show it. They smile eagerly and respond with their whole body.

Developing Intentional Communication—3 to 10 months

Now infants begin to engage in dialogues with others. Mother and baby initiate their own playful sequences of communication, including looking at each other, playing short games, and taking rests. Fathers and siblings do the same.

Emergence of an Organized Sense of Self—9 to 18 months

One-year-old infants can do more things for themselves and take a more active role in the emotional partnership with their mothers and fathers. They can signal their needs more effectively and precisely than before. They soon begin using words to communicate. By now a number of emotions—including anger, sadness, and happiness—have emerged. At the end of this period the infant has a well-developed sense of self.

Creating Emotional Ideas—18 to 36 months

Toddlers can now symbolize, pretend, and form mental images of people and things. They learn about the social world through make-believe and pretend play. Now that they have a sense of self, they can feel the ambivalent needs of autonomy and dependency. During this period toddlers' emotional repertoire expands to include social emotions such as empathy and embarrassment and gradually shame, pride, and guilt. This coincides with the new sense of self and a growing knowledge of social rules.

Emotional Thinking: The Basis for Fantasy, Reality, and Self-Esteem—30 to 48 months

By this time the give-and-take of close relationships with significant others has settled into a kind of partnership. Young children can discern what the caregiver expects of them and they try to modify their behavior to meet those expectations and achieve their own goals.

Source: Adapted from Greenspan & Greenspan, 1985.

The Attachment Process

Because attachment is so crucial to the infant's overall psychosocial development, it's important to examine the mechanisms through which it occurs. Mary Ainsworth defined attachment behaviors as those that primarily promote nearness to a *specific* person (1983). Such behaviors include signaling (crying, smiling, vocalizing), orienting (looking), movements relating to another person (following, approaching), and active attempts at physical contact (clambering up, embracing, clinging). Attachment is mutual and reciprocal—it works both ways and involves sharing experiences in a cooperative manner (Kochanska, 1997). Thus, child-to-caregiver attachment is intertwined with caregiver-to-child attachment.

Ainsworth described these behaviors as criteria of attachment because if they do not occur, attachment can be difficult to establish. Consider, for example, how hard it would be for a mother to develop a sense of emotional closeness to an infant who constantly stiff-arms her instead of embracing her. Or what if an infant rarely smiles or vocalizes in response to the caregiver? Ainsworth and colleagues (1979) have found that when a baby dislikes being touched or has a disability such as blindness, mutual attachment is at risk.

Thus, infant and caregiver alike must behave in ways that foster attachment. Normally the infant's behaviors invite nurturing responses from the caregiver, who not only feeds the infant and cares for the infant's physical needs but communicates with the infant by talking, smiling, and touching. The baby's behavior prompts the caregiver to act in certain ways, and the caregiver's actions prompt the baby as well.

Caregivers also help babies learn to regulate their own emotions. For example, an emotionally available caregiver may respond to the infant in ways that tend to prevent extended crying. Over time the baby may internalize such emotional regulation experiences with the caregiver if these are consistent and the relationship is secure (Emde, 1998).

Is attachment a conditioned response, or are innate needs involved? For a long time developmental psychologists with a conditioning orientation thought that infant-to-caregiver attachment occurred through the fulfillment of the infant's primary needs, such as hunger and thirst. Essentially through classical conditioning in this view, infants learn to associate the caregiver's nearness with the reduction of needs (Sears, 1963). Similarly, psychoanalytic theorists argued that a child's first emotional bonds occur through the gratification of the child's needs. When those needs are met, an infant forms a positive inner image of the mother. However, experimental research with primates indicates that need reduction is only part of how infants form their first attachments, as discussed in "A Matter for Debate" on page 208.

As discussed in Chapter 2, Bowlby (1973) argued that human babies are born with preprogrammed behaviors that function to keep their parents close by and responsive. Such behaviors, in his view, have evolved in humans and other animals partly because they increase the infant's chances of being protected from danger, and therefore surviving, eventually reaching sexual maturity, and passing their genes along to the next generation.

Bowlby proposed that preprogrammed behaviors affect both the infant and the caregiver. Attachment is initiated by those behaviors and is then maintained by pleasurable events, such as physical closeness and warmth between mother and child, reduction of hunger and other drives, and comfort. His theory thus combines heredity and environment in explaining the development

A MATTER FOR DEBATE

GEESE, MONKEYS, AND HUMANS

Half a century ago Konrad Lorenz observed that goslings begin to follow their mother very soon after hatching. They develop a bond that is important in helping the mother protect and train her offspring. Interestingly, Lorenz also found that during their first hours after hatching, orphaned greylag goslings began following *him*, as if he were their mother. The behavior was sometimes annoyingly persistent. Some of Lorenz's greylag geese preferred to spend the night in his bedroom rather than on the banks of the Danube!

The critical period for *imprinting*—forming the bond between goslings and their mother—occurs within hours after hatching, when the gosling is strong enough to move around but before it develops a strong fear of large, moving objects. If imprinting is delayed, the gosling will either fear the parent or simply give up and become limp and listless.

Researchers disagree about the parallels between imprinting in birds and attachment behavior in humans. There is no clear evidence that a critical period exists for human bonding. Parents and infants may be particularly receptive to bonding in the first few days after birth, but this is hardly a critical period. On the other hand, it is clearly necessary for human infants to establish some kind of relationship with one or more major caregivers within the first 8 months or so if normal development is to occur.

Because monkeys have much closer

Orphaned goslings nutured by Konrad Lorenz during the critical imprinting period follow him as if he were their real mother.

biological ties to humans, studies of their social development—and deprivation—are more directly relevant to understanding human development than are studies of goslings. An important series of observations on social deprivation in monkeys began somewhat by accident when Harry Harlow (1959) was studying learning and conceptual development in monkeys. To control the learning environment, Harlow decided to rear each young monkey without its mother, thus ruling out her influence as a teacher and model. Unexpectedly, Harlow found that separation from the mother had a disastrous effect on the young monkeys. Some

died. Others were frightened, irritable, and reluctant to eat or play. Obviously, the monkeys needed something more than regular feeding to thrive and develop.

Harlow and colleagues next conducted experiments with artificial *surrogate* mothers (Harlow & Harlow, 1962). For each infant monkey there was a wire surrogate with a bottle from which the monkey was fed, as well as a terrycloth-covered surrogate from which it was not fed. In spite of the feeding provided by the wire surrogate, the young monkeys showed a distinct preference for the terrycloth form: They spent more time clinging and vocalizing to it, and they ran to it when they were frightened. As a result, Harlow proposed that *contact-comfort* is an important factor in early attachment.

Monkeys who were reared with surrogates still didn't develop normally, however. As adults they avoided or attacked other monkeys and did not engage in normal sexual activity. Subsequent research indicates, however, that peer contact among infant monkeys can compensate for the deprivation (Suomi & Harlow, 1972). Infant monkeys who are reared at first with surrogate mothers and are later given an opportunity to play with younger, normally reared infant monkeys develop reasonably normal social behavior. Thus, mutually responsive social interaction is crucial for normal development in monkeys, and it seems plausible to generalize this conclusion to humans.

and maintenance of attachment. According to Bowlby, the infant's attachment to the primary caregiver becomes internalized as a working model—or scheme—by the end of the first year. The infant uses the model to predict and interpret the mother's behavior and respond to it. Once the model has been formed, the infant tends to hold on to it even when the caregiver's behavior changes. For example, a mother who provides little early nurturance because of prolonged illness may later be rebuffed by the infant when she recovers, because the infant's working model includes prior feelings of rejection. It is then harder for the mother to be responsive because of the infant's behavior (Bretherton, 1992).

In sum, Bowlby and Ainsworth were convinced that the nature of the parent-child interaction that emerges from the development of attachment in the first 2 years of life forms the basis for all future relationships. This view also closely parallels Erikson's theory of early psychosocial development, discussed later in the chapter.

Emotional Communication and Attachment

The attachment behaviors of both mother and infant evolve gradually and constitute a *dynamic* system in which the behaviors of the infant reciprocally influence those of the mother and vice versa (Fogel et al., 1997). For example, a sociable and easy baby who seeks close contact and derives pleasure from it can encourage even the most tentative new mother. In contrast, an often-fussy, difficult baby interrupts a caretaker's efforts at soothing or verbal give-and-take (Belsky, Rovine, & Taylor, 1984; Lewis & Feiring, 1989).

To learn more about the two-way affective (emotional) communication system that defines the infant's interaction with the primary caregiver during the first 6 months of life, Edward Tronick and colleagues (Tronick, 1989; Weinberg & Tronick, 1996) devised a now-classic laboratory experiment that focused on the mutual expectations of parents and infants. In the original version of what is called the "still-face" experiment, parents were first asked to sit and play with their 3-month-old infants in their usual manner. Play patterns differed markedly among parent-infant pairs, but in each case, at some point the infants would turn away or close their eyes before returning to the fun.

After 3 minutes the experimenter asked the parent to stop communicating with the infant. The parent was instructed to continue looking at the infant but to put on a blank, still face. The infants responded with surprise and tried to engage the parent with smiles, coos, and general activity, but the parent maintained the blank expression. Within a few minutes the infants' behavior began to deteriorate. They looked away, sucked their thumbs, and looked pained. Some began to whimper and cry, whereas others had involuntary responses such as drooling or hiccuping. Thus, although the parent was still present and attending, he or she was suddenly and unexpectedly unavailable emotionally and the infants had difficulty coping with the change. This experiment provided a clear demonstration of the strength and importance of emotional communication between caregivers and infants as young as 3 months of age. According to Tronick (1989), emotional communication is a major determinant of children's emotional development. When the bidirectional, reciprocal communication system fails—as it does, for example, when the primary caregiver is chronically depressed or ill—the infant cannot achieve his or her interactive goals.

In the years since Tronick's innovation, numerous still-face experiments have been conducted with a diverse array of purposes, such as comparing infant reactions to mothers versus fathers (Braungart-Rieker, Garwood, Powers, & Notaro, 1992), preterm versus full-term infants' reactions (Segal et al., 1995), and infants' reactions to the still face versus to a still mobile they had previously been able to move by kicking (Shapiro, Fagen, Prigot, Carroll, & Shalan, 1998). The still-face paradigm has also been used to assess the effects of differing caregiving practices across cultures, typically finding little in the way of differences in infants' reactions (e.g., Kisilevsky et al., 1998), to demonstrate negative effects of prenatal cocaine exposure on infant emotionality (Bendersky & Lewis, 1998), and to assess the quality of early infant-caregiver attachment (Cohn, Campbell, & Ross, 1991). The still face has proved to be a robust research paradigm indeed.

At about 7 months, infants become wary of strangers. This stranger-anxiety is a landmark in the infant's social development.

stranger anxiety and separation anxiety An infant's fear of strangers or of being separated from the caregiver. Both occur in the second half of the first year and indicate, in part, a new cognitive ability to respond to differences in the environment.

discrepancy hypothesis A cognitive theory stating that around 7 months, infants acquire schemes for familiar objects. When a new image or object is presented that differs from the old one, the child experiences uncertainty and anxiety.

social referencing Subtle emotional signals, usually from the parent, that influence the infant's behavior.

Stranger Anxiety, Separation Anxiety, and Attachment

A key landmark in the development of the attachment relationship is the appearance of **stranger anxiety and separation anxiety.** Pediatricians and developmentalists often make little distinction between the two, referring to both as "7-months anxiety" because they typically appear suddenly at about that age. Babies who have been smiling, welcoming, friendly, and accepting toward strangers suddenly become shy and wary of them. At the same time, some infants become extremely upset by being left alone in a strange place, even for a moment. Although many babies do not experience intense stranger and separation anxiety, for those who do, such reactions often continue throughout the rest of the first year and much of the second year.

The Discrepancy Hypothesis Most developmentalists see stranger and separation anxiety as a correlate of the infant's cognitive development. As cognitive processes mature, infants develop schemes for what is familiar and notice anything that is new and strange. They distinguish caregivers from strangers and become keenly aware when the primary caregiver is absent. Thus, according to the **discrepancy hypothesis,** they experience anxiety when they become capable of detecting departures from the known or the expected (Ainsworth, Blehar, Waters, & Wall, 1978). The anxiety is based on the infant's new awareness that the caregiver's presence coincides with safety. Things seem secure when familiar caregivers are present but uncertain when they are absent.

Some developmentalists believe that by 9 months the anxiety reaction is further complicated by learning. Gordon Bronson (1978) observed that 9-month-old babies sometimes cry when they first notice a stranger, even before the stranger comes close. This implies that they may have had negative experiences with strangers and anticipate another disturbing encounter, but the learning process may be more subtle than that. Perhaps the mother signals her baby by her facial expression or tone of voice. In one study (Boccia & Campos, 1989), a group of mothers of 8- to 9-month-old babies were trained to knit their eyebrows, widen their eyes, pull down their lips, and otherwise demonstrate worry while greeting a stranger with a troubled "Hello." A second group was trained to show pleasure with a smile and a cheery "Hello." As predicted, the infants accurately picked up their mothers' signals: Infants whose mothers displayed pleasure smiled more and cried less when the stranger picked them up than did infants whose mothers displayed worry. Emotional signaling by the mother or other caregiver is called **social referencing;** we discuss this process in more detail later in the chapter. Through such signaling, parents can assist their infants and toddlers in adjusting to strangers and strange situations by monitoring their own emotional reactions and giving the children time to acclimate (Feiring, Lewis, & Starr, 1984).

Stranger anxiety is also a milestone in social development (Bretherton & Waters, 1985). Once children learn to identify the caregiver as a source of comfort and security, they feel free to explore new objects while in the caregiver's reassuring presence. Children who fail to explore, preferring instead to hover near their mother, miss out on new learning. On the other hand, infants who are too readily comforted by strangers or show wariness when returned to their mother may also be maladjusted (Sroufe & Fleeson, 1986). The latter children may suffer pervasive and unresolved anxiety about their caregivers that can interfere with emotional development.

Stranger anxiety and separation anxiety can also be used to assess the *quality* of infant-to-caregiver attachment, as we see later in the chapter.

CONTENT CHECK
SOCIAL AND EMOTIONAL DEVELOPMENT IN INFANCY

True–False (answers are on the Companion Website)

1. Attachment refers exclusively to the feelings the baby has toward the parents.
2. Attachment develops gradually during the first two years of life and beyond.
3. Virtually all babies experience intense stranger and separation anxiety.
4. According to the discrepancy hypothesis, infants experience anxiety when they become capable of detecting that something is wrong in their environment.

Thinking Critically

How might attachment be a consequence both of preprogrammed behaviors and conditioning?

Patterns of Early Relationships

Infants all over the world normally show similar responses to their social environments; they gradually establish attachment relationships with their primary caregivers. Although the sequence of development of these first relationships is fairly consistent across cultures, the details vary dramatically, depending on the personality of the parents, their culturally based child-rearing practices, and the temperament and personality of the children.

Cultural values play a particularly important role. For example, a study of mother-infant interactions among middle-class U.S. Anglo and Puerto Rican mothers and their firstborn infants during feeding, social play, teaching, and free play showed that Anglo mothers emphasized socialization goals that fostered individualism. Puerto Rican mothers fostered goals more consistent with a family unity orientation (Harwood, Schoelmerich, Schulze, & Gonzales, 1999).

How do we assess the quality of the relationship between the infant and the primary caregiver? Researchers in Western cultures have focused on security of attachment, responsiveness of the mother and its effects on the infant, mutual relationships with key caregivers, and multiple versus exclusive attachments. For perspective, however, it is worthwhile to take a cross-cultural view of attachment. In the United States and much of Western Europe, child development experts have assumed that a single primary relationship—usually with the mother—is ideal for healthy infant development. The relationship is mutually responsive and is characterized by game playing and interactive dialogues.

This is not the norm in many other cultures. In some, for example, infants have close physical contact with caregivers—including being carried in a back sling and co-sleeping with a parent or another adult—but do not have frequent face-to-face interactions. In some cultures, a primary adult-infant relationship is supplemented by many other relationships. Grandmothers, aunts, fathers, siblings, and neighbors take turns caring for the infant. To the extent that these relationships are reasonably consistent, healthy attachment emerges. Thus, although the quality of relationships is important, many cultural and subcultural variations can foster healthy attachment.

Children who spend long hours strapped to their mother's backs form strong attachments.

Quality of Attachment

Ainsworth's *strange-situation test* (Ainsworth & Bell, 1970) is used to assess the quality of infant attachment to the primary caregiver. The test is a kind of minidrama with a simple cast of characters: the mother (or other caregiver), her 1-year-old baby, and a stranger. The setting is an unfamiliar playroom that contains toys. Table 6–2 summarizes the eight scenes involved in the test and what is observed during each scene.

Using the strange-situation test, Ainsworth found two basic types of attachment. Between 60 and 70% of U.S. middle-class babies displayed the first: **secure attachment.** They can separate themselves fairly easily from their mother and go exploring in the room, even when the stranger is present. Although they may become upset when their mother leaves, they greet her warmly and become calm quickly when she returns. Correlational research by Ainsworth indicates that securely attached infants had warm, affectionate, and responsive interactions with their mothers in the 12 months prior to the tests. Follow-up studies indicate that securely attached children are more curious, sociable, independent, and competent than their peers at ages 2, 3, 4, and 5 (Matas, Arend, & Sroufe, 1978; Sroufe, Fox, & Paneake, 1983; Waters, Wippman, & Sroufe, 1979). They also conform to Erikson's predictions regarding the effects of an early sense of trust on later development.

The remaining infants—about a third—displayed **insecure attachment,** which takes three distinct forms (Ainsworth et al., 1978; Main & Solomon, 1990). In one, **resistant attachment,** the child becomes angry when the mother leaves and avoids her when she returns. In another, **avoidant attachment,** the child responds to the mother ambivalently, simultaneously seeking and reject-

secure attachment A strong emotional bond between child and caregiver that develops as a result of responsive caregiving.

insecure attachment The result of inconsistent or unresponsive caregiving.

resistant attachment Insecure attachment characterized by anger and avoidance of the mother.

avoidant attachment Insecure attachment characterized by ambivalence toward the mother.

Table 6–2   Ainsworth's Strange-Situation Paradigm*

Episode	Events	Variables Observed
1	Experimenter introduces parents and baby to playroom and then leaves.	
2	Parent is seated while baby plays with toys.	Parent as a secure base
3	Stranger enters, seats self, and talks to parent.	Reaction to an unfamiliar adult
4	Parent leaves; stranger responds to baby and offers comfort if upset.	Separation anxiety
5	Parent returns, greets baby, and offers comfort if needed; stranger leaves.	Reaction to reunion
6	Parent leaves room; baby is alone.	Separation anxiety
7	Stranger enters and offers comfort.	Ability to be soothed by stranger
8	Parent returns, greets baby, and offers comfort if needed; tries to reinterest baby in toys.	Reaction to reunion

*While each episode lasts for about 3 minutes, the separation episodes may be cut short if the baby becomes too distressed.

Source: Ainsworth et al., 1978.

ing affection and not becoming upset when the mother leaves the room. In the third, **disorganized/disoriented attachment,** the child behaves in contradictory and confused ways—such as avoiding the mother's gaze while being held or coming to her with no visible emotionality. All three forms are often associated with unresponsive, indifferent, or perhaps resentful caregiving during the first year of life.

Longitudinal follow-ups contrasting the secure and insecure attachment have found dramatic differences in personality and social development as early as 18 months of age (Arend, Gore, & Sroufe, 1979; Bretherton & Waters, 1985; Sroufe, 1977). Securely attached infants are more enthusiastic, persistent, and cooperative than infants in the three insecure categories. By age 2 they are also more effective in coping with peers. They spontaneously invent more imaginative and symbolic play. Later, in elementary school, children who have experienced secure attachment during infancy persist in their work longer, are more eager to learn new skills, and exhibit more highly developed social skills in interacting with adults and peers—consistent with Erikson's stages of autonomy versus shame and doubt, and initiative versus guilt.

Numerous other studies have yielded similar findings (see Belsky & Rovine, 1988, 1990). Although the evidence is largely correlational—which means that we can't say absolutely that responsive caregiving *causes* secure attachment and its later benefits—it does strongly point in that direction. Securely attached children do even simple things—like exploring playrooms—better than children who are insecurely attached. They maneuver around the furniture, find their way to interesting toys, and position themselves comfortably for play with greater ease than insecurely attached children (Cassidy, 1986). Also, securely attached 3-year-olds tend to be better liked by their peers (Jacobson & Wille, 1986). In contrast, insecurely attached 2-year-olds exhibit hyperactivity or chronic stress reactions that may interfere with brain development. For example, in rats chronic stress disturbs the development of those parts of the brain involving fearfulness and vigilance, learning, memory, and attention focusing. Generalizing to humans, it may be that secure attachment provides a kind of buffer against these disturbances, whereas insecure attachment leaves the brain open to insults that lead to long-term anxiety, timidity, and learning difficulties (Wright, 1997). Behavioral problems may also be linked to insecure attachment. Besides being at increased risk for insecure attachment, the children of depressed caregivers display higher levels of hostile-aggressive behavior during preschool years than their securely attached peers (Cicchetti, Rogosch, & Toth, 1998). Insecure attachment may also intensify feeding problems, leading to malnutrition (Chatoor, Ganiban, Colin, Plummer, & Harmon, 1998). Research on a young low-income urban population in Chile suggested that a significant association may exist between maternal sensitivity, insecure attachment, and chronic malnutrition among young children (Valenzuela, 1997).

Correlational research notwithstanding, we can safely conclude that a warm, supportive relationship between caregiver and infant leads to higher levels of cognitive competence and greater social skills (Olson, Bates, & Bayles, 1984). It promotes active exploration and early mastery of object play and the social environment. From the beginning, the quality of the relationship between caregiver and infant provides the foundation for many aspects of child development.

What Constitutes Responsive Caregiving Numerous studies have shown that the mother's sensitivity to her baby's signals and her overall responsiveness have important implications for the social and personality development of

disorganized/disoriented attachment Insecure attachment characterized by contradictory behavior and confusion regarding the mother.

the child (De Wolff & van Ijzendoorn, 1997). In early studies of children in Uganda, for example, Ainsworth (1967) found that the children with the strongest attachment behavior had a highly responsive relationship with their mothers. In the United States, she reported that securely attached 1-year-olds had mothers who were more responsive to their cries, more affectionate, more tender, more competent in providing close bodily contact, and more likely than mothers of insecure 1-year-olds to synchronize their rate of feeding and their play behavior with the baby's own pace (Ainsworth et al., 1978). Since then researchers have consistently found that infants who were securely attached at age 1 had mothers who were more responsive to their physical needs, distress signals, and attempts to communicate with facial expressions or vocalizations (Bornstein, 1989). In turn, because of the long-range importance of early attachment, considerable attention in the years since Ainsworth's pioneering research has been focused on evaluating infant and caregiver risk factors (Morton & Browne, 1998; Zeanah, Boris, & Larrieu, 1998) and to developing early intervention strategies (Lieberman & Zeanah, 1999; Svanberg, 1998).

Does this mean that a mother must respond to every little thing her infant does? Of course not. Even highly responsive mothers don't respond 100% of the time. Marc Bornstein and Catherine Tamis-LeMonda (1989) found that mothers' responsiveness varies according to the situation. When infants are in distress, for example, the typical responsive mother responds quickly about 75% of the time. In contrast, mothers respond differently to bids for attention, vocalization, and smiling. Some mothers respond to these cues as little as 5% of the time; others respond almost 50% of the time. Moreover, different mothers respond in different ways—some with physical play, others with vocal imitation, and still others with touching, playing, patting, and feeding.

Mutual Dialogues and Attachment Many researchers have studied the two-way affective communication system between mother and infant, discussed earlier in the context of the still-face experiment. Heinz Schaffer (1977) was an early investigator of the way in which **mutuality,** or **interactive synchrony,** develops between infant and caregiver. He observed that most infant behavior

mutuality or interactive synchrony The patterns of interchange between caregiver and infant in which each responds to and influences the other's movements and rhythms.

Early mutuality and signaling lay the foundation for long-term patterns of interactions.

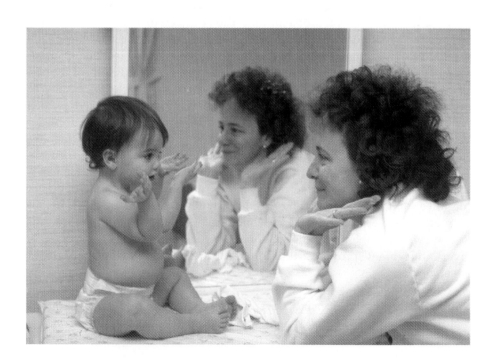

follows an alternating on-off pattern. For example, while visually exploring new objects, babies stare at them and then look away. Some caregivers respond to these patterns more skillfully than others. Films of some mothers face-to-face with their 3-month-old infants reveal a pattern of mutual approach and withdrawal; they take turns looking and turning, touching and responding, vocalizing and answering. Synchrony between infant and caregiver during the first few months is a good predictor of secure attachment at age 1, as well as more sophisticated patterns of mutual communication at that age (Isabella, Belsky, & Von Eye, 1989).

Caregivers do not merely respond to the child's behavior. They also change the pace and nature of the dialogue with a variety of techniques: introducing a new object, imitating and elaborating on the infant's sounds or actions, making it easier for the child to reach something of interest. By monitoring the baby's responses, caregivers gradually learn when the child is most receptive to new cues. It takes months for this mutual process to develop fully.

Some techniques seem to be especially effective in developing synchrony (Field, 1977; Leitch, 1999; Paulby, 1977). For example, Tiffany Field compared infant reactions to three different maternal behaviors: the mother's spontaneous behavior, her deliberate attempts to catch and hold the child's attention, and her imitations of the child. The infants responded most to the imitations, perhaps because of the slowed-down, exaggerated nature of imitative action. The closer the similarity between maternal and infant behavior, the less discrepancy babies have to deal with; thus, the more attentive they will be. Further, each mother carefully observed her infant's "gaze-away" point. Field suggested that respecting the child's need for pauses in the action is one of the earliest rules of "conversation" that a responsive caregiver must learn.

Some parents overstimulate their infants despite signals of resistance from the babies such as turning away, hiding their faces, or closing their eyes. Some parents continue the stimulation until the child actually cries. Other parents understimulate their infants. They often ignore their babies' smiles and babbling or other bids for attention. An infant whose cues for attention are ignored may cry or soon give up trying. Still other parents have mixed patterns of sensitivity. Sometimes they overstimulate, sometimes they understimulate. They regularly misidentify the infant's cues. This pattern is particularly common in abusive mothers (Kropp & Haynes, 1987), depressed mothers (Field, 1986; Teti, Gelfand, Messinger, & Isabella, 1995), some adolescent mothers (Lamb, 1987), and mothers whose temperament is very different from that of their child (Weber, Levitt, & Clark, 1986). Relatively short maternal leave in combination with factors such as maternal depression is also associated with inappropriate maternal sensitivity (Clark, Hyde, Essex, & Klein, 1997).

The behavior of a sensitive and responsive mother changes as the infant grows older (Crockenberg & McCluskey, 1986). Indeed, some developmentalists use the term **scaffolding** to describe the mother's or father's role in progressively structuring the parent-child interaction (Ratner & Bruner, 1978; Vandell & Wilson, 1987). That is, parents provide the framework within which they interact with their infant. With a younger child, they use games like imitation or peekaboo. As the child grows older, the games become more sophisticated. The child learns increasingly complex rules of social interaction—rules of pacing and give-and-take, rules of observing and imitating, how to maintain the game, and so on.

Early mutuality and signaling lay the foundation for long-standing patterns of interaction. This is illustrated in studies of maternal responses to crying. Mothers who respond promptly and consistently to their infant's crying in the

scaffolding The progressive structuring by the parents of parent-child interactions.

first few months are more likely to have infants who cry *less* by the end of the first year. A quick response gives babies confidence in the effectiveness of their communications and encourages them to develop other ways of signaling their mother (Bell & Ainsworth, 1972). On the other hand, if responses to crying are inconsistent, infants may fail to develop confidence and later may cry more, be more insistent, or be less responsive themselves.

During the second year, mutuality blossoms into a variety of behaviors. For example, some securely attached toddlers spontaneously exhibit sharing behavior, both with parents and with other children—showing a toy, placing it in someone's lap, or using it to invite another child to play. In general, whether or not children are born "selfish," the quality of early parent-child interactions has a profound influence on behaviors such as sharing and helping.

Multiple Attachments Versus Exclusivity Infants who have a relatively exclusive relationship with one parent tend to exhibit more intense stranger and separation anxiety. They also show these anxieties at an earlier age than do infants whose relationship with the parent is not exclusive (Ainsworth, 1967). A child who is constantly with the parent and sleeps in the same room exhibits dramatic and intense separation reactions. By contrast, a child who has more than one caregiver from birth tends to accept strangers or separation with far less anxiety (Maccoby & Feldman, 1972).

Is attachment impaired if caregiving involves too many different people? Every year millions of U.S. children receive care from many different people in nurseries and day-care centers. If the *quantity* of attachments is a factor, children who spend less time with their parents might suffer.

Research generally indicates, however, that day care and multiple caregivers do not necessarily produce adverse effects on attachment (but see "A Matter for Debate" on page 233). These children form multiple attachments (Clarke-Stewart & Fein, 1983; Welles-Nystrom, 1988) that can vary in quality just as child-parent attachment can.

When toddlers first attend a day-care program, they often experience separation distress, especially if they're between 15 and 18 months old. Some toddlers adjust more readily than others. Toddlers who have had an exclusive relationship with one person have the most difficulty. Those who have already had too many separations and too many caregivers also display separation distress. Adjustment is easiest for toddlers who have had some experience with other caregivers and have had a moderate degree of separation experience (Jacobson & Wille, 1984).

Besides becoming attached to their mothers, children form attachments with fathers, siblings, and other family members, as we discuss later in the chapter. They also form important attachments with peers. The power of peers as attachment figures was revealed in Anna Freud's famous study (Freud & Dann, 1951) of six German-Jewish orphans who were separated from their parents at an early age during World War II. They were placed in a country home at Bulldog Banks, England, which had been transformed into a nursery for war children. They had previously been in large institutions, so this was their first experience in a small, intimate setting. At first the children were hostile toward their adult caregivers or ignored them, showing much more concern for one another. For example, when a caregiver accidentally knocked over one of the smaller children, two other children threw bricks at her and called her abusive names. The orphans also depended on each other when frightened, which clearly illustrated the strength of their attachment to each other.

Effects of Abuse and Neglect **Child abuse** refers to physical or psychological injuries that are *intentionally* inflicted by an adult, as discussed further in Chapter 8. It is distinguished from child neglect in that the latter is usually unintentional. **Child neglect** involves the failure of a caregiver to respond to or care for children. Though not as serious as abuse, it can nonetheless cause children to suffer or die, also as discussed in Chapter 8. The deliberate nature of child abuse, however, is more horrifying—whether it takes blatant physical forms such as violent punishment or sexual abuse or subtler psychological forms such as ridicule and direct attacks on the child's self-concept and self-esteem.

Neglect is a factor in **failure-to-thrive syndrome,** in which infants are small and emaciated, appear sick, and are unable to digest food properly. Failure-to-thrive can occur as a result of malnutrition, but in many cases it appears to be because of lack of affection and attention—including poor-quality (or nonexistent) attachment. Often there is disruption in the home and the social environment. The infants are often listless and withdrawn, perhaps immobile. They avoid eye contact by staring with a wide-eyed gaze, turning away, or covering their face or eyes. By definition, infants with failure-to-thrive syndrome weigh in the lower 3% of the normal weight range for their age group and show no evidence of disease or abnormality that would explain their failure to grow. Such infants may exhibit developmental retardation, which can be reversed with appropriate feeding and attention (Barbero, 1983; Drotar, 1985).

Child abuse also interferes with attachment (Morton & Browne, 1998). When abuse begins in infancy, it betrays the nurturant relationship on which the infant depends and may have devastating effects throughout life. Studies have shown that toddlers who have suffered physical maltreatment and insecure attachment experience distortions and delays in the development of their sense of self and in their language and cognitive development. When infants are securely attached during the first year, abuse during the second year is less damaging (Beeghly & Cicchetti, 1994) though equally regrettable. Other studies point to a potentially malignant combination of negligent or inconsistent mothering and a biologically or temperamentally vulnerable infant. In combination, the result is an infant who shows insecure attachment and experiences frequent distress and episodes of angry behavior—along with later maladjustment (Cassidy & Berlin, 1994). Abuse is sometimes related to an intrusive, interfering style of caregiving that ignores the baby's wishes and disrupts the baby's activities. One study found that when a mother's style of interaction with her 6-month-old infant is highly intrusive and persistent, the child may later demonstrate poor academic, social, emotional, and behavioral skills (Egelund, Pianta, & O'Brien, 1993).

In some cases mothers of failure-to-thrive and abused or neglected infants are themselves physically ill, depressed or otherwise mentally disordered, or inclined toward alcohol or other drug abuse. Such parents often experienced similar deprivation as infants. Some studies show that many abusive or neglectful parents themselves had negative early childhood experiences themselves; that is, they too were abused or neglected (e.g., Hall, Sachs, & Rayens, 1998). Certainly, not all people who were abused as children grow up to abuse their children, but too often the cycle is repeated.

Preventing Maltreatment and Encouraging Resiliency As indicated, abused and neglected babies are at risk for physical, cognitive, and emotional impairments. Interventions that encourage resiliency may include the presence of

child abuse Intentional psychological or physical injuries inflicted on a child.

child neglect Failure of caregiver to respond to or care for a child.

failure-to-thrive syndrome A condition in which infants are small for age and often sick as a result of malnutrition or unresponsive caregiving.

alternate caregivers, social support measures, and home visits (Lowenthal, 1999). Alternate caregivers such as grandparents, other relatives, or foster or adoptive parents can offer babies the safe and secure nurturance necessary for them to begin to recover from the neglect or abuse by the mother or other caregiver.

Parenting skills programs appear to be especially helpful while also reducing family stress and pathology (Barnett, Manley, & Cicchetti, 1993) as are therapeutic techniques. A National Clinical Evaluation study examined the outcomes of 19 separate projects that trained teachers to use therapeutic techniques with maltreated children between the ages of 18 months to 8 years, and it was found that about 70% of these children improved in their social-emotional, adaptive, and cognitive skills (Daro, 1993). Informal support networks can consist of family members, neighbors, and friends, peer support groups, and neighbors. Both informal and formal social support interventions can help dysfunctional families end the cycle of abuse or neglect that adversely affects the baby as well as other children (Barnett, 1997; Dunst, Trivette, & Deal, 1988).

Attachment and Infants with Special Needs

Infants who cannot see cannot search their caregivers' faces or smile back at them. Infants who cannot hear may appear to be disobedient. Infants with other severe disabilities cannot respond to signals the way normal babies do. Disabilities that are evident from birth, such as Down syndrome and cerebral palsy, create serious adjustment problems for all concerned. Formerly, researchers ignored how infants affect caregivers and concentrated instead on the impact of caregivers' behavior on infants. In recent decades, however, researchers have devoted more attention to the child's role in the relationship.

Infants Who Can't See   Visual communication between caregiver and child is normally a key factor in the establishment of attachment. Caregivers depend heavily on subtle responses from their infants—looking back, smiling, and visually following—to maintain and support their own behavior. They may feel that a blind infant is unresponsive. It is essential that a parent and an unseeing child establish a mutually intelligible communication system that compensates for the child's disability.

In early life, one of the normal infant's best-developed resources for learning is the visual-perceptual system. Babies look at and visually follow everything new, and they have distinct visual preferences. As noted, they especially like looking at human faces. Blind infants, however, cannot observe the subtle changes in caregivers' facial expressions or follow their movements. Thus, they fail to receive the kinds of information that sighted babies use in formulating their own responses.

Caregivers of sighted infants rely on visual signals of discrimination, recognition, and preference. Otherwise competent blind infants do not develop signals for "I want that" or "Pick me up" until near the end of the first year. Thus, the first few months of life are extremely difficult for both caregiver and infant. The child's seeming lack of responsiveness can be emotionally devastating for the caregiver. The danger is that communication and mutuality will break down and that the caregiver will tend to avoid the child (Fraiberg, 1974). Blind babies do not develop a selective, responsive smile as early as sighted children do; they do not smile as often or as ecstatically. They have fewer facial expressions (Troester & Bambring, 1992). Yet they rapidly develop a large, expressive vocabulary of hand signals. Eventually they are able to direct these signals to unseen people and objects. Training parents and caregivers of blind infants to watch for and interpret hand signals greatly enhances parent-child interaction, attachment formation, and subsequent socialization (Fraiberg, 1974), as do other home-based interventions with parents (Beelmann & Bambring, 1998).

Infants Who Can't Hear   The developmental difficulties of deaf-but-sighted infants follow a different pattern. In the first few months of life, their well-developed visual sense generally makes up for the problems imposed by deafness. After the first 6 months, however, communication between parent and infant can begin to break down. The child's responses are not complete enough to meet parents' expectations. To make matters worse, the discovery that the child is deaf often doesn't occur until the second year, by which time the child has already missed a great deal of communication via language. One of the first indications of hearing impairment in 1-year-olds is seeming disobedience, as well as startled reactions when people approach (the child simply doesn't hear them coming). In 2-year-olds, there may be temper tantrums and frequent disobedience owing to failure to hear what the parents want. This may be accompanied by an overall failure to develop normal expectations about the world.

The diagnosis of deafness may come as a shock to parents who have been talking to the child all along. Like parents of blind children, parents of deaf children need special training and counseling (Hadadian, 1995; Robinshaw, 1994). Without careful attention during infancy, deafness can result in poor communication during the early childhood years and beyond, later leading to severe social, intellectual, and psychological problems (Meadow, 1975).

Infants with Severe Disabilities   When an infant is born with a severe disability such as cerebral palsy, there is a high risk of parental rejection, withdrawal, and depression. A severely disabled infant strains marital ties and may trigger a variety of disturbances in other children in the family. Childcare workers can help with a family's early adjustment problems, and they should be consulted from birth. Early success or failure in coping with initial traumas can greatly affect parents' ability to make wise decisions about childcare and education (Turnbull & Turnbull, 1990).

Children with severe disabilities also pose adjustment problems for siblings and grandparents. Grandparent support and involvement is positively related to the closeness of affectional ties with both grandchildren and their parents. Grandparents with higher educational levels also interact more positively with severely disabled grandchildren (Fingerman, 1998).

CONTENT CHECK
PATTERNS OF EARLY RELATIONSHIPS

True–False (answers are on the Companion Website)

1. The strange-situation test assesses the quality of the infant's attachment to the primary caregivers.
2. Highly responsive mothers tend to have more communicative and later more independent children.
3. The behavior of a sensitive mother remains unchanged as the baby grows older.
4. It is always healthier for infants to have exclusive rather than multiple attachments.
5. Child abuse rarely interferes with attachment.

Thinking Critically

How do children with disabilities pose special problems in the establishment of attachment?

Fathers, Siblings, and the Family System

Most children develop within a social context that encourages early attachment to the father, as well as to siblings, grandparents, and other family members who are regularly present. In other words, the infant's emotional development often doesn't depend on the strengths and weaknesses of a single attachment.

Fathers

Much has been learned from research on fathers and fathering in the United States. For some time now, fathers have been spending more time with their infants than they did in the past (Pleck, 1985; Ricks, 1985). They provide routine child care and can bathe, diaper, feed, and rock as skillfully as mothers. Fathers in general can be as responsive to the infant's cues as mothers (Parke, 1981), and infants can become as attached to their fathers as to their mothers. Infants can also experience the same level of separation anxiety as with their mothers (Hock & Lutz, 1998). Moreover, as might be expected, fathers who spend more time taking care of young children form stronger attachments to them, and the children benefit (Ricks, 1985). Despite these shared capabilities, however, most fathers still don't take *primary* responsibility for infant care. As a result, the father's relationship with the infant is often different from the mother's.

Fathering Styles The father's role in child rearing continues to evolve as more and more mothers work outside the home. However, some traditional differences in how fathers and mothers interact with their infants persist. For example, mothers are likely to hold infants for caretaking purposes; fathers are more likely to hold infants during play (Parke, 1981). Fathers are also more physical and spontaneous. Play between fathers and infants occurs in cycles, with peaks of excitement and attention followed by periods of minimal activity. In contrast, mothers engage their infants in subtle, shifting, gradual play, or initiate conventional games such as pat-a-cake. Fathers tend toward unusual,

Fathers today are taking a more active role in caring for infants.

vigorous, and unpredictable games, which infants find highly exciting (Lamb & Lamb, 1976). This changes, though, when the father is the primary or sole caregiver: Of necessity, he acts more like a traditional mother (Field, 1978). Surprisingly, recent research also suggests that older fathers are more likely to behave like traditional mothers when playing with their children, whereas younger fathers are more likely to conform to the traditional "father" role (Neville & Parke, 1997).

As infants grow older and require less direct care, father-infant interaction is likely to increase. Fathers may engage in more rough-and-tumble play and interact more frequently with the young child in public places such as zoos or parks (Lewis, 1987).

Fathers who frequently interact with their infants, are responsive to their signals, and become significant figures in their children's world are likely to develop into forceful agents of socialization. As the child grows older, the father becomes an important and positive role model. In contrast, fathers who are inaccessible to their infants may have difficulty establishing strong emotional ties later on, although even fathers who do not live with their families can remain involved with their children, visiting and playing with them and providing emotional support (Stier & Tienda, 1993). It is even possible that inaccessible fathers will have a negative influence as the child grows older (Ricks, 1985). Fathers' alcoholism has also been associated with more negative father-infant interaction, characterized by diminished paternal sensitivity and responsiveness. In such situations, the risks for later maladjustment among children are apparent as early as infancy (Eiden, Chavez, & Leonard, 1999).

Fathers who have the most positive influence in their young children's lives not only spend time with them but are also sensitive to their wants, cries, and needs (Easterbrooks & Goldberg, 1984; Parke, 1981). Indeed, today many U.S. fathers are broadening their parenting role, even during infancy (Garbarino, 2000; Lamb, 1997; Lamb, Pleck, & Levine, 1987).

Fathers and the Family System   There are both social and psychological reasons why fathers usually are not equal partners in infant care. In one study, mothers and fathers were recruited from a childbirth class in which the fathers were active participants and were expected to share in the care of the infant. It did not work out that way, however (Grossman, Pollack, & Golding, 1988). Soon after childbirth both the mothers and the fathers rated the fathers as less competent in most infant-care skills. As a result, the fathers tended to be relegated to the role of helper. Indeed, no father in the study ever mentioned the reverse situation, in which the mother helped the father. The more competent adult—the mother—generally took primary responsibility for infant care and became more adept at meeting the baby's needs and interpreting his or her signals. In general, fathers' back-seat role may be related to feelings of incompetence in caring for the child (Entwisle & Doering, 1988).

Most couples work through their differing responses to infant care by selecting complementary roles for the father and the mother. Those who aren't successful, however, tend to become impatient with each other, and the father takes on the role of reluctant and occasional helper who plays with the child but does little else.

Whether as partner or as helper, the father's influence on the infant (and the family) is considerable. Numerous studies indicate that the father's emotional support of the mother during pregnancy and early infancy is important in the establishment of positive relationships. The absence of the father during infancy places considerable stress on the family system (Lewis, 1987). Although in our culture the father often remains a secondary caregiver, he plays an important part in a complex system of interactions.

The addition of an infant, especially a firstborn child, affects the marriage itself. Studies have shown that the birth of the first child can place profound stress on the marital relationship. A newborn makes heavy demands on the time and energy of both parents. Complementary roles need to be established, child-care arrangements made, and decisions reached about the mother's return to work. The stress on the marriage may be greater if the infant is demanding, is frequently sick, or has a disability. It is possible for stress to bring the couple closer together (Turnbull & Turnbull, 1990), but if the marriage was vulnerable at the start, stress may instead create increased dissatisfaction and turmoil. Contrary to some people's folk wisdom, having a baby is often not the solution to a marriage that's on the rocks—it can make things worse.

Siblings

Siblings form significant and long-lasting attachments to each other beginning in infancy, although younger siblings are often more attached to older siblings than the reverse (Lewis, 1987). Infants often form very strong attachments to an older sibling and are upset when they are separated from him or her even overnight (Dunn & Kendrick, 1979).

Often, older siblings are important social models. Children learn how to share, cooperate, help, and empathize by watching their older brothers or sisters. They learn appropriate gender roles and family customs and values. In some cultures the older sibling is the principal caretaker of the younger child (Whiting & Whiting, 1975). In many families the positive aspects of sibling roles—helping, protecting, and providing an ally—last throughout life.

It is therefore somewhat surprising that the negative aspects of sibling relationships have received more research attention than the positive aspects (Lewis, 1987). Two negative aspects of sibling relationships are **sibling rivalry** and the **dethroning of the older sibling.** With the birth of a new infant, parents pay less attention to and have less time and energy for the firstborn child. The way they handle these changes influences the degree of strife, competition, and rivalry that develops between siblings (Dunn & Kendrick, 1980; Lewis, 1987; Lewis, Feiring, & Kotsonis, 1984). For example, if parents attempt to enlist the older sibling in the care of the newborn, an alliance is often created both between the siblings and between the older sibling and the parents. The mother and father and the older child may refer to the newborn as "our baby." In general, if parents set aside special time for the first child after the birth of a second child, it is more likely that the firstborn child will feel special rather than disregarded.

Grandparents

In many cultures, including the United States, grandparents see their adult children and grandchildren at least weekly. In families where both parents work, grandparents frequently are the primary caregivers; they also often serve as babysitters. Grandparents can be particularly important to the stability of single-parent households, in which one out of every five U.S. children now live, and to the 60% of all families with children under age 3 whose mothers are in the labor force (U.S. Census Bureau, 1997). Grandparents' roles are usually different from parents' roles, however, and different attachment relationships are formed. Grandparents frequently offer more approval, support, empathy, and sympathy, and use less discipline. The relationship tends to be more playful and relaxed (Lewis, 1987). Grandparents also have more time to tell the child

sibling rivalry Strife and competition between siblings, such as for parental attention.

dethroning of the older sibling Loss of being the center of attention when a younger sibling is born.

In families where both parents work, grandparents may be the primary caregivers for much of the time.

stories about "way-back-when," which can help create a sense of family identity and tradition.

This said, in the United States of today grandparents often find themselves having to balance multiple roles and possibly role conflict. Typically, at the onset of grandparenthood, grandparents are married and employed. They may also have living parents and may have to balance care responsibilities for their parents with those for their grandchildren (Szinovacz, 1998). A considerable proportion of U.S. families now also include stepgrandparents, which adds even more complexity to the caretaking mix (Johnson, 1988). Finally, although there appears to be considerable heterogeneity among grandparents of varying races, ethnicities, and genders, there are differences. For example, in the United States, a higher proportion of black grandmothers assume primary responsibility for grandchildren at some point in their lives than do white grandmothers (Szinovacz, 1998).

CONTENT CHECK

FATHERS, SIBLINGS, AND THE FAMILY SYSTEM

True–False (answers are on the Companion Website)

1. Fathers are less responsive to their infants' cues than are mothers.
2. Fathers who interact frequently and responsively with their infants are likely to become positive role models as the child grows older.
3. The addition of a firstborn child typically places considerable stress on the parents' marriage.
4. Initially, a baby tends to form weak attachments with older siblings.
5. Because grandparents' roles are different from those of parents, different attachment relationships are typically formed.

Thinking Critically

Have researchers been misleading by focusing more on the negative and less on the positive effects of sibling relationships? Why or why not?

Personality Development in the Second Year of Life

The ways in which we convey culture to our children, beginning in infancy, are far from subtle. Almost from birth we try to instill attitudes and values about bodily functions—the acceptability of erotic self-stimulation, the degree and kinds of physical contact that are acceptable—as well as the goodness or badness of their behaviors and their basic nature as human beings. Culturally based attitudes and values are communicated through specific child-rearing practices and have a wide-ranging effect on personality development.

It is in the context of broad, cross-cultural child-rearing patterns that we can see how differing practices affect sociocultural development. Four important aspects of infant development are how trust and nurturance develop; how children receive culturally laden signals through social referencing; how parents respond to children's attempts at autonomy; and how child-rearing practices affect infants' self-awareness and sense of self.

Trust, Nurturance, and a Secure Base

The development of trust marks the first stage of Erikson's theory of psychosocial development and occurs during the first year of life. It is during this stage that infants learn whether they can depend on the people around them and whether their social environment is consistent and predictable. If we examine child-rearing practices in other cultures, we see dramatic differences in approaches to the development of trust.

A basic sense of trust is conveyed to the infant through the mother's (or other primary caregiver's) nurturing behavior, that is, her responsiveness to the infant's needs. Through their reactions to feeding, weaning, and comfort-seeking behaviors, mothers and other caregivers convey their values and attitudes. From these reactions children learn whether they are considered good or bad, when to feel anxious or guilty, and when to feel comfortable and secure. In all, they learn a great deal more than merely whether they should suck their thumbs or carry a security blanket.

Feeding and Comforting   Researchers who study the development of trust focus on how feeding fits into the overall pattern of nurturant care. Feeding, whether by breast or bottle, allows for a special closeness between mother and child as it expresses the mother's sensitivity and responsiveness.

In some cultures the transition period between the infant's birth and separation from the mother lasts 3 years or more. Feeding is an integral part of the prolonged relationship. Children may sleep close to their mothers, be carried around during most of the first year, and be breast-fed until the age of 3 (Richman et al., 1988). In other cultures—especially in the United States—some infants are weaned almost immediately and placed in a separate bedroom.

In Italy, nurturance of the infant is a social affair. Mothers and infants are rarely alone. Mothers do most of the feeding, dressing, and cleaning of their infants in an indulgent and caring fashion, but family members, friends, and neighbors also contribute. In one study, people other than the mother tended to the baby—through hugging, talking, teaching, and even teasing—70% of the time, even when the mother was present. The U.S. observer was especially surprised at the amount of teasing that occurred, even when the infant became upset and cried. Pacifiers were held just out of reach; adults said, "Here comes

Daddy!" only to laugh and declare "He isn't here any more!" Infants were jiggled and pinched to wake them up when adults wanted to play with them. Yet the infants learned to cope remarkably well and developed trust in the adults (New, 1988).

Much research has been devoted to thumb sucking and other self-comforting behaviors, but remarkably few conclusions have been reached about these behaviors. For the most part, sucking seems to be a natural need. Yet parents respond to it in a wide variety of ways (Goldberg, 1972; Richman et al., 1988). In Europe in the early twentieth century, for example, thumb sucking was considered a dirty habit that was harmful to a child's general personality development. Elaborate devices, vile-tasting applications, and sleeves were used to prevent it.

That era is clearly over. Today some children are given a pacifier on the assumption that they can give it up more easily than thumb sucking. Most children who use either thumbs or pacifiers give them up as regular comfort devices by the end of early childhood. For those who remain avid thumb suckers or comfort seekers, it is assumed that they have other needs that are not being met. For example, some children may continue sucking their thumbs simply because of the extra attention they receive when parents try to dissuade them from doing it.

Social Referencing and Cultural Meaning

An important area of parental influence is social referencing. When infants are not sure whether a situation is safe or unsafe, good or bad, they often look to the parent for emotional signals. For example, in Chapter 5 we saw the effectiveness of social referencing in encouraging or discouraging an infant to cross the visual cliff, and earlier in this chapter we saw how social referencing can affect children's behavior toward a stranger. Infants look for emotional signals in many circumstances, including how far to wander away from the mother and whether or not to explore a strange object. Infants reference fathers as well as mothers. Although they look more at mothers than at fathers when both are present, the father's signals seem to be equally effective in regulating behavior (Hirshberg & Svejda, 1990).

What are the consequences of one parent's encouraging the child to explore an unusual object while the other parent frowns and appears worried? In a study of 1-year-olds (Hirshberg, 1990), parents were coached to give either consistent or conflicting emotional signals. The infants adapted much more easily to consistent emotional signals—either both parents happy or both parents fearful—than to conflicting ones. In fact, when they were given conflicting facial responses—say, "happy" from the mother and "afraid" from the father—the infants expressed their confusion with a wide range of anxious behaviors. Some sucked their thumbs or rocked in an agitated way; others avoided the situation altogether; still others seemed disoriented. Thus, even 1-year-olds are remarkably sensitive to emotional signals from their parents.

Through social referencing and selective attention, parents teach infants as young as 1 year of age the values of their culture. Communication of cultural meaning has been demonstrated in a series of studies of the !Kung San, a hunter-gatherer culture in Botswana (Bakeman & Adamson, 1990). For the !Kung San, sharing is highly valued. When cultural anthropologists looked at mothers and their 10- to 12-month-old infants, they were surprised to find that, in contrast to many U.S. parents, the !Kung San parents seemed to pay no attention to the infant's exploration of objects. They did not smile or talk about the objects, nor did they punish their children as they picked up twigs, grass, parts of food, nut shells, bones, and the like. Instead, they said the equivalent of "He's teaching himself." However, the adults paid close attention to the sharing of objects, with commands like "Give it to me" or "Here, take this."

Parents also convey cultural meaning by including toddlers in social interactions, even though the toddlers are often peripheral to the ongoing social life of the family and community. Barbara Rogoff and colleagues (Rogoff, Mistry, Goncu, & Mosier, 1993) visited four communities—a Mayan Indian town in Guatemala, a middle-class urban community in the United States, a tribal village in India, and a middle-class urban neighborhood in Turkey—to study how adults help toddlers learn appropriate social behavior. Sometimes toddlers were given direct instruction and help, but often they learned through their own keen observation, imitation, and participation in adult activities. Thus, through guided participation adults bridge the gap created by the child's limited knowledge of events, and structure small tasks that are within the group's activity. For example, at dinner time toddlers may eat with the family (finger foods instead of adult foods), imitate the conversation and gestures of adults and older siblings, enjoy good feelings and laughter, and be encouraged to take small adult-like actions like lifting a cup for a toast.

Autonomy, Discipline, and Prosocial Behavior

When infants are a year old their parents have already taught them some guidelines for acceptable behavior, especially with regard to dependency and their need for physical closeness. In the second year caregivers must cope with a whole new set of issues. Toward the end of the second year, many toddlers experience increased emotional conflict between their increasing need for autonomy and their obvious dependence and limited skills.

The changes that occur in children at this age were observed at length in a classic study by Margaret Mahler and colleagues (Mahler, Pine, & Bergman, 1975). They noted an extraordinary ambivalence in 18-month-old children. The toddlers were torn between a desire to stay close to their mother and a desire to be independent. Their new sense of separateness seemed to frighten them. They tried to deny it by acting as if their mothers were extensions of themselves. For example, a child might pull the mother's hand in an effort to have her pick up an object the child wanted. In addition, the toddlers experienced a wider range of emotions and were developing new ways of dealing with them, such as suppressing crying. The way parents deal with the conflict between autonomy and dependence is expressed in their approach to discipline.

Discipline What limits should a parent or caregiver set on a child's behavior? Some parents, afraid that any kind of control over their children's behavior will interfere with creative exploration and independence, passively stand by while their 2-year-olds do whatever they please—in *your* home as well as their own. Discipline, when it comes, is often harsh, reflecting the adults' sense of frustration. Other parents, determined not to "spoil" their children and convinced that 2-year-olds should act like responsible little adults, set so many limits on behavior that their children literally cannot do anything right. Although it is easy to see the errors in these extremes, it is not easy to provide guidelines that work for every situation. For example, adults who encourage exploration and manipulation sooner or later may have to cope with a child who wants to stick a fork into an electrical outlet. Obviously, guidelines must be tempered with common sense and must consider children's needs for safety, independence, and creative expression.

Parental feedback helps children see how their actions affect others. Children need feedback if they are to become sensitive to the needs of others. Feedback might consist of praise for good behavior, such as "What a good helper you are." Or it might take the form of mild scolding, such as "Don't do that, it hurts your brother." The key to feedback is that it should focus on the *behavior*—not the child—as the object of criticism.

Children who have a strong attachment relationship and whose needs are met through loving interaction with an adult are neither spoiled by attention nor frightened or threatened by reasonable limits. They are stronger and more confident because they have a secure base from which to venture forth into independent activities. The secure-base phenomenon is robust indeed and has been demonstrated across many cultures in addition to the U.S., including China, Germany, Japan, and Israel (Posada et al., 1995). The researchers also found, however, that across cultures mothers differ with regard to what they perceive as the "ideal" child in this respect, such as what constitutes appropriate proximity to the mother and how much physical contact is preferable.

Going to the potty with a book. Does she plan to be there for a while?

Toilet Training Although much early theory and research, inspired by Freudian theory, focused on the methods and presumed long-range effects of toilet training, recent studies view it as part of a cluster of child-rearing issues. Toilet training is only one aspect of behavior that is affected by adult attitudes toward children's explorations, the way children handle their own body, and children's needs for autonomy. By itself, it is not a major issue in social and personality development.

Those who are severe and harsh in toilet training are usually just as strict about other behaviors that require self-mastery and independence, such as feeding, dressing, and general exploration. Some adults demand that a child have early and total bowel and bladder control; they regard "accidents" as intolerable. Such parents are also likely to be severe when their child breaks a plate, plays in the dirt, and explores new places and objects. This strict discipline can have pronounced effects on personality development, creating a child who is inhibited and fearful of anything new.

Development of Prosocial Behavior Many studies have focused on the development of **prosocial behaviors** such as empathy, cooperation, sharing, and general concern about the well-being of others. Between 18 and 24 months toddlers begin to cooperate, share, help, and respond empathically to emotional distress in others. For example, they may offer their teddy bear to a crying child. The development of empathy in particular may be related to the toddler's developing sense of self, as Carolyn Zahn-Waxler and colleagues explain:

As children begin to differentiate self and other during the second year of life and hence to develop understanding of others as separate beings, their emotional involvement in another's distress begins to be transformed from personal self-distress to sympathetic concern for the victim. (Zahn-Waxler, Radke-Yarrow, Wagner, & Chapman, 1992, p. 126)

These researchers also believe that the roots of empathy in toddlers are linked to secure attachments and to how the child is treated when hurt or in need of help. For example, greater maternal warmth is positively associated with increases in the child's empathy during the second year of life. In contrast, children of mothers who control with anger tend to show decreased empathy (Azar, 1997).

Concern for others does not emerge smoothly. Often toddlers are confused when they see others in distress. They don't know how to react and may even

prosocial behavior Helping, sharing, or cooperative actions that are intended to benefit others.

laugh. In one series of studies (Radke-Yarrow, Zahn-Waxler, & Chapman, 1983), mothers were asked to pretend that they had just hurt themselves. At 21 months, toddlers were confused and anxious about the mother's distress. However, 3 months later some of the toddlers had learned soothing, comforting behaviors by observing the behavior of their mothers, who regularly responded with empathy when the child was in distress.

In studies of cooperation in simple tasks, almost no 12-month-old infants cooperate with each other. At 18 months, cooperation is infrequent and appears accidental. At 24 months, with a little coaching, nearly all toddlers can cooperate (Brownell & Carriger, 1990).

Development of the Self

Many theories of adult and child development emphasize the individual's *self-concept*—his or her perception of personal identity. Self-concept is viewed as an integrator, a filter, and a mediator for much of human behavior. That is, people tend to behave in ways that are consistent with their self-image and self-concept.

At first, infants cannot differentiate between themselves and the world around them. Gradually, however, they begin to realize that they are separate and unique beings. Much of infancy is devoted to making this distinction. From 3 to 8 months infants actively learn about their bodies. First, they discover their hands, their feet, and some of the things they can do with them. Later, they use their hands to explore and manipulate objects and see what happens. At 7 or 8 months, as indicated, they become wary of strangers. They also become capable of delaying their actions for a short time. Infants now become more deliberate in testing and exploring their own responses and events they cause to happen. Also, by observing and imitating the behavior of people around them, infants begin to learn how they should behave.

Between 12 and 18 months, infants are hard at work learning social expectations and what happens when they test or explore the social world. By the end of this period, they clearly recognize themselves in pictures and in the mirror (see Table 6–3 for an overview of stages in self-recognition), and they are ready for more detailed socialization (Lewis & Feinman, 1991). Finally, from 18 to 30 months children learn a great deal about themselves. They learn about their gender, their physical features and characteristics, their goodness and badness, what they can and cannot do. With the growing sense of self come more emotional reactions to others, sometimes in the form of temper tantrums. As toddlers become more aware of their own feelings, they react more personally to frustration and hurt and may respond with intense emotion (Dunn & Munn, 1985).

Michael Lewis (1995) studied the development of "self-conscious" emotions such as pride, shame, guilt, and embarrassment that begin to appear after the infant's first birthday. Such emotions depend on a fairly well-developed understanding of social rules along with a sense of self, as indicated by their displaying joy when they succeed and distress when they fail (Stipek, Recchia, & McClintic, 1992). That is, the infant must be able to determine how personal behavior compares to the standards set by the culture, along with whether she or he is succeeding or failing at meeting those standards.

Awareness of sex roles begins to develop at around 21 months (Goldberg & Lewis, 1969). Girls and boys begin to exhibit gender-specific behaviors. Boys are likely to disengage themselves from their mothers, whereas girls seek greater closeness to them and have more ambivalent feelings about being separate. This behavior seems to be linked to awareness of gender differences.

Table 6-3   Who Is That Baby in the Mirror?

At 9 months, an infant studies "that baby" in the mirror. At about 18 months, infants make the amazing discovery of an independent self.

During the first 2 years, infants make giant leaps in self-knowledge. From experiments involving infants of various ages looking at themselves in the mirror, it appears that self-knowledge develops in the following stages:

Before 8 months

Infants appear to be attracted to the image of an infant in the mirror, but it is unclear whether they recognize it as their own image. Sometimes infants 6 to 8 months old will recognize that their own movements correspond with the movements they observe in the mirror.

Between 8 and 16 months

Infants can tell the difference between their own image and the images of others who are clearly different from themselves, such as an older child. During this period infants begin to associate specific features with their sense of self. Nevertheless, an infant will sometimes crawl around the mirror to try to find the "other" baby. If a researcher puts a dot of red rouge on the infant's nose, the infant notices it but points to the nose in the mirror and not to his or her own nose.

At About 18 months

Toddlers no longer need environmental clues to make the connection between the baby in the mirror and themselves. That is, they recognize that the image they see is their own image. Now, if the researcher puts a dot of red rouge on the toddler's nose, there is a classic reaction. The infant points to her own nose, turns her head away from the mirror, drops her eyes, smiles, and looks embarrassed.

By Age 2

Self-knowledge expands to include awareness of activities as well as appearance. A 2-year-old who preens in front of a mirror is engaging in a self-admiring activity (Cicchetti & Beeghly, 1990).

Primary source: Lewis & Brooks-Gunn, 1979.

By the end of the second year, children's language is filled with references to themselves. Children know their names and use them, often describing their needs and feelings in the third person: "Terri wants water." The words "me" and "mine" take on new significance, and the concept of ownership is clearly and strongly acted out. Even in families that emphasize sharing and minimize ownership, toddlers can be extremely possessive. It may be that they develop the concept of ownership in rounding out their understanding of self. Logically, sharing and cooperation come more easily once toddlers are confident about what is theirs.

In sum, self-awareness is a function of self-exploration, cognitive maturation, and reflections about self. Toddlers can frequently be heard talking to and admonishing themselves ("No, Lee, don't touch") or rewarding themselves ("Me good girl!"). They incorporate cultural and social expectations into their reflections as well as into their behavior, and they begin to judge themselves and others in light of these expectations. If they enjoy consistent, loving interaction with the caregiver in an environment that they are free to explore and can begin to control, they learn to make valid predictions about the world around them. Gradually they develop a perception of self—hopefully as acceptable, competent individuals. Table 6–4 summarizes factors in personality development during infancy.

Table 6–4 Selected Factors in Personality Development During Infancy

Temperament

At birth, children display behavioral styles that can influence how their parents react to and care for them, in turn reciprocally influencing the children's personality development. Some infants are *easy*, some are *difficult*, and some are *slow to warm up*.

Attachment

Responsive caregiving fosters *securely attached* infants who later are highly curious, sociable, independent, and competent during early childhood. Unresponsive or indifferent caregiving fosters *insecurely attached* infants who later are less enthusiastic, persistent, and cooperative compared to securely attached infants.

Neglect and Abuse

Infants and toddlers who suffer neglect and physical abuse experience distortions and delays in developing a sense of self and self-control, also social skills. As adolescents and adults, they are more inclined toward mental disorders and alcohol or other drug abuse and may become child abusers themselves.

Siblings

In addition to parents, older siblings are often attachment objects for infants and toddlers and can serve as important role models. On the positive side, young children learn to share, cooperate, and empathize by observing their older siblings. On the negative side, sibling rivalry may disrupt the family, and older siblings may model undesirable behaviors for young children.

Social Referencing

Personality development and behavior are strongly influenced by emotional and other signals parents provide for their children in social situations. Cultural values and meanings are also conveyed through social referencing.

Parental Discipline

Especially during toddlerhood, how parents balance the child's attempts at autonomy with necessary discipline and limits is important. Either extreme—placing too few or too many limits—can interfere with healthy personality development.

Self-Concept

Personality revolves around a sense of self or personal identity. Children and adults tend to behave in ways that are consistent with their self-concept, which is based in part on gender, physical abilities, and physical appearance. In turn, even young children reflect on matters such as whether they are good or bad, how others view them, and whether they are acceptable, competent human beings, in forming their self-concept.

CONTENT CHECK
PERSONALITY DEVELOPMENT IN THE SECOND YEAR

True–False (answers are on the Companion Website)

1. The crisis of autonomy versus shame and doubt marks the first stage of Erikson's psychosocial development.
2. It is through social referencing that parents teach the infant the values of their culture.
3. By the end of the first year, infants begin to show prosocial behaviors.
4. One of the main tasks of infancy involves developing a sense of self as an independent being.

Thinking Critically

How does the particular society in which the infant is raised influence personality development?

Parental Employment

In exploring the implications of parental employment, we often refer to the employment of mothers. The reason is simple: Traditionally, in most societies, the mother has had the primary responsibility for caregiving. However, an increasing number of fathers are taking on this responsibility. They may do so for a variety of reasons, including a divorce that grants them custody, illness or death of the mother, a situation in which the mother can better support the family, and the recognition that the father can be an effective, nurturing parent.

The Social Ecology of Child Care

The **social ecology of child care** refers to the environment in which child care takes place, including government policy and support, community approval or disapproval, and cost. Not unexpectedly, the social ecology of child care differs from one country to another. In Sweden, for example, a large-scale study found that 85% of mothers with children under school age work part time or full time outside the home. In such a situation, there is an enormous need for child care, which is met by a publicly funded child-care system (Andersson, 1989; Hwang & Broberg, 1992). Child care is provided for every family that requests it. There are day-care centers as well as family-based day-care providers, called *day mothers*. Both the day-care centers and the day mothers are licensed and regulated. There is also a system of open preschools where mothers or day mothers may take children to play with other children and receive advice and support.

By comparison, parents in the United States receive little public support. They are financially responsible for providing whatever supplemental child care they need and are assisted in this responsibility only if their income is low. Because about 60% of U.S. mothers of infants and toddlers work outside the home, many families face the difficult task of finding suitable child care at an affordable price. (Figure 6–1 shows the percentages of U.S. working mothers with children under age 5 for selected years.) Infant day care is one of the most expensive and least available child-care options, often straining the finances of many working parents (Galinsky & Stein, 1990).

social ecology of child care
The totality of the environment in which child care occurs, within and beyond the home.

Figure 6-1 U.S. Labor Force Participation Rates for Wives with Husband Present by Age of Child, 1975-1996

Source: U.S. Census Bureau, 1997.

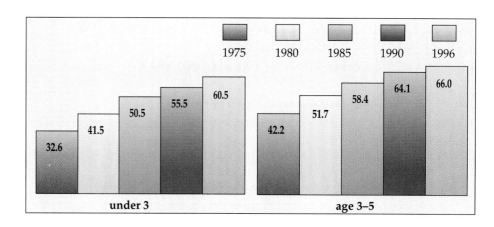

About 3 out of 4 infants and toddlers in the United States receive care from someone other than their parents. About 25% percent are enrolled in nursery schools or group settings, with the rest cared for by relatives or other caregivers (see Figure 6–2). It is clear that U.S. parents are willing to use both formal and informal child-care arrangements.

Infant Day Care

In the United States, under the current Family and Medical Leave Act, employers must provide 12 weeks beginning at childbirth. Mothers (or fathers who take on the primary caregiving role) who return to work after only 12 weeks must arrange for the safe and reliable supervision of their children. Some hire a relative or friend or use an unlicensed "sitter" from their neighborhood. Others seek licensed, high-quality day-care centers, which not only can be costly, but often have waiting lists. Still others seek local "family" day-care homes, which may or may not employ adequately trained personnel.

Both family day-care homes and well-run day-care centers are capable of fostering healthy development in infants and toddlers. Numerous studies have found that children ranging in age from 3 to 30 months developed at least as well in a quality group-care situation as children from similar backgrounds who were reared at home (Clarke-Stewart, 1982; Kagan, 1978; National Institute of Child Health and Human Development, NICHD, 1997). However, Swedish children who begin day care before age 1 have generally been found to rate *more* favorably and perform better in elementary school than children who are

Figure 6-2 U.S. Child-Care Arrangements for Children Under 5 Years of age

Source: U.S. Census Bureau, 1995.

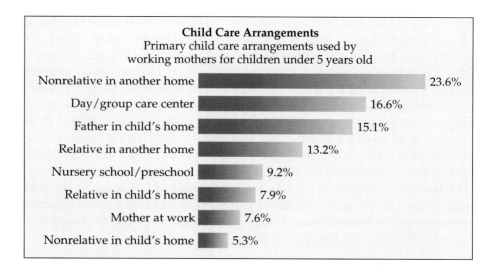

A MATTER FOR DEBATE

EARLY INFANT DAY CARE

In the mid-1980s Jay Belsky published a startling warning to parents and infant-care professionals. After reviewing studies that compared children who had begun day care in their first year with children who started later, he cautiously concluded that entry into day care during the first year is a "risk factor" for the development of insecure attachments in infancy and increased aggressiveness, noncompliance, and withdrawal in early childhood and later (Belsky, 1986, 1988, 1990).

The report drew immediate and intense reactions from many researchers, day-care workers, and parents. If it were true that infants are at risk when both parents work and place their infants in early alternative care, there would be serious implications for all concerned. Clearly, the lifestyle of dual-income parents was being challenged. Some day-care workers felt personally insulted; some instead suggested that the possibility of harm attributable to less than ideal day-care arrangements deserved closer scrutiny (Miringoff, 1987). Other experts warned of a hasty conclusion drawn from diverse studies conducted under a variety of circumstances (Chess, 1987).

Before the 1980s, Belsky noted, virtually all research was done in high-quality, research-oriented centers that were often affiliated with universities. As a result, there was little evidence to suggest that nonparental care was a problem. In fact, infants in high-quality centers tended to show better social, cognitive, and emotional development than home-reared infants. Only recently had researchers studied infants in a wide range of nonparental care arrangements of varying quality. In addition, a more representative cross-section of families were studied, including single-parent families, families at risk for abuse or neglect, and dual-parent families at all socioeconomic levels.

When Belsky looked closely at such studies as well his own, he concluded that there were some disturbing commonalities. Among children who had nonparental care starting in the first year and for more than 20 hours per week, more were insecurely attached to their mothers—even when the non-parental caregiver was a neighbor or relative at home with her own child. In his interpretation, the proportion of infants who were insecurely attached was nearly double (Belsky, 1986; Belsky & Rovine, 1988, 1990a).

Other researchers have reached different conclusions from the same studies. The quality of alternative care, for example, appears to be more important than the number of hours spent in the alternative care setting. Infants who receive low-quality care or experience changes in their primary caregiver are particularly vulnerable. Also, when families that are under stress place their infants in a low-quality care arrangement, the risk to the child's well-being is greater (Phillips, McCartney, Scarr, & Howes, 1987). The same researchers also found no significant differences in quality of attachment between day-care children and home-care children (based on a meta-analysis of 14 prior studies), as did a replication by other researchers of four studies cited by Belsky (Roggman, Langlois, Hubbs-Tait, & Rieser-Danner, 1994).

Finally, a large-scale study by the NICHD (1997) concluded that age of entry into day care and amount of day care *by themselves* were not good predictors of quality of attachment. The NICHD researchers did find, however, that low maternal responsiveness and sensitivity in combination with poor quality day care or extensive day care were associated with insecure attachment. However, in an extensive review of the literature on nonparental child care, Michael Lamb (1996) concluded that age of entry is important, along with the quality of the care and the temperament of individual children.

Thus, the picture is a complex one—much more so than Belsky's conclusions implied—and one that will undoubtedly continue to be a matter for debate.

reared at home by parents. In the study cited earlier, they were more competent on cognitive tests of reasoning and vocabulary and were rated by teachers as better in school subjects like reading and arithmetic and as more socially competent than their home-reared peers (Andersson, 1989). Some researchers in the United States have found similar but smaller positive effects on cognitive or social development for children in early group care (Clarke-Stewart & Fein, 1983). However, the effects on infant-caregiver attachment in particular may be a different matter, as discussed in "A Matter for Debate," above).

Positive outcomes don't apply where the day-care services that are available to many U.S. families are not of good quality. In these, staff members are often poorly trained and poorly paid, staff turnover rates are high, and child-to-staff ratios are high. Such facilities rarely admit researchers, but one study (Vandell & Corasaniti, 1990) was able to assess third graders after the fact in an area characterized by poor-quality day care. The children who had been in day care displayed highly significant and pervasive negative effects compared to children reared at home: Extensive day care was associated with lower ratings on peer relations, work habits, and emotional health, also lower scores on standardized tests. The day-care children also later earned lower grades in school. Some had serious behavior problems, including extreme aggressiveness. It was not possible to determine conclusively that the infant care alone caused these problem behaviors, but the results were highly suggestive.

Other research confirms that how infants fare in day care is influenced by their gender, the family's economic status, and—most importantly—the quality of care the infant receives. Children of poverty seem to do better when cared for by their mothers or grandmothers; in more affluent families, girls do better with baby sitters and boys do better with their mothers (Baydar & Brooks-Gunn, 1991). Higher quality infant care also has been linked to greater maternal sensitivity, whereas more child-care hours are associated with slightly less sensitive mothering (NICHD, 1999).

Two Child-Care Adaptation Models   What is it that causes difficulty for some infants who receive nonparental care after the first year? Researchers suggest two models of adaptation (Jaeger & Weinraub, 1990), which, although based on research specifically with mothers, can be applied to fathers as well. According to the *maternal separation model*, the infant experiences daily, repeated separations from the mother as either maternal absence or maternal rejection. The infant begins to doubt the mother's availability or responsiveness. It is the absence of the mother that leads to insecurity.

In the *quality of mothering model*, it is not maternal employment or separation per se that determines the infant's reactions. Instead, the key factor is how maternal employment affects maternal behavior. The employed mother can't be as sensitive and responsive a caregiver as she might be if she had more time and practice, and the result is insecurity in the infant. Research based on the quality-of-mothering model focuses on the competing demands of the mother's work and family, the quality of the child care (and whether she has to worry about it), the characteristics of the infant, and whether the mother thinks her

The day care services available to many families are not ideal, like this overcrowded infant center. However, what is perceived as overcrowding may vary from culture to culture.

infant is sturdy and capable of coping with the situation. Researchers are also examining the general quality of the mother's life and the satisfaction she experiences in her various roles, as well as any role conflict, marital strain, and fatigue she may experience. If the mother feels strong separation anxiety when she leaves her child each day, the child tends not to do well (S. L. McBride, 1990; Stifter, Coulehan & Fish, 1993).

CONTENT CHECK
PARENTAL EMPLOYMENT

True–False (answers are on the Companion Website)

1. The social ecology of child care refers to the environment beyond the family in which child care occurs.
2. In the United States most infants and toddlers receive care from someone besides their parents.
3. An infant's gender has no effect on the day care the infant receives.
4. According to the quality of mothering model, maternal separation negatively impacts on the infant's ability to cope.

Thinking Critically

Why is early infant day care controversial?

CHAPTER 6 REVISITED

- Enculturation and socialization interact with temperament to help shape personality.

- Some infants are born with an easy temperament, some with a difficult temperament, and some with a slow-to-warm-up temperament.

Social and Emotional Development in Infancy

- Researchers have identified six stages in the emotional development of children in infancy and early childhood.

- In Ainsworth's view, attachment behaviors promote nearness to specific individuals; both infant and caregiver must behave in ways that foster attachment.

- According to Bowlby, human babies are born with preprogrammed behaviors that promote attachment.

- The attachment behaviors of both mother and infant evolve gradually and reciprocally.

- Stranger anxiety and separation anxiety appear at about 7 months and vary considerably in intensity from one child to another.

- The discrepancy hypothesis is one explanation for stranger anxiety and separation anxiety.

- Social referencing profoundly affects infants' emotional reactions.

Patterns of Early Relationships

- Ainsworth's strange-situation test is used to assess the quality of infant attachment to caregivers.

- Secure attachment is associated with responsive caregiving.

- Insecure attachment takes three forms: resistant, avoidant, and disorganized/disoriented, each of which is associated with unresponsive, indifferent, or resenting caregiving.

- Mothers and other caregivers who are more verbally responsive and attentive to their infants tend to have children who are communicative and later more autonomous.

- By monitoring the baby's responses, caregivers gradually learn when the child is most receptive to new cues; the closer the similarity between caregiver and infant behavior, the more attentive babies will be.

- Parents progressively structure their relationship with their child through scaffolding.

- Early mutuality and signaling lay the foundation for long-standing patterns of interaction.

- Day care and multiple caregivers may have no adverse effects on attachment; adjustment to day care is easiest for toddlers who have had some experience with multiple caregivers.

- Lack of caregiver affection and attention can produce failure-to-thrive syndrome.

- Child abuse during infancy can result in insecure attachment and developmental delays.

- When an infant cannot see, there is a danger that communication and mutuality will break down; caregivers can be trained to watch for and interpret infants' hand signals.

- When an infant cannot hear, communication may break down when the infant's responses do not meet parents' expectations; special training for parents helps here as well.

Fathers, Siblings, and the Family System

- Fathers can be as responsive to infants as mothers, and infants can become as attached to their fathers as they are to their mothers.

- Fathers are more likely to hold infants during play and tend to be more physical and spontaneous.

- Fathers who are significant figures in their children's world become important positive role models.

- Most couples develop complementary infant-care roles.

- The birth of the first child can place profound stress on the marital relationship.

- Siblings form significant and long-lasting attachments to each other beginning in infancy.

- Two negative aspects of sibling relationships are sibling rivalry and the dethroning of the older sibling.

- Compared to parents, grandparents frequently offer more approval, support, empathy, and sympathy, and use less discipline.

Personality Development in the Second Year

- According to Erikson, the development of trust versus mistrust marks the first stage of psychosocial development.

- Infants acquire a sense of trust as a result of responsive caregiving.

- Social referencing is an important source of information for infants.

- Through social referencing and selective attention, parents teach infants the values of their culture.

- Toward the end of the second year, toddlers experience increased emotional conflict between their greater need for autonomy and their remaining dependence and limited skills.

- Parental discipline should be tempered with common sense and must consider children's needs for safety, independence, and creative expression.

- Prosocial behaviors begin to develop between 18 and 24 months.

- At first infants cannot differentiate between themselves and the world around them, but they gradually realize that they are separate and unique beings.

- Self-awareness is a function of self-exploration, cognitive maturation, and reflections about self.

Parental Employment

- The social ecology of child care can profoundly affect child development.

- Parents in the United States receive little public support; they use both formal and informal child-care arrangements.

- Both family day-care homes and well-run day-care centers are capable of fostering healthy development in infants and toddlers.

- How infants fare in day care is influenced by their gender, the family's economic status, and the quality of care the infant receives.

- Two explanations for why some infants experience difficulty with nonparental care after the first year are the maternal separation model and the quality of mothering model.

KEY TERMS

personality
temperament
stranger anxiety and separation
  anxiety
discrepancy hypothesis
social referencing
secure attachment

insecure attachment
resistant attachment
avoidant attachment
disorganized/disoriented
  attachment
mutuality or interactive synchrony
scaffolding

child abuse
child neglect
failure-to-thrive syndrome
sibling rivalry
dethroning of the older sibling
prosocial behavior
social ecology of child care

EARLY CHILDHOOD: PHYSICAL, COGNITIVE, AND LANGUAGE DEVELOPMENT

7

CHAPTER OUTLINE

CHAPTER PREVIEW

Do you know:

1. The ways in which a child's *body* loses the look of infancy during early childhood?

2. What the *brain growth spurt* is and why theorists call the first several years of life a *window of opportunity*?

3. What brain *lateralization* is and how it proceeds?

4. How *gross-motor* and *fine-motor* development proceed during early childhood?

5. The difference between *intrinsic* and *extrinsic* motivation?

6. How a *preoperational* child's thinking differs from that of older children and adults?

7. Why *symbolic representation* is so important to cognitive and language development?

8. How Piaget assessed *differences* in the thinking of preoperational children and older children and why he may have *erred* in his conclusions?

9. How the *information-processing model* of memory works and how young children's memory is *limited* compared to older children and adults?

10. What evidence there is that young children devise *their own rules* for language from what they hear being spoken around them?

11. How young children's *conversational skills* develop?

12. What *subdialects* are and how they differ from true *dialects*?

13. Whether *bilingualism* is good or bad for a young child?

14. What kinds of *play* young children engage in and how these are important to learning and cognitive development?

These are the main topics of Chapter 7.

As relative newcomers to our world, 2- to 6-year-olds often demonstrate their thinking in ways that are both amusing and thought provoking. Consider the following excerpt from *Winnie-the-Pooh*, which captures the child's cognitive and social egocentrism in early childhood—that is, the child's tendency to see and interpret things primarily from his or her own point of view:

> One day when he was out walking, he came to an open place in the middle of the forest, and in the middle of this place was a large oak-tree, and, from the top of the tree, there came a loud buzzing-noise.
>
> Winnie-the-Pooh sat down at the foot of the tree, put his head between his paws and began to think.
>
> First of all he said to himself: "That buzzing-noise means something. You don't get a buzzing-noise like that, just buzzing and buzzing, without its meaning something. If there's a buzzing-noise, somebody's making a buzzing-noise, and the only reason for making a buzzing-noise that *I* know of is because you're a bee."
>
> Then he thought another long time, and said: "And the only reason for being a bee that I know of is making honey."

And then he got up, and said: "And the only reason for making honey is so as *I* can eat it." So he began to climb the tree.

He climbed and he climbed and he climbed, and as he climbed he sang a little song to himself. It went like this:
"Isn't it funny
How a bear likes honey?
Buzz! Buzz! Buzz!
I wonder why he does?"

A. A. Milne (1926/1961), pp. 5–7

Such attitudes reveal a great deal about children. During early childhood, children's errors indicate that there's an enormous distance to be covered between the ages of 2 and 6 in developing the thought processes necessary for formal schooling. Young children change gradually and develop into concept-forming, linguistically competent realists. They discover what they can and cannot control. They generalize from experience. Their reasoning changes from forming simple concepts to using the beginnings of logic.

They also acquire the language necessary to express their needs, thoughts, and feelings. Language develops rapidly in interaction with cognitive and social development. In the initial days of early childhood, children manage with two- or three-word "sentences" based on their limited and at times idiosyncratic grammar; in contrast, 6-year-olds speak in complete sentences with essentially correct grammatical structure. As young children learn syntax and vocabulary, they also absorb culturally appropriate social values such as politeness, obedience, and gender roles. Thus, language is a bridge between infancy and childhood: Children come to understand and communicate their wants, needs, and observations, and others respond to them accordingly.

Accompanying cognitive and linguistic development are rapid and dramatic changes in children's appearance and physical competence. Chubby toddlers with large heads and short limbs become slimmer 6-year-olds with smoother coordination and increased strength. Children refine their ability to skip and run and develop the fine motor skills they need to write their alphabet, dress themselves, or place puzzle pieces in the right places.

The developmental strides children make in thinking, language, and motor skills during early childhood are intricately interrelated. As children become physically stronger and more capable, they are motivated to use their developing skills to explore and learn. Exploration leads to further skill development. Thus, the ways in which children behave and think—and the ways in which their brains develop—form an integrated and dynamic system (Diamond, 2000; Johnson, 2000; Thelen, 1992; Thelen & Smith, 1996). Although an understanding of the intricacies of this integration is still in a sense in its infancy, we encounter examples at numerous points in the chapter.

Physical Development

Between the ages of 2 and 6, a child's body loses the look of infancy as it changes in size, body proportions, and shape. At the same time, rapid brain development leads to more sophisticated and complex learning abilities and refinement of gross and fine motor skills.

Body Size and Proportions

A visit to a pediatrician's office often includes an evaluation of the child's height and weight. Although children vary considerably, extreme deviations from the average for a given age can indicate developmental problems. Developmental psychologists share pediatricians' interest in the physiological aspects of growth but also focus on the relationship between growth and the acquisition of new skills.

It cannot be overemphasized that generalized statements about growth may or may not apply to individual children. Each child's physical growth is the result of genetics, nutrition, and the opportunity to play and exercise. As we saw in Chapter 4, prolonged deprivation of essential nutrients can have pronounced effects on children's physical and motor development. Sustained periods of malnutrition during early childhood limit children's cognitive development both directly and indirectly. The situation is much more complex than a simple malnutrition, then brain damage, then delayed cognitive development scenario (Brown & Pollitt, 1996). Malnutrition does directly produce brain damage that is sometimes reversible, sometimes not. At the same time, however, it sets off a dynamic and reciprocal process in which, for example, the child becomes lethargic and only minimally explores and learns from the environment—thus interfering with cognitive development. It also produces delayed physical growth and development of motor skills that lower parental expectations and in turn delay cognitive development.

Body Proportions   Throughout childhood body proportions change dramatically, as shown in Figure 7–1. For example, at birth the head comprises one-quarter of overall body length. By age 16 the head has doubled in size, but now it accounts for only one-eighth of body length. Elongation of the lower body and legs accelerates as children begin to lose the "baby fat" associated with infancy and toddlerhood. From age 2 to age 6 the rate of growth slows compared to the first two years of life. Healthy children may grow in spurts during early childhood but gain an average of 4½ pounds (2 kilograms) per year and grow almost 3 inches (7.6 centimeters) taller each year. As with other aspects of physical development, however, it's important to remember that children vary

Figure 7–1   Changing Body Proportions in Girls and Boys from Birth to Maturity

Source: Nichols, B. (1990). Moving and learning: The elementary school physical eduation experience. St. Louis, MO: Times Mirror/Mosby College Publishing.

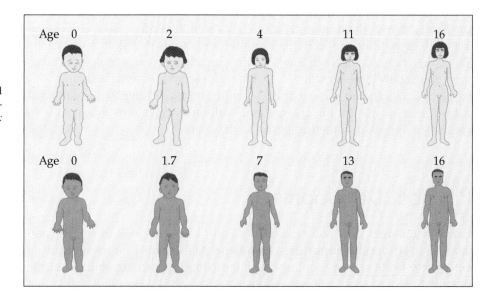

widely in growth rates and gains during early childhood and parents should not attempt to "accelerate" growth through overfeeding or overexercising their children.

In young children the center of gravity is higher than in adults; children carry a greater proportion of their weight in their upper body. Being top-heavy makes it more difficult to control the body. In early childhood, children lose their balance more easily and have difficulty coming to a quick stop without tipping forward. It is also hard for them to catch a large ball without falling backward (Nichols, 1990). The center of gravity gradually descends to the pelvic area as body proportions continue to change.

Skeletal Maturation As the skeletal system matures, bones develop and harden through *ossification*, in which soft tissue or cartilage is transformed into bone. Skeletal age is determined by bone maturation and can be measured by X-rays of the wrist bones. Skeletal age may vary by as much as 2 years in either direction with respect to chronological age. For example, the skeletal age of a 6-year-old may range from 4 to 8 years (Nichols, 1990).

X-ray of a 2-year-old's hand and wrist.

Brain Development

Rapid changes in body size and proportion are obvious signs of growth, but unseen changes are also taking place in the brain. By age 5 a child's brain is nearly the size of an adult's. Brain development makes possible increasingly complex learning, problem solving, and language use; in turn, sensory-perceptual and motor activity create and strengthen neural connections. The myriad neural connections that are formed throughout the lifespan are the physical basis of learning, memory, and knowledge in general.

The development of **neurons**—the 100 to 200 billion specialized cells that make up the nervous system—begins during the embryonic period and is essentially complete by birth. *Glial cells*, which insulate the neurons and improve the efficiency of transmission of neural impulses, continue to grow rapidly throughout the second year. Rapid growth in the size of neurons, the number of glial cells, and the complexity of *synapses* (neural interconnections) produce a **brain growth spurt** during infancy and toddlerhood, which continues (although at a slower rate) well into early childhood . The brain growth spurt is a period of considerable **plasticity** or flexibility, during which children can more readily recover from brain injury than at later ages, although plasticity does continue into adulthood (Nelson & Bloom, 1997).

Maturation of the brain and central nervous system also includes **myelination**—the formation of sheathing cells that "insulate" the neurons and make transmission of neural impulses much more efficient (Cratty, 1986). Myelination of neurons for motor reflexes and vision begins in early infancy. It is followed by myelination of neurons for the complex motor activities and then those controlling eye-hand coordination, attention span, memory, and self-control. Myelination of the central nervous system closely parallels the development of cognitive and motor abilities during the early childhood years and beyond.

At the same time, specializations as a result of each child's unique experiences increase the numbers of synapses of some neurons and eliminate or "prune" synapses of others. As explained by Alison Gopnik and colleagues (Gopnik, Meltzoff, & Kuhl, 1999), neurons in the brain of a newborn average about 2,500 synapses, increasing to a peak of about 15,000 each by age 2 to 3 years—which is in turn many more than in the brain of an adult. In their words,

neurons The cells that make up the nervous system. They form prenatally and continue to grow and branch throughout life barring pruning.

brain growth spurt Rapid growth during infancy in the size of neurons, the number of glial cells, and the complexity of synapses.

plasticity Flexibility of the brain during the brain growth spurt that allows children to more readily recover from brain injury.

myelination The formation of the myelin sheath covering the fast-acting central nervous system pathways. This sheath increases the speed of transmission and the precision of the nervous system.

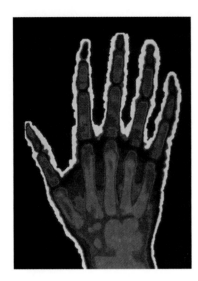

X-ray of a 6-year-old's hand and wrist. Note the greater degree of ossification in the older child's bones.

cerebral cortex The surface of the brain.

lateralization The process whereby specific skills and competencies become localized in particular hemispheres of the brain.

What happens to all these connections as we get older? Brains don't just steadily make more and more connections. Instead, they make many more connections than they need and then get rid of lots of them. It turns out that deleting old connections is just as important as adding new ones. The synapses that carry the most messages get stronger and survive, while weaker synaptic connections are cut out. . . . Between about age ten and puberty, the brain will ruthlessly destroy its weakest connections, preserving only those that experience has shown to be useful. (pp. 186–187)

Not surprisingly, increased knowledge about early brain development has led many theorists to the conclusion that interventions aimed at children who are at risk for cognitive impairment and developmental delays, because of poverty and intellectually impoverished home environments, should start as early as possible. Traditional Head Start programs, for example, start during what some call the "window of opportunity" for brain development—the first 3 years of life. As Craig and Sharon Ramey and colleagues have noted (Ramey, Campbell, & Ramey, 1999; Ramey & Ramey, 1998), major projects that instead enroll children during early infancy have had much greater impact than interventions begun later. They and other authors also note, of course, that quality is everything (Burchinal et al., 2000; Ramey & Ramey, 1998). Bringing infants to centers has been found to be associated with better outcomes (NICHD, 2000), and the approach should be intensive, also comprehensive in addressing areas such as nutritional and other health needs, social as well as cognitive development, and family functioning as well as child functioning. The magnitude of benefits, as Ramey and Ramey (1998, p. 112) put it, depends on a program's

■ Cultural and developmental appropriateness
■ Timing
■ Intensity
■ Breadth
■ Responsiveness to individual risk or impairment

This is not to say that the first 3 years constitute a critical period and that the window somehow "closes" after that. Quality interventions begun after age 3 do still help, and as various theorists have pointed out (e.g., Bruer, 1999), learning and corresponding brain development continue throughout the lifespan. Our increasing knowledge of early brain development simply points out the importance of the first 3 years for all children, whether they are at risk, and researchers have a long way to go in specifying precisely what experiences are important and when during this period.

Lateralization The surface of the brain, or **cerebral cortex** (Latin for "bark"), is divided into two hemispheres—the left and the right. In processing information and controlling behavior, the hemispheres specialize; this is called **lateralization.** In the 1960s Roger Sperry and colleagues verified the presence of lateralization by studying the effects of surgery designed to reduce major epileptic seizures. They found that severing the neural tissue that connects the two hemispheres (the *corpus callosum*) could reduce seizures while leaving intact most abilities needed for daily functioning, although it did create a person with two largely independent hemispheres that couldn't communicate with each other (Sperry, 1968). Nowadays, seizure-related surgery is much more specific and refined.

The left hemisphere controls motor behavior for the right side of the body, and the right hemisphere controls the left side (Cratty, 1986; Hellige, 1993). In some aspects of functioning, however, one hemisphere may be more active. Figure 7–2 illustrates some of these functions for a right-handed person; in left-handed people, some functions may be reversed. Bear in mind, however, that in normal people the *entire* brain is involved in most functioning (Hellige, 1993). Lateralized (or otherwise specialized) functions simply indicate a greater degree of activity in one area than in others.

Taking into account how children's skills develop, it is not surprising that the hemispheres develop at different rates (Thatcher, Walker, & Guidice, 1987). For example, language develops very rapidly from age 3 to age 6, and the left hemisphere of most children shows accelerated growth during that period. In contrast, their right hemisphere matures more slowly during early childhood; its growth accelerates during middle childhood. Lateral specialization continues throughout childhood and into adolescence.

Handedness   Researchers have long been intrigued by right- or left-hand preference, which is a function of lateralization. The majority of people are right-handed and therefore display strong left-hemisphere dominance. Even when a strong preference exists, however, young children can learn to use their nonfavored hand—a flexibility that decreases with age. Research on hemisphere dominance indicates, that for the majority of right-handed people language is highly localized in areas of the left hemisphere. For the remaining 10% or so of the population who are left-handed, language is often shared by the two sides of the brain, suggesting that the brains of left-handed people may be less lateralized in general (Hiscock & Kinsbourne, 1987). Additional evidence is provided by the observation that left-handed people are more likely to be *ambidextrous*—capable of using either hand with good coordination and fine motor skills.

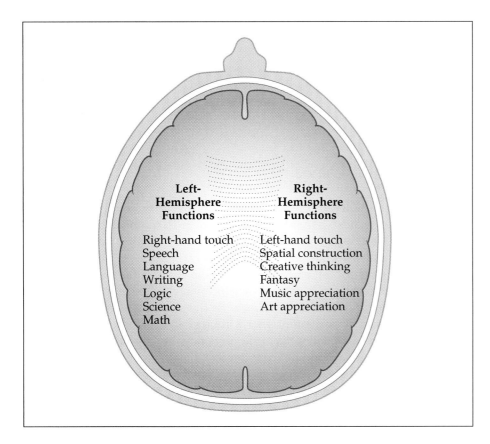

Figure 7-2   The Functions of the Right and Left Cerebral Hemispheres

Source: Shea, C. H., Shebilske, W. L., and Worchel, S. 1993. Motor Learning and Control, *Englewood Cliffs, NJ: Prentice-Hall, p. 38.*

It has long been known that in most children, handedness is established by early to middle childhood (Gesell & Ames, 1947); recent research suggests that it is present in some children as early as 20 months of age (Tirosh, Stein, Harel, & Scher, 1999). In addition to brain maturation, hand preference may reflect pressures by parents and teachers, toward use of the "socially preferable" right hand. The prevailing opinion, however, is that hand preference should be allowed to develop naturally, without coercion. This would be especially important if, as many researchers believe, handedness may have a genetic basis and therefore be prewired (Bryden, Roy, McManus, & Bulman-Fleming, 1997; McKeever, 2000).

The majority of 3- to 5-year-olds also show a well-established foot preference that is further refined during middle childhood. Researchers suggest that because "footedness" is less socially influenced than handedness—parents may force a left-handed child to be right-handed—failure to develop foot preference may actually be a more sensitive indicator of developmental delays associated with establishing preference (Bradshaw, 1989; Gabbard, Dean, & Haensly, 1991).

CONTENT CHECK
PHYSICAL DEVELOPMENT

True–False (answers are on the Companion Website)

1. Malnutrition during early childhood usually causes irreversible brain damage.
2. Skeletal age is determined by the extent of bone ossification.
3. Throughout the lifespan, the average number of synapses between neurons continues to increase.
4. With regard to brain development, the first three years of life are a window of opportunity that essentially closes after that.
5. Handedness is a result of lateralization.

Thinking Critically

How is the relationship between early childhood nutrition and brain development a dynamic process?

Motor Skills Development

Children's motor skills improve markedly during early childhood (Clark & Phillips, 1985). The most dramatic changes are in gross motor skills such as running, hopping, and throwing. In contrast, fine motor skills such as writing and handling eating utensils develop more slowly.

However, distinguishing perceptual-motor development from overall cognitive development is difficult. Almost everything a child does during the early years of life involves interaction between the two, along with social and emotional development. For example, when a young child walks on a log, the child not only learns how to balance but also experiences the cognitive concept "narrow" and the emotional concept "confidence."

Some developmental sequences involve what is called **functional subordination.** Actions that are initially performed for their own sake later become integrated into more complex, purposeful skills. A child's early markings with

functional subordination The integration of a number of separate simple actions or schemes into a more complex pattern of behavior.

Table 7-1 Motor Development During Early Childhood

2-Year-Olds	3-Year-Olds	4-Year-Olds	5-Year-Olds
Walk with wide stance and body sway.	Keep legs closer together when walking and running.	Can vary rhythm of running.	Can walk a balance beam.
Can climb, push, pull, run, hang by both hands.	Can run and move more smoothly.	Skip awkwardly; jump.	Skip smoothly; stand on one foot.
Have little endurance.	Reach for objects with one hand.	Have greater strength, endurance, and coordination.	Can manage buttons and zippers; may tie shoelaces.
Reach for objects with two hands.	Smear and daub paint; stack blocks.	Draw shapes and simple figures; make paintings; use blocks for buildings.	Use utensils and tools correctly.

crayon and paper, for example, are an end in themselves. Later, putting marks on paper becomes functionally subordinated to more complex skills such as writing and creating designs.

The roots of complex behavior and thought are not always as obvious. We return to this issue after we survey gross and fine motor development during the early childhood period. Table 7–1 summarizes the major motor developmental achievements of the early childhood years. Again, note that the age designations are strictly averages; individual children can vary considerably from these norms.

Gross Motor Skills

Compared to infants, 2-year-olds are amazingly competent, but they still have a long way to go. They can walk and run, but they're still relatively short and round. They walk with a wide stance and a swaying gait. Toddlers also tend to use both arms (or legs) when only one is necessary. When handed a cookie, for example, a 2-year-old is likely to extend both hands.

By age 3 children's legs stay closer together during walking and running, and they no longer need to pay attention to what their legs and feet are doing (Cratty, 1970). Thus, their gross motor behavior is showing signs of **automaticity**—the ability to perform motor behaviors without consciously thinking about them (Shiffrin & Schneider, 1977). Three-year-olds run, turn, and stop more smoothly than 2-year-olds do, although their ankles and wrists are not as flexible as they will be by age 4 or 5. They are also more likely to extend only the preferred hand to receive an object such as a cookie.

By age 4 children can vary the rhythm of their running. Many 4-year-olds can also skip (though awkwardly) and execute a running jump or a standing broad jump; 5-year-olds can skip smoothly, walk along a balance beam confidently, stand on one foot for several seconds, and imitate dance steps. Many 5-year-olds can throw a ball overhead and catch a large ball thrown to them (Cratty, 1970), although such skills continue to be refined over the next several years (Robertson, 1984).

Whereas 3-year-olds may push a doll carriage or a large truck for the fun of pushing it, 4-year-olds functionally subordinate their pushing to fantasy play or games, although they may continue to perform some motor activity for its own sake.

automaticity The ability to perform behaviors with little or no conscious attention devoted to them.

Children's overall activity level peaks between the ages of 2 and 3, gradually declining in the remaining years of early childhood. The decline is earlier for girls than for boys, which is why boys may have more trouble sitting still in kindergarten than girls do (Eaton & Yu, 1989).

Fine Motor Skills

Fine motor skills require the coordinated and dexterous use of hand, fingers, and thumb. Abilities involving the hands and fingers result from a series of overlapping processes beginning before birth. (Recall, for example, how an infant's grasp reflex evolves into a voluntary grasp and then a pincer grasp.) Near the end of the third year, new manual abilities emerge as manual schemes become integrated and coordinated with other motor, perceptual, or verbal behaviors. Fine motor skills also begin to display automaticity. For example, 4-year-olds can carry on a dinner conversation while manipulating a fork or other eating utensil (Cratty, 1986). Despite their increasing competence, however, young children still have difficulty with precise fine motor movements. This is linked to the immaturity of the child's central nervous system (myelination is still in progress) as well as to the child's limited patience and relatively short attention span.

As children gain fine motor skills, they become increasingly competent in taking care of themselves and carrying out their daily activities. From 2 to 3 years of age, for example, children can put on and remove simple items of clothing. They can handle large zippers and use chopsticks or a spoon effectively.

A 3- to 4-year-old child can fasten and unfasten items of clothing and independently "serve" food—though sometimes making a mess while doing so. By the time children are 4 to 5 years old, they can dress and undress themselves without assistance and use eating utensils well. Five- to 6-year-olds can tie a simple knot, and 6-year-olds who wear shoes with laces can usually tie them—although many still find it difficult and may ask for help instead.

Learning and Motor Skills

The motor skills that young children learn first are usually everyday actions such as cutting with scissors or other implements, skipping, and jumping. Such skills increase the young child's ability to move around, perform self-care, and be creative. Some young children also learn more highly skilled activities, such as gymnastics, playing the piano, or even riding horses or other animals.

Researchers have identified a number of important conditions for motor learning. These include readiness, practice, attention, competence, motivation, and feedback. *Readiness* is generally required for learning any new skill—cognitive or motor. A certain level of maturation and certain basic skills must be present before the child can profit from training. Although it can be difficult to know just when a child is "ready," classic studies in Russia and the United States have indicated that if children are introduced to new motor learning at the optimal point of readiness, they learn quickly and with little training or effort (Lisina & Neverovich, 1971). Children want to learn, enjoy the practice, and are excited about their successes. Children frequently give clues to when they have reached optimal readiness for a given skill: Watch for them to begin imitating the behavior on their own.

Practice is also essential to motor development. Children cannot master climbing without actually climbing. They can't learn to throw an object unless they practice throwing. When children live in limited, restricted environments, their development of motor skills lags. Children who lack objects to play with, places to explore, tools to use, or people to imitate will have trouble develop-

For a young child to learn a highly skilled activity like playing the piano, certain conditions have to be in place, including readiness, motivation, and attention.

ing motor skills. On the other hand, given a rich, active environment, children tend to pace their own learning appropriately. They imitate behaviors, often repeating them endlessly. They do things like repeatedly pouring water from one container to another to explore the concepts of "full" and "empty," "fast" and "slow." Such self-designed and self-paced schedules of learning are often more efficient than lessons programmed by adults (Karlson, 1972).

Motor learning is also enhanced by *attention*, which requires an alert and engaged state of mind. How can children's attention be improved? Young children can't simply be told what to do and how to do it. Instead, 2- and 3-year-old children learn new motor skills most efficiently by being led through activities. Exercises and games can be used to teach them to move their arms and legs in special ways. Such techniques show that children between the ages of 3 and 5 focus their attention most effectively through active imitation. Only when children have reached age 6 or 7 can they attend closely to verbal instructions and follow them reasonably well, at least while participating in familiar tasks and activities (Zaporozlets & Elkonin, 1971).

In a classic review of the theories of Freud, Piaget, and others, Robert White developed the concept of *competence motivation* (1959). This is reflected in the observation that children (and adults) often attempt things just to see if they can do them, to perfect their skills, to test their muscles and abilities, and to enjoy how it all feels. Children run, jump, climb, and skip for the sheer pleasure and challenge of it. In other words, children often engage in **intrinsically motivated behavior**, behavior that is performed for its own sake, with no identifiable goal except perhaps competence and mastery. In contrast, **extrinsically motivated behavior** is performed to gain reinforcement.

Finally, the ongoing *feedback* children receive for their efforts helps them acquire and refine motor skills. Parents and peers tell them how well they're doing and encourage them to do more. Feedback can also come from the behavior itself. For example, when climbing a play ladder or a small tree, children may derive pleasure from the tension in their muscles and from the experience of being up high and seeing things that are not visible from the ground. Parents and teachers can be particularly helpful by highlighting such internal feedback. Specific statements like "Now you have a strong grip on the bar" are more helpful than general praise such as "What a good job you're doing climbing that ladder."

intrinsically motivated behavior Behavior performed for its own sake, with no particular goal.

extrinsically motivated behavior Behavior performed to obtain rewards or avoid adverse events.

CONTENT CHECK
MOTOR SKILLS DEVELOPMENT

True–False (answers are on the Companion Website)

1. Learning to write is a skill that displays functional subordination.
2. As development proceeds, both gross-motor and fine-motor skills display automaticity.
3. Readiness is important for learning some motor skills but not for others.
4. Competence motivation is an example of intrinsic motivation.

Thinking Critically

Why is it difficult to unscramble the interplay of motor skills development and cognitive development?

Cognitive Development

When we look at all the developmental changes that occur during early childhood, it is often difficult to disentangle the contributions of increasing physical competence from those of cognitive development—in accord with systems theory. Children often use their bodies as a means of testing their developing knowledge and understanding. For example, a child who throws stones of varying sizes into the river is learning some basics about weight, force, angles, and trajectories.

Decades after his initial research, Piaget's theory still provides an important base for understanding cognitive development, although other theories challenge some of Piaget's conclusions about young children's cognitive abilities and how they develop—as well as how to view their cognitive abilities in the first place. We begin with Piaget's observations about early childhood and then consider other perspectives.

An Overview of Preoperational Thinking

Recall from Chapter 2 that Piaget described cognitive development in terms of discrete stages through which children progress on their way to understanding the world. According to Piaget, children actively construct a personal understanding. They build their own reality through experimentation; they are like little scientists working diligently to figure out how the world works. They explore their surroundings and comprehend new information on the basis of their current level and ways of understanding. When they encounter something familiar, they assimilate it. When they encounter something new, they accommodate their thinking to incorporate it.

During the *preoperational stage*, children continue to expand their understanding of the world by using their growing language and problem-solving skills. According to Piaget, however, young children have not yet achieved the cognitive abilities necessary to understand logical operations and interpret reality more fully. Such operations include cause and effect, perceptions of reality, time and space, and most concepts of number. These will be acquired during the next stage—the *concrete operational stage* (Chapter 9). The cognitive skills and understanding acquired during the preoperational stage lay the groundwork.

In Piaget's view, children enter the preoperational stage with only rudimentary language and thinking abilities and leave it asking sophisticated questions such as "Where did Grandma go when she died?"

What is preoperational thinking like? Let's consider the question in conjunction with the dramatic cognitive advances children make during this stage.

Preoperational Substages and Thought The preoperational period lasts from age 2 to about age 7 and is divided into two parts—the *preconceptual period* (age 2 to about age 4) and the *intuitive or transitional period* (about age 5 to age 7).

The preconceptual period is highlighted by increasingly complex use of symbols and symbolic (pretend) play. Previously a child's thinking was limited to the immediate physical environment. Now symbols enable the child to think about things that are not immediately present. The child's thinking is more flexible (Siegler, 1991). Words now have the power to communicate, even in the absence of the things they name.

Preoperational children, however, still have difficulty with major categories of reality. They don't distinguish between mental, physical, and social reality. For example, their thinking displays *animism*: They may think that anything that moves is alive—the sun, the moon, clouds, an automobile or a train. They also display *reification*: Objects and people in their thoughts and dreams are real to them; they represent things as real as those actually present in the child's environment. Such approaches to thinking stem partly from another characteristic of young children's thinking: **egocentrism.** This term refers to the child's tendency to see and understand things in terms of her or his personal point of view—very much like Winnie-the-Pooh at the beginning of the chapter. During early childhood, children are thought to be unable to separate the realm of personal existence from everything else (Siegler, 1991).

In the intuitive or transitional period, children begin to separate mental from physical reality and to understand causation apart from social norms. For example, before this stage children may think that everything was created by their parents or some other adult. Now they begin to grasp the significance of other forces. Intuitive children understand multiple points of view and relational concepts, though in an inconsistent and incomplete way. Compared to older children, they are unable to perform many basic mental operations. Rational thinking increases during this period, but children are also willing to use magical thinking to explain things. Although 4- to 6-year-olds basically understand that an adult cannot be transformed into a child and that people can't pass through solid objects, the majority will change their opinion if an adult relates a fairy tale as if it were true (Subbotsky, 1994).

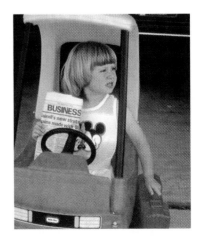

Preschoolers develop the ability to use symbols to represent actions, events, and objects—one of the milestones in cognitive development. This young businesswoman is reading her newspaper during her commute to work.

Symbolic Representation The most dramatic cognitive difference between infants and 2-year-olds is in their use of *symbolic representation*. As defined in Chapter 5, this term refers to the use of actions, images, or words to represent objects and events. The difference can be seen most clearly in language development and symbolic play (Flavell, Miller, & Miller, 1993). Two-year-olds can imitate past events, roles, and actions. A young child might use gestures to act out an extensive sequence of events such as a car ride. Given props, young children may act out a family dinner or a story from a favorite book or folk tale.

The ability to employ numbers to represent quantity is another use of symbolic representation. Still another is the acquisition of skills in drawing and artistic representation, which begins during the preoperational stage.

How does symbolic representation develop? Donald Marzolf and Judy De-Loache (1994) performed a series of experiments on young children's understanding of spatial representations. They found that early experiences with symbolic relations contribute to the child's readiness to recognize that one object may stand for another. One study (DeLoache, 1987) revealed that children's understanding of some symbolic relationships occurs fairly suddenly. For example, although 2½-year-olds do not understand the relationship between a scale model of a room and the actual room it represents, 3-year-olds easily see the connection. The younger child's failure may involve inability to understand that a scale model is *both* an object and a symbol of something else.

Although symbolic representation starts at the end of the sensorimotor period, it continues to be refined; a child is much better at symbolization at age 4 than at age 2. In one experiment (Elder & Pederson, 1978), researchers found that the younger children—2½-year-olds—needed props similar to real objects for their pretend games. In contrast, 3½-year-olds could represent objects with quite different props or act out a situation without props. They could pretend that a hairbrush was a pitcher or even pretend to use a pitcher with no props at all, whereas 2½-year-olds could not.

Thought processes become more complex with the use of symbols (Piaget, 1950, 1951). Children show that they perceive similarities between two objects

egocentrism A self-centered view of the world; perceiving everything in relation to yourself.

by giving the objects the same name. They become more aware of the past and form more expectations for the future. They distinguish between themselves and the person they are addressing. Symbolic representation may help children in social interactions as well (Fein, 1981): It may help them become more sensitive to the feelings and viewpoints of others. This sensitivity, in turn, helps them make the transition to less egocentric and more *sociocentric* thinking. Such socially oriented thought, however, requires many more years to mature.

Limitations on Preoperational Thinking

In spite of the development of symbolic representation, preoperational children have a long way to go before they are logical thinkers. Their thought processes are limited in many ways, as evidenced by observations of their behavior and especially by experiments designed to test the limits of their thinking. The limitations on children's thinking include concreteness, irreversibility, egocentrism, centration, and difficulties with concepts of time, space, and sequence.

Concreteness The thinking of preoperational children is *concrete.* Preoperational children can't deal with abstractions well. They are concerned with the here-and-now and with physical things that they can easily represent mentally.

Irreversibility Young children's thinking is *irreversible.* That is, children see events as occurring in only one direction. Preoperational children cannot imagine how things might return to their original state or how relationships can exist in two directions. Consider the following dialog between an adult and a 3-year-old girl:

"Do you have a sister?"
"Yes."
"What's her name?"
"Jessica."
"Does Jessica have a sister?"
"No."

Here, the relationship is solely one way; the younger girl knows that she has a sister but does not yet recognize that she is Jessica's sister.

Egocentrism As noted earlier, preoperational children's thought is egocentric and centered on their own perspective, so that it's hard for them to take another person's point of view. Preoperational children concentrate on their own perceptions and assume that everyone else's outlook is the same as theirs. Piaget (1954) used the "mountains problem" illustrated in Figure 7–3 to study children's egocentrism. The child sits at one side of a table that has a plaster model of a group of mountains on it. The child is shown pictures taken from the four possible views of the model—the child's and the three other seats at the table. When asked to select a picture that corresponds to his or her own view, most preoperational children can easily do so. However, when asked to select the picture representing the view of a doll placed in one of the other seats, most cannot.

Centration Preoperational children's thought also tends to focus on only one aspect or dimension of an object or situation to the exclusion of others. This limitation—called *centration*—can be seen in *class inclusion* problems. For example, when preoperational children are shown a collection of wooden beads, some red and some yellow, and asked whether there are more red beads or more

Figure 7-3 A View of the "Mountains" Problem

wooden beads, they apparently cannot simultaneously consider the color of the beads and what the beads are made of.

Time, Space, and Sequence A 3-year-old may be able to say, "Grandpa will come visit next week." Even 2-year-olds use words that seem to indicate a knowledge of time and space, such as "later," "tomorrow," "last night," "next time," and "far away." However, a child of 2 or 3 apparently has very little appreciation of what the words really mean. "Noon" may mean lunchtime, but if lunchtime is delayed an hour, it is still noon to the child. Upon waking from a nap, a child may not even know whether it is the same day. Conceptualizing days, weeks, and months is difficult for preoperational children, as is acquiring the more general concept that time exists along a continuum of past, present, and future.

Stated differently, young children have little idea of cause-and-effect sequences. In fact, their early use of the words "cause" and "because" may have nothing to do with the adult understanding of the terms. The same is true of the word "why"—a 4-year-old's favorite question. Consider this dialog:

"Why do we drink out of bottles *and* cans?"

"Because some things are better in bottles, some in cans."

"But juice comes in bottles and cans too! Why?"

"Well, sometimes it's cheaper in cans."

"Why?"

"Go wash up for dinner, we'll talk about it later!"

Meanwhile, the child may have been concerned with the appearance of the containers all along—not the real "why."

Understanding of spatial relations also develops during early childhood. The meanings of words such as "in," "out," "near," "far," "over," "under," "up," and "down" are learned directly through the child's experiences with his or her own body (Weikart, Rogers, & Adcock, 1971). David Weikart and colleagues suggested that the usual progression is for children to learn a concept first with their bodies (crawling under a table) and then with objects (pushing a toy truck under a table). Later they learn to identify the concept in pictures ("See the boat go under the bridge!").

Table 7-2 summarizes selected characteristics of preoperational thinking.

Conservation

Piaget's **conservation** problems have been offered as evidence for the limitations of preoperational thinking. The term *conservation* refers to understanding that changing the shape or appearance of objects and materials doesn't change their volume, mass, number, or the like. The following are examples.

conservation The understanding that changing the shape or appearance of objects doesn't change their amount.

Table 7–2 Selected Characteristics of Preoperational Thinking

Preconceptual Period

Animism	Believes that most things that move are alive	Sun, moon, cars, trains, etc. are seen as living creatures
Reification	Believes that objects and people in thoughts and dreams are real	A monster in a dream actually lurks under the bed.
Egocentrism	Sees and understands things from her or his own point of view	"If I can see it, you must be able to see it too."

Intuitive Period

Symbolic representation	Uses actions, images, or words to represent objects and events	Blocks represent houses; names represent things
Sociocentric thinking	Begins to be able to understand others' points of view	"Maybe you don't want to play what I want to play."

Limitations of Preoperational Thinking

Concreteness	Cannot deal with abstractions	Thinking tends to be in the here-and-now, not oriented toward what might be
Irreversibility	Can't see changes as reversible; one reason for not being able to conserve	"I have a brother, but he doesn't have any sisters or brothers."
Centration	Can't focus on more than one aspect of a problem at a time; another reason for not being able to conserve	Thinking focuses on one dimension and ignores others

Conservation of Volume   Piaget observed that preoperational children do not conserve volume, as indicated by his classic liquid/beakers problem (see Figure 7–4). The child is first presented with two identical beakers containing the same amount of liquid. When asked, "Are they the same?" the child readily says, "Yes." Then, *as the child watches*, the contents of one of the original beakers is poured into a tall, slender beaker. Now the child is asked, "Are they the same, or are they different?" Preoperational children tend to say that they're different, perhaps even adding that the taller beaker contains more liquid. Centration apparently gets in the way, in that the child attends to only one dimension, such as height, and doesn't realize that a compensating change occurs in the beaker's width. For the child, it's a *perceptual* problem, not a logical one—the child simply focuses on the here-and-now, and in effect, the state of the liquids before the pouring is a different problem than the state

Figure 7–4 The Classic "Liquid/Beakers" Problem

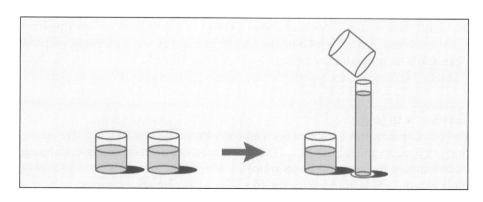

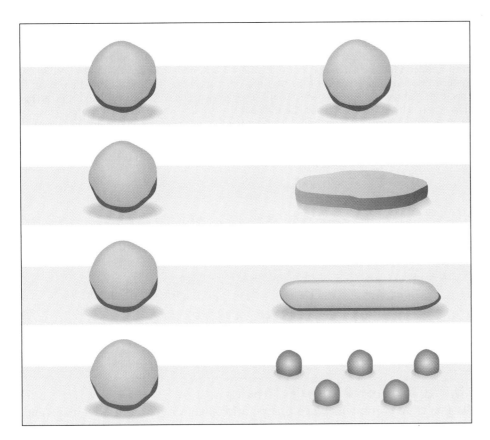

Figure 7–5   Conservation of Mass Problems
In this conservation experiment, a child is shown two identical balls of clay. One ball remains the same, while the other is transformed into various shapes.

of the liquids afterward. In other words, from the child's point of view, the pouring is irrelevant.

Irreversibility is a factor too: It doesn't occur to the child that the liquid in the taller beaker could be poured back into the original one and therefore must be the same—again, the child lacks the necessary logical approach.

Conservation of Mass   Figure 7–5 shows tests for conservation of mass, which illustrate preoperational thinking very similar to that revealed by the liquid/beakers problem. Here a child is presented with two identical balls of clay. As the child watches, one ball is transformed into various shapes while the other ball remains untouched. Consider the case in which the ball is rolled into a longish sausage shape: Because of centration, the child might say either that the sausage contains more clay or that it contains less, depending on whether the child attends to length or height. As before, the child, caught up in the here-and-now, fails to realize that the process is reversible.

Conservation of Number   The development of numerical abilities is an especially intriguing area—both because of the amount of formal education we invest in teaching children to use numbers and the many essential applications of numbers in everyday life. A number-conservation task is shown in Figure 7–6. The researcher first places six candies in each of two rows, one above the other and spaced in the same way. After the child agrees that the two rows contain the same number of candies, the experimenter removes one of the candies from one row and spreads out the remaining candies. To conserve number, the child must recognize that the longer row actually contains one fewer candy despite its "wider" appearance. Children younger than age 5 or 6 are often fooled and judge that the longer row contains more candies.

Figure 7–6 **A Conservation of Numbers Problem**

When shown the arrangement of candies in the top two rows and asked whether one line has more or both lines are the same, the 4- or 5-year-old will generally answer that both lines contain the same number of candies. Using the same candies, those in the lower row were pushed closer together, and one candy was removed from the upper row, but the line was spread out so that it was longer. The child has watched this operation and has been told that he or she may eat the candies in the line that contains more. Even preoperational children, who can count, will insist that the longer line has more, although they have gone through the exercise of counting the candies in each line.

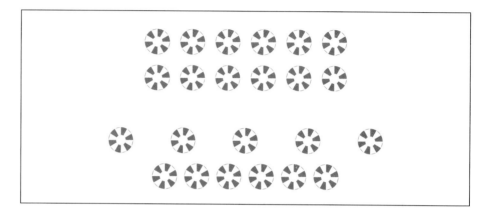

Limitations of Piaget's Theory

Do Piaget's experiments place preoperational children at a disadvantage and underestimate their cognitive abilities? In some respects, research indicates that they definitely do. For example, although preoperational children do tend to be egocentric and preoccupied with their own perspective on things, in some situations they can take another person's point of view. When Piagetian problems are presented in such way that they "make sense," they become clear even to young preoperational children (Donaldson, 1978); conversely, the misleading nature of many of Piaget's questions can lead even adults astray (Winer, Craig, & Weinbaum, 1992). For example, in one classic series of studies, preoperational children who couldn't solve the mountains problem were instead asked if a naughty boy could hide so that he would not be seen by a police officer. Although none of the children in the study had ever actually hidden from the police, they had all played hide-and-seek and had no difficulty taking the naughty boy's point of view. Even 3-year-olds were successful at this (Hughes & Donaldson, 1979). Young children are also better than Piaget thought at taking other's perspectives in the context of understanding their feelings and intentions (Lillard & Currenton, 1999).

Numerous studies have also shown that preoperational children at least occasionally attend to more than one dimension at a time and think in terms of transformations instead of concrete beginning and end states—thus in effect displaying elements of conservation. These simply aren't their *dominant* modes of thinking (Siegler & Ellis, 1996). Similarly, Rochel Gelman and colleagues have demonstrated that preoperational children are also more competent in using numbers than Piaget believed (Gelman & Gallistel, 1986). For example, young children display two important types of numerical skills: *number-abstraction abilities* and *numerical-reasoning principles*. Number-abstraction abilities refer to cognitive processes that children use in counting; even a 3-year-old might count the number of cookies on a table and accurately arrive at "four." Numerical reasoning principles are cognitive processes by which children determine the correct way to operate on or transform an array (Flavell et al., 1993).

For example, a child might know that the only way a number of objects can be increased is by adding an object. Not until children gain more advanced reasoning abilities can they formally add, subtract, multiply, and divide (Becker, 1993), but as summarized by Arthur Baroody (2000), 3- to 5-year-olds display a goodly array of premathematical abilities and concepts—quite contrary to what Piaget thought.

Beyond Piaget: Social Perspectives

As discussed in Chapter 2, some developmentalists view cognitive development from a very different perspective. Rather than seeing children as active scientists, they emphasize their social nature and dispute Piaget's view of the child as a solitary explorer attempting to make sense of the world on her or his own. Active exploration is not excluded, but the child more often acquires cognitive abilities through interactions with more experienced people—parents, teachers, and older children. In the course of these interactions parents and others also pass on society's rules and expectations (Bruner & Haste, 1987). According to the social perspective, the ways in which adults demonstrate how to solve problems help children learn to think. All cultures initiate children into myriad activities through guided participation. When young children help tidy up the home or join in singing their national anthem, specific aspects of culture are transmitted from the more experienced members (adults) to the less experienced members (children). Katherine Nelson argued that knowledge of events is the key to understanding the child's mind (1986). Whereas Piaget focused on what young children *don't* know, Nelson was interested in what they *do* know and what they learn from daily experiences. She viewed the child's knowledge of and participation in routine daily activities as material both for the child's mental life and for the development of cognitive abilities. Thus, the child's understanding of the world is embedded in cultural knowledge.

Vygotsky's zone of proximal development (Chapter 2) includes the view that children develop through participation in activities that are slightly beyond

These children have learned birthday rituals through guided participation.

their competence, given the assistance of others who are more skilled and knowledgeable (Cole, John-Steiner, Scribner, & Souberman, 1978). Social play is important as a means of moving children toward more advanced levels of social and cognitive skills (Berk, 1994a; Nicolopoulou, 1993). Play also provides an excellent opportunity to study the way children learn in widely diverse cultures (Rogoff, 1993). We return to the relationship between play and learning later in the chapter.

CONTENT CHECK
COGNITIVE DEVELOPMENT

True–False (answers are on the Companion Website)

1. Animism is a preoperational child's belief that people and objects in thoughts and dreams are real.
2. Abilities pertaining to symbolic representation are highly refined by the end of the preconceptual period.
3. Piaget's "mountains" problem is used to assess egocentrism.
4. Piaget's "liquid/beakers" problem is used to assess conservation.
5. Research generally indicates that Piaget's problems underestimate the cognitive abilities of preoperational children.

Thinking Critically

In Piaget's view, how do irreversibility and centration interfere with preoperational children's thinking on conservation tasks?

Memory and Cognitive Development

Memory is central to cognitive development. Perceiving selectively, reasoning, classifying, and generally progressing toward more complex concepts all occur along with the maturation and development of memory processes, which change rapidly over the first years of life and reach essentially adult capabilities by about age 7 (Gathercole, 1998). We begin with an overview of the information-processing model of memory introduced in Chapter 2. Then we look at research on developmental changes (and limitations) in memory during early childhood.

Memory Processes

When visual sensory information enters an adult human "computer," the *sensory register* retains that information very briefly—often much less than a second—before it is either replaced by new information or passed along for further processing. Auditory sensory memory lasts longer—up to 3 seconds or so.

Information that we attend to passes to **short-term memory (STM),** also known as *working memory*, for processing. This is essentially "consciousness"— what you're thinking about at a given moment, what's in your mind right now. In the absence of *rehearsal* (repeating something to yourself, such as a new phone number long enough to dial it or directions to a new destination long enough to get there), information remains in STM for about 15 to 30 seconds. If

short-term memory (STM)
Temporary or working memory, where information is conciously processed.

you repeatedly rehearse or otherwise make an effort to remember the information, it passes to **long-term memory (LTM).** Most researchers regard LTM as permanent and based on structural changes in the brain such as the creation of new synapses. Thus, barring brain damage, long-term memories are potentially accessible throughout life and constitute the cumulative store of knowledge that we regularly access both in recognizing the familiar and learning about the new (Atkinson & Shriffrin, 1971; Hagen, Longeward, & Kail, 1975).

Memory can consist of images, actions, or words. Thus, researchers often refer to visual, motor, and verbal (semantic) memory. Visual memory is the first to develop. Yet if asked to remember our very early years, most people can't remember much before age 3 or so. This presumably has something to do with encoding, but researchers aren't sure exactly what processes are involved. Verbally encoded recollections that can be described appear after age 4 to 6. One reason for this is that the development of language may enable preoperational children to encode new information better.

Recognition and Recall

Studies of children's memory skills in early childhood have focused on two basic memory abilities. **Recognition** refers to the ability to identify objects or situations as having previously been seen or experienced. For example, children may recognize a picture or a person they have seen before even though they may not be able to tell us much about the memory. **Recall** refers to the ability to retrieve long-term memories with little in the way of cues or prompts; recall is much harder both for children and for adults. For example, a child might be asked to tell a story from memory. Or you might be asked to relate everything you've learned so far in this chapter. Both tasks would be quite difficult.

Researchers have found that young children perform quite well on recognition tasks but that their recall performance is poor, although both forms of remembering improve between the ages of 2 and 5. In a recognition task in which many objects were shown only once to children between the ages of 2 and 5, even the youngest children could correctly point to 81% of them as having been seen before; the older children recognized 92% of the objects. However, when children between the ages of 2 and 4 were asked to recall objects by naming them, 3-year-olds could name only 22% of the items and 4-year-olds only 40% (Myers & Perlmutter, 1978). Young children are clearly better at recognition than recall but may perform better on the latter if their caregivers routinely ask questions that require recall (Ratner, 1984).

Rehearsal and Organization

It has been generally assumed that young children's difficulties with recall are attributable to limited strategies for encoding and retrieval (Flavell, 1985; Fletcher & Bray, 1997; Myers & Perlmutter, 1978), in conjunction with limited attention span and working memory. In early childhood, children don't spontaneously organize or mentally rehearse information the way older children and adults do. If you ask an adult to memorize a list such as "cat, chair, airplane, dog, desk, car," the adult automatically classifies the items as "animals," "furniture," and "vehicles" and rehearses the items within each category; young children do not. Children age 6 and older also improve in their ability to recall information when they are trained in memory strategies, but it is difficult to teach younger children to organize and rehearse information spontaneously.

Infants and young children do use some memory strategies. In one study, 18- to 24-month-old toddlers watched an experimenter hide a Big Bird replica

long-term memory (LTM)   Permanent memory, where, barring brain damage, memories are potentially accessible throughout life and constitute our cumulative store of knowledge.

recognition   The ability to correctly identify items previously experienced when they appear again.

recall   The ability to retrieve information with or without cues.

under a pillow and were told to remember where Big Bird had been hidden because they would later be asked where it was. The experimenter then distracted the children with other toys for several minutes. During the delay the children frequently interrupted their play to talk about Big Bird, point at the hiding place, stand near it, or even attempt to retrieve Big Bird, clearly indicating that they were trying to remember its location (DeLoache, Cassidy, & Brown, 1985). In another study, the researchers determined that young children group spatial information—but not conceptual information—into categories while trying to remember the information (DeLoache & Todd, 1988). For example, when very young children were asked to remember the location of a hidden object, they frequently used rehearsal-like verbalizations such as referring to the hidden toy, the fact that it was hidden, the hiding place, and their having discovered it. The researchers in both studies concluded that such behaviors may be precursors to more mature strategies for keeping material in short-term memory (Flavell et al., 1993).

Some researchers have focused on teaching young children memory strategies such as sorting, naming, or categorizing. The children learned more advanced memory techniques and retained them for several days, but then they ceased using them, possibly because they forgot them or simply became bored with the activity. Learning advanced memory strategies also appeared to have little effect on the children's recall (Lange & Pierce, 1992). Similar results have been found in studies of mothers who use memory strategies to teach young children skills such as wrapping gifts or naming characters in stories. Young children employ simpler and fewer techniques than their mothers (Harris & Hamidullah, 1993), and often don't apply them spontaneously.

Overall, such studies demonstrate that with carefully planned learning experiences and instructional techniques, young children may learn cognitive skills beyond their current repertoire. But the learning doesn't endure—either because children cannot fit the skills comfortably into their current set of abilities or because they are too busy learning about the world in other, more comfortable ways. Interestingly, when researchers compared a group of children who were asked to "remember" toys to another group who were asked to "play with" the toys, the children involved in active play demonstrated better memory (Newman, 1990). The finding suggests that the active play contributes to children's mental organization. Indeed, a growing body of research has focused on the role of the physical and social contexts in children's ability to remember. Two-year-olds who engage in and talk about an activity in a naturalistic setting such as the home demonstrate increased memory competence. However, when formal strategies such as rehearsal are simply taught and replace informal contextual interactions, children's memory performance actually declines (Fivush & Hudson, 1990).

Event Scripts and Sequential Understanding

It is becoming increasingly clear that young children can remember information that is ordered *temporally*, that is, in a time sequence. They can structure a series of occurrences into an ordered, meaningful whole. In one study, children were asked to describe how they had made objects from clay 2 weeks earlier (Smith, Ratner, & Hobart, 1987). When the children were given the opportunity to make the same objects again, they could describe how they had worked step by step. Apparently young children can organize and remember sequences of actions even after a single experience with them.

Young children are aware that an occasion such as a birthday party is composed of an orderly progression of events: a beginning, when the guests arrive with presents; a series of events in the middle, including playing games, singing "Happy Birthday," blowing out the candles, and eating cake and ice cream; and an end, when the guests leave. Children can also remember the elements of repeated events, such as dinner time, nap time, play time, and so on. It is as if they develop *scripts* for routine events (Mandler, 1983; Nelson, Fibush, Hudson, & Lucariello, 1983). When mothers talk to their young children about objects and events that are not immediately present, such as describing errands to be done, they help their children develop scripts and thereby remember events in a series (Lucariello & Nelson, 1987). Younger children remember events only in the order in which they actually occur, however. Only when young children become extremely familiar with an event can they reverse the order of steps (Bauer & Thal, 1990). Scripts are therefore a *mnemonic*—a memory aid—used to remember sequences of events. They "may be the young child's most powerful mental tool for understanding the world" (Flavell et al., 1993, p. 85).

CONTENT CHECK
MEMORY AND COGNITIVE DEVELOPMENT

True–False (answers are on the Companion Website)

1. Rehearsal both retains information in STM and transfers information to LTM.
2. Compared to recall memory, recognition memory is harder both for children and for adults.
3. During early and middle childhood, children's tendency to rehearse spontaneously steadily improves.
4. During early childhood, children generally do not employ event scripts.

Thinking Critically

Why is memory so important to cognitive development?

Language Development and Culture

Throughout early childhood children rapidly expand their vocabularies, their use of grammatical forms, and their understanding of language as a sociocultural activity. In this section we look at young children's expanding grasp of grammar, words, and concepts; the influence of parents' speech; and the characteristics of children's conversations, including the social context of language. We also discuss two particularly important cultural aspects of language development: ethnic subdialects and bilingualism.

An Expanding Grammar

One of the more influential works on language acquisition was written by Roger Brown (1973). Brown and his colleagues recorded the speech patterns of three young children named Adam, Eve, and Sarah. Using **mean length of**

mean length of utterance (MLU)   The average length of the sentences that a child produces.

utterance **(MLU)** as the primary measure of the children's language acquisition, Brown identified five distinct, increasingly complex stages in language development. Although the three children progressed at different rates, the order was similar for each, as it is for most children. Certain skills and rules are mastered before others, and certain errors are peculiar to specific stages.

Stage 1 The first stage is characterized by two-word utterances, in the form of telegraphic speech and pivot and open words as discussed in Chapter 5. However, Brown went beyond structure to focus on the meanings children attempt to convey with word order and position—concepts such as that objects exist, they disappear and recur, and people possess them.

Stage 2 This stage of language acquisition is characterized by utterances that are slightly longer than two words. In very early childhood, children begin to generalize the rules of *inflection* to words that they already know. For example, they can form the regular past tense of many verbs, such as "play/played," and the regular plurals of many nouns. Are they simply imitating the speech of others, or are they using linguistic rules? According to classic research, the latter seems to be the case (Berko, 1958). In early childhood, children reveal a surprising grasp of rules for conjugating verbs and forming plurals and possessives. Indirect evidence for this is their tendency to **overregularize** inflections. Whereas they previously used the irregular verbs they were hearing in everyday speech, they now temporarily overapply inflection rules to *all* verbs. English-speaking children use past-tense constructions such as "goed" instead of "went," "breaked" instead of "broke," "seed" instead of "saw." Their tendency to overregularize is quite resistant to correction by parents and teachers. Only later do they return to irregular forms that depend on rote learning (Marcus et al., 1992).

Stage 3 Now children learn to modify simple sentences. They create negative and imperative forms, ask yes-no questions, and depart in other ways from the simple statements of earlier stages. The negative form is an excellent example of how complex language learning can be. Earlier, children negated by putting the negative word at the beginning of an utterance, as in "no pocket," "no more," and "no dirty." By the third stage, however, they use auxiliary verbs and embed negatives in sentences. They easily use sentences such as, "Susan didn't try" and "Demetrius won't quit."

However, young children still don't comprehend the passive voice. For example, if 3-year-olds are given stuffed animals and asked to act out "The girl chases the boy" and "The boy chases the girl," they have no trouble doing so. But when told "The girl helps the boy" and "The boy is helped by the girl," children often don't recognize that the intent is the same.

Stages 4 and 5 In the fourth and fifth stages children learn to deal with increasingly sophisticated language elements. They begin to use subordinate clauses and fragments within compound and complex sentences. By the age of 4½, children have a good grasp of correct syntax, but they continue to refine it in the years to come.

More Words and Concepts

Throughout early childhood children learn words rapidly—often at a rate of two or three a day. Some words have meaning only in context—for example, "this" and "that." Some words express relationships between objects: "softer," "lower," "shorter." Frequently children understand one concept, such as

overregularize To generalize language principles and misuse words; typically by preschool children who are rapidly expanding their vocabularies.

"more," much earlier than they know the word or the concept that contrasts with it, such as "less." A 3-year-old may easily be able to tell you which dish has more candy but not which dish has less. Often, too, young children want to say things but don't know the right word, so they invent a word. They use nouns in place of verbs, as in "Mommy, pencil it" for "Mommy, write it." At least through age 3, children also have difficulty with pronouns. For example, a child might say "us need to take a nap." Even when corrected, such errors persist until age 4 or 5, sometimes longer.

The Influence of Parents' Language Use

Every culture transmits language to its children. Many methods of talking and relating to infants facilitate language development. Researchers studying U.S. children have found that caregivers ask questions to check children's understanding, expand children's utterances, and make ritualized use of play speech. Adults often speak for their children; that is, they express the child's wants, wishes, and actions in correct language. The child's language develops most from everyday communication with adults who seek to communicate—that is, to understand and to be understood (Schacter & Strage, 1982).

However, it is not entirely clear how parents' language use and children's language development interact. Individual differences in children's language development are inherited to some extent and are also influenced by the child's environment. For example, twins often display delayed language development, which might suggest a genetic basis. Yet it may be that they receive significantly less verbal input than nontwins because mothers of twins must divide their attention between two children. In addition, twins sometimes communicate with each other using a "primitive" language all their own (Tomasello, Mannle, & Kruger, 1986).

When parents speak with their children, they communicate far more than words, sentences, and syntax. They demonstrate how thoughts are expressed and ideas are exchanged. They teach the child about categories and symbols, about how to translate the complexities of the world into ideas and words. Conceptual tools provide a scaffold for the child to use in understanding the world and expressing her or his place in it (Bruner & Haste, 1987).

Studies have also shown that reading picture books to children can facilitate language learning. This is especially true when parents ask open-ended questions that encourage the child to expand the story and when they respond appropriately to the child's attempts to answer the questions (Whitehurst, Falco, Lonigan, & Fischel, 1988).

Language and Gender Language is also one of the ways in which children learn who they are and how they should relate to other people. Gender is a case in point. Assumptions about gender are often culturally embedded in parents' thinking and cause them to talk differently to male and female children (Lloyd, 1987). However, language development may also be influenced by factors inherent in the sex-typed toys children play with. In one study (O'Brien & Nagle, 1987) researchers analyzed the language used by mothers and fathers while playing with their toddlers with toys such as vehicles or dolls. Playing with dolls elicited more verbal interaction, whereas playing with vehicles involved little talking—whether the parents were playing with daughters or sons. Thus, children who play with dolls may have more opportunities to learn and practice language than do children who play with other toys. Then, because boys and girls play with sex-stereotyped toys starting at age 2, girls may experience

IN THEORY, IN FACT

WHEN CHILDREN TALK TO THEMSELVES, IS IT A SIGN OF IMMATURITY?

Josh is alone in his room playing a game in which he tries to fit pieces into a puzzle. If we were observing him, we might overhear him say to himself, "This piece doesn't fit. Where's a round one? No, it doesn't. It's too big. This one is small. . . ." Children between the ages of 4 and 8 have been observed talking to themselves about 20% of the time in schools that permit it (Berk, 1994b). Why do children talk to themselves? Is it a good thing or a bad thing?

Psychologists call talking aloud to oneself *private speech*. All people, young and old, talk to themselves. However, young children engage in private speech aloud and in public settings. Young children even sing to themselves about what they are doing—songs that are generated spontaneously. They also talk aloud to themselves far more often than adults do. Jean Piaget made early observations of private speech by young children and suggested that it simply indicated immaturity; social speech was more mature because it required consideration of the listener's perspective. He called children's self-talk *egocentric speech* (Piaget, 1926).

Other theorists and researchers have raised questions about Piaget's explanation. They have found that the

Often young children talk out loud while they work or play. Sometimes the talk is pretend dialogue, but more often it fulfills other functions.

amount of private speech varies a great deal, depending on the situation, and that even the youngest children use far more social speech than private speech. Perhaps private speech serves a distinct and separate purpose.

Vygotsky (1934/1987) observed that private speech often mirrors adult social speech and helps develop inner thought and self-direction. More recently, researchers have identified three

stages in the development of children's private speech. In its earliest stage, private speech occurs *after* an action—"I made a big picture." In the second stage, self-talk *accompanies* actions—"It's getting darker and darker with lots of paint." In the third stage, it *precedes* an action—"I want to make a scary picture with dark paint." Private speech, then, corresponds to the developing thought processes in a child's mind. In the third stage, when speech comes before behavior, the child is planning a course of action. The changes in private speech thus illustrate the development of thought processes in guiding behavior and accompanying linguistic development (Berk, 1992; Winsler, Diaz, & Montero, 1997).

Some studies have failed to demonstrate a relationship between private speech and the development of cognitive abilities, but these were done in school settings where children were discouraged from talking while doing things. Other research shows that when children are given tasks and encouraged to speak, they often talk to themselves (Frauenglass & Diaz, 1985). Researchers have also found that children in comfortable school environments tend to use more private speech if adults are not present.

more sophisticated early language environments—which might help explain why girls develop verbal skills somewhat ahead of boys.

Children's Conversations

Young children do more than say words and simple sentences. They have conversations with adults and other children, and even with themselves (see "In Theory, In Fact," above). Their conversations typically follow certain patterns.

Monitoring the Message   First, children realize that it's necessary to get the other person's attention. A child who is just learning the art of conversation may yank on another child's clothing. As time passes, the child may instead say something like "Know what?" Children also discover that conversation means taking turns. They learn that conversations have a beginning, a middle, and an end. Eventually they learn to talk about the same subject and to monitor whether the other person is listening and understanding, and to make nonverbal sounds or nod to indicate their own understanding (Garvey, 1984).

If you listen to younger children's conversations, however, the first thing you'll notice is they don't run smoothly. Very young children's conversations are often **collective monologues**—two children may know that they need to take turns speaking, but they may be talking about entirely different, unrelated subjects. Later, when talking about the same subject, children often stop abruptly to see if the other person is listening. They pause and repeat and correct themselves, all of which is a normal part of developing effective communication (Garvey, 1984; Reich, 1986). Even school-age children sometimes have considerable difficulty communicating what they want to say to a listener, and first- and second-grade children have difficulty comprehending each other fully (Beal, 1987).

Finally, children must learn to adjust their conversations to reduce social friction, conflict, and embarrassment. Adjustment means using courtesy markers like "please" and "thank you," paying attention, and selecting suitable topics and the proper forms of address and phrasing. It also means being aware of the social status of the other person. At the same time that children learn the meaning and syntax of language, they also learn **pragmatics,** the social and cultural aspects of language. They learn that language expresses status, roles, and values. They learn that the specific words, syntax, tone of voice, and mode of address used depend on the relationship between speaker and listener. They learn to talk in one way to younger children, in another way to their peers, and in still another way to older children or adults. They are aided by reminders such as, "Don't talk to your grandmother like that" (Garvey, 1984). In general, young children are quick to learn nuances of speech and conform to social status. They are also quick to perceive degrees of status and the appropriate speech behavior in a wide variety of social settings.

Cross-cultural research has shown that pragmatics of speech differ throughout the world in accord with the cultural values that parents communicate to their children (Shatz, 1991). For example, researchers studying differences between German and middle-class U.S. child-rearing practices noted that German parents tended to speak to their children in more authoritative, dominating ways than did the U.S. parents. The U.S. parents focused more on satisfying their children's desires and intentions. The societal values that underlie these tendencies are communicated, in part, through the use of *modal* verbs. Verbs such as "must," "may," "might," "can," "could," and "should" express cultural concepts such as necessity, possibility, obligation, and permission. Thus, German mothers focused more on necessity ("You will have to tell me what you want") and obligation ("You must pick up your toys"). In contrast, the U.S. mothers emphasized intention ("I'm going to take you to the movies") and possibility ("That might happen"). Young children then adopt such tendencies in their own speech (Shatz, 1991).

In another cross-cultural study, Judy Dunn and Jane Brown (1991) examined how the child-rearing language used by parents in Pennsylvania differs from that used in Cambridge, England with regard to societal values. When the researchers focused on how "prescriptive" messages were sent, they found that U.S. mothers tended to define acceptable or unacceptable behavior in terms of their children's specific actions (mother to child: "Don't do that in here!"). In contrast, English mothers tended to discuss their children's behavior in terms of societal norms (Child to mother: "I want to kick you! Mother to child: "You mustn't kick people"). In addition, English mothers were much more likely than U.S. mothers to use evaluative words ("bad," "good"). Such language differences clearly reflect cultural values: Whereas parents in the United States focus more on personal actions, parents in the United Kingdom focus more on complying with norms.

These girls are playing pretend. One of them is having a conversation with the help of the telephone. Through play, children can practice their conversational skills; for example, they learn to take turns speaking.

collective monologues Children's conversations that include taking talking turns, but not necessarily about the same topic.

pragmatics The social and practical aspects of language use.

Subdialects

Often children are presented with more than one form of a primary language because of subcultural differences within a society. This is especially true in the United States, where numerous racial/ethnic groups and distinct social and economic classes coexist. Subcultural differences can produce **subdialects**— variations of a language that can usually be understood by most speakers, though at times with difficulty. In contrast, true *dialect* differences occur when speakers of a language group often cannot understand each other, as is the case with American English versus British English in terms of pronunciation, inflection, and vocabulary.

The status of Black English (which also has its own regional variations) has been debated for decades. Before linguists studied it systematically, Black English was considered to be simply poor English. Experts have now long agreed that it is one of many legitimate subdialects of American Standard English (which here refers to that used in the United States). That is, it is simply different—as opposed to deficient or substandard (Williams, 1970).

Black English has its own rules and is frequently employed in richly expressive ways (Labov, 1970). Linguists have found that the so-called errors made by speakers of Black English are better viewed as alternative grammatical forms. For example, the word "be" in Black English, as used in the sentence "I be sick," expresses an ongoing rather than a transitory condition. The situation expressed concisely by "I be sick" might be rephrased in American Standard English as "I have been sick and still am feeling sick." Similar considerations apply to Hispanic English and its variations, to variations of English used by Native Americans and peoples of differing Asian ancestry, and to the many regional variations of "white" English—all of which are subdialects of American Standard English.

What position should schools take regarding subdialects? When, for example, Hispanic English is the primary language spoken in the child's home environment and by the child, its use at school can be an important mode of self-expression. At the same time, most children who speak Hispanic English or one of the many other American English subdialects will ultimately have to use American Standard English in addition to the language they learned at home. Ideally, speakers of subdialects become competent in the mainstream language while retaining their own distinct linguistic identity.

Bilingualism

Language is not only a means of communication. It is also a symbol of social or group identity. Thus, language conveys attitudes and values and contributes to socialization. A child who grows up hearing two languages and becomes bilingual goes through both a linguistic and a socializing process (Grosjean, 1982).

The status of bilingualism in different nations is strongly affected by issues of social class and political power. In Europe, for example, bilingualism is associated with being a cultured "citizen of the world." In the United States, bilingualism is more often associated with first- or second-generation immigrant status, which is not always viewed positively by the majority. Although cultural pluralism has become more widely accepted, the millions of U.S. children growing up in bilingual environments still experience considerable pressures to conform.

Learning two languages during infancy and early childhood would appear to be a complex task: two systems of rules, two sets of vocabulary, and different pronunciation. Many children who are bilingual in their earliest years nevertheless show little confusion between the rules of the two languages by age 3 (e.g.,

subdialects Subcultural language differences; speakers of subdialects can usually understand each other.

Nicoladis, 1999), although they sometimes use words in the two languages interchangeably. Thus, some psycholinguists theorize that the young child uses a single, "hybrid" language system and only later is able to distinguish between two languages. Other evidence, however, indicates that bilingual children use two separate language systems even as infants (Genesee, 1989). It is also noteworthy that speaking a native language at home and a second language at school apparently doesn't interfere with either—if anything, it improves a child's usage and grasp of both (Winsler, Díaz, Espinosa, & Rodriguez, 1999).

Does learning two languages during early childhood interfere with a child's cognitive development? Early studies in the United States and the United Kingdom concluded that learning two languages at too young an age was detrimental to cognitive development. In this research, bilingual children scored lower on standardized tests than did monolingual English-speaking children. Most such studies, however, did not take into account the socioeconomic level of either the children or their parents. In other words, the scores of the bilingual children may have been lower for other reasons, such as poverty, poor schooling, or lack of familiarity with their new culture.

Most researchers believe that linguistically, culturally, and probably cognitively, it is an advantage to grow up bilingual (e.g., Diaz, 1985; Goncz, 1988). On each count, children are exposed to different ways of thinking about and doing things that may later make them more flexible and therefore more adaptive to our changing world.

CONTENT CHECK

LANGUAGE DEVELOPMENT AND CULTURE

True–False (answers are on the Companion Website)

1. Overregularization occurs after young children have begun to master the basics of inflection.
2. Typically, beginning in early childhood, parents actively teach their children correct syntax.
3. Young children's first conversations tend to be collective monologues.
4. Black English is best characterized as a separate dialect from American Standard English.
5. Research generally indicates that growing up bilingual is detrimental to language development.

Thinking Critically

What evidence is there that language development during early childhood is a result of heredity and environment in interaction?

Play and Learning

Every aspect of development during early childhood is enhanced through play. Play is children's unique way of experiencing the world and practicing and improving their skills, and it is found in all cultures.

Play satisfies many needs in a child's life: to be stimulated and diverted, to express natural exuberance, to experience change for its own sake, to satisfy curiosity, to explore, and to experiment under risk-free conditions. Play has been called the "work of childhood" because of its central role in the young child's development. It promotes the growth of sensory-perceptual capabilities and physical skills while providing endless opportunities to exercise and expand intellectual skills. Play is different from any other kind of activity. By its very nature, it is often not directed toward goals; it is intrinsically rewarding. As Catherine Garvey (1990) pointed out, play is behavior that is engaged in simply for pleasure, has no purpose other than itself, is chosen by the player(s), requires players to be actively engaged, and is related to other areas of life—that is, it promotes social development and enhances creativity. In other words, in a very real sense, play is developmental business.

Kinds of Play

The ways children play change developmentally. Younger children play with other children, talk about familiar activities, and borrow and lend toys. At first their play has a haphazard quality and doesn't include setting goals or making rules. As they become older, children play together and help each other in activities that do have goals. Young children like to build and create with objects and to take on roles and use props (Isenberg & Quisenberry, 1988).

Each kind of play that researchers have identified has its own characteristics and potential functions. Following are some of the major forms of children's play.

Sensory Pleasure The aim of this kind of play is sensory experience in and of itself. Young children may endlessly splash water, chew grass, bang pots, and pluck flower petals simply to experience new sounds, tastes, odors, and textures. Sensory play teaches children essential facts about their bodies and the qualities of things in their environment.

Play with Motion Running, jumping, twirling, and skipping are just some of the countless forms of play with motion that are enjoyed for their own sake. Play involving the continuously changing sensation of movement is one of the

Play with motion.

earliest forms—infants rock back and forth or blow bubbles with their food. Infants frequently engage in movement routines that not only are exciting and stimulating but also give them practice in body coordination. Play with motion is often initiated by an adult or older child and thus gives infants some of their earliest social experiences. Children typically do not initiate or share this kind of activity with other children until about age 3 (Garvey, 1990).

Rough-and-Tumble Play   Parents and teachers may try to discourage the rough-and-tumble, mock-fighting play that young children are fond of. They may try to reduce aggression and real fighting among children. However, rough-and-tumble is *play* fighting, not real fighting. Research suggests that it provides real benefits, within limits. Not only does it offer a chance to exercise and release energy, but it helps children learn to handle their feelings, control their impulses, and avoid behaviors that are inappropriate in groups. Moreover, it helps children learn to distinguish between pretend and real (Pellegrini, 1987). Rough-and-tumble play is observed in cultures throughout the world (Boulton & Smith, 1989), and boys are more likely to engage in such play than girls are.

Language play.

Play with Language   Young children love to play with language. They experiment with its rhythm and cadences. They mix up words to create new meanings. They play with language to poke fun at the world and to verify their grasp of reality. They use it as a buffer against expressions of anger. The primary function of language—meaningful communication—tends to be lost in language play. Children concentrate on the language itself, playfully manipulating its sounds, patterns, and meanings for their own amusement.

Judith Schwartz (1981) provided some classic examples of language play in English. Sometimes children play with sound and rhythm, regularly repeating letters and words in a steady beat: *La la la / Lol li pop / La la la / Lol li pop.* They also make patterns with words as if practicing a grammatical drill: *Hit it. / Sit it. / Slit it. / Mitt it.* Or, *There is the light. / Where is the light? / Here is the light.* Why do children play with language? Partly because it's simply funny. Other people laugh when a young child says something like "I'm gonna telly 'cause you put jelly in my belly and made me smelly."

Playing with language also gives young children practice in mastering the grammar and words they're learning. By ages 3 and 4, children are using some basic linguistic rules and structures of meaning. They ask questions such as "Couldn't table legs be fitted with shoes?" and "Since there is running water, is there sitting water?" (Chukovsky, 1963; Garvey, 1977). Children also use language to control their experiences. Older children use language to structure their play. They create sometimes elaborate rituals that must be followed: Always do this first, then this, before that—and do it all in highly specific ways. By following the rituals carefully, they control the experience (Schwartz, 1981).

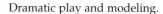
Dramatic play and modeling.

Dramatic Play and Modeling   An important kind of play involves taking on roles or imitating models: in industrialized nations, playing house, mimicking a parent going to work, pretending to be a nurse, astronaut, or truck driver. Such play, called *dramatic play*, involves not only imitation of whole patterns of behavior but also considerable fantasy and novel ways of interaction. Children learn various social relationships, rules, and other aspects of their culture through dramatic play. Dramatic play also interacts with the beginnings of literacy (J. I. Davidson, 1996).

Games, Rituals, and Competitive Play   As children grow older, their play develops rules and specific goals. Children make decisions about taking turns, set up guidelines about what is and what is not permitted, and enjoy situations

A CLOSER LOOK

PRETEND AND REAL

Adults might be tempted to dismiss young children's pretend play as unimportant, perhaps even unhealthy. Quite the reverse is true, according to research.

When children are involved in pretend play they often display two levels of meaning—the level of the reality-based meaning and the level of the pretend meaning. We've long known that children maintain two frames of meaning: a real frame and a play frame (Bateson, 1955). For example, when in the real frame, children playing cops and robbers know that they are actually children. Yet they are deep in the pretend frame too. When there are disagreements, children often "break frame" to resolve their disputes before returning to the pretend frame.

Pretend play becomes increasingly sophisticated during early childhood (Rubin et al., 1983). Children make greater and greater leaps from the real to the pretend meaning of an object or action, and they extend the duration and complexity of their pretend roles and activities. The ability to tell the difference between fantasy and reality continues to develop, however; 4- to 6-year-olds sometimes actually believe that what they imagine is real (Harris, Brown, Marriott, Whittall, & Harmer, 1991).

Young children are capable of various types of pretense (Lillard, 1993). They can pretend about the identity or characteristics of themselves, another person, an object, an event or action, or a situation. As children become older, they rely less on concrete props. Another developmental change is growing flexibility in using self versus another as either the actor or the recipient of action. At first, in solitary play, the child is both the agent and the recipient; the child pretends to go to sleep and covers up. Later, the child uses an object as the active agent—a doll lies down and goes to sleep as though it were doing this itself.

There seems to be a relationship between pretend play and distinctions between appearance and reality. Children who have had lots of practice with pretend play at age 3 and 4 are better able to understand that objects can look like something else (Flavell, Flavell, & Green, 1987; Flavell, Green, & Flavell, 1986). Children who are experienced at pretend play are also better at taking someone else's perspective or understanding someone else's feelings. Researchers suggest that seemingly innocent make-believe play provides key experiences for children's development of structured (organized) knowledge (Flavell, 1985; Garvey, 1977).

in which someone wins and someone loses. Although the intricate rules of many adult games are beyond most young children, they can cope with the rituals and rules of simpler games like tag and hide-and-seek. Such games help them develop cognitive skills such as learning rules, understanding cause and effect, realizing the consequences of various actions, and learning about winning and losing (Flavell et al., 1993; Kamii & DeVries, 1980).

Play and Cognitive Development

Play promotes cognitive development in many ways. Preoperational children use play to learn about their physical surroundings. Although young children are often egocentric, they use dramatic play to master symbolic representation and increase their social knowledge.

Exploring Physical Objects When young children play with physical objects—sand, stones, and water, for example—they learn the properties and physical laws that govern these objects. When playing in sand, a child learns that different objects leave different marks. When bouncing a ball, a child learns that throwing the ball harder will make it bounce higher. By engaging in constructive play, children acquire bits of information that they use to build their knowledge. Greater knowledge, in turn, gives them increasingly higher levels of understanding and competence (Forman & Hill, 1980). Gradually, they learn to compare and classify events and objects, and they develop a better understanding of concepts such as size, shape, and texture. In addition, through active play children develop skills that make them feel physically confident and self-assured (Athey, 1984).

Play and Egocentrism The egocentrism that Piaget ascribed to preoperational children is particularly evident in their play with others. Two-year-olds will watch other children and seem interested in them, but they usually will not approach them. If they do approach, the interaction typically centers on playing with the same toy or object—not with the other child (F. P. Hughes, 1991). Children 2 years old and younger may seem to be playing together but are almost always playing out separate fantasies.

Dramatic play reflects greater social maturity. The play of 3-year-olds shows a better understanding of others' views, which allows the children to be better at role-playing games. In role playing, success depends on cooperation among the players; if children don't act out their parts, the game doesn't work.

In one early study (Shatz & Gelman, 1973) researchers asked 4-year-olds to describe to 2-year-olds how a specific toy worked. Even 4-year-olds understood the need to address younger children in simpler terms. The researchers found that 4-year-olds spoke slowly, used short sentences, employed many attention-getting words such as "look" and "here," and frequently repeated the child's name. Four-year-olds did not speak to older children or adults in that way, consistent with our earlier discussion of pragmatics.

As with all behaviors, however, social maturity is relative. At the age of 3 or even 4, children can still be very stubborn and negative, but they are more likely to conform to others' expectations. Other people are more important to 3-year-olds than they were a year earlier, and the children therefore seek out more social interaction. By now they are more interested in the effects of their behaviors on the world around them and gain considerable satisfaction from showing things they make to others (F. P. Hughes, 1991).

Dramatic Play and Social Knowledge Older preoperational children test their social knowledge in dramatic play. Through imitation, pretending, and role taking, dramatic play promotes the growth of symbolic representation. It also enables children to project themselves into other personalities, experiment with different roles, and experience a broader range of thought and feeling (see "A Closer Look," p. 270). Role playing thus leads to better understanding of others as well as a clearer definition of self (Fein, 1984).

Role playing allows children to experiment with behaviors and to experience the reactions and consequences of those behaviors. For example, children who play hospital with dolls, friends, or alone will play many different roles: patient, doctor, nurse, visitor. In acting out these roles, they may be motivated by real fears and anxieties about illness and dependence on others. Whatever the dramatic situation, role playing allows children to express intense feelings (such as anger or fears), helps them resolve conflicts (such as between them and parents or siblings), and helps them resolve those feelings and conflicts in ways they can understand.

The Role of Peers Given the opportunity, children in general often spend more time interacting directly with each other than with adults. Children play with siblings and other children at home, in the neighborhood, and at school. In many cultures the significance of children's interactions with other children is even greater than it is in U.S. middle-class culture (Rogoff, 1990). In some societies younger children are cared for largely by 5- to 10-year-old children (Watson-Gegeo & Gegeo, 1989). Children may carry a younger sibling or cousin around on their backs or hips, thus enabling the younger children experience the sights and sounds of the community (Rogoff, 1990).

Informal neighborhood groups often include children of various ages. Mixed-age peer groups can offer older children the opportunity to practice teaching and child care with younger children, and younger children can imitate and practice role relations with older children (Whiting & Edwards, 1988). The play activities of mixed-group children may encourage the development of new ways of thinking and problem solving.

CONTENT CHECK
PLAY AND LEARNING

True–False (answers are on the Companion Website)

1. Most children's play is extrinsically motivated.
2. Most experts agree that rough-and-tumble play among young children should be discouraged.
3. Of the various forms of young children's play, dramatic play is the most important in transmission of norms and culture.
4. Role playing is a form of dramatic play.

Thinking Critically

How is young children's play important to their cognitive development?

CHAPTER 7 REVISITED

Physical and motor skills development, cognitive development, and language development are an integrated, dynamic system.

Physical Development

■ Children vary considerably in their rate of physical development; only extreme deviations from average are potentially diagnostic.

■ Malnutrition during early childhood can interfere with cognitive development both directly and indirectly.

■ Rate of physical growth slows during early childhood (although temporary growth spurts may occur); bodily proportions continue to change in the direction of adult proportions.

■ By age 5 a child's brain is approaching the size of an adult's.

■ The brain growth spurt continues from infancy into early childhood and is marked by considerable plasticity.

■ Myelination of central nervous system neurons parallels cognitive and motor skills development.

■ The average number of synapses per neuron increases from birth to a peak at age 2 to 3, after that age the number is gradually reduced by pruning; deleting old synapses is as important as adding new ones.

■ Some view the first 3 years of life as a window of opportunity for brain development.

■ Lateralization of some brain functions occurs rapidly during early childhood, whereas other lateralization occurs during middle childhood; handedness is a function of early lateralization.

Motor Skills Development

■ In general, gross motor skills develop faster than fine motor skills; some skills development is based on functional subordination.

■ Automaticity of gross motor skills begins to become apparent by age 3; automaticity of fine motor skills by about age 4.

■ Readiness, practice, attention, competence, motivation, and feedback are important factors in motor learning.

■ Achieving motor competence and mastery are often intrinsically motivated.

Cognitive Development

■ Piaget divided the preoperational stage into the preconceptual period and the intuitive or transitional period.

■ In Piaget's view, preoperational children's thinking is different from that of older children and adults; examples are animism, reification, and egocentrism.

- Symbolic representation continues to refine during early childhood.

- Limitations on preoperational children's thinking also include concreteness, irreversibility, centration, and immature understanding of time, space, and sequence.

- Piaget's research indicated that preoperational children do not conserve volume, mass, number, and other physical properties of objects; irreversibility and centration explain this in part.

- Subsequent research often indicates that Piaget underestimated the abilities of preoperational children, perhaps because the problems he used to test their abilities were misleading.

- Social perspectives on cognitive development emphasize the importance of guided participation by older children and adults.

Memory and Cognitive Development

- The information-processing model incorporates transfer from a sensory register to STM or working memory to LTM, using a computer analogy.

- Rehearsal both retains information in STM and transfers it to LTM.

- Recognition memory is better than recall memory both for children and adults; both forms of memory improve during early childhood as children eventually learn to rehearse and organize information spontaneously.

- Even young children are capable of remembering temporal ordering of information and simple event scripts; this improves steadily during early childhood.

Language Development and Culture

- Brown's MLU is one reliable measure of children's progress in language development; MLU increases throughout early childhood and beyond.

- Brown proposed five distinct stages of language development during early childhood; overregularization occurs during the second.

- Caregivers and other adults markedly influence the rate and quality of children's early language development, although genetics may play a role as well.

- Children's conversations begin with learning to monitor the message, although their earliest conversations are often collective monologues.

- As conversational skills continue to develop, children soon begin to acquire pragmatics that reflect context and culture.

- Subdialects can usually be understood by most speakers of a primary language; true dialects often cannot be.

- Black English, along with various forms of Hispanic, Native American, Asian, and white English, are subdialects of American Standard English.

- Bilingual children often experience pressures to conform to the primary language of a society, but learning two languages apparently is neither difficult nor detrimental to their language development.

Play and Learning

- Play enhances most aspects of a child's development as well as satisfying natural needs; in most cases play is intrinsically motivated.

- Major forms of play include sensory pleasure; play with motion; rough-and-tumble play; play with language; dramatic play; and games, rituals, and competitive play.

- Dramatic play is especially important to cognitive development, social skills development, and many other aspects of development.

KEY TERMS

neurons	automaticity	recognition
brain growth spurt	intrinsically motivated behavior	recall
plasticity	extrinsically motivated bahavior	mean length of utterance (MLU)
myelination	egocentrism	overregularize
cerebral cortex	conservation	collective monologues
lateralization	short-term memory (STM)	pragmatics
functional subordination	long-term memory (LTM)	subdialects

EARLY CHILDHOOD: PERSONALITY AND SOCIOCULTURAL DEVELOPMENT

8

CHAPTER OUTLINE

Developmental Issues and Coping Patterns
- Fear and Anxiety
- Emotion Regulation and Self-Regulation
- Developmental Conflicts

Aggression and Prosocial Behavior
- Aggression
- Prosocial Behavior

Peers, Play, and Development of Social Skills
- Play and Social Skills
- Popularity and the Development of Social Skills
- The Role of Imaginary Companions

Understanding Self and Others
- Self-Concept
- Self and Gender
- Gender and Socialization
- Social Concepts and Rules

Family Dynamics
- Parenting Styles
- Child Abuse
- Explanations of Child Abuse
- Discipline and Self-Regulation
- Sibling Dynamics

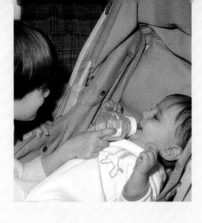

CHAPTER PREVIEW

Do you know:

1. What *fears* and *anxieties* young children commonly display?

2. How parents and teachers can help children *cope* with early childhood fears and anxieties?

3. What *defense mechanisms* children commonly use?

4. The extent to which young children are capable of *emotion regulation* and *self-regulation*?

5. How young children learn to reconcile their needs for *dependence* versus *independence* and Erikson's sense of *initiative* versus *guilt*?

6. The relationship between *frustration* and *aggression*?

7. What effects *punishment* can have on young children's aggression?

8. How parents and others sometimes *model* aggression?

9. What parents and other caregivers can do to foster the development of *empathy* and *prosocial behavior* in young children?

10. The stages of *social play* that occur during early childhood?

11. That many young children have *imaginary companions* and what roles these play?

12. How *self-concept* develops during early childhood?

13. How *gender identity* develops during early childhood?

14. What *androgyny* is and why it apparently is healthy?

15. How parental control and parental warmth interact to produce *authoritative, authoritarian, permissive,* and *indifferent* parenting styles?

16. What *effects* each of these parenting styles tends to have on children?

17. The extent of physical and psychological *child abuse,* the *effects* of abuse on children, and what factors increase the chances that parents will abuse their children?

18. How *sibling dynamics* work and what effects *birth order* has?

These are the main topics of Chapter 8.

Early childhood is a time when the pace of children's learning about their social and cultural world accelerates just as their overall cognitive development does. Ideally, children learn what constitutes good and bad behavior; how to handle their feelings, wants, and needs in socially appropriate ways; and what their family, community, and society at large expect of them. They begin to acquire the norms, rules, and mores of their culture. At the same time, they develop a keen and perhaps lasting concept of self.

Normally, children's self-control and social competence improve dramatically from age 2 to age 6. Although 2-year-olds have all the basic emotions of 6-year-olds (and adults), they express them differently. During the "terrible twos" children can truly be difficult (often unintentionally), but they are often wonderfully charming and affectionate as well. Immediate gratification is the rule, however; deviations from it can produce dramatic emotional outbursts. If a mother promises her 2-year-old an ice cream cone, the 2-year-old wants it *now,* not after the mother has a chat with a friend whom she happens to meet in front of the ice cream parlor. Expressions of dependency are also direct and physical. In unfamiliar settings, 2-year-olds stay close to their mother or father, perhaps clinging. If they venture away, they often return to the parent, using her or him as a "secure base." If they are forcibly separated from the parent, they may throw themselves on the floor and howl in protest. Anger in particular is expressed in physical ways. Instead of expressing themselves verbally, 2-year-olds may kick or bite.

In contrast, 6-year-olds are much more verbal and thoughtful; they are less quick to anger, and they control themselves better. They cope with anger and frustration in far more diverse ways. For example, 6-year-olds can vent anger by kicking a door or a teddy bear rather than a brother or sister or a parent's shin. Some can even hold in their anger and not express it outwardly at all. Some can assume an assertive posture to defend their rights or can use fantasy to see themselves through unpleasant situations. Six-year-olds are also much less likely to kick and howl. Instead, they talk out their anger or fear, or express it indirectly—for example, by being uncooperative and grumpy. By age 6 most children's coping skills are quite refined, and they have their own personal styles.

Personality development, socialization, and enculturation in early childhood are complex; it is no wonder that theorists disagree about the major influences and crucial interactions that take place, as well as about how to study them. Three major theoretical perspectives have governed much research on these issues. As we see—in keeping with the eclectic approach—each has its merits.

Psychodynamic perspectives emphasize the child's feelings, drives, and developmental conflicts. Freud emphasized that young children must learn to cope with powerful innate emotions in socially acceptable ways. Erikson emphasized the growth of autonomy and the need to balance it with dependence on parents during this period.

In contrast, *social-learning perspectives* emphasize links between cognition, behavior, and the environment. The child's behavior is shaped by external rewards and punishments, as well as by role models. Rewards and can also be internal, in that children may behave in ways that augment self-esteem and pride and a sense of accomplishment.

Finally, *cognitive-developmental perspectives* emphasize children's thoughts and concepts as organizers of their social behavior. Young children develop increasingly complex concepts; they learn what it means to be a girl or a boy, a sister or a brother. They also learn about culturally appropriate gender schemes: They judge what behaviors are appropriate for boys and for girls, and they accept or perhaps reject them.

Developmental Issues and Coping Patterns

Children must learn to manage a wide range of feelings or emotions. Some of these are good—such as joy, affection, and pride. Others—such as anger, fear, anxiety, jealousy, frustration, and pain—obviously are not. Whether the feelings are good or bad, however, young children must acquire some means of moderating their feelings and expressing them in socially acceptable ways.

Young children must also find ways of resolving developmental conflicts. They must learn to deal with their dependence on others and find ways to relate to the authority figures in their lives. They must deal with their need for autonomy—the strong drive to do things for themselves, to master their physical and social environments, to be competent and successful. How children master these tasks has been explored extensively by psychodynamic theorists, especially Erikson. As Erikson suggested, children who are unable to resolve these early psychosocial conflicts may have difficulty with adjustment later in life (Erikson, 1964).

The sense of personal and cultural identity that children form between the ages of 2 and 6 is accompanied by many strong feelings. Finding acceptable ways of coping with feelings of fear and anxiety, distress and anger, affection and joy, and sensuality and sexual curiosity is no easy task, and children often experience conflict while doing so.

Fear and Anxiety

One of the most important forces that children must learn to deal with is the stress caused by fear and anxiety. The two emotions are not synonymous. **Fear** is a response to a specific stimulus or situation: A child may fear the dark or lightning and thunder, or have a phobia of big dogs or high places. In contrast, **anxiety** is a more generalized emotional state. Although some children may become anxious in specific situations, those who are characterized as "anxious" experience regular and continuing feelings of apprehension and unease, often without knowing why. A move to a new neighborhood or a sudden change in parental expectations, such as the beginning of toilet training, may induce anxiety that seems to come from nowhere. Many psychologists believe that anxiety inevitably accompanies the socialization process as children attempt to avoid the pain of parental displeasure and discipline (Wenar, 1990).

Causes of Fear and Anxiety　Fear and anxiety can have many causes. Young children may be afraid that their parents will leave them or stop loving them. Parents usually act in a loving and accepting manner, but sometimes they withdraw their love, attention, and protection as a means of punishment. Withdrawal of love threatens children and makes them feel anxious. Anticipation of other types of punishment, especially physical punishment, is another source of anxiety for young children. Two-year-olds sometimes have no realistic idea of how far their parents will go in punishing them. When an exasperated parent shouts, "I'm going to break every bone in your body!" the child may not fully appreciate that the threat is an empty one.

Fear and anxiety may be increased or even created by the child's imagination. For example, children often imagine that the birth of a new baby will cause their parents to reject them. Sometimes anxiety results from children's awareness of their own unacceptable feelings—anger at a parent or other caregiver, jealousy of a sibling or a friend, or a recurrent desire to be held like a baby.

The sources of some fears are easily identified—fear of the doctor who gives inoculations and dread inspired by the smell of a hospital or the sound of a dentist's drill, plus apprehension over a wide variety of real dangers the world sometimes serves up. Other fears are harder to understand. Many young children develop a fear of the dark that is related more to fantasies and dreams than to real events in the child's life. Sometimes the fantasies stem directly from developmental conflicts with which a child is currently struggling; for example, fearsome imaginary tigers or ghosts may arise from the child's struggle with dependency and autonomy.

A classic study of children's fears (Jersild & Holmes, 1935) found that younger children were most likely to be afraid of specific objects or situations,

autonomy　The strong desire to do things for yourself, to master physical and social environments, and to be competent and successful.

fear　A state of arousal, tension, or apprehension caused by a specific, identifiable circumstance.

anxiety　A feeling of uneasiness, apprehension, or fear that has a vague or unknown source.

such as strangers, unfamiliar things, the dark, loud noises, or falling. In contrast, children aged 5 or 6 were more likely to fear imaginary or abstract things—monsters, robbers, death, being alone, or being ridiculed. Fifty years later researchers found most of the same fears in young children, except that fear of the dark, of being alone, and of unfamiliar things now appear at earlier ages (Draper & James, 1985).

In today's world there are many sources of fear, anxiety, and stress. Some are a normal part of growing up, such as being yelled at for accidentally breaking something or being teased by an older sibling. Others are more serious: internal stresses like illness and pain and the chronic long-term stresses created by unfavorable living environments—poverty, parental conflict or drug use, dangerous neighborhoods (Greene & Brooks, 1985). Some children must cope with major disasters or terrors, such as earthquakes, floods, and wars. Severe or long-term stressful situations can drain the psychological resources of even the most resilient child (Honig, 1986; Rutter, 1983).

Although we naturally try to avoid and minimize fear and anxiety, it's important to bear in mind that these are normal feelings that are necessary to development. In mild forms, they can be a spur to new learning. Many kinds of fear are necessary for our very survival in a world full of potentially dangerous things such as hot fireplaces or appliances, fast-moving cars and trucks, and a goodly assortment of things that can threaten our lives—including other people.

Coping with Fear and Anxiety How can we help children cope with fear and anxiety? Using force or ridicule is likely to have negative results, and ignoring children's fears will not always make them go away. Instead, at least when their fears are mild, children can be gently and sympathetically encouraged to confront and overcome them. Parents can help by demonstrating that there is little to fear. For example, to help a child who is afraid of night-time "robbers," parents can have the child watch while they check the locks on all the doors and otherwise verify the home's security. With fears that have acquired true phobia status, however, children (and adults as well) may need professional treatment such as **systematic desensitization.** In this procedure,

systematic desensitization In behavior therapy, a technique that gradually reduces an individual's anxiety about a specific object or situation through relaxation.

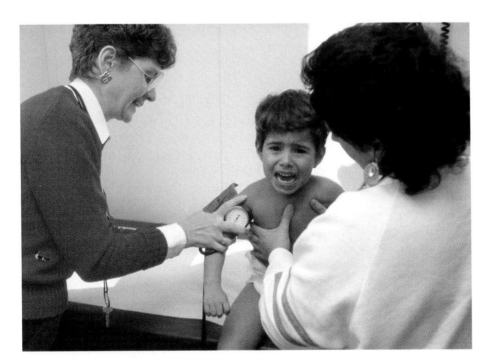

No child really enjoys going to the doctor. Often a trip to the doctor's office is linked in a child's mind with a painful injection.

after learning certain relaxation techniques the person works through a "hierarchy" that begins with minimally fearsome versions of the object or situation and eventually progresses to the real thing. For example, a child who is afraid of dogs might practice staying relaxed while looking at a simple drawing of a dog, then at a more detailed drawing, then at a photograph, and eventually at a real dog. An even more effective procedure is participant modeling, which grew out of Bandura's research on children and imitation (Chapter 1). In this procedure (Bandura & Adams, 1977), clients first watch a model engage in the designated behavior without harm and are then encouraged to engage in the behavior themselves. For a child with a fear of dogs, the goal would be to approach the dog gradually and eventually pet it the way the model has been doing. In this case, in Bandura's view, the child who succeeds in petting the dog acquires a sense of "self-efficacy" where dogs are concerned and no longer fears or avoids them. This is similar to the story of the little train: In many situations, if you *think* you can, then you *can.*

Often the best way to help children cope with anxiety is to reduce unnecessary stress in their lives. When children show unusually high levels of tension or have frequent temper tantrums, it's helpful to simplify their lives by sticking to daily routines, specifying clearly what is expected of them, and helping them anticipate special events such as visits by friends and relatives. Other helpful strategies include reducing their exposure to parental fighting or violent television programs and protecting them from being teased or tormented by neighborhood bullies or gangs.

Not all life stresses can be avoided or minimized, of course. Children must learn to cope with the birth of a sibling, moving to a new home, or entering day care, as well as perhaps with divorce, the untimely death of a parent, or natural disasters. Under such circumstances parents and teachers are encouraged to do the following (Honig, 1986):

1. Learn to recognize and interpret stress reactions in their children.
2. Provide a warm, secure base to help children regain confidence.
3. Allow opportunities for children to discuss their feelings—a shared trauma is easier to handle.
4. Temporarily allow immature behavior, such as thumb sucking, cuddling a blanket, fussing, or sitting on laps.
5. Help children give meaning to the event or circumstance by providing explanations appropriate to their age level.

Children also develop their own means of coping with fears and anxiety. For example, quite normal 2- to 4-year-olds often display highly repetitive, ritualized behaviors that in adults would be deemed "obsessive-compulsive" (Evans et al., 1997). A child who is afraid of the dark, for example, might develop a highly specific ritual for saying good night to parents in a certain order and with an exact number of kisses or hugs, thus reducing anxiety about going to bed.

Defense Mechanisms   In response to more generalized feelings of anxiety—especially those that arise in the intense emotional climate of the family and involve issues of morality or sex roles—children learn strategies called **defense mechanisms.** In psychoanalytic theory, a defense mechanism is a way of reducing or at least disguising anxiety. We often employ defense mechanisms in coping with anxiety and frustration. For example, we may use *rationalization* when we don't get something we want. If you don't get that promotion you were hoping for, you might rationalize away your disappointment by telling yourself that you wouldn't have liked the increased responsibility anyway. If a

defense mechanisms   The psychodynamic "tricks" that individuals use to reduce tensions that lead to anxiety.

child isn't invited to a party, the child might rationalize that he or she wouldn't have had a good time at the party anyway. Common defense mechanisms—many of which were clarified or first identified by Freud's daughter Anna in her work with children—are listed in Table 8–1. By age 5 or 6 most children have learned to use such ways of coping.

Table 8–1   Selected Defense Mechanisms Used by Children

Identification

The process of incorporating the values, attitudes, and beliefs of others. Children adopt the attitudes of powerful figures, such as parents, in order to become more like these figures—more lovable, powerful, and accepted—which helps reduce the anxiety they often feel about their own relative helplessness.

Denial

Refusal to admit that a situation exists or that an event happened. Children may react to an upsetting situation such as the death of a pet by pretending that the pet is still living in the house and sleeping with them at night.

Displacement

Substituting something or someone else for the real source of anger or fear. For example, Tyler may be angry with his baby sister, but he can't hit her—perhaps he can't even admit to himself that he wants to hit her. So instead he torments the family dog or cat.

Projection

Attributing undesirable thoughts or actions to someone else and in the process distorting reality. "She did it, not me" is a projective statement. " He wants to hurt me" may seem more acceptable than "I want to hurt him." Projection thus sets the stage for a distorted form of "self-defense": "If he wants to hurt me, I'd better do it to him first."

Rationalization

Persuading yourself that you don't want what you can't have. Even relatively young children are capable of talking themselves out of things. A child who doesn't get in-

vited to a party might decide, "Oh, well. I wouldn't have had a good time anyway." Rationalization is a common defense mechanism that continues to develop and be refined well into adulthood.

Reaction formation

Behaving in ways opposite to your inclinations. When children have thoughts or desires that make them anxious, they may react by behaving in a contradictory way. For example, they might like to cling to their parents but instead they push them away and behave with exaggerated independence and assertiveness.

Regression

Returning to an earlier or more infantile form of behavior as a way of coping with a stressful situation. Perhaps when frustrated an 8-year-old suddenly reverts to sucking her thumb and carrying around her "blankie"—behaviors that were given up years before.

Repression

An extreme form of denial in which the person *unconsciously* erases a frightening event or circumstance from awareness. There is no need to rely on fantasy because the child literally does not consciously remember that the event ever occurred.

Withdrawal

Simply removing yourself from an unpleasant situation. This is a very common defense mechanism in young children. It is the most direct defense possible. If a situation seems too difficult, the child withdraws from it either physically or mentally.

Source: Adapted from Freud, A., 1946.

Historical and Cultural Influences   As a result of differences in cultural and family backgrounds, children experience fear and anxiety about different things. A hundred years ago, children were afraid of wolves and bears. Fifty years ago, they worried more about goblins and "bogeymen." Nowadays their nightmares are populated with extraterrestrials and killer robots. There are also striking cultural differences in the way children express their fears, indeed whether they express their fears at all. In contemporary Western culture, showing fear is generally frowned upon. Children are supposed to be brave; most parents worry about a child who is unusually fearful. In contrast, traditional Navajo parents believe that it is healthy and normal for a child to be afraid; they consider a fearless child foolhardy. In one study, Navajo parents reported an average of 22 fears in their children, including fears of supernatural beings. In contrast, a group of white parents from rural Montana reported an average of only 4 fears in their children (Tikalsky & Wallace, 1988).

Emotion Regulation and Self-Regulation

Western societies also expect children to inhibit the display of other emotions, both negative and positive, such as anger and distress, affection and joy, sensuality and sexual curiosity. Most parents expect their children to learn what Claire Kopp (1989) called *emotion regulation,* which means dealing with emotions in socially acceptable ways.

In turn, Kopp called children's growing ability to control their overall behavior *self-regulation:* Ideally, children adopt and internalize a composite of specific standards for behavior, such as safety concerns and respect for the property of others. *Compliance,* a component of self-regulation, refers to obeying the requests of caregivers. During toddlerhood, parents' requests, such as "stay indoors" or "pick up your toys," may be met with crying. During the third year, crying occurs infrequently, but "resistive behavior" such as refusal to obey requests increases and peaks. By age 4, resistance declines. Kopp argued that resistance does not decline simply because language skills and communication between child and parents are improving; instead, a 4-year-old's cognitive skills have improved to a point where the child can convey personal needs in more socially acceptable and less emotional ways.

Emotion regulation is a normal part of children's development, especially during the first 8 years of life (Bronson, 2000). Feelings of *shame* and *guilt,* which may have their origins during the second and third years of life (Hoffman, 1998), appear to be important factors affecting emotional regulation in early childhood. Contemporary developmentalists view shame as a more painful and intense emotion than guilt because it goes to the core of the child's sense of identity (Tangney, 1998). Shame is associated with the desire to undo aspects of the self. Guilt, in contrast, involves the desire to undo certain behaviors. Guilt is thus more distinct from the self and therefore shouldn't affect the person's core identity (Niedenthal, Tangney, & Gavanski, 1994). In spite of the difference in intensity, however, researchers have found that both boys' and girls' shame and guilt are directly related to their emotion regulation (Rothbart, Ahadi, & Hershey, 1994).

Otherwise, children who fail to learn the bounds of acceptable behavior may develop mild to severe emotional problems, such as disruptive behaviors, personality disorders, and autism (Cole, Michel, & Teti, 1994).

Distress and Anger Children learn very early that open displays of negative feelings are unacceptable in public places—including nursery schools and day-care centers (Dencik, 1989). As children grow older, their parents' expectations for emotional regulation increase: It's okay for babies to cry when they're hungry, but it is not okay for 6-year-olds to do so. Children who do not learn such lessons at home are at risk of being socially rejected outside the home. In particular, children who cry a lot are likely to be unpopular with their peers (Kopp, 1989).

Learning to manage anger is even more important. In one longitudinal study, children who were still having temper tantrums at age 10 were tracked into adulthood (Caspi, Elder, & Bem, 1987). The researchers found that the children tended to be unsuccessful as adults as a result of their continuing outbursts of anger. They had difficulty holding jobs, and their marriages often ended in divorce.

Learning to manage negative emotions is not the same as not having them—negative emotions are an inevitable part of life. Children can come to accept their angry feelings as a normal part of themselves while at the same time learning to control or redirect their reactions to such feelings. They may use anger as a motivating force, as a way of overcoming obstacles, or as a means of standing up for themselves or others.

Affection and Joy   In many cultures children must also learn to restrain their positive emotions. Spontaneous feelings such as joy, affection, excitement, and playfulness are dealt with quite differently by 2-year-olds and 6-year-olds. Just as 2-year-olds are direct in expressing distress, they are also likely to openly display positive feelings—they freely jump up and down or clap their hands when excited. As early socialization continues, and depending upon their culture, children may be required to learn to subdue such open expressiveness. Spontaneous joy and affection may become embarrassing because they are considered babyish. Children may be required to limit their spontaneity to acceptable occasions such as parties and games.

Sensuality and Sexual Curiosity   Two-year-olds are very sensual creatures. They like the feel of messy, gooey things. They are conscious of the softness or stiffness of clothes against their skin; they are fascinated by sounds, lights, tastes, and smells. Consistent with psychoanalytic theory, such sensuality is primarily oral during infancy, but eventually a fascination with the genital regions develops. Masturbation and sex play are quite common during early childhood, although children in most Western cultures quickly learn not to display such behaviors when adults are present. As children discover that self-stimulation is pleasurable, most develop active curiosity about their bodies and ask many sex-related questions that you as an adult may find difficult to answer in a way that you deem appropriate—but that also varies from one culture to another.

How culture and family members react to a child's developing sensuality and sexual curiosity can have a powerful effect, just as the reactions of others can affect the way a child handles hostility and joy. Until more modern times

Young children are very open about showing positive feelings like joy. But by the age of 6 they have learned to somewhat mask even these feelings.

parents in the United States were advised to prevent their children from engaging in sexual exploration (Wolfenstein, 1951), and many parents still do. Whether openly or in private, however, sensual exploration is a natural and vital part of experience, beginning in early childhood and continuing into adolescence and adulthood.

Developmental Conflicts

Trying to express their feelings in socially acceptable ways is not the only task children face during early childhood. Developmental conflicts also arise as children adjust to their own changing needs. Young children are pulled in one direction by their need for autonomy and in another direction by their continuing dependence on their parents. They must also deal with issues of mastery and competence.

Autonomy and Connectedness   Young children constantly struggle with themselves and others. Out of the close sense of "connectedness" most 2-year-olds have with their caregivers emerges a new sense of autonomy—the conviction that they can do *it* (whatever *it* is) themselves. Ambivalence between the opposing forces of autonomy and connectedness is characteristic of early childhood.

Although dependence and independence are commonly considered opposite types of behavior, things aren't necessarily that simple for young children. Independence follows a complex trajectory during early childhood. Whereas infants are usually fairly cooperative, everything changes at about age 2. Many children now become quite uncooperative, the hallmark of the "terrible twos." Temper tantrums become common. In Western cultures, when 2-year-olds are asked to do something, they may show their independence by saying "No!" As they get older, however, they tend to become compliant and cooperative again. Three-year-olds are more likely to do what their parents tell them and less likely to break rules when their parents aren't looking, perhaps as a result of their developing sense of morality (Emde & Buchsbaum, 1990; Howes & Olenick, 1986).

One study (Craig & Garney, 1972) traced developmental trends in expressions of dependency by observing how children at ages 2, 2½, and 3 maintained contact with their mothers in an unfamiliar situation. The 2-year-olds spent most of their time physically close to their mothers, staying in the same part of the room and looking up often to make sure that their mother was still there. The older children (2½- and 3-year-olds) neither stayed as close to their mother nor checked as often to see if she had left the room. The older the child, the more the child maintained verbal rather than physical contact. All three age groups made a point of drawing attention to their activities, but the older children were more inclined to demonstrate them from afar.

Mastery and Competence   Early childhood is a time for children to discover their own bodies and learn to control them. If they are successful in doing things for themselves, they become self-confident. If their efforts at autonomy are frustrated by criticism or punishment, they think that they have failed and feel ashamed and doubtful about themselves (Erikson, 1964; Murphy, 1962; White, 1959).

In Erikson's third stage, *initiative versus guilt,* the primary developmental conflict from age 3 to age 6 directly involves mastery and competence. Initiative refers to the purposefulness of young children as they ambitiously explore their surroundings. They eagerly learn new skills, interact with peers, and seek the guidance of parents in their social interactions. For most children, guilt is inevitable too, as when they go against their parents' wishes in exploring their world.

All children need to feel a sense of mastery over their environment. This feeling of mastery may lead to chaos at times, but it is still a key aspect of development.

The key is to achieve a balance between initiative and guilt. As Erikson pointed out, excessive guilt can dampen the child's initiative, especially if parents harshly suppress or criticize their children's natural curiosity. Children's self-confidence and initiative-taking breaks down, resulting in timidity and fearfulness that can remain a part of personality for life.

The conflict between initiative and guilt is an extension of the toddler's struggle with autonomy. Toddlers gain control and competence starting with their own bodies—feeding, dressing, toileting, handling objects, and getting around. Ideally, they learn how things work, what social situations and relationships mean, and how to influence people in constructive and appropriate ways. Concepts of right and wrong, good and bad, become important; labels such as "baby" or "brat" can have devastating effects. For the most part, the job of a parent or teacher is to guide and discipline the child without creating too much anxiety or guilt. In the often confusing and complex social world of early childhood, initiative can lead either to success and feelings of competence or to failure and feelings of frustration.

Learning Competence   What happens when children's attempts at mastery or autonomy meet with constant failure or frustration? What happens when children have little or no opportunity to try things on their own, or when their environment is so chaotic that they can't see the consequences of their acts? All children need to master their environment and feel competent and successful. If they do not, they may give up trying to learn and become passive in their interactions with the world. Many studies have shown that such children fail to develop an active, exploratory, self-confident approach to learning; they lack *learning competence* (White & Watts, 1973). Moreover, when children are made to feel anxious about their need for autonomy, they generally learn to deny, minimize, or disguise their needs.

Some children are restricted in their drive toward autonomy. Children who are physically disabled or chronically ill may have little opportunity to test their skills in mastering the environment (Rutter, 1979). Children who grow up in dangerous or crowded surroundings and have to be restrained for their own safety, or who are supervised by excessively vigilant caregivers, may also develop exaggerated passivity or anxiety (Zuravin, 1985).

CONTENT CHECK
DEVELOPMENTAL ISSUES AND COPING PATTERNS

True–False (answers are on the Companion Website)

1. *Systematic desensitization* is a technique employed to treat children's anxieties.
2. Young children have conflicting pulls between autonomy and mastery.
3. Popular preschoolers tend to be more creative than their unpopular peers.
4. Preschoolers' development of *gender schemes* depends on their level of cognitive development.
5. Children of permissive parents tend to be extremely well adjusted.

Thinking Critically

What are the merits and shortcomings of each of the three major theoretical perspectives on development during early childhood?

Aggression and Prosocial Behavior

Young children must also learn to control their aggressive tendencies and engage in positive behaviors such as helping and sharing. Whereas Freud considered aggression to be an inherent drive, the social-learning perspective is quite different. In this view, whether we are born with aggressive tendencies or not, actual aggressive behavior varies considerably from one person to the next as a result of reinforcement, punishment, and imitation of models. Behaviors such as helping and sharing are similarly affected by learning, even though we may also have inherent tendencies in this respect. Thus, the focus of research on both negative and positive behaviors is directed at studying how children are influenced by interactions with parents, siblings, peers, and others.

A young child's social repertoire is also strongly affected by play and other peer interactions. Although theorists disagree about the ultimate origins and purposes of play, it is clear that play enhances social skills by giving children practice in getting along with others.

Aggression

In the language of social psychology, **hostile aggression** is behavior that is intended to harm another or establish dominance over another. For example, a child hits or pushes another child down as an act of revenge. **Instrumental aggression** involves harm caused as a byproduct of some goal-directed behavior. A child pushes another child down while trying to grab a toy; the resulting harm is unintentional. Both forms of aggression differ from **assertiveness**, which does not involve harm and instead takes forms such as standing up for your rights.

Aggression may be physical or verbal. It may be directed at people or "displaced" onto animals or objects. In young children aggression is a common response to anger and hostility. Aggression has also been found to be associated with children's shame, more so that with their guilt (Ferguson, Eyre, Stegge, Sorenson, & Everton, 1997). Whatever its causes, physical aggression typically increases at the beginning of early childhood and then declines as verbal aggression begins to replace it (Achenbach, Howell, Quay, & Conners, 1991; Parke & Slahy, 1983). The decline in aggression is also associated with children's growing ability to resolve conflicts in nonaggressive ways—through negotiation, for example—and with their improving experience in *how* to play (Shantz, 1987). In addition, by the age of 6 or 7, children are less egocentric and better able to understand another child's point of view. This helps in two ways: Children are less likely to misinterpret another child's behavior as aggression that might invite retaliation, and they are better able to empathize with how another child feels when harmed.

Frustration and Aggression Learning theorists once argued that *frustration*—a typically angry state produced when goals are blocked or thwarted—leads to aggression. Can frustration cause aggression? Of course, whenever someone does something that makes you angry and you retaliate verbally or even physically, frustration leads to aggression. However, the learning theorists' *frustration-aggression hypothesis* (Dollard, Doob, Miller, Mowrer, & Sears, 1939) has long since been shown to be incorrect. This hypothesis stated that *all* aggression is derived from frustration, and that sooner or later all frustration results in some form of aggression, either direct or disguised. The aggression might be directed toward the source of the frustration, or it might be displaced

hostile aggression Aggression that is intended to harm another person.

instrumental aggression Aggression that is not intended to harm, but is instead incidental to gaining something from another person.

assertiveness Standing up for and defending your rights.

onto another person or object—for example, a parent scolds a child and takes away a toy, and a little while later the child kicks the family pet.

The frustration-aggression hypothesis was challenged by a classic study of the behavior of young children in a frustrating situation (Barker, Dembo, & Lewin, 1943). The children were given access to attractive toys, which were then removed and placed behind a wire screen; the toys thus remained visible but beyond reach. How did the children react? A few did display aggressive behaviors. Others, however, simply tried to leave the room, or waited patiently, or turned their attention to something else. Some engaged in behaviors such as thumb sucking.

The other half of the frustration-aggression hypothesis—the idea that all aggression is derived from frustration—has been similarly discredited (Dollard & Miller, 1950). Aggression can occur as a result of imitation, as we saw in Bandura's classic experiment on observational learning in Chapter 1. Simply rewarding children for aggressive behavior causes it to increase (Parke & Slahy, 1983). Thus, frustration can lead to aggression, and vice versa, but aggression can occur for many other reasons as well.

The mother's pointing finger tells the story about the child's behavior.

Punishment and Aggression   Punishment can also create a tendency to behave aggressively—especially if the punishment is harsh and frequent. If children are punished for aggressive acts, they will avoid these behaviors—at least in the presence of the person who has punished them. Ironically, however, they may become more aggressive in general. For example, their aggression at home may decrease, but they may become more aggressive at school. They may express aggression in different ways, such as tattling or name-calling. Adults who use physical punishment to curb a child's aggression also provide a model of aggressive behavior. One U.S. study (Strassberg, Dodge, Pettit, & Bates, 1994) found that young children who received spankings at home were more aggressive than children who did not. Moreover, the more often the children were spanked, the more aggressive they were. In other words, a young child who is spanked may learn that if someone is smaller than you, it's okay to use force.

Modeling and Aggression   As noted earlier, observing aggressive models can strongly influence antisocial behavior. Imitation of models is more likely to occur when the observers sense a similarity between themselves and the model, or when the model is perceived as powerful or competent (Eisenberg, 1988). Thus, boys are more likely to imitate other boys or men than to imitate girls or women. Children are also more likely to imitate other children who have dominant personalities—that is, who are socially powerful (Abramovitch & Grusec, 1978). Well-liked children dominate their peers through the force of their personalities, not through physical aggression. In contrast, children dislike physically aggressive playmates (Ladd, Price, & Hart, 1988).

Not all models come from the child's immediate environment, of course; many varieties of potentially powerful models appear on television.

Television is not merely an electronic toy or a casual means of entertainment. It is a pervasive influence that has a major impact on family relationships and especially children. In 1950, only 1 family in 20 had a TV set. Ten years later, about 90 percent of U.S. homes had TV sets. Today virtually every home in the United States, Western Europe, and Japan has at least one TV set; many homes have several, and many even have one for each member of the household.

As noted by Aletha Huston and colleagues, "Although estimates of children's viewing time vary widely (from 11 to 28 hours a week), they all indicate that American children spend more time watching television than in any other activity except sleep" (Huston, Watkins, & Kunkel, 1989, p. 424).

Before entering formal schooling, U.S. children are likely to have watched about 4,000 hours of television (Levin, 1993; Walsh, 1994). For better or worse, television programming has become a major socializing force in the United States (Comstock, 1993), in other industrialized nations, and throughout much of the rest of the world.

The wide-ranging influence of television—plus the Internet—has been and continues to be a major focus of developmental research. For example, researchers have looked at the effects on children's imagination, personality, and multicultural awareness, as well as their eating habits and overall health (Singer & Singer, 2000). Much of this research continues to assess the effects of media violence. For example, TV entertainment directed toward young audiences often includes "for fun" violence—as in cartoons (Levin, 1998). Moreover, TV news shows expose children to violence in the real world—and more than two-thirds of U.S. households have the television on when news programs are on, such as at the evening meal. Many researchers have concluded that exposing children to large doses of casual violence on the TV screen teaches them to think of aggression as a commonplace and acceptable way of dealing with frustration and anger. Others have taken the opposite view, arguing that viewing violent acts on television may serve as a substitute for overt aggression, thus providing *catharsis* (Chapter 2). Research evidence does not support the older view. Many subsequent studies have shown that exposure to televised violence produces a significant increase in the aggressiveness of viewers (Huston et al., 1989). Beyond overall aggressiveness, children also become desensitized to the effects of violence and learn to justify behaving violently when they believe they are right (Levin, 1996).

Many other aspects of televised program content affect children negatively. Often certain kinds of people are presented in a stereotyped fashion: Members of minority groups may be depicted in unfavorable ways; women may be shown in passive, subordinate roles; and older people may be made to appear senile or burdensome. If unsupervised, young children may be exposed to considerable and increasingly graphic sexual content. In all, children can easily develop unrealistic social beliefs and concepts by watching television. Even their overall view of the world may be affected. One study found that heavy television viewing causes people to see the world as a mean and threatening place—probably because there are far more frightening incidents on television than occur in most people's everyday experience (Rubinstein, 1983).

For some children, habitual viewing of aggressive programs may also be combined with an environment in which many role models—parents, siblings, or friends—are also aggressive or antisocial. This combination seems to increase aggressive behavior, especially in children with behavioral or emotional problems (Huesmann, Lagerspetz, & Eron, 1984).

Concerned about the effects of television violence on chidren, the U.S. government passed the 1996 Telecommunications Act, which required that starting in 1998 new TV sets be equipped with a microchip device called the V-chip. Parents can now program their TV sets to block out shows they don't want their children to watch. Knowing what to block out, however, often requires a program rating system. Thus, in 1996 the television industry voluntarily introduced the TV Parental Guidelines ratings, which went into effect the following year.

Despite numerous studies that have identified negative effects of television viewing, television can also have a positive influence on children's thoughts and actions. Television can teach children many forms of *prosocial* behavior, as discussed in the next section. Carefully designed children's programs inter-

Figure 8-1 The Availability of Television Around the World

Source: U.S. Census Bureau, 1997.

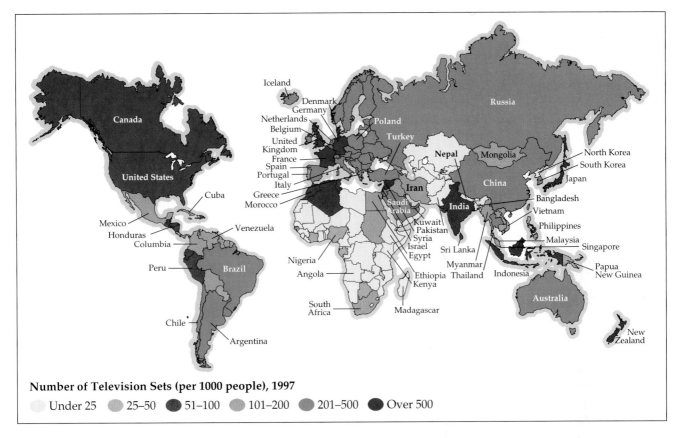

Number of Television Sets (per 1000 people), 1997

● Under 25 ● 25–50 ● 51–100 ● 101–200 ● 201–500 ● Over 500

weave themes such as cooperation, sharing, affection, friendship, persistence at tasks, control of aggression, and coping with frustration. Children who watch such programs, even for relatively short periods, become more cooperative, sympathetic, and nurturant (Stein & Friedrich, 1975).

Just how many television sets are there? Figure 8–1 gives a global view. Social learning also takes place via a wide array of other media, including radio, music, and other sources as illustrated in Figure 8–2.

Prosocial Behavior

Prosocial behavior is defined as actions that are intended to benefit others, with no anticipation of external rewards (Eisenberg, 1988). Such actions, which include comforting, sympathizing, assisting, sharing, cooperating, rescuing, protecting, and defending (Zahn-Waxler & Smith, 1992), mostly fit the definition of *altruism*—unselfish concern for the welfare of others. Prosocial behavior also frequently involves some cost, sacrifice, or risk to the individual. Prosocial behavior is not just a set of social skills, however. When fully developed, it is accompanied by feelings of friendship, caring, and warmth—including empathy with regard to the feelings of others (Zahn-Waxler & Smith, 1992). For example, if a child watches a person who is sad and the child consequently also feels sad, the child is experiencing empathy (Eisenberg, 2000).

Prosocial behavior begins to develop in early childhood and may be displayed by children as young as age 2. Parents exert a powerful influence on the development of prosocial behaviors, as do siblings. Young children who have

Figure 8-2   Media Usage, United States (hours per person per year)*

Source: U.S. Census Bureau, 1997.

*1998, projected.

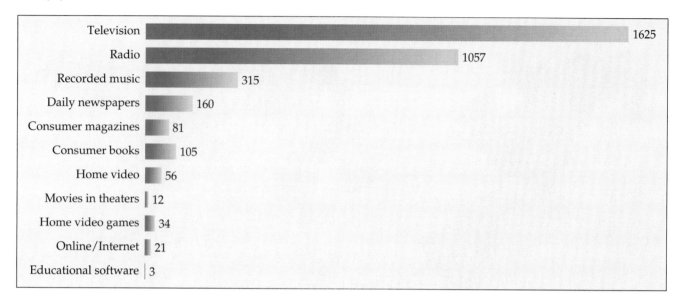

secure relationships with their caregivers are more likely to attempt to comfort younger siblings than children who have insecure relationships (Teti & Ablard, 1989). Signifiers of empathy such as facial, behavioral, and physiological reactions to seeing others in need or distress have also been linked to prosocial behavior (Hastings & Zahn-Waxler, 1998). There are limits to young children's ability to empathize, share, and cooperate, however; prosocial behavior continues to develop into middle childhood and adolescence and beyond.

Whether behavior is considered socially appropriate depends on the situation and on the standards of the family and the culture. Aggression is not always bad, altruism not always appropriate. Unaggressive soldiers would be useless in combat; altruistic ball players would never win a game. Overly altruistic people also may be intrusive, moralistic, and conforming (Bryan, 1975).

Conditioning, Learning, and Prosocial Behavior   Because reward and punishment affect aggression, it is natural to assume that they also affect helping and sharing behaviors. However, it has been difficult to prove that this is true. One problem is that researchers are understandably reluctant to conduct experiments in which prosocial behavior is punished. Another is that experiments in which prosocial behavior is rewarded are often inconclusive because the results may be due to modeling: When experimenters give a reward, they are also modeling the act of giving (Rushton, 1976). Even so, one study found that 4-year-old children who were given many chores to do at home were more likely to be helpful outside the home. Interestingly, the most helpful children in this study were ethnically black males. The experimenters hypothesized that because more of the black children came from single-parent homes, their caregivers had turned to their sons for help and emotional support. Thus, these children had learned helping and comforting behaviors very early in life (Richman et al., 1988).

Two other approaches to enhancing prosocial behavior are *role playing* and *induction.* In the former, children are encouraged to act out roles as a way of helping them see things from another person's point of view. In the latter, children are given reasons for behaving in positive ways; for example, they may be told what consequences their actions will have for others. In one early experiment (Staub, 1971) both procedures were employed with kindergarten children. Role playing increased the children's willingness to help others, and its effects lasted as long as a week. In contrast, induction had little or no effect, perhaps because the children didn't pay much attention to a lecture from an unfamiliar experimenter. Other research has shown that when induction is employed by parents or other familiar people children can become more prosocial (Eisenberg, 1988).

Prosocial behaviors such as cooperation also change with age. Millard Madsen (1971; Madsen & Shapira, 1970) found that U.S. children become less cooperative and more competitive as they grow older. When playing a game that can be won only if the two players cooperate (see Figure 8–3), 4- and 5-year-olds often cooperated. Older children, however, tended to compete with each other; as a result, neither player won. In studies of Mexican children and children raised in Israeli kibbutzim, however, researchers found that older children were more likely to cooperate, presumably because their cultures emphasize group goals more than individual achievement. Madsen suggested that many U.S. children are reared to be competitive and learn this value so completely that they are often unable to cooperate even when they could benefit from doing so.

Modeling and Prosocial Behavior   Many studies have demonstrated the influence of modeling on prosocial behavior. In a typical experiment a group of children observe a person performing a prosocial act, such as putting toys or money into a box designated for "needy children." After watching the generous model, each child is given an opportunity to donate something. Researchers usually find that children who witness another person's generosity become more generous themselves (Eisenberg, 1988). Prosocial models are also more effective when the model is perceived as nurturant or has a special relationship with the child, but note again that models often appear in movies and on TV.

Figure 8–3   **Madsen's Game**

In Madsen's game, two children sit at opposite ends of a game board that features a cup at each end, a gutter down each side, and a marble holder with a marble inside. To play the game, the children move the marble holder by pulling on strings; if the holder is moved over a cup, the child earns the marble as it drops into the cup. The children must cooperate to earn marbles; if they both pull on the strings at the same time, the marble holder comes apart, and the marble rolls into the gutter.

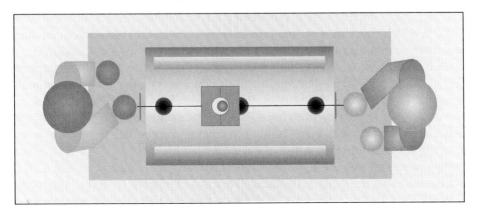

CONTENT CHECK
AGGRESSION AND PROSOCIAL BEHAVIOR

True–False (answers are on the Companion Website)

1. Verbal aggression begins to replace physical aggression as early childhood unfolds.
2. Frustration always causes aggression in young children.
3. Punishment can cause young children to become more aggressive.
4. Young children are more likely to learn aggression than prosocial behavior as a result of modeling.
5. Role-playing is a technique that discourages prosocial behavior.

Thinking Critically

Does social-learning theory adequately explain the development of aggression and prosocial behavior in preschoolers? Why or why not?

Peers, Play, and Development of Social Skills

Children influence one another in many ways. They provide emotional support in a variety of situations. They serve as models, reinforce behavior, and encourage complex, imaginative play. They also encourage—or discourage—both prosocial and aggressive behaviors.

Children help one another learn a variety of physical, cognitive, and social skills (Asher, Renshaw, & Hymel, 1982; Hartup, 1983). For example, young boys playing aggressively may first imitate characters seen on television and then imitate each other. They continue to respond and react to each other in a way that supports and escalates the play, a form of *social reciprocity* (Hall & Cairns, 1984).

Play and Social Skills

A classic study of peer relations (Parten, 1932–33) identified five developmental levels of social interaction in young children: (1) *solitary play;* (2) *onlooker play,* in which a child simply observes other children; (3) *parallel play,* in which children play alongside each other but do not directly interact; (4) *associative play,* in which children share materials and interact but do not coordinate their activities within a single theme; and (5) *cooperative play,* in which children engage in a single activity together—such as building a house with blocks or playing hide-and-seek. Two-year-olds mostly engage in onlooker and parallel play, whereas 4- and 5-year-olds show increasing periods of associative and cooperative play. Children at ages 5, 6, and 7 can interact for relatively long periods while sharing materials, establishing rules, resolving conflicts, helping one another, and exchanging roles.

Beginning around age 4, children often engage in *social pretend play,* which involves imagination and the sharing of fantasies in accordance with agreed-upon rules. According to Vygotsky (as discussed in Chapter 2), it is

U.S. children become more competitive in their play as they grow older.

partly through social pretend play that children learn cooperation and other social skills along with the ability to think about and regulate their own behavior. Pretend play offers many opportunities for discussion, reflective thought, and joint problem solving. Together, children negotiate mutually acceptable activities and construct the play framework. For example, if two 5-year-olds pretend that they are astronauts, both children share their limited knowledge and develop play sequences in a cooperative fashion (Berk, 1994a; Goncu, 1993; Kane & Furth, 1993). There are also pronounced cultural variations in styles and meanings of social play, as discussed in "A Closer Look," page 294.

Popularity and the Development of Social Skills

When we observe children in nursery schools, day-care centers, or kindergartens, it is apparent that some children are popular with their peers and others are not. Popularity can be remarkably stable over the years: Children who are rejected by their peers in early childhood are likely to be rejected in middle childhood as well. They are also more likely to have adjustment problems in adolescence and adulthood (Parker & Asher, 1987). It is therefore important to understand what social skills are involved in popularity and to identify unpopular children early to teach them the skills they lack.

Popular children are more cooperative and generally display more prosocial and other-oriented behaviors during play with their peers; these behaviors are summarized in Table 8–2 (Asher, 1983; Asher et al., 1982). Such behaviors are also good predictors of social status in the first grade (Putallaz, 1983).

In contrast, unpopular, rejected children may be either more aggressive or more withdrawn. They may also simply be "out of sync" with their peers' activities and social interactions (Rubin, 1983). Which comes first: Do rejected children engage in negative behaviors because they are rejected, or are they rejected because of their negative behaviors? Why do some children lack the social skills that make others popular? Abuse or neglect during early

A CLOSER LOOK

CULTURAL VARIATIONS IN THE MEANING OF PLAY

Play has long been recognized as important to cognitive development. Play is also a primary vehicle for practicing the values, behaviors, and roles of society. Through play, for example, children act out themes, stories, or episodes that express their understanding of their culture (Nicolopoulou, 1993).

Children in all cultures develop and learn in social contexts that include older peers and adults who pass on their cultural heritage. When children pretend, the roles they imitate "channel" their behavior. For example, a child playing "father" or "mother" parallels the parent's behavior as the child understands it. When a little girl plays mother, she attends to and makes explicit her understanding of the rules embedded in the role of mother (Nicolopoulou, 1993; Oppenheim, Emde, & Warren, 1997). Because the role of mother—and other major social roles and values—differs from one culture to another, we would expect to find that the specifics of play also vary across cultures (e.g., see Farver & Shin, 1997). This appears to be the case even though play itself is found in all cultures.

Even in cultures in which there is little time for play, children frequently create play situations by integrating chores and fun. Kenyan Kipsigis children, for example, play tag while tending herds, or climb trees while watching younger siblings (Harkness & Super, 1983). Work songs are common among Amish children as they collectively wash potatoes or shuck peas. Children in countries that are at war play games of war.

There are vast differences in the amount and type of play observed both across and within cultures. In some cultures, children's games are simple; in others, they are complex and elaborate. In some cultures, competitive games are virtually nonexistent and cooperative games are the rule. For example, the day nurseries of the former Soviet Union emphasized collective play in the form of group games, also complex toys that required more than one child to make them work (Bronfenbrenner, 1970). In cultures in which daily survival depends on motor skills, games of physical skill are generally the only forms of competition. For example, in hunting-and-gathering societies where machetes are used to cut through dense undergrowth, playful competition in speed of machete use is the norm. In other societies, foot races, competitive tracking, and spear-throwing contests are the main types of play (L. A. Hughes, 1991).

Table 8–2   Characteristics of Popular Children in Kindergarten

Initiate activity by moving into the group slowly, making relevant comments and sharing information

Sensitive to the needs and activities of others

Don't force themselves on other children

Content to play alongside other children

Possess strategies for maintaining friendships

Show helpful behavior

Are good at maintaining communication

Are good at sharing information

Are responsive to other children's suggestions

Possess strategies for conflict resolution

When faced with conflict, are less likely to use aggressive or physical solutions

Source: Asher (1983), Asher et al., (1982).

childhood can be a factor. Research indicates that young children who are physically maltreated by their caregivers are more likely to be rejected by their peers. Unable to form effective peer relationships, abused children are often more disliked, less popular, and more socially withdrawn than children who aren't abused, and the extent to which they are rejected by peers increases with age (Dodge, Pettit, & Bates, 1994). Less dramatic but nonetheless potentially important contributors to unpopularity include being "sheltered" and allowed little interaction with peers, being singled out as "different" by peers, or simply getting off to a bad start when first entering a group-care setting. Remember too, as discussed earlier, that highly aggressive children are unlikely to be popular.

Given that peer relations are a significant socializing influence in the lives of children, and that the success of these relations depends on the development of social skills, it is important to help children during early childhood, when rejection first occurs (Asher, 1990). Adults can help in at least two ways. First, they can teach social skills directly, through modeling and induction. Second, they can offer and encourage opportunities for successful social experiences with peers. Especially in group-care settings, adults can draw unpopular children into group activities and help them learn how to get along with others. Children need opportunities to play with other children, as well as appropriate space and play materials. Dolls, clothes for dress-up activities, toy cars and trucks, blocks, and puppets promote cooperative play and offer opportunities for interaction. With young children, adult caregivers must be available to help initiate activities, negotiate conflicts, and provide social information (Asher et al., 1982).

The Role of Imaginary Companions

Many young children create **imaginary companions** and playmates who become a regular part of their daily routines. An imaginary companion is an invisible character that may seem quite real to the child (Taylor, Cartwright, & Carlson, 1993). Children give these characters names, mention them in their conversations, and play with them. Imaginary companions help children deal with fears, provide companionship during periods of loneliness, and provide reassurance.

Research indicates that as many as 65% of young children have imaginary companions. Normally, creating imaginary friends is associated with positive personality characteristics. For example, compared with children who don't have imaginary companions, those who do have such companions have been found to be more sociable and less shy, have more real friends, be more creative, and participate more in family activities (Mauro, 1991). Imaginary companions also seem to help children learn social skills and practice conversations. Children who have imaginary companions will play happily with peers and will be cooperative and friendly with both peers and adults (Singer & Singer, 1990).

Finally, there may be cognitive as well as emotional benefits to having an imaginary companion. It is possible that children who are adept at imagination and fantasy are better at mastering symbolic representation and the real world. Pretending may facilitate children's understanding that their mental images are distinct from external objects.

imaginary companions Companions children "make up" and pretend are very real.

Understanding Self and Others

So far we have focused mostly on specific types of behavior—how children learn to share or be aggressive or handle feelings. But children also act in a more comprehensive way. They put together various specific behaviors to create overall patterns of behavior that are appropriate for their gender, family, and culture. As children grow older they become less dependent on the rules, expectations, rewards, and punishments of others, and more capable of making judgments and regulating their behavior on their own. Cognitive-developmental theorists believe that the integration of patterns of social behavior coincides with the development of a concept of self, which includes gender schemes and social concepts that help mediate the child's behavior.

Self-Concept

Even a 2-year-old has some understanding of self. As we saw in Chapter 6, by 21 months a child can recognize herself in the mirror; if she sees a red mark on her nose, she may show embarrassment. The language of 2-year-olds is full of assertions of possession, which imply "me" versus "you." In one study of 2-year-olds playing in pairs, most of the children began their play with numerous self-assertions. They defined their boundaries and their possessions—"my shoe, my doll, my car." Assertiveness can be viewed as a cognitive achievement, not mere selfishness: Children are increasing their understanding of self and others as separate beings (Levine, 1983). A review of studies of children's self-concepts and social play concluded that the children who are most social also have more fully developed self-concepts (Harter, 1983). Thus, self-understanding is closely linked to the child's understanding of the social world.

During early childhood children develop certain generalized attitudes about themselves—a sense of well-being, for example, or a feeling that they are "slow" or "bratty." Many of these ideas begin to emerge very early and at a nonverbal level. Children may develop strong anxieties about some of their feelings and ideas while being quite comfortable with others. They also begin to develop ideals, and they begin measuring themselves against who they think they ought to be. Often children's self-evaluations are direct reflections of what other people think of them. Imagine a lovable 2-year-old with a talent for getting into mischief, whose older siblings call him "Bad Buster" whenever he gets

Older preschoolers tend to describe themselves according to their activities such as "I stand on my head."

into trouble. By the age of 7 the child might be making a conscious effort to maintain his reputation for being bad. Early attitudes thus can eventually become basic elements of a person's self-concept.

Young children are fascinated with themselves; many of their activities and thoughts center on learning about themselves. They compare themselves to other children in terms of height, hair color, family background, and likes or dislikes. They compare themselves to their parents and imitate their parents' behavior. As part of their drive to find out about themselves, young children ask a variety of questions about where they came from, why their feet grow, whether they are good or bad, and on and on.

Awareness of how you appear to others is a key step in the development of self-knowledge and self-concept. Young children tend to define themselves in terms of physical characteristics ("I have brown hair") or possessions ("I have a ball"). In the United States, older children are more likely to describe themselves in terms of their activities: "I walk to school," "I play ball" (Damon & Hart, 1982). They also define themselves through their interpersonal relationships and experiences. According to Peggy Miller and colleagues (Miller, Mintz, Hoogstra, Fung, & Potts, 1992), young children commonly describe themselves through stories about their families. Children's tendency to portray themselves through their social connections increases during early childhood. In turn, personal storytelling by parents can be an important means of conveying moral and social standards to children (Miller, Wiley, Fung, & Liang, 1997).

As children learn who and what they are and begin to evaluate themselves as active forces in the world, they put together a cognitive theory or *personal script* about themselves that helps to regulate their behavior. In other words, human beings apparently need to feel that they are consistent and do not act randomly: Even as children, we try to bring our behavior in line with our beliefs and attitudes.

Self and Gender

Sex is genetically determined and biological; *gender* is culturally based and therefore acquired, as discussed in Chapter 6. Some theorists suggest that sex determines dramatically differences in intellect, personality, adult adjustment, and style biologically. In everyday language, think how often you hear statements like "Women are . . ." and "Men are . . . ," which clearly indicate underlying beliefs in built-in, immutable differences between the sexes.

The alternate view is that men and women differ primarily because of the way they are treated by their parents, teachers, friends, and culture from early childhood on—in other words, they differ because of differences in their environment. But when we argue about whether heredity or environment is more important in determining gender-specific behaviors, we are actually missing the point. Genetics and culture may each set limits on **gender roles**—what is appropriate for a male or a female to be and do—but they interact like two strands of a rope. In addition, children play an active role in developing their own personal sense of gender, as we see in this chapter and in later chapters.

In early childhood, children typically begin to acquire the social behaviors, skills, and roles that their culture deems appropriate for their sex. For perspective, let's look first at some differences between the sexes that set the stage for this process, for better or for worse.

Male-Female Differences During Childhood Male babies, on average, are born slightly longer and heavier than female babies. Newborn girls have slightly more mature skeletons and are a bit more responsive to touch. As

gender roles Roles we adopt as a result of being psychologically female or male.

toddlers, again strictly on average, boys are more aggressive and girls have a slight edge in verbal abilities. In the United States, by age 8 to 10 boys begin to outperform girls in mathematics. By age 12 the average girl is well into adolescence, whereas physically the average boy is still a preadolescent (Chapter 11).

Equally important are areas in which girls and boys do *not* differ. One literature review (Ruble, 1988) revealed many areas in which gender differences are not found. For example, there are no consistent differences in sociability, self-esteem, motivation to achieve, or even rote learning and certain analytical skills.

Finally, actual differences between boys and girls are small, and there is considerable overlap between the sexes—for example, many girls are more aggressive than many boys, and many boys aren't as good at math as many girls. It's also important to note that many studies conducted in the mid-1980s found less significant gender differences than those reported in earlier studies (Halpern, 1986; Ruble, 1988). These findings suggest that cultural changes—specifically, changed views of gender-appropriate behavior—have influenced the social roles open to girls and boys, and later, to women and men.

Gender and Socialization

Gender has at least two interrelated components: gender-related behaviors and gender concepts. Social-learning theorists focus on how gender-specific behaviors are learned and combined to create gender roles.

In most cultures, children display gender-specific behaviors by age 5; many children learn some of those behaviors by age 2½ (Weinraub et al., 1984). In U.S. nursery schools, for example, girls are often observed playing with dolls, helping with snacks, and showing interest in art and music; boys build bridges, engage in rough-and-tumble play, and play with cars and trucks (Pitcher & Schultz, 1983), although more nursery schools now take an egalitarian approach.

In turn, young children often exaggerate gender-specific behaviors and rigidly conform to **gender-role stereotypes**—fixed ideas about female and male behavior. Such stereotypes imply a belief that "feminine" and "masculine" are two distinct and mutually exclusive categories. This belief appears in nearly every culture, although cultures vary considerably in the specific attributes they ascribe to males and females. In the United States, for example, traditional parents expect their male children to be "real boys"—reserved, forceful, self-confident, tough, realistic, and assertive—and their female children to be "real girls"—gentle, dependent, high-strung, talkative, frivolous, and impractical (Bem, 1975; Williams, Bennett, & Best, 1975). In traditional families children are pressured to conform to these gender stereotypes, regardless of their natural dispositions.

How are gender attributes learned? As with aggressive behavior and prosocial behavior, rewards, punishment, and modeling that are appropriate for the child's gender begin early. In one study (Smith & Lloyd, 1978), mothers were observed interacting with 6-month-old infants who were not their own. Sometimes baby girls were presented to the mothers as boys, sometimes boys were presented as girls; sometimes the babies were presented in accordance with their actual sex. Invariably the mothers encouraged babies whom they thought were boys to walk, crawl, and engage in physical play. Girls were handled more gently and encouraged to talk.

As children grow older, parents often react more favorably when they engage in behavior that is appropriate to their sex. Fathers may be especially important in the development of the child's gender role (Parke, 1981). Even more than mothers, fathers teach specific gender roles by reinforcing femininity in daughters and masculinity in sons.

gender-role stereotypes Rigid, fixed ideas of what is appropriate female or male behavior.

Gender Schemes   Most experts agree that the development of **gender schemes**—gender-based cultural standards or stereotypes—depends in part on the child's level of cognitive development and in part on aspects of the culture that the child attends to (Levy & Carter, 1989). That is, children progressively become more capable of understanding what it means to be a girl or a boy, and as they do, they elaborate their knowledge of what is culturally "appropriate" for females and males.

Children develop gender schemes directly, from what they are taught and from the models they see around them, and indirectly from stories, movies, and television. Studies of stereotypical models in television programs indicate that over the years the gender roles conveyed by these models have been quite traditional (Signorelli, 1989). Even studies of children's elementary school reading books, conducted in 1972 and again in 1989, indicated a preponderance of gender-stereotyped roles (Purcell & Sewart, 1990). Nor have such differences disappeared in the years since (e.g., Tepper & Cassidy, 1999). It is therefore not surprising that children's concepts about gender are often stereotyped.

As we saw, children learn some aspects of gender roles by imitating significant others and by being reinforced for gender-appropriate behavior. Children are also active participants in this process and are selective about what they imitate and internalize as they acquire **gender identity**—our sense of who we are as males and females. Research suggests that children's developing understanding of gender-related schemes helps determine what attitudes and behaviors they learn. Moreover, gender-related schemes and a sense of gender identity develop in predictable ways during early childhood. By about age 2½ most children can readily label people as boys or girls, or men or women, and they can accurately answer the question "Are you a boy or a girl?" (Thompson, 1975). However, even though they can easily discriminate between females and males, they may be confused about what this distinction means. Many 3-year-olds believe, for instance, that if a boy puts on a dress he becomes a girl. They may not realize that only boys can become fathers and only girls can become mothers. By age 5 to 7 children understand that their gender is stable and permanent. Thus, children acquire **gender constancy**—the understanding that girls invariably become women, boys become men, and gender is consistent over time and situations (Kohlberg, 1966; Shaffer, 1988; Stangor & Ruble, 1987)(see Table 8–3).

During early childhood, children also acquire a sense of the meaning underlying gender stereotypes. In research settings 4-year-olds offer fierce toy bears to boys and fluffy toy kittens to girls; this suggests that the cultural associations of objects and qualities with one gender or the other do not depend solely on observing or being taught *specific* associations—such as that dolls are for girls and trucks are for boys. Instead, children readily generalize what *classes* of toys are appropriate for each gender. As one group of researchers concluded: "Children, even at these early ages, may have begun to connect certain qualities with males and other qualities with females" (Fagot, Leinbach, & O'Boyle, 1992, p. 229).

Many cognitive-developmental psychologists believe that children are intrinsically motivated to acquire values, interests, and behaviors consistent with their gender—a process called **self-socialization.** Children develop rigid concepts of "what boys do" and "what girls do." For example, boys play with cars and don't cry; girls play with dolls and like to dress up. Typically, a child will be more interested in the details of behaviors that are gender-appropriate and less so in gender-inappropriate behaviors (Martin & Halverson, 1981).

Are young children better at attending to and remembering things that are consistent with their gender schemes? Research indicates that they are. In

Children's developing understanding of gender-appropriate behavior and gender schemes often involve modeling and dramatic play.

gender schemes   Cognitive standards (including stereotypes) as to what behavior and attitudes are appropriate for males and females.

gender identity   The knowledge of who you are as male or female and the ability to make that judgment about other people.

gender constancy   The older child's understanding that gender is stable and stays the same despite changes in superficial appearance.

self-socialization   When children are intrinsically motivated to acquire values, interests, and behaviors consistent with their sex.

Table 8-3 **The Development of Gender Schemes Across Early Childhood**

Level of Schemes	Approximate Age	Characteristics of Behavior
Gender identity	2 to 5 years	By 2½ children can label people as boys or girls; are confused about the meaning of being a boy or girl; believe gender is changed by surface appearance—for example, changing clothes changes gender.
Gender constancy	5 to 7 years	Children can understand that gender is stable and permanent; boys grow up to become daddies or men, girls grow up to become mommies or women; gender is consistent over time and situations.

memory tests, for example, girls tend to remember more "girl" items, boys more "boy" items. Children make memory errors when a story violates their gender stereotypes. For example, they may remember that a boy was chopping wood when in fact a girl was. Such results indicate that children's developing gender concepts have a powerful influence on their attention and learning (Martin & Halverson, 1981). When concepts of gender stability and consistency are developing, children tend to have stereotyped concepts of gender-appropriate behavior that organize and structure their behavior and feelings. If stereotypes are violated, children may feel embarrassed, anxious, or uncomfortable—although they may also be amused, depending on the situation.

Androgyny In U.S. culture parents and teachers have traditionally been urged to help children establish clear, gender-specific behavior by the time they entered elementary school. Research suggests, however, that exaggerated gender-specific behavior severely limits the emotional and intellectual development of both women and men (Bem, 1985).

Sandra Bem and colleagues have argued that "feminine" and "masculine" are not opposite ends of a single dimension. They are two separate dimensions, which means that it's possible for a person to be high or low on either or both. Stated differently, desirable masculine and feminine traits can easily exist in the same person regardless of gender. Both men and women are capable of being ambitious, self-reliant, and assertive (traditional masculine roles), as well as affectionate, gentle, sensitive, and nurturant (traditional feminine roles). Such a blend of traits in either a woman or a man is called **androgynous personality.** Depending on the situation, androgynous men can be independent and assertive, yet able to cuddle an infant or offer a sensitive ear to another person's troubles. Likewise, androgynous women can be assertive and self-reliant, yet expressive and nurturant when warranted.

Androgynous personality is formed by specific child-rearing practices and parental attitudes that encourage desirable cross-gender behaviors. Traditionally, parents have accepted more cross-gender behavior in girls than in boys (Martin, 1990). Lifelong androgynous gender identities that combine aspects of both traditional masculinity and femininity are most likely to develop when such behavior is modeled and accepted. It helps for the same-sex parent to provide a model of the cross-sex behavior and for the opposite-sex parent to reward the pattern (Ruble, 1988). Dad can vacuum the rug, clean bathrooms, and

androgynous personality
Characteristic of a person who is high in both desirable masculine and femine traits.

mend clothing, just as Mom can mow the lawn, repair appliances, and take out the trash.

Social Concepts and Rules

Young children busily sort things out, classify behaviors as good or bad, and attempt to find meaning in the *social* world—just as they do with regard to the physical world. Central to the development of social concepts and rules is internalization: Ideally, children learn to incorporate the values and moral standards of their society into their self-concept. Some values are related to appropriate gender-role behavior, some to moral standards, and some simply to customary ways of doing things.

How do children internalize values and rules? At first they may simply imitate verbal patterns: A 2-year-old says "No, no, no!" as she marks on the wall with crayons. She continues doing what she wants to do, but at the same time she shows the beginnings of self-restraint by telling herself that she shouldn't be doing it. In a few months she should have developed enough self-control to arrest such impulses. Cognitive theorists point out that children's attempts to regulate their own behavior are influenced not only by their developing self-concept but also by their developing social concepts. Such concepts reflect increased understanding about others as well as about self. For example, a young child may be learning what it means to be a big sister or brother or to be a friend. The child is also learning about concepts such as fairness, honesty, and respect for others. Many such concepts are far too abstract for young children, but they struggle to understand them anyway.

Young children learning about social concepts often ask, "Why did he or she do that?" The answers often involve attributions about personality and character. For example, the question "Why did Kevin give me his cookie?" may be answered with "Because Kevin is a nice boy." As children grow older, they become progressively more likely to see other people—as well as themselves—as having stable character attributes (Miller & Aloise, 1989). Caregivers can encourage children to be helpful or altruistic by teaching them that they are kind to others because they want to be—because they are "nice" people (Eisenberg, Pasternack, Cameror, & Tryon, 1984; Grusec & Arnason, 1982; Perry & Bussey, 1984).

At the same time, young children must learn to understand the *minds* of others—what others intend, what others feel and want. As proposed by Angeline Lillard and Stephanie Curenton (1999), "The development of social understanding is so important to human development and it begins so early that psychologists are beginning to think of it as an innate potential, like the ability to learn language" (p. 52). Understanding what others are thinking is particularly relevant to forming early friendships and minimizing disputes, discussed next.

Children's Friendships Social concepts and rules surrounding children's friendships have been studied extensively. Children do not acquire a clear understanding of friendship until middle childhood; notions of mutual trust and reciprocity are too complex prior to this. . However, young children do behave differently with friends than with strangers, and some 4- and 5-year-olds can maintain close, caring relationships over an extended period. They may not be able to verbalize what friendship is, but they follow some of its implied rules (Gottman, 1983). In one study, for example, young children who watched puppet scenarios involving either a friend or an acquaintance in trouble reacted differently depending on which character was involved. They responded with more empathy to the friend and showed greater willingness to help the friend (Costin & Jones, 1992).

Children's Disputes   When children argue with peers, siblings, and parents, they often demonstrate a surprisingly sophisticated level of social understanding and an ability to reason from social rules and concepts. Children as young as 3 years of age can justify their behavior in terms of social rules ("Now it's my turn!") or the consequences of an action ("Stop, you'll break it if you do that!") (Dunn & Munn, 1987). A close look at children's verbal disputes in early childhood demonstrates systematic development in their understanding of social rules, their understanding of another person's perspective, and their ability to reason from social rules or from the consequences of their actions (Shantz, 1987).

CONTENT CHECK
UNDERSTANDING SELF AND OTHERS

True–False (answers are on the Companion Website)

1. Young children tend to define themselves in terms of their activities.
2. Internalization is a process by which young children acquire self-concept and gender identity.
3. By the end of early childhood, children have a relatively clear understanding of friendship.
4. Gender constancy is attained by the beginning of early childhood.
5. Traditionally, U.S. parents have accepted more cross-gender behavior in girls than in boys.

Thinking Critically

What links are there between patterns of social behavior and the development of self-concept?

Family Dynamics

Many family dynamics—parenting styles, number and spacing of children, interactions among siblings, discipline techniques—affect development during early childhood. Development is also influenced by the structure and circumstances of the family, such as whether there are two parents or only one, whether family members are employed, whether grandparents or other relatives live in the household, and whether the family lives in a comfortable house in the suburbs or a crowded apartment in the city.

Parenting Styles

Just as each individual is unique, each family is unique. Parents use their own versions of child-rearing techniques, depending on the situation, the child, the child's behavior at the moment, and the culture. Ideally, parents place reasonable limits on the child's autonomy and instill values and self-control while being careful not to undermine the child's curiosity, initiative, and growing sense of competence. Crucial dimensions in parenting are control and warmth.

Parental control refers to how restrictive the parents are. Restrictive parents limit their children's freedom; they actively enforce compliance with rules and see that children fulfill their responsibilities. In contrast, nonrestrictive parents

Authoritative parents encourage the developing autonomy of their children while at the same time setting reasonable limits.

are minimally controlling, make fewer demands, and place fewer restraints on their children's behavior and expression of emotions. *Parental warmth* refers to the amount of affection and approval the parents display. Warm, nurturing parents smile at their children frequently and give praise and encouragement. They limit criticism, punishment, and signs of disapproval. In contrast, hostile parents criticize, punish, and ignore their children, rarely expressing affection or approval. Parental control and warmth directly affect children's aggressiveness and prosocial behavior, their self-concepts, their internalization of moral values, and their development of social competence (Maccoby, 1984).

Four Parenting Styles Diana Baumrind (1975, 1980) used these dimensions in classifying parenting styles. She identified three distinct patterns of parenting: *authoritative, authoritarian,* and *permissive.* To complete the picture, we also include *indifferent* parenting (Maccoby & Martin, 1983). These are summarized in Table 8–4. Bear in mind that these are general tendencies, not absolutes; parenting style can vary from one situation to the next.

Authoritative parents combine a high degree of control with warmth, acceptance, and encouragement of autonomy. Although they set limits on behavior, the limits are reasonable, and the parents provide explanations appropriate to the child's level of comprehension. Their actions do not seem arbitrary or unfair; as a result, their children more willingly accept restrictions. Authoritative parents also listen to their children's objections and are flexible when it is appropriate. For example, if a young girl wants to visit at a friend's house beyond the hour when she is normally expected to be home, authoritative parents might ask her why, what the circumstances will be (such as whether the friend's parents be there), and whether it will interfere with responsibilities such as homework or chores. If there are no problems, the parents might allow the small deviation from the rule.

Authoritarian parents are highly controlling and tend to show little warmth toward their children. They adhere rigidly to rules. In the situation just described, their response to their daughter's request would probably be refusal

authoritative parents Those parents who use firm control with children but encourage communication and negotiation in rule setting within the family.

authoritarian parents Those parents who adhere to rigid rule structures and dictate rules to children; in this situation, children contribute little to the family's decision-making process.

Table 8-4 Parenting Styles Based on Warmth and Control

Authoritative	Moderately high control	Accept and encourage the growing autonomy of their children.
	High warmth	Have open communication with children; flexible rules; children found to be the best adjusted—most self-reliant, self-controlled, and socially competent; better school performance and higher self-esteem.
Authoritarian	High control	Issue commands and expect them to be obeyed.
	Low warmth	Have little communication with children; inflexible rules; allow children to gain little independence from them; children found to be withdrawn, fearful, moody, unassertive, and irritable; girls tend to remain passive and dependent during adolescence; boys may become rebellious and aggressive.
Permissive	Low control	Have few or no restraints on child; unconditional love by parents.
	High warmth	There is communication from child to parent; much freedom and little guidance for children; no setting of limits by parents; children tend to be aggressive and rebellious; also tend to be socially inept, self-indulgent, and impulsive; in some cases, children may be active, outgoing, and creative.
Indifferent	Low control	Set no limits for children; lack affection for children.
	Low warmth	Focus on stress in their own lives; no energy left for their children; if indifferent parents also show hostility (as neglectful parents do), children tend to show high expression of destructive impulses and delinquent behavior.

accompanied by statements like "A rule is a rule" or "Because I said so!" If the child argues or resists, the parents might become angry and impose punishment—often physical. Authoritarian parents issue commands and expect them to be obeyed; they avoid lengthy verbal exchanges with their children. They behave as if their rules are set in concrete and can't be changed, which can make the child's attempts at autonomy highly frustrating.

Permissive parents show a great deal of warmth and exercise little control, placing few or no restraints on their children's behavior. The issue of staying out later than usual would probably not even arise because there would be few curfews in the first place, along with no fixed times for going to bed and no rule that the child must always keep her parents informed of her whereabouts. Rather than asking her parents if she can stay out later than usual, the young girl might simply tell her parents what she plans to do, or perhaps just let them find out about it afterward. When permissive parents are annoyed or impatient with their children, they often suppress these feelings. According to Baumrind (1975), many permissive parents are so intent on showing their children "unconditional love" that they fail to perform other important parental functions—in particular, setting necessary limits on their children's behavior.

Indifferent parents neither set limits nor display much affection or approval—perhaps because they don't care or because their own lives are so stressful that they don't have enough energy left over to provide guidance and support for their children.

Effects of Different Parenting Styles As indicated by Baumrind (1972, 1975) and other researchers, authoritarian parents tend to produce withdrawn, fearful children who are dependent, moody, unassertive, and irritable. As adolescents, these children—especially boys—may overreact to the restrictive, punishing environment in which they were reared and become rebellious and aggressive.

Although permissiveness in parenting is the opposite of restrictiveness, it does not necessarily produce the opposite results: Children of permissive parents may also be rebellious and aggressive. In addition, they tend to be self-

permissive parents Those parents who exercise little control over their children but are high in warmth.

indifferent parents Parents who are minimally interested in their role as parents or in their children; they exercise little control over and demonstrate little warmth toward their children.

indulgent, impulsive, and socially inept, although some may instead be active, outgoing, and creative (Baumrind, 1975).

Children of authoritative parents have been found to fare well in most respects. They are most likely to be self-reliant, self-controlled, and socially competent. In the long run these children develop higher self-esteem and do better in school than children reared with the other parenting styles (Buri, Louiselle, Misukanis, & Mueller, 1988; Dornbusch, Ritter, Leiderman, Roberts, & Fraleigh, 1987).

The worst outcome is found in children of indifferent parents. When permissiveness is accompanied by hostility and lack of warmth, the child feels free to give rein to even the most destructive impulses.

Still, the effects of parenting styles can vary considerably across cultures and subcultures, and we can't say that any one style is universally "best" (Darling & Steinberg, 1993). Moreover, the methods by which authoritative parents convey standards for behavior can vary considerably across cultures. Some research also indicates that certain elements of the authoritarian style have advantages. Traditional Chinese parents, for example, are often described as authoritarian and highly controlling, yet the "training" approach they take to childrearing fosters high academic achievement (Chao, 1994).

"Traditional Parents"   In two-parent families each parent may have a different parenting style. For example, in what has been called the *traditional style,* parents conform to traditional male and female stereotypes. The father may be quite authoritarian, the mother more nurturant and permissive (Baumrind, 1989). Here the impact of either parenting style is balanced by that of the other parent.

Negotiation of Shared Goals   Eleanor Maccoby (1980) looked at styles of parenting from a perspective similar to Baumrind's, but she expanded the dimensions of the model to include the effects of children's behavior on their parents. Parents, of course, are in a better position than children to control the home environment. But the reciprocal interaction between parents and children affects the climate of family life. In some families, the parents are highly controlling. At the other extreme, the children are in control.

Ideally, neither parents nor children dominate the family all the time. Maccoby (1980) focused on the ways in which parents and children interact. As children grow older, parents need to negotiate with them in making decisions and defining rules. Rather than simply establishing rules and requiring compliance, it is better to help the child develop his or her own ways of thinking problems through and learning the give-and-take of getting along with others—in a warm, supportive atmosphere. Thus, the family relationship evolves; children exert more self-control and self-responsibility as they grow older.

Through long-term dialogue and interaction, parents and children come to agree on what Maccoby calls *shared goals.* The result is a harmonious atmosphere in which decisions are reached without much struggle for control. Families that achieve such a balance have a fairly high degree of intimacy, and their interactions are stable and mutually rewarding. Families that are unable to achieve shared goals must negotiate everything—from what to have for supper to where to go on vacation. This too can be an effective family style, despite the need for constant discussion.

If either the parents or the children dominate the situation, negotiation is difficult and the family atmosphere becomes unstable. Parents who continue to be highly controlling tend to produce preadolescent children who concentrate on avoiding control. They stay away from home as much as possible. On the other hand, when the children are in control, the parents may avoid the family situation as much as possible. Either extreme weakens the socialization process during middle childhood and adolescence, making it more difficult for children to effect a smooth transition from dependence on the family to independence and close peer friendships.

Child Abuse

As noted in Chapter 6, one of the most serious and disturbing examples of parent-child interactions is child abuse. Regardless of the child's age, an abusing parent destroys the expectations of love, trust, and dependence that are so essential to healthy personality and social development. Severe developmental problems frequently result.

It can be difficult to draw the line between child abuse and acceptable punishment, partly because the distinction varies according to community and cultural standards. Historically, as discussed in Chapter 1, many cultures condoned, even encouraged, physical mistreatment that is now generally considered shocking and brutal. Harsh physical punishment was at one time viewed as necessary in disciplining and educating children. Some cultures imbued certain forms of physical cruelty, such as foot binding, skull shaping, or ritual scarring, with deep symbolic meaning and reverence. Because children were viewed as property, parents had the legal right to treat them any way they saw fit (Radbill, 1974).

Today, deliberately causing serious injury or death to a child is a serious crime—a felony with consequences ranging from removal of the child from the parents to imprisonment or capital punishment. But, sadly, child abuse is still not uncommon.

Physical Abuse   In the United States, official reports of child abuse and neglect total about 1 million a year; three children die every day as a result of physical abuse or neglect. These figures may be appalling but they are not unique to the United States; similar rates have been found in Western nations such as Canada, Australia, Great Britain, and Germany (Emery, 1989).

Physical abuse most often occurs at the hands of the child's parents, both mothers and fathers. When someone other than a parent is responsible, however, male abusers outnumber females by four to one. The proportion of male *sexual* abusers is even higher—nearly 95%. Sexual abuse of little girls usually is not committed by the child's own father. Stepfathers are five times more likely to abuse female children than are biological fathers (Wolfe, Wolfe, & Best, 1988). Sexual abuse is more often inflicted on girls, physical abuse more often on boys. Younger children sustain more serious injuries than older ones; about half of cases involving serious injury or death involve children under the age of 3 (Rosenthal, 1988). Of those who survive, many suffer traumatic brain injuries that can have permanent detrimental effects on potentially any aspect of development and functioning—especially if the trauma occurs during infancy or toddlerhood (Lowenthal, 1998).

Psychological Abuse   Physical abuse is always accompanied by psychological components that may be even more damaging than the physical abuse itself (Emery, 1989). Psychological abuse takes six distinct forms (Hart, Germain, & Brassard, 1987); these are summarized in Table 8–5. Psychological abuse is so common that virtually no one grows up without experiencing some form of it. Fortunately, however, in most cases the abuse is not intense or frequent enough to do permanent damage (Hart et al., 1987).

Effects of Child Abuse   Sexual and other physical abuse have long-term effects on the child's emotional well-being. Children's self-esteem can be

Table 8–5   Forms of Psychological Child Abuse

Rejection

Actively refusing the requests or needs of a child in a way that implies strong dislike.

Denial of emotional responsiveness

Passive withholding of affection that involves behaviors such as coldness or failing to respond to the child's attempts to communicate.

Degradation

Humiliating children in public or calling them names like "dummy." Children's self-esteem is lowered by frequent assaults on their dignity or intelligence.

Terrorization

Being forced to witness the abuse of a loved one or being threatened with personal abuse. A child who suffers regular beatings or is told "I'll break every bone in your body" is being terrorized. A more subtle form of terrorism occurs when a parent abandons a misbehaving child on the street.

Isolation

Refusing to allow a child to play with friends or take part in family activities. Some forms of isolation, such as locking a child in a closet, may also be terrorization.

Exploitation

Taking advantage of a child's innocence or weakness. The most obvious example of exploitation is sexual abuse.

irreparably damaged, and they may find it difficult to trust anyone because of the fear of exploitation and pain. Thus, abused children tend to isolate themselves and may display highly aggressive behaviors when approached (Hart & Brassard, 1991; Haskett & Kistner, 1991; Mueller & Silverman, 1989). In addition, abused children tend to have more school-related problems than children raised in nonabusive homes (Hanson, Conaway, & Christoher, 1989; Vondra, Barnett, & Cicchetti, 1990). Adolescents and adults who were abused as children are at greater risk of psychological problems, including depression, alcoholism, and drug abuse (Schaefer, Sobieraj, & Hollyfield, 1988). Their incidence of suicide attempts is also higher than average.

Abused children also have trouble controlling their emotions and behavior and tend to be less socially competent than children who are not abused (Shields, Cicchetti, & Ryan, 1994). When researchers conducted a longitudinal study of a sample of physically abused 5-year-olds, they found that the children were less popular and more socially withdrawn than their nonabused peers and that such peer-related problems increased during each of the five years of the study (Dodge, Pettit, & Bates, 1994).

Researchers also speculate that a history of family conflict involving verbal and physical abuse may have a cumulative impact on children's reaction to anger, even when the anger does not directly involve them (Hennessy, Rabideau, Cicchetti, & Cummings, 1994). Abused children are caught in damaged relationships and aren't socialized in positive, supportive ways. They may learn defiance, manipulation, and other problem behaviors as ways of escaping abuse; they may learn to exploit, degrade, or terrorize. They may also come to *expect* interpersonal relationships to be painful—with pervasive, long-term consequences.

Explanations of Child Abuse

Historically, research on child abuse has centered on three theoretical explanations: psychiatric, sociological, and situational (Parke & Collmer, 1975). Let's look briefly at each of these.

Psychiatric Explanations The psychiatric model focuses on the personality and family background of the parents. The basic view is that abusive parents are sick and in need of psychiatric treatment, although researchers have not found a particular cluster of personality or other traits associated with child abuse. Child abusers come from all walks of life.

One consistent finding, however, is many child abusers were themselves abused as children (Ney, 1988). Although it remains unclear how child abuse is passed from one generation to the next, a plausible explanation is that adults who were abused as children pattern their abusive parenting behavior after role models—their parents—in the same way that acceptable behaviors are learned during childhood. For example, their parents may have taught them that needs like dependency or autonomy are unacceptable—that crying or asking for help is useless or inappropriate. To underscore that, consider a child who became distressed when his father quit beating him. The child asked the social worker, "How come Daddy doesn't love me any more?" Thus, children absorb such lessons at an early age, and when they become parents they apply what they learned to their own children.

Sociological Explanations An aspect of U.S. culture that may be related to child abuse is violence. The United States ranks higher in murders and other violent crimes than all other industrialized nations. Violent television programming suggests that violence is an acceptable way to resolve conflicts. Also significant is that when physical spouse abuse occurs, physical child abuse is also likely. Child abuse is also linked to the widespread acceptance of physical punishment as a form of discipline; 93% of all U.S. parents spank their children, although the majority do it sparingly and within acceptable limits. In comparison, more peaceful societies that tend to use love-oriented disciplinary techniques have less overall violence and child abuse (Parke & Collmer, 1975).

Although physical abuse of children is found at all socioeconomic levels, it is more likely in poverty-stricken homes (e.g., Black, 2000). This may be partly because abuse in middle-class homes is less likely to come to the attention of authorities. It is also true, however, that general family stresses such as those associated with poverty increase the risk of child abuse.

Unemployment is another risk factor. In periods of high unemployment, male violence against wives and children increases. Fathers or mothers who are suddenly and unexpectedly out of work may begin to abuse their children. Aside from the financial problems, unemployment lowers the parent's social status and self-esteem. An unemployed father may try to compensate by wielding authority at home through physical domination.

Social isolation is another common characteristic of families in which child abuse occurs. These parents are often isolated from relatives, friends, and other support systems. They have difficulty sustaining friendships and rarely belong to social organizations. Thus, they may have no one to ask for help when they need it, and they may take out their frustrations on their children.

Situational Explanations Like the sociological model, the situational model looks at environmental factors. Here, however, the emphasis is on interactions among family members and the recognition that children are active participants in the process (Parke & Collmer, 1975). When we examine the child's role in abusive families, we find that parents usually single out one child for mistreatment. Infants and very young children are the most frequent targets. Those with physical disabilities or mental disorders or difficult temperaments are at especially high risk. Infants who cry constantly can drive parents to the breaking point. Or there may simply be a mismatch between the parent's expectations and the child's characteristics. For example, a mother who wants to touch and comfort her child may have a child who doesn't like to be touched. Another possibility is that the parent has unrealistic views of what kinds of behavior are appropriate in a child (Parke & Collmer, 1975; Vasta, 1982). For example, a father may become angry when his 3-year-old fails to clean up.

Although each approach sheds light on possible causes of child abuse, none tells us how to stop it. Programs for preventing child abuse focus on giving parents social support and teaching them better methods of discipline. Although these programs usually reduce the level of abuse, approximately one in four participants continues to abuse their children (Ferleger, Glenwick, Gaines, & Green, 1988). Criminal prosecution of offenders and removal of the child from the home are sometimes the only alternatives.

Discipline and Self-Regulation

As noted, disciplinary techniques have varied widely in different historical periods. Just as there have been periods when harsh physical punishment was in vogue, there have been periods of relative permissiveness. Methods of disciplining children—setting rules and limits and enforcing them—are subject to changes in fashion just as other aspects of culture are. The child-rearing literature of the 1950s and early 1960s, for example, warned against strong, overbearing disciplinary methods. Parents worried about stifling their children's emotions and turning them into anxious and repressed adults. Then the trend changed: The literature of the 1970s and 1980s emphasized that children need external social control, firmness, and consistency to feel safe and secure.

The 1990s continued the trend toward firm parental control. Of course, children's need for affection and approval also continues to be recognized (Perry & Bussey, 1984). Parents are advised to follow these guidelines:

1. Foster an atmosphere of warmth, caring, and mutual support among family members. Affection tends to be reciprocated, and children who are generally happy show more self-control, maturity, and prosocial behavior.
2. Concentrate more on promoting desirable behaviors than on eliminating undesirable ones. Deliberately suggest, model, and reward children's helping and caring behaviors.
3. Set realistic expectations and demands, firmly enforce demands, and above all, *be consistent.*
4. Avoid unnecessary use of power, including use of force and threats to control children's behavior. The assertion of power fosters similar behavior in children and may cause anger, bitterness, and resistance.
5. Help children gain a sense of control over themselves and their environment.
6. Use verbal reasoning (induction) to help children understand social rules.

To this list we might add: Tell children personal stories and fables that exemplify social and moral values (Miller et al., 1997).

In sum, children need to know the consequences of their behavior, including how other people will feel. They also need opportunities to discuss or explain their actions to their parents. Such interchanges help them develop a sense of responsibility for their behavior. In the long run, self-regulated behavior is

IN THEORY, IN FACT

TEACHING CHILDREN SELF-REGULATION

In raising healthy and achieving children, isn't it enough for parents to be warm, loving, and in control? Evidently not, according to research by John Gottman and colleagues Lynn Katz and Carole Hooven (Gottman, Katz, & Hooven, 1996). The researchers found that the way parents deal both with their own and their children's emotions may strongly affect not only the children's psychological and physical health but also their academic achievement. Regardless of their IQs, children whose parents had taught them how to cope emotionally had longer attention spans, scored higher on reading and math achievement tests, exhibited fewer behavior problems, and had slower heart rates; in addition, urine samples from these children contained smaller amounts of stress hormones.

Four types of parents were identified: those who helped their children think about their emotions and express them constructively, those who ignored their children's feelings of anger or sadness, those who disapproved of their children's having such feelings, and those who believed that the parental role consisted of simply accepting all their children's emotions. Children of parents in the first category scored highest both intellectually and physically. The researchers proposed that their findings can help parents teach children better ways of coping with their emotions. As Gottman explained, "So much of the popular parenting literature is oriented toward getting obedience, control, and consistent discipline. But so little really talks about how to make an emotional connection with the child." One father, for example, held his daughter in his arms or tried to distract her by putting her in front of the TV when she was upset and sad. Although the father was concerned, he was not actively helping his daughter understand and control her feelings of sadness. A more effective approach would be to ask the child what is making her sad and what she can do about it to make her feel better. Similarly, if a boy is jealous of his brother, a parent could talk with him about what is making him jealous and say, "You can't hit your brother, but you can talk to me about it when you're jealous."

determined by children's understanding of the situation in addition to parental warmth and control (also see "In Theory, In Fact" above).

Sibling Dynamics

Siblings are the first and closest peers who affect children's personality development. Sibling relationships provide experiences that are different from parent-child interactions . The down-to-earth openness of brothers and sisters gives them a chance to experience the ups and downs of human relationships on the most basic level. Siblings can be devotedly loyal to each other, despise each other, or form an ambivalent love-hate relationship that may continue for life. Young children may engage in sibling rivalry that leads to arguments and hitting, but brothers and sisters are actually more likely to give each other affection and friendship and have enormous influence on what the other does. Even when children are far apart in age, they are directly affected by the experience of living with others who are both equal (as children in the same family) and unequal (differing in age, size, sex, competence, intelligence, attractiveness, and so on). Indeed, siblings are important in helping each other identify social concepts and social roles by prompting and inhibiting certain patterns of behavior (Dunn, 1983, 1985).

Judy Dunn (1993) described five major dimensions of sibling relationships: rivalry, attachment, security, connectedness (including self-disclosure and humor), and shared fantasy. With regard to attachment security, for example, some toddlers and older children are so attached to their siblings that they miss them terribly when they are absent, are delighted when they appear, and join forces with them to explore the world in novel and imaginative ways. Sibling attachment may be as strong as child-to-parent attachment. Or, in contrast, siblings may have little to do with each other and lead separate emotional lives.

Families provide a powerful context for learning attitudes, beliefs, and appropriate behavior—sometimes down to the last detail of posture and dress.

How does birth order, or **sibling status,** affect each child's personality? Although personality theorists have devoted much speculation to the effects on personality of being the oldest, youngest, or middle sibling, no consistent personality differences appear to result solely from birth order. This doesn't mean, of course, that all children in a family will be similar in personality. Siblings raised in the same family are likely to have very different personalities—often as different as those of unrelated children (Plomin & Daniels, 1987).

One reason for personality differences is that children *need* to establish distinct identities for themselves. Thus, if an older sibling is serious and studious, a younger one may be boisterous. A girl who has four sisters and no brothers may carve out her own niche in the family by taking on a masculine role. Another reason is shared versus nonshared experiences (Chapter 3). Although siblings in the same family share many experiences, including living in the same home with the same set of parents, they also have many nonshared experiences and relationships. As Robert Plomin (1990) explained, DNA, not shared experiences, runs in families. Environmental effects are specific to each child rather than common to the entire family.

Some nonshared experiences are linked to birth order. For example, a firstborn son may receive more favorable treatment than his brothers and sisters. Other nonshared experiences, such as illness, changes in family finances, and peer and school relationships, have nothing to do with birth order (Bower, 1991a).

Although birth order seems to have few if any predictable effects on personality, many studies have found that the oldest child does have some advantages. On average, firstborns have higher IQs and achieve more in school and in their careers. "Only" children are also high achievers, although their IQs tend to be slightly lower on average than that of the oldest child in a family of two or three children (Zajonc & Markus, 1975). One possible explanation for this is that only children lack the opportunity to serve as teachers for their younger siblings, which can enhance intellectual development (Zajonc & Hall, 1986).

Average differences in IQ based on birth order tend to be small, however, and—as with gender differences—they tell us nothing about individual children. Larger and more consistent differences appear when researchers look at family size. The more children there are in a family, the lower their IQs tend to be and the less likely they are to graduate from high school. This remains the case even when other factors are taken into account (Blake, 1989). Family structure (whether there are two parents or one) and income can also have strong effects on IQ and achievement—effects that are noticeably greater than those of birth order or number of siblings (Ernst & Angst, 1983).

Older siblings are powerful models; children who have older same-sex siblings tend to show stronger gender-typed behavior than those with older siblings of the opposite sex (Sutton-Smith & Rosenberg, 1970). The spacing between siblings also affects sibling status. Siblings who are closer in age have more intense relationships (Sutton-Smith & Rosenberg, 1970).

The effects of birth order vary across cultures, however. Robert LeVine (1990) noted that the concept of birth order has vastly different implications for a family in a "high-fertility" agrarian society like Kenya than it does for a family in the United States. In many agrarian societies several families share communal living quarters, with the result that children of several mothers are raised together. The firstborn child in a U.S. family usually is at least temporarily the only child in the home and has his or her own room and possessions, with liberal access to parents for conversation and games. In contrast, firstborn children in agrarian cultures live with older children from other families, who function much like older siblings, caring for and socializing the young. As a

sibling status   Birth order.

result, said LeVine, "the early social experience of only or firstborn children in agrarian societies is rarely as differentiated from that of later-borns as it is in middle-class America" (LeVine, 1990, p. 105).

CONTENT CHECK
FAMILY DYNAMICS

True–False (answers are on the Companion Website)

1. Authoritative parenting is best for all children.
2. Psychological abuse is as bad for children as physical abuse is.
3. The majority of child-abusing parents are mentally disordered.
4. In promoting self-regulation, parents should set consistent expectations and demands.
5. Firstborn and only children are usually significantly more intelligent than later-born children.

Thinking Critically

Where would you draw the line between acceptable discipline and child abuse? Why?

CHAPTER 8 REVISITED

Psychodynamic, social-learning, and cognitive-developmental perspectives emphasize different developmental processes during early childhood.

Developmental Issues and Coping Patterns

■ Young children's fears tend to be specific and their anxieties tend to be general.

■ Children's fears and anxieties may arise both from external and internal causes; most are a normal part of growing up.

■ Research has found that young children are most likely to be afraid of strangers, unfamiliar things, the dark, loud noises, or falling.

■ Systematic desensitization and participant modeling are techniques for treating children's phobias.

■ Where applicable, reducing the stresses a child is experiencing helps reduce fear and anxiety.

■ Children also develop their own means of dealing with fear and anxiety; even very young children use defense mechanisms.

■ Western societies expect children to acquire progressively greater emotion regulation and self-regulation, both for negative and for positive emotions.

■ Feelings of guilt and shame interact with a child's emotion regulation.

■ Sensuality and sexual curiosity are normal during early childhood.

■ Developmental conflicts during early childhood include autonomy versus connectedness and initiative versus guilt; autonomy and initiative are directly involved in acquiring mastery and competence.

Aggression and Prosocial Behavior

■ Young children may display both hostile and instrumental aggression; each of these differs from assertiveness.

■ Physical aggression declines across early childhood as verbal aggression replaces it.

■ Frustration sometimes leads to aggression and aggression is sometimes caused by frustration.

■ Physical punishment can make children more aggressive, as can exposure to violence and aggressive models in person or on television; in the United States, the latter prompted government action in the 1990s.

■ Altruism, empathy, and other aspects of prosocial behavior can be learned through conditioning, also through modeling; two techniques that can enhance prosocial behavior are role-playing and induction.

■ Prosocial behaviors such as cooperation vary considerably across cultures.

Peers, Play, and Development of Social Skills

■ Play tends to develop in an orderly sequence of stages: solitary play, onlooker play, parallel play, associative play, and cooperative play.

■ Social pretend play becomes evident in the middle of early childhood, and its forms and meanings vary across cultures.

■ Being unpopular during early childhood can have effects that persist into middle childhood and beyond; unpopular children are often aggressive or withdrawn.

■ Popular children tend to be cooperative and display a wide range of other prosocial behaviors.

■ Imaginary companions are common in early childhood; young children who have imaginary companions tend to be more sociable and creative.

Understanding Self and Others

■ Self-concept is present at the beginning of early childhood and progressively becomes more intricate and refined with age.

■ Self-concept is acquired in part through self-comparisons with others; younger children define themselves more in terms of physical characteristics as compared to others, older children more in terms of their activities.

■ Gender differences result from genetics and environment in interaction; early gender differences tend to be small and there is much overlap between females and males.

■ Gender-specific behaviors and gender stereotypes appear very early in childhood; many are learned in the same ways as aggressive or prosocial behaviors.

■ Gender identity develops first; gender constancy develops later, toward the end of early childhood.

■ People with an androgynous personality display both desirable masculine and feminine traits.

■ Social concepts and rules become internalized as a result of modeling and imitation, and also as a result of children's active efforts to acquire them.

■ An understanding of friendship begins in early childhood but is not complete until middle childhood or beyond.

Family Dynamics

■ Parental control and warmth interact to determine four authoritative, authoritarian, permissive, or indifferent parenting styles; each has markedly different effects on children, although they vary somewhat across cultures and it is not possible to say that one is universally best.

■ Negotiation of shared goals between parents and children is generally regarded as a positive process.

■ Physical child abuse and psychological child abuse are both damaging to the child in many ways and can have lasting effects; psychological abuse takes six distinct forms.

■ There are psychiatric, sociological, and situational factors that increase the risk of child abuse; child abusers come from all socioeconomic levels.

■ Approaches to disciplining children have changed historically; recommended approaches now include warmth, emphasizing desirable behaviors more than undesirable ones, being consistent, minimizing the use of force, helping children gain a sense of control, and using induction.

■ Sibling rivalry is less likely than sibling friendship; siblings may argue, but they also tend to become strongly attached to each other.

■ Sibling status or birth order have not been found to have consistent effects on personality, although first-borns and only children do on average have slightly higher IQs; birth-order effects vary considerably across cultures.

KEY TERMS

autonomy
fear
anxiety
systematic desensitization
defense mechanisms
hostile aggression
instrumental aggression

assertiveness
imaginary companions
gender roles
gender-role stereotypes
gender schemes
gender identity
gender constancy

self-socialization
androgynous personality
authoritative parents
authoritarian parents
permissive parents
indifferent parents
sibling status

MIDDLE CHILDHOOD: PHYSICAL AND COGNITIVE DEVELOPMENT

315

CHAPTER PREVIEW

Do you know:

1. That the brain shows an initial *growth spurt* during middle childhood and approaches the size of an adult's by the end of the period?

2. That the *strength* and *motor abilities* of girls and boys are comparable during middle childhood?

3. Why a significant percentage of U.S. children are *obese* during this period?

4. That at the same time as obesity in U.S. children has been increasing, *physical fitness* has been on the *decline?*

5. That *accidents* cause more deaths among children during this period than the seven other major causes *combined?*

6. What differences exist between *preoperational* and *concrete-operational* thought and how they are assessed?

7. How *Piaget's theory* has been applied to *elementary education?*

8. That a number of highly significant improvements in *memory skills* and *metacognition* occur during middle childhood?

9. How *literacy* and *sociocultural context* interact?

10. The difference between *criterion-referenced tests* and *norm-referenced tests?*

11. How *intelligence testing* began and where it is today?

12. That there are many different and often-conflicting theories of what *intelligence* is?

13. What *adjustments* children have to make upon entering school?

14. What factors at home and at school help determine children's *academic success?*

15. How schools sometimes foster *skill differences* as a result of *gender stereotypes?*

16. What constitutes *mental retardation* and what people at different levels are capable of accomplishing?

17. What constitutes a *learning disorder* and what problems children with learning disorders have both in and out of school?

18. What constitutes *Attention-deficit/Hyperactivity disorder* and how it is treated?

These are the main topics of Chapter 9.

Middle childhood—in Western nations, the age range from about 6 to 12—is an exciting time for learning and refining skills from reading and writing and arithmetic to playing ball and dancing. Children focus on testing themselves, on meeting their own challenges as well as those imposed by their world. The child who is successful will become capable and self-assured; the child who is unsuccessful may develop feelings of inferiority or a weak sense of self. Erikson called middle childhood the period of *industry*, which nicely captures the spirit of the age range—the word is derived from the Latin for "to build."

In this chapter we look at ways in which children build both physical and cognitive competencies. We also look at schooling and developmental problems encountered in middle childhood, including how academic and intellectual development are measured and current approaches to understanding learning disorders and mental retardation.

It's important to remember that physical, cognitive, and psychosocial factors interact to produce individual development. In part because neurological functioning improves (through myelination of the reticular formation), children can focus their attention for longer periods. Because their cognitive skills improve, children can anticipate the moves of others and plan strategies. These and other changes influence their choices of activities as well as their successes or failures.

Physical and Motor Development

During the elementary school years, children refine their motor abilities and become more independent. Given appropriate opportunities or training, children can learn to ride a bicycle, jump rope, swim, dance, write, or play a musical instrument. Group sports like baseball, basketball, soccer, and the many variations of football become important as children's coordination and physical abilities improve. In this section we survey changes in physical characteristics and motor skills in middle childhood, along with important health-related issues such as obesity, physical fitness, and accidents and injuries. Then we look at physical environments at school and at home that promote healthy activity and exercise.

Physical Growth and Change

Growth is slower and steadier during middle childhood than during the first 2 years of life. The average 6-year-old weighs 45 pounds (20.4 kilos) and is 3½ feet (just over a meter) tall. Gradual, regular growth continues until about age 9 for girls and age 11 for boys; at that point, the "adolescent growth spurt" begins (Chapter 11). The changes in body size and proportion that are typical of middle childhood are illustrated in Figure 9–1. Note, however, that there is

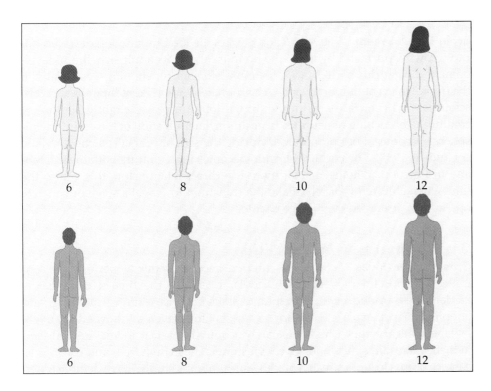

Figure 9–1 Changes in Body Size and Proportion During Middle Childhood. Broad variations in growth patterns occur during middle childhood. The illustrated changes are typical.

wide variability in the timing of growth; not all children mature at the same rate. Activity level, exercise, nutrition, genetic factors, and gender interact dynamically to determine growth. For example, girls tend to be slightly shorter and lighter than boys until age 9, after which their growth accelerates because their growth spurt begins earlier. Moreover, some girls and boys are structurally smaller than others. Such differences may affect the child's body image and self-concept, which is yet another way in which physical, social, and cognitive development interact.

Internal Changes

Skeletal Maturation Bones grow longer as the body lengthens and broadens; sometimes these changes cause growing pains. Episodes of stiffness and aching caused by skeletal growth are particularly common at night. Rapidly growing children experience such pains as early as age 4; other children don't experience them until adolescence. In either case children may need reassurance that they're experiencing a normal response to growth (Nichols, 1990; Sheiman & Slomin, 1988). Parents should also be aware that because the skeleton and ligaments of the school-age child are not mature, overly stringent physical training may cause injuries. In the United States, for example, it is common for Little League pitchers to injure their shoulders and elbows. Wrist, ankle, and knee injuries are also associated with vigorous sports.

Beginning at age 6 or 7, children also lose their primary or "baby" teeth. When the first permanent teeth emerge, they appear too big for the child's mouth until facial growth catches up. Two noticeable landmarks of middle childhood are the toothless smile of a 6-year-old and the "beaver-toothed" grin of an 8-year-old.

Fat and Muscle Tissue After about 6 months of age, fat deposits gradually decrease until age 6 to 8; this decrease is more marked in boys. In both sexes, muscles increase in length, breadth, and width (Nichols, 1990). The strength of girls and boys is comparable throughout middle childhood.

Brain Development Between 6 and 8 years the forebrain undergoes a temporary growth spurt, and by age 8 the brain is 90% of its adult size. Brain development during this period produces more efficient functioning—especially in the frontal lobes of the cortex, which is intimately involved in thought and consciousness. The surface area of the frontal lobes increases slightly because of continuing branching of neurons. In addition, lateralization of the brain's hemispheres becomes more pronounced during the school years (Thatcher, Walker, & Guidice, 1987). The corpus callosum becomes more mature both in structure and in function. Whether or not there is a direct relationship, this is also the time when children typically make the transition to Piaget's stage of concrete operations, discussed later in the chapter.

Development of Motor Skills

Gross Motor Skills School-age children become better at performing controlled, purposeful movements (Nichols, 1990). By the time a child enters kindergarten around age 5, locomotive skills such as running, jumping, and hopping are well in place. They are executed with an even rhythm and relatively few mechanical errors. Children's newly acquired physical abilities are reflected in their interest in sports and daredevil stunts. They climb trees and use logs as balance beams to cross streams or gullies. Numerous studies have demonstrated how motor development progresses during middle childhood. At age 7, a boy

By middle childhood children are developing the fine motor skills required to draw, write, paint, cut, and shape materials like clay and papier-mâché.

can typically throw a ball about 34 feet. By age 10, he can probably throw it twice as far; by age 12, three times as far. Accuracy improves as well. Girls make similar progress in throwing and catching, although at each age their throwing distance is, on average, shorter than that of boys (Williams, 1983).

However, differences in motor skills before puberty are more a function of opportunity and cultural expectations than of differences attributable to sex (Cratty, 1986; Nichols, 1990). These differences are closely linked to the time a child spends practicing a skill. Girls who participate in Little League develop longer, more accurate throws than girls who sit on the sidelines. Boys and girls who play soccer and other sports develop skills at a similar pace.

Fine Motor Skills   Fine motor skills also develop rapidly during middle childhood, growing out of skills taught in nursery schools and day-care centers. Preschool teachers help build writing readiness as they offer children opportunities to draw, paint, cut, and mold with clay. Thus, children discover how to draw circles, then squares, and then triangles. Each increasingly complex shape requires greater hand-eye coordination, which leads to the ability to write. Most of the fine motor skills required for writing develop between the ages of 6 and 7, although some quite normal children cannot draw a diamond or master many letter shapes until age 8.

Ideally, children develop mastery over their bodies and at the same time gain feelings of competence and self-worth that are essential to good mental health. Controlling their bodies also helps them win the acceptance of peers. Awkward, poorly coordinated children are often left out of group activities and may continue to feel rejected long after their awkwardness disappears. Table 9–1 summarizes physical changes during middle childhood.

Health, Fitness, and Accidents

Middle childhood can be one of the healthiest periods in life. Although minor illnesses such as ear infections, colds, and upset stomachs are prevalent in younger children, most 6- to 12-year-olds experience few such illnesses. This is

Table 9-1 **Physical Development During Middle Childhood**

5- TO 6-YEAR-OLDS
- Steady increases in height and weight
- Steady growth in strength for both boys and girls
- Growing awareness of the placement and actions of large body parts
- Increased use of all body parts
- Improvement in gross motor skills
- Performance of motor skills singly

7- TO 8-YEAR-OLDS
- Steady increase in height and weight
- Steady increase in strength for both boys and girls
- Increased use of all body parts
- Refinement of gross motor skills
- Improvement in fine motor skills
- Increasing variability in motor skill performance but still performed singly

9- TO 10-YEAR-OLDS
- Beginning of growth spurt for girls
- Increase in strength for girls accompanied by loss of flexibility
- Awareness and development of all body parts and systems
- Ability to combine motor skills more fluidly
- Balance improvement

11-YEAR-OLDS
- Girls generally taller and heavier than boys
- Beginning of growth spurt for boys
- Accurate judgment in intercepting moving objects
- Continued combination of more fluid motor skills
- Continued improvement of fine motor skills
- Continued increasing variability in motor skill performance

partly a result of greater immunity due to previous exposure, and partly because most school-age children have somewhat better nutrition, health, and safety habits than younger ones (O'Connor-Francoeur, 1983; Starfield, 1992). Minor illnesses and disorders do occur, however. For example, myopia (nearsightedness) is often diagnosed during middle childhood. By the sixth grade 25% of white middle-class children have been fitted with glasses or contact lenses.

It has been suggested that minor illnesses such as colds play a positive role in children's psychological development (Parmelee, 1986). Although common illnesses disrupt school, family social roles, and work schedules, children and their families generally recover quickly. In the process, children learn how to cope with stress. They also develop a realistic understanding of the role of "being sick" and therefore learn to empathize with others who get sick.

Obesity Obesity is a common problem during middle childhood in developed nations and in some developing ones. Seriously overweight as a child is defined by the NCHS as weighing the same as or more than 95% of children of the same age, and in the mid-1990s almost 14% of U.S. children ages 6 to 11 fell into this category—a huge increase from the mid-1960s, when the incidence was only 5% (NCHS, 1999). Childhood obesity clearly is a growing problem, and nearly 70 percent of children who are obese at ages 10 to 13 will continue to be seriously overweight as adults (Epstein & Wing, 1987). Obesity predisposes them to heart disease, high blood pressure, diabetes, and numerous other medical problems.

Genetic factors apparently play an important role in obesity. A child with one obese parent has a 40% chance of becoming obese, and the proportion leaps to 80% if both parents are obese. Further evidence for genetic factors is that adopted children more closely resemble their biological parents than their adoptive parents with regard to body weight (Rosenthal, 1990; Stunkard, 1988).

Genetics is not the whole story, however, and should not be used as an "excuse" for being overweight. Environmental factors are also involved, as can be seen in the increase in obesity among U.S. children. One environmental factor is television viewing (Flodmark, 1997), which has increased steadily over the same period. Children who spend a lot of time sitting in front of TV sets don't get the exercise they need to develop physical skills or burn excess calories. At the same time, if they spend their viewing hours munching the snacks and drinking the sweetened beverages they see advertised on TV, they lose their appetite for more nutritious, less fattening foods (Dietz, 1987). Home computers have a similar impact in that many children spend inordinate amounts of time playing computer games, exchanging e-mail, visiting chat rooms, and "surfing the Net."

Another important factor is parental encouragement of overeating. Beginning in infancy, some parents overfeed their children either as a way of calming them or because the parents believe that a healthy baby should be round and plump. Later, parents may encourage their children to eat as a way of coping with frustration or anxiety, or regularly offer them treats as a way of reinforcing them for desired behaviors—thus fostering a habit of overeating.

Even seriously overweight children should not be placed on drastic weight-loss programs, however. They need a balanced, nutritious diet to support their energy level and growth. Parents should instead try to encourage overweight children to develop better eating habits that they can maintain. In particular, children should increase their intake of healthful foods, such as fruits and vegetables, and decrease their intake of foods that are high in fats, such as pizza. Equally important is physical activity to develop muscles and burn calories. Successful weight-loss programs may involve treating the parents as well as the children (Epstein, Valoski, Wing, & McCurley, 1990), because obese parents may be less concerned about obesity in their children and may also model bad eating and exercise habits.

Overweight children face far fewer medical risks than overweight adults, but their obesity can still have serious social and psychological consequences. Peers may reject or stereotype them and call them names. The result can be a negative self-image that may make overweight children even more reluctant to play with peers and engage in physical activities and sports that might help them lose weight—thus creating a "vicious circle" that helps maintain high weight levels.

Physical Fitness   Health is often measured in terms of the absence of illness. A better measure is *physical fitness*—optimal functioning of the heart, lungs, muscles, and blood vessels. Physical fitness does not require that children become star athletes. It simply requires that they engage in regular exercise that involves four aspects of conditioning: flexibility, muscle endurance, muscle strength, and cardiovascular efficiency. Some activities help more than others. Basketball, soccer, tennis, bicycling, and swimming exercise the whole body continuously, in contrast to football and baseball, in which players are often idle (Nichols, 1990).

As obesity among U.S children has been increasing, physical activity and exercise have been on the decline. Given the number of hours school-age children spend watching television and playing video games, it is not surprising that many live sedentary lives. In addition, "latchkey" children (those who must care for themselves after school) may not be allowed to play outside for safety reasons—a situation that reduces their activity level still further.

Physical Education in Schools   Although we generally think of school in terms of cognitive or social development, schools also promote physical and motor development. Elementary schools include physical education, partly because physical activity in childhood often sets a pattern for lifelong activity. *Physical education* is defined as a program of carefully planned and conducted motor activities that prepare students for skillful, fit, and knowledgeable performance (Nichols, 1990). It can be carried out in different school settings: classroom, gymnasium, multipurpose room, playground, or playing field.

Because of the poor average level of physical fitness in the U.S. population, national health objectives call for increasing children's participation in daily physical education classes and regular physical activity and provide guidelines for schools and communities. Such programs may assist in increasing children's overall physical activity and eventual interest in fitness as adults. A national health objective therefore calls for programs that engage students in active physical exercise—preferably lifelong activities such as jogging and swimming—for at least 50% of the time devoted to physical education (CDC, 1997b).

Because their improved mobility exposes school-age children to greater accident risk, they often need guidance on ways to protect themselves from injury.

Accidents and Injuries   As children grow in size, strength, and coordination, they engage in increasingly dangerous activities such as climbing, cycling, skateboarding, and rollerblading. Many participate in team sports that employ potentially harmful projectiles and bone-breaking body contact and falls (Maddux, Roberts, Sledden, & Wright, 1986). From infancy on, children's need to exercise their newfound skills often conflicts with their need for protection against the dangers associated with many physical activities. In addition, children's risk of harming themselves typically exceeds their ability to foresee the consequences of their actions (Achenbach, 1982). Parental warnings against riding a bicycle or skateboard on a busy street may be ignored or forgotten in the excitement of play.

Accidents—especially motor vehicle accidents—cause more child deaths than seven other major causes of death combined: pneumonia/influenza, heart diseases, congenital anomalies, cancers, suicide, and homocide (see Figure 9–2 for incidences of each). Notably, according to the NCHS (1999), since 1980 the incidence per 100,000 for each of the causes listed in the table showed significant declines except two: Homicides increased slightly, and suicides more than doubled. Actual *rates* increased in all categories. Overall, about half of all childhood deaths result from injuries and accidents. Accidents are also the leading cause of physical disability in childhood.

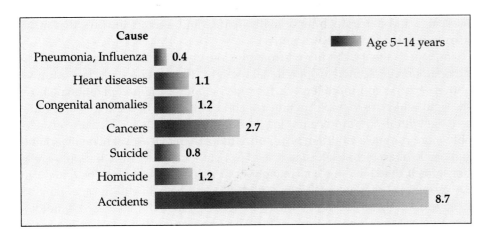

Figure 9–2 **Major Causes of U.S. Deaths, Ages 5–14 (in thousands of deaths per year).**

Source: Hoyert, Kochanek, & Murphy, 1999.

CONTENT CHECK
PHYSICAL AND MOTOR DEVELOPMENT

True–False (answers are on the Companion Website)

1. For the most part, children mature at the same rate during middle childhood.
2. Strength and motor development during middle childhood is a function of opportunity and practice, not gender.
3. About one-third of U.S. children are seriously overweight.
4. Diseases and congenital anomalies account for the majority of deaths and disabilities among U.S. children.

Thinking Critically

How does internally driven physical and motor development interact with external factors?

Cognitive Development

Here we return to the two major approaches to studying cognition, this time with respect to middle childhood: cognitive-developmental theory and information-processing theory. Metacognition and factors in acquiring literacy are considered as well.

Piaget and Concrete Operational Thinking

The thinking of a 12-year-old child is very different from that of a 5-year-old. This is partly because of the larger body of knowledge and information that a 12-year-old has accumulated, but it is also due to the different ways in which children think and process information. In Piaget's terms, middle childhood is characterized by *concrete operational thought*.

Cognitive Abilities A large part of cognitive development occurs in schoolrooms, beginning at age 5 to 7 in most cultures. At those ages many cognitive, language, and perceptual-motor skills mature and interact in ways that make learning easier and more efficient.

In Piaget's theory, the period from age 5 to age 7 marks the transition from preoperational to concrete operational thought: Thought becomes less intuitive and egocentric and more logical. Toward the end of the preoperational stage, the rigid, static, irreversible qualities of children's thought begin to "thaw out," as Piaget put it. Children's thinking becomes reversible, flexible, and considerably more complex. Children now notice more than one aspect of an object and can use logic to reconcile differences. They can evaluate cause-and-effect relationships if they have the concrete object or situation in front of them and can see changes as they occur. When a piece of clay looks like a sausage, they no longer find it inconsistent that the clay was once a ball or that it can be molded into a new shape, such as a cube. The emerging mental ability to go beyond the immediate situation or state lays the foundation for systematic reasoning in the concrete operational stage and, later, in the formal operational stage. Table 9–2 contrasts the basics of preoperational and concrete operational thought.

An important difference between preoperational and concrete operational thought can be illustrated by school-age children's use of logical inference (Flavell, 1985). Recall Piaget's liquid/beakers conservation problem (Chapter 7). Preoperational children consistently judge that a tall, narrow glass holds more liquid than a short, wide one, even though both quantities of liquid have been shown to be identical at the start. In contrast, concrete operational children recognize that both containers must hold the same amount of liquid. They begin to think differently about states and transformations and can remember how the liquid appeared before it was poured into the tall, thin container. They can think about how its shape changed as it was poured from one glass into the other, and can imagine the liquid being poured back. They also understand that changes in one dimension such as height can be compensated for by changes in

Table 9–2 Preoperational Versus Concrete Operational Thought

Stage	Age	The Child's Thinking Is:
Preoperational	2 to 5–7 years	Rigid and static
		Irreversible
		Focused on the here and now
		Centered on one dimension
		Egocentric
		Focused on perceptual evidence
		Intuitive
Concrete operational	5–7 to 12 years	Flexible
		Reversible
		Not limited to the here and now
		Multidimensional
		Less egocentric
		Marked by the use of logical inferences
		Marked by the search for cause-and-effect relationships

Figure 9-3   Piaget's Matchstick Problem
Concrete operational children realize that the six matchsticks in the zigzag top row
will make a longer line than the five matchsticks in the straight bottom row. Younger
children will say that the bottom row is the longest because they tend to center only
on the end points of the two lines and not on what lies between them.

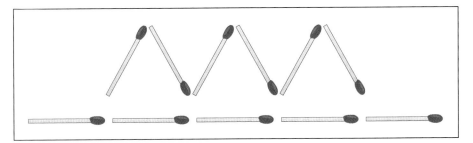

another such as width. Respectively, their thinking is both reversible and decentered.

In addition, concrete operational children know that differences between
similar objects can be measured. In Piaget's (1970) matchstick problem, illlus-
trated in Figure 9–3, children are shown a zigzag row of six matchsticks and a
straight row of five matchsticks placed end to end. When asked which row has
more matchsticks, preoperational children center only on the distance between
the end points of the rows and therefore pick the "longer" row with five matchsticks. Concrete operational children, however, can take into account what lies
between the end points of the rows and therefore correctly choose the one with
six matchsticks.

Unlike preoperational children, concrete operational children can also theorize about the world around them. They think about and anticipate what will
happen; they make guesses about things and then test their hunches. They may
estimate, for example, how many more breaths of air they can blow into a bal-
loon before it pops, and may keep blowing until they reach that goal. However,
their ability to theorize is limited to objects and social relationships that they
can see or concretely imagine. They don't develop theories about abstract concepts, thoughts, or relationships until they reach the stage of formal operations
around age 11 or 12.

The transition from preoperational to concrete operational thought does not
happen overnight. It requires years of experience in manipulating and learning
about objects and materials in the environment. According to Piaget, children
learn concrete operational thought largely on their own. As they actively explore their physical environment, asking themselves questions and finding the
answers, they acquire more complex, sophisticated forms of thinking.

Piaget and Education   Infants benefit from stimulation that is slightly ahead of
their developmental level. Some researchers believe that appropriate training can
also accelerate the cognitive development of preoperational children, hastening
their entry into concrete operational thinking. Training is of course most effective
when children have reached a state of readiness.

Many of the basic concepts presented by Piaget have been applied to education, especially in the areas of the sciences and math. One such application includes the use of concrete objects for teaching 5- to 7-year-olds. By combining,
comparing, and contrasting objects (e.g., blocks and rods of different shapes and
sizes, seeds that grow in sand, water, or soil), children discover similarities, differences, and relationships.

Figure 9–4 Spatial Arrays

Some possible spatial arrays of 16 cubes. By arranging the cubes in different ways, a teacher can help young schoolchildren understand the number concept of 16.

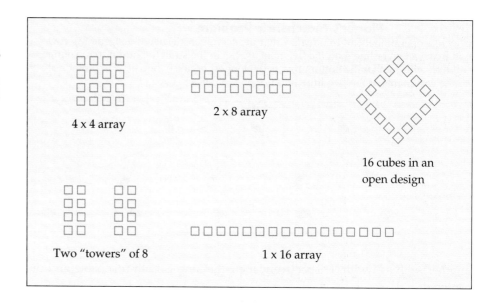

4 x 4 array

2 x 8 array

16 cubes in an open design

Two "towers" of 8

1 x 16 array

An example of this technique is arranging objects in simple patterns (see Figure 9–4). In introducing first- or second-graders to the number concept of 16, a teacher might present several different spatial arrays of 16 cubes—grouped into two towers of 8, one row of 16, four rows of 4, and so on. The teacher might then give verbal cues to help the children conserve, pointing out that the number of cubes remains the same even though the length and width of the rows change.

There are many other applications of Piaget's concepts. For example, addition and subtraction involve an understanding of reversibility (5 + 8 = 13; 13 − 5 = 8). Again, children can learn most readily by manipulating real objects. Parents and teachers who understand the basic principles of Piaget's theory of cognitive development can develop effective educational lessons and organize them into a logical sequence. Piagetian concepts have also been applied to social studies, music, and art.

Piaget's theory therefore extends to learning as a component of cognitive development. Children are active learners who construct their own theories about how the world operates, and they are self-motivated to change their theories when pieces of information do not fit (Bruner, 1973). Educational psychologists warn against structuring education in ways that encourage children to seek praise from teachers rather than solve problems for their own sake. They emphasize that children's interest in learning depends on the intrinsic rewards they find in the encounter with the subject matter itself. Children gain confidence from mastering problems and discovering principles, and they learn by *doing*—just as adults do (Gronlund, 1995).

Educators also point out that, all too often, teachers fall into the trap of telling instead of showing. Some teachers remove the real-life, concrete context of many subjects. They present rules for children to memorize by rote without motivating the children to understand the rules. Children are then left with a body of arid facts and principles without the ability to apply these beyond the immediate situation. Children need to learn by actively exploring ideas and relationships and solving problems in realistic contexts.

Piaget was a remarkable observer of young children's cognitive development, as we've seen. There are simply some aspects of cognitive development that he didn't assess, and these are also important for learning—both formal and informal. Many of these are in the area of information-processing.

When spelling a word, children need to retrieve the proper letters from their memory.

Information Processing

Recall that information-processing theorists see the human mind as analogous to a computer. Thus, the focus shifts to cognitive functions such as attention and problem solving, along with two crucial functions that show considerable development during middle childhood: memory and metacognition.

Memory   A number of significant developments occur in the memory abilities of concrete operational children. Preoperational children do well at recognition tasks but poorly at recall tasks; they have trouble using memory strategies like rehearsal (Chapter 7). Early in the period of concrete operations (between the ages of 5 and 7), children's ability to recall lists of items improves significantly. Most children begin making conscious efforts to memorize information. They look at material to be remembered and repeat it over and over. Later they organize material into categories, and eventually they may create stories or visual images to help them remember particular items. The increasingly deliberate use of memory strategies makes an older child's recall more effective and efficient (Flavell, 1985).

To put it another way, elementary schoolchildren learn **control processes**—strategies and techniques that enhance memory. Following are examples of such processes, with indications of the ages at which they develop.

1. *Rehearsal:* At first, children rehearse simply by saying items to themselves over and over, one at a time. At about age 9, however, they begin to group or "chunk" items together (Ornstein, Naus, & Liberty, 1975; Ornstein, Naus, & Stone, 1977). This improves their ability both to hold information in short-term memory and to transfer it to long-term memory.

2. *Organization:* Another major development in the use of memory strategies is the ability to organize. Younger school-age children tend to relate words by simple association (such as the arrangement of words in a list); older children organize groups of words by common features and meaning. For example, apples, pears, and grapes are "fruit." Children who group words into categories can remember more items than those who do not. However, children

control processes   Higher cognitive processes that enhance memory.

seldom use organizational strategies on their own before about age 9 (Bjork-lund, 1988).

3. *Semantic elaboration:* It is clear that elementary-school children can often re-member what they infer from statements in addition to what is actually said to them. In a classic series of studies by Scott Paris and colleagues, children were given sentences like "Her friend swept the floor." They were then asked whether the friend had a broom. Eleven-year-olds were able to infer the presence of a broom; 7-year-olds were not (Paris, Lindauer, & Cox, 1977). Semantic elaboration involves the use of logical inferences to reconstruct an event, as opposed to simply recalling an "imperfect," unedited copy (Flavell et al., 1993).

4. *Mental imagery:* Younger children can be taught to remember unusual mate-rial by constructing images or "pictures" in their minds. Older children are more likely to construct such images on their own, and their images tend to be more vivid (Siegler, 1986).

5. *Retrieval:* Often, when younger children try to spell a word, they search their memory for the proper letters. They may know the letter the word begins with, but they need to sound out possibilities for the rest of the word. Older children become much better at retrieval strategies (Flavell et al., 1993).

6. *Scripts:* Memory for routine events may be organized in the form of more so-phisticated scripts. This has the advantage that an event that occurs over and over again need not be stored separately in memory each time. It can be re-membered in the form of a standard sequence of events, along with fill-in "slots" for aspects that vary. For example, the script for a school morning might specify the events that typically occur on such a morning: get up, get dressed, eat breakfast, go to school. The slots would be filled with variable items, such as which clothes are worn, what's for breakfast, and what form of transportation is used to get to school (Nelson & Gruendel, 1986). By age 4 or 5, children apparently use specific scripts for familiar routines, but dur-ing middle childhood they become capable of "merging" specific scripts into broader categories (Case, 1996).

Metacognition   Metacognition refers to the sophisticated intellectual processes that enable children to monitor their own thinking, memory, knowl-edge, goals, and actions; in other words, metacognition is "thinking about thinking." During middle childhood, children develop metacognitive abilities that they use in planning, making decisions, and solving problems.

In a well-known description of metacognition, Flavell (1985) cited the fol-lowing example: Preschool and elementary-school children were asked to study a group of items until they were certain that they could remember them perfectly. When the elementary-aged children said that they were ready, they usually were: When tested, they remembered each item without error. In con-trast, the younger children often said that they were ready when in fact they were not. Despite their good intentions, they did not have sufficient cognitive abilities to complete the task *and* know when they had completed it; they could not monitor their own intellectual processes. The ability to monitor thinking and memory begins at about age 6 and emerges more fully between the ages of 7 and 10. Even then, however, metacognition is better when the material to be learned is typical or familiar (Hasselhorn, 1992).

Like other aspects of cognitive ability, metacognitive skills continue to de-velop into adolescence. Just as a 9-year-old has greater metacognitive ability than a 4-year-old, a 15-year-old's self-monitoring skills far surpass those of a 9-year-old.

metacognition   The process of monitoring your own thinking and memory.

Language and Literacy

Oral and written language skills become much more refined during middle childhood. As their vocabulary continues to expand, children master increasingly complex grammatical structures and more sophisticated language usage. For example, they begin to use and understand the passive voice, although their syntax may still be shaky. They can also infer that sentences like "John was watched as he walked along the beach" include participants who are not explicitly named.

Literacy   Although oral language development is often dramatic, it frequently takes a back seat to the development of *literacy*—skills in reading and writing. Younger children focus on learning to produce and understand spoken language; older children learn to read and write. Reading includes learning phonetics and how to decode the alphabet, and writing includes refining the fine motor skills needed to form letters, but there's much more. Reading requires the ability to elicit *meaning* from print and writing requires the ability to convey meaning in print. Both reading and writing are forms of symbolic communication that also involve attention, perception, memory, and other cognitive processes.

Through symbolic communication, children learn to relate the external world to their inner thoughts and feelings. "Members of a culture share common ways of infusing various forms (such as sounds, actions, marks on paper, and monuments in the park) with meaning," commented Anne Haas Dyson (1993, p. 25), a researcher in the field of literacy development. "These symbols—these connections between forms and meanings—connect us to others and, at the same time, organize our own feelings, experiences, and thoughts."

Reading and writing are natural outgrowths of the child's growing language skills. The recognition that oral and written language learning are interconnected has led to the *whole-language* approach to literacy (Fields & Spangler, 1995). Rather than looking for a distinct point at which children develop reading and writing readiness, whole-language theorists focus on the concept of "emergent" literacy: The skills associated with oral and written language acquisition begin to develop in infancy and gradually improve over a period of years (Teale & Sulzby, 1986). Thus, the stories that an infant can only listen to, the "writing" that a toddler does with a crayon, and the preschooler's "reading" from memory that occurs in early childhood are all precursors to reading and writing. Parents and teachers can encourage the development of literacy by providing a rich home and school environment (see Table 9–3 for details).

The development of reading and writing skills during middle childhood is a complex, multidimensional process that also emerges out of a sociocultural context. Children learn to read and write in the context of relevant social situations. They acquire the basics of literacy while interacting with their parents, siblings, teachers, and peers. The interactions differ, as do the contributions each interaction makes to the child's growing literacy. Parents, for example, may make their greatest contributions by having conversations with their children rather than focusing exclusively on print-related activities (Snow, 1993). Similarly, children respond differently when they are actively engaged with their peers in learning to read than when they are working with a teacher (Daiute, Campbell, Griffin, Reddy, & Tivnan, 1993). Teachers help children learn the knowledge and skills they need to become expert readers and writers, but peer interactions give children the opportunity to discuss ideas and problems spontaneously. When children work with each other on a collaborative basis, they also tend to talk more than when they work with a teacher.

Table 9–3 Conditions That Promote Literacy

1. A print-rich environment
- adults who read for their own purposes
- adults who write for their own purposes
- frequent story-time experiences
- dictation experiences
- high-quality literature
- contextualized print
- functional print
- answers to questions about print

2. A rich oral language environment
- adult language models
- adults who listen to children
- free exploration of oral language
- peer conversation
- dramatic play roles
- experiences for vocabulary enrichment
- vocabulary information as requested

3. Firsthand experiences of interest
- play
- daily living
- field trips
- nature exploration

4. Symbolic representation experiences
- dramatic play
- drawing and painting
- music and dance

5. Pressure-free experimentation with writing
- drawing
- scribbling
- nonphonetic writing
- invented spelling

6. Pressure-free exploration of reading
- reading from memory
- reading with context clues
- matching print to oral language

Source: From *Let's Begin Reading Right: Developmentally Appropriate Beginning Literacy*, Third Edition, by M. V. Fields and K. L. Spangler, p. 104. Copyright © 1995 by Prentice-Hall. Reprinted by permission.

Taken together, children's social interactions lay the groundwork for literacy in a much more important way than merely mastering units of written language. Just as communication or problem solving occurs in social context, children learn to read and write in a social environment. When problems of literacy occur, educators take into consideration the family, peer, and teacher relationships that make up the child's social world (Daiute, 1993).

CONTENT CHECK
COGNITIVE DEVELOPMENT

True–False (answers are on the Companion Website)

1. The thinking of concrete operational children is both reversible and decentered.
2. Much of Piaget's theorizing about concrete operations has been discredited and therefore has not been applied to education.
3. During middle childhood children become better at memory strategies and elaboration, but their use of mental imagery remains very limited.
4. During middle childhood most children become capable of metacognition.
5. Whole-language theorists focus on emergent literacy.

Thinking Critically

How does a child's acquisition of literacy interact with sociocultural context?

Intelligence and Achievement

In the 1940s and 1950s achievement, personality, and career aptitude tests were widely administered to U.S. schoolchildren. As a result, school files were filled with test scores that often varied in accuracy and significance. In the 1960s many parents and educators became alarmed at what they considered the abuse of school-based tests. Although intelligence, achievement, and diagnostic tests are still widely used, educators are now more aware of the dangers of misinterpreting (or overinterpreting) test results and labeling children incorrectly. Indeed, whether the label is accurate or not, the very fact of being labeled as *retarded* or *dyslexic* (as defined later in the chapter) can haunt the child for life and create a "self-fulfilling prophecy" that prevents the child from obtaining a quality education (Howard, 1995; Tobias, 1989).

When used appropriately, however, tests are vital educational tools. They identify what children can and cannot do, allowing teachers to prescribe steps in learning that are tailored to the individual child. Preferably, a child is not simply labeled as "superior" or a "slow learner" but instead is assessed with regard to specific behaviors and skills.

In addition to classroom observation and "diagnostic" lessons, children are given **criterion-referenced tests** that measure the extent to which they have mastered specific skills and objectives (Glaser, 1963). Because criterion-referenced tests focus on the specific achievements of an individual, they differ radically from the more familiar **norm-referenced tests,** which compare children's scores to those of other children of the same age. Most IQ and general achievement tests are norm-referenced, meaning that they are first given to a large sample of people and standardized with regard to procedures and scoring criteria. Whereas a criterion-referenced math test describes a child's accuracy and speed in specific math skills, a norm-referenced test assesses whether a child is performing at a level that is higher or lower than average. A norm-referenced test might identify a child as being in the bottom 10% of the class in math skills, yet reveal little about what the child actually knows, why the child answers specific items incorrectly, or what skills the child needs to acquire.

criterion-referenced tests Tests that evaluate an individual's performance in relation to mastery of specified skills or objectives.

norm-referenced tests Tests that compare an indiviual's performance with performances of others in the same age group.

Intelligence Testing

Perhaps no issue in developmental psychology has been more controversial than intelligence and intelligence testing. The academic debate has often gone public because of the broad impact intelligence test scores can have on educational and social opportunities and because intelligence tests are administered widely and taken seriously in the United States and other industrialized nations. When young children are labeled on the basis of intelligence test scores, the results can be far reaching. Children's scores may affect the extent and quality of their education, determine the jobs they can obtain as adults, and have a lasting impact on self-image. Why is intelligence in such high regard? What is being measured in the first place? In this section we look at attempts to measure intelligence and then consider how to define it.

The Stanford-Binet Test   The first comprehensive intelligence test was designed in the early twentieth century by Alfred Binet, a psychologist who was commissioned by the French government to devise an objective method for identifying children who weren't doing well in school. In 1916 a U.S. version of Binet's test was created by Lewis Terman and colleagues at Stanford University and referred to as the Stanford-Binet test. This individually administered test gained wide acceptance during the 1940s and 1950s and—in its modern form, the Stanford-Binet Intelligence Scale, Fourth Edition (SB-IV)—is still widely used.

Binet's initial concept of intelligence focused on complex intellectual processes such as judgment, reasoning, memory, and comprehension. Through extensive trial and error, he developed test items involving problem solving, word definitions, and general knowledge that appeared to differentiate children according to *mental age* (MA). For example, if more than half of all 5-year-olds but fewer than half of all 4-year-olds could define the word *ball*, that would be an item on the test for 5-year-olds (Binet & Simon, 1905, 1916).

The Intelligence Quotient   According to this formula, a 4-year-old who could answer questions at the level of a 5-year-old would have a mental age of 5, and this was as far as Binet went in developing his early tests. (Remember, his purpose was to test schoolchildren and determine which ones were not progressing well.) However, later test researchers developed a formula for expressing the child's intellectual level that made it possible to compare children of different *chronological age* (CA). This measure, **the intelligence quotient (IQ),** was obtained as follows:

$$IQ = MA \ / \ CA \times 100$$

Thus, an average 4-year-old should score an MA of 4 on the test; then her or his IQ would be 100 ($4/4 \times 100 = 100$). An above-average 4-year-old with an MA of 5 would obtain an IQ of 125 ($5/4 \times 100 = 125$); a below-average child with an MA of 3 would have an IQ of 75.

intelligence quotient (IQ)   An individual's mental age divided by chronological age, multiplied by 100 to eliminate the decimal point.

deviation IQ   The approach that assigns an IQ score by comparing an individual's raw score with the scores of other subjects of the same age range.

The Wechsler Tests   There were problems with the "ratio" approach, however. The formula worked reasonably well with children and adolescents whose cognitive abilities were continuing to improve in predictable ways, but it was difficult to assess adult intelligence by this means. What kinds of test items would uniformly and fairly assess the mental age of a 30-year-old compared to that of a 40-year-old? Because of this drawback, IQ is now assessed by **deviation IQ.** This measure was developed primarily by David Wechsler and applied to IQ tests that he and colleagues developed for early childhood, childhood and adolescence, and adulthood—currently the Wechsler Preschool and

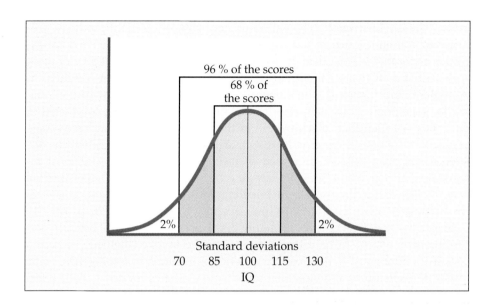

Figure 9–5   **Distribution of IQ in the General Population**

Primary Scale of Intelligence—Revised (WPPSI-R), the Wechsler Intelligence Scale for Children—Third Edition (WISC-III), and the Wechsler Adult Intelligence Scale—Third Edition (WAIS-III). An individual who takes the test obtains a score that is compared statistically to the scores of other people in the same age range. In other words, today's IQ tests (including the SB-IV) are norm-referenced, as discussed earlier.

Figure 9–5 illustrates the distribution of deviation IQ scores in the general population, based on the numbering system of the widely used Wechsler IQ tests. Note the familiar "bell-shaped" curve: IQ is assumed to be normally distributed around an average of 100, with about two-thirds of the general population scoring between 85 and 115 and almost 96% of the population scoring between 70 and 130. That leaves roughly 2% scoring below 70, which is one criterion for mental retardation, and roughly 2% scoring above 130, which is a popular cutoff point for "giftedness."

IQ test scores are by no means the whole story, however. Even though the modern versions of the Stanford-Binet and Wechsler tests provide "subscores" on performance in specific areas such as language and math abilities, the consensus is that they do not measure all of what we commonly think of as intelligence. They primarily measure abilities associated with academic performance, which is appropriate; that's what intelligence tests were originally designed for. A related point is that the tests measure an individual's intellectual abilities only at the time when they are administered; in other words, they measure *current* intellectual functioning. A popular misconception is that they assess intellectual *potential*, which is definitely not the case. Thus, as noted earlier, labeling children as "bright" or "dull" on the basis of IQ scores can be misleading and even detrimental to the child—IQ scores can change substantially over time as a function of schooling and other cognitive experiences, yet an early label may persist in spite of such change.

The Nature of Intelligence

The development of sophisticated models for testing and measuring intelligence naturally stimulated inquiry into what intelligence actually is. Here are some of the highlights of the continuing debate.

Innate Versus Learned?   The nature-nurture controversy still produces fireworks in academic journals and the popular press. Arthur Jensen (1969), for example, generated a great deal of controversy when he stated that 80% of what is measured on IQ tests is inherited and only 20% is determined by a child's environment, and further that intelligence is racially determined, with the intellectual gene pool of blacks inferior to that of whites. In research conducted in the 1960s self-identified black people in the United States in fact on average scored 10 to 15 points lower on IQ tests than did self-identified whites. The difference has progressively decreased in recent years, however, and most researchers now agree that "adjustments for economic and social differences in the lives of black and white children all but eliminate differences in the IQ scores between these two groups" (Brooks-Gunn, Klebanov, & Duncan, 1996, p. 396).

Jensen's research has been thoroughly discredited and need not be discussed further here, except to note that the criticism he invoked helped produce a backlash with regard to the possible genetic contribution to intelligence. Some researchers even took the view that there is no evidence for any genetic effect on IQ (Kamin, 1974). Yet Jensen and colleagues persist (e.g., Nyborg & Jensen, 2000). To be fair, prominent developmental researcher Sandra Scarr (1998) pointed out that Jensen's research has made major contributions with regard to his honesty and integrity—which is striking, given the professional rejection he has experienced all along the way. At the same time, however, this does not make his conclusions more credible.

The current view is more balanced: The consensus is that genetic and environmental factors are about equally important in determining intelligence, and that this too is a dynamic, reciprocal process. For further consideration of environmental factors that influence intellectual development and achievement, see "A Closer Look" on the facing page.

General and Specific Abilities   Some intelligence tests define intelligence as a single, unitary attribute; most instead define it as a composite of abilities. The WISC-III, for example, has separate subtests for information, comprehension, mathematics, vocabulary, digit span, picture arrangement, and others. These yield a Verbal IQ score, a Performance (nonverbal) IQ score, and a Full-Scale IQ score that combines the two. The SB-IV takes a similar approach in breaking down general intelligence into separate components.

Howard Gardner has been a prominent proponent of the view that intelligence consists of independent abilities (Gardner, 1983; Gardner & Walters, 1993). On the basis of studies of neurology, psychology, and human evolutionary history, he originally identified seven distinct intelligences: *linguistic, logical-mathematical, spatial, bodily-kinesthetic, musical, interpersonal,* and *intrapersonal,* later adding *naturalist* for a total of eight. Naturalist intelligence represents ". . . The ability to recognize and classify plants, minerals, and animals, including rocks and grass and all variety of flora and fauna" (Gardner, as stated in an interview by Kathy Checkly, 1997, p. 9). In other words, paraphrasing Gardner, we need to know which animals to hunt and which animals to run away from. People vary considerably in this kind of intelligence, and Gardner saw it as distinct from the rest because of its impact on survival. It is easy to see how such intelligence could have evolved.

Thus, although a particular child may be below average in the academic intelligence measured by most IQ tests, he or she may be high in other types of intelligence, such as the ability to understand the feelings and motivations of others. Of course, it's also important to consider whether the child actually *uses* her or his different types of intelligence (Hatch, 1997).

In schools today, skills that are not easily measured, like the ability to appreciate art, tend to be ignored.

A CLOSER LOOK

SOUTHEAST ASIAN REFUGEES AND ACADEMIC ACHIEVEMENT

The scholastic success of certain Asian children in science and math in particular is widely recognized. Schools in Japan and Taiwan, for example, have longer years and more rigorous work requirements than do U.S. schools. Is that all there is to it?

An answer to this question may be found by studying Southeast Asian "boat people" who immigrated to the United States in the late 1970s and early 1980s. At first glance it might seem that the children of these refugee families would be doomed to failure in U.S. schools. Devastating economic and political circumstances forced their families to flee their countries. The children often went for months, even years, without formal schooling while living in relocation camps. Many suffered hunger and physical trauma. In addition, they had little knowledge of English.

Nevertheless, in a study of 200 Southeast Asian families who had been in the United States an average of 3½ years, researchers found that the children had surprisingly high grade-point averages and math test scores. Despite their many disadvantages, the majority of the children adapted to their urban schools and quickly began to achieve at or above their grade level (Kaplan, Choy, & Whitmore, 1992).

What factors were responsible for these children's academic success? Parental encouragement and dedication to learning were especially significant. Parents helped their children overcome poor English skills, initial poverty, and the often disruptive environment of urban schools. They had a strong tradition of collective family responsibility. Parents and children alike expressed their obligations, not only to each member of the family but also to the family's overall success. The children's academic achievement was highly valued because it was linked to the future success of the entire family.

Nowhere was the family's commitment to academic excellence more obvious than in attitudes toward homework. During the evenings homework was the dominant family activity. Despite their weak English skills, parents set standards and goals for the evening's activity and did many of the children's chores so that they could study. Older siblings helped younger ones. This sibling involvement indicates how a large family can encourage academic success in its members, in contrast to the lower educational achievement typically encountered in large, poverty-stricken U.S. families.

In about half of the families, the parents read aloud to their children regularly. Children whose parents read to them got higher grades, whether the reading was in English or in their native language. Reading aloud fosters shared knowledge, strengthens emotional ties, and maintains an environment in which learning and discussion are valued. The more successful refugee families also displayed egalitarianism in gender roles. Husbands helped with the dishes and laundry. Both boys and girls were expected to help with chores. Both boys and girls were expected to go to college.

Finally, the families believed that their efforts would enable them to achieve change or desired goals—not just immediately but also in the future. They did not depend on luck or fate for their success.

Robert Sternberg (1985) inaugurated another perspective in his "triarchic" (three-part) concept of intelligence. According to Sternberg, *contextual intelligence* involves adaptation to the environment and what we might call "common sense"; *experiential intelligence* involves the ability to cope with new tasks or situations as well as with old ones; and *componential intelligence* corresponds roughly to the abilities measured by commonly employed IQ tests. In the years since 1985, Sternberg and colleagues have applied triarchic theory to diverse topics such as teaching for intelligence in schools (Sternberg, 1988a), the relationship of intelligence to creativity (Sternberg & Lubart, 1993), what constitutes common sense (practical intelligence) and how to test it (Sternberg, Wagner, Williams, & Horvath, 1995), and how intelligence varies within cultures (Sternberg, 1999)—to name a few. In his recent "theory of successful intelligence" (1999), the emphasis on practical aspects of intelligence in living and achieving remains, as summarized in Table 9–4.

Limitations of Testing   Schools use many kinds of tests to assess students' skills and competencies. Their tendency to concentrate on measurable abilities reflects the popularity of behavioral objectives, meaning the specific kinds of knowledge and skills that a student is expected to display after a specified

Table 9–4   **Elements of Sternberg's Successful Intelligence**

Definition of successful intelligence
  The ability to achieve success in life
  According to one's personal standards
  Within one's sociocultural context
Types of processing skills contributing to successful intelligence
  Analytical
  Creative
  Practical
Uses of processing skills for successful intelligence
  Adaptation to environments
  Shaping of environments
  Selection of environments
Mechanisms for utilization of processing skills in successful intelligence
  Capitalization on strengths
  Correction of weaknesses
  Compensation for weaknesses

Source: Sternberg, R. J. (1999). The theory of successful intelligence. *Review of General Psychology, 3,* 292–316.

Copyright © 1999 by the Educational Publishing Foundation. Reprinted with permission.

amount of instruction. In a very real sense, the tests provide a way of testing schools as well as students. At various points during each academic year, schools are expected to provide objective data on what their students are learning. As valuable as this approach can be in keeping schools up to par, however, placing too much emphasis on a school's success can mean that children spend much of the school day focusing on the particular competencies that are measured by the tests. As a result, less tangible competencies, ways of thinking, and personality traits may be overlooked. Tests do not tell the whole story about ability, and some personal qualities and skills are difficult or impossible to measure.

There is also the question of possible cultural bias in the tests themselves. To demonstrate the absurdity of culturally linked intelligence tests, Stephen Jay Gould (1981) gave a class of Harvard students a nonverbal test of intelligence designed for World War I army recruits. (A sample of the test is shown in Figure 9–6.) He found that many of his students could not identify a horn as the missing part of a Victrola record player (item 18), despite the test makers' claim that the subjects' "innate" intelligence would guide them to the correct answer.

For many years, minority groups have objected to having their skills and abilities measured by tests that assume wide exposure to the dominant culture; they feel that the tests are unfair to people from different subcultural backgrounds. Support for this view is provided by a study of ethnically black and "interracial" children who had been adopted by white middle-class parents. The IQ scores and school achievements of these children were well above

Figure 9-6 The Army Beta Mental Test
This is part 6 of the Army Beta mental test given to recruits during World War I. (Answers: 1. mouth; 2. eye; 3. nose; 4. spoon in right hand; 5. chimney; 6. left ear; 7. filament; 8. stamp; 9. strings; 10. rivet; 11. trigger; 12. tail; 13. leg; 14. shadow; 15. bowling ball in man's right hand; 16. net; 17. left hand; 18. horn of Victrola; 19. arm and powder puff in mirror image; 20. diamond.)

average—and well above those of children with similar backgrounds but different cultural experiences (Weinberg, 1989). Research also suggests that minority children may be victims of a self-fulfilling prophecy. They acquire low expectations about their academic performance on tests designed primarily for white students and the low expectations further lower their self-confidence and, hence, their test scores. To be fair, in recent years designers of tests such as the Stanford-Binet and the Wechsler tests have gone to great lengths to eliminate as much cultural bias as possible and have incorporated representative samples of minorities during standardization, but the tests are still slanted toward the mainstream culture and its language.

It is not always necessary to use tests to assess children's progress. Teachers, parents, and caregivers can learn a lot by informally observing what children do and say. By merely listening as a child reads a book, a skilled teacher can determine much about the child's progress toward reading mastery.

CONTENT CHECK
INTELLIGENCE AND ACHIEVEMENT

True–False (answers are on the Companion Website)

1. The SB-IV and the WISC-III are criterion-referenced tests.
2. The SB-VI and the WISC-III are based on deviation IQ.
3. The consensus is that genetics and environment contribute about equally to intelligence.
4. Sternberg's triarchic theory specifies eight different forms of intelligence.
5. Modern IQ tests are thoroughly culturally fair.

Thinking Critically

What are the advantages and disadvantages of intelligence testing?

Learning and Thinking in School

Where they exist, formal schools play a crucial role in children's development. At school, children test their intellectual, physical, social, and emotional competencies to find out whether they can meet the standards set for them by their parents, their teachers, and society in general. They also gain confidence in their ability to master their world and develop good relationships with peers.

On beginning school, children encounter demands and expectations that differ markedly from those they have faced at home. Children vary greatly in how well they adapt to these demands, in their ability to use critical thinking, in their overall success in school, and in the role their parents play in helping them learn. Around the world, children also vary widely with regard to opportunities to attend school and the extent to which they take (or are allowed to take) advantage of it (see Figure 9–7).

Figure 9–7   Primary School Enrollment Around the World

Source: UNICEF, 1995.

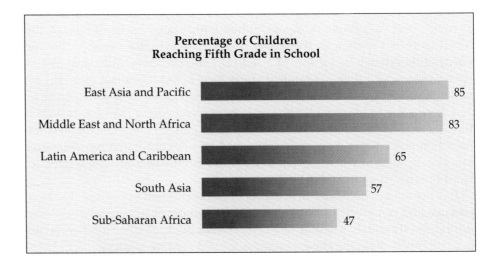

Percentage of Children Reaching Fifth Grade in School

East Asia and Pacific	85
Middle East and North Africa	83
Latin America and Caribbean	65
South Asia	57
Sub-Saharan Africa	47

New Demands and Expectations

Children entering school are separated from their parents, some for the first time, and they must learn to trust unfamiliar adults. At the same time, greater independence is expected of them. No longer can a little boy yell to his mother, "Put on my boots!" The teacher expects him to do it himself, just as the teacher expects little girls to do things for themselves. Even in small classes, children must now compete for adult attention and assistance.

Regardless of the school, there is always a gap between what is expected at home and what is expected in the classroom. The greater the gap, the more difficult the child's adjustment will be. Children who have just begun to internalize the rules of family life are suddenly expected to adapt to a new set of standards. Their success will depend on their family background, the school environment, and their own individuality. How well a child has coped with dependency, autonomy, authority, aggression, and conscience will influence his or her adjustment to school. Although teachers recognize that the inner resources of a child who has just started school may be shaky, they nonetheless insist that the child adapt—and quickly.

From the first day of school, children are expected to learn the complex social rules that govern the social life of the classroom. Relations with classmates involve finding the right balance between cooperation and competition. Similarly, relations with teachers involve achieving a compromise between autonomy and obedience.

Some schools have elaborate codes of behavior: Children must listen when the teacher speaks, line up to go outside for recess, obtain permission to go to the bathroom, and raise a hand before speaking. Initially, a great deal of class time may be spent enforcing such rules. Public school classrooms have been studied with respect to how much time teachers spend on the following activities: (1) teaching facts or concepts; (2) giving directions for a particular lesson; (3) stating general rules of behavior; (4) correcting, disciplining, and praising children; and (5) miscellaneous activities (Sieber & Gordon, 1981). The results were startling: In a half-hour lesson, it was not unusual for a teacher to spend only 10 to 15% of the time on academic work (categories 1 and 2). Research indicates that children learn more in classes in which time on task is maximized— that is, in which the teacher spends at least half the time on actual teaching and less on such concerns as maintaining order (Brophy, 1986). Time and energy invested in socializing children to the specific demands of the classroom is only indirectly connected to intellectual or social growth.

Developing Competent Learners and Critical Thinkers

In a rapidly changing world there is much to learn and little time to learn it. With knowledge becoming obsolete literally overnight, people need to become lifelong learners who can integrate and organize barrages of changing information. Thus, many educators are no longer focusing on having children memorize disconnected facts and principles but instead are helping children become self-directed, competent learners and critical thinkers.

Educational psychologists recommend a range of teaching strategies to develop student thinking. Children need to develop six kinds of thought (A. Costa, 1985). We might call these the six Rs:

1. Remembering: Recalling a fact, idea, or concept.
2. Repeating: Following a model or procedure.
3. Reasoning: Relating a specific instance to a general principle or concept.

4. Reorganizing: Extending knowledge to new contexts and devising original solutions to problems.
5. Relating: Connecting newly acquired knowledge with past or personal experience.
6. Reflecting: Exploring the thought itself and how it occurred.

Teaching students to develop critical thinking is more difficult than simply imparting facts and principles (A. Costa, 1985). To develop reasoning, for example, teachers must challenge students with interesting problems and materials. The goal is to increase curiosity, foster questioning, develop related concepts, encourage evaluation of alternatives, and help students construct and test hypotheses.

In the latter part of the 20th century U.S. schools placed greater emphasis on teaching learning and thinking skills; tailoring instruction to the child's individual learning style and developmental level; and fostering independent, self-regulated, self-paced learning. One way of achieving such goals is to assign students small-group projects and activities. When small-group instruction is done effectively, children experience cooperative rather than competitive learning. Cooperative learning techniques have been found to increase overall performance (Johnson & Johnson, 1994a; 1994b). It has also been found to raise the self-esteem of female students significantly more than when individual-centered teaching strategies are employed (Slavin, 1995). However, despite the success of these strategies, most students in U.S. classrooms still don't perform as well in math and science as students in Japan and China (Stevenson, Chen, & Lee, 1993).

Success in School

Success in school is influenced by many factors. Children who are in poor health, do not get enough to eat, are preoccupied with problems at home, or have low self-esteem don't fare as well. Self-perceived competence may also affect school performance. In one study, 20% of school-age children under-

To do well in school, children need a healthy diet.

estimated their actual abilities, set lower expectations for themselves, and were surprised when they made high grades (Phillips, 1984).

According to David McClelland (1955), the reason that some children achieve more than others may stem from the values of the culture in which they are reared. After comparing several cultures during different periods of history, McClelland concluded that **achievement motivation**—persistence toward success and excellence—is an acquired, culturally based drive. In any given society at any time, some groups value achievement more highly than others. Different cultures or subcultures may also value different kinds of achievement; one group may stress educational goals; another may place more value on social success. Children whose parents stress values that are different from those of the school may bring less motivation to academic tasks.

Gender Differences and School Success   Success in school is also influenced by gender differences. A pioneering review of the literature on gender differences (Maccoby & Jacklin, 1974) found that—on average—girls tend to outperform boys in verbal skills and boys tend to do better in quantitative and spatial tasks. There are many possible reasons for this. For example, there may be small sex differences in relevant brain development (Kimura, 1992), but different social expectations for boys and girls profoundly influence their behavior. As Carol Gilligan (1987) pointed out, girls in middle childhood who are self-confident and have a strong sense of identity sometimes confront major obstacles to their intellectual development during the preadolescent and adolescent years. As their bodies mature, they must reconcile their notions of what it means to be a woman with what they observe around them. Attractiveness and fitting in may become more important than academic achievement. To put it another way, girls may find themselves "dumbing down" to be popular in a traditionally male-dominated society.

In addition, the broader society has traditionally defined mathematics and science as male-oriented and literature and language as female-oriented. Many adults—even teachers—may therefore assume that boys will do better in math and put more effort into teaching math to boys than to girls. Classroom-based

achievement motivation   A learned drive involving persistence toward success and excellence.

Girls who do well in mathematics during middle childhood may put less effort into this subject when they become adolescents because of societal stereotypes that mathematical thinking is typically more "masculine" than "feminine."

gender bias that is a direct result of the different ways in which teachers perceive girls and boys is examined in greater detail in "In Theory, In Fact" below.

Research indicates that while gender differences still emerge on standardized tests, they have been declining in some respects (Feingold, 1988). For example, in studying the results of the Preliminary Scholastic Aptitude Test (PSAT) between 1960 and 1983, researchers found significant gender differences. On average, girls scored higher than boys in grammar, spelling, and perceptual speed; boys scored higher in spatial visualization, high school mathematics, and mechanical aptitude. No differences were found in verbal reasoning, arithmetic, and figural reasoning. However, the gender gap remained constant at higher levels of performance in high school mathematics. Negative experiences in the classroom and at home, combined with outmoded yet still widely accepted stereotypes of males and females, do much more to produce gender differences than actual brain physiology.

Parental Influences on School Success   Parents can play a large role in creating a supportive environment and encouraging the development of specific skills that help children succeed. On the negative side, children from homes characterized by severe marital distress, parental criminality or psychiatric disorder, or overcrowding, along with intermittent placement in foster care, are at special risk for school failure (Sameroff, Seifer, Baldwin, & Baldwin, 1993).

If we look at the parents of children who succeed in school, we find behaviors that almost any parent can practice, regardless of economic circumstances.

IN THEORY, IN FACT

GENDER EQUALITY IN THE CLASSROOM

In an incident at an exclusive New York City private school, several first-grade boys told the girls in their class that they were "sexy babes" and suggested to them, "Let's do sexy." When parents learned that the teacher had done little more than tell the girls to ignore the comments, some went to the principal, and others spoke privately to the parents of the boys involved. As one mother explained, "I was upset that my daughter was getting the message that boys were stronger and more aggressive and that she's a victim."

Although the principal contended that teachers at the school treated boys and girls equally and that great pains were taken to create a gender-equal environment, she formed a committee to study whether anything at the school contributed to the boys' behavior. Meanwhile, the teacher explained to the boys why their comments were offensive and that it is important to treat each other with respect.

Unfortunately, this was not an isolated incident. Parents and educators across the country are becoming increasingly aware of gender inequality in their children's classrooms. A 1992 report entitled *How Schools Shortchange Girls,* issued by the American Association of University Women, described ways in which girls' self-esteem and school performance fall precipitously during adolescence. *Failing at Fairness: How America's Schools Cheat Girls*, by Myra and David Sadker (1995), also raised awareness of school-based gender inequality. The Sadkers, professors of education at American University in Washington, DC, have studied the issue for over 20 years. They advise parents who are worried about gender bias to visit their children's schools and observe the behaviors of both teachers and students, looking for the following:

1. Do teachers call on girls as much as on boys?
2. Do they display the work of both sexes equally?
3. Do they offer greater assistance to girls while allowing boys to solve problems on their own?
4. Do they punish girls and boys for the same reasons?
5. Do girls stand back while boys perform hands-on work in science labs?
6. Are there girls-only and boys-only lines or teams?
7. Do girls participate in sports at recess?
8. Are any girls team captains?
9. Can children of both sexes name 10 famous women in American history? (If not, the school may have a gender-biased curriculum.)

Primary source: Rubenstein, 1994, p. C4.

Children who perform well in school tend to have parents who strongly value education and encourage their child's academic self-esteem.

Researchers have long known that parental factors associated with children's success at school include (Hess & Holloway, 1984):

1. Parents of successful children have realistic beliefs about their children's current abilities but also have high expectations for the future. These parents help their children develop self-confidence by encouraging them to perform age-appropriate tasks both at school and at home.
2. Parent-child relationships are warm and affectionate, and parents have discipline and control strategies that are authoritative rather than authoritarian (see Chapter 8). Parents place limits on their children's behavior, but the children feel safe and accepted.
3. Finally, and perhaps most important, parents talk to their children. They read to them, listen to them, and have regular conversations with them. They support and enrich their children's exploration and inquiry, acting as role models in the process.

To this we might add parental admonitions to the effect of "Do your homework!"

In general, children tend to succeed academically when their parents provide support and guidance. This supportive atmosphere is common among Southeast Asian families. The parents value learning and hard work and believe that children can succeed at any task through determination and effort (Kaplan et al., 1992). Similarly, the parents of U.S. black children who excel academically tend to stress the importance of education and encourage the development of self-esteem and belief in personal efficacy—ability to get things done. At the same time, they acknowledge that their children may encounter racial prejudice and discrimination and try to prepare them to cope with it (Patterson, Kupersmidt, & Vaden, 1990).

Although poverty and minority status may be major factors lowering children's intellectual performance, it is not only poor, often-minority children who have school problems. Middle- and upper-income families may also have underachieving children. Parents who emphasize fun, excitement, or material possessions tend to have children who perform more poorly in school than children of parents who value educational achievement (Kaplan et al., 1992).

CONTENT CHECK
LEARNING AND THINKING IN SCHOOL

True–False (answers are on the Companion Website)

1. For most children, the transition to formal schooling is relatively simple and easy.
2. Rote memory remains a primary emphasis in elementary education.
3. Achievement motivation is an acquired drive that can vary considerably from one child to the next.
4. Gender differences in academic skills are primarily a function of schooling and differing learning experiences.
5. One of the most important things parents can do to help their children in school is to talk and read to them regularly.

Thinking Critically

What aspects of modern schooling foster the critical thinking we're asking you to do here?

Developmental Disorders

Mental Retardation

In Chapters 3 and 4 we discussed four general causes of mental retardation: genetic anomalies, prenatal exposure to diseases and drugs, anoxia at birth, and extreme malnutrition before birth or during infancy. We have also seen that the family or other caregiving environment can have either a facilitating or debilitating effect on a child's intellectual development. In this section we survey mental retardation, noting that it often goes undetected until age 5 or 6 when the child enters formal schooling.

The *Diagnostic and Statistical Manual* (DSM-IV) of the American Psychiatric Association (American Psychiatric Association, 1994), based on guidelines originally developed by the American Association on Mental Deficiency (now the American Association on Mental Retardation), lists three criteria that a child must meet to be diagnosed as mentally retarded:

1. Significantly subaverage intellectual functioning based on IQ test scores.
2. Significantly impaired adaptive behaviors in areas such as self-care, self-direction, and general functioning at home and in the community.
3. Onset before age 18.

There are four levels of mental retardation: *mild* (IQ of about 55 to 70), *moderate* (40 to 55), *severe* (25 to 40), and *profound* (below 25). What are mentally retarded children (and adults) like at each level? It's important to remember that they are individuals just like intellectually normal or above-average people. Nevertheless, their level of impairment does produce certain common characteristics. Also note, with regard to the normal distribution on page 333, that there are many more mentally retarded persons at the higher than at the lower levels.

mental retardation Significantly subaverage intellectual functioning and self-help skills, with onset prior to age 18.

Mildly mentally retarded children are generally "educable" and attend public schools, although they're often placed in special education classes. They can learn to read, and in time many can achieve at least an elementary school education and corresponding social skills. Most can also hold a job, although they may require continuing support and assistance.

Moderately mentally retarded children were once inappropriately labeled as merely "trainable," but they too can benefit to some extent from academic and vocational education. They often can care for themselves with supervision, learn to get around in their neighborhood, and support themselves at jobs that don't exceed their limited mental and social capabilities.

Severely and profoundly retarded children don't fare as well. They often require close supervision and generally are not able to perform more than the simplest of tasks. They are capable of learning limited self-care, but they generally don't profit from training or education beyond a preschool level and are unlikely to be able to support themselves. Severely and profoundly retarded individuals can still adapt to structured home and community settings, however, and are not merely "custodial" or "vegetative" as they were once labeled. Known neurological defects and a variety of physical disabilities often accompany their mental retardation—hence the term *biological* mental retardation. The contrasting term, *psychosocial* retardation, is applied to people in the mild-to-moderate range and is thought to arise more from social and environmental factors than from neurological problems. In actuality, however, in about 30 to 40% of cases the cause or causes cannot be clearly determined (American Psychiatric Association, 1994).

Is there hope for mentally retarded children? Indeed there is. With help, many will grow up to lead happy, productive, and in many respects normal lives. At least at the higher levels, many will also marry and have normal children.

Learning Disorders

Learning disorders, also termed *learning disabilities,* involve difficulty in acquiring specific academic skills but not others. The child may have average or above-average general intellectual ability, yet be markedly substandard in a particular area such as reading. Such a child's overall academic achievement often suffers—a child who can't read adequately, for example, is at a major disadvantage in all areas of schooling and will eventually encounter vocational difficulties as well. Perhaps understandably, the school dropout rate for older children with unremediated learning disorders is much higher than the rate for the general student population.

Children with learning disorders often have no more in common than the label itself. In school systems today, children with normal intelligence and no sensory or motor defects are considered learning disordered when they require special attention in the classroom—that is, when they have trouble learning to read, write, spell, or do arithmetic. For reasons that remain unclear, up to 80% of learning-disordered children are boys.

The *DSM-IV* (American Psychiatric Association, 1994) recognizes three main categories of learning disorders: *reading disorder* (dyslexia); *disorder of written expression* (dysgraphia), which can involve anything from spelling and handwriting to syntax; and *mathematics disorder* (dyscalculia), which can involve anything having to do with recognizing mathematical symbols and performing mathematical operations. Each category typically also involves poor perceptual skills.

Day after day, learning-disordered children are unable to do things that their classmates seem to accomplish effortlessly. With each failure they become

learning disorders Extreme difficulty in learning school subjects such as reading, writing, or math, despite normal intelligence and absence of sensory or motor disabilities.

increasingly insecure about their ability to perform, and their self-esteem suffers. Classmates tend to interact less with a child who doesn't succeed. Children with learning disorders often have difficulty with social as well as academic skills (Kavale & Forness, 1996). They may become increasingly isolated from peers and even from family members, who find life with a learning-disordered child highly stressful (Dyson, 1996). Some children with these disorders become shy and withdrawn; others become boastful; still others are prone to impulsive or angry outbursts. It can be difficult indeed to find ways to help a learning-disordered child develop confidence and experience success in other areas.

The study of learning disorders is a challenging puzzle with a confusing array of expert opinions about their causes, symptoms, and treatments. If there is a consensus, it is that learning disorders are associated with one or more basic mental processes. For example, a learning-disabled child may experience difficulty with attention, memory, perception, or cognitive control processes. Many of the classic controversies about child development are also evident in the questions raised about learning disorders. Is the child abnormal, deficient, or disabled, or is the child just different in temperament and style? Is the problem organic, or is it a result of the home or school environment? Should the child be "treated" medically, "managed" through behavioral programs, or "educated" creatively? One thing is clear, however: The earlier intervention begins, the better the child's chances of later success (see Slavin, 1996).

Reading Disorder Reading disorder or dyslexia is one of the most common types of learning disorders. Because dyslexic children often confuse letters such as *b* and *d*, or read *star* as *rats*, it was long believed that these children simply "see things backward." Very few of them actually have anything wrong with their visual system, however. In other contexts dyslexic children may have no perceptual problems. They have no trouble finding their way around, so they aren't deficient in spatial relationships. They may be exceptionally good at putting together puzzles. Why, then, do they make errors like confusing *b* and *d*? One observation is that these are very common errors for beginning readers. Most children make reversal errors when they first learn to read, but most get through this stage quickly. Dyslexic children somehow remain stuck in the early stages of reading (Richardson, 1992; Vogel, 1989).

Dyslexic children also have problems outside of school. Many have pervasive language problems. They may be delayed in learning to speak, or their speech may be at a lower developmental level than that of their agemates. Their difficulty in naming letters and written words is matched by their difficulty in naming objects or colors; it takes them longer than usual to recall an ordinary word like *key* or *blue*. They also have trouble hearing the two separate syllables in a two-syllable word or recognizing that the spoken word *sat* starts with an *s* sound and ends with a *t* sound (Shaywitz, Shaywitz, Fletcher, & Escobar, 1991; Wagner & Torgerson, 1987).

Although the hypothesized "brain dysfunction" that underlies dyslexia has not yet been identified, it is clear that heredity plays a role in the disorder. Many reading-disordered children have a parent or a sibling with the same problem (Scarborough, 1989). It is also interesting to note that dyslexia tends to run in families that exhibit left-handedness. However, left-handedness itself is only weakly associated with dyslexia; most reading-disordered children are right-handed (Hiscock & Kinsbourne, 1987).

Treatment of dyslexia generally involves intensive remedial work in reading and language, including carefully sequenced tutorial instruction. One approach (Stanton, 1981) emphasizes the need to improve the child's confidence.

Although no single educational plan seems to work with all children, most programs help children learn. Graduates of one especially successful program—a British residential school for dyslexic children—usually can attend college. In contrast, children who attend the least successful programs generally become high school dropouts (Bruck, 1987). Dyslexic children who manage to overcome their disorder may emerge with renewed self-confidence and have successful adult lives. Thomas Edison, Nelson Rockefeller, and Hans Christian Andersen were all dyslexic as children.

Attention-Deficit/Hyperactivity Disorder

Extreme inattentiveness, difficulty sustaining attention or concentrating long enough to follow through on tasks, distractibility, and forgetfulness define **Attention-deficit/hyperactivity disorder (ADHD).** Perhaps contrary to what the term *ADHD* implies, attention deficit is not always associated with hyperactivity, which involves inability to sit still or remain quiet, as well as impulsiveness and impatience, again to extremes. Nor is hyperactivity always associated with attention deficit. However, most children with the disorder display at least some of each aspect of the disorder; hence the combined name.

Researchers have suggested many possible causes of ADHD, including malnutrition, lead poisoning, organic brain damage, heredity, intrauterine abnormalities, prenatal exposure to drugs like crack cocaine, and anoxia during fetal development or childbirth. Many children with symptoms of ADHD (and also learning disorders) experienced some form of birth irregularity, including prematurity (Buchoff, 1990). In addition, studies of identical and fraternal twins suggest that ADHD has a strong genetic link (Gillis, 1992).

Just as there are different possible causes of ADHD, there are also differences in recommended treatments. Many children who display symptoms of ADHD respond to an amphetamine derivative, Ritalin. They calm down in response to a drug that ordinarily speeds up behavior and CNS activity. This has given rise to the hypothesis that ADHD children are either understimulated or unable to focus on tasks because all stimulation comes in at equal levels. Perhaps their high activity level is an attempt to provide more environmental stimulation. In that case, Ritalin lowers children's threshold of sensitivity to events around them. An alternate hypothesis is that by speeding up neural processing Ritalin enables ADHD children to control their overall cognitive functioning better, thereby improving their attention and behavioral control.

Although not all ADHD children benefit from taking Ritalin, and there has been considerable controversy about its overuse with children who are simply overactive and not truly hyperactive, the benefits can outweigh the risk of possible side effects for those who do respond when the treatment program is monitored carefully. Research has consistently shown improvements in these children's school work and family and peer relationships (Campbell & Spencer, 1988).

An alternate form of treatment for children with ADHD is educational management, which takes place both at home and at school. This method restructures the child's environment by simplifying it, reducing distractions, making expectations more explicit, and generally reducing confusion. The specific educational plan depends on the theoretical position of the therapist or educator. One position (Cruickshank, 1977) advocates an instructional program involving various training tasks that require specific skills. Another (Ross, 1977) focuses more on the development of selective attention. A newer approach focuses on finding acceptable and constructive outlets for the boundless energy often associated with ADHD (Armstrong, 1996).

Attention-deficit/hyperactivity disorder (ADHD) An inability to keep focused on something long enough to learn it, often accompanied by poor impulse control.

CONTENT CHECK
DEVELOPMENTAL DISORDERS

True–False (answers are on the Companion Website)

1. People are diagnosed as mentally retarded primarily on the basis of IQ scores.
2. Most mentally retarded persons can become functional and productive members of society.
3. Most children who are diagnosed as having learning disorders are also mentally retarded.
4. Reading disorder is the most common type of learning disorder.
5. Children with ADHD are for the most part untreatable.

Thinking Critically

Why would children with developmental disorders often be viewed negatively and rejected by other children?

CHAPTER 9 REVISITED

Physical and Motor Development

■ There is wide variability in the timing of physical growth and motor development during middle childhood; each process is dynamic.

■ Growing pains in early to later middle childhood are a normal part of development.

■ At about 6 to 8 years of age, the forebrain undergoes a growth spurt that may relate to entrance into Piaget's period of concrete operations.

■ Girls and boys are comparable in strength and motor skill development during middle childhood; the more important thing is practice.

■ Physical motor skills mastery helps produce a psychological sense of mastery as well.

■ Middle childhood is normally a very healthy period; such diseases that children do experience help develop responses to stress.

■ Obesity is a common problem during middle childhood in many nations; causes may be genetic or environmental, and experts advise against severe dieting.

■ As obesity among U.S. children has been increasing, sedentary activities have also been increasing and physical fitness has been decreasing.

■ In the United States, a national physical health objective has emphasized physical education because habits acquired during middle childhood may persist into adulthood.

■ Accidents are by far the leading cause of death or disability in middle childhood.

Cognitive Development

■ Concrete operational thinking is characteristic of middle childhood.

■ Compared to preoperational thinkers, concrete operational thinkers are less intuitive, less egocentric, and more capable of understanding logical cause-and-effect relationships.

■ Concrete operational children are also decentered and capable of reversibility in their thinking, and in concrete situations they can theorize about what will happen.

■ Piaget's theory has been applied extensively in teaching children science and math, where children are encouraged to solve problems on their own.

■ Memory processes that markedly improve during middle childhood include rehearsal, organization, semantic elaboration, mental imagery, retrieval, and the use of scripts; metacognition improves dramatically as well.

■ Becoming literate improves considerably during middle childhood; literacy is intricately involved with sociocultural context.

■ The whole-language approach emphasizes the gradual and progressive emergence of literacy.

Intelligence and Achievement

■ Intelligence and achievement tests have both advantages and disadvantages where education is concerned.

■ Criterion-referenced tests often provide more useful information about children's strengths and weaknesses than norm-referenced tests do.

■ The first intelligence test was developed by Binet and colleagues. It was based on assessing MA; later a comparison of MA to CA was incorporated.

■ On modern norm-referenced tests such as the SB-IV and the WISC-III, the measure is instead deviation IQ.

■ IQ is assumed to be normally distributed with an average is 100; a small percentage of people score high enough to be considered gifted or low enough to be considered mentally retarded, although IQ scores can change.

■ Jensen argued that intelligence is primarily genetic and that some populations are inferior to others; the modern consensus is that intelligence is determined about half and half by genetics and environment.

■ Contemporary theories of intelligence stress that there may be more than one kind, also that practical, everyday intelligence is as important as what is measured by traditional IQ tests; Gardner's theory of multiple intelligences and Sternberg's triarchic theory are examples.

■ Assessing a school's effectiveness by testing its children can have both positive and negative effects.

■ In spite of efforts to improve them, popular IQ tests still favor the majority over minorities.

Learning and Thinking in School

■ Children's initial adjustment to formal schooling can be difficult for a wide variety of reasons, mostly involving new demands and expectations regarding the children's behavior.

■ In developing critical thinking, modern educators still focus on memorization, but also on repeating, reasoning, reorganizing, relating, and reflecting.

■ Tailoring instruction to the child and fostering both independent and cooperative learning are also emphasized by modern educators.

■ Success in school often includes acquiring achievement motivation and overcoming gender stereotypes—especially for girls.

■ Parental factors that are associated with children's success in school include realistic beliefs laced with high expectations, use of authoritative discipline, and talking and listening to their children—plus monitoring them and requiring that they do their homework.

Developmental Disorders

■ Causes of mental retardation vary considerably; to be diagnosed as mentally retarded a child must meet each of three criteria.

■ The DSM-IV specifies four levels of mental retardation: mild, moderate, severe, and profound; persons at the higher levels can nevertheless be productive members of society, and even persons at the lower levels can learn and profit from special training.

■ Learning disorders occur in children who are otherwise normal to above-average; learning disorders involve problems in a specific area of learning.

■ Reading disorder (dyslexia), disorder of written expression (dysgraphia), and mathematics disorder (dyscalculia) are the DSM-IV's main categories of learning disorders; theories vary considerably as to what causes learning disorders.

■ ADHD is a cognitive/behavioral disorder, the causes of which are also poorly understood; it is often treatable by medication or by behavioral interventions.

KEY TERMS

control processes
metacognition
criterion-referenced tests
norm-referenced tests

intelligence quotient (IQ)
deviation IQ
achievement motivation
mental retardation

learning disorders
Attention-deficit/hyperactivity
  disorder

MIDDLE CHILDHOOD: PERSONALITY AND SOCIOCULTURAL DEVELOPMENT

10

CHAPTER PREVIEW

Do you know:

1. What *psychodynamic, cognitive-developmental,* and *social-learning* approaches have to say about development during middle childhood?

2. How a child's *self-concept* and *self-esteem* develop?

3. How components of social cognition such as *social inference* and an understanding of *social responsibility* and *social regulations* develop during middle childhood?

4. What Piaget's concepts of *moral realism* and *moral relativism* refer to?

5. How Kohlberg used *moral dilemmas* to assess child and adult *moral development,* and what stages he found?

6. Why Gilligan objected to Kohlberg's theory and how her theory's *moral caring* orientation differs from Kohlberg's *justice* orientation?

7. Why *parental monitoring* remains important during middle childhood?

8. What factors contribute to *optimal parenting* during this period?

9. In what ways the makeup and functioning of U.S. families *changed* during the latter part of the 20th century?

10. What characterizes *resilient children*?

11. What special stresses occur in *single-parent* families?

12. How children typically react to their parents' *divorce* and what factors help *alleviate* children's negative reactions?

13. How children's understanding of *friendship* develops in stages during middle childhood, and what *functions* friendships serve?

14. How *peer-group status* and *peer-group conformity* affect children?

15. How the existence of *in-groups* and *out-groups* contribute to *prejudice*?

These are the main topics of Chapter 10.

If Shakespeare was right and all the world's a stage, then the stage on which children perform broadens dramatically during middle childhood. The emotional and social attachments of younger children centered primarily on the family; now children move into a the broader world made up of peers, teachers, and other people in the wider community. In industrialized nations, the expansion of the child's world is gradual, yet punctuated with milestones like beginning first grade, joining clubs, and venturing beyond the immediate neighborhood.

As their social world expands, so do children's perspectives on the conflicts and stresses in their own families. Children who experience divorce or life in a single-parent household must find ways of coping, as must children who are abused in families of any composition. Methods of coping in turn influence patterns of social and emotional behavior that help determine personality. Children's growing alliances with peers also influence how they come to see themselves and their place in the world.

In all, broadened experiences teach children about the complexities of family relationships and friendships and the conduct society expects of them. They also prepare children to make moral judgments.

Personality Development in an Expanding Social World

How does a child's personality develop and change during middle childhood? Again the answer depends on your theoretical perspective. In this section we begin with how psychodynamic, cognitive-developmental, and social-learning theories generally apply to middle childhood. We then focus on the child's developing sense of self.

Three Perspectives on Middle Childhood

Freud described middle childhood as a period of *latency*. In his view, the period from age 6 to 12 was a time during which family jealousies and turmoil (along with sexual impulses) became submerged. If so, children could turn their emotional energies toward peer relationships, creative efforts, and learning the culturally prescribed tasks in the school or the community. As noted in Chapter 2, however, Freud had much less to say about the latency period (and the adolescent genital period beyond that) than he did about the first 6 or 7 years of life. It was therefore up to Erikson to expand on Freud's ideas and develop a more comprehensive theory. Unlike Freud, however, Erikson emphasized *psychosocial* factors in personality development.

Erikson proposed that the central focus of middle childhood is the crisis of industry versus inferiority. In middle childhood, with the impetus of formal or informal schooling, much of the child's time and energy is directed toward acquiring new knowledge and skills. Children are better at channeling their energies into learning, problem solving, and achievement. When children succeed in school, they incorporate a sense of industry into their self-image—they come to realize that hard work produces results, and they continue to progress toward mastering their environment. In contrast, children who do not progress toward academic mastery begin to feel inferior compared to their peers. This sense of inferiority can affect personality throughout life if it isn't compensated for later or by ongoing success in other activities that are valued, such as sports, music, or art.

The second theoretical perspective—the cognitive-developmental approach—has been increasingly applied to personality and social development. Piaget and Lawrence Kohlberg, for example, have written extensively about the development of children's concepts about self and **morality**—ideas about fairness and justice, right and wrong, good and bad. Other researchers have focused more broadly on the importance of children's self-concepts as determinants of their behavior.

Finally, social-learning theory has made major contributions to the understanding of how specific behaviors are learned via the family and the peer group. During middle childhood peers increasingly serve as models and reinforce or punish behaviors again with potentially profound effects on personality development.

These perspectives merge to help us understand how children become socialized and enculturated during middle childhood. The ways in which children interact with peers, adults, and family members change: A demanding

morality Ideas about fairness and justice, right and wrong, good and bad.

4-year-old becomes a cooperative 8-year-old, who in turn may become a rebellious 13-year-old. Neither of the three perspectives alone explains all personality and sociocultural development during middle childhood, but taken together they provide a more complete picture.

Self-Concept

Self-concept in particular helps us understand development during middle childhood, in that self-concept interweaves personality and social behavior. Children form increasingly stable pictures of themselves, and self-concept also becomes more realistic. They understand their skills and limitations more accurately, and their understanding of themselves organizes and orients their behavior.

As children grow older, they form more complex pictures of other people's physical, intellectual, and personality characteristics as well as their own. They attribute increasingly specific *traits*—stable personality characteristics—to themselves and others. They try to behave consistently and expect consistency in the behavior of others.

Children continuously compare themselves with their agemates (Marsh, Craven, & Debus, 1991) and draw conclusions such as, "I'm better than Susan at sports, but I'm not as popular as Tanya," or "My writing isn't as good as Jose's, but I'm better than he is at math." As Susan Harter (1982) aptly put it, children's emerging self-concept provides a "filter" through which they evaluate their own behavior and that of others.

Early self-concepts are not always accurate, however. For example, first-graders tend to have more positive perceptions of their abilities and competencies than do older children (Eccles, Wigfield, Harold, & Blumenfeld, 1993). During the elementary school years children also continue to refine their gender stereotypes and at the same time develop greater flexibility in interacting with others (Serbin, Powlishta, & Gulko, 1993).

Self-Esteem   Whereas self-concept involves who you are and what you can do, **self-esteem** adds an evaluative component; it refers to whether you see yourself in a favorable or an unfavorable light—or somewhere in between. High self-esteem means that you basically like yourself and often feel competent in your social and other skills; low self-esteem means that you often dislike yourself and feel incompetent and inferior. Like self-concept, self-esteem has roots in early childhood and is influenced both by the child's experiences with success and failure and by his or her interactions with parents. During the school years self-esteem is significantly correlated with academic achievement. Children who do well in school have higher self-esteem than those who do poorly (Alpert-Gillis & Connell, 1989).

The correlation between self-esteem and academic achievement is far from perfect, however: Many children who don't do well in school nonetheless manage to develop a healthy respect for themselves. If they come from a culture or subculture in which school is regarded as unimportant or irrelevant, their self-esteem won't be related to their academic achievement. Depending on how their parents treat them and what their friends think of them, children who don't do well in some activity, such as sports, can often find other areas in which to excel. A child's self-esteem can also be strongly affected by being viewed positively by family, peers, and the immediate community. This is how many ethnic minority children around the world manage to develop healthy self-esteem despite their continuing encounters with prejudice and bigotry by the majority (Spencer, 1988).

self-esteem   Your attitude toward yourself, which can range from positive (high self-esteem) to negative (low self-esteem).

Development of self-esteem is a reciprocal process. Children tend to do well if they are confident in their own abilities; their success then bolsters and increases their self-esteem. In the same way, a "vicious circle" may set in when children perform poorly because of low self-esteem; because of their poor performance, their self-esteem tends to decrease still further. In all, personal successes or failures can lead children to see themselves as winners or losers, "in" or "out." Fortunately, however, many children who start off with academic or social deficits eventually find something they can do well and thus turn things around.

Many teachers use praise to build self-esteem in their students. Used in moderation and given only for legitimate accomplishments, praise can be quite effective. Too much praise can prevent children from developing an accurate sense of their weaknesses as well as their strengths. They may begin to think, "I am great no matter what I do." This can create confusion and problems in peer and school relations (Damon & Hart, 1992), as well as lead to frustration when achievements do not match expectations. Praise that is unwarranted tends to be ineffective and can even alienate children.

In recent years researchers have warned that when children are told that the most important thing in the world is how highly they regard themselves, they hear an implicit message that they are the center of the universe—which can hinder their progress beyond egocentrism. Further, critics contend that overpraised children don't acquire a real sense of right and wrong. For example, they may deny misdeeds even when caught red-handed because they're convinced of their own rightness (Damon, 1991).

CONTENT CHECK
PERSONALITY DEVELOPMENT IN AN EXPANDING SOCIAL WORLD

True–False (answers are on the Companion Website)

1. Erikson's crisis of industry versus inferiority emphasizes experiences in schooling.
2. With regard to personality development, cognitive-developmental theory emphasizes observational learning.
3. With regard to sociocultural development, social-learning theory emphasizes the role of parents.
4. Self-concept is one important component of self-esteem.

Thinking Critically

How might self-concept be influenced by each of the three major perspectives discussed in this section?

Social Knowledge and Reasoning

Children must come to terms with the subtleties of friendship and authority, expanding or conflicting gender roles, and a host of social rules and regulations. One way they do this is through what we might call "direct socialization" by parents and teachers: rewards for desirable behavior, punishments for undesirable behavior. Another way is through observation and imitation of models. In general, conditioning and observational learning play a large role in helping children understand right and wrong. Children also learn about the social world through processes best viewed as psychodynamic. They develop feelings of anxiety in certain situations, and they learn defense mechanisms to reduce the anxiety.

Central to socialization during middle childhood is *social cognition*: thought, knowledge, and understanding pertaining to the world of self in social interactions with others. The social-cognitive approach shifts the emphasis to what the child thinks, partly as a result of reward, punishment, observation, and psychodynamics, but also partly as a result of what the child actively figures out for herself or himself. First we focus on how social cognition develops during middle childhood; then we consider links to the development of moral reasoning.

Development of Social Cognition

During middle childhood and into adolescence, social cognition becomes an increasingly important determinant of behavior. In middle childhood, children must learn how to deal with the complexities of friendship and justice, social rules and manners, gender-role conventions, obedience to authority, and moral law. Children begin to look at their social world and gradually come to understand the principles and rules that govern it (Ross, 1981). Social-cognitive theorists believe that all knowledge, whether scientific, social, or personal, exists as an organized system or structure, not as unrelated bits and pieces. That is, children's understanding of the world does not develop in a piecemeal fashion; rather, children try to make sense of their experience as an organized whole.

In early childhood, children's understanding of the world is limited by egocentrism. During middle childhood, children gradually develop a less self-centered focus that takes into account what other people think and feel. A primary component of social cognition is **social inference**—guesses and assumptions about what another person is feeling, thinking, or intending (Flavell, 1985; Flavell et al., 1993). A young child, for example, hears Mom laughing and assumes that she is happy. An adult might hear something forced about the mother's laughter and instead infer that she is covering up feelings of unhappiness. Although young children cannot make sophisticated inferences, by age 6 they can usually infer when another person's thoughts differ from their own. Around age 8 they understand that people can think about each other's thoughts. By age 10 they can infer what another person is thinking while at the same time inferring that their own thoughts are the subject of another person's thoughts. A child might think, "Johnny is angry with me, and he knows that I know he's angry." Accuracy in social inference continues to develop through late adolescence (Shantz, 1983).

A second component of social cognition is the child's understanding of **social responsibility.** Children gradually accumulate information and understanding about obligations of friendship (such as fairness and loyalty), respect for authority, and concepts of legality and justice. A third component is the understanding of **social regulations** such as customs and conventions. Many customs are first learned by rote or imitation and applied rigidly. Later, children become more flexible and thoughtful about conforming to the customs of their culture.

Piaget on Moral Reasoning and Judgment

As they grow up, most children somehow learn how to tell good from bad and distinguish between kindness and cruelty, generosity and selfishness. Mature moral judgment involves more than rote learning of social rules and conventions. It involves making decisions about right and wrong.

social inference Guesses and assumptions about what another person is feeling, thinking, or intending.

social responsibility Obligations to family, friends, and society at large.

social regulations The rules and conventions governing social interactions.

There is considerable debate as to how children develop a sense of morality. Social-learning theorists believe that conditioning and observational learning are primarily responsible. Modern psychodynamic theorists believe that morality develops as a defense against anxiety, guilt, and shame. Cognitive-developmental theorists believe that, like intellectual development, morality develops in progressive, age-related stages.

Piaget took the latter view. He started by defining morality as an individual's respect for the rules of social order and sense of justice—justice being a concern for give-and-take and equality among individuals (see Hoffman, 1970). According to Piaget (1932/1965), children's moral sense arises from the interaction between their developing cognitive structures and their gradually widening social experience. The moral sense develops in two stages. At the stage of **moral realism** (early middle childhood), children think that all rules must be obeyed as if they were written in stone. To them rules are real, indestructible things, not abstract principles. Games, for example, must be played strictly according to the rules. A child at this stage also judges the morality of an act in terms of its consequences and is unable to judge intentions. For example, a young child will think that a child who accidentally breaks a stack of dishes while setting a table is much guiltier than a child who intentionally breaks one dish out of anger.

Toward the end of middle childhood, children reach the stage of **moral relativism.** Now they realize that rules are created and agreed upon cooperatively by individuals and that they can be changed as the need arises. This leads to the realization that there is no absolute right or wrong and that morality depends not on consequences but on intentions.

Developing a sense of right and wrong involves understanding social rules and gaining experiences in social relationships.

Kohlberg's Six-Stage Theory

Kohlberg (1981, 1984) expanded Piaget's two stages of moral development into six. In developing his theory, he presented participants (children, adolescents, and adults) with stories about **moral dilemmas** and then asked them questions about the stories to assess the kinds of reasoning they used. The leading character in each story was faced with a moral dilemma, and the subject being interviewed was asked to resolve the dilemma. Here is a classic example:

> In Europe, a woman was near death from a special kind of cancer. There was one drug that the doctors thought might save her. It was a form of radium that a druggist in the same town had recently discovered. The drug was expensive to make, but the druggist was charging 10 times what the drug cost him to make. He paid $200 for the radium and charged $2,000 for a small dose of the drug. The sick woman's husband, Heinz, went to everyone he knew to borrow the money, but he could only get together $1,000, which is half of what it cost. He told the druggist that his wife was dying and asked him to sell it cheaper or let him pay later. But the druggist said, "No, I discovered the drug, and I am going to make money from it." So Heinz got desperate and broke into the man's store to steal the drug for his wife. (Kohlberg, 1969, p. 379)

Should Heinz have stolen the drug? What do you think? Why? Was the druggist right to have charged so much more than it cost to make the drug? Why?

Subjects' answers to such questions provided evidence that moral reasoning develops in an orderly fashion and in distinct stages. Kohlberg defined three broad levels of moral reasoning: *preconventional*, *conventional*, and *postconventional*, as summarized in Table 10–1. Each of these is subdivided into two stages.

moral realism   Piaget's term for the first stage of moral development, in which children believe in rules as real, indestructible things.

moral relativism   Piaget's term for the second stage of moral development, in which children realize that rules are agreements that may be changed, if necessary.

moral dilemmas   In Kohlberg's research, narratives in which participants are asked to judge whether a character's behavior was moral or immoral.

Table 10-1   Kohlberg's Stages of Moral Development

Stage			Illustrative Reasoning
LEVEL I. PRECONVENTIONAL (BASED ON PUNISHMENTS AND REWARDS)	Stage 1	Punishment and obedience orientation	Obey rules in order to avoid punishment.
	Stage 2	Naive instrumental hedonism	Obey to obtain rewards, to have favors returned.
LEVEL II. CONVENTIONAL (BASED ON SOCIAL CONFORMITY)	Stage 3	"Good-boy" morality of maintaining good relations, approval of others	Conform to avoid disapproval or dislike of others.
	Stage 4	Authority-maintaining morality	Conform to avoid censure by legitimate authorities, with resulting guilt.
LEVEL III. POSTCONVENTIONAL (BASED ON MORAL PRINCIPLES)	Stage 5	Morality of contract, of individual rights, and of democratically accepted law	Abide by laws of the land for community welfare
	Stage 6	Morality of individual principles of conscience	Abide by universal ethical principles.

Source: Kohlberg, L., *Stages of Moral Development*. Unpublished doctoral dissertation, University of Chicago, 1958. Used by permission. Also adapted from Kohlberg, L., *The Philosophy of Moral Development*. New York: Harper & Row, 1981.

Note two interrelated trends that characterize progress through the six stages: (1) At first reasoning is based on external consequences, whereas later it is based on internalized moral principles; and (2) at first reasoning is highly concrete, whereas later it is quite abstract.

Support for Kohlberg's theory was provided by studies showing that males, at least in Western societies, generally go through the stages in the predicted order. In a 20-year longitudinal study that began with 48 boys, Kohlberg and his associates found remarkable support for the theory (Colby, Kohlberg, Gibbs, & Lieberman, 1983).

Many objections have been raised to Kohlberg's theory and research, however. Researchers have pointed out that it can be very difficult to follow Kohlberg's procedures exactly and to agree on how a child's response to the test should be scored (Rubin & Trotten, 1977). Others have attacked the theory on grounds of **moral absolutism:** It disregards significant cultural differences that determine what is or is not considered moral in a given culture (Baumrind, 1978; Carlo, Koller, Eisenberg, Da Silva, & Frohlich, 1996; Wainryb, 1995). Kohlberg (1978) himself acknowledged that it is necessary to take into account the social and moral norms of the group to which a person belongs. In particular, he concluded that his sixth stage of moral development may not apply to all people in all cultures.

There are other weaknesses in Kohlberg's theory (Power & Reimer, 1978). Kohlberg's research assesses moral attitudes, not moral behavior, and there can be a great difference between thinking about moral questions and behaving morally. Here's a quick example: In most cultures stealing is wrong and the trait of honesty is highly prized. You, of course, are an honest person. So suppose you see someone on the sidewalk unknowingly drop a quarter. You'll probably call the person's attention to it. Suppose it's a ten-dollar bill. You'll do the same, right? Suppose it's a packet of hundred-dollar bills, and the person looks a bit

moral absolutism   Any theory of morality that disregards cultural differences in moral beliefs.

shady and has already turned the corner and there's no one else around. Ask yourself honestly what you would do. Also ask yourself what an honest but extremely poor and desperate parent would do.

Moral decisions are not made in a vacuum. No matter how high our moral principles may be, when the time comes to act on them, our behavior may not reflect our thoughts or beliefs. Regardless of which view of moral development makes the most sense to you (Piaget's or Kohlberg's, or Gilligan's as discussed next), as William Damon (1999) has argued, it is every bit as important to teach children to *act* on their knowledge of right and wrong as it is to teach them right and wrong in the first place. In turn, it is crucial that people incorporate their moral beliefs and attitudes as a central part of their moral identity—that is, the moral component of a person's self-concept. As noted earlier, self-concept organizes and orients behavior; thus, if moral beliefs are at the core, moral behavior becomes more likely.

How are parents to accomplish this? It isn't simple, but Damon has recommended starting with authoritative parenting with its emphasis on ongoing discussions between parents and children (chapter 8), here with regard to behaving in moral ways. In particular he has recommended encouraging the "right kinds of peer relations," with help and feedback for children when the perhaps inevitable moral conflicts arise.

Gilligan's Alternative View

Carol Gilligan (1982; Gilligan & Attanucci, 1994) proposed that because Kohlberg based his theory entirely on interviews with male subjects, he overlooked the possibility that moral development might proceed differently in females than in males. She challenged Kohlberg on grounds of gender bias, noting that females' response to Kohlberg's moral dilemmas generally place them at lower levels in his model of moral development. According to Gilligan, this difference arises because males and females use different criteria in making moral judgments. In traditional U.S. culture, girls and boys are taught from early childhood to value different qualities. Boys are trained to strive for independence and to value abstract thinking. In contrast, girls are taught to be nurturing and caring and to value relationships with others. Gilligan proposed that there are two distinct types of moral reasoning. One is based primarily on the concept of justice, the other primarily on human relationships and caring. The justice perspective is characteristic of traditional masculine thinking; caring for others is more common in traditionally feminine thought. Traditional men often focus on rights, whereas traditional women see moral issues in terms of concern for the needs of others. However, Gilligan noted that gender differences in moral reasoning (like other gender differences) are not absolute. Some women make moral judgments from a justice perspective, and some men make moral judgements from a caring perspective.

Gilligan's subjects were mostly adolescents and young adults. Other researchers have looked at younger children and failed to find gender differences in moral judgments prior to age 10. However, some 10- or 11-year-old boys give rather aggressive responses to test questions—the sorts of responses that are rarely given by girls. For example, in one study children listened to a story about a porcupine who, needing a home for the winter, moved in with a family of moles. The moles soon found that they were constantly being pricked by the porcupine's sharp needles. What should they do? Only boys responded with suggestions like "Shoot the porcupine" or "Pluck out his quills." Girls tended to look for solutions that would harm neither the moles nor the porcupine—in other words, caring solutions (Garrod, Beal, & Shin, 1989).

Eisenberg's View

Nancy Eisenberg (1989a, 1989b) argued that Kohlberg's mistake was not in placing too much emphasis on abstract justice; it was in making the stages too rigid and absolute. Her position was that children's moral development is not predictable and narrowly determined. Many factors go into children's moral judgments, ranging from the social customs of the culture in which they are reared to how they feel at a particular moment. Children (and adults) are capable of making moral judgments at a higher level one moment and at a lower level the next. They may even make judgments at a higher level for some issues (whether they would help someone who was injured) than for others (whether they would invite someone they didn't like to their home).

With regard to gender differences, Eisenberg also found that between the ages of 10 and 12 girls give more caring and empathic responses than boys. This she attributed to girls maturing more rapidly than boys. By late adolescence, boys catch up. Eisenberg and her colleagues have found few gender differences in the responses of older adolescents (Eisenberg, 1989a; Eisenberg et al., 1987).

CONTENT CHECK
SOCIAL KNOWLEDGE AND REASONING

True–False (answers are on the Companion Website)

1. An understanding of social responsibility is a component of social cognition.
2. In Piaget's theory, moral relativism precedes moral realism.
3. Kohlberg's theory was developed by studying whether participants judged characters such as Heinz to be moral or immoral.
4. In Kohlberg's theory, moral thinking progresses from concrete to abstract and from external to internal.
5. Gilligan's theory emphasizes caring instead of justice.

Thinking Critically

Why does Kohlberg's theory not apply exclusively to males and Gilligan's theory not exclusively to females?

Continuing Family Influences

In spite of the time children spend in school, the family normally continues to be the most important socializing influence. At the same time, their expanding cognitive abilities enable children to learn ever more sophisticated social concepts and rules, whether the rules are taught explicitly or simply implied by the behavior of others.

Social learning occurs in the context of relationships that are sometimes close and secure, sometimes anxiety provoking, and sometimes full of conflict. In this section we examine the family as the context of personality development and socialization. We look closely at the changing forces in family life that affect children, including stress, divorce, and the permanent absence of a parent.

Parent-Child Interactions and Relationships

In middle childhood the overall nature of parent-child interactions changes. Children express less direct anger toward their parents and are less likely to whine, yell, or hit than when they were younger. Parents are less concerned with promoting autonomy and establishing daily routines and more concerned with children's work habits and achievement (Lamb, Hwang, Ketterlinus, & Fracasso, 1999). School-age children need more subtle monitoring of their behavior than previously, but parental monitoring is still very important. Monitoring means knowing where your children are and what they're doing, and also that what they are doing is appropriate—both socially and with regard to schoolwork and other responsibilities. Researchers find that well-monitored children receive higher grades than those who are less monitored (Crouter, MacDermid, McHale, & Perry Jernkins, 1990).

Parents teach the value of warmth and affection by their own behavior.

Optimal Parenting   What is *optimal* parenting? Opinions on this subject have differed over the years. Contemporary research emphasizes that a major goal of parenting is to increase children's **self-regulated behavior**—basically, their ability to control and direct their behavior and meet requirements that parents and others impose upon them. As we saw in Chapter 8, authoritative approaches to discipline are often more successful than other approaches in helping children develop self-regulation. When a parent relies on verbal reasoning and suggestions, the child tends to negotiate rather than react with defiance (Lamb, Ketterlinus, & Fracasso, 1992).

Reasoning is related both to prosocial behavior and to compliance with social rules. Parents who remind their children of the effects of their actions on others tend to have children who are more popular and whose moral standards are more fully internalized. In contrast, when parents simply assert their power over the child (as in authoritarian parenting), their children tend not to develop internalized standards and controls—cultural exceptions notwithstanding. Studies consistently find that children who comply with adults' demands when the adults are present, but not when the adults are absent, are more likely to have parents who used power-assertive techniques.

Parents are more successful in fostering self-regulated behavior if they gradually increase the child's involvement in family decisions. In a series of studies on parental dialogue and discipline, Eleanor Maccoby (1992) concluded that children adjust best when their parents foster what she called **coregulation.** The parents gradually build cooperation and share responsibility in anticipation of the teenage years, by which time they expect their children to make most decisions for themselves. In preparation, they engage in frequent discussions and negotiations with their children. The parents see themselves as building a framework for responsible decision making.

The concept of scaffolding is especially useful in understanding optimal parenting. Children learn about the social world in complex social contexts in which they are accompanied by parents or other, more competent partners (Rogoff, 1990). Imagine a family attending a large wedding. Socially competent parents help their children anticipate what will happen. They may discuss the meaning of the event and specific rituals, cueing their children as to how adults expect them to behave. Only small parts of the broad set of shared meanings of "marriage" and "wedding" are conveyed at one time, ideally at a level just beyond the child's current understanding.

It has been argued that socialization should not be viewed as a process in which control shifts from parents to child as the child becomes more autonomous and self-regulating. Instead, it is a process of mutual or shared coregulation that

self-regulated behavior   Personal behavior controlled and directed by the child.

coregulation   Development of a sense of shared responsibility between parents and children.

will last throughout the participants' lives—or until the relationship ends. Maccoby (1992) suggested that enduring parental influence stems from the strength and health of the parent-child relationship, which is particularly important during middle childhood.

The Changing Nature of the Family

Until recently research on parenting was based primarily on the so-called traditional U.S. family: mother, father, and two or three children. Things have changed. Having children isn't going out of style—there were almost 4 million live births in the United States in 1997 (U.S. Census Bureau, 1999). What has changed is getting married in the first place, as well as the likelihood of staying married. Either way, single parenthood has become commonplace. About one-third of those births were to unmarried mothers—an increase of almost 50% since 1985 (U.S. Census Bureau, 1999). In turn, in 1998 there were nearly 9½ million single parents caring for their own children. Table 10–2 breaks this figure down by age range of the children and whether the single parent was female or male, also whether the parent was employed.

U.S. families have also undergone rapid change with regard to mothers working. Once children enter school, the majority of U.S. mothers enter the paid workforce. In 1948 only 26% of the mothers of school-age children (ages 6–17) worked outside the home; in 1975 the figure was 51% and in 1996 it was over 76% (U.S. Census Bureau, 1997). Since the early 1950s, mothers of school-age children have been more likely to work than married women without children—owing partly to the greater financial needs of families with children, partly to the larger number of single-parent women (Scarr, Phillips, & McCartney, 1989). Figure 10–1 illustrates trends for all women (with or without children) in the U.S. labor force from 1960 to 1998. Note that the percentage of working married women who were living with husbands almost doubled during this period.

Families and Stress   An important consideration in changing families is the stress experienced both by parents and by children. Many life situations are inherently stressful for children and their families, including poverty, divorce, moving to a new town, suffering a serious illness or injury, or growing up in a dangerous neighborhood (see "A Closer Look," page 364). What determines a child's ability to cope constructively with these stresses? One factor is the sheer

Table 10–2   U.S. Single Parents Caring for Their Own Children and Employment Status, 1998 (in Thousands)

	Employed	Unemployed	Total
Own children under age 6			
Single mothers	1,867	1,068	2,935
Single fathers	660	104	764
Own children age 6–17			
Single mothers	3,573	1,065	4,638
Single fathers	913	162	1,075
			9,412

Source: U.S. Census Bureau, 1999.

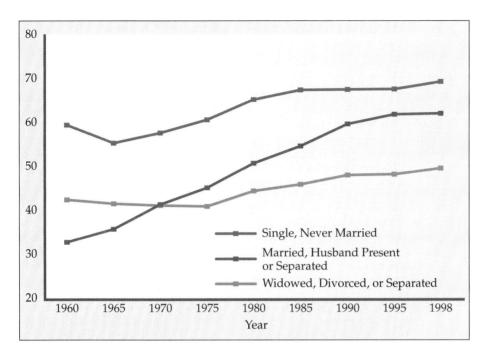

Figure 10–1 **Percentages of Women in the U.S. Civilian Labor Force, 1960–1998.**

Source: U.S. Census Bureau, 1999.

number of stressful situations in a child's life; a child (or adult) who can deal successfully with one stressful event may be overwhelmed if forced to deal with several at the same time (Hetherington, 1984). A second factor is the child's perception or understanding of the event. For example, the first day of school is a major event in a child's life. A child who knows what to expect and who can use this milestone as a sign of increasing maturity will experience less stress in making the transition.

Research clearly indicates that close-knit, adaptable families with open communication patterns and good problem-solving skills are better able to weather stressful events (Brenner, 1984). Social support systems such as neighbors, relatives, friendship networks, or self-help groups are also valuable.

From a different perspective, temperament and early personality characteristics influence children's ability to cope with stressful environments. Over a 30-year period Emmy Werner (1989, 1995) studied a group that she termed **resilient children.** The children had been born on one of the Hawaiian islands and raised in family environments that were marred by poverty, parental conflict or divorce, alcoholism, and mental illness. Yet they developed into self-confident, successful, and emotionally stable adults. Because most children reared under such conditions do not fare nearly as well, Werner was interested in learning how these children managed to thrive in spite of their unfavorable environment. She found that they had been temperamentally "easy" and lovable babies who had developed secure attachments to a parent or grandparent in the first year of life. Later, if that parent or grandparent was no longer available, these children had the ability to find someone else—another adult or even a sibling or friend—who could provide the emotional support they needed. Other researchers have found that positive self-esteem and good self-organization are strongly related to resilience in children—especially those who are maltreated (Cicchetti & Rogosch, 1997).

Coping with Single Parenting About 13% of U.S. families with two parents have incomes below the poverty line, but nearly half of all families headed by single women live in poverty (U.S. Census Bureau, 1997). If a mother did not

resilient children Children who overcome difficult environments to lead socially competent lives.

A CLOSER LOOK

GROWING UP IN DANGER

It was morning, and a 19-year-old gang member who had been gunned down in the Watts neighborhood of Los Angeles lay on the sidewalk in a pool of blood as hundreds of children walked by, lunch boxes and school bags in hand, on their way to the 102nd Street Elementary School. A few months later, children playing in the schoolyard dropped to the ground as five shots nearby claimed another victim. On yet another occasion, an outdoor assembly was disrupted by gunshots and wailing sirens as students watched a neighborhood man scuffle with police officers (Timnick, 1989).

Such experiences are not rare for U.S. children living in inner cities and some suburbs, and children in many other parts of the world. Children often fall asleep to the sound of gunfire. Children as young as age 6 are recruited as drug runners. Some babies' first words and gestures are the names and signs of their parents' gangs (Timnick, 1989). Researchers have found that children growing up in inner-city "war zones"

are often anxious and depressed. Children who experienced violence themselves or witnessed the brutal murder of a parent, sibling, or friend are especially prone to severe psychological distress.

Posttraumatic stress disorder (PTSD; see Chapter 1) was first used to describe the psychological problems exhibited by some war veterans. These veterans had vivid nightmares, flashbacks about combat, and difficulty sleeping, concentrating, and controlling their impulses. They were either withdrawn, aggressive, or both. Research indicates that children living in inner-city war zones have similar behavioral patterns. Many engage in aggressive play, have nightmares, and are troubled by sudden memories that intrude during school or other activities.

Chronic, ongoing violence produces a state of sustained stress. Young children who live with constant violence are fearful, depressed, and anxious (Garbarino, Kostelny, & Dubrow, 1991). Many have trouble concentrating in school and suffer other school-related

problems. They may fear being abandoned and may become overly aggressive and cocky to disguise their fears. Many develop blunted emotions—they're afraid to develop affection for people who may be killed or who may abandon them. In turn, parents are likely to underestimate the extent of their children's psychological distress, either because the children don't talk about their fears or because the parents cannot acknowledge their children's emotional pain, which they feel helpless to remedy (Elkind, 1981).

The American Psychological Association's Committee on Violence and Youth recommends a community approach to the problem of children living in violent surroundings. Programs involving health care, recreation, and vocational training should be built around children's developmental needs. In addition, role models from the community and peer support groups should be available to help children find alternatives to activities involving violence and drug use.

graduate from high school, the likelihood that the family income will be below the poverty level is almost 90% (Children's Defense Fund, 1992).

Children who grow up in poverty in a home headed only by a mother are at risk in many ways (McLoyd & Wilson, 1990). Not having a father lowers a family's social status as well as its economic status. Housing is likely to be crowded; frequent moves are common. Meals may be skimpy and nutritionally poor. Medical care may be lacking. Also, the women who head these homes are often psychologically stressed by their struggle for survival. Many suffer from depression or anxiety, which interferes with their ability to be supportive and attentive parents.

Children who grow up in these homes may be at a disadvantage in a number of ways that affect both their psychological health and their intellectual development. As a result, they are less likely than other children to improve their socioeconomic status when they become adults. They are also more likely to become single parents themselves. Thus, the problems are passed on to the next generation (McLanahan & Booth, 1989).

Researchers have tried to identify factors that can break the cycle of depression and hopelessness that is characteristic of many low-income, single-parent families. They have found, for example, that when mothers in single-parent families work at jobs that they like, their children have greater self-esteem and a greater sense of family organization and togetherness compared to children whose mothers do not work or who work at jobs that they intensely dislike. Working single mothers have an especially strong impact on their daughters, who place greater emphasis on independence and achievement than mothers who do not work (Alessandri, 1992).

Researchers have also examined specific factors in single-parenting that negatively affect children's relationship with their mothers and their feelings about themselves. When Vonnie McLoyd (1994) and colleagues studied how maternal unemployment and work interruption affected a sample of 241 single U.S. black mothers and their children, they found an indirect negative effect on children's well-being. That is, economic hardship took a toll on the mother's psychological functioning, in turn affecting her ability to be an effective parent and therefore the mother-child relationship. The mothers in the study showed symptoms of depression when they were unemployed; when depressed, they tended to punish their children more frequently. In turn, children who were punished frequently showed greater signs of cognitive distress and depression.

What, if anything, can break this cycle of economic hardship, maternal depression, and psychological consequences for children in single-parent families? McLoyd and colleagues found that when mothers perceived that tangible help was available in the form of goods and services—when they knew, for example, that someone outside their family would help them run errands if they were sick—they had fewer depressive symptoms, felt better about their role as mothers, and punished their children less.

Social support helps, but not always. In one study (Chase-Lansdale, Brooks-Gunn, & Zamsky, 1994), the researchers examined the disciplinary styles, problem-solving strategies, and emotionality of U.S. black grandmothers, mothers, and children who shared the same residence. In this built-in support system, a complex interplay of helpful, though sometimes conflicting, parenting was exhibited by both the mothers and the grandmothers. The effects of coresidence on parenting were most likely to be positive when the mothers were in their teens. Older mothers were more likely to provide positive parenting when they did not live in a three-generation household. In addition, part-time grandmothers provided better parenting and social support than grandmothers who lived in the same family unit.

Despite the stresses that single-parent families face, many do succeed. Table 10–3 provides some guidelines for making a single-parent family work.

Children in close-knit adaptable families generally tend to be best-equipped to cope with stressful situations.

Children of Divorce

About half of all U.S. marriages end in divorce; each year over a million U.S. children experience the breakup of their families (U.S. Census Bureau, 1997). Here we look mainly at the effects of divorce on children; we return to the effects on the parents in Chapter 16.

Psychological Consequences of Divorce Family breakup affects children in a number of ways. Both parents strongly influence their children's development; a divorce means that both parents will no longer be equally available to their children. Moreover, usually the family has already been in a state of tension and stress for a long time. The children may have heard the word *divorce* spoken (or shouted) in their homes for months or even years, often accompanied by anger, fights, and crying. Even very young children know when their parents' relationship is disturbed. Children wonder what will happen to them if their parents divorce.

Table 10-3   Seven Guidelines for Single Parenting

1. Accept responsibilities and challenges. Maintain a positive attitude and the feeling that solutions are possible.
2. Give the parental role high priority. Successful single parents are willing to sacrifice time, money, and energy to meet their children's needs.
3. Use consistent, nonpunitive discipline.
4. Emphasize open communication. Encourage trust and open expression of feelings.
5. Foster individuality within a supportive family unit.
6. Recognize the need for self-nurturance. Parents must understand the need to take care of themselves in order to be able to help their children.
7. Emphasize rituals and traditions, including bedtime routines, holiday celebrations, and special family activities.

Source: Adapted from Olson & Haynes, 1993.

When one parent finally leaves, children may fear that the other parent will also abandon them. They may feel sad, confused, angry, or anxious. They may become depressed or disruptive at home or at school. Many children—especially younger ones—feel that they are to blame for the divorce: Were it not for something they did wrong, maybe their parents would still be together. Children may even try to bring their parents back together, perhaps by being very good; they may also fantasize about a reconciliation (Hetherington, 1992; Hetherington, Stanley-Hagan, & Anderson, 1989; Wallerstein, Corbin, & Lewis, 1988). Some parents complicate things even further by not being sure about their divorce at first, perhaps making failed attempts to get back together and falsely raising their children's hopes.

Relationships with both parents change during and after a divorce. Children may become defiant and argumentative; as adolescents, they may disengage themselves emotionally. Often children are forced to serve as sounding boards for their parents, listening to each parent criticize the other at length. They may be at the center of a custody battle and may be asked to choose sides. The parents may compete for their children's affection and try to bribe them with gifts or privileges. Parents often are under considerable stress right after the divorce and may be incapable of providing warmth or control; they may be less affectionate, inconsistent in applying discipline, uncommunicative, or unsupportive. Also, children may become upset when their parents start new relationships. For example, a boy who is living with his mother may take over the role of "man of the house" and feel threatened when a "rival" appears on the scene (Hetherington et al., 1989).

Among the most important factors that determine how children react to divorce are these:

1. *The amount of hostility accompanying the divorce.* If there is a great deal of hostility and bitterness, it is much harder for children to adjust. Parental conflict lowers children's sense of well-being. When parents fight, children develop fear and anger. They are especially vulnerable when they are forced to choose between their parents (Amato, 1993). Ongoing squabbles or legal battles over custody, division of property, child support, visitation, or child-care arrangements make the situation much more difficult for both children and parents (Rutter & Garmezy, 1983).

2. *The amount of actual change in the child's life.* If children continue to live in the same home, attend the same school, and have the same friends after a divorce, their adjustment problems are likely to be less severe. In contrast, if their daily life is disrupted in major ways—moving back and forth from one parent's household to the other's, losing friends, entering a new school— their self-confidence and sense of order are likely to be shaken. The more changes a child is forced to make, especially in the period immediately following the divorce, the more difficult the adjustment (Hetherington & Camara, 1984).

3. *The nature of the parent-child relationship.* Long-term involvement and emotional support from *both* parents help considerably. Some researchers have observed that the nature of ongoing parent-child interactions is much more important than whether both parents are present in the home (Rutter & Garmezy, 1983). In fact, sometimes children of divorce are better off than they would have been had their parents stayed together and continued to argue and fight.

Consequences in Daily Life Immediately after a divorce, children—especially those between the ages of 5 and 7—often appear confused. They exhibit behavioral difficulties at home and at school. Their daily lives and their understanding of their social world are severely disrupted. The long-established patterns of their family life have broken down. Whereas in the past the world was predictable—after work every evening, the entire family sat down to dinner, and bedtime was at 8:00—unpredictability is now the rule. Consequently, children often test the rules to see if the world still works the way it did before. They may have to be told by their mother: "I know it's upsetting that Daddy's not coming home any more. But that doesn't mean you don't have to go to bed at 8:00. You still have to get up early in the morning and go to school. And you still need your rest." Teachers can help by gently reminding the child of the school's rules and expectations and by being emotionally supportive. Children who are seriously hurt by divorce are more likely to repeat a grade or be expelled from school and be treated for emotional and behavioral problems than children of intact families.

Reconstituted Families When the custodial parent remarries and therefore forms a **reconstituted family,** as a majority do nowadays, some children welcome the arrival of the stepparent. For others, though, a parent's remarriage represents yet another difficult adjustment. Children may be distressed because there is no longer any chance of reuniting their parents. They may resent the stepparent's attempts to win their affection or discipline them. They may feel divided loyalties to their original parents and feel guilty about "abandoning" the noncustodial parent by giving affection to the stepparent. Children may also be unhappy about having to "share" their parent with his or her new partner, and they may worry about being "left out" of the new family. Many children have the additional problem of having to learn to live with stepsiblings (Hetherington et al., 1989).

How Enduring Are the Effects of Divorce on Children? As summarized by Mavis Hetherington and Margaret Stanley-Hagan (1999), the negative effects on many children of divorce and the corresponding negative behaviors of these children are minimal and relatively temporary, but many other children suffer emotionally, socially, and academically. Even for children who initially appear to cope well with divorce, serious adjustment problems sometimes emerge later, during adolescence and the attainment of puberty (Chapter 11). "Compared to

reconstituted family Also known as stepfamily; a family where a mother or father with children has remarried to produce a new family.

their peers in nondivorced homes, adolecents in divorced families are two to three times as likely to drop out of school, to become pregnant, or to engage in antisocial and delinquent behavior . . ." (p. 131). Similar problems may persist into young adulthood.

However, as Hetherington and Stanley-Hagan also pointed out, children who move from a disruptive or abusive home environment may instead benefit. And in the long run, most children are quite resilient and adaptive in dealing with their parents' divorce. Once again, it depends to a major extent on how the parents handle the transition and what they do afterward.

CONTENT CHECK
CONTINUING FAMILY INFLUENCES

True–False (answers are on the Companion Website)
1. Helping a child develop self-regulation is a prime concern in optimal parenting.
2. About half of all live births in the United States in 1997 were to unmarried women.
3. Regardless of marital status, the percentage of U.S. women who are employed has increased since 1960.
4. About half of all U.S. marriages end in divorce.
5. Children are always better off if their parents stay together instead of divorcing.

Thinking Critically
What are the most important things parents can do to ease their child or children's distress when the parents divorce?

Peer Relationships and Social Competence

Peer relationships become increasingly important in middle childhood and exert a major influence on social and personality development. In this section we begin with a look at individual friendships, how they form, and how they benefit children. Then we consider peer relationships on a larger scale, with emphasis on peer pressure.

Concepts of Friendship
The ability to infer the thoughts, expectations, feelings, and intentions of others plays a central role in understanding what it means to be a friend. Children who can view things from another person's perspective are better able to develop strong, intimate relationships with others.

Robert Selman (1976, 1981) studied the friendships of children aged 7 to 12. His approach was similar to that used in Kohlberg's studies of moral development: Tell children stories involving a "relationship" dilemma, then ask them questions to assess their concepts of other people, their self-awareness and ability to reflect, their concepts of personality, and their ideas about friendship. Here's an example of the stories Selman used:

Kathy and Debbie have been best friends since they were 5. A new girl, Jeannette, moves into their neighborhood, but Debbie dislikes her because she

Friendship and fun go hand-in-hand.

considers Jeannette a showoff. Later, Jeannette invites Kathy to go to the circus on its one day in town. Kathy's problem is that she has promised to play with Debbie that same day. What will Kathy do?

Such stories raise questions about the nature of relationships, old friendships versus new ones, and loyalty and trust. They require children to think and talk about how friendships are formed and maintained, and about what is important in a friendship. On the basis of the children's responses, Selman (1981) described four stages of friendship; these are summarized in Table 10–4. At the first stage (age 6 and younger), a friend is just a playmate—someone who lives

Table 10-4   Selman's Stages of Friendship Development

Stage	Age	Characteristics
1	6 and under	Friendship is based on physical or geographic factors; children are self-centered, with no understanding of the perspectives of others.
2	7–9	Friendship begins to be based on reciprocity and awareness of others' feelings; it begins to be based on social actions and evaluation by each other.
3	9–12	Friendship is based on genuine give-and-take; friends are seen as people who help each other; mutual evaluation of each other's actions occurs; the concept of trust appears.
4	11–12 and older	Friendship is seen as a stable, continuing relationship based on trust; children can observe the relationship from the perspective of a third party.

Source: Adapted from Selman (1981).

nearby, goes to the same school, or has desirable toys. There is no understanding of the other person's perspective, so Kathy simply goes to the circus. At the second stage (7 to 9), awareness of another person's feelings begins to appear. A child at this stage might say that Kathy could go to the circus with Jeannette and remain friends with Debbie only if Debbie did not object. At the third stage (9 to 12), friends are seen as people who help each other, and the concept of trust appears. The child realizes that the friendship between Kathy and Debbie is different from the friendship between Kathy and Jeannette because the older friendship is based on long-standing trust. At the fourth stage, which was rare among the 11- and 12-year-olds studied, children are fully capable of looking at a relationship from another's perspective. A child at this level might say, "Kathy and Debbie should be able to understand each other and work it out."

Selman argued that the key to developmental changes in children's friendships is the ability to take another person's perspective. Not all researchers agree, however. For example, there is evidence that younger children implicitly know more about the rules and expectations of being a friend than they can explain to an interviewer (Rizzo & Corsaro, 1988). Also, real friendships are more complicated and changing than Selman's model implies. They may involve mutuality, trust, and reciprocity at one time, competitiveness and conflict at another (Hartup, 1996). Conflict in particular may be intrinsic to friendship. Such complexities are not easily handled by a model that looks only at the cognitive aspects of children's friendships and ignores the emotional aspects (Berndt, 1983). Finally, as noted by Willard Hartup (1996), if we are to understand the effects of children's friendships fully, it is also necessary to know something about *who* the children's friends are.

Functions of Friendship

Children and adults alike benefit from having close, confiding relationships. Friendships help children learn social concepts and social skills and develop self-esteem. Friendship provides structure for activity; reinforces and solidifies group norms, attitudes, and values; and serves as a backdrop for individual and group competition (Hartup, 1970, 1996). Children with stable, "satisfying" friendships have better attitudes toward school and achieve more (Ladd, Kochenderfer, & Coleman, 1996).

Friendship patterns shift during childhood (Piaget, 1932/1965). The egocentric pattern of Selman's first stage changes during middle childhood, when children begin to form closer relationships and have "best" friends. In later childhood and adolescence, *group friendships* become common. The groups are generally large, with several boys or girls regularly participating together in various activities.

Children who are friends may complement each other. One may be dominant, the other submissive. One friend may use the other as a model, while the other may enjoy "teaching." Friendship can also be a vehicle of self-expression. Children sometimes choose friends whose personalities are quite different from their own. An outgoing or impulsive child may choose a more reserved or restrained child as a close friend. As a pair, the children may demonstrate more personality traits than either child could alone (Hartup, 1970). Of course, friends are rarely complete opposites. Friendship pairs that last usually have many shared values, attitudes, and expectations. Indeed, the relationship may be egalitarian, with neither friend playing a clear or consistent role.

With a friend, children can share their feelings, their fears, every detail of their lives. Having a best friend to confide in teaches a child how to relate to others openly without being self-conscious. Having friends also allows for sharing secrets, although the kinds of secrets children understand and share (or don't share) change during middle childhood. Younger children are less likely to "keep" secrets from adults (Watson & Valtin, 1997). Otherwise, close friendships are more common among girls; boys tend to reveal less of themselves to their friends (Maccoby, 1990; Z. Rubin, 1980).

Some childhood friendships last throughout life; more often, however, friendships change. Best friends may move away or transfer to another school, and when this happens children may feel a real sense of loss—until they make new friends. Sometimes friends become interested in other people who meet their needs in new and different ways. Sometimes friends just grow apart or develop new interests.

Finally, although research indicates that virtually all children have at least one *unilateral* friendship, many children lack *reciprocal* friendships characterized by give-and-take (George & Hartmann, 1996). Some children are consistently unsuccessful at forming meaningful friendships. Children who are rejected by their peers are at risk for maladjustment later in life, but not all children who are rejected by peers are "friendless." Even a single close friend helps a child cope with the negative effects of being disliked and isolated from peers (Rubin & Coplan, 1992). Research has also shown that many children who are consistently rejected by their peers still believe they have friends, although the friendships are weak and unsatisfying (Parker & Asher, 1993).

Peer Groups

A **peer group** is more than just a group of kids. It is relatively stable and stays together, and its members interact with one another regularly and share values. Group norms govern interactions and influence each member. Finally, there are status differences within the group—some members are leaders, some followers.

Developmental Trends   Peer groups are important throughout middle childhood, but a general shift occurs in both their organization and their significance during the years from 6 to 12.

In early middle childhood, peer groups are relatively informal. They are usually created by the children themselves, they have very few operating rules, and turnover in their membership is rapid. It is true that many of the group's activities, such as playing games or riding bikes, may be carried out according to precise rules. But the structure of the group itself is quite flexible.

The group takes on greater significance for its members when they reach the ages of 10 to 12. Conformity to group norms becomes extremely important, and peer pressure becomes much more effective. Groups also develop a more formal structure. They may have special membership requirements, club meetings, and initiation rites. At this time, also, separation of the sexes becomes especially noticeable. Peer groups are now almost invariably composed of one sex, and groups of different sexes maintain different interests, activities, and styles of interaction (Maccoby, 1990). Strict attitudes about rules, conformity, and sex segregation usually do not diminish until mid-adolescence.

Group Formation   Children are constantly thrown together in schools, camps, and neighborhoods. Groups form quickly. Role differentiation develops within groups, and shared values and interests emerge. Mutual influences and expectations grow, and a feeling of tradition takes shape. This process is almost universal across cultures.

peer group   A group of three or more people of similar age who interact with each other and who share norms and goals.

Peer groups form wherever children with common values, interests, or goals are thrown together.

Classic research on how fifth-grade boys in summer camp form peer groups indicated that groups formed quickly and developed shared values and norms; the boys even named their groups. Most important, when groups competed against each other, feelings of exclusiveness and hostility quickly developed. When the groups were later required to cooperate, hostility was greatly reduced (Sherif, Harvey, White, Hood, & Sherif, 1961). Such findings are typical of how groups form and compete in classrooms, athletic competitions, and neighborhood or ethnic rivalries.

Status Within the Peer Group   If we watch schoolchildren during free time, such as lunch or recess, we can observe the development of roles within groups. One girl is surrounded by children who are eager to get her attention. Another stands on the fringes, ignored. Three boys run by, shouting. A muscular child grabs a smaller child's toy, and the child cries. Scenes like this occur throughout the world, wherever there are children.

Each peer group has some members who are popular and who are not. In addition to factors discussed in Chapter 8, peer acceptance is often related to an individual's overall adjustment—enthusiasm and active participation, ability to cooperate, and responsiveness to social overtures. "Getting in sync" tends to be reinforced because of its effects on self-esteem and social self-confidence. The adjustment of well-liked children is bolstered by their popularity; inept children become even more ill at ease when ignored or rejected by the group.

Academic performance and athletic ability also influence popularity. In general, popular children are brighter than average and do well in school. Slow learners are often made fun of or ignored. Athletic ability is particularly important in settings like camps or playgrounds, where the peer group is involved in sports.

Peer acceptance can be influenced by teacher feedback. In one study (White & Kistner, 1992), a group of first and second graders viewed a videotape of a problem child (an actor) who was rejected by his peers. The positive comments that the teacher made about the child when the video was over encouraged students to change their negative perceptions. Thus, by accepting problem children—but not their problem *behavior*—teachers can influence peer group status.

Popularity is affected by both extreme aggressiveness and extreme timidity. No one likes a bully, so the overly aggressive child is shunned. The child may then become even more aggressive out of frustration or in an attempt to win by force what he or she cannot win by persuasion. Similarly, a timid, anxious child is at risk of becoming a chronic victim, picked on not just by bullies but even by nonagressive children (Dodge, Coie, Pettit, & Price, 1990; Newcomb, Bukowski, & Pattee, 1993; Perry, Williard, & Perry, 1990). Timid children also show little prosocial behavior and suffer the most from peer rejection. They tend to be lonelier and to worry more about their peer relationships than aggressive children who are rejected by peers (Parkhurst & Asher, 1992).

Status within the group affects the way children feel about themselves. In one study (Crick & Ladd, 1993) researchers assessed the feelings of loneliness, social anxiety, and social avoidance reported by a group of third and fifth graders. It was found that the way children feel about themselves and whether they blame themselves or others for what happens to them depend on their experiences with peers. Rejected children reported a higher degree of loneliness and had a greater tendency to blame unsatisfactory relationships on others than did children who were accepted peer-group members. Unpopular children often have traits that make them different from their classmates—obesity, skin of the "wrong" color, or even an unusual name (as discussed in "In

IN THEORY, IN FACT

NICKNAMES

Remember the good old days in grade school, when you were called everything but the name your parents gave you? You may have been lucky enough to have borne the equivalent of "Chief" "Queenie," or "Ace," or unfortunate enough to be called "Dumbo" or "Four-Eyes." Such labels may seem amusing to adults, but they can be painful for children. Nicknames teach children about social status, friendship, and morality.

To better understand the significance of nicknames, Rom Harré (1980) surveyed thousands of youngsters and adults in the United States, Great Britain, Spain, Mexico, Japan, and the Arab nations. They found that children between the ages of 5 and 15 often create separate, secret worlds for themselves and that nicknames may perform important social functions in these worlds. One of the main reasons that children bestow nicknames on each other is to separate "us" from "them." Children who have no nick-

names are considered too insignificant to bother with. They tend to be unpopular and isolated from the rest of the group. As Harré (1980) pointed out, "To be nicknamed is to be seen as having an attribute that entitles one to social attention, even if that attention is unpleasant. Thus, it may be better to be called 'Sewage' than merely 'John'" (p. 81). In other words, having even a bad nickname is better than having no nickname at all.

The "Lamers" and "Chunkies" of the group are used as examples by group leaders to show what people are *not* supposed to be like. They are walking advertisements of violated group standards. Through nicknames, children proclaim what is acceptable to society and what is not. Any behavior, style, or physical characteristic that does not meet society's standards can become the source of a nickname. Thus, when children call others "Stinky" or "Pimplehead," they indicate that they

have internalized adult norms for cleanliness and appearance.

Unfortunately, nicknaming can be very painful. However, children are often willing victims of the process: "It is not necessarily the fattest, stupidest, and dirtiest who acquire the names 'Hippo' or 'Tapeworm-Woman,' but those who willingly bear the humiliation of being symbols of childhood greed, improvidence, and aversion to washing" (Harré, 1980, p. 81).

Children use nicknames differently in various cultures. Nicknames like "The Lame One" or "The Three-Legged One," which poke fun at physical disabilities, are much more common in the Arab nations than in England or Japan. Japanese children are more likely to use animal and insect analogies. In any culture, though, it seems that nicknames help children build the social reality they take with them into adulthood. What's in a name? In the case of nicknames, there's a lot more than you might expect.

Each peer group has members who are popular and members who are not.

Theory, In Fact," page 373). These traits can reduce children's conformity to group standards.

Peer Group Conformity How insistent is the pressure to conform to group standards? Conforming to the peer group can be a normal, healthy, and often desirable behavior. As part of their daily behavior, children conform to peer group standards as well as to adult expectations. But children sometimes conform excessively to group norms—even when these standards are not helpful to the individual child, to the group as a whole, or to the society at large.

Several characteristics are common among highly conforming children. They have feelings of inferiority and low "ego strength" (Hartup, 1970). They tend to be more dependent or anxious than other children and are exceptionally sensitive to social cues for behavior (Graziano, Leone, Musser, & Lautenschlager, 1987). They also tend to *self-monitor* what they do and say very closely. They are especially concerned with how they appear to others, and constantly compare themselves to their peers.

Of course, peer pressure can be positive as well as negative. Studies have shown, for example, that peer group influence can encourage academic motivation. When peer group formation was studied in classes of fourth and fifth graders, researchers found that peer groups tend to be composed of students with similar motivations regarding school (Kindermann, 1993). Thus, because peer group members identify with each other, the peer group can foster learning and academic success. Children are actually more likely to conform to peer pressure when it is positive than when it involves misbehavior such as stealing, drinking, or using illegal drugs. When peer pressure involves antisocial acts, boys are more likely than girls to yield to it (Brown, Clasen, & Eicher, 1986). Children who are unsupervised after school also tend to conform to antisocial peer pressure more than those who are monitored by adults (Steinberg, 1986).

Conformity is especially meaningful to children during late middle childhood, when they begin moving beyond the security of family life. Preadolescents typically have a strong need to belong, to feel accepted, and to be part of a group. These needs coexist with an equally strong need for autonomy or mastery. Children try to exert some control over their social and physical environments, to understand the rules and limits, and to find a place within these limits. Thus, they become very involved in making rules and learning rituals.

Unfortunately, peer groups sometimes breed conformity that manifests itself in prejudice toward people who are different. The final section of the chapter examines how prejudice develops during middle childhood, with emphasis on the development of what has historically been called "racial" prejudice. Such prejudice of course remains very real even though "race" itself has no scientific basis (Chapter 3). Here we use the preferable term *ethnicity*, which also broadens the discussion. In the United States, although the spotlight and most of the research has been on white prejudice toward blacks, a great many other targets of prejudice exist as well—nor are whites the only people who exhibit prejudice.

In-Groups, Out-Groups, and Prejudice

prejudice A negative attitude formed without adequate reason and usually directed toward people because of their membership in a certain group.

discrimination Treating others in a prejudiced manner.

Prejudice means having negative attitudes toward people because of their membership in a group that is defined on the basis of ethnicity, religion, or some other noticeable set of attributes. Prejudice implies an *in-group*—people who believe they possess desirable characteristics—and an out-group—people who are different and undesirable. **Discrimination** means acting on the basis of prejudice—for example, by not hiring members of a particular ethnic group.

Ethnic awareness begins to develop during the early childhood years. Just as a child learns that she is a girl or that he is a boy, in the United States a black child learns that she or he has darker skin and other differences in physical features compared with many—but not all—whites. Just as a girl learns that her body is different from a boy's before she understands what it means to be female, a black child learns that she is different from white children before understanding what it means to be characterized as black in U.S. society. Thus, she learns first that she is different from white children in appearance, and second that these differences may make her unwelcome or may be held against her. The same principle holds for any child who is different from members of an otherwise homogeneous group who regard the child's differences as important. Thus, a Jewish child growing up in a Catholic neighborhood, a Saudi Arabian child in an Italian neighborhood, a Chinese child in a Japanese neighborhood, or even an Irish-Catholic child in an Irish-Protestant neighborhood goes through this process. What the child does not understand is *why* ethnicity matters so much. Answering that question can be a lifelong task (Spencer, 1988).

Understanding group differences and what it means to be a member of a group requires social cognition, which in turn depends on cognitive development. Thus, a child whose thought is still egocentric and who can focus on only one dimension at a time assumes that people who are similar on one dimension (such as skin color) must be similar on other dimensions as well. As children grow older, they become more skilled at seeing people as multidimensional. In an experiment with English-speaking and French-speaking Canadian children (Doyle, Beaudet, & Aboud, 1988), the researchers found that older children had more flexible attitudes about members of the other language-speaking group. Children capable of concrete operational thought were less likely to attribute negative characteristics to members of the other group than were children still in the preoperational period. Other researchers have found, however, that level of cognitive development is not directly related to children's understanding of their own ethnic identity (Ocampo, Knight, & Bernal, 1997).

Greater ability to see people as multidimensional is offset by the strong tendency of older school-age children to conform to group standards and reject those who are different from them in any way. A study in a California town in which the schools were about half black and half white found that older children were actually less likely than younger ones to have a friend of a different ethnicity. Interethnic friendships declined steadily from the fourth through the seventh grade. The researchers concluded that as children grow older, similarity becomes an increasingly powerful basis for friendship.

There may also be pressure from other members of a peer group to avoid forming friendships with members of a different group (Hallinan & Teixeira, 1987). It works both ways with regard to blacks and whites. Black children who become friendly with white children may be pressured to give up such friendships because they are being "disloyal" to their "race" (Schofield, 1981), and vice versa. Studies have also found that black children who succeed at school—regardless of the school's ethnic composition—may be perceived as being disloyal on grounds that school itself is a "white" institution. They may be taunted by their peers and excluded from group activities.

Ethnic awareness is an important issue during middle childhood. Children absorb the cultural attitudes of those around them. In return for adhering to the standards of their society, children must receive some assurance that they belong to a larger, more powerful group. Yet, in the United States black parents and parents of other ethnicities have faced a majority culture that often places them in conflict. They are expected to teach their children the values of a society that holds them in low esteem. Children naturally sense this conflict, and it can profoundly affect their attitudes toward society.

Peer pressures aggravate this situation. Minority peer groups often have norms that differ widely from those of the majority. A black child growing up in an environment characterized by poverty and a high crime rate belongs to an entirely different culture from that of most middle-class whites—or blacks. The degree of acceptance that black children find in the larger society often depends on their ability to conform to its norms. When these children get together with other members of their ethnic group, adjustment is easier during middle childhood. Group membership tends to improve self-esteem. Still, minority children will inevitably face the problem of reconciling their own self-concepts with the rest of their society's image of them, which can cause conflict, anxiety, or anger at any age.

CONTENT CHECK
PEER RELATIONSHIPS AND SOCIAL COMPETENCE

True–False (answers are on the Companion Website)

1. In middle childhood, children's understanding of friendships proceeds in identifiable stages.
2. Group friendships are more common in the early part of middle childhood.
3. The effects of peer-group pressures are more often negative than positive.
4. The existence of distinct races is a scientifically accepted fact.
5. Children of minority or other groups at risk for prejudice first learn that they are different and then learn that the differences will be held against them.

Thinking Critically

How do in-groups versus out-groups set the stage for prejudice?

CHAPTER 10 REVISITED

In most societies, a child's social world expands considerably during middle childhood.

Personality Development in an Expanding Social World

- With regard to personality development during middle childhood, psychodynamic theorists focus on psychosocial development, cognitive-developmental theorists focus on children's concepts of self and morality, and social-learning theorists focus on the role of observation and reinforcement and punishment.

- During middle childhood, self-concept becomes more realistic, complex, and organized; much of a child's self-concept derives from comparisons between self and others.

- Children develop and maintain good self-esteem in various ways; success at school is an important way for many children.

- Appropriate praise for actual achievements enhances children's self-esteem.

Social Knowledge and Reasoning

- Social cognition is central to socialization; social inference and an understanding of social responsibility and social regulations are components of social cognition.

■ Piaget saw moral development during middle childhood as occurring in two stages: moral realism and moral relativism.

■ Kohlberg used moral dilemmas in developing his theory that moral development occurs in three stages: preconventional, conventional, and postconventional; each has two substages.

■ Kohlberg's theory has been criticized with regard to procedures, moral absolutism, and gender bias.

■ Gilligan's theory of moral development is based on relationships and caring instead of justice.

■ Gender differences in moral judgments tend to decrease with age.

Continuing Family Influences

■ Parental monitoring remains highly important during middle childhood.

■ An important part of optimal parenting is helping children acquire self-regulated behavior and learn coregulation; authoritative parenting and scaffolding foster these.

■ Births to unmarried mothers have increased considerably in the United States in recent years; single parenting has also become frequent.

■ The majority of U.S. mothers of school-age children work.

■ Numerous stresses are associated with living in a single-parent home; many such families live below the poverty line, and the children are less likely to improve their situation when they grow up.

■ In single-parent families, social support and the presence of extended family members to help with childcare lessen the potentially negative effects on parent and child.

■ Many U.S. marriages end in divorce; children often suffer in many ways, refuse to accept the divorce as permanent, and exhibit negative behaviors.

■ Three factors that contribute to how children react to divorce are the amount of hostility accompanying the divorce, the amount of actual change in the child's life, and the nature of the parent-child relationship.

■ Many divorced people remarry and form reconstituted families; children may react positively or negatively to the presence of a stepparent.

Peer Relationships and Social Competence

■ Children's understanding of friendships goes through identifiable stages in middle childhood, although researchers disagree about what underlies these stages.

■ Children's friendships can have many positive effects; early middle-childhood friendships mostly take the form having best friends, with group friendships appearing later.

■ Almost all children have unilateral friendships; many children do not have reciprocal ones.

■ Group norms govern children's peer groups; within peer groups, some children are leaders and some are followers.

■ The nature of peer groups changes across middle childhood; the importance of conformity increases and the groups become more formal.

■ Peer groups include members who are popular and members who are not; numerous characteristics of a child and the child's behavior determine popularity and peer group status.

■ The existence of in-groups and out-groups sets the stage for prejudice and discrimination.

■ Ethnic awareness develops in early childhood, before a child realizes or understands what the child's ethnicity may bring with it in the form of prejudice.

■ As peer group pressures to conform increase across middle childhood, interethnic friendships tend to decrease and prejudice tends to increase.

KEY TERMS

morality	moral relativism	resilient children
self-esteem	moral dilemmas	reconsituted family
social inference	moral absolutism	peer group
social responsibility	moral identity	prejudice
social regulations	self-regulated behavior	discrimination
moral realism	coregulation	

ADOLESCENCE: PHYSICAL AND COGNITIVE DEVELOPMENT

11

CHAPTER OUTLINE

Adolescence Today

Physical Development and Adjustment
- Physical Growth and Change
- Puberty
- Body Image and Adjustment

Sexual Attitudes and Behavior
- The Sexual "Revolution"
- Masturbation
- Gender Differences in Sexual Expression
- Factors Influencing Early Sexual Relationships
- Sexual Abuse of Adolescents
- Teenage Parents

Cognitive Changes in Adolescence
- Abstract Thinking
- Information Processing
- Scope and Content of Thought

CHAPTER PREVIEW

Do you know:

1. That many cultures have clear-cut *rites of passage* that mark the transition from adolescence to adulthood?

2. How U.S. adolescents tend to occupy their own *developmental niche* and what the implications of this are?

3. How *hormones* influence the biological changes that accompany entrance into adolescence and puberty and what *glands* produce these hormones?

4. How the *timing* of adolescent maturation differs for *girls* and for *boys?*

5. What marks *attainment of puberty* for males and for females?

6. That adolescents tend to become intensely concerned with *self-image* and especially *body image?*

7. The symptons and suspected causes of *anorexia nervosa* and *bulimia nervosa?*

8. How *early* versus *late maturation* affects girls and boys *differently?*

9. The history of the U.S. *sexual revolution*, where things stand today, and what role the spread of STDs has played?

10. What factors influence *teenage sexual activity?*

11. The extent to which U.S. adults report having been *sexually abused* as children or adolescents, how this abuse typically occurs, and what its *long-range effects* are?

12. The extent of *teenage pregnancy* in the United States and elsewhere, and why the U.S. rate is *higher?*

13. What constitutes Piaget's *formal operational thinking* and what new cognitive abilities emerge?

14. What advances in *information-processing skills* typically accompany adolescence?

15. How the *scope* and *content* of thought typically changes during adolescence?

16. That adolescence often includes a temporary return to *egocentrism?*

17. How the *imaginary audience* and the *personal fable* often affect adolescent behavior?

18. How *moral development* proceeds during adolescence?

These are the main topics of Chapter 11.

In the United States and other industrialized nations, adolescence often extends over a period of a decade or more. Both the beginning and the end of adolescence are often ambiguous. Children frequently begin to act like adolescents before they start to change physically. And how can we define when an adolescent truly becomes an adult? Perhaps the best indicator of adulthood is emotional maturity rather than more obvious criteria such as completing an education, earning a living, marrying, or becoming a parent (Baldwin, 1986); however, emotional maturity is also difficult to define.

Despite mixed opinions about its boundaries, there's complete agreement that the prolonged transitional period from childhood to adulthood is a modern phenomenon found mainly in developed nations. As discussed in Chapter 1, adolescence historically was a much shorter stage. This is still true in parts of some developing nations, where young people go through a symbolic ceremony, name change, or physical challenge at puberty, and that's mostly it. Such transition rituals are called **rites of passage.** An apprenticeship of a year or two may follow, and by age 16 or 17 the young person achieves full, unqualified adulthood. Such a relatively rapid transformation is possible because the skills necessary for adult life in less complex societies can be mastered without a lengthy education. Still, the need for some period of transition is recognized everywhere; no society demands that a child become an adult overnight, and no society fails to recognize the attainment of adulthood. Becoming an adult member of society is a universal milestone.

Adolescence Today

To understand adolescents and what adolescence is, it helps to be aware of the special developmental niche in which today's adolescents live. One factor is age segregation: U.S. adolescents interact mostly with other adolescents and much less with younger children or adults. This is largely because they choose to do so, perhaps because they don't want to be considered children by virtue of associating with them, or perhaps because they want to figure out things for themselves without the constraints often imposed by adults.

Age segregation can have negative effects. Being separated from younger children deprives adolescents of opportunities to guide and tutor those who are less knowledgeable than themselves, the only exceptions being the limited periods they may spend caring for younger siblings or working as baby-sitters or camp counselors. Separation from the adult world means that adolescents miss opportunities to serve apprenticeships—to learn jobs by working alongside older, experienced people. Adolescents are separated for many hours every day from the major activities, customs, and responsibilities of society, except for the limited time they may spend helping their parents with chores or working at after-school jobs.

Prolonged economic dependence is another characteristic of adolescence. In a society like the United States, adolescents often depend on financial support from their parents while they acquire the extended education necessary for jobs requiring technologically sophisticated skills. For those who don't obtain sufficient education, the low-level jobs available to them are usually neither interesting nor financially rewarding. Either way, adolescents often become frustrated and restless with their place in the world. It remains the case that adolescence is in some respects a time of restricted rights and opportunities and prescribed roles. Others, like Erikson (see Chapter 12), take a more positive view, seeing adolescence as a time when individuals are allowed to explore and experiment with various roles before taking on the responsibilities of the adult world.

Adolescents are also affected by the events of the time in which they live. Every era has its wars, religious movements, and economic ups and downs. Adolescents are especially vulnerable to such crises. The state of the world affects adolescents much more than it does younger children. Adolescents and young adults fight in wars, participate in riots, and put their energies into movements for social reform. Adolescents and young adults support radical political and religious movements with their idealism. They lose their jobs during economic downturns and are hired during economic booms. Today's adolescents are affected not only by local and regional crises but also by crises in distant parts of the world.

rites of passage Symbolic events or rituals to mark life transitions, such as from childhood to adult status.

Finally, the mass media have specific effects on adolescents. As we have seen repeatedly, theories of human development emphasize the importance of an emotionally supportive and responsive environment. Individuals of any age learn best when they can act on their environment, perceive the consequences of their actions, and have some power to cause change. But there is no way to alter events portrayed by television and other mass media. It seems that adolescents, with their rapidly developing physical and cognitive capacities, are particularly vulnerable to the passive role of mass-media consumer. They accept tragedy and brutality in a matter-of-fact way; perhaps they develop a thirst for excessive stimulation. Perhaps they model their behavior on the trite or bizarre events they see portrayed. Perhaps they become absorbed with the often angry, socially deviant worlds portrayed by hip-hop and heavy metal music in particular. The list of potentially harmful—or at least counterproductive—influences is endless.

CONTENT CHECK

ADOLESCENCE TODAY

True–False (answers are on the Companion Website)

1. Adolescents today tend to live in a separate developmental niche.
2. Many U.S. adolescents experience prolonged economic dependence on their parents.
3. In contrast to younger children, adolescents are only minimally influenced by the events and role models they see portrayed on television.

Thinking Critically

What are the pros and cons of the age segregation that characterizes adolescence in industrialized nations?

Physical Development and Adjustment

Physiologically, adolescence ranks with the fetal period and infancy as a time of extremely rapid biological change. Adolescents, however, have the pains and pleasures of observing the process; they watch themselves with alternating feelings of fascination, delight, and horror as their bodies change. Surprised, embarrassed, and uncertain, they constantly compare themselves with others and revise their self-images. Both sexes anxiously monitor their development—or lack of it—basing their judgments on both knowledge and misinformation. They compare themselves with the prevailing ideals for their sex; in fact, trying to reconcile differences between the real and the ideal is a major problem for adolescents. How parents react to their child's physical changes can also have a profound impact on the adolescent's adjustment.

Physical Growth and Change

The biological hallmarks of adolescence are a marked increase in the rate of growth, rapid development of the reproductive organs, and the appearance of secondary sex characteristics such as body hair, increases in body fat and

The onset of puberty requires considerable adaption whether to a suddenly crackly voice, longer legs, or unfamiliar passions or feelings.

muscle, and enlargement and maturation of genitalia. Some changes are the same for boys and girls—increased size, improved strength and stamina—but most changes are sex-specific.

Hormone Changes The physical changes that occur upon entry into adolescence are controlled by **hormones,** biochemical substances that are secreted into the bloodstream in minute amounts by internal organs called *endocrine glands.* Hormones that eventually trigger adolescent growth and change are present in trace amounts from the fetal period on, but their production greatly increases at about age 10½ for girls and age 12 to 13 for boys—although as always where ages are concerned, with considerable variability. Then comes the **adolescent growth spurt,** a period of rapid growth in physical size and strength accompanied by changes in body proportions. Especially for girls, the growth spurt is a sign of entry into adolescence; the more noticeable changes associated with **puberty** (sexual maturity) follow the growth spurt by about a year (see Figure 11–1).

The growth spurt is typically accompanied by clumsiness and awkwardness as children learn to control their "new" bodies. Some of the clumsiness is also because the growth spurt isn't always symmetrical; one leg may temporarily be longer than the other, one hand larger than the other. As you might imagine, the growth spurt is accompanied by a ravenous appetite as the body seeks the nutrients necessary for such rapid growth. Another change is an increase in the size and activity of *sebaceous* (oil-producing) glands in the skin, which can cause a teenager's face to break out in acne. A new kind of sweat gland also develops in the skin, resulting in a stronger body odor.

Subtle changes preceding the growth spurt may include an increase in body fat; some preadolescents become noticeably pudgy. In both males and females fat is deposited in the breast area; this is permanent in females but temporary in males. As the growth spurt kicks in, boys generally lose most of the extra fat, whereas girls tend to keep it.

Both sexes display wide variability in the timing of the hormone changes associated with entry into adolescence. As discussed later in this section, there are

hormones Biochemical secretions of the endocrine glands that are carried by the blood or other body fluids to a particular organ or tissue.

adolescent growth spurt The sudden increase in rate of growth that accompanies the entrance into puberty.

puberty The attainment of sexual maturity in males and females.

Figure 11-1 Growth Rates and Sexual Development During Puberty

The peak in the line labeled "height spurt" represents the point of most rapid growth. The bars below represent the average beginning and end of the events of puberty.

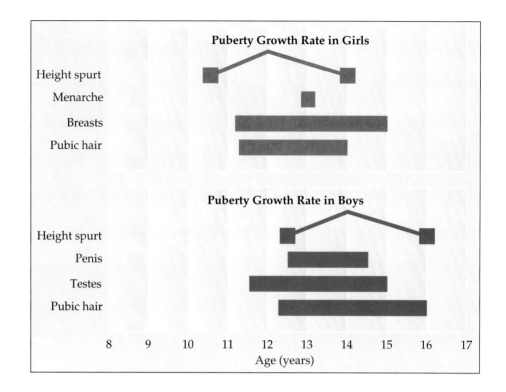

"early maturers" and "late maturers," and the timing of maturation can have pronounced effects on adjustment. "Male" and "female" hormones are present in members of both sexes, but males begin to produce more of the hormones called *androgens,* of which the most important is **testosterone,** and females begin to produce more of the hormones **estrogen** and **progesterone** (Tanner, 1978).

Each hormone influences a specific set of targets or *receptors.* For example, the secretion of testosterone causes the penis to grow, the shoulders to broaden, and hair to grow in the genital area and on the face. Similarly, estrogen causes the uterus and breasts to grow and the hips to broaden. Receptor cells are sensitive to minute quantities of the appropriate hormones, even though the hormones are present only in amounts comparable to a pinch of sugar dissolved in a swimming pool (Tanner, 1978).

The endocrine glands secrete a delicate and complex balance of hormones. Maintaining the balance is the job of two areas of the brain: the *hypothalamus* and the *pituitary gland.* The hypothalamus is the part of the brain that, among other many functions, initiates growth and eventual reproductive capability during adolescence. The pituitary, located on the underside of the brain, is a "master gland" that produces several varieties of hormones. These include *growth hormone,* which controls the overall growth of the body, as well as some secondary *trophic* hormones. Trophic hormones stimulate and regulate the functioning of other glands, including the sex glands—the ovaries in females and the testes in males. In females, the sex glands secrete estrogens and regulate ovulation; in males, the sex glands secrete androgens and produce sperm. Hormones secreted by the pituitary gland and the sex glands have emotional as well as physical effects on adolescents, although the emotional effects aren't usually as profound as some people think (see "In Theory, in Fact," page 385.)

testosterone A male sexual hormone.

estrogen A female sexual hormone.

progesterone A female sexual hormone.

IN THEORY, IN FACT

ARE ADOLESCENTS VICTIMS OF RAGING HORMONES?

In most cultures adolescence—whether brief or extended—is marked by major changes in behavior and appearance. Historically, many of these changes have been described as negative and attributed to biological factors—especially hormones. Adolescents have been portrayed as victims of their own "raging hormones." Is this a realistic portrayal?

From a physiological perspective, hormones act on the brain in two ways. First, sex hormones can influence personality and behavior through their early influence on brain development. Such effects are permanent and therefore are not affected by changes in hormone levels during puberty. Second, hormones may activate specific behaviors through their effects on the nervous system. These effects tend to be immediate or only slightly delayed. Physical and sexual maturation result from interactions among the hormonal levels, health factors, and genetic makeup of the developing person.

Researchers have found only a very limited *direct* relationship between hormone levels during adolescence and the following behaviors (Buchanan, Eccles, & Becker, 1992):

Moodiness
Depression
Restlessness and lack of
    concentration
Irritability
Impulsiveness
Anxiety
Aggression and behavior problems

It should also be recognized that not all adolescents exhibit dramatic changes in these behaviors, even though they all experience increases and fluctuations in hormone levels. It is therefore likely that other factors are involved. Among these are changing roles, social or cultural expectations, specific situations in the home or school, and even the influence of the media.

If there are problems in the family during early and middle childhood, for example, they may become worse during adolescence. Adolescents in dysfunctional families may have problems with inappropriate sexual behavior, running away, aggression, and drug use. In contrast, if parent-child relationships are good before adolescence, they generally remain good throughout adolescence and the parents continue to have a positive influence on their children (Buchanan et al., 1992).

This is not to say that hormones have no effect on behavior, just that their effect is moderated or exacerbated by psychological and social factors. For example, in one study, testosterone level was found to be a strong predictor of sexual activity among 12- to 16-year-old girls (Udry, 1988). But its effect was reduced or eliminated by having a father in the home or by the girl's participation in sports. Fathers who are present tend to raise girls' self-esteem in ways that lessen their need to be sexually active. In conjunction with the mother's guidance and role modeling, fathers are also more likely to create situations that stress relationships rather than sexual behavior alone. Environmental factors can readily override hormonal effects on behavior. Researchers therefore conclude that the notion that raging hormones are a direct cause of adolescent behaviors is a myth.

Puberty

As noted, puberty refers to the attainment of sexual maturity and the ability to have children. For females, the approach of puberty is marked by the first menstrual period, or **menarche,** although contrary to popular belief, the first ovulation may occur a year or more later (Tanner, 1978). For boys, puberty is marked by the first emission of semen containing viable sperm cells.

In earlier times, puberty occurred later than it does now. In the 1880s, for example, the average age at puberty was 15½ for girls (Frisch, 1988), and the social transition from youth to adulthood followed closely behind—in contrast to what happens today.

Sexual Maturation in Males   In males the first indication of puberty is accelerating growth of the testes and scrotum. The penis undergoes a similar acceleration in growth about 1 year later. In the meantime, pubic hair begins to appear but does not mature completely until after genital development is complete. During this period there are also increases in the size of the heart and lungs. Because of the presence of testosterone, boys develop more red blood cells than girls. The extensive production of red blood cells may be one factor in the average superior strength and athletic ability of adolescent boys. The first

menarche   The time of the first menstrual period.

One reason girls often feel more mature than boys their own age is that the female growth spurt during puberty occurs about 2 years before the male growth spurt.

emission of semen may take place as early as age 11 or as late as age 16. A boy's first ejaculation usually occurs during the growth spurt and may be a result of masturbation or come in a "wet dream." These first emissions generally do not contain fertile sperm (Money, 1980).

Characteristically, descriptions of adolescent boys include their awkwardly cracking voices. The actual voice change takes place relatively late in the sequence of pubertal changes, however, and in many boys it occurs too gradually to constitute a developmental milestone (Tanner, 1978).

Sexual Maturation in Females   In girls the "breast buds" are usually the first signal that changes leading to puberty are under way. The uterus and vagina also begin to develop, accompanied by enlargement of the labia and clitoris.

Menarche, which is the most dramatic and symbolic sign of a girl's changing status, actually occurs late in the sequence, after the peak of the growth spurt. It may occur as early as age 9½ or as late as age 16½; in the United States the average age at menarche for girls is about 12½. In other parts of the world menarche occurs considerably later: The average girl in former Czechoslovakia has her first period at age 14; among the Kikuyu of Kenya the average age is 16; and for the Bindi of New Guinea it is 18 (Powers, Hauser, & Kilner, 1989). Menarche typically occurs when a girl is nearing her adult height and has stored some body fat. For a girl of average height, menarche typically occurs when she weighs about 100 pounds (Frisch, 1988).

The first few menstrual cycles vary greatly from one girl to another; they also tend to vary from one month to another. In many cases the early cycles are irregular and *anovulatory*—that is, a mature ovum is not produced (Tanner, 1978). However, it is thoroughly unwise for a young teenage girl to assume that she is infertile. (We return to the subject of teenage pregnancy later in the chapter.)

Menstruation is accompanied by menstrual "cramping" in nearly half of all teenage girls (Wildholm, 1985). Premenstrual tension is common and is often accompanied by irritability, depression, crying, bloating, and breast tenderness.

Table 11–1 summarizes physical changes associated with puberty for girls and for boys.

Body Image and Adjustment

As mentioned earlier, adolescents continually appraise their changing bodies. Are they the right shape and size? Are they coordinated or clumsy? How do they compare with the ideals portrayed by their culture?

Table 11-1   Typical Physical Changes in Adolescence

Changes in Girls	Changes in Boys
• Breast development	• Growth of testes and scrotal sac
• Growth of pubic hair	• Growth of pubic hair
• Growth of underarm hair	• Growth of facial and underarm hair
• Body growth	• Body growth
• Menarche	• Growth of penis
• Increased output of oil and sweat-producing glands	• Change in voice
	• First ejaculation of semen
	• Increased output of oil- and sweat-producing glands

Adolescents belong to what sociologists call a **marginal group**—a group between cultures or on the fringe of a dominant culture—that typically exhibits an intensified need to conform. Adolescents can be extremely intolerant of deviation, whether in body type (being too fat or too thin) or timing (maturing late or early). The mass media contribute to this intolerance by presenting stereotypical images of attractive, exuberant youths who glide through adolescence without pimples, braces, awkwardness, or weight problems. Because many adolescents are extremely sensitive about their appearance, discrepancies between their less-than-perfect self-image and the glowing ideals they see in the media often foster considerable anxiety and self-doubt.

Concern with Body Image   During middle childhood, children become keenly aware of different body types and ideals and gain a fairly clear idea of their own body type, proportions, and skills. In adolescence, body type receives even closer scrutiny. Some young people subject themselves to intense dieting, while others engage in rigorous regimens of physical fitness and strength training. For boys, the primary concern is physical strength (Lerner, Orlos, & Knapp, 1976). Height and muscles are most important. Girls, in contrast, worry about being too fat or too tall. They focus on weight largely because of their concern with social acceptance. Thus, many normal, even lean, adolescent girls consider themselves overweight. When carried to an extreme, such concerns can lead to eating disorders, particularly **anorexia nervosa** and **bulimia nervosa** as described in "A Closer Look," page 388.

Height, weight, and complexion are major sources of concern for 10th graders of both sexes. Most wish for one or more physical changes in themselves. Such self-consciousness diminishes in late adolescence. One longitudinal study found that satisfaction with body image is lowest for girls at age 13 and for boys at age 15; then it rises steadily. At every age from 11 to 18, however, it is lower for girls than for boys (Rauste-von Wright, 1989). For adolescent girls, having a positive body image is directly correlated with whether their mothers have a positive body image (Usmiani & Daniluk, 1997).

There are some interesting differences in the changes adolescent girls and boys would like to make in their bodies. Girls want specific changes: "I would make my ears lie back" or "I would make my forehead lower." Boys are less precise. A boy might say: "I'd make myself look handsome and not fat. I'd change my whole physical appearance so that I'd be handsome and with a good build." Both sexes worry about their skin, however: Almost half of all adolescents voice concerns about pimples and blackheads.

Early and Late Maturers   The effects of timing of maturation have engrossed researchers almost as much as adolescence itself. Although many teenagers have a fairly positive attitude toward their own rate of maturation (Pelletz, 1995), ill-timed maturation can be a problem. This is especially true for late-maturing boys. Because girls mature on average 2 years earlier than boys, a late-maturing boy is last of all to begin the growth spurt and reach puberty. Thus, he is smaller and less muscular than his agemates, which puts him at a disadvantage in most sports and many social situations. Other children and adults tend to treat a late maturer as though he were a younger child, and the late maturer has lower social status among his peers and is perceived as less competent by adults (Brackbill & Nevill, 1981).

Sometimes this perception becomes a self-fulfilling prophecy and the boy reacts with childish dependence and immature behavior. In other cases the boy may overcompensate by becoming highly aggressive. In contrast, early-maturing boys tend to gain social and athletic advantages among their peers

marginal group   A group between cultures or on the fringe of a dominant culture.

anorexia nervosa   An eating disorder in which a person is obsessed by thoughts of an unattainable image of "perfect" thinness. Can result in death.

bulimia nervosa   An eating disorder characterized by binging and purging.

A CLOSER LOOK

ANOREXIA NERVOSA AND BULIMIA NERVOSA

Victims of the disorder known as anorexia nervosa can literally starve themselves to death. Obsessed by thoughts of food and an unattainable image of "perfect" thinness, they refuse to eat and may also engage in behaviors such as purging and abusing laxatives. Even though they may feel that they are becoming increasingly attractive, they actually become emaciated and physically ill. In the United States today there are more than 100,000 people with anorexia (10 times as many as there were two decades ago); 10,000 to 15,000 will die because of medical problems associated with the disorder.

Most anorexics are women under age 25. Although the disorder has no single identifiable cause, many anorexics are apparently victims of Western culture's obsession with thinness and its emphasis on feminine attractiveness (Nagel & Jones, 1992). Constantly getting the message that thin is beautiful and fat is repugnant, they fear that the curves and added weight that come with adolescence will make them unattractive and undesirable. Family pressures to remain thin or be attractive may make matters worse. A father who teasingly tells his daughter that she is putting on a few extra pounds may in-crease her negative self-concept and contribute to the disorder.

To date there is no cure for anorexia nervosa and no generally accepted method of treatment. Some therapists take a behaviorist approach, rewarding their patients with praise and approval when they eat. Others attempt to analyze childhood problems that they believe may cause the disease. Still others focus on the patient's feelings and attitudes about food and eating and body image. However, regardless of the theoretical orientation of the therapist, hospitalization with intravenous feeding may be required to reverse the life-threatening weight loss that anorexics often experience. The goal of all therapy with anorexics is to help them learn to separate their feelings about food from their feelings about themselves, and to develop a sense of self-worth and autonomy.

Bulimia nervosa has some things in common with anorexia, but it is classified as a separate disorder in the DSM-IV. A major difference is that people with bulimia typically don't lose weight and actually are often slightly overweight. Although they are terribly anxious about weighing too much—like anorexics—bulimics have a peri-odic uncontrollable urge to eat, especially sweets and salty snacks. Bulimics on a "binge" consume huge quantities of carbohydrates in a very short time, usually an hour or two. They then feel despondent and out of control. To compensate, they purge or take laxatives.

Like anorexics, most bulimics are female. Bulimia usually afflicts people in late adolescence (in contrast, many people who develop anorexia are in their early or mid-adolescence). Some researchers have estimated that about 20% of college-age women engage in bulimic eating patterns (Muuss, 1986).

Although bulimia does not have fatal consequences, it is highly self-destructive and requires treatment. Bulimics develop gastrointestinal disorders, ulceration of the throat and mouth and erosion of teeth caused by frequent passage of stomach acids through purging, and sometimes hernias caused by purging. Fortunately, bulimics tend to be more responsive to treatment than anorexics. Antidepressant drugs are often helpful in treating this disorder—even among patients who show no signs of depression—suggesting that a biochemical abnormality may be involved (Walsh, 1988).

and enjoy a positive self-fulfilling prophecy. From middle childhood on, early-maturing boys are likely to be the leaders of their peer groups (Weisfeld & Billings, 1988).

Early maturation is a mixed blessing for girls. Late maturation can be advantageous in that the girl matures at about the same time as most of her male peers. She is therefore in a better position to share their interests and privileges. She may be more popular with her peers than are early-maturing girls. On the other hand, early-maturing girls are taller and more developed than all of their peers, both male and female. One effect is that they have fewer opportunities to discuss their physical and emotional changes with friends. Another is that they are significantly more likely to experience psychological distress over their changes (Ge, Conger, & Elder, 1996) and be teased by peers. They may also be considered "easy" by older boys. But there are compensations. After a difficult period of initial adjustment, early-maturing girls frequently feel more attractive, are legitimately more popular with older boys, and are more likely to date than their late-maturing agemates (Blyth, Bulcroft, & Simmons, 1981).

Girls' Reactions to Menarche   Menarche is a unique event, a milestone on the path to physical maturity. It occurs without warning and is heralded by a

With regard to body image, boys tend to be concerned more with exercises to increase physical strength, girls more with exercises that help control weight.

bloody vaginal discharge. In some parts of the world it has major religious, cultural, or economic significance and may trigger elaborate rites and ceremonies. Although there is no such drama in the United States, menarche still holds considerable significance for girls and their parents (Greif & Ulman, 1982).

Studies of adolescent girls confirm that menarche is a memorable event. Only girls who were not informed about it in advance by their parents or who experienced it very early describe it as traumatic. Some girls who receive information about menarche from men react negatively to the experience. But most girls are well informed by their mothers or other female relatives about what to expect, and they report a positive reaction to menarche—a feeling that they are coming of age (Ruble & Brooks-Gunn, 1982).

CONTENT CHECK
PHYSICAL DEVELOPMENT AND ADJUSTMENT

True–False (answers are on the Companion Website)

1. Increases in body fat characteristically precede the growth spurt both in girls and in boys.
2. The same hormones trigger entrance into puberty for boys and for girls.
3. Menarche marks the beginning of fertility in girls.
4. Emission of viable sperm cells marks the beginning of fertility in boys.
5. Overall, both early-maturing boys and girls have the advantage over their late-maturing counterparts.

Thinking Critically

What are the consequences of the intense concern with body image most adolescents display?

Sexual Attitudes and Behavior

During middle and late childhood, children associate mostly in same-sex peer groups. At puberty, however, the biological changes experienced by adolescents are usually accompanied by interest in members of the opposite sex and a need to integrate sexuality with other aspects of the personality. During adolescence, therefore, young people begin forming relationships in which sex plays a central role. In some cases, adolescents are attracted to members of their own sex (Chapter 13) and may feel distinctly different from most of their peers. In addition, how adolescents feel about their bodies is influenced by their personal history of physical contact—nurturing or abusive—and the attitudes of respect, caring, or manipulation that went with those experiences.

The Sexual "Revolution"

Historical changes in social attitudes are clearly visible in the way people respond to sexuality. In large part, adolescents view themselves in terms of the cultural norms of the time and place in which they live. Their sexual behavior varies accordingly, as does that of young adults.

Before the mid-1960s, most young people felt that premarital sex was immoral, although peer pressure often impelled older adolescent boys to gain sexual experience before marriage. Girls, in contrast, were under pressure to remain chaste until marriage. By the late 1960s and early 1970s, sexual attitudes had changed considerably, partly because of the development and widespread distribution of birth control pills, partly because of the "free love" movement that accompanied protests against the Vietnam War and against "the establishment" in general. In a study of adolescent sexual attitudes during that era (Sorensen, 1973), the majority of adolescents did not think of premarital sex as inherently right or wrong but instead judged it on the basis of the relationship between the participants. A majority rejected the traditional double standard that gave sexual freedom to boys but not to girls. Almost 70% agreed that two people should not have to marry to have sex or live together. About 50% approved of **same-sex orientation** or same-sex sexual activity. At the same time, 80% stated that they had never engaged in sexual activity with a member of their own sex and would never want to. In all, their attitudes were quite different from those of their much more conservative parents.

By the late 1970s the sexual "revolution" was in full swing. In 1979 Catherine Chilman reviewed the findings of numerous studies and reported an increasing trend toward sexual liberalization, reflected both by an increase in sexual activity among adolescents and by a change in societal attitudes. Society at large—not just young people—had become more accepting of a wide range of sexual behaviors, including masturbation, same-sex sexual activity, and unmarried couples having sex (Dreyer, 1982). In another study (Hass, 1979), 83% of the boys and 64% of the girls interviewed approved of premarital intercourse; 56% of the boys and 44% of the girls reported actually having had intercourse.

Note that there was relatively little difference between the responses of boys and girls, consistent with the continuing decline in the double standard. The sexual revolution affected girls' behavior much more than it did boys': Even in the 1940s, 1950s, and 1960s, between one-third and two-thirds of teenage boys reportedly had already lost their virginity—a statistic comparable to that reported in the 1970s. In contrast, the proportion of 16-year-old girls reporting having lost their virginity rose from 7% in the 1940s to 33% in 1971 and 44% in 1982 (Brooks-Gunn & Furstenberg, 1989).

same-sex orientation Sexual attraction toward members of one's own sex.

The sexual revolution was accompanied by a variety of problems. For one, large numbers of adolescents were having sexual intercourse without using birth control. As a result, the rate of pregnancy among teenage girls tripled between 1940 and 1975. Another problem was the spread of sexually transmitted diseases (STDs) at epidemic proportions—first syphilis, gonorrhea, and genital herpes, later HIV/AIDS (also see Chapter 13). Although AIDS is still rare among adolescents (because it often takes years for symptoms to appear and therefore goes undetected), teenagers have a high rate of other STDs. In the United States, for example, one in seven teenagers has an STD (Quadrel, Fischoff, & Davis, 1993). In addition, although few teenagers suffer from full-blown AIDS, an increasing number are HIV positive. It is believed that many of the approximately 30,000 young adults age 20 to 29 diagnosed with AIDS in 1996 probably were infected with the virus while they were adolescents (U.S. Census Bureau, 1997).

The sexual revolution began to decline in the 1980s. Young people became more cautious about sexual activity, and monogamy—or at least "serial" monogamy—became fashionable again. During the 1980s, when adolescents were asked what they thought of the sexual attitudes of the 1960s and 1970s, a sizable proportion viewed them as irresponsible. College students were also again more likely to consider sexual promiscuity undesirable (Leo, 1984; Robinson & Jedlicka, 1982).

The late 1980s saw a continuation of the trend toward more conservative attitudes about sexual matters (Murstein, Chalpin, Heard, & Vyse, 1989). Although young people still considered sex an essential part of romance, they were generally not in favor of casual sex (Abler & Sedlacek, 1989). Attitudes toward same-sex orientation and sexual activity also began to turn more negative again (Williams & Jacoby, 1989). This increase in "homophobia" (fear or dislike of people who have same-sex relations or orientation is attributable in part to fear of sexually transmitted diseases, especially HIV/AIDS—even though, worldwide, the disease is now spread primarily through *heterosexual* contact.

Masturbation

In adolescence, girls spend more time fantasizing about romance as an outlet for their sexual impulses; boys are more likely to masturbate. But masturbation and fantasizing are common in both sexes. According to one early study, about one-half of adolescent girls and three-quarters of boys masturbate (Hass, 1979); the rates may be higher now. Social-class differences play a part too, or at least they did in the past. Enjoyment of fantasies during masturbation was reportedly more common in middle-class males, whereas guilt over the "unmanliness" of masturbation was of greater concern to working-class males. These differences have been gradually disappearing, however (Dreyer, 1982), as have male-female differences in attitudes toward masturbation.

Gender Differences in Sexual Expression

Class differences in sexual behavior have traditionally been less significant among females, partly because of the limited roles that were available to women in the past. Girls were discouraged from overt sexuality; instead, they received early training in enhancing their desirability in subtle ways, evaluating potential mates, and "holding out" until marriage. Dating and courtship then provided the setting in which members of each gender learned from each other about desires and expectations. In the United States femininity formerly connoted passivity, nurturance, and ability to fit in. Girls were to remain flexible enough to conform to the value systems of potential spouses. Now girls are encouraged to acquire skills that they can employ to support themselves regardless of their future marital plans, and expression of sexuality by members of both genders is encouraged by the media.

The expression of sexuality for each gender always depends on the society's prevailing norms; it changes as these norms change. Some societies reserve sexuality exclusively for procreation. At the other extreme, some view restrictions on sex as silly or even as a crime against nature.

Factors Influencing Early Sexual Relationships

Although societal attitudes toward sexual behavior have become more conservative again, at least in the United States, teenagers continue to be highly active sexually. The age at which they first have sex still varies by gender; it also varies by ethnic group. In 1990 the Centers for Disease Control and Prevention reported the results of a national survey of high school students. Among people who identify themselves as white, over 60% of boys and just under 60% of girls have had intercourse by age 18. Sexual activity begins at an earlier age for men and women who identify as black, also for people who identify as Hispanic—except for Hispanic women. (Michael, Gagnon, Laumann, & Kolata, 1994) (see Figure 11–2).

Several factors influence adolescent sexual behavior, including education, psychological makeup, family relationships, and biological maturation. Let's consider these factors in more detail.

Education Education is related to sexual behavior partly because those who attain higher levels of education more frequently come from the middle and upper middle classes, which tend to have more conservative views about sex. This is especially true for adolescents who emphasize careers, intellectual pursuits, and educational goals. Another factor is the relationship between sexual behavior and academic success in high school: Good students are less likely to initiate sexual activity at an early age (Miller & Sneesby, 1988). Perhaps adolescents who are failing academically turn to sexual activity (and drugs, which lower inhibitions about sex) as an alternate means of gratification. In the past, this may have been more true for girls than for boys because girls had fewer op-

Figure 11–2 Age and First Sexual Intercourse

Source: Michael, Gagnon, Laumann, and Kolata, 1994.

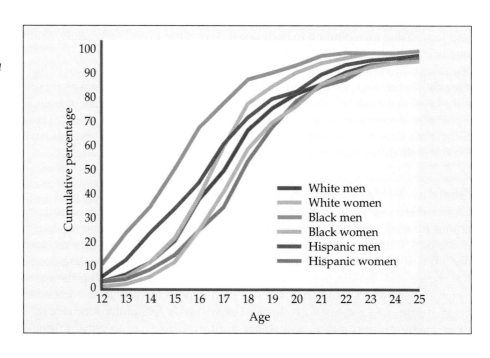

portunities for achievement in nonacademic areas such as sports. With the current emphasis on opportunities for women in all aspects of society, including sports, this situation may be changing.

Education is also the way most teenagers learn about sex nowadays; in the past they generally learned about it from their parents or peers. What children learn about sex in school depends to a large extent on their culture, although in most societies that provide advanced schooling sex education has become a standard part of the curriculum.

Psychological Factors   To some extent the psychological factors associated with early sexual experience are different for males and females. Sexually experienced male adolescents tend to have relatively high self-esteem, while sexually experienced females tend to have low self-esteem. However, for both sexes early sexual activity has been found to be associated with other problem behaviors, such as drug use and delinquency (Donovan, Jessor, & Costa, 1988).

Family Relationships   A number of studies have found that parent-child interactions influence adolescent sexual behavior. Both overly restrictive and overly permissive parenting are associated with earlier sexual activity in adolescents; moderate restrictiveness tends to work best with this age group (Miller, McCoy, Olson, & Wallace, 1986). Another significant factor is communication between parents and offspring: Adolescents who are sexually active are more likely to report poor communication with their parents. In contrast, "quality" parent-child communication has been found to be correlated with adolescent sexual abstinence (Miller, Norton, Fan, & Christopherson, 1998). Good parent-child relationships, however, will not necessarily prevent young people from experimenting with sex (Chilman, 1979).

Research suggests that the changing structure of U.S. families also influences adolescent sexual behavior. The higher divorce rate and the larger number of single-parent families are social realities that affect teenage sexual activity. In general, male and female teenagers from two-parent families have less and later sexual experience than those from single-parent families (Young, Jensen, Olsen, & Cundick, 1991).

Biological Factors   The biological factors that influence early sexual behavior constitute an important area of research that has frequently been overlooked. For example, adolescents may become sexually active earlier today than in the past because of the decline in the average age at which puberty occurs. This is consistent with the observation that individuals who mature early are likely to engage in sexual activity at a younger age than those who mature late (Miller et al., 1998). There's a major exception, however: Although boys reach sexual maturity about 2 years later than girls, they report losing their virginity about a year earlier (Brooks-Gunn & Furstenberg, 1989). However, because sexual activity is a status symbol for many boys, it is likely that such research includes some exaggeration.

Sexual Abuse of Adolescents

Unfortunately, for a significant number of children and adolescents at all socioeconomic levels, their first sexual experiences occur without their consent; they are sexually abused or exploited. Reported cases probably represent only a small fraction of the actual number of such incidents. In one study, a large random sample of women was interviewed about their sexual experiences in childhood and adolescence (Russell, 1983). The researchers found that 32% had been sexually abused at least once before age 18, and 20% had been victimized before age 14. Fewer than 5% of these women had reported the incidents to the police, although nowadays reporting is much more likely.

The impact of sexual abuse on children depends on a variety of factors, including the nature of the abusive act, the age and vulnerability of the victim, whether the offender is a stranger or a family member, whether there was a single incident or an ongoing pattern of abuse, and the reactions of adults in whom the child confides (Kempe & Kempe, 1984). The impact on the individual's identity and self-esteem often lasts throughout life.

The most common form of sexual abuse occurs between a young adolescent girl and an adult male relative or family friend (Finkelhor, 1984). A stepfather or the mother's boyfriend is more likely to be the culprit than the girl's natural father (Wolfe et al., 1988). The abuse often continues and becomes a secret between the abuser and the victim. Sometimes the victim's mother is unaware that the abuse is taking place. At other times, the mother steadfastly refuses to believe her child's claims, or if she does believe them, does nothing to protect her against further abuse.

Sexually abused and traumatized adolescent girls often feel guilty and ashamed, yet powerless to avoid the abuse. They may feel isolated and alienated from their peers and distrustful of adults in general. Some have academic problems, others have physical complaints, and still others become sexually promiscuous. Some girls turn their anger inward, becoming depressed or contemplating suicide (Brassard & McNeill, 1987). Some inappropriately blame themselves for having "enticed" the abuser.

In general, these girls' attitudes about intimate relationships become distorted. As adults, they have difficulty establishing normal sexual relationships; they may even have difficulty establishing normal relationships with their own children. Many have distorted views of sexuality and are actually more likely than nonabused women to marry abusive men. When abuse begins in their own family—say, between their husband and daughter—they may deny the problem or feel powerless to do anything about it (Kempe & Kempe, 1984).

Sexual abuse also involves young boys, mainly in same-sex encounters. The abusers usually are not family members; the abuse takes place outside the home. Molestation by an adult male is especially traumatic for boys; they feel ashamed that they were forced to engage in same-sex acts and were powerless to defend themselves against their attacker (Bolton, Morris, McEacheron, 1989).

Teenage Parents

The proportion of babies born to U.S. adolescents overall has declined since the 1960s, as has the proportion born to adolescents outside of marriage (Ventura et al., 2000; Henshaw, 1998), but many thousands of teenage girls still become pregnant. About 50% of the pregnancies end in miscarriage or abortion; the other 50% result in delivery (Alan Guttmacher Institute, 1994; Brooks-Gunn & Furstenberg, 1989; Sonenstein, 1987). In 1998 there were about 380,000 babies born to unmarried mothers age 15–19; an additional 9,000 were born to unmarried mothers under age 15 (Ventura et al., 2000). In each case, the rate for teenagers who identified as black or Hispanic was more than twice that for teenagers who identified as white, which logically in part reflects socioeconomic-status differences in rates of sexual activity as noted earlier.

Why Teenagers Become Pregnant There is a great deal of sexual activity among U.S. teenagers. Teenagers in most Western European nations are equally active, but the pregnancy rates in those nations are much lower (Coley & Chase-Lansdale, 1998; Hechtman, 1989). Why so many more girls in the United States become pregnant is a major cause of concern. One basic factor seems to be that U.S. adolescents are less likely to use contraception. Another likely factor is that there is less social stigma attached to births outside of marriage than

It is generally difficult for teenage mothers to care for the needs of an infant as well as their own developmental needs.

there was in the past. Instead of expelling pregnant teenagers from high school, many school systems now have special programs to help young mothers complete their education. Nowadays, many young and unmarried mothers receive support both from their families and the fathers of their children. Finally, some teenage girls wish to have and keep children because of their own need to be loved. These young mothers have usually been deprived of affection and expect children to supply what they have missed.

About 3 out of 10 sexually active U.S. adolescents do not use contraceptives (Fielding & Williams, 1991), a figure that has varied little throughout the 1990s (NCHS, 2000a). The most common reasons are ignorance about the facts of reproduction, unwillingness to accept responsibility for sexual activity, or a generally passive attitude toward life (Dreyer, 1982)—coupled with a belief that "it can't happen to me." The double standard continues to play a role too: Both sexes tend to view the male as the sexual initiator and the female as the one who is responsible for setting limits on sexual activity. At the same time, adolescents tend to believe that it is more proper for a female to be "swept off her feet by passion" than to prepare for sex by taking contraceptive precautions (Goodchilds & Zellman, 1984; Morrison, 1985), which has become less likely in recent years but is still the case for adolescents with traditional attitudes. An important point is that studies have shown that sexually active teenagers who attend sex education classes are more likely to use contraceptives than those who do not attend such classes (Fielding & Williams, 1991).

Effects of Early Parenthood What is the impact of early parenthood on a teenage girl's later development? Teenage mothers may drop out of school and therefore work at lower-paying jobs, experience greater job dissatisfaction, and become dependent on government support (Coley & Chase-Lansdale, 1998). Adolescent mothers also must deal with their own personal and social development while trying to adapt to the needs of an infant or small child (Rogel & Peterson, 1984).

The effects of parenthood on the lives of teenage boys may also be negative and long-lasting. Because of the pressures they feel to support their new family, many teenage fathers also tend to leave school and take low-skilled, low-paying jobs. As the years pass, they are more likely to have marital problems (Card & Wise, 1978).

Often adolescents who become pregnant encounter strong disapproval at home. Yet if they do not marry, they may have no choice but to continue living at home in a dependent situation during and after their pregnancy. Thus, some teenagers are motivated to get married in order to set up their own households. But marriage is not necessarily the best solution to an adolescent mother's problems. Some researchers believe that even though early motherhood obstructs adult growth, in many cases it is preferable to early motherhood combined with early marriage. Adolescent marriage is more likely to lead to dropping out of high school than is adolescent pregnancy. Similarly, those who marry young are more likely to divorce than those who bear a child and marry later.

Children of teenage parents are at a disadvantage compared to children of older parents. They may suffer from their parents' lack of experience in handling adult responsibilities and caring for others. Because young parents are often stressed and frustrated, they are more likely to neglect or abuse their children. Children of teenage parents more often exhibit slow development and cognitive growth (Brooks-Gunn & Furstenberg, 1986). If poverty, marital discord, and poor education exist simultaneously in the family, and if they persist over time, the child's chances of developing these and also emotional problems increase (McLoyd, 1998).

Some teenage parents, however, do an excellent job of nurturing their young while continuing to grow toward adulthood themselves—given assistance.

A CLOSER LOOK

HELPING TEENAGE MOTHERS IN THE CONTEXT OF POVERTY

What characteristics are crucial if teenage mothers are to escape from poverty? According to Judith Musick (1994), young mothers who free themselves and their children from poverty achieve a strong sense of self-worth, self-efficacy, and personal responsibility. "In a context where many forces act to divert young women and hold them back," said Musick, "only those with steady will and self-determination keep moving forward against the tide" (p. 7).

Teenage mothers face enormous obstacles. Many have grown up in disorganized families and are continually reexposed to this negative influence, making it more difficult for them to change their lives. Musick explained: "Chronic disorganization takes on a life of its own within a family; an enduring mode of transmitting cycles of inadequacy from generation to generation, unnoticed and unbroken" (1994, p. 1).

Teenage mothers with a strong sense of self-worth define a special role for themselves as protectors of their children. A young mother living in a Chicago housing project defined her parenting role as follows:

No way would I send my children through these buildings at five years old. . . . So many kids get snatched off. . . . Not only will somebody snatch them, the older kids, they take their money. They beat them up. All kinds of things. . . . Maybe I'm over protective. . . . Mine wouldn't be doing it. (Musick, 1994, p. 6)

At the same time that a mother is protecting her children from harm, she must also nurture their cognitive and psychosocial development and instill in them a sense of self-worth. Unfortunately, noted Musick, many adolescent mothers are unable to dedicate themselves to fostering their children's well-being. This is especially true when adolescent mothers are involved in destructive, violent relationships with a series of men on whom they are financially dependent. Thus, even when a young mother wants to improve the quality of her life, her relationships may stand in the way.

The more effective programs for teenage mothers work on many levels. They include education or work training as well as guidance in improving parenting skills and family relationships. They offer counseling to help teenage mothers with problem solving, as well as direct help with matters such as housing, meal preparation, child care, and other aspects of daily life. Some programs focus on the teenager's need to develop and mature as a person. The program may provide role models, mentoring, and guidance, or simply a view of a wider world beyond the home and community.

Do intervention programs help? According to Musick, the results so far have been modest, mainly because these programs must compete against the powerful negative forces that shape the lives of these young women. However, one thing is fairly certain: Intervention programs can help only those who discover a sense of self-worth and are willing to make an effort on their own to climb out of poverty.

Helping young parents and their offspring thrive and become productive remains an overriding social concern and challenge, as discussed in "A Closer Look," page 396.

CONTENT CHECK
SEXUAL ATTITUDES AND BEHAVIOR

True–False (answers are on the Companion Website)

1. During the sexual revolution, both females and males became more liberal in their attitudes toward sex.
2. Male and female adolescents are about equally likely to masturbate.
3. More highly educated adolescents and young adults tend to have more conservative attitudes toward sex.
4. Early-maturing adolescents are likely to engage in sex an earlier age than are late maturers.
5. In the United States, the incidence of pregnancy among unmarried adolescent females has risen in recent years.

Thinking Critically

Why didn't the changes in adolescent attitudes toward sex that occurred during the sexual revolution last?

Cognitive Changes in Adolescence

During adolescence there is normally an expansion in the capacity and style of thought that broadens the young person's awareness, imagination, judgment, and insight. These enhanced abilities lead to a rapid accumulation of knowledge that opens up a range of issues and problems that can both enrich and complicate adolescents' lives.

Cognitive development during adolescence is defined by increasingly abstract thinking and increased use of metacognition. Both exert a dramatic influence on the scope and content of an adolescent's memory and problem solving, as well on thinking in social contexts and making moral judgments.

Abstract Thinking

Piaget characterized the abstract thinking of the adolescent as the hallmark of the final stage of cognitive development. Theorists are still arguing about whether the onset of abstract thinking is dramatic and sudden or part of a gradual, continuous process. In this section we take a closer look at this developmental stage.

Formal Operational Thought   In Piaget's developmental theory, the final stage is *formal operational thinking.* This new form of intellectual processing is abstract, speculative, and independent of the immediate environment and circumstances. It involves thinking about possibilities as well as comparing reality with things that might or might not be. Whereas younger children are more comfortable with concrete, observable events, adolescents show a growing inclination to treat everything as a mere variation on what *could* be (Keating, 1980). Formal operational thought requires the ability to formulate, test, and evaluate hypotheses—indeed, in Piaget's theory, logical and systematic hypothesis testing is the hallmark of the formal operational stage. Formal operational thinking also involves manipulation not only of known, verifiable events but also of things that are contrary to fact ("Let's just suppose, for the sake of discussion, that . . .").

Adolescents also show increasing ability to plan and think ahead. In one study (Greene, 1990), the researcher asked 10th graders, 12th graders, college sophomores, and college seniors to describe what they thought might happen to them in the future and to say how old they thought they would be when these events occurred. The older subjects could look further into the future than the younger ones, and the narratives of the older subjects were more specific. Formal operational thought thus can be characterized as a *second-order* process. Whereas the first order of thinking is discovering and examining relationships between objects, the second order involves thinking about one's thoughts, looking for links between relationships, and maneuvering between reality and possibility (Inhelder & Piaget, 1958). In sum, three notable characteristics of adolescent thought are:

1. The capacity to combine relevant variables in finding a solution to a problem.
2. The ability to offer conjecture about what effect one variable will have on another.
3. The ability to combine and separate variables in a hypothetical-deductive fashion ("If X is present, then Y will occur). (Gallagher, 1973)

It is generally agreed that not all individuals become capable of formal operational thought. Moreover, adolescents and adults who attain this level don't always use it consistently. For example, people who find themselves facing unfamiliar problems in unfamiliar situations are likely to fall back on more concrete reasoning. A certain level of intelligence seems to be necessary for formal operational thought. Cultural and socioeconomic factors, particularly educational level, also play a role (Neimark, 1975). The observation that not all individuals achieve formal operational thought has led some developmentalists to suggest that it should be considered an extension of concrete operations rather than a stage in its own right. Piaget (1972) admitted that this may be the case. Nevertheless, he emphasized that elements of this type of thought are essential for the study of advanced science and mathematics.

A Continuous Process or a Dramatic Shift? As we have seen repeatedly, Piaget's notion of dramatic, qualitative shifts in cognitive ability is not shared by all developmental theorists. Some theorists contend that the transition is much more gradual, with shifts back and forth between formal operational thought and earlier cognitive modes. For example, Daniel Keating (1976, 1990) argued that the lines drawn between the thinking of children, adolescents, and adults are artificial; cognitive development is a continuous process, and even young children may have latent formal operational abilities. Some children are able to handle abstract thought. Perhaps better language skills and more experience with the world, instead of new cognitive capability per se, are responsible for the appearance of these abilities in adolescents.

Information Processing

In contrast, information-processing theorists emphasize the adolescent's improvement in metacognition (Chapter 9). Because of their improved skills in thinking about thinking, forming strategies, and planning, teenagers learn to examine and consciously alter their thought processes.

Cognitive development during adolescence thus includes the following:

1. More efficient use of separate information-processing components such as memory, retention, and transfer of information.
2. More complex strategies for different types of problem solving.
3. More effective ways of acquiring information and storing it symbolically.
4. Higher-order executive functions, including planning, decision making, and flexibility in choosing strategies from a broader base of scripts. (Sternberg, 1988b)

In sum, cognitive development, and therefore the growth of intellectual skills, involves both the accumulation of knowledge and the improvement of information processing. The two are interrelated. Problem solving is more efficient and effective when there is a larger store of relevant information. Individuals with more efficient storage and retrieval strategies develop a more complete knowledge base. Adolescents are more efficient and effective in solving problems and making inferences than school-age children, but they also have a broader range of scripts and other schemes to employ in doing so. Remember that preschool children develop simple scripts for everyday activities. In contrast, adolescents develop more complicated scripts for special circumstances (a ball game) or special procedures (the election of a president). When they attempt to solve a problem or understand a social event, they can make inferences about the meaning of such things by relating them to their more elaborate social scripts.

Scope and Content of Thought

Adolescents also use their developing cognitive skills in intellectual and moral pursuits that focus on themselves, their families, and the world. Because of new and improved cognitive skills, adolescents develop a much broader scope and richer complexity in the content of their thoughts. Since the adolescent can now deal with contrary-to-fact situations, reading or viewing science fiction, fantasy, or horror is a popular pastime. Experimentation with the occult, cults, or altered states of consciousness caused by anything from meditation to drug-induced conditions is often intriguing to adolescents. Abstract thinking influences not only those pursuits and the study of science and math but also how adolescents examine the social world.

Examining World and Family   The ability to understand contrary-to-fact situations affects the parent-child relationship. Adolescents contrast their ideal parent with the real parent they see on a daily basis. Often they are critical of all social institutions, including family and especially their parents.

Family bickering therefore tends to escalate during early adolescence. Many researchers believe, however, that the battles that rage over such daily activities as chores, dress, adornments (such as tatoos and jewelry that requires piercing), hair style, schoolwork, and family meals serve a useful purpose. They allow the adolescent to test her or his independence over relatively minor issues and in the safety of the home. Indeed, *negotiation* has become a popular word in the psychology of adolescence. Instead of talking about rebellion and the painful separation of teenagers from their families, many researchers prefer to describe adolescence as a time in which parents and teenagers negotiate new relationships with one another (as with the negotiation of shared goals). Teenagers must gain more independence; the parents must learn to see their child as more of an equal, with the right to differing opinions. For most adolescents the interplay between these competing needs is conducted within a caring, close relationship with their parents. In a recent study, for example, teenagers who had the strongest sense of themselves as individuals grew up in families where the parents offered guidance and comfort but also permitted their children to develop their own points of view (Flaste, 1988).

During middle and late adolescence there may be increasing concern with social, political, and moral issues. Adolescents begin to develop holistic concepts of society and its institutions, along with ethical principles that go beyond those they have experienced in specific interpersonal relationships. Adolescents construct their own beliefs about the political system within a social, cultural, and historical context (Haste & Torney-Purta, 1992). Their understanding of the world becomes increasingly sophisticated over time as they gain experience and can conceptualize more complex theories and scenarios. When conflicts occur, their concepts of civil liberties—including freedom of speech and religion—change (Helwig, 1995).

Adolescents also employ rational analysis of issues in an effort to achieve internal consistency; they evaluate what they have been in the past and what they hope to become in the future. Some of their swings and extremes of behavior occur when they start taking stock of themselves intellectually. They restructure their behavior, thoughts, and attitudes, either toward a new, more individualized self-image or toward greater conformity with group norms.

The improved cognitive abilities that develop during adolescence also help young people make vocational decisions. They analyze both real and hypothetical options in relation to their talents and abilities. Often, however, it is not until late adolescence that vocational choices become based on realistic self-appraisal and attainable career options (Ginsburg, 1972).

Self-Insight and Egocentrism   As noted earlier, an important aspect of formal operational thought is the ability to analyze your own thought processes. Adolescents typically do this a great deal, and in addition to gaining insight into themselves they indirectly gain insight into others. Taking others' thoughts into account, combined with the adolescent's preoccupation with his or her own "metamorphosis," leads to a peculiar kind of egocentrism. Adolescents assume that other people are as fascinated with them as they are with themselves. They may fail to distinguish between their own concerns and those of others. As a result, adolescents tend to jump to conclusions about the reactions of those around them and to assume that others will be as approving or as critical of them as they are of themselves. In particular, research indicates that adolescents are far more concerned than younger children about having their inadequacies revealed to others (Elkind & Bowen, 1979).

An adolescent's idea that she or he is constantly being watched and judged has been dubbed the **imaginary audience** (Elkind, 1967). As a product of the adolescent's self-involved imagination, the imaginary audience shares the adolescent's involvement with personal thoughts and feelings. Adolescents use the imaginary audience to "try on" various attitudes and behaviors. The imaginary audience is also a source of self-consciousness—a feeling of being constantly and painfully on display. Because adolescents are unsure of their identities, they overreact to other people's views in trying to figure out who they are (Elkind, 1967).

At the same time, adolescents are absorbed in their own feelings. They sometimes believe that their emotions are unique and that no one has ever known or will ever know the same degree of agony or ecstasy. As part of this variation of egocentrism, some adolescents develop what David Elkind termed the **personal fable**—the feeling that they are so special that they should be exempt from the ordinary laws of nature, that nothing bad can happen to them, and

imaginary audience   Adolescents' assumption that others are focusing a great deal of critical attention on them.

personal fable   Adolescents' feeling that they are special and invulnerable—exempt from the laws of nature that control the destinies of ordinary mortals.

that they will live forever (Elkind, 1967). These feelings of invulnerability and immortality may be the basis for the risk-taking behavior that is so common during adolescence, as discussed in Chapter 12.

Another popular adolescent idea is the **foundling fantasy** (Elkind, 1974). Adolescents become convinced that their parents have a large number of failings. Then they have trouble imagining how two such ordinary and limited individuals could have possibly produced such a sensitive and unique "me." Because this is obviously not possible, the adolescent must have been a foundling. Fortunately, however, each variation of egocentrism typically starts receding by the age of 15 or 16 as adolescents realize that most people are not paying all that much attention to them and that they are indeed subject to the laws of nature just like everyone else.

In sum, adolescence can be an intellectually intoxicating experience. New powers of thought are turned inward to a close examination of the self and, at the same time, outward to a world that has suddenly grown much more complex.

Continuing Moral Development   As they progress toward adulthood, adolescents are forced to confront aspects of morality that they haven't encountered before. Now that they are capable of having sex, for example, they have to decide what sex means to them and whether to have sex before marriage— along with "how far to go." They have to evaluate the behaviors and attitudes of peers who might be involved with drugs or gangs. They have to decide whether doing well in school is important, how they feel about fitting into a society that measures success largely in terms of wealth and power, and what role, if any, religion will play in their life. As a result, adolescents start considering the broader issues that will define their adult years.

Some of their decisions—including those about sex—have complex, even life-threatening consequences. Rosemary Jadack and her colleagues (1995) investigated the moral reasoning of 18-year-olds and 20-year-olds about sexual behavior that could lead to STDs, including HIV/AIDS. The researchers found that only subjects in their early 20s carefully considered the moral dilemmas associated with STDs. Apparently, even the ability to make moral judgments about life-threatening behaviors takes time to develop.

The thinking of adolescents changes within the context of their developing sense of morality. By the time they reach their teens, a majority of U.S. children have moved beyond Kohlberg's preconventional level of moral development (Chapter 10) and arrived at the conventional level (which is based in large part on social conformity). Most are motivated to avoid punishment, are oriented toward obedience, and are ready to abide by conventional moral stereotypes. They may remain at this "law-and-order" level throughout their lives, especially if they have no reason to move beyond it—in many day-to-day situations, this level of thinking works in the sense that it avoids trouble with society. They may never reach the final stage of moral development, in which morality is seen as derived from personal ethical principles—which can get a person in trouble when those ethical principles are at odds with the demands of society.

Can more advanced moral thinking be learned? In the early days of his theorizing, Kohlberg and others tried setting up experimental moral education classes for children and adolescents from a variety of social backgrounds. The results, even with juvenile delinquents, suggested that higher levels of moral judgment can indeed be taught. The classes centered on discussions of hypothetical moral dilemmas. Adolescents were presented with a problem and asked to give a solution. If the answer was argued at stage 4, the discussion

foundling fantasy   The early adolescent's feeling that her or his parents are so ordinary and limited that they can't possibly be related to a sensitive and unique her or him.

leader suggested a stage 5 rationale to see if the teenager thought it was a good alternative. The students almost always found that slightly more advanced reasoning was more appealing, and through repeated discussions they sooner or later began to form judgments at higher stages (Kohlberg, 1966).

Educators in particular are concerned with how morality develops during childhood and adolescence. They feel that if they could understand it better, they could do something about such problems as delinquency and drug abuse and help create a better social order. According to Kohlberg's framework, presenting a child with increasingly complex moral issues creates *disequilibrium* in the child's mind, forcing the child to think and try to resolve contradictions. Considering moral paradoxes and conflicts requires the child to use higher levels of moral reasoning. However, as noted, it is not always the case that superior moral judgments lead to superior moral behavior.

CONTENT CHECK
COGNITIVE CHANGES IN ADOLESCENCE

True–False (answers are on the Companion Website)

1. A major milestone in the stage of formal operations is the ability to test hypotheses.
2. Sooner or later, all individuals achieve formal operational thinking.
3. Metacognition improves markedly during adolescence.
4. The personal fable is an adolescent's idea that his or her current parents are not his or her real parents.
5. Sooner or later, all individuals attain Kohlberg's postoperational level of moral development.

Thinking Critically

How do improvements in cognition during adolescence alter the ways an adolescent views self and the social world?

CHAPTER 11 REVISTED

■ Cultures in which adolescence is relatively short usually have rites of passage.

■ Becoming an adult member of society is a universal milestone.

Adolescence Today

■ Adolescents have their own developmental niche, characterized by age segregation.

■ In industrialized nations, adolescence is often a prolonged period of economic dependence on parents.

■ Adolescents are markedly influenced by the historical context in which they live and by popular media.

Physical Development and Adjustment

■ A sharp increase in hormones released by the endocrine glands triggers the adolescent growth spurt and later the changes associated with entrance into puberty.

■ Some of the clumsiness displayed by early adolescents is attributable to asymmetry in growth.

■ An increase in body fat just prior to the growth spurt occurs in both females and males; females tend to keep it.

■ In males the androgen testosterone stimulates sexual maturation and changes; in females the hormones are estrogen and progesterone.

- The pituitary gland releases growth hormone and trophic hormones.

- In females, puberty follows menarche by up to a year or more; in males, puberty is marked by emission of viable sperm cells.

- Onset of puberty varies considerably; the average age of onset has declined in modern times.

- In males, the first sign of entrance into puberty is growth of the testes and scrotum; in females, the first sign is usually breast buds.

- Early menstrual cycles are often irregular and accompanied by temporary physical and emotional difficulties.

- Adolescents tend to be keenly focused on body image; boys focus most on strength, girls on weight.

- Anorexia nervosa and bulimia nervosa are more common among young females than among young males.

- Young adolescent males and females alike often would make changes in their bodies if they could.

- Among boys, early maturers tend to have advantages over late maturers; among girls, early maturing is a mix of disavantages and advantages.

Sexual Attitudes and Behavior

- The sexual revolution included increasingly liberal attitudes toward sex and variations in sexual behavior for both females and males; the revolution ended at least in part because of increases in teenage pregnancy and an epidemic of STDs.

- Attitudes toward masturbation have continued to become more liberal; historically, more boys than girls reported masturbating.

- Age of first sexual intercourse varies by gender and degree of academic orientation.

- The relationship between sexual activity and self-esteem varies by gender.

- Parent-child relationships and other family factors can influence the extent to which an adolescent is sexually active.

- Earlier maturers tend to become sexually active earlier; yet boys in general report being sexually active earlier than girls do.

- Sexual abuse is traumatic for both girls and boys; who is most likely to commit the abuse varies by gender.

- In the United States, the proportion of babies born to both married and unmarried adolescents has declined, although hundreds of thousands of babies are still born to unmarried adolescents each year.

- U.S. teenagers are no more sexually active than those in most European nations, but because of differing attitudes on the part of adolescents the U.S. teenage pregnancy rate is much higher.

- Teenage parenting is usually extremely difficult for married and unmarried teens alike and can have far-reaching effects on their lives.

Cognitive Changes in Adolescence

- Formal operational thought is characterized by abstract thinking, logical and systematic hypothesis testing, and increased ability to plan ahead.

- Not all people achieve formal operational thinking; theorists have also questioned whether this is a discrete stage.

- Various aspects of information processing improve considerably during adolescence, as does metacognition.

- Improvements in cognition during adolescence also shape how adolescents view their social world and themselves; in general, their views of institutions, cultural values, and society at large tend to become much more sophisticated and rational.

- The egocentrism of early childhood returns during adolescence, although in a different form; this is associated with beliefs such as the personal fable and ideas such as the foundling fantasy.

- Many people never achieve Kohlberg's highest levels of moral reasoning.

KEY TERMS

rites of passage	estrogen	bulimia nervosa
hormones	progesterone	same-sex orientation
adolescent growth spurt	menarche	imaginary audience
puberty	marginal group	personal fable
testosterone	anorexia nervosa	foundling fantasy

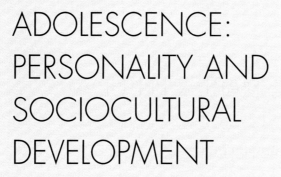

ADOLESCENCE: PERSONALITY AND SOCIOCULTURAL DEVELOPMENT

12

CHAPTER OUTLINE

Developmental Tasks of Adolescence
- Independence and Interdependence
- Identity Formation

Family Dynamics
- Intergenerational Communication
- Changes in Family Composition
- Leaving Home

Relationships During Adolescence
- Social Comparison
- Peer Relationships
- Negotiating the Borders: Peers and Parents

When Adolescence Goes Awry
- Risk-Taking
- Drug Abuse
- Delinquency

Stress, Depression, and Adolescent Coping
- Depression
- Depression and Other Disorders
- Protective Factors and Coping Behaviors

CHAPTER PREVIEW

Do you know:

1. What two major *developmental tasks* adolescents must face?

2. That for most, adolescence is not a period of *Sturm und Drang*?

3. How *dependence, independence,* and *interdependence* interact during adolescence?

4. How Erikson defined *identity formation* and what factors influence it?

5. What James Marcia's *foreclosure, diffusion, moratorium,* and *identity achievement* modes refer to?

6. How *identity status* is involved in adolescent behavior and how it differs by gender?

7. The role that *intergenerational communication* plays in resolving family conflicts?

8. What family factors help prepare an adolescent to *leave home*?

9. How *social comparison* influences adolescent personality development?

10. The distinction between a *clique* and a *crowd* and how peer groups influence adolescent personality and sociocultural development?

11. How adolescent *dating* develops?

12. Why some adolescents often engage in *risk-taking behaviors*?

13. The extent of adolescent *drug use* and how this has changed for various drugs over the years?

14. What propels some adolescents into *delinquent behaviors*?

15. What causes adolescent *depression* and *suicide*?

16. Factors that place an adolescent *at risk* for and factors that help *protect* adolescents from depression and other disorders?

These are the main topics of Chapter 12.

Adolescents frequently display a curious combination of maturity and childishness during their transition to adulthood. The mixture is awkward and sometimes comical, but it serves an important developmental function. How adolescents cope with the stresses created by changing bodies and new roles depends on their personality development in earlier years. To meet new challenges, they draw upon the skills, resources, and strengths they began to develop much earlier.

In the preceding chapter we observed that the transitional period between childhood and adulthood varies considerably from one culture to another. In some societies adult skills are mastered quickly and easily; new adult members are urgently needed and promptly recruited immediately following puberty. In contrast, in industrialized nations successful transition to adult status often requires lengthy education and occupational training. In these societies adolescence often stretches from puberty at least to the late teenage years and often well beyond. Adolescents thus live in an extended period of limbo: Despite their physical and intellectual maturity, many are excluded from meaningful work.

On the one hand, prolonged adolescence gives the young person repeated opportunities to experiment with different adult styles without making irrevocable commitments. On the other hand, a decade of adolescence generates certain pressures and conflicts, such as the need to appear independent and sophisticated while still being financially dependent on one's parents.

Some adolescents experience a great deal of pressure from their parents, who transfer to them their own compulsions to succeed and attain higher social status (Elkind, 1998). Adolescents must cope with these pressures as well as with those that come from within themselves. They must also accomplish significant developmental tasks and weave the results into a coherent, functioning identity. In this chapter we look at how young people cope with the dilemmas of adolescence and the resulting triumphs and setbacks. We examine how young people adopt values and form loyalties and become more mature. Involved are parents and peers—including crowds, cliques, and intimate friends—and choices as wide and varied as society itself. Also involved are stresses and maladaptive coping patterns that sometimes lead to risk-taking behaviors, drug abuse, delinquency, and even depression and suicide.

Developmental Tasks of Adolescence

Each period in life presents developmental challenges and difficulties that require new skills and responses. Most theorists agree that adolescents must confront two major tasks:

1. Achieving autonomy and independence from their parents (although the form this takes varies across cultures).
2. Forming an identity, which means creating an integrated self that harmoniously combines different elements of the personality.

In Western nations, adolescence has traditionally been viewed as a period of "storm and stress," a dramatic upheaval of emotions and behavior. The term derives from a German literary movement of the late eighteenth and early nineteenth centuries (**Sturm und Drang**). It was adopted by Anna Freud as a label for the emotional state that she believed to be characteristic of adolescence. She went so far as to say, "To be normal during the adolescent period is by itself abnormal" (1958, p. 275). She and other Freudians and neo-Freudians argued that the onset of biological maturation and increased sexual drive produces pronounced conflicts between adolescents and their parents, their peers, and themselves.

Are adolescents habitually troubled? Some are, but we now know that most are not. The majority are well adjusted and have no major conflicts with their parents, peers, or selves. Only an estimated 10 to 20% experience psychological disturbances, a percentage comparable to that of adults in the general population (Powers et al., 1989).

Independence and Interdependence

In the prevailing view, adolescents use conflict and rebelliousness as means of achieving autonomy and independence from their parents. Especially since the mid-1960s, the media have focused on the "generation gap" and turbulent conflicts between parents and their children. Stories with this theme are dramatic and interesting, but there is limited research evidence to support them. Most research in this area indicates that the degree of conflict between adolescents and their families has been greatly exaggerated.

Although the emotional distance between teenagers and their parents tends to increase in early adolescence (Steinberg, 1988), this does not necessarily lead to rebellion or to rejection of parental values. In a study of 6,000 adolescents in

Contrary to popular belief, adolescence is not inevitably marked by rebellion against parents.

Sturm und Drang   Term used by Anna Freud to describe adolescence as a time of dramatic upheaval of emotions and behavior; German for "storm and stress."

10 diverse nations—Australia, Bangladesh, Hungary, Israel, Italy, Japan, Taiwan, Turkey, the United States, and the former West Germany—Daniel Offer and his colleagues (Offer, Ostrov, Howard, & Atkinson, 1988) administered a questionnaire that focused on how teenagers perceived their family relations. They found that the vast majority of teenagers in each nation got along well with their parents and had positive attitudes toward their families. Only small percentages of respondents endorsed the following negative statements:

> My parents are ashamed of me. (7%)
> I have been carrying a grudge against my parents for years. (9%)
> Very often I feel that my mother is no good. (9%)
> Very often I feel that my father is no good. (13%)
> My parents will be disappointed in me in the future. (11%)

The adolescents' responses differed somewhat from one nation to another, underlining the importance of cultural context in adolescent development. Israeli youth, for example, reported the most positive family relations—probably because of the emphasis placed on family relations by traditional Jewish culture. In general, Offer's findings clearly contradicted the Freudian view of inevitable conflict stemming from biological drives and changes.

Definitions of autonomy that stress freedom from parental influence need to be reconsidered. Independence must take into account the continuing influence of parents during and after adolescence. John Hill (1987) suggested an interesting approach to adolescent independence seeking. He proposed that autonomy be defined as self-regulation. Independence involves making your own judgments and regulating your own behavior, as in the expression, "Think for yourself." Many adolescents learn to do precisely that. They reevaluate the rules, values, and boundaries that they experienced as children at home and at school. Sometimes they encounter considerable resistance from their parents, which may lead to conflict. More often, however, their parents work through the process with them, minimizing areas of conflict and helping them develop independent thought and self-regulated behavior (Hill, 1987).

Becoming an adult is of course a gradual transformation. It requires being simultaneously independent and interdependent. **Interdependence** can be defined as reciprocal dependence. Social relationships are interdependent—as, for example, in the workplace. Bosses depend on their workers to produce; workers depend on their bosses to manage the enterprise. Interdependence thus involves long-term commitments and interpersonal attachments (Gilligan, 1987).

Identity Formation

Before adolescence we view ourselves in terms of an assortment of roles—friend, enemy, student, ball player, guitar player—and in terms of membership in cliques, clubs, or gangs. In adolescence our improved cognitive powers (see Chapter 11) allow us to analyze our roles, identify inconsistencies and conflicts in them, and restructure them in forging an identity. Sometimes we abandon earlier roles; sometimes we establish new relationships with parents, siblings, and peers. Erikson (1968) saw the task of **identity formation** as the major hurdle that adolescents must cross in making a successful transition to adulthood. Ideally, adolescents enter adulthood with a stable and consistent sense of who they are and how they fit into society.

Influences on Identity   Adolescents derive many of their ideas about roles and values from reference groups. **Social reference groups** may consist of individuals with whom adolescents interact often and have close relationships,

interdependence   Reciprocal dependence.

identity formation   Gaining a sense of who you are and how you fit into society.

social reference groups   Narrow or broad groups with which people identify, and in so doing, help define themselves.

or they may be broader social groups with whom they share attitudes and ideals: religious, ethnic, generational, or interest groups, even chat or usenet groups on the Internet. Reference groups, whether broad or narrow, confirm or reject values and sometimes impose new ones.

Adolescents must come to terms with a variety of reference groups. Group memberships that were almost automatic in childhood—in the family, the neighborhood gang, or the religious youth group, for example—are no longer as comfortable or fulfilling as they were earlier. Often an adolescent feels conflicting loyalties to family, peer groups, and other reference groups.

Sometimes adolescents are drawn to the values and attitudes of a special person rather than to those of a group. This significant other may be a close friend, an admired teacher, an older sibling, a movie or sports or music star, or anyone whose ideas and behaviors the adolescent admires. Although the influence of significant others may be felt at any stage of life, it often has its greatest impact during adolescence.

In sum, adolescents are surrounded by a bewildering variety of roles offered by a multitude of reference groups and people. These roles must be integrated into a personal identity, and conflicting ones must be reconciled or discarded. This process is even more difficult when there is conflict between roles (for instance, between being a member of a fun-loving peer group and being a good student) or between significant others (for example, between an older sibling and a romantic partner).

Erikson's Concept of Identity   Erikson spent much of his professional life as a clinical psychologist working with adolescents and young adults. His writings on the process of establishing an "inner sense of identity" have had an enormous impact on developmental psychology. According to Erikson, identity formation is an often lengthy and complex process of **self-definition.** It provides continuity between the individual's past, present, and future. It forms a framework for organizing and integrating behaviors in diverse areas of life. It reconciles the person's own inclinations and talents with earlier roles that were supplied by parents, peers, or society. By helping the individual know where he or she stands in comparison to others, it also provides a basis for social comparisons. Finally, a sense of identity helps give direction, purpose, and meaning to life (Erikson, 1959, 1963, 1968; Waterman, 1985).

Modes of Identity Formation   James Marcia (1966, 1980, 1993) extended Erikson's theory and defined four different states, or modes, of identity formation. The four modes, or "identity statuses," are *foreclosure, diffusion, moratorium,* and *identity achievement.* At issue is whether the individual has gone through a decision-making period called an **identity crisis** and whether the individual has made a commitment to a specific set of choices, such as a system of values or a plan for a future occupation.

Adolescents who are in **foreclosure status** have made commitments without going through much decision making. They have chosen an occupation, a religious outlook, an ideological viewpoint, and other aspects of their identity, but the choices were made early and determined more by their parents or teachers than by themselves. Their transition to adulthood occurs smoothly and with little conflict, but also with little experimentation.

Young people who lack a sense of direction and seem to have little motivation to find one are in **diffusion status.** They have not experienced a crisis, nor have they selected an occupational role or a moral code. They are simply avoiding the issue. For some, life revolves around immediate gratification; others experiment,

self-definition   The complex and lengthy process of an individual forming an identity.

identity crisis   A period of making decisions about important issues, such as "Who am I, and where am I going?"

foreclosure status   The identity status of those who have made commitments without going through an identity crisis.

diffusion status   The identity status of those who have neither gone through an identity crisis nor made commitments.

seemingly at random, with various kinds of attitudes and behaviors (Coté & Levine, 1988).

Adolescents or young adults in **moratorium status** are in the midst of an ongoing identity crisis or decision-making period. The decisions may concern occupational choices, religious or ethical values, or political philosophies. Young people in this status are preoccupied with "finding themselves."

Finally, **identity achievement** is the status attained by people who have passed through an identity crisis and made their commitments. As a result, they pursue work of their own choosing and attempt to live by their own individually formulated moral code. Identity achievement is usually viewed as the most desirable and the most mature status (Marcia, 1980).

Effects of Identity Status   Research indicates that identity status profoundly influences an adolescent's social expectations, self-image, and reactions to stress. Moreover, cross-cultural research in the United States, Denmark, Israel, and other societies suggests that Marcia's four statuses are part of a relatively universal developmental process, at least in cultures characterized by an extended period of adolescence and an individualist orientation. Let's consider next how the four identity statuses interact with some of the problems of adolescence in such cultures.

Anxiety is a dominant emotion for young people in moratorium status because of their unresolved decisions. They often struggle with conflicting values and choices and are constantly faced with unpredictability and contradictions. They are often tied to their parents in an ambivalent relationship: They struggle for freedom yet fear or resent parental disapproval. Many college students are in moratorium status.

In contrast, adolescents in foreclosure status experience a minimum of anxiety. They have more authoritarian values than adolescents in the other statuses, and they have strong, positive ties to significant others. Young men in foreclosure status tend to have lower self-esteem than those in moratorium status and are more easily persuaded by others (Marcia, 1980).

Diffusion status is seen most frequently in teenagers who have experienced rejection or neglect from detached or uncaring parents. They may become dropouts, perhaps turning to alcohol or other drug use as a way of evading responsibility. Diana Baumrind (1991) has shown that drug and alcohol abuse are most common in children of "indifferent" parents (see Chapter 8).

Adolescents who have attained identity achievement have the most balanced feelings toward their parents and family. Their quest for independence is less emotionally charged than that of youths in moratorium, and it is not tainted with the isolation and sense of abandonment that troubles individuals in the diffusion status (Marcia, 1980).

The proportion of people in identity achievement status naturally increases with age. In high school there are far more individuals in diffusion and foreclosure statuses than in moratorium and identity achievement statuses. Identity status may also vary according to what aspect of identity is under consideration: A high school student may be in foreclosure status regarding sex-role preference, moratorium status regarding vocational choice or religious beliefs, and diffusion status regarding political philosophy.

Gender Differences   Marcia and other researchers have noted a marked difference between males and females in the behavior and attitudes associated with the various identity statuses. For example, males in identity achievement and moratorium statuses seem to have a great deal of self-esteem. Females in

moratorium status   The identity status of those who are currently in the midst of an identity crisis.

identity achievement   The identity status of those who have gone through an identity crisis and have made commitments.

these statuses appear to have more unresolved conflicts, especially regarding family and career choices.

Other studies partially confirm the earlier findings but present a more complex picture. Sally Archer (1985), for example, found that for family and career choices, girls in the later high school years are most likely to be in foreclosure status and boys are most likely to be in diffusion status. Further, girls in foreclosure and moratorium statuses express a great deal of uncertainty about reconciling conflicts stemming from their family and career preferences. Although both boys and girls say that they plan to marry, have children, and pursue careers, girls traditionally have been more likely to express concern about possible conflicts between family and career. When asked how much concern they had, 75% of males and 16% of females said none, 25% of males and 42% of females said some, and 0% of males and 42% of females said they felt a lot of concern about potential conflicts between family and career. It has also been found that whereas males primarily develop *intrapersonal* identity, females develop a blend of intrapersonal and *interpersonal* identity (Lytel, Bakken, & Romig, 1997).

In the other major areas of interest—religious and political beliefs—results are mixed. For religion, research indicates no significant gender differences. For political beliefs, there seems to be a significant difference in identity status between older male and female adolescents. Males have more often been found to be in identity achievement status, whereas females are more often in foreclosure status (Waterman, 1985).

Identity Formation, Culture, and Context   As noted in Chapter 2, Erikson's psychosocial theory favors development in Western societies that stress individual accomplishments over group or collective accomplishments. Nowhere is this more evident than in his conceptualization of identity formation during adolescence. The emphasis on becoming a distinct, relatively autonomous individual as opposed to becoming a contributing member of a cooperative group directly bears this out. In collectivist societies, for the most part, the good of the individual is subordinated to the good of the group—where "group" can refer to family, peers, neighborhood, town, or society at large. That is, collectivist societies place much less emphasis on autonomy and much more on a child or adolescent becoming and remaining interdependent with others (Matsumoto, 2000). To be sure, Erikson's theory has been found to have a high degree of universality with regard to each stage's crises per se; but what a given culture views as a *favorable* resolution of each crisis can vary considerably (Matsumoto, 2000). Identity—as well as self-concept— are thus deeply rooted in culture and context (Adams & Marshall, 1997; Portes, Dunham, & Castillo, 2000; Yoder, 2000).

Marcia's conceptualization of adolescent indentity statuses has also been the subject of considerable scrutiny since its inception (Marcia, 1966) and continues to be. Although some have argued that the statuses do not represent a continuum of distinctly different phases or paths toward identity achievement (Meeus, Iedama, Helsen, & Vollebergh, 1999), others have demonstrated that the statuses are at least useful in understanding adolescent states and transitions—again, in societies where a relatively extended period of adolescence exists (Jensen, Kristiansen, & Kroger, 1998; Kroger & Green, 1996; Stegarud, Solheim, Karlsen, & Kroger, 1999). What differs across cultures apparently is not the existence of different adolescent identity statuses. As Alan Waterman has proposed (1999), differences instead occur in the timing of the statuses, the stability of the statuses, and gender differences in the statuses. As various researchers have also found, the relative proportion of adolescents in each identity status differs according to culture and especially ideology and religiosity (e.g., Markstrom-Adams & Smith, 1996; Taylor & Oskay, 1995).

CONTENT CHECK
DEVELOPMENTAL TASKS OF ADOLESCENCE

True–False (answers are on the Companion Website)

1. Adolescence for most is best characterized as a period of storm and stress.
2. Across cultures, most adolescents get along well with their parents.
3. In Erikson's view, the single most important task of adolescence is acheiving autonomy.
4. Marcia's diffusion status is the least adaptive of the four identity statuses.
5. The effects of identity status differ for females and males.

Thinking Critically

How does adolescent identity formation differ in individualist versus collectivist cultures?

Family Dynamics

Throughout the process of identity formation, adolescents are forced to assess their own values and behaviors in relation to those of their family. In turn, the most important tasks of parenthood often seem paradoxical. On the one hand, successful parents provide their children with a sense of security and roots in an environment in which the children feel loved and accepted. On the other hand, successful parents encourage their children to become self-directing adults who can function independently in society.

How parents interact with their adolescents affects the adolescents' moves toward adulthood in dramatic ways. Family systems are dynamic: Behavioral changes in one family member influence every other member of the family. Because adolescence is a time of significant and often dramatic change, the family as a social system also changes, as does the nature of intergenerational communication.

Intergenerational Communication

The adolescent's emerging need for autonomy and self-definition normally leads to at least some conflict within the family and an increased need to talk with parents about certain issues. Adolescents remain very much influenced by their families, although their ties to the family may become strained. Studies have consistently shown that there is much less conflict between adolescents and their families than was previously believed. Surveys report serious conflicts in only 15 to 25% of families. Most conflicts revolve around such ordinary issues as family chores, curfew hours, dating, grades, personal appearance, and eating habits. Conflicts between parents and adolescents about basic economic, religious, social, and political values are much less common (Hill, 1987). The rel-

In general, the greater involvement of mothers in their adolescent children's daily life activities such as homework tends to make this a relationship more complex than the adolescents' relationship with their fathers.

atively few adolescents who form truly independent opinions about ideological matters generally do so late in high school or in college (Waterman, 1985).

Generally, early adolescence is more conflict-laden than later adolescence. When teenagers and their parents are older, both are better able to come to grips with potentially difficult autonomy and separation issues. It is important for parents and adolescents alike to realize that if they can maintain communication and share views during adolescence, the difficult issues can be negotiated successfully.

Mothers and fathers influence their teenagers in different ways. Although there is little difference between how adolescent males and females describe their family relations (Hauser et al., 1987; Youniss & Ketterlinus, 1987), there is considerable difference between the behavior and roles of mothers and those of fathers (Steinberg, 1987a). Traditionally, fathers tend to encourage intellectual development and are frequently involved in discussing and solving family problems. As a result, both boys and girls generally discuss their ideas and concerns with their fathers (Hauser et al., 1987). Adolescents' involvement with their mothers is far more complex. Mothers and adolescents are more likely to interact in areas such as household responsibilities, homework, discipline both in and out of the home, and leisure activities (Montemayor & Brownlee, 1987). Although these interactions may cause greater strain and conflict between mothers and their children, they also tend to create greater closeness (Youniss & Ketterlinus, 1987).

Parenting Styles   In Chapter 8 we discussed the influences of different parenting styles on children's psychological makeup. These influences continue into adolescence. The authoritative parenting style is most likely to result in normal or healthy adolescent behavior (Baumrind, 1991; Hill, 1987), characterized by responsible, independent actions and good self-acceptance and self-control. In contrast, adolescents who have experienced authoritarian parenting may be dependent and anxious in the presence of authority figures, or may become defiant and resentful. The often-but-not-universally negative impact of authoritarian parenting also holds up for ethnic groups, as does the positive impact of authoritative parenting (Lamborn, Dornbusch, & Steinberg, 1996).

The warmth and the confident control provided by authoritative parents is reassuring to most adolescents. The parent provides the experimenting adolescent with a safety net. The consequences of failure are not irreparable because the parents help pick up the pieces. Authoritative parenting also takes into account the adolescent's increased cognitive ability. For the first time, both parents and children can communicate using the same or similar levels of reasoning and logic (Baumrind, 1987).

Family Alliances   Family alliances also play a powerful role in communication. Like parenting styles, they begin to shape behavior long before adolescence. An older brother who dominated his younger brother during childhood will probably have the same influence in adolescence; a daughter who was "Daddy's girl" at age 6 will probably remain close to her father when she is 16.

Although alliances between various family members are natural and healthy, it is important that parents maintain a united front and a distinct boundary between themselves and their children. Parents also need to work together to nurture and discipline their children; a close bond between a child and one parent that excludes the other parent can be disruptive. The excluded parent loses stature as a socializing agent and an authority figure. Problems also arise from other kinds of imbalance, such as the absence of one parent because of divorce or separation. When an adolescent is testing new roles and struggling to achieve a new identity, parental authority may be severely tested in a single-parent home.

Changes in Family Composition

The effects of families in transition, discussed in earlier chapters, also continue into adolescence.

It is interesting to observe how changes in U.S. families have affected adolescents' responsibility for household chores. One study yielded some surprising findings (Benin & Edwards, 1990). Teenagers in dual-income families tend to help less around the house than those in families in which the mother is a homemaker. Moreover, the demands made on adolescents are divided along gender lines. Although sons in dual-income households spend only one-third as much time on chores as sons in traditional families, daughters in dual-income families spend one-fourth *more* time on chores than daughters in traditional families. In contrast, full-time homemakers expect their teenage sons and daughters to do an equal amount of work around the house. Why? The researchers suggest that working mothers may trust their daughters more than their sons to complete their assigned chores while unsupervised and therefore give them a larger workload. Homemakers may succeed in getting their sons to do an equal amount of work by monitoring them closely.

How do adolescents respond to the stresses and pressures associated with changes in family composition? Some take on added responsibilities. Others externalize their negative feelings and conflicts by becoming involved in antisocial, noncompliant behavior. Still others disengage themselves from the family by focusing on activities involving peers.

Leaving Home

For all concerned, making adjustments as adolescents become increasingly independent and prepare to leave home is not an easy task. Parents and children must renegotiate roles. Adolescents need different support than younger children because they explore their independence more actively. Separateness and self-assertion are not harmful characteristics; they are crucial to development. Some families encourage these characteristics; others oppose them.

Researchers have identified three dimensions of family functioning that are relevant here: *cohesion*, *adaptability*, and *quality of communication* (Barnes & Olsen, 1985). During the separation process, it helps if families have moderate but not extreme levels of cohesion and adaptability. It's best if families are somewhat flexible and adaptable, but not so loosely structured as to be chaotic. Also, families should be cohesive but not "smothering." Families adapt best if they can negotiate changes rationally, taking each member's wants and needs into consideration. Family cohesiveness can be maintained when parents and the departing adolescent can deal with one another as individuals and establish reciprocal relationships (Grotevant & Cooper, 1985). Open communication helps preserve family cohesiveness because it enables family members to talk things out and minimize friction.

Some studies suggest that fathers play a key role in helping adolescents find the right balance between separateness and connectedness, a balance that extends to the time when they are ready to leave home. Fathers who emphasize separateness give their adolescents the "space" they need to form their own identity and begin to take responsibility for their own actions. Adolescents generally have fewer conflicts with their fathers than with their mothers, which suggests that fathers tend to interfere less and have greater respect for their adolescent's independence. Thus, instead of expending energy opposing their fathers, many adolescents are free to pursue their own interests (Shulman & Klein, 1993).

Helping adolescents form their own identity and separate themselves from their parents may be more difficult in single-parent households. In such cases the involvement of another adult, such as a grandparent, aunt, uncle, or teacher, makes the transition easier for both the parent and the adolescent (Dornbusch et al., 1985).

CONTENT CHECK
FAMILY DYNAMICS

True–False (answers are on the Companion Website)

1. Serious conflicts between adolescents and their parents occur in a majority of families.
2. Mothers and fathers influence their adolescent children in much the same ways.
3. Usually, authoritative parenting fosters the best adolescent development.
4. Daughters in dual-income families tend to spend less time on chores than daughters in single-income families.
5. Adolescents tend to have fewer conflicts with their mothers than with their fathers.

Thinking Critically

In what ways is good intergenerational communication especially important?

Relationships During Adolescence

As individuals become more independent of their families, they depend increasingly on friendships to provide emotional support and serve as testing grounds for new values (Douvan & Adelson, 1966; Douvan & Gold, 1966). Close friends in particular help in identity formation. To accept her or his identity, the adolescent must feel accepted and liked by others.

During adolescence the importance of peer groups increases enormously. Teenagers seek support from others in coping with the physical, emotional, and social changes of adolescence. Understandably, they are most likely to seek support from peers, who are going through the same experiences. In a study of how much time adolescents spend with peers versus parents (Csikszentmihalyi & Larson, 1984), high school students were given electronic pagers and were beeped at different times during the day and evening. On each of these occasions there were to call the researchers and report what they were doing. As expected, the students spent significantly more of their free time with friends and classmates than with their families (including parents and siblings)—about 50% versus about 20%. They spent the rest of their free time alone.

Peer networks are essential to the development of social skills. The reciprocal equality that characterizes teenage relationships also helps develop positive responses to the various crises young people face (Epstein, 1983; Hawkins & Berndt, 1985). Teenagers learn from their friends and agemates the kinds of behavior that will be socially rewarded and the roles that suit them best. *Social competence* is a major element in a teenager's ability to make new friends and maintain old ones (Fischer, Sollie, & Morrow, 1986).

Social competence is based in part on the adolescent's ability to make *social comparisons*. Social comparisons enable the adolescent to form a personal identity and to evaluate characteristics of others. On the basis of these evaluations, adolescents choose close and intimate friends and sort through the cliques and crowds that are part of their environment. Adolescents are also faced with analyzing the often conflicting values of peers, parents, and others. Here we look at these processes in some detail.

Social Comparison

Social comparison is the process we all use to evaluate our abilities, behaviors, personality characteristics, appearance, reactions, and general sense of self in comparison to those of others, and it takes on tremendous importance during adolescence. Social comparison begins in early childhood, but it takes different forms during the adolescent years (Seltzer, 1989). During early adolescence, teenagers spend their time and energy defining themselves in a diverse "peer arena" made up of many different kinds of young people; they use this arena to explore and define who they are and who they want to become. They focus on their appearance and on personality characteristics that make them popular, such as a sense of humor and friendliness. This process involves a wide circle of acquaintances but few close friends; many of their relationships lack intimacy. Teenagers need time by themselves during this stage to sort out the different messages they receive, consolidate their identity, and develop a secure sense of self.

Social comparison changes during later adolescence. Teenagers now seek friends with whom they share similar characteristics as they substitute the quality provided by a few close friendships for a larger quantity of relatively loose friendships. Intimacy in same-sex friendships increases (Atwater, 1992; Seltzer, 1989; Shulman, Laursen, Kalman & Karpovsky, 1997).

Between ages 12 and 17, adolescents are increasingly likely to agree with statements like "I feel free to talk with my friend about almost anything" and

social comparison Evaluating yourself and your situation relative to others.

Peers serve as audience, critic, and emotional support for their friends' ideas, innovations, and behavior.

"I know how my friend feels about things without his or her telling me." Most adolescents report that they have one or two "best friends" as well as several "good friends." These friendships tend to be stable and usually last for at least a year. Not surprisingly, the stability of relationships also increases as adolescence progresses. Teenagers tend to choose friends on the basis of shared interests and activities, with equality, commitment, and especially loyalty playing major roles. Disloyalty is one of the main reasons teenagers cite for ending a friendship (Hartup, 1993).

As friendships become more intimate, teenagers tend to turn to close friends instead of to their parents for advice. As Table 12–1 shows, adolescents are likely to ask their peers for advice on many matters. However, they continue to seek advice from their parents on such matters as education, finances, and career plans (Sebald, 1989).

Peer Relationships

Identifiable trends occur in the development of peer relationships during adolescence, including dating. Pressures from peers may also conflict with the desires and demands of parents.

Cliques, Crowds, and Loners   There are two basic types of peer groups, distinguished by size. The larger type, with perhaps 15 to 30 members, is called a **crowd;** the smaller type, which might have as few as 3 members or as many as 9, is called a **clique,** and is more cohesive. Peer crowds typically have cliques

crowd   Adolescent peer group with about 15 to 30 members.

clique   Adolescent peer group with about 3 to 9 members.

Table 12-1   **Percentages of Teenagers Seeking Advice from Peers on Specific Issues**

Issues	Girls	Boys
What to spend money on	2	19
Whom to date	47	41
Which clubs to join	60	54
Where to get advice on personal problems	53	27
How to dress	53	43
Which courses to take at school	16	8
Which hobbies to take up	36	46
How to choose the future occupation	2	0
Which social events to attend	60	66
Whether to go to college	0	0
What books to read	40	38
What magazines to buy	51	46
How often to date	24	35
Whether to participate in drinking parties	40	46
How to choose a future spouse	9	8
Whether to go steady	29	30
How intimate to be on a date	24	35
Where to get information about sex	44	30

Adapted from Sebald, H. (1989, Winter). "Adolescents' Peer Orientation: Changes in the Support System During the Past Three Decades." *Adolescence*, pp. 940–941.

As adolescence proceeds, cliques expand to include both males and females.

within them. Clique members share similar backgrounds, characteristics, interests, or reputations; examples include "jocks," "populars," "brains," and "druggies" (Brown & Lohr, 1987; Dunphy, 1963, 1980). During early adolescence, cliques tend to be all male or all female; later, teenagers become involved in opposite-sex cliques as well. This change coincides with the beginning of dating. Small same-sex cliques merge or relate to other same-sex groups, expand to include opposite-sex groups, and finally reemerge as groups that include both males and females (Atwater, 1992; Dunphy, 1980).

Although about 80% of adolescents belong to identifiable groups, 20% don't and are therefore "loners." Most of us think of being alone as a sad state of affairs that no one would willingly choose, but this isn't necessarily the case. For example, creative work such as painting, composing music, or writing requires solitude. Creative people want to be alone much of the time. Solitude may have many other positive attributes as well. Some people experience a sense of renewal or healing when alone. Also, many seek solitude for the same reasons as the artist or writer—they can think best while alone and can work through their problems (Marcoen, Goossens, & Caes, 1987). In each case the aloneness is *voluntary*—an opportunity for creativity, relief from pressures, or psychological renewal.

Sometimes, however, adolescents wind up as loners because they feel that they're different and strange and can't really "belong." That can happen for many reasons, but a striking one is having grown up in a markedly different neighborhood, city, or region of the country. An extreme example—having lived overseas in childhood and then returning to the United States is discussed in "A Closer Look," page 419. Also on the negative side, *involuntary* aloneness imposed by others through arguments and rejection can bring on severe feelings of isolation and depression (Marcoen et al., 1987).

Dating   At the same time that the intimacy of same-sex friendships is increasing, friendships with members of the opposite sex are being formed. Close re-

A CLOSER LOOK

REPATRIATED ADOLESCENTS

At any given time, roughly a quarter of a million U.S. children and adolescents live overseas with their families, go to U.S.-sponsored or international schools, and are part of what are in effect small U.S. communities living in the midst of local cultures that are often quite different from their own. What is it like when they are repatriated—that is, when they and their families eventually return to the United States?

This experience, often termed *re-entry*, has been compared to coming back to the earth from outer space. It is often stressful and psychologically difficult for adolescents—especially if they have spent extended portions of their childhood periods. They feel different and may even look different; they find it hard to answer questions like "Where are you from?" They experience "re-

verse culture shock" when they encounter aspects of U.S. culture that are unfamiliar to them. It can take months, even years, to learn how to fit in and feel comfortable.

For adolescents who have this experience, identity formation may be particularly difficult. They may have to retrace the steps toward identity achievement outlined by Erikson and Marcia. And they are frequently treated as outsiders by peers. It is difficult for them to gain acceptance in already established crowds or cliques, especially if their outlooks and values are very different from those of their peers. Thus, at least for a time, they often become loners. Some will never feel that they truly belong.

On the positive side, repatriated adolescents often have a much more re-

alistic view of the United States and how its actions and policies affect other nations and peoples. Moreover, they often feel like "global citizens," avoiding the ethnocentric view of many citizens that the United States is the center of the universe. The skills they developed while living overseas—such as language ability and the ability to bridge cultural gaps—stand them in good stead as they pursue careers in such fields as intercultural counseling and international relations. In the long run, then—after their difficult period of adjustment—they may actually become better citizens than many who have not had an opportunity to view their nation from the outside.

Source: Smith, 1994.

---

lationships with opposite-sex friends are reported at an earlier age by girls than by boys (Sharabany, Gershoni, & Hoffman, 1981); this is probably because puberty occurs earlier in girls than in boys.

During early adolescence, most interactions with the opposite sex take place in group settings. Many 14- or 15-year-olds prefer group contact to the closer relationship of dating. In the United States, "just hanging out" (sitting around and chatting in a pizzeria, standing on a street corner, milling around a shopping mall) is a popular pastime throughout adolescence, and it becomes increasingly "coeducational" as adolescence progresses. This type of interaction is often the first step in learning how to relate to the opposite sex. Early adolescence is a stage of testing, imagining, and discovering what it's like to function in mixed groups and pairs. It gives adolescents a trial period to collect ideas and experiences from which to form basic attitudes about gender roles and sexual behavior without feeling pressured to become too deeply involved.

Bruce Roscoe and colleagues (Roscoe, Diana, & Brooks, 1987) noted seven important functions dating serves. These are summarized in Table 12–2, and it should be noted that they can be applied to same-sex dating as well as to opposite-sex dating—as can the following developmental trends noted by the researchers. Younger adolescents tend to think in terms of immediate gratification; they consider recreation and status to be the most important reasons for dating. Young adolescents look for dates who are physically attractive, dress well, and are liked by others. Older adolescents are less superficial in their attitudes toward dating; they are more concerned about personality characteristics and the person's plans for the future. Older adolescents consider companionship and mate selection important reasons for dating.

Table 12-2 Functions of Dating

Recreation: An opportunity to have fun with a person of the opposite sex.

Socialization: An opportunity for persons of opposite sexes to get to know each other and to learn how to interact appropriately.

Status: An opportunity to increase status by being seen with someone who is considered desirable.

Companionship: An opportunity to have a friend of the opposite sex with whom to interact and to share experiences.

Intimacy: An opportunity to establish a close, meaningful relationship with a person of the opposite sex.

Sex: An opportunity to engage in sexual experimentation or to obtain sexual satisfaction.

Mate selection: An opportunity to associate with members of the opposite sex for the purpose of selecting a husband or wife.

In addition, an interesting gender difference emerges for both younger and older adolescents: Females consider emotional intimacy more important than sex; males consider sex far more important than intimacy—consistent with the views of evolutionary psychologists as noted in Chapter 2.

In general, adolescents tend to select friends and dating partners who are similar to themselves in terms of social class, interests, moral values, and academic ambitions (Berndt, 1982). They become increasingly aware of peer groups and are very concerned about whether their group is "with it" or "out of it." Adolescents know which kind of group they belong to and consider its effect on their status and reputation. Teenagers who belong to high-status groups tend to have high self-esteem (Brown & Lohr, 1987). Also teenagers who have a strong sense of ethnic identity tend to have higher self-esteem than those who do not (Martinez & Dukes, 1997).

Negotiating the Borders: Peers and Parents

As we've seen, the backdrop for adolescents' relationships with their peers is their relationships with their families. Adolescents respond to their peers in the context of the cultural practices they grew up with at home, including their parents' socioeconomic status, occupation, and ethnic and religious background. Inevitably, there will be some difference between the world views of family members and those of peers. All teenagers must "negotiate the border" between differing world views in defining their own identities.

For some adolescents this task is especially difficult. For example, Hindu adolescents whose parents have immigrated to the United States from India face a double set of standards, many of which are in direct conflict. They must decide how to dress and wear their hair—in the traditional way, perhaps demanded by their parents, or in a way that conforms to that of their new U.S.-born peers. When one researcher investigated how Hindu adolescents handle this conflict (Miller, 1995), she found that such conflicts are more serious for girls than for boys. Girls must choose between strict Hindu standards, which require extreme modesty in attire and long, braided hair, and the more liberal clothing and hairstyles that are popular in the United States. Miller reported that time and again the influence of the peer group was stronger than that of parents. Even at events held at religious temples, some adolescent girls wore shorts while their parents wore the traditional sari or kurta/pajama wear. Similarly, Hindu adolescent girls in the United States frequently wear their hair short and unbound.

Conflicts also occur when Hindu values about dating and premarital sex clash with the more liberal values of the U.S. adolescent culture. As Indian psychoanalyst Sudhir Kakar (1986) explains,

> In sexual terms, the West is perceived as a gigantic brothel, whereas the "good" Indian woman is idealized nostalgically in all her purity, modesty, and chastity. For Indians living in the West, this idealization and the splitting that underlies it are more emotionally charged and more intense than would be the case in India itself. The inevitable Westernization of wives and daughters is, therefore, the cause of deep emotional stress in men, and of explosive conflicts in the family. (p. 39)

The difficult act of negotiating the borders between parental and peer values and practices is of course common to all adolescents, not just new immigrants. Some urban adolescents, for example, must negotiate between a peer culture that glorifies drugs and crime and parental values that stress working within the system and obeying the rules. For adolescents who are still in the process of defining themselves, there is a tendency to draw the borders too narrowly or to adhere slavishly to a narrow set of peer prescriptions for behavior, dress, and all the other things that matter so much to adolescents.

CONTENT CHECK
RELATIONSHIPS DURING ADOLESCENCE

True–False (answers are on the Companion Website)

1. Social comparison intensifies during adolescence.
2. Loners are almost always losers.
3. Younger adolescents are more likely than older ones to seek immediate gratification in dating.
4. Adolescents who have a strong sense of ethnic identity tend to have higher self-esteem than those who don't.

Thinking Critically

In what ways are peer relationships extremely important during adolescence?

When Adolescence Goes Awry

Experimenting with different attitudes and behaviors, defining and redefining oneself, and gradually moving away from parental control are hallmarks of adolescence that serve an important and healthy purpose—they help transform a child into an adult. These same tendencies, however, can yield extremely unhealthy behaviors during adolescence—such as risk-taking in general and drug use in particular. In this section we look at these and other aspects of the "down side" of adolescence, along with some of their causes.

Risk-Taking

Many adolescents continue to engage in unprotected sex, sometimes with multiple partners and with outcomes ranging from unwanted pregnancy to life-threatening diseases as noted in the preceding chapter. Many also abuse drugs. Teenagers are notorious for reckless driving and a variety of other dangerous activities. Violence, often gang-related, continues at an alarming rate.

Naturally, some teenagers are more prone to engage in high-risk activities than others, often engaging in more such activities as they get older (Jessor, 1992). For other teenagers, the increase in energy and intellectual curiosity that accompanies adolescence is harnessed in different ways, perhaps in sports, or put to constructive rather than potentially destructive uses. For example, many teenagers become involved in social activism, engaging in environmental clean-ups, helping to build houses for poor families, or working with sick children. It is important to keep in mind that only a minority of adolescents engage in destructive high-risk behaviors.

Adolescents engage in high-risk behaviors for a variety of reasons. They may get into trouble because they don't understand the risks they're taking. They may have too little information; the warnings they receive from adults may be ineffective, or they may choose to ignore them. Many researchers believe that adolescents who take risks underestimate the likelihood of bad outcomes; in other words, they see themselves as invulnerable. They focus mainly on the anticipated benefits of high-risk behaviors, such as higher status with some peers. This explanation is consistent with Elkind's concept of the personal fable (Chapter 11), in which adolescents believe that they won't get hurt, sick, or pregnant as a result of their behavior (Buis & Thompson, 1989).

The results of over two decades of research on adolescent risk-taking point to multiple causes for these behaviors (see Figure 12–1). Factors producing high-risk behaviors are divided into five domains: biology/genetics, the social environment, the perceived environment, personality, and actual behavior. These domains interact to cause adolescents to engage in high-risk behaviors or lifestyles. Note that both hereditary and social-environmental factors contribute. For example, a child with a family history of alcohol or other drug use might be predisposed to such behavior, experience environmental poverty and deviant role models, and be more like to engage in drug-related behavior than a child who doesn't experience each domain.

How can parents prevent adolescents from engaging in dangerous activities? Many families become involved in their children's schools, contact public officials and teachers when their child is having trouble, and take action to prevent drug use and other destructive behaviors at home. Some families move their child to a safer environment, such as a private school, to avoid negative neighborhood or peer group influences (Jessor, 1993). In general, when adolescents develop self-esteem, a sense of competence, and a sense of belonging to a stable family and social order, they are less likely to engage in high-risk behaviors (Jessor, 1993; Quadrel et al., 1993). However, there is no truly safe environment, and no child is completely invulnerable to the destructive forces that are ubiquitous in U.S. society. In the remainder of this section we will take a closer look at some of these forces, beginning with perhaps the most destructive of all: drugs.

Drug Abuse

A pervasive high-risk behavior during adolescence and young adulthood is the use and and therefore the abuse of alcohol and other drugs—in the United States, even drugs that are legal for adults are not for most adolescents. Of all the legal and illegal drugs that are widely available in this country, nicotine (cig-

Figure 12-1   A Conceptual Framework for Adolescent Risk Behavior

Source: "Risk Behavior in Adolescence: A Psychosocial Framework for Understanding and Action," (p. 27) by Richard Jessor, 1992, in Adolescents at Risk: Medical and Social Perspectives, *edited by D. F. Rogers and E. Ginzberg. Reprinted by permission of Richard Jessor.*

BIOLOGY/ GENETICS	SOCIAL ENVIRONMENT	PERCEIVED ENVIRONMENT	PERSONALITY	BEHAVIOR

Risk factors
  Family history
    of alcoholism
 	
Protective factors
  High intelligence
	Risk factors
	  Poverty
	  Normative
	    anomie
	  Racial inequality
	  Illegitimate
	    opportunity
	
	Protective factors
	  Quality schools
	  Cohesive family
	  Neighborhood
	    resources
	  Interested adults
		Risk factors
		  Models for
		    deviant behavior
		  Parent-friend
		    normative conflict
		
		Protective factors
		  Models for
		    conventional
		    behavior
		  High controls against
		    deviant behavior
			Risk factors
			  Low perceived
			    life chances
			  Low self-esteem
			  Risk-taking
			    propensity
			
			Protective factors
			  Value on
			    achievement
			  Value on
			    health
			  Intolerance of
			    deviance
				Risk factors
				  Problem drinking
				  Poor school work
				
				Protective factors
				  Church
				    attendance
				  Involvement in
				    school and
				    voluntary clubs

RISK & PROTECTIVE FACTORS

ADOLESCENT RISK BEHAVIORS/LIFESTYLES

Problem behavior	Health-related behavior	School behavior
Illicit drug use	Unhealthy eating	Truancy
Delinquency	Tobacco use	Dropout
Drunk driving	Sedentariness	Drug use at school
	Nonuse of safety belt	

RISK BEHAVIORS

HEALTH/LIFE-COMPROMISING OUTCOMES

Health	Social roles	Personal development	Preparation for adulthood
Disease/illness	School failure	Inadequate self-concept	Limited work skills
Lowered fitness	Social isolation	Depression/suicide	Unemployability
	Legal trouble		Amotivation
	Early childbearing		

RISK OUTCOMES

arettes) and alcohol (beer, wine, or liquor) have the highest potential for abuse—they're easily and cheaply obtained, and many adults serve as models for their use. Aside from the effects of these drugs, and in spite of public-service messages and education to the contrary, many adolescents consider smoking and drinking "safe" habits that make them look more adult. Marijuana, cocaine, amphetamine stimulants, heroin, and *hallucinogenic drugs* such as lysegic acid diethylamide (LSD) are also widely available in inner cities and suburbs and outlying areas alike. Given limited funds, some adolescents (and younger children) also resort to "huffing" volatile inhalants such as glues and even gasoline.

As described in Chapter 1, the National Household Survey on Drug Abuse (NHSDA), conducted annually by the Substance Abuse and Mental Health Services Administration (SAMSHA), assesses the extent of drug use and abuse in age ranges beginning at age 12. Although most experts agree that the survey underestimates actual drug use, it nonetheless provides a clear picture of *trends*

Figure 12–2 Current Illicit Drug Use, by Age, 1985 and 1991–1999
Current drug use means at least once in the month preceding the interview.

Source: SAMSHA, 1997, 2000.

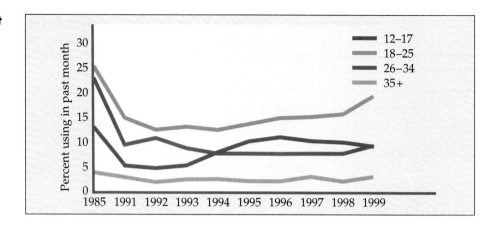

over the years, as illustrated in Figure 12–2. Aside from the alarmingly high percentages for persons ages 12 to 17 and 18 to 25, note the rise in illicit drug use in these age groups in the early 1990s—which then more or less stabilized for ages 12 to 17 but continued to rise for ages 18 to 25 over the remainder of the decade. Table 12–3 presents trends in drug use among 12- to 17-year-olds by type of drug.

Tobacco Cigarettes remain an alluring symbol of maturity to some teenagers, despite overwhelming evidence that cigarette smoking is a serious health hazard and the increasingly negative image associated with smoking in the minds of many adults. Smoking increases heart rate, constricts blood vessels, irritates the throat, and deposits foreign matter in sensitive lung tissues—thus limiting lung capacity. Years of smoking can lead to premature heart attacks, lung and throat cancer, emphysema, and other respiratory diseases. Even moderate smoking shortens a person's life by an average of 7 years (Eddy, 1991).

Tobacco smoking by U.S. adolescents showed a sharp decline in the 1970s and 1980s, but since then it has remained relatively stable. About 16% of adolescents reported "current" smoking (at least once within the past month) in 1999. In the past, boys began smoking earlier than girls and smoked more. Since the 1970s, however, more adolescent girls than boys have reported daily smoking. More than half of both boys and girls who smoke begin by the ninth grade, sometimes as a result of peer pressure. In the years just after high school,

Table 12–3 Percentages of Adolescents Age 12 to 17 Reporting Current Alcohol and Other Drug Use, 1985 and 1991–1999

	1985	1991	1992	1993	1994	1995	1996	1997	1998	1999
Any alcohol	41	27	21	24	22	21	19	20	19	19
"Heavy" alcohol	8	7	6	7	3	3	3	3	3	4
Cigarettes	29	21	18	19	19	20	18	20	18	16
Marijuana	10	5	5	5	6	8	7	9	8	7
Cocaine	3	1	1	1	1	1	1	1	1	1
Any illicit drug	13	6	5	6	8	11	9	11	10	9

Current drug use means at least once in the month preceding the interview.
Source: SAMSHA, 1997, 2000.

Many cigarette ads still target teenagers.

many light smokers begin smoking more heavily. As adults, many continue to smoke because nicotine is a highly addictive drug.

Perhaps not surprisingly, smoking is highly correlated with adolescent use of other drugs as illustrated in Figure 12–3. For example, of the adolescents classified as current smokers, about 55% also use alcohol at least occasionally, compared with only 10% of nonsmokers.

Alcohol   Alcohol is a CNS depressant with effects similar to those of sleeping pills or tranquilizers. When alcohol is consumed in small amounts, the psychological effects include reduced inhibition and self-restraint, a heightened feeling of well-being, and an accelerated sense of time. Many drinkers use alcohol to ease tension and facilitate social interaction—which it does, but only up to a point. Larger doses distort vision, impair motor coordination, and slur speech;

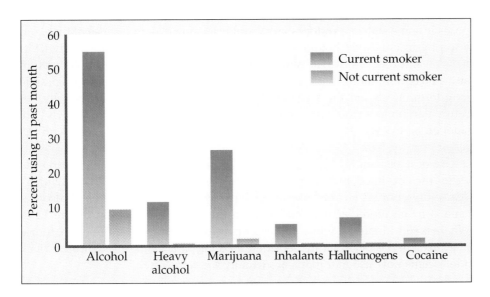

Figure 12–3 Use of Alcohol and Illicit Drugs by Smokers and Nonsmokers Age 12 to 17, 1996

Source: SAMSHA, 1997.

still larger doses lead to loss of consciousness or even death. These effects depend not only on the amount of alcohol consumed but also on individual levels of tolerance for the substance. Long-term habitual use of alcohol increases tolerance but eventually causes damage to the liver and brain. Gender is a factor too: Females don't metabolize alcohol out of their system as rapidly as males, so smaller amounts on average make females relatively more inebriated—although again depending upon an individual's tolerance level.

Like cigarettes, a powerful factor in teenage alcohol use is the notion that alcohol consumption is a symbol of adulthood and social maturity. In 1999 there were about 10½ million current drinkers in the 12 to 20 age range (SAMSHA, 2000). By early adolescence more than half of U.S. teenagers have used alcohol; the proportion grows to 92% by the end of high school (Newcomb & Bentler, 1989). Although only 1 in 20 high school seniors reports drinking every day, heavy drinking on weekends has become quite common among adolescents. Fully 35% of high school seniors report having had five or more drinks in a row at least once in the past 2 weeks, and 32% report that most or all of their friends get drunk at least once a week. Young adults who can drink legally tend to consume more alcohol because they may drink on a more regular basis at bars and social gatherings. These patterns of alcohol consumption have remained relatively stable in recent years, with only a slight decline since the 1980s.

Alcohol consumption by young people varies according to age, ethnic and religious background, locality, and gender. For example, the pattern of occasional heavy drinking ("binge" drinking) is highest for those in the 7 years immediately after high school (about 38%); for males (49% versus 28% for females); for noncollege youth; and for those who live in cities rather than in rural areas (SAMSHA, 2000).

The typical alcohol-abusing adolescent is a male with low grades and a family history of alcohol abuse. He is likely to have friends who also drink; he may also use other drugs. Many alcohol abusers have serious psychological problems such as depression, a poor sense of identity, lack of goals, or a tendency to constantly seek new sensations and experiences. In addition, poor self-efficacy and low personal competence are predictors of adolescent alcohol use (Scheier & Botvin, 1998).

Marijuana After alcohol and nicotine, marijuana is the most widely used drug in the United States. This drug, which is illegal (except for medicinal purposes in some states), produces mild euphoria and an altered sense of time, but also physical and psychological symptoms in those who use it regularly (Witters & Venturelli, 1988). The short-term effects include impaired coordination and perception, along with a rise in heart rate and blood pressure. Possible long-term effects are the same as those of smoking cigarettes, especially because marijuana is smoked without filtering; marijuana "joints" or "bowls" are smoked all the way because of the cost of the drug, with harsh effects on the respiratory system.

Use of marijuana by adolescents and young adults rose sharply during the 1970s, then declined, but began to rise again in the 1990s—about 7% of 12 to 17-year-olds reported current use in 1999 (SAMSHA, 2000). Marijuana also became a much more "egalitarian" drug in the 1990s, as shown in Figure 12–4. Whereas self-identified white adolescents were significantly more likely to use marijuana in the 1980s, white, self-identified Hispanic, and self-identified black adolescents now use marijuana at virtually the same rate.

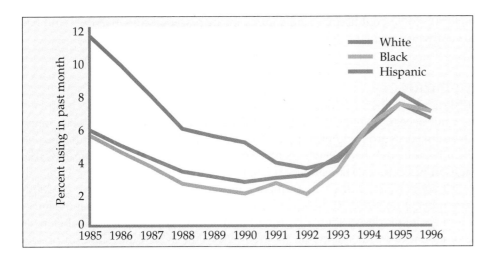

Figure 12-4 Current Marijuana Use by Ethnicity, Age 12 to 17, 1985–1996
Current drug use means at least once in the month preceding the interview.

Source: SAMSHA, 1997.

Cocaine Cocaine is an extract of the coca plant and is medically classified as a CNS stimulant, although it is legally classified as a narcotic. It is highly addictive in any form—powder, which is sniffed or injected in solution, or "crack," which is usually smoked. Crack is the most addictive form. Crack smokers experience the greatest initial "rush" of exhilaration; they also feel the most intense craving as the dose wears off. The full range of physical and psychological risks of cocaine use has not been studied fully, but the known risks include death from stroke, heart attack, or respiratory failure (Kaku, 1991; Witters & Venturelli, 1988). Using cocaine in conjunction with other drugs, such as alcohol and heroin, is popular and obviously increases the risks.

Because cocaine is very expensive, its use has never been common among adolescents; it is more likely to be used by young adults who can afford it, although it is also associated with prostitution at all ages. In fact, crack cocaine use is heavily implicated in the transmission of HIV/AIDS because some users engage in prostitution to support their habit; in addition, unprotected sex with multiple partners is routine in "crack houses."

As indicated in Table 12–3, cocaine use by younger adolescents has always been minimal and remained stable at about 1% during the 1990s. This is consistent with the observation that adolescents' attitudes toward cocaine use going into the 1990s had undergone a striking change: 97% disapproved of regular use of the drug (Newcomb & Bentler, 1989).

Heroin Heroin is a central nervous system depressant that alleviates pain, produces strong feelings of euphoria, and therefore is highly addictive. It is usually injected for maximum effect, although it can also be sniffed or smoked. As with cocaine, heroin use is relatively low among adolescents; however, heroin use showed a steady increase among high school seniors during the 1990s (University of Michigan, 2000). Among adolescents between the ages of 12 and 17, heroin use increased from 1994 to 1998, but that tapered off in 1999 (SAMSHA, 2000).

Other Drugs According to the University of Michigan's Monitoring the Future study (2000), an annual survey of junior high and high school students, hallucinogen use (including LSD) increased steadily in the 1990s but leveled off from 1997 on. Adolescent use of "designer" drugs such as ecstasy ("X") and other amphetamine derivatives has also been on the rise with a strong increase in 2000. Adolescent use of volatile inhalants increased in the early 1990s but has recently declined.

Delinquency

Risk-taking sometimes takes the form of delinquent behavior, which often—but not necessarily—goes hand in hand with drug use. Delinquent acts range in seriousness from shoplifting and vandalism to robbery, rape, and murder. People under age 16 or 18 who commit criminal acts are called **delinquents;** the age cutoff varies by state and by the nature of the crime.

At some point in their lives, most children engage in some form of delinquent behavior. Shoplifting is very common, as are minor acts of vandalism—damage to or desecration of property. Whether individuals are labeled as delinquent depends mainly on the frequency with which they commit misdemeanors or felonies and, of course, on whether they're arrested.

Statistically, delinquency rates are highest in poor urban areas, although this may be due in part to the tendency of police to make more arrests in those areas. Delinquency is also more likely among ethnic groups that have only recently been assimilated into urban life, either from other cultures or from rural areas—especially if they form gangs. Young males from single-parent homes headed by a mother are more likely to engage in delinquent behavior, regardless of the family's socioeconomic level. It is not merely the absence of a male role model that is responsible; an adolescent boy with a stepfather is as likely to get into trouble as one who lives with his mother alone (Steinberg, 1987b).

Sociologists and psychologists explain delinquentbehavior in different ways. Sociological statistics and theories link delinquency to factors in the youth's social environment, but they do not address psychological factors. Psychological theories maintain that environmental factors alone do not explain why adolescents commit crimes. Individuals are not delinquent because they are poor or live in a city. They may be delinquent because they are unable or unwilling to adjust to society or develop adequate self-control or outlets for anger or frustration. Some adolescents also become delinquent mainly because they are members of delinquent peer groups (Vitaro, Tremblay, Kerr, Pagani, & Bukowski, 1997).

The distinction between sociological and psychological causes of delinquency is artificial, however (Gibbons, 1976). As we have seen, sociological factors often lead to psychological consequences, and vice versa. Sociological influences such as crowding, mobility, and rapid change are linked to psychological problems. Like the other patterns we have studied in this chapter, delinquency is a form of adjustment to the social and psychological realities of adolescence—an extreme adjustment that society disapproves of. Delinquency may satisfy the need for self-esteem; it provides acceptance and status within deviant peer groups (such as gangs) and a sense of autonomy. Some delinquents engage in high-risk behaviors just for thrills.

In addition to individual factors, the mass media may be implicated in the development of violent or delinquent behaviors among vulnerable teenagers. Movies, for example, may affect troubled adolescents through social learning. Identification with a violent movie and its characters may lead to imitation of the characters' behaviors with regard to assault and battery, stealing, using and selling drugs, even "copy-cat" acts of violence.

delinquents People under age 16 or 18 who commit criminal acts.

CONTENT CHECK
WHEN ADOLESCENCE GOES AWRY

True–False (answers are on the Companion Website)

1. At one time or another, most adolescents engage in destructive high-risk behaviors.
2. Genetics is the primary cause of adolescent risk-taking behavior.
3. Teenage smokers are much more likely than nonsmokers to use other drugs as well.
4. Minority adolescents are much more likely than whites to use marijuana.
5. The prevailing veiw is that sociological and psychological factors interact to determine adolescent delinquency.

Thinking Critically

Why would adolescent drug use often be associated with deliquency?

Stress, Depression, and Adolescent Coping

Many articles and discussions about adolescents are filled with dramatic rhetoric. One article may claim that all adolescents are depressed or rebellious or potential runaways; another may state: "Wait until your child turns 12; then the parenting fun *really* begins!" Two problems arise from such overstatements of the psychological traumas of adolescence. First, all adolescents are labeled as experiencing psychological distress, which is not the case. Second, adolescents who need help are not taken seriously because their behavior and feelings are considered part of a normal developmental phase (Connelly, Johnston, Brown, Mackay, & Blackstock, 1993). Clearly, it is important to distinguish between normal adolescents and those who are experiencing real psychological distress. In this section we look at adolescent depression and other stress-related disorders, the factors that help protect adolescents from these disorders or make them vulnerable to them, and common coping responses.

Depression

In general, studies of psychiatric disorders during adolescence have found a fairly low incidence of moderate to severe depression, but in those who are affected the symptoms may be life-threatening (Peterson, Compas, Brooks-Gun, Stemmler, Ey, & Grant, 1993). In a recent study, for example, although the results show an increase in depression during the teenage years, the percentage experiencing depression is consistently low, peaking at age 16 and again at age 19 (see Table 12–4).

Symptoms vary by gender. Troubled boys are likely to engage in antisocial behaviors like delinquency and drug abuse. Troubled girls are more likely to direct their symptoms inward and become depressed (Ostrov, Offer, & Howard, 1989). Overall, depression is about twice as common in female adolescents (and adults) as in males. Although the reasons for these gender differences aren't clear, psychologists believe that they may be related to the substantial drop in self-esteem that sometimes occurs in girls when they enter junior high school

Table 12–4   Percentage of Adolescent Students Experiencing Depression, by Age and Gender

SEVERITY	13	14	15	16	17	18	19	TOTAL
Males								
None to mild	96%	97%	93%	88%	93%	94%	89%	93%
Moderate to severe	4%	3%	7%	12%	7%	6%	11%	7%
Female								
None to mild	93%	90%	89%	84%	87%	87%	82%	88%
Moderate to severe	7%	10%	11%	16%	13%	13%	18%	12%

The "Age" header spans columns 13 through 19.

Source: Connelly, Johnston, Brown, Mackay, & Blackstock, 1993.

(Bower, 1991b; Orenstein, 1994). As we have seen, girls are pressured by peers and the media to become more attractive and to value relationships above achievements (Connelly et al., 1993). In general, the combination of less effective coping styles and greater challenges may increase the likelihood of depression for girls as they move through adolescence.

Researchers have also found ethnic and other group differences in the incidence of depression in adolescence. For example, teenagers categorized as white or Asian are more likely to show symptoms of depression when under stress than are those categorized as black or Hispanic. Native American teens have elevated rates of depression. Same-sex-oriented adolescents also show higher rates of depression and are two to three times more likely to commit suicide than heterosexual adolescents (Connelly et al., 1993), presumably because of the negative social pressures they often encounter as a minority. Factors in adolescent suicide are discussed in more detail in "A Closer Look," page 431.

Depression and Other Disorders

In a recent review of the research literature on depression, Dante Cicchetti and Sheree Toth (1998) note that understanding childhood and adolescent depression requires understanding the interrelationships among biological, psychological, social-systems components. Several such interrelationships are discussed here.

Depression in adolescence often occurs at the same time as other disorders in response to internal and external stresses. Thus, depression and anxiety disorders often occur together, and so do depression and conduct disorders. Boys are more likely to be disruptive when depressed, whereas depressed girls are more likely to develop eating disorders such as anorexia or bulimia (Connelly et al., 1993), discussed in the preceding chapter. A high proportion of adolescents of either sex who attempt suicide are depressed, both before and after the attempt. Depression, thoughts of suicide, and substance abuse are also interrelated (Kandel, Raveis, & Davies, 1991).

On the other hand, poor body image may lead to eating disorders and then to depression. An elevated risk of depression has been found to be associated with illness, and this too can work in either direction—chronic illness is de-

A CLOSER LOOK

WHAT CAUSES ADOLESCENT SUICIDE?

In recent years, public concern over the increasing rate of adolescent suicide has led to increased suicide prevention efforts at the local, state, and federal levels. The concern is justified. In 1992, 4,693 adolescents and youth between the ages 15 and 24 and 314 children under age 15 committed suicide (National Center for Health Statistics, 1995). Suicide is the third leading cause of death among adolescents, behind accidents and homicide, and the statistics probably underestimate the actual number of suicides. Suicide tends to be underreported because of religious taboos against it and concern for the feelings of other family members (Garland & Zigler, 1993). Surveys of high school students have found that from 54 to 62.6% of students have either engaged in suicidal behavior or thought about suicide (Meehan, Lamb, Saltzman, & O'Carroll, 1992).

RISK FACTORS

Studies of adolescents who have attempted suicide, together with "psychological autopsies" of successful suicides, have revealed certain risk factors. Although many adolescents who experience of these risk factors do not contemplate or attempt suicide, these factors can provide early warnings that suicide is a possibility. Generally accepted risk factors for adolescent suicide include the following (see Norton, 1994, for a review of risk factors and warning signs):

1. A previous suicide attempt (the best single predictor).
2. Depression, including strong feelings of helplessness and hopelessness (perhaps the next best predictor).
3. Other psychiatric problems, such as conduct disorder or antisocial personality.
4. Abuse of alcohol and other drugs.
5. Stressful life events, such as serious family turmoil, divorce, or separation.
6. Access to and use of firearms.

In general, adolescents who attempt suicide are not responding to one particular upsetting event. Instead, suicides generally occur within the context of long-standing personal or family problems, although the attempt itself may be done on impulse (Curran, 1987).

Elkind (1998) attributed the dramatic increase in adolescent suicides to increased pressure on young children to achieve and be responsible at earlier ages. Others have blamed the mass media: There is a significant increase in adolescent suicidal behavior following television or newspaper coverage of suicides. Fictional stories about suicide have also been found to be associated with an increase in suicidal behavior (Garland & Zigler, 1993). "Copycat suicides" are particularly likely in adolescence, when individuals are most vulnerable to the belief that the future is beyond their control or is unlikely to meet their dreams.

PREVENTION EFFORTS

Crisis intervention services and telephone hotlines have been established throughout the nation to help prevent suicide. There are over 1,000 suicide hotlines available to adolescents. A rel-atively new approach, preventive education, is usually directed at secondary school students, their parents, and educators. These programs typically include a review of the statistics on suicide, the warning signs for suicide, a list of community resources and how to contact them, and the listening skills needed to convince a suicidal friend or family member to seek help (Garland & Zigler, 1993).

The American Psychological Association has developed a suicide prevention program (Garland & Zigler, 1993) that includes the following recommendations:

1. Professional education for educators, health workers, and mental health workers.
2. Restricting access to firearms by passing strict gun control laws.
3. Suicide education for media personnel to ensure correct information and appropriate reporting.
4. Identification and treatment of at-risk youth.

Given the severity of the problem, a comprehensive program such as this may offer the best means of preventing adolescent suicide. Prevention, of course, must be followed by treatment. Through psychotherapy, adolescents with suicidal tendencies gain insight into their problems and develop coping strategies. Therapy also helps troubled teenagers feel better about themselves and develop increased self-efficacy. Treatment may also include antidepressive medications such as Elavil, Tofranil, and Prozac (Shuchman & Wilkes, 1990).

pressing, and depression can increase vulnerability to illness. Depression may also cause other problems because of its impact on interpersonal functioning, and vice versa. Poor social functioning may worsen the parent-child relationship during adolescence and may also affect friendships and romantic relationships. For example, pregnancy is three times more likely among depressed teenage girls than among those who are not depressed (Horowitz, Klerman, Sungkuo, & Jekel, 1991).

Protective Factors and Coping Behaviors

The biological changes of puberty, as well as the social changes related to the move from elementary school to middle and high school, all demand extensive psychological adjustment. Here we look at risk factors, protective factors, and coping behaviors.

Risk Factors   Factors that place adolescents at risk for depression and stress reactions include the following:

1. Negative body image, which is believed to lead to depression and eating disorders.
2. Increased capacity to reflect about oneself and the future, which can lead to depression as adolescents dwell on negative possibilities.
3. Family dysfunction or parental mental health problems, which can lead to stress reactions and depression as well as conduct disorders.
4. Marital discord or divorce and economic hardship in the family, which lead to depression and stress.
5. Low popularity with peers, which is related to depression in adolescence and is among the strongest predictors of adult depression.
6. Low achievement in school, which leads to depression and disruptive behavior in boys but does not appear to affect girls.

In the United States, many girls emerge from early adolescence with a poor self-image, relatively low expectations of life, and much less confidence in themselves and their abilities than is true of boys (American Association of University Women, 1991; Orenstein, 1994; Zimmerman, Copeland, Shope, & Dielman, 1997). At age 9 a majority of girls feel positive about themselves, but by the time they reach high school less than a third feel that way. Although boys lose some self-esteem during the middle school years, their loss isn't nearly as great as that of girls.

There are significant ethnic differences in this loss of self-esteem: It appears to be largely a phenomenon found among those who identify as white. Surveys indicate that ethnically black adolescent girls seem to derive self-esteem from their families and communities rather than from their experiences in school. Black girls may be surrounded by strong women whom they admire. In addition, black parents often emphasize to their children that there is nothing wrong with them, only with the way the world treats them. White girls, on the other hand, may overreact to social cues in schools where boys are favored, as noted in earlier chapters. By the age of 15 or 16, many white girls are filled with self-doubt. When they have problems with academic subjects such as math, they are more likely to blame themselves, whereas boys are more likely to blame the course or the teacher (Daley, 1991). As Carol Gilligan put it,

> This [research] makes it impossible to say that what happens to girls is simply a matter of hormones. . . . If that was it, then the loss of self-esteem would happen to all girls and at roughly the same time. This work raises all kinds of issues about cultural contributions and it raises questions about the role of the schools, both in the drop of self-esteem and in the potential for intervention. (As quoted by Daley, 1991)

Protective Factors   There are three sets of counterbalancing factors that help adolescents cope with the transitions of this period. First, good relationships with parents and peers serve as buffers against stress. The importance of protective, supportive relationships cannot be overstated. Second, a particular area of competence or expertise, such as in sports, music, a craft, or an academic subject, can give the teenager with a basis for realistic self-confidence. Finally, a role that includes responsibility for others (perhaps team members or younger siblings) can help an adolescent set priorities and respond to challenges or crises with greater resilience.

Coping Responses   Adolescents use a variety of coping responses to deal with the stress of their daily lives. Positive coping strategies, such as careful planning and organization, setting priorities, or finding a close friend or confidante, can help relieve moderate stress. When an adolescent is under heavy stress, the use of more negative defensive strategies increases. In general, research has found that substance use, diversions, and rebelliousness are major ways in which adolescents cope with stress. Students at all levels report drinking alcohol, smoking cigarettes, and using drugs to reduce feelings of stress. The diversions they report include shopping, taking a hot bath or shower, going out with friends, sleeping, watching television, and eating. These activities do not deal with problems directly, but at least they divert attention from them. In all, few adolescents who are under extreme stress feel that they can deal with the stress directly—they often lack the personal resources (Mates & Allison, 1992).

CONTENT CHECK
STRESS, DEPRESSION, AND ADOLESCENT COPING

True–False (answers are on the Companion Website)

1. Depression is more frequent among adolescent females than adolescent males.
2. Rates of depression vary little across ethnic groups.
3. Typically, depression among adolescents is caused by poor body image.
4. Both girls and boys experience a significant decline in self-esteem as they enter adolescence.

Thinking Critically

Why is suicide often associated with depression?

CHAPTER 12 REVISITED

Developmental Tasks of Adolescence

■ The two major tasks of adolescence are achieving autonomy and forming an identity.

■ Adolescence is not a time of Sturm und Drang for most.

■ Cross-cultural research indicates that the majority of adolescents around the world get along well with their parents.

■ Becoming an adult is best described as occurring through a process of interdependence.

■ Identify formation is strongly influenced by social reference groups.

■ Erikson's theory of identity formation emphasizes self-definition.

■ Marcia's extension of Erikson's theory notes four identity statuses: *foreclosure, diffusion, moratorium,* and *identity achievement.*

■ Anxiety differs across the identity statuses; there are also gender differences in the statuses affect adolescents.

Family Dynamics

■ Conflicts between adolescents and their parents are usually minor; good intergenerational communication helps resolve family conflicts.

■ Mothers and fathers influence their adolescents differently by stressing the importance of different behaviors and goals.

■ Authoritative parenting usually works best in helping children navigate adolescence.

■ Household responsibilities and chores differ between single- and dual-income families, also by gender of the child.

■ Beyond achieving a sense of identity, achieving a balance between separateness and connectedness is helpful as an adolescent prepares to leave home.

Relationships During Adolescence

■ Adolescents spend significantly more time with members of their peer groups than with family.

■ Peer groups are essential to the development of social skills; ideally, through peer group interactions adolescents develop a sense of social competence.

■ Social comparison intensifies during adolescence; aside from its effects on personality development, it is also involved in the formation of friendships.

■ Cliques and crowds are two basic types of adolescent peer groups.

■ A significant percentage of adolescents are loners who do not belong to peer groups; being a loner can come about in various ways.

■ Hanging out in groups is often a precursor to actual dating; dating in turn serves a number of functions important to development.

■ Belonging to a high-status peer group or to an ethnic peer group often enhances self-esteem.

■ Adolescents often have to negotiate between peer group and parental requirements.

When Adolescence Goes Awry

■ A minority of teenagers often engage in potentially destructive risk-taking behaviors; many more spend their time constructively.

■ Reasons for engaging in risk-taking behaviors vary considerably; the personal fable often plays a role.

■ A conceptual framework for adolescent risk-taking emphasizes the interaction of biological/genetic, social-environmental, perceived-environmental, personality, and behavioral factors.

■ In the United States, nicotine and alcohol have the highest potential for abuse by adolescents.

■ Adolescent use of illicit drugs declined going into the 1990s, but then at least temporarily increased; adolescent smoking and use of alcohol remained relatively stable but high in the 1990s.

■ Adolescents who smoke are much more likely to use other drugs as well.

■ Various statistics show that alcohol remains a very popular drug for U.S. adolescents, although its use varies according to numerous personal and sociocultural factors.

■ Marijuana use ranks third among adolescents; the incidence of its use varies little across ethnic groups.

■ Adolescent use of other drugs popular with older persons has always been minimal because their cost.

■ Delinquents commit more than their share of serious crimes; sociological and psychological factors are contributors.

Stress, Depression, and Adolescent Coping

■ Depression occurs at a relatively low but significant rate during adolescence; its incidence and the behaviors associated with it vary according to the adolescent's age, gender, sexual orientation, and ethnicity.

■ Depression is often associated with suicide or suicide attempts, also with other disorders such as anorexia and bulimia; however, what causes what in depression is often difficult to determine.

■ Family, social, and personal factors place an adolescent at risk for depression; loss of self-esteem during adolescence is an important personal factor, gender is another.

■ A good family relationship, a sense of expertise in something, and a sense of responsibility for others are protective factors with regard to the effects of stress and depression.

■ Adolescents use a variety coping methods in dealing with stress or depression; many are maladaptive, others are merely diversions.

KEY TERMS

Sturm und Drang
interdependence
identity formation
social reference groups
self-definition

identity crisis
foreclosure status
diffusion status
moratorium status
identity achievement

social comparison
crowd
clique
delinquents

YOUNG ADULTHOOD: PHYSICAL AND COGNITIVE DEVELOPMENT

13

CHAPTER OUTLINE

Perspectives on Adult Development
- Age Clocks and Social Norms
- Contextual Paradigms or Approaches

General Physical Development
- Strength and Stamina
- Fitness and Health

Sex and Sexuality
- Sexual Attitudes and Behavior
- Fertility
- Sexual Responsiveness
- Same-Sex Orientation and Sexual Activity
- Sexually Transmitted Diseases and Social Change

Cognitive Continuity and Change
- Cognitive Growth or Decline?
- "Stages" of Thought in Young Adulthood
- Flexibility in Intelligence

Seasons and Tasks of Adult Development
- Havighurst's Developmental Tasks
- Erikson's Developmental Tasks
- Levinson's Seasons of a Man's Life
- Levinson's Seasons of a Woman's Life
- Gould's Transformations

CHAPTER PREVIEW

Do you know:

1. How *age clocks* and *social norms* define adult periods such as young adulthood?

2. That *biological age* in interaction with *social age* and *psychological age* provides a more accurate picture of a person's maturity?

3. What changes occur in *strength*, *stamina*, and *perceptual* and *motor skills* during adulthood, and when they peak?

4. That improvements in *exercise* and *diet* are why athletes continue to break past records?

5. That death rates are *lower* for young adults than for any other adult age group, and what the *leading causes of death* are?

6. That the majority of people in the United States have very few *sex partners* during their lifespan?

7. How adult *attitudes toward sex* have changed over the years?

8. That orgasms are not crucial to having a *satisfying sex life?*

9. The distinctions between *lesbian*, *gay*, and *bisexual*, and that sexual activity with a member of the same sex doesn't necessarily equate with being *same-sex oriented?*

10. What identifiable stages are there in adult *cognitive development?*

11. What *dialectical thinking* is?

12. That some view *cognitive flexibility* as a hallmark of adult thinking?

13. The role of *systems of meaning* in adult cognitive development?

14. What *developmental tasks* theorists believe adults must face?

15. What the *seasons* of a person's life are, and what men and women have in common and how they differ?

16. How a person's *assumptions*, *ideas*, *myths*, and *world view* change during adulthood?

These are the main topics of Chapter 13.

Development continues throughout life. Although some theorists argue that there are recognizable developmental stages in adulthood, the developmental processes that occur during the adult years differ from those that occur during childhood and adolescence. Changes in adult thought, personality, and behavior are much less a result of chronological age or specific biological changes than of personal, social, and cultural forces or events. The social milestones and cultural demands of the young adult may support, expand, or disrupt behavior patterns laid down in the adolescent years. Decisions must be made and problems solved on a daily basis. A hallmark of maturity is increasing ability to respond to change and adapt to new conditions. Positive resolution of contradictions and difficulties is the basis for mature adult activity (Datan & Ginsberg, 1975). Not all adults progress the same way or structure their lives the same way. Pathways can diverge considerably during adulthood, and adults therefore have less in common than children.

As we see, however, there are some commonalities in the developmental processes of adulthood. Although there are no adult physical markers comparable to pubescence, and no clear-cut cognitive stages, we do have culturally defined *social* milestones to go by, such as roles and relationships that are part of the cycles of family and career. Social and emotional development is blended with the gradual physical changes that take place during the adult years, as well as with the individual's growing body of knowledge, skills, and experience—all of which may be influenced by sudden, traumatic events that can occur on both a personal and a sociocultural level.

The timing of social milestones such as marriage, parenting, and career choice varies widely from one individual to another and from one culture to another. The ways in which different people react to these events, as well as the nature of the roles they must play vary according to the demands and restrictions of the culture. Some social events—and the transitions that surround them—are *normative;* others are *idiosyncratic.* Normative events and transitions occur at relatively specific times and are shared with most people in a particular age cohort. Such events aren't usually associated with extreme, acute stress. There is time for planning, and social support and cultural meaning are often available to provide guidance. Examples of such events include looking for a first job and moving out of the parental home.

In contrast, idiosyncratic events and transitions can happen at any time. Examples include losing a job, having a spouse die suddenly, contracting a major illness, or—on a happier note—winning the lottery. Because these events often are not anticipated or emotionally shared with others, they create considerable stress and a need for major reorganization of the person's life both personally and socially.

In this chapter, in addition to exploring physical and cognitive development in young adulthood, we lay the groundwork for the chapters that follow. We examine fundamental concepts and theories of adult development, looking at how theorists define adulthood. Next we turn more specifically to young adulthood, first in terms of physical development and then in terms of cognitive functioning from the perspectives of both continuity and change. We examine whether there are identifiable stages of adult cognitive development, along with characteristics of adult cognition—which interacts with social and personality development. Finally, we look at some of the developmental tasks of young adulthood.

Perspectives on Adult Development

As discussed in Chapter 1, we conventionally divide the adult years into young adulthood (the 20s and 30s), middle adulthood (the 40s and 50s), and later adulthood (age 60 or 65 and up). We have also noted that what age means to a given individual can vary considerably. How can we classify and study adult development if so much of it is based on individual behavior and judgment? In the absence of markers other than arbitrary age ranges, we turn to the concepts of *age clocks* and *social norms.*

Age Clocks and Social Norms

It is difficult if not impossible to pinpoint stages of adult development solely on the basis of age, so researchers devised the concept of the **age clock** (Neugarten, 1968). Age clocks are a form of internal timing; they let us know if we are progressing through life too slowly or too quickly. For example, a 35-year-old who is still in college might be considered to be lagging behind his or her peers; a 35-year-old who is thinking about retirement might be considered to be far ahead of them. Age clocks let us know when certain events in our life should

age clock A form of internal timing used as a measure of adult development; a way of knowing that we are progressing too slowly or too quickly in terms of key social events that occur during adulthood.

Although age clocks let us know when events generally should occur, they are more flexible than previously. Many people, like this woman, are returning to school in their 30s or even later.

biological age A person's position with regard to his or her expected lifespan.

social age An individual's current status as compared with cultural norms.

psychological age An individual's current ability to cope with and adapt to social and environmental demands.

contextual paradigms The view that numerous environmental, social, psychological, and historical factors interact to determine development.

occur, relative to our culture. If these events happen earlier or later than expected, we may experience distress and less peer support than when we accomplish things according to schedule.

In other words, we have built-in expectations, constraints, and pressures for various periods of life that we apply to ourselves and others. Although these boundaries sometimes have a biological or psychological basis—a woman normally can't conceive after menopause; an older man might not welcome the rigors of rearing an infant—the boundaries are more often socially based. For example, if we observe a couple proudly introducing their newborn child, we will probably have quite different reactions depending on whether the couple is in their 20s or their 40s. We will interpret the motivations of the couple differently, and we may also behave differently toward them. To complicate matters further, the behaviors expected of an individual and the reactions of others can vary considerably according to historical and cultural contexts, as discussed in "A Closer Look," page 441.

In examining cultural changes in the United States over recent decades, Bernice and Dail Neugarten (1987) suggested that there has been a "blurring of traditional life periods," with the result that age clocks are more flexible now than they were in earlier decades. "Nontraditional" students return to school at age 35, 45, or even older; many couples postpone having their first child until they are in their mid to late 30s; marriage, divorce, and remarriage occur throughout the lifespan, not just during early adulthood. In many respects, the United States has become an "age-irrelevant" society in which members of a given adult age cohort may be involved in vastly different activities and life events.

Three Components of Age   It is important to keep in mind that an adult's *chronological age* (number of years of life) has relatively little meaning by itself. **Biological age** is a preferable way of looking at things, in interaction with **social age** and **psychological age** (Birren & Cunningham, 1985). Biological age, which is the person's position with regard to his or her expected lifespan, varies tremendously from one individual to another. A 40-year-old with emphysema and a severe heart condition who is likely to die in the near future differs greatly in biological age from a healthy 40-year-old who can expect to live another 35 years or more. In turn, social age refers how an individual's current status compares to cultural norms. A 40-year-old married person with three children is developmentally different from a 40-year-old single person who engages in casual dating and doesn't plan to have children. Finally, psychological age refers to how well a person can adapt to social and other environmental demands. It includes such things as intelligence, learning ability, and motor skills, as well as subjective dimensions like feelings, attitudes, and motives.

What is maturity? Although biological, social, and psychological age combine to determine maturity, certain psychological characteristics are the primary ingredients. Although they vary somewhat according to the culture, they include physical and social independence and autonomy; independent decision making; and some degree of stability, wisdom, reliability, integrity, and compassion. Different investigators put different characteristics into the blend, and different cultures make different demands, with the result that there is no universal definition of maturity.

Contextual Paradigms or Approaches

A *paradigm* is a hypothetical model or framework, or, more simply, a systematic way of looking at things. **Contextual paradigms** for human development seek to describe and organize the effects of different kinds of forces on development.

A CLOSER LOOK

HISTORY, CULTURE, AND THE LIFE COURSE

The study of adult development is in many ways a study of the life course—the ways in which an individual's personal biography intertwines with the historical period in which she or he lives and with the person's place in the social system. Research reveals that social, cultural, and historical factors affect crucial transitions in an adult's life in dramatic ways and that these factors help define personal expectations (Hagestad, 1990; Stoller & Gibson, 1994).

It is important, therefore, to examine how historical factors define the demographic conditions of a period and influence the normal expectations and life scripts of people living in that period. It is clear that an ethnically black woman born in poverty in 1950 will have a very different life course than an ethnically white woman born into a socially well-connected family in an affluent section of the city. It is also clear that a black woman born in 1870 had a very different life course than a black woman born 100 years later. Perhaps the most important historical change affecting the life course is the increasing length of the lifespan. Whereas in 1900 only about 14% of U.S. women reached age 80 or older, by 1980 more than half

of them expected to reach that age (Watkins, Menken, & Bongaarts, 1987). In Germany in 1600, nearly half of all children never reached adulthood, with the result that for centuries "it took two infants to make one adult" (Imhof, 1986). These changes affect how families experience a child's death. Losing a child was once a normal and expected event; it is now an abnormal part of the social script. In 1800, by the time an average woman reached age 35 in 1800, she had lost one-third of her children. In 1990, less than 1% of 35-year-old women had lost a child. As a result, the death of a child is now a shattering personal loss instead of an event that touches almost every woman's life at one time or another.

Historical periods also affect the "time budgets" of adulthood, with the result that today's adults spend their lives in very different ways than those of earlier periods. When Ellen Gee (1986, 1987, 1988) studied the demographic conditions prevailing in 1830, she found that after a woman married, 90% of her life was spent raising children. In contrast, in 1950 the percentage had dropped to 40%. Another interesting observation was that in 1860 only 16% of

50-year-olds had living parents, whereas by 1960 the figure had risen to 60%.

The death of a parent is a more age-graded transition today than ever before; that is, it occurs during predictable times in the lifespan. The death of parents now occurs significantly later in a child's life and is likely to be encountered during a relatively narrow band of time (Winsborough, 1980). As a result, it is common to hear the Baby Boomers referred to as the "sandwich" generation because they are responsible both for raising children and for caring for aging, often infirm, parents.

When the effects of factors such as gender, race, socioeconomic status, personality, and intelligence are considered in addition to historical periods, each individual's life course is unique. Nevertheless, researchers remain fascinated with discernible patterns shared by members of the same adult cohorts. They wonder how these patterns will evolve over the next 100 years as medicine and technology prolong life and reduce disease and suffering, as gender roles continue to change, and as ethnic minorities become an ever-larger part of the "gorgeous mosaic" of the U.S. population.

The term *context* is used here the way it has been used at other points in the text: We speak of the environmental context, the social context, the psychological context, and the historical context, each of which influences development in interaction with the others.

Context is a large part of what make us unique as individuals: No two individuals experience exactly the same combination of contexts. Contextual paradigms attempt to pull the various contexts together into an orderly package and thereby provide insights into both commonalities and idiosyncrasies in development. They focus on developmental forces as a whole, whether those forces are within or external to the individual, meaning biological/maturational or experiential/historical (Dixon, 1992). The contrasting (and outdated) approach is to view development from only one perspective at a time, excluding all the rest.

Needless to say, contextual approaches are complex. They also apply throughout the lifespan, beginning in early childhood. At no point, however, do contextual considerations become more important than in adult development, when, as noted earlier, pathways of life begin to diverge markedly compared to those of childhood and adolescence.

CONTENT CHECK
PERSPECTIVES ON ADULT DEVELOPMENT

True–False (answers are on the Companion Website)

1. Age clocks are primarily cultural in nature.
2. Chronological age is the best way to determine where a person is with respect to the lifespan.
3. Contextual paradigms focus on development forces as a whole.

Thinking Critically

Why is it difficult to define the beginning and end of young adulthood?

General Physical Development

In part, our responses to life events are determined by our physical capacity—our health, fitness, strength, and stamina. Almost every aspect of physical development reaches its peak in early adulthood. Most young adults are stronger and healthier than they have ever been or will ever be.

Strength and Stamina

In young adulthood—the 20s and 30s—most people enjoy peak vitality, strength, and endurance compared to people in other age ranges. This is a normative, age-graded expectation, as discussed in Chapter 3. Most cultures capitalize on these prime years by putting professional apprentices through grueling regimens of internships, bar exams, and dissertation defenses; sending the young to do battle; idolizing young athletes and fashion models; and expecting women to have children.

For the most part, organ functioning, reaction time, strength, motor skills, and sensorimotor coordination are at their maximum between the ages of 25 and 30; after that they gradually decline. However, the decline that occurs during the 30s and 40s is less than most people imagine. As Figure 13–1 illustrates, the major functional drop-off of most of the body's biological systems occurs after about age 40. Thus, although the decline from peak performance that occurs after the mid-20s may be important to star athletes, it barely affects the rest of us. Not all systems are at their peak between 25 and 30, however. Visual accommodation, for example, declines gradually but steadily beginning in middle childhood, and visual acuity begins a very slow decline from about age 20 that accelerates markedly after about age 40 (Meisami, 1994).

Declines in physical skills and capabilities are most noticeable in emergency situations and at other times when physical demands are extreme (Troll, 1985). For example, when a woman is in her late 30s, a pregnancy draws more heavily on her reserve physical stamina than if she were in her 20s. In addition, it may take longer for the older woman to return to normal after the child is born. Similarly, it is easier for a 25-year-old man to work at more than one job to get his family through a financial crisis than it is for a 40-year-old.

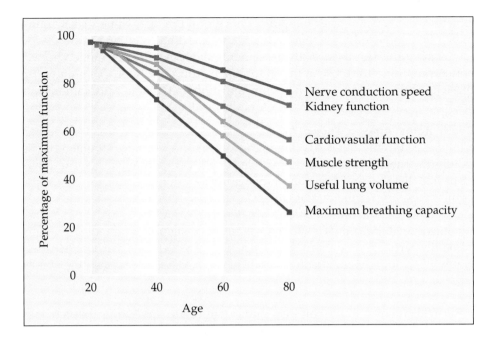

Figure 13-1 **Average Declines in Biological Systems**
These declines can be improved dramatically by health and fitness practices, including regular exercise.

Source: Adapted from J. Fries and Crapo. Vitality and Aging. San Francisco, W. H. Freeman and Company, 1981.

Fitness and Health

By and large, young adulthood is a healthy period. This is especially true for people who follow a sensible diet, get regular exercise, avoid tobacco and other drugs, and consume alcohol in moderation, if at all. Compared to older adults, young adults also are least likely to be overweight.

The health and exercise habits formed during young adulthood often persist throughout the adult years. Many of these patterns have beneficial effects, which we examine in greater depth in Chapter 15. Although attitudes and behaviors related to health and fitness can change at any point, people often tend to resist such change making it especially important to establish good health habits in young adulthood.

Physical Fitness   Many athletes reach their peak skills and conditioning during young adulthood. Between ages 23 and 27 the *striated* (voluntary) muscles, including the biceps and triceps, achieve their maximum physical strength (Hershey, 1974). Peak leg strength comes between the ages of 20 and 30, peak hand strength at about age 20 (Buskirk, 1985). Of course, the age at which athletes reach their peak *performance* varies according to the sport (Fries & Crapo, 1981). Swimmers generally peak during adolescence, runners and tennis players in their early 20s (Schulz & Salthouse, 1999). In contrast (and with some notable exceptions), golfers tend to perform best in their late 20s and on into their 30s. Major league baseball players generally peak around age 27–30, although the players with the greatest ability may peak several years after that (Schulz, Musa, Staszewski, & Siegler 1994).

In recent decades improvements in exercise and diet have added so much to adult fitness that older adults are now capable of higher performance levels than adults in their prime a century ago. When Anders Ericsson (1990) compared the winning times of younger runners in the 1896 Olympics with the best performances of "master" athletes aged 50 to 69 in 1979, he found that the older

Today, HIV infection, resulting in AIDS is the leading cause of death among males between 25 and 44.

athletes were usually faster than the younger gold medal winners. For example, in 1896 the winning time for a marathon was 2 hours 59 minutes; in 1979, the winning time for master athletes running the same distance ranged from 2 hours 25 minutes for those in the 50 to 54 age group to 2 hours 53 minutes for those aged 65 to 69. In general, better nutrition and training throughout the adult years more than compensates for advanced age.

Death Rates Among Young Adults Death rates are lower for U.S. young adults than for any other *adult* age group. Today few younger women die in childbirth. Tuberculosis is no longer a leading killer of young adults, and diseases like diabetes and heart and kidney disease are often manageable over a normal lifespan. Yet the rate of *preventable* deaths during young adulthood remains high. Deaths attributable to accidents, HIV/AIDS, and stabbings and shootings (including police shootings) still pose significant threats to young adults in particular. Here are some specifics (U.S. Census Bureau, 1999) (see Figure 13–2 for a comparison of each major cause of death among young adults):

- As with infants, older children, and adolescents, the leading preventable cause of death among both males and females ages 25 to 44 is accidents; in turn, the rate for males approached twice that for females; here, the rate for males is about three times that for females.
- For both males and females ages 25 to 44, the second leading preventable cause of death is HIV/AIDS; here, the rate for males is over four times that for females.

Disease, Disability, and Physical Limitations Although death rates for young adults are much lower than those for other adult age groups, it has long been known that many of the diseases that will cause trouble later in life begin during young adulthood (Scanlon, 1979). Young adults may feel no symptoms,

Figure 13–2 Major Causes of U.S. Deaths, Age 25–44 (in Thousands of Deaths per Year).

Source: U.S. Census Bureau, 1999.

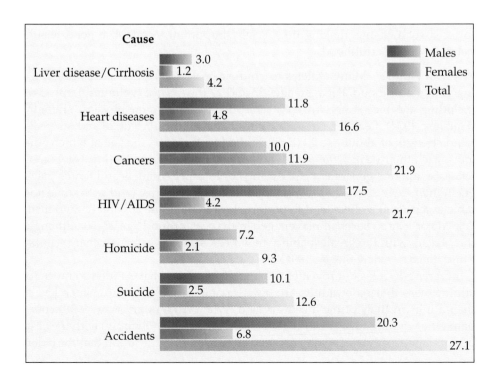

A CLOSER LOOK

COPING WITH PHYSICAL DISABILITY IN YOUNG ADULTHOOD

Most young adults are in their physical prime. They enjoy peak strength, stamina, and energy. They are generally in good health and have few illnesses. If they are physically fit, they enjoy the self-esteem and sense of efficacy and competence that go along with their physical prowess. What about young adults who are physically disabled? How do they adjust psychologically while their agemates are performing at optimal levels?

Adjusting to a physical disability is difficult at any age. However, late adolescence and young adulthood can be a particularly difficult period (Wright, 1983). At this stage in life, individuals normally are developing intimate relationships and making major decisions such as choosing an occupation. Physically disabled people may become overwhelmed by their limitations during this future-oriented period.

There are at least three factors that influence how people adapt to physical disabilities (Wright, 1983). First, it is important to understand the disability and its limitations. Any disability is defined by the interaction between the individual's abilities and the environmental task—a simple analogy is that if you can't speak Japanese, you will be functionally disabled in a Japanese classroom. The second aspect of adaptation to a physical disability involves coping with the attitudes and values of others and their social expectations. Physically disabled people are often stereotyped and must deal with prejudices and other undesirable attitudes in the minds of others. They may be pitied or demeaned, or looked upon as passive and incompetent. There is often a sweeping set of generalizations that may be applied to any physically disabled individual regardless of the particular disability.

Finally, coping with a physical disability involves coping with an array of hopes, fears, dreams, frustrations, lost opportunities, guilt, and anger. When a person becomes disabled suddenly, perhaps because of an accident, there may initially be a crisis period accompanied by grief and mourning as well as shock and disbelief. There will be periods of anger and frustration as the disabled person attempts to cope with everyday tasks that are easy and routine for others. There is likely to be further anger and frustration at unnecessary social obstacles imposed by others who are prejudiced toward people with disabilities or avoid them for other reasons such as being uncomfortable around them.

In the process, some individuals adopt a definition of themselves as "physically challenged" rather than disabled. This attitude is particularly common among disabled athletes. Simply by changing the definition and the terminology, it is sometimes easier to see the specific physical obstacle as a challenge to be overcome, perhaps with the help of others, rather than as a label or category that defines the person. Unfortunately, however, the term "challenged" has become somewhat of a cliché and is often used in a derogatory way in jokes.

Young adults with physical disabilities have been in the forefront of efforts to change social attitudes and laws that affect all those disabled people. In the United States in 1990, as a result of their actions and those of other interested individuals and groups, the Americans with Disabilities Act (ADA) was passed. This law makes it illegal to discriminate against individuals with disabilities in employment, public accommodations, transportation, and telecommunications. Among other things, it requires companies to make "reasonable accommodations" for the needs of disabled employees so that they can do work for which they are trained; if that isn't possible, they must be trained for comparably skilled work. Most important, people cannot be fired because of a disability alone; the ADA demands a policy of inclusion rather than exclusion.

but lung, heart, and kidney diseases, as well as arthritis, joint and bone problems, atherosclerosis, and cirrhosis of the liver, may be in their initial stages. Diseases and disorders that do yield symptoms during young adulthood include multiple sclerosis and rheumatoid arthritis, stress-linked diseases such as hypertension, ulcers, and depression, and some genetically based diseases such as diabetes or sickle cell anemia.

Sometimes sociocultural factors lead to disease or even death. In times of war, young adults are killed or permanently disabled. In urban areas with high crime rates, youths are often victims of homicide or drug abuse. Most recently, the AIDS epidemic has hit young adults at disproportionate rates, sometimes stemming from HIV infection during adolescence (Chapter 11). Individual psychological development and adjustment is especially difficult when a young adult's physical condition counteracts normal biological changes. In general, any physical disability or disease is likely to affect both biological age and social age expectations (see "A Closer Look," above).

CONTENT CHECK
GENERAL PHYSICAL DEVELOPMENT

True–False (answers are on the Companion Website)

1. For most people, strength, organ functioning, and perceptual and motor skills peak at about age 30 to 35.
2. Most athletes' strength and stamina peak in their 20s.
3. Strength and stamina decline noticeably after about age 40.
4. The leading cause of death among U.S. young adults is HIV/AIDS, followed closely by accidents.
5. Many diseases of older age are contracted during young adulthood.

Thinking Critically

Aside from improvements in exercise and diet, what other factors might be involved in athletes continuing to break past records?

Sex and Sexuality

Most young adults are also more fertile than they have ever been or will ever be. As a rule, they are also more sexually active and responsive and have a clear sense of sexual identity.

Sexual Attitudes and Behavior

Researchers at the University of Chicago conducted a random survey on the sexual habits of nearly 3,500 U.S. participants aged 18 to 59 (Laumann, Gagnon, Michael, & Michaels, 1994; Michael et al., 1994). Bearing in mind the usual problems associated with surveys on sensitive matters such as sex, such as underreporting of socially "undesirable" behaviors (see Chapter 1) and overreporting of desirable ones, their findings included the following:

■ The vast majority of people are monogamous. More than 8 out of 10 have just one sexual partner a year (or no partner at all). Over the course of a lifetime, a typical woman has just two partners; a typical man has six.
■ There are three basic patterns of sexual relations: One-third have sex at least twice a week, one-third several times a month, and one-third a few times a year or not at all.
■ Married couples have the most sex and are most likely to have orgasms during sex. Only 1 out of 4 single people has sex twice a week; nearly 2 out of 5 married people do.
■ Contrary to popular stereotypes, there are only very minor variations across ethnic groups with regard to frequency of sex.

Earlier researchers noted important changes in U.S. marital sexual behavior in the past several decades. The median duration of intercourse has increased markedly, suggesting that partners are experiencing greater enjoyment, relaxation, and mutuality during intercourse (Hunt, 1974). It appears that attitudes and priorities have changed. More couples seek to maximize the pleasure of the entire act rather than reaching release quickly. Flexibility has also increased; intercourse now may include previously "undesirable" acts such as initiation of sex by the woman, masturbation, and oral sex (Hunt, 1974; McCary, 1978).

Trends in adult sexual behavior have shifted considerably over the decades. In 1937 and again in 1959, only 22% of the U.S. population condoned premarital sex for both men and women. In the 1974 survey (Hunt, 1974), 75% of the men approved of premarital sex for men and over 50% found it acceptable for women. Some behaviors have not increased significantly, however; these include mate swapping, group sex, and extramarital sex. The double standard persisted into the 1970s, with 50% of college men approving of premarital sex for women but 75% still preferring a virgin bride (McCary, 1978).

Although sexuality is certainly more open and accepted now than it was before the 1960s, it appears that college students engaged in less sexual intercourse during the 1980s than during the 1960s and 1970s. For example, one study reported that in 1978, 51% of sophomore women were engaging in sex at least once a month, but in 1983 the figure had fallen to 37% (Gerrard, 1987). The continuing shift toward more conservative sexual behavior among college women is almost certainly attributable in part to increased fear of sexually transmitted diseases. It may also reflect the growing self-assurance of young women, who feel less compelled to have sex merely to "please" their boyfriends. Women are more likely to follow their own belief systems rather than those imposed upon them by others (Gerrard, 1987).

Fertility

During the young adult years a woman's supply of ova remains relatively stable. Females are born with their lifetime supply of about 400,000 ova, which are released monthly, beginning soon after menarche and ending at menopause. This process is relatively stable between the ages of 25 and 38. After age 38, however, there is a rapid decline in the number and regularity of ova released. This does not mean that older women can't or shouldn't become pregnant. On the contrary: Increasing numbers of women are choosing to have children in their late 30s and early 40s, when they are more secure emotionally and financially, and perhaps well established in a career. Genetic screening procedures such as amniocentesis and chorionic villus sampling (Chapter 4) help make late pregnancies less risky.

Men produce sperm continually from puberty on. Most men remain fertile throughout their later adult years (Troll, 1985), although seminal emissions contain progressively fewer viable sperm. Only during adolescence and the early adult years are both men and women are at their peak levels of fertility.

Sexual Responsiveness

The dominant pattern of sexual intimacy between men and women in the 1990s appeared to be one of increased communication and mutual satisfaction. Yet a frequent finding of studies of sexual attitudes and behavior has been a marked difference in the patterns of male and female satisfaction. In the 1970s (Hite, 1976; Hunt, 1974; McCary, 1978), research indicated that for some couples men routinely achieved physical gratification but women did not. Women complained that men were in too much of a hurry, were rough and perfunctory, and failed to appreciate the erotic and romantic importance of gentle, slow arousal. Men complained that women were frigid and unresponsive. It appeared that sexual intimacy was not always as mutually satisfying as the popular media presented it.

In the 1990s, the key components of sexual intimacy between men and women became greater communication and mutual satisfaction.

Figure 13–3 Three Measures of Sexual Satisfaction with Primary Partner

Source: From Sex in America *by Robert T. Michael et al. Copyright © 1994 by CSG Enterprises, Inc., Edward O. Laumann, Robert T. Michael, and Gina Kolata. By permission of Little, Brown and Company (Inc.).*

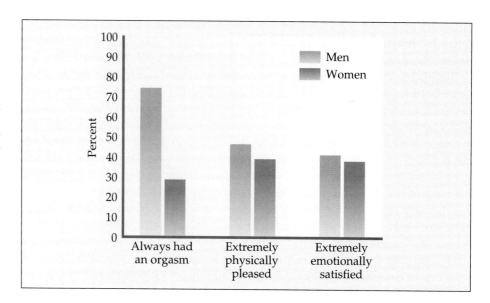

The University of Chicago study suggested otherwise (Laumann et al., 1994; Michael et al., 1994). As Figure 13–3 indicates, large percentages of married or cohabiting men and women reported being extremely physically and emotionally satisfied by sex with their primary partner. Notably, less than 30% of the women reported always having an orgasm (consistent with earlier research), which led the authors to conclude that "Despite the fascination with orgasms, despite the popular notion that frequent orgasms are essential to a happy sex life, there was not a strong relationship between having orgasms and having a satisfying sexual life" (Michael et al., 1994). In addition, as you might expect, the highest frequencies of sexual activity regardless of marital status were reported by people in their 20s and 30s. We return to how sexuality changes with age in Chapter 15.

Sexual Orientation

Sexuality clearly does not permeate our existence to the extent Freud proposed (Chapter 2), but few would deny that it is still an important part of out lives. In turn, **sexual orientation**—which refers to which sex you are physically attracted to as well as which sexual partners you might wish to become emotionally involved with—is a distinct part of most people's self-concept and sense of identity. Just as we develop perspectives on who we are with regard to ethics, religious and philosophical beliefs, vocation, and goals in life (Chapter 12), we develop a perspective on who we are sexually.

Negotiating sexual identity formation and the relationships that accompany it can be difficult for anyone in a society as diverse as the United States, where what are considered appropriate gender attributes and behaviors vary considerably and continue to be in a state of transition. This is offset for the majority of adolescents and young adults, for whom there is at least one aspect of sexual identity that seems stable and serves as a reference point: "I am a woman and I'm attracted to men," or "I am a man and I'm attracted to women." This in turn tends to receive considerable acceptance and support from family and peers. However, for a small but significant minority who discover in themselves a *same-sex orientation* altogether or in part, sexual identity formation is often extremely difficult (Carrion & Lock, 1997). Realizing that you are sexually and romantically attracted to members of your own sex—that is, that you are

sexual orientation Which sex you are physically and perhaps romantically attracted to.

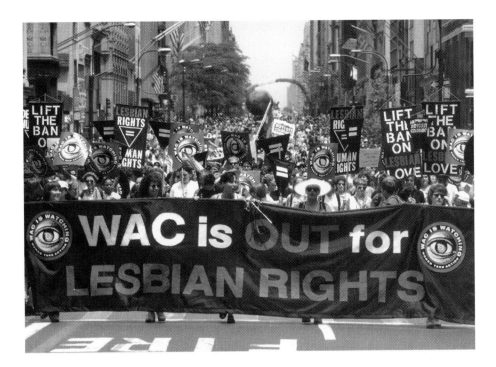

Part of the Annual Gay Parade down New York City's Fifth Avenue.

potentially a **lesbian** female, a **gay** male, or to varying degree a **bisexual** person of either sex—tends to be accompanied by feelings of being "different" in some important way, an intense "self-questioning" process, and an inner struggle to reconcile this aspect of yourself with your overall identity as a person (Carrion & Lock, 1997; Diamond, 1998; Patterson, 1995b). Moreover, as many authors have noted, gay, lesbian, and bisexual adolescents and adults who "come out" and openly acknowledge their sexual orientation face a gamut of negative reactions from the much larger heterosexual majority that can have markedly detrimental effects on psychosocial development.

This **homophobia** remains pervasive in the United States. It is not a true phobia and is perhaps better called *sexual prejudice* (Herek, 2000), but the term continues to be used both in everyday language and in professional journals—as does the somewhat ill-defined term *homosexual*. Homophobia refers to a set of sharply negative attitudes that can include unreasoned fear, but also unreasoned and intense loathing, revulsion, and anger directed toward people entirely on the basis of their same-sex-orientation. Both by family, peers, and society at large, openly same-sex oriented people are often blatantly scorned, shunned, condemned as immoral, and discriminated against (Nichols, 1999; Patterson, 1995b). For example, one large-scale study of gay men, lesbian women, and bisexual persons in a California city (Herek, Gillis, & Cogan, 1999) found that about one quarter of the men and one fifth of the women had in the year prior to the study experienced "hate crime" victimization—such as verbal harassment, being threatened with violence, being chased or followed, having an object thrown at them, or being spat on. Much worse treatment—including beatings and murders—surfaces regularly in the media.

Obviously, we shouldn't assume that all or even most U.S. heterosexuals are homophobic—the extent of homophobia simply isn't known. Nor should we assume that homophobia and subtler forms of sexual prejudice and discrimination are confined to any particular segment of the heterosexual population, such as less-educated or less-enlightened people. For example, one study found significantly sexually prejudiced attitudes among second-year medical students

lesbian A woman with a sexual orientation toward other women.

gay A man with a sexual orientation toward other men.

bisexual A person who is attracted both to men and to women.

homophobia Prejudice, aversion, fear, and other negative attitudes by heterosexuals toward homosexuals.

(Klamen, Grossman, & Kopacz, 1999), with 9% endorsing the outdated belief that homosexuality is a mental disorder. (It was removed from classification as a mental disorder over three decades ago.) Similarly, the APA's Division 44 Committee on Lesbian, Gay, and Bisexual Concerns Joint Task Force (2000), in establishing guidelines for psychotherapy with lesbian, gay, and bisexual clients, cited numerous studies indicating "heterosexist" bias among clinical psychologists and other therapists. Beyond that, the very need for detailed guidelines is evidence in itself, and such bias is especially surprising given the high priority the APA has given to the egalitarian issues in general for decades (also see APA, 1994).

Other authors have pointed out that although recent textbooks in psychology and sociology no longer *explicitly* characterize homosexuality as a disorder, many still *implicitly* do so in the way in which the topic is discussed (Weitz & Bryant, 1997). As for the population at large, the only consistently identified factor associated with sexual prejudice is that heterosexual men are likely to have much more negative attitudes toward same-sex-oriented people than are heterosexual women, especially where the targets are gay men (e.g., Heaven & Oxman, 1999; Kite & Whitley, 1996).

What kind of backdrop does this provide for adolescent and young adult development? A harsh one, so harsh that many nonheterosexual adolescents conceal their sexual orientation except among their closest friends or partners, perhaps choosing to come out later as young adults in college or in urban settings. There they predictably still experience significant abuse and rejection by homophobics but are likely to find companionship and support among others like themselves, along with a significant number of heterosexuals who are not homophobic. Understandably, some come out only to their closest confidants and not to the broader public. This is especially likely if they choose a vocation that places them among coworkers who are openly homophobic.

Who Are Same-Sex-Oriented People?   The best answer is people like anyone else in most respects, with the usual personal life satisfactions and life disappointments. They form friendships that deepen in young adulthood and that may or may not involve sex, they seek out and form intimate relationships that may or may not last, they pursue goals in life and succeed or fail and move on. The apparent dichotomy between being homosexual and being heterosexual is not real; gay, lesbian, and bisexual people are as individual as anyone. There are some important differences, however, that revolve around *feeling* and *being* different in a way that the larger U.S. society deems important not to be. The homosexual experience is distinct, as is the black experience and the experience of other groups who suffer or have suffered at the hands of a majority.

There are also some demographic differences, as illustrated in Figure 13–4. A higher proportion attend or complete college than do not, and a higher proportion live in large cities than in other locales—again where they are more likely to encounter compatible friends and partners.

Finally, there are some clear psychological differences that again appear directly attributable to the effects of living in a society replete with homophobia. Among lesbian, gay, and bisexual adolescents in particular, distress, depression, substance abuse, and suicidal risk are substantially higher than among heterosexual adolescents (Faulkner & Cranston, 1998; Remafedi, 1999; Remafedi, French, Story, Resnick, & Blum, 1998; Safren & Heimberg, 1999); these findings readily extend to young adults in transition. Researchers have also found that by young adulthood, some same-sex-oriented individuals *internalize* the larger society's prejudiced views of them, with the effect that they accept

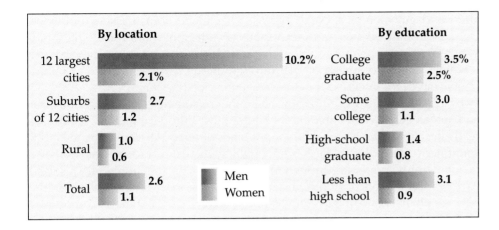

Figure 13–4

Demographic Differences Between People Who Reported Having Same-Sex Partners in the Preceding Year, Men and Women

Source: Laumann et al., The Social Organization of Sexuality. *Copyright © 1994 by the University of Chicago Press. Reprinted with permission.*

and live with a sense of shame and lowered self-esteem as a result of their sexual orientation (Allen & Oleson, 1999).

Otherwise, the popular conception that gay men are "effeminate" and lesbian women are "macho" is for the most part a myth. As noted by Michael Bailey and colleagues on the basis of a series of large-scale studies (Bailey, Kim, Hills, & Linsenmeier, 1997), there is wide variation among lesbians and gays with regard to both adherence to traditional gender stereotypes and preferred masculinity or femininity in partners. Gay men may appear feminine, but they may also appear as masculine as any strongly sex-typed heterosexual male. Lesbian women may appear masculine, but they may also appear as feminine as any strongly sex-typed heterosexual female. In turn, the researchers found a general (but not universal) tendency for lesbian women to prefer feminine partners and gay men to prefer masculine partners. However, research along these lines should *not* be taken to mean that same-sex-oriented people are stereotypically masculine or feminine to an extent greater than in the general population. There is also no reason to rule out *androgyny* (Chapter 8) among lesbian women, gay men, and bisexual persons, although research on this issue is noticeably lacking.

What Are the Origins of Same-Sex Orientation? The best answer to this question is clearly, "We don't know," beyond the likelihood that sexual orientation in general is a complex result of heredity and environment in interaction—as with other traits. In an extensive review of the literature, Baumrind (1995) noted that theorists remain sharply divided on the relative contributions of biology and social learning; there is evidence for each position, but much of the evidence is inconclusive. In sum she noted, ". . . with the exception of the few clear biological anomalies that result in cross-gender structural anomalies, it is impossible to disentangle the biological and the psychological contributions to the behavioral differences that constitute sexual orientation." Other researchers have reiterated this observation (e.g., Cohler & Galatzer-Levy, 2000; Schueklenk & Ristow, 1996), adding that it is much more important to understand what it means to be a member of the homosexual minority than it is to understand where homosexuality comes from.

Sexually Transmitted Diseases and Social Change

As noted, HIV/AIDS is the second leading cause of death for men ages 25 to 44. However, the response to the AIDS epidemic has not always been constructive. At first many heterosexuals ignored the threat of AIDS because it appeared to

For both young homosexuals and heterosexuals, there is now caution and concern about multiple sexual partners.

affect only gay men (because of increased likelihood of torn tissues and blood contact during anal sex) and intravenous (IV) drug users (through sharing of syringes). The gay community, too, responded with resistance and denial. Early warnings about the spread of HIV through unsafe sex were labeled as homophobic messages intended to set the stage for violating their rights.

By 1984, however, everyone was beginning to take the epidemic seriously. It had spread across the United States and to most European nations, having already decimated the young adult populations of many African countries—as it continues to do today. It affected not only gay men and IV drug users but also people with hemophilia (through blood transfusions containing HIV), sexual partners of bisexuals or IV drug users, and babies born to mothers who had the disease. What's more, it was estimated that perhaps 10% of the gay community in San Francisco and twice that many in New York were infected with the virus. These facts—together with the long latency period between HIV infection and development of AIDS symptoms, which makes HIV less likely to be detected—led to more serious action. Medical research on AIDS took on greater urgency, and the gay community began to educate its members and to promote safer sexual practices.

Social change does not happen smoothly, however. Many HIV-positive people continued to infect others; they also avoided HIV testing. In the late 1980s the heterosexual community was still far behind the gay community in responding to the epidemic, even though by then AIDS was being transmitted primarily through heterosexual activity. Sporadic incidents of panic and discrimination against individuals who had AIDS, who might have AIDS, or who might contract AIDS because of their lifestyle received more attention from the press than the educational information needed to reduce the spread of the disease.

During the second half of the 1980s and in the 1990s, sexual behavior of both heterosexuals and gays continued to change. Today most young people report

Table 13-1 Major Sexually Transmitted Diseases Other than HIV/AIDS (1996, United States, all Ages)

Chlamydia

Causes urinary tract infections in men; also responsible for testicular infection. In women, chlamydia can cause inflammation of the cervix and fallopian tubes. Although the infection is easily treated with antibiotics, failure to treat it may result in permanent damage, including infertility. Approximately half a million new cases of chlamydia occur each year.

Gonorrhea

Can cause sterility and other chronic problems if left untreated or if treated at an advanced stage. Over 300,000 new people are infected with gonorrhea each year.

Herpes

A group of viruses that includes herpes simplex virus, types I and II, and affects about half a million new people a year. Although there is no cure for herpes, there are treatments that can limit the severity of outbreaks.

Syphilis

Can cause severe health problems, including sterility and even death if left untreated. Pregnant women with untreated syphilis can infect their developing fetus. Now affects about 47,000 new people each year.

Source: U.S. Census Bureau, 1999.

exercising greater caution in their sexual activities. In the University of Chicago study, 76% of those who reported having five or more sex partners in the past year claimed either to be decreasing their sexual activity, being tested for HIV regularly, or always using condoms (Laumann et al., 1994). Prostitution without condoms has also sharply declined. Some observers have even suggested that U.S. society has entered a period of new restraint comparable to the 1950s.

Other Sexually Transmitted Diseases In addition to AIDS, over 20 different organisms cause STDs that affect millions of sexually active adolescents and adults each year (Stevens-Long & Commons, 1992). The effects include urinary tract infections, gonorrhea, syphilis, and herpes, as described in Table 13–1.

CONTENT CHECK
SEX AND SEXUALITY

True–False (answers are on the Companion Website)

1. More than 8 of 10 U.S. adults have no more than one sexual partner per year.
2. Behaviors such as mate swapping and extramarital sex increased significantly in the latter 20th century.
3. It is essential that people regularly have orgasms if they are to view their sex life as satisfactory.
4. All people who engage in same-sex sexual activity are same-sex oriented.
5. Same-sex-oriented men are primarily responsible for the continuing spread of HIV/AIDS.

Thinking Critically

In what ways did attitudes toward sexuality in general change in the latter 20th century?

Cognitive Continuity and Change

At the same time that the body is reaching its physical peak, so is cognitive functioning. Stages of cognitive development are relatively clear in childhood and adolescence; they are not easily defined in adulthood. Theorists disagree over whether the concept of stages even applies in adulthood. Thus, in the absence of a universally accepted theory, exploring cognitive development in adulthood involves assessing different theoretical perspectives that address specific aspects of the evolution of adult intellectual functioning.

Cognitive Growth or Decline?

An obvious consequence of learning, memory, problem solving, and other cognitive processes we use as we grow older is that we accumulate a broader knowledge base; we know more about ourselves and the physical and social world around us. What changes occur in what we call intelligence or cognitive capacity, or in intellectual competence? Is there continued cognitive *development* after adolescence?

The evidence is not clear, especially with regard to timing. Early theorists and researchers argued that intellectual capacities peak during the late teens or early 20s, but it is now clear that this conclusion was based on misinterpretation of the limited research findings available at the time. In a study conducted during World War I, for example, all draftees took a group intelligence test called the Army alpha. The younger recruits—those between the ages of 15 and 25—did better on average than the older ones. Several other studies conducted in the 1930s and 1940s produced somewhat similar results. Older people scored consistently lower than younger people. What was wrong with this research? The problem began with the Army alpha itself, which was a "quick" paper-and-pencil test designed to assess large numbers of recruits as efficiently as possible, not necessarily as accurately as possible; also, it emphasized verbal skills over basic reasoning skills. In all, because the research used a cross-sectional design, the tests were measuring age-cohort differences instead of developmental differences (see Chapter 1). Stated differently, older adults had different historical contexts (especially lower educational levels) that caused them on average to score lower on the tests—quite apart from how intelligent they might actually have been.

In the late 1940s, when researchers began using better IQ tests and longitudinal designs, quite a different picture emerged. Individuals usually showed some increase in intelligence test performance through their 20s and 30s, leveling off at around age 45 (Whitbourne, 1986b). Longitudinal studies also suggest that continuing education tends to increase IQ test scores in adulthood (Schaie, 1983), which makes sense when we remember that IQ tests primarily assess academic skills and knowledge.

What specific cognitive abilities increase in young adulthood? Some skills peak in the late teens and early 20s; they include speed-related performance, rote memory, and the manipulation of matrices and other patterns. This may have a biological basis, or it may be because many young people are full-time students who practice, develop, and rely on these skills on a daily basis. Note, too, that specific disciplines are associated with specific reasoning skills. Psychology majors, for example, tend to develop probabilistic reasoning because of their frequent use of statistical procedures; in contrast, humanities majors tend to develop skills in written analysis and exposition. In any case, people in their 30s, 40s, 50s, and beyond perform better with training in specific cognitive skills such as approaches to reasoning and processing information (Willis, 1990).

Similarly, skills that are exercised frequently are maintained better than those that aren't. Architects, for example, retain their visual-spatial skills at above-average levels for longer periods (Salthouse, Babcock, Skovronek, Mitchell, & Palmon, 1990; Salthouse & Mitchell, 1990). Other cognitive abilities, especially judgment and reasoning, normally continue to develop throughout the lifespan. However, it still isn't clear which cognitive abilities change and in what ways. We return to these issues in Chapters 15 and 17.

"Stages" of Thought in Young Adulthood

Are there stages of cognitive development after adolescence and the achievement of formal operational thought? Are there qualitative differences between the way an adult understands the world and the way an adolescent understands it? In 1970 William Perry conducted a classic study of change in the thought processes of 140 Harvard and Radcliffe students during their 4 years in college that sheds some light on these questions. At the end of each year the students were asked questions about how they made sense of their college experiences—how they interpreted those experiences, what those experiences meant to them. Of particular interest was how the students came to grips with the many conflicting points of view and frames of reference they encountered in their studies.

The results provided evidence for stages of cognitive development. At first the students interpreted the world and their educational experiences in authoritarian, dualistic terms. They were seeking absolute truth and knowledge. The world could be divided into good and bad, right and wrong. The faculty's role was to teach them, and they would learn through hard work.

Inevitably, however, the students were confronted with differences of opinion, uncertainty, and confusion. Perhaps professors presented subject matter in ways that encouraged students to figure out things for themselves. Or perhaps the professors themselves didn't have all the answers. Gradually, in the face of contradictory points of view, the students began to accept and even respect diversity of opinion. They began to adopt the perspective that people have a right to hold different opinions, and they began to understand that things can be seen in different ways, depending on context. This relativistic perspective, however, eventually gave way to a stage in which the students made personal commitments and affirmations to particular values and points of view, although they did so in a testing, exploratory manner at first.

In sum, the students moved from a basic dualism (e.g., truth versus falsehood) to tolerance for many competing points of view (conceptual relativism) to self-chosen ideas and convictions. Perry viewed this aspect of intellectual development as characteristic of young adults.

Beyond Formal Operations   Other theorists have elaborated on the types of thinking that are characteristic of young adulthood. Klaus Riegel (1973, 1975) emphasized understanding of contradictions as an important achievement of adult cognitive development and proposed a fifth stage of cognitive development, which he called **dialectical thinking.** The individual considers and contemplates, then attempts to integrate opposing or conflicting thoughts and observations. One particularly important aspect of dialectical thinking is the integration of the ideal and the real. According to Riegel, this ability is the strength of the adult mind. Riegel also pointed out, with respect to contextual paradigms, that the process is ongoing and dynamic—never static.

Both Perry's and Riegel's studies were based primarily on young adults in college. The changes they observed may have been specifically related to college experiences rather than to the more general experiences of young adulthood. Another theorist, Gisela Labouvie-Vief (1984), emphasized "commitment and responsibility" as the hallmark of adult cognitive maturity. In her view, the course of cognitive development should involve both the evolution of logic, as described by Piaget, and the evolution of self-regulation from childhood well into adulthood. She recognized that logic may reach its final stage in adolescence with the development of formal operational thought. Like Perry and Riegel, however, she argued that individuals need exposure to complex social issues, different points of view, and the practicalities of life in the real world if they are to escape from dualistic thinking. She described a somewhat longer process of evolution in which adults become truly autonomous and can handle the contradictions and ambiguities of their life experiences. Adult cognitive maturity is marked by the development of independent decision-making skills (Labouvie-Vief, 1987).

Flexibility in Intelligence

Not all researchers believe that there is a fifth stage of cognitive development. Some focus on how adults use whatever intelligence they have acquired to meet life's demands and how cognitive functioning evolves in the face of new

dialectical thinking   Thought that seeks to integrate opposing or conflicting ideas and observations.

In Schaie's acquisition period, young adults use their intellectual abilities to choose a lifestyle and pursue a career.

experiences that force us to change our "systems of meaning." Let's look at each of these approaches.

Schaie's Stages of Adult Thinking   Warner Schaie (1986) proposed that the distinctive feature of adult thinking is the flexible way in which adults use the cognitive abilities they already possess. He suggested that during childhood and adolescence we acquire increasingly complex structures for understanding the world. The powerful tools of formal operational thinking are the key achievement of this period, which he called the *acquisition* period. In young adulthood we use our intellectual abilities to pursue a career and choose a lifestyle; Schaie called this the *achieving* period. We apply our intellectual, problem-solving, and decision-making abilities toward accomplishing goals and a life plan—aspects of cognition that do not show up on traditional IQ tests.

Individuals who successfully do this acquire a certain degree of independence and move on to another phase in the application of cognitive skills, a period involving *social responsibility*. In middle age, according to Schaie, we use our cognitive abilities to solve problems for others in the family, in the community, and on the job. For some people these responsibilities may be quite complex, involving the understanding of organizations and different levels of knowledge. Such individuals exercise their cognitive abilities in *executive* functions in addition to assuming social responsibilities. Finally, in the later years the nature of problem solving shifts again. The central task is one of *reintegrating* the elements experienced earlier in life—making sense of your life as a whole and exploring questions of purpose. For Schaie, then, the focus of cognitive development in adulthood is not expanded capacity or a change in cognitive structures. Instead, it is the flexible use of intelligence at different stages of the lifespan (see Figure 13–5).

Systems of Meaning   Several theorists view adulthood as a time of continued change and growth. A leader in this field has been Robert Kegan (1982, 1995), who drew upon various developmental theories to present an integrated

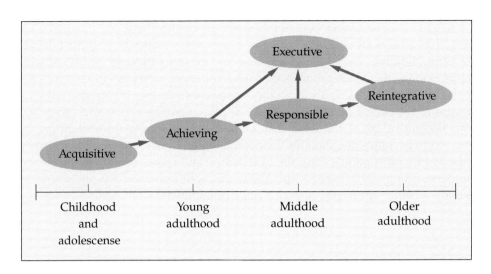

Figure 13-5 Schaie's Stages of Adult Cognitive Development

Source: Adapted from Schaie, 1986.

perspective on the evolving, cognitive self. Much of Kegan's theorizing was influenced by the work of Jane Loevinger (1976), who attempted to describe how individuals form a consistent idea of themselves and whether such self-concepts might develop in a sequence of predictable stages. Loevinger combined psychoanalytic theory and aspects of Kohlberg's theory of moral development with a variety of research findings to create a new model of personality development. She also developed a series of tests to determine whether the model fits actual experience.

Like Loevinger, Kegan emphasized the importance of meaning. The developing individual is continually differentiating the self from the world and at the same time integrating the self into the broader world. Kegan is also one of the few theorists who has looked at both female and male tendencies in development. Kegan's stages of development are summarized in Table 13-2.

In particular, Kegan emphasized that we continue to develop **systems of meaning** well into adulthood. Such systems can take many forms: religious, political, cultural, personal. We actively construct systems of beliefs and values through experience, and in turn they shape our experiences, organize our thoughts and feelings, and underlie our behavior.

systems of meaning Belief systems that shape our experiences, organize our thoughts and feelings, and help determine our behavior.

Table 13-2 Kegan's Stages of the Cognitive Self

Stage	Illustrative Behavior
0. Incorporative (Infancy)	No separation of self and other.
1. Impulsive (2–7 years)	Impulsive behavior, self-centered (similar to Loevinger's Impulsive stage).
2. Imperial (7–12 years)	Strives for independence, works toward achievement and skill building.
3. Interpersonal (13–19 years)	Restructuring of relationships; some marked sex differences.
4. Institutions (early adulthood)	Reintegration of the interconnectedness of the evolving self.
5. Interindividual (adulthood)	

Source: Adapted from Kegan, 1982.

Kegan's theory is too complex to present adequately here, but the basics are as follows. He built on the tradition of Piaget and theories of cognitive development, defining several levels or stages of "meaning making" that yield systems of meaning. As we progress through adulthood, each individual's systems of meaning become more idiosyncratic, yet have some things in common with the meaning systems of others at the same developmental level. At each stage the old becomes part of the new, just as children's concrete understanding of the world becomes raw data for their formal operational thought. For theorists like Kegan, most people continue to structure and restructure their systematic understanding of themselves and the world well into their 30s and even beyond—a rather optimistic view of adult development.

CONTENT CHECK
COGNITIVE CONTINUITY AND CHANGE

True–False (answers are on the Companion Website)

1. Contemporary research indicates that most cognitive abilities peak during a person's late teens or early 20s.
2. In Perry's stage theory of adult cognitive development, the highest stage found was tolerance for competing points of view.
3. Dialectical thinking is part of formal operational thinking.
4. In Schaie's theory, young adulthood is characterized by cognitive processes that center around achieving.
5. In Kegan's theory, young adult cognition tends to focus on institutions.

Thinking Critically

Why are longitudinal designs better for studying changes in cognitive abilities across the lifespan?

Seasons and Tasks of Adult Development

Various researchers have examined the interweaving of adult intellectual competence, personal needs, and social expectations in attempting to define stages or periods of adult development. The data underlying their theories often come from extensive interview studies of particular age cohorts. Specific developmental periods emerge, based on "crises" or conflicts that we all supposedly experience. Thus, the theories often provide insightful descriptions of the issues and concerns of adulthood, but how broadly and universally they apply to adult development remains open to question. "Milestones" in particular should be viewed as tentative.

Also note that the theories or frameworks presented here go well beyond young adulthood; as we see in later chapters.

Havighurst's Developmental Tasks

In 1953, Robert Havighurst (1900–1991) wrote a classic and very pragmatic description of development over the lifespan. He saw adulthood as a series of periods in which certain developmental tasks must be accomplished; these are summarized in Table 13–3. In a sense, the tasks provide the broad context in which development takes place. They are demands that shape our use of intelligence. In young adulthood, the tasks mostly involve starting a family and establishing a career. In middle adulthood, they center on maintaining what was established earlier and adjusting to physical changes as well as to changes in the family. In the later years, still other adjustments must be made, as we return to in Chapter 18.

Do these concepts still apply to adult development in this millennium? Yes, but not for all people. For many, the developmental tasks of middle adulthood include settling into a single lifestyle or starting a family and raising young children, learning to live with a new mate after a divorce, or beginning a new occupation or facing early retirement as a result of corporate "downsizing." Although most Western people's lives still conform to the timing of Havighurst's developmental tasks, there are more exceptions now than ever before. Again

Table 13–3 Havighurst's Developmental Tasks

Tasks of Early Adulthood

1. Selecting a mate
2. Learning to live with a marriage partner
3. Starting a family
4. Rearing children
5. Managing a home
6. Getting started in an occupation
7. Taking on civic responsibility
8. Finding a congenial social group

Tasks of Middle Adulthood

1. Achieving adult civic and social responsibility
2. Establishing and maintaining an economic standard of living
3. Developing adult leisure-time activities
4. Assisting teenage children to become responsible and happy adults
5. Relating oneself to one's spouse as a person
6. Accepting and adjusting to the physiological changes of middle age
7. Adjusting to aging parents

Tasks of Older Adulthood

1. Adjusting to decreasing physical strength and health
2. Adjusting to retirement and reduced income
3. Adjusting to death of spouse
4. Establishing an explicit affiliation with one's age group
5. Meeting social and civic obligations
6. Establishing satisfactory physical living arrangements

Source: *Human Development and Education,* by Robert J. Havighurst. Copyright © 1953 by Longman, Inc. Reprinted by permission of Longman, Inc., New York.

Young adults who are successful tend to be practical, organized individuals with an integrated personality.

we see how the particular path an individual takes depends in large part on his or her cultural environment.

Erikson's Developmental Tasks

Many theorists look to Erikson's theory of psychosocial stages in defining the central developmental tasks of adulthood. Recall from Chapter 2 that Erikson's theory includes eight psychosocial stages (crises) and that each stage builds on the one before. Adult development depends on resolution of the problems of earlier periods—issues of trust and autonomy, initiative and industry. In adolescence, the central issues to be resolved were identity achievement versus identity confusion. These can persist into young adulthood and give a sense of continuity to adult experiences (Erikson, 1959). Individuals define and redefine themselves, their priorities, and their place in the world.

The crisis of **intimacy versus isolation** is the issue that is most characteristic of young adulthood. Intimacy involves establishing a mutually satisfying, close relationship with another person. It represents the union of two identities without the loss of each individual's unique qualities. By contrast, isolation involves inability or failure to achieve mutuality, sometimes because the individual's identity is too weak to risk a close union with another person (Erikson, 1963).

Erikson's theory is basically a stage theory, but he applied it in a much more flexible fashion (Erikson & Erikson, 1981). Like Havighurst's theory, it can be considered normative. Issues of identity and intimacy are present throughout life, again with emphasis on life in industrialized nations. Major events such as a death in the family may create simultaneous identity and intimacy crises as a person struggles with the loss and tries to redefine her- or himself in the absence of an intimate partner. Moving to a new town, starting a new job, and going back to college are major changes that require psychosocial adjustment. Erikson's theory therefore provides guidelines for issues that may have to be resolved again and again throughout life. After a major move to a new area of the country, for example, it may be necessary to "back up" all the way to reestablishing trust, developing autonomy, and rediscovering competence and industry before you can truly feel like an adult again.

Hence, for many contemporary thinkers both identity and intimacy processes are central to an understanding of adult development (Whitbourne, 1986b). However, intimacy and identity achievement may be specific to Western culture. For example, graduate students who come to the United States from collectivist societies may find independent identity and more intimacy in their marriage to be very unfamiliar concepts.

Levinson's Seasons of a Man's Life

Daniel Levinson (1978, 1986) conducted an intensive study of adult development in the United States; the participants were 40 men aged 35 to 45, drawn from different ethnic and professional groups. Over a period of several months, interviews were conducted in which the men introspected about their feelings, attitudes, and life experiences. Along with the men's reconstructed biographies, Levinson and colleagues also studied the biographies of great figures such as Dante and Gandhi for clues to patterns of adult growth. Objective tests and scales were not used, however. In all, Levinson's approach was not unlike that of Freud (Chapter 2), and his theory should be viewed accordingly. Levinson's theory is also oriented toward traditional male-female roles and relationships; whether it extends beyond these is debatable.

The researchers identified three major eras in the adult male life cycle, which were later found to be comparable for women—as discussed in the next sec-

intimacy versus isolation Crisis in young adulthood characterized by the conflict between establishing a mutually satisfying relationship with another person as opposed to failing to achieve mutuality.

tion. Each extends for roughly 15 to 20 years (see Figure 13–6). During each era the person constructs what Levinson calls a **life structure.** This is the pattern underlying a person's life. It serves both as a boundary between the inner person and the outside world and as a means by which the person deals with the outside world. The life structure is composed mainly of the person's social and environmental relationships, including what the individual gains from and must contribute to each relationship. The relationships may be with individuals, groups, systems, or even objects. For most men, relationships at work and within the family are central. At specific ages people begin to question their existing life structure. They then construct a new structure that is consistent with their current needs, which dominates until the person "outgrows" it and starts the process again.

Although Levinson was interested primarily in the midlife decade from age 35 to age 45, he found that maturation and adjustment at this stage is largely dependent on the individual's growth in a *novice* phase that extends from age 17 to age 33 (not labeled in the figure). In the United States, this is the time when young men resolve adolescent conflicts, create a place for themselves in adult society, and commit themselves to stable, predictable patterns of behavior and life. Within the novice phase, Levinson saw three distinct periods: early adult transition (about ages 17 to 22); entering the adult world (ages 22 to 28);

life structure   The overall pattern that underlies and unifies a person's life

Figure 13–6   Levinson's Seasons of a Person's Life

Source: Adapted from Levinson, 1986.

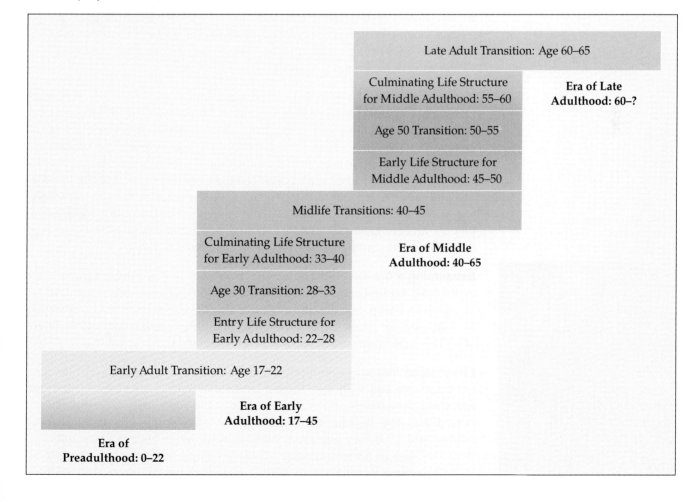

and the age-30 transition (ages 28 to 33). Developmental "crises" then occur when people have difficulty making the transitions.

To achieve complete entry into adulthood, according to Levinson, a young man must master four developmental tasks: (1) defining a "dream" of what adult accomplishment will consist of, (2) finding a mentor, (3) developing a career, and (4) establishing intimacy. Let's take a closer look at each of these tasks.

Defining a Dream At the beginning of the novice phase, a man's dream of adult accomplishment is not necessarily linked to reality. It may consist of a specific goal such as winning a Pulitzer Prize, or a grandiose role such as becoming a movie producer, business tycoon, or famous writer or athlete. Some men have more modest aspirations, such as being a master craftsman, village philosopher, or loving family man. The most important aspect of the dream is its ability to inspire a man in his present endeavors. Ideally, the young man begins to structure his adult life in realistic, optimistic ways that will help him realize this dream. Hopeless fantasies and utterly unattainable goals are not conducive to growth.

Besides being unrealistic, the dream may not be realized because of lack of opportunity, parental pressures in other directions, individual traits such as passivity and laziness, or special skills that the person lacks and can't acquire. Consequently, a young man may enter and master an occupation that is beneath his dream, one that holds no magic for him. According to Levinson, such decisions bring about continual career conflicts and are responsible for lack of excitement and limited investment in work. Levinson proposed that those who struggle to achieve at least some semblance of their dream are more likely to achieve a sense of fulfillment. Also note that the dream itself undergoes change. A young man who enters the early adult transition hoping to become a basketball star may later find satisfaction as a coach, thus incorporating some but not all elements of his dream.

Finding a Mentor In pursuing their dream, young people can be aided enormously by mentors. A mentor can instill self-confidence by sharing and approving of the dream as well as imparting skills and wisdom. As a sponsor, the mentor may influence advancement of the apprentice's career. The major function of the mentor, however, is to provide a transition from the parent-child relationship to the world of adult peers. The mentor must be sufficiently parental and authoritative, yet sufficiently sympathetic to overcome the generation gap and establish a peer bond. Gradually, the apprentice may acquire a sense of autonomy and competence; he may eventually overtake the mentor. Frequently, the mentor and young man drift apart at this point.

Developing a Career Besides forming the dream and acquiring a mentor, the youth faces a complex process of career formation that goes well beyond the selection of an occupation. Levinson viewed this developmental task as spanning the entire novice phase as the young man attempts to define himself vocationally. (This topic is discussed more fully in Chapter 14).

Establishing Intimacy Similarly, the formation of intimate relationships does not begin and end with the "marker" events of marriage and the birth of the first child. Both before and after these events, the young man is learning about himself and how he relates to women. He must ascertain what he likes about women and what they like about him; he must define his inner strengths and vulnerabilities in sexual intimacy. Although some self-discovery along these lines takes place in adolescence, young men often are still puzzled about these

Signs of successful career development.

women into the workforce at all levels. By middle adulthood, the traditional women were no longer the best adjusted in the study. Instead, they were more dependent or overcontrolled than the less traditional women. Apparently, being in congruence with societal roles is important to individual well-being. The roles open to young adult women today usually combine career and family. Young men, on the other hand, still are typically expected to pursue a career and not make a full commitment to homemaking (Kalleberg & Rosenfeld, 1990).

Gould's Transformations

Researchers on the course of development during adulthood are often faced with the difficult task of deciding how to organize extensive biographical data. The results depend in part on the focus and interests of the investigator. In his original study, Levinson obtained 15 hours of biographical interviews from 40 men. He chose to look at various aspects of the process of establishing a career and a lifestyle.

Roger Gould (1978) had a more cognitive focus. He was interested in the individual's assumptions, ideas, myths, and world views during different periods of adulthood. Gould's studies of U.S. adults included both women and men. He and his colleagues examined the life histories of a large group of women and men aged 16 to 60. On the basis of these profiles they developed descriptions of the way people look at the the world around them that are characteristic of different adult stages. For Gould, growth is best seen as a process of casting off childish illusions and false assumptions in favor of self-reliance and self-acceptance. Like Kegan, he believed that an individual's system of meaning-making shapes his or her behavior and life decisions.

According to Gould, from age 16 to age 22 the major false assumption to be challenged is: "I'll always belong to my parents and believe in their world." To penetrate and discard this illusion, young adults must start building an adult identity that their parents cannot control or dominate. Young people's sense of self, however, is still fragile at this point, and self-doubt makes them highly sensitive to criticism. Young adults also begin to see their parents as imperfect and fallible people rather than the all-powerful, controlling forces they once were.

Between the ages of 22 and 28, young adults often make another false assumption that reflects their continuing doubts about self-sufficiency: "Doing things my parents' way, with willpower and perseverance, will bring results. But if I become too frustrated, confused, or tired, or am simply unable to cope, they will step in and show me the right way." To combat this notion, the young adult must accept full responsibility for her or his own life, surrendering the expectation of continuous parental assistance. This involves far more than removing yourself from a mother's or father's domination; it requires the active, positive construction of an adult life. Conquering the world on your own also diverts energy from constant introspection and self-centeredness. Gould found that the predominant thinking mode during this period progresses from flashes of insight to perseverance, discipline, controlled experimentation, and goal orientation.

From age 28 to age 34, a significant shift toward adult attitudes occurs. The major false assumption during this period is: "Life is simple and controllable. There are no significant coexisting contradictory forces within me." This impression differs from those of previous stages in two important respects: It indicates a sense of competence and an acknowledgment of limitations. Enough adult understanding has been achieved to admit inner turmoil without calling strength or integrity into doubt. Talents, strengths, and desires that were suppressed during the 20s because they didn't fit into the unfolding blueprint of adulthood may resurface. Gould cited the examples of an ambitious young partner in a prestigious law firm who begins to consider public service, and a suave, carefree single person who suddenly realizes that having many intimate relationships is not satisfying because of some inadequacy of his or her own. (This development closely resembles Levinson's prediction about the dream: Those who ignore and suppress it in young adulthood will be haunted by this unresolved conflict later in life.)

Even those who have fulfilled youthful ambitions still experience some doubt, confusion, and depression during this period. They may begin to question the very values that helped them gain independence from their parents. Growth involves breaking out of the rigid expectations of the 20s and embracing a more reasonable attitude: "What I get is directly related to how much effort I'm willing to make." Individuals cease to believe in magic and begin to put their faith in disciplined, well-directed work. At the same time, they begin to cultivate the interests, values, and qualities that will endure and develop throughout adult life.

The years between 35 and 45 bring full involvement in the adult world. Parents no longer have control over people at this age, and their children have not yet effectively challenged them. They are, as Gould said, "in the thicket of life." At the same time, they experience time pressure and fear that they won't accomplish all of their goals. The physical changes of middle adulthood frighten and dismay them; reduced career mobility makes them feel penned in. The drive for stability and security, which was paramount when they were in their 30s, is replaced by a need for immediate action and results. There can be no more procrastination. The deaths of their parents and their awareness of their own mortality bring them face to face with the frequent unfairness and pain of life. In acknowledging the ugly side of human existence, they let go of their childish need for safety. They also become free at last to examine and discard

Table 13-4   Selected Theorists' Views of the Major Tasks of Adulthood

Erikson	Continuing to develop a sense of identity; resolving intimacy versus isolation
Gould	Casting off erroneous assumptions about dependency and accepting responsibility for one's life; developing competence and acknowledging personal limitations
Havighurst	Starting a family and establishing a career
Kegan	Structuring and restructuring personal systems of meaning
Labouvie-Vief	Developing autonomy and independent decisionmaking
Levinson	Developing an early life structure and making the age-30 and other transitions; includes defining a dream, finding a mentor, developing a career, and establishing intimacy with a special partner
Perry	Progressing from dualistic thinking to relativistic thinking
Riegel	Achieving dialectical thinking
Schaie	Flexibly applying intellectual abilities to accomplishing personal and career goals—the *achieving* period.

the sense of their own worthlessness and wickedness left over from childhood. This, Gould proposed, represents a full, autonomous adult consciousness.

In closing, it is important to remember that theories that emphasize periods or stages are valuable in understanding adult development but should not be interpreted too rigidly, for several reasons. First, the notion of stages tends to obscure the stable aspects of personality during adulthood. Second, these theories pay little attention to the unpredictability of life events (Neugarten, 1979). Third, thus far most participants in studies of adult development have been men, and much of the research has concentrated on the same age cohorts—individuals born in the first half of the twentieth century.

Differing theoretical views of the major tasks of adulthood are summarized in Table 13–4.

CONTENT CHECK
SEASONS AND TASKS OF ADULT DEVELOPMENT

True–False (answers are on the Companion Website)
1. Havighurst's theory is primarily based on resolving intimacy versus isolation.
2. With regard to Levinson's seasons of a person's life, both men and women define a dream and look for a mentor.
3. With regard to Levinson's seasons of a person's life, both men's and women's adult development is best organized around chronological age.
4. In Gould's theory, the emphasis is upon adults achieving self-reliance and self-acceptance.

Thinking Critically
What do each of the theories discussed in this section have in common? How do they differ?

CHAPTER 13 REVISITED

- Beginning with young adulthood, chronological age is of relatively little use in studying development.

- The important events and milestones of adulthood may be normative or idiosyncratic and depend upon culture.

Perspectives on Adult Development

- Age clocks reflect when certain achievements should occur within a given cultural context.

- In the United States, many traditional observations about adult development have become blurred.

- Biological, social, and psychological age in interaction give a better picture of an adult's development than does chronological age.

- There is no universal definition of maturity.

- Contextual paradigms are yet another way of looking at adult development.

General Physical Development

- Young adulthood is a time of peak strength, stamina, and most perceptual and motor skills; the major drop-off doesn't come until about age 40.

- Young adulthood is generally a healthy period; health and exercise habits that develop during this period tend to persist for life.

- With some exceptions, most athletes peak in their 20s; improved exercise and diet have resulted in athletes continuing to break established records.

- In young adulthood, the leading preventable cause of death is accidents; second is HIV/AIDS.

- Young adults may acquire diseases but show no symptoms until later life.

Sex and Sexuality

- Most people in the United States are monogamous and have few sexual partners throughout their lives.

- Married or cohabiting couples have the most sex and are likely to experience the greatest satisfaction, but this does not necessarily mean having regular orgasms.

- Changes in U.S. adult attitudes across the latter part of the 20th century included increased emphasis on satisfaction and more flexibility.

- In the United States, frequency of sexual behavior peaked in the 1960s and 1970s then declined.

- Females ovulate regularly during young adulthood, until they approach menopause in middle adulthood; males produce viable sperm through their lifespans after reaching puberty.

- In the past, sexual intimacy among U.S. women and men was often not mutually satisfying; this changed considerably by the 1990s.

- Sexual orientation helps define sexual identity, which is in turn part of a person's identity as a whole.

- Sexual identity formation can be especially difficult for gay, lesbian, and bisexual adolescents, who often do not come out until young adulthood.

- In the United States, pervasive homophobia and the abuse and discrimination that may accompany it are the primary sources of difficulty for same-sex-oriented people.

- Homophobic people come from all walks of life, including the professions; heterosexual males tend to have more intense homophobic attitudes than heterosexual females.

- Lesbian, gay, and bisexual people share much with people in general, although they are in part distinctly different because of their homosexual experience; they also have a higher rate of psychological disorders and are at greater risk for suicide as a result of others' homophobia.

- Origins of same-sex orientation are as yet unclear, but most likely involve heredity and environment in interaction.

- In the United States, HIV/AIDS may have begun primarily as a same-sex or IV drug user problem; it is now transmitted primarily through heterosexual relations and occurs throughout the U.S. population.

Cognitive Continuity and Change

- It is clear that people continue to acquire a larger knowledge base during young adulthood and beyond; researchers disagree on what other cognitive changes take place.

- Early research found early cognitive decline because of the cohort effect; longitudinal research later demonstrated that cognitive decline in most areas occurs much later and more gradually.

- In Perry's research, college students began as dualistic thinkers, then progressed to conceptual relativism and finally to self-chosen convictions.

- Riegel emphasized dialectical thinking as a fifth stage of cognitive development beyond formal operations.

- Labouvie-Vief emphasized the evolution of logic and self-regulation as aspects of young adult cognitive development, resulting in independent decision-making skills.

- Schaie emphasized achieving in young adulthood, social responsibility and executive functions in middle adulthood, and reintegration in older adulthood—each of which involves flexible use of intelligence.

- Loevinger and later Kegan emphasized systems of meaning, on which Kegan based his child and adult stages of development.

Seasons and Tasks of Adult Development

- Havighurst based his theory of adult development on tasks that must be accomplished; these are no longer as clear-cut or broadly applicable today.

- Erikson stressed the crisis of intimacy versus isolation during young adulthood.

■ Levinson's seasons of a man's life are based on chronological age; developmental issues that occur during these stages include defining a dream, finding a mentor, developing a career, and establishing intimacy.

■ Levinson's seasons of a woman's life are defined similarly but the developmental issues take different forms; researchers also believe that a woman's stage in the family cycle is more relevant that her chronological age.

■ Gould's transformations are based on developmental changes that eventually result in an accurate understanding of the world and at the same time self-reliance and self-acceptance.

KEY TERMS

age clock
biological age
social age
psychological age
contextual paradigms

sexual orientation
lesbian
gay
bisexual
homophobia

dialectical thinking
systems of meaning
intimacy versus isolation
life structure

YOUNG ADULTHOOD: PERSONALITY AND SOCIOCULTURAL DEVELOPMENT

14

CHAPTER PREVIEW

Do you know:

1. That there is an interrelationship between *self, family,* and *work?*

2. What Maslow's *self-actualization* refers to and how it relates to other needs?

3. Why Rogers saw *conditions of worth* and *unconditional positive regard* as crucial?

4. How *adult friendships* form and what functions they serve?

5. What's involved in the development of intimate relations according to Sternberg's *triangular theory of love?*

6. How the couple formation process is an expression of *intimacy?*

7. What's involved in the *transition to parenthood?*

8. That parenthood develops in identifiable *stages?*

9. The similarities and differences in the child-rearing challenges faced by *married* and *single* parents?

10. The main factors that influence *occupational choice?*

11. The major challenges for young adults when they *enter* the workforce?

12. How work has different *meanings* for different people?

13. How *myths* and *stereotypes* affect women in the workplace?

14. The special characteristics of and the difficulties faced by *dual-earner families?*

These are the main topics of Chapter 14.

In this chapter, we focus on the importance of relationships and work. Erikson emphasized achieving intimacy, and later generativity, which includes productive work of any kind. Other theorists have talked about affiliation and achievement; still others about acceptance and competence. Clearly, a successful journey through adulthood is intimately tied to a person's involvement with a career and, for most people, with a romantic partner and a family.

In this chapter, we focus on the importance of love and work in development during early adulthood. With regard to love, crucial social contexts are the family and evolving personal lifestyles. We look at the various ways in which adults establish intimate relationships and use these relationships to structure and restructure their sense of identity. With regard to work, we focus on how adults apply their energy and skills and pursue their ambitions. Work shapes our lifestyles, friendships, prestige, and socioeconomic status, as well as our attitudes and values. Ideally, work challenges us and helps us grow. It requires us to solve problems. It can be a means for finding pleasure, satisfaction, and fulfillment. On the downside, it can cause frustration, boredom, worry, humiliation, and a sense of hopelessness. It can create stress and damage health. Either way, however, work is a central context for and contributor to adult development.

Continuity and Change

Socialization continues into young adulthood and beyond; we become socialized to new roles within the contexts of work, independent living, sustained intimacy with another person, marriage, and family. Many people assume new roles in their community as well by joining clubs, civic groups, and religious institutions.

Is it the same for personality? Do we continue to develop and change during early adulthood and beyond? Many theorists think so, as discussed in the preceding chapter. The role changes of young adulthood constitute transitions and turning points in our lives (Clausen, 1995), and we are changed by them. We see things differently; we behave differently; we adjust our beliefs, attitudes, and values in accordance with the roles and contexts we experience. That indeed is personality development—although the changes are subtler and less systematic than those of childhood and adolescence, and there is much continuity as well. *Stable* personality, however, typically is not achieved until the latter part of young adulthood or in early middle adulthood. Even then, personality is not cast in concrete: Abrupt changes in family, social, or vocational contexts can influence personality at any point in the lifespan.

Self, Family, and Work

Adult development can be described in the context of three separate but interacting systems that focus on various aspects of the self. These involve the development of the personal self, the self as family member (adult child, member of a couple, and parent), and the self as worker (Okun, 1984) (see Figure 14–1). Interactions abound. For example, research has shown that the more positive a father's work experience, the higher his self-esteem and the more likely he is to have an accepting, warm, and positive parenting style (Grimm-Thomas & Perry-Jenkins, 1994).

These systems change as a result of events and circumstances and as a result of interactions with the broader community and culture. As discussed in Chapter 2, Urie Bronfenbrenner's (1979, 1989) ecological systems model presents development as a dynamic, multidirectional process involving the individual's immediate surroundings, the social environment, and the values, laws, and customs of the culture in which the individual lives. These interactions and the personal changes that emerge from them occur throughout the lifespan.

The Personal Self

There are many conceptualizations of self, as we have seen in previous chapters with regard to childhood and adolescence. A classic formulation of what is important to the adult self is that of Abraham Maslow (1908–1970). Maslow's theory has distinct developmental overtones. Instead of stages, however, it emphasizes *needs* that each individual must meet in striving to reach her or his unique potential and sense of self. The goal is **self-actualization,** which means full development and utilization of talents and abilities (Maslow, 1954, 1979). Self-actualization is at the top of Maslow's classic "hierarchy of needs," which is often illustrated as a pyramid as in Figure 14–2. **Humanistic psychologists**

self-actualization Realizing one's full unique potential.

humanistic psychology The view that humans actively make choices and seek to fulfill positive personal and social goals.

Figure 14–1 **Domains of Self**

The three domains of adult development involve dynamic interactions among the self as an individual, a family member, and a worker. These interactions take place in the broad context of community and culture.

Source: Adapted from Okun, B. (1984). Working With Adults: Individual and Family Career Development. Monterey, CA. Brooks/Cole.

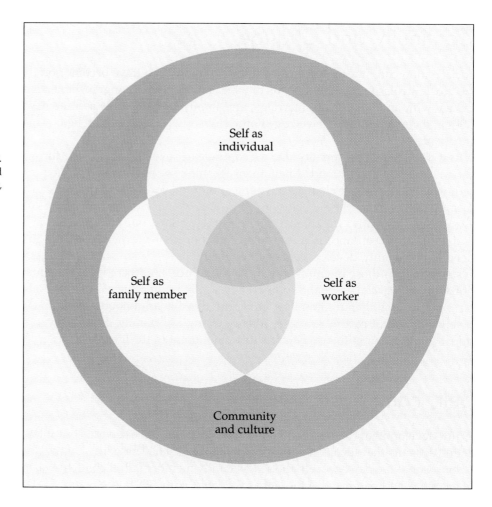

Figure 14–2 **Maslow's Hierarchy of Needs**

Although higher needs are no less important than lower needs, individuals must satisfy lower needs, such as those for survival and safety, before meeting higher needs such as belongingness and esteem. Throughout life, adults must work out their needs for self-actualization in order to develop their fullest potential.

Source: Adapted from Maslow, 1954.

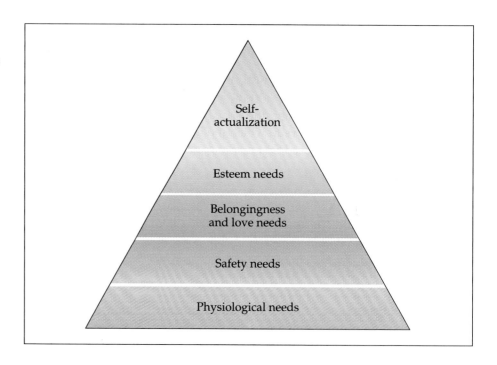

like Maslow maintain that we actively make choices about our own lives. We are influenced by our experiences with others, but we also determine the directions we take and strive to achieve our own goals (May, 1986/1987).

This need for self-actualization can be expressed or pursued only after lower needs such as those for food and shelter and safety have been met. People living in conditions of deprivation or terror are not likely to be concerned with achieving their full potential. People also need to love and feel loved and to "belong" in contexts such as family and community. Beyond that, we need self-esteem; we need positive responses from others, which can range from simple confirmation of our personality, skills, and accomplishments by family and friends to acclamation and fame in society at large. We also seek to satisfy higher cognitive and aesthetic needs.

What are self-actualizers like? They tend to be realistic, have a good sense of humor, be creative, be productive, and have a positive self-concept. But they aren't necessarily perfect. They can be cranky, absentminded, and single-minded in pursuit of their unique potential. Also, they aren't necessarily happy all the time, although they do have *peak experiences* in which they feel extremely good about themselves and their place in the world. A person can only begin the journey toward self-actualization in young adulthood; it is a lifelong quest that can never be fully satisfied.

Carl Rogers (1902–1987), another humanistic psychologist, approached these issues from the viewpoint of a psychotherapist. He was attempting to discover the causes of his patients' anxieties, low self-esteem and sense of self-worth, and interpersonal difficulties. For him, the core of human nature consists of healthy and constructive impulses (1980). At birth, we are prepared to be "good" both as individuals and as members of society, but as we develop, society often "corrupts" us. Various significant others, beginning with our parents, impose **conditions of worth** on us: Do this, don't do that, or you will be a worthless human being. An individual who internalizes such conditions develops low self-esteem, a sense of failure, and recurrent anxiety and despair. The internalized conditions become standards of perfection that can never be attained. Rogers proposed that we should view ourselves and others with **unconditional positive regard,** by which he meant being warmly accepting without reservations or conditions. As a parent, love your child unconditionally, regardless of his or her behavior. When the child misbehaves, punish if necessary, but never attack the child's sense of being loved and having worth as a person.

Modern perspectives on the personal self emphasize identity, much as Erikson did. In the words of Susan Whitbourne and Loren Connolly (1999), "Identity is defined as the individual's self-appraisal of a variety of attributes along the dimensions of physical and cognitive abilities, personal traits and motives, and the multiplicity of social roles including worker, family member and community citizen." In particular, identity is not static during young adulthood and later life. As the authors noted, ongoing experiences may be assimilated or may force accommodations in identity, analogous to the processes proposed by Piaget with regard to cognitive development (Chapter 2). In turn, it appears that there are three basic identity styles among adults in each age range: those who are predominantly assimilative and unrealistically prefer to see themselves as unchanging, those who are predominantly accommodative and too changeable as a result of experiences, and those who are balanced and realistically "integrate" both positive and negative experiences into their

conditions of worth Conditions others impose upon us if we are to be worthwhile as human beings—conditions that are often impossible to fulfill.

unconditional positive regard Rogers' proposition that we should warmly accept another person as a worthwhile human being, without reservations or conditions.

identities—the latter being the healthiest approach (Whitbourne & Connolly, 1999).

Self as Family Member

Any individual views his or her family as an extremely important context for adult development. In one national survey, women and men of all ages said that their family roles were very important in defining who they are (Beroff, Douvan, & Julka, 1981). In a more detailed study of adult identity, fully 90% of the men and women who were interviewed indicated that their family roles and responsibilities were the most important components in defining who they were (Whitbourne, 1986a; Whitbourne & Ebmeyer, 1990; VanManen & Whitbourne, 1997). They talked about their roles as parents, spouses, siblings, and children, about family tasks and responsibilities, about closeness, communication, companionship, and personal fulfillment. Broadly speaking, they talked about the people they had become within these family relationships and experiences. Very few men and women defined themselves primarily in terms of their career rather than their family.

Young adults, whether married, cohabiting, or single, are often in transition, moving from the family they grew up in to the family they may create. Some years ago, Lois Hoffman (1984) identified four aspects of this process that are still worth considering. The first is *emotional independence*, in which the young adult becomes less dependent on the parents for social and psychological support. The second form is *attitudinal independence*. The young adult develops attitudes, values, and belief systems that may differ from those of the parents. *Functional independence*, the third form, refers to the young adult's ability to support herself or himself financially and take care of day-to-day problems. Finally, *conflictual independence*—which can occur at any point along the way—involves separating from parents without feelings of guilt or betrayal.

Studies of college students (Lapsley, Rice, & Shadid, 1989) indicate substantial progress in each form of independence over the college years. Substantial functional dependence often remains, however, even in the senior year. Many students still rely on their parents financially. Finally, young adults who fail to complete the separation process, especially with regard to conflictual independence, are more likely to develop psychological adjustment problems (Friedlander & Siegel, 1990; Lapsley et al., 1989).

Self as Worker

Children are often asked, "What do you want to be when you grow up?" Many of our thoughts and fantasies are occupied by this question, which we may continue asking ourselves well beyond childhood. In adulthood, how we answer the question contributes greatly to our identity—who we are and who we are not.

Whatever our occupation, we carry with us the attitudes, beliefs, and experiences of our jobs. We are members of a corporation, a profession, a trade or craft, perhaps a union. Work often defines our status, income, and prestige. It defines our daily schedule, social contacts, and opportunities for personal development.

What does work give people in return for the time and energy they devote to it? Industrial/organizational psychologists note that for some people work is merely a means of survival. It provides them with money to feed, clothe, and shelter themselves and their families, and they "live their lives" away from their jobs. For other people, work provides a chance to be creative or pro-

Because low-ceiling jobs often offer less intrinsic satisfaction, work friendships may be an especially important source of extrinsic satisfaction.

ductive; offers welcome challenge and stimulates growth; and provides an opportunity to gain self-esteem or respect. For still others, work is an addiction—"workaholics" are driven to perform and define their lives in terms of their work.

When researchers ask adults what is important to them about their work, there are two typical kinds of answers. On the one hand, people talk about the characteristics of their job together with the particular abilities they possess to do the work. These are **intrinsic factors of work.** People who focus on intrinsic factors might describe their work in terms of its challenge or interest and talk about their work competence and achievements. On the other hand, some people focus on **extrinsic factors of work.** These include salary and status, the comfort or convenience of the work environment and hours of work, the adequacy of supervision and other employer practices, the attitudes and support of coworkers, and the opportunities for advancement (Whitbourne, 1986a).

What workers say about their jobs depends in part on the job. Many, many jobs in our society offer little challenge and opportunity for personal growth, and the people who perform them can only talk about extrinsic factors and financial survival. The fortunate workers whose jobs do provide for intrinsic factors and who do talk about them tend, on average, to report more job satisfaction and higher motivation and personal involvement in their jobs. These workers also are more likely to define their identity largely in terms of their work or career. They are aware of and do not wish to lose the personal satisfaction they derive from work.

Figure 14–3 presents a model of how intrinsic work motivation is tied to identity as a competent worker. When a worker is intrinsically motivated, there is more job involvement, better job performance, and stronger identity as a competent worker. This in turn increases intrinsic work motivation, although the cycle can go in a negative direction as well. For example, feeling

intrinsic factors of work Satisfaction workers obtain from doing the work in and of itself.

extrinsic factors of work Satisfaction in the form of pay, status, and other rewards for work.

Figure 14-3 The Interaction Between Intrinsic Work Motivation and Worker Identity

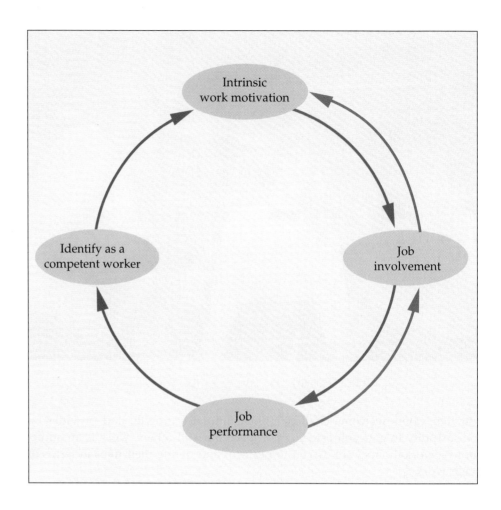

incompetent or overwhelmed decreases intrinsic motivation, job involvement, and job performance (Maehr & Breskamp, 1986; Whitbourne, 1986b).

Friendships can be important extrinsic factors in the workplace. Friendships formed on the job may be especially important to people in "low-ceiling" jobs (Kanter, 1977), where the pay may be adequate but there is no ladder of success to climb; instead, there is a "ceiling" beyond which the worker can't advance. Socializing with fellow employees may add meaning to such a job. Women in particular may find social relationships at work important (Repetti, Matthews, & Waldron, 1989). These relationships provide emotional support and may be one reason why women who work outside of the home typically have better mental and physical health than those who do not. (This point is discussed more fully later in the chapter.)

Other extrinsic factors are related to health. When high job demands are combined with unclear supervision, stress and the risk of heart attacks increase (Repetti et al., 1989). Thus, extrinsic factors are important not only to job satisfaction but also to overall physical and mental health.

Finally, attitudes and values toward work began shifting during the 1980s. The majority of workers no longer defined themselves exclusively or even primarily with respect to work. Far more workers sought a balance among family, work, and personal interests and pastimes (Derr, 1986; Whitbourne, 1986b). Nevertheless, the majority of respondents reported high levels of personal satisfaction in their work. In this study, intrinsic rewards outweighed extrinsic rewards.

CONTENT CHECK
SELF, FAMILY, AND WORK

True–False (answers are on the Companion Website)

1. Humanistic psychologists believe adults actively make choices about their own lives.
2. Young adults are often in transition between the family they grew up in and the family they will create.
3. In terms of job satisfaction, intrinsic factors of work are more important than extrinsic factors of work.
4. Friendships are particularly important to people in "high-ceiling" jobs.

Thinking Critically

Why can young adults only start but not complete the journey to self-actualization?

Forming Close Relationships

Finding a partner, building a close emotional bond, making a long-term commitment—these are important tasks for most young adults. Yet, the multiple patterns and styles of relationships defy a simple analysis. Here we survey assorted perspectives.

Adult Friendships

As noted by Beverly Fehr (1996), friendships are a core aspect of adult life. Although as Fehr put it, "There are as many definitions of friendship as there are social scientists studying the topic," there are some things that friendships have in common. Close friends are people whom we trust and rely on in times of difficulty, who are always ready to help, and whom we enjoy spending time with. Like romantic relationships, friendships are usually characterized by positive emotional attachment, need fulfillment, and interdependence (Brehm, 1992). We return to adult friendships in Chapter 16; for now, note that friendship also includes elements that are closely akin to those of love.

Sternberg's Triangular Theory of Love

Robert Sternberg's triangular theory of love (1986, 1997) demonstrates the complexities of achieving love relationships. Sternberg suggested that love has three components, as illustrated in Figure 14–4. First, there is **intimacy,** the feeling of closeness that occurs in love relationships. Intimacy is the sense of being connected or bonded to the loved one. We want to do things to make life better for people we love. We genuinely like them and are happiest when they are around. We count on them to be there when we need them, and we try to provide the same support in return. People who are in love share activities, possessions, thoughts, and feelings. Indeed, sharing may be one of the most crucial factors in turning a dating relationship into a loving, marriage or marriage-like relationship.

    Passion is the second component of love. This refers to physical attraction, arousal, and sexual behavior in a relationship. Sexual needs are important but are not the only motivational needs involved. For example, needs for

intimacy   The feeling of closeness that occurs in love relationships.

passion   The second component of love that refers to physical attraction, arousal, and sexual behavior in a relationship.

Figure 14–4 Sternberg's Triangular Theory of Love.

Source: Sternberg, 1986; adapted from Feldman, 1998.

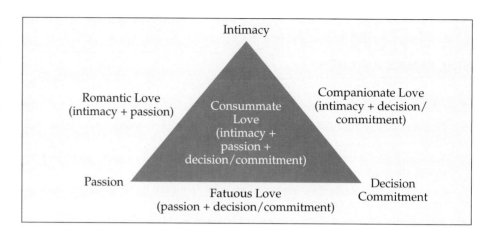

self-esteem, affiliation, and nurturance may also play a role. Sometimes intimacy leads to passion; at other times passion precedes intimacy. In still other cases there is passion without intimacy or intimacy without passion (as in a sibling relationship).

The final component of Sternberg's love triangle is **decision/commitment.** This component has both short- and long-term aspects. The short-term aspect is the decision or realization of being in love. The long-term aspect is a commitment to maintain that love. Again, the relationship between decision/commitment and the other components of love can vary. To demonstrate the possible combinations, Sternberg (1986) developed the taxonomy of love relationships shown in Table 14–1. Clearly, those of us who are interested in marriage hope for a relationship marked by consummate love. But more than one couple has mistaken infatuation for love, and in many marriages passion ebbs and the relationship becomes essentially nonromantic.

Intimacy can be destroyed by denial of feelings, particularly anger. Fear of rejection also blocks intimacy, especially when it leads to a false identity de-

decision/commitment The realization of being in love and making a commitment to maintain it.

According to Sternberg, intimacy is a key characteristic of a love relationship.

CHAPTER 14 YOUNG ADULTHOOD: PERSONALITY AND SOCIOCULTURAL DEVELOPMENT ■ 481

Table 14-1 Taxonomy of Kinds of Love Based on Sternberg's Triangular Theory

| KIND OF LOVE | Component | | |
	INTIMACY	PASSION	DECISION/COMMITMENT
Liking	+	–	–
Infatuated love	–	+	–
Empty love	–	–	–
Romantic love	+	+	–
Companionate love	+	–	+
Fatuous love	–	+	+
Consummate love	+	+	+

Note: + = component present; – = component absent. These kinds of love represent limiting cases based on the triangular theory. Most loving relationships fit between categories because the various components of love are expressed along continuums, not discretely.
Source: Sternberg, 1986.

signed to cater to another person rather than fulfill important personal needs. Traditional courtship and dating patterns may even discourage intimacy if they involve only ritual exchanges and facades. Some behaviors are even more harmful to intimacy: Casual sex, brutal candor, and contrived aloofness are not fertile ground for intimacy.

Couple Formation and Development

Couple formation and development are a major part of adult development. Individuals achieve part of their personal identity as a member of a relatively stable couple. It is therefore important to understand how people choose their mates and why some decide to marry and others to cohabit.

When Arland Thornton (1989) analyzed how attitudes and values about family life changed from the late 1950s to the mid-1980s, he found a dramatic and pervasive weakening of the norms requiring couples to marry, remain married, have children, engage in intimate relations only within the marriage, and maintain separate roles for males and females. The power of socially shared beliefs that individuals "ought to" or "should" follow certain patterns in marriage and family formation has diminished. Still, whereas there is greater acceptance of different family patterns, most people still choose a traditional family lifestyle—one that includes marriage and parenthood.

Marital Choice How do people choose their marital partners? Do they make this all-important choice on the basis of similarity, choosing partners who are "like" them? Or do more complex emotional and environmental factors steer them toward a certain kind of person? Over the years a number of theorists have tried to answer these questions. If nothing else, their conclusions show that marital choice is a far more complex issue than it might appear to be at first glance.

Freud was one of the early theorists who speculated about why people marry. A cornerstone of his psychoanalytic theory was the love attraction that children feel toward the opposite-sex parent (Chapter 2), which they later "transfer" to a socially acceptable object—their potential mate. (Hence, perhaps, the old song that goes, "I want a girl just like the girl that married dear old Dad.") As with many other aspects of Freud's theory, however, conclusive research evidence is lacking.

The *instrumental theory of mate selection* developed by Richard Centers (1975) also focused on gratification of needs, but it stated that some needs (such as sex and affiliation) are more important than others and that some needs are more appropriate for men and others for women. According to Centers, people are attracted to others with similar or complementary needs.

The *stimulus-value-role theory* developed by Bernard Murstein (1982, 1999) stated that mate selection is motivated by each partner's attempt to get the best possible deal. Each person examines the assets and liabilities of the other partner to determine whether the relationship is worthwhile. This takes place during three stages of courtship. During the *stimulus* stage, when a man and woman meet or see each other for the first time, they make initial judgments about each other's appearance, personality, and intelligence. If the mutual first impressions are favorable, the couple progresses to the second stage of courtship, *value-comparison*. During this stage their conversations reveal whether their interests, attitudes, beliefs, and needs are compatible. During the final *role* stage, the couple determines whether they can function in compatible roles in a marriage or similarly long-term relationship.

According to one classic study of seriously involved college-age couples over a period of 6 months (Adams, 1979), initial attraction is based on fairly superficial qualities such as physical appeal, gregariousness, poise, and shared interests. The relationship is reinforced by the reactions of others (including being labeled as a couple) and by feeling comfortable in each other's presence. The couple then enters a stage of commitment and intimacy, which leads to deeper attraction and involvement. Each person examines the other's viewpoints and value systems in making a commitment. At this point the couple often feels prepared to make decisions about marriage.

Finally, there's the *family system perspective* (McGoldrick, 1988), which emphasizes that couple formation involves the development of a new structure as well as a process of getting to know each other. Negotiating boundaries is crucial to couple formation. Gradually, a couple redefines their relationships with others—their family and friends—as well as with each other. Many informal shifts in relationships occur. In addition, more formal events such as the marriage ritual establish specific boundaries for the couple.

Marriage takes different forms in different cultures, but it is a major milestone in adult development in virtually all cultures.

Marriage The United States is a nation of subcultures with many different patterns of adult lifestyles. Yet monogamous marriage is by far the most popular and most frequently chosen lifestyle. Over 90% of men and women will marry at some point in their lives. Many cultures approve of sexual intimacy only within the confines of marriage. Preparation for marriage may involve elaborate rituals of dating, courtship, and engagement. The bond is symbolized by a wedding rite; subsequently, the new roles of husband and wife in relation to each other and the rest of society are defined. The community sanctions the union, which is expected to provide emotional sustenance, sexual gratification, and financial security for young couples and their families. Cultures (and individuals) vary considerably, however, in the extent to which sexual fidelity is expected.

In traditional Arab cultures, for example, the transition to married life is carefully orchestrated by older relatives. As soon as girls reach puberty, maintaining chastity through constant family vigilance takes on an urgent, life-or-death quality. All contact with men—including the fiancé—is forbidden once he has been selected. Young men are also excluded from the courtship process. Older relatives of the young man screen eligible young girls and their families. Male elders conduct bride-price negotiations. To conserve family assets and protect family honor, "cousin marriages" with the daughter of the father's brother are strongly favored. In this manner, a family can be sure that the young bride will be chaperoned and guarded in an acceptable manner (Goode, 1970).

Although most U.S. marriages are free of such prenuptial investigation and negotiation, there remain strong constraints for relationships that violate social, economic, religious, or ethnic boundaries. Community groups and social institutions, as well as parents, often frown on "mixed" marriages of any kind. Mixed marriages are becoming more socially acceptable, however. As of 1996, for example, there were 1,260,000 "interracial" couples in the United States (U.S. Census Bureau, 1997).

Alternatives to Formal Marriage Depending on the couple, cohabiting or "living together" may or may not be similar to marriage. It lacks the social approval and legalized responsibilities of traditional marriage but offers greater freedom for the partners to design their roles as they see fit. It is characterized by an overt acknowledgment that the couple is not married. Accurate statistics are hard to come by because of the reluctance of some couples to proclaim their relationship, and also because of the often transient nature of cohabitation. The U.S. Census Bureau nonetheless documents a large increase in the number of couples openly acknowledging cohabitation, especially young adults. For the population as a whole, cohabitation increased almost eightfold from 1970 to 1996, from 523,000 to 3,958,000 couples (U.S. Census Bureau, 1997). Among people under age 25, a 15-fold increase was reported—from 55,000 couples in 1970 to 816,000 in 1996. Most cohabiting couples (64%) have no children, but that leaves more than a million such households that do include children. Most cohabitors are young adults; 59% are between ages 25 and 44 (U.S. Census Bureau, 1997). As cohabitation without marriage becomes increasingly acceptable, marriage may become less important as a means of formally sanctioning sex (Thornton, 1989).

It has been estimated that about one-third of all cohabiting couples eventually marry—if they legally can. Although the great majority of such couples plan to marry, they feel less urgency than those who have never cohabited. Cohabiting couples who eventually marry do not necessarily communicate better or find greater satisfaction in marriage than couples who do not live together before marriage (Demaris & Leslie, 1984). Because cohabiting couples who do not marry typically break up, it is rare to find a long-established cohabiting couple. Philip Blumstein and Pepper Schwartz (1983) could not locate enough heterosexual cohabitors who had been together for more than 10 years to permit data analysis, although they did find enough gay and lesbian couples who had been together this long. The latter finding is undoubtedly related to laws against homosexual marriage. To date, one state has legalized same-sex marriages and another has allowed them by court order. Legislation or lawsuits are pending in many other states. Same-sex marriages are legal in several Scandinavian countries (McWhirter & Mattison, 1996).

IN THEORY, IN FACT

SINGLES

In many historical periods, remaining single was often an unfortunate result of disaster or war. It was also considered a sign of abnormality or immaturity, and to an extent it still is. Some married people hold stereotyped images of singles, such as "swingers" and "losers." Swingers supposedly live wild, exciting lives with few restraints. The stereotyped loser is a physically unattractive person with no compensating personality or intellectual characteristics, who would like to get married but can't find anyone who's willing. Is there any truth to the stereotypes?

Sometimes there is. There are individuals who fit the descriptions, at least for a while; but people change. A real understanding of singlehood, however, requires placing it in a historical perspective. Periodically, large groups of people have remained single. During the late 1930s, for example, when the country was recovering from the Great Depression, fewer people married, and those who did marry did so at later ages. This trend continued during World War II, when millions of temporarily single women joined the labor force while their boyfriends or husbands were overseas fighting and dying. After the war the picture changed dramatically. By the mid-1950s, only 4% of marriage-age adults remained single, and the age at first marriage was the youngest on record. Remaining single became popular once again in the 1970s and 1980s: The marriage rate among single people under 45 years of age fell to equal the post-Depression low. In 1996, 26.8% of the population over 18 years of age was single, 2.7% widowed, and 8.4% divorced (U.S. Census Bureau, 1997).

The choice of a single lifestyle may also be deliberate—a balance between freedom and constraint, self-sufficiency and interdependence. Some commentators worry about the trend toward fewer marriages and more divorces. Are we as a society too fascinated with freedom and autonomy at the expense of interpersonal obligations (Weiss, 1987)? More than one observer has expressed fears about the effects of our individualistic lifestyles and our emphasis on free choice at the expense of transgenerational ties and interdependent roles (Hunt & Hunt, 1987).

Many singles choose the single life as a way of enjoying intimate relationships while avoiding the possible constraints and problems of marriage. They do not want to feel trapped by a mate who stands in the way of their own personal development. Nor do they want to feel bored, unhappy, angry, sexually frustrated, or lonely with a person from whom they have grown apart. Watching the marriages of their friends fall apart, they feel that the single life is a far better choice.

Living together in an informal arrangement entails many of the same relationship-building tasks that newlyweds face. Conflicts must be resolved through a complex process of "negotiation and collective bargaining" (Almo, 1978). Constant and effective communication is essential. As in marriage, good communication is a constant struggle. In fact, it may be even more important and more difficult within the vague boundaries of cohabitation.

Finally, a couple that lives together must deal with issues of commitment, fidelity, and permanence. Both men and women in cohabiting relationships are more likely than married people to have affairs outside the relationship (Blumstein & Schwartz, 1983). This may contribute to the greater tension reported by cohabiting heterosexual couples compared with married heterosexual, gay, or lesbian couples (Kurdek & Schmitt, 1986). According to one study (Almo, 1978), couples find it difficult to deal explicitly with such concerns even though the partners have strong feelings about each other. Most couples make a definite, if unspoken, commitment to each other before moving in together. That commitment is based on a mutual desire for some kind of permanence that will allow them to plan for the future but retain flexibility. They may or may not require sexual exclusivity and fidelity. Some couples view outside relationships as taboo. Others explicitly agree that each partner may pursue other relationships, although this arrangement is usually desired by one partner and acquiesced to by the other.

An alternative to marriage or cohabitation is remaining single, as discussed in "In Theory, In Fact," above.

CONTENT CHECK
FORMING CLOSE RELATIONSHIPS

True–False (answers are on the Companion Website)

1. Sternberg's three components of a love relationship are intimacy, passion, and romantic love.
2. Among the seven types of love, according to Sternberg, is empty love.
3. In general, most people choose their marital partners mainly on the basis of sexual attraction.
4. Cultures vary greatly in expectations concerning marital fidelty.
5. Men and women in cohabiting relationships are more likely than married people to have affairs outside the relationship.

Thinking Critically

Which theory describing mate selection do you think best describes what's involved? Why?

Parenthood and Adult Development

Parenthood imposes new roles and responsibilities on both the mother and the father. It also confers a new social status on them. The actual birth brings an onslaught of physical and emotional strains—disruption of sleep and other routines, financial drain, increased tension, and conflicts of various kinds. The mother is tired, the father feels neglected, and both partners feel that their freedom has been curtailed. The closeness and companionship of husband and wife can be diluted by the introduction of a new family member, and the focus of either or both partners may shift to the baby.

The challenges and demands of parenthood are a major developmental phase for the parents as individuals and for the couple as a system (Osofsky & Osofsky, 1984). Nor is there a single path to parenthood, as we see.

The Family Life Cycle

Families go through a predictable family life cycle marked by specific events (Birchler, 1992). The first milestone occurs when the individual leaves his or her family of origin. Separation may come at the time of marriage, or earlier if the individual opts for independence and lives alone or with others. The second milestone is usually marriage, with all the attendant adjustments of establishing a relationship with a new individual and a new family network—the spouse's. The third milestone is the birth of the first child and the beginning of parenthood, which is referred to as the establishment of a family or simply as the transition to parenthood. There are other milestones, such as the first child's enrollment in school, the birth of the last child, the departure of the last child from the family, and the death of a spouse.

During the past 50 to 100 years, family life cycles have changed in timing as well as in nature. Not only are more people living longer, but their ages at various points in the family cycle and the length of time between milestones have changed. For example, the time between the last child leaving and the parent's retirement or death has increased and continues to do so.

The Transition to Parenthood

The transition to parenthood is one of the major periods in the family life cycle. Often there is considerable family and cultural pressure to have a child—a change that is irrevocable. In contrast to those of marriage by itself, many of the roles and responsibilities of parenting endure despite changing life circumstances. Parenthood calls for numerous adaptations and adjustments. Newlywed couples often enjoy a relatively high standard of living when both spouses are working and there is no child to provide for. They buy cars, furniture, and clothes. They eat out often and enjoy numerous recreational activities. This all comes to an abrupt end with the arrival of the first child (Aldous, 1978, 1996; Klein & Aldous, 1988).

Effects of the transition to parenthood on specific domains of personal and family life include the following (Cowan & Cowan, 1992):

■ *Changes in identity and inner life*: Each parent's sense of self changes, along with assumptions about how family life works.
■ *Shifts in roles and relationships within the marriage*: The division of labor between the parents changes at a time when both are stressed by sleep disruptions and by not being able to be alone together as much as they would like.
■ *Shifts in generational roles and relationships*: The transition affects grandparents as well as parents.
■ *Changing roles and relationships outside the family*: Outside changes affect the mother most, as she is likely to put her career on hold, at least temporarily.
■ *New parenting roles and relationships*: The couple must navigate the new responsibilities associated with raising a child.

During the wife's pregnancy, both spouses can offer emotional support to each other.

Although they share many concerns, fathers and mothers also display different reactions to the arrival of the first child. Women characteristically adjust their lifestyles to give priority to parenting and family roles. Men, on the other hand, more often intensify their work efforts to become better or more stable providers. When the child arrives, there are new stresses and challenges, and the role changes are rapid. Both parents experience new feelings of pride and excitement coupled with a greater sense of responsibility that can be overwhelming. Some men are envious of their partner's ability to reproduce and of the close emotional bond established between mother and infant. Couples need to find time for each other and for other interests. Sexual problems, less communication and sharing of interests, and increased conflict occur in many marriages after the birth of a child (Osofsky & Osofsky, 1984).

The arrival of the first child usually constitutes a transition rather than a crisis, however (Entwisle, 1985). Most couples say that they experienced only slight difficulty adjusting. For example, most mothers do not experience postpartum depression (Chapter 4). Instead they experience 2 to 3 days of much milder "baby blues." Perhaps 10% to 20% of new mothers do not even experience that (O'Hara, Zekoski, Philipps, & Wright, 1990). In addition, one study (Belsky & Rovine, 1990b) reported that 20% to 35% of couples experience increased marital satisfaction.

A variety of factors influence how well new parents adjust to their roles. Social support, especially from the husband, is crucial to a new mother (Cutrona & Troutman, 1986). Marital happiness during pregnancy is another important

Parents may be better at dealing with children at one stage of development than at another.

factor in the adjustment of both husband and wife (Wallace & Gotlib, 1990). In fact, the father's adjustment is strongly affected by the mother's evaluation of her marriage and pregnancy (Wallace & Gotlib, 1990).

Parental self-esteem can be an issue too, in that parents with higher self-esteem are more likely to adjust well (Belsky & Rovine, 1990b). The baby's characteristics are also important. For example, parents of "difficult" babies (see Chapter 6) often report a decline in marital satisfaction (Belsky & Rovine, 1990b; Crockenberg, 1981).

Coping with Children's Developmental Stages

The demands on parents vary at each period in the family life cycle. A young infant requires almost total and constant nurturance, which some parents provide more easily than others. Some parents are overwhelmed by the infant's intense dependency. Some can't bear to hear an infant cry. The baby's wails may trigger feelings of helplessness, even anger, in the father or mother.

Each critical period for the child produces or reactivates a critical period for the parents. According to one theory (Galinsky, 1980), there are six separate stages of parenthood. In the *image-making stage*, from conception to birth, couples create images of the kind of parents they will be and measure their anticipated performance against their own standards of perfection. In the *nurturing stage*, from birth to about 2 years (specifically, until the child starts saying "No!"), parents become attached to their baby and try to balance the baby's needs with the emotional commitment and time they devote to spouse, job, friends, and parents. During the *authority stage*, the time roughly between the child's second and fifth birthdays, parents begin to question the kind of parents they have been and will be. Growth comes when parents realize that they, along with their child, sometimes fall short of their images of perfection.

During the *interpretive stage*—the middle childhood years—parents reexamine and test many of their long-held theories. When their children become teenagers, parents pass through the *interdependence stage*, in which they must redefine the authority relationship they have with their nearly grown children.

They may find themselves competing with or comparing themselves with their children. Finally, during the *departure stage* when grown children leave home, parents not only have to "let go" but must also face the difficult and sometimes unpleasant task of taking stock of their experiences as parents. During each stage, parents must be able to resolve their own conflicts at a new and more advanced level of integration; otherwise they may be unable to cope with their feelings. Unresolved tensions may interfere with the marriage relationship or with the ability to function well as parents.

Parents who are unable to deal effectively with children at one stage may be quite good at dealing with them at another stage. For example, parents who have a lot of difficulty with an infant may cope quite effectively with a preschool child or adolescent. The reverse may also be true; the parent who is quite at ease with a helpless baby may have problems with an increasingly independent teenager.

At each phase in the family life cycle, parents not only have to cope with the new challenges and demands of their changing and developing children; they must also renegotiate their own relationship (McGoldrick, 1988). Couples must establish ways of making decisions and resolving conflicts that will maintain the integrity and respect of each partner. Systems in which one person is always dominant and the other is always passive tend to dissolve over time. The new pressures created by adolescent rebellion and the quest for independence, for example, require that the couple adapt the family system to make room for the nearly autonomous child. The family system that is too rigid or too unstructured doesn't cope well with the child's emerging needs.

Coping with Single Parenthood

The pressures of parenthood are particularly acute for single parents, the overwhelming majority of whom are working mothers. Single-parent families are becoming increasingly common in the United States. In the mid-1970s, one of every seven children spent part of childhood without a father in the home. Since then, single-parent families have increased at a rate 10 times faster than traditional two-parent families. The trend is greatest among young women. In 1995, almost one-third of all families were maintained by single mothers (U.S. Census Bureau, 1997).

For perspective, in 1999 about 1,115,000 marriages ended in divorce. In the same year, the divorce rate per 1000 was 4.1, over 12% lower than it was in 1979 and 1981, which were peak years for divorce (Clarke, 1995; NCHS, 2001). For every three marriages that succeed, two are expected to fail (Clarke, 1995). Failures are concentrated in the first 7 years of marriage, with divorcing couples having a median marriage duration of 7.2 years. Although divorce can happen at any age, they are more likely in young adulthood. In 1995, for example, the divorce rate for men was 32.8 per 1000 married men in the 15 to 19 age group and 50.2 per 1000 for men in the 20 to 24 age group (see Figure 14–5).

Single-Mother Families What's responsible for the exploding number of single-parent families headed by women? There are a number of factors. In the 1960s and 1970s, the main cause was the rising divorce rate, accompanied by the tradition of awarding custody of the children to the mother. The next greatest increase was in unmarried mothers. In 1998, 32.8% of all births were to unmarried women; for women who indicated that they were black, the figure was 69.1% (NCHS, 2000b). Third, there was a substantial increase in the number of mothers who were separated from their spouses but not divorced.

Figure 14–5   Age-Specific Divorce Rates for Men and Women, United States

Divorce rates peak for men and women in early adulthood and then decline steadily throughout middle and old age.

Source: NCHS, 1995.

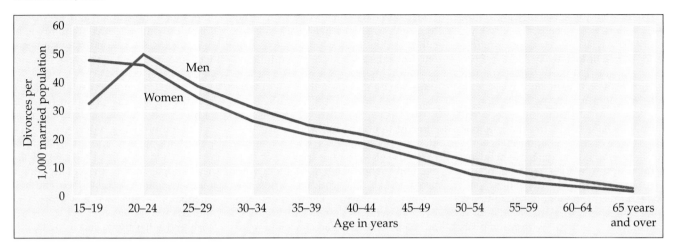

Researchers have long pointed to improved social and economic conditions for women as an important factor in these changes. They conclude that better job opportunities and improved status have enabled mothers and children to survive without their husbands and fathers, at least in the short run. Indeed, for many single mothers the status is only temporary because a large percentage eventually remarry. And for many single parents, staying single is a viable option.

Single parenthood can be an exhausting struggle, even in middle- and working-class families. Single parents experience frequent and destructive levels of stress (McAdoo, 1995). Single mothers consistently earn less than single fathers. For women without education, making ends meet is extremely difficult. For those who formerly depended on public assistance, welfare reform has brought new demands and pressures, as discussed in "A Matter for Debate," page 490.

Single-mother homes are more numerous and more often below the poverty level among people who identify as black. Fully 58% of all black families with children under 18 years are headed by single women (U.S. Census Bureau, 1997). Although less than 3% of all families in poverty remain in poverty indefinitely, 62% of them are black (Klein & Rones, 1989). The majority of black children will spend at least half of their childhood in poverty (Ellwood & Crane, 1990). In 1994, the median family income for single-mothers who identify as white was only about 65% of that for white married couples. All of this indicates the special hardships faced by black single parents.

On the other hand, black and Hispanic people who live in poverty are also more likely to live in intergenerational households (Harrison et al., 1990; Jackson, Antonucci, & Gibson, 1990). These extended families most often include one of the single mother's parents in addition to other family or nonfamily members. Thus, additional financial, psychological, and social resources are available to the single mother and she may feel less isolated and overwhelmed. There will also be less general housework to do if other members of the household contribute, but there is a downside: Living with her parents makes it significantly less likely that the mother will receive public assistance (Folk, 1996).

A MATTER FOR DEBATE

THE IMPACT OF WELFARE REFORM ON U.S. SINGLE PARENTING

The Personal Responsibility and Work Opportunity Reconciliation Act (PRWORA) was enacted by Congress and signed into law in August 1996. This was the first major welfare reform effort in the 60 years since passage of the Aid to Families with Dependent Children (AFDC) program. The intent of the PRWORA was to change public assistance into a system that helps welfare mothers become independent, self-sufficient workers instead of encouraging them to be dependent, passive aid recipients who tended to pass their dependency along to the next generation. Exactly how to accomplish this was to be determined by the states, within guidelines that (1) set a relatively tight schedule for implementation of state programs (2) establish immediate and lifetime limits on a mother's receipt of welfare payments, and (3) most important, required the mother to work to receive payments and other assistance. The intent, in other words, was to reverse the welfare/poverty cycle.

How well the welfare reform act is faring is unclear at this point; the results are still coming in. Suffice it to say—largely on the basis of anecdotal evidence—that it appears to be working better in some states than in others, and better for some mothers than for others. For example, for mothers who are semi-skilled and have some work history, the transition to employment isn't as difficult as it is for those who are capable of only unskilled labor and have little or no work history. At the outset, most states have focused on the easier cases; the difficult ones are yet to come.

It is possible, however, to discuss some of the problems welfare has created for single mothers, who constitute over 90% of welfare recipients. Of crucial importance is the question of who takes care of the children while the mothers are at work. For mothers who live in extended families, as discussed on page 489, satisfactory child care arrangements can often be made within the home. For two-parent welfare families, alternating shifts are a possibility. For single mothers who are on their own, the transition is proving more difficult. Day care facilities are limited, and most have long waiting lists as a result of the PRWORA—up to several months in many communities. In turn, federal funds to assist with child care are limited—and day care can be very expensive. An additional problem for unskilled single mothers in particular is that whatever jobs they can find often involve working at times when day care centers aren't open. Entry-level positions in factories, warehouses, and service industries (such as building cleaning and maintenance and food preparation and service in fast-food outlets) often require night and weekend work; but day care centers cater to 9-to-5 employees who are at home on weekends.

Finally, for mothers who do solve child care problems and find full-time employment, the job is typically paid the minimum wage, which is still well below the poverty line for a family of three (Children's Defense Fund, 1998). The simple fact is that many single mothers cannot support their children adequately even when they work, and the disparity between what people earn and what they can buy with it is increasing (Children's Defense Fund, 1998). What will happen to single mothers, working or not, when their Temporary Cash Assistance (TCA) runs out? Will their children have to be placed in foster care? Will the states start making exceptions—which they can do under extenuating circumstances—at such a rate that the outcome will resemble the former welfare system? Or will increasing numbers of single mothers and their children become destitute and homeless as suggested by Bassuk and colleagues (Bassuk, Browne, & Buckner, 1996)?

It all remains to be seen. The only certainty is that welfare as we knew it is history; what is much less clear is exactly what we have replaced it with.

Single-Father Families Although it is still true that only a small proportion of fathers gain custody of their children after divorce, the number is growing and is at least 10%. Another 16% participate in joint custody settlements (NCHS, 1995).

Single fathers experience many of the same problems and tensions as single mothers. However, they are usually better off financially (Hetherington & Camara, 1984). One profile of single fathers revealed that many had taken on extensive parenting roles before the divorce (Pichitino, 1983). Most single fathers maintain high levels of emotional involvement with their children, are heavily invested in and committed to their care, and worry about failing them or not spending enough time with them. However, their parenting experience does not always prepare them for the demands they face when they must maintain a job and a family simultaneously. Many single fathers have the same feelings of loneliness and depression that single mothers have. Single fathers also find, as do single mothers, that it is difficult to maintain an active circle of friends and other sources of emotional support (Pichitino, 1983).

Gay and Lesbian Families   Families with same-sex parents are relatively new on the scene, and less research has been conducted on the dynamics of their family life. However, in a review of the existing literature, Charlotte Patterson (2000) did find an overall picture of positive adjustment in the face of adversity. In all probability, as with lesbian and gay individuals, future research will find both commonalities and distinct differences compared to other kinds of families. As Judith Stacey (1998) has noted, there is much to be learned by studying the varied experience of lesbian and gay families.

There is however a growing body of research on the effects on children of having a gay or lesbian couple as parents. How do same-sex couples come to have children? Despite the prejudices of the larger society, they may be awarded custody after divorcing a heterosexual partner, they may adopt children or serve as foster parents, and in the case of lesbian women, they may bear children through donor insemination (Baumrind, 1995). In turn, as noted by Baumrind (1995), much of the research on potential long-range effects on children in particular is as yet inconclusive, in part because of reliance on relatively small "samples of convenience." From research that has been conducted, however, it appears that few if any detrimental effects occur and in particular that such children are no more likely than the general population to develop a same-sex orientation themselves (Bailey, Bobrow, Wolfe, & Mikach, 1995; Flaks, Ficher, Masterpasqua, & Joseph, 1995; Patterson, 1995a). In particular, one extensive review (Fitzgerald, 1999) found that the sexual orientation of the parents is only minimally associated with successful development on the part of the child in areas such as intelligence, emotionality, and behavior. There may also be some benefits: Such children may be more tolerant of and accepting toward others (Baumrind, 1995), which logically follows from the stigmatization they may experience from peers with heterosexual parents.

Single parenting is no easier for fathers than for mothers.

CONTENT CHECK
PARENTHOOD AND ADULT DEVELOPMENT

True–False (answers are on the Companion Website)

1. During the last 50 years, family life cycles have changed in timing and in nature.
2. Typically, the birth of a first child constitutes a crisis for the family.
3. Parents may deal with their children at one developmental stage better than at another.
4. The majority of single parents are working mothers.
5. Single fathers generally experience fewer problems and tensions than single mothers do.

Thinking Critically

How does parenthood constitute a major developmental phase for parents both as individuals and as a couple?

The Occupational Cycle

An adult's working life follows what is called the **occupational cycle.** The cycle begins in adolescence with thoughts and experiences that lead to a choice of occupation; it continues with pursuit of the chosen career; and it ends with retirement from the workforce. The cycle isn't usually that simple, however, and it doesn't always run smoothly. An adult must make important choices throughout her or his working life, choices that can include changing careers more than once. In any career there are moments of doubt and crisis, and special events such as receiving a promotion or being fired can affect the course of an individual's career.

To a great extent, people's work influences their attitudes and lifestyle. Their work may determine whether they will lead mobile or relatively settled lives, the kind of community they will live in, and the kind of home and standard of living they will have. Work may also contribute to their friendships, opinions, prejudices, and political affiliations.

In this section we examine the stages individuals go through in their vocational lives, some factors that affect occupational choice and preparation, and the process of entering the workforce and consolidating and maintaining, or perhaps changing, a career.

Stages of Vocational Life

According to Robert Havighurst (1964), the occupational cycle starts in middle childhood. He divided the cycle into a series of stages based on how people are involved with work at various times in their lives, with emphasis on the acquisition of attitudes and work skills. The stages are as follows:

1. *Identification with a worker* (ages 5 to 10): Children identify with working fathers and mothers and the idea of working enters their self-concept.
2. *Acquiring basic habits of industry* (ages 10 to 15): Students learn to organize their time and efforts so as to accomplish tasks like schoolwork or chores. They also learn to give work priority over play when necessary.
3. *Acquiring an identity as a worker* (ages 15 to 25): People choose their occupation and begin to prepare for it. They acquire work experience that helps them choose their career and get started in it.
4. *Becoming a productive person* (ages 25 to 40): Adults perfect the skills required for their chosen occupation and move ahead in their career.
5. *Maintaining a productive society* (ages 40 to 70): Workers are now at the high point of their career. They begin to pay attention to and give time to civic and social responsibilities related to and beyond their jobs.
6. *Contemplating a productive and responsible life* (age 70 on): Workers are now retired. They look back on their careers and contributions, hopefully with satisfaction (see also Erikson's stage of *integrity versus despair* in Chapter 18).

Although Havighurst's model is useful, it doesn't always apply in today's rapidly changing, highly technological society. Not everyone goes through a single, forward-moving set of stages and a single occupational cycle. Young people often change jobs frequently before they make a major occupational commitment; many adults make one or more major midcareer shifts. These shifts may be the result of factors beyond the person's control, such as when a company downsizes and lays off the worker or when the worker's job simply becomes obsolete. Alternatively, the shifts may result from personal career reevaluation, as when a person hits a "ceiling" and can progress no further in

occupational cycle A variable sequence of periods or stages in a worker's life, from occupational exploration and choice, through education and training, novice status, promotions and more experienced periods.

his or her present occupation, or perhaps simply "burns out" and feels compelled to find something else to do.

Occupational Choice and Preparation

Why does one person become an accountant, another a police officer, another a doctor, another a plumber or electrician? A multitude of factors influence the choice of an occupation, including socioeconomic status, ethnic background, intelligence, skills, gender, and parents' occupations. Here, we look specifically at gender and ethnicity, parental attitudes, self-concept, personality traits, and practical considerations.

Gender and Ethnicity   As Table 14–2 indicates, people who identify as black, along with women of all ethnicities, are overrepresented in lower-status, lower-paying jobs and underrepresented in more highly paid professions (see also Walsh, 1997). Researchers explain these discrepancies in two ways. One

Career choice is often a defining feature in self-concept.

Table 14–2   **Representation in Various Occupations of Women of all Ethnicities and People Who Identify Themselves as Black or Hispanic, United States, 1996**

OCCUPATION	Percentage of Total		
	WOMEN	BLACK	HISPANIC
Total percent employed*	46.2	10.7	9.2
Architects	16.7	2.7	4.3
Engineers	8.5	4.2	3.8
Registered nurses	93.3	8.6	2.6
Teachers, college and university	43.5	6.5	4.1
Teachers, prekindergarten and kindergarten	98.1	13.6	5.8
Teachers, elementary school	83.3	9.9	4.8
Social workers	68.5	22.6	7.7
Secretaries	98.6	9.3	6.2
Duplicating, mail, and other office machine operators	63.6	13.2	13.1
Mail clerks	49.3	29.8	11.1
Data entry keyers	84.5	17.0	10.8
Teachers' aides	92.1	15.9	14.4
Private household cleaners and servants	93.6	18.5	32.4
Correctional institution officers	21.7	22.1	8.4
Dental assistants	99.1	6.2	11.2
Nursing aides, orderlies, and attendants	88.4	33.2	8.1
Maids and housemen	81.8	29.6	21.1
Janitors and cleaners	34.9	21.1	19.7
Automobile mechanics	1.2	7.6	13.9
Pressing machine operators	76.3	22.7	38.4
Farmworkers	18.8	3.4	37.3

*Civilian noninstitutionalized population 16 years old and over.
Source: U.S. Census Bureau, 1997.

explanation is that individuals make early choices that ultimately determine what occupations they can or cannot pursue. For example, blacks are less likely to finish high school than whites, and those who drop out cannot compete for the jobs that require a high school or college education. Women limit their choices when they question their competence in the sciences and avoid careers in technology-based fields such as engineering. Some women choose careers that will give them the flexibility to raise a family. They may choose part-time work; move in and out of the job market during their child-rearing years; and look for jobs involving limited stress and time pressure—which also have limited career and financial potential (Council of Economic Advisers, 1987; Kalleberg & Rosenfeld, 1990). Role modeling by parents may also influence career choice. Once they are established, such job-limiting patterns can be self-perpetuating.

A second explanation for these occupational patterns is discrimination. Blacks and women may be subtly (or not so subtly) channeled into some jobs rather than others, in spite of federal equal opportunity requirements. The better positions still tend to be given to men more frequently than to women—even when women have equal skills (Heilman, 1995). Promotions also may not be equally available. Such discrimination is illegal, but as affirmative action and employment "quotas" have come under increasing pressure, it has become easier for employers to hire or promote in discriminatory ways for "legitimate" reasons—such as exaggerated performance reviews. Thus, the education and skills that predict high salaries for white men do not result in equally high salaries for blacks and women (Ferber, Green, & Spaith, 1986; Klein & Rones, 1989).

Formal and Informal Preparation Before entering the workforce, people acquire certain skills, values, and attitudes, both formally and informally. Formal occupational preparation includes structured learning in high school, vocational training programs, and college, as well as on-the-job training (OJT). Informal occupational preparation takes subtler forms: It involves adopting the attitudes, norms, and role expectations that are appropriate to a particular job. Long before we begin formal preparation, we are acquiring informal norms and values from our parents and teachers, members of the trades and professions, even television and movie portrayals. We learn by observing others and from our day-to-day experiences. Informal socialization is so pervasive that it often determines our choice of the formal steps taken to prepare for a career.

For many people, college is considered a mandatory step in preparing for a career, although educational attainment (especially college) and other job-related training varies considerably across nations (see Table 14–3). In many areas of college work, particularly in the liberal arts, little or no training is specifically aimed at developing marketable skills. Liberal arts curricula try to develop basic communication skills, expose students to a variety of ideas and perspectives, and develop analytical skills. Although they are essential to intellectual maturity, these skills are not directly related to specific job titles—except perhaps for future teachers of these skills. In contrast, programs such as engineering, health sciences, business, and education provide substantive knowledge and practical skills. They usually attract motivated, determined students who have already defined their goals.

Some Practical Issues The preceding sections explain in part how occupational choices are made. But practical issues often are equally or even more important than these factors. In times of recession and high unemployment, for example, people may not have much choice and may be forced to focus on simply finding some kind of job that will make ends meet. Under such condi-

Table 14-3   Educational Attainment and Other Job-Related Training Across Selected Industrialized Nations (Percent Distribution, Persons Age 25–84)

NATION	TOTAL	Educational Attainment			
		EARLY CHILDHOOD, PRIMARY, AND LOWER SECONDARY EDUCATION ONLY	UPPER SECONDARY EDUCATION ONLY	NONUNIVERSITY TERTIARY EDUCATION ONLY	UNIVERSITY EDUCATION ONLY
Australia	100	50	27	10	13
Austria	100	32	60	2	6
Belgium	100	51	27	12	10
Canada	100	26	28	29	17
Denmark	100	40	40	6	14
Finland	100	36	44	9	11
France	100	33	50	8	9
Germany	100	16	62	10	13
Greece	100	55	27	6	12
Ireland	100	55	27	10	9
Italy	100	67	26	—	8
Netherlands	100	40	38	—	21
New Zealand	100	43	34	14	9
Norway	100	19	53	11	16
Portugal	100	81	8	3	7
Spain	100	74	11	4	11
Sweden	100	28	46	14	12
Switzerland	100	18	61	13	8
Turkey	100	60	13	—	7
United Kingdom	100	26	54	9	12
United States	100	15	53	8	24

NATION	Participation in Job-Related Continuing Education and Training			
	YEAR	TOTAL	MALE	FEMALE
United States	1995	34	31	36
Australia	1993	38	37	40
Belgium	1994	3	3	2
Canada	1993	28	27	30
Denmark	1994	15	13	18
Finland	1993	41	38	44
France	1994	40	38	43
Germany	1994	33	35	31
Greece	1994	1	1	1
Ireland	1994	4	3	6
Italy	1994	1	1	2
Spain	1994	3	2	4
Sweden	1995	44	40	47
Switzerland	1993	38	42	34
United Kingdom	1994	13	12	14

Source: U.S. Census Bureau, 1997.

tions it is not uncommon to hear about individuals who want to be architects or musicians but instead wind up as civil servants or hospital workers, depending on what jobs are available. In extreme cases, you find people with college degrees sacking groceries and mowing lawns. The need to support a spouse or children may also cause people to look for a job in a different field than they would choose if they did not have these constraints. An aspiring painter, for example, may get by with advertising or public relations work (or even house painting), with little time left for artistic pursuits.

Finally, many people let family pressures determine their choice of a career. Some children are "groomed" to take over family businesses or to follow in a parent's footsteps, even though they might have preferred to pursue a different career. Alternatively, people without definite plans or with varied interests and abilities may take any job that is available and frequently change jobs.

Gaining a Place in the Workforce

Having made at least tentative occupational choices and acquired appropriate training or education, young adults are ready to enter the workforce. This involves an adjustment period that can be eased somewhat by the assistance of a mentor. It also involves a growing sense of loyalty and commitment. To set the stage, however, let's first consider how attitudes about work have changed in recent decades.

Changing Attitudes About Work   Before the 1970s, a coherent value system dominated the attitudes of most U.S. workers (Yankelovich, 1981). The old value system had several distinct components. It was considered desirable for women to stay home if their husbands could afford it, and many husbands were strongly opposed to the idea of wives working outside the home. In turn, men often tolerated unsatisfying jobs for the sake of economic security. The main motivations for workers were money, status, and achieving the "American dream": Work hard, own your home, and retire comfortably. If you did your job well, society—including your company—would provide for you.

This value system has eroded considerably in recent decades. The civil rights movement, the Vietnam War, the counterculture, the women's movement, Watergate, and other social phenomena challenged the old order. Many young adults entering the work force view work in very different ways, primarily as a means to an end. Another factor is the corporate downsizing that began in the late 1980s, which left millions of workers uncertain about their future. In industries as unrelated as banking and steel, workers no longer believe that companies have any loyalty to their employees, and they realize that they may suddenly be unemployed through no fault of their own. They also realize that they are responsible for advancing their own career and cannot depend on the corporation for anything—such as a long-term career path and retirement benefits or short-term benefits such as health insurance.

Forced by circumstances to reassess what work means to them, many young adults attempt to find work that they can do at home. This new pattern is largely the result of modern technology. Architects, writers, and computer programmers, among others, are working at home thanks to computers, e-mail, fax machines, cellular phones, and conference calls. *Someone* has to actually go to the factory or office, however. What they find there, especially if they're young adults entering the workforce, can be quite different from what they might expect.

Expectation Meets Reality   When young adults start working, they may experience what could be termed *reality shock*. During adolescence and preparation for a career, people often have high expectations about what their work

A formal system of mentor relationships might help more young women obtain managerial, executive, and administrative positions.

will be like and what they will accomplish. When the training ends and the job begins, novices quickly learn that some of their expectations were unrealistic. Their training may be inadequate to the actual work; many employers view novices as people who have yet to be trained. The work may be dull and mechanical, supervisors unfair, and peers difficult to work with. The goals of the job may be lost in a maze of bureaucratic politics, or subject to the whims of superiors. The shock of reality may result in a period of frustration and anger as the young worker adjusts to the new situation.

The Role of Mentors   Gradually, the entry phase gives way to growing competence and autonomy. Remember that Levinson emphasized the role of mentors, who help younger workers acquire appropriate values and norms. In the context of work, apprentices acquire skills and self-confidence with the help of mentors. They soon establish themselves and may begin to outperform their mentors and break away from them. Later, they acquire authority over others and serve as mentors themselves.

Several authors have noted the positive role of good mentors in the development of young workers (e.g., Corzine, Buntzman, & Busch, 1994), especially in the era of downsizing. Mentors perform teaching and training roles. They sponsor the young workers' advancement. They serve as models for social as well as work-related behavior. Generally, they ease the transition to independent work status. In executive and academic careers, male workers frequently report having a mentor. However, the number of available upper-level mentors available is very limited, and women executives may have particular difficulty finding them. Some women find male mentors, or their husbands serve as mentors, but that kind of relationship can become complicated, as we saw in Chapter 13. If the woman's career threatens to reduce the amount of time devoted to her husband and family, the husband often becomes less supportive of the wife's career development (Roberts & Newton, 1987). In an effort to help more women achieve executive, administrative, and managerial roles, some have suggested that one of the most successful strategies would be to promote a formal, company-based system of mentor relationships (Corzine et al., 1994).

Consolidation, Maintenance, and Change   For those who conform to the classic occupational cycle, the midcareer period is a time of consolidation—settling down and coming to grips with the realities of one's occupational situation. For the men studied by Levinson (1978), the late 30s was a time of establishing a niche in society, forgetting about attractive alternative careers, and striving for advancement. This involved striving to be as good as possible at their chosen profession. It also involved attempting to create some stability at work and in life in general. For some, it involved increasing responsibility and prestige, drawing away from the mentor, and becoming autonomous.

Climbing the ladder of success generally is not as easy as anticipated. The higher you climb, the less room there is for advancement. Hence, by their early 40s many workers are disillusioned and somewhat cynical. The original dream is gone; they face lower levels of accomplishment. The study of AT&T managers discussed earlier found such a pattern at midcareer. Although some managers had reached upper-management levels, many were still at low- or middle-management levels and had downgraded their goals and aspirations. Indeed, many reported that further advancement in their careers was not crucial to their life satisfaction and that other areas of their lives—such as family and personal pursuits—had become more important (Bray & Howard, 1983). The high-level managers in the AT&T study, however, rated work as crucial to their sense of self and overall life satisfaction.

In sum, the classic occupational cycle is no longer the dominant pattern, even for white-collar managers and executives. Only a minority of workers now stay with the same company throughout their careers. Many people change jobs within a field, looking for better pay, more responsibility, promotion, or better working conditions. So-called "headhunters" earn fees by enticing talented and accomplished workers—especially managers and those with skills that are in high demand, such as computer programming—to move to another company. In addition, an increasing number of people are making career shifts and changing fields to pursue different interests. Some workers don't experience much occupational stability at all, and they may encounter frequent or protracted periods of unemployment and career crisis—often accompanied by financial, social, and adjustment problems.

CONTENT CHECK
THE OCCUPATIONAL CYCLE

True–False (answers are on the Companion Website)

1. Havighurst's model of the *occupational cycle* describes perfectly today's technological work world.
2. Blacks and women are still overrepresented in lower-status jobs.
3. Practical factors are the most important of all factors influencing occupational choices.
4. Most young adults experience reality shock when they first begin working.
5. Finding a mentor is equally difficult for young male and young female workers.

Thinking Critically

Which of these factors do you think are the most important influences on occupational choice? Why?

Work and Gender

For women, occupational career patterns have often been interrupted rather than continuous. Indeed, in the 21st century the most common occupational pattern for both women and men in midlife will probably be one of change rather than consolidation and maintenance of one vocation. Whereas some women follow the same path as men in their working lives, the majority try to combine work and family roles by taking a more flexible approach to their careers. Some stop working during their child-rearing years; others work part-time; and still others find a way to continue earning money by working at home.

In this section, we look at work from the perspective of gender, paying special attention to how women combine work and family roles. We examine how women's work patterns differ from what was once considered the norm for all workers but actually applied only to men. We also consider what work really means to women—despite stereotypes to the contrary. Finally, we look at what it means to be a member of a dual-earner couple. Let's begin with some dramatic statistics on women's growing presence in the workforce.

A Changing Statistical Picture

One of the most notable developments in the employment world is the great increase in the percentage of women in the U.S. workforce in recent decades. In 1950, about one in three women age 16 and older were in the labor force; by 1998, the figure had risen to three in five (U.S. Department of Labor, 2000a). The increase has been most dramatic for white women. It has been less so for black women, who have always worked in greater numbers out of greater economic necessity. In all, less than 11% of married women are full-time homemakers.

Women have made advances in the professions. For example, in the United States in the year 2000, about 28% of physicians, 50% of medical scientists, 30% of lawyers and judges, 53% of economists, and 65% of psychologists were women (U.S. Department of Labor). These figures are generally two to three times higher than they were a quarter of a century ago. Of the overall category "professional specialty" as designated by the U.S. Department of Labor (which includes the preceding and over 30 others), almost 54% were women—making them the majority. The data do however include "traditional" women's professions such as nurses and school teachers, which have extremely high percentages as indicated in Table 14–2.

Nevertheless, by far the largest number of women are still limited to lower-paying "women's jobs" such as nursing, primary and secondary school teaching, and secretarial/clerical work (Matthews & Rodin, 1989) (again see Table 14–2). One out of every two women is employed in low-paying, low-advancement jobs. Moreover, women still make less money than men—about 75 cents for every dollar men earn. Among full-time permanent employees, the median salary for white women is only about 74% of that for white men, and for black women the figure drops to about 67% (U.S. Census Bureau, 1997).

Changes in Work Patterns

Paid employment for women is not a new phenomenon, of course. Women have always worked outside the home, especially during periods of economic hardship. Many worked in factories and offices during the two World Wars when large numbers of male workers were overseas fighting. Before the rise of

For women who are not career oriented, self-esteem seems related more to family life than to full-time employment.

industrialism in the early 1800s, men and women often combined their efforts in family businesses and farms (as some still do). Not until the late nineteenth century did men come to be regarded as the "natural" providers for their families (Bernard, 1981). They worked at jobs outside the home while their wives cared for the children and the home. In the 1970s, however, the picture changed again as more and more women entered the workforce and established careers.

Women who work outside the home do not necessarily follow the same career patterns that men do. Although there are no formal theories dealing with women's career development, it is clear that women follow a greater *variety* of patterns. An increasing number of women follow the traditional male pattern of pursuing a career without interruption. Others plan to stop work and have children when their careers are well established. Women who wish to devote themselves exclusively to raising a family in early adulthood sometimes establish careers outside the home after the last child has entered first grade, or perhaps even later, when the child enters college. The average woman can devote 10 years to full-time child care while her children are young and still have 35 years left to enter the workforce, establish a career, or pursue other interests (Daniels & Weingarten, 1982). Most women still interrupt work at least temporarily to take care of children, however, whereas men rarely do so (Kalleberg & Rosenfeld, 1990). These interruptions may contribute to the wage gap between men and women.

The Many Meanings of Work

Like men, women participate in the world of work for many reasons. The primary reason is economic necessity. Single mothers are often the sole source of income for their families. Even many married couples could not make ends meet without income from both spouses. Female factory and mill workers, for example, contribute almost as much money to the family as their husbands (Thompson & Walker, 1989). Like men, however, many women find satisfaction and fulfillment in employment outside the home. They find their work interesting and challenging; they consider it an opportunity for self-direction or increased responsibility; they like the benefits of salary, greater future security, and the possibility of advancement (Whitbourne, 1986a).

There are some differences, however. In some studies, women more often report that the opportunity to interact with people—as clients, coworkers, supervisors—is a particularly important reason for working outside the home. For some women, interpersonal relations at work are particularly important in helping define their own self-concept (Forrest & Mikolaitis, 1986).

Whatever the reasons, working women tend to be both physically and psychologically healthier than nonworking women (Baruch & Barnett, 1986; A. McBride, 1990; Repetti et al., 1989; Rodin & Ickovics, 1990). They suffer fewer heart attacks and ulcers and have higher self-esteem. Unmarried women reap the most benefits, but married women gain as well, especially if their husbands are supportive of their career. Either way, women who enjoy their work benefit more. This may be one reason that professional women actually gain more physical and psychological benefits than do clerical workers, despite the greater responsibilities and stresses of their jobs. Given the potential role strains, family problems, and stress, it is surprising that there is virtually no evidence indicating detrimental effects of employment, regardless of the types of work.

There is a more dramatic contrast between career-oriented and noncareer-oriented women. Some women find homemaking meaningful and fulfilling; others consider it sheer drudgery. In one survey (Pietromonaco, Manis, & Markus, 1987), reports on self-esteem, life satisfaction, and self-perception differed dramatically between career-oriented and noncareer-oriented women. Those who described themselves as career oriented and were employed full time were much happier. Those who were temporarily unemployed or were working at part-time jobs or jobs that underutilized their skills were much less happy and had lower self-esteem and poorer self-concepts. The results were quite different for women who described themselves as noncareer-oriented. Their self-esteem and life satisfaction were not related to whether they were employed full time or part time. They agreed with such statements as "I cannot imagine having a fully satisfying life without having children" or "I would not take a job that would interfere with the things I like to do with my family."

Myths and Stereotypes That Affect Women's Employment

Although there are real differences in the ways in which men and women approach work, there are also persistent myths and stereotypes that deny women's real motivations and can delay or block their career advancement. One such myth is that women in managerial, professional, or technical positions are less willing to take risks or make the sacrifices associated with career advancement. Another is that women do not want, need, or expect the same salaries as men, even when they accept a promotion. In reality, it has repeatedly been found that many women are quite similar to men in their attitudes about risk taking, salaries, and advancement (Rynes & Rosen, 1983). Nor do women have less motivation to achieve or less specific career plans than men. Although women in traditionally "female" fields such as education, social work, and nursing are sometimes less ambitious and expect to make accommodations to fulfill marriage and family responsibilities, women in traditionally "male" professions such as business, law, and medicine have career plans that are very similar to those of men pursuing the same careers.

Dynamics of Dual-Earner Couples

The dramatic increase in the number of women in the work force has led to an increasingly common phenomenon known as the **dual-earner couple** or *dual-earner marriage* which is now the norm. A dual-earner couple is defined as one in which the husband works full time and the wife works 20 or more hours per week. Today millions of women fully share the provider role with their husbands.

There are obvious advantages to dual-earner marriages. A higher total income makes possible a higher standard of living. There is more money for daily necessities, emergencies, a better place to live, a better education for the children. For college-educated dual-earner couples in particular, perhaps the most important benefit is the wife's equal chance to gain self-fulfillment through a job or career.

There are stresses and role conflicts too, of course. These stem in part from the need to juggle the roles of the wife as a worker, the husband as a worker, and both partners as family members. At times one role may require more time and energy than the others. During early adulthood, for example, the needs of

dual-earner couple A married or unmarried couple sharing a household, in which both contribute to family income as members of the paid labor force.

young children and the struggle to establish a career often collide, forcing the couple to set priorities and resolve conflicts.

Husbands in dual-earner families often report more marital dissatisfaction than other husbands (Staines, Pottick, & Fudge, 1986). Many dual-earner couples report experiencing severe role conflicts in their attempts to meet both work and family responsibilities. The conflicts stem from job demands, work hours, family and work scheduling conflicts, and family crises. Although both men and women in dual-earner couples experience these conflicts, women report higher levels of conflict between work and family roles. The role conflict experienced by professional women is particularly acute when they work long hours and are under time pressures (Guelzow, Bird, & Koball, 1991). For both partners, dissatisfaction and stress can be eased somewhat by a flexible work schedule that allows them to take care of family needs (Guelzow et al., 1991).

Domestic tasks—especially child care—are shared more equally in some dual-earner families than in others. However, women who work still tend to have the primary responsibility for housework and child care (Barnett & Baruch, 1987; Kalleberg & Rosenfeld, 1990). This is true when the children are infants as well as when they are in school, and it remains true in spite of the recently enacted federal law requiring that companies offer their employees, both male and female, a minimum 12 weeks of **family leave.** It is true whether the woman is working full time or part time. Indeed, some people have suggested that working mothers really have two full-time jobs—that when they come home from work they begin a "second shift" (Hochschild, 1989). Many are up at 6 in the morning, in the workplace by 9, and back home at 6 or 7 in the evening. During the evenings and weekends they face a mountain of household chores—everything from child care to cooking to laundry to cleaning.

It would seem logical and fair to assume that dual-earner couples should share household chores equally, but that is rarely the case. Study after study has shown that even when both spouses are employed full time, women continue to do the lion's share of the housework (Berk, 1985; Pleck, 1985). Research consistently indicates that husbands of employed women do not spend significantly more time doing housework than husbands of women who are not employed outside the home (Ferber, 1982). Other studies have shown that the amount of work men do around the house decreases as their income increases (Antial & Cottin, 1988; Smith & Reid, 1986).

Men who have positive attitudes about sharing the provider role are more likely to share household chores than men who resent their wife's income-earning role (Hood, 1986; Perry-Jenkins & Crouter, 1990). "Who does what and how much" around the house apparently is only part of the story, however (Perry-Jenkins & Folk, 1994). Where overall marital satisfaction is concerned, how fair each spouse *perceives* the distribution of labor to be can be as important as the actual amount of housework each spouse does (Blair & Johnson, 1992; Thompson, 1991; Wilkie, Ratcliff, & Ferree, 1992).

There are other strains in dual-career marriages. Although social attitudes now favor women in the workforce, there is still some disapproval of mothers who work full time when they have very young children. Some working women experience negative reactions from friends, neighbors, and colleagues. Some experience considerable role conflicts themselves. Their ambivalence is accentuated when they have difficulty finding adequate, affordable day care for their children. Women may feel particularly uneasy about leaving an infant in someone else's care, yet may be subject to financial pressures that require them to do so as soon as possible. Federal law does not require that workers be

family leave Leave required by law to deal with family affairs and problems, especially those involving taking care of children.

paid while on family leave. Larger companies tend to provide pay during family leave, but many smaller ones do not.

The ambivalence many women feel about their dual roles may be a result of gender socialization. Historically, women were expected to be less active than men, to focus on marriage, and not to develop a work or career orientation (Hansen, 1974). Alternatively, working women's ambivalence toward their roles may be attributable to the day-to-day pressures created by attempting to satisfy two competing sets of demands. In that case, role conflict is a result of the circumstances of dual-earner couples and not a psychological "problem."

Women who pursue professional or managerial careers face additional strains. There are strains in the marriage when decisions must be made about whose career takes precedence—especially during promotions or transfers. Since men generally have greater earning power, favoring the husband's career may maximize the family's income and standard of living but place obstacles in the path of the woman's career development.

Again, despite all the strains, women can gain substantial benefits from working. The job satisfactions described earlier often spill over into the families of working women, especially if the women have high-status jobs. This enables the family to adjust better to the woman's limited flexibility and time as well as to the increased pressure inherent in dual-earner families. It may also be one reason why most studies have found that dual-career marriages are no less happy than other marriages. In fact, several studies have found higher levels of marital satisfaction among employed wives than among nonemployed wives in both working-class and professional families (Walker & Wallston, 1985). Why might working women benefit despite the strains? One possibility is social support. Women can turn to their colleagues at work for friendship, advice, and emotional bolstering. Work may also provide an alternative source of self-esteem and even a sense of control when things are going poorly at home (Rodin & Ickovics, 1990). Thus, work may serve as a buffer against stresses experienced at home.

CONTENT CHECK
WORK AND GENDER

True–False (answers are on the Companion Website)

1. The number of women in the workplace has slowed in the last decade because of economic prosperity.
2. Women working outside the home now basically follow the same career patterns as men do.
3. Working women are physically and psychologically healthier than nonworking women.
4. Women and men in *dual-earner families* share equally the responsibility for household tasks and raising children.
5. Women pursing or in managerial positions have the least strain of all working women.

Thinking Critically

How do common myths and stereotypes continue to hold back women's advancement in the workplace?

CHAPTER 14 REVISITED

Continuity and Change

- The role changes of young adulthood are subtler and less systematic than those of childhood and adolescence.

- Adult development occurs in the context of personal self, self as family member, and self as worker.

- According to Maslow, every individual strives toward self-actualization; the need for self-actualization can be pursued only after lower needs are met.

- According to Rogers, society corrupts the individual by imposing conditions of worth; the alternative is unconditional positive regard.

- Young adults are often in a period of transition toward greater emotional, attitudinal, functional, and conflictual independence.

- Some people focus on intrinsic factors of work, others focus on extrinsic factors; friendships can be important extrinsic factors in the workplace.

Forming Intimate Relationships

- Friendships are a core aspect of adult life.

- According to Sternberg's triangular theory of love, love has three components: intimacy, passion, and decision/commitment.

- Three theories of attraction and mate selection are complementary needs theory, stimulus-value-role theory, and family systems theory.

- Monogamous marriage is by far the most popular form in the United States; it is symbolized by a wedding rite and sanctioned by the community.

- Cohabiting has become increasingly popular; about one-third of cohabiting couples eventually marry.

Parenthood and Adult Development

- The family life cycle has predictable stages: The individual leaves and marries, has a first child, and has a last child; the last child departs, and the spouse dies.

- The transition to parenthood calls for numerous adaptations and adjustments.

- Mothers characteristically adjust their lifestyles to give priority to parenting; men more often intensify their work efforts.

- Social support, marital happiness during pregnancy, parental self-esteem, and the baby's characteristics influence how the new parents adjust.

- Six stages of parenthood have been identified: the image-making stage, the nurturing stage, the authority stage, the interpretive stage, the interdependence stage, and the departure stage.

- At each stage, parents must cope with new challenges and demands of children and renegotiate their own relationship.

- The pressures of parenthood are particularly intense for single parents.

- Black single-mother homes are more likely to be poverty level; if present, extended family members help compensate.

- Single fathers experience the same problems and tensions as single mothers, except for often being better off financially.

The Occupational Cycle

- Traditionally, the occupational cycle begins with thoughts and experiences that lead to a choice, continues with pursuit of the chosen career, and ends with retirement; but things have changed.

- According to Havighurst, the occupational cycle consists of identification with a worker, acquiring basic habits of industry, acquiring an identity as a worker, becoming a productive person, maintaining productivity, and contemplating a productive and responsible life.

- Factors that influence occupational choice include socioeconomic status, ethnic background, intelligence, skills, gender, and parents' occupations.

- Black people and women are overrepresented in lower-status, lower-paying jobs and underrepresented in more highly paid professions for a variety of historical reasons.

- According to self-concept theory, people seek careers that fit their self-concept. Trait theory is similar, but it investigates objectively measured personality traits.

- Occupational preparation tends to be both formal and informal.

- Practical issues also affect occupational choice.

- In recent decades workers have come to realize that they are increasingly on their own where careers are concerned.

- When young adults start working, they often find that their expectations are not matched by reality and may react negatively.

- Mentors can play a positive role in the development of young workers.

- Maintaining a sense of excitement and commitment to work throughout adulthood is essential to mature job satisfaction.

- The midcareer period is a time of consolidation and coming to grips with reality.

Work and Gender

- Although women have entered the workforce in large numbers and have made significant advances, by far the largest number of women are still limited to lower-paying jobs; women also still make less money than men for the same jobs.

- Women who work outside the home follow a greater variety of career patterns than men do.

- Many women work or return to work out of economic necessity; many others find satisfaction and fulfillment in employment outside the home.

- Working women tend to be both physically and psychologically healthier than nonworking women.

- Women often suffer from the effects of erroneous myths and stereotypes regarding risk taking, salaries, advancement, and motivation.

- Dual-earner couples have higher incomes, but they must juggle roles and set priorities.

- Even when both spouses are employed full time, women are likely to do most of the housework, which amounts to a "second shift."

- Some working women experience considerable role conflicts because of child care, gender socialization, and competing sets of demands.

KEY TERMS

self-actualization	intrinsic factors of work	decision/commitment
humanistic psychology	extrinsic factors of work	occupational cycle
conditions of worth	intimacy	dual-earner couple
unconditional positive regard	passion	family leave

MIDDLE ADULTHOOD: PHYSICAL AND COGNITIVE DEVELOPMENT

15

CHAPTER PREVIEW

Do you know:

1. That developmental theorists differ considerably over what constitutes *middle adulthood*?

2. That *economic conditions, social class,* and *historical context* affect how people view middle adulthood?

3. The differences between the *transition model* and the *crisis model* of midlife, and the *myths* associated with the latter?

4. The short-term and long-term *physical* and *emotional changes* that are associated with middle age?

5. What happens during *menopause*?

6. What the term *climacteric* refers to?

7. What happens to *sexuality* and *sexual* activity during middle adulthood?

8. The major *diseases* that affect middle adults and the connection between their onset and poor health habits?

9. What the leading causes of *death* in middle adulthood are?

10. How *stressful life events* affect health in middle adulthood?

11. The differences between *fluid intelligence* and *crystallized intelligence* and how they change during middle age?

12. The implications of *changes in intellectual functioning* for middle adults?

13. How *declarative* and *procedural* knowledge contribute to *expertise* and help compensate for cognitive decline?

14. How cognitive functioning, technological change, and professional obsolescence *interact*?

These are the main topics of Chapter 15.

We have looked at childhood, adolescence, and young adulthood. We have seen the developmental steps through which a child becomes an adult, an individual with a relatively stable outlook and personality. We have noted the social milestones that mark the adolescent's entry into the world of the adult—moving away from home, getting married, becoming a parent, establishing a career. What's next?

Middle adulthood (arbitrarily considered to begin at age 40), along with older adulthood, may constitute 50% or more of a person's lifespan. Does it pose new challenges, or is it merely a time in which to live out the decisions made earlier in life, possibly making a few corrections and adjustments here and there? How much continuity is there during these years? Are Tanya Harris or Justin Jones the same people at age 50 that they were at age 30? If not, what makes them change, how much, and in what ways? Do they embrace new experiences and accumulate wisdom, or do their perspectives and opinions narrow? What role does their inevitable biological decline play in their psychological functioning?

As in young adulthood, the theme of the middle years is continuity and change—there is some of each. We begin with an overview that includes exposing popular myths about middle-aged people, such as the midlife "crisis."

Then we look at changes in sensorimotor skills and other biological factors, as well as both biological and psychological aspects of sexuality. Health and disease are considered next. Finally, we take a detailed look at what happens to intelligence and cognitive skills during middle age, with emphasis on which skills decline and which ones do not.

Development in Middle Adulthood

When do people start thinking of themselves as "middle-aged"? What cues tell them that they are no longer exactly young, and how do they react to this realization? There are many signals of middle age. By popular convention, middle adulthood covers roughly the years from age 40 to age 60 or 65. On a person's fortieth birthday it is common practice to proclaim the milestone loudly, tell jokes about being "over the hill," send disparaging greeting cards, and maybe put up a sign and flamingo the person's lawn. In U.S. culture, turning 40 is often heralded as the beginning of the end.

Developmental theorists tend to see middle adulthood as a cultural construction of the 20th century (Moen & Wethington, 1999). As for when it begins and ends, much depends on the life experiences the person is going through: Does a 43-year-old woman with a newborn baby think of herself as middle-aged? Does a 41-year-old man in a job-training program consider himself in the middle years of his career—and life—or does he view himself as making a new start? Health is a factor too: How much do 40-year-olds who are physically fit and full of vim and vigor have in common with 40-year-olds who have "let themselves go" through alcohol or drug use and lack of exercise?

Moreover, the period defined as middle adulthood may begin earlier or later, and be longer or shorter for different people because there are so many different cues associated with aging (Neugarten & Brown-Rezanka, 1996). Some cues have to do with social and family status. Middle adulthood is an in-between period, a bridge between two generations. People in midlife are aware of being separate not only from youngsters and young adults but also from older people, especially retirees. Some people feel that they are middle aged when their children begin to leave home. Other cues may be physical and biological. A woman may suddenly realize that her son is taller than she is; a man may find that a certain skill, such as drawing or playing the piano, is hampered by the beginnings of arthritis.

There are also psychological cues, most of which involve issues of continuity and change. People realize that they have made certain basic decisions about their career or family that are now fairly set and remain to be played out or fulfilled. The future is never certain, but it no longer holds as many different possibilities as it once did. Cues also come from people's careers; their advancement at work may have stopped. They may have reached a position of seniority, or they may realize that they have reached a plateau well below their original goal.

Prime Time or the Beginning of the End?

How do people feel about being middle-aged? Theorists and middle-aged people themselves do not agree on whether this is a time of new fulfillment, stability, and potential leadership or a period of dissatisfaction, inner turmoil, and depression. Economic conditions, social class, and the times in which people

Upon entry into middle age, many people may slightly reduce their physical activity.

live affect how they view middle adulthood. Many realize that they are no longer young, yet they feel satisfied and believe that they are now in the "prime of life." Middle-aged people often feel "safe," settled, and secure (Helson, 1997). For many, physical abilities may be slightly diminished, but experience and self-knowledge allow them to manage their own lives to a greater extent than at any other age. They can make decisions with ease, expertise, and self-confidence that were previously beyond their grasp. This is why the 40- to 60-year-old age group has been called the **command generation,** and why most of the decision makers in government, corporations, and society at large are middle-aged. In the United States today's generation of adults in midlife are better educated and healthier than ever before. Many of them report a strong sense of self-efficacy, at least in some important areas of their lives (Clark-Plaskie & Lachman, 1999).

Of course, many middle-aged people do not make weighty decisions and run corporations or government agencies. Many do not feel that they even control their own lives, let alone those of others. Some people lose their vitality after age 40. Else Frenkel-Brunswik (1963), for example, did not see middle-aged people as the command generation. Instead, she saw the period as one of declining activity whose onset, around the age of 48, is usually marked by both psychological and biological crises. Levinson (1978, 1996) and his colleagues also contended that "the midlife transition is a time of moderate to severe crisis" for both men and women.

Most people experience a sense of ambivalence during middle adulthood (Chiriboga, 1981; Sherman, 1987). It may be the prime of life with respect to family, career, or creative talents, but most people are also keenly aware of their own mortality and have recurrent thoughts about how their time is running out—also that the years seem to pass more quickly. Some people in midlife become preoccupied with questions of creativity and ongoing contributions to the next generation, with fears of stagnation or lost opportunities, and with concerns about maintaining intimate relationships with family and friends. With each major event—birth, death, job change, divorce—adults

command generation The generation of middle-aged people, who make most of the decisions that affect our lives.

reexamine the meaning of their lives (Sherman, 1987). This applies to events that happen to them as well as events that happen to others around them. For some, the theme of middle adulthood becomes "Whatever we do must be done now" (Gould, 1978). How people interpret this sense of urgency, together with the particular events they experience, determines whether middle adulthood is a period of gradual transition and reassessment or a period of crisis.

Midlife Crisis and Related Myths

Although some researchers have proposed that adults perceive middle age as "a period in which some hopes are blighted, some opportunities are seen as forever lost" (Clausen, 1986), a substantial and persuasive body of research indicates the opposite. Studies have shown that most adults experience the middle years simply as years of gradual transitions—both positive and negative—associated with growing older. Whereas the crisis model links the normative developmental changes of the period to predictable crises, the **transition model** rejects the idea that midlife crisis is the norm (Helson, 1997; Hunter & Sundel, 1989; Rosenberg, Rosenberg, & Farrell, 1999).

According to the transition model, development is marked by a series of expected major life events that can be anticipated and planned for. Although the transitions associated with these events can be difficult both psychologically and socially, most people adapt successfully because they know that these life changes are coming. For example, knowing that she will probably retire sometime in her sixties, a 40-year-old small-business owner makes regular deposits into a tax-deferred individual retirement account (IRA). By the time she's 50, she may have found the ideal home to retire in, and she regularly discusses her retirement plans with her spouse and children. Thus, individuals who expect to confront change during their middle years are not likely to wait for these changes to hit them over the head before acting. Through anticipation, they can plan for these life events and avoid midlife crises (Clausen, 1986; Troll, 1985).

The **crisis model** also has certain methodological weaknesses that limit its appeal. Many of the studies that support it were based on clinical populations rather than on normal samples, which reflect the overall adult population more accurately. Moreover, the classic studies of Levinson (1978) and Gould (1978) focused exclusively on middle-class white males. For example, Levinson and his colleagues (1978) found that at about the age of 40, a man may begin to question, or at least put into perspective, the "driven" life he has been leading. If he has been successful in reaching his goals, he may suddenly ask, "Was it worth the struggle?" If he has not achieved what he wanted in life, he may become keenly aware that he does not have many more chances to change things. Thus, he questions his entire life structure, including both work and family relationships (Levinson, 1986). Women—and their unique midlife concerns— were excluded from this and other classic studies of the middle years. Indeed, some researchers question whether such male themes as "anguish over mortality and over the inadequacy of one's achievements" even apply to women (Baruch & Brooks-Gunn, 1984). They also question whether the negative impact of major life events such as menopause and the "empty nest" have been exaggerated.

Middle adulthood, then, is a time when people begin to take stock of their lives. Some may feel effective, competent, and at the peak of their powers

transition model   The view that changes in midlife are gradual.

crisis model   The view that changes in midlife are abrupt and often stressful.

(Chiriboga, 1981). Others may find it painful to examine their lives. Although age-graded influences such as graying hair, an expanding midsection, or menopause may combine with nonnormative events such as divorce or unemployment to precipitate a crisis, if any of these influences is anticipated or regarded as a normal event, it is less likely to lead to a crisis (Neugarten & Brown-Rezanka, 1996).

Still, it is difficult for many adolescents and young adults to think of middle age as anything but a giant black hole in which they will spend at least 20 years of their lives. By middle age, they argue, growth and development are over. So are youthful dreams and passions about career and relationships, as well as the plans and strategies to make them happen. Whereas youth is about hope, middle age is about being stuck in a quagmire. Wrong, said Ronald Kessler, a sociologist and fellow at the MacArthur Foundation Research Network on Successful Midlife Development:

> The data show that middle age is the very best time in life. When looking at the total U.S. population, the best year is 50. You don't have to deal with the aches and pains of old age or the anxieties of youth: Is anyone going to love me? Will I ever get my career off the ground? Rates of general distress are low—the incidences of depression and anxiety fall at about 35 and don't climb again until the late sixties. You're healthy. You're productive. You have enough money to do some of the things you like to do. You've come to terms with your relationships, and the chance of divorce is very low. Midlife is the "it" you've been working toward. You can turn your attention toward being rather than becoming. (quoted in Gallagher, 1993)

Kessler also believed that midlife crisis is the exception rather than the rule. The overwhelming majority of people shift gently into midlife as they trade their youthful goals of fame, wealth, accomplishment, and beauty for more realistic expectations. A 42-year-old tennis player, accomplished enough to be ranked among the top 100 players in his state as an adolescent, has accepted that he will never make it to Wimbledon and has instead become a high school physical education teacher or a tennis pro. A politician with youthful aspirations to run for the U.S. Senate settles for being the mayor of her small town. Such "redirection" involves measuring ourselves against people with similar goals and accomplishments. When facing trouble, mature people are likely to compare themselves to people who are worse off. Thus, a middle-aged couple whose house was just flooded and their belongings destroyed may compare themselves with neighbors who experienced the same fate but who are also unemployed.

Those who are most likely to experience a midlife crisis tend to avoid introspection and use denial to avoid thinking about their changing bodies and lives. As a result, a 45-year-old who thinks he is still a great athlete may be emotionally devastated when his 15-year-old son beats him at basketball. "Such individuals have to work hard to maintain their illusions," said Kessler. "They spend a lot of energy on the cognitive effort of self-delusion, until reality finally intervenes" (Gallagher, 1993). Kessler also believed that midlife crises are more common among the affluent than among poor or working class people. Apparently, it is easier to delude yourself about the realities of middle adulthood when money in the bank shields you from the burdens and struggles of life.

CONTENT CHECK
DEVELOPMENT IN MIDDLE ADULTHOOD

True–False (answers are on the Companion Website)

1. Developmental theorists agree that middle adulthood spans the years 40 through 60–65.
2. Middle adulthood is a bridge between generations.
3. According to Levinson, the midlife transition is for most adults a time marked by severe crisis.
4. According to the transition model, midlife crisis is not the norm.
5. According to Kessler, midlife crisis is more common among the poor than among the affluent.

Thinking Critically

What factors influence whether people experience or do not experience a midlife crisis?

Physical Continuity and Change

The most obvious changes associated with the middle years are physical ones. It is generally during middle adulthood that people receive the first clear reminders that their bodies are aging.

"Age is like love; it cannot be hid," wrote a 17th-century dramatist. For many middle-aged people, there is a "moment of truth" when the mirror reveals new wrinkles, midriff bulge, a receding hairline, or gray hair at the temples that no longer seems distinguished—just depressing. These warning signals are more disturbing to some than to others, depending on their attitudes toward aging and eventually dying. Are these signs of maturity or of decline? Some obvious biological events, such as menopause for women, increased difficulty in achieving erection for men, and decreasing visual acuity for both sexes, are events that require a change in self-image or activities and must be incorporated into a satisfactory lifestyle (Newman, 1982; Timiras, 1994). Most physical abilities peak during adolescence or early adulthood and level off in middle adulthood; then the first signs of physical decline begin to appear. As we examine these changes, however, bear in mind that people age and develop at different rates. Many factors influence aging. By taking these into account, people can often ease the process and alleviate many of its unpleasant effects.

Changes in Capabilities

Some physical decline or slowing down is likely to occur during middle adulthood (Birren, Woods, & Williams, 1985; Birren & Fisher, 1995). This decline involves sensory and motor skills as well as the body's internal functioning.

Sensation   Visual capabilities are fairly stable from adolescence through the 40s or early 50s; then visual acuity declines (Kline & Schieber, 1985). A partial exception is nearsightedness: People often see distant objects better in middle adulthood than they could as young adults. Hearing typically becomes less acute after age 20 and declines gradually, especially with regard to high-frequency sounds. This hearing loss is more common in men than in women, a fact that may be attributable to environmental factors in jobs such as construction work, that include sustained exposure to loud or high-frequency noises. In any case, it is rarely severe enough to affect normal conversation in middle adulthood (Olsho, Harkins, & Lenhardt, 1985). Taste, smell, and sensitivity to pain decline at different points in middle adulthood, although these changes are more gradual and less noticeable than visual or auditory changes (Bartoshuk & Weiffenbach, 1990). Sensitivity to temperature changes remains high in middle adulthood (Newman, 1982).

Motor Skills and Reaction Time   Reaction time and sensorimotor skills are likely to slow down. Reaction time drops off slowly throughout adulthood and more quickly during older adulthood. Motor skills may decline, but actual performance remains constant, probably as a result of continuing practice and experience (Newman, 1982; Stones & Kozme, 1996). For example, someone who chops firewood or plays tennis every day will experience little decline in performance during middle adulthood. Learning new skills, however, gradually becomes more and more difficult as middle adulthood progresses.

Internal Changes   Internal changes begin to occur as well. The nervous system begins to slow down, particularly after age 50. The skeleton stiffens and shrinks a bit over the course of adulthood; gravity gradually takes its toll and the person becomes shorter in stature. Skin and muscles begin to lose elasticity and wrinkles develop. There is a tendency to accumulate more subcutaneous fat, especially in areas like the midriff. The heart pumps an average of 8% less blood to the body for each decade after the beginning of adulthood, and by middle adulthood the opening of the coronary arteries is nearly one-third less than it is in the 20s. Lung capacity decreases as well. Because endurance depends on the amount of oxygen supplied to body tissues, people generally can't perform as much sustained hard labor in middle adulthood as they can in young adulthood (Siegler, Kaplan, Von Dras, & Mark, 1999). These trends in cardiovascular functioning are likely, although the extent depends on lifestyle.

Menopause and the Climacteric

For women, the most dramatic internal change is **menopause**—cessation of ovulation and menstruation—which is an event with varied physical and psychological implications. Menopause is part of the **climacteric,** which refers to the overall complex of physical and emotional effects that accompany hormonal changes in middle adulthood. Because of its broad implications for women's lives, we devote this section to both the immediate and long-term physical and emotional changes associated with menopause. Although there is no comparable "male menopause," despite its occasional coverage in the popular media, many professionals believe that men also undergo biological changes in middle adulthood that are accompanied by emotional readjustments and changes in sexual behavior. We consider these changes as well.

Physical Changes and Symptoms   On average, women experience their last menstrual period between ages 45 and 55, although for some women it may occur somewhat earlier or considerably later (Avis, 1999; Carlson, Eisentat & Zoporyn, 1996). Ovulation and the menstrual cycle become erratic at first, then stop altogether. At the same time, less estrogen is produced and the reproductive

menopause   The permanent end of menstruation; it occurs in middle adulthood and may be accompanied by physical symptoms and intense emotional reactions, more so in some women than in others.

climacteric   The broad complex of physical and emotional symptoms that accompany reproductive changes in middle adulthood, affecting both men and women.

system "shuts down." Slowly the uterus shrinks; there is a gradual reduction in breast size as glandular tissue atrophies and is replaced with fat tissue. Menopause is accompanied by physical symptoms such as hot flashes and night sweats and, less frequently, headaches, dizziness, palpitations, and pain in the joints. However, research indicates that hot flashes and night sweats are the only one of these symptoms that are directly caused by menopause—specifically, by the decrease in estrogen levels. In the United States, 70 to 81% of women report hot flashes during menopause. Night sweats are reported by 50 to 60% of women (Carlson et al., 1996; Avis 1999), and may be extensive enough to cause insomnia. The other symptoms, such as the headaches and pains that some women experience, tend to occur mainly in women who have a history of the problem or are experiencing a particularly intense menopause. In all, only about one-fifth of women who report such symptoms rate them as bothersome (Avis, 1999).

Many menopausal and post-menopausal women feel happy, now that their active mothering is drawing to an end, to have more time to themselves.

Immediate Emotional Effects   For some women, the physical changes are accompanied by emotional changes such as feelings of depression and a sense of being somehow less feminine because their reproductive function is gone. In particular, women who have not had children and had not completely made up their minds about childbearing may experience a sense of regret or loss, depression. Most women, however, do not encounter such difficulties during menopause (Avis, 1999). Indeed, some researchers report a *decrease* in emotional difficulties during and after menopause compared with the years immediately preceding it.

In general, considerable research indicates that most women do not respond negatively to menopause in either the short run or the long term (Avis, 1999; Neugarten, 1967; Neugarten, Wood, Kraines, & Loomis, 1968). Half of the menopausal and postmenopausal women in one survey reported that the change was "easy" or at least "moderately easy" (Goodman, 1980). Many women feel freer and more in control of their own lives, with a sense of elation because they no longer need to be concerned with menstrual periods or the possibility of pregnancy. At the same time, their active mothering role is usually ending, and they will have more time for themselves. Even women who are not particularly pleased about menopause tend not to be worried or distressed—they simply take it in stride. During this period of their lives women are more likely to be worried about becoming widows than about passing through menopause (Neugarten, 1967).

The cultural context of menopause can also affect the woman's feelings about herself, her behavior, and her actual physical symptoms. In the words of Margaret Lock (1993), menopause and other universal aging experiences are "the products . . . of an ongoing dialectic between biology and culture in which both are contingent." In some castes in India, for example, menopause traditionally brings with it a new positive status for the woman. She is no longer required to remain isolated from much of society, associating only with her husband and immediate family. She may enjoy the company of both men and women in a greater variety of social circumstances. In one study of a group of Indian women, none reported the range of symptoms often associated with menopause—such as excessive moodiness, depression, or headaches (Flint, 1982). Some researchers have suggested that the excessive focus on youth and attractiveness in Western cultures may contribute to the symptoms that some women in these cultures experience during menopause.

Long-Term Effects   The estrogen loss that accompanies menopause has two, possibly three, long-term effects. The two clear-cut effects are changes in bone mass and in the genitals. The more controversial one is increased risk of coronary disease.

The mineral mass of bones peaks between the ages of 25 and 40 and then remains steady for several years. Both men and women experience a loss in bone mass as they age, but the loss is about twice as great in women and occurs more rapidly (Asso, 1983; Avis, 1999). As a result, bone fractures are much more common in older women than in older men. Women's loss of bone mass accelerates greatly after menopause, apparently owing to estrogen deprivation. In the United States, **osteoporosis,** the medical term for loss of bone mass and increased bone fragility (regardless of the cause), affects 25 million people—most of whom are woman. Nearly half of all postmenopausal women over the age of 50 will experience a bone fracture related to osteoporosis (McBean, Forgac, & Finn, 1994).

The second well-established long-term physical change involves the genitals. Vaginal atrophy occurs as a result of decreased estrogen. The tissues of the vagina, as well as the labia and other surrounding tissues, shrink and become thinner and drier. The vagina becomes shorter and narrower, and less lubrication occurs during intercourse. These and other changes may cause pain or bleeding during intercourse (Asso, 1983).

Such changes do not mean that intercourse is no longer possible, however. The changes are gradual, so a menopausal or immediately postmenopausal woman can easily continue intercourse. Lubricating cream or jelly can be used. Hormone replacement therapy (HRT) will alleviate and even reverse many of these symptoms (Avis, 1999), although it is not a panacea—as discussed in "In Theory, In Fact" on the facing page.

The more controversial long-term effect concerns the relationship between menopause and cardiovascular disease and heart attacks. Women have a much lower rate of cardiovascular disease than men until menopause; then the rate for women rises nearly as high as the male rate. However, it remains unclear whether this is because of menopausal changes per se; it could have to do with other aspects of the aging process.

Changes in Men   For men there is no single, relatively abrupt event comparable to menopause (Masters, Johnson, & Kolodney, 1982). We do know, however, that men undergo changes in sexual interest and activity, generally in their late 40s. As with women, the amount of change varies widely and depends on the individual's personality and lifestyle as well as on cultural factors. Some changes in men are a result of biological factors, especially decreased production of androgens such as testosterone. Unlike estrogen, however, which decreases dramatically during menopause, androgens decline very gradually over a longer period. Even so, men occasionally experience symptoms such as impotence, frequent urination, and ulcers. Some experience loss of self-confidence; others become irritable, fatigued, and depressed. Some of these symptoms may be related to changes in hormone levels, but many are probably attributable to psychological stresses such as job pressures, boredom with a sexual partner, family responsibilities, or fear of ill health.

Sexuality in the Middle Years

As we've seen, the physiological and psychological changes associated with middle adulthood markedly affect sexual functioning in both men and women. How people respond to midlife changes has a major influence on their sexual satisfaction.

Frequency of sexual activity—as well as the number of different sexual partners a person is likely to have—generally slows down in middle adulthood

osteoporosis   Loss of bone mass and increased bone fragility in middle adulthood and beyond.

IN THEORY, IN FACT

HORMONE REPLACEMENT THERAPY AND OTHER TREATMENTS

Hormone replacement therapy, in the form of either estrogen or progesterone supplements or a combination of the two, is used to treat the short- and long-term effects of menopause (Dan & Bernhard, 1989). Hormone therapy helps alleviate symptoms such as hot flashes and appears to be of some value in slowing or even stopping the progress of bone loss, although it will not reverse damage already done. During the first 5 years after menopause, bone loss is linked almost entirely to withdrawal of estrogen, and only estrogen replacement therapy slows this loss (McBean et al., 1994).

Hormone replacement therapy is also associated with reduced incidence of coronary heart disease, as well as fewer deaths associated with cardiovascular disease. In a longitudinal study of over 121,000 nurses, medical researchers found that replacement hormone users have a signficantly lower risk of death from heart disease, at least in the early years. The benefits decline with long-term use, but ". . . the benefits of estrogen use appear to far outweigh the risks" in the short run (Grodstein et al., 1997). It is not clear, however, whether estrogen replacement therapy helps women cope with the emotional symptoms that often accompany menopause.

On the down side, hormone replacement therapy in the form of estrogen alone may be associated with an increased overall risk of cancer, especially uterine cancer (N. E. Davidson, 1996). Studies also suggest a specific link between long-term use and increased risk of breast cancer (Grodstein et al., 1997; see also Avis, 1999). Although the evidence remains inconclusive (Petrovitch, Masaki, & Rodriguez, 1997). It is believed that using a combination of estrogen and progesterone minimizes these risks and may increase the estrogen's ability to prevent osteoporosis; progesterone also minimizes the uterine bleeding associated with intermittent use of estrogen alone (*Journal of the American Medical Association*, 1996). In all cases, however, the particular combination of hormone-replacing agents must be carefully tailored to the individual. In addition, feminists argue that defining menopause as a *de facto* "disease" requiring long-term treatment "medicalizes" a normal developmental process and turns an otherwise healthy population of women into patients (Gonyea, 1998).

There are partial alternatives to HRT. Evidence is mounting that increased calcium intake may also reduce the bone loss associated with osteoporosis. Adequate calcium during childhood and early adulthood helps build the bone mass needed throughout life. Studies have shown that older postmenopausal women who consume 800 milligrams of calcium a day have less bone loss than similar women who consume less than 400 milligrams of calcium a day. However, calcium's positive effects are not seen in the 5 years immediately following menopause. Other drugs to prevent or minimize postmenopausal osteoporosis are currently being developed (Mestel, 1997; Rizzoli & Bonjour, 1997).

Finally, regular weight-bearing exercise throughout life helps increase bone density and may reduce the risk of osteoporosis. Postmenopausal women who exercise increase their strength, stability, flexibility, and balance and are less likely to fall and suffer bone fractures (McBean et al., 1994). Among the exercises believed to increase bone mass are running, tennis, weight training, and low-impact aerobics. To be effective, these exercises must be performed at least three times a week for 30 to 45 minutes. However, the bone mass gained through exercise may be lost when exercise is discontinued. According to research physiologist Barbara Drinkwater, "We are sometimes told that exercise will put bone in our bank. I think it's more like putting bone in our savings and loan associations" (Skolnick, 1990).

(Laumann et al., 1994; Michael et al., 1994). Nevertheless, many healthy individuals can—and do—enjoy satisfying sex lives until age 70 and beyond, and frequency of sexual behavior knows no ethnic bounds. Physiological changes account for some of the slowdown, but sexual activity may also drop off in the middle years because of ill health. Health problems that inhibit sexual activity include physical conditions such as hypertension, diabetes, and coronary artery disease, and emotional problems such as depression. In addition, medications used to treat these illnesses may have adverse effects on sexual activity. For example, the biochemicals used in the treatment of coronary artery disease may cause impotence as a side effect. Similarly, tranquilizers tend to reduce sexual desire.

Lack of opportunity is also a factor. The time pressures associated with the middle years may interfere with sexual interest. The pressures of career and

Although sexual capabilities decline during middle adulthood, sexual and romantic interests continue both for women and men.

family leave many couples with little time or energy for sex. For many people, interpersonal and family problems further interfere with sexual interactions (Weg, 1989).

For many adults, sexuality is redefined during the middle years to place more emphasis on **sensuality,** which includes a range of physical expressions that may or may not lead to a sexual act. Hugging, hand holding, and touching and stroking are as much expressions of mature sexuality as they are of caring and affection (Weg, 1989). For women, physiological changes associated with menopause do not eliminate the ability to function sexually. However, more time may be needed to achieve orgasm. A similar slowdown occurs in men, who may take longer to achieve an erection and reach organism. Thus, because both men and women require more time during sex, the result is often a more sharing kind of lovemaking—in contrast to lovemaking in former years, which may have been directed more urgently toward orgasm (Weg, 1989). One compensation is that middle-aged men often can maintain erection for a longer time (Masters et al., 1982).

On the down side, there is often an increase in sexual anxiety and dissatisfaction among middle-aged men (Featherstone & Hepworth, 1985). In addition to job stresses and boredom with a long-term sexual partner, poor physical conditioning may affect men's sexual activity. Men who are anxious about sex and have even a single episode of impotence or partial erection may start believing that age has diminished their sexual ability. To protect themselves from additional "failures," they avoid sex—or perhaps turn to an affair, often with a younger woman.

One pattern consistently emerges, however. Middle adults who engage in sex infrequently often mistakenly believe that others around them are enjoying active, fulfilling sex lives; many men also believe that there is a male "seven-year-itch" that others around them are pursuing even though they're not (Michael et al., 1994). Such misconceptions can compound their own dissatisfaction. Indeed, as Robert Michael and colleagues have pointed out, media give the impression that everyone is doing it all the time, both within

sensuality Hugging, touching, stroking, and other behaviors that may or may not lead to sex.

TABLE 15-1   Physical Changes of Middle Adulthood

Sensation

Decline in visual acuity, except for distant objects. Hearing loss, especially for high-frequency sounds.

Decline in taste, smell, and sensitivity to pain.

Reaction time

Slow decline in reaction time.

Internal changes

Slowing of the nervous system.

Stiffening and shrinking of the skeleton.

Loss of elasticity in skin and muscles; development of wrinkles.

Accumulation of subcutaneous fat.

Decrease in heart and lung capacity.

Sex-related changes in women

Menopause (cessation of ovulation and menstruation).

Reduced production of estrogen.

Shrinking of uterus and reduction of breast size.

Hot flashes; night sweats.

Loss of bone mass (osteoporosis).

Vaginal atrophy.

Sex-related changes in men

Gradual decline in production of androgens.

Increased difficulty in achieving erection.

their marriage and extramaritally as well. Not so. The results of their broad-scale survey "support an extraordinarily conventional view of love, sex, and marriage," with monogamy predominant and many people having sex relatively infrequently.

Table 15–1 summarizes selected physical changes of middle adulthood.

CONTENT CHECK
PHYSICAL CONTINUITY AND CHANGE

True–False (answers are on the Companion Website)

1. During middle adulthood sensory and motor skills fall off sharply.
2. The *climacteric* is part of *menopause*.
3. Most women respond negatively to menopause.
4. At midlife men generally experience decreased production of androgens such as testosterone.
5. For both men and women frequency of sexual activity tends to decline during middle adulthood.

Thinking Critically

During middle age do you think people are declining or simply reaching their maturity? Why?

Health and Disease

Associated with the normal physical changes that occur during the middle years are changes in health, some of which are linked to the diseases associated with middle adulthood. As the body ages, it becomes increasingly vulnerable to disease. Middle-aged people often become more aware of their own mortality as they or their friends become ill. In this section we look at the major diseases that affect people in their middle years; the cumulative effects of good or poor health habits; the relationships among ethnicity, poverty, and health; and the link between stress and disease. First, however, let's consider some statistics on the good news.

The Good News About Aging and Health

The large-scale Baltimore Longitudinal Study of Aging (as summarized by Nancy Shute, 1997) reported the following positive findings:

- Many losses of function associated with aging can be stopped or slowed.
- Even past age 70, only 20 to 30% of people have symptoms of heart disease.
- Much of the cognitive decline that older people experience (discussed later in the chapter) is attributable to treatable diseases.
- It's actually healthy to gain a pound or so a year from age 40 on—middle-agers should avoid obesity, of course, but being concerned about losing 5 or 10 pounds is trivial.
- Finally, an aside: People don't get crankier as they age. Cranky older folks were just as cranky when they were young.

Major Diseases of Middle Adulthood

The leading cause of death for U.S. adults in middle adulthood is cancers. During middle adulthood, people increasingly begin to die as a result of this and heart diseases as well (U.S. Census Bureau, 1999). Certain diseases become major problems, and some of them affect one sex more than the other (see Figure 15–1). Throughout much of the lifespan, the death rate of men at any particular age is about twice that of women of the same age. This is partly because men are more likely to work in dangerous occupations. Psychological factors contribute too: Men are likely to be less concerned about their health than women because they have been taught that it is masculine to ignore pain, and they may be less likely to visit a doctor when ill or for a checkup. It is also possible that men have a higher genetic predisposition to certain diseases than women do.

Some diseases of middle adulthood are less serious but nonetheless cause considerable discomfort and interfere with daily living. Arthritis, for example, troubles many middle-aged people of both sexes.

Cumulative Effects of Health Habits

Fortunately, most middle-aged people will not suffer serious, life-threatening forms of any disease. The life expectancy for individuals who make it to age 45 in the United States is about 80 years (Anderson, 2001). Over 80% of people who reach age 45 survive and remain in reasonably good health at least until age 65. Various researchers have noted that although the average lifespan has not increased much beyond 85 years for any subset of the population, a sizable proportion maintain relatively good health in middle adulthood.

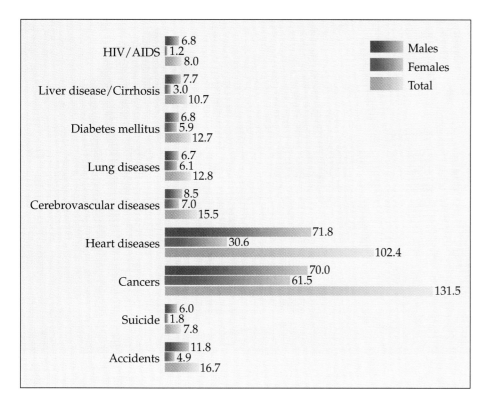

Source: U.S. Census Bureau, 1999.

HIV/AIDS   6.8 / 1.2 / 8.0
Liver disease/Cirrhosis   7.7 / 3.0 / 10.7
Diabetes mellitus   6.8 / 5.9 / 12.7
Lung diseases   6.7 / 6.1 / 12.8
Cerebrovascular diseases   8.5 / 7.0 / 15.5
Heart diseases   71.8 / 30.6 / 102.4
Cancers   70.0 / 61.5 / 131.5
Suicide   6.0 / 1.8 / 7.8
Accidents   11.8 / 4.9 / 16.7

Males / Females / Total

Good Health Habits   In part, longevity is attributable to good health habits. With a balanced and nutritious diet, a reasonable amount of exercise, and regular health care, many people will experience an active and extended adulthood (Fries & Crapo, 1981; Siegler & Costa, 1985). Indeed, many health experts believe that by following a program of regular exercise, lessened stress, and good diet, people can slow the aging process and continue to function with youthful vitality and a sense of well-being through middle adulthood and beyond (Fries & Crapo, 1981). Numerous studies have shown that exercise before and during middle adulthood can increase physical capacities and endurance (Weg, 1983). Certain kinds of exercise—especially aerobic exercises—are designed to increase heart and lung capacity, thus supplying the body with more oxygen and, in turn, more energy. Even short-term, mild exercise training programs for formerly sedentary older adults produce impressive gains in strength and heart and lung functioning. Regular exercise can also slow the deterioration of muscle tissue, reduce body fat, help prevent deterioration of the joints, and combat some kinds of arthritis.

Poor Health Habits   The cumulative effects of poor health habits during early adulthood take their toll in middle adulthood. Most chronic disorders begin to develop long before they are diagnosed. Chief among these are conditions related to cigarette smoking. Smoking contributes to cancer (of the lung, mouth, pharynx, larynx, esophagus, colon, stomach, pancreas, uterine cervix, kidney, ureter, and bladder), respiratory and cardiovascular diseases, arteriosclerosis, hypertension, and other diseases (Merrill &Verbrugge, 1999). Of the more than 2 million deaths in the United States in 1990, 20% (400,000) were caused by smoking-related illnesses. Among people between the ages of 35 and 64, smoking is responsible for more than 25% of all deaths. This should be no surprise; in addition to nicotine there are 42 other substances in cigarette smoke that can cause cancer (Bartecchi, Mackenzie, & Schrier, 1995).

Middle-aged people who exercise tend to maintain their youthful vitality and sense of well-being.

The long-term effects of alcohol abuse become apparent in middle age.

Despite 40 years of media campaigns about the dangers of smoking, about one out of four U.S. adults continues to smoke. Although the percentage has dropped significantly since 1985, when about 36% of adults over age 35 smoked, health officials are concerned that the percentage of smokers in the 1990s has only shown minor declines to 25% in 1998 (SAMSHA, 2000). This is despite continuing efforts to alert the public to smoking-related health risks. The continuing popularity of smoking can be traced in part to the effectiveness of tobacco manufacturers' marketing programs, including the increasing prevalence of discount brands that have made cigarettes more affordable. In 1987, these brands accounted for only 10% of the market; 6 years later, their market share had risen to 36%. Demographic groups that are disproportionately affected by the lure of cigarette smoking include minority groups, people with the least education, and those living below the poverty level (Bartecchi et al., 1995).

Regular smoking is just one habit that can lead to chronic disorders. Heavy use of any drug, including alcohol, has long-term consequences. As the liver and kidneys age, they become less efficient at clearing unusual amounts of drugs from the body. Cumulative damage to these two organs begins to become apparent in middle adulthood (Rowe, 1982). In 1990, alcohol consumption was linked to approximately 100,000 preventable deaths in the United States; illicit use of other drugs was linked to 20,000 deaths (Bartecchi et al., 1995).

The long-term effects of smoking, alcohol abuse, and habitual use of other drugs are often compounded by other long-term habits, such as poor nutrition and lack of regular exercise. Table 15–2 summarizes some of the lifestyle habits and other factors that contribute to chronic disorders.

Stress and Health

Increasing evidence shows that the way people live has a marked effect on their health. Stress in particular plays a role in many of the diseases of middle adulthood. In the case of heart disease, for example, there is a complex interrela-

Table 15–2   Disease Conditions and Lifestyles

Disorders/Diseases	Lifestyle Factors
Diseases of the heart and cirulatory system	High-fat, refined-carbohydrate, high-salt diet; overweight; sedentary lifestyle; cigarette smoking; heavy drinking, alcoholism, unresolved, continual stress; personality type
Strokes	Sedentary lifestyle; low-fiber, high-fat, or high-salt diet; heavy drinking, alcoholism (which contribute to athero-sclerosis, arteriosclerosis, and hypertension, risk factors for cerebrovascular accidents)
Osteoporosis and dental and gum diseases	Malnutrition—inadequate calcium, protein, vitamin K, fluoride, magnesium, and vitamin D; lack of exercise; immobility; for women, low estrogen
Lung diseases such as emphysema	Cigarette smoking; air pollution; stress; sedentary habits
Obesity	Low caloric output (sedentary lifestyle), high caloric intake; high stress levels; heavy drinking, alcoholism; low self-esteem
Cancer	Possible correlation with personality type; stress; exposure to environmental carcinogens over a long period of time; nutritional deficiencies and excesses; radiation; sex steroid hormones; food additives; cigarette smoking; occupational carcinogens (for example, asbestos); viruses; reduced immunity
Dementia and other forms of memory loss	Malnutrition; long illness and bed rest; drug abuse; anemia; other organ system disease; bereavement; social isolation
Sexual dysfunction	Ignorance (the older individual and society at large); societal stereotypic attitudes; early socialization; inappropriate or no partner; drug effects (for example, antihypertensive drugs); long periods of abstinence; serious disease

Source: From *Aging: Scientific Perspectives and Social Issues*, 2nd edition, by D. W. Woodruff and J. E. Birren. Copyright © 1983. Reprinted with permission of Brooks/Cole, an imprint of the Wadsworth Group, a division of Thomson Learning. Fax 800 730-2215.

tionship among lifestyle, personality, genetic factors, and stress. Because men experience heart disease more often than women, most studies of stress and coronary disease have focused on men.

An important question is what kinds of stress are dangerous. Is just being middle-aged stressful enough? What about the need to redefine goals, adjust to changing family roles, relinquish power to younger competitors, or cope with the first signs of biological aging? Table 15–3 lists potentially stressful events that people encounter throughout life. To determine the stress values in the table, each situation was rated by individuals of all ages for the amount of stress it produced. The death of a spouse, for example, was judged to be the highest stress producer and was assigned a value of 100. At the other extreme, a change in eating habits was rated as only mildly disruptive and assigned a value of only 15. Because middle adulthood is a time when people do lose spouses through death, divorce, and separation, and suffer changes such as

Table 15-3 Stress Scale for Life Events

Event	Value	Event	Value
Death of spouse	100	Pregnancy	40
Son or daughter leaving home	29	Change in recreational habits	19
Divorce	73	Sex difficulties	39
Trouble with in-laws	29	Change in church activities	19
Marital separation	65	Addition to family	39
Outstanding personal achievement	28	Change in social activities	18
Jail term	63	Business readjustment	39
Spouse begins or stops work	26	Mortgage or loan under $10,000 [as of 1967]	17
Death of close family member	63	Change in financial status	38
Starting or finishing school	26	Change in sleeping habits	16
Personal injury or illness	53	Death of close friend	37
Change in living conditions	25	Change in number of family gatherings	15
Marriage	50	Change to different line of work	36
Revision of personal habits	24	Change in eating habits	15
Being fired from work	47	Change in number of marital arguments	35
Trouble with boss	23	Vacations	13
Marital reconciliation	45	Mortgage or loan over $10,000 [as of 1967]	31
Change in work hours, conditions	20	Christmas season	12
Retirement	45	Foreclosure of mortgage or loan	30
Change in residence	20	Minor violation of the law	11
Change in family member's health	44	Change in work responsibilities	29
Change in schools	20		

Source: The Social Readjustment Rating Scale, by T. H. Holmes and R. H. Rahe, *Journal of Psychosomatic Research*, 1967, *11*(2), 213–218. Copyright 1967, Pergamon Press, Ltd. Reprinted with permission.

early retirement and illness, it's easy to see that the middle years have the potential for extremely high stress levels.

Stress is not caused solely by life events, however. How an individual perceives and interprets an event plays an important role as well. Researchers have repeatedly pointed out that the same event may cause considerable distress for one person but be viewed as a positive "challenge" by another (Chiriboga & Cutler, 1980; Lazarus, 1981, 1999, 2000). Occasional exposure to stressful events may be an important stimulus to continuing personality development. Another factor is that if an event is anticipated or expected, it may be less stressful than if it occurs suddenly and without warning. Yet another is that the effects of stressful events are *additive*: If several stressful events occur at the same time, the impact is much worse than if only one or two occur. To put it another way, the impact of a particular stressful events depends on what other conditions are present at the time (such as concerns about money, legal problems, or family life), how seriously the event affects daily routines, and to what extent the event is a personal hazard. Richard Lazarus (1981) suggested that an accumulation of little hassles sometimes is more stressful in the long run than major life changes (see "In Theory, In Fact," on facing page).

IN THEORY, IN FACT

LITTLE HASSLES AND STRESS

Have you ever felt like exploding when life's little hassles get to be too much, such as when your friendly neighborhood dry cleaner burned a hole in your new suit or when you spent an hour watching the tail lights of the car in front of you instead of the first act of a hit play you had waited months to see? Minor blowups, frustration, and anger have long been thought to be consequences of petty annoyances like these. However, according to Richard Lazarus (1981) and his colleagues at the University of California at Berkeley, the effects of little hassles may be far more serious.

To test this premise and determine whether pleasant, satisfying, and uplifting experiences counterbalance the negative effects of daily hassles, the researchers studied 100 men and women between the ages of 48 and 52 for 1 year. At the beginning of the study, each person filled out a 24-item life events scale, similar to the one presented in Table 15–3. On a monthly basis, they also completed a 117-item "hassle" checklist and a 135-item "uplift" checklist. To learn how the hassles and uplifts affected the participants' health, questionnaires measuring physical and mental health were completed at the beginning and end of the year, along with other measures of health changes.

The results of this study raise serious doubts about the belief that major life events are the main sources of stress. According to Lazarus, everyday hassles predict a person's physical and mental health far better than major life

events. Study participants who were overburdened with hassles had more mental and physical health problems than those whose lives were relatively calm. In contrast, people who experienced major life events such as divorce or the death of a close relative showed no serious health problems during the period of the study. Participants whose mental and physical health were affected by major life events had experienced these events during the 2½ years before the study began. Thus, although there is a link between major life events and long-term health, little hassles seem to determine well-being in the short term.

This is not to say that major life events and hassles are unrelated. Divorce, the death of a spouse, or even marriage can have a ripple effect that creates a seemingly inexhaustible supply of little hassles. A man who divorces after 30 years of marriage may find, for example, that he has difficulty coping with cooking his own meals, cleaning his own house, and having no readily available sex partner. Of course, not everyone responds to daily frustrations in the same way. Personality and coping style affect the way we respond. In addition, Lazarus found that frequency, duration, and intensity of stress interact to determine whether we feel overwhelmed. Misplace a wallet or a purse or get a splinter in your foot; then you'll be less prepared to cope with a notice from the bank that a check bounced.

Do the small uplifts of life help? Do news of a raise or the good feelings we get from our families offset the pressures that everyday hassles cause? Unfortunately, the study found that daily uplifts do little to compensate.

Lazarus's Top 10 Hassles and Uplifts

Hassles
1. Concern about weight
2. Health of a family member
3. Rising prices of common goods
4. Home maintenance
5. Too many things to do
6. Misplacing or losing things
7. Yard work or outside home maintenance
8. Property, investment, or taxes
9. Crime
10. Physical appearance

Uplifts
1. Relating well with your spouse or lover
2. Relating well with friends
3. Completing a task
4. Feeling healthy
5. Getting enough sleep
6. Eating out
7. Meeting responsibilities
8. Visiting, phoning, or writing someone
9. Spending time with family
10. Home pleasing to you

Source: Reprinted with permission from *Psychology Today* magazine. Copyright © 1981, Sussex Publishers, Inc.

Ethnicity, Poverty, and Health

Minority groups and the poor bear the heaviest burden of disease and death. This burden is present throughout life, but it is especially evident during the middle and older years. In large part, poor health in these populations is linked to a higher incidence of unhealthy behaviors, including smoking, drinking, and drug abuse, as well as obesity. The consequences are devastating. For example, in the 45- to 64-year-old group, the death rate for people who consider themselves black is nearly twice the rate for people who consider themselves white (Kovar, 1992; NCHS, 1995), although higher murder rates in some lower-income black neighborhoods are also a factor.

In addition to homicides, statistics show that black people are more likely to die from heart disease, hypertension, cancer, diabetes, accidents, and AIDS than are whites. Similarly, people who consider themselves Hispanic have higher death rates from infectious and parasitic diseases, diabetes, hypertension, and AIDS than whites do (NCHS, 1990a, 1995).

A number of social factors are responsible for these differences. Although medical and lifestyle interventions can reduce the effects of many diseases, Hispanic and black people tend to underutilize the health care system until they are in a state of emergency (and therefore won't be turned away from hospital emergency rooms). Higher levels of poverty, along with lack of health insurance, discourage some members of these groups from taking advantage of health screenings, physical examinations, and other early detection methods (Harlan, Bernstein, & Kessler, 1991; Kravitz, Pelaez, & Rothman, 1990). Hispanics in particular are less likely to have private health insurance than either whites or blacks and twice as many Hispanics as whites use hospital emergency rooms as their primary source of health care. Hispanic people's access to preventive health care is also made more difficult by cultural and language barriers. Studies have shown that English-speaking Hispanics are more likely to have a regular source of medical care than Hispanics who speak only Spanish (Council on Scientific Affairs, 1991).

Poor health habits that lead to increased risk factors are inextricably linked to a sense of hopelessness and to life in difficult social conditions (Williams, 1992). Cigarettes, alcohol, drugs, and overeating help people cope with daily stresses, which is one reason why the incidence of such bad habits is higher in minority groups. Thus, there is a trade-off: Although these health habits may have negative long-term consequences, they provide the poor and disadvantaged with immediate physiological and psychological compensations that enable them to cope with the stresses of their daily lives (Williams, 1992).

CONTENT CHECK
HEALTH AND DISEASE

True–False (answers are on the Companion Website)
1. Most losses of function associated with aging are irreversible.
2. During middle age people increasingly die because of disease.
3. Good health habits contribute to longevity whereas bad health habits have the opposite effect.
4. All stress is harmful to health.

Thinking Critically

Why do minority groups and the poor have more health problems than others during middle adulthood? What might be done to change this?

Cognitive Continuity and Change

Longitudinal studies have repeatedly indicated that aging is accompanied by decline in cognitive functioning, but we now know that the decline is much more gradual than researchers assumed as recently as 20 years ago. Serious cognitive decline occurs later than was previously thought, and then only in certain areas of intellectual functioning. Some aspects of intelligence actually increase during middle adulthood and beyond, especially for college-educated adults who remain active (Schaie, 1983, 1995). Contrary to the stereotype that intellectual development peaks in adolescence or young adulthood, the development of some cognitive abilities continues throughout the middle years, especially in areas related to work and daily living (Willis, 1989).

Fluid Versus Crystallized Intelligence

One way of looking at cognitive changes in middle and older adulthood was proposed by Raymond Cattell (1965) and later studied by researchers such as John Horn (1982). **Fluid intelligence** and **crystallized intelligence** both contribute to IQ test scores, but they can be analyzed separately. Fluid intelligence consists of abilities that we apply to new learning, including memorizing, reasoning inductively, and perceiving new relationships between objects and events. The term *fluid intelligence* is a metaphor suggesting that these basic processes "flow into" various other intellectual activities, including recognizing, learning, analyzing, and solving problems (Horn, 1982; Neugarten, 1976). Fluid intelligence has been thought to increase until late adolescence or early adulthood and then decline gradually throughout the remainder of the lifespan, paralleling changes in the efficiency and integrity of the nervous system (Horn, 1982).

In contrast, *crystallized intelligence* is the knowledge that comes with education and life experiences in general; it is the body of knowledge and information that a person accumulates over the years. As with fluid intelligence, it is used in finding new relationships, making judgments, and analyzing problems, but it differs in that previously learned strategies are employed to a greater extent. People acquire this form of intelligence through formal education as well as daily contact with their culture. Unlike fluid intelligence, crystallized intelligence tends to increase over the lifespan in people who are free from brain damage, as long as they remain alert and capable of taking in and recording information (Neugarten, 1976). When people are tested for skills involving this kind of intelligence, they often score higher in their 50s than they do in their 20s. This helps explain why scholars and scientists, whose work is based on a great deal of accumulated knowledge and experience, are usually more productive in their 40s, 50s, and even 60s and 70s, than they were in their 20s (Dennis, 1966; Simonton, 1990). Thus, in a sense, increasing crystallized intelligence compensates for declining fluid intelligence.

Research Problems   What evidence is there for the decline in fluid intelligence and the increase in crystallized intelligence? This isn't an easy research problem, and, as with all research problems, the results depend on how we study it. In Chapter 1 we discussed some of the differences between longitudinal and cross-sectional studies. Remember that longitudinal studies involve repeated measures of the same individuals over time, whereas cross-sectional studies involve measures of different individuals of different ages. In studying intelligence in adulthood, Horn and Donaldson (1980) used a cross-sectional approach with several different types of tests. As shown in Figure 15–2, measures of vocabulary, general information, and an element called *experiential evaluation* were much higher for individuals in their 40s and 50s than for individuals in their 20s and 30s. On the other hand, measures of figural relations and inductive reasoning were much lower for people in their 50s and 60s than for younger people (Horn & Donaldson, 1980).

fluid intelligence   Abilities involved in acquiring new knowledge and skills.

crystallized intelligence   Accumulated knowledge and skills based on education and experience.

Figure 15–2 A Cross-Sectional Comparison of Changes in Intellectual Abilities with Age

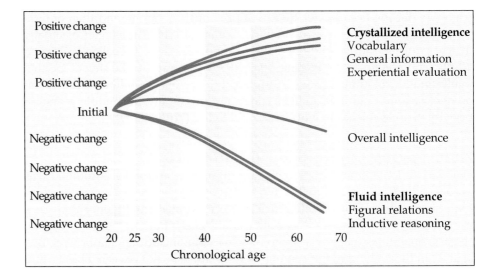

However, in a cross-sectional study the individuals at each age level are from different cohorts. They were born in different eras and have had different life experiences. Younger cohorts are better educated, have better health, and have had better nutrition over a longer period. Older cohorts have been educated in a very different fashion than the younger cohorts. They may have had an education that emphasized certain types of intellectual abilities over others; for example, in the early twentieth century educators placed much more emphasis on rote memorization of facts than on understanding what was being memorized.

So what happens when we use a longitudinal approach? The results vary somewhat from one study to the next, but in well-educated populations many of the tested abilities generally continue to rise. According to a broad-based study conducted by Warner Schaie (1983, 1995), it appears that several different kinds of intellectual abilities, both fluid and crystallized, either increase or are maintained throughout much of adulthood, declining only after age 60. Recall, however, that there are problems with extended longitudinal studies as

According to Lazarus, a pleasing home environment is one of life's top emotional uplifts.

well. It is difficult to get subjects to come back and be tested again and again—some refuse to participate further; some become ill; some die. Comparisons of people who continue participating with those who drop out indicate that the dropouts score lower, on average, at the earlier testings. Therefore, the increase in certain scores may be because of the loss of a disproportionate number of low scorers.

What if we look at individual changes rather than at averages? By and large, we find that between 45% and 60% of people maintain a stable level of overall intellectual performance—both fluid and crystallized—well into their 70s. Some people (10 to 15%) often show increases in performance until their mid-70s. A slightly larger group (roughly 30%) declines, at least by the time they reach their 60s.

Individuals thus vary considerably in intellectual growth and decline. Some show declines in word fluency and numerical reasoning, but not in other cognitive areas. A few remain stable or actually show increases on tests that involve verbal and numerical skills. Notably, inductive reasoning does not seem to decline any more dramatically than other abilities (Schaie, 1983; Willis & Schaie, 1999). In all, losses during middle adulthood are very limited. Indeed, there are often increases in full-scale intelligence test scores until the late 30s or early 40s, followed by a period of relative stability until the middle 50s or early 60s. On average, it now appears that only word fluency and numerical reasoning show any statistically significant declines before age 60 (Schaie, 1990; Willis & Schaie, 1999).

Implications for Intellectual Functioning Thus, it appears that many adults maintain a high level of functioning across a broad spectrum of intellectual abilities throughout middle adulthood. There are also wide individual differences. Some of the abilities that are classified as fluid intelligence do decline somewhat more rapidly in some individuals, but such declines are not an inevitable consequence of aging. In one study, the decline was clearly found to be related to the complexity of individuals' lives. People who had more opportunity for environmental stimulation, greater satisfaction with life, less noise in their environment, an intact family, a lot of social interaction, and ongoing cultural influences showed longer maintenance of and even increases in intellectual abilities (Schaie, 1983).

There is one factor that does seem to decline in middle adulthood, however. Skills that require speed become increasingly difficult as people grow older—various psychomotor processes gradually begin to slow down because of physical/neurological decline. Middle-aged adults compensate for declines in speed with increases in efficiency and general knowledge (Salthouse, 1990). Intellectual activities that are well practiced and used regularly in daily problem solving or in work settings are maintained at high levels of efficiency.

People adapt their intellectual development to meet environmental demands. To succeed at a particular job or within a certain social network, a person may emphasize the development of some skills while neglecting others (Lerner, 1990). This may be one reason why many middle-aged and older people perform more poorly than young adults on tests of abstract reasoning (Labouvie-Vief, 1985). They tend to place problems in context and make them concrete, thinking in terms of practical meaning and downplaying abstract reasoning—to the detriment of their test scores.

It is clear that one of the central influences on cognition in middle adulthood is the wealth of past life experience. Thus, if you think about it, it's a bit odd to conduct learning and memory studies comparing college students and older people on tests that use exclusively novel tasks and new, perhaps meaningless information, as most studies do. They do so, however, to avoid confounding accumulated knowledge with "basic" abilities to think and reason. College students are in a period of life in which coping with new information is an important adaptive skill. People in middle adulthood function best when they can use the wealth of background and experience they have accumulated (Labouvie-Vief, 1985). Thus, rather than measuring the cognitive capacities of middle-aged adults according to strategies appropriate to young adults, perhaps we should measure adult cognition in terms of experience and expertise (Salthouse, 1987).

Experience and Expertise

So some aspects of cognitive functioning do gradually decline starting in middle adulthood; how is it that so many of us—especially those in leadership positions—remain competent at work? How do aging experts differ from youthful novices? Given that the person remains intellectually active, age brings *more* knowledge—both **declarative** (factual) and **procedural** (action or "how-to" information)—through deliberate practice and refinement of skills.

Expertise, then, compensates for cognitive decline in middle adulthood. Extensive research supports this view. Expert knowledge is better organized; there are more interconnections between units of information, such as schemas. Expert skills display more in the way of *automaticity* (Chapter 7), thus freeing up conscious brain power at the same time that certain abilities in memory and concentration may be declining. Experts quickly and easily recognize patterns and link these to appropriate procedures and responses (Glaser, 1987). This applies across the board, to experts as diverse as physicists, computer programmers, musicians, bridge players, cooks, and gardeners.

Although experts remember relevant and crucial information better, however, they do not differ from novices in recalling material that is unorganized,

declarative knowledge Factual knowledge; knowing "what."

procedural knowledge Action knowledge; knowing "how to."

Experience is one factor that enables middle-aged adults to continue being productive.

unstructured, or unrelated to a particular problem. A study of chess players illustrates this point. Subjects were classified as older versus younger and as expert versus intermediate in ability, and there were two tasks. The subjects were first shown chess boards with a game in progress and asked to remember the position of every piece. The younger chess players did better on this task than the older ones, but skill level was not a factor. Then the subjects were asked to make an appropriate move. The experts (both old and young) were much better at this task because they did not need to remember where all the pieces were to make a good move. Experts' memory was selective and organized, and focused on connections between the patterns of the pieces and the appropriate moves (Charness, 1981; Salthouse, 1987).

Experience, then, doesn't guarantee the maintenance of a particular skill—the older chess players could not remember the position of every piece. Older typists are slower under controlled conditions; older architects suffer losses in visual-spatial skills (Salthouse et al., 1990). But experience compensates. The more experienced architect knows almost automatically which building materials will work best. The older typist may read longer spans of words, thereby maintaining speedy typing. These compensations allow adults in their middle and later years to remain productive at work (Salthouse, 1990). The opportunities provided by the environment to develop and practice these compensations clearly influence functioning. These findings show that development often involves a trade-off: As one skill declines, another improves (Baltes, 1987).

In sum, elements of expertise include continuing development of competence; knowledge and skills that are specific to a particular area or field; knowledge that is highly procedural or goal-oriented; rapid recognition that minimizes the need for an extensive memory search; and generalized thinking and problem-solving skills (Glaser, 1987). Again, extended experience tends to increase not only the amount of information but also its organization. Individuals continually restructure their knowledge system to make it more cohesive, correct, and accessible. This may be true for common knowledge, such as how to use the Yellow Pages, or for occupational knowledge, such as how to perform a technical procedure more efficiently. Cognitive tests rarely measure experiential influences on the knowledge and problem solving of older adults (Salthouse, 1987).

Cognitive Skills in Context

For most middle-aged adults, the context for continued development of cognitive skills is the workplace. Adults' cognitive abilities are closely linked to the demands of their job. Those who are continually challenged by complexity in their work achieve higher scores on tests of intellectual flexibility than those who perform routine work (Kohn, 1980; Schooler, 1990). That is, adults with a high degree of *occupational self-direction*—regular use of thought, initiative, and independent judgment—also have a high degree of intellectual flexibility (Schooler, 1987).

Increasingly, workers need flexibility in today's workplace. Technological change demands that most of us learn new skills, either to keep our jobs or to find new ones (see "A Closer Look, Back to School at Middle Age," page 532). Middle-aged adults who have the cognitive ability and skill to learn new tasks and the flexibility to take on more challenging assignments are better able to meet the demands of a changing workplace (Willis, 1989). This is especially true in fields such as medicine, engineering, and computer technology, in which

A CLOSER LOOK

BACK TO SCHOOL AT MIDDLE AGE

Visualize a "typical" college student. What do you see? A young adult? Someone who has gone straight from high school to college? Someone who is still supported by his or her parents during an "extended adolescence"? Someone who is a full-time student? The answer is not necessarily any of the above. Although today's college campuses are filled with 18- to 22-year-olds, they are also filled with older, nontraditional students who return to school. More than 2.8 million people over age 35 are attending college—in 2-year programs, 4-year programs, and graduate school. From 1980 to 1995, the number of students over age 35 increased by 46% (U.S. Census Bureau, 1997).

This dramatic trend coincides with the recognition that humans are lifelong learners with cognitive abilities that adapt to life's demands. Despite societal stereotypes that the time for education is over after adolescence and young adulthood, middle-aged adults often need to gain the information and skills required to meet the changing demands of their jobs (Willis, 1989). This is as true for bankers as it is for computer scientists, both of whom work in fields that have changed radically in recent years.

Although some middle-aged students are there for self-enrichment or to complete the education they abandoned earlier, many are there because they have to be. Some are unemployed—victims of corporate downsizing. Others, both men and women, are moving into the job market after spending many years at home as full-time parents. A financial planner who stopped working for 5 years to raise her daughter may need to be recertified before a firm will hire her. Even adults who worked part-time during their child-rearing years may have to return to school to acquire the knowledge and skills they need to qualify for a full-time job. This is especially true in fields with a high degree of professional obsolescence. Whatever the reason for their return, however, studies show that the majority of middle-aged students are conscientious about their work. They attend classes regularly and get better grades, on average, than other segments of the college student population.

Returning to school requires many adjustments, and usually the support of other family members. It also involves a personal assessment of one's skills and abilities. The student role is generally very different from other roles that middle-aged adults have assumed; considerable adaptation may be necessary to become a student who is subordinate to younger faculty members. Mature adults also find themselves among a large number of students who are considerably younger than they are,

and the age difference may be disconcerting. Self-doubt is also common when the older student returns to the school environment and must perform unfamiliar tasks in a prescribed fashion.

In the past, colleges and universities sometimes made it difficult for older students to succeed (Women's Reentry Project, 1981). Some middle-aged adults had trouble arranging time for other responsibilities because of rigid, full-time class schedules. Appropriate counseling was not always available, and the older part-time student often found that transferring credits, obtaining financial aid, and even gaining admission were geared exclusively to the needs of 18- to 22-year-old full-time students.

Nowadays the situation has changed at most colleges. With the realization that nontraditional students are here to stay and that they are increasingly important in maintaining enrollments, many colleges and universities have made substantial adjustments to meet their needs. Some schools have evening programs for nontraditional students; others attempt to incorporate them into the mainstream by offering a full program of day, evening, and weekend courses that are available to all students, both traditional and nontraditional.

knowledge quickly becomes obsolete as new requirements and changes in the disciplines occur. With regard to computers in particular, keeping up with hardware, operating systems, and new programs is almost a full-time job in itself. In fact, as much as half of a computer scientist's knowledge may be obsolete within only 2 to 3 years (Cross, 1981).

The concept of obsolescence is particularly important in middle adulthood because formal schooling typically ends years earlier, yet the length of time most adults are involved in active work has increased dramatically in the last century. In today's rapidly changing workplace, obsolescence is almost inevitable if workers don't adapt to new technology and methods. Whereas in

1900 the average adult spent 21 years in the labor force, by 1980 that figure had jumped to 37 years. In addition, the work years are now marked by multiple job changes requiring the latest knowledge and skills. As a result, "the relevant knowledge one needs in one's career cannot be fully obtained in the years of formal schooling. The individual must continue to update throughout the adult years" (Willis, 1987). Fortunately, continued cognitive development is possible in middle adulthood in areas of ability that are "exercised" regularly on the job, especially in careers that involve complex decision making and independent judgment—both of which can foster cognitive development (Willis, 1989).

Functional Changes in Cognition

Another way to look at adult cognitive development is to consider *functional* changes. Schaie (1977/1978) has suggested that it is the function, not the nature, of intelligence that changes over time. Recall from Chapter 12 that the young adult is in the *achieving* stage. Intelligence is used primarily to solve real-life problems with long-term implications, such as selecting a job or a spouse. In middle adulthood we enter the *responsibility* stage. Now responsibilities to spouse, children, coworkers, and the community play a major role in decision making. For some middle-aged people, this stage takes a somewhat different form and is called the *executive* stage, which applies to people managers, government officials, and corporate executives, whose decisions affect many people's lives.

In older adulthood, the uses of intellect shift again. In the *reintegrative* stage, people get back in touch with their own interests, values, and attitudes. They may balk at performing tasks such as IQ tests, which have little relevance for daily living. They can think abstractly, but they don't typically engage in solving such problems just for the sake of doing them, as young adults might.

Thus, intellectual changes especially during the middle years mainly consist of orientation and emphasis in how intelligence is applied; definitely not intellectual decline.

CONTENT CHECK
COGNITIVE CONTINUITY AND CHANGE

True–False (answers are on the Companion Website)

1. During midlife fluid intelligence increases whereas crystalized intelligence decreases.
2. Many people maintain a high level of cognitive functioning throughout middle age.
3. Expertise can never compensate for cognitive decline during middle age.
4. Extended experience tends to increase the amount of information but not its organization.
5. According to Schaie, the function but not the nature of intelligence changes over time.

Thinking Critically

What factors contribute to maintaining good cognitive functioning during middle adulthood?

CHAPTER 15 REVISITED

Development in Middle Adulthood

■ Developmental theorists differ considerably on the question of when middle adulthood begins and when it ends.

■ Cues associated with aging include social and family status, physical and biological changes, and psychological changes.

■ Economic conditions, social class, and historical context affect how people view middle adulthood.

■ Most people experience a sense of ambivalence during middle adulthood.

■ Some theorists believe that most adults experience a midlife crisis; other emphasize the transition model.

■ Middle adulthood is a time when people begin to take stock of their lives, for better or for worse.

■ Those who are most likely to experience a midlife crisis tend to avoid introspection and use denial.

Physical Continuity and Change

■ The most obvious changes associated with the middle years are physical ones.

■ Most sensory capabilities decline during the latter part of middle age.

■ Reaction time and sensorimotor skills slow down, continuing practice and experience compensate.

■ The nervous system slows down, the skeleton stiffens and shrinks, and muscles lose elasticity.

■ For women, the most dramatic internal change is menopause, which is part of the climacteric.

■ Menopause can be accompanied by physical and emotional symptoms, but most women do not respond negatively to menopause.

■ Estrogen loss produces osteoporosis, plus thinning and drying of vaginal tissue and an increased risk of coronary disease.

■ For men, there is no single event comparable to menopause, but men do undergo changes.

■ Frequency of sexual activity gradually slows down in middle age; for many adults sexuality is redefined to place more emphasis on emotional closeness and warmth.

Health and Disease

■ Many losses of function can be slowed; much of the cognitive decline is attributable to treatable diseases.

■ In part, longevity is attributable to good health habits.

■ Poor health habits during early adulthood take their toll in middle age.

■ Stress plays a major role in many of the diseases of middle age.

■ Poor health in minority groups is linked to a higher incidence of unhealthy behaviors; minorities also tend to underutilize the health care system.

Cognitive Continuity and Change

■ Unlike fluid intelligence, crystallized intelligence tends to increase over the lifespan as long as the person remains alert and capable of taking in and remembering information.

■ Many people maintain a stable level of overall intellectual performance well into their 70s, but individuals vary considerably.

■ Environmental stimulation, satisfaction with life, an intact family, and similar factors help maintain intellectual abilities.

■ Skills that require speed become increasingly difficult as people grow older.

■ Expertise compensates for cognitive decline in middle age.

■ Elements of expertise include competence, specific knowledge and skills, procedural knowledge, rapid recognition, and generalized thinking and problem-solving skills.

■ For most middle adults, the context for continued development of cognitive skills is the workplace; intellectual flexibility is increasingly necessary in the modern workplace.

■ According to Schaie, cognitive development in middle adulthood involves the responsibility stage and perhaps executive functions.

KEY TERMS

command generation

transition model

crisis model

menopause

climacteric

osteoporosis

sensuality

fluid intelligence

crystallized intelligence

declarative knowledge

procedural knowledge

MIDDLE ADULTHOOD: PERSONALITY AND SOCIOCULTURAL DEVELOPMENT

16

CHAPTER PREVIEW

Do you know:

1. What *developmental tasks* define middle adulthood?

2. What Erikson's *generativity versus absorption* refers to and how complex this can be?

3. The similarities and differences between *men's and women's reactions* to middle age?

4. Why middle adults are called *kinkeepers*?

5. What's involved in *launching* adolescents into the real world?

6. What the *empty nest* entails?

7. What the *most common attitude* that middle-aged children have toward their parents is?

8. The kinds of difficulties middle-adult parents often confront in dealing with *aging parents*?

9. What becoming a *grandparent* involves?

10. What *real* and *symbolic roles* middle-aged grandparents fulfill?

11. What differences there are between *friendships* in early and later middle age?

12. The difficulties posed by *divorce* in middle adulthood?

13. Why *reconstituted families* experience more adjustment problems than original families do?

14. The differences between contemporary occupational patterns during midlife and the *traditional* occupational cycle?

15. What's involved in coping with *midlife job loss, job burnout,* and *job stress*?

These are the main topics of Chapter 16.

I n *Over Our Heads* is the title of a book by Robert Kegan (1995). He used this phrase to describe the complexity of adult roles and responsibilities in the modern world. As the comments on the book jacket state, "If contemporary culture were a school, with all the tasks and expectations meted out by modern life as its curriculum, would anyone graduate?" This view is especially apt during middle adulthood, which is a time when adults try to make sense of the continually changing demands of parenting, the shifting roles in intimate relationships, and the changing world of work, as well as issues in the world at large, such as racism, sexism, and emerging technologies—altogether a bewildering array of concerns.

Although it can be argued that there is little firm ground on which to stand during middle adulthood as life events race by and trigger a continual stream of social and cognitive changes, it can also be argued that the middle adult years are a period of continuity in personality and outlook. Even when we experience an onslaught of external changes and major life events, internal change can be gradual.

It is in the context of continuity and change during the middle years that reflection and reassessment occur. Between the ages of 40 and 65, we mentally rewrite our autobiographies as we go. We review our life scripts as we experience major events and transitions (the death of a parent, a friend's serious illness, a new job, the birth of a midlife baby, the "launching" of the youngest child into high school or college). We take stock, contemplate our own mortality (especially when a relative or friend dies or becomes critically ill), and sort out our values in a continuing attempt to decide what really matters in life. As we reflect, we think less about how long we've lived and more about how much time we have left.

These reflections and reassessments take place within the context of three interconnecting worlds: self, family, and work (see Chapter 14). Each adult expresses his or her development uniquely in each of these areas. For example, those who choose to have a child at 40, to enter and leave the workforce many times during a career, or to divorce and remarry will have vastly different lifestyles and experiences than those who have children early, have a steady career, and maintain a lifelong commitment to one spouse.

This chapter examines the complexity of psychosocial development during middle age, focusing on interpersonal relationships and work. Change and the need to adjust to it are constant during this period, as is a reordering of our notion of the way things ought to be. For example, it is during middle adulthood that many families must adjust to the aftermath of divorce, the demands of stepfamilies, and unemployment. We begin by looking at personality continuity and change during the middle years.

Personality Continuity and Change

In discussing the events of adulthood, most theories refer to role shifts, marker events, milestones, critical issues, and developmental tasks. The specific expression of these elements of continuity and change is tied to the family life cycle and to a model of development based on the timing of events. Certain developmental tasks define middle age, although the tasks of early and late adulthood may be mingled with those of middle adulthood. These tasks also differ for women and men.

The Tasks of Middle Adulthood

Numerous recent studies have provided evidence that the course of midlife is extremely diverse and varied (Lachman & James, 1997) and at times tumultuous (Moen & Wethington, 1999). In other words, middle-aged adults "grow" too, often as a result of physical and social stressors (Chiriboga, 1996; Fiske & Chiriboga, 1990).

Carl Jung (1875–1961) was one of the first theorists to emphasize the second half of life: He believed that older people mainly need to find meaning in their lives (1931/1960). Since then, various models of adult development have been proposed that emphasize how much more complex the middle and later years can be. Most middle-aged people have adolescent or young adult children and aging parents (Troll, 1989, 1996). However, an increasing number of people, including those in their 40s with very young children, experience many normative life events at a later age than most others in their generation. Having young children in middle adulthood is particularly common among career women who decide late in life to become mothers and among divorced men who marry younger women who want children of their own. In other cases, people in middle adulthood adopt their young grandchildren because their adult children can't or won't care for them. Either way, these middle-aged adults tend to share activities and establish friendships with others who are at the same stage of the family life cycle, even though they are older chronologically.

Generativity Versus Self-Absorption   According to Erikson (1981), the basic issue facing people at this time of life is *generativity versus self-absorption*. With regard to generativity, Erikson suggested that people act within three domains: a *procreative* one, by giving and responding to the needs of the next generation; a *productive* one, by integrating work with family life and caring for the next generation; and a *creative* one, by contributing to society on a larger scale. For both men and women, generativity may be expressed through prosocial community activities, work, immersion in parenting, and caring for other loved ones (Peterson & Klohnen, 1995). For many, generativity is expressed across multiple roles, including both family and work roles (MacDermid, Heilbrun, & Gillespie, 1997).

The alternative is self-absorption and a sense of stagnation and boredom. Some people fail to find value in helping the next generation and have recurrent feelings of living an unsatisfying life. They also lack much in the way of accomplishments, or devalue whatever accomplishments they have.

Havighurst's model as it applies to middle adulthood (Chapter 13) is distinctly similar to Erikson's. Both emphasize the importance of establishing increasingly complex relationships with others and adjusting to the many changes that middle adulthood brings. According to Erikson, however, the most important responsibilities of this period are derived from the simple fact of being literally "in the middle" of life, sandwiched between an older generation and a younger one. We return to the implications of this later in the chapter.

Peck's Extension of Erikson's Theory   As summarized in Chapter 2, Erikson described a lifelong process of development consisting of 8 stages. We have dealt with the first 6 earlier and cover the seventh here. But the later years present other important issues as well. Robert Peck (1968) was especially concerned with expanding Erikson's picture of the second half of the lifespan.

In middle age, some people may rearrange their priorities, for example, an individual may decide to switch careers—to be an artist rather than an accountant, a teacher rather than an advertising executive.

Peck's main criticism of Erikson is that the 8 stages place too much emphasis on childhood, adolescence, and young adulthood. The 6 developmental issues of those periods—trust versus mistrust, autonomy versus shame and doubt, initiative versus guilt, industry versus inferiority, ego identity versus ego diffusion, and intimacy versus isolation—all pose important crises that each individual must resolve in the early years. Peck suggests that far too many new issues and tasks arise in the middle and older years to be summed up in two stages: generativity versus self-absorption and later *integrity versus despair* (when older people look back evaluate their lives; see Chapter 18).

During these later years, all of the earlier issues and their resolutions reappear from time to time—especially during times of stress or change. A sudden physical impairment such as a heart attack may revive struggles with autonomy and dependence in a 45-year-old. The death of a spouse may renew strong intimacy needs in the survivor. In fact, each major life adjustment may necessitate reevaluations and revisions of earlier solutions. Erikson believed that when we are uprooted by such major life circumstances as the death of a spouse, we *must* revisit issues of basic trust, autonomy, initiative, identity, and intimacy before we can pursue adult generativity.

In accounting for the special challenges of adult life, Peck proposed seven issues or conflicts of adult development; these are summarized in Table 16–1. The first four issues are particularly important in middle adulthood; the latter three become important in older adulthood, although the individual is already beginning to deal with them during middle adulthood.

Like Erikson's stages, none of Peck's issues are strictly confined to middle adulthood or older adulthood. The decisions made early in life act as building blocks for all the solutions of the adult years, and middle-aged people are already starting to resolve the issues of older adulthood. In fact, research suggests that the period from age 50 to age 60 is often a critical time for making adjustments that will determine the way people live out the rest of their lives.

Personal Reactions to Middle Adulthood

In middle adulthood both men and women reassess their goals and reflect on whether their original goals have been met. They made choices and established themselves in careers in young adulthood, but by middle adulthood they often take a second look at their choices. Most people then realize that they have made career choices that they must live with for better or worse. Some who are dissatisfied with their work or are unemployed or have not advanced as far as they had hoped become bitter and discouraged. Others simply rearrange their priorities. For example, some people at midlife may decide to direct more attention to family and other interpersonal or even moral commitments and less to occupational development (Fiske & Chiriboga, 1990).

Men's Reactions to Middle Age   In one study of attitudes toward family, work, and physical self (Farrell & Rosenberg, 1981), researchers interviewed 300 middle-aged men. They found that men react to middle adulthood in individual ways but with some similarities. Most of the men felt committed to both work and family. Most had developed a routine way of life that helped them cope as problems arose. Many had to face the same problems: caring for aging and dependent parents, dealing with adolescent children, coming to terms with personal limitations, and recognizing increasing physical vulnerability—issues that are as relevant today as then, and for both men and women.

Table 16-1 Peck's Issues (Conflicts) of Adult Development

Middle Adulthood

Valuing wisdom versus valuing physical powers

As physical stamina and health begin to wane, people must shift much of their energy from physical activities to mental ones.

Socializing versus sexualizing in human relationships

This, too, is an adjustment imposed by social constraints as well as by biological changes. Physical changes may force people to redefine their relationships with members of both sexes—to stress companionship rather than sexual intimacy or competitiveness.

Cathectic (emotional) flexibility versus cathectic impoverishment

Emotional flexibility underlies the various adjustments that people must make in middle age as families split up, friends move away, and old interests cease being the central focus of life.

Mental flexibility versus mental rigidity

Individuals must fight the inclination to become too set in their ways or too distrustful of new ideas. Mental rigidity is the tendency to become dominated by past experiences and former judgments—to decide, for example, that "I've disapproved of Republicans (or Democrats or Independents) all my life, so I don't see why I should change my mind now."

Older Adulthood

Ego differentiation versus work-role preoccupation

If people define themselves exclusively in terms of job or family, such events as retirement, a change in occupation, or divorce, or a child leaving home will create a gulf in which they are likely to flounder. Ego differentiation means defining yourself as a person in ways that go beyond what work you do or what family roles you fulfill.

Body transcendence versus body preoccupation

This centers on the individual's ability to avoid becoming preoccupied with the increasing aches, pains, and physical annoyances that accompany the aging process.

Ego transcendence versus ego preoccupation

This is particularly important in old age. It requires that people not become mired in thoughts of death (the "night of the ego," as Peck calls it). People who age successfully transcend the prospect of their own mortality by becoming involved in the younger generation—the legacy that will outlive them.

Source: Adapted from Peck, 1968.

Although men's psychological well-being has traditionally been linked to their job roles, it is now clear that family relations at midlife are extremely important as well. In the words of the researchers,

> Our contact with families demonstrated the ways in which a man's experience at midlife is very much dependent on the culture and structure of his family. The changing relationships to wife and children act as precipitants

for development in men. . . . This interlocking of individual and family developmental processes is a critical element in men's experience at midlife. (Farrell & Rosenberg, 1981)

Indeed, midlife has been characterized as the "prime" of fathers, as their influence over their young adult children tends to increase (Nydegger & Mitteness, 1996). Other research supports the importance of family to men during midlife. In one study, the quality of men's marital and parental roles significantly predicted their level of psychological distress and affected how much distress they experienced on the job (Barnett & Pleack 1992).

From the foregoing research, it appears that there are four general paths in middle adulthood for men. The first is that of the **transcendent-generative man.** He does not experience a midlife crisis and has found adequate solutions to most problems of life, so midlife can be a time of fulfillment and accomplishment. The second path is that of the **pseudo-developed man.** This man copes with problems by maintaining the facade that everything is under control even when it isn't; underneath, he feels lost, confused, or bored. A **man in midlife crisis**—the third path—is confused and feels that his whole world is disintegrating. He is unable to meet demands and solve problems. For some men, this may be a temporary phase; for others, it may be the beginning of a continuous decline. The final path is that of the **punitive-disenchanted man,** who has been unhappy or alienated for much of his life and also displays signs of a midlife crisis and inability to cope with problems.

It should be noted that U.S. society has traditionally forced men to conform to one standard of success and masculinity and that most men still try to conform to this standard. A number of the problems men experience at midlife come from having to cope with the idea that they have not lived up to this standard or that they have had to put aside many of their other interests and desires in trying to reach the standard. Only a few men manage to avoid at least some feelings of failure, self-estrangement, or loss of self-esteem in middle adulthood.

Women's Reactions to Middle Age   Women, too, often experience difficult transitions and reassessments. Although there are wide individual differences, again there are some common patterns. Traditionally, women define themselves more in terms of the family cycle than by their place in the career cycle. One study of midwestern women (Reinke, Ellicott, Harris, & Hancock, 1985) found that the women tended to report major life transitions at three points in the family cycle. Fully 80% reported major role changes associated with the birth of their children and their early child-rearing years in young adulthood. Two other major transitions occurred in midlife. About 40% reported a major transition when their children left home, although very few described the transition as particularly traumatic. The final major transition (33% of the women) was menopause.

From a different perspective and on the basis of more recent research, Terri Apter (1995) identified four "types of midlife women" in a sample of 80 women between the ages of 39 and 55. **Traditional women** (18 of the 80 studied), having previously defined themselves in terms of family roles, had relatively little difficulty shifting into the role of mature woman responsible for her own future. Their main issues were concerns about past compromises and unused potential. **Innovative women** (24), who had pursued careers, were beginning to view the climb to the top as too demanding and were reassessing "the work

In our society, women are usually judged by their looks, and in order to be considered attractive, they must appear youthful. It is not surprising, then, that researchers report a high incidence of depression in middle-aged women.

transcendent-generative man A man for whom middle age is a time of well-being, fulfillment, and accomplishment.

pseudo-developed man   A middle-aged man who maintains a facade that everything is well when it isn't.

man in midlife crisis   A middle-aged man undergoing feelings of confusion and disintegration.

punitive-disenchanted man   A man whose earlier sense of unhappiness or alienation continues into middle age and is accompanied by a midlife crisis.

traditional woman   In Apter's research, a woman who has previously defined herself in terms of family and who easily makes the transition to middle age and maturity.

innovative woman   In Apter's research, a woman who has devoted herself to a career and begins to reassess her life in middle age.

they had done on themselves" in their pursuits and the effects it had. **Expansive women** (18) made marked changes in their goals in midlife in an attempt to expand their horizons. They were going back to school, some to qualify for new kinds of work, or they were turning hobbies into vocations. Finally, there were **protesters** (13), who had been thrust into a premature adulthood during late adolescence and were attempting to postpone midlife as long as possible. Apter noted, however, that only a small minority of the women had much trouble with the transition to midlife.

The timing-of-events model of development applies especially to women during middle adulthood. That is, the timing of key events in the family life cycle and careers defines women's status, lifestyle, and options at middle adulthood—their major activities, their pleasures and stresses, their friends and colleagues. A woman who postpones marriage and childbearing until she is 40 usually does so to pursue a career. Once her child is born, she may enter and leave the workforce many times during her child-rearing years. Her decision to combine family with a full-blown career may reduce her chance of poverty in older adulthood (Baruch & Brooks-Gunn, 1984). The timing of events also defines the specific nature of role conflicts and role strains (see Chapter 14). Common *role conflicts* for middle-aged women involve finding time for both family and career. For example, how does a busy executive cook an evening dinner while at the same time meeting business deadlines that may require overtime work? **Role strain** is associated with an overload of demands within the same role, such as when a mother tries to give each of her three teenage children the attention they need and feels incapable of fully satisfying any of them (Lopata & Barnewolt, 1984, Spurlock, 1995).

Women react more strongly than men to the physical changes of aging. In the United States, women who appear youthful are often judged as more attractive than older women. Some women perceive wrinkles, graying hair, and other signs of aging as indications that they are no longer sexually desirable. As we saw in Chapter 15, some women also react negatively to menopause and regret losing the capacity to bear children.

Ethnically black women share many of the reactions of ethnically white women to middle adulthood, as the following description indicates:

> We are never-married, married, separated and/or divorced, and widowed. . . . Some of us may be more preoccupied about our weight, age spots, and dry skin than we were about color in our adolescence. At middle age, many of us are more concerned about the thinning of our hair than about its texture. Others are taking the physical signs of middle age in stride, and fret little, if any, about the natural youthfulness of some of our sisters. We are represented in the statistics of the depressed and well-adjusted. Some of us are involved in midcareer changes; others are adjusting to early retirement. We are represented among blue- and white-collar workers, as well as among the self-employed in both stable and unstable businesses. (Spurlock, 1984, p. 246)

Despite the similarities between black women and white women, the combined effects of ethnicity and gender create meaningful differences for black women in middle adulthood. Memories of past discrimination engender anger in some, psychological denial in others. In addition, socioeconomic factors funnel many middle-aged black women into low-paying, dead-end jobs and often into poverty. Many suffer health problems associated with limited access to health care (Spurlock, 1984).

expansive woman   In Apter's research, a woman who makes major life changes to expand her horizons in middle age.

protesting woman   In Apter's research, a woman who experienced premature adulthood and tries to postpone middle age.

role strain   An overload of demands within a given role, such as mother or father.

CONTENT CHECK
PERSONALITY CONTINUITY AND CHANGE

True–False (answers are on the Companion Website)

1. According to Erikson, the main issue facing middle adults is generativity versus boredom.
2. According to Peck, the issues and tasks of middle adulthood are more complex than those suggested by Erikson.
3. For men at midlife, career is more important than family relationships.
4. The timing-of-events model applies especially to women at midlife.
5. Ethnicity and socioeconmic factors create some differences in how women experience middle adulthood.

Thinking Critically

In what ways may developmental conflicts that characterize earlier stages of development reappear in midlife?

Family and Friends: Interpersonal Contexts

For both men and women, interpersonal relationships are crucial during the middle adult years. It can be argued that the key element that defines middle adulthood is relationships with family members and friends. We begin by looking at the complex and changing relationships between middle-aged people and their young adult children, including the task of launching children into their own independent lives and the (typically easier) task of adjusting to a home without children. We then turn to relationships between middle-aged people and their aging parents, also to their new role of grandparent. Finally, we examine the importance of relationships with friends.

The Generation That Runs Things

Middle-aged people act as a bridge between the younger generation (which usually means their children) and the older generation (their aging parents). As they adjust to their changing roles in these relationships, they often gain a new perspective on their own lives. They are now the generation that must run things. This new responsibility entails taking stock. They may regret goals not achieved and may have to acknowledge that some goals will never be reached. More than any other group, middle adults must live in the present. Young people can look ahead, and older people often look back; people in their middle years, with shifting responsibilities to two generations as well as to themselves, must live in the here and now. As they do so, they serve as family **kinkeepers** (Richlin-Klonsky & Bengston, 1996). They are the ones who maintain family rituals, celebrate achievements, keep family histories alive, reach out to family members who are far away, and gather the family together for holiday celebrations—all of which helps keep the family close.

kinkeeper The role assumed by middle-aged people that includes maintaining family rituals, celebrating achievements and holidays, and keeping family histories alive.

At this point in their lives, many middle-aged parents must begin to let go of their teenage children so that they may start the process of entering the adult world.

Relationships with Adult Children

Relationships with adult children include launching the children into their own independent lives and adjusting to life without them. They also involve learning to relate to adult children in a reciprocal way.

Launching Adolescents and Young Adults   Redefinition of the parent-child relationship begins with the **launching of adolescents** into the adult world. Some families are good at letting go. Adolescents on the verge of assuming responsible adult roles are best supported by parents who maintain a dialogue with them but increasingly trust and respect their judgments, decisions, and progress toward maturity. Parents must learn to let go, up to a point, and accept who their children really are.

There is no doubt that the launching of adolescents is an important transition for the parents (Harris et al., 1986). Although many women report unhappiness during this transition, the source of their dissatisfaction is more commonly related to work or marriage than to the children's departure (Harris et al., 1986). Men may also feel torn as the children leave home, especially if they feel that they somehow missed seeing their kids grow up (L. Rubin, 1980).

Parents repeatedly say that although they are glad they had children, the increase in freedom, privacy, and discretionary income once the children are gone make this a pleasant time of life (Alpert & Richardson, 1980; Cooper & Guttman, 1987). Women especially benefit from being freed from daily parenting responsibilities and report greater assertiveness and freedom to explore their own interests.

Because of the high divorce rate in the United States, many parents are raising children alone, at least temporarily (Bray & Hetherington, 1993). Others have chosen to be single parents without marrying in the first place. Single parents may find themselves in sharp conflict or shifting relationships with their adolescent children (Alpert & Richardson, 1980). Some studies suggest that this may be particularly true when the children are preadolescents. During this period, there may be almost daily conflicts over rights and responsibilities (Smetana, 1988). When children marry, parents are suddenly confronted with a new family member in the form of a son- or daughter-in-law. This abrupt demand for intimacy with someone who may be a total stranger is another common adjustment that must be made during this period (Neugarten, 1976).

Finally, it should be noted that not all children who are launched into the world manage to stay there the first time or two out. Because of aborted marriages, job loss, and the difficulty of earning enough to live independently in today's world, many adult children "bounce" and return home to recuperate before giving the outside world another try. A few even return home with the intent to stay. How does a returning adult child affect parents? In general, negatively. Aside for issues as simple as having to share space and resources with another adult, a young adult's return to dependency tends to violate parents' expectations about their children's development and thereby lower parental satisfaction and put strain on the parent-child relationship (Aquilino, 1996). Moreover, the return often happens as the parents are trying to deal with their own midlife issues, complicating matters further.

The "Empty Nest"   After successfully launching their last child, parents turn to roles and interests beyond the sometimes all-encompassing role of parenthood. This is becoming more important as people live longer. For example, among U.S. adults, a women who was 40 in 1998 could expect to live another 41.1 years and a man who was 40 could expect to live another 36.4 years

launching of adolescents   Parents' letting go of children so that they can assume responsible adult roles.

(Anderson, 2001). Given this life expectancy, parents who remain married can anticipate spending a lengthy period together after the launching of the last child. This stage of the family life cycle, sometimes referred to as the **empty nest,** can be difficult if the partners have grown apart over the years, developed different interests, and become unaccustomed to spending much time together.

Many middle-aged couples, however, have a history of mutual parenting that includes shared traditions, values, and experiences. Even couples who no longer enjoy the high level of companionship that is characteristic of early marriage may have a strong emotional support system and be materially and functionally interdependent. They have a home and its furnishings and have grown accustomed to their daily routines. Marital satisfaction in this later period is not necessarily based on the same patterns of interaction or solutions to joint problems as it was in earlier phases of the family cycle (Troll, 1985), and it is quite possible to "survive and thrive" after launching children (Lauer & Lauer, 1999).

Mutually Reciprocal Relationships   By middle adulthood the relationship between parents and their children is more reciprocal than it has ever been before. The relationship evolves into one in which two adults interact on a more equal basis than was possible when the young adult was a child. The shift to a reciprocal relationship rarely takes place suddenly or smoothly; it usually occurs in a series of jolts over a period of years. In turn, the nature of the parenting relationship can make this shift easier or harder. If the parenting relationship was authoritarian, the roles and obligations tend to be formal, rigid, and resistant to change. Middle-aged parents and their young adult children may have to struggle for years to create a reciprocal relationship, if indeed they ever do.

Adult children often feel the need to distance themselves, at least for a while, from their parents—and from perceived parental judgment—before they can see their parents in a realistic way. When this happens, middle-aged parents may feel cut off or unappreciated. It is often during times of family crisis—the death or illness of a family member, financial hardship, divorce, or unemployment—that adult children and their parents find ways to renegotiate their relationship so that they can interact with each other in new, more reciprocal ways. In some families this process can take many years; in others mutual respect emerges as adolescence wanes.

Relationships with Aging Parents

In 1900, one in four children experienced the death of a parent before they were 15 years old. In the 1980s, fewer than 1 in 20 children did. Conversely, in 1980, 40% of people in their late fifties had at least one surviving parent (Brody, 1985). Estimates indicate that of the women born in the 1930s, fully one-quarter will have living mothers when they turn 60 (Gatz, Bengtson, & Blum, 1990), and these numbers are continuing to rise. As a result, middle-aged adults will need to adjust to the changing needs and roles of an aging parent. When parents are in good health and can live independently, the relationship is often characterized by reciprocity; the parent and adult child help each other in concrete ways. The relationship changes when parents become ill or too frail to live on their own—indeed, the primary reason for "re-forming" a shared household is disability on the part of the parent (Brody, Litvin, Hoffman, & Kloban, 1995b).

How adult children behave toward their parents depends to a large extent on their life experiences and, more specifically, on their stage in the family life cycle. A 42-year-old woman with grown children who is at the peak of her professional life and living 1000 miles away from her parents must take a different approach to them than a woman of similar age who is a full-time homemaker living near

empty nest   The period in the family life cycle that occurs after the last child has left home.

her parents. The backdrop for adult-parent relationships is the repertoire of beliefs and practices that has defined their unique relationship over the years. With time come diverse strategies and understandings between parent and child that ultimately lead to different patterns of interaction and coping. Moreover, the degree to which children are called on to help their parents varies from one individual to another and from one family to another (Stueve & O'Donnell, 1984).

As you read about the evolving relationships between middle-aged adults and their aging parents, keep in mind that gender differences often affect these relationships. "Daughters of aging parents are different from sons of aging parents; the difference even depends on whether the aging parent is a father or a mother" (Troll, 1989). Traditionally, the primary parent-child relationship at this stage of life generally involves the daughter as caregiver. Ethnic and social class may also influence intergenerational relationships.

Reciprocal Exchange of Assistance   Most middle-aged people have ongoing relationships with their aging parents that include regular contact, shared memories, and reciprocal exchange of assistance. Numerous surveys have revealed lasting social, emotional, and material exchanges between adult children and their parents (Stueve & O'Donnell, 1984; Troll & Fingerman, 1996). Many older parents provide financial assistance to their middle-aged children and to their grandchildren (Giordano & Beckman, 1985), at least in middle- and upper-middle-class families. In ethnically black families the older generation more often does not have the financial resources to contribute (Jackson et al., 1990). On the other hand, they are more likely to provide social support and perhaps caregiving services to their children—especially those who are coping with single parenthood.

In all, contrary to widespread public opinion, it appears that most middle-aged people remain quite concerned about and close to both their parents and their children (see "In Theory, In Fact," on facing page). Table 16–2 summarizes various myths with regard to intergenerational estrangement during midlife.

Role Reversals   With age, role reversals gradually take place for middle adults and their parents. Middle adults become the generation in charge—working, raising children, and generally functioning as the "doers" in society.

Table 16–2   Some Midlife Intergenerational Myths

1. Midlife men and women live as far apart from their children and their parents as they can.
2. Midlife men and women rarely visit or receive visits from their adult children or their parents.
3. Midlife men and women rarely phone (or get phone calls) or write (or receive letters) from their adult children or their parents.
4. Midlife men and women abandon their parents when they get old and sick.
5. Midlife parents and their adult children are more likely to stay in touch and feel close if they share values and personality.
6. Grandparents feel they know how to raise their grandchildren better than their children are doing and are eager to interfere.
7. Extensive extended family contact is deleterious to mental health.

Source: From *Midlife Myths: Issues, Funding, and Practice Implications* by S. Hunter and M. Surdel, eds. Reprinted by permission of the author.

IN THEORY, IN FACT

BETWEEN TWO GENERATIONS

Middle-aged people are often described as being "caught in the middle" between the conflicting needs of their young adult children (and perhaps their children's children) and their aging parents. When middle-aged people find themselves in this situation, they supposedly choose to focus on their own needs and have little contact with either the younger or the older generation.

Despite the prevalence of this belief, research on intergenerational relationships has shown that it is more fiction than fact. In the words of Lillian Troll (1989), "The myth that parents and their adult children are essentially estranged from each other in today's Western society is so widespread and persistent that it is difficult to convince the general public that it is untrue." Intergenerational myths can make it harder for middle-aged people to perceive positive feelings about family members as normal, so it is important to examine where the truth lies.

Despite the widespread belief that estrangement and isolation are the norm and contact is held to a minimum, surveys show that middle-aged children are likely to live relatively close to their parents and see or speak with them on a regular basis. However, this does not mean that the generations are likely to share a home. Because independence is valued by each generation, fewer than 10% of aging parents share a home with their middle-aged children, and many do so only when economic hardship or physical disability gives them little choice.

Most middle-aged parents also have regular contact with their grown children, and this contact is likely to increase when problems arise for either the children or the parents. However, although family members tend to come together to support one another during

Usually, middle-aged women assume most of the responsibilities for the care of aging parents.

times of crisis, they are likely to return to their normal interaction patterns after the crisis is over (Belsky & Rovine, 1984; Morgan, 1984).

When the generations come together, they try to help each other in concrete ways. When help is needed—and given—it is in the context of a mutual, reciprocal relationship whose balance changes over time. During an individual's early adult years, most of the help given during times of illness flows from parent to child. During middle adulthood, the flow often shifts toward the older generation as adults are forced to take care of their aging parents. The responsibility—and burden—of caring for both young and old usually falls on the "woman in the middle" (Brody, 1985), who may have to juggle the needs of her aging parents,

her young adult children, her marriage, and the health of her husband, as well as her own career and personal needs. Most women manage to meet these responsibilities but have little time left for themselves.

Relationships between the middle generation and their children and parents are often characterized by attempts to influence behavior (Hagestad, 1985). In most cases such attempts are directed at children rather than parents, and regardless of the target, the advice is usually intended to be practical. Attempts to change poor health habits are common to all generations as the middle-aged, their parents, and their children try to persuade each other to stop smoking, eat sensibly, see their doctor regularly, and take their medications.

Their parents, if they are still living, may be in poor health, retired, and in need of financial aid. Over a period of years power gradually and naturally shifts to their middle-aged child. Unless both generations realize that this role reversal is an inevitable part of the life cycle, it can cause resentments on both sides and lead to conflicts (Albert & Brody, 1996; Gould, 1978; Neugarten, 1976).

Some adult children do not look after their aging or ill parents; instead they abandon them to nursing homes and other impersonal social services. However, they are by far the minority. Today people are living longer after the onset of chronic diseases or disabilities, and few people reach the end of life without experiencing a period in which they are dependent on their children. The responsibility of long-term care for parents has become more the norm than the exception. One study (Marks, 1996) found that 1 in 5 adults aged 35 to 64 had cared for a relative or a friend in the last year. Several studies conducted in the 1970s demonstrated that 80 to 90% of medically related and personal care, household tasks, and transportation and shopping for aging parents was managed by family members, not the social system (Brody, 1985).

Family members react to emergencies, but they also respond to the need for long-term assistance of the chronically disabled (Matthews & Rosner, 1988). In the Long-Term-Care Survey of caregivers of very frail older persons, 75% of the daughter caregivers provided daily assistance. Only 10% of the caregivers used formal services (Stone, Cafferata, & Sangl, 1987). Families also provide social support, affection, and a sense of having someone to rely on. It is also true, however, that family resources can become exhausted or the parent can become so debilitated that family members must turn over primary responsibility to someone else, such as a nursing home. Nevertheless, conservative estimates indicate that well over 5 million people in the United States are involved in parent care at any given time (Brody, 1985).

Daughters are much more likely than sons to provide care for aging parents (Brody, Kleban, Johnsen, Hoffman, & Schoonover, 1987; Gatz et al., 1990; Spitze & Logan, 1990). The same applies to daughters-in-law (Globerman, 1996), but there are fewer differences between working and nonworking women (Brody & Schoonover, 1986). Working daughters provide comparable amounts of help with tasks such as shopping, transportation, and emotional support. One survey indicated that nonemployed daughters are more likely to help with cooking and personal care. Substantial numbers of working daughters also change their work schedules to accommodate their parents' needs (Brody et al., 1987). Surveys also indicate that 20 to 30% of caregiver daughters had rearranged their schedules to provide care. In fact, caring for ill relatives is the second most common reason given by middle-aged women for leaving the workforce (the first is problems with their own health).

Siblings may work together to care for their ailing parents (Goetting, 1982). The distribution of labor between the siblings is not always equal, however, with daughters again more likely than sons to provide care. In fact, parents expect more assistance from daughters than from sons (Brody, Johnsen, & Fulcomer, 1984). If there are two daughters and only one of them works outside the home, the unemployed one will provide more of the daily care and assistance in last-minute emergencies (Matthews, Werkner, & Delaney, 1989). Nevertheless, the working daughter is expected to make significant contributions, typically providing aid in the evenings and on weekends.

How a daughter responds to the needs of her aging parents depends to a large extent on her life circumstances, including her age (is she in her 30s, 40s, or 50s?), her position in the family life cycle (does she have grown children or is she raising preschoolers?), and her involvement in the workforce (does she have a full-time job or is she a full-time homemaker?) (Stueve & O'Donnell, 1984). Daughters may experience physical strain as a result of their caregiving efforts. However, when daughters have dependent children of their own, they experience less strain and a greater sense of well-being than those without dependent children (Stull, Bowman, & Smerglia, 1994). Married daughters also fare best by far, conpared to divorced or never-married daughters (Brody, Litvin, Hoffman, & Kleban, 1995a; Brody et al., 1995b), given help and support from their husband's and children.

In sum, responsibility for parent care is both rewarding and stressful. For some, it creates tension between dependence and independence. It may reactivate old dependency conflicts or other relationship problems between parent and child or between siblings. Old loyalties and alliances or rivalries sometimes reappear. The need to care for parents also foreshadows the future of the caregivers, who will be dependent on their children when they become old. It may be a preview and model for relinquishing autonomy, control, and responsibility. These internal conflicts—together with the very real demands on time and freedom, competing responsibilities, and interference with lifestyle, and social and recreational activities—can create a stressful environment. It is remarkable that 80 to 90% of middle-aged adults persist in the tasks and responsibilities of parental care. Indeed, some women practically make a career of serving as caregivers to one aging relative after another. Despite the extent of their caregiving, however, fully three-fifths of caregiving women in one study reported that they felt guilty about not doing enough, and three-quarters of them agreed that nowadays middle-aged children do not take care of their older parents to the extent that they did in the past (Brody, 1985).

Introduction to Grandparenting

Many people in middle adulthood find themselves in the new role of grandparent. Grandparenting is highly satisfying for many people; they can help raise a new generation without having the daily responsibilities of a parent and without being involved in the intense relationships and conflicts that may develop between parent and child.

The majority of people in the United States become grandparents in middle age; minorities and women tend to become grandparents somewhat earlier than whites and men (Szinovacz, 1998). If their adult children divorce or encounter other problems, some grandparents become full-time surrogate parents to their grandchildren; others care for their grandchildren part time even though they themselves may still be working full-time (Szinovacz, 1998). Thus, in many ways, the concept of a U.S. grandparent has evolved from that of an old person in a rocking chair to that of an active, involved family member (Troll, 1989).

Although grandparenting is a highly individualized activity, there are some distinct roles that grandparents can play, depending on their relationships with their grandchildren (Troll, 1980). If a single mother or both parents work, grandparents can take care of children during the day. Some grandparents become "fun people" to their grandchildren, taking them on trips, shopping, or to interesting places. In certain ethnic groups a grandfather maintains his status and position as formal head of the family. And increasingly, in cases where parents either can't or don't want to rear their children, grandparents take their place (Morrow-Kondos, Weber, Cooper, & Hesser, 1997).

One author suggested that there are four important, yet often largely symbolic, roles that grandparents fulfill (Bengston, 1985).

1. *Being there*: Sometimes grandparents describe their most important role as simply being there. They are a calming presence in the face of family disruption or external catastrophe. They provide an anchor of stability to both grandchildren and parents. Sometimes they even act as a deterrent to family disruption.

2. *Family national guard:* Some grandparents report that their most important function is to be available in times of emergency. During these times they often need to go well beyond the role of simply being there and actively manage the grandchildren.

3. *Arbitrator:* Some grandparents see their role as one of imparting and negotiating family values, maintaining family continuity, and helping out in times of conflict. Although there are often differences in values between generations, some grandparents see themselves as better able to handle the conflicts between their adult children and their grandchildren because of their relative distance and greater experience.

4. *Maintaining the family's biography:* Grandparents can provide a sense of continuity for the family, teaching grandchildren about the heritage and traditions of their family.

Each of these roles may be either real or symbolic. Sometimes family values are maintained more because adult children and grandchildren worry about how a grandparent might react than through actual intervention by the grandparent (Bengtson, 1985). For example, a grandchild may choose not to marry outside her ethnic or religious group because of the way her grandparents might respond.

Friendships: A Lifelong Perspective

Although many important life stages are defined by family relationships, many people in midlife rely more on friends than on family. Although the majority of people marry and raise children, a significant and growing number remain single or raise children by themselves. For them friendships are often a central part of life. Such important life tasks as establishing intimacy, for example, must be accomplished through friendships rather than through marriage and family.

In later middle age, friends become appreciated for what makes them unique.

For older people whose children are grown or who are widowed, friendship often fills many vital emotional needs.

In a 12-year study by Marjorie Fiske and colleagues (1990), people at four different stages of life were interviewed about their attitudes toward friendship and the kinds of friendships they had. The study involved high school students, newlyweds, people in early middle adulthood, and people in late middle adulthood. Most middle-aged people reported that they had several friends with whom they had been close for at least 6 years, whereas adolescents and newlyweds tended to have more short-term friendships. When asked what qualities were important in real friendships and what qualities characterized an ideal friend, people at all four life stages had similar views. Reciprocity was considered very important, with a strong emphasis on helping and sharing. People saw their friends as similar to themselves in many ways and stressed the importance of shared experiences and being able to communicate well. Sex differences were more significant than age differences. Women responded in more detail than men and seemed to be more deeply involved in their friendships. Women considered reciprocity most important in their close friendships; men tended to choose their friends on the basis of similarity. It should be noted, however, that many of today's middle-aged people are baby boomers who grew up in a time of relaxed norms regarding friends and acquaintances; thus, as Rebecca Adams and Rosemary Blieszner (1998) have suggested, middle-age friendships today are now much more heterogeneous with regard to ethnicity and gender.

In general, the most complex friendships occurred among the late-middle-aged group. In early middle adulthood, people were more involved with their families and jobs. They had less time to devote to friends. On the other hand, by late middle adulthood highly complex and multidimensional relationships were the rule. People at this stage were likely to appreciate the unique characteristics of their friends. This may be a result of certain personality shifts during middle adulthood. Jung described the period from age 40 to age 60 as a time of inner awareness, when people turn away from the activities of the conscious mind and confront the unconscious. It is possible that as people become aware of the subtleties of their own natures, they also begin to appreciate complexity in others more than they did earlier in life (Fiske & Chiriboga, 1990).

CONTENT CHECK

FAMILY AND FRIENDS: INTERPERSONAL CONTEXTS

True–False (answers are on the Companion Website)

1. A major midlife transition involves launching their adolescent children into the adult world.
2. In middle adulthood, the relationship between parent and child tends to become less reciprocal as the adolescent's gaze is increasingly centered outside the family.
3. Today adult male and female siblings tend to equally share the responsibilities in caring for aged parents.
4. Grandparenting is a new role that typically occurs during middle adulthood.
5. During midlife, people tend to rely more on family than on friends.

Thinking Critically

Why might we characterize middle adults as the generation that runs things?

The Changing Family

Increasingly, as we have seen in earlier chapters, family relationships must be viewed in the context of a changing family unit characterized by divorce, remarriage, and reconstituted families. Here we look at the impact of the changing family on middle-aged adults.

No one—not even the most radical social critic—would claim that the traditional nuclear family is dead or even dying. But few families still fit the traditional mold in which the father works and the mother stays home to care for the children. Just as individuals are tailoring their lifestyles to suit their own needs and priorities, the idea of the family is adapting to changes in the social and personal needs and priorities of its members. As shown in Figure 16–1, marital (and therefore family) status in the U.S. population has changed markedly in recent decades: There are fewer married couples and more single and divorced people.

Divorce and Remarriage

As discussed in Chapter 14, for every three marriages that succeed, two fail. Although divorce is much more likely during young adulthood, it still occurs at significant rates in middle adulthood and beyond (see Figure 14–5, p. 489). What are some of the reasons that people divorce, and what happens when so many of them remarry?

Why Couples Divorce Marriages rarely fall apart suddenly. More often a breakup is the culmination of a long process of emotional distancing. The final months of the marriage are usually remembered as unhappy by both partners, although the eventual decision to divorce is usually made by one partner. The wife usually raises the issue first. Wives often are dissatisfied with a marriage earlier than husbands, and they are much more often the initiators of divorce (Kincaid & Caldwell, 1995).

In middle adulthood, couples get divorced for many of the same reasons that younger couples do. They want more from their marriage than they are

Figure 16–1 The Changing Marital Status of the U.S. Population, Age 18 and Over, 1970–1996 (In Percent)

Source: U.S. Census Bureau, 1997.

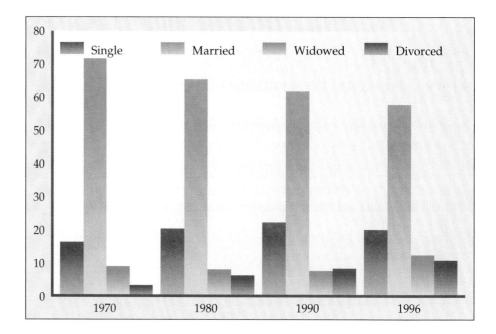

currently getting, and divorce appears preferable to continuing an unhappy relationship (Gigy & Kelly, 1992; Kincaid & Caldwell, 1995). In addition, if the marriage is shaky, the empty nest stage of the family life cycle may create a personal or marital crisis. Couples observe that it's no longer necessary to stay together for the sake of the children; they may wonder whether they want to spend the rest of their lives together. In addition, divorce is often associated with misconceptions about marriage. Churches, lawyers, marriage counselors, the media, family, and friends all pay homage to myths about what marriage is supposed to be. These myths often include unrealistic expectations that set the stage for failure.

Myths About Marriage, Divorce, and Remarriage   In 1999 about 2.4 million people in the United States got married and 1.6 million got divorced (NCHS, 2001). In other words, about two-thirds as many individuals divorced each other as married. Traditionally, over 40% of contemporary marriages involve the remarriage of one or both individuals, and almost half of all remarriages end in divorce (Coleman & Ganong, 1985). What are the reasons for this persistently high rate of marital failure?

There are, of course, many explanations. One of the most interesting is the argument that too many couples are swayed by myths about marriage and remarriage. A *myth* is defined as an oversimplified or downright erroneous belief that guides perceptions and expectations. Jessie Bernard (1981) provided a fascinating comparison of eight myths about marriage and divorce. Marilyn Coleman and John Ganong (1985; also see Ganong & Coleman, 1997) followed up with a corresponding analysis of myths about remarriage. These are summarized in Table 16–3.

Coping with Life After Divorce   When marriages fail, divorced people must pick up the pieces and start again. Especially when there are children, going on with life can be complicated indeed, as discussed in Chapter 14. The family as a system must make serious adjustments in practical living.

Mavis Hetherington and colleagues (Hetherington, Cox, & Cox, 1978) studied 96 divorced couples with children during a 2-year period and have conducted numerous studies in the years since (e.g., see Hetherington, 1999). The 1978 study is representative: Many of the divorced men and women suffered from a wide range of problems that they had not encountered while they were married. The practical problems of organizing and maintaining a household plagued many divorced men, who were accustomed to having their wives perform these tasks. Financial hardship was also reported by both men and women. With two households to support instead of one, some men found that their incomes were spread too thin to make ends meet. Many took a second job or worked overtime to make extra money. Women who had been homemakers before their divorce usually suffered financial strain—especially if their husbands failed to make court-ordered alimony or child support payments. Strapped by these new economic burdens, many women were forced to spend less time with their children and had little or no time for themselves.

Divorce can be particularly difficult in middle adulthood because the partners have grown accustomed to their way of life. The new financial and social circumstances that result from divorce may be wrenching to people in middle adulthood, especially if they are forced to concentrate on developmental tasks (going back to school, finding a new job, dating) that are considered more appropriate for people in early adulthood.

Disruption of the marital relationship, whether through divorce or death, is a stressful event. There is often grief and mourning over the loss of an intimate

Table 16-3 Myths of Marriage, Divorce, and Remarriage

Marriage

Everything will work out well if we love each other.

Always consider the other person first.

Emphasize the positive; keep criticisms to oneself.

If things go wrong, focus on the future.

See oneself as part of a couple first and then as an individual.

What's mine is yours.

Marriage makes people happier than they were before marriage.

What is best for the children will be best for us.

Divorce

Because we no longer love each other, nothing can work out any more.

Always consider oneself first.

Emphasize the negative and criticize everything.

If things go wrong, focus on the past.

See oneself as an individual first and then as part of a couple.

What's yours is mine.

Divorce makes people unhappy.

What is best for us must be devastating for the children.

Remarriage

This time we'll make it work by doing everything right.

Always consider everyone first.

Emphasize the positive and overlook the negative.

If things go wrong, think of what went wrong in the past and make sure it does not happen again.

Depending on one's personality, one might duplicate the marriage or divorce myth and see oneself either as part of a couple first or as an individual first.

What's mine is mine and what's yours is yours.

Marriage makes people significantly happier than they were before marriage.

What is best for us must be harmful to the children.

Sources: Bernard, 1981; Coleman & Ganong, 1985.

relationship, even when it was an unhappy one—people usually have second thoughts about whether they should have divorced. There is disruption of normal routines and patterns. There is the new independence and autonomy, whether welcome or unwelcome, as well as sheer loneliness at times. There are, however, marked differences between divorce and widowhood, as we see in Chapter 18.

Most people who are experiencing divorce perceive it as a kind of failure. For the partner who did not make the decision to divorce, there is often a feeling of rejection. Feelings of humiliation and powerlessness are not uncommon.

Even if the marriage was unsatisfactory, the final decision comes as a shock. For the partner who makes the decision, the stress is often higher during the agonizing months or years before the separation. The spouse who initiates the divorce may feel sadness, guilt, and anger, but there is at least a compensating sense of control. She or he has also rehearsed and mentally prepared for the separation (Kelly, 1982), which may come as a complete surprise to the other partner.

Starting a New Life Establishing a new lifestyle after divorce is easier for some people than for others. For some, the freedom from constraint, obligation, and emotional turmoil is a welcome relief. Women especially are likely to feel that they have a "new chance" after a divorce (Caldwell, Bloom, & Hodges, 1984; Kelly, 1982). For others, the idea of living alone is frightening. After a long period of marriage, older women often experience considerable difficulty relinquishing their previous role. In the past, women often had more difficulty than men maintaining friendships with their married peers and in managing financial and legal matters such as obtaining credit cards or securing a bank loan or mortgage. That has changed, but many divorced women still lack enough income to obtain credit. Individuals who married young have never been on their own and have little experience in coping with the independence that now confronts them. These newly single people often underestimate the problems of adjusting to being alone. Finally, regardless of the duration of the marriage, recently divorced men and women have higher rates of alcoholism, physical illness, and depression, sometimes as a direct result of the life changes resulting from separation.

Most divorced individuals experience considerable improvement in well-being within 2 or 3 years of the final separation (Spanier & Furstenberg, 1982). Divorced women are likely to have greater self-esteem (Wallerstein & Blakeslee, 1989). Divorced people with the strongest sense of well-being are likely to remarry within 3 or 4 years. In fact, divorced men have the highest rate of remarriage among all single groups. Overall, divorced men are three times as likely as divorced women to remarry. After age 40, most divorced men remarry, compared to only a third of divorced women (Spanier & Furstenberg, 1982). Many middle-aged men marry younger women and start a second family. Divorced people who develop new intimate relationships are more likely to experience a positive adjustment after divorce, partly because their new relationships diminish their attachments to their ex-spouse (Tschann, Johnston, & Wallerstein, 1989).

A sizable minority of divorced people remain bitter and isolated even 10 years after the divorce. Some men virtually lose contact with their children and, despite adequate resources, refuse to help cover costs such as college expenses (Wallerstein & Blakeslee, 1989). Some divorced women use their children as "weapons" against their ex-husbands, in an effort to produce guilt and shame.

Because divorce is so common, some researchers have studied why couples stay together instead of why they divorce (e.g., Lauer & Lauer, 1985; Lauer, Lauer, & Kerr, 1990). Although middle-aged men and women cite different reasons for remaining married, both list "My spouse is my best friend" as their primary reason. Interestingly, the top seven reasons listed by men and women who have been married for 15 years or more are the same:

- My spouse is my best friend.
- I like my spouse as a person.
- Marriage is a long-term commitment.

■ Marriage is sacred.
■ We agree on aims and goals.
■ My spouse has grown more interesting.
■ I want the relationship to succeed.

Although most happily married couples in the study were satisfied with their sex lives, it was not a primary factor in their happiness or marital satisfaction. Men listed satisfaction with sex as the 12th most important reason for staying together; women listed it as 14th.

Middle-aged people who remain married or remarry report higher levels of general happiness and satisfaction than those who are single. Marriage helps older people deal with stressful life events such as retirement, loss of income, illness, and disability. These positive effects stem from the sense of intimacy, interdependence, and belonging that marriage brings (Gilford, 1986).

Reconstituted Families

When divorced or widowed people with children remarry, they form **reconstituted or blended families,** also known as stepfamilies. These families present many more role adjustment problems for both stepparents and stepchildren than primary families do. With little preparation to handle their new roles and little support from the society around them, stepparents often find that achieving a satisfactory family relationship is harder than they ever imagined. Done properly, however, remarriage can reduce stress—particularly for the parent who has custody of the child (Furstenberg, 1987). A partner who is willing to share financial responsibilities, household tasks, child-rearing decisions, and so on can offer welcome relief to a divorced parent. Men who remarry, however, may have to deal with additional pressures if they are expected to provide financial support to two households.

In any event, second marriages are different from first marriages (Visher & Visher, 1998). They operate within a more complex family organization—stepchildren, ex-spouses, and former in-laws, for example—that can cause con-

reconstituted or blended family   A family in which partners with children have remarried or formed a cohabiting relationship.

Most stepparents and children ultimately make a positive adjustment to each other.

siderable conflict (Coleman & Ganong, 1996). Yet second marriages are often characterized by more open communication, greater acceptance of conflict, and more trust that any disagreements that arise can be resolved satisfactorily (Furstenberg, 1987).

Reconstituted Families in Perspective   There is a tendency to think that the current high divorce rate and the resulting high remarriage rate have created an entirely new phenomenon, but this is not the case. In fact, the current remarriage rate closely parallels remarriage rates in Europe and the United States in the seventeenth and eighteenth centuries. There is, however, a major difference. Today, most stepfamilies are created as a result of a marriage-divorce-remarriage sequence. In the past, most stepfamilies were a result of a marriage-death-remarriage sequence (Ihinger-Tallman & Pasley, 1987).

The difference between these two types of stepfamilies is, of course, the presence of a living former spouse. Contact with that former spouse often continues and may include shared custody, financial support, and visitation. In some families it is difficult to maintain distance, resolve conflicts, and avoid feelings of rejection by one spouse or the other. For the children, remarriage often creates a situation characterized by ambivalence, conflict, uncertainty, and divided loyalties. It is therefore not surprising that previously widowed stepparents often report more positive relationships with each other and with their children following remarriage than do previously divorced stepparents (Ihinger-Tallman & Pasley, 1987).

Learning to Live in a Reconstituted Family   The expectation that stepfamilies can simply pick up where the primary family left off is unrealistic and inevitably leads to frustration and disappointment. Both stepparents and stepchildren need time to adjust to one another—to learn about and test each other's personalities. To do this, the best advice is that stepparents try to establish a position in the children's lives that is different from the one held by the missing biological parent. If they try to compete with the child's real parent, they're more likely to fail.

When asked what the greatest difficulties are in a stepparent-stepchild relationship, most stepparents mention discipline, adjusting to the habits and personalities of the children, and gaining the children's acceptance (Kompara, 1980). Stepmothers often have more problems than stepfathers in adjusting to their new roles. Partly because of the stereotype of the "wicked stepmother" and partly because stepmothers spend more time with children than stepfathers do, stepmothers sometimes must overcome tremendous odds if they are to succeed.

There is also the popular stereotype of the stepchild. Stepchildren are seen as neglected, perhaps abused, and definitely not loved as much as the "real" child. Surveys of the general public and even of professionals who help stepfamilies find that these stereotypes are fairly widespread (Coleman & Ganong, 1987). Fairy tales like those of Cinderella and Hansel and Gretel reinforce the stereotypes. In reality, such stereotypes are inaccurate. When such a situation does exist (and it often does not), the stepparent is not always to blame. The children themselves may stand in the way. If they haven't accepted the divorce or loss of their biological parent, are used as pawns in a bitter, angry divorce, or hold an idealized view of the missing parent, children may reject the stepparent's love and make family harmony impossible.

Taking time to develop mutual trust, affection, a feeling of closeness, and respect for the child's point of view often helps in forming a workable relationship. Girls are likely to have greater difficulty forming a good relationship with a stepfather than boys are (Hetherington, 1992). This may be because the girl had a close relationship with her mother before the divorce and sees the stepfather as an intruder. Boys, on the other hand, often have tumultuous, conflictual relationships with their stepmothers.

Even though stepparents rarely duplicate the idealized biological parent's place in the child's life, they can often provide a loving, nurturant, and secure environment—one that is often more satisfactory than the one the child experienced before the divorce. Indeed, most stepparents and stepchildren eventually make positive adjustments (Clingempeel & Segal, 1986; Visher & Visher, 1998). This adjustment is more likely to occur if the stepfamily creates a new social unit that extends the characteristics of the children's biological family to include new relationship and communication styles, methods of discipline, and problem-solving strategies (Paernow, 1984; Pasley & Ihinger-Tallman, 1989; Whiteside, 1989).

CONTENT CHECK
THE CHANGING FAMILY

True–False (answers are on the Companion Website)

1. The reasons for divorce in middle adulthood are often the same as for divorce in young adulthood.
2. Adjusting to divorce in middle adulthood can be especially difficult because partners have to break up customary patterns of life.
3. Middle-adult couples who remain married or remarry are less happy than peers who remain single.
4. For children, parental remarriage often creates conflict and ambivalence.
5. Stepfathers tend to have more problems adjusting to their new role in a reconstituted family than do stepmothers.

Thinking Critically

In what ways are divorce, remarriage, and the creation of a stepfamily especially difficult in midlife?

Occupational Continuity and Change

Middle age is also a time when long-term career goals may be met, midcourse corrections may be needed, or disappointments become obvious. It is also a time when job-related stress can reach its peak.

Until recently it was thought that a person's working life consisted of—or should consist of—entering a particular occupation or career as a young adult and remaining in that occupation until retirement. Obviously, this "preferred" career course required a thoughtful choice of occupation and careful preparation at the outset. Once a person had begun a job, he or she was expected to lay the foundation for a lifetime career and climb the ladder of success as quickly as possible.

This scenario has changed considerably, partly because of the realization that adult development may produce many shifts in attitudes, career needs, and goals. Moreover, in today's technologically advanced and economically unsta-

A MATTER FOR DEBATE

DOWNSIZING AND OUTSOURCING

Corporate restructuring can take many forms as upper management attempts to minimize costs and maximize profits (often earning huge year-end bonuses for themselves in the process). *Downsizing* is one approach: Jobs are eliminated, workers are laid off permanently, and the remaining workers are expected to do more, work harder, and put in longer hours. *Outsourcing* is another: Work that was previously performed in-house is farmed out to other companies, which often hire some of the same people who were doing the work before but reduce their benefits (especially retirement plans) and eliminate their job security. As with downsized workers, outsourced workers are also expected to work harder and increase their productivity, expectations that greatly increase job stress (Gowing, Kraft, & Quick, 1997).

For those who are laid off as a result of corporate restructuring, joblessness is far more than an economic misfortune. It can be a psychological catastrophe for the unemployed and their families. It can cause illness, divide families, and create feelings of worthlessness and lack of self-esteem. For many, unemployment represents more than just loss of income. Unemployed

workers commonly report an increased incidence of headaches, stomach problems, and insomnia. They also smoke, drink, and worry a lot more than they did when they were working (Liem, 1981). Men who were socialized to be the family breadwinner are especially hard hit by unemployment. They suffer more depression and anxiety and have a higher incidence of psychotic behavior than men who are employed (Liem, 1981). Beyond that, illness, suicide, alcoholism, divorce, and even crime occur at epidemic rates among the unemployed. Left without a job, many workers feel that they have nothing to look forward to. They miss their coworkers and the routine of going to work. For many, the sense of hopelessness grows worse every time they are rejected for a new job. When this happens often enough, the worker may totally withdraw from the labor force. The rejection that unemployed workers feel may be exacerbated if friends and neighbors avoid them.

What about workers who survive restructuring? Constantly unsure of their future ("I might be the next to go"), and with greater demands placed on them, they are subject to many potential sources of stress (Burke &

Nelson, 1997). They experience role confusion, work overload, more office politics and conflicts, increased conflict between their job and their personal/family life, and in general a tense climate at work—with accompanying symptoms such as dizziness, stomach problems, and high blood pressure. Their job satisfaction wanes, and they may become angry, cynical, and depressed; their company loyalty is likely to evaporate.

What will be the long-run effects of the increasing trend toward downsizing and outsourcing? For now, that remains a matter for debate. At present unemployment is low, corporate profits and the stock markets are up, and the economy is generally viewed as healthy—with much of that health attributed to corporate restructuring. It's worth noting, however, that a similar condition existed around the beginning of the 20th century, when workers had few federally mandated rights and were exploited in every way imaginable.

We might well wonder whether downsizing and outsourcing are the modern world's way of turning back the clock. What do you think?

ble world, jobs change so quickly or are eliminated in such numbers that the one-career pattern no longer applies to most people. As Phyllis Moen put it, "The ground is shifting beneath them as the nature of work, family, careers, and retirement is being reconfigured" (1998). Downsizing and outsourcing are taking their toll on U.S. workers (see "A Matter for Debate," above). People frequently change employers or change positions within a company.

Although most people do not make truly dramatic changes once their careers have been established, it is now considered unusual for individuals to begin and end their working lives in the same job or career. This is especially true for women who interrupt their careers to spend a decade or more raising a family. At middle age they are ready to channel their energies into another form of generativity. It is in the workplace that these women gain a new sense of accomplishment and form meaningful, sustaining relationships. With this in mind, we examine the process of career reassessment that often takes place during middle adulthood, as well as responses to job change and stress.

Midcareer Reassessment

As we have seen, when we look at the work histories of individuals in the past several decades, it seems that the occupational life cycles described by Havighurst (Chapter 14) overlook a period of serious career reassessment or reexamination that often occurs at midlife, a time when workers report lower well-being than either younger or older workers (Warr, 1992). Reassessment occurs for a number of reasons. Two prominent ones are that workers find that they are not being promoted as rapidly as they had expected and that a job may turn out to be less desirable than anticipated. Middle-aged people who experience major midlife transitions are more likely to make dramatic changes in their occupation. Levinson (1978) found that adults in their 40s may experience a shift in their values and goals that leads them to consider changing the course of their career. Levinson explained the occurrence of this change in terms of the reappearance of the dream—the inspiration, ideals, and goals of youth. Research suggests that adults cope with this reassessment period best if they realistically and systematically assess their own abilities and the pluses and minuses of their current occupational position (Okun, 1984).

Eugene Thomas (1979) suggested that certain societal conditions permit people who experience such dramatic alterations in their values and attitudes to act on them. People now live longer and can work longer, so when their responsibilities to their children end, they are free to make changes that may even reduce their income or transform their way of living. When both spouses work, one spouse may continue to earn income while the other makes a career change. Thomas cites the greater tolerance for deviations from traditional social norms (including the wife supporting the husband), which makes it easier for people to act upon their new-found beliefs and ideals.

Still, only a minority of people make dramatic career shifts during midlife (Levinson, 1983). One reason they make such shifts is that they feel that their abilities are underutilized at their current job, perhaps because of changes in the job or because there are fewer challenges once a person has developed a high level of expertise. Another reason is **job burnout**—a feeling of being unable to endure the job any more, accompanied by a strong sense of dread each morning when it's time to go to work. Burnout is not restricted to middle adulthood, of course (Stagner, 1985). Indeed, the entire process of reappraising your life structure, including work, is not restricted to middle adulthood (Levinson, 1986).

Job Change and Stress

For many people, career changes are not welcome and may not go smoothly. Occupational instability can be harmful. Workers who move through predictable, on-schedule events in the course of their lives generally experience less stress than those who must cope with unpredictable, off-schedule ones. Careers in which progress and promotions do not occur as expected, forced career shifts or sudden unemployment may cause high levels of stress, anxiety, and disequilibrium. Other off-time events encountered by middle-aged workers may include the need to return to school to prepare for new careers, or long periods away from work to upgrade their skills to continue progressing in their present careers.

Job Loss People who get fired, are laid off indefinitely, or experience forced retirement often face emotional problems that may outweigh the problem of loss of income (again see "A Matter for Debate, page 561). Many people's self-

job burnout The emotional exhaustion that often affects people particularly in high-stress professions and trades.

concept is destroyed and their self-esteem shattered. Individuals often react to career loss in ways that are similar to the grief response triggered by the death of a loved one. The pattern of grieving that may follow sudden, involuntary job loss begins with initial shock and disbelief, followed by anger and protest. Some people even go through a bargaining stage similar to that experienced by terminally ill patients, in which they plead (with employers, spouses, or God) for more time, a second chance, and so on. This stage may be followed by depression, loneliness, or physical ailments. Jobless workers may feel panic, guilt about the loss, or resentment, and may be unable to participate in their normal activities, even though these are unrelated to work. Occasionally they even "go postal"—an unfortunate term that refers to highly publicized postal workers who have sought murderous revenge on those whom they perceived as responsible for their job loss, along with anyone else who happened to be around at the time.

For middle adults, job loss may be far more difficult to cope with than for young adults, as more of the older person's identity tends to be invested in the job.

Once the grief and anger reactions have passed, the person can begin to accommodate the loss, develop hope, and redirect her or his energies toward finding another job or career. However, job loss may be more difficult to resolve for middle-aged people than for young adults. First, it is likely that the middle-aged individual has more of his or her identity invested in the job. Second, older people are likely to face age discrimination both in hiring and in training programs—in spite of federal laws barring such discrimination. Third, whatever job the worker can find is likely to have a lower salary and status than the previous one (Kelvin & Jarrett, 1985; Sinfeld, 1985). People who have worked their way up the job hierarchy in a company to a position that is beyond their educational qualifications are particularly vulnerable to reduced salary and loss of status because their skills are often specific to that particular company.

In general, those who cope best with job loss try to take it in stride and not turn their anger inward by blaming themselves or considering themselves professional and personal failures. Additional factors that determine how well people cope with job loss are summarized in Table 16–4.

Job Burnout Burnout, as noted earlier, is a psychological state of emotional exhaustion, often accompanied by extreme cynicism, that is especially prevalent among individuals in the helping professions (Schaufeli, Maslach, & Marek, 1993). Social workers, police officers, nurses, therapists, teachers, and others who must work in close personal contact with those whom they serve—often in strained, tension-filled situations—are especially at risk. In a different sense, burnout also applies to the effect on people who have worked hard and spent all their energies toward reaching a virtually impossible goal—and failed (Freudenberger & Richelson, 1980). Workers in low-status, subordinate positions who cannot respond to maltreatment they sometimes experience on the job may also suffer burnout (Holt, 1982).

By and large, people in the helping professions who suffer job burnout are idealistic, highly motivated, extremely competent workers who finally realize that they cannot make the difference they once thought they could. Here, the general cause of burnout is lack of rewards in a work situation in which great effort has been expended and high hopes originally predominated (Chance, 1981). It is also important to note as Christina Maslach and colleagues have emphasized, that burnout in the helping professions and other settings is primarily the fault of the organization—not the individual (e.g., Maslach & Goldberg, 1998; Maslach & Laiter, 1997).

People who experience burnout often start out with high ideals and the best of intentions. In the course of their work, they realize that they are having little

Table 16-4 Factors in Coping with Job Loss

Physical health

One of the first ways of coping with losing a job is to find another one, and it is easier for individuals to present themselves effectively during job interviews if they are in good health. Being in good physical condition also adds to the ability to handle the stress, unforeseen challenges, and fatigue associated with losing a job.

Physical and financial resources

Losing a job places greater stress on individuals who have no financial resources than on those who can pay their bills while they are looking for work. Those without financial resources may be forced to sell their house and scale down their lifestyle—all of which adds to the stress created by the job loss.

Specific skills

People with marketable job skills will probably have less difficulty finding a job than those with inadequate or outmoded training.

Social support

An individual who is surrounded by a loving, supportive family can often cope better with job loss than someone who is alone or has troubled family relations.

Cognitive understanding of events

The ability to understand the reasons behind a job loss (was it corporate downsizing, poor performance, or a personality clash?) helps the individual handle the dislocation and gather the energy to search for a new job. This ability comes partly from education and past experience.

Anticipation and preparation

An aerospace engineer who understood the implications of the dismantling of the Soviet Union and the end of the cold war could anticipate the possibility of job loss and train for employment in related fields well in advance of being laid off. People who can't or don't anticipate job loss are left with fewer options.

Personality factors

Personality traits such as flexibility, openness to experience, and resilience prepare the individual to handle the pressures associated with finding a new job.

Life history

Individuals who have lost jobs before and have lived through periods of unemployment may react differently to a job loss than those who have never had these experiences.

effect on the people they are trying to aid or that the problems they are trying to solve are so overwhelming and the tasks so difficult that they can never succeed. The problems that some have chosen to tackle—poverty, educational failure, disease and disease prevention, family violence, drug abuse—are difficult or impossible to solve. Plus, the people they try to help may resent their efforts. To make matters even worse, they may also be forced to spend hours filling out forms to comply with institutional, state, and federal regulations, a thankless task that takes considerable time and energy away from helping people.

Early warning signs of burnout include increasingly frequent anger, frustration, and despair. Work becomes a burden that the individual can no longer handle. Burned-out workers may even turn on the people they are supposed to help, or withdraw from emotional involvement into cold detachment. Physical exhaustion, psychosomatic illnesses, low morale, mediocre performance, and absenteeism commonly accompany burnout (Schaufeli et al., 1993).

There is little anyone can do to eliminate the causes of burnout without completely transforming society and the situations in which people work. Workers can, however, avoid or at least minimize burnout by learning to be realistic in their approach to their work and their goals, promoting changes in their job requirements or work flow, attempting to keep the rest of their life separate from their work (i.e., not taking their work troubles home with them), and developing interests outside of their jobs. That's actually good advice for all workers, not just potential burnout victims.

Job Stress in Context   Job stress is not simply a function of what goes on in the workplace. Both men and women have a large number of work and family roles that sometimes compete with one another. A subtle form of discrimination is sometimes practiced in the workplace when only women are thought to have such competing roles; sometimes it is feared that women will bring their family problems to work, and therefore that they are less qualified than men to hold responsible jobs. Thus, they may quit or find themselves under too much stress to deal effectively with the demands of work. Some authors suggest that if we include the multiplicity of work and family roles in our models of work stress, we rediscover men's roles as fathers and husbands. With this type of model, men as well as women could feel free to acknowledge and deal with family-based as well as work-based sources of stress, and organizations could make adjustments to adapt to the conflicting demands of work and family (Baruch, Biener, & Barnett, 1987).

CONTENT CHECK
OCCUPATIONAL CONTINUITY AND CHANGE

True–False (answers are on the Companion Website)

1. In midlife, job-related stress may reach its peak.
2. Midlife is often a period of job stability.
3. The pattern of grieving after job loss frequently tends to be similar to that following the death of a loved one.
4. People in corporate executive positions are most vulnerable to job burnout.
5. Women have far more competing work and family roles that conflict with each other than do men.

Thinking Critically

Why does midlife tend to be a period of career reassessment for both men and women?

CHAPTER 16 REVISITED

Personality Continuity and Change

■ The course of midlife is extremely diverse and varied, and the middle and later years can be very complex because of both adolescent or young adult children and aging parents.

■ According to Erikson, the basic issue facing people at this time of life is generativity versus self-absorption, within three domains: procreative, productive, and creative.

■ Peck proposed that the issues and tasks of middle and older adulthood are more numerous than suggested by Erikson; he proposed four additional conflicts of middle adulthood and three of older adulthood.

■ Middle adult men feel committed to both work and family, yet have to face caring for aging parents, dealing with adolescent children, and coming to terms with personal limitations and increasing physical vulnerability.

■ Middle-adult men face four paths: transcendent-generative, pseudo-developed, midlife crisis, or punitive-disenchanted.

■ Traditionally, women define themselves in terms of the family cycle more so than the career cycle. Four types of midlife women are: traditional, innovative, expansive, and protesters.

■ Common stresses for middle-adult women involve family and career, plus role strain.

Family and Friends: Interpersonal Contexts

■ Midlife people act as a bridge between the younger and older generations, as kinkeepers, maintainers of family rituals, celebrators of achievements, and family historians.

■ An important transition is launching children, which has its pros and cons.

■ After successfully launching their last child, parents tend to turn to roles and interests other than parenthood as they experience the empty nest.

■ The relationship between parents and their children becomes more reciprocal; how adult children behave toward their parents depends to a large extent on their life experiences and their stage in the family life cycle.

■ Most middle adults have an ongoing relationship with their aging parents.

■ With age, role reversals gradually take place; middle adults become the generation in charge.

■ Many middle adults take responsibility for the long-term care of their parents; daughters are much more likely than sons to do so.

■ The majority of people in the United States become grandparents in middle adulthood; four of their important roles are providing stability, being available in times of emergency, acting as arbitrator, and maintaining the family's biography.

■ Friendships during middle adulthood often fill many vital emotional needs.

The Changing Family

■ Divorce usually occurs as the culmination of a long process of emotional distancing; divorce is also associated with unrealistic expectations about marriage.

■ Divorced people suffer from a wide range of problems; divorce can be particularly difficult in middle adulthood.

■ Establishing a new lifestyle after divorce is easier for some than for others.

■ Most divorced people individuals feel much better within 2 or 3 years of the final separation; some remain bitter and isolated indefinitely.

■ Middle adults who remain married or remarry report higher levels of general happiness and satisfaction than those who are single.

■ Remarriage often creates a reconstituted or blended family, which may pose role adjustment problems and conflicts for both stepparents and stepchildren.

■ The greatest difficulties in a stepparent-stepchild relationship are discipline, adjusting to the habits and personalities of the children, and gaining the children's acceptance. Taking time to develop mutual trust, affection, and respect often helps.

Occupational Continuity and Change

■ Adult development may produce many shifts in attitudes, career needs, and goals; the one-career pattern no longer applies to most people.

■ A period of serious career reassessment or reexamination often occurs at midlife.

- Middle adults who experience major midlife transitions are more likely to make dramatic changes in their occupations.

- People who get fired, are laid off indefinitely, or experience forced retirement often face emotional difficulties similar to grief.

- Those who cope best with job loss try to take it in stride and not turn their anger inward by blaming themselves or considering themselves failures.

- Job burnout is a psychological state of emotional exhaustion, often accompanied by extreme cynicism, that is especially prevalent among individuals in the helping professions.

KEY TERMS

transcendent-generative man
pseudo-developed man
man in midlife crisis
punitive-disenchanted man
traditional woman

innovative woman
expansive woman
protesting woman
role strain
kinkeeper

launching of adolescents
empty nest
reconstituted or blended family
job burnout

OLDER ADULTHOOD: PHYSICAL AND COGNITIVE DEVELOPMENT

17

CHAPTER PREVIEW

Do you know:

1. Why most stereotypes associated with aging are *myths*?

2. That many of these myths are *positive*?

3. How great the differences are in how cultures view *older adulthood*?

4. How *categorizing* older adults into a single group negatively impacts on them?

5. That older adulthood actually consists of four distinct *periods*?

6. What *physical changes* are associated with aging and what factors are involved in these changes?

7. What *chronic problems* older adults encounter?

8. How *poor nutrition* and *misuse of prescribed medication* increase the health problems of older adults?

9. How heredity and environment *interact* in the aging process?

10. The differences between *stochastic* and *preprogrammed* theories of aging?

11. The *cognitive changes* associated with later adulthood?

12. The primary and secondary processes that affect cognitive decline, including *dementia* and *Alzheimer's disease*?

13. The ways older people can *compensate* for declines in cognitive functioning?

These are the main topics of Chapter 17.

Some years ago, Don and his 77-year-old father Horace were huffing and puffing up a hilly trail in a high-altitude national park; they were passed by two much younger men who were briskly taking the hill in stride. As the young men went by, one of them glanced back and then said to the other, "Man, I sure don't want to get old." Horace immediately responded, with a twinkle in his eye, "Neither do I!" Age is relative; how old you are depends a lot on how old you *think* you are.

Older adulthood is an important period in its own right. It begins in the early 60s for most people, and for some it may span 40 years or more. In some societies, people in their older adult years are recognized as elders and awarded high status. In contrast, Western societies seem to have only recently rediscovered this large and growing segment of the population, often somewhat disparagingly called "senior citizens."

In this chapter we look at the physical and intellectual development that occurs in older adulthood, along with individual reactions to predictable developmental changes. Although it may seem odd to use the term *development* in the chapter title, the term actually refers to both growth and decline as a result of the influences of heredity and environment.

Aging Today

What is it like to grow old? For many people, the prospects are so grim that they never want to find out. In fact, many younger people seem to view older adulthood as a state of marginal existence. They fear the losses of energy, control, flexibility, sexuality, physical mobility, memory, and even intelligence that they think go hand in hand with aging. We start by examining some of the stereotypes of older adults and the impact that these have on everyone concerned. Then we take a decade-by-decade look at some of the actual characteristics of older adults.

Ageism and Stereotypes

Older people are often stereotyped in Western nations. Polls of the U.S. population, including older adults, have documented both negative and positive images of older people (see Table 17–1). Such stereotypes make it difficult to see older people accurately, to understand them as the varied individuals they really are. Stereotypes may even lead to attitudes and policies that discourage older adults from active participation in work and leisure activities. Studies also indicate that there are gender differences in people's perceptions of aging. For example, in a survey of popular movies over the last several decades, Doris Bazzini and colleagues (Bazzini, McIntosh, Smith, Cook, & Harris, 1997) found that older women are more often portrayed as unattractive, unfriendly, and unintelligent than are older men.

The Error of Generalizing from the Few to the Many   Objectively, the situation of some older persons seems unfulfilling. On average, today's older adults have a lower educational level than the younger population. Some nursing homes have become notorious for taking advantage of older people, giving them just enough care for survival and little reason to live and thrive. Aside from stories about nursing home abuses, newspapers are also filled with gruesome stories about older women being mugged and robbed and even raped by vicious young people, and about desperate older people shoplifting hamburger meat or living on canned dog food. Until aggressive advocacy groups like the Gray Panthers began to voice the needs of older people and the American Association of Retired Persons (AARP) began organizing resources to help older adults, most people assumed that older people were not even able to speak for themselves. There has also been such a lack of interest in older people that almost no research was conducted on them until the past four decades. Bernice Neugarten (1970) used the word **ageism** to describe this attitude of indifference and neglect. No wonder older adulthood has often seemed to be a horrible fate in Western nations.

Do the stereotypes of the past still exist now that people over age 65 have become a significant and growing minority and public awareness of them has greatly increased? At California State University, 160 students were asked a series of questions about what old people are like (Babladelis, 1987). They estimated that 30% of the U.S. population was old and in need of services. They thought that the word *old* should apply to people over age 60. They reported that although they had family members and neighbors who were old, they were "reluctant to spend time with old people." They reported having a concerned, dutiful attitude toward them, but that old people had a lot of undesirable characteristics—such as being senile, self-centered, boring, and too

ageism In Western societies, a widely prevalent attitude that overvalues youth and degrades older persons.

Table 17-1 **Common Misperceptions About the Elderly Based on Stereotypes**

Examples of Misperceptions Based on Negative Stereotypes

Most older people are poor.

Most older people are unable to keep up with inflation.

Most older people are ill-housed.

Most older people are frail and in poor health.

The aged are impotent as a political force and require advocacy.

Most older people are inadequate employees; they are less productive, efficient, motivated, innovative, and creative than younger workers. Most older workers are accident-prone.

Older people are mentally slower and more forgetful; they are less able to learn new things.

Older people tend to be intellectually rigid and dogmatic. Most old persons are set in their ways and unable or unwilling to change.

A majority of older people are socially isolated and lonely. Most are disengaging or disengaged from society.

Most older people are confined to long-term-care institutions.

Examples of Misperceptions Based on Positive Stereotypes

The aged are relatively well off; they are not poor but in good economic shape. Their benefits are generously provided by working members of society.

The aged are a potential political force that votes and participates in unity and in great numbers.

Older people make friends very easily. They are kind and amiable.

Most older people are mature, experienced, wise, and interesting.

Most older people are good listeners and are especially patient with children.

A majority of older people are very kind and generous to their children and grandchildren.

Source: S. Lubomudrov (1987). Congressional Perceptions of the Elderly: The Use of Stereotypes in the Legislative Process. *Journal of Gerontology, 27*, 77–81. Copyright © The Gerontological Society of America.

talkative. They viewed old people as generally physically disabled. Even though many of these students had grandparents in their 60s who were quite vigorous, their attitudes about the old had not changed dramatically from similar attitudes prevailing in the late 1970s (Babladelis, 1987).

In general, and especially in the United States, people of all ages tend to assign more negative stereotypes to older people and more positive ones to younger people (Hummert, Garstka, Shaner, & Strahm, 1995; Hummert, Mazloff, & Henry, 1999). Negative attitudes and stereotypes about older people are not necessarily the rule, however. Several studies have found that attitudes toward older people are often ambivalent, if not contradictory. Older people are often seen as both wise and senile, both kind and grouchy, and both concerned for others and inactive and unsociable (Crockett & Hummert, 1987). Thus, the stereotypes just presented are a mosaic of fact and fantasy. Some problems are only loosely associated with aging; failing health and loneliness do not have to be part of aging any more than acne and awkwardness have to be part of adolescence. The population over age 65 has its marathoners and executives as well as its shut-ins and bench-sitters. Negative stereotypes not only instill fear of aging in the young but also have a powerful grip on older people. Polls have shown that most older adults have a much higher opinion of their own economic and social condition than does the general public. At the same time, however, they often believe that they are among the lucky few who have escaped the misery of aging in the United States.

A Sociocultural Perspective   People have not always dreaded getting old. In many of the world's religions, elders are considered to possess great wisdom. Among Native Americans throughout the hemisphere, older people have traditionally been venerated as wise elders, transmitters of culture, and a storehouse of historical lore. In China, Japan (Maeda, 1992), and other Asian nations, older people are venerated and respected in a tradition known as **filial piety.** In Japan, for example, more than three out of four older adults live with their children, and respect is demonstrated through a variety of everyday activities. At home, meals are prepared with everyone's tastes in mind, and in public, people bow with respect when they pass an older person. However, although respect for older people remains strong in Japan, it is more pronounced among middle-aged and rural people than young adults and urban residents (Palmore & Maeda, 1985).

In many non Western societies, including China, Japan, and other Asian nations, older people tend to be venerated and respected.

In colonial times prior to the establishment of the United States, the Biblical tradition of veneration for elders was a powerful cultural influence. Long life was viewed as an outward manifestation of divine grace and favor, the reward for an extraordinarily upright life. Benjamin Franklin played a major role in drafting the Constitution not only because he was a shrewd parliamentarian but also because he was over 80 years old at the time and was viewed as "crowned" with the glory of his years. From a pragmatic point of view, reverence for age was powerful because so few people managed to achieve it. The demographic contrast between then and now is startling; in the colonial period, the median age of the population was 16 and only 2% reached the age of 65. Some accounts of early colonists describe adults in their 30s as wrinkled, balding, or gray (Fischer, 1978).

Today, the median age of the U.S. population is 35.7 and climbing (U.S. Census Bureau, 1999). Approximately 1 in 8 people is 65 or older. As a result of the aging of the baby boomers and the trend toward lower birth rates and declining death rates, the percentage of the population over age 65 will rise dramatically in the next three decades. According to U.S. Census Bureau projections, by the year 2030 1 out of every 5 people will be 65 or older (see Table 17–2). Modern medicine helps many people survive serious illnesses and injuries, and some people continue to live despite severe impairments. However, many other older people are vigorous, involved, and independent. Clearly, we are witnessing the emergence of an unprecedented group of healthy, educated, retired or partly retired older people, at least in the developed nations. Figure 17–1 shows population pyramids for men and women in selected nations (shaded areas represent percentages in the paid labor force). Note in particular the much larger number of people in the 65 and older age range in developed nations like the United States.

Four Decades of Later Life

Nowadays in the United States, an average 60-year-old can expect to live about another 22 years; those who are now 75 years old can look forward to about 11 more years (Anderson, 2001). Thus, the period beyond 60 has become a

filial piety   The veneration given the elderly in Asian and other cultures. This respect is manifested in cultural traditions as well as everyday encounters.

Table 17-2   Aging of the Population: Percentage of the Population 65 Years of Age and Over

Actual		Projected	
YEAR	**TOTAL**	**YEAR**	**TOTAL**
1950	8.1%	2000	12.8%
1960	9.2	2010	13.4
1970	9.8	2020	16.3
1980	11.3	2030	20.1
1990	12.5		

Source: U.S. Census Bureau, 1997.

significant part of the lifespan. However, individuals in later adulthood are not a homogeneous group. A currently employed or newly retired and relatively hardy 65-year-old may be caring for an 85- or 90-year-old parent who may be quite frail. These people are members of two separate generations; they are clearly different cohorts with respect to historical events. In addition, many older people behave more like younger people. Medical advances as well as cultural factors influence the way older people live. Today, many active 70-year-olds are doing things that people in their 50s did just 30 years ago (Neugarten & Neugarten, 1987).

Irene Burnside and colleagues (Burnside, Ebersole, & Monea, 1979) analyzed older adulthood in terms of four decades of later life. Let's look at the major features of each decade.

"Young-Old": 60 to 69   This decade marks a major transition. In our 60s, most of us must begin to adapt to a new role structure (Havighurst, 1972). Income is often reduced by retirement or reduced hours of work—whether voluntarily or otherwise—and some friends and colleagues die. Society frequently reduces its expectations of people in their 60s, demanding less energy, independence, and creativity. Burnside lamented this social response, believing that it demoralizes older adults, especially those who remain healthy and vigorous (1993). Many people in their 60s accept these expectations and respond by slowing the pace of their life, thereby creating a self-fulfilling prophecy.

Physical strength does wane somewhat, and reduced strength may pose problems for industrial workers who are still on the job. Yet many people in their 60s have plenty of energy and seek out new and different activities. Many recently retired people are healthy, hardy, and well educated. They may use their new leisure time for self-enhancement or for community or political activities. Some enjoy regular athletic and sexual activity. Some retirees are determined to remain givers, producers, and mentors. They become volunteer executives in small businesses, visitors to hospitals, or foster grandparents.

There is tremendous variation in this age group with regard to retirement. Whereas most people retire at around age 65, others retire at age 55 and still others at age 75. Retirement decisions in any decade depend on such issues as health, energy level, and type of work. (As noted in an earlier chapter, those who perform hard physical labor are likely to be forced to retire much earlier than those who do white-collar work.) The decision to retire also depends on interpersonal factors such as the health of a spouse and the relocation of friends, as

Figure 17-1 **Population Pyramid for Selected Nations**

Source: U.S. Census Bureau, 1990.

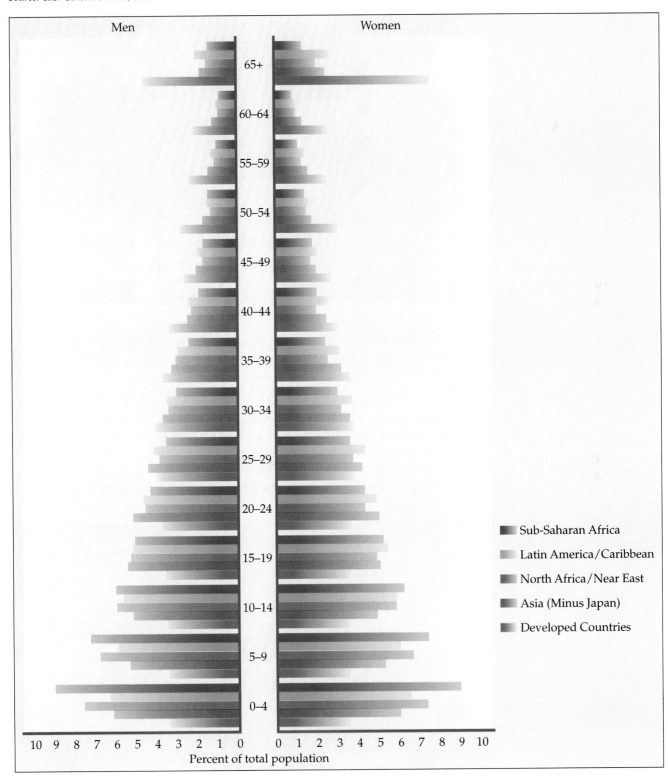

Many recently retired people become involved in community or political activities during their new leisure time.

well as "environmental" issues such as family finances (Quinn & Burkhauser, 1990). Whereas one 68-year-old with little savings may be forced to continue working to pay the bills, another may be able to retire in comfort on a pension and invested savings supplemented by Social Security or other benefits.

"Middle-Aged-Old": 70 to 79 A bigger shift occurs in our 70s than in the previous two decades. According to Burnside, the major developmental task of people in their 70s is to maintain the personality integration they achieved by their 60s. Many people in their 70s (**septuagenarians**) suffer loss and illness. More friends and family members die. Along with a contracting social world,

septuagenarians People in their 70s.

Most people over 70 maintain their independence by living in their own homes.

many must cope with reduced participation in formal organizations. They often exhibit restlessness and irritability. Their own health problems tend to become more troublesome during this decade. There is often a decline in sexual activity for both men and women, in many cases because of the loss of a sexual partner. Despite these losses, many septuagenarians are able to avoid the more serious effects of the disabilities that often accompany advanced age. Often those who have suffered heart attacks, strokes, or cancer survive—most without serious disability—because of improved medical care and healthier lifestyles (see Figure 17–2) (Note that this figure is limited to patterns of death and disability for women because they far outnumber men in the later decades.)

"Old-Old": 80 to 89   Although age is certainly one of the markers of the transition from young-old to old-old, it is not the only one. Being in one's 80s has been poignantly described as a "gradual process which begins the very first day one begins to live in his [or her] memories" (Burnside et al., 1979).

Most people in their 80s (**octogenarians**) experience increased difficulty in adapting to and interacting with their surroundings. Many need a streamlined, barrier-free environment that offers both privacy and stimulation. They need help in maintaining social and cultural contacts.

Most, but not all, 85-year-olds are frail. But frailty does not necessarily imply disability or total dependence. Although 25% of U.S. people currently in this age group were hospitalized for some time in the previous year, only 10% are seriously disabled. Most people over age 85 live in their own homes; only 19% reside in nursing homes (NCHS, 1999). Nevertheless, caring for frail older people is increasingly a matter of international concern. We consider social policy and frail older persons in more detail in Chapter 18.

People over 85 make up the fastest-growing group in the U.S. population, and **centenarians** (people over 100) are the fastest-growing segment worldwide (see "A Closer Look," on page 578). In the United States in 1980, there were 2.24 million people over age 85; in 1998, there were 4.05 million—over two-thirds of whom were women (U.S. Census Bureau, 1999). By 2040, because of the baby

octogenarians   People in their 80s.

centenarians   People over age 100.

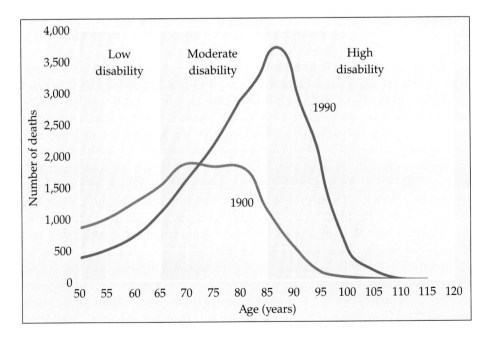

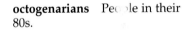

Figure 17–2   Deaths by Age, U.S. Females
Patterns of disability and death are changing. Because of healthier lifestyles and improved medical care, people are living longer than ever before with heart disease, stroke, and cancer. As a result of extended life, people 85 years and older may live with a high level of disability.

Source: From "The Aging of the Human Species" by S. Jay Olshansky, Bruce A. Carnes, and Christine K. Cassel. Copyright © 1993 by Scientific American, Inc. All rights reserved.

A CLOSER LOOK

CENTENARIAN CENTURY?

You may be surprised to learn that the age group 100 and older is the fastest-growing segment of the world's population. In 1998, the United Nations' Population Division reported that about 135,000 people around the world were 100 years old or over. Of these, the U.S. Census Bureau estimated that there were about 59,000 U.S. centenarians, about 83% of whom were woman (U.S. Census Bureau, 2001). For the year 2050 centenarians are projected to reach 2.2 million worldwide and 834,000 in the United States (Volz, 2000).

What's behind these statistics? It's a decreasing mortality rate attributable to improved public health, wider distribution of health information through the media, and medical advances such as the development of antibiotics and vaccines to combat previously terminal illnesses, along with better sanitation and higher living standards. Physical exercise is another key factor, as is mental exercise—education itself and the desire never to stop learning help extend life. Education seems especially vital as it relates to increased opportunity for higher economic and health status.

Because, until recently, the number of centenarians has been so small, they have been a virtually ignored segment of society. The situation is changing as social scientists and health care specialists are turning their attention to life styles of centenarians. What has emerged so far is that many people in their late 90s or 100s are, contrary to popular belief, leading active healthy lives until their death, with their cognitive skills declining only minimally.

Researchers also are continuing to work on finding genetic keys to slowing or reversing the aging process. Others have found amazing absences of Alzheimer's and dementia. Results like these have led Harvard researcher Thomas Perls to speculate that the good brain health among centenarians may be "a survival of the fittest phenomenon." Another surprising discovery is the association of late motherhood with longer lives. Women who had children in their 40s were substantially represented among female centenarians in suburban Boston (Perls, 1995). These women's late maternal age may be an indicator of the slow aging of their reproductive system and as such a predictor of their living to very old age.

For centenarians-in-the-making, Walter Bortz, former president of the American Geriatrics Society, suggested following what he called the DARE guidelines—diet, attitude, renewal, and exercise. The value of diet and exercise has been linked to longevity, but attitudes may be equally crucial—that is, maintaining an optimistic belief you will reach 100 and the idea that very old age is entirely possible for you to achieve may actually help you to achieve it. Similarly, your capacity to renew yourself and to pick yourself up after the inevitable losses associated with aging may also increase your possibility of becoming a member of that rapidly expanding club, the centenarians.

Primary source: Wagner, 1999.

---

boom, the number of people over age 85 is expected to swell to between 8 million and 13 million (U.S. Census Bureau, 1995).

"Very Old-Old": 90 and Over   There are fewer data on people over age 90 (**nonagenarians**) than on 60-, 70-, or 80-year-olds. It is difficult to obtain accurate information about the health and social circumstances of people in this age group.

Although health problems become more severe, nonagenarians can successfully alter their activities so as to make the most of what they have. One practicing psychiatrist in her 90s advised creating new fields of activity by removing the competitive element of earlier years. She emphasized the advantages of older adulthood, such as freedom from work pressures and responsibilities (Burnside et al., 1979). The changes that shape life in our 90s occur gradually and over a long period. If previous crises have been resolved in satisfactory ways, this decade can be joyful, serene, and fulfilling. It is also noteworthy that people who survive to their 90s are often healthier, more agile, and more active than people 20 years younger (Perls, 1995; Bould & Longino, 1997); the reason is that they have survived the diseases and other afflictions that cause some people to die in their 70s and 80s.

To reiterate, "the aged" are not a single cohesive group but, rather, a collection of subgroups, ranging from the active 65-year-old to the frail nonagenarian. Each group has its unique problems and abilities. To an extent, many share age-related difficulties of reduced income, failing health, and loss of loved ones.

nonagenarians   People in their 90s.

But *having* a problem is not the same as *being* a problem. The all-too-popular view of people over age 65 as needy, unproductive, and unhappy is an inaccurate one indeed.

CONTENT CHECK
AGING TODAY

True–False (answers are on the Companion Website)

1. People generally assign more negative stereotypes to older people and more positive ones to younger people.
2. Society often reduces its expectations for people in their 60s.
3. Many people in their 70s must deal with loss and illness.
4. Most people in their 80s are totally dependent on others.
5. People in their 90s are usually sick and are no longer able to be physically or socially active.

Thinking Critically

What are the harmful effects of both negative and positive stereotypes on older people?

Physical Aspects of Aging

The physical aspects of aging determine many of the changes and limitations that occur in later adulthood. Physical aging is universal. It comes sooner for some people and later for others, but it is inevitable. All bodily systems age, even under optimal genetic and environmental circumstances, although they do not age at the same rate. Yet for most bodily systems the processes of aging begin in early and middle adulthood. Many of the effects of aging are not noticed until later adulthood because aging is gradual and most physical systems have considerable reserve capacity. Most individuals do not experience interruptions in daily living or major health problems until well into their 70s. With regard to life expectancy, Figure 17–3 shows that both black men and white men tend to have shorter lifespans than women, and that white women have the longest life expectancy of all.

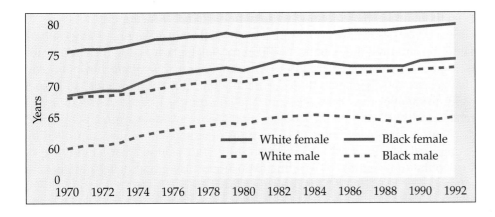

Figure 17–3 Life Expectancies by Gender and Ethnicity 1970–1992

Source: NCHS, 1995.

The sensory and systemic slowdowns that we will examine here commonly accompany age, but not all older people show these signs of aging. Studies have found that people who remain physically fit and active can perform as well as younger people who are not physically fit (Birren et al., 1980). In addition, we cannot say that the predictable biological course of nature is the only explanation for physical aging. Many people who become partially or completely deaf in older adulthood do so because of experiences earlier in life—such as a firecracker that went off close to their ear or frequent attendance at loud music concerts. Similarly, for most sensory deficiencies and defects of the internal organs, individual experiences begin the process of decline. Lifelong smokers may develop breathing problems in later years. An older woman with back trouble may have suffered strain as a young mother when she lifted her children. A 65-year-old man with heart trouble may have had early warning signs with a brief illness at age 40. Thus, not all of the changes that come with age are part of a normal aging process. The kind of life individuals have led and the illnesses and accidents they have experienced all contribute. These factors are sometimes called **pathological aging factors** (Elias & Marshall, 1987). Some experts believe that the cumulative effects of disease and accidents are so much a part of life that it is impossible to separate them from the normal aspects of aging (Kohn, 1985).

We begin this section by looking at some of the more common physical changes that are the result of aging. Then we discuss some diseases and personal habits that contribute to physical decline.

The Changing Body

Our bodies change in a number of ways during older adulthood. Specifically, changes occur in appearance, the senses, muscles, bones, mobility, and internal organs. Daily cycles change as well, though not always as a result of aging per se—as discussed in "In Theory, In Fact," on facing page.

Appearance A look in the mirror provides clear evidence of the aging process. The gray hair, the aging skin, a shift in posture, and deepening wrinkles are telltale signs. The skin becomes drier, thinner, and less elastic. In earlier years, wrinkles were formed by the use of particular muscles; "laugh lines" are an example. In older age, wrinkles are caused partly by loss of fat tissue under the skin and partly by the decrease in the skin's elasticity. The skin may take on the crisscrossed look of soft, crumpled paper or fine parchment (Rossman, 1977). There may be an increase in warts on the trunk, face, and scalp. Small blood vessels often break, producing tiny black-and-blue marks. Age spots may appear; these brown areas of pigmentation are popularly called "liver spots" even though they have nothing to do with the liver's functioning.

Some changes in appearance are a result of the normal aging that we all experience, although they can be modified by genetic factors. Identical twins, for example, show very similar patterns of aging. For many people, however, skin changes are closely related to exposure to wind, climate, abrasions, and especially ultraviolet rays from the sun. The sun diminishes the skin's ability to renew itself; a "healthy tan" leads to thin, wrinkled skin for some people and skin cancer for others. Some of these signs of aging skin can be controlled by eating well, staying healthy, and protecting your skin against lengthy exposure to the sun—either by avoiding exposure or using high-level sunblocking lotions.

pathological aging factors
Cumulative effects of diseases and accidents that may accelerate aging.

IN THEORY, IN FACT

SLEEP PATTERNS OF OLDER ADULTS

Is insomnia as normal among older adults as white hair and wrinkles? Changes in sleep patterns are, but insomnia is not. Although about half of people over the age of 65 who live at home and about two-thirds of those in nursing homes and other long-term care facilities suffer from sleep problems, these problems are not an inevitable part of aging (Becker & Jamieson, 1992). They may be linked to a primary sleep disorder, an illness, or even medication. Depending on the problem, older insomniacs can often be helped.

Sleep problems must first be viewed in the context of the normal changes in sleep that occur as we age. According to researchers, the following sleep patterns are typical in individuals between the ages of 60 and 80 (Bachman, 1992; Becker & Jamieson, 1992):

- Older people average between 6 and 6½ hours of sleep a night, although many remain in bed for up to 8 hours.
- Although many older people sleep more than younger adults, the amount of nightly sleep that older people get varies from fewer than 5 hours to more than 9 hours. Many older people have trouble going to sleep and may toss and turn for up to 30 minutes before falling asleep.
- After older people fall asleep, they experience significantly more early awakenings than younger people. It is considered normal for older people to spend up to 20% of their time in bed awake and to compensate by spending more time in bed.
- A change in the distribution of sleep stages results in an increase in stage 1 sleep (light sleep) and a decrease in stages 3 and 4 sleep (deep sleep). Thus, even when sleep occurs, generally it is not deep, satisfying sleep.

Adjustment sleep disorders occur in about one-third of older people, many of whom have a prior history of sound sleep. In these cases insomnia is related to recent stresses in the older person's life, such as a recent hospitalization, retirement, or the death of a spouse or close friend. The individual reacts to these problems by being unable to fall asleep or to remain asleep for extended

Changes in sleep patterns in older people are normal, but sleep disturbances are not.

periods. Deprived of sleep, they may be irritable, anxious, or lethargic during the day and worried about their sleeplessness at night, which makes falling asleep even harder. Adjustment sleep disorder generally disappears over time as the older person learns to deal with the stress that causes it.

Poor sleep hygiene—sleep-related habits and behaviors that are incompatible with sleep—is another cause of insomnia. For example, individuals who drink caffeinated beverages before bedtime, who work until bedtime, or who watch the clock may experience heightened arousal, which is incompatible with sleep. Going to bed at irregular hours may also worsen the problem. Many older adults who experience these problems become preoccupied by their inability to sleep. They attempt to nap during the day or drink coffee to stay awake—both of which make the insomnia worse. Problems related to inadequate sleep hygiene can often be remedied by behavior modification. For example, individuals are encouraged to go to sleep at regular hours and to avoid caffeine.

Psychophysiologic insomnia is sometimes linked to adjustment sleep disorders and poor sleep hygiene. Individuals suffering from psychophysiologic insomnia associate bedtime and the bedroom with mental and physical arousal and high levels of

frustration. Philip Becker and Andrew Jamieson, psychiatrists who specialize in sleep disorders, explained:

> These sleep disturbances continue as a result of conditioned, learned arousal, even after normal coping and sleep habits are reestablished. Following her retirement, one of our older patients began lying in bed to plan her investments. Twelve months later, she successfully invested her money but could not fall asleep until after 1 A.M. To her surprise, however, she was able to fall asleep quickly in a motel room. Without realizing it, she had associated her bed and bedtime with thinking and problem solving rather than with rapid sleep onset. (Becker & Jamieson, 1992, pp. 48–49)

Behavioral therapies that stress positive sleep hygiene are often used to treat psychophysiologic insomnia.

Insomnia in older people is sometimes linked to a variety of psychiatric disorders, including major depression and anxiety. In these cases appropriate medication may help alleviate the symptoms. Insomnia is also linked to symptoms of medical illness. The pain of arthritis, for example, may interrupt sleep. In addition, medications designed to treat medical disorders may have the unfortunate side effect of disturbing sleep.

Finally, sleep disturbances are also related to sleep apnea and periodic limb movements. *Sleep apnea* is an interruption in breathing that lasts at least 10 seconds and occurs at least 5 times per hour. Individuals suffering from this disorder may be plagued by loud snoring, restless sleep, daytime sleepiness, and depression. *Periodic limb movements* are repeated jerks of the legs that arouse the sleeper. Individuals suffering from these disorders often benefit from medical treatment.

In sum, although severe sleep problems are not an inevitable part of growing old, they occur frequently in older people and should be viewed as problems that can often be treated successfully.

The Senses The senses—hearing, vision, taste, and smell—generally become less efficient as we age. Many older people find that it takes longer to perceive and process an event through the sensory systems (Hoyer & Plude, 1980; Ross et al., 1997). However, although each kind of sensory decline described here is common among older individuals, not all older people are affected. Again, there is wide variation in the overall aging process.

Hearing deficits are quite common. In fact, hearing impairments hamper daily living for as many as a third of all older people (Fozard, 1990). These impairments are usually mild to moderate and often involve detecting voices in the midst of background noise (Olsho et al., 1985). In addition, there is hearing loss in the higher-frequency tones—those that occur in speech sounds such as *s*, *sh*, *ch*, and *f*, as well as in the lower-frequency tones (Schneider & Pichora-Fuller, 2000). Sometimes, hearing aids are helpful in dealing with these problems, but often they are frustrating as well. Most hearing aids amplify all sound frequencies, including background noise, and therefore do not provide much help in picking out the details of what someone is saying. With or without hearing aids, older individuals with hearing loss may appear inattentive or embarrassed when in fact they simply can't understand what is being said. Others withdraw or become suspicious of what they cannot hear.

Several kinds of visual impairments are common in aging individuals. The ability to focus on objects declines as the lenses of the eyes become less flexible and able to accommodate (Schneider & Pichora-Fuller, 2000). Depth perception may also be affected by loss of flexibility in the lens. Another problem associated with aging is that the lens may become cloudy and may eventually develop a **cataract**—an almost complete blockage of light and visual sensation. Yet another problem is **glaucoma,** an increase of pressure within the eyeball that can result in damage and gradual loss of vision. Fortunately, most cataracts can be removed through outpatient laser surgery, and glaucoma can often be treated with medication. Subtler problems like loss of flexibility in the lens are less easily remedied (Kline & Schieber, 1985).

Older individuals often lose some **visual acuity**—the ability to distinguish fine detail. It is not uncommon for older people to have difficulty perceiving visual details—whether it's reading names or numbers on mailboxes, distinguishing a staircase from a confusing carpet pattern, or simply reading a newspaper (Perlmutter, 1978; Perlmutter et al., 1987; Schneider & Pichora-Fuller, 2000). This may be due partly to the inflexibility of the lens and partly to the loss of visual "receptor" cells in the rear of the eye. Visual acuity can be increased with corrective lenses, including bifocals and trifocals (Kline & Schieber, 1985). Surgical procedures to improve visual acuity still incorporate a high degree of risk, however.

From a perceptual viewpoint, many older people also have trouble ignoring irrelevant stimuli. For example, detecting a particular road sign in a crowded display of signs becomes more difficult with age. *Redundancy*, in the form of repeated, standard signs that convey the same instructions, helps older adults understand visual signals (Allen, Madden, Groth, & Crozier, 1992). Still, sooner or later there usually comes a point when older adults should avoid driving because of limited visual acuity (and reaction time), not an easy transition in areas where people lack alternative means of transportation.

In contrast, the sense of taste shows considerable stability even during advanced aging. The ability to taste sugar is particularly consistent (Bartoshuk & Weiffenbach, 1990). However, there appears to be some decline in the ability to detect and distinguish among bitter tastes (Spitzer, 1988). People with compli-

cataract Clouding of the lens of the eye that obstructs vision.

glaucoma Increased, potentially damaging pressure within the eye.

visual acuity The ability to distinguish fine detail.

cations such as **hypertension** (high blood pressure) have more trouble distinguishing among different tastes. Medications associated with aging may also be a factor, although Mary Spitzer (1988) has hypothesized that higher sensory thresholds may be involved as well. With regard to salt in particular, older people need more salt to taste it at all. However, increased consumption of salt may contribute to increased hypertension.

Aging people also have difficulty distinguishing tastes within blended foods. This appears to be attributable more to a decline in the sense of smell than to a decrease in taste sensitivity (Bartoshuk & Weiffenbach, 1990). The sense of smell often shows a marked decline compared with that of taste.

Muscles, Bones, and Mobility   Muscle weight—and therefore strength and endurance—decreases with age. The structure and composition of muscle cells change; body weight may be lower than it was in early and middle adulthood owing to loss of muscle tissue, unless increased fat tissue compensates for the loss.

Muscle function is affected by the changing structure and composition of the skeleton. Older adults are usually an inch or more shorter than they were in early adulthood as a result of compression of cartilage in the spine (a long-term effect attributable to the effects of gravity), as well as because of osteoporosis changes in posture (Whitbourne, 1999). The bones become weaker, hollower, and more brittle. Because they are more porous, they are more likely to fracture and take longer to mend (see Chapter 15). Older women are particularly susceptible to this condition (Belsky, 1984). To make things worse, the tendency to fall increases because of changes in the *vestibular system* that regulates balance (Ochs, Newberry, Lenhardt, & Harkins, 1985). The sensitivity of vestibular sensory receptors, which detect bodily movement and changes in position, declines markedly in older adulthood. An estimated 33% of individuals over age 65 and 40% of those over age 80 fall at least once a year (Simoneau & Leibowitz, 1995).

In general, muscle reaction and functioning slows down and it takes longer for a muscle to achieve a state of relaxation and readiness after being exerted. Muscles also function less efficiently if the cardiovascular system doesn't deliver enough nutrients or if it does not remove toxic waste products well, which can result both from aging and from poor health habits earlier in life. The blood vessels become less elastic; some become clogged. Consequently, there is less blood flow to the muscles. Decreased lung functioning may reduce the supply of oxygen to the muscles as well as to the brain. Fine motor coordination and speed of reaction time therefore decrease as well (Botwinick, 1984; Rogers & Fisk, 2000).

Studies have shown that high-intensity exercise training—within age-appropriate limits—helps counteract muscle weakness and related physical frailty in very old people. For example, in a study of 63 women and 37 men with an average age of 87 years, regular exercise increased muscle strength by more than 113% (Fiatarone et al., 1994). Similarly, a 3-year study conducted by the National Institute on Aging and the National Center for Nursing Research showed how strength and balance exercises can benefit frail people in their 80s and 90s. Those who engaged in muscle-building exercises were able to double and even triple their strength and, for the first time in years, perform many strength-related tasks without assistance (Krucoff, 1994).

Internal Organs   The heart is a highly specialized muscle that suffers from some of the same problems as other muscles during aging. The heart also depends on the efficiency of the cardiovascular system, which can develop a

hypertension   Abnormally high blood pressure, sometimes accompanied by headaches and dizziness.

variety of problems associated with aging. The result is decreased blood flow to and from the heart and increased recovery time after each heart contraction (Timiras, 1978). In turn, decreased or disrupted blood flow to the brain (as in fibrillation) can cause cognitive impairment (Sabatini et al., 2000).

The lungs of older people often have less capacity for oxygen intake. Of course, much lung trouble may be attributable not to the normal aging process but to prolonged damage caused by smoking and air pollution.

The reserve capacity of the heart, lungs, and other organs also decreases with age. During early adulthood, these organs can function at between 4 and 10 times their normal level when under stress. Reserve capacity drops slowly but steadily in middle adulthood and beyond. Older people may not notice the diminished capacity in day-to-day living, but they may realize it when, for example, they attempt to shovel snow after the first storm of the season. Diminished reserve capacity may be especially severe in extreme heat or cold. Many older people adapt more slowly to cold environments than they did when they were younger, and they may chill more easily, with a resulting low body temperature that is a serious health risk. Thus, older people often complain of being cold, and they are, even at temperatures that younger people find normal or on the warm side. Older people often have similar difficulty coping with heat, particularly if they exert themselves, as in mowing the lawn on a hot summer day. Nevertheless, older adults can often perform many of the tasks they did when they were younger as long as they do them more slowly, take frequent breaks, and consume extra liquids such as water and nutrient-replenishing products such as sports drinks.

The immune system also changes during later adulthood; production of antibodies peaks during adolescence and then starts to decline. The result: By older adulthood, people have less protection against microorganisms and disease (La Rue & Jarvik, 1982). This is why annual flu shots are often routinely recommended for older people (and not-so-old people as well). Influenza can be lethal to older people, not only by itself but also because it makes the individual vulnerable to secondary bacterial infections such as pneumonia.

Health, Disease, and Nutrition

Most older people, however, report having good to excellent health most of the time. They may be forced to adapt to the slow development of arthritis or to the side effects of medication to control high blood pressure and other disorders, but they usually can do this easily. Health-related changes that occur during later adulthood fall into three general categories: They may be chronic; they may be related to changing nutritional needs; or they may involve misuse of prescribed medications.

Chronic Health Problems When health problems occur, they may become chronic—that is, lasting and recurrent. One major difference between childhood and late adulthood is in the incidence of acute versus chronic diseases. In childhood, acute diseases—which last a brief time and often climax with a fever and a rash—are very common. Older adults, however, often suffer from chronic conditions—illnesses that occur repeatedly and never go away. In the United States, the most common chronic conditions are arthritis, heart problems, and hypertension (NCHS, 1999), as well as the visual and hearing impairments discussed previously. Accidental falls also produce chronic effects. In all, chronic diseases and impairments touch the lives of a substantial number of older adults, with 79% of noninstitutionalized people over age 70 reporting at least

In the United States, although it is not uncommon for older people to be overweight and undernourished, it is important to note that many others are well nourished.

one of seven common chronic conditions. The most common chronic condition is arthritis, reported by 63% of women and 50% of men over age 70.

To a great extent, this increase in health problems reflects the body's decreased ability to cope with stress, including the stress of disease. A disease that a young person can handle easily—for example, a respiratory infection—may linger on in an older person and cause permanent damage. Ironically, as the ability to cope with stress declines with age, the number of stressful events in the person's life tends to increase (Timiras, 1978). Aside from health problems, stress comes about as a result of life-cycle crises such as retirement and widowhood.

Socioeconomic factors, ethnicity, and sex all play a part in the occurrence of illness among older adults. In fact, in people over age 25, the number of days of restricted activity due to sickness is more highly correlated with socioeconomic background than with age (Kimmel, 1974). Similar data exist for the leading causes of death among older people. The majority of deaths in U.S. adults age 65 or older are attributable to three categories: cardiovascular disease, cancer, and cerebrovascular disease (U.S. Census Bureau, 1999). The rates for women are higher than for men in each category except cancer. The rate of cardiovascular disease for whites is twice as high as the rate for Asians (NCHS, 1990a).

Nutrition Some of the poor health of older adults is attributable to poor diet or improper nutrition. Because of their reduced physical activity and their slowdown in body metabolism, older adults do not require as much food as younger adults. In fact, by the time they reach age 65, individuals require at least 20% fewer calories than younger adults. But they still need nearly as many basic nutrients. As a result, it is not unusual for older U.S. adults to be both overweight and undernourished. Some older people are anemic and malnourished because they are too poor, uninformed, or depressed to buy and consume sufficient quantities of nutritious food. The most common deficiencies are in iron, calcium, and vitamins A and C.

Much of the problem lies in overconsumption of fats. As the body ages, it becomes less able to use the various kinds of fat that are present in many foods. Fat that is not used is stored in special *lipid* cells and within the walls of the arteries. There it may harden and form plates that reduce the flow of blood. This condition, called **atherosclerosis** or hardening of the arteries, is responsible for many of the heart conditions that are prevalent among older people. Atherosclerosis is so common in older people in the United States and Western Europe that it is almost considered a normal part of aging. The condition is rare, however, in some non-Western countries with radically different diets (Belsky, 1984).

Thus, with age, bodily changes require changes in diet. As noted earlier and in Chapter 15, the bones of older adults become fragile and porous. Over the years, bones lose more calcium than they can absorb from food. To counteract this loss, middle-aged and older people are advised to supplement their diets with calcium. Also, the muscle tone of the intestines decreases with age, often causing constipation and a temptation to rely on laxatives—which can be extremely habit-forming. Nutritionists recommend that older people suffering from constipation add high-fiber foods such as bran to their diets and drink plenty of water to maintain proper bowel function.

Misuse of Prescribed Medication Serious intentional drug abuse is not a major problem among older adults. In fact, the most popular "recreational drug" used by this age group is alcohol, and by and large, older U.S. adults

atherosclerosis Hardening of the arteries, which is a common condition of aging caused by the body's increasing inability to use excess fats in the diet. These fats are stored along the walls of arteries and restrict the flow of blood when they harden.

are more moderate drinkers than members of younger age groups (SAMSHA, 2000). Nevertheless, some researchers are convinced that as much as one-third of older adults are hospitalized because of overuse, misuse, or abuse of drugs (Poe & Holloway, 1980). Why? For many older people, the problem may relate to changes in body chemistry that result in reduced need for a particular prescription drug, a condition that may go undetected for months or even years. In addition, older people often take combinations of medications for different conditions, and those who are experiencing cognitive decline may simply become confused as to when and how much of each medication to take. They may also fail to mention all of their medications to nurses or physicians. In turn, some physicians may prescribe inappropriately: A recent study (Spore, Mor, Parrat, Hawes, & Hiris, 1997) found that among older people in residential facilities some 20 to 25% had at least one inappropriate prescription.

Interactions between medications can have toxic effects. In fact, there have been cases of octogenarians who enter the hospital with numerous symptoms and a depressed level of functioning, suggesting that they are close to death. Yet when certain medications are given in reduced dosages or completely withheld, some of these patients return to a level of functioning that they have not enjoyed for years (Poe & Holloway, 1980).

Drug effects may produce symptoms that mimic **dementia.** The various forms of dementia (including dementia associated with Alzheimer's disease, as discussed later in the chapter) have in common cognitive deficits such as impaired memory and learning ability, deterioration of language and motor functions, progressive inability to recognize familiar people and objects, and frequent confusion (American Psychiatric Association, 1994). Personality changes often accompany dementia. Tranquilizers such as Valium or Librium and cardiac medication such as digitalis can produce dementia-like disorientation and confusion (Rudd & Balaschke, 1982; Salzman, 1982). Another factor contributing to involuntary abuse of drugs is that older people have greater difficulty clearing drugs through declining organ systems such as the liver and kidneys, with the effect that larger amounts of drugs remain in their systems longer.

dementia A disorder that produces the confusion, forgetfulness, and personality changes that may be associated with older age.

CONTENT CHECK
PHYSICAL ASPECTS OF AGING

True–False (answers are on the Companion Website)

1. Pathological factors affect the ways people age.
2. Generally, all senses become less efficient as people age.
3. People who are in their 80s are too old to benefit from strength and balance exercises.
4. As people age, the reserve capacity of their hearts, lungs, and other organs diminishes.
5. Older adults tend to suffer more from acute than from chronic health problems.

Thinking Critically

How do improper nutrition and misuse of prescribed medication negatively impact on the life of older adults?

Causes of Aging

Aside from the effects of stress, disease, poor nutrition, and so on as contributors to aging, what about normal aging processes? What is the physiology of aging? What happens to cells and organs, and can that process be slowed or stopped by advances in medical science or environmental controls? Many plausible theories have been proposed, but none is conclusive. Some are too complex for a full treatment here, so we limit our discussion to the central issues. We begin by examining hereditary and environmental factors associated with aging; then we look at theories of aging.

Hereditary and Environmental Factors

Many kinds of aging are observed in nature: Many plants flower, go to seed, die, and regenerate annually according to a preprogrammed genetic code; trees grow until they can no longer raise nutrients and fluid to their highest points—a lifespan of many years, predictable according to the species. In lower mammals, aging and death usually occur at about the same time as loss of fertility; as soon as the younger generation is successfully launched into the world, the parent generation dies. Humans and other primates (as well as elephants) are among the few exceptions to this rule. The human life cycle extends well beyond reproductive capacity, which ends roughly at age 50 for women and perhaps not at all for men.

It is clear from studies across species that each plant or animal's characteristic lifespan has a hereditary component. In humans, the genetic influence is particularly striking in studies of identical twins. Identical twins grow bald, accumulate wrinkles, and shrink in stature at the same rate, despite long separations that may expose them to markedly different environmental influences. Identical twins who die of natural causes often die at about the same time. Fraternal twins, on the other hand, may age at different rates and have thoroughly dissimilar lifespans. For the hereditary components in the aging process to be completely expressed, however, all other factors such as stress, accidents, and diseases would have to be held constant. Because this is impossible, we must consider other processes, both inside and outside the body, that determine how much of the genetic potential will be fulfilled—along with whether we can extend that potential.

In addition to those discussed previously, there are a number of reversible and permanent external factors that lengthen or shorten life expectancy. For example, rural life adds several years to the lifespan compared with city life, as does being married compared with being single. Obesity has a consistently negative effect, taking several years off the lives of people who are 25% overweight and about 15 years off the lives of those who are 67% overweight.

Theories of Aging

How does aging actually happen? Does the "genetic clock" simply run down, or is the process more one of wear and tear? **Senescence,** or normal aging, refers to the universal biological processes of aging; it does not include the effects of disease.

The majority of theories of aging can be grouped into two categories—the stochastic theories and the preprogrammed or "clock" theories.

Stochastic Theories According to **stochastic theories of aging,** the body ages as a result of random assaults from both the internal and external environments (Schneider, 1992). These theories, which are sometimes called *wear-and-tear*

senescence The normal aging process, not connected with the occurrence of disease in the individual.

stochastic theories of aging Theories suggesting that the body ages as a result of random assaults from both internal and external environments.

theories, compare the human body to a machine that simply wears out as a result of constant use and accumulated cellular insults and injuries. In one such theory, for example, it is thought that as cells age, they are less efficient in disposing of wastes. Extra substances, particularly a fatty substance called *lipofusein*, accumulate, especially in blood and muscle cells. Eventually these substances take up space and slow down normal cell processes. Most gerontologists, however, think that the accumulation of chemicals such as lipofusein is a result rather than a cause of aging.

A more popular stochastic theory involves the action of pieces of molecules called *free radicals.* In the course of normal use of oxygen for virtually every cellular process, small, highly charged, unpaired electrons are left over. These free radicals react with other chemical compounds in the cell and may interrupt normal cell functioning. Normally, the cell has repair mechanisms that reduce the damage done by free radicals. But after a major injury such as a heart attack or exposure to radiation, substantial free radical damage occurs. Researchers have explored the effects of some dietary substances, such as vitamins C and E, that seem to reduce the effects of free radicals. Research on these and other dietary supplements has been promising but remains experimental (Cantuti-Castelvetri, Shukitt-Hale, & Joseph, 2000; Harman, Holliday, & Meydani, 1998).

There are still other stochastic theories. Damage might be done to DNA in the genes, for example. It is known that the ultraviolet light in sunshine can damage the DNA in skin cells. Usually, when the genes in a cell are damaged, the cell either repairs itself or dies and is replaced. In older people such repairs are less efficient and damage tends to remain. Perhaps aging is nothing more than a decline in self-repair capacity.

Wear and tear affects tissues and systems as well. Sometimes connective tissue, or the cross-links between cells, is affected. It loses some of its flexibility and become rigid. In aging, the immune system also becomes less efficient. Sometimes the immune cells attack their own body's healthy cells, as in *rheumatoid arthritis* or certain kidney ailments. Still, the processes described by stochastic theories, though fairly common, might be a result of some deeper aging process rather than the cause of aging itself.

In sum, although stochastic theories are appealing, they do not fully explain aging. They do not, for example, explain why the functions of the body's internal "repair shop" decline. In addition, they do not explain why exercise—a potential form of wear and tear—can have beneficial rather than negative effects.

Biological Clock Theories The second general type of theory of aging focuses on genetic programming. Preprogrammed theories of aging suggest that the programmed actions of specific inherited genes determine aging. It is believed that approximately 200 human genes determine the average lifespan of a human being (Schneider, 1992). The notion of biological clocks is associated with that of programmed aging. The idea is that there are built-in timers, or clocks, that are set to go off according to a schedule. These clocks may be located in each cell or in the brain. At the cellular level, it has been found that particular kinds of cells seem to be preprogrammed to divide (and therefore replace damaged or worn out cells) only a certain number of times. For example, some human embryo cells divide only about 50 times. Even if you freeze these cells after 30 divisions, when you thaw them they will divide only another 20 times. The maximum number of reproductions varies in different types of cells and in different species. Individuals may also vary in the potential number of cellular reproductions for different kinds of cells.

Another biological clock theory suggests that there is some sort of pacemaker, or timer, housed in the hypothalamus and the pituitary gland. In this view, the pituitary gland releases a hormone shortly after puberty that begins the process of decline throughout the rest of the lifespan at a programmed rate.

Biological clocks in humans appear to control the female menstrual cycle, which begins at around age 12 and ends somewhere around age 50. A biological clock also appears to control the human immune system, which gains strength until age 20 and then gradually weakens. Some theorists suggest that this decline in immune function is linked to many age-related conditions, including susceptibility to cancer and infections like influenza and pneumonia, as well as to alteration in the walls of the blood vessels and arteriosclerosis (Schneider, 1992).

In sum, no single theory can explain aging. A combination of theories works better, and future discoveries will undoubtedly contribute further to our understanding of the normal aging process. Researchers are also keenly interested in studying ways to slow the process so that we can all live longer. Some of this research is disease-related. The study of the relationship between childhood cancer or juvenile arthritis and premature aging is an example. Other research is aimed at helping people live a healthy, disease-free life until close to the end of their natural lifespan. However, despite recent advances, the likelihood of dramatically extending the normal lifespan seems a long way off.

CONTENT CHECK
CAUSES OF AGING

True–False (answers are on the Companion Website)
1. Heredity is more important than environment in the aging process.
2. Senescence refers to the biological processes of aging, including the affects of disease.
3. Stochastic theories of aging assert that people age because of random assaults from the internal and external environments.
4. Stochastic theories do not explain why as people age the body's internal repair shop works less well than formerly.
5. Preprogrammed theories focus on genetic programming to explain the aging process.

Thinking Critically
In what ways do heredity and environment interact during the aging process?

Cognitive Changes in Advanced Age

Having examined various processes and theories of aging, we next take a close look at changes that occur in cognition as a result of aging.

Many people assume that older people's intellect automatically decays. For example, if a young or middle-aged man prepares to leaves a party and doesn't remember where he left his coat, people think nothing of it. If the same forgetfulness is observed in an older person, however, people shrug their shoulders and say, "Her memory is going" or "He's losing his mind." Here we consider facts and fictions about cognitive changes associated with advanced age, and how older adults cope with those changes.

Cognition in the Later Years

As noted in Chapter 15 with regard to fluid and crystallized intelligence, there is some controversy over the extent of decline in intellectual functioning as a result of normal aging. However, it is agreed that most mental skills remain relatively intact. Extensive research has demonstrated that age-related decline in memory is not as general or as severe as was previously thought (Perlmutter et al., 1987; Zachs, Hasher, & Li, 2000). Many of the memory problems that some older people suffer are not the inevitable consequences of age but are due to other factors, such as depression, inactivity, or side effects of prescription drugs. When cognitive decline does occur—and there is a well-documented decline in the *speed* of cognitive processing—there are compensations. The effect is that any loss normally has very little effect on daily living (Perlmutter et al., 1987; Salthouse, 1985, 1990). Let's look at selected cognitive changes as they relate to speed of performance, memory, and the development of wisdom.

Speed of Cognition Older adulthood brings a decline in the speed of both mental and physical performance (Birren et al., 1985). Many studies have shown that intellectual functions that depend heavily on speed of performance decline in older people (Salthouse, 1985, 1995). Older people have slower reaction times, slower perceptual processing, and slower cognitive processes in general (McDowd & Shaw, 2000). Although some of this slowness is clearly attributable to aging, some may be due to the fact that older people value accuracy more than younger people do. When tested, older people make fewer guesses and try to answer each item correctly. Also, they may be less familiar with some of the tasks used in testing situations. For example, older people are often compared with college students in tests of recall of nonsense syllables. Students regularly practice learning new vocabularies for examinations, but older people usually have not engaged in such practice for a long time. On many such tasks, older people are sometimes slower because they haven't practiced the relevant cognitive skills recently, and therefore such comparisons are unrealistic and lead to inaccurate conclusions (Labouvie-Vief, 1985). Thus, although the decline in cognitive processing associated with aging is real, much of it appears to be exaggerated.

Studies of performance on standard memory tasks typically reveal a difference in speed between the performances of 30- and 70-year-olds. In relatively simple cognitive tasks, such as those that ask participants to compare the size of different objects, older people take approximately 50% longer to complete the task than younger people. As cognitive problems become more complex—requiring, for example, simultaneous comparisons of size and location—older adults require about twice as much time as younger adults to complete the task (Baltes, 1993).

There are, however, certain compensations that older people use to make up for their loss of speed. In one study, older typists did just as well as younger typists despite seemingly slower visual processing and reaction time and reduced dexterity. Why? When the researcher limited the number of words that the typists could read ahead, the older typists slowed down considerably and the younger ones were much less affected. It appears that older typists had learned to look farther ahead and thereby type quickly (Salthouse, 1985). With fairly limited training, older people are often able to compensate for loss of speed on such tasks and in many cases to recover much of their former speed (Willis, 1990; Willis & Nesselroade, 1990).

Memory Perhaps no single aspect of aging has been studied more thoroughly than memory. Recall the information-processing model of memory discussed in Chapter 7. Information is first fleetingly retained in sensory memory in the form of visual or auditory images, then transferred to short-term memory for organization and encoding, and finally transferred to long-term memory for retention. In studies of adult memory we also find evidence of even more permanent, or *tertiary* memory, which holds extremely remote information. Each of these presumed levels of memory has been studied in some detail (Poon, 1985).

Sensory storage is very brief visual or auditory memory that holds sensory input for fractions of a second while the information is being processed. It appears that older individuals are able to pick up and hold slightly less sensory information than young adults. On average, they have a slightly shorter perceptual span, particularly when two things are happening at once. It is not clear why this is so. Is there a decline in the visual or auditory system? Is there less selective attention or pattern recognition? Or is there perhaps less motivation to succeed in these very precise tasks? In any case, it is unlikely that the modest sensory memory loss observed in later adulthood has much effect on daily living. An older person can often compensate by looking at or listening to things longer (Poon, 1985), although this isn't always possible: Highway signs that whiz by can create difficulty for older drivers, who require relatively more sensory input for skilled performance (Fozard, 2000).

Most mental skills remain relatively intact in older people.

Short-term memory, which is limited-capacity storage that holds things that are "in mind" at the moment, also changes little with age. Most studies find no significant difference between older and younger adults in short-term memory capacity per se.

When it comes to *long-term memory*, however, most studies show clear age differences. In studies of learning and recall, older people often remember fewer items on a list or fewer details in a design. But are these differences due to the storage capacity of the older person or to the processes of learning or remembering (that is, the *transfer* of information from short-term to long-term memory)? In some memory studies, it appears that older individuals are less efficient in organizing, rehearsing, and encoding material to be learned—all of which are short-term memory functions. Yet, with careful instruction and a little practice, older people improve markedly (Willis, 1990). Even people near age 80 show some benefits from training in how to organize and rehearse information for permanent retention (Poon, 1985; Willis & Nesselroade, 1990).

The effectiveness of such training is not unlimited, however. Even after memory training, individuals in their 70s may not reach the same levels as young adults (Campbell & Charness, 1990). In some studies comparing older and younger people, the training actually increased the gap in performance because young adults made even greater gains than older adults (Kleigl, Smith, & Baltes, 1990). This may imply that older adults may have less reserve capacity (Baltes, 1987) than young adults, at least in some skills. In other words, older adults have less room for improvement and less plasticity in their thinking.

Paul Baltes (1993) demonstrated the limitation of reserve capacity in older adults a study in which young adult and older adult participants with similar educational backgrounds were asked to remember long lists of words, such as 30 nouns, in correct order. Realizing that under normal conditions most people can remember a string of only about 5 to 7 words presented at a rate of about 2 words per second, the researchers trained the participants to use a mnemonic device—that is, a memory strategy—known as the *method of loci*. In this strategy, participants associate items to be remembered with objects in a setting that is very familiar to them, such as a room or the neighborhood they live in. They then form bizarre or humorous mental images as an aid to recall. When asked to recall the items, they easily remember the familiar objects and then the associated items on the list.

The researchers found that healthy older adults could apply the method of loci fairly well. However, there were clear age-related performance differences. These involved both speed and accuracy of performance. For example, even after 38 training sessions, most older adults failed to reach the level of performance achieved by young adults after only a few training sessions. In fact, the researchers found no participants over age 70 who performed above the average for the young adults.

There are other age differences in performance of long-term memory tasks. Older participants tend to do better on recognition tasks than on recall of such things as vocabulary lists (Craik & McDowd, 1987). They tend to be somewhat selective in what they retain. They may balk at memorizing useless word lists but do very well in the comprehension of paragraphs (Meyer, 1987). One study found that older people remembered interesting metaphors such as "the seasons are the costumes of nature" better than college students did. They did not try to reproduce the sentence exactly; rather, they understood and remembered its meaning (Labouvie-Vief & Schell, 1982). In other words, older people tend to remember what appears to them to be useful and important. This reminds us, then, that development and behavior occur in context, and that even as we age, environmental demands and opportunities shape our skills and abilities (Lerner, 1990).

Tertiary memory, or memory for extremely remote events, appears to remain fairly intact in older adults. Indeed, in some studies, older adults are better at recalling details of historical events than younger adults. This is especially true of historical events that the older adults experienced but the young adults learned about secondhand. It is also consistent with the ease with which older adults can often vividly describe memorable events of their childhood.

In sum, very few significant age differences are found in each of the memory stages except long-term memory, and the differences found in this stage depend on several factors. Older individuals may do poorly if the memory task requires unusual organizational and rehearsal techniques that are not well practiced. Most will improve, however, if they are taught organization and memory strategies. Memory in older people is also selective. More interesting and meaningful material is remembered more easily. In all, the notion of major memory decline associated with aging is best categorized as a myth.

Wisdom   Although the mechanics of memory are somewhat stronger in young adults than in older adults, the reverse is often true with regard to **wisdom**—expert knowledge that focuses on the "fundamental pragmatics of life" and involves judgment and advice on crucial life issues (Staudinger & Pasupathi, 2000). "To understand wisdom fully and correctly probably requires more wisdom that any of us have," wrote Robert Sternberg (1990). Nevertheless, Paul Baltes has proposed that the expert knowledge associated with wisdom can be classified into five categories: factual knowledge, procedural knowledge, lifespan contextualism, value relativism, and uncertainty (see Figure 17–4). At the very least, wisdom is a cognitive quality founded on crystallized, culture-based intelligence (see Chapter 15) that is related to experience and personality. Remember that crystallized intelligence stems from the knowledge and information an individual gathers about the world and human relationships throughout life.

According to Baltes (1993; also see Baltes, 2000), wisdom has five general characteristics. First, it appears to focus on important and difficult matters that are often associated with the meaning of life and the human condition. Second, the level of knowledge, judgment, and advice reflected in wisdom is superior. Third, the knowledge associated with wisdom has extraordinary scope, depth, and balance and is applicable to specific situations. Fourth, wisdom combines

wisdom   An expert knowledge system focusing on the pragmatics of life that involves excellent judgment and advice on critical life issues, including the meaning of life and the human condition; wisdom represents the capstone of human intelligence.

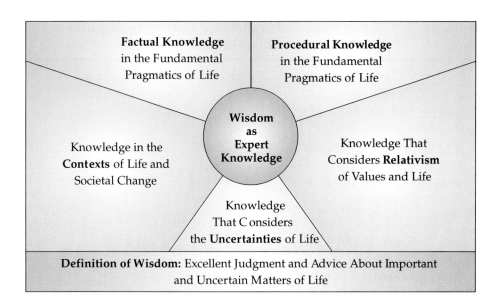

Figure 17–4   A Model of Wisdom

Source: Baltes, 1993.

mind and virtue (character) and is employed for personal well-being as well as for the benefit of humankind. Fifth, though difficult to achieve, wisdom is easily recognized by most people.

To measure the body of knowledge associated with wisdom, Baltes (1993) asked research participants to consider dilemmas like this one: A 15-year-old girl wants to get married right away. What should she do? Baltes asked participants to "think aloud" about this problem. Their thoughts were taped, transcribed, and evaluated on the basis of the degree to which they approached the five criteria of wisdom-related knowledge: factual knowledge, procedural knowledge, lifespan contextualism, value relativism, and recognition and management of uncertainty. Participants' answers were rated to evaluate how much and what kind of wisdom-related knowledge they had. The various criteria and the evaluation are summarized in Table 17–3.

According to Baltes, there are two reasons why growing old might increase the quantity and quality of an individual's wisdom-related knowledge and make a high score more likely than a low one. First, it takes years of experience in diverse life circumstances to fully understand and work with wisdom-enhancing factors. This experience comes with age. Second, as adults age, they develop personal attributes that are conducive to the development of wisdom. These attributes involve personality and cognitive growth. However, the development of wisdom is not irreversible. The losses in cognitive processing experienced by very old people may limit their wisdom or their ability to apply it, especially in old-old age (Staudinger & Pasupathi, 2000).

Cognitive Decline

Despite the retention of memory skills and the development of wisdom in many older adults, some individuals experience a marked decline in cognitive functioning. This decline may be temporary, progressive, or intermittent. It is relatively minor and fleeting in some cases, severe and progressive in others.

Cognitive decline may have primary or secondary causes. Among the primary causes of decline are Alzheimer's disease and strokes. However, it should be remembered that most cognitive decline is not intrinsic to the aging process itself; rather, it is attributable to other factors such as failing health, poor formal education, poverty, or low motivation. These secondary causes of decline deserve consideration as well, although they can be difficult to distinguish from

Table 17–3 Use of the Wisdom-Related Criteria to Evaluate Discourse about Life Matters

Example: A 15-year-old girl wants to get married right away. What should one/she consider and do?

Factual knowledge:

__Who, when, where?

__Examples of possible different situations

__Multiple options (forms of love and marriage)

Procedural knowledge:

__Strategies of information search, decision making, and advice giving

__Timing of advice, monitoring of emotional reactions

__Cost/benefit analysis: scenarios

__Means-ends analysis

Lifespan contextualism:

__Age-graded (e.g., issues of adolescence), culturally graded (e.g., change in norms), idiosyncratic (e.g., terminal illness) contexts across time and life domains

Value relativism:

__Separating personal values from those of others

__Religious preferences

__Current/future values

__Cultural-historical relativism

Uncertainty:

__No perfect solution

__Optimization of gain/loss ratio

__Future not fully predictable

__Backup solutions

Illustration of Two Extreme Responses (Abbreviated)

Low score

A 15-year-old girl wants to get married? No, no way; marrying at age 15 would be utterly wrong. One has to tell the girl that marriage is not possible. (After further probing) It would be irresponsible to support such an idea. No, this is just a crazy idea.

High score

Well, on the surface, this seems like an easy problem. On average, marriage for 15-year-old girls is not a good thing. I guess many girls might think about it when they fall in love for the first time. And, then, there are situations where the average case does not fit. Perhaps in this instance, special life circumstances are involved, such that the girl has a terminal illness. Or this girl may not be from this country. Perhaps she lives in another culture and historical period. Before I offer a final evaluation, I would need more information.

Source: Adapted from Baltes, 1993.

primary causes. Let's begin our consideration of cognitive decline with its ultimate manifestation, dementia.

Dementia As noted earlier, dementia refers to the chronic confusion, forgetfulness, and accompanying personality changes that are sometimes associated with advanced age. It can have many causes, the primary of which is Alzheimer's disease. Many people fear dementia in the mistaken belief that it is an inevitable curse of growing old. To them, growing old means losing emotional and intellectual control and becoming a helpless, useless person who becomes a "burden" on his or her family.

According to gerontologists, the actual incidence and nature of dementia have been exaggerated and distorted. Far from being inevitable, only 2 to 4% of people over 65 have dementia associated with Alzheimer's disease, and other types are rare (American Psychiatric Association, 1994). Unfortunately, however, a recent community-based survey indicates that the rate increases dramatically with advanced aging. The Boston-based survey indicated that nearly 20% of the 75- to 84-year-olds tested appeared to suffer from dementia in the form of Alzheimer's disease. The rate among community dwellers 85 years old and older approached 50% (Evans et al., 1989).

People who suffer from dementia have a limited ability to grasp abstractions; they may lack ideas, repeat the same statements over and over again, think more slowly than normal people, and be unable to pay attention to those around them. They also lose their train of thought in the middle of a sentence. Memory for recent events may be impaired. A person suffering from dementia may clearly recall a childhood event but be unable to remember something that happened an hour ago. Because of these symptoms of mental deterioration, the person may be unable to cope with such routine tasks as keeping clean and groomed. Operating within the confines of a shrinking mental world, he or she can no longer think, behave, or relate to people normally (Craik & Salthouse, 2000; American Psychiatric Association, 1994).

Unfortunately, the label *senile* is all too often attached to older people who show even the slightest signs of confusion, mental lapses, or disoriented behavior, even though these problems may be attributable to a number of other causes. A clear diagnosis is difficult, given the wide range of secondary causes. Improper nutrition, as well as chronic insufficient sleep related to illness, anxiety, depression, grief, or fear, can distort thinking in young as well as old people. Heart or kidney problems that cause changes in normal body rhythms or metabolism, or the accumulation of toxic body wastes may also affect the ability to think clearly. Confusion, agitation, and drowsiness can also be induced by drugs used to treat other illnesses. In each of these cases, when the physical or emotional illness is treated effectively, the senility-like symptoms disappear (Kastenbaum, 1979).

Primary Causes of Decline As noted earlier, the leading primary cause of dementia and other forms of cognitive decline is Alzheimer's disease. Alzheimer's disease is also the eighth leading cause of death among people age 65 and older.

Alzheimer's disease involves a progressive deterioration of brain cells, beginning in the outer cerebral cortex. Autopsies have revealed a characteristic pattern of damaged areas that look like little bits of braided yarn. While the patient is alive, the diagnosis of Alzheimer's disease is based on patterns of regressive memory loss and disorientation.

The causes of Alzheimer's disease are not yet known, although the high incidence of the disease in some families has led researchers to suspect a genetic

Alzheimer's disease A disease that causes dementia due to a progressive deterioration of brain cells, especially those in the cerebral cortex.

cause (Miller, 1993), and an assortment of potential candidates have been identified (e.g., see Abate, Ferrari-Ramondo, & Di Iorio, 1998; Felician & Sandson, 1999). In turn, pharmacological treatments that arrest or at least alleviate some of the symptoms of Alzheimer's disease continue to be developed (Felician & Sandson, 1999; Mayuex & Sano, 1999).

Whatever its causes, the effects of Alzheimer's disease are devastating both to the patient and his or her family. Generally, the first symptoms are forgetfulness and minor disruptions in speech. In the beginning, only little things are forgotten; as the disease progresses, places, names, and routines may not be recalled; and finally, even events that may have just occurred are forgotten. The forgetful phase is followed by a sense of confusion. It is much more difficult to plan and perform even simple routines; for example, it is hard to get something to eat because you can't find the refrigerator. This loss of contact with the routine and familiar aspects of life causes serious disorientation, confusion, and anxiety. At this point it becomes clear that the person cannot be left alone because of the potential for injury. Finally, full dementia sets in. The patient is unable to complete the simplest tasks, such as dressing or even eating. Familiar people are not recognized; even a devoted spouse who has cared for the patient through years of decline may be perceived as a complete stranger.

Alzheimer's disease typically has a substantial impact on the patient's family. Within a few years an independent, cognizant adult becomes childlike and requires 24-hour care and supervision. In the early stages, adaptations are relatively easily. The environment can be simplified and objects—even furniture—can be labeled. The person can still be alone, at least for short periods, and things like a sandwich prepared earlier by a family member may prevent an accident in the kitchen at mealtime. Later, when 24-hour care becomes necessary, major adaptations must be made. Aside from practical matters, family members often must deal with grief and despair and perhaps with anger and frustration. Feelings of resentment, guilt, embarrassment, and isolation are likely. Although such feelings are understandable, family members must continue to consider the feelings of the patient. In addition, the support of other families with similar experiences is particularly helpful (Cohen & Eisdorfer, 1986; Haley et al., 1996). Often the difficult decision to place the person in a nursing home must be made. Sometimes this decision is easier in the final stages if the person seems not to know where he or she is, even at home with familiar family members. Sometimes, too, the simpler, more predictable environment of the institution makes life easier for an Alzheimer's patient (but see "In Theory, In Fact" in Chapter 18, page 618).

Strokes, including ministrokes, are another primary cause of dementia. This form of cognitive decline is sometimes called multi-infarct dementia (MID). An *infarct* is an obstruction of a blood vessel that prevents a sufficient supply of blood from reaching a particular area of the brain. This causes destruction of brain tissue and is commonly referred to as a stroke or ministroke. If these events are very small and temporary, they are referred to as *transient ischemic attacks* (TIAs). Often the person is not even aware that the event has occurred. As the name implies, MID is caused by a series of events that damage brain tissue.

Often the underlying cause of ministrokes and the resulting destruction of brain tissue is atherosclerosis—the buildup of fatty plates on the lining of the arteries. People who have atherosclerosis or existing heart problems, hypertension, or diabetes are at particular risk for strokes. Those at risk are advised to pay attention to measures to improve their circulation, such as moderate exercise, and to control their hypertension and diabetes through diet and medication.

Secondary Causes of Decline Psychological expectations, mental health, and other factors can profoundly influence cognitive functioning in older adults.

stroke Blockage of blood to the brain, which can cause brain damage.

At any age, our beliefs or judgments about our own abilities have an effect on how well we perform. Some older adults fully believe that they are going to lose their memory and become less able to do things than they were in the past. They expect to be helpless and dependent on others and to lose control of their lives. Older people often imagine that their fate will rest in the hands of luck, chance, or powerful others. In a self-fulfilling prophecy, individuals who have these expectations become less competent and less in control. They have less self-esteem and show less persistence and effort. On the other hand, if they can be convinced that they can take more control of their lives and that cognitive loss is not inevitable, they often improve markedly (Perlmutter et al., 1987).

An individual's mental health directly affects his or her performance on cognitive tasks. Depression is a common psychological reaction in older adulthood, partly because of the loss of loved ones and friends; many old people have several such experiences. Depression causes reduced concentration and attention and, hence, lowers the overall level of cognitive functioning.

There are a number of other secondary factors that cause cognitive decline (Perlmutter et al., 1987). Some of the more important ones include the following:

- Physical fitness affects mental tasks as well as physical tasks. On a wide range of tests of cognitive functions, individuals who are more physically fit perform at a higher level.
- Nutritional deficits such as anemia, vitamin deficiencies, or chorine deficiency result in poor performance on intellectual tasks. Chorine, which is found in meat, fish, and egg yolks, is used by the brain to manufacture acetylcholine, a chemical that is essential for efficient neural processing.
- Use of alcohol over an extended period—even in moderate amounts—results in reduced short- and long-term memory. More extensive drinking tends to interfere with daily functioning, also with adequate nutrition. Both directly and indirectly, alcohol use impairs mental functions even when the person is not under the influence.
- Prescription and over-the-counter drugs, ranging from sleeping pills to pain relievers and drugs for hypertension, have side effects that reduce alertness and attention. Drugs are not always easily cleared from the kidneys or liver. As an individual grows older, smaller doses of a drug may be just as potent as large ones. Sometimes a reduction in the amount of a drug used can dramatically improve mental functioning.
- Disuse of mental functioning. After periods of prolonged illness, social isolation, or depression, some individuals do not return to their former level of mental functioning. The old adage "Use it or lose it" holds true in such cases.

Compensating for an Aging Mind

Research conducted by Baltes (1993) focused on the mechanisms that older adults use to coordinate the gains and losses of an aging mind. These mechanisms are especially important as biological and health-related losses shift the balance of cognitive functioning. The model that Baltes developed is based on "selective optimization with compensation." He used the following example to describe how this adaptive process works:

When the concert pianist Rubinstein was asked, in a television interview, how he managed to remain such a successful pianist in his old age, he mentioned three strategies: (1) In old age he performed fewer pieces, (2) he now practiced each piece more frequently, and (3) he introduced more ritardandos in his playing before fast segments, so that the playing speed sounded

Even moderate drinking over extended time causes impairment of primary and secondary memory.

faster than it was in reality. These are examples of selection (fewer pieces), optimization (more practice), and compensation (increased use of contrast in speed). My contention is that this is the kind of life knowledge that is another facet of the pragmatics of the aging mind. (Baltes, 1993, p. 590)

Baltes contended that as older adults recognize their objective and subjective cognitive losses, as well as the changing balance between gains and losses, they reorganize and adjust their sense of self in response. This readjustment, Baltes proposed, may explain why most older adults do not experience a major reduction in their sense of either subjective well-being or personal control. Other research supports this view. For example, factors such as higher education (Liebovici, Ritchie, & Ledesert, 1996) and sustained overall activity level (Christensen et al., 1996) help a person compensate for and minimize some aspects of cognitive decline in very old adulthood.

CONTENT CHECK
COGNITIVE CHANGES IN ADVANCED AGE

True–False (answers are on the Companion Website)

1. In old age memory loss is universally severe.
2. In old age the speed of mental and physical performance declines.
3. Long-term memory falls off sharply in old age.
4. Symptoms of *Alzheimer's disease* include regressive memory loss and disorientation.
5. Secondary factors such as depression may negatively affect cognitive functioning in old age.

Thinking Critically

Is cognitive decline inevitable in older adulthood age? Why or why not?

CHAPTER 17 REVISITED

Aging Today

■ Stereotypes about older people and ageism make it difficult to understand them as the varied individuals they really are; people of all ages tend to assign more negative stereotypes to older people and more positive ones to younger people.

■ In some cultures and historical eras, older people have been respected as wise elders and transmitters of culture and lore.

■ The median age of the U.S. population is increasing.

■ Older adulthood can be viewed as consisting of four decades: young-old, middle-aged-old, old-old, and very old-old, each of which has differing characteristics.

Physical Aspects of Aging

■ Many effects of aging are not noticed until later adulthood; aging is gradual and most physical systems have reserve capacity.

■ Not all older people show the same signs of aging; physically fitness and activity cause variations.

■ Pathological factors contribute directly to changes during older age.

■ Signs of aging include gray hair, less elastic skin, a shift in posture, and deepening wrinkles.

■ The senses generally become less efficient with age, as does information processing.

- Hearing deficits are common but are usually mild to moderate.
- Visual impairments are common during older age; these include cataracts, glaucoma, decreased ability to focus, and decreased visual acuity.
- The sense of taste shows considerable stability into old age.
- Muscle weight decreases with age; bones become weaker, hollower, and more brittle.
- High-intensity exercise training helps counteract muscle weakness and related physical frailty in very old people.
- The cardiovascular system becomes less efficient with age, and the capacity of the lungs decreases; reserve capacities are also reduced, as is the immune system.
- Older people are more likely to have chronic health problems than acute illnesses.
- Some of the poor health of older adults may be because of improper nutrition; excess fat consumption results in atherosclerosis.
- Overuse, misuse, or abuse of drugs causes health problems in older people.

Causes of Aging

- Genetic components, stress, accidents, and diseases play a role in aging.
- Senescence refers to the universal biological processes of aging.
- Theories of aging fall into two basic categories: stochastic theories and preprogrammed or biological clock theories.

Cognitive Changes in Advanced Age

- Most mental skills remain relatively intact in older adulthood, although there is a decline in the speed of cognitive processing.
- Sensory storage and short-term memory change little with age, but transfer to long-term memory normally declines; tertiary memory remains fairly intact in older adults.
- Gaining wisdom is a positive aspect of aging that often increases the quantity and quality of an individual's understanding.
- Among the primary causes of cognitive decline in older adults are Alzheimer's disease and strokes. Secondary causes include poverty or failing health.
- Dementia and accompanying personality changes are sometimes associated with older adulthood; confusion, mental lapses, or disoriented behavior may be attributable to other causes, such as physical or emotional illnesses that can be treated.
- About half of people diagnosed as having dementia suffer from Alzheimer's disease; the eventual result is severe disorientation and death from failure of crucial bodily systems.
- Strokes or ministrokes are another primary cause of dementia.
- Psychological expectations, mental health, and other factors can profoundly influence cognitive functioning in older adults.
- Other factors that can cause cognitive decline include lack of physical fitness and good nutrition, excessive use of alcohol, side effects of prescribed medication, and disuse of mental functioning.

KEY TERMS

ageism
filial piety
septuagenarians
octogenarians
centenarians
nonagenarians

pathological aging factors
cataract
glaucoma
visual acuity
hypertension
atherosclerosis

dementia
senescence
stochastic theories of aging
wisdom
Alzheimer's disease
stroke

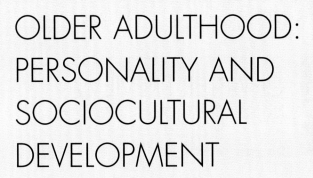

OLDER ADULTHOOD: PERSONALITY AND SOCIOCULTURAL DEVELOPMENT

18

CHAPTER PREVIEW

Do you know:

1. What a *status passage* is?

2. How older adults maintain a relatively consistent *identity*?

3. What Erikson's crisis of *integrity versus despair* involves?

4. How theorists differ concerning the issue of *continuity and change* in adjustment to older adulthood?

5. How *personality type* and *coping styles* affect adjustment to aging?

6. What's involved in *successful* aging?

7. Why *retirement* is an important status passage?

8. What *physical, economic,* and *social* conditions influence adjustment to retirement?

9. How *gender* affects adjustment to retirement?

10. How to *prepare* for retirement and what *options* there are?

11. What patterns of *family* and *personal relationships* contribute to the stresses and satisfactions of old age?

12. What adjustments an older *widow* or *widower* must make?

13. What role *sibling relationships* play during later life?

14. What social programs successfully address the needs of *frail older persons*?

15. How older people themselves are an *important resource* in meeting their own needs and those of peers?

These are the main topics of Chapter 18.

A major change in role and social position is called a **status passage.** Changes in status occur throughout the lifespan. The adolescent becomes a young adult; the young adult enters middle adulthood; in each case the individual takes on enlarged roles and responsibilities, typically with gains in status and power. The status passage into older adulthood, however, is quite different. The transition to retirement, to becoming a widow or widower, or to failing health may result in loss of power, responsibility, and autonomy.

On the positive side, retiring can yield new freedom to pursue personal interests, and becoming a great-grandparent can provide the opportunity to spend more time with loved ones. Thus, the way a person interprets status passages and the changes that accompany them is often at least as important as the events themselves. The effect of many life events of later adulthood depends in large part on the meaning attached to them. You may view retirement as signaling the end of your usefulness or productiveness in the workforce, perhaps the end of a major part of your identity—whether as a truck driver, a dentist, a dancer, or a corporate executive. You may view retirement quite differently if you have spent the last 30 to 40 years hating your job and everything about it. In this case retirement may mean release from tedium, drudgery, and subservience to authority. (Indeed, one factor that predicts successful adjustment to retirement is "dislike of your job.") Similarly, becoming a widower or widow may bring a sudden release from the toil of caring for a chronically ill spouse, along with new freedoms. It may also mean no longer having to live with

status passage A change in the role and position that occurs when an individual enters adolescence, becomes a parent, retires, or becomes a widow or widower.

602

someone you've disliked for many years but been unwilling to divorce. On the other hand, it can bring considerable and enduring grief over the loss.

Illness and physical disabilities are among the most difficult circumstances that we may have to cope with in later adulthood. Even here, however, there is wide variation in styles of coping. As one older man commented, "I don't get around the way I used to, but I've never enjoyed my garden like I have these last few years, and that last grandchild is a sheer joy."

When journalist Gail Sheehy interviewed U.S. adults in their 60s and 70s, she found that many of the respondents continued to see life as full of potential rather than limitations. They anticipated a life "in which they can concentrate on becoming better, stronger, deeper, wiser, funnier, freer, sexier, and more attentive to living the privileged moments" (Sheehy, 1995). In their 60s, many older adults experienced a wonderful combination of good health and freedom from work and worry. In their 70s and beyond, these same adults fine-tuned their priorities and focused on what they could do rather than on what they could not do any longer.

Here we explore the status changes that mark later adulthood with regard to personality, adjustment to developmental tasks such as retirement, and family relationships with grandchildren and great-grandchildren. We also look at topics such as caring for an ill spouse, adjusting to being a widow or widower, and reaffirming relationships with siblings and friends. Finally, we consider in detail how older people are affected by social policy in such areas as health care and housing.

Personality and Aging

It is easy to overgeneralize about personality, life satisfaction, and developmental tasks in later adulthood. Recall from the last chapter that there are many differences between the vigorous, healthy, recently retired young-old, the often frail old-old, and those in between. Each individual, regardless of age, also has a unique pattern of attitudes, values, and beliefs about old age and about himself or herself, along with a pattern of life experiences that reinforces that pattern. Yet, given all the differences, there are still some events and concerns that are common to most people in later life. How these are dealt with plays a major role in successful aging.

Developmental Tasks in Older Adulthood

At the outset, it is helpful to return to Erikson's theory to look for central developmental tasks. In his view, people who can face and cope with such tasks maintain better mental health.

Maintaining Identity   One of the central tasks from adolescence on is maintaining a relatively consistent identity. As the term is used here, *identity* refers to the reasonably consistent set of concepts that a person has about his or her physical, psychological, and social attributes. For theorist Susan Whitbourne and colleagues (Whitbourne & Connolly, 1999), the process of maintaining a consistent identity is a lot like Piaget's ongoing process of adaptation (Chapter 2): It involves assimilating new events and changing circumstances into existing self-concepts, and accommodating major life events or threats that cannot be readily assimilated. In the face of a major chronic illness, for example, physical, psychological, and social aspects of self-concept are threatened and may require considerable accommodation.

Ideally, according to Whitbourne, individuals maintain a balance between assimilation and accommodation. Refusal to accommodate may mean that the individual is denying reality. Such a person may be defensive and rigid and may unjustifiably blame other people. On the other hand, accommodating too readily can make a person hysterical, impulsive, or hypersensitive. In all, maintaining a balance between consistency of identity and openness to new experiences is an important developmental task of older adulthood, just as it is in earlier periods of the lifespan.

For the very old, maintaining a sense of consistency in personal identity may be particularly important. In one study of over 600 individuals, mostly in their 70s and 80s, who experienced major changes in their health and living arrangements (Lieberman & Tobin, 1983), the researchers found that accommodating was an enormously difficult task, especially for those who were frail and highly dependent on others. Those who were most successful in adapting managed to do so by maintaining and "validating" their identities. In spite of the adversity, they were able to say, "I am who I have always been." How were they able to do this in the face of very real shifts in their lives and physical abilities? Generally, they shifted from thinking about the present to thinking about the past. For example, one woman at first described herself by saying, "I am important to my family and friends; you should see how many birthday cards I got." Two years later, after some major changes in her life, she instead defined herself by saying, "I think I am important to my family; I have always done the best I could for my family, and they appreciate it." Her past became evidence that allowed her to maintain a concept of her present personal identity that was in accordance with the person she used to be (Ruth & Coleman, 1995).

Integrity Versus Despair　The final stage in Erikson's theory is the psychosocial conflict of *integrity versus despair*. In his view, older people ponder whether their lives have fulfilled their earlier expectations. Those who can look back and feel satisfied that their lives have had meaning and that they have done the best they could develop a strong sense of personal integrity. Those who look back and see nothing but a long succession of wrong turns, missed opportunities, and failures develop a sense of despair. Ideally, resolution of this conflict involves a preponderance of integrity tinged with realistic despair (Erikson, Erikson, & Kivnick, 1986), which is an aid to wisdom (see Chapter 17). Wisdom enables older adults to maintain dignity and an integrated self in the face of physical deterioration and even impending death.

Part of the adjustment to old age includes the psychological need to reminisce and reflect on past events. Older people often spend time searching for themes and images that give their lives meaning and coherence. Sometimes they need to sort out and make sense of episodes and situations in their past (Neugarten, 1976). Some people ruminate over what sort of legacy they will leave, what contributions they have made, and how the world will remember them—whether through works of art, social service, their accomplishments at work, the children they bore and raised, or the material wealth they will pass along to their children or to society. Many look to their children and grandchildren as a legacy in whom traces of their own personality and values will live on.

An 85-year-old woman eloquently expressed some of the musings, sighings, and expressions of minor regrets that are typical of this process:

If I had my life to live over, I'd dare to make more mistakes next time. I'd relax. I'd limber up. I'd be sillier than I've been this trip. I'd take fewer things seriously. I'd take more chances. I'd take more trips. I'd climb more mountains and swim more rivers. I'd eat more ice cream and less beans. I'd perhaps have more actual troubles, but I'd have fewer imaginary ones.

You see, I'm one of those people who live sensibly and sanely hour after hour, day after day. Oh, I've had my moments and if I had it to do over again, I'd have more of them. In fact, I'd try to have nothing else. Just moments, one after another, instead of living so many years ahead of each day. I've been one of those persons who never goes anywhere without a thermometer, a hot water bottle, a raincoat, and a parachute. If I had it to do again, I would travel lighter than I have.

If I had my life to live over, I would start barefoot earlier in the spring and stay that way later in the fall. I would go to more dances. I would ride more merry-go-rounds. I would pick more daisies. (Burnside, 1979, p. 425)

Continuity and Change in Older Adulthood

As we have seen in earlier chapters, most contemporary theorists tend to see development as a lifelong phenomenon; thus, adjustment to old age is an extension of earlier personality styles. Even in older adulthood, however, theorists differ on the issue of continuity and change.

"Stage" theorists believe that new life structures or organizations emerge in old age, built on the earlier stages. Levinson (1978, 1986, 1996), for example, believed that there is a period of transition (ages 60 to 65) that links the individual's previous life structure to that of late adulthood. Erikson saw ego integrity (or its counterpart, despair) as the outcome of a long process of development (Erikson et al., 1986). Peck (1968) viewed old age in terms of the resolution of the conflict between *ego transcendence* (acheiving a state of mind that goes beyond one's prospects of dying) and *ego preoccupation* (with dying) (see Chapter 16).

Other theorists see even more continuity between previous adjustment and reactions to aging. Robert Atchley (1989) suggested that continuity provides people with an identity, a sense of who they are. People strive to be consistent in their behavior because it makes them feel more secure. Consistency enables people to say things like "I would never do that" or "That's just like me" with confidence. Similarly, there are external pressures for consistency. Other people expect us to we behave in a similar way in various kinds of situations, and become uncomfortable if we are often unpredictable. Atchley was quick to emphasize, however, that continuity does not mean that there are no changes at all. Certainly, people's roles, abilities, and relationships all change. This requires them to make certain alterations in their behaviors, their expectations, even their values. Atchley proposed that these changes are in line with a relatively constant "inner core" that we use to define ourselves.

Personality   As adults, do we fit the following pronouncement by William James that "In most of us, by the age of thirty, the character has set like plaster, and will never soften again . . ." (cited in Costa & McCrae, 1994)?

Apparently we do. Several longitudinal studies have looked at the maintenance of basic personality traits or types over the decades in adulthood, and they have the kind of found continuity described by James. In one study, Paul Costa and Robert McCrae (1985) assessed three aspects of personality in a group of 2000 adult men. First, they looked at *neuroticism*—the amount of anxiety, depression, self-consciousness, vulnerability, impulsiveness, and hostility the men displayed. By and large, they found no real changes in the men's neuroticism over a 10-year period. Those who were highly neurotic tended to complain about their health; smoke heavily; have problems with drinking, sex, and finances; and feel generally dissatisfied with their lives. In particular, those who were high in neuroticism tended to be hypochondriacs, in accordance with one popular stereotype of older people. The evidence, however, showed that they had probably been hypochondriacs all their lives (Costa & McCrae, 1985).

Second, the researchers looked at *extraversion* versus *introversion*. Extraverted people are assertive and outgoing; they seek excitement and activity. Introverted people are more inclined to be shy and keep to themselves. The men in the study who were highly extraverted tended to stay that way. They were also happier and more satisfied with their lives than those who were highly introverted. There was a minor shift toward introversion, however, when circumstances required the men to become more dependent upon others. Other researchers have studied extraversion and introversion over longer periods and have found that many of their subjects become more introverted in old age.

The third dimension studied was *openness to experience*. The men who were open to new experiences had a wider range of interests. They tended to experience events intensely, whether the events were positive or negative. Men who were open to experience also showed more life satisfaction than those who were more defensive, cautious, and conforming. This aspect of personality also remained consistent from middle to later adulthood.

Many such studies show general consistency in personality (Labouvie-Vief & Diehl, 1999). Even the oldest old have organized, coherent, integrated patterns or beliefs about themselves (Troll & Skaff, 1997), and they tend to act in ways that are consistent with their self-image. When they are able—despite major life changes—to judge themselves as having acted in accordance with their self-concept, by and large they express more life satisfaction and self-esteem. Self-concept is, of course, vulnerable to life events and major changes in health, finances, social involvement, social class, sex, housing conditions, and marriage. Major changes in self-concept can, in turn, affect a person's sense of well-being (Thomae, 1980). Yet, aging per se seems to have no direct effect on self-concept.

Although few universal personality changes occur in later life, some researchers have studied whether any distinct pattern of personality change occurs as people grow older. One longitudinal study (Gutmann, 1964) used the Thematic Apperception Test (TAT), in which subjects tell stories about ambiguous pictures and researchers infer attitudes and feelings from the stories. The question was whether any consistent changes would occur over the 20-year period of the study. The researchers found that 40-year-old men tended to view their environment as being within their control, rewarding boldness and risk taking; they saw themselves as equal to the challenges presented by the outside world. In contrast, 60-year-old men saw the world as more complex and dangerous, no longer within their power to be changed according to their will. They instead saw themselves as accommodating and conforming to their environment.

Coping Styles Whereas the research just discussed suggests that coping skills decline during old age, other research puts a different spin on the changes, indicating that people become more mature in their coping skills (Vaillant, 1977). For example, they show increases in the use of wise detachment and humor in the face of stress. Still others have argued that there are age-related differences in coping but that they are determined by the different stressors faced by older versus younger adults (Folkman, Lazarus, Pimley, & Novacek, 1987). Stressors that present positive challenges (for example, a promotion at work) become less frequent with age. Although losses don't increase appreciably with age, it may be that the losses experienced by older adults are more centrally related to their identity and, hence, more threatening. Similarly, the nature of daily hassles—which also create stress—also varies with age (Folkman et al., 1987).

Some theorists, beginning with Jung (1931/1960), have suggested that men's and women's coping styles change in different ways. Men seem to move from an active to a passive style. After a lifetime of responsibility and decision making, they feel free to express more of the complexity of their personalities—including traits that are traditionally considered feminine (Gutmann, 1994). Very old men move beyond passivity to a style called **magical mastery,** in which they deal with reality through projection and distortion. As women age, they seem to become more aggressive, instrumental, and domineering—in accordance with masculine stereotypes. Perhaps both sexes respond to being liberated from the **parental imperative,** the social pressures for women to conform to nurturing roles and for men to be financially responsible and to suppress any traits that conflict with that role.

Cross-sectional research has also indicated that there are age-related changes in coping styles. Susan Folkman and her colleagues (1987) found that younger adults are more likely to use active, problem-focused coping styles, whereas older adults are more passive and focused on emotions. For example, an older woman might downplay the importance of the traffic accident she just had, or might view it in a more positive light by saying "I really needed to get rid of that car anyway" or "At least no one was injured." A younger woman might instead handle the situation by confronting the other driver, getting his or her name and address, contacting the insurance company, and getting estimates to repair the damage. As in all cross-sectional research, the differences could also be attributable to cohort differences (see Chapter 1). Generally, however, longitudinal research has also tended to find continuity in coping styles as people age (e.g., McCrae, 1989).

In sum, adjustments in later life are often very similar to the adjustments that occur in earlier life. People develop an identity; they create themes that they carry with them through life. When they reach old age, their reactions to aging and to new situations will be highly individual and consistent with the identity and themes they have created for themselves throughout their lives. Personality development in old age, then, consists of personal interpretation of events and reactions to events in keeping with the individual's past reactions (Ryff, 1985).

Most older people must cope with a sense of their own vulnerability.

Successful Aging

Eventually, many older individuals must confront the problems of sensory decline or ill health, both in themselves and in friends and relatives. Many must confront the realities of lower status or productivity and reduced income. The longer they live, the more likely they are to experience the death of friends and family members, including their spouse. For some, the problems are overwhelming. They become preoccupied with their health, restricted circumstances, hardships, and increasing lack of autonomy.

What, then, is successful aging? First, note that the preceding description is not the predominant pattern in later adulthood. All too often, stereotypical thinking about aging paints a bleak picture that many older people themselves accept and conform to. In reality, the great majority of older people perceive themselves in quite different, more positive ways. One survey, for example, noted that although many older people agreed that "life is really tough for most

magical mastery   A lifestyle of very old men characterized by coping via projection and distortion of reality.

parental imperative   Traditional pressures for women to be nurturers and men to be providers.

A CLOSER LOOK

AGING IN THE U.S. BLACK COMMUNITY

There is a paradox between the plight of many older ethnically black people in the United States and their remarkable ability to sustain themselves psychologically as they age. No one can dispute that black adults are more likely than whites to live in poverty, have less education, be single mothers, and experience substandard medical care. Yet survey after survey has shown that many older blacks have resources that enable them to cope with aging—often more effectively than their white counterparts.

Researchers have identified two key factors that are largely responsible for the staying power of many black people: (1) prayer and affiliation with a church and (2) help from family and friends. "The adaptive value of these two strategies," said researcher Rose Gibson (1986), "may make blacks' entry into old age more transition than crisis."

Gibson based her conclusion on an analysis of the 1957 and 1976 versions of the *Americans View Their Mental Health* surveys, which asked respondents of differing ethnicities how they handled problems or worries. Several important findings emerged.

The surveys showed the importance of prayer in the lives of many blacks. Black peoples' responses to the surveys indicated that they were much more likely than whites to turn to prayer as a source of help and comfort. This was true in both 1957 and 1976, when blacks indicated that they used prayer more often than they used any other single coping strategy. By 1976, however, there was a significant lessening in prayer among middle-aged black people. Whereas in 1957 a clear majority of middle-aged blacks continued to turn to prayer as they grew older, in 1976 far fewer (27.3%) of their middle-aged counterparts prayed as a way of coping with problems.

Black peoples' reliance on prayer can be explained in part by the role of the church in the black community. Many look to the church for a range of social services as well as religious activity. Research has shown that they are more likely than whites to rely on their church for practical assistance, especially when the rest of the community offers little help (Haber, 1984). As a result, older black people perceive the church as providing practical support while family members provide emotional support (Walls, 1992). Those who receive strong support from their church and their families are also more likely to report a sense of well-being than those who receive moderate support.

The surveys also showed a pattern among blacks of seeking informal help from varied family members and friends. Whereas in both 1957 and 1976 whites were much more likely than blacks to turn to an internal network in times of worry, the helper they chose was likely to be a spouse or another family member. In contrast, blacks were more likely to turn to friends for help in 1957 and to combinations of family members in 1976. According to Gibson (1986), "The use of multiple family members for help with worries seems to increase as blacks move from middle to old age." This informal social support network plays a crucial role in the lives of low-income, older black people, who rely on second- and third-generation adult kin for the physical and emotional help they need during their later years (Luckey, 1994).

Thus, although older ethnically black people tend to endure many more hardships over their lifetimes and have fewer economic resources to sustain them in old age, they find enormous comfort and sustenance in family and friends and in prayer. However, it is important to remember that this sense of psychological well-being is no substitute for adequate economic and social support. Despite inner peace, their lives continue to be marred by limited resources (Gibson, 1986).

---

people over 65," they and their friends were, for some reason, exceptions to the rule (Harris & Associates, 1978).

As noted by Paul and Margaret Baltes (1990), the Roman statesman Cicero (106–43 BC) produced perhaps the first essay on positive aspects of aging. He contended that in advanced age it is finally possible for a person to enjoy life and contemplation without being distracted by "bodily pleasures." Life satisfaction and adjustment in older adulthood actually depend on a number of factors, but such satisfaction has little relationship to age itself. Health is the most important factor. After that, money, social class, marital status, adequacy of housing, amount of social interaction, and even transportation are important factors that influence whether older adults feel satisfied with their lives. Earlier life satisfaction also influences feelings of satisfaction in later adulthood. Although life satisfaction itself is comparable in young and old adults, the sources of satisfaction may change. Younger adults gain the most satisfaction from achievements and advances in work, self-development, and other areas; older adults may be satisfied simply to maintain their ability to function (Bearon, 1989). In addition, many older people look to religion and an extended social network for support and validation, as discussed in "A Closer Look," on facing page.

Life satisfaction in later adulthood is also determined by how older people define positive functioning. In a study of 171 middle-aged and older adults, Carol Ryff (1989) found that both cohorts defined psychological well-being in terms of an "other" orientation—being a caring, compassionate person and having good relationships with others. Older subjects also pointed to acceptance of change as an important quality of positive functioning.

When Ryff and colleagues (Heidrich & Ryff, 1993b) tried to determine why many older people maintain a positive outlook in spite of failing health and declining abilities, they found that social comparison plays a crucial role. Social comparison means evaluating yourself and your own situation relative to that of others. Older adults compared their situations to those of other older people around them and modified their perspectives accordingly. In particular, older women facing health problems frequently engaged in social comparison. The more positive the comparisons, the better the women's mental health—even in the face of severe physical problems. Interestingly, the women who were in poorest health showed the strongest effects of social comparison and achieved a degree of psychological adaptation comparable to that of healthy women— they came to perceive themselves as better off than they actually were. Another study (Heidrich & Ryff, 1993a) found that social comparison and social integration—maintenance of meaningful roles, normative guidelines, and reference groups—offset the negative effects of poor physical health and had a positive impact on maintaining well-being and minimizing psychological distress.

In sum, maintaining activities you're good at and actively compensating for any physical or mental decline you experience are important factors in successful aging (Schulz & Heckhausen, 1996; also see Chapter 17). Stated somewhat differently, successful aging involves avoiding disease and disability, maintaining physical and cognitive functioning, and especially staying engaged in social and productive activities (Rowe & Kahn, 1997). Old age, then, is very much what you yourself make of it.

CONTENT CHECK
PERSONALITY AND AGING

True–False (answers are on the Companion Website)

1. A key developmental task for the very old involves the maintenance of a sense of a consistent personal identity.
2. According to Erikson, the psychosocial conflict characteristic of older adulthood is that of integrity versus ego transcendence.
3. Older adulthood is a time when many universal personality changes occur.
4. Coping skills tend to decline substantially in old age.
5. Social comparison is an important factor in determining a positive or negative outlook in old age.

Thinking Critically

In what ways is old age very much what an individual makes of it?

Retirement: A Major Change in Status

One of the primary tasks of older adulthood is adjusting to retirement. Historically, this adjustment affected men much more than women because of men's greater participation in the workforce. In the past 30 years, however, the gender difference has changed dramatically as increasing numbers of women have entered and remained in the workforce all the way to retirement. In the past, also, retirement was the culmination of a long and stable career. That, too, has changed (Chapter 16). Nowadays, a great many workers do not stay in the same job and work for the same company throughout their working years, and this often has a negative impact on their social and economic circumstances after retirement (Hayward, Friedman, & Chen, 1998). Indeed, one of the most important considerations in how people fare after retirement is whether they actually choose to retire (Reitzes, Mutran, & Fernandez, 1996), as opposed to being forced to retire because of their age, because of being squeezed out by a younger person, or as a result of corporate downsizing.

Either way, however, retirement is the most significant status change of later adulthood. Work provides a structure for living, a daily schedule. It provides coworkers and other people to interact with regularly. Work also provides roles and functions and thereby contributes to personal identity. Thus, retirement may require considerable adjustment.

Retirement does not just involve dealing with greatly increased free time. An individual must work out choices, negotiations, and coping patterns consistent with his or her personal set of meanings; in effect, each person constructs his or her own social reality for retirement. How easily the individual adopts the new role depends on a number of factors. If the shift to retirement is sudden and dramatic, or if an individual's identity has been closely tied to an occupational role, the transition will probably be very difficult.

Physical, Economic, and Social Conditions

The pattern of and adjustment to retirement are the results of many factors: physical health, economic status, the attitudes of others, and the need for work-related fulfillment. As we also see, men and women often face different circumstances when they retire.

Physical Health An important consideration that influences the way a person reacts to retirement is health. A great number of older people leave the workforce—willingly or otherwise—because of ill health. One study of a large group of men who were about to retire (Richardson, 1999) found that healthy men who wanted to retire fared the best. Those in ill health fared poorly, whether or not they wanted to retire. This may be because retirement frequently occurs more suddenly for people in ill health (Ekerdt, Vinick, & Bosse, 1989). They may therefore be less prepared financially and psychologically than those who have time to anticipate and plan for retirement. Moreover, their health expenses may create a financial burden, especially if they have a disability. Overall, for two-thirds of retired U.S. adults age 65 or older, Social Security benefits are their major source of income; for one-third, the benefits are virtually their only income (Social Security Administration, 2000). Disabled retirees rely much more on these benefits than other retirees do.

Attitudes often change in the first few years of retirement (Levy, 1978). It was found that healthy men who are unwilling to retire quickly become dissatisfied; they withdraw socially and tend to be bitter and angry. They eventually tend to

Of those who retire, people healthy generally fare better than those retiring because of poor health.

recover, however, and gradually take on attitudes similar to those of people who want to retire. In contrast, those who are ill when they retire show little improvement in attitude over time, even if they had looked forward to retirement.

Economic Status   Economic status is another major factor that affects a retiree's adjustment to a new way of life. Contrary to what you might think, most older people in the United States have sufficient financial assets to live on. In terms of net worth, older adults tend to be wealthier than young adults. Still, some 1 out of 10 adults age 65 or older live below the poverty line (NCHS, 1999). This is a lower rate than among young adults, but it masks the circumstances of certain subgroups of older people. Single people are much more likely to be poor than those who are married. Members of minority groups are more likely to be poor. For example, about 24% of older adults who consider themselves Hispanic are below the poverty line (NCHS, 1999). Women are more likely than men to be poor. Among older women who identify as white, over 11% live in poverty, compared to less than 6% of men. Those suffering the discrimination that often comes with being both female and a member of a minority group are the most likely to be poor. Almost 29% of older women who identify as black are impoverished, as are over 26% who identify as Hispanic (NCHS, 1999). Moreover, older adults are less likely than young adults to escape poverty. This is particularly true when the older person has been poor for more than 3 years. Whereas the majority of young adults living in poverty will improve their situation, only 5% of older adults will do so (Coe, 1988).

Need for Work-Related Fulfillment   As discussed earlier, an individual's lifelong attitude toward work also affects his or her feelings about retirement. In some segments of the United States, there is an almost religious devotion to work. Many people have invested so much time and energy in their jobs that their overall sense of self-worth and self-esteem depends on the work they do. For many, leisure activities are superficial and therefore lack meaning. In a very real sense, retirement for such men means stepping out of their previous life. Disengagement is especially hard for people who have never found satisfaction outside of their jobs in the form of hobbies, reading, continued education, or involvement in civic organizations. The problem tends to be worse for the less educated, the financially strained, and those with few social or political involvements, but professionals or business executives may also have difficulty finding something to do with their greatly increased leisure time. This is one reason why substantial numbers of people continue to work part time after retiring (Quinn & Burkhauser, 1990).

Gender Differences in Retirement Until the past decade, studies that include both men and women (and in some cases women only) reported findings similar to those of earlier studies that included only men: Factors such as good health, economic security, and higher educational level predict a positive adjustment to retirement for women as well as men (Atchley, 1982; Block, 1981; Hatch, 1992). Unfortunately, however, many women receive lower salaries and are often less financially secure than men after retirement—particularly if they are single or recently widowed or divorced. In addition, women's satisfaction after retirement can be markedly reduced if the retirement was forced upon them because of the need to care for an ailing spouse or parent.

Otherwise, it is popularly thought that women adjust to retirement more easily than men because many women have had interrupted work histories and therefore have experience with being unemployed. This view, however, is not entirely supported by research evidence. Indeed, in one study, women who had a continuous work history for an extended portion of their adult lives adapted more easily to retirement (Block, 1981). On average, the women with continuous work experience had greater financial security and were better prepared for retirement than those who had intermittent experience in the workforce.

Deciding to Retire

Retirement is not necessarily hazardous to your health, of course. In fact, fully a third of retirees report improvement in their mental and physical health in the period immediately after retirement. Another 50% report no change. Overall, many recent retirees experience an increase in life satisfaction (Ekerdt, 1987).

Preparing for Retirement As noted, adjusting to retirement is easier if you are prepared for it. In one view (Thompson, 1977), preparing for retirement consists of three elements:

1. *Decelerating*: As people grow older, they begin to let go or taper off their work responsibilities to avoid a sudden drop in activity at retirement.
2. *Retirement planning*: People plan specifically for the life they will lead after retirement.
3. *Retirement living*: People come to grips with concerns about stopping work and think about what it will be like to live as a retired person.

Some companies provide retirement counselors who can guide people through the process and help them determine the best time to retire. Several specific factors are considered (Johnson & Riker, 1981). How long has the potential retiree worked? Does the retiree have adequate savings and income, a place to live, and plans for further work or activities after retirement? Is he or she old enough to consider retirement? Some retirement counselors refer to the answers to these questions as an index of **retirement maturity**—how prepared a person is to retire. In general, people with a higher degree of retirement maturity have more positive attitudes toward retirement and an easier time adjusting to it.

retirement maturity How prepared a person is to retire.

Retirement Options Of course, complete withdrawal from the workforce is not the only option for people in later adulthood. Some experts suggest that society may face a work shortage in the future (Forman, 1984), that we may be needlessly losing talented and productive workers, and that the increase in the number of full-time retirees may put severe strains on the pension plans of the future (Wojahn, 1983). Therefore, creative solutions such as part-time, perhaps less physically demanding work options are needed for older people. Although formerly there was little or no financial incentive for older workers to remain in the labor force, recent changes in Social Security regulations have made it less costly for older people to continue to work part time (Quinn & Burkhauser, 1990).

Pilot programs to employ retired people have been remarkably successful. For example, retired businesspeople have been hired to train young and inexperienced workers. Another approach trains older people to work with handicapped children. Numerous other options have been explored (Donovan, 1984; Kieffer, 1984). When we look at how retirement has changed in the past 50 years and how it is likely to change in the years ahead, it becomes clear that retirement must be viewed in a historical context. Whereas in 1950 about half of all men over age 65 were still working, in 1995 only about 12% of this age group still had a job or were looking for work (Quinn & Burkhauser, 1990; Kaye, Lord, & Sherrid, 1995). Increases in Social Security benefits, retirement funds, and pensions are partially responsible for many early-retirement decisions. Those who continue working after retirement are more likely to be employed part-time or self-employed than younger workers (Quinn & Burkhauser, 1990).

However, if these economic trends continue, fewer people may have the option of early retirement in the years to come. Experts predict that many of the 76 million baby boomers will be forced to continue working to age 70 and beyond because they cannot afford to retire. According to the federal Committee for Economic Development, a combination of factors is putting pressure on baby boomers to remain employed. These include the government's decision to raise the minimum age for Social Security retirement benefits, the uncertain future of the Social Security system, and Baby Boomers' notoriously poor rates of savings (Kaye et al., 1995).

CONTENT CHECK
RETIREMENT: A MAJOR CHANGE IN STATUS

True–False (answers are on the Companion Website)

1. Retirement is a more significant status change for older men than for older women.
2. Poor health is one of the main reasons why older people retire.
3. Women with continuous work experience tend to adjust better to retirement than women with intermittent work experience.
4. Preparing for retiring involves decelerating, retirement planning, and retirement living.
5. Pilot programs to employ retired people have mostly proved to be unsuccessful.

Thinking Critically

What are the best ways people can plan for retirement and how can society at large help?

Older couples, without the responsibilities of work and children, often report increased life satisfaction and harmony.

Family and Personal Relationships

An age-related status change equal in importance to retirement involves changes in family and personal relationships, often including coping with illness and death and making a new life as a widow or widower.

As in any period of life, the social context of family and personal relationships helps define our roles and responsibilities and our life satisfactions. In today's world, this social context is shifting for older adults much as it is for younger adults. Divorce and remarriage are more common. Kinship relations with grandchildren and stepgrandchildren are more complicated. There is also a wider range of single lifestyles. Nevertheless, close interpersonal relationships continue to define many of the stresses and satisfactions of life in later adulthood. We explore these relationships first by focusing on the "postparental" period and then by examining the role of many older people as caregiver to an ill or dying spouse. The importance of support from siblings and friends is also considered.

When Parenting Is Over

Marital satisfaction often changes during the postparental period, as do relationships with children and grandchildren. For most older adults, the direct responsibilities of parenting are over (assuming that they had children). On average, older married couples report being more satisfied with their marriage after the children leave home. There may be some initial difficulty in adjusting to each other as a couple, but most couples who remain married report less stress and increased feelings of satisfaction and harmony (Lee, 1988; Olson & Lavee, 1989). Couples who report greater than average satisfaction are also likely to be those whose marriage is at the emotional center of their lives. Marriage now brings them more comfort, emotional support, and intimacy. Happy marriages that survive into later adulthood characteristically are more egalitarian and cooperative. There is reasonable equality with regard to love, status, and money (Reynolds, Remer, & Johnson, 1995). Traditional gender roles also become less important.

Relationships with Children and Grandchildren Despite high mobility and social change, most older adults report having relatively frequent contact with their children and grandchildren—if not in person, at least by phone. Typically, they still feel responsible for helping their children as needed, although they are also anxious not to interfere (Blieszner & Mancini, 1987; Greenberg & Becker, 1988; Hagestad, 1987). Aside from advice—whether solicited or not—parents often provide their adult children with various forms of assistance, such as money and babysitting.

Grandparenthood (Chapter 16) is often seen as one of the most satisfying roles of older age. Studies have shown that many grandparents develop strong, companionable relationships with their grandchildren. These bonds are based on regular contact and are the basis for close, loving relationships (Cherlin & Furstenberg, 1986).

In the United States, over 40% of older people have great-grandchildren (Doka & Mertz, 1988). In general, great-grandparents are also pleased with their role and attach emotional significance to it. The role can provide a sense of personal and family renewal, a new diversion in their lives, and a proud marker of longevity (Doka & Mertz, 1988). Thus, great-grandparents may be given a special status in the family.

Still, kinship patterns have undergone stress and change in the past few decades. The high rates of divorce and remarriage have made those patterns more complex. It is therefore not surprising that grandparents often report greater closeness to their grandchildren in situations in which their adult child is the custodial parent. Some grandparents feel that they have a particularly important role in helping to maintain stability and a sense of values during periods of family disruption (Johnson & Barer, 1987).

Caring for an Ill Spouse

Although most older people do not need much help with daily living, those who do tend to rely heavily on their families (Gatz et al., 1990; Stone et al., 1987). If there is a surviving spouse, she or he is the most likely caregiver, with wives being more likely to play this role than husbands. This means, of course, that the caregiver is also likely to be old and have health problems.

Caregiver wives often report more stress than caregiver husbands, although some studies find that the differences are small (Miller, 1990). There are probably many contributing factors; research suggests that gender-role changes that occur in old age may be involved (Pruchno & Resch, 1989). As men become more oriented to the family, they may actually be more interested in providing such care than women, who may feel that they have already spent most of their lives taking care of other people. It is also possible, however, that the differences in caregiver stress and strain are due to factors such as women's greater willingness to admit to having health or psychological problems (Miller, 1990).

Caring for someone with Alzheimer's disease entails unique strains. It is particularly stressful when the afflicted person's behavior becomes disruptive or socially embarrassing (Deimling & Bass, 1986). Moreover, these caregivers tend to have smaller support systems than people who are caring for physically but not mentally impaired older persons (Birkel & Jones, 1989). Even organized respite programs do not seem to be particularly helpful (Lawton, Brody, & Saperstein, 1989). In spite of the stresses and strains, however, caregivers often report considerable gratification from providing care for a person who has meant so much to them (Motenko, 1989).

Widows and Widowers

In later adulthood it is all too common to suffer the loss of a close family member, friend, or spouse, a loss that is usually marked by grief and bereavement, followed by a long period of readjustment (as discussed in Chapter 19). At the same time, men and women who experience the death of their spouse also assume a new status in life—that of widower or widow. For many, this is a very difficult transition involving major changes in daily life patterns and the risk of social isolation. For others, it may provide a long-awaited opportunity to assume control of their lives, especially if they have been caring for an ill or frail spouse.

There are more than five times more older-adult widows than widowers in the United States—some 9.2 million in all as of 1992 (see Figure 18–1). In addition, most older men are married, whereas most older women are not. By age 85, four out of every five women are widows (U.S. Census Bureau, 1993). These numbers are due in part to longevity. On average, older widows survive about 50% longer than older widowers after the spouse's death (Burnside, 1979).

Living Arrangements   The statistics just discussed spell loneliness for many older people, but a woman's experience of forced independence is often quite different from a man's. As with divorce, after the death of a spouse women of

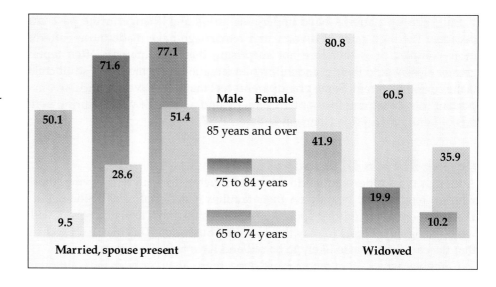

Figure 18-1   Marital Status of Older Persons by Age and Gender, United States (in Percent)
There are far more widows than widowers in the elderly U.S. population.

Source: U.S. Census Bureau, 1993.

all ages are less likely than men to remarry; on average, older-adult women are more than eight times less likely to remarry than older-adult men (Burnside, 1979a). This is partly because U.S. cultural attitudes traditionally favored the pairing of older men and younger women, which is also one of the reasons for the disproportionate number of widows in the first place: On average, women live longer than men do. Of U.S. women over age 65, nearly half are widowed and more than 40% live alone; another 40% live with their husbands. Of U.S. men over 65, only 15% are widowed and less than 20% live alone; the large majority are still married and living with their wives. Among the oldest-old (people in their 80s), one study found that only 10% of the women were married and about two-thirds lived alone; in contrast, 50% of the men were married and less than half lived alone (Barer, 1994). In all, some 9.5 million older adults live alone, and 8 out of 10 are women (see Figure 18–2). The morbid preoccupation

Figure 18-2   Noninstitutional Living Situations of Older Persons by Age and Gender, United States (in Thousands)
Living arrangements for the elderly differ considerably for men and women.

Source: U.S. Census Bureau, 1993.

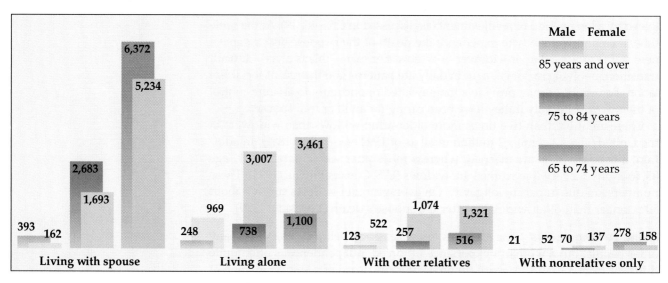

about becoming widows sometimes seen in middle-aged and older married women therefore has roots in reality.

There are many practical and psychological realities that widows and widowers must face if they live alone. They must run errands, maintain social contacts, and make financial decisions on their own. Some may welcome the opportunity; others may have difficulty because their spouses have always taken care of certain matters, such as finances.

Social Support Many potential support systems are available for widows and widowers, including family, friends, work associates (or former ones), and participants in leisure activities. In the United States, the majority of older adults have at least one child living within 10 miles of them, and adult children who have moved away often return when their parents need help (Lin & Rogerson, 1995). Both mothers and fathers are likely to receive assistance from their children, especially if they have daughters (Spitze & Logan, 1989, 1990). A widowed father may see his children less often than a widowed mother, although the difference is typically small (Spitze & Logan, 1989). In the immediate aftermath of the spouse's death, there is increased contact, help, and perception of kinship obligations. Relationships between the surviving parent and his or her children may be disrupted. In time, however, mother-child relationships usually improve or remain close, with exchanges of help and finances. Father-child relationships are less predictable and may be affected negatively. In such cases the wife often becomes the family's kinkeeper (Aquilino, 1994).

Widows may have an easier time than widowers in maintaining a social life because wives traditionally maintain communication with family members and initiate social activities with friends (Stevens, 1995). Widowers are therefore more likely to become isolated from the couple's previous social contacts. They are also generally less active in social organizations than widows. Finally, widowers are prone to certain sexual problems following bereavement. Attempts to end prolonged sexual inactivity, particularly when a wife dies after a long illness, may cause intense guilt and in turn may bring about a form of impotence known as **widower's impotency** (Comfort, 1976).

In general, then, the ways in which men and women adapt to widowhood differ significantly. According to the results of two studies conducted in the Netherlands in which older men and women who had been widowed for 3 to 5 years and were living alone were interviewed, widowers generally have greater income, education, freedom from health problems, and access to more partner-like relationships than do widows. However, they have more trouble coping emotionally than widows, who tend to have a broader support network that includes close female friends, children, and helpful neighbors (Stevens, 1995). The loneliest widows are those who have few or no children, were widowed suddenly and early, and have been widowed for less than 6 years (Lopata, Heinemann, & Baum, 1982).

Siblings and Friends

In later adulthood, many people report increased contact with and concern for siblings. Relationships that were quite distant in the busy, middle part of adult life are sometimes renewed and revitalized. Siblings share living quarters, provide comfort and support in times of crisis, and nurture each other in times of ill health. They are valuable companions for the kind of reminiscing that leads to ego integrity. They may also work together to organize and provide help to an ailing parent (Goetting, 1982). Siblings are also important to a widow's recovery from bereavement after the death of her husband, and to her subsequent

widower's impotency A form of impotence men sometimes experience after the death of their wife. Often accompanied by guilt.

IN THEORY, IN FACT
EMOTIONAL STABILITY IN LATER LIFE

Traditional views of old age have focused on the narrowing of the individual's emotional and social world. Recent research, however, is encouraging a revised notion of people's emotional capabilities in later life, in which this life-stage is seen as one of continued emotional growth. Based on this research, new psychological models propose that emotional well-being declines only in the period preceding death, at the point when cognitive and physical problems seriously impact on critical areas of functioning (Baltes, 1998). Prior to this, older people tend to experience increased satisfaction with interpersonal relationships (Diener & Suh, 1997). Accounting at least partly for this finding are greater complexity of emotional experience and better regulation of emotions experienced in daily life. More specifically, awareness of the fragility of human life and long-term relationships with family and friends is keener than at any other stage in the lifespan, leading to greater investments in emotionally close relationships (Carstensen & Charles, 1998).

It remains the case that social networks are more constricted in old age. However, very close relationships continue and do not diminish in intensity (Lang & Carstensen, 1994). What does seem to account for the diminished size of social networks is the loss of acquaintance relationships as people increasingly focus on connections that are meaningful to them—in preference to acquaintances or unfamiliar people. This preference has also been replicated across cultures. For example, in one study researchers found that in Hong Kong older people showed a greater preference for familiar social partners than did younger subjects (Fung, Carstensen & Lutz, 1999). The sense in old age that time is fleeting also deepens and makes for more complex emotionality, in which sadness is a significant component. For example, each visit with an intimate friend is pervaded by a sense that this may be one of the last occasions to be together. The rich mix of sadness and joy resulting from this kind of awareness often causes older people to report that life has never been better (Carstensen & Charles, 1998).

All this suggests that older adults can still experience emotions as they did in young adulthood. Older people show no reduction in their capacity to feel positive emotions such as happiness and joy (Lawton, Parmelee, Katz, & Nesselroade, 1996). Negative emotions, in contrast, while undiminished in intensity, surface less frequently than previously. Other aspects of emotionality like excitement and sensation seeking are relatively reduced. In addition, and consistently in studies across cultures, older adults report fewer mood swings, less agitation, and more ability to control their emotions than young adults (Gross et al., 1997), which contributes to a greater sense of well-being.

well-being. Research has shown that the support a widow receives from her siblings depends on a variety of factors, including the sex, marital status, and proximity of her siblings as well as the proximity of her own children. Sometimes the most helpful relationships are those between a widow and her married sisters (O'Bryant, 1988).

Sibling relationships are not always smooth and congenial, of course. Nevertheless, at least a modicum of kinship responsibility among siblings is a common part of the social network of older adults. It is particularly important for single adults or for older individuals who need care and assistance but do not have grown children who can help.

As discussed in Chapter 16, friendships also provide considerable stability and life satisfaction for both married and unmarried individuals. Still, most studies that compare friendships and family relationships find clear distinctions. Most older adults think of kinship relationships as permanent. We can call upon kin for long-term commitments; we cannot make quite the same demands on a friendship. The prevailing view is that friends will help in handling an immediate emergency such as a sudden illness, but long-term responsibilities should be handled by kin (Aizenberg & Treas, 1985). Friends can, however, take on special importance for adults who lack siblings. Friendships are also an important source of social support for older adults living in retirement communities (Potts, 1997). For more on emotionality and friendships in older adulthood, see "In Theory, In Fact" above.

CONTENT CHECK
FAMILY AND PERSONAL RELATIONSHIPS

True–False (answers are on the Companion Website)

1. Grandparenthood is one of the most satisfying roles of older adulthood.
2. Caring for an ill spouse generally tends to be too much for an older caregiver to handle.
3. With modern advances in medical technology, older husbands no longer die sooner than older wives.
4. Older men cope better with widowhood than do older women.
5. In older adulthood, concern for siblings tends to increase.

Thinking Critically

How do close interpersonal relationships define many of the stresses and satisfactions of later adulthood?

U.S. Social Policy and Older Adulthood

Although personality stability and change, retirement, and family and personal relationships are issues that older adults face as individuals, the needs of older adults have social policy implications as well.

Social policy that affects older adults is influenced by the demographic composition of the population. These policies are most important to older adults who are frail, who often must rely on others for their care. Often, social policy translates into lifestyle options for older persons.

The Demographics of Aging

As Figure 18–3 shows, the demographics of the older adult population in the United States have changed dramatically since 1900 and will continue to change as we move toward 2050. Whereas in 1900 there were only 3.1 million older people in the United States—about 1 in 25 in the general population—in 1990 there were 31.1 million—about 1 in every 8 people. By 2050, this segment of the population is expected to grow to about 79 million people and represent 1 in every 5 people (U.S. Census Bureau, 1993). Many of these older people are expected to remain healthy into their 70s and beyond.

As noted in Chapter 17, the fastest-growing group in the U.S. population is age 85 and older, and the number will increase markedly in the decades to come. Although most people believe that this demographic shift will place enormous financial strains on the health-care system, and particularly on Medicare, current data indicate that the oldest old may actually be healthier than people in the young-old age group. Richard Suzman of the National Institute on Aging explained: "There seems to be a selection process, and once you're over the hump, you start a less steep trajectory of disablement" (cited in Angier, 1995). Moreover, the oldest old usually die quickly as a result of such illnesses as pneumonia and are less likely to suffer prolonged hospitalizations than people in their 60s and 70s.

When researchers at the Health Care Financing Administration calculated the impact of increased longevity on Medicare spending, they found that

Figure 18–3 Past and Projected Population by Age and Gender, United States (In Millions)

Over the last one hundred and the next fifty years, the older-adult population of the United States grows from one in twenty-five to one in five.

Source: U.S. Census Bureau, 1993.

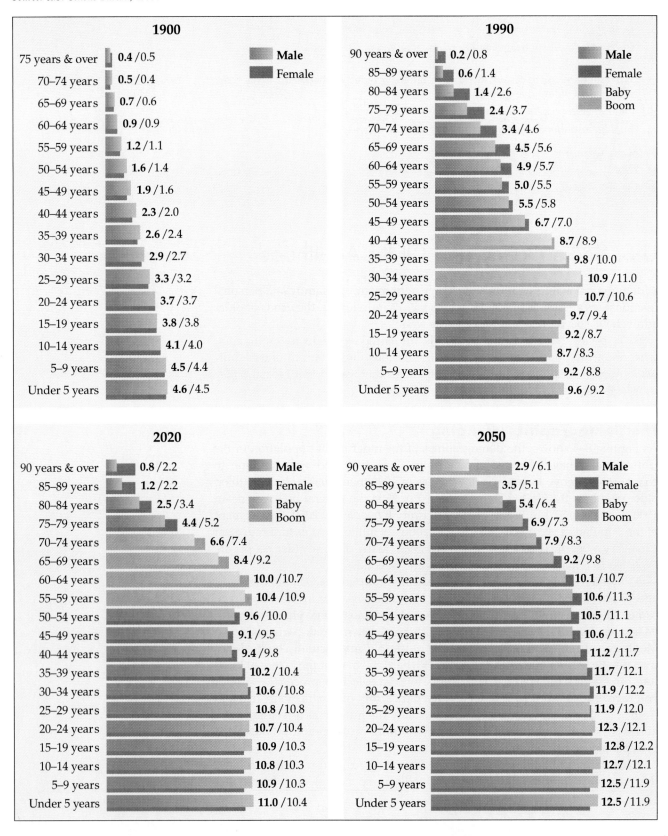

improved life expectancy had only a small financial impact on the system. Instead, it is the sheer size of the baby boom cohort—the vast numbers of people who will reach age 65 over the next decades—that is expected to drive up annual Medicare costs by about $98 billion (Angier, 1995).

Although today most older people are white, this group will become more ethnically diverse in the years ahead. By 2050, the percentage of white older adults is expected to decline from its 1990 level of 87% to 67% as other groups come to represent a significantly larger share of the older population (see Figure 18–4).

As the older population grows, more attention is being given to the quality of services available to the aged. Only a small fraction of the total number of older people are frail and in need of extensive services. However, despite their small numbers, these people are often the most vulnerable members of society. Social services are needed to address their specific needs.

Frail Older Adults

In the 1970s, much public attention focused on the poverty, ill health, and inadequate living conditions of older people and the limited social services available to them. Many services were improved. Although poverty still exists among older adults, most older individuals are guaranteed a minimum annual income and basic health-care services. Far more low-income housing units were allocated to older people, and some communities have developed a range of social services for them.

It has been more difficult to identify the next level of problems and to develop possible solutions. For example, living in near poverty isn't much less depressing than living in poverty. Public housing does not always meet the needs of older people. Some may lack the opportunity to share living space with others; in other cases it might not be safe to walk in the corridors of community projects. Also, transportation can become a major problem for those who must stop driving because of failing vision or slow reaction time.

About one-third of noninstitutionalized U.S. older adults receive help in daily living from one or more caregivers (NCHS, 1999) (also see "A Closer Look, p. 623). Only about 4% of people over age 65 are in nursing homes; about half of these people are over age 85 (NCHS, 1999). Those who end up in nursing

For the elderly, living in near poverty may be just as depressing as living in poverty.

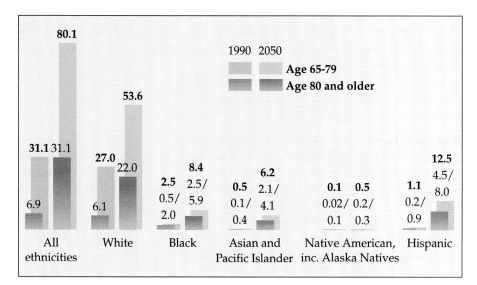

Figure 18–4 Past and Projected Population Age 65 and Over by Age and Self-Identified Ethnicity, United States (in Millions)
The U.S. elderly population will become more ethnically diverse in the years ahead.

Source: U.S. Census Bureau, 1993.

homes are likely to be single and suffering from mental impairment (Birkel & Jones, 1989; NCHS, 1999).

Social programs for frail older persons are not fine-tuned to meet the needs of the individual. Critics have often warned that people sometimes opt for nursing home placement when other services might be more appropriate. We are anxious to avoid medical and economic catastrophes for older adults, but we have difficulty with the range of lesser services that might help the individual maintain a higher quality of life and prevent catastrophe (Brody, 1987). Other critics warn that we must remember that aging per se is not the problem—older individuals with physical and mental disabilities need to be treated for those disabilities. Similarly, some older individuals lack the social support of family or friends, display unusual behavior patterns, or have trouble with self-care; they need help in those areas in particular, not necessarily complete nursing home care. They may need education, counseling, legal aid, social networking, or just more interesting things to do.

The institutional care received by older people varies widely in quality. Although there are many well-planned and caring institutions, in the past few years many nursing homes have been exposed as boring, meaningless places where people often have little to do but wait for the end of their lives. Thus, people who are about to enter an institution often feel great anxiety and dread, and their children often feel guilty. People entering nursing homes may also exhibit many characteristics of people who are already institutionalized, such as apathy, passivity, bitterness, or depression. They are facing a break with the continuity of their lives, losing their independence, becoming separated from many of their possessions and familiar routines. Once they do enter an institution, they may find that their identity is further submerged (they are now "Honey" or "Dearie" instead of Mr. or Mrs. or Ms. Somebody), and they may have to conform to unfamiliar and unpleasant daily routines (Kastenbaum, 1979).

Lifestyle Options for Older Adults

As we have seen, older people constitute a remarkably varied group; they are not a single, uniform mass of humanity. Catch-all phrases such as "the elderly" and "senior citizens" are inadequate to describe the multitude of individual qualities found in aging individuals. Moreover, the period of old age covers a long span of time. Consequently, there are sharp differences between the young-old, who are recently retired and are often healthy and vigorous, and the old-old, who are more likely to experience ill health, restricted mobility, and social isolation. Social policies designed to assist older people must take account of this diversity if they are to be effective.

Social policies center on caregiving and living facilities and other services that provide older adults with the assistance they need to live with dignity. The push for recognition comes from older people themselves.

Day Centers for Older Adults   Of individuals over age 65, 1 in 4 can expect to be disabled to such an extent that **institutionalization**—long-term, typically permanent, placement—will be necessary. Far more will need limited health, social, and living assistance. Day centers are one option (Irwin, 1978). They provide an attractive alternative to nursing homes for those who need care on a limited basis. To families who are willing to care for their older relatives in the evenings and at night, day centers offer periods of relief and the opportunity to maintain a normal working schedule. Consider the case of a 77-year-old stroke

institutionalization   Long-term, usually permanent placement in an institution.

A CLOSER LOOK

CARING FOR FRAIL OLDER PERSONS

How best to care for the frailest and oldest members of society is a concern shared by older adults, family members, and policymakers throughout the world. As the focus of public policy, care of older people has undergone dramatic changes in thinking and implementation over the past decade in such countries as Great Britain, Sweden, Denmark, the Netherlands, and Australia. The purpose of these policy changes has been to reduce costs to taxpayers and improve the effectiveness and efficiency of elder care.

Pressure from the users of elder-care services—older people themselves—is especially potent in countries with organized senior citizen groups. In Sweden, for example, 30% of all older adults belong to pensioners' associations that make their members' voices heard at both the national and local levels. Even in countries with few organized groups, government officials have gotten the message that they must listen to what older people and their families want and adapt existing programs to fit their needs. In general, after listening to constituents' voices, policymakers have embraced three goals that are changing the nature of elder care.

The first goal is to do as much as possible to keep older adults integrated into society while at the same time trying to improve the quality of their life and the care they receive. This involves improving care in nursing homes and other residential facilities. It also involves trying to make existing residential facilities less restrictive than and, when possible, moving older people out of these facilities into home and day-care situations. Bleddyn Davies (1993), who has analyzed the elder-care policies of various nations, commented on this trend:

> The official authors of policy documents the world over seem to be working hard to express the same sentiments, sometimes using almost the same words. The English version is typical: One of the three main aims of the comprehensive new policy is "to enable persons as far as possible to live in their own homes or in a homelike environment in the local community." (Davies, 1993)

The goal of caring for older people in their own homes entails a second goal: to recognize the burdens and stresses experienced by caregivers and devise programs to help avoid caregiver burnout. Policy statements from Great Britain give high priority to providing practical support to caregivers. In Sweden, legislation requires that local governments listen to what caregivers say and provide support for their efforts. Since 1989 part of this support has been given in the form of up to 30 days' paid leave, reimbursed through sick-leave insurance policies. Both Great Britain and Australia have elevated the issue of rest for long-time caregivers to a national concern.

Naturally, these ambitious goals result in higher costs for taxpayers. Limiting these costs and improving the effectiveness and efficiency of elder care programs is the third policy goal. In the Netherlands, for example, a committee on health care financing was charged with the task of providing "strategies for volume and cost containment against the background of an aging population" (Dekker, 1987). Similarly, the Australian Aged Care Reform Strategy is committed to efficient and equitable use of public funds.

In most nations, meeting the evolving needs of frail older adults and their caregivers requires major changes in societal assumptions, behaviors, and practices. Meeting these needs also requires overcoming public resistance to allocating scarce resources to elder care at the expense of other social programs.

victim. She lived with her daughter and son-in-law but spent her days in a Baltimore day center, where she received therapy, kept busy, and made new friends. Her morale and temperament improved dramatically after only a few weeks of attendance and made her family's burden of care much lighter. Note, however, that the cost of day centers often is not covered by health insurance policies, even though these centers are more cost-effective than nursing homes. Thus, they may be prohibitively expensive for many families.

Other Options   For older people in good health, there are various other options. Retirement communities allow older people to live together and share interests and activities in safe surroundings. One drawback is that they isolate older adults from the rest of the world, a situation that most older people do not like—and do not have to face in many parts of the world beyond the United States. U.S. polls show that most older people want to spend their postretirement years in their own communities and preferably in their own homes (Lord, 1995).

There is great diversity among older people with many adopting active lifestyles.

Other ideas are being tried by organizations such as the Gray Panthers and the Quakers. One successful experiment is the Life Center operated by the Quakers in Philadelphia. Here, older people live in a large converted house with students and people in other age groups. Costs, housework, and meals are shared, and the resulting sense of community keeps older people in the mainstream of life. Home sharing has also worked for older adults in such varied locations as Boulder, Colorado, and Rochester, Vermont (Lord, 1995).

Community Services An array of services is increasingly being made available to older people: various modes of transportation, including door-to-door service and escort services in dangerous neighborhoods; "meals on wheels" services; in-home care, including both homemakers and health professionals; friendly visitors; telephone reassurance; cultural services, such as bookmobiles and other library programs and free or reduced-price admission to museums and concerts; opportunities to serve as foster grandparents or in some other volunteer capacity, possibly even work for pay; and free legal assistance.

Many communities and religious groups have also established senior centers at which older people can participate in varied activities, attend classes and parties, and receive needed services. Other communities have experimented with community care programs in which people who would otherwise be institutionalized receive around-the-clock care in a private home.

Progress Through Self-Help Although society is finally beginning to pay more attention to the needs of older people, older people themselves are an important resource for meeting their own needs and those of others. Older people are often unaware of the services and benefits already available to them. Better use of the media could inform them of their rights and opportunities. Even more effective as a means of self-help are activist organizations like the Gray Panthers (actually a coalition of older people and young people) and the AARP, which bring older people together as a political and social force. These groups rightly see older people as a largely untapped resource in the United States.

Members of these and other groups are working for more rights for older people both in the workplace and in society as a whole. Their work has led to greater autonomy and better living conditions both for older people and for other members of society. One badly disabled older woman made a great impact in Philadelphia by publicly demonstrating that the urban transportation system could not accommodate the weak or the old. The most serious shortcoming found was that the steps for getting onto buses were too high. Efforts like this have led to the use of "kneeling buses" and special vans for the handicapped. Finally, organizations like the Gray Panthers and AARP are giving older people a better self-image—something long neglected in a world that equates youth with beauty, maturity with power, and age with obsolescence.

With a little flexibility in social policy and creative solutions to health, mobility, and social needs, numerous other adaptive living styles may be developed. A larger population of older people does not necessarily mean a larger burden on the younger adult population. The financial and creative resources of this segment of the population may more than pay for itself.

CONTENT CHECK
U.S. SOCIAL POLICY AND OLDER ADULTS

True–False (answers are on the Companion Website)

1. Demographics influences the social policy affecting older adults.

2. In the United States, the fastest growing segment of the older population is age 80 and older.

3. Despite criticism to the contrary, social programs for frail older persons generally tend to meet individual needs.

4. For most people over age 65, institutionalization will be necessary.

5. Options for older persons in good health include retirement communities and the use of an increasing variety of community services.

Thinking Critically

How are older people themselves an important resource in providing for their own needs and for those of other older individuals?

CHAPTER 18 REVISITED

Personality and Aging

■ According to Erikson, a central developmental task from adolescence on is maintaining a relatively consistent identity; for the very old, maintaining personal identity may be particularly important.

■ The final stage in Erikson's theory is the psychosocial conflict of integrity versus despair; part of the adjustment to old age includes the need to reminisce and reflect on past events.

■ Levinson said that there is a period of transition that links an individual's previous life structure to that of late adulthood.

■ People strive to be consistent in their behavior.

■ Personality characteristics such as neuroticism, extraversion versus introversion, and openness to experience remain consistent from middle to older adulthood.

■ Some studies suggest that coping skills decline during older adulthood; others indicate that people become more mature in their coping styles.

■ Stereotypical thinking about aging paints a bleak picture that many older people themselves accept; however, most older people perceive themselves in positive ways.

■ Life satisfaction and adjustment in older adulthood depend on factors other than age.

■ Social comparison plays a crucial role in the outlook of older people.

Retirement: A Major Change in Status

■ One of the most important considerations in how people fare after retirement is whether they actually choose to retire; retirement is the most significant status change of later adulthood.

■ An important factor in reactions to retirement is health; economic status is another.

■ An individual's lifelong attitude toward work affects feelings about retirement.

■ On average, women with continuous work experience have greater financial security and are better prepared for retirement than those with intermittent work.

■ Preparation for retirement consists of decelerating, retirement planning, and retirement living. Some companies provide retirement counselors.

■ Talented and productive workers may be lost to retirement; solutions such as part-time, less demanding work options are needed for older people.

Family and Personal Relationships

■ Interpersonal relationships continue to define many of the stresses and satisfactions of life in later adulthood.

■ On average, older married couples report being more satisfied with their marriage after the children leave home; happy marriages characteristically are more egalitarian and cooperative.

■ Most older adults report having relatively frequent contact with their children and grandchildren.

■ Grandparenthood is seen by many as one of the most satisfying roles of older age.

■ Older people who need help with daily living tend to rely heavily on their families; a surviving spouse is the most likely caregiver, although caregiver wives often report more stress than caregiver husbands.

■ Caring for someone with Alzheimer's disease entails unique strains and stresses.

■ Becoming a widow or widower is a difficult transition involving major adjustments.

■ Men are more likely than women to remarry after the death of a spouse, so more older women face the difficulties of living alone.

■ Social support systems available for widows and widowers include family, friends, work associates, and participants in leisure activities.

■ Widows may have an easier time than widowers in maintaining a social life; widowers are more likely to become isolated.

■ In later adulthood many people report increased contact and concern for siblings.

■ Friendships provide considerable stability and life satisfaction for both married and unmarried older individuals.

U.S. Social Policy and Older Adults

■ The fastest-growing segment of the older adult population is age 85 and up; many of the oldest-old may be healthier than young-old people.

■ Older people are projected to become more ethnically diverse in the years ahead.

■ Many noninstitutionalized older adults receive help in daily living from unpaid caregivers; others live in residential-care homes in the community; only a small percentage are in nursing homes.

■ Social programs for frail older persons are not fine-tuned to meet their needs.

■ Although about 1 in 4 individuals can expect to be disabled to the extent that institutionalization will be necessary, far more will need limited health, social, and living assistance that can be provided by day centers.

■ For older people in good health, retirement communities are an option; however, most older adults want to spend their postretirement years in their own homes, and social services are increasingly available to help them do so.

■ Activist organizations like the AARP bring older people together as a political and social force.

KEY TERMS

status passage

magical mastery

parental imperative

retirement maturity

widower's impotency

institutionalization

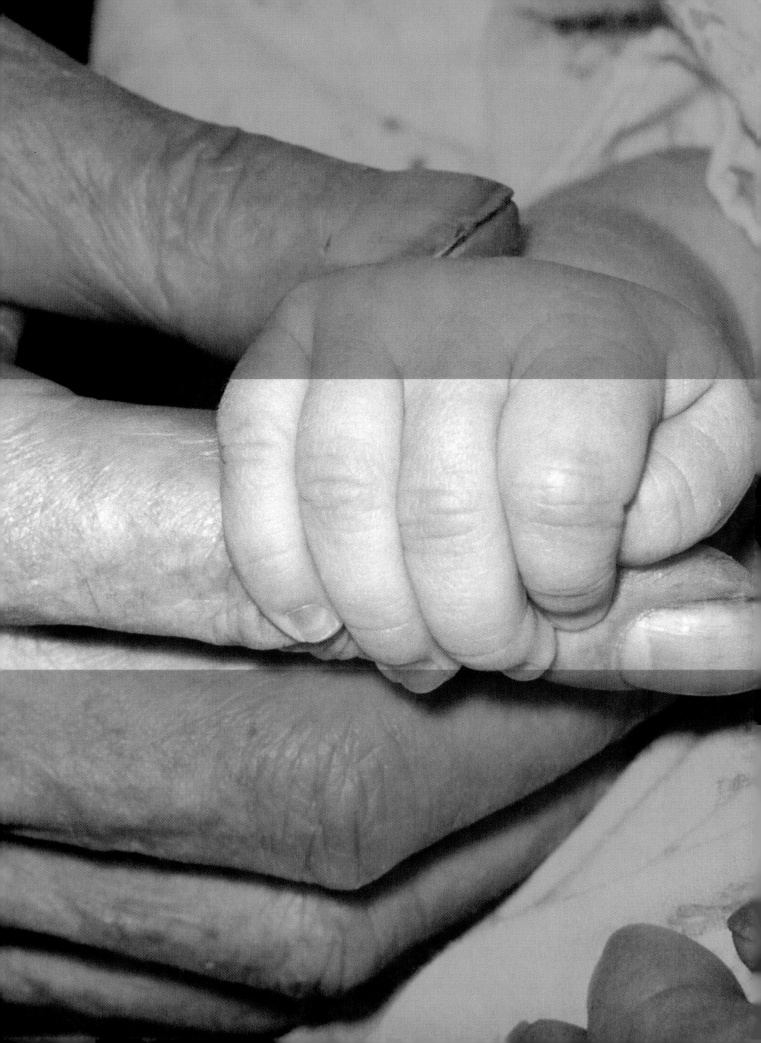

DEATH AND DYING

CHAPTER PREVIEW

Do you know:

1. What *death* really is?

2. About differences between *earlier attitudes* toward death and dying, *contemporary views*, and how the United States and other societies have changed them?

3. The extent to which people engage in *denial* where death is concerned?

4. How *older* and *younger people* view death and dying differently?

5. That death is the final stage of *development*?

6. That there are five identifiable *stages* in facing death?

7. What *alternatives* there are in dying?

8. That middle and older adults often commit *suicide*?

9. How hospices and hospitals differ in their approach to the dying?

10. That many people now demand a *right to die*?

11. The difference between *active euthanasia*, *passive euthansia*, and *assisted suicide*?

12. Why a *living will* and a *medical power of attorney* are important?

13. Why *grieving* is important and how it works?

14. How attitudes toward dying *differ across cultures*?

These are the main topics of Chapter 19.

"Life is short. Shorter for some than for others," observed Gus, a leading character in the TV movie *Lonesome Dove*. To that—for most people—we might add the following points: (1) No matter how long you live, it will not be long enough, and (2) when the end arrives, it will seem to have arrived suddenly and abruptly.

Death is the ultimate milestone, the end of life as we know it. Physiologically, death is an irrevocable cessation of life functions. Psychologically, of course, death has intense personal significance to the dying person as well as to his or her family and friends. To die means to cease experiencing, to leave loved ones, to leave unfinished business, and to enter the unknown (Kalish, 1987). Bear in mind, however, that death is a *natural* event—whether it occurs prematurely because of disease or accident or at the end of a full and rich lifespan. All creatures die; death is as much a part of development as is living (DeSpelder & Strickland, 1999).

A person's death is also deeply embedded in a cultural context. There are collective meanings, many of which are expressed in the culture's literature, arts, music, religion, and philosophy. In most cultures, death is also associated with particular rituals and rites. Depending on your culture—in conjunction with your personal beliefs and interpretations—death may be an event to be feared, dreaded, abhorred, and postponed as long as possible. Alternatively, many cultures and religions view death more as a transition than as an end, a passage into another life and, it is hoped, a better world or a higher plane of existence. For some individuals, death may be a welcome relief from the extreme suffering that can accompany disease or aging. For others—such as those who commit suicide—it may be a final, desperate escape from a life replete with pain and misery. Death indeed has many meanings.

If we knew more about the experience of dying and the process of grief and bereavement, would we be better able to help people cope with the tragedies in their lives as well as with the triumphs? Historically, developmental psychologists ignored the subject of death. Granted, it isn't easy to study, and perhaps they thought it inappropriate to scrutinize the attitudes and reactions of individuals who were dying. In recent decades, however, death has been studied thoroughly. In this chapter, we take a look at some of the things that have been discovered about death and consider some of the ways in which this knowledge might be applied. We examine the thoughts and fears that surround death, the process of confronting your own death, the societal and individual search for a humane death, and the process of grief and bereavement. We consider both normal death in older adulthood and death at younger ages. In closing, we also consider what it means to complete the life cycle.

Thoughts and Fears of Death

Birth and death are both natural events; they constitute the beginning and end of a life. However, their emotional impact and personal meanings are vastly different. Birth is usually anticipated with excitement and optimism; death is usually avoided, even by those who believe in an afterlife. Sometimes people deny the reality of death.

Denial of Death

Several authors have suggested that the U.S. technological, youth-oriented society has a curious habit of denying and avoiding death while, at the same time, being strangely preoccupied with it—especially in the media, although there we are detached from it and don't usually think about it happening to us as well. People tend to believe that murders and fatal accidents happen only to *other* people.

People also tend to sidestep the subject of death when with someone who is dying. To illustrate this point, one author (Kalish, 1985) told a tale of being invited to cocktails and dinner at the home of a friend. Upon entering the dining room, the man notices with astonishment that there is a brown horse sitting quietly on the dining room table. He turns to look at the reactions of the other guests and the host; all of their faces express shock and confusion. But no one wants to embarrass the host by mentioning something that is so obviously discomforting. The dinner proceeds, with long silences that are broken only by innocuous and inconsequential conversation. Is this, the author asked, analogous to what goes on when a person is dying and no one will speak with him or her about it?

In earlier historical periods, death was a familiar event. It usually occurred at home, with family members caring for the dying person until the end. Even after death, the details of preparing the body for burial and performing the final rituals were family and community events. With regard to burial in particular, family members and friends even opened and closed the grave.

In the 20th century, however, death became something of a technological marvel. In Western nations, most people now die in hospitals, with medical staff attending to their needs and family members standing by. Professional morticians prepare the body for the final rituals and burial, and the body is presented for final viewing in a funeral home. Contact with the dying person before and after death is greatly restricted. Thus, some have suggested that we live in an era of "invisible death." Moreover, they wonder whether people have deceived themselves into believing that death is just another problem to deal with, such as a disease for which a cure has yet to be found (Ariès, 1981).

Denial is a common mechanism for coping with stress—the person simply refuses to see or accept reality—and it can greatly interfere with coping. Actively coping with the reality of death means taking realistic precautions about the hazards of living without restricting ourselves unnecessarily. We must be able to accept the limitations of life and our own vulnerability. Some experts suggest that if U.S. culture could deal more directly with death, it might present fewer distorted images of death to its children (Pattison, 1977).

Some researchers believe that the cultural taboo in the United States against discussing death is weakening, however. Books, articles, and death education classes are available that may change people's attitudes. Even members of the medical profession, who confront death and dying on a daily basis, need educational programs and seminars on how to cope with their feelings about it. In the mid-1960s, when Elisabeth Kübler-Ross began her study of the dying process (discussed in the next section), she noted considerable resistance and denial on the part of hospital staff members (Kübler-Ross, 1969). Once a diagnosis of terminal illness was made, both nurses and doctors paid less attention to the patient, seemingly avoiding all but the most necessary contact. They talked to the patient less, provided less in the way of routine care, and usually didn't tell the patient that he or she was in a terminal state—even when the patient asked. Patients were also discouraged from discussing their feelings about dying.

Today this has changed (Kastenbaum, 1998). All nursing programs and many programs for doctors include seminars on death education, which stress maintaining contact with the patient and respecting the patient's "right to know." It is now recognized that medical professionals who understand the dying process are better able to set realistic goals for "good" outcomes, in which the patient dies with dignity, has a chance to express final sentiments to family and friends, and faces death in a manner consistent with his or her lifestyle.

Preoccupation with Death

Are older people more fearful about or preoccupied with death than younger people? Are healthy people and those who feel more in control of their lives less fearful of death? Psychoanalytic theory asserts that anxiety or fearfulness at the prospect of your own death is normal; however, this may not be universally true. Moreover, individuals who experience significant anxiety about death differ in how they deal with it. Some people find meaning and purpose in life and incorporate the knowledge that they will die into that meaning. Religious fanatics who sacrifice themselves for their cause (as in suicide bombings) are an extreme of such a "solution." In contrast, an existentialist or a devout atheist who believes in no afterlife may be terrified by the prospect of the perceived finality of death—although this is not always the case; it is possible for people who do not believe in an afterlife to be reconciled to death as a natural, perhaps even peaceful state. In the latter view, where there is nothingness there can also be no stress or pain, nor is it possible afterwards to "worry" about being dead.

For the wide range of individuals who fall somewhere between these extremes, researchers find that personal and cultural meanings of death often

Older people, when confronted with the question what they would do if they had only 6 months to live, often focus on spending time with their families.

play a key role in determining whether individuals are fearful or preoccupied with thoughts of their own death. Studies have found that older adults actually tend to be somewhat less anxious about death than younger people, that individuals with a strong sense of purpose in life fear death less, and that although some older people think about death often, they feel surprisingly calm at the prospect of it (Kastenbaum, 1998). Religious beliefs are also a factor: Research has repeatedly shown that people with strong religious convictions and a deep belief in an afterlife experience less depression and anxiety about death (Alvarado, Templer, Bresler, & Thomas-Dobson, 1995). However, it is the personal conviction itself that is the important thing; attempting to lower your anxiety about dying by increasing your religious participation and forcing yourself to believe "is not a guaranteed remedy."

When young people are asked how they would spend their 6 remaining months of life if that was all they had, they describe activities such as traveling and trying to do things that they have wanted to do but not yet had a chance to do. Older people have different priorities. Sometimes they talk about contemplation, meditation, and other inner-focused pursuits. Often they talk about spending time with their families and those closest to them (Kalish, 1987; Kalish & Reynolds, 1981). Indeed, in a comprehensive set of interviews with a large group of older adult volunteers, only 10% answered yes to the question "Are you afraid to die?" (Jeffers & Verwoerdt, 1970). Many participants did report, however, that they were afraid of a prolonged and painful death.

Although older people generally report low levels of anxiety about death, not all older people feel this way. There are substantial individual differences with regard to anxiety about death (Stillion, 1985). Is there a pattern that identifies those who will be most or least anxious? The research findings are difficult to interpret. In some studies, those who are psychologically well adjusted and who seem to have achieved Erikson's stage of personality integrity are the least anxious. In other studies, older individuals who are both physically and mentally healthy and feel in control of their own lives are the most anxious. Nor is anxiety about death a constant. Often, for example, individuals experience high anxiety about death when they are diagnosed as having a potentially fatal disease, but gradually become less anxious over a period of several weeks or months thereafter (Belsky, 1984). Death anxiety appears to be only one symptom in an ongoing process of establishing and accepting the meaning of death in the context of the meaning of life.

CONTENT CHECK
THOUGHTS AND FEARS OF DEATH

True–False (answers are on the Companion Website)
1. Before the 20th century, death usually occurred at home.
2. Today's technological society tends to both deny death and be preoccupied with it.
3. Cultural taboos against death are weakening.
4. Older people are more preoccupied with death than are younger people.
5. Substantial differences in attitudes concerning death exist among older people.

Thinking Critically
What is the role of psychological denial in coping with dying?

Confronting Your Own Death

As people grow older or become ill, they realize that death is no longer a distant event. Young people have the luxury of pushing such thoughts into the background, but in illness or in older adulthood, thoughts of death are unavoidable. How do people react to this final stage of development? Many experience an orderly series of stages of adjustment to dying, which ultimately includes acceptance of death. This is not true of everyone, however, as we see in this section.

Death as the Final Stage of Development
People who are not faced with the prospect of immediate death can spend more time adjusting to the idea. They often spend their last years looking back and reliving old pleasures and pains. According to one theorist (Butler, 1968; 1980–1981), this life review is a very important step in the lifelong growth of the individual. At no other time is there as strong a force toward self-awareness as in older adulthood. The process often leads to real personality growth; individuals resolve old conflicts, reestablish meaning in life, and even discover new things about themselves. Only in coping with the reality of approaching death can we make crucial decisions about what is important and who we really are. Death lends the necessary perspective (Kübler-Ross, 1975). Paradoxically, then, dying can be "a process of re-commitment to life" (Imara, 1975).

As in earlier periods of life, the task of finding meaning and purpose involves active restructuring of philosophical, religious, and pragmatic thoughts and beliefs (Sherman, 1987). In 1974, when author Ernest Becker was hospitalized in the last stages of terminal cancer, he was interviewed about what he was feeling. During his life he had written a great deal about facing up to death, so he was aware of what he was experiencing on many levels. Becker had passed through several stages in adjusting to his own death, and by the time of the interview, he had apparently reached a final stage, one of transcendence. His own resolution was a religious one: "What makes death easier [is] to know that . . . beyond what is happening to us there is the fact of the tremendous creative energies of the cosmos that are using us for some purposes we don't know" (cited in Keen, 1974). Other individuals may use a quite different approach in coming to grips with their own death, and beliefs pertaining to death vary considerably across cultures and religions. In any case, however, Becker's testimony is a persuasive argument for allowing people to work out their own personal resolution and face death in dignity and peace.

Stages of Adjustment

Elisabeth Kübler-Ross (1969) was one of the first researchers to study death and dying. She focused on relatively short-term situations in which death becomes an imminent possibility—such as when a person is diagnosed as having a terminal illness. Through extensive interviews with such people, she identified five stages in the process of adjusting to the idea of death: denial, anger, bargaining, depression, and acceptance. The following are brief descriptions of these stages:

■ In the *denial* stage, the person rejects the possibility of death and searches for other, more promising opinions and diagnoses.
■ Once the person realizes that she or he actually will die, there is anger, resentment, and envy; this is the *anger* stage. The person is frustrated because plans and dreams will not be fulfilled.
■ In the *bargaining* stage the person looks for ways to buy time, making promises and negotiating with his or her God, doctors, nurses, or others for more time, as well as for relief from pain and suffering.
■ When the bargaining fails or time runs out, helplessness and hopelessness take hold. The person is now in the *depression* stage and mourns both for the losses that have already occurred and for the death and separation from family and friends that will soon occur.
■ In the final stage, *acceptance*, the person accepts the fact of imminent death and awaits it calmly.

Although the stages described by Kübler-Ross are common reactions to impending death and therefore are helpful in understanding how dying people feel, they are not universal. Not all people go through all the stages, and only a few go through them in the specified order. Many factors influence a person's reactions, including culture, personality, religion, personal philosophy, and the length and nature of the terminal disease. Some people remain angry or depressed until the end; others welcome death as a release from pain. People cope with death in individual ways and should not be forced into a set pattern of stages. Instead, as Robert Kastenbaum (1998, 2000) has long advocated, people should be allowed to follow their own paths to dying. If they want, they should talk about their feelings, concerns, and experiences; have their questions answered; set their lives in order; see relatives and friends; and forgive or ask forgiveness for quarrels or petty misdeeds. These actions, Kastenbaum suggested, are more important to the individual than experiencing broad emotional states in a particular order. Figure 19–1 includes practical suggestions for caregivers attempting to provide support for dying loved ones.

Figure 19-1 Your Caring Presence: Advice on Providing Effective Support for Others

Source: The Centre for Living with Dying.

1. Be honest about your own concerns and feelings.
2. When in doubt, ask:

   How is it for you?

   How do you feel now?

   Can you tell me more?

   What do you need?

   How can you take care of yourself?
3. Stay in the present. How do you feel RIGHT NOW? What do you need RIGHT NOW?
4. Listening is healing. You don't have to make it better.
5. People in crisis need to know that they have decision-making power. Point out alternatives.
6. Offer any practical assistance that you feel comfortable giving.

Alternative Trajectories

Often the course of the illness itself affects reactions to the dying process. If death is sudden, there is little time for life review and integration. An illness that causes considerable pain or limited mobility or requires frequent and complex medical intervention may leave a person little time or energy to adjust to death. It would be a mistake for medical personnel or family members to assume that a person is in the anger stage when, in fact, the reaction is directly related to the person's physical condition or medical treatment (Kastenbaum & Costa, 1977).

Nowhere are reactions to the dying process more strongly influenced by the nature of the illness than in the case of AIDS, a disease that is often transmitted sexually and is therefore surrounded by strong emotions among those afflicted and those closest to them. Author Fenton Johnson (1994) focused on the themes of memory and forgiveness that "lie at the heart of any community" and yet are challenged by this disease. He explained:

> The wisest people I know, HIV-positive or negative, live not in denial [of death] but in acceptance—a state not of forgive and forget but of forgive and remember. The most difficult and necessary of the mourner's tasks are these contradictory imperatives: forgive and remember, accept and never shut up (1994, p. 15).

The prolonged dying process experienced by many AIDS patients makes acceptance and forgiveness difficult for those who must cope with the emotions that surround dying. This difficulty is heightened in some segments of the Hispanic and black communities because many individuals who succumb to AIDS are young adults. In addition, grieving for the deaths of others while dealing with their own illness eliminates the time and energy necessary to go through the traditional stages associated with accepting death (Horn, 1993).

Just as there are numerous and unique life trajectories in adult development, there is also a wide range of dying trajectories. The commonly accepted ideal trajectory is to be healthy to age 85 or more, put your affairs in order, and die suddenly and without pain (Kalish, 1985), perhaps while asleep. Indeed, surveys show that far more people would prefer a sudden death—particularly the young (Kalish, 1985).

When there is an illness with an expected trajectory, family members as well as the dying individual adjust and adapt to the presumed "time left to live." For many, there are tasks to be completed, arrangements to be made, things to be said—the unfinished business of living. Some people attempt to influence the expected trajectory by accepting treatment or rejecting it, exerting their "will to live," or resigning themselves to the inevitable. Many individuals need to maintain some control and dignity in this final trajectory. All search for a humane way to die.

Suicide   Suicide is surprisingly common in U.S. middle-aged and older people. Although the most highly publicized suicides are those of young adults, adolescents, and even schoolchildren, by far the greatest number of suicides occur among people over age 45; of this group, most occur among those age 65 and older (U. S. Census Bureau, 1997). Four times as many men as women commit suicide. The rate for men rises steadily with age, reaching a peak among those over age 80 (Manton, Blazer, & Woodbury, 1987). Both white and minority men show dramatic increases in suicide during older adulthood (Manton et al., 1987). These statistics do not take into account the more passive forms of suicide, such as simply letting yourself die, which is called **submissive death,** or indirect forms, such as excessive drinking, smoking, or drug abuse, which is called **suicidal erosion.** Yet another indirect form of suicide is "going postal" and gunning down a group of innocent bystanders, which typically results in the perpetrator being killed as well.

Suicide among the elderly is almost always a result of "vital losses," such as employment difficulties, retirement shock, or becoming a widow or widower. Both widows and widowers therefore are at higher risk for suicide than the general population (Li, 1995). The risk falls off sharply after the first year of bereavement but remains higher than average for several years. There is another important factor besides retirement and widow- or widowerhood. Older people who are chronically lonely or have a history of emotional instability—especially those with deep-seated anxieties and feelings of inferiority—are highly prone to suicide.

One of the most effective means of improving the mental health of widows and widowers and helping to meet their social needs is self-help groups. Individuals who participate in such groups may find comfort in sharing their fears and feelings with others. The groups also provide a protective setting in which to form new relationships and try out new roles, so that people become less isolated and better able to help themselves. Systematic study of participants in formal support groups has repeatedly demonstrated positive outcomes for most participants (e.g., Levy, Derby, & Martinkowski, 1993; Lund, Caserta, & Dimond, 1993).

submissive death   Suicide in the form of simply letting yourself die.

suicidal erosion   An indirect form of suicide through excessive drinking, smoking, or other drug abuse.

CONTENT CHECK
CONFRONTING YOUR OWN DEATH

True–False (answers are on the Companion Website)

1. Many older people experience orderly stages of adjustment to dying.
2. According to Kübler-Ross, the five stages of adjusting to the idea of death are denial, anger, bargaining, frustration, and acceptance.
3. The course of illness may influence how a person reacts to dying.
4. A wide range of dying trajectories exist.
5. Suicide among the elderly is most often a response to poor living conditions.

Thinking Critically

In what sense can death be considered a stage of growth?

The Search for a Humane Death

As we have seen, a great deal of study has been conducted on the experience of dying; former ignorance and neglect of the subject are giving way to a more realistic view. It may be a long time, however, before society's general attitude toward death catches up to the advanced thinking of some theorists. We are remarkably good at providing health care to dying patients, in the form of medication and life-support systems, but we are poor at dealing head-on with their worries and thoughts. The terminally ill are sometimes treated as somehow less than human by those around them. They may be isolated from their loved ones in a sterile environment; decisions are made for them without regard for their wishes. They still often are not told what their treatments are for, and if they become upset or rebellious they may be sedated. Compared with the terrifyingly cold atmosphere of the hospital, an old-fashioned death at home, where the dying person is surrounded by familiar faces and objects, seems almost a luxury.

Doctors and other health-care professionals have at least become more honest with dying patients about their condition. Along these lines, it is suggested that dying patients should be given some measure of autonomy. Having a say in how much pain medication or sedatives they receive, for example, can give them a sense that they still control some aspects of their lives. This is very important for patients who may otherwise feel that they are being swept along by forces beyond their control. In fact, some research indicates that almost any animal—be it a rat, a dog, or a cockroach—often simply relinquishes life if it feels that it has lost control (Seligman, 1974). In one experiment in which rats were put in water to see how long they could swim, some lasted as long as 60 hours, whereas others sank below the surface and drowned almost instantly. What caused the different reactions? The rats that died quickly had been restrained for an extended period before being put in the water; this caused them to feel helpless, so they simply gave up. Those that kept on struggling had not been restrained and therefore tried their best to survive. A similar thing happens when people are put in nursing homes or hospitals prematurely and feel that they can no longer control their own lives in any meaningful way. They respond by giving up the struggle. In contrast, individuals who have spent a lifetime controlling their environment may try to control the hospital or nursing staff. Although these patients may not be cooperative or easy to get along with, they do tend to live longer (Tobin, 1988).

We have already seen that only a relatively small proportion of older persons report fearing death. Yet they often report other fears about the dying process. They do not want a long, painful terminal period, and they do not want to be dependent on others. Also, they fear the loss of their mind as well as their dignity. Some even talk about wanting a "good death," not an agonizing, degrading one. The quest for a good death has led to several proposed changes in how services are provided to the dying. These changes include hospice care and the right to die.

In hospices, death is seen as a normal stage of life to be faced with dignity.

hospice A philosophy that involves care, counseling, support, and other assistance for dying people and their families.

Hospice

The notion that dying people should maintain some control over their life and, for that matter, over their death, has given rise to the development of hospices for the dying. **Hospice** is designed to help terminally ill patients live out their days as fully and independently as possible by giving needed support both to patients and to their families. The first hospice for the dying was started in England in 1967 as an inpatient program. The idea spread to the United States in 1974, with the launching of a hospice program in New Haven, Connecticut, and it caught on rapidly. Four years later, there were some 200 hospice programs in 39 states and the District of Columbia in various stages of planning and implementation (Abbott, 1978); there are currently more that 3,100 hospice programs throughout the United States (Hospice Foundation of America, 1999).

Some hospices are independent, but most are part of comprehensive health-care organizations. The comprehensive program usually includes an inpatient unit, home-care programs with a variety of home-based services, medical and psychological consultation, and ongoing medical and nursing services that relieve pain and help control symptoms. Notably, hospice is not a "place"; it is a philosophy. Eighty percent of hospice care is provided either in homes or in nursing homes (Hospice Foundation of America, 1999).

A law enacted in 1982 helped make hospice services more affordable and available to dying patients. Under Public Law 97–248, individuals covered by the Social Security system can receive home services for as much as two periods of 3 months each. These services include involvement of the regular physician, home nursing care, psychological counseling, nutrition evaluation, respite care, spiritual guidance, home support services, legal and financial advice, occupational, physical, and speech therapy, and bereavement care for the family. Not only is this kind of home service welcomed by the patient, but in many cases it is much more cost-effective than hospitalization (Cloud, 2000).

Hospitals are devoted to life and life support; hospital personnel tend to see death as the "enemy." Sometimes the care they give to the dying reflects this attitude, as noted earlier. The hospice concept, however, views death not as a failure but as a normal and natural stage of life to be approached with dignity. Death is as natural as birth, and like birth, sometimes requires assistance. Hospices are designed to provide that assistance and comfort. Their first aim is to manage pain of all sorts: physical, mental, social, and spiritual. Beyond that, they try, to the extent possible, to respect the dying person's rights with regard to choices about death (DeSpelder & Strickland, 1995). In addition, they help the family understand the dying person's experience and needs, and they keep lines of communication open so that the dying member feels less isolated. Hospice contact with the family continues up to and beyond death, extending throughout the period of bereavement.

The Right to Die

If, as many people believe, death is a natural, essentially positive experience, do we have the right to tamper with it? Do we rob people of a dignified death if we artificially maintain their bodily systems beyond the point at which they can ever recover? Is there a time when a person is "meant" to die, when it would be better to let nature take its course? Do we prolong life because we fear death, even though the patients themselves may be ready to die? These questions have received a great deal of attention in recent years, and many people now demand a **right to die.**

The idea of letting nature take its course—or even lending a helping hand—is of course not entirely new. *Euthanasia*, or mercy killing, was practiced in ancient Greece and probably earlier. Reportedly, one of the more notable "victims" of euthanasia in this century was Sigmund Freud. In 1939, the 83-year-old Freud, who had been suffering from cancer of the jaw for 16 years, decided that he had had enough: "Now it is nothing but torture, and makes no

right to die The view that death is a right to be exercised at the individual's discretion.

In contemporary American society, Dr. Jack Kevorkian has publicized the moral, ethical, and legal issues involved in active euthanasia.

sense any more" (cited in Shapiro, 1978). He had previously made a pact with his physician to administer a lethal dose of morphine should Freud decide that he could no longer bear his intense pain and frustration. He then asked that the agreement be put into effect, and the doctor honored his wish (Shapiro, 1978).

In Freud's case, nature was not simply allowed to take its course; positive steps were taken to bring about death. This is generally called **active euthanasia**, although many would consider the term euphemistic. In U.S. society, such an act is considered murder, pure and simple—although it is sometimes treated with leniency (Shapiro, 1978). This is especially true in cases in which the final act of euthanasia is carried out by the dying person, so that it legally can be considered a suicide. Termed **assisted suicide,** this is what happens in the widely publicized cases of terminally ill patients being provided with "death machines" that allow the patient to self-administer a lethal drug, as discussed in "A Matter for Debate" on page 642.

Passive euthanasia involves withholding (or disconnecting) life-sustaining equipment so that death will come about naturally. Passive, voluntary euthanasia has become a conspicuous issue, because of medical advances in the ability to sustain life—in some cases almost indefinitely. Indeed, a major issue is how to determine when to disconnect life support machines. Table 19–1 lists the Harvard Criteria for defining death. These have been widely used as a foundation for legal definitions of death. Although they seem straightforward and irrefutable, however, the criteria do not fully resolve all of the issues (Kastenbaum, 1998). For example, do functioning and blood flow have to be absent in all areas of the brain for the person to be considered dead, or is cessation of activity in the cerebral cortex sufficient? Such questions are most likely to be raised—and the criteria are most likely to be invoked—when there are differing opinions among family members or medical staff and a judge is asked to make the decision as to whether to terminate life support (Robbins, 1986).

One example of an effort to ensure some individual autonomy in the last stages of life is a **living will,** such as the one prepared by Concern for Dying, an Educational Council (see Figure 19–2). This document informs your family,

active euthanasia Taking positive steps to bring about another person's death, as in cases of terminal illness. In the United States, active euthanasia is murder.

assisted suicide Providing a terminally ill patient with the means to end his or her own life.

passive euthanasia Withholding or disconnecting life-sustaining equipment so that death can occur naturally.

living will An advance directive signed by a person indicating that the person does not wish that extraordinary measures be employed to sustain life in case of terminal illness.

Table 19-1   The Harvard Criteria for Determination of a Permanently Nonfunctioning (Dead) Brain

Unreceptive and unresponsive: No awareness is shown for external stimuli or inner need. The unresponsiveness is complete even under the application of stimuli that ordinarily would be extremely painful.

No movements and no breathing: There is a complete absence of spontaneous respiration and all other spontaneous muscular movement.

No reflexes: The usual reflexes that can be elicited in a neurophysiological examination are absent (for example, when a light is shined in the eyee, the pupil does not constrict).

A flat electroencephalogram (EEG): Electrodes attached to the scalp elicit a printout of electrical activity from the living brain. These are popularly know as brain waves. The respirator brain does not provide the usual pattern of peaks and valleys. Instead, the moving automatic stylus records essentially a flat line. This is taken to demonstrate the lack of electrophysiological activity.

No circulation to or within the brain: Without the oxygen and nutrition provided to the brain by its blood supply, functioning will soon terminate. (Precisely how long the brain can retain its biability, the ability to survive, without circulation is a matter of much current investigation and varies somewhat with conditions.)

Source: Kastenbaum, 1998.

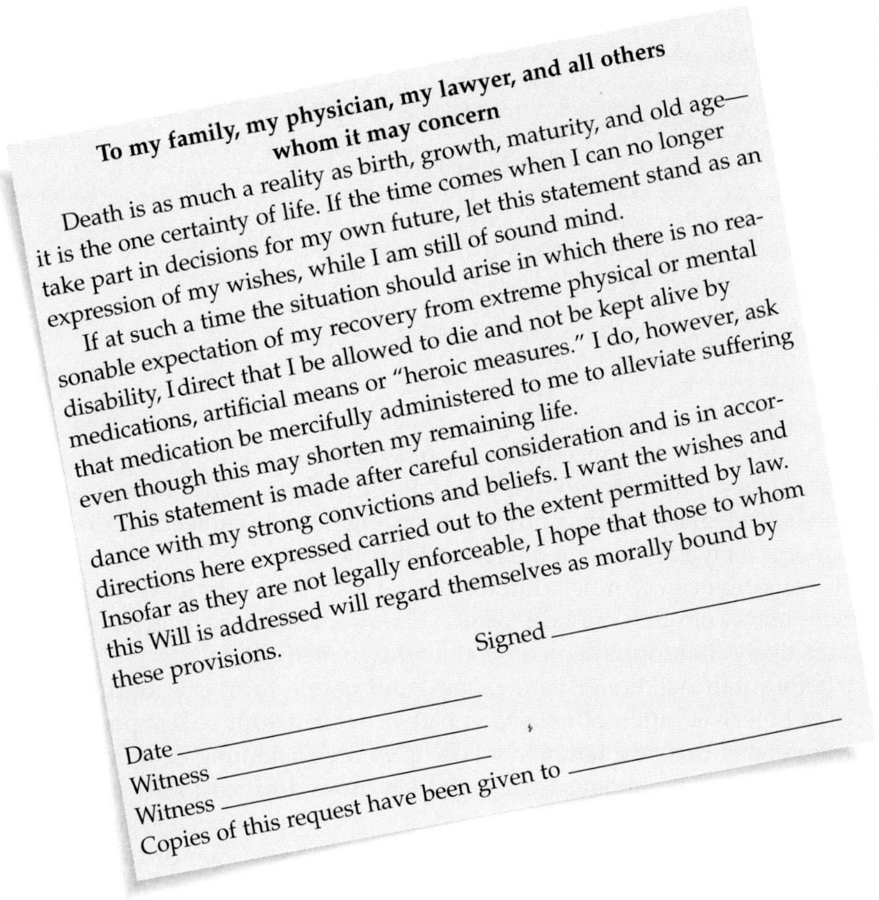

To my family, my physician, my lawyer, and all others whom it may concern

Death is as much a reality as birth, growth, maturity, and old age— it is the one certainty of life. If the time comes when I can no longer take part in decisions for my own future, let this statement stand as an expression of my wishes, while I am still of sound mind.

If at such a time the situation should arise in which there is no reasonable expectation of my recovery from extreme physical or mental disability, I direct that I be allowed to die and not be kept alive by medications, artificial means or "heroic measures." I do, however, ask that medication be mercifully administered to me to alleviate suffering even though this may shorten my remaining life.

This statement is made after careful consideration and is in accordance with my strong convictions and beliefs. I want the wishes and directions here expressed carried out to the extent permitted by law. Insofar as they are not legally enforceable, I hope that those to whom this Will is addressed will regard themselves as morally bound by these provisions.

Signed _____

Date _____
Witness _____
Witness _____
Copies of this request have been given to _____

Figure 19–2   A Living Will

This is a formal request prepared by Concern for Dying, and Educational Council. It informs the signer's family, or others who may be concerned, of the signer's wish to avoid the use of "heroic measures" to maintain life in the event of irreversible illness.

A MATTER FOR DEBATE

ASSISTED SUICIDE

According to John Horgan, staff writer for *Scientific American* (1997), polls indicate that a majority of people in the United States now support the right of a patient to receive a lethal drug from their physician if they wish. Some health-related professional organizations also endorse this view. On the other hand, the majority of such organizations, including the American Medical Association (AMA), strongly oppose suicide with the assistance of a physician. What are some of the issues?

Proponents of assisted suicide argue that a significant number of people die in pain and agony after lengthy battles with diseases such as cancer and AIDS. In spite of major advances in the management of pain, modern narcotics often do not eliminate it. Moreover, current laws often prohibit doctors from prescribing excessive dosages of painkillers. Bear in mind that an individual's tolerance for narcotics increases with sustained use, requiring ever-increasing dosages—which render the patient immobile and unconscious much of the time. Thus, for many terminally ill patients the quality of life declines rapidly.

Advocates of assisted suicide question the point of it all. Why not instead allow the patient to choose a quick, easy, "good death"? In addition, they note that "hastening death" in less dramatic ways than openly assisted suicide is a common practice with terminally ill patients. In other words, the equivalent of assisted suicide is already widespread, just as abortion was widespread even before its legalization. Currently in the United States, physician-assisted suicide is legal only in Oregon.

Opponents of assisted suicide argue that it constitutes a form of euthanasia. They are extremely wary of the precedent that would be set by legalization of assisted suicide. For example, would the next step be death for patients with nonterminal but nonetheless incurable and debilitating diseases such as major mental disorders? Who would make the decision in such cases, given that the mentally disordered patient is incapable of informed consent? Would family members have this right? In all, given assisted suicide as a "foot in the door" for euthanasia, where would we draw the line?

In the forefront of most discussions of assisted suicide is Jack Kevorkian, a former physician whose license was revoked, who has assisted numerous such patients and been acquitted of wrongdoing in each such case for which he has been prosecuted. Kevorkian has openly advocated euthanasia, not just for the dying but also for the disabled, the mentally ill, and infants with birth defects, among others (Betzold, 1997). Who would make the final decision in such cases? Kevorkian believes that it should be made by doctors, an idea that many people, both in the medical community and in society at large, also find alarming. Critics also contend that at least some of Kevorkian's patients have not been terminally ill (see Gutmann, 1996).

Thus, the debate continues. Legislative action, state referendums, and court challenges continue. Civil and criminal prosecutions of those who openly help patients commit suicide will no doubt continue as well. Moreover, although hospices increasingly offer services that offset much of the pain, misery, and isolation that often accompany dying (see page 638), it remains true, as Joe Loconte (1998) put it, that "Too many people in America are dying a bad death." To this we might add that far too many people in America are *afraid* of dying a bad death, which makes better death care—whatever its form—an issue that deserves thoughtful consideration.

For Kevorkian, however, the saga appears to be over for now. On videotape, he administered a lethal dosage himself—thus, for the first time as far as we know, performing active euthanasia. He was subsequently convicted of second-degree murder in April, 2000 and is currently imprisoned and on appeal.

or others who may be concerned, of your wish to avoid the use of "heroic" or "extraordinary" measures to maintain your life in the event of irreversible illness. It is not legally binding, but it is a starting point in protecting a loved one who might then allow you to die naturally at home.

The situation can be much different if you have been admitted to a hospital, nursing home, or other medical facility. Requirements vary from state to state, but it is likely that forms signed by at least two medical doctors will be necessary before staff will honor your request and not perform extraordinary measures or otherwise attempt to keep you alive against your will. If possible, it is also preferable that you not be hooked up to life-sustaining equipment in the first place; getting unhooked can be much more difficult to accomplish. Finally, while you are still of sound mind, it is a very good idea to have a notarized, **medical power of attorney.** This grants a loved one or other trusted person the power to authorize or *not* authorize life-sustaining procedures on your behalf should you become mentally incapacitated during a protracted

medical power of attorney A legal document by which a person authorizes another to make life-or-death medical decisions.

illness—particularly an illness such as Alzheimer's disease, in which dementia can precede loss of crucial bodily functions by years.

CONTENT CHECK
THE SEARCH FOR A HUMANE DEATH

True–False (answers are on the Companion Website)

1. Hospices are designed to help the terminally ill live out their remaining time as fully and independently as possible.
2. In contrast to hospices, hospitals regard death as both painful and inevitable.
3. In the United States, active euthanasia is considered murder.
4. Most people today demand a right to die.
5. A living will represents a person's effort to preserve individual autonomy in the last stages of life.

Thinking Critically

How has the quest for a humane death changed the ways services are provided to the dying?

Grief and Bereavement

What about those who are left behind? Often, surviving family members and close friends must make major adjustments to a loved one's death, beginning during the dying process. For them, life must go on.

Family members and close friends must make short- and long-term adjustments to the death of a loved one. Short-term adjustments include initial emotional reactions to the personal loss—often called **grief work**—plus the practical matters of funeral arrangements, financial matters, and legal proceedings. Long-term adjustments, particularly for a widow or widower, include changes in life patterns, routines, roles, and activities that may be necessary to cope with the social void left by death, as discussed in the preceding chapter. Each of these adjustments may require more time and involvement than anticipated. The grieving process may also differ from one culture to another, and it often involves differing rituals and customs. As we also see, grieving may be especially difficult when a child dies.

Grieving

Is it actually necessary to grieve? Do sorrow and mental anguish serve some essential function? What is the purpose of grief work?

The prevailing view is that certain psychological tasks need to be accomplished after the loss of a loved one. The survivor needs to accept the reality of the loss and the pain associated with it. In addition, the survivor must rechannel the emotional energy that he or she had previously invested in the relationship with the deceased person.

Many experts hesitate to define specific phases of grieving, on grounds that it might encourage people to "force" what are actually widely varying patterns

grief work Dealing with emotional reactions to the loss of a loved one.

of grieving into some prescribed sequence (Gallagher, 1987). Experts who do address patterns in grieving note that initial reactions often include shock, numbness, denial, and disbelief. There may be anger; there may be attempts to blame someone or something. The shock phase often lasts for several days, sometimes much longer. Especially after a sudden, unanticipated death, the people closest to the deceased may participate in the funeral ceremonies and burial in a robot-like fashion, not yet fully believing that the loss has occurred.

In the second phase, survivors may experience active grief in the form of weeping or other expressions of sorrow. They may yearn or pine for the deceased person. Some people have symptoms such as feelings of weakness or emptiness, as well as appetite loss and sleep disturbances. Often, they lose interest in normal pursuits and become preoccupied with thoughts of the deceased. They may have the full range of symptoms associated with depression.

Eventually, however, most survivors begin to recover. They adjust to their new life circumstances. They "let go" of the loved one, invest time and energy in new relationships, and reconstruct an identity apart from the relationship with the deceased. This does not, however, mean that they forget the loved one and cease to think about him or her; instead, what seems to happen is that the emotional pain associated with thoughts of the loved one gradually diminishes.

As noted, there are many patterns of grieving; these depend on personality, age, sex, and cultural traditions, as well as on the quality of the relationship with the deceased. In addition, there are factors than can aid the recovery process. If the death is preceded by a long illness or loss of functioning, for example, the survivors can, to some extent, prepare themselves for the loss; they experience **anticipatory grief.** Perhaps feelings of loss, guilt, or missed opportunities are discussed with the dying person. Anticipatory grief, however, will not eliminate postdeath grieving. Indeed, it may not even reduce the intensity of postdeath grief (Rando, 1986). It can, however, make the effects of the death less overwhelming because plans and adjustments can be made in advance, making it somewhat easier to cope with the grief. On the other hand, if an illness lasts for more than about 18 months, the emotional drain of caring for the person tends to outweigh any benefits of anticipatory grief. Moreover, when an illness is prolonged, the survivor may become convinced that the terminally ill person will not really die, that he or she has "beaten the odds." In such cases the person's eventual death can be even more shocking than a sudden death would have been (Rando, 1986).

Social support also plays a role in grieving. Theoretical models of stress and coping frequently note the value of a strong social-support system in successfully negotiating life crises. Yet, not all social support is equally helpful (Bankoff, 1986; Morgan, 1989). In one study, about 40% of the comments made by widows about their postbereavement social relationships were negative (Morgan, 1989). Another point is that support from peers, especially those who have also experienced the loss of their spouse, seems to be more helpful than family support. Widowhood self-help support groups can also be of value (Morgan, 1989). Similarly, parents who have lost a child often find it comforting to interact with others whose children have died (Edelstein, 1984).

There are circumstances in which grief may be particularly overwhelming. For example, older people who happen to experience the loss of several friends or family members in a relatively short span of time may experience **bereavement overload.** Bereavement overload also affects gay and minority communities that may lose many of their members to AIDS. Depression then becomes a serious risk during bereavement, especially for men (Stroebe & Stroebe, 1987).

anticipatory grief Emotionally preparing yourself for the death of a loved one, as in cases of prolonged terminal illness.

bereavement overload A stress reaction experienced by people who lose several friends or loved ones during a short period of time. Often characterized by depression.

So does abuse of alcohol and other drugs, again especially among men. Physical health may also be affected; recently bereaved individuals visit their physicians more frequently than people who are not experiencing bereavement (Mor, Sherwood, & Gutkin, 1986). It is possible, however, that such visits are for routine care that was neglected while the bereaved person served as a caregiver to the deceased. Many of these visits may also be linked to depression more than to physical illness per se (Mor et al., 1986).

Bereavement in Cross-Cultural Perspective

Are there universal grief responses after the death of a loved one? Studies have shown that some responses that were long thought of as the norm (1) may not be shared by a majority of bereaved people, (2) may be culturally bound, and (3) may not even be healthy adaptations. When Margaret Stroebe and colleagues (Stroebe, Gergen, Gergen, & Stroebe, 1992) explored the universality of grief responses, they found that responses are both historically and culturally determined. Although the modern Western view of grief requires that people engage in "proper grieving" by recovering from their grief as quickly as possible and returning to normal functioning, many non-Western cultures stress a continuing bond with the deceased. In Japan, mourners traditionally have an altar in their home dedicated to the family's ancestors. They offer food at the altar and talk to the ancestors, who they believe are accessible to them. In Egypt, mourners are encouraged to express their grief through emotional outpourings. In Mexico, there is a traditional celebration of ancestors (see "A Closer Look, *Todos Santos*—The Day of the Dead," page 646).

Similarly, whereas current Western thought about grief emphasizes a rational response as the means of returning to normal functioning, grief was viewed differently during the 19th-century Romantic period. Stroebe and colleagues explained:

> Because close relationships were matters of bonding in depth, the death of an intimate other constituted a critical point of life definition. To grieve was to signal the significance of the relationship, and the depth of one's own spirit. Dissolving bonds with the deceased would not only define the relationship as superficial, but would deny as well one's own sense of profundity and self-worth. It would make a sham of a spiritual commitment and undermine one's sense of living a meaningful life. In contrast with the breaking bonds orientation of modernism, romanticism valor was found in sustaining these bonds, despite a "broken heart" (Stroebe et al., 1992, p. 1208).

Stroebe and colleagues pointed out that despite the modern Western emphasis on "breaking bonds," many widows and widowers tend to maintain their ties to the deceased just as the bereaved did during the Romantic age. Widows and widowers may "sense" their spouse's presence for years after he or she has died, and the deceased continues to have a strong psychological influence on the survivor's life.

Other theorists (Wortman & Silver, 1989) took issue with contemporary views of bereavement that focus on immediate, intense emotionality. They disputed the popular view of bereavement, which states that distress or depression is inevitable; that failure to experience distress is pathological; that "working through" a loss is important; and that the bereaved should have an expectation of recovery. For example, they cited studies showing that despite the belief that individuals who are depressed after a loss adapt more successfully than those who experience no depression, people with the greatest degree

A CLOSER LOOK

TODOS SANTOS—THE DAY OF THE DEAD

The strength of cultural influences on bereavement and death is clearly seen in traditional Mexican culture. During the festival of *Todos Santos* (All Saints), Mexicans from every walk of life—the rich and the poor, the educated and the illiterate, the urban and the rural—stop their worldly business to remember and respect the dead. This commemoration contrasts sharply with bereavement practices in most of the United States, which seem to be motivated more by anxiety and discomfort than by celebration and remembrance.

Todos Santos stems from a belief that death is a natural element of the life cycle—an element to be celebrated with a community festival (Cohen, 1992). The celebration combines pre-Columbian customs and beliefs of Indian cultures with those of Catholic Spain.

At the center of the celebration are community altars that beckon the an-

cestors to return. Each family has its own altarpiece, known as an *ofrenda*, to honor and remember deceased family members. Each *ofrenda* includes the favorite food and drink of the deceased, as well as articles of the deceased's clothing and personal belongings. Special offerings are made for the souls of deceased children. These offerings are prepared in miniature and include ample sweets. After the souls of the dead have made their presence felt, the living take part in the celebration. Family members consume some of the food and drink, share some with neighbors and friends, and place a final offering on the graves of the deceased. What might these customs mean? In the words of one observer,

> This joyful sharing creates a form of communal reciprocity: it helps connect the community with their dead and, in turn, creates a

symbolic presence of the deceased within the community. (Cohen, 1992, p. 108)

Rather than being shielded from the realities of death, Mexican children are at the center of the *Todos Santos* festivities. They help prepare the *ofrenda* and take part in graveside celebrations. They help decorate the graves with brightly colored flowers and light candles of remembrance. From this, children learn that death is a natural part of life and is not to be feared. Thus,

> In many [cultures], death is . . . not regarded as a termination but as an elevation to another level of existing. It is an event initially tinged with uncertain emotions, but ultimately one to be celebrated as the dead are reaccommodated as ancestors. (Carmichael & Sayer, 1991, p. 7)

In Mexico, this reaccommodation has the status of a national tradition.

---

of distress and depression are likely to still be the most distressed 1 or 2 years later. Similarly, they identified **chronic grief,** or failure to ever recover from a loss, as a pathological mourning process that is clearly identifiable in many grievers.

A lengthy longitudinal study of the bereavement response (Cleiren, 1993) focused on the loss reactions, health, and social functioning of 309 family members who were immediate relatives of people who had died from suicides, traffic accidents, or long-term illnesses. The study, known as the *Leiden Bereavement Study* after the Dutch town in which it was conducted, found wide variations in bereavement responses based on the meaning of the relationship before the death, the nature of the death, whether there was an opportunity to anticipate the death, and the practical support received by the bereaved person after the death occurred.

Thus, grief reactions differ markedly from person to person and from culture to culture. There is no universal or "right" way to grieve, although societal expectations are powerful influences that can make it appear that there is.

Rituals and Customs

The customs and rituals of death in the United States have changed considerably throughout history. It used to be customary, for example, for a widow to wear black and refrain from most social activities for up to a year. This symbolized her presumed and expected emotional distress. Other people were signaled to provide comfort and support, and the culture allowed for a long period of adaptation (Ariès, 1981). The opposite is true in much of contemporary

chronic grief A pathological mourning process in which the person never overcomes the grief.

Western culture; normally, the survivor is expected to return to normal living in a few days.

Funerals and memorial services can impart a sense of order, decorum, and continuity. They can reaffirm the values and beliefs of the individuals and the community as well as demonstrate the support of family and friends. The deceased person's life can be reviewed and celebrated in a public, shared forum. Sometimes, however, the public ceremonies clash with the values and experiences of the survivors, leaving them feeling further isolated. Sometimes, too, the rituals and institutions are too distant from the personal lives of the participants to be meaningful. Yet, it is hard for most of us to conceive of following a loved one's death with no ritual whatsoever; rituals make the end "official."

When a Child Dies

Many aspects of grief and bereavement may be intensified when a child dies, although as some researchers have pointed out, there is considerable variability in grieving here as well (Dijkstra & Stroebe, 1998). There may also be confusion, guilt, and attempts to assign blame for the loss (Miles, 1984). The brothers and sisters of a dying child may be particularly confused and disoriented. Death is often seen as a punishment of some sort—to the child who died, to the parent, or to the surviving brothers or sisters—or perhaps they simply resort to platitudes such as "God moves in mysterious ways" to reconcile themselves to their loss. Often parents who are coping with their own grief may be unable to help the other children in the family or even to answer a child's questions on an appropriate developmental level. Many siblings do not disclose their secret fears, feelings of guilt, or misunderstandings, and yet many of the thoughts and feelings that arise during such a family crisis may last a lifetime (Coleman & Coleman, 1984).

When a child dies slowly of a terminal illness, there are other issues to deal with. What should the dying child be told? How can the child be helped to confront death? How do the parents deal with their feelings of failure, guilt, and helplessness? Often medical caregivers become personally involved in the

Funerals can help survivors by providing, among other things, a sense of continuity and closure.

child's hopes for recovery. They, too, experience feelings of failure and anticipatory grief. There is a tendency for all involved to deny these painful feelings.

A crisis of values is not uncommon among survivors after the death of a child. Certainly the child did not deserve to die. The survivors struggle to reevaluate their most closely held beliefs and values—especially religious ones—at the same time that they are suffering from numerous symptoms of sorrow and depression (Kushner, 1981). Those who find some way to resolve such issues often report sensing a deeper meaning in their own lives; those who do not resolute them may live out a lifetime of despair. In the case of unnecessary fatal accidents, they may also find meaning and resolution in joining advocacy groups such as Mothers Against Drunk Driving (MADD), which seek to prevent needless child deaths in the future.

CONTENT CHECK
GRIEF AND BEREAVEMENT

True–False (answers are on the Companion Website)
1. After the death of a loved one, survivors need to accept the reality of the loss and the accompanying pain.
2. Many patterns of grieving exist.
3. Many non-Western cultures stress quick recovery from grief.
4. Rituals such as funerals and memorials impart a sense of order, decorum, and continuity.
5. Grief and bereavement are especially intense after the death of a child.

Thinking Critically
Is grieving a necessary process? Why or why not?

Completing the Life Cycle

Ultimately, whether death involves a child, a frail, elderly adult, or anyone in between, it marks the completion of the individual's life cycle. We close the chapter (and the book) with some thoughts about what this completion means.

Each individual life cycle is embedded in a cultural and historical context. Birth, first steps, first words, schooling, coming of age, finding a mate, working, building a family, finding wisdom, and facing your own mortality are common tasks, but they are played out against a rich tapestry of individual biological and cultural patterns—that is, heredity and environment in interaction. The social sciences have much to say about some common patterns and influences and their timing, but the community of which the individual is a member has much to say about what it all means.

Some cultural practices make the links between death, birth, and the life cycle explicit. In traditional Chinese culture, for example, when a grandparent dies, a grandchild of the appropriate age may be urged to marry or to have a child. In Jewish culture, it is the custom to name a newborn child after a deceased member of the immediate family; renewal and continuity are thus celebrated in the new birth. Hence, what seem like polar opposites—birth and death—are linked as part of a continuous family thread.

Whatever the cultural backdrop, death and its prospects often give life new meaning for the individual and the community. As we try to make sense of a particular person's life and death, we reassess our own priorities and values. The death of a community leader or public figure may sharpen individual and community values. Yet, quite ordinary deaths often help just as much in defining the meaning of courage, loyalty, kindness, or virtue in lasting and personal ways.

Otherwise, as noted at the beginning of the chapter, death—regardless of its circumstances—is a part of nature. It is undeniable and clear-cut. It happens to all of us and every member of every other species as well. What lies beyond death for any individual will always be debated and probably never be known scientifically; but what lies beyond death for us as human beings is new life for those who follow.

CHAPTER 19 REVISITED

Thoughts and Fears of Death

- In the United States, the tendency has been to deny death while at the same time being preoccupied with it.

- In earlier historical periods death was a familiar event that usually occurred at home; in the 20th century, most people died in hospitals.

- Actively coping with the reality of death means taking realistic precautions.

- In the past there was considerable resistance to discussing dying, but this changing.

- Personal and cultural meanings of death often play a key role in determining whether individuals are fearful or preoccupied with thoughts of their own death.

Confronting Your Own Death

- People who are not faced with the prospect of immediate death can spend more time adjusting to it.

- Finding meaning and purpose in life involves active restructuring of philosophical, religious, and pragmatic thoughts and beliefs.

- Kübler-Ross identified five stages in the process of adjusting to the idea of death: denial, anger, bargaining, depression, and acceptance, but these are not universal.

- Reactions to dying are strongly influenced by the nature of the illness, especially in the case of AIDS; many AIDS patients experience a prolonged dying process that makes acceptance and forgiveness difficult.

- Suicide is common in middle-aged and older people; submissive death and suicidal erosion are other trajectories.

- Suicide among older people is almost always a result of loss of spouse.

The Search for a Humane Death

- The modern view is that dying patients should be informed of their condition and given autonomy.

- Hospices are designed to help terminally ill patients live out their days as fully and independently as possible; their goals include managing pain of all sorts and respecting the dying patient's wishes.

- Many people now demand a right to die, perhaps through passive euthanasia, assisted suicide, or even active euthanasia.

- A living will is a document the states that signer's wish to avoid the use of "heroic" or "extraordinary" measures to maintain life in the event of irreversible illness; a medical power of attorney is advisable as well.

Grief and Bereavement

- Family and friends must make short- and long-term adjustments to the death of a loved one. The short-term adjustments include initial emotional reactions, often called grief work. Long-term adjustments include changes in routines, roles, and activities.

- Certain psychological tasks need to be accomplished after the loss of a loved one. These include accepting the reality of the loss and rechanneling the emotional energy previously invested in the deceased.

■ Initial reactions to death are many; these may be followed by active grieving.

■ If the death is preceded by a long illness or loss of functioning, the survivors may experience anticipatory grief.

■ Social support, especially from peers, can be helpful in coping with grief.

■ People who experience several losses within a relatively short span of time may experience bereavement overload.

■ Grief responses are both historically and culturally determined.

■ Some theorists dispute the popular view of bereavement.

■ Chronic grief, or failure to ever recover from a loss, has been identified as a pathological mourning process.

■ Funerals and memorial services can impart a sense of order and continuity.

■ Many aspects of grief and bereavement are intensified when a child dies, especially if the death is sudden or unexpected.

Completing the Life Cycle

■ Each individual life cycle is embedded in a cultural and historical context; biological and cultural patterns interact throughout the cycle.

■ Death and its prospects often give life new meaning.

KEY TERMS

submissive death
suicidal erosion
hospice
right to die
active euthanasia

assisted suicide
passive euthanasia
living will
medical power of attorney

grief work
anticipatory grief
bereavement overload
chronic grief

Glossary

accommodation Piaget's term for the act of changing our schemas when a new object or event does not fit.

achievement motivation A learned drive involving persistence toward success and excellence.

active euthanasia Taking positive steps to bring about another person's death, as in cases of terminal illness. In the United States, active euthanasia is murder.

adaptation In Piaget's theory, the process by which infant schemes are elaborated, modified, and developed.

adolescent growth spurt The sudden increase in rate of growth that accompanies the entrance into puberty.

affordances The different opportunities for interaction offered by a perception; for example, halls are for moving through.

afterbirth The third and last stage of childbirth, typically occurring within 20 minutes after delivery, during which the placenta and the umbilical cord are expelled from the uterus.

age clock A form of internal timing used as a measure of adult development; a way of knowing that we are progressing too slowly or too quickly in terms of key social events that occur during adulthood.

age of viability The age (at about 24 weeks) at which the fetus has a 50-50 chance of surviving outside the womb.

ageism In Western societies, a widely prevalent attitude that overvalues youth and degrades older persons.

alleles A pair of genes, found on corresponding chromosomes, that affect the same trait.

altruism Self-sacrifice without self-interest.

Alzheimer's disease A disease that causes dementia due to a progressive deterioration of brain cells, especially those in the cerebral cortex.

amniocentesis The withdrawal and analysis of amniotic fluid with a syringe to obtain cells for testing.

amniotic fluid Fluid that cushions and helps protect the embryo or fetus.

amniotic sac A fluid-filled membrane that encloses the developing embryo or fetus.

androgynous personality Characteristic of a person who is high in both desirable masculine and femine traits.

anorexia nervosa An eating disorder in which a person is obsessed by thoughts of an unattainable image of "perfect" thinness. Can result in death.

anoxia Lack of oxygen; can cause brain damage.

anticipatory grief Emotionally preparing yourself for the death of a loved one, as in cases of prolonged terminal illness.

anxiety A feeling of uneasiness, apprehension, or fear that has a vague or unknown source.

Apgar Scoring System A standard scoring system that allows hospitals to evaluate an infant's condition quickly and objectively.

assertiveness Standing up for and defending your rights.

assimilation In Piaget's theory, the process of making new information part of existing schemas.

assisted suicide Providing a terminally ill patient with the means to end his or her own life.

atherosclerosis Hardening of the arteries, which is a common condition of aging caused by the body's increasing inability to use excess fats in the diet. These fats are stored along the walls of arteries and restrict the flow of blood when they harden.

attachment The emotional bond that develops between child and caregivers. The infant's first bond is usually characterized by strong interdepence, intense mutual feelings, and vital emotional ties.

Attention-deficit/hyperactivity disorder (ADHD) An inability to keep focused on something long enough to learn it, often accompanied by poor impulse control.

authoritarian parents Those parents who adhere to rigid rule structures and dictate rules to children; in this situation, children contribute little to the family's decision-making process.

authoritative parents Those parents who use firm control with children but encourage communication and negotiation in rule setting within the family.

automaticity The ability to perform behaviors with little or no conscious attention devoted to them.

autonomy The strong desire to do things for yourself, to master physical and social environments, and to be competent and successful.

autosomes All chromosomes except those that determine sex.

avoidant attachment Insecure attachment characterized by ambivalence toward the mother.

baby biography Recording mini-milestones of child development, such as the ages when the child discovers parts of the body, creeps, sits upright, or walks.

base pairs A "rung" in the DNA ladder; the base adenine pairs only with the base thymine, the base cytosine pairs only with the base guanine.

base A nitrogen-carbon-hydrogen component of nucleotides.

behavior genetics The study of relationships between behavior and genetic makeup.

behavior modification A method that uses conditioning procedures such as reinforcement, reward, and shaping to change behavior.

bereavement overload A stress reaction experienced by people who lose several friends or loved ones during a short period of time. Often characterized by depression.

bioecological model A model that emphasizes that human development is a dynamic, reciprocal process that begins with genetic endowment and unfolds as a result of interactions with various levels of the environment.

bioinformatics   A discipline that combines biology and computer science.

biological age   A person's position with regard to his or her expected lifespan.

birthing center   Place designed to accommodate the entire birth process, from labor through delivery and recovery.

bisexual   A person who is attracted both to men and to women.

blastula   The hollow, fluid-filled sphere of cells that forms soon after conception.

brain growth spurt   Rapid growth during infancy in the size of neurons, the number of glial cells, and the complexity of synapses.

breech presentation   The baby's position in the uterus such that the head will emerge last. Assistance is usually needed in such cases to prevent injury to the infant, producing anoxia.

bulimia nervosa   An eating disorder characterized by binging and purging.

case study   The compilation of often large and intricate amounts of information on an individual, family, or community through interviews, observations, and formal testing.

cataract   Clouding of the lens of the eye that obstructs vision.

cells   The smallest self-contained structures in the human body.

centenarians   People over age 100.

cephalocaudal trend   The sequence of growth that occurs first in the head and progresses downward.

cerebral cortex   The surface of the brain.

cesarean section   Surgical procedure used to remove the baby and the placenta from the uterus by cutting through the abdominal wall.

child abuse   Intentional psychological or physical injuries inflicted on a child.

child neglect   Failure of caregiver to respond to or care for a child.

chorionic villus sampling (CVS)   In this procedure, cells are drawn from the membranes surrounding the fetus, either with a syringe or with a catheter. Because more cells are collected in this procedure than in amniocentesis, the test can be completed more quickly.

chromosome   Chain of genes, visible under a microscope.

chronic grief   A pathological mourning process in which the person never overcomes the grief.

chronosystem   Part of Bronfenbrenner's model of the socio-cultural environment; the fluid back-and-forth interactions among the four systems (microsystem, mesosystem, exosystem, (macrosystem) across time.

classical conditioning   A type of learning in which a neutral stimulus, such as a bell, comes to elicit a response, such as salivation, by repeated pairings with an unconditioned stimulus, such as food.

climacteric   The broad complex of physical and emotional symptoms that accompany reproductive changes in middle adulthood, affecting both men and women.

clique   Adolescent peer group with about 3 to 9 members.

codominance   Where neither the dominant nor recessive allele is dominant and the resulting phenotype is a blend of the two; an example is the AB blood type.

cognitive domain   Segment of development that includes acquiring skills in perceiving, thinking, reasoning, problem solving, as well as the intricate development and use of language.

cognitive-developmental theory   An approach that focuses on the development of thinking, reasoning, and problem solving.

cohort effects   Sociocultural differences between people of different age groups.

collective monologues   Children's conversations that include taking talking turns, but not necessarily about the same topic.

collectivist (culture)   A culture where the group takes precedence over the individual. Cooperation and group achievement are stressed over competition and individual achievement.

command generation   The generation of middle-aged people, who make most of the decisions that affect our lives.

conditions of worth   Conditions others impose upon us if we are to be worthwhile as human beings—conditions that are often impossible to fulfill.

confounding   The problem of not being able to tell if effects noticed between cohorts are due to developmental or historical factors.

congenital anomalies   Also called birth defects; abnormalities resulting from genetic and chromosomal problems as well as exposure to toxins, disease, and such during the prenatal period.

conscious mind   What we are aware of and thinking about at any given time.

conservation   The understanding that changing the shape or appearance of objects doesn't change their amount.

content   The meaning of any written or spoken message.

context   The particular setting or situation in which development occurs; the "backdrop" for development.

contextual paradigms   The view that numerous environmental, social, psychological, and historical factors interact to determine development.

contextualism   The view that environmental, social, psychological, and historical factors interact to determine development.

contingency   A relationship between behavior and its consequences.

control processes   Higher cognitive processes that enhance memory.

coregulation   Development of a sense of shared responsibility between parents and children.

correlation   A mathematical statement of the relationship or correspondence between two variables.

covert behavior   Behavior that cannot be seen or measured with instrumentation.

crisis model   The view that changes in midlife are abrupt and often stressful.

criterion-referenced tests   Tests that evaluate an individual's performance in relation to mastery of specified skills or objectives.

critical period   The only span of time when a particular environmental factor can have an effect.

cross-sectional design   A method of studying development in which a sample of individuals of one age are compared with one or more samples of other age groups.

crowd Adolescent peer group with about 15 to 30 members.

crystallized intelligence Accumulated knowledge and skills based on education and experience.

culture The beliefs, norms, practices, language, ethnicity, and other aspects of personal and group identity shared by interacting people.

death instincts According to Freud, the processes involved in each person's eventual death, plus aggression and destructiveness.

decision/commitment The realization of being in love and making a commitment to maintain it.

declarative knowledge Factual knowledge; knowing "what."

defense mechanisms According to Freud, the cognitive "tricks" that individuals use to reduce tensions that lead to anxiety.

defense mechanisms The psychodynamic "tricks" that individuals use to reduce tensions that lead to anxiety.

deferred imitation Imitating something that happened hours or even days earlier.

delinquents People under age 16 or 18 who commit criminal acts.

dementia A disorder that produces the confusion, forgetfulness, and personality changes that may be associated with older age.

deoxyribonucleic acid (DNA) A large, complex molecule composed of carbon, hydrogen, oxygen, nitrogen, and phosphorus. It contains the genetic code that regulates the functioning and development of an organism.

dependent variable The variable in an experiment that changes as a result of manipulating the independent variable.

dethroning of the older sibling Loss of being the center of attention when a younger sibling is born.

development The changes over time in the physical structure, thought, or behavior of a person as a result of both biological and environmental influences.

developmental neuroscience The study of the development of brain structures and the relations betweeen brain structures and functions and behavior.

developmental niche Interaction of components such as everyday physical and social settings, childcare and child-rearing customs, and the overall psychology of caregivers that determines the unique world of each child.

deviation IQ The approach that assigns an IQ score by comparing an individual's raw score with the scores of other subjects of the same age range.

dialectical thinking Thought that seeks to integrate opposing or conflicting ideas and observations.

diffusion status The identity status of those who have neither gone through an identity crisis nor made commitments.

discrepancy hypothesis A cognitive theory stating that around 7 months, infants acquire schemes for familiar objects. When a new image or object is presented that differs from the old one, the child experiences uncertainty and anxiety.

discrimination Treating others in a prejudiced manner.

disorganized/disoriented attachment Insecure attachment characterized by contradictory behavior and confusion regarding the mother.

dizygotic (fraternal) twins Twins resulting from the fertilization of two separate ova by two separate sperm.

dominant In genetics, one gene of a gene pair that will cause a particular trait to be expressed.

dual-earner couple A married or unmarried couple sharing a household, in which both contribute to family income as members of the paid labor force.

eclectic Accepting and using those parts of diverse theories that work; being willing and able to draw upon works from a broad range of theoretical perspectives.

ecological systems theory A theory of child development in which the growing child actively restructures aspects of the environment in which he or she lives while simultaneously being influenced by these environments and their relationships.

ego According to Freud, the conscious, reality-oriented component of personality.

egocentrism A self-centered view of the world; perceiving everything in relation to yourself.

embryo From the Greek term "swell."

embryonic period The second prenatal period, which lasts from implantation to the end of the second month after conception. All the major structures and organs of the individual are formed at this time.

empty nest The period in the family life cycle that occurs after the last child has left home.

episiotomy An incision to enlarge the vaginal opening.

Eros Life instincts.

estrogen A female sexual hormone.

ethnocentric bias The tendency to assume that our own beliefs, perceptions, customs, and values are correct and normal and that those of others are inferior or abnormal.

ethnocentrism The tendency to assume that our own beliefs, perceptions, customs, and values are correct or normal and that those of others are inferior or abnormal.

ethology The study of patterns of animal behavior, especially behavior that is guided by instinct.

event-related potential (ERP) method A method for testing infants whereby electrodes carefully positioned on the head obtain a graph of brain-wave activity, which is then used to study perceptual and other capabilities and specifics of brain function in response to different kinds of stimulation.

evolution The process through which species change across generations.

evolutionary psychology The study of inherited psychological characteristics.

exosystem Third level of Bronfenbrenner's model of the sociocultural environment; social settings or organizations beyond an individual's immediate experience that affect the individual.

expansive woman In Apter's research, a woman who makes major life changes to expand her horizons in middle age.

experimental design A broad term referring to the many considerations necessary for conducting meaningful and valid experiments.

expressive jargon The babbling produced when an infant uses inflections and patterns that mimic adult speech.

external validity The extent to which an experiment corresponds to what happens in the real world.

extrinsic factors of work Satisfaction in the form of pay, status, and other rewards for work.

extrinsically motivated behavior Behavior performed to obtain rewards or avoid adverse events.

failure-to-thrive syndrome A condition in which infants are small for age and often sick as a result of malnutrition or unresponsive caregiving.

fallopian tubes Two passages that open out of the upper part of the uterus and carry ova from the ovary to the uterus.

false labor Also called Braxton-Hicks contractions; contractions that may diminish if the mother walks around.

family leave Leave required by law to deal with family affairs and problems, especially those involving taking care of children.

fear A state of arousal, tension, or apprehension caused by a specific, identifiable circumstance.

fetal alcohol effects (FAE) Similar to FAS though milder abnormalities due to drinking during pregnancy.

fetal alcohol syndrome (FAS) Congenital abnormalities, including small size, low birth weight, certain facial characteristics, and possible mental retardation, resulting from maternal alcohol consumption during pregnancy.

fetal monitor The external monitor records the intensity of uterine contractions and the baby's heartbeat by means of two belts placed around the mother's abdomen. The internal monitor consists of a plastic tube containing electrodes, that is inserted through the vagina and attached to the baby's head.

fetal period The final period of prenatal development, lasting from the beginning of the second month after conception until birth. During this period, all organs mature and become functional.

fetus French for "pregnant" or "fruitful."

filial piety The veneration given the elderly in Asian and other cultures. This respect is manifested in cultural traditions as well as everyday encounters.

fine motor skills Competence in using the hands and fingers.

fixation According to Freud, and "arrestment" in development that causes the adult to continue to seek gratification in ways that are appropriate only for children.

fluid intelligence Abilities involved in acquiring new knowledge and skills.

fontanelles The soft, bony plates of the skull, connected only by cartilage.

foreclosure status The identity status of those who have made commitments without going through an identity crisis.

form The particular symbol used to represent content.

foundling fantasy The early adolescent's feeling that her or his parents are so ordinary and limited that they can't possibly be related to a sensitive and unique her or him.

functional subordination The integration of a number of separate simple actions or schemes into a more complex pattern of behavior.

gametes Reproductive cells (sperm and ova).

gay A man with a sexual orientation toward other men.

gender constancy The older child's understanding that gender is stable and stays the same despite changes in superficial appearance.

gender identity The knowledge of who you are as male or female and the ability to make that judgment about other people.

gender roles Roles we adopt as a result of being psychologically female or male.

gender schemes Cognitive standards (including stereotypes) as to what behavior and attitudes are appropriate for males and females.

gender-role stereotypes Rigid, fixed ideas of what is appropriate female or male behavior.

gene imprinting A phenomenon in which gene expression and phenotype depend on which parent the genes come from; examples are Prader Willi syndrome (PWS) and Angelman syndrome (AS).

gene therapy An approach to establishing cures for genetic disorders that can be applied at any point from altering the molecular structure of DNA to altering the process of protein synthesis.

genes The basic units of inheritance.

genetic counseling A widely available resource that can help potential parents evaluate genetic risk factors in childbearing and enable them to make intelligent decisions.

genotype The genetic makeup of a given individual.

germinal period After conception, the period of very rapid cell division and initial cell differentiation lasting for approximately two weeks.

glaucoma Increased, potentially damaging pressure within the eye.

grief work Dealing with emotional reactions to the loss of a loved one.

gross motor skills Those skills that involve the larger muscles or the whole body and that show refinement as well.

gross-to-specific trend The tendency to react to body stimuli with generalized, whole-body movements at first, with these responses becoming more local and specific later.

guided participation Vygotsky's concept that we develop understanding and expertise mainly through apprenticeship with more knowledgeable learners.

habituation method To study infant perceptual capabilities, researchers habituate infants to certain stimuli and then change the stimuli.

habituation Ceasing to attend to respond to repetitive stimulation; occurs at several levels from sensation to perception to higher cognition.

heritability The extent to which a trait is inherited versus acquired, thus presuming a genetic basis.

heterozygous Referring to the arrangement in which the two alleles for a simple dominant-recessive trait differ.

holophrastic speech In the early stages of language acquisition, the young child's use of single words to convey complete thoughts.

homophobia Prejudice, aversion, fear, and other negative attitudes by heterosexuals toward homosexuals.

homozygous Referring to the arrangement in which the two alleles for a simple dominant-recessive trait are the same.

hormones Biochemical secretions of the endocrine glands that are carried by the blood or other body fluids to a particular organ or tissue.

hospice A philosophy that involves care, counseling, support, and other assistance for dying people and their families.

hostile aggression Aggression that is intended to harm another person.

humanistic psychology The view that humans actively make choices and seek to fulfill positive personal and social goals.

hypertension Abnormally high blood pressure, sometimes accompanied by headaches and dizziness.

id According to Freud, the primitive, hedonistic component of personality.

identity achievement The identity status of those who have gone through an identity crisis and have made commitments.

identity crisis A period of making decisions about important issues, such as "Who am I, and where am I going?"

identity formation Gaining a sense of who you are and how you fit into society.

imaginary audience Adolescents' assumption that others are focusing a great deal of critical attention on them.

imaginary companions Companions children "make up" and pretend are very real.

inclusive fitness The concept that evolutionary survival of the fittest comes about through both direct and indirect fitness, where adaptive characteristics are passed along to the next generation and biological relatedness also plays a part.

incomplete dominance Where people with a single recessive gene for a trait show some of the trait along with other normal manifestations; an example is sickle-cell anemia.

independent variable The variable in an experiment that is manipulated in order to observe its effects on the dependent variable.

indifferent parents Parents who are minimally interested in their role as parents or in their children; they exercise little control over and demonstrate little warmth toward their children.

individualist (culture) A culture where competition predominates over cooperation and personal achievement

is typically valued more highly than group achievement; individual freedom and choice receive strong emphasis.

information-processing theory A theory of human development that uses the computer as an analogy for the way the human mind receives, analyzes, and stores information.

informed consent A clear statement of the procedures and risks, as well as the obligations of both the participants and the researchers.

initial labor The first stage of labor, during which the cervical opening of the uterus begins to dilate to allow for passage of the baby.

innovative woman In Apter's research, a woman who has devoted herself to a career and begins to reassess her life in middle age.

insecure attachment The result of inconsistent or unresponsive caregiving.

instinct Behavior that occurs in all normal members of a species, under the same conditions, and in the same way.

Institutional Review Boards (IRBs) Screening committees of research institutions that evaluate all research projects relative to potential harm to participants.

institutionalization Long-term, usually permanent placement in an institution.

instrumental aggression Aggression that is not intended to harm, but is instead incidental to gaining something from another person.

intelligence quotient (IQ) An individual's mental age divided by chronological age, multiplied by 100 to eliminate the decimal point.

interdependence Reciprocal dependence.

internal validity Conducting an experiment so as to allow researchers to draw meaningful information about cause-and-effect relationships.

intimacy versus isolation Crisis in young adulthood characterized by the conflict between establishing a mutually satisfying relationship with another person as opposed to failing to achieve mutuality.

intimacy The feeling of closeness that occurs in love relationships.

intrinsic factors of work Satisfaction workers obtain from doing the work in and of itself.

intrinsically motivated behavior Behavior performed for its own sake, with no particular goal.

job burnout The emotional exhaustion that often affects people particularly in high-stress professions and trades.

karyotype A photograph of a cell's chromosomes arranged in pairs according to size.

kinkeeper The role assumed by middle-aged people that includes maintaining family rituals, celebrating achievements and holidays, and keeping family histories alive.

kwashiorkor Type of severe malnutrition caused by insufficient protein. In first three years of life, this can be highly damaging in the long run because brain development is affected.

laboratory observation The method in which researchers set up controlled situations designed to elicit the behavior of interest.

language acquisition device or LAD Chomsky's term for an innate set of mental structures that aid children in language learning.

lateralization The process whereby specific skills and competencies become localized in particular hemispheres of the brain.

launching of adolescents Parents' letting go of children so that they can assume responsible adult roles.

law of effect A principle of learning theory stating that a behavior's consequences determine the probability of its being repeated.

learning disorders Extreme difficulty in learning school subjects such as reading, writing, or math, despite normal intelligence and absence of sensory or motor disabilities.

learning The basic developmental process of change in the individual as a result of experience or practice.

lesbian A woman with a sexual orientation toward other women.

life instincts According to Freud, impulses having to do with obtaining food, water, and other necessities of survival.

life structure The overall pattern that underlies and unifies a person's life.

living will An advance directive signed by a person indicating that the person does not wish that extraordinary measures be employed to sustain life in case of terminal illness.

longitudinal design A study in which the same participants are observed continuously over a period of time.

long-term memory (LTM) Permanent memory, where, barring brain damage, memories are potentially accessible throughout life and constitute our cumulative store of knowledge.

macrosystem Outermost level of Bronfenbrenner's model of the sociocultural environment; the values, laws, and customs of the society in which the individual lives.

magical mastery A lifestyle of very old men characterized by coping via projection and distortion of reality.

man in midlife crisis A middle-aged man undergoing feelings of confusion and disintegration.

marasmus Type of malnutrition caused by insufficient total quantity of food where muscles waste away and stored fat is depleted. If duration is short, no long-term negative effects result.

marginal group A group between cultures or on the fringe of a dominant culture.

mean length of utterance (MLU) The average length of the sentences that a child produces.

medical power of attorney A legal document by which a person authorizes another to make life-or-death medical decisions.

meiosis The process of cell division in reproductive cells that results in gametes with an infinite number of different chromosomal arrangements.

menarche The time of the first menstrual period.

menopause The permanent end of menstruation; it occurs in middle adulthood and may be accompanied by physical symptoms and intense emotional reactions, more so in some women than in others.

mental retardation Significantly subaverage intellectual functioning and self-help skills, with onset prior to age 18.

mesosystem Second level of Bronfenbrenner's model of the sociocultural environment; the interrelationships of two or more microsystems.

metacognition The process of monitoring your own thinking and memory.

microsystem First level of Bronfenbrenner's model of the sociocultural environment; the activities, roles, and interactions of an individual and his or her immediate setting.

midwife A woman experienced in childbirth, with or without training, who assists with home delivery.

mitosis The process of ordinary cell division that results in two cells identical to the parent.

monozygotic (identical) twins Twins resulting from the division of a single fertilized ovum.

moral absolutism Any theory of morality that disregards cultural differences in moral beliefs.

moral dilemmas In Kohlberg's research, narratives in which participants are asked to judge whether a character's behavior was moral or immoral.

moral realism Piaget's term for the first stage of moral development, in which children believe in rules as real, indestructible things.

moral relativism Piaget's term for the second stage of moral development, in which children realize that rules are agreements that may be changed, if necessary.

morality Ideas about fairness and justice, right and wrong, good and bad.

moratorium status The identity status of those who are currently in the midst of an identity crisis.

mutuality or interactive synchrony The patterns of interchange between caregiver and infant in which each responds to and influences the other's movements and rhythms.

myelination The formation of the myelin sheath covering the fast-acting central nervous system pathways. This sheath increases the speed of transmission and the precision of the nervous system.

"natural" or prepared childbirth Childbirth based on procedures developed by Fernand Lamaze, a French obstetrician.

natural selection Survival of the fittest.

naturalistic or field observation The method in which researchers go into everyday settings and observe and record behavior while being as unobtrusive as possible.

negative punishment Also called omission training; a subject's behavior results in something desirable or pleasant being taken away and the behavior decreases.

negative reinforcement Also called escape or active avoidance training; a subject's behavior results in something unpleasant or aversive being taken away or simply not occurring. Behavior increases.

neonate Baby in the first month of life.

neurons The cells that make up the nervous system. They form prenatally and continue to grow and branch throughout life barring pruning.

nonagenarians People in their 90s.

nonnormative influences Individual environmental factors that do not occur at any predictable time in a person's life.

normative age-graded influences The biological and social changes that normally happen at predictable ages.

normative history-graded influences The historical events, such as wars, depressions, and epidemics, that affect large numbers of individuals at the same time.

norm-referenced tests Tests that compare an indiviual's performance with performances of others in the same age group.

novelty paradigm A research plan that uses infants' preferences for new stimuli over familiar ones to investigate their ability to detect small differences in sounds, patterns, or colors.

nucleotides Building blocks of DNA.

object permanence According to Piaget, the beginning realization in infants at about 8 months that objects continue to exist when they are out of sight.

occupational cycle A variable sequence of periods or stages in a worker's life, from occupational exploration and choice, through education and training, novice status, promotions and more experienced periods.

octogenarians People in their 80s.

Oedipus complex According to Freud, during the phallic stage, a boy develops lustful desires for his mother and then a fear that his father will castrate him for those desires; a girl develops lustful desires for her father, but without the driving force of castration anxiety.

operant conditioning A type of conditioning that occurs when an organism is reinforced or punished for voluntarily emitting a response.

operational definitions The actual procedures researchers use to represent variables.

osteoporosis Loss of bone mass and increased bone fragility in middle adulthood and beyond.

overextensions The young child's tendency to overgeneralize specific words, as when a child uses "chihuahua" as the term for all dogs.

overregularize To generalize language principles and misuse words; typically by preschool children who are rapidly expanding their vocabularies.

overt behavior Behavior that can be observed and measured objectively.

ovulation The release of an ovum into one of the two fallopian tubes; occurs approximately 14 days after menstruation.

parental imperative Traditional pressures for women to be nurturers and men to be providers.

partial reinforcement A procedure in which only some responses are reinforced; produces much stronger habits than continuous reinforcement.

passion The second component of love that refers to physical attraction, arousal, and sexual behavior in a relationship.

passive euthanasia Withholding or disconnecting life-sustaining equipment so that death can occur naturally.

pathological aging factors Cumulative effects of diseases and accidents that may accelerate aging.

peer group A group of three or more people of similar age who interact with each other and who share norms and goals.

perception The complex process by which the mind interprets and gives meaning to sensory information.

perinatology A branch of medicine that deals with childbirth as a span of time including conception, the prenatal period, and the first few months of life.

permissive parents Those parents who exercise little control over their children but are high in warmth.

personal fable Adolescents' feeling that they are special and invulnerable—exempt from the laws of nature that control the destinies of ordinary mortals.

personality domain Segment of development that includes acquiring relatively stable and enduring traits and a sense of self as an individual.

personality Characteristic beliefs, attitudes, and ways of interacting with others.

phenotype In genetics, those traits that are expressed in the individual.

phobia Unreasonable fear of an object or situation.

physical domain Segment of development involving changes in shape and size, brain structure, sensory capabilities, and motor skills.

pincer grasp The method of holding objects, developed at around the age of 12 months, in which the thumb opposes the forefinger.

pivot grammar A two-word, sentence-forming system used by 1½- and 2-year-olds that involves action words or possessives (pivot words) in combination with open words, which are usually nouns.

placenta A disk-shaped mass of tissue that forms along the wall of the uterus through which the embryo receives nutrients and discharges waste.

plasticity Flexibility of the brain during the brain growth spurt that allows children to more readily recover from brain injury.

polygenic inheritance The overall system of interactions among genes and gene pairs.

positive punishment Also called passive avoidance; a subject's behavior results in something aversive being presented or happening and the behavior decreases.

positive reinforcement Also called reward training; a subject receives rewards for behavior and the behavior increases.

pragmatics The social and practical aspects of language use.

preference method A research plan that gives infants a choice between stimuli to look at or listen to. If an infant consistently spends more time attending to one of the two stimuli, the preference indicates that the infant can both perceive a difference

prejudice A negative attitude formed without adequate reason and usually directed toward people because of their membership in a certain group.

preterm status An infant born before a gestation period of 35 weeks.

primitive reflexes Reflexes that do not have apparent survival value but may have been important at some point in our evolutionary history.

procedural knowledge Action knowledge; knowing "how to."

productive language The spoken or written communication of preschool children.

progesterone A female sexual hormone.

prosocial behavior Helping, sharing, or cooperative actions that are intended to benefit others.

proteins Molecules that perform a diverse array of crucial functions in the human body; examples include ezymes, hemoglobin, collagen, and hormones.

protesting woman In Apter's research, a woman who experienced premature adulthood and tries to postpone middle age.

proximodistal trend The sequence of growth that occurs from the midline of the body outward.

pseudo-developed man A middle-aged man who maintains a facade that everything is well when it isn't.

psychoanalysis Freud's view of human nature as motivated by innate biological drives and inner dynamics.

psychodynamic approach The theory that focuses on the often-subtle inner workings of the mind as they play out against external reality.

psychological age An individual's current ability to cope with and adapt to social and environmental demands.

psychosexual stages Freud's stages of personality development in terms if erogenous zones.

psychosocial theory In Erikson's departure from Freud's theory, which emphasizes stages throughout the lifespan and social interactions as primary.

puberty   The attainment of sexual maturity in males and females.

punitive-disenchanted man   A man whose earlier sense of unhappiness or alienation continues into middle age and is accompanied by a midlife crisis.

questionnaire   A paper-and-pencil method that asks questions about past or present behavior, attitudes, preferences, opinions, feelings, and so on.

random assignment   Placing subjects in groups with the hope that these groups will be roughly equivalent, e.g., by drawing names from a container.

random sample   A sample selected in such a way that any member of a population has an equal chance of being selected.

recall   The ability to retrieve information with or without cues.

receptive language   The repertoire of words and commands that a child understands, even though she or he may not be able to use them.

recessive   In genetics, one of a gene pair that determines a trait in an individual only if the other member of that pair is also recessive.

recognition   The ability to correctly identify items previously experienced when they appear again.

recombinant DNA technology   An assortment of highly sophisticated procedures in which DNA is extracted from cell nuclei and cut into segments. The resulting fragments are then joined to self-replicating elements, forming, in essence, functional gene clones. These are then placed in host bacterial cells to be maintained and cultured.

reconstituted family   Also known as stepfamily; a family where a mother or father with children has remarried to produce a new family.

reconstituted or blended family   A family in which partners with children have remarried or formed a cohabiting relationship.

replication (replicate)   Systematic repetitions of an experiment to determine if findings are valid and generalizable.

representative sample   A sample that accurately mirrors a population.

repression   According to Freud, the mechanisms by which the ego "parks" unacceptable and inexpressible impulses, peceived guilts over misdeeds, and other personally distressing ideas in the unconscious, where they remain without the person's awareness but continue to trouble the individual all the same.

resilient children   Children who overcome difficult environments to lead socially competent lives.

resistant attachment   Insecure attachment characterized by anger and avoidance of the mother.

retirement maturity   How prepared a person is to retire.

right to die   The view that death is a right to be exercised at the individual's discretion.

rites of passage   Symbolic events or rituals to mark life transitions, such as from childhood to adult status.

role strain   An overload of demands within a given role, such as mother or father.

same-sex orientation   Sexual attraction toward members of one's own sex.

scaffolding   The progressive structuring by the parents of parent-child interactions.

schemes or schemas   Piaget's term for mental structures that process information, perceptions, and experiences; the schemes of individuals change as they grow.

secure attachment   A strong emotional bond between child and caregiver that develops as a result of responsive caregiving.

self-actualization   Realizing one's full unique potential.

self-concept   Your perception of your personal identity.

self-definition   The complex and lengthy process of an individual forming an identity.

self-efficacy   What we as individuals are capable of doing in a given situation.

self-esteem   Your attitude toward yourself, which can range from positive (high self-esteem) to negative (low self-esteem).

self-regulated behavior   Personal behavior controlled and directed by the child.

self-socialization   When children are intrinsically motivated to acquire values, interests, and behaviors consistent with their sex.

senescence   The normal aging process, not connected with the occurrence of disease in the individual.

sensation   The translation of a stimulus by a sense organ.

sensitive or optimal periods   The times during which certain types of learning and development occur best and most efficiently, but not exclusively.

sensorimotor period   Piaget's first period of cognitive development (from birth to about 2 years).

sensuality   Hugging, touching, stroking, and other behaviors that may or may not lead to sex.

septuagenarians   People in their 70s.

sequential-cohort design   Research design where several overlapping cohorts of different ages are studied longitudinally.

sex chromosomes   The twenty-third chromosome pair, which determines sex.

sex-linked inheritance   Traits determined by genes on the twenty-third chromosome pair.

sexual orientation   Which sex you are physically and perhaps romantically attracted to.

shaping   Systematically reinforcing successive approximations to a desired behavior.

shared meanings   Vygotsky's concept that we understand our world by learning both simple and complex concepts of the culture of others around us.

short-term memory (STM)   Temporary or working memory, where information is conciously processed.

sibling rivalry   Strife and competition between siblings, such as for parental attention.

sibling status   Birth order.

single nucleotide polymorphisms (SNPs)   Nucleotide variations that occur on average about every 1,250 base pairs.

single-subject design   An approach whereby one subject at a time—rat, pigeon, chimpanzee, or human—is exposed to contingencies that are expected to alter or affect behavior.

small-for-date   A full-term newborn who weighs less than 5½ pounds.

social age An individual's current status as compared with cultural norms.

social cognition Thought, knowledge, and understanding that involve the social world.

social comparison Evaluating yourself and your situation relative to others.

social ecology of child care The totality of the environment in which child care occurs, within and beyond the home.

social inference Guesses and assumptions about what another person is feeling, thinking, or intending.

social reference groups Narrow or broad groups with which people identify, and in so doing, help define themselves.

social referencing Subtle emotional signals, usually from the parent, that influence the infant's behavior.

social regulations The rules and conventions governing social interactions.

social responsibility Obligations to family, friends, and society at large.

society An organized group of interacting people.

sociocultural domain Segment of development comprised of socialization and enculturation.

spontaneous abortions Miscarriage; expulsion of the developing child before it is viable.

stages Discrete periods proposed to have abrupt transitions from one to the next.

status passage A change in the role and position that occurs when an individual enters adolescence, becomes a parent, retires, or becomes a widow or widower.

stochastic theories of aging Theories suggesting that the body ages as a result of random assaults from both internal and external environments.

stranger anxiety and separation anxiety An infant's fear of strangers or of being separated from the caregiver. Both occur in the second half of the first year and indicate, in part, a new cognitive ability to respond to differences in the environment.

strict behaviorism The view that only observable, measurable behavior can be studied scientifically.

stroke Blockage of blood to the brain, which can cause brain damage.

structuralists Cognitive-developmental psychologists concerned with the structure of thought and the way in which the mind operates on information.

Sturm und Drang Term used by Anna Freud to describe adolescence as a time of dramatic upheaval of emotions and behavior; German for "storm and stress."

subdialects Subcultural language differences; speakers of subdialects can usually understand each other.

submissive death Suicide in the form of simply letting yourself die.

suicidal erosion An indirect form of suicide through excessive drinking, smoking, or other drug abuse.

superego According to Freud, the conscience component of personality, which includes the ego ideal.

surprise paradigm A research technique used to test infants' memory and expectations. Infants cannot report what they remember or expect, but if their expectations are violated, they respond with surprise.

survey A questionnaire administered to a large group.

survival reflexes Reflexes necessary for adaptation and survival, especially during the first few weeks before the higher brain centers begin to take control.

symbolic representation The use of a word, picture, gesture, or other sign to represent past and present events, experiences, and concepts.

systematic desensitization In behavior therapy, a technique that gradually reduces an individual's anxiety about a specific object or situation through relaxation.

systems of meaning Belief systems that shape our experiences, organize our thoughts and feelings, and help determine our behavior.

telegraphic speech The utterances of 1½- and 2-year-olds that omit the less significant words and include the words that carry the most meaning.

temperament Inborn behavioral styles.

teratogen Toxic agent of any kind that potentially causes abnormalities in the developing child.

testosterone A male sexual hormone.

Thanatos Death instincts.

traditional childbirth Hospital labor and delivery.

traditional woman In Apter's research, a woman who has previously defined herself in terms of family and who easily makes the transition to middle age and maturity.

transcendent-generative man A man for whom middle age is a time of well-being, fulfillment, and accomplishment.

transition model The view that changes in midlife are gradual.

ultrasound A technique that uses sound waves to produce a picture of the fetus in the uterus.

umbilical cord The "rope" of tissue connecting the placenta to the embryo; this rope contains two fetal arteries and one fetal vein.

unconditional positive regard Rogers' proposition that we should warmly accept another person as a worthwhile human being, without reservations or conditions.

unconscious mind According to Freud, the part of the personality that governs most of our behavior without our direct awareness.

use The way in which a speaker employs language to give it one meaning as opposed to another.

uterus The area that contains and nourishes the embryo and fetus (discussed later in the chapter).

visual acuity The ability to distinguish fine detail.

widower's impotency A form of impotence men sometimes experience after the death of their wife. Often accompanied by guilt.

wisdom An expert knowledge system focusing on the pragmatics of life that involves excellent judgment and advice on critical life issues, including the meaning of life and the human condition; wisdom represents the capstone of human intelligence.

zone of proximal development Vygotsky's concept that children develop through prticipation in activities slightly beyond their competence with the help of adults or older children.

zygote The first cell of a human being that occurs as a result of fertilization; a fertilized ovum.

Bibliography

ABATE, G., FERRARI-RAMONDO, V., & DI IORIO, A. (1998). Risk factors for cognitive disorders in the elderly: A review. *Archives of Gerontology & Geriatrics, Supl. 6,* 7–15.

ABBOTT, J. W. (1978). Hospice. *Aging, 5* (3), 38–40.

ABEL, E. L. (1995). An update on incidence of FAS: FAS is not an equal opportunity birth defect. *Neurotoxicology and Teratology, 17,* 437–443.

ABEL, E. L. (1997). Maternal alcohol consumption and spontaneous abortion. *Alcohol and Alcoholism, 32,* 211–219.

ABLER, R. M., & SEDLACEK, W. E. (1989). Freshman sexual attitudes and behaviors over a 15-year-period. *Journal of College Student Development, 30,* 201–209.

ABRAMOVITCH, R., & GRUSEC, J. E. (1978). Peer imitation in a natural setting. *Child Development, 49,* 60–65.

ACHENBACH, T. M. (1982). *Developmental Psychopathology.* New York: Wiley.

ACHENBACH, T. M., HOWELL, C. T., QUAY, H. C., & CONNERS, C. K. (1991). National survey of problems and competencies among four-to-sixteen-year olds. *Monographs of the Society for Research in Child Development, 56,* v–120.

ADAMS, B. B. (1979). Mate selection in the United States: A theoretical summarization. In W. Butt, R. Hill, I. Nye, & I. Reis (Eds.), *Contemporary theories about the family* (Vol. 1). New York: Free Press.

ADAMS, D. (1983). *The psychosocial development of professional black women's lives and the consequences of career for their personal happiness.* Unpublished doctoral dissertation. Wright Institute, Berkeley, CA.

ADAMS, G. R., & MARSHALL, S. K. (1996). A developmental social psychology of identity: Understanding the person-in-context. *Journal of Adolescence, 19,* 429–442.

ADAMS, R. G., & BLIESZNER, R. (1998). Baby boomer friendships. *Generations, 22,* (1), 70–75.

ADAMS, R. J., & COURAGE, M. L. (1995). Development of chromatic discrimination in early infancy. *Behavioural Brain Research, 67,* 99–101.

ADAMS, R. J., COURAGE, M. L., & MERCER, M. E. (1995). Systematic measurement of human neonatal color vision. *Vision Research, 34,* 1691–1701.

ADOLPH, K. E. (1997). Learning in the development of infant locomotion. *Monographs of the Society for Research in Child Development, 62* (3).

AFRICA NEWS SERVICE. (July 14, 2000). 1,800 infants get HIV daily.

AINSWORTH, M. D. (1967). *Infancy in Uganda: Infant care and the growth of love.* Baltimore: Johns Hopkins University Press.

AINSWORTH, M. D., & BELL, S. M. (1970). Attachment, exploration, and separation: Il-

lustrated by the behavior of one-year-olds in a strange situation. *Child Development, 41,* 49–67.

AINSWORTH, M. D., BLEHAR, M., WATERS, E., & WALL, S. (1978). *Patterns of attachment.* Hillsdale, NJ: Erlbaum.

AINSWORTH, M. D. S. (1983). Patterns of infant–mother attachment as related to maternal care. In D. Magnusson & V. Allen (Eds.), *Human development: An interactional perspective.* New York: Academic Press.

AINSWORTH, M. D. S., & BOWLBY, J. (1991). An ethological approach to personality development. *American Psychologist, 46,* 333–341.

AINSWORTH, M. D. S., BLEHAR, M. C., WATERS, E., & WALL, S. (1979). *Patterns of attachment: A psychological study of the strange situation.* Hillsdale, NJ: Erlbaum.

AIZENBERG, R., & TREAS, J. (1985). The family in late life: Psychosocial and demographic considerations. In J. Birren & K. W. Schaie (Eds.), *Handbook of the psychology of aging* (2nd ed.). New York: Van Nostrand Reinhold.

AJDUKOVIC, M., & AJDUKOVIC, D. (1998). Impact of displacement on the psychological well-being of refugee children. *International Review of Psychiatry, 10,* 186–195.

ALAN GUTTMACHER INSTITUTE (1994). *Sex and America's teenagers.* New York.

ALBERT, S. M., & BRODY, E. M. (1996). When elder care is viewed as child care: Significance of elder's cognitive impairment and caregiver burden. *American Journal of Geriatric Psychiatry, 4,* 121–130.

ALDOUS, J. (1978). *Family careers: Developmental change in families.* New York: Wiley.

ALDOUS, J. (1996). *Family careers: Rethinking the developmental perspective.* Thousand Oaks, CA: Sage.

ALESSANDRI, S. M. (1992). Effects of maternal work status in single-parent families on children's perception of self and family and school achievement. *Journal of Experimental Child Psychology, 54,* 417–433.

ALLEN, D. J., & OLESON, T. (1999). Shame and internalized homophobia in gay men. *Journal of Homosexuality, 37,* 33–43.

ALLEN, M., DONOHUE, P., & DUSMAN, A. (1993). The limits of viability—Neonatal outcome of infants born at 22 to 25 weeks' gestation. *New England Journal of Medicine, 329,* 1597–1601.

ALLEN, P. A., MADDEN, D. J., GROTH, K. E., & CROZIER, L. C. (1992). Impact of age, redundancy, and perceptual noise on visual search. *Journals of Gerontology, 47,* 69–74.

ALLGAIER, A. (1978). Alternative birth centers offer family-centered care. *Hospitals, 52,* 97–112.

ALMO, H. S. (1978). Without benefit of clergy: Cohabitation as a noninstitutionalized marriage role. In K. Knafl & H. Grace

(Eds.), *Families across the life cycle: Studies from nursing.* Boston: Little, Brown.

ALMQVIST, KJERSTIN, & BRANDELL-FORSBERG, M. (1997). Refugee children in Sweden: Post-traumatic stress disorder in Iranian preschool children exposed to organized violence. *Child Abuse and Neglect, 21,* 351–366.

ALPER, J. S. (1996). Genetic complexity in single gene diseases: No simple link between genotype and phenotype. *British Medical Journal, 312,* 196–197.

ALPERT, J. L., & RICHARDSON, M. (1980). Parenting. In L. W. Poon (Ed.), *Aging in the 1980s.* Washington, DC: American Psychological Association.

ALPERT-GILLIS, L. J., & CONNELL, J. P. (1989). Gender and sex-role influences on children's self-esteem. *Journal of Personality, 57,* 97–113.

ALVARADO, K. A., TEMPLER, D. I., BRESLER, C., & THOMAS-DOBSON, S. (1995). The relationship of religious variables to death depression and death anxiety. *Journal of Clinical Psychology, 51,* 202–204.

AMATO, P. R. (1993). Children's adjustment to divorce: Theories, hypotheses, and empirical support. *Journal of Marriage and the Family, 55,* 23–38.

AMERICAN ACADEMY OF PEDIATRICS (AAP) (1992). Positioning and SIDS. *Pediatrics, 89,* 1120–1126.

AMERICAN ACADEMY OF PEDIATRICS (AAP) (1996). *Policy statement: Drug-exposed infants.* Washington, DC.

AMERICAN ACADEMY OF PEDIATRICS (AAP) (1999). The lure of technology. *Pediatrics, 103,* 1037.

AMERICAN ASSOCIATION OF UNIVERSITY WOMEN (1991). *Shortchanging girls, shortchanging America: Executive Summary.* Washington, DC: American Association of University Women Educational Foundation.

AMERICAN PSYCHIATRIC ASSOCIATION (1994). *Diagnostic and statistical manual of mental disorders* (4th ed.). Washington, DC.

ANDERSEN, A. N., WOHLFAHRT, P. C., CHRISTENS, J. O., OLSEN, J., & MELBYE, M. (2000). Maternal age and fetal loss: Population based register linkage study. *British Medical Journal, 320,* 1708–1712.

ANDERSON, R. N. (2001). United States life tables, 1998. *National Vital Statistics Reports, 48* (18), 1–35. Hyattsville, MD: National Center for Health Statistics.

ANDERSSON, B.-E. (1989). Effects of public daycare: A longitudinal study. *Child Development, 60,* 857–866.

ANGIER, N. (1995). If you're really ancient, you may be better off. *New York Times, 44* (June 11), E1, E5.

ANTIAL, J. K., & COTTIN, S. (1988). Factors affecting the division of labor in households. *Sex Roles, 18,* 531–553.

APTER, T. E. (1995). *Secret paths: Women in the new midlife*. New York: Norton.

AQUILINO, W. S. (1994). Late life parental divorce and widowhood: Impact on young adults' assessment of parent–child relations. *Journal of Marriage and the Family, 56,* 908–922.

AQUILINO, W. S. (1996). The returning child and parental experience at midlife. In C.D. Ryff & M. M. Seltzer (Eds.), *The parental experience in midlife*. Chicago: University of Chicago Press.

ARCHER, S. L. (1985). Identity and the choice of social roles. In A. S. Waterman (Ed.), *New Directions for Child Development, 30,* 79–100. San Francisco: Jossey-Bass.

AREND, R. A., GORE, F. L., & SROUFE, L. A. (1979). Continuity of individual adaptation from infancy to kindergarten. *Child Development, 50,* 950–959.

ARIÈS, P. (1962). *Centuries of childhood: A social history of family life.* New York: Vintage Books.

ARIÈS, P. (1981). *The hour of our death.* New York: Knopf.

ARIÈS, P. (1989) Introduction. In R. Chartier (Ed.) *A history of a private life, Vol. 3: Passions of the Renaissance.* Cambridge, MA: Belknap Press of Harvard University Press.

ARMSTRONG, T. (1996). A holistic approach to attention deficit disorder. *Educational Leadership, 53,* 34–36.

ASHER, S. R. (1983). Social competence and peer status: Recent advances and future directions. *Child Development, 54,* 1427– 1434.

ASHER, S. R. (1990). Recent advances in the study of peer rejection. In S. R. Asher & J.D. Coie (Eds.), *Peer rejection in childhood.* New York: Cambridge University Press.

ASHER, S. R., RENSHAW, P. D., & HYMEL, S. (1982). Peer relations and the development of social skills. In W. W. Hartup (Ed.), *The young child: Reviews of research* (Vol. 3). Washington, DC: National Association for the Education of Young Children.

ASLIN, R. (1987). Visual and auditory development in infancy. In J. D. Osofsky (Ed.), *Handbook of infant development* (2nd ed.). New York: Wiley.

ASLIN, R. N., & SMITH, L. B. (1988). Perceptual development. *Annual Review of Psychology, 39,* 435–473.

ASLIN, R. N., PISONI, D. V., & JUSCZYK, P. W. (1983). Auditory development and speech perception in infancy. In P. H. Mussen (Ed.), *Handbook of child psychology* (Vol. 2). New York: Wiley.

ASSO, D. (1983). *The real menstrual cycle.* Chichester, UK: Wiley.

ASTLEY, S. J., CLARREN, S. K., LITTLE, R. E., SAMPSON, P. D., & DALING, J. R. (1992). Analysis of facial shape in children gestationally exposed to marijuana, alcohol and/or cocaine. *Pediatrics, 89,* 67–77.

ATCHLEY, R. C. (1982). The process of retirement: Comparing women and men. In M. Szlnovacy (Ed.), *Women's retirement: Policy implications of recent research.* London: Sage.

ATCHLEY, R. C. (1989). A continuity theory of normal aging. *The Gerontologist, 29,* 183–190.

ATHEY, I. J. (1984). Contributions of play to development. In T. D. Yawkey & A. D. Pellegrini (Eds.), *Child's play.* Hillsdale, NJ: Erlbaum.

ATKINSON, R. C., & SHIFFRIN, R. M. (1971). The control of short-term memory. *Scientific American, 225,* 82–90.

ATWATER, E. (1992). *Adolescence* (3rd ed.). Englewood Cliffs, NJ: Prentice Hall.

AVIS, N. E. (1999). Women's health at midlife. In S. L. Willis & J. D. Reid (Eds.), *Life in the middle: Psychological and social development in middle age.* San Diego: Academic Press.

AZAR, B. (1997). Defining the trait that makes us human. *APA Monitor, 28,* (11), 1, 15.

BABLADELIS, G. (1987). Young persons' attitudes toward aging. *Perceptual and Motor Skills, 65,* 553–554.

BACHMAN, D. L. (1992). Sleep disorders with aging: Evaluation and treatment. *Geriatrics, 47,* 41–52.

BAILEY, J. M., BOBROW, D., WOLFE, M., & MIKACH, S. (1995). Sexual orientation of adult sons of gay fathers. *Developmental Psychology, 31,* 124–129.

BAILEY, J. M., KIM, P. Y., HILLS, A., & LINSENMEIER, J. A. W. (1997). Butch, femme, or straight acting? Partner preferences of gay men and lesbians. *Journal of Personality and Social Psychology, 73,* 960–973.

BAILLARGEON, R. (1987). Object permanence in three-and-a-half- and four-and-a-half-month-old infants. *Developmental Psychology, 23,* 655–674.

BAILLARGEON, R. (1993). The object concept revisited: New directions in the investigation of infants' physical knowledge. In C. E. Granrud (Ed.), *Visual perception and cognition in infancy.* Hillsdale, NJ: Erlbaum.

BAILLARGEON, R. (1994). How do infants learn about the physical world? *Current Directions in Psychological Science, 3(5),* 133–140.

BAILLARGEON, R., & DeVOS, J. (1991). Object permanence in young infants: Further evidence. *Child Development, 62,* 1227–1246.

BAKEMAN, R., & ADAMSON, L. B. (1990). !Kung infancy: The social context of object exploration. *Child Development, 61,* 794–809.

BAKER, O. (1999). Faulty gene underlies retardation. *Science News, 1999, 156,* 214–215.

BALDWIN, B. A. (1986). Puberty and parents: Understanding your early adolescent. *PACE, October,* 15–19.

BALTES, M. M. (1998). The psychology of the oldest-old: The fourth age. *Current Opinion in Psychiatry, 11,* 411–418.

BALTES, P. B. (1987). Theoretical propositions of life-span developmental psychology: On the dynamics of growth and decline. *Developmental Psychology, 23,* 611–626.

BALTES, P. B. (1993). The aging mind: Potential and limits. *The Gerontologist, 33,* 580–594.

BALTES, P. B., & BALTES, M. M. (1990). Psychological perspectives on successful aging: The model of selective optimization with compensation. In P. B. Baltes & M. M. Baltes, (Eds.), *Successful aging: Perspectives from the behavioral sciences.* New York: Press Syndicate of the University of Cambridge.

BALTES, P. B., & STAUDINGER, U. M. (2000). Wisdom: A metaheuristic (pragmatic) to orchestrate mind and virtue toward excellence. *American Psychologist, 55,* 122–136.

BANDURA, A. (1965). Influence of models' reinforcement contingencies on the acquisition of imitative responses. *Journal of Personality and Social Psychology, 1,* 589–595.

BANDURA, A. (1969). *Principles of behavior modification.* New York: Holt, Rinehart and Winston.

BANDURA, A. (1977). *Social learning theory.* Englewood Cliffs, NJ: Prentice Hall.

BANDURA, A. (1997). *Self-efficacy: The exercise of control.* New York: Freeman.

BANDURA, A., & ADAMS, N. E. (1977). Analysis of self-efficacy theory of behavioral change. *Cognitive Therapy & Research, 1,* 287–310.

BANKOFF, E. (1986). Peer support for widows: Personal and structural characteristics related to its provision. In S. Hobfoll (Ed.), *Stress, social support, and women.* Washington, DC: Hemisphere.

BANKS, M. S., & SALAPATEK, P. (1983). Infant visual perception. In P. H. Mussen (Ed.), *Handbook of child psychology* (4th ed.). New York: Wiley.

BANKS, M., & DANNEMILLER, J. (1987). Infant visual psychophysics. In P. Salapatek & L. Cohen (Eds.), *Handbook of infant perception, Vol. 1: From sensation to perception.* New York: Academic Press.

BARBERO, G. (1983). Failure to thrive. In M. Klaus, T. Leger, & M. Trause (Eds.), *Maternal attachment and mothering disorders.* New Brunswick, NJ: Johnson & Johnson.

BARER, B. M. (1994). Men and women aging differently. *International Journal of Aging and Human Development, 38,* 29–40.

BARKER, R. G., DEMBO, T., & LEWIN, K. (1943). Frustration and regression. In R. G. Barker, J. S. Kounin, & H. F. Wright (Eds.), *Child behavior and development.* New York: McGraw-Hill.

BARNES, H. L., & OLSEN, D. H. (1985). Parent-adolescent communication and the circumplex model. *Child Development, 56,* 438–447.

BARNETT, D. (1997). The effects of early intervention on maltreating parents and their children. In M. J. Guralnick (Ed.), *The effectiveness of early intervention.* Baltimore: Brooks.

BARNETT, D., MANLEY, J. T., & CICCHETTI, D. (1993). Defining child maltreatment: The interface between policy and research. In D. Cicchetti & S. Toth (Eds.) *Child abuse, child development, and social policy.* Norwood, NJ: Ablex.

BARNETT, M., & PLEACK, M. (1992). Men's multiple roles and their relationship to men's psychological distress. *Journal of Marriage and the Family, 54,* 358–367.

BARNETT, R., & BARUCH, G. (1987). Social roles, gender, and psychological distress. In R. Barnett, L. Biener, & G. Baruch (Eds.), *Gender and stress.* New York: Free Press.

BARON, N. S. (1992). *Growing up with language: How children learn to talk.* Reading, Ma.: Addison-Wesley Publishing Co.

BAROODY, A. J. (2000). Does mathematics instruction for three- to five-year-olds really make sense? *Young Children, 55* (4), 61–67.

BARR, H., DARBY, B., STREISSGUTH, A., & SAMPSON, P. (1990). Prenatal exposure to alcohol, caffeine, tobacco, and aspirin:

Effects on fine and gross motor performance in 4-year-old children. *Developmental Psychology, 26,* 339–348.

BARR, R., DOWDEN, A., & HAYNE, H. (1996). Developmental changes in deferred imitation by 6– to 24–month-old infants. *Infant Behavior and Development, 19,* 159–170.

BARTECCHI, C. E., MACKENZIE, T. D., & SCHRIER, R. W. (1995). The global tobacco epidemic. *Scientific American, 272* (5), 44–51.

BARTLETT, D. (1997). Primitive reflexes and early motor development. *Journal of developmental and behavioral pediatrics, 18,* 151–157.

BARTON, S. (1994). Chaos, self-organization, and psychology. *American Psychologist, 49,* 5–14.

BARTOSHUK, L. M., & WEIFFENBACH, J. M. (1990). Chemical senses and aging. In E. L. Schneider & J. W. Rowe (Eds.), *Handbook of the biology of aging* (3rd. ed). San Diego: Academic Press.

BARUCH, G. K., BIENER, L., & BARNETT, R. (1987). Women and gender in research on work and family stress. *American Psychologist, 42,* 130–135.

BARUCH, G., & BARNETT, R. (1986). Role quality, multiple role involvement, and psychological well-being in midlife women. *Journal of Personality and Social Psychology, 51,* 578–585.

BARUCH, G., & BROOKS-GUNN, J. (1984). The study of women in mid-life. In G. Baruch & J. Brooks-Gunn (Eds.), *Women in midlife.* New York: Plenum.

BASSUK, E. L., BROWNE, A., & BUCKNER, J. C. (1996). Single mothers and welfare. *Scientific American, 275* (4), 60–67.

BATEMAN, D., NG, S., HANSEN, C., & HEAGARTY, M. (1993). The effects of interuterine cocaine exposure in newborns. *American Journal of Public Health, 83,* 190–194.

BATESON, G. (1955). A theory of play and fantasy. *Psychiatric Research Reports, 2,* 39–51.

BAUER, P. J., & THAL, D. J. (1990). Scripts or scraps: Reconsidering the development of sequential understanding. *Journal of Experimental Child Psychology, 50,* 287–304.

BAUMRIND, D. (1972). Socialization and instrumental competence in young children. In W. W. Hartup (Ed.), *The young child: Reviews of research* (Vol. 2). Washington, DC: National Association for the Education of Young Children.

BAUMRIND, D. (1975). *Early socialization and the discipline controversy.* Morristown, NJ: General Learning Press.

BAUMRIND, D. (1978). A dialectical materialist's perspective on knowing social reality. In W. Damon (Ed.), *New Directions for Child Development, 2.* San Francisco: Jossey-Bass.

BAUMRIND, D. (1980). New directions in socialization research. *American Psychologist, 35,* 639–650.

BAUMRIND, D. (1987). A developmental perspective on adolescent risk-taking in contemporary America. In C. E. Irwin, Jr. (Ed.), *New Directions for Child Development, 37,* 93–125. San Francisco: Jossey-Bass.

BAUMRIND, D. (1989). *Rearing competent children.* In W. Damon (Ed.), *Child development today and tomorrow.* San Francisco: Jossey-Bass.

BAUMRIND, D. (1991). The influence of parenting style on adolescent competence and substance use. *Journal of Early Adolescence, 11,* 56–95.

BAUMRIND, D. (1995). Commentary on sexual orientation: Research and social policy implications. *Developmental Psychology, 31,* 130–136.

BAYDAR, N., & BROOKS-GUNN, J. (1991). Effects of maternal employment and child-care arrangements on preschoolers' cognitive and behavioral outcomes: Evidence from the children of the National Longitudinal Survey of Youth. *Developmental Psychology, 27,* 932–945.

BAZZINI, D. G., MCINTOSH, W. D., SMITH, S. M., COOK, S., & HARRIS, C. (1997). The aging woman in popular film: Underrepresented, unattractive, unfriendly, and unintelligent. *Sex Roles, 36,* 531–543.

BEAL, C. R. (1987). Repairing the message: Children's monitoring and revision skills. *Child Development, 58,* 401–408.

BEARON, L. (1989). No great expectations: The underpinnings of life satisfaction for older women. *The Gerontologist, 29,* 772–776.

BECKER, J. (1993). Young children's numerical use of number words: Counting in many-to-one situations. *Developmental Psychology, 29,* 458–465.

BECKER, P. M., & JAMIESON, A. O. (1992). Common sleep disorders in the elderly: Diagnosis and treatment. *Geriatrics, 47,* 41–52.

BECKWITH, L., & COHEN, S. E. (1989). Maternal responsiveness with preterm infants and later competency. In M. H. Bornstein (Ed.), *New directions for child development, 43.* San Francisco: Jossey-Bass.

BEEGHLY, M., & CICCHETTI, D. (1994). Child maltreatment, attachment, and self system: Emergence of an internal state lexicon in toddlers at high social risk. *Development and Psychopathology, 6,* 5–30.

BEELMANN, A., & BRAMBRING, M. (1998). Implementation and effectiveness of a home-based early intervention program for blind infants and preschoolers. *Research in Developmental Disabilities, 19,* 225–244.

BELL, S. M., & AINSWORTH, M. D. (1972). Infant crying and maternal responsiveness. *Child Development, 43,* 1171–1190.

BELLER, F., & ZLATNIK, G. (1994). Medical aspects of the beginning of individual lives. In F. K. Beller & R. F. Weir (Eds.), *The beginning of human life.* Dordrect, The Netherlands: Kluwer.

BELSKY, J. (1984). *The psychology of aging: Theory and research and practice.* Monterey, CA: Brooks/Cole.

BELSKY, J. (1986). Infant day care: A cause for concern? *Zero to Three, 6* (5), 1–7.

BELSKY, J. (1988). The "effects" of infant day care reconsidered. *Early Childhood Research Quarterly, 3,* 235–272.

BELSKY, J. (1990). Developmental risks associated with infant day care: Attachment insecurity, noncompliance, and aggression? In S. Chehrazi (Ed.), *Psychosocial issues in day care.* Washington, DC: American Psychiatric Press.

BELSKY, J., & ROVINE, M. (1984). Social-network contact, family support, and the transition to parenthood. *Journal of Marriage and the Family, 46,* 455–462.

BELSKY, J., & ROVINE, M. (1988). Nonmaternal care in the first year of life and the security of infant–parent attachment. *Child Development, 59,* 157–167.

BELSKY, J., & ROVINE, M. (1990a). Q-sort security and first-year nonmaternal care. In K. McCartney (Ed.), *New directions for child development, 49.* San Francisco: Jossey-Bass.

BELSKY, J., & ROVINE, M. (1990b). Patterns of marital change across the transition to parenthood: Pregnancy to three years postpartum. *Journal of Marriage and the Family, 52,* 5–19.

BELSKY, J., ROVINE, M., & TAYLOR, D. (1984). The Pennsylvania infant and family development project III. The origins of individual differences in infant–mother attachment: Maternal and infant contributions. *Child Development, 58,* 718–728.

BEM, S. (1985). Androgyny and gender schema theory: A conceptual and empirical integration. In T. B. Sondegegger (Ed.), *Nebraska Symposium on Motivation, 1984: Psychology and gender.* Lincoln: University of Nebraska.

BEM, S. L. (1975). Androgyny vs. the tight little lives of fluffy women and chesty men. *Psychology Today, 9* (9), 59–62.

BENDERSKY, M., & LEWIS, M. (1998). Arousal modulation in cocaine-exposed infants. *Developmental Psychology, 34,* 555–564.

BENGSTON, V. L. (1985). Diversity and symbolism in grandparents' role. In V. L. Bengston & J. F. Robertson (Eds.), *Grandparenthood.* Beverly Hills, CA: Sage.

BENIN, M. H., & EDWARDS, D. A. (1990). Adolescents' chores: The differences between dual- and single-earner families. *Journal of Marriage and the Family, 52,* 361–373.

BENNETT, J. C. (1991). The irrationality of the catharsis theory of aggression as justification for educators' support of interscholastic football. *Perceptual and motor skills, 72,* 415–418.

BENNETT, S. C., ROBINSON, N. M., & SELLS, C. J. (1983). Growth and development of infants weighing less than 800 grams at birth. *Pediatrics, 71,* 319–323.

BERG, C. J., ALTRASH, H. K., KOONIN, L. M., & TUCKER, M. (1996). Pregnancy-related mortality in the United States, 1987–1990. *Obstetrical Gynecology, 88,* 161–167.

BERGER, L. M., & WALDFOGEL, J. (2000). Prenatal cocaine exposure: Long-run effects and policy implications. *Social Science Review, 74,* 28–43.

BERK, L. E. (1992). Children's private speech: An overview of theory and the status of research. In R. M. Diaz & L. E. Berk (Eds.), *Private speech: From social interaction to self-regulation.* Hillsdale, NJ: Erlbaum.

BERK, L. E. (1994a). Vygotsky's theory: The importance of make-believe play. *Young Children, 50* (1), 30–38.

BERK, L. E. (1994b). Why children talk to themselves. *Scientific American, 271,* (1), 78–83.

BERK, S. F. (1985). *The gender factory: The apportionment of work in American households.* New York: Plenum.

BERKO, J. (1958). The child's learning of English morphology. *Word, 14,* 150–177.

BERKOWITZ, L. (1970). Experimental investigations of hostility catharsis. *Journal of Consulting and Clinical Psychology, 35,* 1–7.

BERNARD, J. (1981). The good-provider role: Its rise and fall. *American Psychologist, 36,* 1–12.

BERNDT, T. J. (1982). The features and effects of friendship in early adolescence. *Child Development, 53,* 1447–1460.

BERNDT, T. J. (1983). Social cognition, social behavior, and children's friendships. In E. T. Higgins, D. Ruble, & W. Hartup, *Social cognition and social development: A socio-cultural perspective.* Cambridge, MA: Cambridge University Press.

BEROFF, J., DOUVAN, E., & JULKA, R. (1981). *The inner American: A self-portrait from 1957–1976.* New York: Basic Books.

BETZHOLD, M. (1997). The selling of Dr. Death. *New Republic, 297* (4), 22–28.

BIELBY, W., & BARON, J. (1986). Sex segregation within occupations. *American Economic Review, 76,* 43–47.

BINET, A., & SIMON, T. (1905). Methodes nouvelles pour le diagnostic du niveau intelectual des anormaux. *L'Annee Psychologique, 11,* 191–244.

BINET, A., & SIMON, T. (1916). *The development of intelligence in children.* Baltimore: Williams & Wilkins.

BIRCHLER, G. R. (1992). Marriage. In V. B. Van Hasselt & M. Hersen (Eds.). *Handbook of social development: A lifespan perspective.* New York: Plenum.

BIRKEL, R., & JONES, C. (1989). A comparison of the caregiving networks of dependent elderly individuals who are lucid and those who are demented. *The Gerontologist, 29,* 114–119.

BIRREN, J. E., & CUNNINGHAM, W. R. (1985). Research on the psychology in aging: Principles and experimentation. In J. E. Birren & K. W. Schaie (Eds.), *Handbook of the psychology of aging* (2nd ed.). New York: Van Nostrand Reinhold.

BIRREN, J. E., & FISHER, L. M. (1995). Aging and speed of behavior: Possible consequences for psychological functioning. *Annual Review of Psychology, 46,* 329–353.

BIRREN, J. E., WOODS, A. M., & WILLIAMS, M. V. (1985). Behavioral slowing with age: Causes, organization, and consequences. In L. W. Poon (Ed.), *Aging in the 1980s.* Washington, DC: American Psychological Association.

BJORKLUND, D. F. (1988). Acquiring a mnemonic: Age and category knowledge effects. *Journal of Experimental Child Psychology, 45,* 71–87.

BJORKLUND, D. F. (1997). The role of immaturity in human development. *Psychological Bulletin, 122,* 153–169.

BLACK, M. M. (2000). The roots of child neglect. In R. M. Reece (Ed.), *Treatment of child abuse: Common ground for mental health, medical, and legal practitioners.* Baltimore, MD: Johns Hopkins University Press.

BLAESE, R. M. (1997). Gene therapy for cancer. *Scientific American, 276* (6), 111–115.

BLAIR, S. L., & JOHNSON, M. P. (1992). Wives' perceptions of fairness of the division of labor: The intersection of housework and ideology. *Journal of Marriage and the Family, 54,* 570–581.

BLAKE, J. (1989). Number of siblings and educational attainment. *Science, 245,* 32–36.

BLIESZNER, R., & MANCINI, J. (1987). Enduring ties: Older adults' parental role and responsibilities. *Family Relations, 36,* 176–180.

BLOCK, M. R. (1981). *Effect of work pattern on women's satisfaction with retirement.* Unpublished doctoral dissertation. University of Maryland.

BLOOM, L. (1970). *Language development: Form and function in emerging grammars.* Cambridge, MA: MIT Press.

BLOOM, L. (1993). *The transition from infancy to language: Acquiring the power of expression.* New York: Cambridge University Press.

BLOOM, L., LIFTER, K., & BROUGHTON, J. (1985). The convergence of early cognition and language in the second year of life: Problems in conceptualization and measurement. In M. Barrett (Ed.), *Children's single-word speech.* New York: Wiley.

BLUMSTEIN, P., & SCHWARTZ, P. (1983). *American couples.* New York: Morrow.

BLYTH, D., BULCROFT, A. R., & SIMMONS, R. G. (1981). *The impact of puberty on adolescents: A longitudinal study.* Paper presented at the annual meeting of the American Psychological Association, Los Angeles.

BOCCIA, M., & CAMPOS, J. J. (1989). Maternal emotional signals, social referencing, and infants' reactions to strangers. In N. Eisenberg (Ed.), *New Directions for Child Development, 44.* San Francisco: Jossey-Bass.

BOLTON, F. G., MORRIS, L. A., AND MCEACHERON, A. E. (1989). *Males at risk: The other side of child sexual abuse.* Newbury Park, CA: Sage.

BOOTHBY, N. G., & KNUDSEN, C. M. (2000). Children of the gun. *Scientific American, 282,* (6), 60–65.

BORNSTEIN, M. H. (Ed.) (1989). *Maternal responsiveness: Characteristics and consequences.* San Francisco: Jossey-Bass.

BORNSTEIN, M. H., & ARTERBERRY, M. E. (1999). Perceptual development. In M. H. Bornstein & M. E. Lamb (Eds.), *Developmental psychology: An advanced textbook* (4th ed.). Mahwah, NJ: Erlbaum.

BORNSTEIN, M. H., & O'REILLY, A. W. (1993). The role of play in the development of thought. In M. H. Bornstein and A. W. O'Reilly (Eds.), *New directions for child development, 59.* San Francisco: Jossey-Bass.

BORNSTEIN, M. H., & TAMIS-LEMONDA, C. S. (1989). Maternal responsiveness and cognitive development in children. In M. H. Bornstein (Ed.), *New directions for child development, 43.* San Francisco: Jossey-Bass.

BOTWINICK, J. (1984). *Aging and behavior: A comprehensive integration of research findings* (3rd ed.). New York: Springer.

BOUCHARD, T. J. (1999). Genes, environment, and personality. In S. J. Ceci & W. M. Williams (Eds.), *The nature-nurture debate: The essential readings.* Malden, MA: Blackwell.

BOULD, S., & LONGINO, C. F., JR. (1997). Women survivors: The oldest old. In J. M. Coyle (Ed.), *Handbook on women and aging.* Westport, CT: Greenwood.

BOULTON, M., & SMITH, P. K. (1989). Issues in the study of children's rough-and-tumble play. In M. N. Block & A. D. Pelligrini (Eds.), *The ecological content of children's play.* Norwood, NJ: Ablex.

BOUTWELL, J., & KLARE, M. T. (2000). A scourge of small arms. *Scientific American, 282,* (6), 48–53.

BOWER, B. (1991a). Same family: Different lives. *Science News, 139,* 375–478.

BOWER, B. (1991b). Emotional aid delivers labor-saving results. *Science News, 139,* 277.

BOWER, T. G. R. (1971). The object in the world of the infant. *Scientific American, 224* (4), 30–38.

BOWLBY, J. (1969/1980). *Attachment and loss, Vol. 1: Attachment.* New York: Basic Books.

BOWLBY, J. (1973). *Attachment and loss, Vol. 2: Separation.* New York: Basic Books.

BRACE, C. L. (1995). Race and political correctness. *American Psychologist, 50,* 725–726.

BRACKBILL, Y., & NEVILL, D. (1981). Parental expectations of achievement as affected by children's height. *Merrill-Palmer Quarterly, 27,* 429–441.

BRACKBILL, Y., MCMANUS, K., & WOODWARD, L. (1985). Medication in maternity: Infant exposure and maternal information. *International Academy for Research on Learning Disabilities Monographs, Series Number 2.* Ann Arbor: University of Michigan Press.

BRADSHAW, J. (1989). *Hemispheric specialization and psychological function.* New York: Wiley.

BRAINE, M. D. S. (1963). The ontogeny of English phrase structure: The first phase. *Language, 39,* 1–13.

BRASSARD, M. R., & MCNEILL, L. E. (1987). Child sexual abuse. In M. Brassard, R. Germain, & S. Hart (Eds.), *Psychological maltreatment of children and youth.* New York: Pergamon.

BRAUNGART-RIEKER, J., GARWOOD, M. M., POWERS, B. P., & NOTARO, P. C. (1992). Infant affect and affect regulation during the still-face paradigm with mothers and fathers: The role of infant characteristics and parental sensitivity. *Developmental Psychology, 34,* 1428–1437.

BRAY, D. W., & HOWARD, A. (1983). The AT&T longitudinal studies of managers. In K. W. Schaie (Ed.), *Longitudinal studies of adult development.* New York: Guilford.

BRAY, J. H., & HETHERINGTON, E. M. (1993). Families in transition: Introduction and overview. *Journal of Family Psychology, 7,* 3–8.

BRAZELTON, T. B. (1969). *Infants and mothers: Differences in development.* New York: Dell.

BRAZELTON, T. B. (1973). *Neonatal behavioral assessment scale.* London: Heinemann.

BRAZELTON, T. B., & NUGENT, J. K. (1995). *The newborn behavioral assessment scale.* London: McKeith Press.

BREHM, S. (1992). Intimate relationships. New York: McGraw-Hill.

BRENNER, A. (1984). *Helping children cope with stress.* Lexington, MA: Heath.

BRETHERTON, I. (1992). Attachment and bonding. In V. B. Van Hasselt & M. Hersen (Eds.), *Handbook of social development: A lifespan perspective.* New York: Plenum Press.

BRETHERTON, I., & WATERS, E. (Eds.) (1985). Growing points of attachment. *Monographs of the Society for Research in Child Development, 50* (1–2).

BRIGGS, G. C., FREEMAN, R. K., & YAFFE, S. J. (1986). *Drugs in pregnancy and lactation* (2nd ed.). Baltimore, MD: Williams & Wilkins.

BRITANNICA BOOK OF THE YEAR (1997). Chicago: Encyclopaedia Britannica.

BRODY, E. M. (1985). *Parent care as a normative family stress.* Donald P. Kent Memorial Lecture, presented at the 37th annual scientific meeting of the Gerontological Society of America, San Antonio, Texas.

BRODY, E. M., LITVIN, S. J., HOFFMAN, C., & KLEBAN, M. H. (1995a). Marital status of caregiving daughters and co-residence with dependent parents. *Gerontologist, 35,* 75–85.

BRODY, E. M., LITVIN, S. J., HOFFMAN, C., & KLEBAN, M. H. (1995b). On having a "significant other" during the parent care years. *Journal of Applied Gerontology, 14,* 131–149.

BRODY, E., & SCHOONOVER, C. (1986). Patterns of parent-care when adult daughters work and when they do not. *The Gerontologist, 26,* 372–381.

BRODY, E., JOHNSEN, P., & FULCOMER, M. (1984). What should adult children do for elderly parents? Opinions and preferences of three generations of women. *Journal of Gerontology, 39,* 736–746.

BRODY, E., KLEBAN, M., JOHNSEN, P., HOFFMAN, C., & SCHOONOVER, C. (1987). Work status and parent care: A comparison of four groups of women. *The Gerontologist, 27,* 201–208.

BROMAN, S. (1986). Obstetric medication: A review of the literature on outcomes in infancy and childhood. In Michael Lewis (Ed.), *Learning disabilities and prenatal risk.* Urbana: University of Illinois Press.

BRONFENBRENNER, U. (1970). *Two worlds of childhood: U.S. and U.S.S.R.* New York: Russell Sage Foundation.

BRONFENBRENNER, U. (1979). *The ecology of human development.* Cambridge, MA: Harvard University Press.

BRONFENBRENNER, U. (1989). Ecological systems theory. In R. Vasta (Ed.), *Annals of Child Development, Vol. 6.* Greenwich, CT.: JAI Press.

BRONFENBRENNER, U., & EVANS, G. W. (2000). Developmental science in the 21st century: Emerging questions, theoretical models, research designs, and empirical findings. *Social Development, 9,* 115–125.

BRONFENBRENNER, U., & MORRIS, P. A. (1998). The ecology of developmental processes. In R. M. Lerner (Ed.), *Handbook of child psychology* (5th ed., Vol. 1). New York: Wiley.

BRONSON, G. (1978). Aversion reactions to strangers: A dual process interpretation. *Child Development, 49,* 495–499.

BRONSON, M. B. (2000). *Self-regulation in early childhood: Nature and nurture.* NY: The Guilford Press.

BROOKS-GUNN, J., & FURSTENBERG, F. F., JR. (1986). The children of adolescent mothers: Physical, academic, and psychological outcomes. *Developmental Review, 6,* 224–251.

BROOKS-GUNN, J., & FURSTENBERG, F. F., JR. (1989). Adolescent sexual behavior. *American Psychologist, 44,* 249–257.

BROOKS-GUNN, J., BERLIN, L. J., LEVENTHAL, T., & FULIGNI, A. S. (2000). Depending on the kindness of strangers: Current national data initiatives and developmental research. *Child Development, 71,* 257–268.

BROOKS-GUNN, J., KLEBANOV, P. K., & DUNCAN, G. J. (1996). Ethnic differences in children's intelligence test scores: Role of economic deprivation, home environment, and maternal characteristics. *Child Development, 67,* 396–408.

BROPHY, J. (1986). Teacher influences on student achievement. *American Psychologist, 41,* 1069–1077.

BROUDE, G. J. (1995) *Growing up: A cross-cultural encyclopedia.* Santa Barbara, CA: ABC-CLIO.

BROWN, A. S., SUSSER, E. S., BUTLER, P. D., ANDREWS, R. R., KAUFMANN, C. A., & GORMAN, J. M. (1996). Neurobiological plausibility of prenatal nutritional deprivation as a risk factor for schizophrenia. *Journal of Nervous & Mental Disease, 184,* 71–85.

BROWN, B. B., & LOHR, M. J. (1987). Peer-group affiliation and adolescent self-esteem: An integration of ego-identity and symbolic-interaction theories. *Journal of Personality and Social Psychology, 52,* 47–55.

BROWN, B. B., CLASEN, D. R., & EICHER, S. A. (1986). Perceptions of peer pressure, peer conformity dispositions, and self-reported behavior among adolescents. *Developmental Psychology, 22,* 521–530.

BROWN, J. L., & POLLITT, E. (1996). Malnutrition, poverty and intellectual development. *Scientific American, 276* (2), 38–43.

BROWN, R. (1973). *A first language: The early stages.* Cambridge, MA: Harvard University Press.

BROWNELL, C. A., & CARRIGER, M. S. (1990). Changes in cooperation and self-other differentiation during the second year. *Child Development, 61,* 1164–1174.

BRUCK, M. (1987). The adult outcomes of children with learning disabilities. *Annals of Dyslexia, 37,* 252–263.

BRUER, J. T. (1999). *The myth of the first three years: A new understanding of early brain development and lifelong learning.* New York: Free Press.

BRUNER, J. (1983). *Child's talk.* New York: Norton.

BRUNER, J. S. (1973). *Beyond the information given: Studies in the psychology of knowing.* New York: Norton.

BRUNER, J., & HASTE, H. (Eds.) (1987). *Making sense: The child's construction of the world.* London: Methuen.

BRUSCHWEILER-STERN, N. (1997). Imagining the baby, imagining the mother: Clinical representations of perinatology. *Ab Initio: The Brazelton Institute Newsletter, 4,* 1–5.

BRYAN, J. H. (1975). Children's cooperation and helping behaviors. In E. M. Hetherington (Ed.), *Review of child development* (Vol. 5). Chicago: University of Chicago Press.

BRYDEN, M. P., ROY, E. A., MCMANUS, I. C., & BULMAN-FLEMING, M. B. (1997). On the genetics and measurement of human handedness. *Laterality, 2,* 317–336.

BUCHANAN, C. M., ECCLES, J. S., & BECKER, J. B. (1992). Are adolescents the victims of raging hormones: Evidence for activational effects of hormones on moods and behavior at adolescence. *Psychological Bulletin, 111,* 62–107.

BUCHOFF, R. (1990). Attention deficit disorder: help for the classroom teacher. *Childhood Education, 67* (2), 86–90.

BUIS, J. M., & THOMPSON, D. N. (1989). Imaginary audience and personal fable: A brief review. *Adolescence, 24,* 773–781.

BULTERYS, M. G., GREENLAND, S., & KRAUS, J. F. (1990). Chronic fetal hypoxia and sudden infant death syndrome: Interaction between maternal smoking and low hematocrit during pregnancy. *Pediatrics, 86,* 535–540.

BURCHINAL, M. R., ROBERTS, J. E., RIGGINS, R., JR., ZEISEL, S. A., NEEBE, E., & BRYANT, D. (2000). Relating quality of center-based care to early cognitive and language development longitudinally. *Child Development, 71,* 339–357.

BURI, J. R., LOUISELLE, P. A., MISUKANIS, T. M., & MUELLER, R. A. (1988). Effects of parental authoritarianism and authoritativeness on self-esteem. *Personality and Social Psychology Bulletin, 14,* 271–282.

BURKE, R. J., & NELSON, D. (1997). Mergers and acquisitions, downsizing, and privatization: A North American perspective. In M. K. Gowing, J. D. Kraft, & J. C. Quick (Eds.), *The new organizational reality: Downsizing, restructuring, and revitalization.* Washington, DC: American Psychological Association.

BURNSIDE, I. M. (1979). The later decades of life: Research and reflections. In I. M. Burnside, P. Ebersole, & H. E. Monea (Eds.), *Psychosocial caring throughout the life span.* New York: McGraw-Hill.

BURNSIDE, I. M. (1993). Healthy older women—in spite of it all. In J. D. Garner & A. A. Young (Eds.), *Women and healthy aging: Living productively in spite of it all.* New York: Harrington Park/Haworth.

BURNSIDE, I. M., EBERSOLE, P., & MONEA, H. E. (Eds.) (1979). *Psychosocial caring throughout the life span.* New York: McGraw-Hill.

BUSHMAN, B. J., BAUMEISTER, R. F., & STACK, A. D. (1999). Catharsis, Aggression, and Persuasive Influence: Self-fulfilling or self-defeating prophecies? *Journal of Personality and Social Psychololgy, 76,* 367–376.

BUSHNELL, E., & BOUDREAU, J. P. (1993). Motor development and the mind: The potential role of motor abilities as a determinant of aspects of perceptual development. *Child Development, 64,* 1005–1021.

BUSKIRK, E. R. (1985). Health maintenance and longevity: Exercise. In C. E. Finch & E. L. Schneider (Eds.), *Handbook of the biology of aging* (2nd ed.). New York: Van Nostrand Reinhold.

BUSS, D. M. (1999). *Evolutionary Psychology: The New Science of the mind.* Boston: Allyn and Bacon.

BUTLER, R. N. (1968). The life review: An interpretation of reminiscence. In B. L. Neugarten (Ed.), *Middle age and aging.* Chicago: University of Chicago Press.

BUTLER, R. N. (1980–1981). The life review: An unrecognized bonanza. *International Journal of Aging & Human Development, 12,* 35–38.

CALDWELL, R. A., BLOOM, B., & HODGES, W. (1984). Sex differences in separation and divorce: A longitudinal perspective. In A. Rickel, M. Gerrard, & I. Iscoe (Eds.), *Social and psychological problems of women.* Washington, DC: Hemisphere.

CAMPBELL, J. I., & CHARNESS, N. (1990). Age-related declines in working-memory skills: Evidence from a complex calculation task. *Developmental Psychology, 26,* 879–888.

CAMPBELL, M., & SPENCER, E. K. (1988). Psychopharmacology in child and adolescent psychiatry: A review of the past five years. *Journal of the American Academy of Child and Adolescent Psychiatry, 27,* 269–279.

CAMPOS, J. J., LANGER, A., & KROWITZ, A. (1970). Cardiac responses on the visual cliff in prelocomotor human infants. *Science, 170,* 196–197.

CANTUTI-CASTELVETRI, I., SHUKITT-HALE, B., & JOSEPH, J. A. (2000). Neurobehavioral aspects of antioxidants in aging. *International Journal of Developmental Neuroscience, 18,* 367–381.

CAPELLI, C. A., NAKAGAWA, N., & MADDEN, C. M. (1990). How children understand sarcasm: The role of context and intonation. *Child Development, 61,* 1824–1841.

CARD, J. J., & WISE, L. L. (1978). Teenage mothers and teenage fathers: The impact of early childbearing on the parents' personal and professional lives. *Family Planning Perspectives, 10,* 199–205.

CARLO, G., KOLLER, S. H., EISENBERG, N., DA SILVA, M. S., & FROHLICH, C. B. (1996). A cross-national study on the relations among prosocial moral reasoning, gender role orientations, and prosocial behaviors. *Developmental Psychology, 32,* 231–240.

CARLSON, K. J., EISENSTAT, S. A., & ZOPORYN, T. (1996). *The Harvard guide to women's health.* Cambridge, MA: Harvard University Press.

CARMICHAEL, E., & SAYER, C. (1991). *The skeleton at the feast: The day of the dead in Mexico.* London: British Museum Press.

CARPENTER, G. (1974). Mother's face and the newborn. *New Scientist, 61,* 742–744.

CARRION, V. G., & LOCK, J. (1997). The coming out process: Developmental stages for sexual minority youth. *Clinical Child Psychology and Psychiatry, 2,* 369–377.

CARSTENSEN, L. L., & CHARLES, S. T. (1998). Emotion in the second half of life. *Current Directions in Psychological Science, 7,* 144–149.

CASE, R. (1996). Reconceptualizing the nature of children's conceptual structures and their development in middle childhood. *Monographs of the Society for Research in Child Development, 61,* 1–26.

CASPI, A., ELDER, G. H., JR., & BEM, D. J. (1987). Moving against the world: Life-course patterns of explosive children. *Developmental Psychology, 23,* 308–313.

CASSIDY, J. (1986). The ability to negotiate the environment: An aspect of infant competence as related to quality of attachment. *Child Development, 57,* 331–337.

CASSIDY, J., & BERLIN, L. J. (1994). The insecure/ambivalent pattern of attachment: Theory and research. *Child Development, 65,* 971–991.

CATTELL, R. B. (1965). *The scientific analysis of personality.* Baltimore, MD: Penguin.

CELERA GENOMICS CORPORATION (2000). Celera Genomics launches SNP reference database product with more than 2.8 million SNPs. Press release.

CENTERS FOR DISEASE CONTROL AND PREVENTION (CDC). (1995). *Monthly Vital Statistics Reports, 43 (6).* Washington, DC.

CENTERS FOR DISEASE CONTROL AND PREVENTION (CDC). (1996). Status report on the childhood immunization initiative: Reported cases of selected vaccine-preventable diseases—-United States. *Morbidity and Mortality Weekly Report, 45,* 667–671.

CENTERS FOR DISEASE CONTROL AND PREVENTION (CDC). (1997a). Status report on the childhood immunization initiative: Reported cases of selected vaccine-preventable diseases—United States. *Morbidity and Mortality Weekly Report, 46,* 667–671.

CENTERS FOR DISEASE CONTROL AND PREVENTION (CDC). (1997b). *Guidelines for school and community health programs to promote lifelong physical activity among young people.* Hyattsville, MD.

CENTERS FOR DISEASE CONTROL AND PREVENTION (CDC). (1999a). Healthier mothers and babies—1900–1999. *Morbidity and Mortality Weekly Report, 48,* 849–857.

CENTERS FOR DISEASE CONTROL AND PREVENTION (CDC). (1999b). Progress in reducing risky infant sleeping positions—13 states, 1996–1997. *Morbidity and Mortality Weekly Report, 48,* 878–886.

CENTERS FOR DISEASE CONTROL AND PREVENTION (CDC). (2000a). Birth defects. Internet document. CDC home page: www.cdc.gov

CENTERS FOR DISEASE CONTROL AND PREVENTION (CDC). (2000b). Contribution of assisted reproduction technology (ART) and ovulation-inducing drugs to triplet and higher-order multiple births—United States, 1980–1997. *Morbidity and Mortality Weekly Report, 49,* 529–556.

CENTERS FOR DISEASE CONTROL AND PREVENTION (CDC). (2000c). *National Vital Statistics Reports, 48 (11).* Washington, DC.

CENTERS, R. (1975). *Sexual attraction and love: An instrumental theory.* Springfield, IL: Thomas.

CHANCE, P. (1981). That drained-out, used-up feeling. *Psychology Today, 15 (1),* 88–95.

CHAO, R. K. (1994). Beyond parental control and authoritarian parenting style: Understanding Chinese parenting through the cultural notion of training. *Child Development, 65,* 1111–1119.

CHAPMAN, K. L., & MERVIS, C. B. (1989). Patterns of object-name extension in production. *Journal of Child Language, 16,* 561–571.

CHARNESS, N. (1981). Search in chess: Age and skill differences. *Journal of Experimental Psychology: Human Perception and Performance, 7,* 467–476.

CHASE-LANSDALE, P. L., BROOKS-GUNN, J., & ZAMSKY, E. S. (1994). Young African-American multigenerational families in poverty: Quality of mothering and grandmothering. *Child Development, 65,* 373–393.

CHASNOFF, I. J. (1989). Cocaine, pregnancy and the neonate. *Women and Health, 5,* 33.

CHASNOFF, I. J., ANSON A., HATCHER R., STENSON H., KAI, I. K., & RANDOLPH, L. A. (1998). Prenatal exposure to cocaine and other drugs: Outcome at four to six years. *Annals of the New York Academy of Science, 846,* 314–328.

CHATOOR, I., GANIBAN, J., COLIN, V., PLUMMER, N., & HARMON, R. (1998). Attachment and feeding problems: a reexamination of nonorganic failure to thrive and attachment insecurity. *Journal of the American Academy of Child and Adolescent Psychiatry, 37,* 1217–1224.

CHAVEZ, A., MARTINEZ, C., & SOBERANES, B. (1995). Effects of early malnutrition on late mental and behavioral performance. *Developmental Brain Dysfunction, 8,* 90–102.

CHECKLY, K. (1997). The first seven...and the eighth. *Educational Leadership, 55,* (1), 8–13.

CHEOUR-LUHTANEN, M., ALHO, K., SAINIO, K., RINNE, T., & REINIKAINEN, K. (1996). The ontogenetically earliest discriminative response of the brain. *Psychophysiology, 33,* 478–481.

CHERLIN, A., & FURSTENBERG, F. F. (1986). Grandparents and family crisis. *Generations, 10 (4),* 26–28.

CHESS, S. (1987). Comments: "Infant day care: A cause for concern." *Zero to three, 7 (3),* 24–25.

CHICCHETTI, D., & ROGOSCH, F. A. (1997). The role of self-organization in the promotion of resilience in maltreated children. *Development and Psychopathology, 9,* 797–815.

CHILDREN'S DEFENSE FUND (1991). *The state of America's children, 1991.* Washington, DC.

CHILDREN'S DEFENSE FUND (1992). *The state of America's children, 1992.* Washington, DC.

CHILDREN'S DEFENSE FUND (1998). *The state of America's children, 1998.* Washington, DC.

CHILDREN'S DEFENSE FUND (2000). *The state of America's children yearbook, 2000.* Washington, DC.

CHILMAN, C. (1979). *Adolescent sexuality in changing American society.* Washington, DC: U.S. Government Printing Office.

CHIRIBOGA, D. A. (1981). The developmental psychology of middle age. In J. Howells (Ed.), *Modern perspectives in the psychiatry of middle age.* New York: Brunner/Mazel.

CHIRIBOGA, D. A. (1996). In search of continuities and discontinuities across time and culture. In V. L. Bengtson (Ed.), *Adulthood and aging: Research on continuities and discontinuities.* New York: Springer-Verlag.

CHIRIBOGA, D. A., & CUTLER, L. (1980). Stress and adaptation: Life span perspectives. In L. W. Poon, (Ed.), *Aging in the 1980s.* Washington, DC: American Psychological Association.

CHOMSKY, N. (1959). Review of *Verbal Behavior* by B. F. Skinner. *Language, 35,* 26–58.

CHRISTENSEN, H., KORTEN, A., JORM, A. F., HENDERSON, A. S., SCOTT, R., & MACKINNON, A. J. (1996). Activity levels and cognitive functioning in an elderly community sample. *Age and Ageing, 25,* 72–80.

CHUKOVSKY, K. (1963). *From two to five.* Berkeley: University of California Press.

CICCHETTI, D., & BEEGHLY, M. (1990). Perspectives on the study of the self in transition. In D. Cicchetti & M. Beeghly (Eds.), *The self in transition: Infancy to childhood.* Chicago: University of Chicago Press.

CICCHETTI, D., ROGOSCH, F. A., & TOTH, S. (1998). Maternal depressive disorder and contextual risk: Contributions to the development of attachment insecurity and behavior problems in toddlerhood. *Development and Psychotherapy. 10,* 283–300.

CICCHETTI, D., & TOTH, S. L. (1998). The development of depression in children and adolescents. *American Psychologist, 53,* 221–241.

CIESIELSKI, K. T., LESNIK, P. G., BENZEL, E. C., & HART, B. L. (1999). MRI morphometry of maillary bodies, caudate nuclei, and prefrontal cortices after chemotherapy for childhood leukemia: Multivariate models of early and late developing memory subsystems. *Behavioral Neuroscience, 113,* 439–450.

CLARK, E. V. (1983). Meaning and concepts. In P. H. Mussen (Ed.), *Handbook of child psychology* (4th ed., Vol. 4). New York: Wiley.

CLARK, E. V. (1987). The principle of contrast: A constraint on acquisition. In B. Macwhinner (Ed.), *Mechanisms of language acquisition.* Hillsdale, NJ: Erlbaum.

CLARK, J. E., & PHILLIPS, S. J. (1985). A developmental sequence of the standing long jump. In J. E. Clark & J. H. Humphrey (Eds.), *Motor development: Current selected research.* Princeton, NJ: Princeton Book Company.

CLARK, K. (1957). *Present threats to children and youth.* Draft report, manuscript in the office of the National Committee on the employment of youth, New York City, May 31.

CLARK, R., HYDE, J. S., ESSEX, M. J., & KLEIN, M. H. (1997). *Child Development, 68,* 364–383.

CLARK-PLASKIE, M., & LACHMAN, M. E. (1999). The sense of control in midlife. In S. L. Willis & J. D. Reid (Eds.), *Life in the middle: Psychological and social development in middle age.* San Diego: Academic Press.

CLARKE, S. C. (1995). Advance report of final divorce statistics, 1989 and 1990. *Monthly Vital Statistics Reports, 43* (9). Hyattsville, MD: National Center for Health Statistics.

CLARKE-STEWART, K. A. (1982). *Daycare.* Cambridge, MA: Harvard University Press.

CLARKE-STEWART, K. A., & FEIN, G. C. (1983). Early childhood programs. In M. Haith & J. Campos (Eds.), *Handbook of child psychology, Vol. 2: Infancy and developmental psychobiology* (4th ed.). New York: Wiley.

CLAUSEN, J. A. (1986). *The life course: A sociological perspective.* Englewood Cliffs, NJ: Prentice Hall.

CLAUSEN, J. A. (1995). Gender, contexts, and turning points in adults' lives. In Moen, P., Elder, G. H., & Luscher, K. (Eds.), *Examining lives in context: Perspectives on the ecology of human development.* Washington, DC: American Psychological Association.

CLEIREN, M. (1993). *Bereavement and adaptation: A comparative study of the aftermath of death.* Washington, DC: Hemisphere Publishing.

CLIFTON, R. K., ROCHAT, P., ROBIN, D. J., & BERTHIER, N. E. (1994). Multimodal perception in the control of infant reaching. *Journal of Experimental Psychology: Human Perception and Performance, 20,* 876–886.

CLINGEMPEEL, G., & SEGAL, S. (1986). Stepparent–stepchild relationships and the psychological adjustment of children in stepmother and stepfather families. *Child Development, 57,* 474–484.

CLOUD, J. (2000). A kinder, gentler death. *Time, 156* (12), 60–67.

COE, R. (1988). A longitudinal examination of poverty in the elderly years. *The Gerontologist, 28,* 540–544.

COHEN, D., & EISDORFER, K. (1986). *The loss of self: A family resource for the care of Alzheimer's disease and related disorders.* New York: Norton.

COHEN, L. B., & GELBER, E. R. (1975). Infant visual memory. In L. B. Cohen & P. Salapatek (Eds.), *Infant perception: From sensation to cognition* (Vol. 1). New York: Academic Press.

COHEN, L. H., FINE, B. A., & PERGAMENT, E. (1998). An assessment of ethnocultural beliefs regarding the causes of birth defects and genetic disorders. *Journal of Genetic Counseling, 7,* 15–29.

COHEN, N., & ESTNER, L. (1983). *Silent knife: Caesarean prevention and vaginal birth after Caesarean.* South Hadley, MA: Bergin & Garvey.

COHEN, S. (1992). Life and death: A cross-cultural perspective. *Childhood Education, 69* (2), 107–108.

COHLER, B. J., & GALATZER-LEVY, R. M. (2000). *The course of gay and lesbian lives: Social and psychoanalytic perspectives.* Chicago: University of Chicago Press.

COHN, J. F., CAMPBELL, S. B., & ROSS, S. (1991). Infant response in the still-face paradigm at 6 months predicts avoidant and secure attachment at 12 months. *Development & Psychopathology, 3,* 367–376.

COLBY, A., KOHLBERG, L., GIBBS, J., & LIEBERMAN, M. (1983). A longitudinal study of moral development. *Monographs of the Society for Research in Child Development, 48.*

COLE, M. (1999). Culture in development. In M. Bornstein & M. Lamb (Eds.), *Developmental psychology: An advanced textbook* (4th ed.). Mahwah, NJ: Erlbaum.

COLE, M., JOHN-STEINER, V., SCRIBNER, S., & SOUBERMAN, E. (Eds.) (1978). *Mind in society: The development of higher psychological processes, L. S. Vygotsky.* Cambridge, MA: Harvard University Press.

COLE, P. M., MICHEL, M. K., & TETI, L. O. (1994). The development of emotion regulation and dysregulation: A clinical perspective. In N. A. Fox (Ed.), *Monographs of the Society for Research in Child Development, 59,* (2–3), 73–100.

COLEMAN, F. W., & COLEMAN, W. S. (1984). Helping siblings and other peers cope with dying. In H. Wass & C. A. Corr, *Childhood and death.* Washington, DC: Hemisphere.

COLEMAN, M., & GANONG, L. (1985). Remarriage myths; Implications for the helping professions. *Journal of Counseling and Development, 64,* 116–120.

COLEMAN, M., & GANONG, L. (1987). The cultural stereotyping of stepfamilies. In K. Pasley & M. Ihinger-Tallman (Eds.), *Remarriage and stepparenting: Current research and theory.* New York: Guilford.

COLEMAN, M., & GANONG, L. H. (1997). Stepfamilies from the stepfamily's perspective. *Marriage & Family Review, 26,* 107–121.

COLES, R. (1980). *Children of crisis: Privileged ones.* Boston: Atlanta-Little, Brown.

COLEY, R. L., & CHASE-LANSDALE, P. L. (1998). Adolescent pregnancy and parenthood: Recent evidence and future directions. *American Psychologist, 53,* 152–166.

COLLIE, R., & HAYNE, H. (1999). Deferred imitation by 6- and 9-month-old infants: More evidence for declarative memory. *Developmental Psychobiology, 35,* 83–90.

COLUMBIA UNIVERSITY COLLEGE OF PHYSICIANS AND SURGEONS (1985). *Complete home medical guide.* New York: Crown.

COMFORT, A. (1976). *A good age.* New York: Crown.

COMMITTEE ON LESBIAN, GAY, & BISEXUAL CONCERNS TASK FORCE (2000). Guidelines for psychotherapy with lesbian, gay, and bisexual clients. *American Psychologist, 55,* 1440–1451.

COMSTOCK, G. (1993). The medium and the society: The role of television in American life. In G. L. Berry & J. K. Asamen (Eds.), *Children & television: Images in a changing sociocultural world.* Thousand Oaks, CA: Sage.

CONNELLY, B., JOHNSTON, D., BROWN, I. D. R., MACKAY, S., & BLACKSTOCK, E. G. (1993). The prevalence of depression in a high school population. *Adolescence, 28,* 149–158.

CONNOR, E. M., SPERLING, R. S., GELBER, R., KISELEV, P., SCOTT, G., O'SULLIVAN, M. J., VANDYKE, R., BEY, M., SHEARER, W., JACOBSON, R. L., JIMENEZ, E., O'NEIL, E., BAZIN, B., DELFRAISSY, J., CULNANE, M., COOMBS, R., ELKINS, M., MOYE, J., STRATTON, P., & BALSEY, J. (1994). Reduction of maternal-infant transmission of human immunodeficiency virus type I with zidovudine treatment. *The New England Journal of Medicine, 331,* 1173–1180.

COONTZ, S. (2000). *The way we never were: American families and the nostalgia trip.* New York: Basic Books.

COOPER, K., & GUTTMAN, D. (1987). Gender identity and ego mastery style in middle-aged, pre- and post-empty nest women. *The Gerontologist, 27,* 347–352.

COOPER, P. G. (1999a). What is external fetal monitoring? *Clinical Reference Systems,* November 1, 535.

COOPER, P. G. (1999b). What is internal fetal monitoring? *Clinical Reference Systems,* November 1, 791.

CORZINE, J. B., BUNTZMAN, G. F., & BUSCH, E. T. (1994). Mentoring, downsizing, gender and career outcomes. *Journal of Social Behavior & Personality, 9,* 517–528.

COSTA, A. (Ed.) (1985). *Developing minds: A resource book for teaching thinking.* Washington, DC: Association for Supervision and Curriculum Development.

COSTA, P. T., JR., & McCRAE, R. R. (1985). Hypochondriasis, neuroticism, and aging: When are somatic complaints unfounded? *American Psychologist, 40,* 19–28.

COSTA, P. T., JR., & MCCRAE, R. R. (1989). Personality continuity and the changes of adult life. In M. Storandt & G. R. VandenBos (Eds), *The adult years: Continuity and change*. Washington, DC: American Psychological Association.

COSTA, P. T., JR., & MCCRAE, R. R. (1994). Set like plaster? Evidence for the stability of adult personality. In T. F. Heatherton, & J. L. Weinberger (Eds.), *Can personality change?* Washington, DC: American Psychological Association.

COSTIN, S. E., & JONES, D.C. (1992). Friendship as a facilitator of emotional responsiveness and prosocial interventions among young children. *Developmental Psychology, 28,* 941–947.

COTÉ, J. E., & LEVINE, C. (1988). A critical examination of the ego identity status paradigm. *Developmental Review, 8,* 147–184.

COUNCIL OF ECONOMIC ADVISERS (1987). *The economic report of the president.* Washington, DC: U.S. Government Printing Office.

COUNCIL ON SCIENTIFIC AFFAIRS (1991). Hispanic health in the United States. *Journal of the American Medical Association, 365* (2), 248–252.

COWAN, C. P., & COWAN, P. A. (1992). *When partners become parents: The big life change for couples.* New York: Basic Books.

COWLEY, S. J. (1997). Of presentations and language. *Language & Communication, 17,* 279–300.

CRAIG, G. J., & GARNEY, P. (1972). *Attachment and separation behavior in the second and third years.* Unpublished manuscript. University of Massachusetts, Amherst.

CRAIK, F. I. M., & MCDOWD, J. M. (1987). Age differences in recall and recognition. *Journal of Experimental Psychology: Learning, Memory, and Cognition, 13,* 474–479.

CRAIK, I. M., & SALTHOUSE, T. A. (Eds.) (2000). *Handbook of aging and cognition* (2nd ed.). Mahwah, NJ: Erlbaum.

CRATTY, B. (1986). *Perceptual and motor development in infants and children.* Englewood Cliffs, NJ: Prentice Hall.

CRATTY, B. J. (1970). *Perceptual and motor development in infants and children.* New York: Macmillan.

CRICK, N. R., & LADD, G. W. (1993). Children's perceptions of their peer experiences: Attributions, loneliness, social anxiety, and social avoidance. *Developmental Psychology, 29,* 244–254.

CROCKENBERG, S. (1981). Infant irritability, mother responsiveness, and social support influences on the security of infant–mother attachment. *Child Development, 52,* 857–865.

CROCKENBERG, S., & MCCLUSKEY, K. (1986). Change in maternal behavior during the baby's first year of life. *Child Development, 57,* 746–753.

CROCKETT, W. H., & HUMMERT, M. L. (1987). Perceptions of aging and the elderly. In K. W. Schaie & K. Eisdorfer (Eds.), *Annual review of gerontology and geriatrics* (Vol. 7). New York: Springer-Verlag.

CROSS, K. P. (1981). *Adults as learners.* San Francisco: Jossey-Bass.

CROUTER, A. C., MACDERMID, S. M., MCHALE, S. M., & PERRY-JENKINS, M. (1990). Parental monitoring and perceptions of children's school performance and conduct in single- and dual-earner families. *Developmental Psychology, 26,* 649–657.

CRUICKSHANK, W. M. (1977). Myths and realities in learning disabilities. *Learning Disabilities, 10,* 57–64.

CSIKSZENTMIHALYI, M., & LARSON, R. (1984). *Being adolescent.* New York: Basic Books.

CULLITON, B. J. (2000). The heart, the moon, and the genome. Celera Genomics Corporation press release.

CUMMINGS, M. R. (2000). *Human heredity: Principles and Issues.* Pacific Grove, CA: Brooks/Cole.

CUNNINGHAM, H. (1996). The history of childhood. In C. P. Hwang, M. E. Lamb, & I. E. Siegel (Eds.), *Images of childhood.* Mahwah, NJ: Lawrence Erlbaum.

CURRAN, D. K. (1987). *Adolescent suicidal behavior.* Washington, DC: Hemisphere.

CURTIN, S. C., & PARK, M. M. (1999). Trends in the attendant, place and timing of births, and in the use of obstetric interventions: United States, 1989–97. *National Vital Statistics Reports, 47* (27). Hyattsville, MD: National Center for Health Statistics.

CUTRONA, C., & TROUTMAN, B. (1986). Social support, infant temperament, and parenting self-efficacy: A mediational model of postpartum depression. *Child Development, 57,* 1507–1518.

DAIUTE, C. (1993). Synthesis. In C. Daiute (Ed.), *New directions for child development, 61.* San Francisco: Jossey-Bass.

DAIUTE, C., CAMPBELL, C. H., GRIFFIN, T. M., REDDY, M., & TIVNAN, T. (1993). Young authors' interactions with peers and a teacher: Toward a developmentally sensitive sociocultural literacy theory. In C. Daiute (Ed.), *New directions for child development, 61.* San Francisco: Jossey-Bass.

DALEY, S. (1991). Girls' self-esteem is lost on the way to adolescence, new study finds. *New York Times Magazine, 140* (Jan. 9), B1, B6.

DALMAN, C., ALLEBECK, P., CULLBERG, J., GRUNEWALD, C., & KOESTER, M. (1999). Obstetric complications and the risk of schizophrenia: A longitudinal study of a national birth cohort. *Archives of General Psychiatry, 56,* 234–240.

DAMON, W. (1991). *The moral child: Nurturing children's natural moral growth.* New York: Free Press.

DAMON, W. (1999). The moral development of children. *Scientific American, 281,* (2), 72–78.

DAMON, W., & HART, D. (1982). The development of self-understanding from infancy through adolescence. *Child Development, 53,* 841–864.

DAMON, W., & HART, D. (1992). Self understanding and its role in social and moral development. In M. H. Bornstein & M. E. Lamb (Eds.), *Developmental psychology: An advanced textbook* (3rd ed.). Hillsdale, NJ: Erlbaum.

DAN, A. J., & BERNHARD, L. A. (1989). Menopause and other health issues for midlife women. In S. Hunter & M. Sundel (Eds.), *Midlife myths: Issues, findings, and practice implications.* Newberry Park, CA: Sage.

DANIELS, P., & WEINGARTEN, K. (1982). *Sooner or later: The timing of parenthood in adult lives.* New York: Norton.

DARLING, N., & STEINBERG, L. (1993). Parenting style as context: An integrative model. *Psychological Bulletin, 113,* 487–496.

DARO, D. (1993). Child maltreatment research: Implications for program design. In D. Cicchetti & S. Toth (Eds.), *Child abuse, child development and social policy.* Norwood, NJ: Ablex.

DARWIN, C. (1859/1958). *The origin of species: by means of natural selection or the preservation of favoured races in the struggle for life.* New York: New American Library.

DATAN, N., & GINSBERG, L. (Eds.) (1975). *Lifespan developmental psychology.* New York: Academic Press.

DAVIDSON, J. I. (1996a). *Emergent literacy and dramatic play in early education.* New York: Delmar.

DAVIDSON, N. E. (1996b). Current controversies: Is hormone replacement therapy a risk? *Scientific American, 275,* (3), 101.

DAVIES, B. (1993). Caring for the frail elderly: An international perspective. *Generations, 17* (4), 51–54.

DAWKINS, J. L., TYLDEN, E., COLLEY, N., & EVANS, C. (1997). Drug abuse in pregnancy: Obstetric and neonatal problems—Ten years' experience. *Drug and Alcohol Review, 16,* 25–31.

DE BOYSSON-BARDIES, B., HALLE, P., SAGART, L., & DURAND, C. (1989). A crosslinguistic investigation of vowel formants in babbling. *Journal of Child Language, 16,* 1–17.

DE HAAN, M., & NELSON, C. A. (1999). Brain activity differentiates face and object processing in 6–month-old infants. *Developmental Psychology, 35,* 1113–1121.

DE VILLIERS, P. A., & DE VILLIERS, J. G. (1979). *Early language.* Cambridge, MA: Harvard University Press.

DE VILLIERS, P. A., & DE VILLIERS, J. G. (1992). Language development. In M. H. Bornstein & M. Lamb (Eds.), *Developmental psychology: An advanced textbook* (3rd ed.). Hillsdale, NJ: Erlbaum.

DE WOLFF, M. S., & VAN IJZENDOORN, M. H. (1997). Sensitivity and attachment: A meta-analysis on parental antecedents of infant attachment. *Child Development, 68,* 571–591.

DECASPER, A. J., & FIFER, W. P. (1987). Of human bonding: Newborns prefer their mothers' voices. In J. Oates and S. Sheldon (Eds.), *Cognitive development in infancy.* Hove, UK: Erlbaum.

DECASPER, A. J., LECANUET, J.-P., BUSNEL, M.-C., & GRANIER-DEFERRE, C. (1994). Fetal reactions to recurrent maternal speech. *Infant Behavior and Development, 17,* 159–164.

DECASPER, A. J., & SPENCE, M. J. (1986). Prental maternal speech influences newborn's perception of speech sounds. *Infant Behavior and Development, 9,* 133–250.

DEIMLING, G., & BASS, D. (1986). Symptoms of mental impairment among elderly adults and their effects on family caregivers. *Journal of Gerontology, 41,* 778–784.

DEKKER, R. (1987). *Willingness to change.* The Hague: Ministry of Welfare, Health and Cultural Affairs.

DELOACHE, J. S. (1987). Rapid change in the symbolic functioning of young children. *Science, 238,* 1556–1557.

DELOACHE, J. S., & TODD, C. M. (1988). Young children's use of spatial categorization as a mnemonic strategy. *Journal of Experimental Child Psychology, 46,* 1–20.

DELOACHE, J. S., CASSIDY, D. J., & BROWN, A. L. (1985). Precursors of mnemonic strategies in very young children's memory. *Child Development, 56,* 125–137.

DEMARIS, A., & LESLIE, G. (1984). Cohabitation with a future spouse: Its influence upon marital satisfaction and communication. *Journal of Marriage and the Family, 46,* 77–84.

DEMAUSE, L. (1974). The evolution of childhood. In L. deMause (Ed.) *The history of childhood.* New York: Psychohistory Press.

DENCIK, L. (1989). Growing up in the post-modern age: On the child's situation in the modern family, and on the position of the family in the modern welfare state. *Acta Sociologica, 32,* 155–180.

DENNIS, W. (1966). Creative productivity between the ages of 20 and 80 years. *Journal of Gerontology, 21,* 1–8.

DENT-READ, C., & ZUKOW-GOLDRING, P. (1997). Introduction: Ecological realism, dynamic systems, and epigenetic systems approaches to development. In C. Dent-Read & P. Zukow-Goldring (Eds.), *Evolving explanations of development: Ecological approaches to organism-environment systems.* Washington, DC: American Psychological Association.

DERR, C. B. (1986). *Managing the new careerists.* San Francisco: Jossey-Bass.

DESPELDER, L. A., & STRICKLAND, A. L. (1995). *The path ahead: Readings in death and dying.* Mountain View, CA: Mayfield.

DESPELDER, L. A., & STRICKLAND, A. L. (1999). *The last dance: Encountering death and dying* (5th ed.). Mountain View, CA: Mayfield.

DEVLIN, B., DANIELS, M., & ROEDER, K. (1997). The heritability of IQ. *Nature, 388,* 468–471.

DIAMOND, A. (2000). Close interrelation of motor development and cognitive development and of the cerebellum and prefrontal cortex. *Child Development, 71,* 44–56.

DIAMOND, L. M. (1998). Development of sexual orientation among adolescent and young adult women. *Developmental Psychology, 34,* 1085–1095.

DIAZ, R. M. (1985). Bilingual cognitive development: Addressing three gaps in current research. *Child Development, 56,* 1376–1388.

DIENER, E., & SUH, M.E. (1997). Subjective well-being and age: An international analysis. In K. W. Schaie & M. P. Lawton (Eds.), *Annual review of gerontology and geriatrics: Vol. 17. Focus on emotion and adult development.* New York: Springer-Verlag.

DIETZ, W. H., JR. (1987). Childhood obesity. *Annals of the New York Academy of Sciences, 499,* 47–54.

DIJKSTRA, I. C., & STROEBE, M. S. (1998). The impact of a child's death on parents: A myth (not) disproved? *Journal of Family Studies, 4,* 159–185.

DIMATTEO, M. R., MORTON, S. C., LEPPER, H. S., & DAMUSH, T. M. (1996). Cesarean childbirth and psychosocial outcomes: A meta-analysis. *Health Psychology, 15,* 303–314.

DITZION, J. S., & WOLF, P. W. (1978). Beginning parenthood. In Boston Women's Book Collective (Ed.), *Ourselves and our children.* New York: Random House.

DIVISON 44 COMMITTEE ON LESBIAN, GAY, AND BISEXUAL CONCERNS JOINT TASK FORCE (2000). Guidelines for psychotherapy with lesbian, gay, and bisexual clients. *American Psychologist, 55,* 1440–1451.

DIXON, R. A. (1992). Contextual approaches to adult intellectual development. In R. J. Sternberg & C. A. Berg (Eds.), *Intellectual development.* New York: Cambridge University Press.

DODGE, K. A., COIE, J. D., PETTIT, G. S., & PRICE, J. M. (1990). Peer status and aggression in boys' groups: Developmental and contextual analyses. *Child Development, 61,* 1289–1309.

DODGE, K. A., PETTIT, G. S., & BATES, J. E. (1994). Effects of physical maltreatment on the development of peer relations. *Development and Psychopathology, 6,* 43–55.

DODWELL, P., HUMPHREY, G. K., & MUIR, D. (1987). Shape and pattern perception. In P. Salapatek & L. Cohen (Eds.), *Handbook of infant perception, Vol. 1: From sensation to perception.* New York: Academic Press.

DOKA, K., & MERTZ, M. (1988). The meaning and significance of great-grandparenthood. *The Gerontologist, 28,* 192–197.

DOLE, A. A. (1995). Why not drop *race* as a term? *American Psychologist, 50,* 40.

DOLLARD, J., & MILLER, N. E. (1950). *Personality and psychotherapy: An analysis in terms of learning, thinking, and culture.* New York: McGraw-Hill.

DOLLARD, J., DOOB, L. W., MILLER, N. E., MOWRER, O. H., & SEARS, R. R. (1939). *Frustration and aggression.* New Haven: Yale University Press.

DONALDSON, M. (1978). *Children's minds.* New York: Norton.

DONOVAN, J. E., JESSOR, R., & COSTA, F. M. (1988). Syndrome of problem behavior in adolescence: A replication. *Journal of Consulting and Clinical Psychology, 56,* 762–765.

DONOVAN, R. (1984). Planning for an aging work force. *Aging, 47,* 4–7.

DORNBUSCH, S. M., CARLSMITH, J. M., BUSHWALL, S. J., RITTER, P. L., LEIDERMAN, H., HASTORF, A. H., & GROSS, R. T. (1985). Single parents, extended households, and the control of adolescents. *Child Development, 56,* 326–341.

DORNBUSCH, S. M., RITTER, P. L., LEIDERMAN, P. H., ROBERTS, D. F., & FRALEIGH, M. J. (1987). The relation of parenting style to adolescent school performance. *Child Development, 58,* 1244–1257.

DOUVAN, E., & ADELSON, J. B. (1966). *The adolescent experience.* New York: Wiley.

DOUVAN, E., & GOLD, M. (1966). Modal patterns in American adolescence. In L. W. Hoffman & M. L. Hoffman (Eds.), *Review of child development research* (Vol. 2). New York: Russell Sage Foundation.

DOYLE, A. B., BEAUDET, J., & ABOUD, F. (1988). Developmental patterns in the flexibility of children's ethnic attitudes. *Journal of Cross-Cultural Research, 19,* 3–18.

DRAPER, T. W., & JAMES, R. S. (1985). Preschool fears: Longitudinal sequence and cohort changes. *Child Study Journal, 15,* 147–155.

DREYER, P. H. (1982). Sexuality during adolescence. In B. Wolman (Ed.), *Handbook of developmental psychology.* Englewood Cliffs, NJ: Prentice Hall.

DROEGE, R. (1982). *A psychosocial study of the formation of the middle adult life structure in women.* Unpublished doctoral dissertation. California School of Professional Psychology, Berkeley.

DROTAR, D. (Ed.). (1985). *New directions in failure to thrive: Implications for research and practice.* New York: Plenum.

DUNN, J. (1983). Sibling relationships in early childhood. *Child Development, 54,* 787–811.

DUNN, J. (1985). *Sisters and brothers.* Cambridge, MA: Harvard University Press.

DUNN, J. (1986). Growing up in a family world: Issues in the study of social development of young children. In M. Richards & P. Light (Eds.), *Children of social worlds: development in a social context.* Cambridge, MA: Harvard University Press.

DUNN, J. (1993). *Young children's close relationships: Beyond attachment.* Newberry Park, CA: Sage.

DUNN, J., & BROWN, J. (1991). Becoming American or English? Talking about the social world in England and the United States. In M. H. Bornstein, (Ed.), *Cultural approaches to parenting.* Hillsdale, NJ: Erlbaum.

DUNN, J., & KENDRICK, C. (1979). Interaction between young siblings in the context of family relationships. In M. Lewis & L. Rosenblum (Eds.), *The child and its family: The genesis of behavior* (Vol. 2). New York: Plenum.

DUNN, J., & KENDRICK, C. (1980). The arrival of a sibling: Changes in interaction between mother and first-born child. *Journal of Child Psychology, 21,* 119–132.

DUNN, J., & MUNN, P. (1985). Becoming a family member: Family conflict and the development of social understanding in the second year. *Child Development, 56,* 480–492.

DUNN, J., & MUNN, P. (1987). Development of justification in disputes with mother and sibling. *Developmental Psychology, 23,* 791–798.

DUNPHY, D. C. (1963). The social structure of urban adolescent peer groups. *Sociometry, 26,* 230–246.

DUNPHY, D. C. (1980). Peer group socialization. In R. Muuss (Ed.), *Adolescent behavior and society* (3rd ed.). New York: Random House.

DUNST, C., TRIVETTE, C., & DEAL, A. (1988). *Enabling and empowering families.* Cambridge, MA: Brookline Books.

DWYER, T., PONSONBY, A. B., NEWMAN, N. M., & GIBBONS, L. E. (1991). Prospective cohort study of prone sleeping position and sudden infant death syndrome. *The Lancet, 337,* 1244–1247.

DYSON, A. H. (1993). A sociocultural perspective on symbolic development in primary grade classrooms. In C. Daiute (Ed.), *New directions for child development, 61.* San Francisco: Jossey-Bass.

DYSON, L. L. (1996). The experiences of families of children with learning disabilities: Parental stress, family functioning, and sibling self-concept. *Journal of Learning Disabilities, 29,* 280–286.

EAKINS, P. S. (Ed.) (1986). *The American way of birth.* Philadelphia: Temple University Press.

EASTERBROOKS, M. A., & GOLDBERG, W. A. (1984). Toddler development in the family: Impact of father involvement and parenting characteristics. *Child Development, 55,* 740–752.

EATON, W. O., & YU, A. P. (1989). Are sex differences in child motor activity level a function of sex differences in maturational status? *Child Development, 60,* 1005–1011.

ECCLES, J., WIGFIELD, A., HAROLD, R. D., & BLUMENFELD, P. (1993). Age and gender differences in children's self- and task perceptions during elementary school. *Child Development, 64,* 830–847.

EDDY, D. M. (1991). The individual vs. society: Is there a conflict? *Journal of the American Medical Association, 265,* 1446–1450.

EDELSTEIN, L. (1984). *Maternal bereavement.* New York: Praeger.

EGELUND, B., PIANTA, R., & O'BRIEN, M. A. (1993). Maternal intrusiveness in infancy and child maladaptation in early school years. *Development and Psychopathology, 5,* 359–370.

EICHORN, D. (1979). Physical development: Current foci of interest. In J. D. Osofsky (Ed.), *Handbook of infant development.* New York: Wiley.

EIDEN, R.D., CHAVEZ, F., & LEONARD, K.E. (1999). Parent-infant interactions among families with alcoholic fathers. *Development & Psychopathology, 11,* 745–762.

EIMAS, P. D. (1974). Linguistic processing of speech by young infants. In R. L. Schiefelbusch & L. L. Lloyd (Eds.), *Language perspectives: Acquisition, retardation, and intervention.* Baltimore: University Park Press.

EIMAS, P. D. (1975). Speech perception in early infancy. In Lin L. B. Cohen & P. Salapatek (Eds.), *Infant perception: From sensation to cognition* (Vol. 2). New York: Academic Press.

EIMAS, P. D. (1999). Segmental and syllabic representations in the perception of speech by young infants. *Journal of the Acoustical Society of America, 105,* 1901–1911.

EIMAS, P. D., & QUINN, P. C. (1994). Studies on the formation of perceptually-based categories in young infants. *Child Development, 65,* 903–917.

EISENBERG, N. (1988). The development of prosocial and aggressive behavior. In M. Bornstein & M. Lamb (Eds.), *Developmental psychology: An advanced textbook* (2nd ed.). Hillsdale, NJ: Erlbaum.

EISENBERG, N. (1989a). *The development of prosocial moral reasoning in childhood and mid-adolescence.* Paper presented at the biennual meeting of the Society for Research in Child Development, Kansas City.

EISENBERG, N. (1989b). The development of prosocial values. In N. Eisenberg, J.

Reykowski, & E. Staub (Eds.), *Social and moral values: Individual and social perspectives.* Hillsdale, NJ: Erlbaum.

EISENBERG, N. (2000). Emotion, regulation, and moral development. *Annual Review of Psychology, 51,* 665–697.

EISENBERG, N., PASTERNACK, J. F., CAMEROR, E., & TRYON, K. (1984). The relation of quantity and mode of prosocial behavior to moral cognitions and social style. *Child Development, 55,* 1479–1485.

EISENBERG, N., SHELL, R., PASTERNACK J., BELLER, R., LENNON, R., & MATHY, R. (1987). Prosocial development in middle childhood: A longitudinal study. *Developmental Psychology, 23,* 712–718.

EISENMAN, R. (1995). Why pychologists should study race. *American Psychologist, 50,* 42–43.

EKERDT, D. (1987). Why the notion persists that retirement harms the health. *The Gerontologist, 27,* 454–457.

EKERDT, D., VINICK, B., & BOSSE, R. (1989). Orderly endings: Do men know when they will retire? *Journals of Gerontology, 44,* S28–S35.

ELBERS, L., & TON, J. (1985). Play pen monologues: The interplay of words and babbles in the first words period. *Journal of Child Language, 12,* 551–565.

ELDER, G. H. (1998). The life course as developmental theory. *Child Development, 69,* 1–12.

ELDER, G. H., CASPI, A., & BURTON, L. M. (1988). Adolescent transition in developmental perspective: Sociological and historical insights. In M. R. Gunnar & W. A. Collins (Eds.), Development during the transition to adolescence. Hillsdale, NJ: Erlbaum.

ELDER, J. L., & PEDERSON, D. R. (1978). Preschool children's use of objects in symbolic play. *Child Development, 49,* 500–504.

ELIAS, J. W., & MARSHALL, P. H. (Eds.). (1987). *Cardiovascular disease and behavior.* Washington, DC: Hemisphere.

ELKIND, D. (1967). Egocentrism in adolescence. *Child Development, 38,* 1025–1034.

ELKIND, D. (1974). *Children and adolescents: Interpretive essays on Jean Piaget.* New York: Oxford University Press.

ELKIND, D. (1981). *The hurried child.* Reading, MA: Addison-Wesley.

ELKIND, D. (1998). *All grown up and no place to go: Teenagers in crisis* (rev. ed.). Reading, MA: Perseus.

ELKIND, D., & BOWEN, R. (1979). Imaginary audience behavior in children and adolescents. *Developmental Psychology, 15,* 38–44.

ELLWOOD, D., & CRANE, J. (1990). Family change among black Americans: What do we know? *Journal of Economic Perspectives, 4,* 65–84.

EMDE, R. N. (1998). Early emotional development: New modes of thinking for research and intervention. In Warhol, J. G. (Ed.), *New perspectives in early emotional development.* St. Louis, MO: Johnson & Johnson Pediatric Institute.

EMDE, R. N., & BUCHSBAUM, H. K. (1990). "Didn't you hear my Mommy?" Autonomy with connectedness in moral self-emergence. In D. Cicchetti & M. Beeghly

(Eds.), *The self in transition: Infancy to childhood.* Chicago: University of Chicago Press.

EMERY, R. E. (1989). Family violence. *American Psychologist, 44,* 321–328.

ENTWISLE, D. (1985). Becoming a parent. In L. L'Abate (Ed.), *The handbook of family psychology and therapy* (Vol. 1). Homewood IL: Dorsey.

ENTWISLE, D. R., & DOERING, S. (1988). The emergent father role. *Sex Roles, 18,* 119–141.

EPSTEIN, J. L. (1983). Selecting friends in contrasting secondary school environments. In J. L. Epstein & M. L. Karweit (Eds.), *Friends in school.* New York: Academic Press.

EPSTEIN, L. H., & WING, R. R. (1987). Behavioral treatment of childhood obesity. *Psychological Bulletin, 101,* 331–342.

EPSTEIN, L. H., VALOSKI, A., WING, R. R., & MCCURLEY, J. (1990). Ten-year follow-up of behavioral, family-based treatment for obese children. *Journal of the American Medical Association, 264,* 2519–2523.

ERICSSON, K. A. (1990). Peak performance in sports. In P. B. Baltes & M. M. Baltes (Eds.), *Successful aging: Perspectives from the behavioral sciences.* New York: Cambridge University Press.

ERIKSON, E. H. (1950). *Childhood and society.* New York: Norton.

ERIKSON, E. H. (1959). The problem of ego identity. In E. H. Erikson (Ed.), *Identity and the life cycle: Selected papers (Psychological Issues Monographs, No. 1).*

ERIKSON, E. H. (1964). *Childhood and society* (2nd ed.). New York: Norton.

ERIKSON, E. H. (1968). *Identity, youth, and crisis.* New York: Norton.

ERIKSON, E. H. (1981). On generativity and identity. *Harvard Educational Review, 51,* 249–269.

ERIKSON, E. H. (1984). Reflections on the last stage—and the first. *Psychoanalytic study of the child, 39,* 155–165.

ERIKSON, E. H., & ERIKSON, J. M. (1981). Generativity and identity. *Harvard Educational Review, 51,* 249–269.

ERIKSON, E. H., ERIKSON, J., & KIVNICK, H. (1986). *Vital involvement in old age.* New York: Norton.

ERNST, C., & ANGST, J. (1983). *Birth order: Its influence on personality.* New York: Springer-Verlag.

EVANS, D. W., LECKMAN, J. F., CARTER, A., REZNICK, J. S., HENSHAW, D., KING, R. A., & PAULS, D. (1997). Ritual, habit, and perfectionism: The prevalence and development of compulsive-like behavior in normal young children. *Child Development, 68,* 58–68.

EVANS, D., FUNKENSTEIN, H., ALBERT, M., SCHERR, P., COOK, N., CHOWN, M., HEBERT, L., HENNCKENS, C., & TAYLOR, D. (1989). Prevalence of Alzheimer's disease in a community population of older people. *Journal of the American Medical Association, 262,* 2551–2556.

FAGAN, J. F., III. (1977). Infant recognition memory: Studies in forgetting. *Child Development, 48,* 66–78.

FAGEN, J., PRIGOT, J., CARROLL, M., PIOLI, L., STEIN, A., & FRANCO, A. (1997). Auditory context and memory retrieval in young infants. *Child Development, 68,* 1057–1066.

FAGOT, B. I., LEINBACH, M. A., & O'BOYLE, C. (1992). Gender labeling, gender stereotyping and parenting behaviors. *Developmental Psychology, 28,* 225–231.

FANTZ, R. L. (1958). Pattern vision in young infants. *Psychological Record, 8,* 43–47.

FANTZ, R. L. (1961). The origin of form perception. *Scientific American, 204 (5),* 66–72.

FANTZ, R. L., ORDY, J. M., & UDELF, M. S. (1962). Maturation of pattern vision in infants during the first six months. *Journal of Comparative and Physiological Psychology, 55,* 907–917.

FARBER, J. (1970). *The student as nigger.* New York: Pocket Books.

FARRELL, M. P., & ROSENBERG, S. D. (1981). *Men at midlife.* Boston: Auburn House.

FARVER, J. A. M., & SHIN, Y. L. (1997). Social pretend play in Korean- and Anglo-American preschoolers. *Child Development, 68,* 544–556.

FAULKNER, A. H., & CRANSTON, K. (1998). Correlates of same-sex sexual behavior in a random sample of Massachusetts high school students. *American Journal of Public Health, 88,* 262–266.

FEATHERMAN, D., HOGAN, D., & SORENSON, A. (1984). Entry into adulthood: Profiles of young men in the fifties. In *Lifespan development and behavior* (Vol. 6). New York: Academic Press.

FEATHERSTONE, M., & HEPWORTH, M. (1985). The male menopause: Lifestyle and sexuality. *Maturitas, 7 (3),* 235–246.

FEDOR-FREYBERGH, P., & VOGEL, M. L. V. (1988). *Prenatal and perinatal psychology and medicine.* Carnforth, UK: Parthenon.

FEHR, B. (1996). *Friendship processes.* Thousand Oaks, CA: Sage.

FEIN, G. G. (1981). Pretend play in childhood: An integrated review. *Child Development, 52,* 1095–1118.

FEIN, G. G. (1984). The self-building potential of pretend play, or "I gotta fish all by myself." In T. D. Yawkey & A. D. Pellegrini (Eds.), *Child's play.* Hillsdale, NJ: Erlbaum.

FEINGOLD, A. (1988). Cognitive gender differences are disappearing. *American Psychologist, 43,* 95–103.

FEIRING, C., LEWIS, M., & STARR, M. D. (1984). Indirect affects and infants' reactions to strangers. *Developmental Psychology, 20,* 485–491.

FELGNER, T. (1997). Nonviral strategies for gene therapy. *Scientific American, 276 (6),* 102–106.

FELICIAN, O., & SANDSON, T. A. (1999). The neurobiology and pharmacotherapy of Alzheimer's disease. *Journal of Neuropsychiatry & Clinical Neurosciences, 11,* 19–31.

FENSON, L., DALE, P. S., REZNICK, S., BATES, E., THAL, D. J., & PETHICK, S. J. (1994). Variability in early communicative development. *Monographs of the Society for Research in Child Development, 59 (5).*

FERBER, M. (1982). Labor market participation of young married women: Causes and effects. *Journal of Marriage and the Family, 44,* 457–468.

FERBER, M., GREEN, C., & SPAITH, J. (1986). Work power and earnings of women and men. *American Economic Review, 76,* 53–56.

FERGUSON, T. J., EYRE, H. L., STEGGE, H., SORENSON, C. B., & EVERTON, R. (1997). *The distinct roles of shame and guilt in childhood psychopathology.* Paper presented at the biennual meeting of the Society for Research in Child Development, Washington, DC.

FERLEGER, N., GLENWICK, D. S., GAINES, R. R. W., & GREEN, A. H. (1988). Identifying correlates of reabuse in maltreating parents. *Child Abuse and Neglect, 12,* 41–49.

FIATARONE, M. A., O'NEILL, E. F., RYAN, N. D., CLEMENTS, K. M., SOLARES, G. R., NELSON, M. E., ROBERTS, S. B., KEHAYIAS, J. J., LIPSITZ, L. A., AND EVANS, W. J. (1994). Exercise training and nutritional supplementation for physical frailty in very elderly people. *New England Journal of Medicine, 330,* 1769–1775.

FIELD, T. M. (1977). Effects of early separation, interactive deficits, and experimental manipulations on infant–mother face-to-face interaction. *Child Development, 48,* 763–771.

FIELD, T. M. (1978). Interaction behaviors of primary vs. secondary caretaker fathers. *Developmental Psychology, 14,* 183–184.

FIELD, T. M. (1979). Interaction patterns of preterm and term infants. In T. M. Field (Ed.), *Infants born at risk.* New York: Spectrum.

FIELD, T. M. (1986). Models for reactive and chronic depression in infancy. In E. Tronick & T. M. Field (Eds.), *New directions for child development, 34.* San Francisco: Jossey-Bass.

FIELD, T. M. (1991). Quality infant day-care and grade school behavior and performance. *Child Development, 62,* 863–870.

FIELD, T. M., WOODSON, R., GREENBERG, R., & COHEN, D. (1982). Discrimination and imitation of facial expressions by neonates. *Science, 218,* 179–181.

FIELDING, J. E., & WILLIAMS, C. A. (1991). Adolescent pregnancy in the United States: A review and recommendations for clinicians and research needs. *American Journal of Preventive Medicine, 7,* 47–51.

FIELDS, M. V., & SPANGLER, K. L. (1995). *Let's begin reading right: Developmentally appropriate beginning literacy* (3rd ed). Englewood Cliffs, NJ: Merrill.

FINGERMAN, K. L. (1998). The good, the bad, and the worrisome: Emotional complexities in grandparent's experiences with individual grandchildren. *Family Relations, 47,* 403–412.

FINKELHOR, D. (1984). *Child sexual abuse: New theory and practice.* New York: Free Press.

FISCHER, D. H. (1978). *Growing old in America.* New York: Oxford University Press.

FISCHER, J. L., SOLLIE, D. L., & MORROW, K. B. (1986). Social networks in male and female adolescents. *Journal of Adolescent Research, 6,* 1–14.

FISCHMAN, M. W. (2000). Informed consent. In B. D. Sales & S. Folkman (Eds.), *Ethics in research with human participants.* Washington, DC: American Psychological Association.

FISKE, M., & CHIRIBOGA, D. A. (1990). *Change and continuity in adult life.* San Francisco: Jossey-Bass.

FITZGERALD, B. (1999). Children of lesbian and gay parents: A review of the literature. *Marriage and Family Review, 29,* 57–75.

FIVUSH, R., & HUDSON, J. A. (1990). *Knowing and remembering in young children.* New York: Cambridge University Press.

FLAKS, D. K., FICHER, I., MASTERPASQUA, F., & JOSEPH, G. (1995). Lesbians choosing motherhood: A comparative study of lesbian and heterosexual parents and their children. *Developmental Psychology, 31,* 105–114.

FLASTE, R. (1988). The myth about teenagers. *New York Times Magazine, 137* (October 16), 19, 76, 82, 85.

FLAVELL, J. H. (1963). *The developmental psychology of Jean Piaget.* Princeton, NJ: Van Nostrand.

FLAVELL, J. H. (1985). *Cognitive Development* (2nd ed.). Upper Saddle River, NJ: Prentice Hall.

FLAVELL, J. H., FLAVELL, E. R., & GREEN, F. L. (1987). Young children's knowledge about the apparent-real and pretend-real distinctions. *Developmental Psychology, 23,* 816–822.

FLAVELL, J. H., GREEN, F., & FLAVELL, E. R. (1986). Development of knowledge about the appearance-reality distortion. *Monographs of the Society for Research in Child Development, 212.*

FLAVELL, J. H., MILLER, P. H. & MILLER, S. A. (1993). *Cognitive Development.* Englewood Cliffs, NJ: Prentice Hall.

FLETCHER, K. L., & BRAY, N. W. (1997). Instructional and contextual effects on external memory strategy use in young children. *Journal of Experimental Child Psychology, 67,* 204–222.

FLINT, M. (1982). Male and female menopause: A cultural put-on. In A. Voda, M. Dennerstein, & S. O'Donnel (Eds.), *Changing perspectives in menopause.* Austin: University of Texas Press.

FLOCCIA, C., CHRISTOPHE, A., & BERTONCINI, J. (1997). High-amplitude sucking and newborns: The quest for underlying mechanisms. *Journal of Experimental Child Psychology, 64,* 175–198.

FLODMARK, C.-E. (1997). Childhood obesity. *Clinical Child Psychology & Psychiatry, 2,* 283–295.

FOGEL, A., DICKSON, K. L., HSU, H., MESSINGER, D., NELSON-GOENS, G. C., & NWOKAH, E. (1997). Communication of smiling and laughter in mother-infant play: Research on emotion from a dynamic systems perspective. In K. C. Barrett (Ed.), *The communication of emotion: Current research from diverse perspectives.* San Francisco: Jossey-Bass.

FOLK, K. F. (1996). Single mothers in various living arrangements: Differences in economic and time resources. *American Journal of Economics and Sociology, 55,* 277–291.

FOLKMAN, S. (2000). Privacy and confidentiality. In B. D. Sales & S. Folkman (Eds.), *Ethics in research with human participants.* Washington, DC: American Psychological Association.

FOLKMAN, S., LAZARUS, R., PIMLEY, S., & NOVACEK, J. (1987). Age differences in stress and coping processes. *Psychology and Aging, 2,* 171–184.

FORMAN, B. I. (1984). Reconsidering retirement: Understanding emerging trends. *The Futurist, 18* (June), 43–47.

FORMAN, G. E., & HILL, F. (1980). *Constructive play: Applying Piaget in the preschool.* Monterey, CA: Brooks/Cole.

FORREST, L., & MIKOLAITIS, N. (1986). The relational component of identity: An expansion of career development theory. *The Career Development Quarterly, 35* (2), 76–85.

FOZARD, J. L. (1990). Vision and hearing in aging. In J. E. Birren & K. W. Schaie (Eds.), *Handbook of the psychology of aging* (3rd ed.). New York: Academic Press.

FOZARD, J. L. (2000). Sensory and cognitive changes with age. In K. W. Schaie & M. Pietrucha (Eds.), *Mobility and transportation in the elderly, Societal impact on aging series.* New York: Springer-Verlag.

FRAIBERG, S. H. (1974). Blind infants and their mothers: An examination of the sign system. In M. Lewis & L. Rosenblum (Eds.), *The effect of the infant on its caregiver.* New York: Wiley.

FRAUENGLASS, M. H., & DIAZ, R. M. (1985). Self-regulatory functions of children's private speech: A critical analysis of recent challenges to Vygotsky's theory. *Developmental Psychology, 21,* 357–364.

FREEMAN, S. F. N., & HODAPP, R. M. (2000). Educating children with Down syndrome. Linking behavioral characteristics to intervention strategies. *Down Syndrome Quarterly, 5,* 1–9.

FRENKEL-BRUNSWIK, E. (1963). Adjustments and reorientation in the course of the life span. In R. G. Kuhlen & G. G. Thompson (Eds.), *Psychological studies of human development* (2nd ed.). New York: Appleton-Century-Crofts.

FREUD, A. (1946). *The ego and the mechanisms of defence.* NY: International Universities Press.

FREUD, A. (1958). Adolescence. In *Psychoanalytic study of the child* (Vol. 13). New York: International Universities Press.

FREUD, A., & DANN, S. (1951). An experiment in group up-bringing. In R. S. Eisler, A. Freud, H. Hartmann & E. Kris (Eds.), *The psychoanalytic study of the child* (Vol. 6). New York International Universities Press.

FREUD, S. (1920/1922). *Beyond the pleasure principle.* London: The International Psycho-Analytical Press.

FREUD, S. (1923/1960). *The ego and the id.* New York: Norton.

FREUD, S. (1924/1964). *A general introduction to psycho-analysis.* New York: Washington Square Press.

FREUDENBERGER, H., & RICHELSON, G. (1980). *Burnout: The high cost of high achievement.* New York: Anchor Press/Doubleday.

FRIED, P. A., & OXORN, H. (1980). *Smoking for two: Cigarettes and pregnancy.* New York: Free Press.

FRIED, P. A., WATKINSON, B., & GRAY, R. (1998). Differential effects on cognitive functioning in 9- to 12-year-olds prenatally exposed to cigarettes and marihuana. *Neurotoxicology and Teratology, 20,* 293–306.

FRIEDLANDER, M., & SIEGEL, S. (1990). Separation-individuation difficulties and cognitive-behavior indicators of eating disorders among college women. *Journal of Counseling Psychology, 37,* 74–78.

FRIEDLER, G. (1996). Paternal exposures: Impact on reproductive and developmental outcome: An overview. *Pharmacology, Biochemistry, and Behavior, 55,* 691–700.

FRIEDMANN, T. (1997). Overcoming the obstacles to gene therapy. *Scientific American, 276 (6),* 96–101.

FRIES, J. F., & CRAPO, L. M. (1981). *Vitality and aging.* San Francisco: Freeman.

FRISCH, R. E. (1988). Fatness and fertility. *Scientific American, 258* (3) 88–95.

FUNG, H., CARSTENSEN, L. L., & LUTZ, A. (1999). The influence of time on social preferences: Implications for life-span development. *Psychology and Aging, 14,* 595–604.

FURST, K. (1983). *Origins and evolution of women's dreams in early adulthood.* Unpublished doctoral dissertation. California School of Professional Psychology, Berkeley.

FURSTENBERG, F. F., JR. (1987). The new extended family: The experience of parents and children after remarriage. In K. Pasley & M. Ihinger-Tallman (Eds.), *Remarriage and stepparenting: Current research and theory.* New York: Guilford.

GABBARD, C., DEAN, M., & HAENSLY, P. (1991). Foot preference behavior during early childhood. *Journal of Applied Developmental Psychology, 12,* 131–137.

GALINSKY, E., & STEIN, P. J. (1990). The impact of human resource policies on employees. *Journal of Family Issues, 11,* 368–383.

GALINSKY, E. (1980). *Between generations: The six stages of parenthood.* New York: Times Books.

GALLAGHER, D. (1987). Bereavement. In G. L. Maddox, R. C. Atchley, & R. J. Corsini (Eds.), *The encyclopedia of aging.* New York: Springer-Verlag.

GALLAGHER, J. M. (1973). Cognitive development and learning in the adolescent. In J. F. Adams (Ed.), *Understanding adolescence* (2nd ed.). Boston: Allyn & Bacon.

GALLAGHER, W. (1993). Midlife myths. *Atlantic, 271* (May), 51–55, 58–62, 65, 68–69.

GALLER, J. R. (1984). *Human nutrition: A comprehensive treatise (Vol. 5): Nutrition and behavior.* New York: Plenum.

GANONG, L. H., & COLEMAN, M. (1994). *Remarried family relationships.* Thousand Oaks, CA: Sage.

GANONG, L. H., & COLEMAN, M. (1997). How society views stepfamilies. *Marriage and Family Review, 26,* 85–106.

GARBARINO, J. (2000). The soul of fatherhood. *Marriage and Family Review, 29*(2–3), 11–21.

GARBARINO, J., KOSTELNY, K., & DUBROW, N. (1991). What children can tell us about living in danger. *American Psychologist, 36,* 376–383.

GARBARINO, J., SEBES, J., & SCHELLENBACH, C. (1984). Families at risk for destructive parent–child relations in adolescence. *Child Development, 55,* 174–183.

GARDINER, H. W., MUTTER, J. D., & KOSMITZKI, C. (1998). *Lives across cultures: Cross-cultural human development.* Boston: Allyn and Bacon.

GARDNER, H. (1973). *The quest for mind: Piaget, Levi-Strauss, and the structuralist movement.* New York: Random House.

GARDNER, H. (1983). *Frames of mind.* New York: Basic Books.

GARDNER, H., & WALTERS, J. (1993). A rounded version. In H. Gardner (Ed.), *Multiple intelligences: The theory in practice.* New York: Basic Books.

GARDNER, J. M., & KARMEL, B. Z. (1984). Arousal effects on visual preference in neonates. *Developmental Psychology, 20,* 374–377.

GARLAND, A. F., & ZIGLER, E. (1993). Adolescent suicide prevention: Current research and social policy implications. *American Psychologist, 48,* 169–182.

GARROD, A., BEAL, C., & SHIN, P. (1989). *The development of moral orientation in elementary school children.* Paper presented at the biennial meeting of the Society for Research in Child Development, Kansas City.

GARTNER, A. (1984). Widower self-help groups: A preventive approach. *Social Policy, 14* (3), 37–38.

GARVEY, C. (1977). *Play.* Cambridge, MA: Harvard University Press.

GARVEY, C. (1984). *Children's talk.* Cambridge, MA: Harvard University Press.

GARVEY, C. (1990). *Play.* Cambridge, MA: Harvard University Press.

GATHERCOLE, S. E. (1998). The development of memory. *Journal of Child Psychology and Psychiatry and Allied Disciplines, 39,* 3–27.

GATZ, M., BENGTSON, V., & BLUM, M. (1990). Caregiving families. In J. Birren & K. W. Schaie (Eds.), *Handbook of the psychology of aging* (3rd ed.). San Diego: Academic Press.

GE, X., CONGER, R. D., & ELDER, G. H., JR. (1996). Coming of age too early: Pubertal influences on girls' vulnerability to psychological distress. *Child Development, 67,* 3386–3400.

GEARY, D. C., & BJORKLUND, D. F. (2000). Evolutionary developmental psychology. *Child Development, 71,* 57–65.

GEE, E. M. (1986). The life course of Canadian women: A historical and demographic analysis. *Social Indicators Research, 18,* 263–283.

GEE, E. M. (1987). Historical change in the family life course of Canadian men and women. In V. Marshall (Ed.), *Aging in Canada* (2nd ed.). Markham, ON: Fitzhenry & Whiteside.

GEE, E. M. (1988). *The changing demography of intergenerational relations in Canada.* Paper presented at the annual meeting of the Canadian Association of Gerontology, Halifax.

GELIS, J. (1989) The child: From anonymity to individuality. In R. Chartier (Ed.) *A history of a private life, Vol. 3: Passions of the Renaissance.* Cambridge, MA: Belknap Press of Harvard University Press.

GELMAN, R., & GALLISTEL, C. R. (1986). *The child's understanding of number.* Cambridge, MA: Harvard University Press.

GELMAN, S. A. (1998). Categories in children's thinking. *Young Children, (1),* 20–26.

GENESEE, F. (1989). Early bilingual development: One language or two? *Journal of Child Language, 16,* 161–179.

GEORGE, T. P., & HARTMANN, D. P. (1996). Friendship networks of unpopular, average, and popular children. *Child Development, 67,* 2301–2316.

GERRARD, M. (1987). Sex, sex guilt, and contraceptive use revisited: The 1980s. *Journal of Personality and Social Psychology, 52,* 975–980.

GESELL, A. (1940). *The first five years of life: The preschool years.* New York: Harper & Brothers.

GESELL, A., & AMES, L. B. (1947). The development of handedness. *Journal of Genetic Psychology, 70,* 155–175.

GIBBONS, D. C. (1976). *Delinquent behavior* (2nd ed.). Englewood Cliffs, NJ: Prentice Hall.

GIBSON, E. J., & WALK, R. D. (1960). The "visual cliff." *Scientific American, 202 (4),* 64–71.

GIBSON, E., & WALKER, A. S. (1984). Development of knowledge of visual–tactile affordances of substance. *Child Development, 55,* 453–456.

GIBSON, R. C. (1986). Older black Americans. *Generations, 10 (4),* 35–39.

GIGY, L., & KELLY, J. B. (1992). Reasons for divorce: Perspectives of divorcing men and women. *Journal of Divorce and Remarriage, 18,* 169–187.

GILFORD, R. (1986). Marriages in later life. *Generations, 10 (4),* 16–20.

GILLIGAN, C. (1982). *In a different voice: Psychological theory and women's development.* Cambridge, MA: Harvard University Press.

GILLIGAN, C. (1987). Adolescent development reconsidered. In C. E. Irwin, Jr. (Ed.), *New Directions for Child Development, 37,* 63–92. San Francisco: Jossey-Bass.

GILLIGAN, C., & ATTANUCCI, J. (1994). Two moral orientations: Gender differences and similarities. In B. Puka (Ed.), *Caring voices and women's moral frames: Gilligan's view.* New York: Garland.

GILLIS, J. J. (1992). Attention deficit disorder in reading-disabled twins: Evidence for a genetic etiology. *Journal of Abnormal Child Psychology, 20,* 303.

GINSBURG, E. (1972). Toward a theory of occupational choice: A restatement. *Vocational Guidance Quarterly, 20,* 169–176.

GIORDANO, J., & BECKMAN, K. (1985). The aged within a family context: Relationships, roles, and events. In L. L'Abate (Ed.), *The handbook of family psychology and therapy* (Vol. 1). Homewood, IL: Dorsey.

GLASER, R. (1963). Instructional technology and the measurement of learning outcomes: Some questions. *American Psychologist, 18,* 519–521.

GLASER, R. (1987). Thoughts on expertise. In C. Schooler & K. W. Schaie (Eds.), *Cognitive functioning and social structure over the life course.* Norwood, NJ: Ablex.

GOETTING, A. (1982). The six stations of remarriage: Developmental tasks of remarriage after divorce. *Family Relations, 31,* 213–222.

GLOBERMAN, J. (1996). Daughters- and sons-in-law caring for relatives with Alzheimer's disease. *Family Relations, 45,* 37–45.

GOLDBERG, S. (1972). Infant care and growth in urban Zambia. *Human Development, 15,* 77–89.

GOLDBERG, S. (1979). Premature birth: Consequences for the parent–infant relationship. *American Scientist, 67,* 214–220.

GOLDBERG, S., & LEWIS, M. (1969). Play behavior in the year-old infant: Early sex differences. *Child Development, 40,* 21–31.

GOLDBERG, S., LOJKASEK, M., GARTNER, G., & CORTER, C. (1989). Maternal responsiveness and social development in preterm infants. In M. H. Bornstein (Ed.), *New directions for child development, 43.* San Francisco: Jossey-Bass.

GOLDIN-MEADOW, S., & MYLANDER, C. (1984). Gestural communication in deaf children: The effects and noneffects of parental input on early language development. *Monographs of the Society for Research in Child Development, 49* (3–4).

GOLDSTEIN, A. P. (1999). Aggression reduction strategies: Effective and ineffective. *School Psychology Quarterly, 14,* 40–58.

GOLINKOFF, R. M., & HIRSH-PASEK, K. (1999). *How babies talk: The magic and mystery of language in the first three years of life.* New York: Dutton.

GONCU, A. (1993). Development of intersubjectivity in social pretend play. *Human Development, 36,* 185–198.

GONCZ, L. (1988). A research study on the relation between early bilingualism and cognitive development. *Psychologische-Beitrage, 30,* 75–91.

GONYEA, J. G. (1998). Midlife and menopause: Uncharted territories for Baby Boomer women. *Generations, 21, (2),* 87–89.

GOODCHILDS, J. D., & ZELLMAN, G. L. (1984). Sexual signalling and sexual aggression in adolescent relationships. In N. M. Malmuth & E. D. Donnerstein (Eds.), *Pornography and sexual aggression.* New York: Academic Press.

GOODE, W. J. (1970). *World revolution and family patterns.* New York: Free Press.

GOODLIN, R. C. (1979). History of fetal monitoring. *American Journal of Obstetrics and Gynecology, 133,* 323–347.

GOODMAN, M. (1980). Toward a biology of menopause. *Signs, 5 (4),* 739–753.

GOODWIN, J. M., & SACHS, R. G. (1996). Child abuse in the etiology of dissociative disorders. In L. K. Michelson & W. J. Ray (Eds.), *Handbook of dissociation: Theoretical, empirical, and clinical perspectives.* New York: Plenum.

GOPNIK, A., MELTZOFF, A. N., & KUHL, P. K. (1999). *The scientist in the crib: Minds, brains, and how children learn.* New York: Morrow.

GOTTMAN, J. M. (1983). How children become friends. *Monographs of the Society for Research in Child Development, 48.*

GOTTMAN, J. M., KATZ, L. F., & HOOVEN, C. (1996). Parental meta-emotion philosophy and the emotional life of families: Theoretical models and preliminary data. *Journal of Family Psychology, 10,* 243–268.

GOULD, R. L. (1978). *Transformations, growth and change in adult life.* New York: Simon & Schuster.

GOULD, S. J. (1981). *The mismeasure of man.* New York: Norton.

GOWING, M. K., KRAFT, J. D., & QUICK, J. C. (Eds.) (1997). Foreword to *The new organizational reality: Downsizing, restructuring, and revitalization.* Washington, DC: American Psychological Association.

GRANTHAM-MCGREGOR, S., POWELL, C., WALKER, S., CHANG, S., & FLETCHER, P. (1994). The long-term follow-up of severely malnourished children who participated in an intervention program. *Child Development, 65,* 428–439.

GRATCH, G., & SCHATZ, J. (1987). Cognitive development: The relevance of Piaget's infancy books. In J. Osofsky (Ed.), *Handbook of infant development* (2nd ed.). New York: Wiley.

GRAZIANO, W. G., LEONE, C., MUSSER, L. M., & LAUTENSCHLAGER, G. J. (1987). Self-monitoring in children: A differential approach to social development. *Developmental Psychology, 23,* 571–576.

GREB, A. (1998). Multiculturalism and the practice of genetic counseling. In D. L. Baker, J. L. Schuette, & W. R. Ulhlman, (Eds.), *A guide to genetic counseling.* New York: Wiley-Liss.

GREEN, R. G., STONNER, D, & SHOPE, G. L. (1975). The facilitation of aggression by aggression: Evidence against the catharsis hypothesis. *Journal of Personality and Social Psychology, 31,* 721–726.

GREEN, R. M. (2000). Should we be working toward human cloning for infertility treatment? *Contemporary OB/GYN, 45 (5),* 51–54.

GREENBERG, J., & BECKER, M. (1988). Aging parents as family resources. *The Gerontologist, 28,* 786–791.

GREENBERG, M., & MORRIS, N. (1974). Engrossment: The newborn's impact upon the father. *American Journal of Orthopsychiatry, 44,* 520–531.

GREENE, A. L. (1990). Great expectations: Construction of the life course during adolescence. *Journal of Youth and Adolescence, 19,* 289–303.

GREENE, A. L., & BROOKS, J. (1985). *Children's perceptions of stressful life events.* Paper presented at the biennual meeting of the Society for Research in Child Development, Toronto.

GREENSPAN, S., & GREENSPAN, N. (1985). *First feelings.* New York: Penguin.

GREENSPAN, S.I., & LEWIS, N.B. (1999). *Building healthy minds: The six experiences that create intelligence and emotional growth in babies and young children.* Cambridge, MA: Perseus.

GREENWOOD, S. (1984). *Menopause, naturally: Preparing for the second half of life.* San Francisco: Volcano Press.

GREIF, E. B., & ULMAN, K. J. (1982). The psychological impact of menarche on early adolescent females: A review of the literature. *Child Development, 53,* 1413–1430.

GRIMM-THOMAS, K., & PERRY-JENKINS, M. (1994). All in a day's work: Job experiences, self-esteem, and fathering in working-class families. *Family Relations, 43,* 174–181.

GRODSTEIN, F., STAMPFER, M. J., COLDITZ, G. A., WILLETT, W. C., MANSON, J. E., JOFFE, M., ROSNER, B., FUCHS, C., HANKINSON, S. E.,

HUNTER, D. J., HENNEKENS, C. H., & SPEIZER, F. E. (1997). Postmenopausal hormone therapy and mortality. *New England Journal of Medicine, 336,* 1769–1775.

GRONLUND, G. (1995). Bringing the DAP message to kindergarten and primary teachers. *Young Children, 50* (5), 4–13.

GROSJEAN, F. (1982). *Life with two languages: An introduction to bilingualism.* Cambridge, MA: Harvard University Press.

GROSS, J. J., CARSTENSEN, L. L., PASUPATHI, M., TSAI, J., GOETESTAM-SKORPEN, C., & HSU, A. Y. C. (1997). Emotion and aging: Experience, expression, and control. *Psychology & Aging, 12,* 590–599.

GROSSMAN, F. K., POLLACK, W. S., & GOLDING, E. (1988). Fathers and children: Predicting the quality and quantity of fathering. *Developmental Psychology, 24,* 82–91.

GROTEVANT, H. D., & COOPER, C. R. (1985). Patterns of interaction in family relationships and the development of identity exploration in adolescence. *Child Development, 56,* 415–428.

GRUSEC, J. E., & ARNASON, L. (1982). Consideration for others: Approaches to enhancing altruism. In S. Moore & C. Cooper (Eds.), *The young child: Reviews of research* (Vol. 3). Washington, DC: National Association for the Education of Young Children.

GUELZOW, M. G., BIRD, G. W., & KOBALL, E. H. (1991). An exploratory path analysis of the stress process for dual-career men and women. *Journal of Marriage and the Family, 53,* 151–164.

GUNNAR, M. R. (1989). Studies of the human infant's adrenocortical response to potentially stressful events. In M. Lewis & J. Worobey (Eds.) *New Directions for Child Development, 45.* San Francisco: Jossey-Bass.

GUTMANN, D. L. (1964). An exploration of ego configurations in middle and later life. In B. L. Neugarten (Ed.), *Personality in middle and late life: Empirical studies.* New York: Atherton Press.

GUTMANN, D. L. (1975). Parenthood: A key to the comparative study of the life cycle. In N. Datan & L. H. Ginsberg (Eds.), *Life-span developmental psychology: Normative life crises.* New York: Academic Press.

GUTMANN, D. L. (1994). *Reclaimed powers: Men and women in later life.* Evanston, IL: Northwestern University Press.

GUTMANN, S. (1996). Death and the maiden. *New Republic, 249* (4), 20–31.

HABER, D. (1984). Church-based programs for black caregivers of noninstitutionalized elders. *Journal of Gerontological Social Work, 7,* 43–49.

HADADIAN, A. (1995). Attitudes toward deafness and security of attachment relationships among young deaf children and their parents. *Early Education and Development, 6,* 181–191.

HAGEN, J. W., LONGEWARD, R. H. J., & KAIL, R. V., JR. (1975). Cognitive perspectives on the development of memory. In H. W. Reese (Ed.), *Advances in child development and behavior* (Vol. 10). New York: Academic Press.

HAGESTAD, G. O. (1985). Continuity and connectedness. In V. L. Bengston & J. Robert-

son (Eds.), *Grandparenthood.* Beverly Hills, CA: Sage.

HAGESTAD, G. O. (1987). Able elderly in the family context: Changes, chances, and challenges. *The Gerontologist, 27,* 417–422.

HAGESTAD, G. O. (1990). Social perspectives on the life course. In R. H. Binstock & L. K. George (Eds.), *Handbook of aging and the social sciences* (3rd ed.). New York: Academic Press.

HALEY, W. E., ROTH, D. L., COLETON, M. I., FORD, G. R., WEST, C. A. C., COLLINS, R. P., & ISOBE, T. L. (1996). Appraisal, coping, and social support as mediators of well-being in Black and White family caregivers of patients with Alzheimer's disease. *Journal of Consulting & Clinical Psychology, 64,* 121–129.

HALL, L. A., SACHS, B., & RAYENS, M. K. (1998). Mothers' potential for child abuse: The roles of childhood abuse and social resources. *Nursing Research, 47,* 87–95.

HALL, W. M., & CAIRNS, R. B. (1984). Aggressive behavior in children: An outcome of modeling or social reciprocity? *Developmental Psychology, 20,* 739–745.

HALLINAN, M. T., & TEIXEIRA, R. A. (1987). Students' interracial friendships: Individual characteristics, structural effects, and racial differences. *American Journal of Education, 95,* 563–583.

HALPERN, D. F. (1986). *Sex differences in cognitive abilities.* Hillsdale, NJ: Erlbaum.

HANNAH, M., & HANNAH, W. (1996). Caesarean section or vaginal birth for breech presentation at term: We need better evidence as to which is better. *British Medical Journal, 312,* 1433–1434.

HANSEN, L. S. (1974). Counseling and career (self) development of women. *Focus on Guidance, 7,* 1–15.

HANSON, D., CONAWAY, L. P., & CHRISTOHER, J. S. (1989). Victims of child physical abuse. In R. T. Ammerman & M. Hersen (Eds.), *Treatment of family violence.* New York: Wiley.

HARKNESS, S., & SUPER, C. M. (1983). *The cultural structuring of children's play in a rural African community.* Paper presented at the annual meeting of the Association for the Anthropological Study of Play, Baton Rouge, LA.

HARLAN, L. C., BERNSTEIN, A. B., & KESSLER, L. G. (1991). Cervical cancer screening: Who is not screened and why? *American Journal of Public Health, 81,* 885–890.

HARLOW, H. F. (1959). Love in infant monkeys. *Scientific American, 201* (6), 68–74.

HARLOW, H. F., & HARLOW, M. K. (1962). Social deprivation in monkeys. *Scientific American, 208* (5), 137–146.

HARMAN, D., HOLLIDAY, R., & MEYDANI, M. (Eds.) (1998). *Towards prolongation of the healthy life span: Practical approaches to intervention.* New York: New York Academy of Sciences.

HARRÉ, R. (January 1980). What's in a nickname? *Psychology Today, 13 (1),* 78–84.

HARRIS, B. (1979). Whatever happened to Little Albert? *American Psychologist, 34,* 151–160.

HARRIS, L., & ASSOCIATES (1978). Myths and realities of life for older Americans. In R. Gross, B. Gross, & S. Seidman (Eds.), *The*

new old: Struggling for decent aging. Garden City, NY: Anchor Press/Doubleday.

HARRIS, P. L., BROWN, E., MARRIOTT, C., WHITTALL, S., & HARMER, S. (1991). Monsters, ghosts and witches: Testing the limits of the fantasy–reality distinction in young children. *British Journal of Developmental Psychology, 9,* 105–123.

HARRIS, R., ELLICOTT, A., & HOMMES, D. (1986). The timing of psychosocial transitions and changes in women's lives: An examination of women aged 45 to 60. *Journal of Personality and Social Psychology, 51,* 409–416.

HARRIS, Y. R., & HAMIDULLAH, J. (1993). Maternal and child utilization of memory strategies. *Current Psychology: Developmental, Learning, Personality, Social, 12,* 81–94.

HARRISON, A. O., WILSON, M. N., PINE, C. J., CHAN, S. Q., & BURIEL, R. (1990). Family ecologies of ethnic minority children. *Child Development, 61,* 347–362.

HART, S. N., & BRASSARD, M. R. (1991). Psychological maltreatment: Progress achieved. *Development and Psychopathology, 3,* 61–70.

HART, S. N., GERMAIN, R. B., & BRASSARD, M. R. (1987). The challenge: To better understand and combat psychological maltreatment of children and youth. In M. R. Brassard, R. Germain, & S. N. Hart (Eds.), *Psychological maltreatment of children and youth.* New York: Pergamon.

HARTER, S. (1982). The perceived competence scale for children. *Child Development, 53,* 87–97.

HARTER, S. (1983). Developmental perspectives on the self system. In P. H. Mussen (Ed.), *Handbook of child psychology* (4th ed., Vol. 4). New York: Wiley.

HARTER, S. (1988). Developmental processes in the construction of the self. In T. D. Yawkey & J. E. Johnson (Eds.), *Integrative processes and socialization: Early to middle childhood.* Hillsdale, NJ: Erlbaum.

HARTUP, W. W. (1970). Peer interaction and social organization. In P. H. Mussen (ed.), *Carmichael's manual of child psychology* (3rd ed., Vol. 2). New York: Wiley.

HARTUP, W. W. (1983). Peer relations. In P. H. Mussen (Ed.), *Handbook of child psychology* (4th ed., Vol. 4). New York: Wiley.

HARTUP, W. W. (1989). Social relationships and their developmental significance. *American Psychologist, 44,* 120–126.

HARTUP, W. W. (1993). Adolescents and their friends. In B. Laursen (Ed.), *New Directions for Child Development, 60,* 3–19. San Francisco: Jossey-Bass.

HARTUP, W. W. (1995). Personality development in social context. *Annual Review of Psychology, 46,* 655–687.

HARTUP, W. W. (1996). The company they keep: Friendships and their developmental significance. *Child Development, 67,* 1–13.

HARWOOD, R. L., SCHOELMERICH, A., SCHULZE, P. A., & GONZALEZ, Z. (1999). Cultural differences in maternal beliefs and behaviors: A study of middle-class Anglo and Puerto Rican mother-infant pairs in four everyday situations. *Child Development, 70,* 1005–1016.

HASKETT, M. E., & KISTNER, J. A. (1991). Social interactions and peer perceptions of young physically abused children. *Child Development, 62,* 979–990.

HASS, A. (1979). *Teenage sexuality: A survey of teenage sexual behavior.* New York: Macmillan.

HASSELHORN, M. (1992). Task dependency and the role of category typicality and metamemory in the development of an organizational strategy. *Child Development, 63,* 202–214.

HASTE, H., & TORNEY-PURTA, J. (Eds.) (1992). The development of political understanding: A new perspective. In H. Haste & J. Torney-Purta (Eds.), *New directions for child development, 56.* San Francisco: Jossey-Bass.

HASTINGS, P.D., & ZAHN-WAXLER, C. (1998). *Psychophysiological and socialization predictors of empathy and externalizing problems in middle childhood.* Paper presented at the annual convention of the American Psychological Association, San Francisco.

HATCH, L. R. (1992). Gender differences in orientation toward retirement from paid labor. *Gender and Society, 6,* 66–85.

HATCH, T. (1997). Getting specific about multiple intelligences. *Educational Leadership, 54,* 26–29.

HAUSER, S. T., BOOK, B. K., HOULIHAN, J., POWERS, S., WEISS-PERRY, B., FOLLANSBEE, D., JACOBSON, A. M., & NOAM, G. (1987). Sex differences within the family: Studies of adolescent and parent family interactions. *Journal of Youth and Adolescence, 16,* 199–220.

HAVIGHURST, R. J. (1953). *Human development and education.* New York: Longman.

HAVIGHURST, R. J. (1964). Stages of vocational development. In H. Borow (Ed.), *Man in a world at work.* Boston: Houghton Mifflin.

HAVIGHURST, R. J. (1972). *Developmental tasks and education* (3rd ed.). New York: McKay.

HAWKINS, J. A., & BERNDT, T. J. (1985). *Adjustment following the transition to junior high school.* Paper presented at the biennial meeting of the Society for Research in Child Development.

HAYNE, H., & ROVEE-COLLIER, C. (1995). The organization of reactivated memory in infancy. *Child Development, 66,* 893–906.

HAYNE, H., BONIFACE, J., & BARR, R. (2000). The development of declarative memory in human infants: Age-related changes in deferred imitation. *Behavioral Neuroscience, 114,* 77–83.

HAYWARD, M. D., FRIEDMAN, S., & CHEN, H. (1998). *Journals of Gerontology, 53,* S91–S103.

HAZEN, N. L., & LOCKMAN, J. J. (1989). Skill in context. In J. J. Lockman & N. L. Hazen (Eds.), *Action in social context: Perspectives on early development.* New York: Plenum.

HEAVEN, P. C. L., & OXMAN, L. N. (1999). Human values, conservatism and stereotypes of homosexuals. *Personality and Individual Differences, 27,* 109–118.

HEBB, D. O. (1966). *A textbook of psychology.*

HECHTMAN, L. (1989). Teenage mothers and their children: Risks and problems: A review. *Canadian Journal of Psychology, 34,* 569–575.

HEIDRICH, S. D., & RYFF, C. D. (1993a). Physical and mental health in later life: The self-system as mediator. *Psychology and Aging, 8,* 327–338.

HEIDRICH, S. D., & RYFF, C. D. (1993b). The role of social comparisons processes in the psychological adaptation of elderly adults. *Journals of Gerontology, 48,* 127–136.

HEILMAN, M. E. (1995). Sex stereotypes and their effects in the workplace: What we know and what we don't know. *Journal of Social Behavior and Personality, 10,* 3–26.

HEIMANN, M., & MELTZOFF, A. N. (1996). Deferred imitation in 9– and 14–month-old infants: A longitudinal study of a Swedish sample. *British Journal of Developmental Psychology, 14,* 55–64.

HELLIGE, J. B. (1993). Unity of thought and action: Varieties of interaction between the left and right cerebral hemispheres. *Current Directions in Psychological Science, 2,* 21–25.

HELMS, J. E., & TALLEYRAND, R. M. (1997). Race is not ethnicity. *American Psychologist, 52,* 1246–1247.

HELSON, R. (1997). The self in middle age. In M. E. Lachman & J. B. James, (Eds.), *Multiple paths of midlife development.* Chicago: University of Chicago Press.

HELSON, R., & PICANO, J. (1990). Is the traditional role bad for women? *Journal of Personality and Social Psychology, 59,* 311–320.

HELWIG, C. C. (1995). Adolescents' and young adults' conceptions of civil liberties: Freedom of speech and religion. *Child Development, 66,* 152–166.

HENDRICKS, M.D., LARSEN, R., & SUAREZ, L. (1999). Folic acid for healthy babies: a primer (Pub. No. 99–0093). Hyattsville, MD: National Center for Environmental Health.

HENNESSY, K. D., RABIDEAU, G. J., CICCHETTI, D., & CUMMINGS, E. M. (1994). Responses of physically abused and nonabused children to different forms of interadult anger. *Child Development, 65,* 815–828.

HENSHAW, S. K. (1998). *U.S. teenage pregnancy statistics.* New York: The Alan Guttmacher Institute.

HEREK, G. M. (2000). The psychology of sexual prejudice. *Current Directions in Psychological Science, 9,* 19–22.

HEREK, G. M., GILLIS, J. R., & COGAN, J. C. (1999). Psychological sequelae of hate-crime victimization among lesbian, gay, and bisexual adults. *Journal of Consulting and Clinical Psychology, 67,* 945–951.

HERNANDEZ, D. J. (1994). Childrens changing access to resources: A historical perspective. *Social Policy Report: Society for Research in Child Development, 8(1),* 1–3.

HERSHBERGER, S. L., PLOMIN, R., & PEDERSEN, N. L. (1995). Traits and metatraits: Their reliability, stability, and shared genetic influence. *Journal of Personality and Social Psychology, 69,* 673–685.

HERSHEY, D. (1974). *Life-span and factors affecting it.* Springfield, IL: Charles C Thomas.

HESS, R. D., & HOLLOWAY, S. D. (1984). Family and school as educational institutions. In R. D. Parker (Ed.), *Review of Child Development Research 7: The Family.* Chicago: University of Chicago Press.

HETHERINGTON, E. M. (1984). Stress and coping in children and families. In A. Doyle, D. Gold, & D. Moskowitz (Eds.), *New direc-*

tions for child development, 24. San Francisco: Jossey-Bass.

HETHERINGTON, E. M. (1992). Coping with marital transitions: A family systems perspective. *Monographs of the Society for Research in Child Development, 57,* 1–14.

HETHERINGTON, E. M. (Ed.) (1999). *Coping with divorce, single parenting, and remarriage: A risk and resiliency perspective.* Mahwah, NJ: Erlbaum.

HETHERINGTON, E. M., & BALTES, P. B. (1988). Child psychology and life-span development. In E. M. Hetherington, R. Lerner, & M. Perlmutter (Eds.), *Child development in life-span perspective.* Hillsdale, NJ: Erlbaum.

HETHERINGTON, E. M., & CAMARA, K. A. (1984). Families in transition: The process of dissolution and reconstitution. In R. D. Parke (Ed.), *Review of child development research* (Vol. 7). New York: Russell Sage Foundation.

HETHERINGTON, E. M., & STANLEY-HAGAN, M. (1999). The adjustment of children with divorced parents: A risk and resiliency perspective. *Journal of Child Psychology and Psyciatry, 40,* 129–140.

HETHERINGTON, E. M., COX, M., & COX, R. (1978). The aftermath of divorce. In J. H. Stevens & M. Athews (Eds.), *Mother–child, father–child relationships.* Washington, DC: National Association for the Education of Young Children.

HETHERINGTON, E. M., STANLEY-HAGAN, M., & ANDERSON, E. R. (1989). Marital transitions: A child's perspective. *American Psychologist, 44,* 303–312.

HILL, J. P. (1987). Research on adolescents and their families past and present. In C. E. Irwin, Jr. (Ed.), *New Directions for Child Development, 37,* 13–32. San Francisco: Jossey-Bass.

HIRSH-PASEK, K., & GOLINKOFF, R. M. (1996). *The origins of grammar.* Cambridge, MA: MIT Press.

HIRSHBERG, L. M. (1990). When infants look to their parents: II. Twelve-month-olds' response to conflicting parental emotional signals. *Child Development, 61,* 1187–1191.

HIRSHBERG, L. M., & SVEJDA, M. (1990). When infants look to their parents: I. Infants' social referencing of mothers compared to fathers. *Child Development, 61,* 1175–1186.

HISCOCK, M., & KINSBOURNE, M. (1987). Specialization of the cerebral hemispheres: Implications for learning. *Journal of Learning Disabilities, 20,* 130–142.

HITE, S. (1976). *The Hite report.* New York: Macmillan.

HO, D. Y., & SAPLOSKY, R. M. (1997). Gene therapy for the nervous systems. *Scientific American, 276 (6),* 116–120.

HOBBES, C. J., WYNNE, J. M., & GELLETLIE, R. (1995). Leeds inquiry into infant deaths: The importance of abuse and neglect in sudden infant death. *Child Abuse Review, 4,* 329–339.

HOCHSCHILD, A. (1989). *The second shift.* New York: Avon Books.

HOCK, E., & LUTZ, W. (1998). Psychological meaning of separation anxiety in mothers and fathers. *Journal of Family Psychology, 2,* 41–55.

HOFFMAN, L. (1984). Psychological separation of late adolescents from their parents. *Journal of Counseling Psychology, 31,* 170–178.

HOFFMAN, M. L. (1970). Moral development. In P. H. Mussen (Ed.), *Carmichael's manual of child psychology* (3rd ed., Vol. 2). New York: Wiley.

HOFFMAN, M. L. (1981). Is altruism part of human nature? *Journal of Personality and Social Psychology, 40,* 121–137.

HOFFMAN, M. L. (1982). Development of prosocial motivation: Empathy and guilt. In N. Eisenberg (Ed.), *The development of prosocial behavior.* San Diego: Academic Press.

HOFFMAN, M. L. (1990). Empathy and justice motivation. *Motivation and Emotion, 14,* 151–171.

HOFFMAN, M. L. (1998). Varieties of empathy-based guilt. In J. Bybee (Ed.), *Guilt and children.* New York: Academic Press.

HOLT, R. R. (1982). Occupational stress. In L. Goldberger & S. Breznity (Eds.), *Handbook of Stress.* New York: Free Press.

HOMGREN, R. A., EISENBERG, N, & FABES, R. A. (1998). The relations of children's situational empathy-related emotions to dispositional prosocial beheavior. *International Journal of Behavior and Development, 22,* 16–19.

HONIG, A. S. (1986). Stress and coping in young children. *Young Children, 41* (5), 50–63.

HOOD, J. C. (1986). The provider role: Its meaning and measurement. *Journal of Marriage and the Family, 48,* 349–359.

HOOK, E. B., & CZEIZEL, A. E. (1997). Can terathanasia explain the protective effect of folic-acid supplementation on birth defects? *The Lancet, 350,* 513–516.

HOPKINS, B. (1991). Facilitating early motor development: An intercultural study of West Indian mothers and their infants living in Britain. In J. K. Nugent, B. M. Lester & T. B. Brazelton (Eds.), *The cultural context of infancy.* Norwood, NJ: Ablex.

HORGAN, J. (1993). Eugenics revisited. *Scientific American, 268* (6), 122–128, 130–131.

HORGAN, J. (1997). Seeking a better way to die. *Scientific American, 276* (5), 100–105.

HORN, J. L. (1982). The theory of fluid and crystallized intelligence in relation to concepts of cognitive psychology and aging in adulthood. In F. I. M. Craik & S. Trehub (Eds.), *Aging and cognitive processes.* New York: Plenum.

HORN, J. L., & DONALDSON, G. (1980). Cognitive development in adulthood. In J. Kagan & O. G. Brim, Jr. (Eds.), *Constancy and change in development.* Cambridge, MA: Harvard University Press.

HORN, M. (1993). Grief re-examined: The AIDS epidemic is confounding the normal work of bereavement. *U.S. News & World Report, 114* (23), 81–84.

HORNEY, K. (1937). *The neurotic personality of our time.* New York: Norton.

HORNSTEIN, N. L., & PUTNAM, F. W. (1996). Abuse and the development of dissociative symptoms and dissociative identity disorder. In C. R. Pfeffer (Ed.), *Severe stress and mental disturbance in children.* Washington, DC: American Psychiatric Press.

HOROWITZ, S. M., KLERMAN, L. V., SUNGKUO, H., AND JEKEL, J. F. (1991). Intergenerational transmission of school age parenthood. *Family Planning Perspectives, 23,* 168–177.

HOSPICE FOUNDATION OF AMERICA (1999). *What is hospice?* Internet document. Hospice Foundation of America home page: www.hospicefoundation.org

HOWARD, J. (1995). You can't get there from here: The need for a new logic in education reform. *Daedalus, 124* (4), 85–93.

HOWELL-WHITE, S. (1997). Choosing a birth attendant: The influences of a woman's childbirth definition. *Social Science and Medicine, 45,* 925–936.

HOWES, C., & OLENICK, M. (1986). Family and child care influences on toddler's compliance. *Child Development, 57,* 202–216.

HOYER, W. J., & PLUDE, D. J. (1980). Attentional and perceptual processes in the study of cognitive aging. In L. W. Poon (Ed.), *Aging in the 1980s.* Washington, DC: American Psychological Association.

HOYERT, D. L., KOCHANEK, K. D., & MURPHY, S. L. (1999). Deaths: Final Data for 1997. *National Vital Statistics Reports, 47* (19). Hyattsville, MD: National Center for Health Statistics.

HUESMANN, L. R., LAGERSPETZ, K., & ERON, L. D. (1984). Intervening variables in the TV violence-aggression relation: Evidence from two countries. *Developmental Psychology, 20,* 746–775.

HUGHES, F. P. (1991b). *Children, play and development.* Boston: Allyn & Bacon.

HUGHES, L. A. (1991a). A conceptual framework for the study of children's gaming. *Play & Culture, 4,* 284–301

HUGHES, M., & DONALDSON, M. (1979). The use of hiding games for studying the coordination of viewpoints. *Educational Review, 31,* 133–140.

HULL, C. L. (1943). *Principles of behavior.* New York: Appleton-Century-Crofts.

HUMANE GENOME ORGANIZATION (HUGO) (2000). Count of mapped genes by chromosome. Internet document. HUGO home page: www.gdb.org

HUMMERT, M. L., GARSTKA, T. A., SHANER, J. L., & STRAHM, S. (1995). Judgments about stereotypes of the elderly. *Research on Aging, 17,* 168–189.

HUMMERT, M. L., MAZLOFF, D., & HENRY, C. (1999). Vocal characteristics of older adults and stereotyping. *Journal of Nonverbal Behavior, 23,* 111–132.

HUNT, J. G., & HUNT, L. L. (1987). Here to play: From families to life-styles. *Journal of Family Issues, 8,* 440–443.

HUNT, M. (1974). *Sexual behavior in the 1970s.* New York: Dell.

HUNTER, S., & SUNDEL, M. (1989). *Midlife myths: Issues, findings, and practice implications.* Newbury Park, CA: Sage.

HUSTON, A. C., WATKINS, B. A., & KUNKEL, D. (1989). Public policy and children's television. *American Psychologist, 44,* 424–433.

HUTCHESON, R. H., JR. (1968). Iron deficiency anemia in Tennessee among rural poor children. *Public Health Reports, 83,* 939–943.

HUTCHINSON, J. (1991). What crack does to babies. *American Educator, 15,* 31–32.

HWANG, C. P., & BROBERG, A. (1992). The historical and social context of child care in Sweden. In M. E. Lamb & K. J. Sternberg (Eds.), *Child care in context.* Hillsdale, NJ: Erlbaum.

IHINGER-TALLMAN, M., & PASLEY, K. (1987). Divorce and remarriage in the American family: A historical review. In R. Pasley & M. Ihinger-Tallman (Eds.), *Remarriage and stepparenting: Current research and theory.* New York: Guilford.

IMARA, M. (1975). Dying as the last stage of growth. In E. Kübler-Ross (Ed.), *Death: The final stage of growth.* Englewood Cliffs, NJ: Prentice Hall.

IMHOF, A. E. (1986). Life course patterns of women and their husbands. In A. B. Sorensen, F. E. Weinert, & L. R. Sherrod (Eds.), *Human development and the life course: Multidisciplinary perspectives.* Hillsdale, NJ: Erlbaum.

INHELDER, B., & PIAGET, J. (1958). *The growth of logical thinking: From childhood to adolescence.* New York: Basic Books.

IRWIN, T. (1978). After 65: Resources for self-reliance. In R. Gross, B. Gross, & S. Seidman (Eds.), *The new old: Struggling for decent aging.* Garden City, NY: Anchor Press/Doubleday.

ISABELLA, R. A., BELSKY, J., & VON EYE, A. (1989). Origins of infant–mother attachment: An examination of interactional synchrony during the infant's first year. *Developmental Psychology, 25,* 12–21.

ISENBERG, J., & QUISENBERRY, N. L. (1988). Play: A necessity for all children. *Childhood Education, 64,* 138–146.

JACKSON, J., ANTONUCCI, T., & GIBSON, R. (1990). Cultural, racial, and ethnic minority influences on aging. In J. Birren & K. W. Schaie (Eds.), *Handbook of the psychology of aging* (3rd ed.). San Diego: Academic Press.

JACOBSON, J., & WILLE, D. (1986). The influence of attachment pattern on developmental changes in peer interaction from the toddler to the preschool period. *Child Development, 57,* 338–347.

JACOBSON, J. L., JACOBSON, S. W., SCHWARTZ, P. M., FEIN, G., & DOWLER, J. K. (1984). Prenatal exposure to an environmental toxin: A test of the multiple effects model. *Developmental Psychology, 20,* 523–532.

JADACK, R. A., HYDE, J. S., SHIBLEY, J., MOORE, C. F., & KELLER, M. L. (1995). Moral reasoning about sexually transmitted diseases. *Child Development, 66,* 167–177.

JAEGER, E., & WEINRAUB, M. (1990). Early non-maternal care and infant attachment: In search of progress. In K. McCartney (Ed.), *New directions for child development, 49.* San Francisco: Jossey-Bass.

JAMES, W. (1890/1950). *The principles of psychology.* New York: Dover.

JEFFERS, F. C., & VERWOERDT, A. (1970). Factors associated with frequency of death thoughts in elderly community volunteers. In E. Palmore (Ed.), Normal aging: Reports from the Duke longitudinal study. Durham, NC: Duke University Press.

JENSEN, A. R. (1969). How much can we boost IQ and scholastic achievement? *Harvard Educational Review, 39,* 1–123.

JENSEN, M., KRISTIANSEN, M. S., & KROGER, J. (1998). Ego identity in cross-cultural context: A comparison of Norwegian and United States university students. *Psychological Reports, 83*, 455–460.

JERSILD, A. T., & HOLMES, F. B. (1935). *Children's fears*. (Child Development Monograph No. 20). New York: Teachers College Press, Columbia University.

JESSOR, R. (1992). Risk behavior in adolescence: A psychosocial framework for understanding and action. *Developmental Review, 12*, 374–390.

JESSOR, R. (1993). Successful adolescent development among youth in high-risk setting. *American Psychologist, 48*, 117–126.

JOHNSON, C.L. (1988). *Ex familia*. New Brunswick, NJ: Rutgers University Press.

JOHNSON, C. L., & BARER, B. M. (1987). Marital instability and the changing kinship networks of grandparents. *The Gerontologist, 27*, 330–335.

JOHNSON, D. W., & JOHNSON, R. T. (1994a). *Learning together and learning alone: Cooperative, competitive, and individualistic learning* (4th. ed.). Boston: Allyn & Bacon.

JOHNSON, F. (1994). Death into life. *New York Times, 144* (Dec. 24), 15.

JOHNSON, M. H. (2000). Functional brain development in infants: Elements of an interactive specialization framework. *Child Development, 71*, 75–81.

JOHNSON, R. B., JR. (1997). Folic acid: New dimensions of an old friendship. In L. A. Barness, *Advances in pediatrics*, Vol. 44. St. Louis, MO: Mosby-Yearbook.

JOHNSON, R. P., & RIKER, H. C. (1981). Retirement maturity: A valuable concept for preretirement counselors. *Personnel and Guidance Journal, 59*, 291–295.

JOHNSON, R. T., & JOHNSON, D. W. (1994b). An overview of cooperative learning. In J. S. Thousand & R. A. Villa (Eds.), *Creativity and cooperative learning: A practical guide to empowering students and teachers*. Baltimore, MD: Brookes.

JONES, A. P., & CRNIC, L. S. (1986). Maternal mediation of the effects of malnutrition. In E. P. Riley & C. V. Vorhees (Eds.), *Handbook of behavioral teratology*. New York: Plenum.

JONES, S. S. (1996). Imitation or exploration? Young infants' matching of adults oral gestures. *Child Development, 67*, 1952–1969.

JORDANOVA, L. (1989). Children in history: Concepts of nature and society. In G. Scarr (Ed.), *Children, parents, and politics*. Cambridge, U.K.: Cambridge University Press.

JOURNAL OF THE AMERICAN MEDICAL ASSOCIATION (1996). Boning up on estrogen: New options, new concerns (editorial). *Vol. 276*, 1430–1432.

JUNG, C. G. (1931/1960). The stages of life. In H. Read, M. Fordham, & G. Adler (Eds.), *The collected works of C. G. Jung* (Vol. 8). New York: Pantheon.

KAGAN, J. (1978). The baby's elastic mind. *Human Nature, 1*, 66–73.

KAGAN, J., ARCUS, D., & SNIDMAN, N. (1993). The idea of temperament: Where do we go from here? In R. Plomin & G. E. McClearn (Eds.), *Nature, nurture, and psychology*. Washington, DC: American Psychological Association.

KAĞITÇIBAŞI, Ç. (1996). *Family and human development across cultures: A view from the other side*. Mahwah, NJ: Lawrence Erlbaum.

KAKAR, S. (1986). Male and female in India: Identity formation and its effects on cultural adapatation in tradition and transformation. In R. H. Brown & G. V. Coelho (Eds.), *Asian Indians in America*. Williamsburg, VA: College of William and Mary Press.

KAKU, D. A. (1991). Emergence of recreational drug abuse as a major risk factor for stroke in young adults. *Journal of the American Medical Association, 265*, 1382.

KALIL, A., & KUNZ, J. (1999). First births among unmarried adolescent girls: Risk and practice factors. *Social Work research, 23*, 197–208.

KALISH, R. A. (1985). *The final transition*. From the *Perspectives on Death & Dying* series. Farmingdale, NY: Baywood.

KALISH, R. A. (1987). Death. In G. L. Maddox, R. C. Atchley, & R. J. Corsini (Eds.), *The encyclopedia of aging*. New York: Springer-Verlag.

KALISH, R. A., & REYNOLDS, D. K. (1981). *Death and ethnicity: A psychological study*. Farmingdale, NY: Baywood.

KALLEBERG, A., & ROSENFELD, R. (1990). Work in the family and in the labor market: A cross-national, reciprocal analysis. *Journal of Marriage and the Family, 52*, 331–346.

KALNINS, I. V., & BRUNER, J. S. (1973). Infant sucking used to change the clarity of a visual display. In L. J. Stone, H. T. Smith, & L. B. Murphy (Eds.), *The competent infant: Research and commentary*. New York: Basic Books.

KAMII, C., & DEVRIES, R. (1980). *Group games in early education*. Washington, DC: National Association for the Education of Young Children.

KAMIN, L. (1974). *The science and politics of IQ*. Hillsdale, NJ: Erlbaum.

KANDALL, S. R., & GAINES, JUDITH (1991). Maternal substance use and subsequent sudden infant death syndrome. *Neurotoxicology and Teratology, 13*, 235–240.

KANDEL, D. B., RAVEIS, V. H., & DAVIES, M. (1991). Suicidal ideation in adolescence: Depression, substance use & other risk factors. *Journal of Youth and Adolescence, 20*, 289–309.

KANE, S. R., & FURTH, H. G. (1993). Children constructing social reality: A frame analysis of social pretend play. *Human Development, 36*, 199–214.

KANTER, R. (1977). *Men and women of the corporation*. New York: Basic Books.

KAPLAN, N., CHOY, M. H., AND WHITMORE, J. K. (1992). Indochinese refugee families and academic achievement. *Scientific American, 266* (2), 36–42.

KAPLAN, R. M., & SINGER, R. D. (1978). Television violence and viewer aggression: A reexamination of the evidence. *Journal of Social Issues, 32*, 35–70.

KARLSON, A. L. (1972). *A naturalistic method for assessing cognitive acquisition of young children participating in preschool programs*. Unpublished doctoral dissertation, University of Chicago.

KASTENBAUM R., & COSTA, P. T. (1977). Psychological perspectives on death. In M. R. Rosenzweig & L. W. Porter (Eds.), *Annual review of psychology* (Vol. 28). Palo Alto, CA: Stanford University Press.

KASTENBAUM, R. (1979). *Growing old: Years of fulfillment*. New York: Harper & Row.

KASTENBAUM, R. J. (1998). *Death, society, and human experience* (6th ed.). Boston: Allyn & Bacon.

KASTENBAUM, R. J. (2000). *The psychology of death* (3rd ed.). New York: Springer-Verlag.

KAVALE, K. A., & FORNESS, S. R. (1996). Social skill deficits and learning disabilities. *Journal of Learning Disabilities, 29*, 226–237.

KAYE, S. D., LORD, M., & SHERRID, P. (1995). Stop working? Not boomers. *U.S News and World Report, 118* (23), 70–72, 75–76.

KEATING, D. (1976). Intellectual talent, research, and development: Proceedings. In D. Keating (Ed.), *Hyman Blumberg Symposium in Early Childhood Education*. Baltimore: Johns Hopkins University Press.

KEATING, D. P. (1980). Thinking processes in adolescence. In J. Adelson (Ed.), *Handbook of adolescent psychology*. New York: Wiley.

KEATING, D. P. (1990). Adolescent thinking. In S. S. Feldman & G. R. Elliott (Eds.), *At the threshold: The developing adolescent*. Cambridge, MA: Harvard University Press.

KEEN, S. (1974). The heroics of everyday life: A theorist of death confronts his own end. *Psychology Today, 7* (11), 71–75.

KEGAN, R. (1982). *The evolving self: Problem and process in human development*. Cambridge, MA: Harvard University Press.

KEGAN, R. (1995). *In over our heads: The mental demands of modern life*. Cambridge, MA: Harvard University Press.

KELLY, J. B. (1982). Divorce: The adult perspective. In B. Wolman (Ed.), *Handbook of developmental psychology*. Englewood Cliffs, N.J.: Prentice Hall.

KELLY, S. J., DAY, N., & STREISSGUTH, A. P. (2000). Effects of prenatal alcohol exposure on social behavior in humans and other species. *Neurotoxicology and Teratology, 22*, 143–149.

KELVIN, P., & JARRETT, J. (1985). *Unemployment: Its social psychological effects*. Cambridge, UK: Cambridge University Press.

KEMPE, R. S., & KEMPE, C. H. (1984). *The common secret: Sexual abuse of children and adolescents*. San Francisco: Freeman.

KENISTON, K. (1975). Youth as a stage of life. In R. J. Havighurst & P. H. Dreyer (Eds.), *Youth: The 74th yearbook of the NSSE*. Chicago: University of Chicago Press.

KERMOIAN, R., & CAMPOS, J. J. (1988). Locomotor experience: A facilitation of spatial cognitive development. *Child Development, 59*, 908–917.

KETT, J. F. (1977). *Rites of Passage: Adolescence in America, 1790 to the present*. New York: Basic Books.

KIEFFER, J. (1984). New roles for older workers. *Aging, 47*, 11–16.

KIMMEL, D. C. (1974). *Adulthood and aging: An interdisciplinary view*. New York: Wiley.

KIMURA, D. (1992). Sex differences in the brain. *Scientific American, 267*, (3), 118–126.

KINCAID, S. B., & CALDWELL, R. A. (1995). Marital separation: Causes, coping, and consequences. *Journal of Divorce and Remarriage, 22,* 109–128.

KINDERMANN, T. A. (1993). Natural peer groups as contexts for individual development: The case of children's motivation in school. *Developmental Psychology, 29,* 970–977.

KINNON, J. B. (1998). Special deliveries: New childbirth options for modern mothers (and fathers) range from high-tech to home again. *Ebony, 53* (7), 40–42.

KISILEVSKY, B. S., HAINS, S. M. J., LEE, K., MUIR, D. W., XU, F., FU, G., ZHAO, Z. Y., & YANG, R. L. (1998). The still-face effect in Chinese and Canadian 3- to 6-month-old infants. *Developmental Psychology, 34,* 629–639.

KITE, M. E., & WHITLEY, B. E., JR. (1996). Sex differences in attitudes toward homosexual persons, behaviors, and civil rights: A meta-analysis. *Personality and Social Psychology Bulletin, 22,* 336–353.

KITZINGER, S. (1981). *The complete book of pregnancy and childbirth.* New York: Knopf.

KLAMEN, D. L., GROSSMAN, L. S., & KOPACZ, D. R. (1999). Medical student homophobia. *Journal of Homosexuality, 37,* 53–63.

KLEIGL, R., SMITH, J., & BALTES, P. (1990). On the locus and process of magnification of age differences during mnemonic training. *Developmental Psychology, 26,* 894–904.

KLEIN, B., & RONES, P. (1989). A profile of the working poor. *Monthly Labor Review, 112* (10), 3–13.

KLEIN, D. M., & ALDOUS, J. (Eds.) (1988). *Social stress and family development.* New York: Guilford.

KLEIN, N., HACK, N., GALLAGHER, J., & FANAROFF, A. A. (1985). Preschool performance of children with normal intelligence who were very low birth weight infants. *Pediatrics, 75,* 531–37.

KLINE, D. W., & SCHIEBER, F. (1985). Vision and aging. In J. E. Baron & K. W. Schaie (Eds.), *Handbook of the psychology of aging* (2nd ed.). New York: Van Nostrand Reinhold.

KLINNERT, M. D., EMDE, R. N., BUTTERFIELD, P., & CAMPOS, J. J. (1986). Social referencing: The infant's use of emotional signals from a friendly adult with mother present. *Developmental Psychology, 22,* 427–432.

KNOBLOCH, H., MALONE, A., ELLISON, P. H., STEVENS, F., & ZDEB, M. (1982). Considerations in evaluating changes in outcome for infants weighing less than 1,501 grams. *Pediatrics, 69,* 285–295.

KOCHANSKA, G. (1997). Mutually responsive orientation between mothers and their young children: Implications for early socialization. *Child Development, 68,* 94–112.

KOHLBERG, L. (1958). *Stages of moral development.* Unpublished doctoral dissertation. University of Chicago.

KOHLBERG, L. (1966). A cognitive developmental analysis of children's sex-role concepts and attitudes. In E. Maccoby (Ed.), *The development of sex differences.* Stanford: Stanford University Press.

KOHLBERG, L. (1969). Stage and sequence: The cognitive-developmental approach to socialization. In D. A. Goslin (Ed.), *Handbook of Socialization Theory & Research.* Chicago: Rand McNally.

KOHLBERG, L. (1978). Revisions in the theory and practice of moral development. In W. Damon (Ed.), *New directions for child development,* 2. San Francisco: Jossey-Bass.

KOHLBERG, L. (1981). *Essays on moral development, Vol. 1: The philosophy of moral development.* New York: Harper & Row.

KOHLBERG, L. (1984). *Essays on moral development, Vol. 2: The psychology of moral development.* New York: Harper & Row.

KOHN, M. L. (1980). Job complexity and adult personality. In N. J. Smelser & E. H. Erikson (Eds.), *Theories of work and love in adulthood.* Cambridge, MA: Harvard University Press.

KOHN, M. L., & SCHOOLER, C. (1983). *Work and personality: Inquiry into the impact of social stratification.* Norwood, NJ: Ablex.

KOHN, R. R. (1985). Aging and age-related diseases: Normal processes. In H. A. Johnson (Ed.), *Relations between normal aging and disease.* New York: Raven.

KOMNER, M., & SHOSTAK, M. (1987). Timing and management of birth among the !Kung: Biocultural interaction and reproductive adaptation. *Cultural Anthropology, 2*(1), 11–28.

KOMPARA, D. R. (1980). Difficulties in the socialization process of stepparenting. *Family Relations, 29,* 69–73.

KOPP, C. B. (1989). Regulation of distress and negative emotions: A developmental view. *Developmental Psychology, 25,* 343–354.

KORTE, D., & SCAER, R. (1990). *A good birth, a safe birth.* New York: Bantam.

KOVAR, M. G. (Ed.) (1992). Mortality among minority populations in the United States. *American Journal of Public Health, 82,* 1168–1170.

KRAVITZ, S. L., PELAEZ, M. B., & ROTHMAN, M. B. (1990). Delivering services to elders: Responsiveness to populations in need. In S. A. Bass, E. A. Kutza, & F. M. Torres-Gil (Eds.). *Diversity in Aging.* Glenview, IL: Scott, Foresman.

KROGER, J., & GREEN, K. E. (1996). Events associated with identity status change. *Journal of Adolescence, 19,* 477–490.

KROPP, J. P., & HAYNES, O. M. (1987). Abusive and nonabusive mothers' ability to identify general and specific emotion signals of infants. *Child Development, 58,* 187–190.

KRUCOFF, C. (1994). Use 'em or lose 'em. *Saturday Evening Post, 226* (2), 34–35.

KÜBLER-ROSS, E. (1969). *On death and dying.* New York: Macmillan.

KÜBLER-ROSS, E. (1975). *Death: The final stage of growth.* Englewood Cliffs, NJ: Prentice Hall.

KUHL, P. K., & IVERSON, P. (1995). Linguistic experience and the "perceptual magnet effect." In W. Strange (Ed.), *Speech perception and linguistic experience: Issues in cross-language research.* Timonium, MD: York Press.

KUHL, P. K., & MELTZOFF, A. N. (1988). Speech as an intermodal object of perception. In A. Yonas (Ed.), *The Minnesota Symposia on Child Psychology, Vol. 20: Perceptual Development in Infancy.* Hillsdale, NJ: Erlbaum.

KUHL, P. K., WILLIAMS, K. A., LACERDA, F., STEVEN, K. H., & LINDBLOM, B. (1992). Linguistic experience alters phonetic percep-

tion in infants by 6 months of age. *Science, 255,* 606–608.

KULIEV, A. M., MODELL, B., & JACKSON, L. (1992). Limb abnormalities and chorionic villus sampling. *The Lancet, 340,* 668.

KURDEK, L., & SCHMITT, J. (1986). Early development of relationship quality in heterosexual married, heterosexual cohabiting, gay, and lesbian couples. *Developmental Psychology, 48,* 305–309.

KUSHNER, H. S. (1981). *When bad things happen to good people.* New York: Schocken Books.

LA RUE, A., & JARVIK, L. F. (1982). Old age and behavioral changes. In B. Wolman (Ed.), *Handbook of developmental psychology.* Englewood Cliffs, NJ: Prentice Hall.

LABOUVIE-VIEF, G. (1984). Logic and self-regulation from youth to maturity: A model. In M. L. Commons, F. A. Richards, & C. Armon (Eds.), *Beyond formal operations: Late adolescence and adult cognitive development.*

LABOUVIE-VIEF, G. (1985). Intelligence and cognition. In J. Birren & K. W. Schaie (Eds.), *Handbook of the psychology of aging* (2nd ed.). New York: Van Nostrand Reinhold.

LABOUVIE-VIEF, G. (1987). Age, ego level, and the life-span development of coping and defense processes. *Psychology & Aging, 2,* 286–293.

LABOUVIE-VIEF, G., & DIEHL, M. (1999). Self and personality development. In J. C. Cavanaugh & S. K. Whitbourne (Eds.), *Gerontology: An interdisciplinary perspective.* New York: Oxford University Press.

LABOUVIE-VIEF, G., & SCHELL, D. A. (1982). Learning and memory in later life. In B. Wolman (Ed.), *Handbook of developmental psychology.* Englewood Cliffs, NJ: Prentice Hall.

LABOUVIE-VIEF, G., HAKIM-LARSON, J., & HOBART, C. J. (1987). Age, ego level, and the life-span development of coping and defense processes. *Psychology & Aging, 2,* 286–293.

LABOV, W. (1970). The logic of nonstandard English. In F. Williams (Ed.), *Language and poverty.* Englewood Cliffs, NJ: Prentice Hall.

LACHMAN, M. E., & JAMES, J. B. (Eds.) (1997). *Multiple paths of midlife development.* Chicago: University of Chicago Press.

LADD, G. W., KOCHENDERFER, B. J., & COLEMAN, C. C. (1996). Friendship quality as a predictor of young children's early school adjustment. *Child Development, 67,* 1103–1118.

LADD, G. W., PRICE, J. M., & HART, C. H. (1988). Predicting preschoolers' peer status from their playground behaviors. *Child Development, 59,* 986–992.

LAGASSE, L. L., VAN VORST, R. F., BRUNNER, S. M., & ZUCKER, M. S. (1999). Infants' understanding of auditory events. *Infant and Child Development, 8,* 85–100.

LAMAZE, F. (1958). *Painless childbirth: Psychoprophylactic method.* London: Burke.

LAMAZE, F. (1970). *Painless childbirth: The Lamaze method.* Chicago: Regnery.

LAMB, M. E. (1987). *The father's role: Cross-cultural perspectives.* New York: Wiley.

LAMB, M. E. (1996). Effects of nonparental child care on child development: An update. *Canadian Journal of Psychiatry, 41,* 330–342.

LAMB, M. E. (1997). *The role of the father in child development* (3rd ed.). New York: Wiley.

LAMB, M. E., HWANG, P. C., KETTERLINUS, R. D., & FRACASSO, M. P. (1999). Parent-child relationships: Development in the context of a family. In M. H. Bornstein & M. E. Lamb (Eds.), *Developmental psychology: An advanced textbook* (4th ed.). Hillsdale, NJ: Erlbaum.

LAMB, M. E., KETTERLINUS, R. D., & FRACASSO, M. P. (1992). Parent-child relationships. In M. H. Bornstein & M. E. Lamb (Eds.), *Developmental psychology: An advanced textbook* (3rd ed.). Hillsdale, NJ: Erlbaum.

LAMB, M. E., PLECK, J. H., & LEVINE, J. A. (1987). Effects of increased paternal involvement on fathers and mothers. In C. Lewis & M. O'Brien (Eds), *Reassessing fatherhood: New observations on fathers and the modern family.* London: Sage.

LAMB, M., & LAMB, J. (1976). The nature and importance of the father–infant relationship. *Family Coordinator, 4,* 379–386.

LAMBORN, S. D., DORNBUSCH, S. M., & STEINBERG, L. (1996). Ethnicity and community context as moderators of the relations between family decision making and adolescent adjustment. *Child Development, 67,* 283–301.

LANDER, E. (1999). Millenium evening at the White House. Whitehead Center for Genome Research press release. Whitehead Institute Internet address: www.wi.mit.edu.

LANG, F.R., & CARTENSEN, L.L. (1994). Close emotional relationships in late life: Further support for proactive aging in the social domain. *Psychology and Aging, 9,* 315–324.

LANGE, G., & PIERCE, S. H. (1992). Memory-strategy learning and maintenance in preschool children. *Developmental Psychology, 28,* 453–462.

LANZA, R. P., DRESSER, B. L., & DAMIANI, P. (2000). Cloning Noah's ark. *Scientific American, 283* (5), 84–89.

LAPSLEY, D., RICE, K., & SHADID, G. (1989). Psychological separation and adjustment to college. *Journal of Counseling Psychology, 36,* 286–294.

LAUER, J. C., & LAUER, R. H. (1985). Marriages made to last. *Psychology Today, 19* (6), 22–26.

LAUER, J. C., & LAUER, R. H. (1999). *How to survive and thrive in an empty nest.* Oakland, CA: New Harbinger.

LAUER, R. H., LAUER, J. C., & KERR, S. T. (1990). The long-term marriage: Perceptions of stability and satisfaction. *International Journal of Aging and Human Development, 31,* 189–195.

LAUERSEN, N. H. (1983). Childbirth with love. New York: Berkley.

LAUMANN, E. O., GAGNON, J. H., MICHAEL, R. T., & MICHAELS, S. (1994). *The social organization of sexuality: Sexual practices in the United States.* Chicago: The University of Chicago Press.

LAWTON, M. P., BRODY, E., & SAPERSTEIN, A. (1989). A controlled study of respite service for care-givers of Alzheimer's patients. *The Gerontologist, 29,* 8–16.

LAWTON, M. P., PARMELEE, P. A., KATZ, I., & NESSELROADE, J. (1996). Affective states in normal and depressed older people. *Journals of Gerontology, 51,* 309–316.

LAZARUS, R. S. (1981). Little hassles can be hazardous to health. *Psychology Today, 15* (7), 58–62.

LAZARUS, R. S. (1999). *Stress and emotion: A new synthesis.* New York: Spring-Verlag.

LAZARUS, R. S. (2000). Toward better research on stress and coping. *American Psychologist, 55,* 665–673.

LEE, G. R. (1988). Marital satisfaction in later life: The effects of nonmarital roles. *Journal of Marriage and the Family, 50,* 775–783.

LEITCH, D. B. (1999). Mother-infant interaction: Achieving synchrony. *Nursing Research, 48,* 55–58.

LEO, J. (1984). The revolution is over. *Time,* (April 9), 74–83.

LERNER, R. (1990). Plasticity, person-context relations and cognitive training in the aged years: A developmental contextual perspective. *Developmental Psychology, 26,* 911–915.

LERNER, R. M. (1998). Theories of human development: Contemporary perspectives. In W. Damon & R. M. Lerner (1998), *Handbook of child psychology* (Vol. 1). New York: Wiley.

LERNER, R. M., ORLOS, J. B., & KNAPP, J. R. (1976). Physical attractiveness, physical effectiveness and self-concept in late adolescence. *Adolescence, 11,* 313–326.

LESTER, B. M., & DREHER, M. (1989). Effects of marijuana use during pregnancy on newborn cry. *Child Development, 60,* 765–771.

LESTER, B., LaGRASSE, L., & BIGSBY, R. (1998). Prenatal cocaine exposure and child development: What do we know and what do we do? *Seminars in Speech and Language, 19,* 123–146.

LEVENTHAL, E.A., LEVENTAL, H., SHACHAM, S., & EASTERLING, D.V. (1989). Active coping reduces reports of pain from childbirth. *Journal of Consulting and Clinical Psychology, 57,* 365–371.

LEVIN, D. E. (1993). *Violence and youth: Psychology's response, Vol. 1: Summary report.* Washington, DC: American Psychological Association.

LEVIN, D. E. (1996). *Physician's guide to media violence.* Chicago: American Medical Assocation.

LEVIN, D. E. (1998). *Remote control childhood: Combatting the hazards of media culture.* Washington, DC: National Association for the Education of Young People.

LEVINE, L. E. (1983). Mine: Self-definition in two-year-old boys. *Developmental Psychology, 19,* 544–549.

LeVINE, R. (1989). Cultural influences in child development. In W. Damon (Ed.), *Child development today and tomorrow.* San Francisco: Jossey-Bass.

LeVINE, R. A. (1990). Enculturation: A biosocial perspective on the development of self. In D. Cicchetti & M. Beeghly (Eds.), *The self in transition: Infancy to childhood.* Chicago: University of Chicago Press.

LEVINSON, D. (1986). A conception of adult development. *American Psychologist, 41,* 3–13.

LEVINSON, D. (1990). *The seasons of a woman's life: Implications for women and men.* Paper presented at the 98th annual convention of the American Psychological Association, Boston.

LEVINSON, D. (1996). *The seasons of a woman's life.* New York: Ballantine.

LEVINSON, D. J. (1978). *The seasons of a man's life.* New York: Knopf.

LEVINSON, H. (1983). A second career: The possible dream. *Harvard Business Review, 61,* 122–129.

LEVY, G. D., & CARTER, D. B. (1989). Gender schema, gender constancy and gender-role knowledge: The roles of cognitive factors in preschoolers' gender-role stereotype attributions. *Developmental Psychology, 25,* 444–449.

LEVY, L. H., DERBY, J. F., & MARTINKOWSKI, K. S. (1993). Effects of membership in bereavement support groups on adaptation to conjugal bereavement. *American Journal of Community Psychology, 21,* 361–381.

LEVY, S. M. (1978). Temporal experience in the aged: Body integrity and social milieu. *International Journal of Aging and Human Development, 9,* 319–343.

LEWIS, M. (1987). Social development in infancy and early childhood. In J. Osofsky (Ed.), *Handbook of infant development.* New York: Wiley.

LEWIS, M. (1995). Self-conscious emotions. *American Scientist, 83,* 68–78.

LEWIS, M. D. (2000). The promise of dynamic systems approaches for an integrated account of human development. *Child Development, 71,* 36–43.

LEWIS, M., & BROOKS-GUNN, J. (1979). *Social cognition and the acquisition of self.* New York: Plenum Press.

LEWIS, M., & FEINMAN, S. (Eds.) (1991). *Social influences and socialization in infancy.* New York: Plenum.

LEWIS, M., & FEIRING, C. (1989). Infant, mother, and mother–infant interaction behavior and subsequent attachment. *Child Development, 60,* 831–837.

LEWIS, M., FEIRING, C., & KOTSONIS, M. (1984). The social network of the young child: A developmental perspective. In M. Lewis (Ed.), *Beyond the dyad: The genesis of behavior.* New York: Plenum.

LEWIS, W. A., & BUCHER, A. M. (1992). Anger, catharsis, the reformulated frustration-aggression hypothesis, and health consequences. *Psychotherapy, 29,* 385–392.

LI, G. (1995). The interaction effect of bereavement and sex on the risk of suicide in the elderly: An historical cohort study. *Social Science and Medicine, 40,* 825–828.

LICKLITER, R., & BAHRICK, L. E. (2000). The development of infant intersensory perception: Advantages of a comparative convergent-operations approach. *Psychological Bulletin, 126,* 260–280.

LIEBERMAN, A. F., & ZEANAH, C. H. (1999). Contributions of attachment theory to infant-parent psychotherapy and other interventions with infants and young children. In J. Cassidy & P. R. Shaver (Eds.), *Handbook of attachment: Theory, research, and clinical applications.* New York: Guilford.

LIEBERMAN, M. A., & TOBIN, S. S. (1983). *The experience of old age: Stress, coping and survival.* New York: Basic Books.

LIEBOVICI, D., RITCHIE, K., & LEDESERT, J. T. (1996). Does education level determine the course of cognitive decline? *Age and Ageing, 25,* 392–397.

LIEM, R. (1981). Unemployment and mental health implications for human service policy. *Policy Studies Journal, 10,* 350–364.

LILLARD, A., & CURENTON, S. (1999). Do young children understand what others feel, want and know? *Young Children, 54* (5), 52–57.

LILLARD, A. S. (1993). Pretend play skills and the child's theory of mind. *Child Development, 64,* 348–371.

LIN, G., & ROGERSON, P. A. (1995). Elderly parents and the geographic availability of their adult children. *Research on Aging, 17,* 303–331.

LIPSITT, L. P., & KAYE, H. (1964). Conditioned sucking in the human newborn. *Psychonomic Science, 1,* 29–30.

LISINA, M. I., & NEVEROVICH, Y. Z. (1971). Development of movements and formation of motor habits. In A. Z. Zaporozlets & D.B. Elkonin (Eds.), *The psychology of preschool children.* Cambridge, MA: MIT Press.

LLOYD, B. (1987). Social representations of gender. In J. Bruner & H. Haste (Eds.), *Making sense: The child's construction of the world.* London: Methuen.

LLOYD, P., & FERNYHOUGH, C. (Eds.) (1999a). *Lev Vygotsky: Critical assessments: Vygotsky's theory* (Vol. I). New York: Routledge.

LLOYD, P., & FERNYHOUGH, C. (Eds.) (1999b). *Lev Vygotsky: Critical assessments: The zone of proximal development* (Vol. III). New York: Routledge.

LOCICERO, A. K. (1993). Explaining excessive rates of Cesareans and other childbirth interventions: Contributions from contemporary theories of gender and psychosocial development. *Social Science and Medicine, 37,* 1261–1269.

LOCK, M. (1993). *Encounters with aging.* Berkeley, CA: University of California Press.

LOCKMAN, J. J., & THELEN, E. (1993). Developmental biodynamics: Brain, body, and behavior connections. *Child Development, 64,* 953–959.

LOCONTE, J. (1998). Hospice, not hemlock. *Policy Review, 88,* 40–48.

LOEVINGER, J. (1976). *Ego development: Conceptions and theories.* San Francisco: Jossey-Bass.

LONGINO, C. F. (1987). *The oldest Americans: State profiles for data-based planning.* Coral Gables, FL: University of Miami Department of Sociology.

LOPATA, H. Z. (1975). Widowhood: Societal factors in life-span disruptions and alterations. In N. Datan & L. H. Ginsberg (Eds.), *Life-span developmental psychology: Normative life crisis.* New York: Academic Press.

LOPATA, H. Z., & BARNEWOLT, D. (1984). The middle years: Changes and variations in social role commitments. In G. Baruch & J. Brooks-Gunn (Eds.), *Women in midlife.* New York: Plenum.

LOPATA, H. Z., HEINEMANN, G. G., & BAUM, J.(1982). Loneliness: Antecedents and copying strategies in the lives of widows. In L. A. Peplau & D. Perlman (Eds.), *Lone-liness: A sourcebook of current theory, research and therapy.* New York: Wiley.

LORD, M. (1995). Feathering a shared nest. *U.S. News & World Report, 118,* (23), 86–88.

LORENZ, K. (1952). *King Solomon's Ring.* New York: Crowell.

LOVAAS, I. (1977). *The autistic child: Language development through behavior modification.* New York: Halsted Press.

LOWENTHAL, B. (1998). Early childhood traumatic brain injuries: Effects on development and interventions. *Early Child Development and Care, 146,* 21–32.

LOWENTHAL, B. (1999). Effects of maltreatment and ways to promote children's resiliency. *Childhood Education, 75,* 204–209.

LOZOFF, B. (1989). Nutrition and behavior. *American Psychologist, 44,* 231–236.

LUBIC, R. W., & ERNST, E. K. (1978). The childbearing center: An alternative to conventional care. *Nursing Outlook, 26,* 754–760.

LUCARIELLO, J., & NELSON, K. (1987). Remembering and planning talk between mothers and children. *Discourse Processes, 10,* 219–235.

LUCAS, V.A. (1993). Birth: Nursing's role in today's choices. *RN, 56* (6), 38.

LUCKEY, I. (1994). African American elders: The support network of generational kin. *Families in Society: Journal of Contemporary Human Services, 75,* 33–36.

LUND, D. A., CASERTA, M. S., & DIMOND, M. F. (1993). The course of spousal bereavement in later life. In M. S. Stroebe & W. Stroebe (Eds.), *Handbook of bereavement: Theory, research, and intervention.* New York: Cambridge University Press.

LYNN, R., & HATTORI, K. (1990). The heritability of intelligence in Japan. *Behavior Genetics, 20,* 545–546.

LYTEL, L., BAKKEN, L., & ROMIG, C. (1997). Adolescent female identity development. *Sex Roles, 37,* 175–185.

MACCOBY, E. E. (1980). *Social development: Psychological growth and the parent–child relationship.* New York: Harcourt Brace Jovanovich.

MACCOBY, E. E. (1984). Socialization and developmental change. *Child Development, 55,* 317–328.

MACCOBY, E. E. (1990). Gender and relationships: A developmental account. *American Psychologist, 45,* 513–520.

MACCOBY, E. E. (1992). The role of parents in the socialization of children: An historical overview. *Developmental Psychology, 28,* 1006–1017.

MACCOBY, E. E., & FELDMAN, S. S. (1972). Mother-attachment and stranger-reactions in the third year of life. *Monographs of the Society for Research in Child Development, 37* (1).

MACCOBY, E. E., & JACKLIN, C. N. (1974). *The psychology of sex differences.* Stanford, CA: Stanford University Press.

MACCOBY, E. E., & MARTIN, J. A. (1983). Socialization in the context of the family: Parent–child interaction. In P. H. Mussen (Ed.), *Handbook of child psychology, Vol. 4: Socialization, personality, and social development.* New York: Wiley.

MACDERMID, S. M., HEILBRUN, G., & GILLESPIE, L. G. (1997). The generativity of employed mothers in multiple roles: 1979 and 1991. In M. E. Lachman & J. B. James (Eds.), *Multiple paths of midlife development.* Chicago: University of Chicago Press.

MACFARLANE, A. (1978). What a baby knows. *Human Nature, 1, (2),* 81–86.

MACKEY, M. C. (1995). Women's evaluation of their childbirth performance. *Maternal-Child Nursing Journal, 23,* 57–72.

MADDEN, J. D., PAYNE, T. F., & MILLER, S. (1986). Maternal cocaine abuse and effect on the newborn. *Pediatrics, 77,* 209–211.

MADDUX, J. E., ROBERTS, M. C., SLEDDEN, E. A., & WRIGHT, L. (1986). Developmental issues in child health psychology. *American Psychologist, 41,* 25–34.

MADSEN, M. C. (1971). Developmental and cross-cultural differences in the cooperative and competitive behavior of young children. *Journal of Cross-Cultural Psychology, 2,* 365–371.

MADSEN, M. C., & SHAPIRA, A. (1970). Cooperative and competitive behavior of urban Afro-American, Anglo-American, Mexican-American, and Mexican village children. *Developmental Psychology, 3,* 16–20.

MAEDA, D. (1992). Aging in Japan. In M. Bergener & K. Hasegawa (Eds.), *Aging and mental disorders: International perspectives.* New York: Springer-Verlag.

MAEHR, M. L., & BRESKAMP, L. A. (1986). *The motivation factor: A theory of personal investment.* Lexington, MA: D. C. Heath.

MAHLER, M., PINE, F., & BERGMAN, A. (1975). *The psychological birth of the human infant: Symbiosis and individuation.* New York: Basic Books.

MAIN, M., & SOLOMON, J. (1990). Procedures for identifying infants as disorganized/disoriented during the Ainsworth Strange Situation. In M. Greenberg, D. Cicchetti, & M. Cummings (Eds.), *Attachment in the Preschool years: Theory, research, and intervention.* Chicago: University of Chicago Press.

MAKIN, J. W., & PORTER, R. H. (1989). Attractiveness of lactating females' breast odors to neonates. *Child Development, 60,* 803–810.

MALLICK, S. K., & MCCANDLESS, B. R. (1967). A study of catharsis of aggression. *Journal of Personality and Social Psychology, 1966,* 591–596.

MANDLER, J. M. (1983). Representation. In J. H. Flavell & E. M. Markham (Eds.), *Handbook of child psychology: Cognitive development* (Vol. 3). New York: Wiley.

MANDLER, J. M. (1988). How to build a baby: On the development of an accurate representational system. *Cognitive Development, 3,* 113–136.

MANDLER, J. M. (1990). A new perspective on cognitive development in infancy. *American Scientist, 78,* 236–243.

MANDLER, J. M. (1992). Commentary. *Human Development, 35,* 246–253.

MANTON, K., BLAZER, D., & WOODBURY, M. (1987). Suicide in middle age and later life: Sex and race specific life table and chart analyses. *Journal of Gerontology, 42,* 219–227.

MARATSOS, M. (1983). Some current issues in the study of the acquisition of grammar. In

J. H. Flavell & E. M. Markham (Eds.), *Handbook of child psychology: Vol. 3, Cognitive Development.* New York: Wiley.

MARCIA, J. (1966). Development and validation of ego-identity status. *Journal of Personality and Social Psychology, 3,* 551–558.

MARCIA, J. (1980). Identity in adolescence. In J. Adelson (Ed.), *Handbook of adolescent psychology.* New York: Wiley.

MARCIA, J. F. (1993). *The status of the statuses.* In J. F. Marcia, A. S. Waterman, D. Matteson, S. L. Archer, & J. Orlofsky (Eds.), *Ego identity.* New York: Springer-Verlag.

MARCOEN, A., GOOSSENS, L., & CAES, P. (1987). Loneliness in pre- through late adolescence: Exploring the contributions of a multidimensional approach. *Journal of Youth and Adolescence, 16,* 561–577.

MARCUS, G. F., PINKER, S., ULLMAN, M., HOLLANDER, M., ROSEN, T. J., & KU FEI, T. J. (1992). Overregularization in language acquisition. *Monographs of the Society for Research in Child Development, 57.*

MARKS, N. F. (1996). Caregiving across the lifespan: National prevalence and predictors. *Family Relations, 45,* 27–36.

MARKSTROM-ADAMS, C., & SMITH, M. (1996). Identity formation and religious orientation among high school students from the United States and Canada. *Journal of Adolescence, 19,* 247–261.

MARSH, H. W., CRAVEN, R. G., & DEBUS, R. (1991). Self-concepts of young children 5 to 8 years of age: Measurement and multidimensional structure. *Journal of Educational Psychology, 83,* 377–392.

MARTIN, C. L. (1990). Attitudes and expectations about children with nontraditional and traditional gender roles. *Sex Roles, 22,* 151.

MARTIN, C. L., & HALVERSON, C. F., JR. (1981). A schematic processing model of sex-typing and stereotyping in children. *Child Development, 52,* 1119–1134.

MARTINEZ, R. O., & DUKES, R. L. (1997). The effects of ethnic identity, ethnicity, and gender on adolescent well-being. *Journal of Youth and Adolescence, 26,* 503–511.

MARZOLF, D. P., & DELOACHE, J. S. (1994). Transfer in young children's understanding of spatial representations. *Child Development, 65,* 1–15.

MASLACH, C., & GOLDBERG, J. (1998). Prevention of burnout: New perspectives. *Applied and Preventive Psychology, 7,* 63–74.

MASLACH, C., & LEITER, M. P. (1997). *The truth about burnout: How organizations cause personal stress and what to do about it.* San Francisco: Jossey-Bass.

MASLOW, A. H. (1954). *Motivation and personality.* New York: Harper & Brothers.

MASLOW, A. H. (1979). *The journals of A. H. Maslow* (R. J. Lowry & B. G. Maslow, Eds.). Monterey, CA: Brooks/Cole.

MASON, D. A., & FRICK, P. J. (1994). The heritability of antisocial behavior: A meta-analysis of twin and adoption studies. *Journal of Psychopathology and Behavioral Assessment, 16,* 301–323.

MASTERS, W. H., JOHNSON, P. E., & KOLODNEY, R. C. (1982). *Human sexuality* (2nd ed.). Boston: Little, Brown.

MATAS, L., AREND, R. A., & SROUFE, L. A. (1978). Continuity of adaptation in the second year: The relationship between quality of attachment and later competence. *Child Development, 49,* 547–556.

MATES, D., & ALLISON, K. R. (1992). Sources of stress and coping responses of high school students. *Adolescence, 27,* 463–474.

MATSUMOTO, D. (2000). *Culture and psychology* (2nd ed.). Belmont, CA: Wadsworth.

MATTHEWS, K., & RODIN, J. (1989). Women's changing work roles: Impact on health, family and public policy. *American Psychologist, 44,* 1389–1393.

MATTHEWS, S. H., & ROSNER, T. T. (1988). Shared filial responsibility: The family as the primary care-giver. *Journal of Marriage and the Family, 50,* 185–195.

MATTHEWS, S., WERKNER, J., & DELANEY, P. (1989). Relative contributions of help by employed and nonemployed sisters to their elderly parents. *Journal of Gerontology, 44,* S36–44.

MATTSON, S. N., & RILEY, E. P. (1998). A review of the neurobehavioral deficits in children with fetal alcohol syndrome or prenatal exposure to alcohol. *Alcoholism: Clinical and Experimental Research, 22,* 279–294.

MAURER, D., & MAURER, C. (1988). *The world of the newborn.* New York: Basic Books.

MAURO, J. (1991). *The friend that only I can see: A longitudinal investigation of children's imaginary companions.* Unpublished doctoral dissertation. University of Oregon.

MAY, ROLLO (1986/1987). *Will, decision and responsibility.* Review of Existential Psychology & Psychiatry (Spec Issue 20), 269–278.

MAYUEX, R., & SANO, M. (1999). Drug therapy: Treatment of Alzheimer's disease. *New England Journal of Medicine, 341,* 1670–1679.

MAZZOCCO, M. M. M. (2000). Advances in research on the fragile X syndrome. *Mental Retardation and Developmental Disabilities Research Reviews, 6,* 96–100.

McADOO, H. P. (1995). Stress levels, family help patterns, and religiosity in middle- and working-class African American single mothers. *Journal of Black Psychology, 21,* 424–449.

McBEAN, L. D., FORGAC, T., & FINN, S. C. (1994). Osteoporosis: Visions for care and prevention—A conference report. *Journal of the American Dietic Association, 94,* 668–671.

McBRIDE, A. (1990b). Mental health effects of women's multiple roles. *American Psychologist, 45,* 381–384.

McBRIDE, S. L. (1990a). Maternal moderators of child care: The role of maternal separation anxiety. In K. McCartney (Ed.), *New directions for child development, 49.* San Francisco: Jossey-Bass.

McCALL, R. B., EICHORN, D. H., & HOGARTY, P. S. (1977). Transitions in early mental development. *Monographs of the Society for Research in Child Development, 42* (3).

McCARTNEY, K., HARRIS, M. J., & BERNIERI, F. (1990). Growing up and growing apart: A developmental meta-analysis of twin studies. *Psychological Bulletin, 107,* 226–237.

McCARY, J. L. (1978). *Human sexuality* (3rd ed.). New York: Van Nostrand Reinhold.

McCLELLAND, D. C. (1955). Some social consequences of achievement motivation. In M.

R. Jones (Ed.), *Nebraska symposium on motivation* (Vol. 3). Lincoln: University of Nebraska Press.

McCRAE, R. R. (1989). Age differences and changes in the use of coping mechanisms. *Journal of Gerontology, 44,* 161–169.

McDOWD, J. M., & SHAW, R. J. (2000). Attention and aging: A functional perspective. In F. I. M. Craik & T. A. Salthouse (Eds.), *Handbook of aging and cognition* (2nd ed.). Mahwah, NJ: Erlbaum.

McFADYEN, A., GLEDHILL, J., WHITLOW, B., & ECONOMIDES, D. (1998). *British Medical Journal, 317,* 694–695.

McGOLDRICK, M. (1988). The joining of families through marriage: The new couple. In E. A. Carter & M. McGoldrick (Eds.), *The changing family life cycle: A framework for family therapy* (2nd ed.). New York: Gardner.

McKEEVER, W. F. (2000). A new family handedness sample with findings consistent with X-linked transmission. *British Journal of Psychology, 91,* 21–39.

McKENNA, J. J. (1996). Sudden infant death syndrome in cross-cultural perspective: Is infant-parent cosleeping protective? *Annual Review of Anthropology, 25,* 201–216.

McLANAHAN, S., & BOOTH, K. (1989). Mother-only families: Problems, prospects, and politics. *Journal of Marriage and the Family, 51,* 557–580.

McLOYD, V. C. (1998). Economic disadvantage and child development. *American Psychologist, 53,* 185–204.

McLOYD, V. C., JAYARATNE, T. E., CEBALLO, R., & BORQUEZ, J. (1994). Unemployment and work interruption among African American single mothers: Effects on parenting and adolescent socioemotional functioning. *Child Development, 65,* 562–589.

McLOYD, V. C., & WILSON, L. (1990). Maternal behavior, social support, and economic conditions as predictors of distress in children. *New directions for child development, 46.* San Francisco: Jossey-Bass.

McNEILL, D. (1972). *The acquisition of language: The study of developmental psycholinguistics.* New York: Harper & Row.

McWHIRTER, D. P., & MATTISON, A. M. (1996). Male couples. In R. P. Cabaj & T. S. Stein (Eds.), *Textbook of homosexuality and mental health.* Washington, DC: American Psychiatric Press.

MEADOW, K. P. (1975). The development of deaf children. In E. M. Hetherington (Ed.), *Review of child development research* (Vol. 5). Chicago: University of Chicago Press.

MEADOWS, D., ELIAS, G., & BAIN, J. (2000). Mothers' ability to identify infant's communicative acts consistently. *Journal of Child Language, 27,* 393–406.

MEEHAN, P. J., LAMB, J. A., SALTZMAN, L. E., & O'CARROLL, P. W. (1992). Attempted suicide among young adults: Progress toward a meaningful estimate of prevalence. *American Journal of Psychiatry, 149,* 41–44.

MEEUS, W., IEDEMA, J., HELSEN, M., & VOLLEBERGH, W. (1999). Patterns of adolescent identity development: Review of literature and longitudinal analysis. *Developmental Review, 19,* 419–461.

MEISAMI, E. (1994). Aging of the sensory systems. In P. S. Timiras (Ed.), *Physiological basis of aging and geriatrics* (2nd ed.). Ann Arbor, IN: CRC Press.

MELTZOFF, A. N. (1988a). Infant imitation and memory: Nine month olds in immediate and deferred tests. *Child Development, 59,* 217–225.

MELTZOFF, A. N. (1988b). Infant imitation after a 1–week delay: Long-term memory for novel acts and multiple stimuli. *Developmental Psychology, 24,* 470–476.

MELTZOFF, A. N., & BORTON, R. W. (1979). Intermodal matching by human neonates. *Nature, 282,* 403–404.

MELTZOFF, A. N., & MOORE, M. K. (1977). Imitation of facial and manual gestures by human neonates. *Science, 198,* 75–78.

MELTZOFF, A. N., & MOORE, M. K. (1989). Imitation in newborn infants: Exploring the range of gestures imitated and the underlying mechanisms. *Developmental Psychology, 25,* 954–962.

MELTZOFF, A. N., & MOORE, M. K. (1997). Explaining facial imitation: A theoretical model. *Early Development and Parenting, 6,* 179–192.

Men, work, and family. Newbury Park, CA: Sage.

MERRILL, S. S., & VERBRUGGE, L. M. (1999). Health and disease in midlife. In S. L. Willis & J. D. Reid (Eds.), *Life in the middle: Psychological and social development in middle age.* San Diego: Academic Press.

MERRIMAN, W. E. (1987). Lexical contrast in toddlers: A re-analysis of the diary evidence. Paper presented at the biennial meeting of the Society of Research in Child Development, Baltimore.

MERVIS, C. B. (1987). Child-basic object categories and early lexical development. In U. Neisser (Ed.), *Concepts and conceptual development: Ecological and intellectual factors in categorization.* London: Cambridge University Press.

MESTEL, R. (1997). A safer estrogen: Would you take it? *Health, 11,* (8), 73–75.

METCOFF, J., COSTILOE, J. P., CROSBY, W., BENTLE, L., SESHACHALAM, D., SANDSTEAD, H. H., BODWELL, C. E., WEAVER, F., & McCLAIN, P. (1981). Maternal nutrition and fetal outcome. *American Journal of Clinical Nutrition, 34,* 708–721.

MEYER, B. J. F. (1987). Reading comprehension and aging. In K. W. Schaie (Ed.), *Annual review of gerontology and geriatrics* (Vol. 7). New York: Springer-Verlag.

MICHAEL, R. T., GAGNON, J. H., LAUMANN, E. O., & KOLATA, G. (1994). *Sex in America: A definitive survey.* Boston: Little, Brown.

MILES, D. R., & CAREY, G. (1997). Genetic and environmental architecture of human aggression. *Journal of Personality and Social Psychology, 72,* 207–217.

MILES, M. S. (1984). Helping adults mourn the death of a child. In H. Wass & C. A. Corr (Eds.), *Childhood and death.* Washington, DC: Hemisphere.

MILLER, B. (1990). Gender differences in spouse caregiver strain: Socialization and role explanations. *Journal of Marriage and the Family, 52,* 311–321.

MILLER, B. C., & SNEESBY, K. R. (1988). Educational correlates of adolescents' sexual attitudes and behavior. *Journal of Youth and Adolescence, 17,* 521–530.

MILLER, B. C., McCOY, J. K., OLSON, T. D., & WALLACE, C. M. (1986). Parental discipline and control attempts in relation to adolescent sexual attitudes and behavior. *Journal of Marriage and the Family, 48,* 503–512.

MILLER, B. C., NORTON, M. C., FAN, X., & CHRISTOPHERSON, C. R. (1998). Pubertal development, parental communication, and sexual values in relation to adolescent sexual behavior. *Journal of Early Adolescence, 18,* 27–52.

MILLER, B. D. (1995). Percepts and practices: Researching identity formation among Indian Hindu adolescents in the United States. In J. J. Goodnow, P. J. Miller, & F. Kessel (Eds.), *New Directions for Child Development, 67,* 71–85. San Francisco: Jossey-Bass.

MILLER, D. W. (1993). Reflections on the psychobiological nature of reality, with a theory about Alzheimer's disease. *Advances, 9,* 69–76.

MILLER, P. (1989). *Theories of developmental psychology* (2nd ed.). New York: Freeman.

MILLER, P. H., & ALOISE, P. A. (1989). Young children's understanding of the psychological causes of behavior: A review. *Child Development, 60,* 257–285.

MILLER, P. J., MINTZ, J., HOOGSTRA, L., FUNG, H. J., & POTTS, R. (1992). The narrated self: Young children's construction of self in relation to others in conversational stories of personal experience. *Merrill–Palmer Quarterly, 38* (1), 45–67.

MILLER, P., WILEY, A. R., FUNG, H., & LIANG, C.-H. (1997). Personal storytelling as a medium of socialization in Chinese and American families. *Child Development, 68,* 557–568.

MILLS, J. L. (1999). Cocaine, smoking, and spontaneous abortion. *New England Journal of Medicine, 340,* 380–381.

MILNE, A. A. (1926/1961). *Winnie-the-Pooh.* New York: Dutton.

MIRINGOFF, N. (1987). A timely and controversial article. *Zero to Three, 7* (2), 26.

MISAGO, C., UMENAI, T., NOGUCHI, M., MORI, T., & MORI, T. (2000). Satisfying birthing experiences in Japan. *The Lancet, 3555,* 2256.

MOEN, P. (1998). Recasting careers: Changing reference groups, risks, and realities. *Generations, 21* (2), 40–45.

MOEN, P., & WETHINGTON, E. (1999). Midlife development in a life course context. In S. L. Willis & J. D. Reid (Eds.), *Life in the middle: Psychological and social development in middle age.* San Diego: Academic Press.

MOERK, E. L. (1989). The LAD was a lady and the tasks were ill-defined. *Developmental Review, 9,* 21–57.

MOLLICA, R. F. (2000). Invisible wounds. *Scientific American, 282,* (6), 54–57.

MOLLICA, R. F., POOLE, C., SON, L., & MURRAY, C. C. (1997). Effects of war trauma on Cambodian refugee adolescents' functional health and mental health status. *Journal of the American Academy of Child and Adolescent Psychiatry, 36,* 1098–1106.

MONEY, J. (1980). *Love and love sickness: The science of sex, gender differences and pair-bonding.* Baltimore: Johns Hopkins University Press.

MONTAGU, A. (1951). Statement on race. New York: Henry Schuman (as cited in Yee et al., 1993).

MONTE, C. F. (1999). *Beneath the mask: An introduction to theories of personality* (6th ed.). New York: Harcourt Brace.

MONTEMAYOR, R., & BROWNLEE, J. R. (1987). Fathers, mothers and adolescents: Gender-based differences in parental roles during adolescence. *Journal of Youth and Adolescence, 16,* 281–292.

MOORE, K. (1988). The developing human: Clinically oriented embryology (4th ed.). Philadelphia: Saunders.

MOR, V., SHERWOOD, S., & GUTKIN, C. (1986). A national study of residential care for the aged. *The Gerontologist, 26,* 405–416.

MORELLI, G. A., ROGOFF, B., OPPENHEIM, D., & GOLDSMITH, D. (1992). Cultural variation in infants' sleeping arrangements. *Developmental Psychology, 28,* 604–613.

MORGAN, D. (1989). Adjusting to widowhood: Do social networks really make it easier? *The Gerontologist, 29,* 101–107.

MORGAN, L. (1984). Changes in family interaction following widowhood. *Journal of Marriage and the Family, 46,* 323–331.

MORRISON, D. M. (1985). Adolescent contraceptive behavior: A review. *Psychological Bulletin, 98,* 538–568.

MORRONGIELLO, B. A., FENWICK, K. D., & CHANCE, G. (1998). Crossmodal learning in newborn infants: Inferences about properties of auditory-visual events. *Infant Behavior and Development, 21,* 543–553.

MORROW-KONDOS, D., WEBER, J. A., COOPER, K., & HESSER, J. L. (1997). Becoming parents again: Grandparents raising grandchildren. *Journal of Gerontological Social Work, 28,* 35–46.

MORTON, N., & BROWNE, K. D. (1998). Theory and observation of attachment and its relation to child maltreatment: A review. *Child Abuse and Neglect, 22,* 1093–1104.

MOTENKO, A. (1989). The frustrations, gratifications, and well-being of dementia caregivers. *The Gerontologist, 29,* 166–172.

MOUNTAIN STATES GENETICS NETWORK (MoSt GeNe) (2000). Indications for genetic counseling referrals. Internet document. MoSt GeNe home page: www.mostgene.org.

MOYER, K. E. (1982). Aggression theories. *Academic Psychology Bulletin, 4,* 415–423.

MUELLER, E., & SILVERMAN, N. (1989). Peer relations in maltreated children. In D. Cicchetti & V. Carlson (Eds.), *Child maltreatment: Theory and research on the causes and consequences of child abuse and neglect.* Cambridge, England: Cambridge University Press.

MUELLER, E., & TINGLEY, E. (1990). The bear's picnic: Children's representations of themselves and their families. In K. McCartney (Ed.), *New directions for child development, 49.* San Francisco: Jossey-Bass.

MURPHY, L. B. (1962). *The widening world of childhood: Paths toward mastery.* New York: Basic Books.

MURPHY, P. A. (1993). Preterm birth prevention programs: A critique of current literature. *Journal of Nurse-Midwifery, 38,* 324–335.

MURRAY, B. (1996a). Judges, courts get tough on spanking. *American Psychologial Association Monitor, 11,* 10.

MURRAY, B. (1996b). British case could set precedent. *American Psychologial Association Monitor, 11,* 10.

MURSTEIN, B. I. (1982). Marital choice. In B. Wolman (Ed.), *Handbook of developmental psychology.* Englewood Cliffs, NJ: Prentice Hall.

MURSTEIN, B. I. (1999). The relationship of exchange and commitment. In J. M. Adams & M. H. Jones (Eds.), *Handbook of interpersonal commitment and relationship stability.* New York: Kluwer Academic/Plenum.

MURSTEIN, B. I., CHALPIN, M. J., HEARD, K. V., & VYSE, S. A. (1989). Sexual behavior, drugs, and relationship patterns on a college campus over thirteen years. *Adolescence, 24,* 125–139.

MUSICK, J. S. (1994). Directions: Capturing the childbearing context. *SRCD Newsletter, 37* (4), 1, 6–7.

MUUSS, R. E. (1986). Adolescent eating disorder: Bulimia. *Adolescence, 21* (8), 257–267.

MYERS, N. A., & PERLMUTTER, M. (1978). Memory in the years from two to five. In P. Ornstein (Ed.), *Memory development in children.* Hillsdale, NJ: Erlbaum.

MYERS, N. A., CLIFTON, R. K., & CLARKSON, M. G. (1987). When they were very young: Almost-threes remember two years ago. *Infant Behavior and Development, 10,* 123–132.

NADEL, L., & ROSENTHAL, D. (Eds.) (1995). *Down syndrome: Living and learning in the community.* New York: Wiley-Liss.

NAEYE, R. L. (1980). Abruptio placentae and placenta previa: Frequency, perinatal mortality, and cigarette smoking. *Obstetrics and Gynecology, 55,* 701–704.

NAEYE, R. L. (1981). Influence of maternal cigarette smoking during pregnancy on fetal and childhood growth. *Obstetrics and Gynecology, 57,* 18–21.

NAGEL, K. L., & JONES, K. H. (1992). Sociological factors in the development of eating disorders. *Adolescence, 27,* 107–113.

NATIONAL CENTER FOR ENVIRONMENTAL HEALTH (NCEH). (1999b). Preventing alcohol-exposed pregnancies among high-risk women in special community-based settings (Pub. No. 99–0302). Hyattsville, MD.

NATIONAL CENTER FOR ENVIRONMENTAL HEALTH (NCEH). (1999a). Folic acid for healthy babies: A primer (Pub. No. 99–0093). Hyattsville, MD.

NATIONAL CENTER FOR HEALTH STATISTICS (NCHS). (1990b). *Health, United States, 1989.* Hyattsville, MD.

NATIONAL CENTER FOR HEALTH STATISTICS (NCHS). (1990a). *Monthly Vital Statistics Reports, 39,* (7), 1–2.

NATIONAL CENTER FOR HEALTH STATISTICS (NCHS). (1993). *Health, United States, 1992.* Washington, DC.

NATIONAL CENTER FOR HEALTH STATISTICS (NCHS). (1995). *Monthly Vital Statistics Reports, 43* (6), 5.

NATIONAL CENTER FOR HEALTH STATISTICS (NCHS). (1999). *Health, United States, 1999.* Hyattsville, MD.

NATIONAL CENTER FOR HEALTH STATISTICS (NCHS). (2000a). *Health, United States, 2000.* Hyattsville, MD.

NATIONAL CENTER FOR HEALTH STATISTICS (NCHS). (2000b). *National Vital Statistics Reports, 48* (3), 44.

NATIONAL CENTER FOR HEALTH STATISTICS (NCHS). (2001). Births, marriages, divorces, and deaths: Provisional data for 1999. *National Vital Statistics Reports, 48* (19), 1–2.

NATIONAL CENTER ON ADDICTION AND SUBSTANCE ABUSE AT COLUMBIA UNIVERSITY. (1996). *Substance abuse and the American Woman: Using the law.* New York.

NATIONAL INSTITUTE OF CHILD HEALTH AND HUMAN DEVELOPMENT (NICHD). (1997). The effects of infant child care on infant-mother attachment security: Results of the NICHD study of early child care. *Child Development, 68,* 860–879.

NATIONAL INSTITUTE OF CHILD HEALTH AND HUMAN DEVELOPMENT (NICHD). (1999). Child care and mother-child interaction in the first 3 years of life. *Developmental Psychology, 35,* 1399–1411.

NATIONAL INSTITUTE OF CHILD HEALTH AND HUMAN DEVELOPMENT (NICHD). (2000). The relation of child care to cogntive and language development. *Child Development, 71,* 960–980.

NEIMARK, E. D. (1975). Intellectual development during adolescence. In F. D. Horowitz (Ed.), *Review of child development* (Vol. 4). Chicago: University of Chicago Press.

NELSON, C. A. (1995). The ontogeny of human memory: A cognitive neuroscience perspective. *Developmental Psychology, 31,* 723–738.

NELSON, C. A., & BLOOM, F. E. (1997). Child development and

NELSON, C. A., & COLLINS, P. F. (1992). Neural and behavioral correlates of visual recognition memory in 4– and 8–month-old infants. *Brain and Cognition, 19,* 105–121.

NELSON, C. A., & DE HAAN, M. (1996). Neural correlates of infants' visual responsiveness to facial expression of emotion. *Developmental Psychobiology, 29,* 577–595.

NELSON, K. (1974). Concept, word and sentence: Interrelations in acquisition and development. *Psychological Review, 81,* 267–285.

NELSON, K. (1981). Individual differences in language development: Implications for development and language. *Developmental Psychology, 17,* 170–187.

NELSON, K. (1986). *Event knowledge: Structure and function in development.* Hillsdale, NJ: Erlbaum.

NELSON, K. (1996). *Language in cognitive development: Emergence of the mediated mind.* New York: Cambridge University Press.

NELSON, K., & GRUENDEL, J. M. (1986). Generalized event representations: Basic building blocks of cognitive development. In A. Brown & M. Lamb (Eds.), *Advances in developmental psychology* (Vol. 1). Hillsdale, NJ: Erlbaum.

NELSON, K., FIBUSH, R., HUDSON, J., & LUCARIELLO, J. (1983). Scripts and the development of memory. In M. T. C. Chi (Ed.), *Trends in memory development research.* Basel, Switzerland: Carger.

NESS, R. B., GRISSON, J. A., HIRSHINGER, N., MARKOVIC, N., SHAW, L. M., DAY, N. L., & KLINE, J. (1999). Cocaine and tobacco use and the risk of spontaneous abortion. *New England Journal of Medicine, 340,* 333–339.

NEUGARTEN, B. (1967). The awareness of middle age. In B. Neugarten (Ed.), *Middle age and aging.* Chicago: University of Chicago Press.

NEUGARTEN, B. L. (1968). Adult personality: Toward a psychology of the life cycle. In B. L. Neugarten (Ed.), *Middle age and aging.* Chicago: University of Chicago Press.

NEUGARTEN, B. L. (1970). The old and the young in modern societies. *American Behavioral Scientist, 14,* 18–24.

NEUGARTEN, B. L. (1976). *The psychology of aging: An overview.* Washington, DC: American Psychological Association.

NEUGARTEN, B. L. (1979). Time, age and the life cycle. *American Journal of Psychiatry, 136,* 887–894.

NEUGARTEN, B. L., & BROWN-REZANKA, L. (1996). Midlife women in the 1980s. In B. L. Neugarten & D. A. Neugarten, *The meanings of age: Selected papers of Bernice L. Neugarten.* Chicago: University of Chicago Press.

NEUGARTEN, B. L., & MOORE, J. W. (1968). The changing age status system. In B. L. Neugarten (Ed.), *Middle age and aging.* Chicago: University of Chicago Press.

NEUGARTEN, B. L., & NEUGARTEN D. A. (1987). The changing meanings of age. *Psychology Today, 21,* 29–33.

NEUGARTEN, B. L., WOOD, V., KRAINES, R., & LOOMIS, B. (1968). Women's attitudes toward the menopause. In B. L. Neugarten (Ed.), *Middle age and aging.* Chicago: University of Chicago Press.

NEVILLE, B., & PARKE, R. D. (1997). Waiting for paternity: Interpersonal and contextual implications of the time of fatherhood. *Sex Roles, 37,* 45–59.

NEW, R. S. (1988). Parental goals and Italian infant care. In R. A. LeVine, P. M. Miller, & M. M. West (Eds.), *New directions for child development, 40.* San Francisco: Jossey-Bass.

NEWCOMB, A. F., BUKOWSKI, W. M., & PATTEE, L. (1993). Children's peer relations: A meta-analytic review of popular, rejected, neglected, controversial, and average sociometric status. *Psychological Bulletin, 113,* 99–128.

NEWCOMB, M. D., & BENTLER, P. M. (1989). Substance use and abuse among children and teenagers. *American Psychologist, 44,* 242–248.

NEWMAN, B. M. (1982). Mid-life development. In B. Wolman (Ed.), *Handbook of developmental psychology.* Englewood Cliffs, NJ: Prentice Hall.

NEWMAN, L. F., & BUKA, S. L. (1991). Clipped wings: The fullest look yet at how prenatal exposure to drugs, alcohol, and nicotine hobbles children's learning. *American Educator, 42,* 27–33.

NEWMAN, L. S. (1990). Intentional and unintentional memory in young children: Remembering vs. playing. *Journal of Experimental Child Psychology, 50,* 243–258.

NEWSWEEK (1999). Learning the killing game. *134,* Sept. 11th., 38.

NEY, P. G. (1988). Transgenerational child abuse. *Child Psychiatry and Human Development, 18,* 151–168.

NICHOLS, B. (1990). *Moving and Learning: The elementary school physical education experience.* St. Louis, MO: Times Mirror/Mosby.

NICHOLS, S. L. (1999). Gay, lesbian, and bisexual youth: Understanding diversity and promoting tolerance in schools. *Elementary School Journal, 99,* 505–519.

NICOLADIS, E. (1999). "Where is my brush-teeth?" Acquisition of compound nouns in a French-English bilingual child. *Bilingualism, 2,* 245–256.

NICOLOPOULOU, A. (1993). Play, cognitive development, and the social world: Piaget, Vygotsky, and beyond. *Human Development, 36,* 1–23.

NIENDENTHAL, P. M., TANGNEY, J. P., & GAVANSKI, I. (1994). "If only I weren't" versus "if only I hadn't": Distinguishing shame and guilt in counterfactual thinking. *Journal of Personality and Social Psychology, 67,* 584–595.

NIGHSWANDER, J. K., & MAYER, G. R. (1969). Catharsis: A means of reducing elementary school students' aggressive behavior? *Personal and Guidance Journal, 47,* 461–466.

NILSSON, L., & HAMBERGER, L. (1990). *A child is born* (rev. ed.). New York: Dell.

NORTON, R. D. (1994). Adolescent suicide: Risk factors and countermeasures. *Journal of Health Education, 25,* 358–361.

NOZYCE, M., HITTELMAN, J., MUENZ, L., DURAKO, S. J., FISCHER, M., & WILLOUGHBY, A. (1994). Effect of perinatally acquired human immunodeficiency virus infection on neurodevelopment during the first two years of life. *Pediatrics, 94,* 883–891.

NUGENT, J. K. (1994). Cross-cultural studies of child development: Implications for clinicians. *Zero to Three,* November, 6.

NUGENT, J. K., & BRAZELTON, T. B. (2000). Preventive infant mental health: Uses of the Brazelton scale. In J. D. Osofsky & H. E. Fitzgerald (Eds.), *Handbook of infant mental health: Vol. 2., Early intervention, evaluation, and assessment.* New York: Wiley.

NUGENT, J. K., GREENE, S., & MAZOR, K. (October 1990). The effects of maternal alcohol and nicotine use during pregnancy on birth outcome. Paper presented at Bebe XXI Simposio Internacional, Lisbon, Portugal.

NYBORG, H., & JENSEN, A. R. (2000). Black-white differences on various psychometric tests: Spearman's hypothesis tested on American armed services veterans. *Personality & Individual Differences, 28,* 593–599.

NYDEGGER, C. N., & MITENESS, L. S. (1996). Midlife: The prime of fathers. In C.D. Ryff & M. M. Seltzer (Eds.), *The parental experiment in midlife.* Chicago: University of Chicago Press.

O'BRIEN, M., & NAGLE, K. J. (1987). Parents' speech to toddlers: The effect of play context. *Journal of Language Development, 14,* 269–279.

O'BRYANT, S. L. (1988). Sibling support and older widows' well-being. *Journal of Marriage and the Family, 50,* 173–183.

O'CONNOR, T. G., PLOMIN, R., CASPI, A., & DEFRIES, J. C. (2000). Are associations between parental divorce and children's adjustment genetically mediated? An adoption study. *Developmental Psychology, 36,* 429–437.

O'CONNOR-FRANCOEUR, P. (1983). *Children's concepts of health and their health behavior.* Paper presented at the biennial meeting of the Society for Research in Child Development, Detroit.

O'HARA, M., ZEKOSKI, E., PHILIPPS, L. H., & WRIGHT, E. (1990). Controlled prospective study of postpartum mood disorders: Comparison of childbearing and nonchildbearing women. *Journal of Abnormal Psychology, 99,* 3–15.

OAKES, L. M., & MADOLE, K. L. (2000). The future of infant categorization research: A process-oriented approach. *Child development, 71,* 119–126.

OAKLEY, A., & RICHARDS, M. (1990). Women's experiences of Caesarean delivery. In J. Garcia, R. Kilpatrick, & M. Richards (Eds.), *The politics of maternity care.* Oxford: Clarendon Press.

OCAMPO, K. A., KNIGHT, G. P., & BERNAL, M. E. (1997). The development of cognitive abilities and social identities in children: The case of ethnic identity. *International Journal of Behavioral Development, 21,* 479–500.

OCHS, A., NEWBERRY, J., LENHARDT, M., & HARKINS, S. (1985). Neural and vestibular aging associated with falls. In J. Birren & K. Schaie (Eds.), *Handbook of the psychology of aging* (2nd ed.). New York: Van Nostrand Reinhold.

OFFER, D., OSTROV, E., HOWARD, K., & ATKINSON, R. (1988). *The teenage world: Adolescents' self-image in ten countries.* New York: Plenum Medical.

OKUM, B. F. (1984). Working with adults: Individual, family and career development. Monterey, CA: Brooks/Cole.

OLDS, D. (1997). Tobacco exposure and impaired development: A review of the evidence. *Mental Retardation and Developmental Disabilities Research Reviews, 3,* 257–269.

OLLER, D. K., & EILERS, R. E. (1988). The role of audition in infant babbling. *Child Development, 59,* 441–449.

OLSHO, L. W., HARKINS, S. W., & LENHARDT, M. L. (1985). Aging and the auditory system. In J. E. Birren & K. W. Schaie (Eds.), *Handbook of the psychology of aging* (2nd ed.). New York: Van Nostrand Reinhold.

OLSON, D. H., & LAVEE, Y. (1989). Family systems and family stress: A family life cycle perspective. In K. Kreppner & R. M. Lerner (Eds.), *Family systems and life-span development.* Hillsdale, NJ: Erlbaum.

OLSON, M. R., & HAYNES, J. A. (1993). Successful single parents. *Families in Society: The Journal of Contemporary Human Services, 74,* 259–267.

OLSON, S. L., BATES, J. E., & BAYLES, K. (1984). Mother–infant interaction and the devel-

opment of individual differences in children's cognitive competence. *Developmental Psychology, 20,* 166–179.

ONLINE MENDELIAN INHERITANCE IN MAN (OMIM) (2000). McKusick-Nathans Institute for Genetic Medicine, Johns Hopkins University (Baltimore, MD) and National Center for Biotechnology Information, National Library of Medicine (Bethesda, MD). Internet address: www.ncbi.nlm.nih.gov/omim

OPPENHEIM, D., EMDE, R. N., & WARREN, S. (1997). Children's narrative representations of mothers: Their development and associations with child and mother adaptation. *Child Development, 68,* 127–138.

ORENSTEIN, P. (1994). *Schoolgirls: Young women, self-esteem, and the confidence gap.* New York: Anchor.

ORNSTEIN, P. A., NAUS, M. J., & LIBERTY, C. (1975). Rehearsal and organizational processes in children's memory. *Child Development, 46,* 818–830.

ORNSTEIN, P. A., NAUS, M. J., & STONE, B. P. (1977). Rehearsal training and developmental differences in memory. *Developmental Psychology, 13,* 15–24.

OSOFSKY, J. D., & OSOFSKY, H. J. (1984). Psychological and developmental perspectives on expectant and new parenthood. In R. D. Parke (Ed.), *The family: Review of child development research* (Vol. 7). Chicago: University of Chicago Press.

OSTROV, E., OFFER, D., & HOWARD, K. I. (1989). Gender differences in adolescent symptomatology: A normative study. *Journal of the American Academy of Child and Adolescent Psychiatry, 28,* 394–398.

Oxford English Dictionary 2 on CD-ROM (1994). Oxford, U. K.: Oxford University Press.

PAERNOW, P. L. (1984). The stepfamily cycle: An experimental model of stepfamily development. *Family Relations, 33,* 355–363.

PAL, S., SHYAM, R., & SINGH, R. (1997). Genetic analysis of general intelligence "g": A twin study. *Personality and individual differences, 22,* 779–780.

PALACIOS, J. (1996). Proverbs as images of children and childrearing. In C. P. Hwang, M. E. Lamb, & I. E. Siegel (Eds.), *Images of childhood.* Mahwah, NJ: Lawrence Erlbaum.

PALKOVITZ, R. (1985). Fathers' birth attendance, early contact and extended contact with their newborns: A critical review. *Child Development, 56,* 392–406.

PALMORE, E., & MAEDA, D. (1985). *The honorable elders revisited: A revised cross-cultural analysis of aging in Japan.* Durham, NC: Duke University Press.

PAPOUSEK, H. (1961). Conditioned head rotation reflexes in infants in the first three months of life. *Acta Paediatrica Scandanavica, 50,* 565–576.

PARIS, S. C., LINDAUER, B. K., & COX, G. I. (1977). The development of inferential comprehension. *Child Development, 48,* 1728–1733.

PARKE, R. D. (1979). Perceptions of father–infant interaction. In J. Osofsky (Ed.), *Handbook of infant development.* New York: Wiley.

PARKE, R. D. (1981). *Fathers.* Cambridge, MA: Harvard University Press.

PARKE, R. D., & COLLMER, C. (1975). Child abuse: An interdisciplinary analysis. In E. M. Hetherington (Ed.), *Review of child development research* (Vol. 5). Chicago: University of Chicago Press.

PARKE, R. D., & TINSLEY, B. J. (1987). Family interaction in infancy. In J. D. Osofsky (Ed.), *Handbook of infant development* (2nd ed.). New York: Wiley.

PARKE, R., & SLABY, R. (1983). The development of aggression. In P. H. Mussen (Ed.), *Handbook of child psychology* (Vol. 4). New York: Wiley.

PARKER, J. G., & ASHER, S. R. (1987). Peer relations and later personal adjustment: Are low-accepted children at risk? *Psychological Bulletin, 102,* 357–389.

PARKER, J. G., & ASHER, S. R. (1993). Friendship and friendship quality in middle childhood: Links with peer group acceptance and feelings of loneliness and social dissatisfaction. *Developmental Psychology, 29,* 611–621.

PARKER, W. A. (1980). Designing an environment for childbirth. In B. L. Blum (Ed.), *Psychological aspects of pregnancy, birthing, and bonding.* New York: Human Sciences Press.

PARKHURST, J. T., & ASHER, S. R. (1992). Peer rejection in middle school: Subgroup differences in behavior, loneliness, and interpersonal concerns. *Developmental Psychology, 28,* 244–254.

PARMELEE, A. H., JR. (1986). Children's illnesses: Their beneficial effects on behavioral development. *Child Development, 57,* 1–10.

PARTEN, M. B. (1932–33). Social participation among preschool children. *Journal of Abnormal and Social Psychology, 27,* 243–269.

PASCALIS, O., DE HAAN, M., NELSON, C. A., & DE SCHONEN, S. (1998). Long-term recognition memory for faces assessed by visual impaired comparison in 3– and 6–month-old infants. *Journal of Experimental Psychology: Learning, Memory, and Cognition, 24,* 249–260.

PASLEY, B. K., & IHINGER-TALLMAN, M. (1989). Boundary ambiguity in remarriage: Does ambiguity differentiate degree of marital adjustment and integration? *Family Relations, 38,* 46.

PASTERNAK, J. J. (1999). *Human molecular genetics: Mechanisms of inherited diseases.* Bethesda, MD: Fitzgerald Science Press.

PATTERSON, C. J. (1995). Families of the lesbian baby boom: Parent's division of labor and children's adjustment. *Developmental Psychology, 31,* 115–123.

PATTERSON, C. J. (1995). Sexual orientation and human development: An overview. *Developmental Psychology, 31,* 3–11.

PATTERSON, C. J. (2000). Family relationships of lesbians and gay men. *Journal of Marriage and the Family, 62,* 1052–1069.

PATTERSON, C. J., KUPERSMIDT, J. B., & VADEN, N. A. (1990). Income level, gender, ethnicity, and household composition as predictors of children's school-based competence. *Child Development, 61,* 485–494.

PATTISON, E. M. (1977). *The experience of dying.* Englewood Cliffs, NJ: Prentice Hall.

PAUL, M. (1997). Occupational reproductive hazards. *The Lancet, 349,* 1385–1389.

PAULBY, S. T. (1977). Imitative interaction. In H. R. Schaffer (Ed.), *Studies of mother–infant interaction.* London: Academic Press.

PECK, R. C. (1968). Psychological developments in the second half of life. In B. L. Neugarten (Ed.), *Middle age and aging.* Chicago: University of Chicago Press.

PEDERSON, D. R., & MORAN, G. (1999). The relationship imperative: Arguments for a broad definition of attachment. *Journal of Family Psychology, 13,* 496–500.

Pediatrics (1979). The fetal monitoring debate, *63,* 942–948.

PELLEGRINI, A. D. (1987). Rough-and-tumble play: Developmental and educational significance. *Educational Psychologist, 22,* 23–43.

PELLETZ, L. (1995). *The effects of an interactive, interpersonal curriculum upon the development of self in seventh-grade girls.* Unpublished doctoral dissertation. University of Massachusetts, Amherst.

PERLMUTTER, M. (1978). What is memory aging the aging of? *Developmental Psychology, 14,* 330–345.

PERLMUTTER, M., ADAMS, C., BARRY, J., KAPLAN, M., PERSON, D., & VERDONIK, F. (1987). Aging & memory. In K. W. Schaie & K. Eisdorfer (Eds.), *Annual review of gerontology and geriatrics* (Vol. 7). New York: Springer-Verlag.

PERLS, T. T. (1995). The oldest old. *Scientific American, 272* (1), 70–76.

PERRY, D. G., & BUSSEY, K. (1984). *Social development.* Englewood Cliffs, NJ: Prentice Hall.

PERRY, D. G., WILLIARD, J. C., & PERRY, L. C. (1990). Peers' perceptions of the consequences that victimized children provide aggressors. *Child Development, 61,* 1310–1325.

PERRY, W. G., JR. (1970). *Forms of intellectual and ethical development in the college years.* NY: Holt, Rinehart & Winston.

PERRY-JENKINS, M., & CROUTER, A. C. (1990). Men's provider-role attitudes: Implications for household work and marital satisfaction. *Journal of Family Issues, 11,* 136–156.

PERRY-JENKINS, M., & FOLK, K. (1994). Class, couples, and conflict: Effects of the division of labor on assessments of marriage in dual-earner families. *Journal of Marriage and the Family, 56,* 165–180.

PETERS, J. A., DJURDJINOVIC, L., & BAKER, D. (1999). The genetic self: The Human Genome Project, genetic counseling and family therapy. *Families, Systems and Health, 17,* 5–25.

PETERSON, A. C., COMPAS, B. E., BROOKS-GUNN, J., STEMMLER, M., EY, S., & GRANT, K. E. (1993). Depression in adolescence. *American Psychologist, 48,* 155–168.

PETERSON, B. E. , & KLOHNEN, E. C. (1995). Realization of generativity in two samples of women at midlife. *Psychology and Aging, 10,* 20–29.

PETROVICH, H., MASAKI, K., & RODRIGUEZ, B. (1997). Update on women's health: Pros and cons for postmenopausal hormone replacement therapy. *Generations, 20,* (4), 7–11.

PHILLIPS, D. (1984). The illusion of incompetence among academically competent children. *Child Development, 55,* 2000–2016.

PHILLIPS, D., McCARTNEY, K., SCARR, S., & HOWES, C. (1987). Selective review of infant day care research: A cause for concern! *Zero to Three, 7* (3), 18–20.

PHILLIPS, R. B., SHARMA, R., PREMACHANDRA, B. R., VAUGHN, A. J., & REYES-LEE, M. (1996). Intrauterine exposure to cocaine: Effect on neurobehavior of neonates. *Infant Behavior and Development, 19,* 71–81.

PIAGET, J. (1926). *The language and thought of the child.* London: Kegan, Paul, Trench & Trubner.

PIAGET, J. (1932/1965). *The moral judgment of the child.* New York: Free Press.

PIAGET, J. (1936/1952). *The origins of intelligence in children.* (M. Cook, Trans.). New York: International Universities Press.

PIAGET, J. (1950). *The psychology of intelligence.* New York: Harcourt Brace.

PIAGET, J. (1951). *Play, dreams and imitation in childhood.* New York: Norton.

PIAGET, J. (1954). *The construction of reality in the child.* New York: Basic Books.

PIAGET, J. (1970). Piaget's theory. In P. H. Mussen (Ed.), *Carmichael's manual of child psychology* (3rd ed., Vol. 1). New York: Wiley.

PIAGET, J. (1972). Intellectual evolution from adolescence to adulthood. *Human Development, 15,* 1–12.

PICHITINO, J. P. (1983). Profile of the single father: A thematic integration of the literature. *Personnel and Guidance Journal, 61,* 295–300.

PIETROMONACO, P., MANIS, J., & MARKUS, H. (1987). The relationship of employment to self-perception and well-being in women: A cognitive analysis. *Sex Roles, 17,* 467–476.

PIETROMONACO, P. R., & BARRETT, L. F. (2000). Attachment theory as an organizing framework: A view from different levels of analysis. *Review of General Psychology, 4,* 107–110.

PINE, J. M., LIEVEN, E. V. M., & ROWLAND, C. F. (1997). Stylistic variation at the "single-word" stage: Relations between maternal speech characteristics and children's vocabulary composition and usage. *Child Development, 68,* 807–819.

PINKER, S. (1997). *How the mind works.* New York: Norton.

PIPER, J. M., BAUM, C., & KENNEDY, D. L. (1987). Prescription drug use before and during pregnancy in a Medicaid population. *American Journal of Obstetrics and Gynecology, 1,* 148–156.

PITCHER, E. G., & SCHULTZ, L. H. (1983). *Boys and girls at play: The development of sex roles.* New York: Praeger.

PLECK, J. H. (1985). *Working wives, working husbands.* Beverly Hills, CA: Sage.

PLOMIN, R. (1990). *Nature and nurture: An introduction to human behavioral genetics.* Pacific Grove, CA: Brooks/Cole.

PLOMIN, R., & DANIELS, D. (1987). Why are children in the same family so different from one another? *Behavioral and Brain Sciences, 10,* 1–60.

PLUMB, J. H. (1971). The great change in children. *Horizon, 15* (1), 4–12.

POE, W., & HOLLOWAY, D. (1980). *Drugs and the aged.* New York: McGraw-Hill.

POLLITT, E. (1994). Poverty and child development: Relevance of research in developing countries to the United States. *Child Development, 65,* 283–295.

POLLITT, E., GORMAN, K. S., ENGLE, P. L., MARTORELL, R., & RIVERA, J. (1993). Early supplementary feeding and cognition: Effects over two decades. *Monograph for the Society of Research in Child Development, 58.*

POLLOCK, L. A. (1983). *Forgotten children: Parent-child relations from 1500–1900.* Cambridge, UK: Cambridge University Press.

POLLOCK, L. A. (1987). *A lasting relationship: Parents and children over three centuries.* Hanover, NH: University Press of New England.

POON, L. (1985). Differences in human memory with aging: Nature, causes and clinical implications. In J. Birren & W. K. Schaie (Eds.), *Handbook of the psychology of aging* (2nd ed.). New York: Van Nostrand Reinhold.

PORTES, P. R., DUNHAM, R., & CASTILLO, K. D. (2000). Identity formation and status across cultures: Exploring the cultural validity of Eriksonian theory. In A. L. Comunian & U. P. Gielen (Eds.), *International perspectives on human development.* Lengerich, Germany: Pabst Science.

POSADA, G., GAO, Y., WU, F., POSADA, R., TASCON, M., SHOELMERICH, A., SAGI, A., KONDO-IKEMURA, K., HAALAND, W., & SYNNEVAAG, B. (1995). The secure-base phenomenon across cultures: Children's behavior, mothers' preferences, and experts' concepts. *Monographs of the Society for Research in Child Development, 60* (2–3), 27–48.

POTTS, M. K. (1997). Social support and depression among older adults living alone: The importance of friends with and outside of a retirement community. *Social Work, 42,* 348–361.

POWER, C., & REIMER, J. (1978). Moral atmosphere: An educational bridge between moral judgment and action. In W. Damon (Ed.), *New directions for child development, 2.* San Francisco: Jossey-Bass.

POWERS, S. I., HAUSER, S. T., & KILNER, L. A. (1989). Adolescent mental health. *American Psychologist, 44,* 200–208.

PROWS, C. A., & HOPKIN, R. J. (1999). Prader Willi and Angelman syndromes: Exemplars of genomic imprinting. *Journal of Perinatal and Neonatal Nursing, 13* (Sept), 76–85.

PRUCHNO, R., & RESCH, N. (1989). Husbands and wives as caregivers: Antecedents of depression and burden. *The Gerontologist, 29,* 159–165.

PRUETT, K. D. (1987). *The nurturing father: Journey toward the complete man.* New York: Warner Books.

PUBLIC HEALTH SERVICE (2000). Healthy people 2000: National health promotion and disease prevention objectives—full report, with commentary. Washington, DC: U.S. Department of Health.

PURCELL, P., & SEWART, L. (1990). Dick and Jane in 1989. *Sex Roles, 22,* 177–185.

PUTALLAZ, M. (1983). Predicting children's sociometric status from their behavior. *Child Development, 54,* 1417–1426.

QUADREL, M. J., FISCHOFF, B., & DAVIS, W. (1993). Adolescent (in) vulnerability. *American Psychologist, 48,* 102–116.

QUINN, J. F., & BURKHAUSER, R. V. (1990). Work and retirement. In R. H. Binstock & L. K. George (Eds.), *Handbook of aging and the social sciences* (3rd ed.). New York: Academic Press.

RADBILL, S. (1974). A history of child abuse and infanticide. In R. Helfer & C. Kempe (Eds.), *The battered child.* Chicago: University of Chicago Press.

RADKE-YARROW, M., ZAHN-WAXLER, C., & CHAPMAN, M. (1983). Children's prosocial dispositions and behavior. In E. M. Hetherington (Ed.), *Handbook of child psychology, Vol. 4: Socialization, personality and social development.* New York: Wiley.

RALOFF, J. (1998). Fetal deaths climb with air pollution. *Science News, 153* (20), 309.

RAMEY, C. T., & RAMEY, S. L. (1998). Early intervention and early experience. *American Psychologist, 53,* 109–120.

RAMEY, C. T., CAMPBELL, F. A., & RAMEY, S. L. (1999). Early intervention: Successful pathways to improving intellectual development. *Developmental Neuropsychology, 16,* 385–392.

RANDO, T. (1986). A comprehensive analysis of anticipatory grief: Perspectives, processes, promises, and problems. In T. Rando (Ed.), *Loss and anticipatory grief.* Lexington, MA: Lexington Books.

RATNER, H. H. (1984). Memory demands and the development of young children's memory. *Child Development, 55,* 2173–2191.

RATNER, N., & BRUNER, J. S. (1978). Games, social exchange and the acquisition of language. *Journal of Child Development, 5,* 1–15.

RAUSTE-VON WRIGHT, M. (1989). Body image satisfaction in adolescent girls and boys: A longitudinal study. *Journal of Youth and Adolescence, 18,* 71–83.

REICH, P. A. (1986). *Language development.* Englewood Cliffs, NJ: Prentice Hall.

REID, M. (1990). Prenatal diagnosis and screening. In J. Garcia, R. Kilpatrick, & M. Richards (Eds.), *The politics of maternity care.* Oxford: Clarendon Press.

REINKE, B. J., ELLICOTT, A. M., HARRIS, R. L., & HANCOCK, E. (1985). Timing of psychosocial changes in women's lives. *Human Development, 28,* 259–280.

REITZES, D. C., MUTRAN, E. J., & FERNANDEZ, M. E. (1996). Does retirement hurt well-being? Factors influencing self-esteem and depression among retirees and workers. *The Gerontologist, 36,* 649–656.

REMAFEDI, G. (1999). Sexual orientation and youth suicide. *Journal of the American Medical Association, 282,* 1291–1292.

REMAFEDI, G., FRENCH, S., STORY, M., RESNICK, M. D., & BLUM, R. (1998). The relationship between suicide risk and sexual orientation: Results of a population-based study. *American Journal of Public Health, 88,* 57–60.

REPETTI, R., MATTHEWS, K., & WALDRON, I. (1989). Employment and women's health: Effects of paid employment on women's mental and physical health. *American Psychologist, 44,* 1394–1401.

RESTAK, R. (1986). *The infant mind.* Garden City, NY: Doubleday.

REYNOLDS, W., REMER, R., & JOHNSON, M. (1995). Marital satisfaction in later life: An examination of equity, equality, and reward theories. *International Journal of Aging and Human Development, 40,* 155–173.

RICHARDSON, S. O. (1992). Historical perspectives on dyslexia. *Journal of Learning Disabilities, 25,* 40–47.

RICHARDSON, V. E. (1999). How circumstances of widowhood and retirement affect adjustment among older men. *Journal of Mental Health and Aging, 5,* 165–174.

RICHLIN-KLONSKY, J., & BENGSTON, V. L. (1996). Pulling together, drifting apart: A longitudinal case study of a four-generation family. *Journal of Aging Studies, 10,* 255–279.

RICHMAN, A. L., LEVINE, R. A., NEW, R. A., HOWRIGAN, G. A., WELLES-NYSTROM, B., & LEVINE, S. E. (1988). Maternal behavior to infants in five cultures. In R. A. LeVine, P. M. Miller, & M. M. West (Eds.), *New directions for child development, 40.* San Francisco: Jossey-Bass.

RICKS, S. S. (1985). Father–infant interactions: A review of empirical research. *Family Relations, 34,* 505–511.

RIEGEL, K. F. (1973). Dialectic operations: The final period of cognitive development. *Human Development, 16,* 346–370.

RIEGEL, K. F. (1975). Adult life crises: A dialectical interpretation of development. In N. Datan & L. H. Ginsberg (Eds.), *Life-span developmental psychology: Normative life crises.* New York: Academic Press.

RIZZO, T. A., & CORSARO, W. A. (1988). Toward a better understanding of Vygotsky's process of internalization: Its role in the development of the concept of friendship. *Developmental Review, 8,* 219–237.

RIZZOLI, R, & BONJOUR, J.-P. (1997). Hormones and bones. *The Lancet, 349* (3), SI20–SI23.

ROBBINS, D. (1986). Legal and ethical issues in terminal illness care for patients, families, care-givers, and institutions. In T. Rando (Ed.), *Loss and anticipatory grief.* Lexington, MA: Lexington Books.

ROBERTS, R., & NEWTON, P. M. (1987). Levinsonian studies of women's adult development. *Psychology and Aging, 2,* 154–163.

ROBERTSON, M. (1984). Changing motor patterns during childhood. In J. R. Thomas (Ed.), *Motor development during childhood and adolescence.* Minneapolis: Burgess.

ROBINSHAW, H. M. (1994). Deaf infants, early intervention and language acquisition. *Early Child Development and Care, 99,* 1–22.

ROBINSON, I. E., & JEDLICKA, D. (1982). Change in sexual behavior of college students from 1965–1980: A research note. *Journal of Marriage and the Family, 44,* 237–240.

ROCHAT, P. (1989). Object manipulation and exploration in 2– to 5–month-old infants. *Developmental Psychology, 25,* 871–884.

ROCHAT, P., GOUBET, N., & SENDERS, S. J. (1999). To reach or not to reach? Perception of body effectiveness by young infants. *Infant and Child Development, 8,* 129–148.

RODIN, J., & ICKOVICS, J. (1990). Women's health: Review and research agenda as we approach the 21st century. *American Psychologist, 45,* 1018–1034.

ROGEL, M. J., & PETERSON, A. C. (1984). Some adolescent experiences of motherhood. In R. Cohen, B. Cohler, & S. Weissman (Eds.), *Parenthood: A psychodynamic perspective.* New York: Guilford.

ROGERS, C. (1980). *A way of being.* Boston: Houghton Mifflin.

ROGERS, W. A., & FISK, D. (2000). Human factors, applied cognition, and aging. In F. I. M. Craik & T. A. Salthouse (Eds.), *Handbook of aging and cognition* (2nd ed.). Mahwah, NJ: Erlbaum.

ROGGMAN, L. A., LANGLOIS, J. H., HUBBS-TAIT, L., & RIESER-DANNER, L. A. (1994). Infant day-care, attachment, and the "file drawer problem." *Child Development, 65,* 1429–1443.

ROGOFF, B. (1990). *Apprenticeship in thinking: Cognitive development in social context.* New York: Oxford University Press.

ROGOFF, B. (1993). Commentary. *Human Development, 36,* 24–26.

ROGOFF, B., MISTRY, J., GONCU, A., & MOSIER, C. (1993). Guided participation in cultural activity by toddlers and caregivers. *Monographs of the Society for Research in Child Development, 58* (8).

ROSCOE, B., DIANA, M. S., & BROOKS, R. H., II. (1987). Early, middle, and late adolescents' views on dating and factors influencing partner selection. *Adolescence, 12,* 59–68.

ROSENBERG, S. D., ROSENBERG, H. J., & FARRELL, M. P. (1999). The midlife crisis revisited. In S. L. Willis & J. D. Reid (Eds.), *Life in the middle: Psychological and social development in middle age.* San Diego: Academic Press.

ROSENSTEIN, D., & OSTER, H. (1988). Differential facial response to four basic tastes in newborns. *Child Development, 59,* 1555–1568.

ROSENTHAL, E. (1990). New insights on why some children are fat offers clues on weight loss. *New York Times, 139,* (Jan 4), B7–B8.

ROSENTHAL, J. A. (1988). Patterns of reported child abuse and neglect. *Child Abuse and Neglect, 12,* 263–271.

ROSENZWEIG, M. R. (1963). The mechanisms of hunger and thirst. In L. Postman (Ed.), *Psychology in the Making: Histories of selected research problems.* New York: Knopf.

ROSKINSKI, R. R. (1977). *The development of visual perception.* Santa Monica, CA: Goodyear.

ROSS, A. O. (1977). *Learning disability, the unrealized potential.* New York: McGraw-Hill.

ROSS, H. S., & LOLLIS, S. P. (1987). Communication within infant social games. *Developmental Psychology, 23,* 241–248.

ROSS, H., & SAWHILL, I. (1975). *Time of transition: The growth of families headed by women.* Washington, DC: Urban Institute.

ROSS, L. (1981). The "intuitive scientist" formulation and its developmental implications. In J. H. Flavell & L. Ross (Eds.), *Social cognitive development.* Cambridge, UK: Cambridge University Press.

ROSS, M. H., YURGELUN-TODD, D. A., RENSHAW, P. F., MAAS, L. C., MENDELSON, J. H., MELLO, N. K., COHEN, B. M., & LEVIN, J. M. (1997). Age-related reduction in functional MRI response to photic stimulation. *Neurology, 48,* 173–176.

ROSSMAN, I. (1977). Anatomic and body-composition changes with aging. In C. E. Finch & L. Hayflick (Eds.), *Handbook of the biology of aging.* New York: Van Nostrand Reinhold.

ROTHBART, M. K., AHADI, S. A., & HERSHEY, K. L. (1994). Temperament and social behavior in childhood. *Merrill-Palmer Quarterly, 36,* 179–192.

ROUG, L., LANDBERG, I., & LUNDBERG, L. J. (1989). Phonetic development in early infancy: A study of four Swedish children during the first eighteen months of life. *Journal of Child Language, 16,* 19–40.

ROVEE-COLLIER, C. (1987). Learning and memory in infancy. In J. Osofsky (Ed.), *Handbook of infant development* (2nd ed.). New York: Wiley.

ROWE, J. W., & KAHN, R. L. (1997). Successful aging. *The Gerontologist, 37,* 433–440.

RUBENSTEIN, A. J., KALAKANIS, L., & LANGLOIS, J. H. (1999). Infant preferences for attractive faces: A cognitive explanation. *Developmental Psychology, 35,* 848–855.

RUBENSTEIN, C. (1994). Helping teachers and schools to nip sex bias in the bud. *New York Times, 143,* (April 28), C4.

RUBIN, K., & TROTTEN, K. (1977). Kohlberg's moral judgment scale: Some methodological considerations. *Developmental Psychology, 13,* 535–536.

RUBIN, K. H. (1983). Recent perspectives on social competence and peer status: Some introductory remarks. *Child Development, 54,* 1383–1385.

RUBIN, K. H., & COPLAN, R. J. (1992). Peer relationships in childhood. In M. H. Bornstein & M. E. Lamb (Eds.), *Developmental psychology: An advanced textbook* (3rd ed.). Hillsdale, NJ: Erlbaum.

RUBIN, K. H., FEIN, G. C., & VANDENBERG, B. (1983). In P. H. Mussen (Ed.), *Handbook of child psychology* (Vol. 4). New York: Wiley.

RUBIN, L. (1980). The empty nest: Beginning or end? In L. Bond & J. Rosen (Eds.), *Competence and coping during adulthood.* Hanover, NH: University Press of New England.

RUBIN, Z. (1980). *Children's friendships.* Cambridge, MA: Harvard University Press.

RUBINSTEIN, E. A. (1983). Television and behavior: Conclusion of the 1982 NIMH report and their policy implications. *American Psychologist, 38,* 820–825.

RUBLE, D. (1988). Sex-role development. In M. Bornstein & M. E. Lamb (Eds.), *Developmental psychology: An advanced textbook* (2nd ed.). Hillsdale, NJ: Erlbaum.

RUBLE, D. N., & BROOKS-GUNN, J. (1982). The experience of menarche. *Child Development, 53,* 1557–1577.

RUDD, P., & BALASCHKE, T. (1982) Antihypertensive agents and the drug therapy of hypertension. In A. Gilman, L. Goodman, T. Rall, & F. Murad (Eds.), *Goodman and Gilman's the pharmacological basis of therapeutics* (7th ed.), 784–805.

RUDOLFSDOTTIR, A. G. (2000). "I am not a patient, and I am not a child": The institutionalization and experience of pregnancy. *Feminism and Psychology, 10,* 337–350.

RUSHTON, T. P. (1976). Socialization and the altruistic behavior of children. *Psychological Bulletin, 83,* 898–913.

RUSSELL, D. (1983). The incidence and prevalence of intrafamilial and extrafamilial sexual abuse of female children. *Child Abuse and Neglect, 7,* 133–146.

RUSSELL, G. W., ARMS, R. L., & BIBBY, R. W. (1995). Canadian's beliefs in catharsis. *Social Behavior and Personality, 23,* 223–228.

RUTH, J., & COLEMAN, P. (1995). Personality and aging: Coping and management of self in later life. In J. E. Birren & K. W. Schaie (Eds.), *Handbook of the psychology of aging* (4th ed.). San Diego: Academic Press.

RUTTER, M. (1979). Protective factors in children's responses to stress and disadvantage. In M. W. Kent & J. E. Rolf (Eds.), *Primary prevention of psychopathology: III. Social competence in children.* Hanover, NH: University Press of New England.

RUTTER, M. (1983). Stress, coping and development: Some issues and questions. In N. Garmezy & M. Rutter (Eds.), *Stress, coping and development in children.* New York: McGraw-Hill.

RUTTER, M., & GARMEZY, N. (1983). Developmental psychopathology. In P. H. Mussen (Ed.), *Handbook of child psychology* (Vol. 4). New York: Wiley.

RYFF, C. D. (1985). The subjective experience of life-span transitions. In A. S. Rossi (Ed.), *Gender and the life course.* New York: Aldine.

RYFF, C. D. (1989). In the eye of the beholder: Views of psychological well-being among middle-aged and older adults. *Psychology and Aging, 4,* 195–210.

RYNES, S., & ROSEN, B. (1983). A comparison of male and female reactions to career advancement opportunities. *Journal of Vocational Behavior, 22,* 105–116.

SABATINI, T., FRISONI, G. B., BARBISONI, P., BELLELLI, G., ROZZINI, R., & TRABUCCHI, M. (2000). Atrial fibrillation and cognitive disorders in older people. *Journal of the American Geriatrics Society, 48,* 387–390.

SACK, W. H., HIM, C., & DICKASON, D. (1999). Twelve-year follow-up study of Khmer youths who suffered massive war trauma as children. *Journal of the American Academy of Child and Adolescent Psychiatry, 38,* 1173–1179.

SADKER, M., & SADKER, D. (1995). *Failing at fairness: How America's schools cheat girls.* New York: Scribner & Sons.

SAFREN, S. A., & HEIMBERG, R. G. (1999). Depression, hopelessness, suicidality, and related factors in sexual minority and heterosexual adolescents. *Journal of Consulting and Clinical Psychology, 67,* 859–866.

SAGI, A., & HOFFMAN, M. L. (1976). Empathic distress in the newborn. *Developmental Psychology, 12,* 175–176.

SAGI, A., & HOFFMAN, M. L. (1994). Empathic distress in the newborn. In B. Puka et al. *Reaching out: Caring, altruism, and prosocial behavior.* New York: Garland.

SALES, B. D., & FOLKMAN, S. (Eds.) (2000). *Ethics in research with human participants.* Washington, DC: American Psychological Association.

SALT, P., GALLER, J. R., & RAMSEY, F. C. (1988). The influence of early malnutrition of subsequent behavioral development VII: The effects of maternal depressive symptoms. *Developmental and Behaviorial Pediatrics, 9,* 1–5.

SALTHOUSE, T. (1985). Speed of behavior and its implications for cognition. In J. E. Birren & K. W. Schaie (Eds.), *Handbook of the psychology of aging* (2nd ed.). New York: Van Nostrand Reinhold.

SALTHOUSE, T. (1987). The role of experience in cognitive aging. In K. W. Schaie & K. Eisdorfer (Eds.), *Annual review of gerontology and geriatrics* (Vol. 7). New York: Springer.

SALTHOUSE, T. (1990). Cognitive competence and expertise in aging. In J. Birren & K. W. Schaie (Eds.), *Handbook of the psychology of aging* (3rd ed.). San Diego: Academic Press.

SALTHOUSE, T., BABCOCK, R., SKOVRONEK, E., MITCHELL, D., & PALMON, R. (1990). Age and experience effects in spatial visualization. *Developmental Psychology, 26,* 128–136.

SALTHOUSE, T., & MITCHELL, D. (1990). Effect of age and naturally occurring experience on spatial visualization performance. *Developmental Psychology, 26,* 845–854.

SALZMAN, C. (1982) A primer on geriatric psychopharmacology. *American Journal of Psychiatry, 139,* 67–74.

SAMEROFF, A. J., SEIFER, R., BALDWIN, A., & BALDWIN, C. (1993). Stability of intelligence from preschool to adolescence: The influence of social and family risk factors. *Child Development, 64,* 80–97.

SCANLON, J. (1979). *Young adulthood.* New York: Academy for Educational Development.

SCARBOROUGH, H. S. (1989). Prediction of reading disability from familial and individual differences. *Journal of Educational Psychology, 81,* 101–108.

SCARR, S., & McCARTNEY, K. (1985). How people make their own environments: A theory of genotype-evironmental effects. *Child Development, 54,* 424–435.

SCARR, S. (1998). On Arthur Jensen's integrity. *Intelligence, 26,* 227–232.

SCARR, S., PHILLIPS, D., & McCARTNEY, K. (1989). Working mothers and their families. *American Psychologist, 44,* 1402–1409.

SCARR, S., & WEINBERG, R. A. (1983). The Minnesota Adoption Studies: Genetic differences and malleability. *Child Development, 54,* 260–267.

SCHACTER, D. L., KAGAN, J., & LEICHTMAN, M. D. (1995). True and false memories in children and adults: A cognitive neuroscience perspective. *Psychology, Public Policy, and Law, 1,* 411–428.

SCHACTER, F., & STRAGE, A. (1982). Adult's talk and children's language development. In S. Moore & C. Cooper (Eds.), *The young child: Reviews of research* (Vol. 3). Washington, DC: National Association for the Education of Young Children.

SCHAEFER, M. R., SOBIERAJ, K., & HOLLYFIELD, R. L. (1988). Prevalence of childhood physical abuse in adult male veteran alcoholics. *Child Abuse and Neglect, 12,* 141–149.

SCHAFFER, H. R. (1977). *Studies in mother–infant interaction.* London: Academic Press.

SCHAIE, K. W. (1977/1978). Toward a stage theory of adult cognitive development. *Journal of Aging and Human Development, 8,* 129–138.

SCHAIE, K. W. (1983). The Seattle longitudinal study: A twenty-one year exploration of psychometric intelligence in adulthood. In K. W. Schaie (Ed.), *Longitudinal studies of adult psychological development.* New York: Guilford.

SCHAIE, K. W. (1986). Beyond calendar definitions of age, period and cohort: The general developmental model revisited. *Developmental Review, 6,* 252–277.

SCHAIE, K. W. (1990). Intellectual development in adulthood. In J. Birren & K. W. Schaie (Eds.), *Handbook of the psychology of aging* (3rd. ed.). San Diego: Academic Press.

SCHAIE, K. W. (1995). *Intellectual development in adulthood: The Seattle longitudinal study.* New York: Cambridge University Press.

SCHARDEIN, J. L. (1976). *Drugs as teratogens.* Cleveland, OH: Chemical Rubber Co. Press.

SCHAUFELI, W. B., MASLACH, C., & MAREK, T. (Eds.) (1993). *Professional burnout: Recent developments in theory and research.* Washington, DC: Taylor & Francis.

SCHEIER, L. M., & BOTVIN, G. J. (1998). Relations of social skills, personal competence, and adolescent alcohol use: A developmental exploratory study. *Journal of Early Adolescence, 18,* 77–114.

SCHLESINGER, J. M. (1982). *Steps to language: Toward a theory of native language acquisition.* Hillsdale, NJ: Erlbaum.

SCHNEIDER, B. A., & PICHORA-FULLER, M. K. (2000). Implications of perceptual deterioration for cognitive aging research. In F. I. M. Craik & T. A. Salthouse (Eds.), *Handbook of aging and cognition* (2nd ed.). Mahwah, NJ: Erlbaum.

SCHNEIDER, E. (1992). Biological theories of aging. *Generations, 16* (4), 7–10.

SCHNEIDER, M. L., ROUGHTON, E. C., & LUBACH, G. R. (1997). Moderate alcohol consumption and psychological stress during pregnancy induce attention and neuromotor impairments in primate infants. *Child Development, 68,* 747–759.

SCHNEIDER, M. L., ROUGHTON, E. C., KOEHLER, A. J., & LUBACH, G. R. (1999). Growth and development following prenatal stress exposure in primates: An examination of ontogenetic vulnerability. *Child Development, 70,* 263–274.

SCHNEIDER, R., & SCHRECK, L. (1999). Birth weight varies by black mothers' place of birth and community's income. *Family Planning Perspectives, 31,* 205.

SCHOFIELD, J. W. (1981). Complementary and conflicting identities: Images and interaction in an interracial school. In S. R. Asher & J. M. Gottman (Eds.), *The development of children's friendships.* New York: Cambridge University Press.

SCHOOLER, C. (1987). Psychological effects of complex environments during the life span: A review and theory. In C. Schooler & K. W. Schaie (Eds.), *Cognitive functioning and social structure over the life course.* Norwood, NJ: Ablex.

SCHOOLER, C. (1990). Psychosocial factors and effective cognitive functioning in adulthood. In J. E. Birren & K. W. Schaie (Eds.), *Handbook of the psychology of aging* (3rd ed.). San Diego: Academic Press.

SCHRECK, L. (1998). After early amniocentesis, chances of fetal loss and foot deformity rise. *Family Planning Perspectives, 30,* 249–250.

SCHUEKLENK, U., & RISTOW, M. (1996). The ethics of research into the cause(s) of homosexuality. *Journal of Homosexuality, 31,* 5–30.

SCHULZ, R., & HECKHAUSEN, J. (1996). A lifespan model of successful aging. *American Psychologist, 51,* 702–714.

SCHULZ, R., & SALTHOUSE, T. (1999). *Adult development and aging: Myths and emerging realities* (3rd ed.). Upper Saddle River, NJ: Prentice Hall.

SCHULZ, R., MUSA, D., STASZEWSKI, J., & SIEGLER, R. S. (1994). The relationship between age and major league baseball performance: Implications for development. *Psychology and Aging, 9,* 274–286.

SCHWARTZ, J. I. (1981). Children's experiments with language. *Young Children, 36,* 16–26.

SCRIMSHAW, N. S. (1997). The relation between fetal malnutrition and chronic disease in later life: Good nutrition and lifestyle matter from womb to tomb. *British Medical Journal, 315,* 825–826.

SEARS, R. R. (1963). Dependency motivation. In M. R. Jones (Ed.), *The Nebraska symposium on motivation* (Vol. 11). Lincoln, NE: University of Nebraska Press.

SEBALD, H. (1989). Adolescents' peer orientation: Changes in the support system during the past three decades. *Adolescence, 24,* 937–946.

SEGAL, L. B., OSTER, H., COHEN, M., CASPI, B., MYERS, M., & BROWN, D. (1995). Smiling and fussing in seven-month-old preterm and full-term Black infants in the still-face situation. *Child Development, 66,* 1829–1843.

SEGAL, N. L. (2000). *Entwined lives: Twins and what they tell us about human behavior.* New York: Dutton.

SEGALL, M. H., DASEN, P. R., BERRY, J. W., & POORTINGA, Y. H. (1999). *Human behavior in global perspective: An introduction to cross-cultural psychology* (2nd ed.). Boston: Allyn and Bacon.

SELIGMAN, M. E. P. (1974). Submissive death: Giving up on life. *Psychology Today, 7* (12), 80–85.

SELIKOWITZ, M. (1997). *Down syndrome: The facts* (2nd ed.). Oxford, UK: Oxford University Press.

SELMAN, R. L. (1976). The development of interpersonal reasoning. In A. Pick (Ed.), *Minnesota symposia on child psychology* (Vol. 1). Minneapolis: University of Minnesota Press.

SELMAN, R. L. (1981). The child as a friendship philosopher. In S. R. Asher & J. M. Gottman (Eds.), *The development of children's friendships.* Cambridge, UK: Cambridge University Press.

SELTZER, V. C. (1989). *The psychosocial worlds of the adolescent.* New York: Wiley.

SERBIN, L. A., POWLISHTA, K. K., & GULKO, J. (1993). The development of sex typing in middle childhood. *Monographs of the Society for Research in Child Development, 58,* 1–73.

SHAFFER, D. R. (1988). *Social and personality development* (2nd ed.). Pacific Grove, CA: Brooks/Cole.

SHANTZ, C. (1983). Social cognition. In P. H. Mussen (Ed.), *Handbook of child psychology* (Vol. 3). New York: Wiley.

SHANTZ, C. U. (1987). Conflicts between children. *Child Development, 51*, 283–305.

SHAPIRO, B., FAGEN, J., PRIGOT, J., CARROLL, M., & SHALAN, J. (1998). Infants' emotional and regulatory behaviors in response to violations of expectancies. *Infant Behavior & Development, 21*, 299–313.

SHAPIRO, M. (1978). Legal rights of the terminally ill. *Aging, 5* (3), 23–27.

SHARABANY, R., GERSHONI, R., & HOFFMAN, J. E. (1981). Girlfriend, boyfriend: Age and sex differences in intimate friendship. *Developmental Psychology, 17*, 800–808.

SHARMA, D., & FISCHER, K. W. (1998). Socioemotional development across cultures. In D. Sharma & K. W. Fischer (Eds.), *New Directions for Child Development, 81*. San Francisco: Jossey-Bass.

SHATZ, C. (1992). The developing brain. *Scientific American, 267* (9), 61–67.

SHATZ, M. (1991). Using cross-cultural research to inform us about the role of language in development: Comparisons of Japanese, Korean, and English, and of German, American English, and British English. In M. H. Bornstein, (Ed.), *Cultural approaches to parenting*. Hillsdale, NJ: Erlbaum.

SHATZ, M., & GELMAN, R. (1973). The development of communication skills: Modifications in the speech of young children as a function of the listener. *Monographs of the Society for Research in Child Development, 38*.

SHAYWITZ, S. E., SHAYWITZ, B. A., FLETCHER, J. M., & ESCOBAR, M. D. (1991). Reading disability in children. *Journal of the American Medical Association, 265*, 725–726.

SHEA, C. H., SHEBILSKE, W. L., & WORCHEL, S. (1993). *Motor learning and control*. Englewood Cliffs, NJ: Prentice Hall.

SHEEHY, G. (1995). *New passages: Mapping your life across time*. New York: Random House.

SHEIMAN, D. L., & SLOMIN, M. (1988). *Resources for middle childhood*. New York, NY: Garland.

SHERIF, M., HARVEY, O. J., WHITE, B. J., HOOD, W. B., & SHERIF, C. W. (1961). *Intergroup conflict and cooperation: The robber's cave experiment*. Norman, OK: University of Oklahoma Press.

SHERMAN, E. (1987). *Meaning in mid-life transitions*. Albany: State University of New York Press.

SHI, R., WERKER, J. F., & MORGAN, J. L. (1999). Newborn infants' sensitivity to perceptual cues to lexical and grammatical words. *Cognition, 72*, B11–B21.

SHIELDS, A. M., CICCHETTI, D., & RYAN, R. M. (1994). The development of emotional and behavioral self-regulation and social competence among maltreated school-age children. *Development and Psychopathology, 6*, 57–75.

SHIFFRIN, R. M., & SCHNEIDER, W. (1977). Controlled and automatic human information processing II: Perceptual learning, automatic attending, and a general theory. *Psychological Review, 84*, 127–190.

SHORE, R. (1997). *Rethinking the brain: New insights in early development*. New York: Families and Work Institute.

SHREEVE, J. (1996). Terms of estrangement. *Discover, 15*, (11), 6–8.

SHUCHMAN, M., & WILKES, M. S. (1990). Dramatic progress against depression. *New York Times Magazine, 140* (Oct. 7), S12.

SHULMAN, S., & KLEIN, M. M. (1993). Distinctive role of the father in adolescent separation–individuation. In S. Shulman & W. A. Collins (Eds.), *New Directions for Child Development, 62*, 41–58. San Francisco: Jossey-Bass.

SHULMAN, S., LAURSEN, B., KALMAN, Z., & KARPOVSKY, S. (1997). Adolescent intimacy revisited. *Journal of Youth & Adolescence, 26*, 597–617.

SHUTE, N. (1997). A study for the ages. *U.S. News and World Report, 122* (22), 67–70, 72, 76–78, 80.

SIEBER, J. E. (2000). Planning research: Basic ethical decision-making. In B. D. Sales & S. Folkman (Eds.), *Ethics in research with human participants*. Washington, DC: American Psychological Association.

SIEBER, R. T., & GORDON, A. J. (1981). Socialization implications of school discipline or how first graders are taught to listen. In *Children and their organizations: Investigations in American culture*. Boston: G. K. Hall.

SIEGLER, I. C., & COSTA, P. T., JR. (1985). Health behavior relationships. In J. E. Birren & K. W. Schaie (Eds.), *Handbook of the psychology of aging* (2nd ed.). New York: Van Nostrand Reinhold.

SIEGLER, I. C., KAPLAN, B. H., VON DRAS, D. D., & MARK, D. B. (1999). Cardiovascular health: A challenge for midlife. In S. L. Willis & J. D. Reid (Eds.), *Life in the middle: Psychological and social development in middle age*. San Diego: Academic Press.

SIEGLER, R. S. (1986). *Children's thinking*. Englewood Cliffs, NJ: Prentice Hall.

SIEGLER, R. S. (1991). *Children's thinking* (2nd ed.). Englewood Cliffs, NJ: Prentice Hall.

SIEGLER, R. S., & ELLIS, S. (1996). Piaget on childhood. *Psychological Science, 7*, 211–215.

SIGNORIELLI, N. (1989). Television and conceptions about sex roles: Maintaining conventionality and the status quo. *Sex Roles, 21*, 341–350.

SIMONEAU, G. G., & LEIBOWITZ, H. W. (1995). Posture, gait, and falls. In J. E. Birren & K. W. Schaie (Eds.), *Handbook of the psychology of aging* (4th ed.). San Diego: Academic Press.

SIMONTON, D. (1990). Creativity and wisdom in aging. In J. Birren & K. W. Schaie (Eds.), *Handbook of the psychology of aging* (3rd ed.). San Diego: Academic Press.

SIMOPOULOS, A. P. (1983). Nutrition. In C. C. Brown (Ed.), *Prenatal Roundtable: Vol. 9, Childhood learning disabilities and prenatal risk*. Rutherford, NJ: Johnson & Johnson.

SINFELD, A. (1985). Being out of work. In C. Littler (Ed.), *The experience of work*. New York: St. Martin's Press.

SINGER, D., & SINGER, J. (Eds.) (2000). *Handbook of children and the media*. Washington, DC: Sage.

SINGER, D. G., & SINGER, J. L. (1990). *The house of make believe: Children's play and developing imagination*. Cambridge, MA: Harvard University Press.

SKINNER, B. F. (1938). *The behavior of organisms*. New York: Appleton-Century-Crofts.

SKINNER, B. F. (1953). *Science and human behavior*. New York: The Free Press.

SKOLNICK, A. (1990). It's important, but don't bank on exercise alone to prevent osteoporosis, experts say. *Journal of the American Medical Association, 263* (13), 1751–1752.

SLADE, P., MACPHERSON, S. A., HUME, A., & MARESH, M. (1993). Expectations, experiences and satisfaction with labour. *British Journal of Clinical Psychology, 32*, 469–483.

SLATER, A., & JOHNSON, S. P. (1998). Visual sensory and perceptual abilities of the newborn: Beyond the blooming, buzzing confusion. In F. Simion & G. Butterworth (Eds.), *The development of sensory, motor and cogntive capacities in early infancy: From perception to cognition*. Hove, UK: Erlbaum.

SLAVIN, R. E. (1995). *Cooperative learning* (2nd ed.). Boston: Allyn & Bacon.

SLAVIN, R. E. (1996). Neverstreaming: Preventing learning disabilities. *Educational Leadership, 53*, 4–7.

SLOBIN, D. I. (1972). Children and Language: They learn the same way all around the world. *Psychology Today, 6* (2), 71–74, 82.

SMETANA, J. (1988). Concepts of self and social convention: Adolescents' and parents' reasoning about hypothetical and actual family conflicts. In M. Gunnar & W. Collins (Eds.), *Minnesota Symposia on Child Development, Vol. 21: Development during the transition to adolescence*. Hillsdale, NJ: Erlbaum.

SMITH, A. D., & REID, W. J. (1986). Role expectations and attitudes in dual-earner families. *Social Casework, 67*, 394–402.

SMITH, B. S., RATNER, H. H., & HOBART, C. J. (1987). The role of cueing and organization in children's memory for events. *Journal of Experimental Child Psychology, 44*, 1–24.

SMITH, C. D. (1994). *The absentee American: Repatriates' perspectives on America*. Bayside, NY: Aletheia.

SMITH, C., & LLOYD, B. (1978). Maternal behavior and perceived sex of infant: Revisited. *Child Development, 49*, 1263–1265.

SMITH, L. B., THELEN, E., TITZER, R., & McLIN, D. (1999). Knowing in the context of acting: The task dynamics of the A-Not-B Error. *Psychological Review, 106*, 235–260.

SMITH, M. B. (2000). Moral foundations of research with human participants. In B. D. Sales & S. Folkman (Eds.), *Ethics in research with human participants*. Washington, DC: American Psychological Association.

SNOW, C. E. (1993). Families as social contexts for literacy development. In C. Daiute (Ed.), *New directions for child development, 61*. San Francisco: Jossey-Bass.

SOCIAL SECURITY ADMINISTRATION (2000). *The future of social security*. Washington, DC: U.S. Government Printing Office.

SOCIETY FOR RESEARCH IN CHILD DEVELOPMENT (SRCD). (1996). Ethical standards for research with children. In *SRCD directory of members*, 337–339.

SOKEN, N. H., & PICK, A. D. (1999). Infants' perception of dynamic affective expressions.

Do infants distinguish specific expressions? *Child Development, 70,* 1275–1282.

SONENSTEIN, F. L. (1987). Teenage childbearing...in all walks of life. *Brandeis Review, 7* (1), 25–28.

SORENSON, R. C. (1973). *Adolescent sexuality in contemporary America: Personal values and sexual behavior, ages 13–19.* New York: World.

SPANIER, G., & FURSTENBERG, E. (1982). Remarriage after divorce: A longitudinal analysis of well-being. *Journal of Marriage and the Family, 44,* 709–720.

SPELKE, E. S (1988). The origins of physical knowledge. In L. Weiskrantz (Ed.), *Thought without language.* Oxford, UK: Clarendon Press / Oxford University Press.

SPENCER, M. B. (1988). Self-concept development. In D. T. Slaughter (Ed.), *New directions for child development, 42.* San Francisco: Jossey-Bass.

SPERRY, R. W. (1968). Hemisphere deconnection and unity in conscious awareness. *American Psychologist, 23,* 723–733.

SPITZE, G., & LOGAN, J. (1989). Gender differences in family support: Is there a payoff? *The Gerontologist, 29,* 108–113.

SPITZE, G., & LOGAN, J. (1990). Sons, daughters, and intergenerational social support. *Journal of Marriage and the Family, 52,* 420–430.

SPITZER, M. (1988). Taste acuity in institutionalized and noninstitutionalized elderly men. *Journal of Gerontology, 43,* 71–74.

SPORE, D. L., MOR, V., PARRAT, P., HAWES, C., & HIRIS, J. (1997). Inappropriate drug prescriptions for elderly residents of board and care facilities. *American Journal of Public Health, 87,* 404–409.

SPRINGER, L., STANNE, M. E., & DONOVAN, S. S. (1999). Effects of small-group learning on undergraduates in science, mathematics, engineering, and technology: A meta-analysis. *Review of Educational Research, 69,* 21–51.

SPURLOCK, J. (1984). Black women in the middle years. In G. Bauch & J. Brooks-Gunn (Eds.). *Women in midlife.* New York: Plenum.

SPURLOCK, J. (1995). Multiple roles of women and role strain. *Health Care for Women International, 16,* 501–508.

SROUFE, L. A. (1977). Wariness of strangers and the study of infant development. *Child Development, 48,* 731–746.

SROUFE, L. A., & FLEESON, J. (1986). Attachment and the construction of relationships. In W. W. Hartup & Z. Rubin (Eds.), *Relationships and development.* Hillsdale, NJ: Erlbaum.

SROUFE, L. A., FOX, N. E., & PANEAKE, V. R. (1983). Attachment and dependency in a developmental perspective. *Child Development, 54,* 1615–1627.

STACEY, J. (1998). Gay and lesbian families: Queer like us. In M. A. Mason & A. Skolnick (Eds.), *All our families: New policies for a new century.* New York: Oxford University Press.

STAGNER, R. (1985). Aging in industry. In J. Birren & K. Schaie (Eds.), *Handbook of the psychology of aging* (2nd ed.). New York: Van Nostrand Reinhold.

STAINES, G., POTTICK, K., & FUDGE, D. (1986). Wives' employment and husbands' attitudes toward work and life. *Journal of Applied Psychology, 71,* 118–128.

STANGOR, C., & RUBLE, D. N. (1987). Development of gender role knowledge and gender consistency. In L. S. Liben & M. L. Signorella (Eds.), *New directions for child development, 38.* San Francisco: Jossey-Bass.

STANTON, H. E. (1981). A therapeutic approach to help children overcome learning difficulties. *Journal of Learning Disabilities, 14,* 220.

STARFIELD, B. (1992). Child and adolescent health status measures. In R. E. Behrman, (Ed.), *The Future of Children.* Los Angeles: Center for the Future of Children of the David and Lucile Packard Foundation.

STAUB, E. (1971). The use of role playing and induction in children's learning of helping and sharing behavior. *Child Development, 42,* 805–816.

STAUDINGER, U. M., & PASUPATHI, M. (2000). Life-span perspectives on self, personality, and social cognition. In F. I. M. Craik & T. A. Salthouse (Eds.), *Handbook of aging and cognition* (2nd ed.). Mahwah, NJ: Erlbaum.

STEGARUD, L., SOLHEIM, B., KARLSEN, M., & KROGER, J. (1999). Ego identity in cross-cultural context: A replication study. *Psychological Reports, 85,* 457–461.

STEIN, A. H., & FRIEDRICH, L. K. (1975). Impact of television on children and youth. In E. M. Hetherington (Ed.), *Review of child development* (Vol. 5). Chicago: University of Chicago Press.

STEIN, Z., SUSSER, M., SAENGER, G., & MAROLLA, F. (1975). Famine and human development: The Dutch hunger winter of 1944–1945. New York: Oxford University Press.

STEINBERG, L. (1986). Latchkey children and susceptibility to peer pressure: An ecological analysis. *Developmental Psychology, 22,* 433–439.

STEINBERG, L. (1987a). Recent research on the family at adolescence: The extent and nature of sex differences. *Journal of Youth and Adolescence, 16,* 191–198.

STEINBERG, L. (1987b). Single parents, stepparents, and the susceptibility of adolescents to antisocial peer pressure. *Child Development, 58,* 269–275.

STEINBERG, L. (1988). Reciprocal relation between parent–child distance and pubertal maturation. *Developmental Psychology, 24,* 122–128.

STEINHAUSEN, H.-C., & SPOHR, H.-L. (1998). Long-term outcome of children with fetal alcohol syndrome: Psychopathology, behavior, and intelligence. *Alcoholism: Clinical and Experimental Research, 22,* 334–338.

STERNBERG, R. J. (1986). A triangular theory of love. *Psychological Review, 93,* 119–135.

STERNBERG, R. J. (1985). *Beyond IQ: A triarchic theory of human intelligence.* Cambridge, UK: Cambridge University Press.

STERNBERG, R. J. (1988a). Applying cognitive theory to the teaching of intelligence. *Applied Cognitive Psychology, 2,* 231–255.

STERNBERG, R. J. (1988b). Lessons from the life span: What theorists of intellectual development among children learn from their counterparts studying adults. In E. M. Hetherington, R. N. Lerner, & M. Perlmutter (Eds.), *Child development.* Hillsdale, NJ: Erlbaum.

STERNBERG, R. J. (1997). Construct validation of a triangular love scale. *European Journal of Social Psychology, 27,* 313–335.

STERNBERG, R. J. (1999a). A triarchic approach to the understanding and assessment of intelligence in multicultural populations. *Journal of School Psychology, 37,* 145–149.

STERNBERG, R. J. (1999b). The theory of successful intelligence. *Review of General Psychology, 3,* 292–316.

STERNBERG, R. J. (Ed.) (1990). *Wisdom: Its nature, origins, and development.* New York: Cambridge University Press.

STERNBERG, R. J., & LUBART, T. I. (1993). Investing in creativity. *Psychological Inquiry, 4,* 229–232.

STERNBERG, R. J., WAGNER, R. K., WILLIAMS, W. M., & HORVATH, J. A. (1995). Testing common sense. *American Psychologist, 50,* 912–927.

STEVENS, N. (1995). Gender and adaptation to widowhood in later life. *Ageing and Society, 15,* 37–58.

STEVENS-LONG, J., & COMMONS, M. L. (1992). *Adult life: Developmental processes* (4th ed.). Mountain View, CA: Mayfield.

STEVENSON, H. W., CHEN, C., & LEE, S. (1993). Mathematics achievement of Chinese, Japanese, and American children: Ten years later. *Science, 259,* 53–58.

STEWART, W. (1977). *A psychosocial study of the formation of the early adult life structure in women.* Unpublished doctoral dissertation. Columbia University, New York.

STIER, H., & TIENDA, M. (1993). Are men marginal to the family? Insights from Chicago's inner city. In J. C. Hood (Ed.), *Men, work, and family.* Thousand Oaks, CA: Sage.

STIFTER, C. A., COULEHAN, C. M., & FISH, M. (1993). Linking employment to attachment: The mediating effects of maternal separation anxiety and interactive behavior. *Child Development, 64,* 1451–1460.

STILLION, J. (1985). *Death and the sexes: An examination of differential longevity, attitudes, behaviors, and coping styles.* Washington, DC: Hemisphere.

STIPEK, D. J., RECCHIA, S., & MCCLINTIC, S. (1992). A developmental analysis of pride and shame. *Human Development, 26,* 42–54.

STOLLER, E. P, & GIBSON, R. C. (1994). *Worlds of difference: Inequality in the aging experience.* Thousand Oaks, CA: Pine Forge Press.

STONE, R., CAFFERATA, G., & SANGL, J. (1987). Care-givers of the frail elderly: A national profile. *The Gerontologist, 27,* 616–626.

STONES, J. J., & KOZMA, A. (1996). Activity, exercise, and behavior. In J. E. Birren & K. W. Schaie (Eds.), *Handbook of the psychology of aging* (4th ed.). San Diego: Academic Press.

STRACHAN, T., & READ, A. P. (1999). *Human molecular genetics* (2nd ed.). New York: Wiley.

STRASSBERG, Z., DODGE, K. A., PETTIT, G. S., & BATES, J. E. (1994). Spanking in the home and children's subsequent aggression toward kindergarten peers. *Development and Psychopathology, 6,* 445–46l.

STRAUSS, R., & GOLDBERG, W. A. (1999). Self and possible selves during the transition to parenthood. *Journal of Family Psychology, 13*, 244–259.

STREISSGUTH, A. P. (1997). *Fetal alcohol syndrome: A guide for families and communities.* Baltimore, MD: Paul H. Brookes.

STREISSGUTH, A. P., BARR, H. M., BOOKSTEIN, F. L., SAMPSON, P. D., & OLSON, H. C. (1999). The long-term neurocognitive consequences of prenatal alcohol exposure: A 14–year study. *Psychological Science, 10*, 186–190

STREISSGUTH, A. P., SAMPSON, P. D., BARR, H. M., DARBY, B. L., & MARTIN, D. C. (1989). I. Q. at age 4 in relation to maternal alcohol use and smoking during pregnancy. *Developmental Psychology, 25*, 3–11.

STROEBE, M., GERGEN, M. M., GERGEN, K. J., & STROEBE, W. (1992). Broken hearts or broken bonds: Love and death in historical perspective. *American Psychologist, 47*, 1205–1212.

STROEBE, W., & STROEBE, M. S. (1987). *Bereavement and health: The psychological and physical consequences of partner loss.* New York: Cambridge University Press.

STUEVE, A., & O'DONNELL, L. (1984). The daughter of aging parents. In G. Baruch & J. Brooks-Gunn (Eds.), *Women in midlife.* New York: Plenum.

STULL, D. E., BOWMAN, K., & SMERGLIA, V. (1994). Women in the middle: A myth in the making? *Family Relations, 43*, 317–324.

STUNKARD, A. J. (1988). Some perspectives on human obesity: Its causes. *Bulletin of the New York Academy of Medicine, 64*, 902–923.

SUBBOTSKY, E. (1994). Early rationality and magical thinking in preschoolers: Space and time. *British Journal of Developmental Psychology, 12*, 97–108.

SUBSTANCE ABUSE AND MENTAL HEALTH SERVICES ADMINISTRATION (SAMSHA). (1997). *The 1996 national household survey on drug abuse.* Washington, DC.

SUBSTANCE ABUSE AND MENTAL HEALTH SERVICES ADMINISTRATION (SAMSHA). (2000). *The 1999 national household survey on drug abuse.* Washington, DC.

SUNDBERG, K., BANG, J., SMIDT-JENSEN, S., BROCKS, V., LUNDSTEEN, C., PARNER, J., & PHILIP, J. (1997). Randomised study of risk of fetal loss related to early amniocentesis versus chorionic villus sampling. *The Lancet, 350*, 697–704.

SUOMI, S. J., & HARLOW, H. F. (1972). Social rehabilitation of isolate reared monkeys. *Developmental Psychology, 6*, 487–496.

SUPER, C. M., & HARKNESS, S. (1986). The developmental niche: A conceptualization at the interface of child and culture. *International Journal of Behavioral Development, 9*, 545–569.

SUPER, C. M., & HARKNESS, S. (1994). The developmental niche. In W. J. Lonner & R. S. Malpass (Eds.), *Psychology and culture.* Boston: Allyn and Bacon.

SUPER, C. M., HERRERA, M. G., & MORA, J. O. (1990). Long-term effects of food supplementation and psychosocial intervention on the physcial growth of Colombian infants at risk of malnutrition. *Child Development, 61*, 29–49.

SUTHERLAND, G. R., & RICHARDS, R. I. (1994). Dynamic mutations. *American Scientist, 82*, 157–163.

SUTTON-SMITH, B., & ROSENBERG, B. G. (1970). *The sibling.* New York: Holt, Rinehart & Winston.

SVANBERG, P. O. G. (1998). Attachment, resilience and prevention. *Journal of Mental Health, 7*, 543–578.

SWANSON, M. W., STREISSGUTH, A. P., SAMPSON, P. D., & OLSON, H. (1999). Prenatal cocaine and neuromotor outcome at four months: Effect of duration of exposure. *Journal of Developmental and Behavioral Pediatrics, 20*, 325–334.

SZINOVACZ, M. E. (1998). Grandparents today: A demographic profile. *The Gerontologist, 38*, 37–52.

TAFT, L. I., & COHEN, H. J. (1967). Neonatal and infant reflexology. In J. Helmuth (Ed.), *The exceptional infant* (Vol. 1). Seattle: Special Child Publications.

TANGNEY, J. P. (1998). How does guilt differ from shame? In J. Bybee (Ed.), *Guilt and Children.* San Diego: Academic Press.

TANNER, J. M. (1978). Foetus into man: *Physical growth from conception to maturity.* Cambridge, MA: Harvard University Press.

TAYLOR, M., CARTWRIGHT, B. S., & CARLSON, S. M. (1993). A developmental investigation of children's imaginary companions. *Developmental Psychology, 29*, 276–285.

TAYLOR, R. D., & OSKAY, G. (1995). Identity formation in Turkish and American late adolescents. *Journal of Cross-Cultural Psychology, 26*, 8–22.

TEALE, W., & SULZBY, T. (1986). *Emergent literacy: Writing and reading.* Norwood, NJ: Ablex.

TELLER, D., & BORNSTEIN, M. H. (1987). Infant color vision and color perception. In P. Salapatek & L. Cohen (Eds.), *Handbook of infant perception, Vol. 1: From sensation to perception.* New York: Academic Press.

TEPPER, C. A., & CASSIDY, K. W. (1999). Gender differences in emotional language in children's picture books. *Sex Roles, 40*, 265–280.

TETI, D. M., & ABLARD, K. A. (1989). Security of attachment and infant–sibling relationships: A laboratory study. *Child Development, 60*, 1519–1528.

TETI, D. M., GELFAND, D. M., MESSINGER, D. S., & ISABELLA, R. (1995). Maternal depression and the quality of early attachment: An examination of infants, preschoolers, and their mothers. *Developmental Psychology, 31*, 364–376.

THABET, A. A. M., & VOSTANIS, P. (1999). Post-traumatic stress reactions in children of war. *Journal of Child Psychology and Psychiatry and Related Disciplines, 40*, 385–391.

THABET, A. A., & VOSTANIS, P. (2000). Post-traumatic stress disorder reactions in children of war: A longitudinal study. *Child Abuse and Neglect, 24*, 291–298.

THATCHER, R. W., WALKER, R. A., & GUIDICE, S. (1987). Human cerebral hemispheres develop at different rates and ages. *Science, 236*, 110–113.

THELEN, E. (1987). The role of motor development in developmental psychology: A view of the past and an agenda for the future. In N. Eisenberg (Ed.), *Comtemporary topics in developmental psychology.* New York: Wiley.

THELEN, E. (1989). The rediscovery of motor development: Learning new things from an old field. *Developmental Psychology, 25*, 946–949.

THELEN, E. (1992). Development as a dynamic system. *Current Directions in Psychological Science, 1*, 189–193.

THELEN, E., & FOGEL, A. (1989). Toward an action-based theory of infant development. In J. J. Lockman & N. L. Hazen (Eds.), *Action in social context: Perspectives on early development.* New York: Plenum.

THELEN, E., & SMITH, L. B. (1994). *A dynamic systems approach to the development of cognition and action.* Cambridge, MA: MIT Press.

THELEN, E., & SPENCER, J. P. (1998). Postural control during reaching in young infants: A dynamic systems approach. *Neuroscience and Biobehavioral Reviews, 22*, 507–514.

THELEN, E., with SMITH, L. B. (1996). *A dynamic systems approach to the development of cognition and action.* Cambridge, MA: MIT Press.

THOMAE, H. (1980). Personality and adjustment to aging. In J. E. Birren & R. B. Sloane (Eds.), *Handbook of mental health and aging.* Englewood Cliffs, NJ: Prentice Hall.

THOMAS, A., & CHESS, S. (1977). *Temperament and development.* New York: Brunner-Mazel.

THOMAS, L. E. (1979). Causes of mid-life change from high status careers. *Vocational Guidance Quarterly, 27*, 202–208.

THOMPSON, A. S. (1977). Notes on career development inventory—adult form. As quoted in R. P. Johnson & H. C. Riker (1981), Retirement maturity: A valuable concept for preretirement counselors. *Personnel and Guidance Journal, 59*, 291–295.

THOMPSON, L. (1991). Family work: Women's sense of fairness. *Journal of Family Issues, 12*, 181–196.

THOMPSON, L., & WALKER, A. J. (1989). Gender in families: Women and men in marriage, work and parenthood. *Journal of Marriage and the Family, 51*, 845–871.

THOMPSON, R. A. (1990). Vulnerability in research: A developmental perspective on research risk. *Child Development, 61*, 1–16.

THOMPSON, S. K. (1975). Gender labels and early sex-role development. *Child Development, 46*, 339–347.

THORNDIKE, E. L. (1911). *Animal intelligence.* New York: Macmillan.

THORNTON, A. (1989). Changing attitudes toward family issues in the United States. *Journal of Marriage and the Family, 51*, 873–893.

TIKALSKY, F. D., & WALLACE, S. D. (1988). Culture and the structure of children's fears. *Journal of Cross-Cultural Psychology, 19*, 481–492.

TIMIRAS, P. S. (1978). Biological perspectives on aging. *American Scientist, 66*, 605–613.

TIMIRAS, P. S. (Ed.) (1994). *Physiological basis of aging and geriatrics.* Boca Raton, FL: CRC Press.

TIMNICK, L. (1989). Children of violence. *Los Angeles Times Magazine*, (Sept. 3), 6–12, 14–15.

TINBERGEN, N. (1963/1996). On aims and methods of ethology. In L. D. Houck & L. C. Drickamer (Eds.), *Foundations of animal behavior: Classic papers with commentaries.* Chicago: University of Chicago Press.

TIROSH, E., STEIN, M., HAREL, J., & SCHER, A. (1999). Hand preference as related to development and behavior in infancy. *Perceptual and Motor Skills, 89,* 371–380.

TOBIAS, S. (1989). Tracked to fail. *Psychology Today, 60* (9), 54–58.

TOBIN, S. S. (1988). The unique psychology of the very old: Implications for practice. *Issues in Aging* (Monograph No. 4). Chicago: Center for Applied Gerontology.

TOMASELLO, M., MANNLE, S., & KRUGER, A. C. (1986). Linguistic environment of one- to two-year-old twins. *Developmental Psychology, 22,* 169–176.

TOOBY, J., & COSMIDES, L. (1989). Evolutionary psychology and the generation of culture: 1. Theoretical considerations. *Ethology and sociobiology, 10,* 29–49.

TROESTER, H., & BRAMBRING, M. (1992). Early social/emotional development in blind infants. *Child: Care, Health & Development, 18* 207–227.

TROLL, L. E. (1980). Grandparenting. In L. W. Poon (Ed.), *Aging in the 1980s.* Washington, DC: American Psychological Association.

TROLL, L. E. (1985). *Early and middle adulthood: The best is yet to come—maybe* (2nd ed.). Monterey, CA: Brooks/Cole.

TROLL, L. E. (1989). Myths of midlife: Intergenerational relationships. In S. Hunter & M. Sundel (Eds.), *Midlife myths: Issues, findings and practice implications.* Newbury Park, CA: Sage.

TROLL, L. E. (1996). Modified-extended families over time: Discontinuity in parts, continuity in wholes. In V. L. Bengtson (Ed.), *Adulthood and aging: Research on continuities and discontinuities.* New York: Springer-Verlag.

TROLL, L. E., & FINGERMAN, K. L. (1996). Connections between parents and their adult children. In C. Magai & S. H. McFadden (Eds.), *Handbook of emotion, adult development, and aging.* San Diego: Academic Press.

TROLL, L. E., & SKAFF, M. M. (1997). Perceived continuity of self in very old age. *Psychology and Aging, 12,* 162–169.

TRONICK, E. Z. (1989). Emotions and emotional communication. *American Psychologist, 44,* 112–119.

TSCHANN, J. M., JOHNSTON, J. R., & WALLERSTEIN, J. D. (1989). Resources, stressors, and attachment as predictors of adult adjustment after divorce: A longitudinal study. *Journal of Marriage and the Family, 51,* 1033–1046.

TSUCHIYA, K. D., FORSYTHE, M., ROBIN, N. H., & TUNNESSEN, W. W. (1998). Fragile X syndrome. *Archives of Pediatrics and Adolescent Medicine, 152,* 89–90.

TURNBULL, A. P., & TURNBULL, H. R., III. (1990). *Families, professionals and exceptionality: A special partnership* (2nd ed.). Columbus, OH: Merrill.

U.S. CENSUS BUREAU (1990). *Current Population Reports.* Washington, DC: U.S. Government Printing Office.

U.S. CENSUS BUREAU. (1993). *We the American elderly.* Washington, DC: U.S. Government Printing Office.

U.S. CENSUS BUREAU. (1995). *Statistical abstract of the United States: 1995.* Washington, DC: U.S. Government Printing Office.

U.S. CENSUS BUREAU. (1997). *Statistical abstract of the United States: 1997.* Washington, DC: U.S. Government Printing Office.

U.S. CENSUS BUREAU. (1999). *Statistical abstract of the United states: 1999.* Washington, DC: U.S. Government Printing Office.

U.S. CENSUS BUREAU. (2001). Centenarians/life expectancy! *Profile America Transcript.* Internet document. U.S. Census Bureau home page: www.census.gov

U.S. DEPARTMENT OF LABOR. (2000a). Changes in women's labor force participation in the 20th century. *Monthly Labor Review: The Editor's Desk* (Feb. 16). Washington, DC.

U.S. DEPARTMENT OF LABOR. (2000b). *Employment and earnings.* Washington, DC.

UDRY, J. R. (1988). Biological predispositions and social control in adolescent sexual behavior. *American Sociological Review, 52,* 841–855.

UHLENBERG, P., COONEG, T., & BOYD, R. (1990). Divorce for women after midlife. *Journal of Gerontology, 45,* 53–61.

UNITED NATIONS CHILDREN'S FUND (UNICEF). (1995). *The progress of nations, 1995: The nations of the world ranked according to their achievements in child health, nutrition, education, family planning, and progress for women.* New York.

UNITED NATIONS CHILDREN'S FUND (UNICEF). (1998). *State of the world's children 1998.* New York.

UNITED NATIONS CHILDREN'S FUND (UNICEF). (2000). *The state of the world's children 2000.* New York.

UNIVERSITY OF MICHIGAN (2000). *The 2000 Monitoring the Future Study.* Ann Arbor, MI.

USMIANI, S., & DANILUK, J. (1997). Mothers and their adolescent daughters: Relationship between self-esteem, gender role identity, and body image. *Journal of Youth and Adolescence, 26,* 45–62.

UZGIRIS, I. C. (1984). Imitation in infancy: Its interpersonal aspects. In M. Perlmutter (Ed.), *Minnesota Symposia on Child Psychology: Vol. 17, Parent–child interaction and parent–child relations.* Hillsdale, NJ: Erlbaum.

VAILLANT, G. E. (1977). *Adaptation to life.* Boston: Little-Brown.

VALENZUELA, M. (1997). Maternal sensitivity in a developing society: The context of urban poverty and infant chromic undernutrition. *Developmental Psychology, 33,* 845–855.

VANDELL, D. L., & CORASANITI, M. A. (1990). Child care and the family: Complex contributions to child development. In K. McCartney (Ed.), *New Directions for Child Development, 49.* San Francisco: Jossey-Bass.

VANDELL, D. L., & WILSON, C. S. (1987). Infants' interactions with mother, sibling and peer: Contrasts and relations between interaction systems. *Child Development, 58,* 176–186.

VANMANEN, K.-J. & WHITBOURNE, S. K. (1997). Psychosocial development and life events in adulthood. *Psychology and Aging, 12,* 239–246.

VASTA, R. (1982). Physical child abuse: A dual-component analysis. *Developmental Review, 2,* 125–149.

VENTER, J. C. (2000). Remarks at the human genome announcement, the White House. Celera Genomics Corporation press release.

VENTURA, S. J., JOYCE, M. M., CURTIN, S. C., MATHEWS, M. S., & PARK, M. M. (2000). Births: Final data for 1998. *National Vital Statistics Reports, 48* (3), 1–12. Hyattsville, MD: National Center for Health Statistics.

VISHER, E. B., & VISHER, J. S. (1983). Stepparenting: Blending families. In H. McCubbin & C. Figley (Eds.), *Stress and the family* (Vol. 1). New York: Brunner/Mazel.

VISHER, E. B., & VISHER, J. S. (1998). Stepparents: The forgotten family members. *Family and Conciliation Courts Review, 36,* 444–451.

VITARO, F., TREMBLAY, R. E., KERR, M., PAGANI, L., & BUKOWSKI, W. M. (1997). Disruptiveness, friends' characteristics, and delinquency in early adolescence: A test of two competing models of development. *Child Development, 68,* 676–689.

VOELKER, R. (1999). Enzyme deficit may cause SIDS. *Journal of the American Medical Association, 282,* 1121.

VOGEL, J. M. (1989). *Shifting perspectives on the role of reversal errors in reading disability.* Paper presented at the biennial meeting of the Society for Research in Child Development, Kansas City.

VOLZ, J. (2000). How to live a century. *Monitor on Psychology, 31* (1), 30.

VON HOFSTEN, C. (1989). Motor development as the development of systems: Comments on the special section. *Developmental Psychology, 25,* 950–953.

VONDRA, J. I., BARNETT, D., & CICCHETTI, D. (1990). Self-concept, motivation, and competence among children from maltreating and comparison families. *Child Abuse and Neglect, 14,* 525–540.

VORHEES, C., & MOLLNOW, E. (1987). Behavioral teratogenesis. In J. Osofsky (Ed.), *Handbook of infant development* (2nd ed.). New York: Wiley.

VYGOTSKY, L. S. (1934/1987). Thinking and speech. In R. W. Rieber & A. S. Carton (Eds.), *The collected works of L. S. Vygotsky, Vol. 1: Problems of general psychology.* New York: Plenum.

VYGOTSKY, L. S. (1935/1978). *Mind in society: The development of higher psychological processes.* M. Cole, V. John-Steiner, S. Scribner, & E. Souberman (Eds.). Cambridge, MA: Harvard University Press.

VYGOTSKY, L. S. (1934/1962). *Thought and Language.* Cambridge, MA: MIT Press.

WAGNER, C.G. (1999). The centenarians are coming! *The Futurist, 33,* (5) 16–23.

WAGNER, R. C., & TORGERSON, J. K. (1987). The nature of phonological processing and its causal role in the acquisition of reading skills. *Psychological Bulletin, 101,* 192–212.

WAINRYB, C. (1995). Reasoning about social conflicts in different cultures: Druze and Jewish children in Israel. *Child Development, 66,* 390–401.

WALDENSTROEM, U. (1999). Experience of labor and birth in 1111 women. *Journal of Psychosomatic Research, 47,* 471–482.

WALFORD, R. L. (1983). *Maximum lifespan.* New York: Norton.

WALKER, L., & WALLSTON, B. (1985). Social adaptation: A review of dual earner family literature. In L. L'Abate (Ed.), *The handbook of family psychology and therapy.* Homewood, IL: Dorsey.

WALKER-ANDREWS, A. S., BAHRICK, L. E., RAGLIONI, S. S., & DIAZ, I. (1991). Infants' bimodal perception of gender. *Ecological Psychology, 3,* 55–75.

WALLACE, P., & GOTLIB, I. (1990). Marital adjustment during the transition to parenthood: Stability and predictors of change. *Journal of Marriage and the Family, 52,* 21–29.

WALLERSTEIN, J., & BLAKESLEE, S. (1989). *Second chances: Men, women, and children a decade after divorce.* New York: Ticknor & Fields.

WALLERSTEIN, J., CORBIN, S. B., & LEWIS, J. M. (1988). Children of divorce: A ten-year study. In E. M. Hetherington & J. Arasteh (Eds.), *Impact of divorce, single-parenting, and stepparenting on children.* Hillsdale, NJ: Erlbaum.

WALLING, A. D. (2000). Is caffeine safe during pregnancy? *American Family Physician, 62,* 1176.

WALLS, C. T. (1992). The role of the church and family support in the lives of older African Americans. *Generations, 16* (3), 33–36.

WALSH, B. T. (1988). Antidepressants and bulimia: Where are we? *International Journal of Eating Disorders, 7,* 421–423.

WALSH, D. (1994). *Selling out America's children: How America puts profits before values—and what parents can do.* Minneapolis: Fairview.

WALSH, M. (1997). Women's place in the American labour force, 1870–1995. Malden, MA: Blackwell.

WANN, D. L., CARLSON, J. D., HOLLAND, L. C., JACOB, B. E., OWENS, D. A., & WELLS, D. D. (1999). Beliefs in symbolic catharsis: The importance of involvement with aggressive sports. *Social Behavior and Personality, 27,* 155–164.

WARR, P. (1992). Age and occupational well-being. *Psychology and Aging, 7,* 37–45.

WATERLOW, J. C. (1994). Causes and mechanisms of linear growth retardation (stunting). *European Journal of Clinical Nutrition, 48,* (Supplement 1), 1–4.

WATERMAN, A. S. (1985). Identity in the context of adolescent psychology. In A. S. Waterman (Ed.), *New Directions for Child Development, 30,* 5–24. San Francisco: Jossey-Bass.

WATERMAN, A. S. (1999). Issues of identity formation revisited: United States and The Netherlands. *Developmental Review, 19,* 462–479.

WATERS, E., WIPPMAN, J., & SROUFE, L. A. (1979). Attachment, positive affect and competence in the peer group: Two studies in construct validation. *Child Development, 50,* 821–829.

WATKINS, S. C., MENKEN, J. A., & BONGAARTS, J. (1987). Demographic foundations of family change. *American Sociological Review, 52,* 346–358.

WATSON, A. J., & VALTIN, R. (1997). Secrecy in middle childhood. *International Journal of Behavioral Development, 21,* 431–452.

WATSON, J. B. (1925). *Behaviorism.* New York: Norton.

WATSON, J. D., & CRICK, F. H. C. (1953). Molecular structure of nucleic acids: A structure for deoxyribose nucleic acid. *Nature, 171,* 737–738.

WATSON-GEGEO, K. A., & GEGEO, D. W. (1989). The role of sibling interaction in child socialization. In P. Zukow (Ed.), *Sibling interaction across cultures: Theoretical and methodological issues.* New York: Springer-Verlag.

WEBER, R. A., LEVITT, M. J., & CLARK, M. C. (1986). Individual variation in attachment security and strange situation behavior: The role of maternal and infant temperament. *Child Development, 37,* 56–65.

WEG, R. B. (1989). Sensuality/sexuality of the middle years. In S. Hunter & M. Sundel (Eds.), *Midlife myths: Issues, findings, and practice implications.* Newbury Park, CA: Sage.

WEIKART, D. P., ROGERS, L., & ADCOCK, C. (1971). *The cognitively oriented curriculum.* Urbana: University of Illinois Press.

WEINBERG, K. M., & TRONICK, E. Z. (1996). Infant affective reactions to the resumption of maternal interaction after the Still-Face. *Child Development, 67,* 905–914

WEINBERG, R. A. (1989). Intelligence and IQ: Landmark issues and great debates. *American Psychologist, 44,* 98–104.

WEINER, D. B., & KENNEDY, R. C. (1999). Genetic vaccines. *Scientific American, 281 (1),* 50–57.

WEINRAUB, M., CLEMENS, L. P., SOCKLOFF, A., ETHRIDGE, T., GRACELY, E., & MYERS, B. (1984). The development of sex role stereotypes in the third year: Relationships to gender labeling, gender identity, sex-typed toy preference and family characteristics. *Child Development, 55,* 1493–1503.

WEISFELD, G. E., & BILLINGS, R. L. (1988). Observations on adolescence. In K. B. MacDonald (Ed.), *Sociobiological perspectives on human development.* New York: Springer-Verlag.

WEISS, R. S. (1987). On the current state of the American family. *Journal of Family Issues, 8,* 464–467.

WEITZ, R., & BRYANT, K. (1997). The portrayals of homosexuality in abnormal psychology and sociology of deviance textbooks. *Deviant Behavior, 18,* 27–46.

WELLES-NYSTROM, B. (1988). Parenthood and infancy in Sweden. In R. A. LeVine, P. M. Miller, & M. M. West (Eds.), *New Directions for Child Development, 40.* San Francisco: Jossey-Bass.

WENAR, C. (1990). Childhood fears and phobias. In M. Lewis & S. M. Miller (Eds.), *Handbook of developmental psychopathology.* New York: Plenum.

WENTWORTH, N., BENSON, J. B., & HAITH, M. M. (2000). The development of infants' reaches for stationary and moving targets. *Child Development, 71,* 576–601.

WERKER, J. F., & TEES, R. C. (1999). Influences on infant speech processing. *Annual Review of Psychology, 50,* 509–535.

WERNER, E. E. (1989). Children of the garden island. *Scientific American, 260* (4), 106–111.

WERNER, E. E. (1995). Resilience in development. *Current Directions in Psychological Science, 4* (3), 81–85.

WESSELLS, M. G. (1997). Armed conflict and children's rights. *American Psychologist, 52,* 1385–1386.

WHITBOURNE, S. K. (1986a). *The me I know: A study of adult development.* New York: Springer-Verlag.

WHITBOURNE, S. K. (1986b). *Adult development* (2nd ed.). New York: Praeger.

WHITBOURNE, S. K. (1999). Physical changes. In J. C. Cavanaugh & S. K. Whitbourne (Eds.), *Gerontology: An interdisciplinary perspective.* New York: Oxford University Press.

WHITBOURNE, S. K., & CONNOLLY, L. A. (1999). The developing self in midlife. In S. L. Willis & J. D. Reid (Eds.), *Life in the middle: Psychological and social development in middle age.* San Diego: Academic Press.

WHITBOURNE, S. K., & EBMEYER, J. B. (1990). *Identity and intimacy in marriage: A study of couples.* New York: Springer-Verlag.

WHITE, B. L., & WATTS, J. (1973). *Experience and environment: Major influences on the development of the young child.* Englewood Cliffs, NJ: Prentice Hall.

WHITE, K. J., & KISTNER, J. (1992). The influence of teacher feedback on young children's peer preferences and perceptions. *Developmental Psychology, 28,* 933–940.

WHITE, R. W. (1959). Motivation reconsidered: The concept of competence. *Psychological Review, 66,* 297–333.

WHITEHURST, G. J., FALCO, F. L., LONIGAN, C. J., & FISCHEL, J. E. (1988). Accelerating language development through picture book reading. *Developmental Psychology, 24,* 552–559.

WHITESIDE, M. F. (1989). Family rituals as a key to kinship connections in remarried families. *Family Relations, 38,* 34–39.

WHITING, B. B., & EDWARDS, C. P. (1988). *Children of different worlds: The formation of social behavior.* Cambridge, MA: Harvard University Press.

WHITING, B. B., & WHITING, J. W. M. (1975). *Children of six cultures: A psychocultural analysis.* Cambridge, MA: Harvard University Press.

WILDHOLM, O. (1985). Epidemiology of premenstrual tension syndrome and primary dysmenorrhea. In M. Y. Dawood, J. L. McGuire, & L. M. Demers (Eds.), *Premenstrual syndrome and dysmenorrhea.* Baltimore, MD: Urban and Schwartzenberg.

WILKIE, J. R., RATCLIFF, K. S., & FERREE, M. M. (1992). *Family division of labor and marital satisfaction among two-earner married couples.* Paper presented at the annual conference of the National Council on Family Relations, Orlando, FL.

WILLIAMS, D. R. (1992). Social structure and the health behavior of blacks. In K. W. Schaie, D. Blazer, & J. S. House (Eds.), *Aging, health behaviors, and health outcomes.* Hillsdale, NJ: Erlbaum.

WILLIAMS, F. (1970). Some preliminaries and prospects. In F. Williams (Ed.), *Language and poverty.* Chicago: Markham.

WILLIAMS, H. G. (1983). *Perceptual and motor development.* Englewood Cliffs, NJ: Prentice Hall.

WILLIAMS, J. D., & JACOBY, A. P. (1989). The effects of premarital heterosexual and homosexual experience on dating and marriage desirability. *Journal of Marriage and the Family, 51,* 489–497.

WILLIAMS, J. E., BENNETT, S. M., & BEST, D. (1975). Awareness and expression of sex stereotypes in young children. *Developmental Psychology, 5,* 635–642.

WILLIS, S. L. (1987). Cognitive training and everyday competence. In K. W. Schaie (Ed.), *Annual review of gerontology and geriatrics* (Vol. 7.). New York: Springer.

WILLIS, S. L. (1989). Adult intelligence. In S. Hunter & M. Sundel (Eds.), *Midlife myths: Issues, findings, and practice implications.* Newbury Park, CA: Sage.

WILLIS, S. L. (1990). Introduction to the special section on cognitive training in later adulthood. *Developmental Psychology, 26,* 875–878.

WILLIS, S. L., & NESSELROADE, C. (1990). Long-term effects of fluid ability training in old-old age. *Developmental Psychology, 26,* 905–910.

WILLIS, S. L., & SCHAIE, K. W. (1999). Intellectual functioning in midlife. In S. L. Willis & J. D. Reid (Eds.), *Life in the middle: Psychological and social development in middle age.* San Diego: Academic Press.

WILLWERTH, J. (1993). "Hello, I'm Home Alone. . . ." *Time, 141* (9), 46–47.

WILMUT, I. (1998). Cloning for medicine. *Scientific American, 279* (6), 58–63.

WILMUT, I., CAMPBELL, K., & TUDGE, C. (2000). *The second creation: Dolly and the age of biological control.* New York: Farrar, Straus and Giroux.

WILSON, E. O. (1975). *Sociobiology: The new synthesis.* Cambridge, MA: Harvard University Press.

WINER, G. A., CRAIG, R. K., & WEINBAUM, E. (1992). Adult's failure on misleading weight-conservation tests: A developmental analysis. *Developmental Psychology, 28,* 109–120.

WINSBOROUGH, H. H. (1980). A demographic approach to the life-cycle. In K. W. Back (Ed.), *Life course: Integrative theories and exemplary populations.* Washington, DC: American Sociological Association.

WINSLER, A., DÍAZ, R. M., ESPINOSA, L., & RODRIGUEZ, J. L. (1999). When learning a second language does not mean losing the first: Bilingual language development in low-income, Spanish-speaking children attending bilingual preschool. *Child Development, 70,* 349–362.

WINSLER, A., DIAZ, R. M., & MONTERO, I. (1997).

The role of private speech in the transition from collaborative to independent task performance in young children. *Early Childhood Research Quarterly, 12,* 59–79.

WITTERS, W., & VENTURELLI, P. (1988). *Drugs and society* (2nd ed.). Boston: Jones & Bartlett.

WITZIG, R. (1996). The medicalization of race: Scientific legitimization of a flawed social construct. *Annals of Internal Medicine, 125,* 675–679.

WOLFE, D. A., WOLFE, V. V., & BEST, C. L. (1988). Child victims of sexual abuse. In V. B. Van-Hasselt, R. L. Morrison, A. S. Bellack, & M. Herson (Eds.), *Handbook of family violence.* New York: Plenum.

WOLFENSTEIN, M. (1951). The emergence of fun morality. *Journal of Social Issues, 7,* 15–25.

WOLFF, P. H. (1966). The causes, controls, and organization of behavior in the neonate. *Psychological Issues, 5* (No. 1, Monograph 17).

WOLFF, P. H. (1969). The natural history of crying and other vocalizations in early infancy. In B. M. Foss (Ed.), *Determinants of infant behavior* (Vol. 4). London: Methuen.

WOMEN'S REENTRY PROJECT (1981). *Obtaining a degree: Alternative options for reentry women.* Washington, DC: Project on the Status and Education of Women.

WORLD HEALTH ORGANIZATION (WHO). (2000). *Malnutrition - The global picture.* Internet document. WHO home page: www.who.int

WORTMAN, C. B., & SILVER, R. C. (1989). The myths of coping with loss. *Journal of Consulting and Clinical Psychology, 57,* 349–357.

WRIGHT, B. (1983). *Physical disability: A psychological approach* (2nd ed.). New York: Harper & Row.

WRIGHT, K. (1997). Babies, bonds and brains. *Discover, 18* (10), 74–75.

WYATT, P. R. (1985). Chorionic biopsy and increased anxiety. *The Lancet, 2,* 1312–1313.

YAMEY, G. (2000). Scientists unveil first draft of human genome. *British Medical Journal, 321,* 7.

YANKELOVICH, D. (1981). *New rules: Searching for self-fulfillment in a world turned upside-down.* New York: Random House.

YEE, A. H., FAIRCHILD, H. H., WEIZMANN, F., & WYATT, G. E. (1993). Addressing psychology's problems with race. *American Psychologist, 48,* 1132–1140.

YODER, A. E. (2000). Barriers to ego identity status formation: A contextual qualification of Marica's identity status paradigm. *Journal of Adolescence, 23,* 95–106.

YONAS, A., & OWSLEY, C. (1987). Development of visual space perception. In P. Salapatek & L. Cohen (Eds.), *Handbook of infant perception* (Vol. 2). New York: Academic Press.

YOUNG, E. W., JENSEN, L. C., OLSEN, J. A., &

CUNDICK, B. P. (1991). The effects of family structure on the sexual behavior of adolescents. *Adolescence, 26,* 977–986.

YOUNG, S. K., FOX, N. A., & ZAHN-WAXLER, C. (1999). The relations between temperament and empathy in 2–year-olds. *Developmental Psychology, 35,* 1189–1197.

YOUNISS, J., & KETTERLINUS, R. D. (1987). Communication and connectedness in mother and father adolescent relationships. *Journal of Youth and Adolescence, 16,* 265–280.

ZACHS, R. T., HASHER, L., & LI, K. Z. H. (2000). Human memory. In F. I. M. Craik & T. A. Salthouse (Eds.), *Handbook of aging and cognition* (2nd ed.). Mahwah, NJ: Erlbaum.

ZAHN-WAXLER, C., & SMITH, K. D. (1992). The development of prosocial behavior. In V. B. Van Hasselt & M. Hersen (Eds.), *Handbook of social development: A lifespan perspective.* New York Plenum.

ZAHN-WAXLER, C., RADKE-YARROW, M., WAGNER, E., & CHAPMAN, M. (1992). Development of concern for others. *Developmental Psychology, 28,* 126–136.

ZAJONC, R. B., & HALL, E. (1986). Mining new gold from old research. *Psychology Today, 20* (2), 46–51.

ZAJONC, R. B., & MARKUS, G. B. (1975). Birth order and intellectual development. *Psychological Review, 82,* 74–88.

ZANDER, L., & CHAMBERLAIN, G. (1999). Place of birth. *British Medical Journal, 318,* 721–723.

ZAPOROZLETS, A. V., & ELKONIN, D. B. (Eds.) (1971). *The psychology of preschool children.* Cambridge, MA: MIT Press.

ZEANAH, C. H., BORIS, N. W., & LARRIEU, J. A. (1997). Infant development and developmental risk: A review of the past 10 years. *Journal of the American Academy of Child & Adolescent Psychiatry, 36,* 165–178.

ZEANAH, C. H., BORIS, N. W., & LARRIEU, J. A. (1998). Infant development and developmental risk: A review of the past 10 years: Erratum. *Journal of the American Academy of Child & Adolescent Psychiatry, 37,* 240.

ZESKIND, P. S., & RAMEY, C. T. (1978). Fetal malnutrition: An experimental study of its consequences on infant development in two caregiving environments. *Child Development, 49,* 1155–1162.

ZIMMERMAN, M. A., COPELAND, L. A., SHOPE, J. T., & DIELMAN, T. E. (1997). A longitudinal study of self-esteem: Implications for adolescent development. *Journal of Youth and Adolescence, 26,* 117–140.

ZUCKERMAN, M. (1990). Some dubious premises in research and theory on racial differences: Scientific, social, and ethical issues. *American Psychologist, 45,* 1297–1303.

ZURAVIN, S. (1985). Housing and maltreatment: Is there a connection? *Children Today, 14* (6), 8–13.

Photo Credits

Mazzaschi/Stock Boston **515** Byron/Monk-meyer Press **518** Myrleen Ferguson/PhotoEdit **521** B. Daemmrich/The Image Works **522** Michael Weisbrot/Stock Boston **528** Bob Daemmrich/Bob Daemmrich Photography, Inc. **530** Rhoda Sidney/Stock Boston

CHAPTER 16

536 PhotoDisc Vol. 2/"People and Lifestyles" **538** David Young-Wolff/PhotoEdit **540** Stacy Pick/Stock Boston **543** Dagmar Fabricius/Stock Boston **546** Michael Newman/PhotoEdit **549** D.Young-Wolff/PhotoEdit **552** Jeff Greenberg/PhotoEdit **558** Joe

Sohm/Unicorn Stock Photos **563** Wayne Floyd/Unicorn Stock Photos

CHAPTER 17

568 PhotoDisc 42/"Everyday Living version 2" **570** Keith Brofsky/PhotoDisc, Inc. **573** Ken Lax/Photo Researchers, Inc. **576 (top)** Myrleen Ferguson/PhotoEdit **576 (bottom)** Bill Bachmann/Stock Boston **581** Marshall Prescott/Unicorn Stock Photos **584** Myrleen Ferguson/PhotoEdit **591** Frank Siteman/Stock Boston **597** Joseph Sohm/Stock Boston

CHAPTER 18

600 PhotoDisc 42/"Everyday Living version 2" **602** Tom McCarthy/PhotoEdit **607** Edward Lettau/Photo Researchers, Inc. **611** Liaison Agency, Inc. **614** Ken Fisher/Stone **621** Andy Levin/Photo Researchers, Inc. **624** Jim Harrison/Stock Boston

CHAPTER 19

628 PhotoDisc Vol. 2/"People and Life-styles" **630** Jane Lewis/Stone **633** D. Young-Wolff/PhotoEdit **638** A. Rodham/Unicorn Stock Photos **640** Richard Sheinwald/AP/Wide World Photos **647** Tony Freeman/PhotoEdit

Name Index

Subject Index

A

Abstract thinking in adolescence, 397–398

Abuse and neglect, effects of on infants and toddlers, 216

Accommodation, 55

Action schemes, 184

Adaptation, 182–183

Adjustment to death, stages of (Kubler-Ross), 635

Adolescence
cognitive changes, 397–402
developmental tasks of, 407–412
family dynamics, 412–415
images of, 12–14
personality and sociocultural development, 405–435
physical and cognitive development, 379–403
physical development and adjustment, 382–389
problems in, 421–429
delinquency, 428
drug abuse, 422–428
risk-taking, 422
relationships during, 415–421
sexual attitudes and behavior, 390–397
stress, depression, and coping, 429–433
typical physical changes in, table, 386

Adolescent developmental tasks, 407–412
identity formation, 408–412
independence and interdependence, 407–408

Adolescent growth spurt, 383

Adoption studies, 94–95

Adult children, relations with in middle adulthood, 546–547

Adult development
perspectives on, 439–442
age clocks and social norms, 439–440
contextual paradigms or approaches, 440–442
seasons and tasks of, 458–467
Erikson's developmental tasks, 460
Gould's transformations, 465–467
Havinghurst's developmental tasks, 458–460
Levinson's seasons of a man's life, 460–463
defining a dream, 462
developing a career, 462

establishing intimacy, 462–463
finding a mentor, 462
Levinson's seasons of a woman's life, 463–465
differing career trajectories, 464
differing dreams, 463–464
differing reevaluation, 464
differing relationships with mentors, 464
women's dreams and social change, 464–465

Adulthood
images of, 14–16
major tasks of, selected theorists' views, table, 466

Affordances, 188

Afterbirth, 138

Age clock, 439–440

Age cohorts, effects of historical events on, table, 107

Ageism and stereotypes, 571–573

Age of viability, 122

Aggression
early childhood, 286–289
frustration and anger, 286–287
modeling and, 287–289
punishment and, 287

Aging
causes of, 587–589
heredity and environmental factors, 587
theories of, 587–589
biological clock, 588–589
stochastic, 587–588
demographics of, 619–621
and older adulthood, 571–579
ageism and stereotypes, 571–573
common misperceptions about elderly, table, 572
generalizing from the few to the many, 571–573
sociocultural perspective, 573
four decades of later life, 573–579
"middle-aged-old," 70–79, 576–577
"old-old," 80–89, 577–578
"very-old," 90 and over, 578–579
"young-old," 60–69, 574–576
physical aspects of, 579–586
changing body, 580–584
appearance, 580
internal organs, 583–584
muscles, bones, and mobility, 583
senses, 582–583
sleep patterns, 581

health, disease, and nutrition, 584–586
chronic health problems, 584–585
misuse of prescribed medications, 585–586
nutrition, 585
successful, 607–609
in U.S. black community, 608

Aging parents, relations with in middle adulthood, 547–551

Aid to Families with Dependent Children (AFDC), 490

Alcohol, 425–426
effects on embryo and fetus, 132–134

Alleles, 81

Altruism, 61, 289

Alzheimer's disease, 595–596

Ambidextrous, 245

American Association of Retired Persons (AARP), 571, 625

American Medical Association (AMA) and assisted suicide, 642

Americans with Disabilities Act, 445

Amniocentesis, 141

Amniotic fluid, 120

Amniotic sac, 120

Anal stage, 44

Androgynous personality, 300

Anorexia nervosa, 387–388

A-not-B error, 185

Anoxia, 135

Anticipatory grief, 644

Anxiety, definition of, 278

Apgar Scoring System, 146

Apnea, 167

Army Beta Mental Test, illustration of, 337

Assertiveness, 286

Assimilation, 55

Assisted suicide, 640, 642

Atherosclerosis, 585

Attachment, 150, 212–219

Attachment process, 207–209

Attention-deficit/Hyperactivity disorder (ADHD), 347

Audition and auditory perception
early development of, 180–181

Automaticity, 247

Autonomy, 278
vs. connectedness, 284

Autosomal disorders, 86–88
Angelman syndrome (AS), 86
Down syndrome, 86
Prader Willi syndrome (PWS), 86
table of examples, 87
trisomy-21. see Down syndrome